Italy

Guide

Travel Guides to Planet Earth!

OPEN ROAD TRAVEL GUIDES – YOUR GUIDES TO PLANET EARTH!

Whether you're going abroad or planning a trip in the United States, take Open Road along on your journey. Our books have been praised by **Travel & Leisure**, **The Los Angeles Times**, **Newsday**, **Booklist**, **US News & World Report**, **Endless Vacation**, **American Bookseller**, **Coast to Coast**, and many other magazines and newspapers!

Don't just see the world – experience it with Open Road!

About the Author

Having spent more than eight years living in Italy and exploring the country, Douglas E. Morris has put his extensive travel experiences down on paper with *Italy Guide*. Morris's other Open Road guides include *Rome Guide* and *Tuscany & Umbria Guide*, and *Become a Travel Writer* available from *fabjob.com*. His guides to Italy give you the most accurate, up-to-date, and comprehensive information about restaurants, nightlife, hotels and sights in Italy.

Doug in Roma!

Open Road - Travel Guides to Planet Earth!

Open Road Publishing has guide books to exciting, fun destinations on four continents. As veteran travelers, our goal is to bring you the best travel guides available anywhere!

No small task, but here's what we offer:

• All Open Road travel guides are written by authors with a distinct, opinionated point of view – not some sterile committee or team of writers. Our authors are experts in the areas covered and are polished writers.

• Our guides are geared to people who want to make their own travel choices. We'll show you how to discover the real destination – not just see some place from a tour bus window.

• We're strong on the basics, but we also provide terrific choices for those looking to get off the beaten path and experience the country or city – not just see it or pass through it.

• We give you the best, but we also tell you about the worst and what to avoid. Nobody should waste their time and money on their hard-earned vacation because of bad or inadequate travel advice.

• Our guides assume nothing. We tell you everything you need to know to have the trip of a lifetime – presented in a fun, literate, nononsense style.

• And, above all, we welcome your input, ideas, and suggestions to help us put out the best travel guides possible.

Guide

Travel Guides to Planet Earth!

Douglas Morris

Open Road Publishing

Open Road Publishing

We offer travel guides to American and foreign locales. Our books tell it like it is, often with an opinionated edge, and our experienced authors always give you all the information you need to have the trip of a lifetime. Write for your free catalog of all our titles.

**Catalog Department, Open Road Publishing
P.O. Box 284, Cold Spring Harbor, NY 11724**

E-mail:
Jopenroad@aol.com

Library of Congress Control Number: 2002090650
ISBN 1-892975-65-3

Acknowledgments

Many people assisted considerably in the development of this book, but I wish to extend special gratitude to my departed parents, Don and Denise, for being the world travelers and citizens of the world that they were. Without them I would never have lived in Italy and developed the experience to write this book. I also wish to thank Heddi Goodrich for her unique insight into Naples. My brother Dan was a valuable resource. Alain deCocke's editorial assistance, in both English and Italian, was much appreciated. I am also indebted to Anamaria Porcaro, Theresa Luis and the MMI class of '76 for their thoughtful insights about how to travel in Italy as women. And most of all this book is better for the invaluable suggestions and feedback offered by our many readers including: Jack and Joan Sawinski, Pamela A. Motta, Donna and Mike Lareau, Steve and Sheila Cech, Hugh L. Curtin, Senator Paul Simon, and many others. Please forgive me if I did not include you here. And please keep your e-mails coming to *Roma79@aol.com*.

Table of Contents

Maps

Sidebars

Chapter 1

If you're looking for a wide variety of entertainment, stunning architecture, passionate people, soul refreshing relaxation, beautiful beaches, unparalleled artwork, dazzling museums, ruins from ancient civilizations, world-class accommodations, superb restaurants, first-rate ski resorts, championship golf courses, wonderful water sports and continuous recreation, then Italy is the place for you! And the food – by far the best and most varied in the world. Created with the freshest ingredients and always with a distinctly local flair, not only is the cooking healthy and nutritious, but the variety of flavors and tastes will tantalize and satisfy like no other cuisine. Not to mention great wines like Chianti, Ruffino, Frascati and many more. Add onto all of that the Italian passion for living, and in Italy you have an ideal vacation destination.

With this Open Road guide, your days and nights in Italy will be filled with all the exciting possibilities the land of *La Dolce Vita* has to offer. I've given you a multiplicity of options for shopping, eating, traveling and much more so that you can tailor the perfect vacation for your particular needs.

It's easy to see why so many Americans choose to visit the boot-shaped peninsula that juts into the Mediterranean. From the big tourist cities of Rome, Florence, and Venice to historic hill towns like Perugia, Ravello and Lucca, small mountain villages like Nocelle, Gubbio or Todi, and the abundant breathtaking coastal resorts, Italy is romantic, beautiful, fun and exciting. If you are looking for an adventure like no other, read on!

Chapter 2

**o
v
e
r
v
i
e
w**

Italy is generally divided into four main parts: northern Italy, central Italy, southern Italy, and the islands.

Northern Italy

Northern Italy is dominated by the lowland formed by the **Po River** and its tributaries. The **Alps** form the northern and western boundaries, and the **Apennines** are the southern boundary. The main ports on northern Italy's eastern side, that which is accessible to the **Adriatic Sea**, is Venezia and Trieste. On the western side there is access to the **Ligurian Sea**, mainly from the port of Genoa. The north of Italy has the largest portion of the nation's population and is the leading agricultural and industrial area. Good climate and soil composition in the north are favorable for farming; and easy access to the rest of Europe has made northern Italy more economically viable and industrially successful than the rest of Italy.

There are a variety of interesting travel locations in the north. Besides **Venice**, with its fairy tale architecture surrounded by the canals that are the city's roads, you can also find the beautiful city of **Trieste**. This attractive location has been lovingly influenced by three different cultures and offers you an alternative destination filled with fine food and accommodating atmosphere. If city life is too hectic, you might want to explore the hiking trails of the **Alps** in the summer, or ski down mountain slopes in the winter. Also in the north are the majority of Italy's golf courses; all of which I've listed are close to the destinations in this book.

If life by the sea is your thing, try the **Italian Riviera**. Filled with all sorts of fun water sports, stunning beaches, and quaint little towns, the seaside resort areas along the Ligurian coast are the ideal place to relax or to sample *La Dolce Vita*. If rustic is more your taste, try the **Cinque Terre**, five little villages cut into the cliffs along the Ligurian coast of the Mediterranean that seem to be withstanding the annual tide of tourists crashing onto Italy's shores. The middle three will give you a glimpse into the past and a respite from the modern world that will refresh and rejuvenate you for years.

Central Italy

Central Italy is that part of the peninsula that includes and extends north of Rome through the Tuscany region. Although only a small part of the area is composed of lowlands, central Italy plays an important role in farming and in some branches of industry, specifically wine growing. **Florence** and **Rome** are the main tourist cities in Central Italy and contain the best museums, the best churches, and the best sights to see, not only in Italy but some would say the world over. Even if you are a seasoned Italy traveler you should make a point of visiting either of these two cities to refresh your memory of the historical and cultural beauty of Italy.

One small overlooked town that shouldn't be missed while in Florence is **Lucca**. One of only two completely walled medieval cities left in Europe, the ramparts and battlements that surround the city have been converted into the most romantic tree-lined walkway you will find anywhere. For romantics, Lucca is a must see.

Another quaint little town, this one a hill town just outside of Rome, is **Frascati**. Every year they have a bacchanalian wine festival celebrating the pressing of the local wine. If you're in Rome during September you have to visit, since Frascati is only a 30 minute train ride away. And if you come any other time of year and want to stay in a small, peaceful, medieval hill town, with wonderful views over the surrounding countryside (vineyards), wonderful little wine bars, plenty of great restaurants, and a quaint ambiance that will be remembered forever, Frascati is the place for you.

And not to be missed but a little more difficult to get to are the quaint and colorful medieval hill towns of **Umbria**. Though strategically located between Rome and Florence, the province of Umbria is on the periphery of the well worn tourist path. Since many of Umbria's cities are not on strategic rail lines, Italy's main form of inter-city transportation, getting to many locations can be time consuming. But once you are here, Umbria is a beautiful slice of mother nature's paradise. Covered with lush green forests, manicured fields and wonderful medieval hill towns like **Perugia**, **Gubbio**, **Assisi**, **Orvieto** and **Todi**, Umbria is an ideal destination. And since it has yet to be overrun by the thundering herd of mass tourism you will have the scenery and history all to yourself.

Southern Italy

Southern Italy is generally considered to be everything south of Rome. In terms of topography and agriculture there are two significant lowland areas in the south. One is surrounding **Naples**, and the other is the province of **Apulia**, the segment of the east coast that includes the heel of the Italian boot. From these two areas most of the south's agricultural output is generated.

Naples is a vast port city that boasts one of the best museums in Italy. It is a vibrant metropolis, as are all ports, and can be a little dicey at times if you're out late at night in the wrong place; but if you look beyond its reputation as being less than meets the eye, and look into its heart, Naples is a fun city to visit. In its old section it has the ambiance of a large medieval city with its tiny streets and shops of skilled artisans practicing crafts you would never have thought still existed. You can find violin makers, doll makers, cabinet makers and similar craftsmen hidden down the side streets and on the second stories of Naples' *centro storico*.

Naples is the perfect stopping-over point on your way to the quaint islands of **Capri**, **Ischia** or **Procida** in the bay of the city; and is the perfect transit stop for visits to **Pompeii** and **Herculaneum**, those ancient cities smothered but preserved by the lava and ash of the local volcano. These two ancient Roman cities have to be visited if you are a student of history. If sunning and funning is more your speed, the towns along the **Amalfi Coast** are a summer vacation paradise. Beautifully set on the hills overlooking the sea, these little towns offer stunning vistas and all types of summer recreation.

Farther south you can find the resting place of **Santa Claus**. Saint Nicholas is buried in the Church of San Nicola deep in the old town of **Bari**. Down in the heel of Italy's boot is the virtually untouristed **Lecce**, which boasts an array of 17th century Baroque architecture. Besides Lecce's architecture, the city is the perfect jumping-off point to explore the **Salentine peninsula**, which is dotted with medieval fortresses and castles. Exploring the base of Italy's heel is like going back in time, but it is an adventure not to be undertaken except by the most experienced travelers. Southern Italy can sometimes be danger-ous if you venture off the beaten coastline and into the hills. In general Italy is 100 time safer than the United States, but when on vacation it is better to be safe than sorry.

The Islands: Sicily & Sardinia

The fourth region of Italy includes its two major islands: **Sicily** and **Sardinia**, as well as the other smaller island groups in the Mediterranean Sea. The only other island of any size, **Elba**, is in the Tyrrhenian Sea with Sardinia. This small isle off the coast of Tuscany once served as Napoleon's place of exile.

Italy's Jubilee Clean-Up

All of Italy has scrubbed itself clean from years of smog and soot; the monuments haven't gleamed like this since they were first built. So if you have ever wanted to come to Rome, now is the time. Rome has also introduced new red buses, complete with air conditioning and much more comfortable seating. Italians have also made everything much more efficient and intuitive for travelers. Florence, Siena, Perugia, and every other Italian city and town have gone through a massive cleansing and re-organization. Rome and all of Italy have never looked better.

Much smaller islands groups are the **Pontine Islands** near Naples; the **Lipari Islands** off northeastern Sicily; and the **Egadi Islands** opposite Sicily's northwestern end.

Sicily is a historian's dream. Since the island was one of ancient Greece's main colonies, here you'll find the most complete Greek ruins outside of Greece, some of which are located just below the town of **Agrigento**. You can also find ancient medieval hill towns like **Erice**, located 80 km west of Palermo, complete with walls, fortress and even an ancient temple dedicated to Venus. Sicily is also a summer sportsman's paradise, and as a result many resorts have sprung up to accommodate this need.

To enjoy summer sports or to get away from it all, try the Lipari Islands (also known as the **Isole Eolie**). Some islands cater to tourists; others have only a few hotels and all the tranquillity you can soak up.

Movies to Set the Scene for Your Trip!

As you're planning your trip, you might want to rent a few movies to get you in the mood for your travels (save the novels for the airplane trips and beach visits!). Some modern classics include:

- **Amarcord**, Fellini's great film about youth and coming of age
- **Christ Stopped at Eboli**, about a sophisticated left-wing doctor sent to a small hill town during the Fascist era
- **Cinema Paradiso**, about growing up in southern Italy
- **The Garden of the Finzi-Cantinis**, tale of what happens to a wealthy Jewish family before and during World War II
- **Caligula**, a bit rough and not for kids, but an interesting take on the debauchery of aristocrats in the Roman Empire
- **Il Postino**, a romantic movie about a postman, a poet, and the island of Procida
- **Life is Beautiful**, a celebration of living, Italian-style, even in the worst of times

Experience History

Home to the ancient world's most powerful empire, Italy is awash in history. Daily life revolves around ruins thousands of years old. Modern buildings incorporate ancient structures into their walls. Medieval streets snake through almost all cities including Rome, Florence, and especially Venice. In Italy you can see the tapestry of history woven directly in front of you. Museums abound with ancient artifacts, beautiful paintings, and stunning sculpture. You can easily spend an entire trip roaming through museums

– or for that matter inside the beautiful churches where you'll see some of the most exquisite paintings and sculptures anywhere on earth!

A Feast for the Eyes!

Even though you could spend an entire trip inside museums or churches, if you decided to do so you would miss out on what makes Italy such a wonderful vacation: its ancient beauty, charm, and ambiance. Being in Italy is like walking through a fairy tale. The old winding streets, twisting around the quaint refurbished buildings, leading to a tiny piazza centered with a sparkling fountain seems like something out of a dream. And you'll find a similar scene in virtually every city you visit in Italy.

If cities are not your cup of tea, you can't surpass the natural beauty of Italy's **Alpine** region, the crystal clear **Northern Lakes**, the pristine southern coastline, or the little villages perched on hills scattered across the land. A feast for the eyes awaits you in Italy.

Food & Wine

But a feast for the eyes is not all you'll get. Italy has, arguably (pipe down, you Francophiles!), the best food you'll find anywhere in the world. In most cases it's simple food, but with a bountiful taste. Take, for example, a Roman favorite: *abbacchio arrosto*. This is a succulent lamb dish slowly cooked over an open flame until the meat is tender and inviting. It is usually accompanied by *patate arrosto*, roast potatoes cooked with rosemary, olive oil, and salt that makes my mouth water just thinking about them.

Since Italy is surrounded on almost all sides by water you can also sample any flavor of seafood imaginable. Usually caught the same day, especially in the small towns along the sea, the seafood in Italy will have you coming back for more.

And don't forget the pasta. You'll find all shapes and sizes covered with sauces of every description and variety. Regions are known for certain pasta dishes and when there you have to sample them all. The area around Bologna is known for the production of the best ham in the world, *Prosciutto di Parma*. To make this ham so succulent, the pigs are fed from the scraps of the magnificent cheese they make in the same region, *Parmigiano Reggiano*. Both of these foods feature prominently in *spaghetti alla bolognese* making it a favorite in the region and throughout Italy.

To wash down all these savory dishes you need look no further than the local wine list. Italian wines may not have a reputation as being as full-bodied and robust as French or California wines, but they have an intimate, down to earth, rustic taste. Order from the wine list or get a carafe of the house wine, which is usually delicious and more often than not comes from the local vineyards located just outside the city.

Open Road's Italy!

Besides offering the many sights to see, museums and churches to visit, and places to go, I've also listed the best sights to see while visiting a certain destination. In conjunction I've detailed for you the best hotels from each star category, as well as the restaurants where you'll find the best atmosphere and most satisfying cuisine. And to help you plan the perfect vacation and find everything the instant you arrive, this book offers you the **most complete set of city maps** you'll find in virtually any travel guide to Italy.

Sporting Activities

If you've noticed your waistband stretching a little from all the wonderful food and wine you've been enjoying, have no fear – Italy has plenty of activities for you to shave off some of those unwanted pounds. A land of sea and mountains, you can find some of the best skiing in the world in the **Alps** as well as wonderfully clear water and beaches all along the **Mediterranean Sea** and the **Adriatic Sea**.

You can go water-skiing, snorkeling, skin diving, sailing or just lie on the beach and sunbathe. Many vacation beaches are topless today, an unheard of activity a decade ago, so you'll be treated to an added adventure either participating or appreciating the presentation.

There are also many top-level golf courses all over Italy, plenty of tennis courts in most major cities, horseback riding in the country, fishing in lakes and sailing in the seas. Italy has it all.

THE ROMAN FORUM, CIRCA 1910

Chapter 3

rome itineraries

If you only have a short period of time in **Rome** and you want to fill it up with the best sights, restaurants, hotels, cafés at which to lounge, and pubs from which you can crawl back to your bed, all you have to do is follow the itineraries listed below. The hotels, sights, and restaurants mentioned are all described in more detail later in the book.

The places listed in these itineraries are among my favorites in Rome, but there were plenty of close calls! So follow my advice if you wish, or plow through the rest of the information included here and find the perfect itinerary tailor made for your needs.

The Perfect Three Days

Day One

This is going to be a somewhat slow day since you'll have just arrived and will be slightly jet-lagged.

- Arrive at Rome's Leonardo da Vinci airport in the morning.
- Take a cab to your hotel shower and unpack.
- To start off your Roman adventure head to the **Spanish Steps**.
- Get your picture taken while you lean over and grab a drink from the fountain in front of the steps.
- Walk to the top of the steps for the magnificent view over the city
- It should be about lunch time now, so walk back down the steps, cross the street, and take a left into the third street at the edge of the piazza, **Via delle Croce**. Follow this to the end, find an outside seat at the superb local restaurant **Otello alla Concordia**, *Via*

Della Croce 81. Tel. 06/679-1178. Try any of their exquisite Roman pasta specialties – *arrabiata, amatriciana*, or *vongole verace*.

• After lunch it should be about nap time. But remember to only take a 2-3 hour nap, wake up right away, take a shower and get out again – otherwise you'll sleep until 10:00pm and be wide awake because jet-lag will have set in.

• Now it's time to explore the streets around the **Piazza di Spagna**, **Via della Croce**, **Via del Corso**, **Via dei Condotti** and admire all the different shops.

• After shopping/exploring, take a small walk (or short cab ride) to **Piazza Navona**.

• Stop at **Le Tre Scalini** and sample some of the world famous Italian *gelato* (ice cream). If you sit at the tables outside the cost will double or triple.

• If some liquid refreshment is more your style, exit the Piazza Navona on the other side, cross the **Via Vittorio Emanuele**, visit the **Campo dei Fiori** (where they have a superb market in the mornings which we'll get to in a few days) and stop in at the **Drunken Ship** for some Guiness, Harp, or Kilkenny. Enjoy the English speaking bartenders, and have a few ales for me.

• From here you are within striking distance of **Trastevere**, the place for Roman nightlife, on the other side the river. Cross the pedestrian bridge **Ponte Sisto** and make your way to **Piazza Santa Maria** in Trastevere.

• If it's too early for dinner (7:30pm or 8:00pm is the beginning time) stop at one of the outdoor cafés and replenish your fluids.

• For dinner stop at **La Canonica** just outside of the piazza. Here you should also try one of the typical Roman pasta specialties, *arrabiata, amatriciana*, or *vongole verace*; as well as some *sogliola alla griglia* (grilled sole) for seconds.

• After dinner, if you're not too tired, let's go to the **Trevi Fountain**. It is beautiful lit up at night. To do so walk down the long road leading to the Piazza, **Via della Lungaretta**, to the large main road **Viale Trastevere**. From here catch a cab to Piazza Colonna, near the fountain. The side streets leading up to the fountain are usually packed and the cab wouldn't be able to move through the crowds anyway. Go across the big road, Via del Corso and take Via di Sabini to the fountain.

Day Two

• Today is museum day. Start off at the best in the city, the **Vatican Museum** and the **Sistine Chapel**. This should take you all morning.

• After your museum visit, instead of a long sit-down meal, on your way to St. Peter's stop at one of the many cafés and order a light snack. This will be a truly authentic way to eat a quick meal in Rome. My suggestion is getting a *Medallione*, a grilled ham and cheese concoction that is tasty and filling.

You don't order at the counter, you first pay for your order with the cashier (order your drink at the same time), then bring the receipt up to the counter and tell the bartender what you'll have. A good tip to leave is about Euro 50 cents.

- After your meal, let's explore **St. Peter's**. Guys will need slacks and cannot wear tank tops for this adventure, and women cannot wear short skirts, shorts or tank top-like shirts either. While here, make a point of walking to the top, or taking the elevator, to get a great view over St. Peter's square.
- Once done here, which should be late afternoon, let's take a brief walk to the **Castel St. Angelo** and explore the ancient armaments museum and fortifications of the fortress that protected the Vatican in the past.
- Now it's time to go home for a 2-3 hour nap, if you need it.
- Dinner tonight is at the nearby **La Buca di Ripetta**, on Via di Ripetta, where you should try either the *Lasagna al Forno, Saltimbocca alla Romana,* or the *Ossobuco di Vitello.*
- After dinner, if you missed the **Trevi Fountain** last night.
- If not, you must return to the **Piazza Navona** to soak up the ambiance there at night with its fountains lit up. Either bring your own bottle of wine and sit at one of the benches or grab a table at one of the cafés and enjoy a beautiful Roman evening.

Day Three
- Time to explore some serious ruins. First stop the Forum on **Via dei Foro Imperiali** Up ahead you'll see the **Colosseum**, our next destination.
- Wander around the forum in the morning. After which head to the Colosseum.
- Lunch will be a wonderful meal at the at fantastic little wine bar **Cavour 313**, located at Via Cavour 313. It is only open from 12:30pm - 2:30pm for lunch so make sure you get there on time.
- After lunch let's walk back down the Via dei Foro Imperiali towards the Piazza Venezia to get to the **Campidoglio**. Remember to find *La Buca della Verita*. The museums on the Campidoglio should take most of the afternoon.
- When completed, make your way to the **Pantheon** (or back to the hotel if you're tired) and sit at one of the outside cafés and savor the sight of one of Rome's oldest buildings in a quaint medieval square. If it is super hot, sit by the pillars at the entrance of the Pantheon since it is always wonderfully cool there.
- Now it's back to the hotel to freshen up for your meal this evening at **La Carbonara** in **Campo dei Fiori**. Remember you were in this piazza on Day One at the Drunken Ship? They make the best *spaghetti alla vongole verace* I've ever had.

• You can stay in Campo dei Fiori for the whole evening and take in the sights and sounds of one of Rome's most popular nighttime piazzas. Most evenings they have live bands playing. You've already been to Navona, Santa Maria in Trastevere, and Trevi, the other three great piazzas where you can get a true taste of Roman nightlife.

The Perfect Four Days

Follow the above itinerary and add Day Four immediately below.

Day Four

• Time to go to church (you don't have to pray if you that's not your thing). To get to these places of worship you're going to need to take the metro and buses or rely on Roman taxis. Our first stop is the cathedral of Rome, which isn't St. Peter's, it is **San Giovanni in Laterano**.
• From here walk back towards the Colliseum on Via San Giovanni in Laterano or grab a quick cab to the **Church of San Clemente.**
• After this small church walk up to **San Pietro in Vincoli** to see some of Michelangelo's beautiful statues.
• From here **Santa Maria Sopra Minerva** is only a hop skip and a jump up the Via Cavour.
• By now you must be exhausted, and hungry, and planning ways to make the travel writer who wrote this itinerary pay. Let me assuage your frustrations by offering the chance for a repast at **Enotecantina** on Via del Croce 76. This is near the Spanish Steps so hop in a cab and direct it there. Your feet will thank me for having you take a cab.
• After lunch, when the stores re-open, let's do some antique and art shopping on the nearby streets of **Via del Babuino** and the **Via Margutta**, Rome's best for antiques.
• You were in this area on day 1. It is Rome's best shopping area. Once again explore the streets around the **Piazza di Spagna**, **Via della Croce**, **Via del Corso**, **Via dei Condotti** and admire all the different shops
• If you sustain yourself until dinner time, we will be going to try the hidden **Al Piccolo Arancio** at Vicolo Scandberg 112 near the Trevi Fountin.
• For an after-dinner snack let's visit the best ice cream parlor in Rome, **San Crispino**, on Via della Panetteria 42. Now its time to wander to the Trevi Fountain and savor the sight one more time.

The Perfect Seven Days

Follow the above itinerary for the first four days, then add Days Five through Seven immediately below.

Day Five

• Now the fun begins. We're going to a terrific town – **Frascati**. If we are lucky and it's September, we may stumble into their wine festival (and definitely stumble out).

- To get to Frascati, go to the train station, buy a ticket, go to track 27, board the small local train (takes 35 minutes and costs Euro [E] 4), and enjoy the scenery along the way.
- Enjoy the views, exploring the winding medieval streets and the relative peace and quiet compared to Rome. Don't forget to search out some of the little wine stores. My favorite is **Cantina Via Campania**.
- For dinner, let's give the wild and raucous **Pergatolo** at Via del Castello 20 a try. If you're into something more sedate, **Zaraza** at Viale Regina Margherita 21 should be your choice.
- Once dinner is done, make your way back to Rome.
- After arriving at the train station, let's go to a nearby Irish pub, **The Fiddler's Elbow** on Via dell'Olmata, that serves up fine ales, an authentic atmosphere, English conversation, and a fun evening to end an adventurous day.

Day Six

- Let's start off the day at the nearby **Mercato de Stampe**, at Piazza Fontanella, which is open from 9:00am–6:00pm Monday through Saturday. Here you can find maps, stamps, books, almost anything on the intellectual side.
- When done here, take a cab or stroll the short distance to the Church of Bones. Yes you heard me correctly. This is **Santa Maria della Concezione** at the foot of the Via Veneto. Here you will find the crypt layered with the bones of the Capuccin monks. Definitely a once in a lifetime sight.
- Mext we'll stop in the **Palazzo Barberini**, located on the Via Quattro Fontane that leads up the hill from the Piazza. This palazzo is the home of the **National Portrait Gallery**.
- After soaking up the art, walk back to the Via Veneto , the street that embodies the good life – *La Dolce Vita*. Halfway up you'll pass by the **American Embassy** on the right hand side.
- Near the top, just off of the Via Veneto, you will find **Giovanni** at Via Marche 64, a great place to eat.
- After your meal, go through the massive gate at the top of the Via Veneto, cross the street and enter the beautiful park, **Villa Borghese**. Take a leisurely stroll through the gardens to the **Galleria Borghese**. This place has beautiful paintings and sculptures galore. Wander ing the park, and savoring the art should take most of the afternoon.
- Dinner tonight is at **Dal Bolognese** in the Piazza del Popolo. Try their *fritto misto*, a fried mix of veggies, cheese, and meat.
- End the evening by going to the top of the **Spanish Steps** for a view over the city at night.

Day Seven
- Assuming today is a Sunday, you must visit the **Porta Portese** market that lines the Tevere every Sunday. Starting at the **Ponte Sublico**, you'll find all sorts of interesting antiques and junk here. A must visit if you're in Rome on a Sunday.
- After the market, it's time to return to the restaurant you have already visited which you liked best. I always do this wherever I travel. It ensures that one of my last meals is going be great, and it makes me feel somewhat like I belong.
- Return to your hotel and pack, and afterwards go for a stroll back the area you liked best. Just like eating at a favorite restaurant, revisiting a favorite place makes you feel connected, and it helps you say good bye.
- End your stroll at the top of the **Spanish Steps** again. Tonight we're going to the terrace restaurant in the **Villa Hassler** for one of the most scenic and romantic you can find in Rome. Try their specialty, *abbacchio al forno*.

Chapter 4

land & people

Land

From the top of the boot to the toe, Italy is a little more than 675 miles (1,090 kilometers) long. The widest part, in the north, measures about only 355 miles (570 kilometers) from east to west. The rest of the peninsula varies in width from 100 to 150 miles (160 to 240 kilometers) making it an easily traveled country, at least side to side. In total the peninsula of Italy fills an area of about 116,000 square miles (300,400 square kilometers).

A mountainous country, Italy is dominated by two large mountain systems – the **Alps** in the north and the **Apennines** which run down the center of the peninsula. The Alps, which are the highest mountains in Europe, extend in a great curve from the northwestern coast of Italy to the point where they merge with Austria and Slovenia in the east. Just west of the port city of Genoa, the **Maritime Alps** are the beginning of the chain. Despite mighty peaks and steep-sided valleys, the Alps are pierced by modern engineering marvels of mountain passes that have allowed commerce between Italy and its northern neighbors to flow freely. These highway and railroad tunnels provide year-round access through the mountains encouraging trade, tourism and transit.

The Apennine mountain system is an eastern continuation of the Maritime Alps. It forms a long curve that makes up the backbone of the Italian peninsula. The Apennines extend across Italy in the north, follow the east coast across the central region, then turn toward the west coast, and, interrupted by the narrow Strait of Messina, continue into Sicily.

There are numerous smaller mountains in Italy, many of volcanic ancestry, most of which are thankfully extinct. But that does not mean mother nature remains dormant in Italy. Because of the volcanic nature of the peninsula, which is caused by the earth plates shifting, Italy is prone to earthquakes. In the summer of 1997 an earthquake hit Umbria and destroyed not only towns and villages but some of Giotto's precious frescoes in the cathedral in Assisi. The region was still active for months and aftershocks were felt in Rome in November of that year. I can personally attest to that since the aftershocks woke me up at 3 o'clock one November morning. There are only two active volcanoes in all of Europe and Italy has both of them, **Mount Vesuvius** near Naples and **Mount Etna** in Sicily. Maybe that has something to do with the heated and passionate Italian temperament?

People

The Italian people are now considered to be one of the most homogeneous, in language and religion, of all the European populations. The only significant minority group is located in the region called **Trentino-Alto Adige**. These Alpine valleys of the north once made up part of the Austrian province of Tyrol, and the several hundred thousand German-speaking residents still refer to their homeland as South Tyrol. The region was incorporated into Italy after World War I, and both Italian and German are official languages in this region. Obviously, the people of the region have developed their own sense of identity – part of, but separate from, the rest of Italy.

One much smaller minority also lives in northern Italy. This group, the **Valdotains**, dwells in the region called **Valle d'Aosta** in the northwestern corner of the country, and also has two official languages, Italian and French.

About 95 percent of the Italian people speak Italian, while members of the two aforementioned groups make up the other 5%. For more than seven centuries the standard form of the language has been the one spoken in Tuscany, the region of central Italy centered around Florence. However, there are many dialects, some of which are difficult even for Italians to understand. Two of these principal dialects, those of Sicily and Sardinia, sound like a foreign language to most Italians. Because of these differences, if you have lived in Italy for a while, it is easy to discern the different accents and dialects and pinpoint where someone is from. Just like it is easy for us to figure out if someone is from New England or the South based on their accent.

But all this is just about where they live and how they speak. What are the Italians like?

Shakespeare was enamored with Italians and things Italian, as is evidenced by having many of his plays take place in Italy. And when he wrote "All the world's a stage," he definitely had Italy in mind. Filled with stunningly beautiful architecture and ancient ruins, Italy's physical landscape is a perfect

backdrop for the play of Italian life. In Italy everyone is an actor, dramatically emphasizing a point with their hands, facial expressions leaving no doubt about what is being discussed and voices rising or falling based on what the scene requires.

Play in the Piazza

Italians are some of the most animated people in the world and watching them is more than half the fun of going to Italy. These people relish living and are unafraid to express themselves. There is a tense, dramatic, exciting directness about Italians which is refreshing to foreigners accustomed to Anglo-Saxon self-control. In Italy most travelers find, without even realizing it was missing, that combination of sensuality, love and sincerity that is so lacking in their own lives.

In every piazza, on every street, there is some act being played. Whether it's two neighbors quarreling, vendors extolling the virtues of their wares, a group of older ladies chatting across the street as they lean out their windows, lovers whispering hands caressing each other as they walk, a man checking his reflection in the mirror primping for all to see, there is something about the daily street scenes all over Italy that make this country seem more alive, more animated than the rest or the world. Italians really know how to enjoy the production of living; and they love to watch these everyday scenes unfold.

Seats are strategically placed in cafés to catch all that occurs. And it is easy, even for the uninitiated, to see what is transpiring a distance away because Italians are so expressive. On the faces of Italians it is easy to read joy, sorrow, hope, anger, lust, desire, relief, boredom, despair, adoration and disappointment as easily as if they were spoken aloud. When Italians visit Northern Europe, England, or America they seem lost since they seldom know what is going on, as everyone is so expressionless.

Fashion, Art & Warfare?

Virtually all Italians share a love for fashion. The Italians are some of the best dressed people in the world, and they love to prance around like peacocks displaying their finery. 'Style over substance' is an adage that well describes Italians; but they live it with such flair that it can be forgiven. Along with the finery they wear, the beauty of the Italian people is unparalleled. All manner of coloration, including the stereotypical sensual brown eyed and brown haired beauties abound. Besides fashion Italians love art. If you ask an Italian to take your photograph expect to be posed and re-posed for at least five minutes. All Italians imagine themselves to be Federico Fellini, the famous film producer. They want to get the light just right, the shading perfect and the framing ideal. They'll pose you until you're almost blue in the face, but you'll get a great picture.

They also love architecture. What happened in the United States where beautiful buildings were destroyed all over the country to erect parking lots would never happen in Italy, where you'll also never see garish strip malls or ugly suburban sprawl. For example, the McDonalds' in Italy do not stand out the way they do in America with the golden arches glowing the location for all to see. The store signs have been blended to the architecture of the building in which they are located. A balance has been found between commercialism and aesthetic appeal that has been forgotten in America.

Their love for style over substance is why Italians have always excelled in activities where appearance is paramount, like architecture, decorating, landscaping, fireworks, opera, industrial design, graphic design, fashion and cinema. It could be conjectured that because of this pursuit of such 'effeminate' pastimes, warfare has never been Italy's forte.

During the Renaissance, battles were mere window dressing. Well paid *condottieri* headed beautifully appointed companies of men, resplendent in their finest silks, carrying colorful flags bearing the emblem of the families who were paying them. Martial music was played, songs were sung, and bloodcurdling cries were bellowed. But there was not much war being made. There were limited casualties, and when blood was shed it was usually by accident. "Armies" would pursue each other back and forth for weeks in a pageantry of color and celebration until a settlement was decided by negotiation, not bloodshed. This may seem to be a ludicrous form of warfare, but it is a brilliant expression of life, and an appreciation for living.

Religion & Family

In all, the best way to describe Italians is that they are fun. They will "live while they have life to live, and love while they have love to give." But they are also very traditional in their religion. As the center of Roman Catholicism, Italy is a shining example of Christian piety, even though many of the saints they worship are only decorated pagan gods dating back to the pre-Christian era. The Pope is revered as if he truly is sitting on the right hand of God. Virtually every holiday in Italy has some religious undertones and the people perform the necessary rites and rituals associated with those holidays with vigor and enthusiasm.

Christmas is a prime example of religion's effect. In Italy it is not as garish and commercial an activity as it is in America. Religion takes precedence over mass consumption. Having a lavish dinner with family and friends is more important than going into debt to show people you love them through product purchases. Most decorations are of religious figures, not the commercial icons like Santa Claus and Rudolph.

Religion may guide the people and present a foundation for living, but the family is paramount. In a society where legal authority is weak, the law is resented and resisted (estimates place the number of people that actually pay income tax at around 20%) and the safety and welfare of each person is mainly due to the strength of the family. Family gatherings, especially over meals are common. Knowing your third cousins is not rare. And many family members live and die all in the same small neighborhoods where they were born, even in the large cities of Florence, Venice, Naples and Rome. Family traditions are maintained, strengthened and passed on. The young interact, learn from, and respect their elders. The family is the core of Italian society, strong and durable; and from it grows a healthy sense of community.

Useful Phrases

If you want to take a few virtual language lessons before you go, visit the *Foreign Language for Travelers* website at *www.travlang.com/languages*. It's helpful and fun.

Pronunciation

Even though Italian is basically pronounced the way you see it, there are few pronuciation idiocyncrasies you should be aware of before attempting to speak the language.

In Italian you pronounce every letter. Vowels are pronounced differently in Italian than in English. In general **e** is pronunced 'ay,' **i** is 'ee,' **a** is 'ah,' **o** is always 'oh,' and **u** is 'oo.' Which would make our vowel list, a-e-i-o-u pronounced ah-ay-ee-o-oo. Alos, an 'e' at the end of a word is always proncounced. And 'e' and 'i' when used with consonants are soft.

Also, and this is important, the second to last syllable is stressed. This is different from English where the first syllable is usually stressed. For example, we pronounce 'rodeo' with the stress on the 'RO' part. The Italians would put the stress on the 'E' part. We would say **RO**deo. They would say rod**E**o. And would pronounced the **e** as 'ay.'

Other than that, Italian is pretty simple. What you see is how it is pronounced. Sure there are exceptions to that rule, but in general simplicity is the rule. Listed below should not be a considered a comprehensive pronunciation guide for each letter, but it should serve you well.

a - as in father

au - as the 'ow' in cow

b - same as in English

c, cca, ca, cco, co, cchi and **cu** - as the hard 'k' in keep

cci, ci and **ce** - as the 'ch' in cheap

(**c** is the toughest letter with many variations, including: **ca** - ka, **ce** - chay, **ci** - chee, **chi** - key, **che** - kay)

d - same as in English

e - as the 'ay' in day

f - same as in English

g, ga, go, gh and **gu** - as the hard 'g' in gate

ge and **gi** - as the soft 'g' in jar

gl - as the 'll' in million

gn - as the 'ni' in onion

h - silent. OK so not everything is as it appears.

i - as the 'ee' in keep

j - in rare appearances is soft like a 'y' in you.

k/l/m/n - same as in English

o - as the 'o' in float

p/q - same as in English

r - same as in English except for a rolling of the letter. Think of cat purring.

s - majority of cases is as the hard 's' in sit. Between two vowels is soft 's' as in hose.

sc, sca, sco, scu - as the hard sound 'sc' in scout

sce and **sci** - as the soft sound 'sh'in sheep

t - same as in English
u - preceded by a cosonant is pronounced as a 'w'
u - all other occurrences pronounced 'oo' (as in an exlamation over fireworks, oooh)
v - preceded by a consonant is pronounced as a 'w. All other times as in English.
z - like the 'ts' sound in cats

Italian is really easy when you grasp the simple pronunciation rules. Yes these rules are different from those in English, but that helps make the Italian language sound so lyrical.

General
• Excuse me, but ....
  Mi scusi, ma .... (This is a good introduction to virtually any and all inquiries listed below. It is a polite way of introducing your questions.)
• Thank you
  Grazie
• Please
  Per favore
• If you are in trouble, yell "Help"
  Aiuto (eyeyootoh)

If you are looking for something, a restaurant, a hotel, a museum, simply ask "where is ...:"
• Where is the restaurant(name of restaurant)
  Dov'é il ristorante_____?
• Where is the hotel (name of hotel)
  Dov'é l'hotel _____?
• Where is the museum (name of museum)
  Dov'é il museo _____?
  Note: *(Dov'é is pronounced "Dove [as in the past tense of dive] -ay")*

Travel-Trains
• Where is track number ...
  Dov'é binnario ...

1	*uno*	11	*undici*
2	*due*	12	*dodici*
3	*tre*	13	*tredici*
4	*quatro*	14	*quatordici*
5	*cinque*	15	*quindici*
6	*sei*	16	*sédici*
7	*sette*	17	*diciassette*

8	*otto*	18	*diciotto*
9	*nove*	19	*dicianove*
10	*dieci*	20	*venti*

- Is this the train for Florence (Roma)?
  E questo il treno per Firenze (Roma)?
- When does the train leave?
  Quando partira il treno?
- When is the next train for Naples/Milan?
  Quando e il prossimo treno per Napoli/Milano?

Travel-Cars
- Where is the next gas station?
  Dov'é la prossima stazione di benzina?
- I would like some oil for my car.
  Voglio un po di olio per il mio automobile.
- Can you change my oil?
  Puo fare un cambio dell'olio per me?
- I need a new oil filter.
  Voglio un nuovo filtro dell'olio.

Travel-Public Transport
- Where is the (name of station) metro station?
  Dov'é la stazione di Metro _____?
- Where can I buy a Metro ticket?
  Dov'é posso prendere un biglietto per il Metro?
- How much is the ticket?
  Quanto costa il biglietto?
- Where is the bus stop for bus number ___.
  Dov'é la fermata per il bus numero ___?
- Excuse me, but I want to get off.
  Mi scusi, ma voglio scendere.
- Where can I catch a taxi?
  Dov'é posso prendere un tassi?

Purchasing
   The following you can usually get at a drug store (*Farmacia*).
- Where can I get...?
  Dov'é posso prendere ...?
- toothpaste
  dentifricio
- a razor
  un rasoio

- some deodorant
  un po di deodorante
- a comb
  un pettine
- rubbers
  dei profilattici
- a toothbrush
  un spazzolino
- some aspirin
  un po di aspirina

The following you can usually get at a *Tabacchaio*:
- stamps
  francobolli
- a newspaper
  un giornale
- a pen
  una penna
- envelopes
  buste per lettere
- some postcards
  dei cartoline

The following you can usually get at an *Alimentari:*
- some mustard
  un po di senape
- some mayonnaise
  un po di maionese
- tomatoes
  tomaté
- olive oil
  olio d'oliva
- I would like ... *Voglio ...*
- 1/4 of a pound of this salami
  un etto di questo salami
- 1/2 of a pound of Milanese salami
  due etti di salami milanese
- 3/4 of a pound of this cheese
  tre etti di questo formaggio
- a small piece of mozzarella
  un piccolo pezzo di mozzarrella
- a portion of that cheese
  una porzione di quel' formaggio

- a slice of ham
  una fetta (or una trancia) di prosciutto
- one roll
  un panino
- two/three/four rolls
  due/tre/quatro panini
- How much for the toothpaste, razor, etc?
  Quante costa per il dentifrico, il rasoio, etc.
- How much for this?
  Quante costa per questo?
- Excuse me, but where I can find a ...?
  Mi scusi, ma dov'é un ... ?
- pharmacy
  Farmacia
- tobacconist
  Tabacchaio
- food store
  Alimentari
- bakery
  Panificio

Communications
- Where is the post office?
  Dov'é l'ufficio postale?
- Where is a post box?
  Dov'é una buca delle lettere
- Where is a public telephone?
  Dov'é una cabina telefonica?
- May I use this telephone?
  Posso usare questo telefono?

Hotel
- How much is a double for one night/two nights?
  Quanto costa una doppia per una notte/due notte?
- How much is a single for one night/two nights?
  Quanto costa una singola per una notte/due notte?
- Where is the Exit/Entrance?
  Dov'é l'uscita/l'ingresso?
- What time is breakfast?
  A che ora e prima colazione?
- Can I get another....for the room?
  Posso prender un altro ... per la camera?

• blanket
  coperta
• pillow
  cuscino
• bed
  letto

Miscellaneous
• Where is the bathroom?
  Dov'é il cabinetto?
• What time is it?
  Che oré sono?
• Sorry, I don't speak Italian.
  Mi scusi, ma non parlo italiano.
• Where can I get a ticket for ...?
  Dov'é posso prendere un biglietto per ...?
• a soccer game
  una partita di calcio
• a basketball game
  una partita di pallacanestro
• the theater
  il teatro
the opera
  l'opera
• You are truly beautiful.
  Tu se veramente bella (spoken to a woman informally)
  lei e veramente bella (spoken to woman formally)
  Tu se veramente bello (spoken to a man)
  lei e veramente bello (spoken to man formally)
• Can I buy you a drink?
  Posso comprarti una bevanda?
• Do you speak any English?
  Parli un po d'Inglese?
• Do you want to go for a walk with me?
  Voi andare a una passeggiata con me?
• Is there anyplace to go dancing nearby?
  Ch'é un posto per ballara vicino?

Chapter 5

A short Italian history is a contradiction in terms. So much has occurred in that narrow strip of land which has affected the direction of the entire Western world, that it is difficult to succinctly describe its history in a brief outline. We've had the Etruscans, Romans, Greeks, 'Barbarian' hordes, Holy Roman Emperors, the Papacy (although not the whole time – the seat of the Catholic Church was moved to Avignon, France from 1305 until 1377), painters, sculptors, the Renaissance, the Medici family, Crusaders, Muslim invaders, French marauders, Spanish conquistadors, Anarchists, Fascists, American soldiers, Communists, Red Brigades, and much more.

What follows is an attempt at a brief outline of the major events on the Italian peninsula, concentrating mainly on the Roman Empire, since we will cover the Renaissance later. I don't claim to be an historian, only a mere *scrittore di guidi di viaggio*, so please accept this brief historical background as a basic foundation for your travel enjoyment.

Etruscans

Long before Romulus and Remus were being raised by a she-wolf to become the founders of Rome, Italy was the home of a people with an already advanced civilization – the **Etruscans**. This powerful and prosperous society almost vanished from recorded history because not only were they conquered by Rome but were also devastated by marauding **Gauls**. During these conquests once from the south, the other from the north, it is assumed that most of their written history was destroyed, and little remains of it today. The **Eugubine Tablets**, the Rosetta Stone for

Central Italy, are the best link we have to understanding the Etruscan language. These tablets have corresponding Umbrian language text, which evolved from the Etruscan, and a corresponding rudimentary form of Latin.

Because of the lack of preserved examples of their language, and the fact that the inscriptions on their monuments has been only partially deciphered, archaeologists have gained most of their knowledge of the Etruscans from studying the remains of their city walls, houses, monuments, and tombs.

From their research, archaeologists have been able to ascertain that the Etruscans were a seafaring people from Asia Minor, and that as early as 1000 BCE (Before the Common Era) they had settled in Italy in the region that is today **Tuscany** and **Lazio**. An area basically from Rome's Tiber River north almost to Florence's Arno River. Their influence eventually embraced a large part of western Italy, including Rome.

As a seafaring people, the Etruscans controlled the commerce of the Tyrrhenian Sea on their western border. After losing control of Rome, they strengthened their naval power through an alliance with Carthage against Greece. In 474 BCE, their fleet was destroyed by the Greeks of Syracuse. This left them vulnerable not only to Rome, but the Gauls from the north. The Gauls overran the country from the north, and the Etruscans' strong southern fortress of **Veii** fell to Rome after a ten-year siege (396 BCE). But as was the Roman way, the Etruscans were absorbed into their society, and eventually Rome adopted many of their advanced arts, their customs, and their institutions.

The Etruscan Kings of Early Rome

When Greece was reaching the height of its prosperity, Rome was just beginning its ascent to power. Rome didn't have any plan for its climb to world domination; it just seemed to evolve. There were plenty of setbacks along the way, but everything seemed to fall into place at the right time; and the end result was that at its apex, Rome ruled most of the known world.

The early Romans kept no written records and their history is so mixed with fables and myths that historians have difficulty distinguishing truth from fiction. The old legends say that **Romulus** founded the city in 753 BCE when the settlements on the seven hills were united. But this date is probably later than the actual founding of the city. As is the case with many emerging societies, the founders are mythical figures, as was Romulus, but there is some evidence that the kings who followed him in the ancient stories actually existed.

Shortly before 600 BCE, Rome was conquered by several Etruscan princes. The Etruscans were benevolent conquerors, an attitude that Rome would itself adopt, and set about improving the native lifestyles to match their own.

The Etruscans built Rome into the center of all Latium, their southern province. Impressive public works were constructed, like the huge sewer

Cloaca Maxima, which is still in use today. Trade also expanded and prospered, and by the end of the 6th century BCE Rome had become the largest and richest city in Italy.

The Native Roman Population Revolts

But in spite of all this progress and development, the old Latin aristocracy wanted their power back from the Etruscans. **Junius Brutus** led a successful revolt around 509 BCE, which expelled the Etruscans from the city. That was when the people of Rome made themselves a **republic**.

Rome's successful thwarting of the Etruscans helped the young republic gain the confidence it needed to begin its long history of almost constant conquest. At the time Rome was only a tiny city-state, much like the city-states that were flourishing at the same time in Greece, with a population of roughly 150,000. But in a few centuries this small republic would eventually rule the known world.

Rome's Early Republic

In the beginnings of early Rome, the **patricians** (Rome's aristocracy) controlled the government and ruled the **plebes** or **plebeians** (Common People). Since they were shut out from the government, their wealthy fellow citizens politically and economically oppressed the plebeians. The internal history of the republic for the next three centuries is mainly a story of how the plebeians wrested reform after reform from the patricians and gained an increasing amount of control over their existence and eventually directed the path of Roman politics.

The impetus that forced the plebes to seek their freedom was the shackle of the patrician's oppression. The wealthy patricians continued to expand their land holdings, taking the best property and increasing their herds until they monopolized the public pasturelands. They also continued the practice of lending money at ruinous interest to the small proprietors, eventually reducing the plebes to abject slavery when they could not pay.

At the same time, the population of Rome was increasing so fast that the arable land and their primitive farming methods could not support the increase in hungry mouths. Also, the burden of constant warfare fell most heavily on the plebeians, who had to leave their subsistence farms to fight the state's battles. This didn't allow them to provide for their families or even begin to pay off the debts they incurred to start farming the land.

To right these wrongs the plebeians went on what today would be called a general strike. In 494 BCE, they marched out of Rome in a body and threatened to make a new city. At the fear of losing its large labor force, the patricians agreed to cancel all debts and to release people who were in prison for debt. By 350 BCE, the plebes gained the ability to participate fully in the Republic's government.

While these important changes were taking place at home, the little city-state had been gradually extending the reach of its power. Compelled at first to fight for its very existence against its powerful neighbors (mainly the Etruscans, Aequians, and Volscians), Rome gradually fought its way into the leadership role of all the Italian peoples, called the **Latin League**. This dependence on military strength to establish then maintain their republic helped develop the patterns necessary for Rome to conquer of the world.

Roman Conquest of Italy

The Latin League started to develop a dislike for the growing power and arrogance of their ally and attempted to break away from its control; but Rome won the two year war that followed (340-338 BCE) and firmly established their dominance. The truce that was made between Rome and the Latin League was broken a few years later (326 BCE) by the **Samnites**, and a wild-fought struggle ensued, with a variety of interruptions, until the decisive battle of **Sentinum** (295 BCE), which made Rome supreme over all central and northern Italy.

Southern Italy, still occupied by a disunited group of Greek city-states, still remained independent. Alarmed at the spread of Roman power, the Greek cities appealed to **Pyrrhus**, king of Epirus in Greece, who heeded their warning and inflicted two telling defeats on the Roman army. He then crossed to Sicily to aid the Greek cities there in eliminating Carthaginian rule. Unfortunately this was a classic example of spreading your forces too thin and trying to fight a war on two fronts. Encouraged by the arrival of a Carthaginian fleet to combat the Greeks, Rome renewed its struggle for the Greek city-states in southern Italy, and in 275 BCE defeated Pyrrhus in the battle of **Beneventum** and a new phrase was born: a Pyrrhic victory – where you win the war but at excessive cost. Eventually, one by one the Greek cities were taken, and just like that Rome was ruler of all Italy.

Keeping the Conquered Lands Happy

Rome gradually wove the lands conquered into the fabric of a single nation, contented and unified. Rome could have exploited the conquered cities of Italy for its own interests, but instead made them partners in the future success of the entire empire.

Rome also set about establishing colonies of its citizens all over Italy. Almost one sixth of all Italy was annexed and distributed among these colonizing Roman citizens. By encouraging this colonization, a common interest in the welfare of Rome spread throughout the Italian peninsula.

The Punic Wars

The previous centuries of warfare had developed Rome into a nation of soldiers. The republic's only remaining rival in the western Mediterranean was the Phoenician colony of **Carthage**. While Rome obviously was the chief land power, Carthage was the established sea power of that era. They were so powerful that Carthage had a policy of sinking any trading vessel of any other city that dared to bid for a share of the rich commerce of the Mediterranean region. Rome could not abide by these restrictions, so a series of **Punic Wars** for Mediterranean supremacy began in 264 BCE.

The courage and endurance of Rome's forces were tested to the utmost in this long and devastating series of wars; but after the battle of **Zama** (202 BCE), Carthage was reduced to the position of a vassal state. In 146 BCE, during the **Third Punic War**, because Carthage was again beginning to flex its military and economic might, Rome once again savagely attacked its rival and razed the city Carthage eliminating them forever as an opposing force.

Winning World Mastery

With the destruction of Carthage, Rome was well on its way to world domination, at least the known world at the time. Emboldened with this sudden rise to power, the new generation of Roman statesmen ignored the just policies of their successful predecessors; and they forced most of the conquered lands to be administered by governors (**proconsuls**), and did not offer these conquered people a real chance to become full Roman citizens. These foreign governors ruled like czars, and through the enormous taxes levied on the local populations, tried to amass in their one year of office enough wealth to last them a lifetime. A situation that did not ingratiate them, or Rome, to the local populations.

From these taxes, incredible amounts of gold, jewelry, and money in the form of taxes poured into Rome from all over the world, and the ancient simplicity of Roman life gave way to luxury. Morals were undermined, and vice and corruption flourished. Vast estates began to be established by buying up the small farms of the common people. And if they weren't taken over, the common peasants were too poor to compete with the hordes of slaves who were brought it to work the great plantations. One after another of the farmers either failed or were bought out, and as a result the streets of Rome grew clogged with ruined farmers, as well as with discharged soldiers and the poor from all over Italy. These people lived on state and private charity, as well as the bribes that political candidates gave them to curry their favor in the next election.

The End of the Roman Republic

As a result of an increasing disparity in income, once again a conflict began to brew between the aristocracy (formerly the Patricians) and the vast, oppressed and poor citizens (formerly the Plebes). A number of brave men tried to step forward and right the wrongs that were occurring, but each person who did ended up assassinated for his efforts.

To try and maintain a semblance of order a law was forcibly passed that transferred supreme power from the people to the **Senate**. The aristocrats, who became Senators, however, were too corrupt and feeble to hold power, and the Roman Republic came to an end. At this time, two brilliant statesmen, **Gaius Julius Caesar** and his great-nephew **Augustus** (**Octavian**), helped save Rome by scrapping the old republican framework and remolded the tottering structure into an empire. All power was gradually concentrated in the hands of a single ruler, who was backed by the might of the Roman Legions.

Two Centuries of Peace & Prosperity

With the establishment of the Empire, two centuries of profound peace ensued, the **Roman Peace** (*Pax Romana*), only broken by small frontier warfare. In the provinces men held power responsibly, because they feared the omnipotent wrath of the emperor, and in Rome literature and civilization flourished. Increasingly the Mediterranean came to resemble one great nation, with paved roads leading from the south of Italy all the way up into what are now France and Germany. After the Roman Empire crumbled, road transportation did not return to the same level of quality until well into the 19th century. Even today fragments of Roman roads and ruins still exist in Britain, aqueducts and bridges can be seen in France, Roman wells are still used in the Egyptian oases of the Sahara Desert, and Roman amphitheaters can be visited in the heart of Tunisia. All over the Mediterranean the influence of Roman remains for all to see.

After two centuries, the pursuit hedonism once again obsessed the people of Rome. The rich amused themselves by giving splendid feasts. The poor had their circuses where free bread and wine was distributed. Slave labor had degraded the once sturdy peasantry to the status of serfs or beggars, and the middle class, who once had been the backbone of the nation, had almost disappeared. A welfare mentality overcame the population. And Roman governors of the provinces once again began to concentrate on siphoning off as much money as possible during their short term of office, instead of keeping abreast of the economic and political climate.

The Fall of the Roman Empire

Political decay, economic troubles, and decadent living were sapping the strength and discipline of the Roman Empire. At this time, German 'barbarians,' who were a violent people living on the fringes of the empire and led by warrior chiefs, began to attack the edges of the empire in the 4th century CE (Common Era). These **Goths, Vandals, Lombards, Franks, Angles, Saxons**, and other tribes defeated unprepared Roman garrison after garrison, and sacking and pillaging the decadent and crumbling empire. In 330 CE, when the Roman emperor **Constantine** moved the capital to **Constantinople** (today's

Istanbul in Turkey), the Western Roman Empire began a gradual decline. Order made way for chaos and rival governors fought over fragments of Italian territory to increase their power.

With the fall of the Western Roman Empire in CE 476, this was the beginning of the period called the **Dark Ages**. They were so called because Roman civilization and law collapse along with its artistic and engineering achievements. Order was lost, well developed distribution trade routes evaporated, people went back to the way life was like prior to Roman rule and in most cases it was a step backward in time. Coordinated agriculture was lost, the roads fell into ruin, irrigation system were not maintained, public health measures were ignored and the resulting poor hygiene set the stage for coming of the Black Plague.

What the 'barbarians' did bring with them, however, an aspect of their freedom and independence that helped shape the future of Western civilization, was their belief that the individual was important, more so than the state. In contrast, the Romans believed in the rule of the state over the people – in despotism, or the concept of a benevolent dictator. The 'barbarians' gave us a rudimentary form of personal rights, including more respect for women, government by the people for the people, and a system of law which represented the needs and wishes of the people being governed. In essence, these 'barbarians' lived under the beginnings of democracy in Europe.

After the Roman Empire

Even **Charlemagne**, who had conquered the Lombard rulers and had himself crowned emperor of the **Holy Roman Empire** in 800 CE, could not stop the disintegration of everything the Roman Empire had built. To maintain a semblance of order, the Holy Roman Empire became a union between the Papacy and Charlemagne in which management of the empire was shared.

But Charlemagne's Holy Roman Empire fell apart after his death, only to be refounded by the Saxon **Otto I** in 962 CE, bringing Italy into a close alliance with Germany. From that time until the 1800s, the Holy Roman Empire took on many shapes, sizes, and rulers. It included at different times France, Germany, Luxembourg, the north of Italy (because the Muslims, and then the Normans had taken control of Italy south of Naples), Austria, Switzerland, and more. It had rulers from the Saxon Line, Franconian Line, Hohenstaufen Line, Luxembourg Line, and the Hapsburg Line. It may have been constantly in flux but it did last over 1,000 years in some shape or form.

While the Holy Roman Empire expanded and contracted, it eventually contracted itself outside of Italy, leaving Italy an amalgamation of warring city-states. Florence, Venice, Milan, and the Papacy became the strongest of these contending powers and they came to dominate the countryside while feudalism declined. They drew their riches from the produce of their fertile river valleys and from profits generated in commerce between the Orient and Europe. This trade flowed in through Venice, Pisa, Genoa and Naples and passed through to other European cities on its way across the Alps.

The Italian Renaissance

Under the patronage of the Papacy and of the increasingly prosperous princes of the city-states, such as the **Medici** of Florence, the scholars, writers, sculptors and painters created the masterpieces of literature, art, and science that made the **Italian Renaissance** one of the most influential movements in history. In this period many splendid churches, palaces, and public buildings were built that still inspire awe in Italians and visitors alike. But at the same time as this resurgence in artistic expression, almost completely lost after the fall of the Roman Empire the dominant city states in Italy – Florence, Pisa, Siena, Venice, Perugia, Milan, the Papal States and more – were filled with social strife and political unrest.

Pawn of Strong Nations

While Italy was being torn by struggles between the local rulers and the Papacy, and among themselves, strong nations were developing elsewhere in Europe. As a result of this, Italy became an area of conquest for the other powers struggling for European supremacy. French and Spanish rivalry over Italy began in 1494. **Charles VIII of France** valiantly fought his way through the peninsula to Naples, but by 1544 **Charles I of Spain** had defeated the French three times and had become ruler of Sicily, Naples, and Milan.

For centuries the city-states of Italy remained mere pawns in other nations' massive chess games of power. Italian city-states passed from one to another of Europe's rulers through war, marriage, death, or treaty. The **Papacy** was, however, usually strong enough to protect its temporal power over the areas in central Italy known as the **States of the Church**, or the **Papal States**.

Spanish & Austrian Rule

For over 150 years (1559-1713), Spain was the dominant power in Italy. Then the **Treaty of Utrecht** (1713) ended the **War of the Spanish Succession** and established the Austrian Hapsburgs in place of the Spanish as Italy's paramount power.

As time went by the Spanish began to feel slighted by the amount of land that had been ceded to Austria, so they sought to take back their former possessions. In 1734 **Don Carlos**, son of Philip V of Spain, conquered Naples and Sicily, and ruled the area as **Charles III of Naples**.

During this time, in the 18th century, enormous wealth was held by the few while the masses lived in squalor. The peasants existed virtually without rights or defenders. In many areas they lived in abject poverty, and as a result crime rates were shockingly high despite harsh laws and punishments.

Ideas of reform coming from other nations found some response among the intellectuals and the middle class, and the concepts of liberty and equality stirring in France gained many Italian supporters. Many Italians were so blinded with these French egalitarian ideals that they offered assistance to a foreigner, **Napoleon Bonaparte**, when he began his conquest of Italy in the 1790s.

Then when Napoleon was defeated, most Italian states went back to their former sovereigns. For example, Venezia (Venice) was re-absorbed into Austrian rule, Naples and Sicily were re-absorbed into Spanish rule, and the city-states in Umbria become once again part of the Papal States. Italy remained a pawn in European politics without a political will of its own.

Movement for Political Unity

Eventually hatred of foreign rule mounted, and with it grew the **Risorgimento**, or movement for political unity. Such secret societies as the Carbonari (charcoal burners, the name given from their use of charcoal burners' huts for meeting places), plotted against the Austrians, but the **Carbonari Revolts** were crushed in 1821 and again in 1831 by Austrian troops.

Then the idealistic republican leader, **Giuseppe Mazzini**, organized his revolutionary society, **Young Italy**, and called upon **Charles Albert**, king of Sardinia-Piedmont and a member of the ancient House of Savoy, to head a movement to liberate Italy. By early 1848, revolts had broken out in many regions, and constitutions had been granted to Naples, Piedmont, and Tuscany. But when Mazzini drove out the pope and set up a short-lived republic in Rome the French came to the pope's aid, and Austria quelled the revolt in the north. Despite this outside interference, the ball was rolling, and when Charles Albert abdicated his rule in Sardinia-Piedmont to his son **Victor Emmanuel II**, the stage was set for a run at independence.

Under the able leadership of the shrewd diplomat **Count Camillo di Cavour**, Victor Emmanuel's minister, Sardinia-Piedmont grew strong in resources and in alliances. Cavour was also aware that no matter how real Italian patriotic fervor was, the country would never be unified without help from abroad, so he cleverly forged an alliance with **Napoleon III** of France. Then in the spring of 1859 Austria was goaded into declaring war against Sardinia-Piedmont and France, and was defeated by the combined French and Italian forces. Italy claimed the lands of Lombardy for a united Italy, but France kept as its bounty the kingdom of Venezia.

To consolidate their power, Cavour and Victor Emmanuel lobbied the peoples of Tuscany, Modena, Parma, and Emilia who eventually voted to cast out their princes and join Sardinia-Piedmont as parts of a unified Italy.

Napoleon III consented to such an arrangement, but only if Savoy and Nice voted to join France. (Politics is too complicated. I'll stick to travel writing).

Garibaldi To The Rescue

The second step toward a united Italy came the next year, when the famous soldier of fortune **Giuseppe Garibaldi** and his thousand red-shirted volunteers stormed the island of Sicily and the rest of the Kingdom of Naples on the mainland. The people everywhere hailed him as a liberator, and the hated Bourbon king was driven out.

In February 1861 **Victor Emmanuel II** was proclaimed king of Italy, and he began working closely with Garibaldi. Now only the Papal States and Venezia remained outside of the new Italian nation. Venezia joined in 1866 after Prussia defeated Austria in alliance with Italy. The Papal States and **San Marino** were now the only entities on the peninsula outside the Italian kingdom. Not yet as small and isolated as it is today, San Marino was then about the size the current region of Lazio making it a valuable prize for a unified Italy.

Vatican Captured - Kingdom of Italy United

Since French troops still guarded the pope's sovereignty, Victor Emmanuel, being the apt pupil of Cavour (who had died in 1861), did not want to attack the French and perhaps undo all that had been accomplished. Then, miraculously in 1870, the **Franco-Prussian War** forced France to withdraw its soldiers from Rome, at which time Italian forces immediately marched in.

Pope Pius IX, in his infinite lack of wisdom and understanding, excommunicated the invaders and withdrew behind the walls of the Vatican. There he and his successors remained 'voluntary prisoners' until the **Concordat of 1929**, or **Lateran Treaty**, between Italy and the Holy See, which recognized the temporal power of the pope as sovereign ruler over Vatican City (all 108.7 acres of it, or about 1/6 of a square mile!). The rest of the Papal States was absorbed into the new unified Italy, as was San Marino, except for the small, fortified town on top of a butte-like hill that remains independent today.

Modern Italy - The Beginning

Staggering under a load of debt and heavy taxation, giant steps needed to still be taken for Italy to survive. Leaders of the various regions, always trying to gain an edge, were in constant disagreement – even in active conflict. At the same time citizens, used to the ultimate control of despotic rule, found it difficult to adopt the ways of parliamentary government. As a result, riots and other forms of civil disorder were the rule in the latter half of the 19th century.

Despite all of these problems, in the typical Italian mode of functioning despite complete political chaos, an army and navy were developed; railroads, ports, and schools were constructed; and a merchant marine was developed. At the same time, industrial manufacturing started to flourish as it was all over the world.

But then, in 1900, **King Umberto I** (son of Victor Emmanuel II) was assassinated by anarchists – in what was to turn out to be a string of assassinations during that time period all over Europe – and his son, **Victor Emmanuel III**, rose to the throne. Although having joined with Germany and Austria in the **Triple Alliance** in 1882, by the early 1900s Italy began to befriend France and England. With Austria's invasion of Serbia in 1914 after the assassination of Archduke Ferdinand of Austria, Italy declared its neutrality despite being Austria's ally. In April 1915, Italy signed a secret treaty with the **Allies** (Russia, France, and England), and the next month it stated that it had withdrawn from the Triple Alliance. On May 23, 1915, the king of Italy declared war on Austria.

When World War I ended in 1918, the old Austro-Hungarian Empire was broken up. Italy was granted territory formerly under Austrian rule, including "unredeemed Italy" of the Trentino in the north and the peninsula of Istria at the head of the Adriatic.

Mussolini & Fascism

The massive worldwide depression after World War I brought strikes and riots, which were fomented by anarchists, socialists, and Communists. The government of Victor Emmanuel III seemed powerless to stop bands of former servicemen lawlessly roaming the country. In these bands, **Benito Mussolini** saw his opportunity to gain power. With his gift of oratory he soon molded this rabble into enthusiastic, organized groups in many communities all over Italy, armed them, and set them to preserving the order which had been had destroyed. These bands formed the nucleus of his black-shirted **Fascist** party, whose emblem was the *fasces*, the bundle of sticks that had symbolized the authority of the Roman Empire.

On Oct. 28, 1922, the **Blackshirts**, meeting in Naples, were strong enough, well enough prepared, and willing to march on Rome and seize the government. The king, fearing civil war and his own life, refused to proclaim martial law, forced the premier to resign, and asked Mussolini to form a shared government. Within a few years Mussolini, *Il Duce* (The Leader), had reorganized the government so that the people had no voice at all. Mussolini first abolished all parties except his own Fascist party, and took from the Chamber of Deputies the power to consider any laws not proposed by him. The king remained as a figurehead because he was revered by the people and had the support of many wealthy and important families. In 1939 when Mussolini replaced the Chamber of Deputies with the Chamber of Fasces and Corporations, composed of all his henchmen, no semblance of popular rule remained.

Intimidation or violence crushed all opposition. Suspected critics of the regime were sentenced to prison by special courts or were terrorized, tortured or murdered by Blackshirt thugs. News was censored and public meetings could not be held without the government's permission. The new Fascist state was based on the doctrine that the welfare of the state is all-important and that the individual exists only for the state, owes everything to it, and has no right of protection against it. It was a return to the despotism of the later Roman Empire.

A Return to The Roman Empire?

Mussolini, like other Italian leaders before him, longed to create a new Roman empire and to bring back Italy's lost glory. So, in 1935, with his large army and recently expanded navy, he attacked and conquered the weak, backward, and poorly defended African country of Ethiopia.

In October 1936, at Mussolini's invitation, the **Rome-Berlin Axis** was formed between Italy and Nazi Germany to oppose the power of France and England. At this time Mussolini was considered the stronger ally of the two. In April 1939, Italy invaded Albania, and which that time Italy and Germany became formal military allies.

But when Germany's program of aggression plunged it into war with England and France on September 3, 1939, Italy at first adopted the position of a non-belligerent. But on June 10, 1940, Italian forces attacked southeastern France in an invasion coordinated with German forces in the north.

Defeat in World War II

Italy lacked the military power, resources, and national will to fight a large-scale modern war. Within six months, Italian armies met defeat in Greece and North Africa. In fact a running joke during World War II was that Italian tanks had only one gear: reverse. Italy then humbly accepted the military assistance of Germany. This soon grew into complete economic and military dependence, and Italy was forced to let Germany occupy it, control its home affairs, and Mussolini became a German puppet.

The end of the war found Italy with the majority of its industry and agriculture shattered. During its occupation, the Germans had almost stripped Italy's industry bare by commandeering supplies. Italian factories, roads, docks, and entire villages were ruined by the Allied bombing raids and during the invasion. To make things worse, as the Germans retreated they had wrecked whatever industries and transportation remained.

Even with the Allies contributing substantial quantities of food, clothing, and other supplies, the people were cold, hungry, and jobless. After the war, the United Nations Relief and Rehabilitation Administration gave more aid to Italy than to any other country. Reconstruction lagged, however, because of internal political turmoil, a situation that has become something of a theme in postwar Italian politics.

Postwar Political Changes

On May 9, 1946, Victor Emmanuel III formally abdicated in favor of his son, who reigned for less than one month as **Umberto II**, because on June 2, 1946, the Italian people voted to found a republic. They then elected deputies to a Constituent Assembly to draft a new constitution.

Finally on February 10, 1947, the peace treaty between Italy and the Allies was ready to be signed. The treaty stripped Italy of its African 'empire' of Libya, Italian Somaliland, and Eritrea. The pact also ceded the Dodecanese Islands to Greece, placed Trieste under UN protection, made minor boundary changes with France, and gave about 3,000 square miles to Yugoslavia, including most of the Istrian peninsula.

Italy had to pay $360 million in reparations, and was also forced to restore independence to Ethiopia and Albania. One lone gain was that **South Tyrol**, which Austria had been forced to cede after World War I, remained with Italy; and eventually, in 1954, **Trieste** was given to Italy through a pact with Yugoslavia.

On January 1, 1948, Italy's newly formed constitution became effective. It banned the Fascist party – though today there are a number of political parties in Italy that go by another name but informally call themselves *Fascisti* – and the monarchy. Freedom of religion was guaranteed, though Catholicism remained the state religion.

But a constitution alone cannot recreate a country. Italian leaders had the double task of creating a stable parliamentary system of government while at the same time restoring the economy. (They still haven't solved the first problem.) The main economic hindrance was the poverty-stricken, agriculturally dependent south contributing little to the improving industrial economy of the north. As a result there were many riots and moments of intense civil unrest.

Land Reform

One of the reasons that the south of Italy was so poor was because much the lands there, as well as in Sicily and Sardinia were among the last aristocratic strongholds of large-scale landowners. The estates of these landowners covered many thousands of acres and employed only small numbers of laborers, mostly at harvest time. These landless peasants, who had no work during much of the year, lived in nearby villages and small towns and barely made ends meet all year. These people either stayed peaceful and subservient, contributed to civil unrest, or emigrated to find better employment and living conditions elsewhere.

In the early 1950s, the Italian parliament passed special land reform laws that divided large private estates into small farms and distributed them to the peasants. The new owners were given substantial government support for their first years on the land, and the previous owners received cash compensation. Thousands of new small farms were created in this way during the 1950s, and farm production, as a result of the land reform and other measures, rose quickly.

The Italian government not only invested large sums of money in land reform but at the same time also started to develop the infrastructure in the south to help the farmers. New roads were built to help carry produce to market, and new irrigation systems, needed during the long, dry summers, were constructed. Warehouses and cold storage facilities for farm products were provided, and the government also helped to introduce new crops.

Chaos Mixed With Stability

Even with the south's new-found prosperity, Italy's economic development was mainly due to spectacular gains in industrial production in the north. But then during the mid-1960s, Italy began to suffer from severe inflation. A government austerity program to combat this trend produced a decline in profits and a lag in investments. To add insult to injury, devastating floods – the worst in 700 years which were caused by severe soil erosion – hit the country in 1966, ravaging one third of the land and causing losses of more than $1.5 billion. To make matters even worse, some of the priceless art treasures of Florence were irreparably damaged when the flood waters poured through that city.

In 1971 Italy had its largest economic recession since the country's post-World War II recovery. Strikes affected nearly every sector of the economy as Italian workers demanded social reforms. The problems of inflation, unemployment, lack of housing, and unfavorable balance of payments continued in the 1970s.

When Italy was about to pull out of its economic problems, political terrorism escalated, culminating in March 1978, when **Aldo Moro**, leader of the Christian Democratic party and former premier, was abducted in Rome by the **Red Brigades**, an extreme left-wing terrorist group. During the two months that Moro was held, Rome was like an armed camp, with military roadblocks everywhere. I was living there at that time and the memory of submachine guns being pointed at me still lingers. Eventually Moro was found murdered and left in the trunk of his car.

In 1980, in Italy's worst natural disaster in more than 70 years, an earthquake killed more than 3,000 persons in the Naples area. As if things could only get worse, in May 1981 a Turkish political dissident tried to kill Pope John Paul II in St. Peter's Square. Also in 1981, a corruption scandal involving hundreds of public servants who were allegedly members of a secret society erupted and brought down the government.

Economic conditions in the early 1980s were affected by growing recession and rising inflation. The Vatican Bank and the Banco Ambrosiano of Milan, Italy's biggest private banking group, were involved in a major banking scandal that forced the liquidation of Banco Ambrosiano in 1982. Two more natural disasters, an earthquake and a landslide, caused widespread damage in the regions of Perugia and Ancona in late 1982.

In 1989, another bank became involved in a scandal when it was revealed that an American branch of the Banca Nazionale del Lavoro had loaned billions of dollars to Iraq. Then severe drought occurred throughout Italy in the winter of 1989 and in Venice some canals were unusable because water levels had dropped so low. And still, into the late 1990s, the Italian government is under intense investigation for rampant corruption which includes officials taking bribes from, or actively colluding with members of the Mafia.

Despite all of this, the Italian economy continues to improve, to the point where it is one of the more successful in Europe. Throughout all of this chaos, Italy perseveres. It's almost as if without a reasonable amount of disorder, Italy could not survive.

Most recently, a separatist political party has emerged, called the **Northern League** (La Lega Nord) is attempting to create the 'federal republic of Padania' in the industrial north of Italy. Founded in 1984, the party is now gaining support and popularity because most northern Italians feel that they pay a disproportionate share of the country's taxes. Taxes which they say go to support the impoverished south and keep the bloated government functioning in Rome.

This idea of splitting Italy in two is not so far fetched when you realize that only in the last century has the peninsula been one unified country. There have always been glaring differences in culture between south and central Italy and their northern cousins. And to emphasize this point, in the last local elections, the Northern League won over 10% of the vote.

What's New?

Italy has raced into the 21st century along with the rest of Europe by adopting a new currency, the **Euro**, which will join the economies of a number of countries and help the Europeans counterbalance the economic power of America and the almighty dollar. The jury is still out on the impact this will have.

To get to the point where they could be included in this economic gambit, Italy had to pass some rather unpopular laws. The ones which were most controversial were the those associated with food production. Italy is home to some of the world's most diverse food products, all made with time-honored tradition, but sometimes these traditions did not meet hygienic standards required by the European Union. Despite the outcry over having to change the way their beloved food is made, since these standards were imposed food poisonings have decreased all over Italy and the quality and taste of the food products have stayed the same.

Immigration is another issue Italy shares with its European brethren. The economies of Third World countries are not keeping pace with those in the First World. As a result all of Europe is experiencing unparalleled immigration pressure from Africa, the Middle East, Asia, and Eastern Europe. Italy is being especially overrun with refugees from the Balkans, who initially came to avoid the recent war there, but are now escaping their stagnant economies as well.

All of these changes seem to have enhanced the pleasant chaos that is life in Italy.

Chapter 6

Climate & Weather

The climate in Italy is as varied as the country itself, but it never seems to get too harsh. As a result any time is a good time to travel to Italy since most of the country has a Mediterranean type of climate, meaning cool, slightly rainy winters and warm, dry summers.

The summers are mild in the north, but winters there tend to be colder because these regions are in or near the Alps. The Alps do play a role in protecting the rest of Italy from cold northern winds. Because Italy is a peninsula and thus surrounded by water, the entire country never seems to get too hot except for the south and Sicily. These regions are very hot in the summer, and in the winter, wetter than normal. Winter temperatures along and near the coasts of southern Italy seldom drop to freezing in winter, and summer temperatures often reach 90 degrees F (32 degrees C) or higher.

Winter is the rainy season, when stream beds that remain empty during much of the year fill to overflowing. In Venice during this time, even a slight rain fall will cause the city to be flooded. Be aware of this when traveling there during this time. In the summer, since they are on the water, Venice can be somewhat muggy.

Rome has the mildest climate all year round, although the *sirocco* – a hot and humid red sand tinged wind blowing from North Africa – can produce stifling weather in August every other year or so. Winters are very moderate with snow being extremely rare. But it is wise to dress warmly.

When to Go

Basically, anytime is good time to travel to Italy. The climate doesn't vary greatly making Italy a pleasant trip any time of year. Then again I'm biased – I spent eight wonderful years in Italy and I think it's fantastic all year. The busiest tourist season is from May to October, leaving the off-season of Spring and Autumn as the choice times to have Italy all to yourself.

I do believe though that the best time to go is the off-season, when there are less tourists around. More specifically, October and November and March and April are perfect times not only because of the weather but also because of the lack of tourists. December is also fun because there are so many festivals during the Christmas season.

Most people come during the summer making many of the most popular tourist cities like Rome, Florence and Venice over crowded. Then in August the entire country literally shuts down, since most Italians abandon the cities to vacation at the beach or in the mountains. Personally I find August a wonderful time to visit too, since the cities become sparse with people. Granted many restaurants, shops and businesses are closed during this time but the country is still as scenic and beautiful.

The summer months though packed with people in the cities are great months to come and visit the hiking trails of the Alps and Appenines. Remember to bring clothing for colder weather even though it is summer.

The sidebar below offers you a breakdown by season of the best regions to visit during those times.

Italy's Four Seasons

Spring – Italy has an early spring. The best places to visit are Florence, around Naples and Sorrento, Sicily, and Rome.

Summer – Summer can be a little hot in certain places, so to cool you down there are plenty of beach resorts along most of Italy's coast, especially in Liguria on the Italian Riviera. But the best place to go is the mountains of Tuscany or the northern regions of Lombardia, Piemonte, or Trentino Alto-Adige. This is not to say that Rome or Venice would not be pleasant, just crowded with tourists and relatively warm.

Autumn – This is a pleasant time to visit Rome and other major central and southern cities, since they are less crowded and much cooler.

Winter – Time for winter sports. You can find ski centers in the Alps as well as the central Apennines near Florence and Rome. Also at this time, the southern regions and Sicily are at their best.

What to Pack

One suitcase and a carry-on should suffice for your average ten day trip. Maybe the best advice for shoppers is to pack light and buy clothes while you're there, since there are countless clothing stores from which you can buy yourself any needed item. Also if you pack light it will be easier to transport your belongings. A suitcase with wheels is important, but since there are endless numbers of stairs even the wheels won't relieve the burden of lifting your bag every once and awhile. And even if there are no stairs, because of the uneven state of Italian pavements, and in some cases non-existent sidewalks, pulling a wheel suitcase can be cumbersome. I prefer a wheeled carry-on, but if you're the rugged type, a back pack is the best choice.

To clean your clothes you can always find a local *Tintoria* (dry cleaner) if your hotel does not supply such a service. If you want to do it yourself, it's best to look for a *Lavanderia* – coin operated laundromat – instead. Remember also to pack all your personal cosmetic items that you've grown accustomed to, since, more than likely, they're not available in Italian stores. The Italian culture just hasn't seemed to grasp the necessity of having 400 types of toothpaste, or 200 types of tampons. If you take medication remember to get the drug's generic name because name brands on medications are different all over the world.

An important item to remember, especially if you're traveling in the winter time, is an umbrella, a raincoat, and water-proof shoes. You never know when the rain will fall in the winter. You should also bring a small pack, or knapsack to carry with you on day trips. A money belt is also advised, because of pick pockets though I've never had any problems. The same can be said for handbags and purses to thwart the potential risk of purse snatchers.

But most importantly, bring a good pair of comfortable walking shoes or hiking boots. A light travel iron is not a bad idea if you cannot abide wrinkles; but a more sensible option is to pack wrinkle free clothes. And in the summer, if you want to get into most of the churches, remember to pack long pants or something to cover your legs. Tank tops and halter top type shirts are also not considered appropriate attire.

And finally, an important item to remember if you are sexually active are condoms. They can be expensive in Italy so remember to bring along your own.

Public Holidays

Offices and shops in Italy are closed on the dates below. So prepare for the eventuality of having virtually everything closed and stock up on picnic snacks, soda, whatever, because in most cities and towns there is no such thing as a 24 hour a day 7-11. The Italians take their free time seriously. To

them the concept of having something open 24 hours a day is, well, a little crazy.
- **January 1**, New Year's Day
- **January 6**, Epiphany
- **April 25**, Liberation Day (1945)
- **Easter Monday**
- **May 1**, Labor Day
- **August 15**, *Ferragosto* and Assumption of the Blessed Virgin (climax of Italian family holiday season. Hardly anything stays open in the big cities through the month of August)
- **November 1**, All Saints Day
- **December 8**, Immaculate Conception
- **December 25/26**, Christmas

Listed below are some dates that may be considered public holidays in different areas of Italy, so prepare for them too:
- **Ascension**
- **Corpus Christi**
- **June 2**, Proclamation of Republic (celebrated on the following Saturday)
- **November 4**, National Unity Day (celebrated on following Saturday)

Local Festival Days & Their Patron Saints

Town	Date	Patron Saint
Venice	April 25	St. Mark
Florence	June 24	St. John the Baptist
Genoa	June 24	St. John the Baptist
Turin	June 24	St. John the Baptist
Rome	June 29	Sts. Peter and Paul
Palermo	July 15	Santa Rosalia
Naples	Sept. 19	St. Gennaro
Bologna	Oct. 4	St. Petronio
Cagliari	Oct. 30	St. Saturnino
Trieste	Nov. 3	San Giusto
Bari	Dec. 6	St. Nicola
Milan	Dec. 7	St. Ambrose

Making Airline Reservations

Since airfares can vary so widely it is advised to contact a reputable travel agent and stay abreast of all promotional fares advertised in the newspapers. Once you're ticketed getting there is a breeze. Just hop on the plane and 6-

8 hours later you're there. Italy's two main international airports are Rome's **Fiumicino** (also known as **Leonardo da Vinci**) and Milan's **Malpensa**, which handle all incoming flights from North America and Australia.

There are other, smaller regional airports in Bologna, Florence, Pisa and Venice that accept flights from all over Europe as well as the United Kingdom, but not from North America or Australia. So, if you are only visiting the fairy tale city of Venice and want to fly almost directly there, contact your travel agent and make sure they get you on an airline, most likely British Air, that will allow for a transfer in London and a connection to Venice.

Fares are highest during the peak summer months (June through mid-September) and lowest from November through March (except during peak Christmas travel time). You can get the best fares by booking far in advance. This will also assure you a good seat. Getting a non-stop flight to Italy at the last minute is simply an impossibility during the high season. If you are concerned about having to change your schedule at the last minute, and do not want to book far in advance, look into some special **travel insurance** that will cover the cost of your ticket under such circumstances. Check with your travel agent about details and pricing since these, like ticket prices, change almost on a daily basis.

Passport Regulations

A visa is not required for US or Canadian citizens, or members of the European Economic Community, who are holding a valid passport, unless that person expects to stay in Italy longer than 90 days and/or study or seek employment. While in Italy, you can apply for a longer stay at any police station for an extension of an additional 90 days. You will be asked to prove that you're not seeking such an extension for study or employment, and that you have adequate means of support. Usually permission is granted almost immediately.

When staying at a hotel, you will need to produce your passport when you register; and most likely the desk clerk will need to keep your passport overnight to transcribe the relevant details for their records. Your passport will most likely be returned that same day. If not, make sure you request it since it is an Italian law that identification papers be carried at all times. Usually a native driver's license will suffice but I always carry my passport. If you are concerned about pickpockets, keep your passport in the front pocket of your pants. I keep mine in a small zip lock bag so it won't get moist with perspiration.

To find out all the information you need to know about applying for a US Passport go to the State Department website at *http://travel.state.gov/passport_services.html.*

If you have failed to renew your passport and you need one right away try **Instant Passport**, *Tel. 800/284-2564, www.instantpassport.com.* They promise to give you 24-hour turnaround from the time they receive your passport pictures and requisite forms. They charge $100 plus overnight shipping on top of all fees associated with passport issuance.

Another company, **American Passport Express**, *Tel. 800/841-6778, www.americanpassport.com*, offers three types of service – expedited (24 hours), express (three to four business days) and regular. Prices range from $245 to $135.

For **Canadian travelers**, the Canadian Passport Office *(www.dfait-maeci.gc.ca/passport/menu.asp)* also offers an excellent web site to help walk you through the steps to apply for the passport. .

For **British travelers**, the United Kingdom Passport Agency *(www.ukpa.gov.uk)* offers a similar level of exemplary service on their web site.

Vaccinations

No vaccinations are required to enter Italy, or for that matter, to re-enter the U.S., Canada, or any other European country. But some people are starting to think it may be wise, especially for Hepatitis A. One of those people is Donna Shipley, B.S.N, R.N. and President of Smart Travel, an international health service organization. She says, "Even though the perception is that Italy is safe and clean, it is still not like North America. In other words it is better to be safe than sorry. Prevention makes sense."

For information about vaccinations contact:
• **Smart Travel**, *Tel. 800/730-3170*

Travel Insurance

This is the most frequently forgotten precaution in travel. Just like other insurance, this is for 'just in case' scenarios. The beauty of travel insurance is that it covers a wide variety of occurrences, such as trip cancellation or interruption, trip delay/missed connection, itinerary change, accident medical expense, sickness medical expense, baggage and baggage delay, and medical evacuation/repatriation. And to get all that for a week long trip will only cost

Registration by Tourists

This is usually taken care of within three days by the management of your hotel. If you are staying with friends or in a private home, you must register in person at the nearest police station within that three day period. Rome has a special police information office to assist tourists, and they have interpreters available: *Tel. 461-950 or 486-609.*

you $25. You'll spend more than that on the cab ride from the airport when you arrive.

For travel insurance look in your local yellow pages or contact the well-known international organization below:

• **Travelex**, *Tel. 800/228-9792*

Customs Regulations

Duty free entry is allowed for personal effects that will not be sold, given away, or traded while in Italy: clothing, bicycle, moped no bigger than 50cc, books, camping and household equipment, fishing tackle, one pair of skis, two tennis racquets, portable computer, record player with 10 records, tape recorder or Dictaphone, baby carriage, two still cameras with 10 rolls of film for each, one movie camera with 10 rolls of film (I suppose they mean 10 cassette tapes now), binoculars, personal jewelry, portable radio set (may be subject to small license fee), 400 cigarettes, and a quantity of cigars or pipe tobacco not to exceed 500 grams (1.1 lbs), two bottles of wine and one bottle of liquor, 4.4 lbs of coffee, 6.6 lbs of sugar, and 2.2 lbs of cocoa.

This is Italy's official list, but they are very flexible with personal items. As well they should be, since technology is changing so rapidly that items not listed last year could be a personal item for most people this year (i.e. Sony Watchmans, portable video games, etc.).

Getting to Italy

Flying to Italy

Alitalia is Italy's national airline. As you probably know, most international carriers have amazing service, pristine environments, serve exquisite food and overall are a joy to travel – but to be honest Alitalia is not one of them. If you want to experience the chaos of Italy at 30,000 feet, fly Alitalia. Despite all of this rhetoric, Alitalia does have the most frequent direct flights from North America to Italy, and as such they are the most convenient carrier to take to Italy.

Airlines

Below is a list of some other major carriers and their flights to Italy:

• **Alitalia**, *Tel. 800/223-5730 in US, www.alitalia.it/eng/index.html. Toll free in Italy 800/1478/65642. Address in Rome – Via Bissolati 13.* Flights from the United States, Canada, and the United Kingdom.

• **Air Canada**, *Tel. 800/776-3000; www.aircanada.com. Toll free in Italy 800/ 862-216. Rome address – Via C. Veneziani 58.* Flights from

Canada to London or Paris, then connections on another carrier to Rome or Milan.

- **American Airlines**, *Tel. 800/433-7300; www.americanair.com. Rome Tel. 06/4274-1240, Via Sicilia 50. Italy E-mail: abtvlaa@tin.it.* Direct flights from Chicago to Milan.
- **British Airways**, *Tel. 800/247-9297; www.british-airways.com. Toll free in Italy 1478/12266. Rome address – Via Bissolati 54.* Connections through London's Heathrow to Rome, Milan, Bologna, Venice, and Palermo.
- **Delta**, *Tel. 800/221-1212; www.delta-air.com. Toll free in Italy 800/864-114. Rome address – Via Po 10.* Direct flights from New York to Rome or Milan.
- **Northwest**, *Tel. 800/2245-2525; www.nwa.com. KLM in Rome 06/652-9286.* Flights to Amsterdam connecting to KLM and onto Rome or Milan.
- **TWA**, *Tel. 800/221-2000; www.twa.com. Toll free in Italy 800/841-843. Rome address – Via Barberini 59.* Direct flights from New York's JFK to Rome or Milan.
- **United**, *Tel. 800/538-2929; www.ual.com. Rome Tel. 06/4890-4140, Via Bissolati 54.* Direct flights from Washington Dulles to Milan.
- **US Airways**, *Tel. 800/622-1015; www.ual.com. Toll free in Italy 800/870-945.* Direct flights from Philadelphia to Rome.

Discount Travel Agents
     The best way to find a travel agency for your travel to Italy is by looking in your local yellow pages; but if you want to get the same flights for less, the three organizations below offer the lowest fares available. I have had the best service and best prices from *www.lowestfare.com*, but the others are good also.
- **Fly Cheap**, *Tel. 800/FLY-CHEAP*
- **Fare Deals, Ltd.**, *Tel. 800/347-7006*
- **Lowestfare.com**, *Tel. 888/777-2222*
- **Airdeals.com**, *Tel. 888/999-2174*

     In conjunction, listed below are some online travel booking services that offer great fares. Online travel searching can be cumbersome, since there is a registration process and each has a different approach to the reservation and booking process. In essence, what you learn from these services is what your travel agent goes through when they work with reservation systems like Apollo, Worldspan and System One. Also, if you shop here to find out what prices and availability are and then book your flights the regular way, from the airline or a live travel agent, these online service do not like that. Some will even terminate your registration if you shop too frequently without buying.

With that said, here are some websites:
• **Internet Travel Network**, *www.itn.net*
• **Preview Travel**, *www.previewtravel.com*
• **Expedia**, *www.expedia.com*
• **Travelocity**, *www.travelocity.com*

Courier Flights

Acting as an air courier – whereby you accompany shipments sent by air in your cargo space in return for discounted airfare – can be one of the least expensive ways to fly. It can also be a little restrictive and inconvenient. But if you want to travel to Italy, at almost half the regular fare, being a courier is for you.

The hassles are (1) that in most cases you have to get to the courier company's offices before your flight, (2) most flights only originate from one city and that may not be the one where you are, (3) since you usually check in later than all other flyers you may not get your choice of seating, (4) you can only use a carry-on since your cargo space is being allocated for the shipment you are accompanying, (5) your length of stay is usually only 7-10 days – no longer, and (6) courier flights don't do companion flights, which means you fly alone.

But contrary to the common impression, as a courier you usually do not even see the goods being transported and you don't need to check them through customs. Also you are not legally responsible for the shipment's contents – that's the courier company's responsibility – according to industry sources and US Customs. All this aside, if you are interested in saving a large chunk of change, give these services a try:
• **Halbart Express**, *Tel. 718/656-8189*
• **Now Voyager**, *Tel. 212/431-1616. Fee of $50*
• **Discount Travel International**, *Tel. 212/362-8113*
• **Airhitch**, *Tel. 212/864-2000; www.airhitch.org.* Air hitching is the least expensive but they are also the most restrictive. You really need to be very flexible, i.e. can travel at the drop of a hat.

For more information about courier flights, listed below are some books you can buy or organizations you can contact:
• **"Insiders Guide to Air Courier Bargains"** *by Kelly Monaghan. Tel. 212/569-1081.* Contact: The Intrepid Traveler, *Tel. 212/569-1081; www.intrepidtraveler.com.* Company is owned by Monaghan.
• **International Association of Air Travel Couriers**, *Tel. 561/582-8320, www.courier.org.*
• **"A Simple Guide to Courier Travel,"** *Tel. 800/344-9375*

Getting To & From the Airports in Rome

Rome's **Fiumicino (Leonardo da Vinci) Airport** has a number of different ways to get there and back. You can take a direct train, a local train, a taxi, a shuttle service, and a a bus for night time arrivals and departures. If you arrive at **Rome' Ciampino Airport** you can choose between bus, taxi, and shuttle services. Please refer to Chapter 13 for Rome's *Arrivals & Departures* section for more details.

Getting To & From the Airports in Milan

To get to and from **Milano Malpensa**, there is a bus from the square beside **Milano Centrale Railway Station** that leaves every 30 minutes, but only in the morning. The only other option is a rather expensive taxi fare.

Milano Linate can be accessed by bus from the square beside **Milano Centrale Railway Station** every 20 minutes. There is also ATM Municipal Bus Service 73 from Piazza San Babila (corner of Corso Europa) every 15 minutes. Duration for both is 30 minutes. Please refer to Chapter 19 for Milan's *Arrivals & Departures* section for more details.

Accommodations

What to Expect at Hotels

Don't be surprised by hotel taxes, additional charges, and requests for payment for extras, such as air conditioning that make your bill larger than expected. Sometimes these taxes/service charges are included in room rates but you should check upon arrival or when you make your reservation. Remember to save receipts from hotels and car rentals, as 15% to 20% of the value-added taxes (VAT) on these services may be refunded if you are a non-resident. For more information, call **I.T.S. Fabry**, *Tel. 803/720-8646* or see Chapter 9, *Shopping*, Tax-Free Shopping section.

The Italian Tourist Board categorizes all of the hotels in Italy with a star rating. A five star deluxe hotel (*****) is the best, a one-star hotel (*) is the least desirable and usually the least expensive too. The term *Pensione* is in the process of being phased out, and these smaller, bed-and-breakfast type inns are being replaced with a designation of one-star (*), two-star (**), or three star (***) hotel.

Making Reservations

I recommend faxing the hotel(s) of your choice inquiring about availability for the dates you are interested in, as well as the rate for those dates. Faxing is preferable to calling since you can quickly and easily communicate your

Diplomatic & Consular Offices In Italy

These are the places you'll need to contact if you lose your passport or have some unfortunate brush with the law. Remember that the employees of these offices are merely your government's representatives in a foreign country, not God. They cannot fix your problems in the blink of an eye, but they will do their best on your behalf.

Embassies & Consulates in Rome
- **Australia** - *Via Alessandria 205, Tel. 06/852-721*
- **Canadian Embassy** - *Via GB de Rossi 27, Tel. 06/445-981*
- **Great Britain** - *Via XX Settembre 80a, Tel. 06/482-5441, www.grbr.it*
- **Ireland** - *Piazza di Campitelli 3, Tel. 06/697-912*
- **New Zealand** - *Via Zara 28, Tel. 06/441-7171, nzemb.roma@flashnet.it*
- **South Africa** - *Via Tanaro 1, Tel. 06/852-541, sae@flashnet.it*
- **United States** - *Via Veneto 199, Tel. 06/46741*

US Consulates
- **Florence** - *Lungarno Amerigo Vespucci 38. 1 50123 Firenze, Tel. 055/239-8276*
- **Genoa** - *Piazza Portello 6, 16124 Genova, Tel. 010/290-027*
- **Milan** - *Via Principe Amadeo 2/10, 20121 Milano, Tel. 02/290-045-59*
- **Naples** - *Piazza della Repubblica, 80122 Napoli, Tel. 081/583-8111*
- **Palermo** - *Via Vaccarini 1, 90143 Palermo, Tel. 091/343-546*

Canadian Consulates
- **Milan** - *Via Vittor Pisani 19, 20124 Milano, Tel. 02/669-7451 and 669-4970 (night line)*

UK Consulates
- **Cagliari** - *Via San Lucifero 87. 09100 Cagliari, Tel. 070/66 27 55*
- **Florence** - *Palazzo Castelbarco, Lungarno Corsini 2, 50123 Firenze, Tel. 055/21 26 94, 28 41 33 and 28 74 49*
- **Genoa** - *Via XII Ottobre 2, 16121 Genova, Tel. 010/48 33-36*
- **Milan** - *Via San Paolo 7, 1-20121 Milano, Tel. 02/80 34 42*
- **Naples** - *Via Francesco Crispi 122. 08122 Napoli, Tel. 081/20 92 27, 63 33 20 and 68 24 82*
- **Palermo** - *Via Marchese di Villabianca 9, 90143 Palermo, Tel. 091/33 64-66*
- **Torino** - *Corso M. d'Azaglio 60. 10126 Torino, Tel. 011/68 78 32 and 68 39 21*
- **Trieste** - *Via Rossini 2, 14132 Trieste, Tel. 040/6 91 35*
- **Venice** - *Accademia 1051, R301 00 Venezia, Tel. 041/272 07*

information, reducing any long distance telephone charges. Obviously if the hotel listed has an e-mail address, that form of communication is preferable.

Also, since most Italians who run hotels speak English, it is possible to write your fax or e-mail in English; but if you want to practice your Italian, they usually appreciate any effort at communicating in their own language. Personally, I write my requests in both English and Italian so that there is no confusion as to the information imparted.

When writing the dates you are interested in, make sure you spell out the month, since here in America we transpose the month and day in numeric dates. For example, in the US January 10, 2001 would appear numerically as 1/10/01. In Europe, it would appear as 10/01/01. See where the confusion could come in?

Expect a reply to your communication within a few days. If you do not get a reply send another message. Sometimes faxes get lost in the night shift. To book your room you will need to send the hotel a credit card number with expiration date in a reply communication. This will ensure that you show up. So if you have to cancel your trip for whatever reason, make sure you contact the hotel and cancel your room – otherwise you will be charged.

Hotel Prices

The prices that are listed sometimes include a range, for example E50-75. The first number in the range indicates what the price is during the off-season, the second price is the going rate during high season. If there is no range, then the hotel doesn't raise its rate for the off-season.

The high season is generally April through September, with Christmas and New Year's week thrown in. Other high seasons will include local festivals, like the **Palio** in Siena or **Calcio in Costume** in Florence. Also, the high season for the ski areas will be winter, not summer, so it is important to inquire up front about what the actual rates will be.

Hotel Prices, Post-Jubilee

In the year 2000, a **Jubilee** celebration year for the Catholic Church, there was a massive influx of tourists. Hotel prices rose accordingly and many have continued to stay in place . The Italians are going to try and make as much money as possible off of this Y2K situation, so be prepared for some of the prices in this book to be a little lower than what are quoted to you by the hotels. That may not be the case, but just to make sure, please confirm the cost of your room beforehand.

Hotel Rating System

The star rating system that the Italian Tourist Board officially uses has little to do with the prices of the hotels, but more to do with the amenities you will find. The prices for each category will vary according to the locale, so if it's a big city, a four star will be super-expensive; if it's a small town, it will be priced like a three star in a big city.

In the ambiguous way of the Italians, nothing is ever as it seems, which means that even the amenities will be different for each star category depending on whether you are in a big city or a smaller town. But basically the list below is what the ratings mean by star category:

*****Five star, deluxe hotel**: Professional service, great restaurant, perfectly immaculate large rooms and bathrooms with air conditioning, satellite TV, mini-bar, room service, laundry service, and every convenience you could imagine to make you feel like a king or queen. Bathrooms in every room.

****Four star hotel**: professional service, most probably they have a restaurant, clean rooms not so large, air conditioning, TV (usually via satellite), mini-bar, room service, laundry service and maybe a few more North American-like amenities. Bathrooms in every room.

***Three star hotel**: a little less professional service, most probably do not have room service, should have air conditioning, TV and mini bar, but the rooms are mostly small as are their bathrooms. Some rooms in small town hotels may not have bathrooms.

Two star hotel: Usually a family run place, some not so immaculate and well taken care of as higher rated hotels. Mostly you'll only find a telephone in the room, and in big cities you'll be lucky to get air conditioning. About 50% of the rooms have either a shower/bath or water closet and sometimes not both together. Hardly any amenities, just a place to lay your head. The exception to this is in small towns, where some two stars are as well appointed as some of the best three stars.

*One star hotel**: Here you usually get a small room with a bed, sometimes you have to share the rooms with other travelers. The bathroom is usually in the hall. No air conditioning, no telephone in the room, just a room with bed. These are what used to be the low-end *pensiones*. Definitely for budget travelers.

Agriturismo

If you have ever wanted to work on a farm, Italy has a well organized system where you can do just that. Initially the idea behind **Agriturismo** started as a way for urban Italians to re-connect with their old towns and villages, and through that to the earth again; but every year it has grown in popularity. Traditionally you would rent rooms in family farmhouses, but some accommodations have evolved into more hotel type, bed-and-breakfast like situations with separate buildings on the farms for agriturists. Since there is such a large demand for agriturism, two separate competing bodies have published directories to assist people trying to reconnect with mother nature.

Both of the books sold by these groups are also available at selected bookstores, like the Feltrinelli Bookstores listed in this guide:

• **Agriturist**, *Via Vittorio Emanuele 89, 00186 Roma, Tel. 06/658-342. Open Monday-Friday 10:00am-noon and Tuesday, Wednesday, Thursday 3:30-5:30pm. Closed Saturday and Sunday.*

• **Turismo Verde** (Green Tourism), *Via Mariano Fortuny 20, 00196 Roma, Tel. 06/361-1051.*

Mountain Refuges

There are a number of mountain refuges (*rifugi*) available for rent in the Alps and Apennines, many of which are run by the **Club Alpino Italiano (CAI)**. If you are a member, you can get maps and information about hiking, and all necessary information about the *rifugi*. The CAI has offices all over Italy, but there is limited centralization of resources and information, and most offices are run by volunteers and/or avid hikers. Contact the CAI offices listed below, or the local tourist office in the city nearby where you want to go hiking, for any available information.

Even if you are not a member, they are usually rather flexible about accommodating your needs. And if they are not, you can join CAI at any of their offices by simply bringing a photo of yourself and E50. With that you will receive a *tessera* (identification document) which is valid for discounts on all CAI merchandise and on stays in the *rifugi* for a year. You can renew by mail.

The *rifugi* are generally dormitory style and meals are available at a cost of around E12 per person. There are private *rifugi* which charge rates comparable to about one or two star hotel accommodations. All rifugi are usually only open from July to September and are booked well in advance.

• **CAI-Milano**, *Via Silvio Pellico 6, Tel. 02/8646-3516.*

• **CAI-Roma**, *305 Corso Vittorio Emanuelle II, 4th floor, Tel. 06/686-1011, Fax 06/6880-3424. Website: www.frascati.enea.it/cai*

Renting Villas & Apartments

One of the best ways to spend a vacation in Italy is in a rented villa in the country or in an apartment in the center of town. It makes you feel as if you actually are living in Italy and not just passing through. Staying in "your own place" gives your trip that little extra sense of belonging.

The best way to find a place of your own in Italy is to contact one of the agencies listed below that specialize in the rental of villas and apartments in Italy:
- **At Home Abroad, Inc.**, *405 East 58th Street, New York, NY 10022. Tel. 212/421-9165, Fax 212/752-1591*
- **Astra Maccioni Kohane** (CUENDET), *10 Columbus Circle, Suite 1220, New York, NY 10019. Tel. 212/765-3924, Fax 212/262-0011*
- **B&D De Vogue International, Inc.**, *250 S. Beverly Drive, Suite 203, Beverly Hills CA. Tel. 310/247 8612, 800/438-4748, Fax 310/247-9460*
- **Better Homes and Travel**, *30 East 33rd Street, New York, NY 10016. Tel. 212/689 6608, Fax 212/679-5072*
- **CIT Tours Corp.**, *342 Madison Ave #207, New York, NY 10173. Tel. 212/ 697-2100, 800/248-8687, Fax 212/697-1394*
- **Columbus Travel**, *507 Columbus Avenue, San Francisco, CA 94153. Tel. 415/39S2322, Fax 415/3984674*
- **Destination Italia, Inc.**, *165 Chestnut Street, Allendale, NJ 07401. Tel. 201/ 327-2333, Fax 201/825-2664*
- **Europa-let, Inc.** *92 N. Main Street or P.O. Box 3537, Ashland, OR 97520. Tel. 503/482-5806, 800/4624486, Fax 503/482-0660*
- **European Connection**, *4 Mineola Avenue, Roslyn Heights, NY 11577. Tel. 516/625-1800, 800/345 4679, Fax 516/625-1138*
- **Four Star Living, Inc.**, *640 Fifth Avenue, New York, NY 10019. Tel. 212/ 518 3690, Fax 914/677-5528*
- **Heaven on Hearth**, *44 Kittyhawk, Pittsford, NY 14534. Tel. 716/381-7625, Fax 716/381-9784*
- **Hidden Treasure of Italy**, *934 Elmwood, Wilmette IL 60091. Tel. 708/853- 1313. Fax 708/853-1340*
- **Hideaways International**, *P.O. Box 1270, Littleton, MA 01460. Tel. 508/ 486-8955, 800/8434433, Fax 508/486-8525*
- **Homes International**, *Via L. Bissolati 20, 00187 Rome, Italy. Tel. 39/06/ 488-1800, Fax 39/06/488-1808. E-mail: homesint@tin.it*
- **Home Tours International**, *1170 Broadway, New York, NY 10001, Tel. 212/6894851, Outside New York 800/367-4668*
- **Interhome Inc.**, *124 Little Falls Road, Fairfield, NJ 07004. Tel. 201/882- 6864, Fax 201/8051 742*
- **International Home Rentals**, *P.O. Box 329, Middleburg, VA 22117. Tel. 703/687-3161, 800/221-9001, Fax 703/687-3352*
- **International Services**, *P.O. Box 118, Mendham, NJ 07945. Tel. 201/545- 9114, Fax; 201/543-9159*
- **Invitation to Tuscany**, *94 Winthrop Street, Augusta, ME 04330. Tel. 207/ 622-0743*
- **Italian Rentals**, *3801 Ingomar Street, N.W., Washington, D.C. 20015. Tel. 202/244-5345, Fax 202/362-0520*

- **Italian Villa Rentals,** *P.O. Box 1145, Bellevue, Washington 98009. Tel 206/ 827-3964, Telex: 3794026, Fax 206/827-2323*
- **Italy Farm Holidays,** *547 Martling Avenue, Tarrytown, NY 10591. Tel. 914/ 631-7880, Fax 914/631-8831*
- **LNT Associates, Inc.,** *P.O. Box 219, Warren, MI 48090. Tel. 313/739-2266, 800/582 4832, Fax 313/739-3312*
- **Massimo Carli,** *Web: www.incentro.it*
- **Overseas Connection,** *31 North Harbor Drive, Sag Harbor, NY 11963. Tel. 516/725-9308, Fax 516/725-5825*
- **Palazzo Antellesi,** *175 West 92nd Street #1GE, New York NY 10025. Tel. 212/932-3480, Fax 212/932-9039*
- **The Parker Company,** *319 Lynnway, Lynn MA 01901. Tel. 617/596-8282, Fax 617/596-3125*
- **Prestige Villas,** *P.O. Box 1046, Southport, CT 06490. Tel. 203/254-1302. Outside Connecticut 800/336-0080, Fax 203/254-7261*
- **Rent a Home International, Inc.,** *7200 34th Avenue. N.W. Seattle, WA 98117. Tel. 206/789-9377, 800/488-RENT, Fax 206/789-9379, Telex 40597*
- **Rentals In Italy,** *Suzanne T. Pidduck (CUENDET), 1742 Calle Corva, Camarillo, CA 93010. Tel. 805/987-5278, 800/726-6702, Fax 805/482-7976*
- **Rent-A-Vacation Everywhere, Inc.** *(RAVE), 585 Park Avenue, Rochester, NY 14607. Tel. 716/256-0760, Fax 716/256-2676*
- **Unusual Villa Rentals,** *Tel. 804/288-2823. Fax 804/342-9016. E-mail: johng@unusualvillarentals.com; www.unusualvillarentals.com*
- **Vacanze In Italia,** *P.O. Box 297, Falls Village, CT 06031. Tel. 413/528-6610, Fax 413/528-6222. E-mail: villrent@taconic.net. Website: www.homeabroad.com*
- **Villas and Apartments Abroad, Ltd.,** *420 Madison Avenue. New York, NY 10017. Tel. 212/759-1025. 800/433-3021 (nationwide), 800/433-3020 (NY)*
- **Villas International,** *605 Market Street, Suite 610, San Francisco, CA 94105. Tel. 415/281-0910, 800/221-2260, Fax 415/281-0919*

Youth Hostels

Youth Hostels (*ostelli per la gioventu*) provide reasonably priced accommodations, specifically for younger travelers. A membership card is needed that is associated with the youth hostel's organization, i.e. a student ID card. Advanced booking is a must during the high season since these low priced accommodations fill up fast. Hundreds of youth hostels are located all over Italy. Contact the Tourist Information office when you arrive in the city to locate them.

Home Exchange

A less expensive way to have "a home of your own" in Italy is to join a **home swapping club**. These clubs have reputable members all over the world. All you'd need to do is coordinate travel plans with a family in a location you'd like to stay in Italy, and exchange houses. This type of accommodation will save you a lot of money.

The best one that we know is **Home Link**, *PO Box, Key West FL 33041, Tel. 305/294-3720, Tel. 800/638-3841, Fax 305/294-1448.*

Getting Around Italy

Italy is connected by an extensive highway system (*Autostrada*), a superb train system, a series of regional airports, and naturally, since Italy is virtually surrounded by water and has a number of islands, a complete maritime service involving ferries, hydrofoils, and passenger liners. The mode of transportation you select will depend on how long you're staying in Italy and where you are going.

In general, if you have plenty of time on your hands, there will be no need to fly around Italy, and travel by train and car will suffice. If you are going to rural, off-the-beaten path locations, you'll need a car, because even if the train did go to where you're going, the *Locale* would take forever since it stops at every town along the way.

By Air

You can fly between many Italian destinations quite easily. If you are on business, using air travel makes sense to fly from Milan to Rome, but not if you are a tourist. You could enjoy a relaxing three hour train ride in the morning to Florence, spend a day shopping and sightseeing, then get on another three hour train ride to Rome and get there in time for dinner. And the entire cost would only be around $100, a lot less than if you had flown.

But if you insist on flying, here is a list of towns that have airports that receive service from the larger venues in Rome and Milan: Alghero, Ancona, Bari, Bologna, Brindisi, Cagliari, Catania, Firenze, Genoa, Lamezia Terme, Lampedusa, Napoli, Olbia, Pantelleria, Pescara, Pisa, Reggio Calabria, Torino, Trapani, Trieste, Venice, Verona.

By Bicycle

You may think that riding a bicycle among Italian drivers would be ludicrous, but they are actually very respectful and courteous of bicyclists. Cycling is a national sport in Italy, so your reception in Italy will be more as a hero than a villain, as you can all too often be viewed in North America. And if you get tired, one benefit of the Italian train system is that many trains have bicycle cars to accommodate travelers such as us. So if you get to one location and feel like you want a breather, or if you want to make better time, you can hop on trains to your next destination.

Another way to hike or bike around Italy is with an organized tour group. Two such organizations are **Ciclismo Classico**, and **BCT Scenic Walking**. They offer magnificent tours all over Italy, from Sardinia to Tuscany, to Venice and beyond. Their guides are extremely knowledgeable and professional and speak impeccable English. And with Ciclismo you stay at fine hotels, eat fantastic food, meet wonderful people, and constantly interact with the locals – all while seeing Italy up close and personal on a bicycle. I find this to be a truly authentic way to appreciate and experience Italy.

To get more information, contact **Ciclismo Classico**, *13 Marathon Street, Arlington MA 02174; Tel. 800/866-7314 or 781/646-3377, Fax 617/641-1512, E-mail:info@ciclismoclassico.com, Web: www.ciclismoclassico.com.* **BCT Tours**, *2506 N. Clark St #150, Chicago, IL 60614. Tel. 800/736-BIKE, Fax 773/404-1833, E-mail: adventure@cbttours. Web: www.cbttours.com.*

If you are an avid hiker, and enjoy seeing a country from the perspective of the back roads or trails, contact this excellent organization, **BCT** (British Coastal Trails) **Scenic Walking**, which offers some great walking tours of Italy, England and the rest of the European continent. **BCT Scenic Tours**, *703 Palomar Airport Road, Suite 200, Carlsbad CA 92009, Tel. 800/473-1210 or 760/431-7306. Web: bctwalk.com.*

By Bus

Most long distance travel is done by train, but the regional bus systems can be beneficial for inter-city trips to smaller towns not serviced by rail lines, and the Pullman buses can be perfect for a very long trip. If you're not a rental car person, and you simply have to get to that beautiful little medieval hill town you saw from the train window, the only way you're going to get there is by regional bus. Also, if you're going from Florence to Bari to catch the ferry to Greece, it is more convenient to catch a direct bus since you won't have to stop in the Rome or Naples train station to pick up other passengers.

Conveniently, most bus stations are next door to or near the train station in most towns and cities. The Italian transportation system is something to be admired since they make it so convenient, and comfortable too. Hopefully one day Americans will wake up and learn that having a multiplicity of transportation options is better than being completely dependent on the automobile. In Italy, most long range buses are equipped with bathrooms and some have televisions on them (not that you'd understand what was on). The regional inter-town buses are a little less comfortable but still palatial compared to the same type of bus in Central America.

I suggest sticking to the trains, unless the trains don't go where you want to go – which is about everywhere.

By Car

The world's first automobile expressways were built in northern Italy during the 1920s. Today, Italy and Germany have the most extensive networks of fast, limited-access highways in Europe. Motorists can drive without encountering traffic lights or crossroads – stopping only for border crossings, rest, or fuel – from Belgium, Holland, France, or Germany across the Alps all the way to Sicily. Unlike in America, where our highways were designed for short trips with access every other mile or less, in Europe the highways are for long distance travel.

Two highway tunnels through the Alps, under the Great St. Bernard Pass and through Mont Blanc, enable motor vehicles to travel between Italy and the rest of Europe via car regardless of weather. The expressways, called *Autostrada*, are superhighways and toll roads. They connect all major Italian cities and have contributed to the tremendous increase in tourist travel.

Driving is a good way to see the variety of Italy's towns, villages, seascapes, landscapes, and monuments. The Italian drivers may be a little *pazzo* (crazy), but if you drive confidently and carefully you should be fine. If you remain aware and keep your eyes on the car in front of you, you should be fine. Still, be alert on Italy's roadways, because Italian drivers are like nothing you have ever experienced.

Driver's Licenses

US, British, and Canadian driving licenses are valid in Italy, but only when accompanied by a translation. This translation is obtainable from **AAA**, the offices of the **Touring Club Italiano** in Italy, at the offices for the **Italian Government Tourist Office**, and at the Italian frontier. Even if your native driver's license is accepted, it is strongly recommended that you apply for and receive an 'International Drivers Permit,' which you can get from the Italian Government Tourist Offices listed below:

• **Touring Club Italiano**, *Via Marsala 8, 00185, Roma. Tel. 06/49 98 99*
• **Italian Government Tourist Office** – in the US: *500 N. Michigan Ave, Chicago, IL 60611, Tel. 312/644-0990; 630 Fifth Ave, Suite 1565, New York, NY 10111, Tel. 212/245-4822, Fax 212/586-9249; 360 Post Street,*

Suite 801, San Francisco CA 94109, Tel. 415/392-6206; in Canada: *Store 56, Plaza 3, 3 Place Ville Marie, Montreal, Quebec, Tel. 514/866 7667. Web: www.italiantourism.com.*

Car Rental

In all major cities there are a variety of car rental locations, and even such American stalwarts as Avis and Hertz (see each city's individual section for specifics). All you need to do to rent a car is contact the agency in question, or have the management of your hotel do it for you. Remember to have had your driver's license translated prior to your arrival (see above). From your car rental place, you will be able to pick up detailed maps of the area in which you want to drive.

Driving through the back roads of Italy can offer you some of the best access to secluded little hill towns, clear mountain lakes, snow capped mountains and more; but it can also be one of the most expensive items on your trip, not only because of the exorbitant cost of the rental itself, but also because of the price of gasoline, which can run up to $6 or more per gallon. Naturally, there are ways to keep the cost down, one of which is to make the best use of your car.

Don't rent a car for your entire trip, allowing it to sit in a garage when you are in a big city and you are getting around on foot or by bus, metro, or taxi. Use a rental car to travel through the isolated hills and valleys in between the big cities and drop off the car once you arrive at your destination. Compared to the cost of the rental, drop-off charges are minimal. And of course, make sure you have unlimited mileage, otherwise the cost will creep up by the kilometer.

But always be aware of the wild Italian drivers. Unless you are from Boston and are used to aggressive driving tactics, driving a car to get around Italy should be avoided. So think twice about renting a car. Italian drivers are like nothing you've ever seen.

Another caveat against car rental is that it will isolate you from many experiences while traveling. Going by train or bus allows you to become a part of the daily lives of the locals. You experience living from their perspective. Behind the glass and steel of an automobile you tend be isolated from pure cultural experiences.

Since 1945 in America we have not really known anything other than getting around by automobile, but in Europe, and especially in Italy, there are a multiplicity of other transportation options, whether it is inter or intra-city. The inter-urban Italian train system is one of the best in the world, and where trains don't go, frequent bus service exists. So think twice about car rental because there are many other transportation options to choose from in Italy, unlike here in America.

If you do choose to rent a car, Hertz and Avis have offices all over Italy. To book a car in advance, contact their toll free numbers: **Hertz**, *Tel. 800/654-3001*; **Avis**, *Tel. 800/331-1084.*

Road Maps

If you're going to be our of Rome you are going to want adequate maps, and the only place to get really good maps is from the **Touring Club Italiano**. Your rental company will supply you something that will enable you to get the car out of their parking lot, but after that you are on your own. My recommendation to you would be to contact the **Touring Club Italiano**, *Via Marsala 8, 00185, Roma, Tel. 06/49 98 99*, well prior to your visit, or visit their store in Rome at *Via del Babuino 19-21, Tel 06/3609-5834* near the Piazza del Popolo. Here you can get all the maps they have available.

By Hiking

If you are an avid hiker, and enjoy seeing a country from the perspective of the backroads or trails, contact this excellent organization, **BCT** (British Coastal Trails) **Scenic Walking**, which offers some great walking tours of Italy, England and the rest of the European continent. **BCT Scenic Tours**, *703 Palomar Airport Road, Suite 200, Carlsbad CA 92009, Tel. 800/473-1210 or 760/431-7306, Web: bctwalk.com.*

By Train

The Italian railroad system is owned by the government and provides convenient and extensive transportation throughout the country. Train is by far the simplest, easiest, and least expensive way to get around Italy. Ferries link the principal islands with the mainland, and those that travel between southernmost Italy and Sicily carry trains as well as cars, trucks, and people. To get schedule and ticket information call the offices for the **Italian Rail Agency** (CIT) in North America, *Tel. 800/248-7245.* A great web site that contains everything you need to know about rail travel in Italy is for the Italian Rail Company (**Ferrovie dello Stato** – FS) at *www.fs-on-line.com.*

The railroad system is more extensive in north and central Italy, but main lines run along both coasts, and other routes cross the peninsula in several places. The **Simplon Tunnel**, one of the world's longest railroad tunnels, connects Italy and Switzerland. Other rail lines follow routes across the Alps between Italy and France, Austria, and Slovenia.

Taking the train is by far the most expedient, most relaxing, and by far the best way to travel throughout Italy. Trains go almost every place you'd like to visit, they are comfortable, run on time, and free you from having to drive. This efficiency of the railway system in Italy can be directly attributed to Mussolini. You may have heard the saying, "He may not have done much else, but he got the trains to arrive on time." Well, it's true.

Eurostar Style

A feather in the cap of the Italian rail system is the **Eurostar trains**. These are very comfortable, luxurious and fast. Travel between Rome and Florence (and Venice and Florence) has been reduced to less than two hours each way. The seats on these trains are large and accommodating in both first and second class. In first class they serve you a snack with free beverage service, and offer you headphones that you can keep. A truly wonderful way to travel. So if you are going by train and want to enjoy luxury on the rails, try the Eurostar. The price might be expensive for some at E55 (about $55) each way, but is well worth it.

When traveling by train, one thing to remember is that you must always stamp your ticket before boarding the train. Otherwise you may incur a fine of E20. The machines to stamp your ticket with the time and date are at the head of every track platform.

Types of Train Tickets

There are two different levels of seating on most every train in Italy: **first class** and **second class**. The difference in price is usually only a few dollars, but the difference in convenience is astounding. First class ticket holders can make reservations in advance, while second class ticket seating is on a first come first serve basis.

In conjunction, the seating quality is light-years apart. An example of the price difference between first class and second when traveling between Rome and Florence is $35 for first class, $22 for second class. But in first class you will have an air-conditioned car and separate cloth seat, while in second class you will have not A/C, and you'll be in a compartment with five other people sitting on sweat-inducing plastic seats.

Ticket Discounts

The Italian Railway System offers a variety of discounts on its tickets. Check out their web site for more details (*www.fs-on-line.com*). These tickets are can be purchased through the Italian Government Travel Offices (see numbers listed above under Driver's License section) and through authorized travel agencies.

• **Silver Card for Seniors**: Available to all people 60 years and older. It allows for a 20% reduction on the basic fare for all first class and second class tickets on national routes. For day trains for inter-city routes the discount is 40%. A one year pass costs E5; A two year pass costs E9; a permanent pass costs E12.

• **Green Card for Youth Travel**: Available to all persons from 12 to 26 years of age. It allows for a 20% reduction on all first and second class tickets. A one year pass costs E5; a two year pass costs E9.
• **Italy Flexi Rail Cards**: An excellent option for rail travel in Italy. There are many rules and regulations associated with these cards, but they do not hinder the bearer in any way. Example of some rules: cannot be sold to permanent residents of Italy, card is not transferable, card must be validated at any Italian State Railway station's ticket office before travel can commence, validation slip must be kept separate from card (kind of like the validation slip for travelers checks), and lost or stolen cards cannot be refunded or replaced unless bearer has validation slip. Rules, rules, rules. Here are the prices for the Flexi Railcards:

Validity	1st Class	2nd Class
• 4 days of travel within 9 days of validity	$170	$116
• 8 days of travel within 21 days of validity	$250	$164
• 12 days of travel within 30 days of validity	$314	$210

• **Italy Rail Card** or the "BTLC Italian Tourist Ticket:" all travel and any type of train is unlimited and free, except for the special **TR450 or Eurostar** trains where a supplemental fee will be required. The time period begins on the first day of its use. Here are the prices for the Unlimited Rail Pass:

Validity	1st Class	2nd Class
• 8 days	$226	$152
• 15 days	$284	$190
• 21 days	$330	$220
• 30 days	$396	$264

Remember to Validate Your Ticket

Whatever train you are taking, whatever type of ticket you have, remember to validate your ticket at the yellow boxes at the station by each track before you board the train. This is true for all tickets except Eurorail passes. If you do not validate your ticket, you can get fined. To validate your ticket, simply push one end into the yellow box and it will automatically date and time stamp it.

Types of Trains

- **Eurostar**: Top notch services and speed. Air-conditioned, comfortable seats, snacks served at your seat and head phones available for use.
- **IC-Intercity**: Both first and second class seating is available with most first class compartments air-conditioned. Dining cars are also available.
- **EC-Eurocity**: These are the trains that are used in international rail service.
- **EXPR-Expresso**: Ordinary express trains usually carry first and second class passengers. No supplemental fare and reservations are necessary, but I recommend you make them. Food and drink service is available. These are the trains to take. Hardly any stops at all. Kind of like the MetroLiner Service on Amtrak between Washington DC and New York.
- **DIR-Diretto**: Semi-express trains that make plenty of stops. They often have second class seating only. During off-peak hours they are not crowded, but at peak hours they're sardine-city.
- **Locale**: These trains stop everywhere on their route and take forever, but to get to rural locations these are the only options.

Train Departure (Partenze) Board Description

- When the train is scheduled to depart
  - Number of the Train
    - Classes of Service available
      - Main Stops and Destinations
- Special Services Available
  - Track from which the train will depart

Ora	Treno	Classi Servizi	Principali Fermate e Destinazione	Servizi Diretti e Annotazione	Bina rio
11:35	9412	1-2	Firenze (13:11) Bologna (14:13)		9

PARTENZE

Boarding the Right Train

When taking a train in Italy the ultimate destination that is listed on the train schedule and the departure listing by the track may not be the same city or town to which you are going. To get to Pisa, for example, sometimes you have to board a train whose ultimate destination is Livorno. To make sure you're boarding the proper train, first ask the information desk in the train station when your train is leaving and which track it is leaving from, then try one of two things (or both):

1. Consult one of the large glass-enclosed schedules (see graphic on page 81) located in the information offices and usually at the head of the tracks. Normally they have a wildly gesturing crowd hovering around them, so you may have to squeeze your way through for a view. Match your intended departure time with the time printed on the sheet. Then check directly to the right of the time to see the list of all the destinations for the train. If the name of your destination is listed, you've found your train. Next write down the ultimate destination of the train so you can check the main board at the station that lists **partenze** (trains leaving) to see which **binnario** (track) you should board.

2. If that still doesn't soothe your concerns, ask someone waiting at the track or inside the train if it is going to your destination. Ask at least two people, since I've had someone erroneously tell me a train doesn't go where I asked. It seems that these people, some of whom have been riding the same train to and from work for forty years haven't bothered to pay attention to where the train actually stops.

Whatever the case, to ask someone politely in Italian whether the train is going to your destination say **"Scusa, ma questo treno va a Lucca?"** ("Excuse me, but does this train go to Lucca?") Obviously substitute the underlined city name for the destination to which you wish to go. This question is asked countless times by many people, including Italians.

Finally, if you're standing on the platform waiting for the train to come and you suddenly see all the Italians moving away en masse, that usually means that the public address announcer just declared a track change. Ask one of the departing Italians "Has the track for the train to Lucca changed?" **(E cambiato il binnario per il treno per Lucca?)** If the answer is yes (si), either get the number and go there or simply follow them, and as you pass the board that lists the trains leaving, you'll see the change already officially noted.

Chapter 7

b a s i c   i n f o r m a t i o n

Business Hours

Store hours vary all over Italy, but as a rule they are open from Monday through Friday, 9:00am to 1:00pm, then re-open at 3:30 or 4:00pm to 7:30/8:00pm, and Saturdays from 9:00am to 1:00pm. In large towns, mainly to cater to tourists, stores are open on Saturday afternoons and Sundays as well. Most stores everywhere else in Italy are closed on Sundays, and everywhere they are closed on national holidays. Don't expect to find any 24-hour convenience stores just around the corner in Italy. If you want some soda in your room after a long day of touring you need to plan ahead.

Food stores (*alimentari*) keep their own hours entirely but generally follow the regular business hours listed above. *Alimentari* also close at least one other day of the week besides Sunday. Usually this day is Thursday (*Giovedi*), but it varies region to region, and even city to city within the region. There is a sign outside each *alimentari* that you can check to see which day they are closed (*chiuso*).

Basically, you must plan on most stores being closed from 1:00pm to 4:00pm, since this is the Italian siesta time. During that time, the only places open are restaurants, and most of those close at 3pm.

Banking

Banks in Italy are open Monday through Friday, 8:30am to 1:30pm and from 2:45pm to 4:00pm, and are closed all day Saturday and Sunday and on national holidays. In some cities the afternoon open hour may not even exist, and in some cities, like Rome, banks may open on Saturday mornings and extend longer on Thursdays. Once again, bank hours, like business hours, vary region to region and even city to city within the region. Check outside of banks for their posted hours of operation. Even if the bank is closed, most travelers' checks can be exchanged for Italian currency at hotels as well as shops and at the many foreign exchange offices in railway stations and at airports.

Shop around for the best exchange rate. Each bank offers a different rate and exchange fee, as do the **Casa di Cambio**, smaller exchange establishments. Sometimes the rate charged to exchange your money is a set fee, which is best when you change a large amount of money. Other places charge a percentage of the total which is generally more beneficial for smaller amounts.

Lost or Stolen Travelers Checks & Credit Cards

The toll free numbers listed below should be called if your credit cards or traveler's checks are stolen:

American Express, Tel. 800/872-000 (travelers checks)
American Express, Tel. 800/874-333 (credit cards)
Diner's Club, Tel. 800/864-064
Mastercard, Tel. 800/870-866
Thomas Cook/Mastercard, Tel. 800/872-050 (traveler's checks)
VISA, Tel. 800/874-155 (traveler's checks)
VISA, Tel. 800/877-232 (credit cards)

Currency - The Euro

On January 1, 2002, the official currency for all participating members of the European Community, to which Italy belongs, became the **Euro**. (In this book the Euro is represented by a capital 'E.') It took about two months to become seamlessly adopted in each participating country, and now the lira is no longer in circulation.

The Euro will have far reaching economic and political effects, but the impact is also grammatical. In most European languages, the name of the old currency was a feminine word, such as the now extinct Italian lira, which ends in an 'a.' But the word 'Euro' is masculine since it ends in an 'o.' Another grammatical conundrum is the plural. In Italian a masculine plural is usually represented by an 'i.' But with the Euro all of Europe has adopted the English way by adding an 's' - i.e. 'Euros.' This is truly a big step for Europe. Everyone, not least of which the United States, is waiting to see the Euro's long-term impact.

Dollar-Euro Exchange Rates

Following is a conversion table showing what one Euro is approximately valued at in US dollars As you can see it is almost a one-to-one transfer which should make purchases easier for us now. We will no longer have to deal with tens of thousand of lire and wonder how much that is in dollars. Now it is straightforward. This rate changes all the time. Please check your local paper for up-to-date exchange rates.

Euro (E)	US Dollar ($)
1	1.01
2	2.01
5	5.03
10	10.06
20	20.12
50	50.29
100	100.59
200	201.17
500	502.93

But enough philoso-babble: the Euro comes in coin denominations of 50, 20, 10, 5, 2 and 1 cent, and bill denominations of 500, 200, 100, 50, 20, 10, 5, 2, and 1 Euro.

Electricity

The standard electric current in Italy is 220v, but check with your hotel before you plug in an appliance to find out what the current is, because it's not always 220v! If you want to use your blow dryer, electric razor, radio, or plug in your laptop you are going to need a hardware adapter to switch your appliance from a two prong to a three prong insert. These can be found at most hardware stores. Also check before you leave to see if your appliance automatically changes the voltage from 110v to 220v. If it doesn't, you will need to purchase a converter.

If you can't find these devices at your hardware store, you can order them from the **Franzus Company**, *Murtha Industrial Park, PO Box, 142, Beacon Falls, CT 06403, Tel. 203/723-6664, Fax 203/723-6666.* They also have a free brochure *Foreign Electricity Is No Deep Dark Secret* that can be mailed or faxed to you.

Express Couriers

• **DHL**, *Toll free in Italy 800/345-345, Fax 06/7932-0051, Via Lucrezia Romana 87a; E-mail: dhl@dhl.com, Website www.dhl.it*
• **UPS**, *Toll free in Italy 800/822-054, Fax 06/5226-8200, Via della Magliana 329.*

Health Concerns

A wonderful "just in case..." option is Personal Physicians Worldwide. This organization can provide you with a list of physicians and hospitals at your destination. If you have a medical condition that may need treatment, or you just want to be safe, they can help. Your personal medical history will be confidentially reviewed by the Medical Director, Dr. David Abramson. He will then contact screened and qualified physicians at your destination to see if they will agree to be available and to care for you if the need arises, while you are in their location.

This is a great service since you never know where you'll be when you need the care of a competent doctor. To find out more information, contact:

• **Personal Physicians Worldwide**, *Tel. 888/657-8114, Fax 301/718-7725; E-mail Myra Altschuler, Director, at myra@personalphysicians.com, or Dr. David Abramson, Medical Director at doctors@personalphysicians.com; Web: www.personalphysicians.com.*

Newspapers & Magazines

At most newsstands in Italy you can find the world renowned *International Herald Tribune*, which is published jointly by The Washington Post and The New York Times and printed in Bologna. You will also be able to find a condensed version of *USA Today*. Besides these two, you can also find newspapers from all over the world at almost any newsstand.

If you want an insight into what may be going on in the English language community of the city you are visiting, simply stop into any local English-language bookstore. There should be a list of local events posted, or itemized in a newsletter.

Pets

If you're bringing your precious pooch (your dog will have to be on a leash and wear a muzzle in public in Italy) or kitty into Italy with you, you must have a veterinarian's certificate stating that your pet has been vaccinated against rabies between 20 days and 11 months before entry into Italy, and that your pet is in overall good health. The certificate must contain the breed, age, sex, and color of your pet and your name and address. This certificate will be valid only for 30 days. The specific forms that the vet needs to fill out are available at all Italian diplomatic and consular offices.

Parrots, parakeets, rabbits, and hares are also subject to health certification by a vet, and will also be examined further upon entry into Italy. Also Customs officials may require a health examination of your pet if you have just come from a tropical region or that they suspect the pet to be ill. All this means that they can do whatever they want whenever they want, so it might be wise to leave your pet at home.

Postal Service

Stamps can be purchased at any post office or *tabacchi*. If you send a letter airmail with insufficient postage it will not be returned to sender, but will be sent surface mail, which could take months. So make sure you have the correct postage. Air mail prices for post cards is E1.3 to the US and Canada. Air mail letters cost 1.5. And if you put your coorespondence in a red post box, remember to put it in the right hand slot which reads *Per tutte le altre desinazione* (for all other destinations other — other than the city where you are).

The main post office in each city is generally open from 8:30am to 6:00 or 7:00pm Monday through Friday and Saturday they close at noon. Smaller post offices are only open from 8:30am to 2:00pm Monday through Friday.

Restaurant Hours

Restraurants in Italy keep rather rigid hours, which are usually 12:30 or 1:00pm for lunch until 3:00 or 3:30pm. The dinner hours start at either 7:30 or 8:00pm and usually run until 10:00pm. Some late night restaurants, stay open until the early morning hours.

Safety & Avoiding Trouble

Italian cities are definitely much safer than any equivalent American city. You can walk almost anywhere without fear of harm, but that doesn't mean you shouldn't play it safe. Listed below are some simple rules to follow to ensure that nothing bad occurs:
• At night, make sure the streets you are strolling along have plenty of other people. Like I said, most cities are safe, but it doesn't hurt to be cautious.
• Always have your knapsack or purse flung over the shoulder that is not directly next to the road. Why? There have been cases of Italians on motor bikes snatching purses off old ladies and in some cases dragging them a few blocks.
• Better yet, have your companion walk on the street side, while you walk on the inside of the sidewalk with the knapsack or purse.
• Better still is to buy one of those tummy wallets that goes under your shirt so no one can even be tempted to purse-snatch you.
• Always follow basic common sense. If you feel threatened, scared, or alone, retrace your steps back to a place where there are other people.

Gypsies

You may have the misfortune of being confronted with a pack of gypsies whose only interest is to relieve you of your wallet and other valuables. These situations are rare but they do happen. Gypsies are not violent, and usually you will only encounter women and children, but they tend to swarm all around you, poke pieces of cardboard in your midsection and generally distract you to the point where they are able to pilfer your pockets, fanny packs, back packs, or knapsacks. So if you are swarmed by gypsies, do not be polite, push back if you need to, make a scene, yell, scream, start running, do anything you can to get out of their midst. Gypsies will not harm you, but if you do not act quickly you will lose your valuables.

Staying out of trouble with the law is paramount, because in Italy you are guilty until proven innocent, unlike in the States where it's the other way around. And most importantly, if arrested you are not simply placed in a holding cell. The Italian officials take you directly to a maximum security prison and lock you up. And that's where you'll stay for as long as it takes your traveling partners to figure out where you are, bribe your case to the top of the local judge's pile, and have your case heard. That whole process can sometimes take months.

So if you like your drinks strong and your nights long, remember to keep your temper in check. And don't even think about smuggling any banned substance into the country, or God forbid, buying something illicit when you're in Italy. If you are approached to buy some hashish or something else, say politely, *No Grazie* (no thank you) and walk away.

Taxis

Taxi service is widely available in all major cities in Italy, and a little less so in smaller cities such as Pisa or Lucca, and almost non-existent in remote towns and villages. Rates are comparable to those charged in your large American cities, which means expensive. Generally taxis locate themselves in special stands located at railway stations and main parts of the city, but many can be waved down as they cruise the streets for fares. At these taxi stands there are usually telephones that you can call directly from your hotel, but remember, in Italy, if called, the meter starts at the point of origin, so you'll be paying the cabby to come pick you up. The same goes for radio taxis if called to come pick you up.

Fares will vary from city to city, but basically when you get in the cab there will be a fixed starting charge of approximately 2,800 to 6,400 lire, and a cost per kilometer of approximately 1,000 to 1,250 lire. If you are stuck in traffic, every minute another Euro 50 cents or so will be added to the fare. Some extra charges may come into play, like the **nighttime supplement** (between 10:00pm and 6:00am), a **Sunday and public holiday supplement**, as well as a **per item luggage charge**. You will also be charged for every piece of luggage. All of these vary from city to city.

On long trips, like from airports, it is advised to agree upon a price before heading out. Ask at the information booth inside each airport what the expected charge should be.

Telephones & Fax

Calling Italy

Even when making local calls the area code must be used. In conjunction, before it was necessary to discard the leading zero of the area code (for example Rome's area code is 06), but now you need to use the leading zero in all area codes.

To dial Rome from the United States, first dial the international prefix, **011**, then the country code, **39**, then the city code for Rome, **06**, then the number you wish to reach.

Long Distance Calling From Italy

The days of the *gettone* phones is long past. Most pay phones in Italy only use **phone cards** (which you can buy in denominations of E2.5, E5 or E7.5) but some use a combination of cards and coins. You can buy phone cards at any *tabacchi* (the stores with the **T** out in front of them), newsstand, post office and some bars. You will need these cards to be able to use public pay phones

Listed below are some of the major telecommunications carriers for North America and their access numbers:

AT&T – *Tel. 172-1011* (a toll free number in Italy) to gain access to an AT&T operator (or English language prompts) for efficient service. You can bill your AT&T calling card, local phone company card, or call direct.

Canada Direct – *Tel. 172-1001* (a toll free number in Italy) and you will be connected to the Canadian telephone network with access to a bilingual operator. You can bill your *Calling Card, Call Me*™ service, your *Hello!* Phone Pass or call collect.

MCI – *Tel. 172-1022* (a toll free number in Italy) for MCI's World Phone and to use your MCI credit card or call collect. All done through English speaking MCI operators.

Sprint – *Tel. 172-1877* (a toll free number in Italy) for access to an English speaking Sprint operator who can charge your phone card or make your call collect.

Modem or Fax Usage In Italy

To connect you modem or fax to the wall you will need an adapter. These too can be bought from a hardware store or from the **Franzus Company** (see above under Electricity). Many hotels in Italy are starting to use the American standard phone plug, so this may not be a concern. When making your reservations, inquire about the type of plugs in use to insure you can communicate with home without a problem.

Phone Cards

An inexpensive option for international calling is to buy an international phone card (*carta telefonica internationale*) which are sold at most *tabacchi*. You can get cards for E10 which have 100 minutes available on them. This translates to about 10 cents a minute, a steal for international calling. These cards can be used in your hotel room or at public phone booths simply by following the directions on the back. This usually entails calling a toll free number, receiving instructions in a variety of languages, including English, punching in the number of your specific card (usually found on the back after rubbing off a covering), then keying in the number you wish to call. Your connection is crisp and clear. Discerning travelers concerned with spending an arm and a leg to call home, use this option.

Time

Italy is **six hours ahead of Eastern Standard Time** in North America, so if it's noon in New York it's 6:00pm in Rome. Daylight savings time goes into effect each year in Italy usually from the end of March to the end of September.

Tipping

Hotels

A service charge of 15-18% is usually added to your hotel bill, but it is customary to leave a little something else, whatever you deem sufficient, but anything over E1-2 per service rendered can be extravagant.

Tipping at the Right Time

Most people tip at the end of a stay in a hotel indicating an appreciation for the services rendered. But if you want to ensure that the services rendered are exemplary, tip in the beginning of your stay. Giving on the spot tips for services rendered usually guarantees the best possible service. Slip a Euro or two to the person who checks you in; leave a Euro on the bed for the maid with a note saying "Grazie" will almost always ensure service above and beyond the call of duty.

Restaurants
A service charge of around 15% is usually automatically added to all restaurant bills. But if you felt the service was good, it is customary to leave a little something. There is no set percentage, and a good rule of thumb is to leave whatever change is returned, as long as it is not above between 5-10%.
The same applies in cafés and bars. For example, around two hundred lire is normal if you're standing at the counter drinking a soda, cappuccino, etc. If you have an alcoholic beverage, something to eat, etc. at the counter, the tip should be Euro 50 cents or more. Leaving change in this manner is a good way to rid myself of burdensome coins.

Theater Ushers
They get E1 or more if the theater is very high class.

Taxis
Give the cabby 5% of the fare, otherwise they just might drive away leaving you without your luggage. (Just kidding).

Sightseeing Guide & Driver
Give E1 minimum per person for half-day tours, and E2 minimum per person for full day tours.

Service Station Attendant
Give Euro 50 cents or more for extra service like cleaning your windshield, or giving you directions while also filling up your tank.

Weights & Measures
Italy uses the metric system, where everything is a factor of ten. The table below gives you a list of weights and measures with approximate values.

Metric Conversions			
Weights			
Italy	14 grams	Etto	Kilo
US	1/2 oz	1/4 lb	2 lb 2oz
Liquid Measure			
Italy	Litro		
US	1.065 quart		
Distance Measure			
Italy	Centimeter	Meter	Kilometer
US	2/5 inch	39 inches	3/5 mile

Websites of Interest

Before you head off to Italy, I've listed some websites below that you may find interesting or useful. Some of them are featured elsewhere in this book.

Airfare
• *www.bestfares.com*
• *www.lowestfare.com*
• *www.cheaptickets.com*
• *www.airdeals.com*
• *www.lastminutetravel.com*

Currency
• *www.oanda.com/converter/travel* – to create a pocket currency conversion chart to bring with you, visit this website

General Information
• *www.italiantourism.com* – website for the Italian government tourist office; filled with lots of great information
• *www.itwg.com* – an all-inclusive website featuring loads of useful information about Italy
• *www.travel.it/welcome.html* – another all encompassing website produced by yet another Italian government agency
• *www.enjoyrome.com* – offers walking tours of Rome
• *www.mondoweb.it/livinginrome* – the complete guide to living in Rome for foreigners

Hotels
• *www.venere.it* – you can get hotel reservations for thousands of hotels all over Italy at this site, including many that are in this book

Language
• *www.travlang.com/languages* – if you want to take a few virtual language lessons before you go, visit the *Foreign Language for Travelers* website
• *www.arcodidruso.com* – Italian language and culture for foreigners

Medical
• *www.personalphysicians.com* – provides you with a list of physicians and hospitals at your destination; if you have a medical condition that may need treatment, or you just want to be safe, they can help

Passport
• *www.instantpassport.com* – this website promises to give you 24-hour turnaround from the time they receive your passport pictures and

requisite forms; they charge $100 plus overnight shipping on top of all fees associated with passport issuance.

• *www.americanpassport.com* – this site offers three types of service: expedited (24 hours), express (three to four business days) and regular; prices range from $245 to $135.

• *www.travel.state.gov* – you can download passport application forms, international travel advisories, and listings of embassies and consulates worldwide

Weather

• *www.washingtonpost.com/wp-srv/weather/historical/historical.htm* – if you want to obtain the average temperature, temperature ranges and rain accumulation totals by month for Rome or other destinations in Italy visit this website

'Where Rome'

This is the title of a good tourist magazine usually found in hotel rooms. In it you can locate all sorts of up-to-date information about events in Rome, new restaurants, cafes, bars, shops etc. If you do not have one at your hotel, you can contact the publishers, *Tel. 06/578-1615*, and pick up a copy or they can tell you where to get one. A great resource for events and current goings-on while in Rome.

Women Travelers

As stated in the Safety section above, Italy is a safe country, but generally women traveling alone will find themselves the recipients of unwanted attention from men. In most cases the attention you receive will be limited to whistles, stares, comments (in Italian which you will probably not understand), catcalls and the like. This may happen whether you are in groups or alone. But usually if you are with a male companion this type of unwanted attention doesn't occur.

If you choose to be alone, whether it's going for a walk, seeing a sight, or stopping for a coffee, don't expect to be alone for long. Since foreign women have a reputation for being easy, ignoring unwanted suitors won't work because they think they can charm their way into your heart and elsewhere. My suggestion is to politely tell them you are waiting for your boyfriend (*aspetto mio fidanzato*) or husband (*marito*). If that doesn't work, raise your voice, look them in the eye angrily and tell them to *lascia mi stare* (lash-ah me star-ay), which means leave you alone.

If these ploys do not work, simply walk away. If the man continues to badger you, find a local policeman for assistance, but always remain in a populated area. In the vast majority of cases there is truly nothing to fear. Most

Italians just want to get lucky and when rebuffed they will go find easier prey. In conjunction, most of the attention falls into the nuisance category, but like I said in the Safety section, please use common sense. Avoid unpopulated areas, avoid walking alone on dark streets, avoid hitchhiking alone and things like that. Just be smart. Italy is much safer than America and is not even remotely as violent, but it's better to be safe than sorry.

In general too, the further south you go, the more you will be hassled. Something about the warm climate must heat the male's blood or stimulate their libido. Also in port cities women traveling alone will be pegged as targets for petty theft. So be extra careful in those types of cities.

And all over the country, when you ride public transportation you may very well be confronted with wandering hands, especially when the bus or train is crowded. To avoid this, keep your back to the wall. If someone does start to fondle your posterior or elsewhere, make a loud fuss – otherwise it will continue unabated.

Yellow Pages

There is an excellent **English Yellow Pages (EYP)** in Italy. It is the annual telephone directory of English-speaking professionals, organizations, services and commercial activities in Rome, Florence, Milan, Naples, Genoa and Bologna. The EYP is a well-known resource and reference source among the international community in Italy, from which you can easily find numbers for airlines and embassies, English-speaking doctors and dentists, international schools and organizations, hotels, moving companies, real estate agents, accountants, attorneys, consultants, plumbers, electricians, mechanics and much more. Listings are complete with address including zip code, phone and fax numbers, e-mail and web sites.

You can find copies at embassies, international organizations (FAO, IFAD, WWF, etc.) schools & universities, social and professional associations, English-language churches, foreign press offices, local events within the expat community and various businesses that deal directly with an international clientele. And copies of it are on sale at most international bookstores. This is a great resource for any resident or visitor to Italy. Their website is *www.eyp.com*.

Chapter 8

Italians are active sports enthusiasts. Besides soccer they participate in skiing, golf, tennis, scuba diving, mountain climbing, hiking, fishing, hunting, and more. Any sport you can play at home you can also enjoy in Italy!

Golf

In the summer you can also enjoy some excellent golf courses. Located all over Italy, except for the poor south, there are plenty of accessible courses around the main tourist areas of Rome, Milan and Florence (see regional chapters for more information). You can also find courses around the many seaside resort areas that dot Italy's coastline.

Since Constatino Rocca choked in the Ryder Cup in 1994 for the whole world to see, and when he made that miraculous putt after chili dipping his chip in the British Open in 1995 on the final hole (he eventually lost to John Daly), Italian golf has started to get recognition. Maybe not the kind of recognition it wants but, nonetheless, the *cognoscenti* have begun to discover some gems of courses all over Italy. It's only natural that a country filled with such natural beauty would provide superb golf.

Hunting & Fishing

If you are looking for the more rustic pursuits like sport fishing and hunting, Italy has lakes, streams and rivers filled with trout. In the **Alpine and Appenine regions** you can actually bag a wild boar *(cinghiale)*, which is on the menu at many northern Italian restaurants. Hunting is popular all over Italy but the seasons vary according to region. Contact the **Italian Government Travel Office** in New York, *Tel. 212/245-4822*, to find information about the hunting and fishing seasons and how to get licenses for each activity.

Skiing

From December through April, ski resorts all over Italy are swarming with people willing to sacrifice life and limb to get the adrenaline flow that only plummeting down a sheer cliff covered with snow can offer them. Most winter sports areas are found in the north of Italy in the Alps; one of the most famous is **Courmayeur**, but there are also some near Rome in the Central Apennines, **Cortina d'Ampezzo** being the most notable.

These same mountain ranges are used as hiking locations during the summer. If you like breathtaking views without the risk of tearing a medial collateral ligament, try hiking the trails of the **Italian Alps** in the summer.

Spectator Sports

If watching from the sidelines is more up your alley, Italy goes **soccer** crazy every Sunday from September to May. Virtually every city and every town has a team that plays professionally. The Italian league is separated into four divisions, or *Serie*. The first division is *Serie A*, which plays the best soccer in the world, and the bottom division is *Serie D*. Some cities have several teams, like Rome which has two *Serie A* teams (Lazio and Roma), three from *Serie C*, and one from *Serie D*. The Serie A and B games are the most fun to go to since the fans are so passionate. Tickets can be hard to come by since the games are so popular, but contact your hotel's concierge and s/he may be able to scrape some up for you.

If you don't want to go to the game you may still choose to go to the stadium, not only to revel in the atmosphere, but also to get some great gifts from the vendors who sell team paraphernalia outside. Certain types of product piracy is legal in Italy, and putting the names and logos of sports teams on unofficial products is one of them. The quality of the shirts, hats, and scarves is just as good and about one fourth the price of the official products.

Another popular spectator sport is **auto** and **motorcycle racing**. At Monza, just outside of Milan, the **Italian Grand Prix** is held every September; and at Imola, near Bologna, you can find the **San Marino Grand Prix** every May. Equally as popular is **cycling**, which culminates in the **Tour d'Italia** in May.

And surprisingly enough, **basketball** and **baseball** both have professional leagues, and most major cities now have teams. Professional baseball has been around for only about twenty five years, and is still at the level of the CBA

(Continental Basketball Association), a minor league in the US, but is starting to catch on in popularity. Ask your concierge about upcoming games.

Tennis

In virtually every city in Italy there are courts that can be rented if you are interested. Italians are passionate tennis fans and if you are in Rome during the summer, the entire city is caught up in the Italian Open tennis tournament. Where available we list places where you can rent tennis courts. But since the Italians seem to build more courts each year, ask your concierge for advice. There are bound to be some whereever you are.

Water Sports

You'll find scuba diving, sailing, snorkeling, and para-sailing along Italy's various coasts. Since the country is surrounded on three sides by water, Italians are fanatical about their water sports and activities, which has started to include topless bathing, an unheard of activity 10 years ago. At some beaches frequented by northern Europeans, there are days when not a suit is in sight.

Chapter 9

s
h
o
p
p
i
n
g

As mentioned in Chapter 7, store hours are usually Monday through Friday 9:00am to 1:00pm, 3:30/4:00pm to 7:30/8:00pm, and Saturday 9:00am to 1:00pm. In major cities like Rome, shops will also open in the afternoons on Saturday, but everywhere in Italy they will be closed on Sunday. This may vary in Milan and/or Turin, where sometimes the lunch break is shorter so shops can close earlier.

The big Italian chain stores are **La Rinascente**, **Coin**, **UPIM**, and **STANDA**. In Coin, UPIM, and STANDA, you will also find supermarkets filled with all manner of Italian delectables. At the end of this chapter I'll make some suggestions about what you could buy at a local Italian *Supermercato* or *Alimentari* (smaller food store) to bring home with you so you can make a fine Italian meal with authentic ingredients!

Besides food and clothing, Italy has a wide variety of handicrafts. Any one of Italy's crafts would be a perfect memento of your stay. Works in alabaster and marble can be readily found in and around Florence, Milan, and Venice. Wood carvings are the specialty of many of the cities in the south, such as Palermo and Messina. Beautiful glasswork is at its best in and around Venice and Pisa. Embroidery and lace work can be found all over Italy, and rugs from Sardinia rival those of most other European countries. Sardinia is also known for its straw bags, hats, and mats, as is Florence.

Exquisite gold and silver jewelry is a specialty of Florence, where, on the Ponte Vecchio, you'll find shop after shop of jewelry stores. In other parts of Tuscany you can find hand-wrought iron work as well as beautiful tiles.

And finally, the main fashion centers in Italy are, of course, Milan, Florence and Rome, with Florence specializing in shoes and gloves, and Milan and Rome everything else. Each regional chapter will describe for you specific places to visit to find the most exquisite and authentic regional handicrafts.

Tax-Free Shopping

Italian law entitles all non-European Union residents to a **VAT (IVA) tax refund** with a minimum purchase exceeding E150. Ask for an invoice (*fattura* in Italian) or a **Tax-Free Check** when completing a purchase. Upon departure from Italy, purchased goods must be shown to a customs agent at the airport or border station and a customs stamp must be obtained no later than three months after the date of purchase. The stamped invoice must be returned to the store or the VAT Refund Companies Office in Italy no later than four months after the date of purchase.

Direct refunds at the airport or the border are offered albeit at a lower rate. There are also a number of tax free services, such as **Cashback, Global Refund Italia, Tax-Free for Tourists**, etc. and each have a different window at the airport. Be aware of this when you make your purchases so that your time spent in lines at the airport getting refunds is lessened. You will usually see the tax back signs in most upscale stores.

Little Italian Stores

Since there are no 24-hour pharmacies or convenience stores that carry everything under the sun like we have in North America, shopping for the basic necessities can be a little confusing. Listed on the next few pages are specific types of shops and what you can find in them.
Cartoleria

Tax Rebate on Purchases

If you acquire products at the same merchant in excess of E150 (about $150), you can claim an **IVA** (purchase tax) **rebate**. You must ask the vendor for the proper receipt **(il ricetto per il IVA per favore)**, have the receipt stamped at Italian customs, then mail no later than 90 days after the date of the receipt back to the vendor. The vendor will then send you the IVA rebate. You can also do this at the airport, but will receive less money in return. If you spend a fair chunk of money in Italy on clothing or other items, this is a good way to get some money back. Also be aware that there is more than one tax free service available.

Shopping at a *cartoleria* brings you face to face with Italian make-work programs, since most are not self-service. Some products you can pick out what you want, others you will have to enlist a stockboy/girl to help you get it. But you don't bring the products up to the register. In most cases you will have the cost of your purchases tabulated for you by the stockperson. You bring this receipt and your desired products up to the register, where another person rings them up for you.

Things sold in cartoleria include:

- pen   *penna*
- pencil   *mattita*
- notebook   *quaderno*
- paper   *carta*
- envelope   *borsa per una lettera*
- binder   *classificatore*
- calendar   *calandra*
- wrapping paper *carta da regalo*

Alimentari

When shopping at an *alimentari* some products are self-service and some have to be prepared for you. Most meats, cheeses and breads are not pre-packaged and therefore you will have to talk to someone behind a glass counter to get you what you want. Other goods, like mustard and water, are self-service. When ordering meats, cheeses or breads, you will get the products and the receipt for the products from the person behind the counter. Bring the receipt and all your other products to the cashier where you pay.

Typical items in alimentari include:

- mustard   *senape*
- mayonnaise   *maionese*
- tomatoes   *tomaté*
- olive oil   *olio d'oliva*
- salami   *salame* (the best types are *Milanese* or *Ungherese*)
- cheese   *formaggio*
- mineral water   *aqua minerale*
- wine (red/white) *vino (rosso/bianco)*
- beer   *birra*
- potato chips   *patate fritte*
- cookies   *biscotti*
- roll   *panino*
- bread   *pane*
- butter   *burro*

Sometimes *alimentari* do not have bread. If that is the case you'll need to find a *panificio* (bakery). Same type of service here as in an *alimentari*.

Farmacia

Shopping in a pharmacy is full service. You do not have access to anything. If you want anything you have to ask the pharmacist or his/her assistant.

This is what you'll buy in farmacia:

• toothpaste	*dentifricio*
• razor	*rasoio*
• deodorant	*deodorante*
• comb	*pettine*
• rubbers	*profilattici*
• toothbrush	*spazzolino*
• aspirin	*aspirina*
• tampon	*tampone*

Tabacchaio

Most everything but the tobacco products and stamps are self-service in a *tabacchaio*.

The tabacchaio sell:

• stamps	*francobolli*
• newspaper	*giornale*
• pen	*penna*
• envelopes	*buste per lettere*
• postcards	*cartoline*
• cigars	*sigaro*
• cigarettes	*sigarette*
• cigarette paper	*cartina*
• pipe tobacco	*tabacco da pipa*
• matches	*fiammiferi*
• lottery ticket	*biglietto di lotteria*
• lighter	*accendino*

Clothing Sizes

The chart below is a comparison guide between US and Italian sizes. Many sizes are not standardized, so you will need to try everything on anyway. Generally if you are above 6'2" and weigh over 200 pounds you may have trouble finding clothing in Italy because the Italians just are not big people. The following conversions should help you out in your shopping quest:

WOMEN'S CLOTHING SIZES

US	2	4	6	8	10	12	14	16
Italy	36	38	40	42	44	46	48	50

Continued

	18	20	24
	52	54	56

WOMEN'S SHOE SIZES

US	5 1/2	6 1/2	7	7 1/2	8	8 1/2	9	10
Italy	35	36	37	38	38 1/2	39	40	41

WOMEN'S HOSIERY SIZES

US	Petite	Small	Medium	Large
Italy	I	II	III	IV

MEN'S SUITES, OVERCOATS, SWEATERS, & PAJAMAS

US	34	36	38	40	42	44	46	48
Italy	44	46	48	50	52	54	56	58

MEN'S SHIRTS

US	14	14 1/2	15	15 1/2	16	16 1/2	17	17 1/2
Italy	36	37	38	39	40	41	42	43

MEN'S SHOES

US	6	6 1/2	7	7 1/2	8	8 1/2	9	9 1/2
Italy	30	40	40 1/2	41	41 1 1/2	42	42 1/2	43

Continued

	10	10 1/2	11-11 1/2
	43 1/2	44-44 1/2	45

MEN'S HATS

US	6 7/8	7	7 1/8	7 1/4	7 3/8	7 1/2	7 5/8	7 3/4
Italy	55	56	57	58	59	60	61	62

CHILDREN'S SIZES

US	1	2	3	4	5	6	7	8
Italy	35	40	45	50	55	60	65	70

Continued

	9	10	11	12	13	14
	75	80	85	90	95	100

CHILDREN'S SHOES

US	4	5	6	7	8	9	10	10 1/2
Italy	21	21	22	23	24	25	26	27
Continued								
	11	12	13					
	28	29	30					

Key Shopping & Bargaining Phrases

Italian	English
Quanto costa?	How much is this?
E Troppo	That's too much
No Grazie	No thank you
Voglio paggare meno	I want to pay less
Che lai questo pui grande?	Do have this in a bigger size?
..... pui piccolo	..... in a smaller size
..... in nero	..... in black
..... in bianco	..... in white
..... in roso	..... in red
..... in verde	..... in green

When to Bargain

In all stores, even the smallest shops, bargaining is not accepted, just like here in North America. But you can bargain at any street vending location, even if they have placed a sign indicating the price. Don't be afraid to bargain, or you'll end up spending more than you (ahem) 'bargained' for.

Most Italian vendors see foreigners as easy marks to make a few more lire because they know it is not in our culture to bargain, while in theirs it is a way of life.

Italian Soccer Attire

If you or someone you know is a soccer nut, you may want to get them a jersey, hat, or scarf from one of the local teams. Most cities and towns in Italy have a soccer team, whether in the **Serie A** (First Division) or in the three lower divisions. The games are played from September to June and are the best places to get low cost, high quality merchandise.

Outside of most games vendors are selling everything from key rings to official soccer jerseys, all at a low price. The Italian soccer teams are starting to open their own stores featuring their specially-licensed products, like **Milan Point**, for one of the teams in Milan, but those prices will be about four times as much as at the stadium.

The best way to bargain, if the street vendor doesn't speak English, is by writing your request on a piece of paper. This keeps it subdued in case you're embarrassed about haggling over money. Basically while in Italy try to let go of that cultural bias. Anyway, you and the vendor will probably pass the paper back and forth a few times changing the numbers before a price is finally agreed upon. And of course, the Italian vendor will be waving his arms about, jabbering away, most probably describing how you're trying to rip him off, all in an effort to get you to pay a higher price. Remember, this is all done in fun – so enjoy it.

What You're Allowed to Bring Back Through Customs

See Chapter 6, *Planning Your Trip,* for more details, but in short you can bring back to the US $400 worth of goods duty free. On the next $1,000 worth of purchases you will be assessed a flat 10% fee. These products must be with you when you go through customs.

You can mail products duty free, providing the total value of each package sent is not more than $50 *and* no one person is receiving more than one package a day. Also, each package sent must be stamped "Unsolicited Gift" and the amount paid and the contents of the package must be displayed. They'll be able to tell you all this again at the post office.

What you cannot bring back to North America are any fruits, vegetables, and in most cases meats and cheeses, even if they're for your consumption alone, and even if they are vacuum sealed. Customs has to do this to prevent any potential parasites from entering our country and destroying our crops. Unfortunately, this means all those great salamis and cheeses you bought at those quaint outdoor food markets and had on one of your picnics will not be let back into North America.

But there are some things you can buy. In most supermarkets you can find salamis and cheeses that have been shrink-wrapped, which customs should let through. At the same time all the hard cheeses, like *Parmigiano Reggiano* and *Pecorino*, will be let through because they have been cured long enough.

Chapter 10

culture & arts

From Etruscans to the Renaissance

Italy is perhaps best known for its great contributions to painting and sculpture; and many art lovers have described the country as one vast museum. Italy gave birth to such world renowned artists as Giotto, Donatello, Raphael, Michelangelo, Leonardo da Vinci, and Botticelli, who are revered the world over.

The oldest works of art in Italy are those of the **Etruscans**, and they date back to the 9th century BCE. This mysterious society's main cities and art centers were in the middle of the peninsula, between Rome and Florence, mainly in the province now know as Tuscany (the region was named after them ... Etruscans ... Tuscany). In Tarquinia, Volterra, Cerveteri, and Veio, the Etruscans have left behind magnificent temples, sculptures, and bronzes as well as other fascinating testimonies to their presence. The best museum collections of Etruscan art can be found in Rome's **Etruscan Museum**, Florence's **Archaeological Museum**, the **Bologna Municipal Museum**, and the **Municipal Museum of Volterra**.

Italy is also known for being a repository of ancient Greek art. During the time of the Etruscans, the Greeks established colonies in the south of modern-day Italy as well as Sicily. Magnificent ruins of temples exist today in some of these ancient Greek colonies: **Syracuse**, **Agrigento**, and **Taormina** in Sicily; and **Paestu** and **Coma** in Campania. There are good collections of Hellenic art in the **National Museum of Naples**, and in the museums in Palermo, Syracuse, Reggio Calabria, Paestum, and Taranto.

After the Greeks and Etruscans, the Roman Empire left its lasting impression all over Italy. There are still roads, bridges, aqueducts, arches, and theaters built by the Romans still in use today, some of which are over 2,000 years old. The most extensive excavations of ancient Roman ruins have been made at the **Forum** in Rome, at **Ostia** near Rome by the beach, and at **Pompeii** and **Herculaneum** - the cities that the volcanic **Mount Vesuvius** buried. For a first-hand, up-front feel of what life was like in the Roman Empire, don't miss these sites.

After the fall of the Roman Empire, the Byzantine Empire ruled many parts of the southern and eastern regions of Italy. This period left behind many churches, with their glorious mosaics, like those of the 6th century in Ravenna near the east coast; as well as the morbid but powerful **catacombs** outside of Rome.

Then after the Dark Ages, when the Roman Empire's progress reverted back to tribalism, the Renaissance came. This artistic period, meaning "re-birth," began in Italy in the 14th century and lasted for two hundred years. The Renaissance left us an extensive array of churches, palaces, paintings, statues, and beautiful city squares in almost every city of Italy. The main cities of Florence, Rome, Venice, Milan, and Naples have most of the treasures and beauty of this period, but smaller towns like Ferrara and Rimini also have their share. The best museums for viewing Renaissance art are the **Uffizzi Gallery** and **Pitti Palace** in Florence, as well as the **Vatican** and **Borghese Galleries** (in the Borghese Gardens just outside the walls) in Rome.

After the Renaissance, **baroque art** became fashionable. And Rome, more than any other Italian city, contains a dazzling array of churches, paintings, and statues recalling the splendor of such famous artists as Bernini, Borromini, and Caravaggio of the late 16th and 17th centuries.

Renaissance Painting

In Italy (with France and Germany soon following suit) during the 14th and 15th centuries, the Renaissance was a period of exploration, invention, and discovery. Mariners from all over Europe set sail in search of new lands. Scientists like **Leonardo da Vinci** studied the mysteries of the world and the heavens. Artists found the human body to be a marvel of mechanics and beauty (but had to secretly study it, as Michelangelo did, lest the Church condemn them for heresy). This was undoubtedly one of Italy's most exciting periods in the history of artistic and scientific advancement.

Many consider the birthplace of Renaissance art to be Florence. It seemed to start with a young painter named **Masaccio**, who began introducing many bold new ideas into his painting. He made his paintings vibrantly interesting by drawing each person completely different from another, as well as making each person as realistic as possible. In conjunction with his ability to express the human form, Masaccio used combinations of colors to give the impression of space and dimension in his landscapes. Now every art student studies how brown makes objects appear closer, and blue makes them appear as if they in the distance.

Paolo Uccello, another Florentine, worked at the same time as Masaccio. A mathematician as well as an artist, he expanded on the mechanical and scientific issues of painting rather than on the human and psychological ones.

One of his paintings, *The Battle of San Romano*, circa 1457, celebrated the victory of Florence over Siena some 25 years earlier, and is a brilliant study in **perspective**. His depiction of objects, men, and horses all help to accentuate the sense of real perspective he was trying to achieve. One technique he used, which is now part of any good art school's curriculum, is **foreshortening**. In the left foreground of *The Battle of San Romano* is a fallen soldier with his feet facing the front of the picture. To give this figure a proper perspective, Uccello had to shorten the perceived length of the body, an extremely difficult task, and one not usually seen in other artists' previous works. In conjunction, Uccello drew roads, fields, etc., going back into the painting towards the horizon, to give the impression of distance. Now these are all well used and rather pedestrian artistic techniques, but back then they revolutionized the art world.

But most definitely three of the most influential Renaissance artists were **Raphael**, **Leonardo da Vinci**, and **Michelangelo**. Raphael was mainly known for his paintings of the Madonna and Child, from which our conceptual image of the Mother of Jesus is largely based. All of his paintings reflect a harmony that leaves the viewer with a warm and positive feeling of contentment.

Leonardo da Vinci is most well known for his *Mona Lisa*, painted in Tuscany in 1505-06 and now hanging in the Louvre, but he was also a versatile architect and scientist as well. Leonardo studied botany, geology, zoology, hydraulics, military engineering, anatomy, perspective, optics, and physiology. You name it, he did it – the original Renaissance Man!

Another versatile artist of the Italian Renaissance, and definitely its most popular then and now – he was always being commissioned to paint or sculpt all the wealthy people's portraits – was Michelangelo Buonarroti. Although he considered himself chiefly a sculptor – he trained as a young boy to become a stone carver – he left us equally great works as a painter and architect. As a painter he created the huge **Sistine Chapel** frescoes, encompassing more than 10,000 square feet in area. As an architect he helped complete the designs for **St. Peter's**, where his world renowned statue, *La Pieta*, currently resides.

Renaissance Sculpture

Besides painting and architecture, **Michelangelo Buonarroti** was also the pre-eminent sculptor of the Renaissance. By the age of 26 he had carved *La Pieta*, his amazing version of Virgin Mary supporting the dead Christ on her knees; and was in the process of carving the huge and heroic marble *David*. He also created the memorable **Medici tombs** in the Chapel of San Lorenzo, Florence. His greatest but lesser known work is his majestic *Moses* designed for the tomb of Pope Julius II, which can be viewed at the basilica of **San Pietro in Vincoli** in Rome.

Even though Michelangelo was commissioned to create many works by the Popes themselves, he had learned his amazing knowledge of the human anatomy by dissecting cadavers in his home town of Florence as a young man, a crime punishable by death and/or excommunication at the time.

During the Renaissance there were many other sculptors of note, but Michelangelo was truly the best. One of the others was **Lorenzo Ghiberti**, who died a few years before Michelangelo was born. For 29 years he labored to produce ten bronze panels, depicting Biblical episodes, for the doors of the Baptistery of Florence. Michelangelo was said to have been inspired to become a great artist because of these beautiful bronze doors.

Music

Italy also has a great tradition in music. Even today, Italian folk music has made a resurgence, mainly because of the theme song for the *Godfather* movie series. Can't you just hear it playing in your head right now?

Besides folk music and Gregorian chants, Italy is known for its opera. If you are an opera fan you cannot miss taking a tour of the world famous **La Scala** in Milan. Getting a ticket to a performance is another matter. But have no fear, if your appetite cannot be sated without the shrill explosion of an *aria* there are other famous opera houses in Italy: **The Opera** in Rome, **The San Carlos** in Naples, **La Fenice** in Venice, **The Reggio** in Turin, **The Communale** in Bologna, **The Petruzzelli** in Bari, **The Communale** in Genoa, and **Massimo Bellini** in Catania (see addresses and phone numbers below).

These are also many opera festivals all over Italy virtually year-round.

Italian Opera

Italian opera began in the 16th century. Over time such composers as Gioacchino Rossini, Gaetano Donizetti, and Vincenzo Bellini created **bel canto** opera – opera that prizes beautiful singing above all else. The best singers were indulged with *arias* that gave them ample opportunity for a prominent display of their vocal resources of range and agility.

Rossini, who reigned as Italy's foremost composer of the early 19th century, was a master of both melody and stage effects. Success came easily, and while still in his teens he composed the first of a string of 32 operas that he completed by the age of 30. Many of these are comic operas, a genre in which Rossini excelled, and his masterpieces in this form are still performed and admired today. Among them is one you probably recognize, *The Barber of Seville* (1816).

Rossini's immediate successor as Italy's leading operatic composer was **Donizetti**, who composed more than 70 works in the genre. A less refined composer than Rossini, Donizetti left his finest work in comic operas, including *Don Pasquale* (1843) and *Lucia di Lammermoor* (1835).

Although he lived for a shorter time than either Rossini or Donizetti and enjoyed a far briefer career, **Bellini** wrote music that many believe surpassed theirs in refinement. Among the finest of his ten operas are *La Sonnambula* (The Sleepwalker, 1831), *Norma* (1831), and *I Puritani* (The Puritans, 1835), all of which blend acute dramatic perceptions with florid virtuosity.

From these roots came Italy's greatest opera composers of all times, **Puccini** and **Verdi**. Giacomo Puccini lived from 1858-1924 and composed twelve operas in all. Considered by many to be a close second to Verdi in skill of composition, Puccini's music remains alive in the popular mind because of enduring works like *Madame Butterfly* and *La Boheme*. Even though Puccini was the fifth generation of musicians in his family, he was mainly influenced to pursue his career after hearing Verdi's *Aida*.

Giuseppe Verdi lived from 1813-1901, and is best known for his operas *Rigoletto* (1851), *Il Trovatore* and *La Traviata* (both 1853), and what could be the grandest opera of them all, *Aida* (1871). Verdi composed his thirtieth and last opera *Falstaff* at the age of 79. Since he mainly composed out of Milan and many of his operas opened at La Scala opera house in that city, today a **Verdi museum** has been established there to honor his work.

Opera, Music, Drama, & Ballet Festivals

As the birthplace of opera, Italy offers visitors a variety of choices during the operatic seasons, which are almost year-round. In the summer months there are wonderful open-air operas presented at the **Terme di Caracalla** (Baths of Caracalla) in the center of Rome near the main train station from July to August, at the **Arena** in Verona from July to August, and at the **Arena Sferisterio** in Macerata in July. In general the opera season lasts from December to June.

Two of the most spectacular festivals for Italian performing arts are the **Maggio Musicale Fiorentino** with opera, concerts, ballet, and drama performances in Florence from May to June, and the **Festival of Two Worlds** with opera, concerts, ballet, drama performances and art exhibits in Spoleto from mid-June to mid-July.

Other events, by their location in Italy, include:
- **Aosta**, mid-July to mid-August: Organ Music Festival
- **Barga (Lucca)**, mid-July to mid-August: Opera Barga
- **Bolzano**, August: International Piano Competition
- **Brescia**, May and June: Piano Festival
- **Catania**, June to September: music and drama performances at the Greek/ Roman theater

- **Cervo (Imperia)**, July and August: Chamber Music Festival
- **Gardone Riviera (Brescia)**, July and August: drama and concerts in the open air theater of the Vittoriale degli Italiani
- **Lucca**, April and June: Sacred Music Festival in a variety of churches
- **Macerata**, July and August: opera and ballet season at the outdoor Arena Sferisterio
- **Marlia (Lucca)**, mid-July to mid-August: Marlia Festival of rare and exotic live performances
- **Martina Franca**, July to August: Festival of the Itria Valley. Southern Italy's top performing arts festival
- **Monreale and Palermo**, October and November: Sacred Music Festival
- **Orta San Giulio (Novara)**, June: Cusius Festival of Early Music which features Gregorian chants, madrigals, cantata, Baroque and Renaissance music, as well as many other more popular works; all performers are in period garb
- **Pavia**, July-August: Concerts on the Certosa. Drama performances outside
- **Perugia**, mid-July to late July: Umbria Jazz Festival. Italy's top jazz festival
- **Pesaro**, mid-August to mid-September: Rossini Opera Festival
- **Ravello**, July: Ravello Classical Music Festival. These take place in the Duomo of Ravello and in the gardens of Villa Rufolo
- **Ravenna**, July and August: Organ Music Festival in the Basilica of San Vitale
- **Ravenna**, mid-July to early August: opera and ballet are performed in the remains of the majestic Rocca di Brancaleone
- **Rome**, June through August: concerts in the Basilica Maxentius
- **Siena**, August: musical weeks
- **Stresa (Novara)**, August to September: musical weeks
- **Taormina (Messina)**, July and August: music and drama festival
- **Torre del Lago Puccini (Lucca)**, August: Puccini opera in the open air theater in Lucca
- **Trieste**, July and August: Operetta Festival
- **Urbino**, August: drama and art exhibitions and concerts in the Renaissance Theater
- **Verona**, June to September: drama festival in the Roman Theater as well as a Shakespearean Festival featuring drama, ballet and jazz
- **Viterbo**, August: Baroque Music Festival

If you wish to obtain tickets to opera performances, concerts, ballet, and other performances you can either write directly to the theater in question or ask your travel agent to obtain the ticket for you. Currently there is no agency in the US authorized to sell concert and/or opera tickets, so this is the only way. When you are in Italy, your hotel should be able to assist you in obtaining tickets for performances in their city.

Addresses & Phone Numbers of Major Opera Houses

Teatro alla Scala, Via Dei Filodrammatici 2, 20121 Milano. Tel 02/861-781 or 861-772, Fax 02/861-778

Teatro dell'Opera, Piazza D. Gigli 1, 00184 Roma. Tel. 060/481-601, Fax 060/488-1253

Teatro La Fenice, Campo S. Fantin 1977, 30124 Venezia. Tel. 041/786-562 or 786-569, Fax 041/786-580

Teatro Communale, Corso Italia 16, 50123 Firenze. Tel. 055/211-158 or 2729236, Fax 055/277-9410

Teatro San Carlo, Via San Carlo 98f, 80132 Napoli. Tel. 081/797-2331 Or 797-2412, Fax 081/797-2306

Teatro Reggio do Torino, Piazza Castello 215, 10124 Torino. Tel 011/88151, Fax 011/881-5214

Teatro Massimo, Piazza Verdi, 90139 Palermo. Tel 091/605-3111, Fax 091/605-3325 or 605-3324

Arena di Verona, Piazza Bra 28, 37121 Verona. Tel. 045/590-109 Or 800-5151, Fax 045/801-1566 or 801-3287

Teatro Comunale, Largo Respighi 1, 41026 Bologna. Tel. 051/529-011 or 529-999, Fax 051/529-934

Teatro Massimo Bellini, Via G. Perrotta 12, 95131 Catania. Tel. 095/321-830; same fax

Regional & National Folk Festivals

Despite the encroachment of the modern world, the traditional festivals and their accompanying costumes and folk music have survived surprisingly well all over Italy. In many cases they have been successfully woven into the pattern of modern life so as to seem quite normal. Despite all possible modern influences these festivals (both secular and religious) have preserved their distinctive character.

Two of the most famous, the secular festivals of the **Palio** in Siena and **Calcio in Costume** in Florence give foreigners a glimpse into the past customs and way of life of medieval Italians. Both of these festivals pit different sections of their respective cities against each other to see who can earn bragging rights for the year. In Siena, a heated horse race takes place in a crowded city square. In Florence the Piazza della Signorina is turned into a veritable battleground when a game that is a cross between boxing, soccer, rugby, and martial arts is played. And what is most impressive of all in these festivals, besides the competition, is the fact that all participants dress in colorful period garb making each city appear to come alive with the past.

Since Italy is the home of the Catholic church, religious festivals also play a large part in Italian life. Particularly interesting are the processions on the occasion of **Corpus Christi, Assumption**, and **Holy Week**. In Italy, holiday times such as Easter and Christmas have not lost their religious intent as they have in most other places, and commercialism takes a back seat to the Almighty. This also means that tradition has not made way for consumerism, allowing us to experience a rich display of costumes, statues, parades, masses and more that evoke a simpler, more peaceful time.

The items below marked by an asterisk are festivals you simply cannot miss; if you can do so, plan your trip around them.

JANUARY
• **New Year's Day**, *Rome*: Candle-lit processional in the Catacombs of Priscilla to mark the martyrdom of the early Christians
• **January 5**, **Rome*: Last day of the Epiphany Fair in the Piazza Navona. All throughout the piazza a fair filled with food stands, candy stands, toy shops opens to the public. Lasts a week. A must see if you are in Rome for the holidays.
• **January 6**, *Piana Degli Albanesi*: Celebration of the Epiphany according to Byzantine rite.

FEBRUARY/MARCH
During February or March in *San Remo*, the Italian Festival of Popular Songs is celebrated.
• **1st half of February**, *Agrigento*: Almond Blossom Festival. Song, dance, costumes, fireworks.
• **Both Months**: *Viareggio, San Remo, Pisa, Turin and some other towns on the Riviera*: Highlight of the carnival celebrations is the procession of spectacular and colorful floats. **Venice*: Carnival in Venice with costume sand masks, with street mimes, music, and fireworks. A fun time.
• **February 24-26**, *Oristano*: "Sa Sartiglia" medieval procession and jousting of masked knights dressed in Sardinian and Spanish costumes.
• **Friday before Shrovetide**, *Verona*: Gnocco (Festival of Bacchus)
• **19 March**, *Many places*: San Giuseppe (St. Joseph's day)

MARCH/APRIL
During March or April, *Rome* celebrates the Festa della Primavera (Spring Festival).
• **1 April**, *San Marino*: Installation of Regents
• **Palm Sunday**, *Many places, particularly Rome and Florence*: Blessings of palms, with procession
• **Wednesday before Easter**, *Many places, particularly Rome*: Mercoledi Santo (lamentations, Miserere)

- **Thursday Before Good Friday**, *Many places, particularly Rome and Florence*: Washing of the Feet, burial of the sacraments
- **Good Friday**, *Many places, particularly Rome and Florence*: Adoration of the Cross. *Taranto*: Procession of the Mysteries (Solemn procession with many beautiful period costumes).
- **Easter Saturday**, *Many places, particularly Rome and Florence*: Lighting of the Sacred Fire
- **Easter Week**, *Assisi*: Celebration of Spring with rites dating back to ancient times.
- **Easter Day**, *Rome*: Papal blessing; *Florence:* Scopplo dei Carro ("Explosion of the Cart" – A pyramid of fireworks is set off in the Cathedral square to commemorate the victorious return of the first Crusade.
- **End of April**, *Taormina*: Costume festival and parade of floats

MAY
- **1 May**, * *Florence*: Calcio in Costume (historical ball game – A Must See; Can't Miss This One)
- **May 2**, *Asti*: Palio San Secondo – 700 year old ceremony with procession in 13th century costumes and flag throwing.
- **During May**, *Florence*: Maggio Musicale (Music festival of May)
- **Beginning of May**, *Cagliari*: Sagra di Sant'Efisio: One of the biggest and most colorful processions in the world. Several thousand pilgrims (wearing costumes from the 17th century) accompany the saint on foot, in carts, or on horses.
- **First Saturday in May**, *Naples*: San Gennaro (feast of St. Januarius)
- **May 7**, *Bari*: Festival of St. Nicholas (procession of fishing boats with people in costumes)
- **Second Sunday in May**, *Camogli (Liguria)*: Sagra del Pesce (fishermen's festival, frying of fish in giant pan)
- **May 15**, *Gubbio (Umbria)*: "Corsa dei Ceri "(procession with candles). Procession in local costumes with tall shrines. They are carried to the church at the top of Mount Ingino.
- **Next to last Sunday in May**, *Sassari*: Sardinian Cavalcade with a traditional procession with over 3,000 people in Sardinian costumes and some naked on horseback.
- **May 26**, *Rome*: San Filippo Neri
- **Last Sunday in May**, * *Gubbio (Umbria):* Palio dei Balestrieri (shooting with crossbows), medieval crossbow contest between Gubbio and Sansepolcro with medieval costumes and arms.
- **Ascension**, *Florence*: Festival of the Crickets. A lot of fun. You get to take home a cricket in a small cage. Something the Chinese do too, but hey, when in Italy ...; *Sassari (Sardinia)*: Cavalcata Sarda (mounted procession)

• **Corpus Christi**, *Many places, particularly Orvieto (Umbria)*: Processions

JUNE
If you're in *Venice*, don't miss the Biannual art exhibition.
• **First Sunday in June**, *Pisa*: Gioco del Ponte – medieval parade and contest for the possession of the bridge; *Either Pisa, Genoa, Venice, or the Amalfi Coast:* Regatta of the maritime republics. Each year the four former maritime republics of Italy meet to battle for supremacy at sea. The friendly contest takes the form of a historic regatta in which longboats representing each of the republics race for first prize: respect. Site changes between the four cities/regions each year.
• **Mid-June**, *Many places*: Corpus Domini (Ascension processions)
• **Mid-June to mid-July**, *Spoleto (Umbria)*: International Festival of Music, Dancing and Drama
• **Sunday after June 22**, *Nola*: The Lily Festival where flower towers are carried in colorful procession by people in costume
• **June 23-24**, *Rome*: Vigilia di San Giovanni Battista (St. John's Eve, fireworks, eating of snails, song competition)
• **June 29**, *Rome*: Santi Pietro e Paulo (feast of Saints Peter and Paul); *Genoa*: "Palio Marinaro dei Rioni." Rowing race in ancient costumes.

JULY
In *Genoa-Nervi*, see the International Ballet Festival in the park of Villa Gropallo.
• **July 2**, *Siena (Tuscany)*: Palio delle Contrade (horse race, historical parade). Also held on August 16th.
• **July 10-15**, *Palermo*: Feat of Saint Rosalia with processions, bands, fireworks etc., all decorated in honor of the patron saint of the city.
• **July 16**, *Naples*: Feast of Santa Maria del Carmine
• **July 19-26**, *Rome*: Festa de' Noantri folklore festival of old Rome in Trastevere, Rome's oldest habitable section, which includes a colorful procession, folk dances, songs, carnival floats, and fireworks. Everybody gets real worked up for this. A must see.
• **Third Saturday in July (from that night to Sunday)**, * *Venice:* Festival of Redentore on the Grand Canal. Procession of Gondolas and other craft commemorating the end of the black plague epidemic of 1575
• **During July/August**, *Verona*: Operatic Festival in Roman amphitheater

AUGUST
• **Beginning of August**, *Assisi*: Perdono (Forgiveness Festival)
• **First Sunday in August**, *Acoli/Piceno*: Joust of the Quintana. Historical pageant with over 1,000 people in 15th century costumes.
• **During August**, *Venice*: Nocturnal Festival on Grand Canal

- **During August/September,** *Venice*: Film Festival
- **First Sunday in August,** *Ascoli Piceno (Marche):* Quintana
- **14 August,** *Sassari (Sardinia):* Festival of Candles
- **15 August,** *Many places*: Assumption (processions and fireworks)
- **16 August,** *Siena (Tuscany)*: Palio delle Contrade (horse-races and processions in medieval costume)
- **Second Sunday in August,** *La Spezia*: Palio del Golfo. Rowing contest over a distance of 2,000 meters
- **August 26 to September 20,** *Strosa (Piedmont)*: Settimane Musicali (musical festival)
- **August 27th to 30th,** *Nuoro*: Feat of the Redeemer. Colorful procession in Sardinian costume.

SEPTEMBER/OCTOBER
- **First Sunday in September,** *Arezzo*: Giostra del Saracino (joust of the Saracen) - Tilting contest from the 13th century with nights; *Venice*: Traditional competition on the canal between two-oar racing gondolas preceded by a procession of Venetian Ceremonial boats from the time of the Venetian Republic.
- **September 5-7,** *Naples*: Madonna della Piedigrotta Folk Song Festival
- **September 7,** *Florence*: Riticolone (nocturnal festival with lanterns)
- **September 8,** *Loreto (Marche)*: Nativity of the Virgin; *Recco (Liguria)*: Nativity of the Virgin (large fireworks display, eating of *focaccia*)
- **Second Sunday in September,** *Foligno (Umbria)*: Giostra della Quintane Revival of a 17th century joust with over 600 knights in costume. A historical procession takes place the night before the joust; **Sansepolcro*: Palio Balestrieri. Crossbow contest between Sanselpolcro and Gubbio using medieval arms and costumes.
- **Second Saturday/Sunday in September on even years,** **Marostica*: Partita a Scacchi con Personaggi Viventi (Living Chess Game). Chess game played in town square by living pawns in period costumes.
- **September 13,** *Lucca (Tuscany)*: Luminara di Santa Croce
- **Mid-September,** *Ravenna*: Dante celebrations; *Asti (Piedmont)*: Palio race
- **September 19,** *Naples*: Festival of San Gennaro. Religious ceremony honoring the patron saint of the city.
- **Third Sunday in September,** *Asti*: Palio – ancient festival with over 800 costumed participants and 100 horses. Procession followed by bareback horse race along with flag throwing extravaganza.
- **October 1,** *San Marino*: Installation of Regents

NOVEMBER/DECEMBER
- **November 22,** *Many places*: Santa Cecilia (St. Cecilia's day)
- **December 10,** *Loreto (Marche)*: Santa Casa (procession)

• **December 25**, *Rome*: Papal blessing
• **Mid-December to mid-January**, Many places: Christmas crib (Nativity Scenes)
• **Mid-December**, *Rome* - Nativity Scene and Huge Christmas Tree in St. Peter's Square

Crafts

Hundreds of thousands of skillful Italian artisans are the heirs to a 2,000-year tradition of craftsmanship. Their products – fashioned of leather, gold, silver, glass, and silk – are widely sought by tourists who flock to Florence, Rome, Milan, and Venice. Cameos made from seashells, an ancient Italian art form, are as popular today as they were in the days of the Roman Empire. The work of Italian artists and artisans is also exported for sale in the great department stores of France, Germany, the United Kingdom, and the United States.

Italian clothing designers are world famous, especially for precise tailoring, unusual knits, and the imaginative use of fur and leather.

The best place to see Italian artisans at work is in the glass blowing factories of Venice. There you'll be amazed at how easily they can manipulate molten balls into some of the most delicate, colorful, and beautiful pieces you've ever seen. Each chapter in this book highlights specific traditional crafts by region.

Literature

Perhaps Italy's most famous author/poet is **Dante Aligheri**, who wrote the *Divine Comedy*, in which he describes his own dream-journey through Hell (*l'Inferno*) Purgatory (*Purgatorio*), and Paradise (*Paradiso*). At the time it was extremely controversial, since it is a poem about free will and how man can damn or save his soul as he chooses, which was contrary to church teachings. Even today it sparks controversy since it seems apparent that Dante's description of Purgatory is actually describing the life we all lead on earth, and shows his belief in reincarnation.

Two other notable Italian writers (you should remember these for quality cocktail party conversation) are **Petrarch**, famous for his sonnets to Laura, a beautiful girl from Avignon who died quite young, and is known as the "First of the Romantics;" and **Boccaccio**, the Robin Williams of his time, except he wrote, not performed, his famous *Decameron*, a charming and sometimes ribald series of short stories told by ten young people in a span of ten days. He was sort of like the Chaucer of Italy.

Among contemporary Italian writers, **Umberto Eco** stands out on his own. You may know two of his books that have been translated into English: *The Name of the Rose* and the more recent *Foucault's Pendulum*. If you are looking for complex, insightful, intriguing, and intellectual reading, Eco's your man. Last but not least, one Italian writer whom children all over the world should know is **Calo Collodi**, who wrote *Pinnochio*.

Shakespeare's Italy

The Immortal Bard chose Italy as the setting for a number of his best-known masterpieces: **Othello** takes place in part in Venice, and features both honorable and conniving Venetians; **Two Gentlemen from Verona** and **Romeo & Juliet** take place in Verona (the latter was pretty much lifted from Luigi da Porto's identical story, and today you can visit Juliet's House in Verona); **The Merchant of Venice** takes place in Venice; **The Taming of the Shrew** concerns the doings of rich Paduans, Pisans, and Veronans;

about half of **A Winter's Tale** takes part in Sicily; all of **Much Ado About Nothing** takes place in Sicily; and **All's Well That Ends Well** has one part set in Florence.

Ancient Rome and the ageless themes of power, love, and intrigue also held great allure for Shakespeare: pick up **Julius Caesar**, **Titus Andronicus**, **Troilius & Cressida**, or **Coriolanus** for some light reading about the tragic nature of the men and women who made the Roman Empire the world's first superpower!

Chapter 11

food & wine

Food

Most Italian food is cooked with the freshest ingredients, making their dishes not only healthy but tasty and satisfying. There are many restaurants in Italy of international renown, but you shouldn't limit yourself only to the upper echelon. In most cases you can find as good a meal at a fraction of the cost at any trattoria. Also, many of the upper echelon restaurants you read about are only in business because they cater to the tourist trade. Their food is acceptable, but doesn't warrant the prices charged. I list the best restaurants in every city, where you can get a wonderful meal every time. As you will notice in each regional chapter, I feature some top-of-the-line restaurants as well as many local places, but each are well off the regular tourist path, and each offers a magnificently Italian experience for your enjoyment.

The traditional Italian meal consists of an antipasto (appetizer) and/or soup, and/or pasta and is called primo, a main course called secondo (usually meat or fish), with separately ordered side dishes of contorni (vegetables) or insalata (salad) which come either verdi (green) or mista (mixed), then dolci (dessert), which can be cheese, fruit, or gelato (ice cream). After which you then order your coffee and/or after dinner drink.

Note: Pasta is never served as an accompanying side dish with a secondo. In Italy, it is always served as a separate course. It is time to forget everything you thought you knew about "Italian" food that was learned at some run-of-the-mill restaurant chain.

Glossary of Italian Eateries

Bar – Not the bar we have back home. This place serves espresso, cappuccino, rolls, small sandwiches, sodas and alcoholic beverages. It is normal to stand at the counter or sit at a table when one is available. You have to try the **Medalione**, a grilled ham and cheese sandwich available at most bars. A little 'pick-me-up' in the morning is **Café Corretto**, coffee 'corrected' with the addition of **grappa** (Italian brandy) or Cognac.

Gelateria – These establishments offer gelato – ice cream – usually produced on the premisés. Italian gelato is softer than American but very sweet and rich.

Osteria – Small tavern-like eatery that serves local wine usually in liter bottles as well as simple food and sandwiches

Panineria – A small sandwich bar with a wider variety than at a regular Italian bar, where a quick meal can be gotten. One thing to remember is that Italians rarely use condiments on their sandwiches. If you want mustard or such you need to ask for it.

Pasticceria – Small pasty shops that sell cookies, cakes, pastries, etc. Carry-out only.

Pizzeria – A casual restaurant specializing in pizza, but they also serve other dishes. Most have their famous brick ovens near the seating area so you can watch the pizza being prepared. There are many excellent featured pizzerias in this book.

Pizza Rustica – Common in central Italy. These are huge cooked rectangular pizzas displayed behind glass. This pizza has a thicker crust and more ingredients than in a regular Pizzeria. You can request as much as you want, since they usually charge by the weight, not the slice.

Rosticceria – A small eatery where they make excellent inexpensive roast chickens and other meats, as well as grilled and roasted vegetables, mainly potatoes. Sometimes they have baked pasta.

Trattoria – A less formal restaurant with many local specialties.

Ristorante – A more formal eating establishment, but even most of these are quite informal at times.

Tavola Calda – Cafeteria-style food served buffet style. They feature a variety of hot and cold dishes. Seating is available. Great places for a quick lunch.

Many North Americans think that there is one type of Italian food, and that's usually spaghetti and meatballs. As a result they don't know what they are missing. Region by region Italy's food has adapted itself to the culture of the people and land. In Florence you have some of the best steaks in the world, in the south the tomato-based pastas and pizzas are exquisite; in Genoa you can't miss the pesto sauce (usually garlic, pine nuts, parmiggiano and basil); and don't forget the seafood all along the coast.

Listed below is a selection of the main regional specialties that you should try. In each regional section, I have itemized for you some of the best places to find these and other dishes.

- **Piemonte** – *fonduta (cheese with eggs and truffles), agnolotti* (cheese stuffed pasta), and chocolates and toffees
- **Lombardia** – *risotto all milanese* (rice with saffron), *minestrone* (stock and vegetable soup), *ossobuco alla milanese* (knuckle of pork dish), *robiola, gorgonzola, stracchino, Bel Paese* (a variety of cheeses)
- **Veneto** – *risi e bisi* (soup with rice and peas), *polenta* (corn meal dish) *zuppa di pesce* (fish soup), *scampi* (shrimp or prawns)
- **Liguria** – *minestrone* (stock and vegetable soup), *pasta al pesto* (pasta with an aromatic garlic basil sauce), *torta Pasqualina* (Easter pie filled with spinach, artichokes, and cheese)
- **Emilia Romagna** – *lasagna verde* (lasagna made with spinach), *cappelletti alla bolognese* (small hats pasta covered with a tomato meat sauce), *scallope* (scallops) *Parmigiano Reggiano* (cheese) and a variety of salamis
- **Toscana** – *bistecca all Fiorentina* (large T-bone steaks grilled), *arista* (roast pork), *cacciucco* (fish soup)
- **Lazio** – *abbacchio arrosto* (roast lamb), *porcetta* (roast pork), and pastas, including *penne all'arrabiata* (literally translated it means angry pasta; a spicy hot, garlic-laden, tomato dish; should not be missed) and *tortellini alla panna* (most of which is cheese stuffed pasta in a heavy cream sauce but sometimes it can be meat stuffed)
- **Campania** – *spaghetti alla vongole verace* (with a spicy garlic oil sauce.), Fantastic pizzas because of their wonderful cheeses (*mozzarella, provola, caciocavallo*)
- **Sicilia** – fresh fruits, pastries like *cannoli alla Siciliana; caponata di melanzane* (eggplant dish), and seafood

Restaurant Listings in This Book

Here's a sample listing which you'll find in this book in each of our *Where to Eat* sections. The number preceding the name of the restaurant tells you where to find it on the accompanying city or town map.

"**3. LA LEPANTO**, *Via Carlo Alberto 135, Tel. 079/979-116. Closed Mondays in the winter. All credit cards accepted. Dinner for two E70.*

A fine place with a quaint terrace located in the heart of the old city, but the preparation of dishes is haphazard. Sometimes it's great, other times so-so. Maybe it's because they try to do too much. The menu is extensive and seems to have everything that surf and turf could offer. I've always been pleased with the *i polpi tiepido con le patate* (roasted octopus in an oil and garlic sauce with roasted potatoes) and the *spaghetti con gamberi e melanzane* (with shrimp and eggplant). For antipasto, try the exquisite *antipasto misto di pesce spada affumicato* (smoked swordfish) or the *insalata mista* (mixed salad) with fresh vegetables from the region."

The restaurant listings indicate which credit cards are accepted by using the following phrases:
- **Credit cards accepted** = American Express and/or Visa or Mastercard
- **All credit cards accepted** = Everything imaginable is accepted, even cards you've never heard of
- **No credit card accepted** = Only cash or travelers checks (if a listing is left without an indication, that means that no credit cards are accepted.)

Each restaurant listing will give a ballpark price for a dinner for two in Euros. For example: "Dinner for two E40." This price represents the cost for two people who choose to eat a full meal of an antipasto, pasta dish and an entrée. In most cases you can get by with one course, which will make the actual price you will pay less than indicated. With the exchange rate at roughly $1=Euro (E)1, for this example the dollar price would be about $40 for the meal.

Wine

Italy is also famous for its wines. The experts say the reds are not robust enough, and the whites are too light, but I'm not an expert. Personally I think Italian wines are great, one and all. Most importantly, to get a good bottle of wine, you don't have to spend a fortune. You can find some excellent wines straight out of vats in small wine stores in every city in Italy.

At any restaurant, all you'll need to order is the house wine to have a satisfying and excellent wine. (*Vino di casa*: House Wine; *Rosso*: Red; *Biancho*: White). But if you're a connoisseur, or simply want to try a wine for which a certain Italian region is known, in the sidebar above you'll find a selected list of wines and their regions (if you like red wine, try the Chianti, and if it's white you prefer, try Verdicchio or Frascati).

Italian Wines by Region

Piemonte – Barolo (red, dry), Barbera (red, dry), and Asti Spumanti (sweet sparkling wine)

Lombardia – Riesling (white, dry), Frecciarossa (rose wines)

Trentino-Alto Adige – Riesling (white, dry), Santa Maddalena (red, semi-dry), Cabernet (red, dry)

Veneto – Soave (white, dry), Valpolicella (red, dry or semi-sweet)

Liguria – Cinqueterre (named after a section of Liguria you must visit. Cinqueterre is five small seaside towns inaccessible by car or train, you have to walk. They're simply gorgeous.)

Emilia Romagna – Lambrusco (red, semi-sparkling, several kinds going from dry to sweet), Sangiovese (red, dry), Albano (white, dry or semi-sweet)

Tuscany – Chianti (red, dry; look for the Chianti Classico. They're the ones with a black rooster on the neck of the bottle)

Marche – Verdicchio (white, dry)

Umbria – Orvieto (white, dry)

Lazio – Frascati (white, dry or semi-sweet), Est Est Est (white, slightly sweet)

Abruzzi – Montepulciano (red, dry)

Sardinia – Cannonau (red, dry to semi-sweet)

Sicily – Etna (red and white, wide variety), Marsala (white, dry or sweet)

Campania, Apulia, Calabria, Basilicata – Ischia (red and white, several varieties), San Severo (red, dry)

Order Like a Native:
Reading an Italian Menu

Here are a few choice words to assist you when you're ordering from a menu while in Italy. Usually, the waiter should be able to assist you, but if not, this will make your dining more pleasurable. You wouldn't want to order octopus, rabbit or horse by surprise, would you?

And if you do not find this list adequate, I can recommend a superb pocket-sized booklet published by Open Road Publishing, *Eating and Drinking in Italy*, by my good friends Andy Herbach and Michael Dillon. You will find these ever so useful guides in any bookstore, online or at their website: *www.eatndrink.com*.

ENGLISH	ITALIAN	ENGLISH	ITALIAN
Menu	*Lista or Carta*	Teaspoon	*Cucchiaino*
Breakfast	*Prima Colazione*	Knife	*Cotello*
Lunch	*Pranzo*	Fork	*Forchetta*
Dinner	*Cena*	Plate	*Piatto*
		Glass	*Bicchiere*
Cover	*Coperto*	Cup	*Tazza*
Spoon	*Cucchiao*	Napkin	*Tovagliolo*

Antipasto

ENGLISH	ITALIAN	ENGLISH	ITALIAN
Soup	*Zuppa*	Broth	*Brodo*
Fish Soup	*Zuppa di Pesce*	Vegetable soup	*Minestrone*
Broth with beaten egg	*Stracciatella*		

Pasta

ENGLISH	ITALIAN	ENGLISH	ITALIAN
Ravioli with meat stuffing	*Agnolotti*	Egg noodles	*Fettucine*
Large rolls of pasta	*Cannelloni*	Potato-filled, ravioli-like pasta	*Gnocchi*
Thin angel hair pasta	*Capellini*	Thin pasta	*Vermicelli*
Little hat pasta	*Capelletti*	Macaroni-like pasta	*Penne*

Eggs *Uova*

ENGLISH	ITALIAN	ENGLISH	ITALIAN
soft-boiled	*al guscio*	hard boiled	*sode*
fried	*al piatto*	omelet	*frittata*

Fish *Pesce*

ENGLISH	ITALIAN	ENGLISH	ITALIAN
Seafood	*Frutti di mare*	Eel	*Anguilla*
Lobster	*Aragosta*	herring	*Aringa*
Squid	*Calamari*	Carp	*Carpa*
Mullet	*Cefalo*	Grouper	*Cernia*
Mussels	*Cozze/Muscoli*	Perch	*Pesce Persico*
Salmon	*Salmone*	Clams	*Vongole*
Octopus	*Polpo*	Bass	*Spigola*
Oysters	*Ostriche*	Mixed fried fish	*Fritto Misto Mare*

Meat *Carne*

ENGLISH	ITALIAN	ENGLISH	ITALIAN
Spring Lamb	*Abbacchio*	Lamb	*Agnello*
Rabbit	*Coniglio*	Chicken	*Pollo*
Small Pig	*Porcello*	Veal	*Vitello*
Steak	*Bistecca*	Breast	*Petto*

Pork	*Maiale*	Liver	*Fegato*
Cutlet	*Costellata*	Deer	*Cervo*
Wild Pig	*Cinghiale*	Pheasant	*Fagione*
Duck	*Anitra*	Turkey	*Tacchino*

Methods of Cooking

Roast	*Arrosto*	Boiled	*Bollito*
On the Fire/	*Ai Ferri*	Spit-roasted	*Al Girarrosto*
Grilled	*Alla Griglia*		
Rare	*Al Sangue*	Grilled	*Alla Griglia*
Well Done	*Ben Cotto*	Medium Rare	*Mezzo Cotto*

Miscellaneous

French fries	*Patate Fritte*	Cheese	*Formaggio*
Butter Sauce	*Salsa al burro*	Tomato and	*Salsa Bolognese*
		Meat Sauce	
Tomato Sauce	*Salsa Napoletana*	Garlic	*Aglio*
Oil	*Olio*	Pepper	*Pepe*
Salt	*Sale*	Fruit	*Frutta*
Orange	*Arancia*	Cherries	*Ciliege*
Strawberry	*Fragola*	Lemon	*Limone*
Apple	*Mela*	Melon	*Melone*
Beer	*Birra*	Mineral Water	*Aqua Minerale*
Orange Soda	*Aranciata*	7 Up-like	*Gassatta*
Lemon Soda	*Limonata*	Juice (of)	*Succo (di)*

Wine	*Vino*		
Red	*Roso*	White	*Bianco*
House wine	*Vino di Casa*	Dry	*Secco*
Slightly Sweet	*Amabile*	Sweet	*Dolce*
Local Wine	*Vino del Paese*	Liter	*Litro*
Half Liter	*Mezzo Litro*	Quarter Liter	*Un Quarto*
A Glass	*Un Bicchiere*		

In all restaurants in Italy there used to be a universal cover charge, *pane e coperto* (literally "bread and cover"), which was different restaurant to restaurant, and in some cases was quite expensive. **Pane e coperto** was tacked on to your bill above and beyond any tip you decided to leave; but in msot cases, many places in Italy has decided that foreigners would not understand what *pane e coperto* is so they have eliminated it. Butm if your bill has an extra E5 or so, that is the pane e coperto, which covers the cost of the basket of bread at your table and gives you the right to sit there.

There will also be a statement about whether service is included, **servizio incluso**, or not, **servizio non incluso**. If service is included it is usually 15% of the bill. If you felt the service was good, it is customary to leave between 5-10% more for the waiter. Another feature on most menus are **piatti di giorno** (daily specials) and **prezzo fisso** (fixed price offerings.) The latter can be a good buy if you like the choices and is usually a better deal than ordering a la carte. If you have trouble reading the menu, ask your waiter for assistance. Usually they will speak enough English to to help. And in many restaurants there are menus in different languages to help you choose the food you want.

Chapter 12

best places to stay

Rome

EDEN, *Via Ludovisi, 49, Tel. 06/474-3551, Fax 06/482-1584. E-mail: Reservations@hotel-eden.it. Web: www.hotel-eden.it/index_e.html. 100 rooms all with private bath. Single E280-495; Double E450-825, Suites E700. Continental breakfast is E14 extra, buffet breakfast is E20.* *****

Located west of Via Veneto in the exclusive Ludovisi section but still in the middle of everything, the Eden is but steps from the famous Via Veneto and Spanish Steps, and the Trevi Fountain is just down the street. The Eden is ideally situated for sightseeing. With a long tradition of excellent service, year after year it maintains its top-ranked exclusivity, attracting all the cognoscenti (those in the know) to its exquisite accommodations. Declared one of the *Leading Hotels of the World*, it has an ultra-sophisticated level of service and comes with amenities virtually unmatched the world over.

Some of the amenities here include the terrace restaurant, which has a spectacular view over the city. Guests and locals alike flock to this restaurant, not just because of the view but because of the excellence of Chef Enrico Derflingher. The former personal chef to the Prince and Princess of Wales, Chef Derflingher prepares food fit for royalty. And after a sumptuous meal you can work it off in their fully appointed gym with everything from cardiovascular equipment to free weights. If you want to stay in the lap of luxury while in Rome, the Eden is the paradise you've been looking for.

LE GRAND HOTEL, *Via Vittorio Emanuele Orlando, Tel. 06/4709, Fax 06/ 474-7307. Web: www.romeguide.it/legrandhotel/legrandhotel.html. Single E195-310; Double E275-450; Suites E950. Extra bed costs E75. Breakfast E20.* *****

Opulence knows no bounds in this extra fine hotel. Located between the Piazza della Repubblica and Piazza San Bernardo, near the American speaking church in Rome, Santa Susanna, this top-class luxury hotel has everything you'd ever need, and the prices to match. The rooms and suites are palatial, some with 16 to 17 foot ceilings, and the bathrooms have every imaginable amenity. The elegance and professional service here are refined including the hairdresser, beauty salons, and sauna. When staying here you will definitely feel like a prince or princess.

Afternoon tea is served downstairs everyday at 5:00pm. They also have a very relaxing but expensive American-style bar. The Grand Hotel has recently undergone an incredible face lift and has returned to its status as a premier hotel, not just in Rome, but the entire world.

VILLA HASSLER, *Piazza Trinita Dei Monti 6, Tel. 06/678-2651, Fax 06/678- 9991. E-mail: hasslerroma@mclink.it. Web: www.hotelhasslerroma.com. All credit cards accepted. 80 rooms all with bath. Single E370-460; Double E500- 660.. Continental breakfast E23 extra. Buffet breakfast E35 extra.* *****

The Villa Hassler may not be as opulent as the Eden, but it is just as refined and equally as elegant. In many travelers' opinions this is the best hotel in Rome, not just because of it's excellent location at the top of the Spanish Steps, but mainly because of the ultra-professional service and amazingly comfortable accommodations. Oil sheiks, movie stars, the nouveau riche, the landed gentry all have made the Hassler home, at one time or another, for over a century. They have a relaxing courtyard and an excellent (but expensive) roof garden restaurant with a superb view of the city.

These same views are shared with a number of the rooms on the upper floors facing the Spanish Steps, so remember to request one of these. Every imaginable amenity awaits you at the Hassler, and in a city filled with great restaurants, they have one of the best. So you don't even have to leave your hotel to have a first class meal. Even if you don't stay here, come to the restaurant, sample the food, and enjoy the superb view.

One of the best, most famous, and ideally located hotels in Rome. If you have the means, I recommend it highly.

BAROCCO, , *Piazza Barberini 9 (entrance on Via della Purificazione 4), Tel. 06/487-2001/2/3, 487-2005, Fax 06/485-994. E-mail: hotelbarocco@holelbarocco.it. Web: www.hotelbarocco.com. 37 rooms all with bath. Single E150-200; Double E240-290. Breakfast included. All credit cards accepted.* ****

A four star of the highest quality, but also one that is the smallest size. This allows for incredibly attentive service which helps to add to your stay. Here you can have an intimate and elegant four-star experience and you won't get lost in the shuffle as you would at a larger hotel. The entrance hall is a tastefully introduction to its elegance with its beautiful photos of Roman scenes.

The rooms are all as refined, even though each room is different from the other. Some of the best have two levels, others have small terraces, and all offer a unique, comfortable and accommodating living experience while in Rome. All rooms come with an electronic safe, TV, A/C and everything else befitting a four star.

Every decoration and piece of furniture is supremely elegant. The bathrooms are a little small but come with hair dryer and courtesy toiletry kit. In the summer, breakfast is served on the roof terrace. A great location for an evening's relaxation. Centrally located with the Trevi Fountain, Spanish Steps, Via Veneto all around the corner. A great place to spend an entire vacation, or simply the last night of a long one. I love this quaint, intimate little place.

LOCARNO, , *Via della Penna 22, Tel. 06/361-0841, Fax 06/321-5249. E-mail: info@hotellocarno.com. Web: www.hotellocarno.com/. All credit cards accepted. 38 rooms all with bath. Single E207; Double E155-230; Suite E245 and up. Breakfast E12.* ***

Though only a three star I simply adore this hotel. The professional service, the ideal location, and the quality of the rooms, all point to a higher star rating. But let it be our little secret that though only a three star, this place offers exemplary accommodations. Situated between the Piazza del Popolo and the Tiber River, in a nice neighborhood of stores, galleries, and restaurant this hotel is wonderfully situated and amazingly comfortable. It has a very relaxing American-style bar, spacious common areas, a small side-garden patio, and a roof terrace where breakfast is served in good weather. In regular weather the downstair solarium/green house is where you will be served.

The rooms are large and tastefully decorated with all possible amenities. Situated on a side street, the Locarno offers a refined respite from the hectic pace of Rome. The best three star Rome has to offer. One that gives the big boys a run for their money.

Florence

HOTEL TORRE DI BELLOSGUARDO, *Via Roti Michelozzi 2, Tel. 055/ 229-8145, Fax 055/229-008. E-mail: torredibellosguardo@dada.it. Web: www.torrebellosguardo.com/. 16 room all with bath. Single E195; Double E265; Suites E275-325. All credit cards accepted.* ****

If you have the means, this is definitely the most memorable place to stay while in Florence. With stunning views over all of Florence, a swimming pool with a bar at which to relax, olive gardens in which to take an evening stroll, the Bellosguardo is like no other hotel in Florence. Housed in a huge old castle that has been separated into only 16 luxury rooms, it goes without saying that the size of accommodations are quite impressive. The interior common areas with their vaulted stone ceilings and arches, as well as staircases leading off into hidden passages, all make you feel as if you've stepped back in time.

The hotel is a short distance outside of the old city walls in the middle of pristine farmland. You will find pure romance, complete peace, and soothing tranquillity all with stunning views of the city of Florence. In fact the hotel is so well thought of that they are booked solid year round, so you have to reserve well in advance. I can't say enough about the Bellosguardo, it is simply something you have to experience. Also, and most importantly, if you aren't already in love, you'll find it or rekindle it in this wonderfully majestic hideaway.

LOGGIATO DEI SERVITI, *Piazza SS. Annunziata 3, Tel. 055/289-593/4, Fax 055/289-595. E-mail: info@loggiatodeiservitihotel.it. Web: www.loggiatodeiservitihotel.it/. All credit cards accepted. 29 rooms all with private bath. Single E139; Double E201; Suite E268-382. Breakfast included. E40 for an extra bed.* ***

Located in a 16th century *loggia* facing the quiet, quaint and colorful Piazza della SS Annunziata, this hotel is filled with charm, character and is a three star of the highest quality. The interior common areas consist of polished terra-cotta floors, gray stone columns and high white ceilings.

The rooms are pleasant and comfortable and are filled with elegant antique furnishings. All are designed to make you feel like you just walked into the 17th century, and it works. But they do have the modern amenities necessary to keep us weary travelers happy, especially the air conditioning in August.

The best room possible would definitely be #30. From here you have unobstructed views of the Duomo, the spire of the Palazzo Vecchio, and Fort Belvedere beyond the Arno. Out the side windows of this unique room, you can look down into the Accademia and the skylight under which the David stands! A special treat for any traveler.

Some rooms face what many believe is one of the most beautiful piazzas in Italy (no cars allowed), while many of the rest face onto a lush interior garden. They are finished renovation on five additional rooms on the third floor, which will be top of the line accommodations. This place only gets better and better. All the bathrooms come with every modern comfort. The service, the accommodations, everything is at the top of the three star category. So, if you want to have a wonderful stay and also to feel as if you've stepped back in time, book a room here. They also have facilities for weddings and business functions.

Venice

HOTEL CIPRIANI, *Fondamenta San Giovanni 10, La Guidecca, Venezia. Tel. 041/520-7744. Fax 041/520-3930. American Express, Diners Club, Mastercard and Visa accepted. 98 rooms all with bath. Single E250-500; Double E380-700. ****

This exquisite hotel occupies three beautiful acres at the east end of La Isola del Guidecca and comes with a swimming pool, saunas, Jacuzzis, a private harbor for yachts, a private launch to ferry guests back and forth from the center, an American-style bar with every drink imaginable, two superb restaurants, and professional staff waiting on you hand and foot. There are sixty rooms overlooking the lagoon, while many of the others look out over the pool. Each room is stunningly appointed with only the best furnishings and every conceivable comfort.

This hotel is probably as close to heaven on earth as you'll find in Venice. The ambiance is exquisite, the service sublime, and the accommodations impeccable. Staying here makes a visit to Venice almost a fantasy.

HOTEL DANIELI, *Riva degli Schiavoni 4196, Venezia. Tel. 041/522-6480, Fax 041/520-0208. American Express, Diners Club, Mastercard and Visa accepted. 235 rooms all with bath. Single E150-300; Double E250-450. Suites E600-1,400. *****

A completely different style of atmopshere than the Cipriani, but still ultra-luxurious. First opened in 1882 with only 16 rooms, the Danieli has expanded to encompass many surrounding buildings. After encompassing all the fine architectural features of each, the Danieli has developed a beguiling, romantic and enticing atmosphere.

The magnificent lobby, which is built around a Gothic courtyard with its intertwining staircases and columns, is truly awe-inspiring. It makes you feel as if you're suddenly thrust back in time into an ancient medieval castle. One of the largest and best hotels in Venice as well as the most romantic, each room comes perfectly appointed with only the best furnishings and all imaginable modern conveniences. And one of the best places for a meal in all of Venice is the rooftop dining room, with its exquisite view of the Lagoon looking towards the Cipriani.

Courmayeur

GALLIA GRAN BAITA, *Strada Larzy, 11013 Courmayeur. Tel. 0165/844-040, Fax 0165/844-805 (US & Canada Tel. 402/398-3200, Fax 402/398-5484; Australia Toll Free 800/810-862; England, Tel. 071/413-8886, Fax 071/413-8883). 50 rooms and 3 junior suites all with bath. Single E75-140; Double E100-250; Suite E350. Breakfast E12 extra. Credit cards accepted.* ****

Even though it was only established in 1994, the Gran Baita has been created with tradition, style, character and ambiance in mind. The entrance hall comes complete with antique furnishings from the 1600s where you are served tea in the afternoons. The rooms are large, comfortable, and accommodating and come richly decorated in coordinated green or yellow color schemes that complement the furnishings well. The marble bathrooms are amazingly appointed and come complete with every imaginable modern convenience.

They have a heated pool for your use, a free shuttle bus to pick you up and drop you off wherever and whenever you choose, a sun room, a workout room, a spa/beauty room that offers everything from being wrapped in seaweed to getting a wax treatment, and they also have baby-sitting services. A great place to stay while in Courmayeur.

Positano - Amalfi Coast

HOTEL LE SIRENUSE, *Via Cristoforo Colombo 30, 84071 Positano. Tel. 089/875-066, Fax 089/811-798. 60 rooms all with bath. Single E200-250. Double E250-320. Credit cards accepted. Breakfast included. Full board E200-280.* *****

Definitely the place to stay in Positano – everything about this hotel is beautiful. Nothing overly fancy, nothing too ostentatious, just simply radiant. The rooms are furnished with antiques but nothing too frilly. The bathrooms are complete with every conceivable comfort. The breakfast buffet is so ample as to dissuade most from lunch. There is a stunningly beautiful pool at your disposal, a sauna, and a small boat to ferry you along the coast. The service is extremely attentive.

Their restaurant is one of the best, if not the best, in the city. Expensive, yes, but when the food is combined with the great views from the terrace, the price is irrelevant. All the food they make here is great, but I believe the chef concocts the best *spaghetti alla vongole* (with spicy clam sauce) in Positano.

Capri - Southern Italy

LA SCALINATELLA, *Via Tragara 10, 80073 Capri. Tel. 081/837-0633, Fax 081/837-8291. 30 rooms, 2 suites, all with bath. Single E150-220; Double 170-320. All credit cards accepted. Closed November to March.* ****

Located on the sea, this small intimate hotel offers you serene ambiance and excellent service, and is the place to stay when on Capri. This four star is run by the same family that operates the Quisisana, except that here you receive much more personal attention since there are only 30 rooms compared to 150. Many prefer the Quisisana, which is considered one of the leading hotels in the world, but for my choice I prefer its sister, La Scalinatella, because of its intimate, romantic charm.

Besides the ample rooms, all with excellent views and decorated with quality furnishings, the hotel has a pool where you can relax or receive your meals. The restaurant, with its stunningly panoramic views, offers warm and welcoming dining experience. This is definitely the most romantic place to stay in Capri.

Umbria - Perugia

RESIDENZA DELL'OSCANA, *06134 Locanda Cenerente - Perugia. 075/ 690-125, Fax 075/690-666, Email: oscano@krenet.it, Web: www.oscano-castle.com & www.assind.krenet.it/oscano/welcome.htm. 100 rooms all with bath. All credit cards accepted. Breakfast included.* **Castle**: *Suite or junior suite on the top floor of the castle is E220; three rooms elsewhere in the castle E170.* **Villa Ada**: *Double E120 per room per night.* **La Macina**: *Weekly rates E320 to E700. Buffet breakfast included and is served in the dining room of the castle.*

Stunning. Incredibly beautiful. Amazing. Like something out of a fairy tale. Simply unbelievable. By far the best place to stay in all of Umbria. If you have a car, and you have the means, this is definitely the place to stay in Umbria. Near Perugia but set deep in the surrounding verdant forested hills, this amazing medieval castle offers an atmosphere of unparalleled charm and ambiance.

There are three locations to choose from: the Castle (a medieval structure complete with towers and turrets that is simply but elegantly decorated and equipped with every comfort); the Villa Ada (a 19th century residence adjoining the castle that is more modern but no less accommodating); and La Macina (a country house down the hill from the other two structures, which comes with complete apartments and an adjacent pool). All three offer the setting for an ideal vacation, but the castle is the place to stay because of its unique, one of a kind, medieval ambiance and charm. A perfect place to spend a honeymoon or simply have the vacation of a lifetime.

Besides the excellent accommodations, you will also find the finest quality cuisine served nightly in the grand hall in the castle. World class chefs cater to your every need as they creatively concoct regional and international dishes from fresh locally grown produce and game. This is a residence and not a hotel, so it does not carry a star rating, but it would easily receive four stars if it decides to allow itself to be regulated by the tourist industry.

Umbria - Orvieto

LA BADIA, *1a Cat., 05019 Orvieto. Tel 0763/301-959 or 305-455, Fax 0763/305-396. All credit cards accepted. Single E140; Double E320.* ****

An unbelievably beautiful 12th century abbey at the foot of Orvieto is now an incredibly beautiful hotel and restaurant. Located only an hour from Rome, you will find one of the most unique and memorable experiences in the entire world. This historic abbey became a holiday resort for Cardinals in the 15th century, and today, through painstakingly detailed renovations, you can stay or dine in incomparable ambiance and charm.

The rooms are immense, the accommodations exemplary, the service impeccable, and the atmosphere like something out of the Middle Ages. For a fairy tale vacation stay here, and make sure that you eat at least once at their soon to be world renowned restaurant that offers refined local dishes — many ingredients culled from owner Count Fiumi's farms and vineyards — in an incredibly historic and romantic atmosphere.

Milan

PRINCIPE DI SAVOIA, *Piazza della Repubblica 17 (near the Giardini Publici). Tel. 02/62-301, Fax 02/659-5838. All credit cards accepted. 285 rooms all with bath. Single E300-360; Double E360-520. All credit cards accepted. Breakfast E15.* *****

This is one of the most elegant and prestigious hotel in of all Italy. Expensive, ritzy, filled with every amenity imaginable, the service is impeccable and caters to your every need. Situated in a neoclassic palazzo that evokes a feeling of refined elegance, this hotel has an historic tradition of accommodating the most dicerning travelers. When in Milan this is a great place to stay, if you have the means.

Recently absorbed into the ITT Sheraton chain, an amazing transformation has been made, while the overall tone and ambiance of elegance remains. While the Principe has always been elegant, Sheraton's influence has dusted off its hidden charm, and polished the ambiance so the true beauty of this hotel can shine through. The rooms are enormous and delicately furnished with beautiful antiques. The bathrooms are awash in marble and every modern convenience. If you have the means, at over 500 square meters, the Presidential suite is the largest in all of Europe.

The hotel comes complete with the Caffé Doney for breakfast, the Galleria restaurant for lunch and dinner, a fitness center with a lap pool and sauna, and a beauty center. You are also afforded courtesy limousine service to the center. When you stay here, you reside in the lap of luxury.

Chapter 13

**r
o
m
e**

Lazio, the province that **Rome** (**Roma**) is in, covers an area of 6,633 square miles, including the provinces of Frosinone, Latina, Roma, and Viterbo, and has a population of over 6 million. Its charms include quaint little seaside resorts nestled in pine groves, pretty lakeside villages, many dominated by castles. There are also exotic skiing resorts, such as Terminillo, only a few hours drive from Rome's center, as well as many beaches, **Lido di Ostia** being one of the best and most easily accessible.

Other than encompassing the national capital, Lazio does not get much respect from the average Italian. Northerners lump it together contemptuously with the southern provinces of Campania and Calabria, and the southern Italians consider it a wasteland of swamps and poor mountain regions inhibiting the entrance to most everyone's destination in the area – Roma.

That is precisely Lazio's identity problem. It is completely overshadowed by Rome, but this was not always the situation. Rome was not always the largest and most powerful city in the region. Prior to the Roman Empire, another culture, the **Etruscans**, dominated the area around Rome. Cervetri and Tarquinia, north of Rome in Lazio, were two of the richest Etruscan cities. Now they are home to magnificent *Necropoli*, cities of the dead. The Etruscans took great care in laying their dead to rest in cemeteries set up like actual towns; and those found in Tarquinia and Cervetri are two of the finest. **Cervetri** is the closest, so this may be the best alternative for a quick day trip.

Besides Rome, the other locations, towns, and cities featured in this chapter include **Vatican City**, **Tivoli Gardens**, **Castel Gandolfo**, **Frascati**, and **Ostia Antica**.

The Eternal City

Rome is the capital of the Republic of Italy, the region of Lazio, and the province of Rome. As such, it has turned into Italy's largest city, with over 6 million people. The **Tiber River (Tevere)**, Italy's third longest (after the Po and the Adige), dissects the middle of Rome.

For a millennium and a half, Rome was the cultural center of Europe. At the time of the Empire, it controlled territory extending from Scotland to North Africa, and from the Atlantic Ocean to the Persian Gulf. During and after the Renaissance (14th century CE), Rome was also a center of artistic expression. **Michelangelo** spent much time here, working on the Sistine Chapel, helping to design St. Peter's, carving the Pieta, and much more. Hundreds of churches were built by the Vatican, and many artists were sponsored to fill them with beautiful works.

Because of this extensive history, dating all the way back to before the time of Christ, Rome has a wide variety of sights to see, which is why many people describe Rome as a living museum. You'll see ancient Roman ruins resting side by side with buildings built three to four centuries ago, and sometimes these ruins having been incorporated into the design of a 'new' building built at the turn of the century.

If You Haven't Done This, You Haven't Been to Rome

Rome has so many options that it's easy to neglect seeing a certain sight, or taking the time to go to a specific restaurant, or making an effort to visit a particular spot late in the evening to enjoy the ambiance and charm. If you do not have the time to sift through the rest of this chapter - which is filled with the most authentic and enjoyable places to stay, eat, and see while in Rome - I have conveniently listed the best of those options below.

Even if you are the furthest thing from being religious, make the effort to see **St. Peter's** and the **Vatican Museum**. This will take the better part of a day if you do a proper tour. No church is more magnificent and no museum is more complete. All others in Rome as well as the rest of Italy, the Uffizzi in Florence excepted, will pale in comparison.

That night, make sure you get to the **Trastevere** district and sample the atmosphere of **La Canonica**, a converted chapel and now a restaurant that also has many tables spilling out along the street. Reserve a spot inside since this may be your last chance to have a meal in a quaint converted chapel. Try their *spaghetti alla carbonara* (with a light cream sauce, covered with ham, peas, and grated parmesan cheese) for *primo* and for your main course sample the light fish dish, *sogliola alla griglia* (grilled Sole). Then sojourn to one of the cafés in the **Piazza Santa Maria** in Trastevere, grab a drink, and savor the evening.

During another day it is imperative that you visit **Piazza Navona** and grab an ice cream at one of the cafés, and either lounge on their terraces or take it with you while you sit on the edge of one of the fountains. The best vantage point is on Bernini's magnificent **Fontana Dei Quattro Fiumi** (Fountain of Four Rivers). The four figures supporting the large obelisk (a Bernini trademark) represent the Danube, the Ganges, the Nile, and the Plata rivers. Notice the figure representing the Nile. It is shielding its eyes from the facade of the church it is facing, **Santa Agnese in Agone**, which was designed by Bernini's rival at the time, Borromini. An ancient artistic quarrel comes to life everyday in Piazza Navona.

From there, only a few blocks away is the quaint piazza **Campo dei Fiori** where you'll find one of Rome's best fruit and vegetable markets every day until 1:00pm, except Sundays. Make sure you get here to shop or just to enjoy the atmosphere of a boisterous Roman market.

There is a restaurant in the square where you should enjoy at least one meal, **La Carbonara**. Even though the name would lead you to believe that the best dish to get is the *spaghetti alla carbonara*, it is my impression that their best dish is the *spaghetti alla vongole verace* (with a spicy oil, garlic, and clam sauce). If you want to sit outside, you'll have to wait until about 2:00pm, because that is when all the debris from the outdoor market has been swept up from the piazza.

Other dishes you need to sample while in Rome are the *penne all'arrabbiata* (literally means angry pasta and is a tubular pasta made with a spicy garlic, oil, and tomato-based sauce), the *tortellini alla panna* (meat or cheese filled pasta in a thick cream sauce), and any *abbacchio* (lamb) or *maiale alla griglia* (grilled pork).

In the evening, don't miss the **Trevi Fountain** all lit up and surrounded by locals and tourists strumming on guitars and drinking wine. It's definitely a party atmosphere. Come here with friends or arrive and meet new ones. For one of your evening meals, there's a place somewhat close by a little past the **Spanish Steps**, where, if you're here in Spring, you should stop for a minute and admire the floral display covering the steps.

At **La Capriciossa** you can sit in a peaceful little piazza just off the Via del Corso, Rome's main shopping street, while you enjoy your meal. They are known for making excellent pizza (only in the evening) as well as preparing perfect Roman pasta dishes and exquisite meat plates. If you haven't already sampled the *penne all'arrabbiata*, do so here, and try the succulent *abbacchio arrosto* (roast lamb), another staple of the Roman diet. And to finish the meal, order a *sambucca con mosce* (this is a sweet liquor with three flies with three coffee beans floating in it). Remember to bite into the beans as you have the sweet liquor in your mouth. The combination of tastes is exquisite.

There is obviously much more to do in Rome than this, but if you only have a little time, make sure you get to the places mentioned above. Then you can say you really have seen Rome.

Arrivals & Departures

By Air

Most travelers will arrive at **Rome's Fiumicino (Leonardo da Vinci) Airport**, which handles most incoming flights from North America, Australia, and the United Kingdom. If you are arriving from other points in Europe you may arrive at Rome's **Ciampino** airport.

Rome's Fiumicino has a dedicated **train** to whisk you directly to the central train station (**Termini**). When you arrive at **Stazione Termini** (Rome's main train station), you catch a taxi to your hotel from the taxi stand in front of the station. Or you can hop on the Metro, which is underneath the train station, or take one of the many city buses located outside the front of Stazione Termini.

If you arrive at Rome's **Ciampino** (which is really only used for flights from European counties), there are dedicated airport buses that leave for the **Anagnina Metro Station** every half an hour. If you rent a car, simply take **Via Appia** all the way into town. For the scenic view get on the **Via Appia Antica** a kilometer or so after passing the **GRA**.

Rome Fiumicino (Leonardo da Vinci) Airport

Direct Link. A train service is available from the airport directly to **Stazione Termini** (Rome's Central Railway Station). The trip costs Euro (E) 8.5 one way and takes 30 minutes. There are trains every half hour. They start operating from the airport to Termini at 7:38am and end at 10:08pm. Returning to the airport the trains also run every half hour, from track 25-29, but start at 6:52am and ends at 9:22pm. Note: You can pick up a schedule for the train when you buy your tickets. This will help you plan for your departure.

Metropolitan Link. There is train service from the Airport to **Stazione Tiburtina** stopping at the following stations: Ponte Galleria, Muratella, Magliana, Trastevere, Ostiense, and Tuscolana. Departures are every 20 minutes from 6:00am to 10:00pm. Trip takes about 45 minutes. Trains are air-conditioned.

Night Time Arrivals and Departures. There is a night bus running between Fiumicino and Tiburtina station, which stops at Termini. From Fiumicino the bus leaves at 1:15am, 2:15am, 3:30am and 5:00am. From Tiburtina station to the airport the bus runs at 12:30am, 1:15am, 2:30am and 3:45am. The trip takes about half and hour.

Car Rental. If you are renting a car, you can get explicit driving directions from your rental company. See the *Renting a Car* section below for more complete information. If they neglect to give you directions, make sure you get on the large road – **SS 201** – leading away from the airport to the **GRA** *(Grande Raccordo Anulare)*, which is Rome's beltway and is commonly known as the **Anulare**, going north. Get off at **SS 1** (**Via Aurelia**) and follow this road all the way into town.

Airport Shuttles. In the past few years a number of shuttle services have sprouted up to ferry tourists back and forth between Rome's airports and downtown. These are great options if you arrive into either Roman airport, need a ride to Rome and don't want to pay an arm and leg to a taxi. Listed below are two of the best:

• **Airport Shuttle** – *Tel. 06/4201-4507, Web: airportshuttle.it, E-mail: airportshuttle@airportshuttle.it. Office hours 6:30am-10:30pm, 7 days a week. No credit cards. Cash only. E28 for one or two passengers. For service between 8pm and 8am it's 30% more. Pick-up service at Ciampino or Fiumicino add an additional E12. Fluent English spoken.*

• **Airport Connection Services** – *Tel. 06/338-3221. Available 7:00am to 7:00pm. Major credit cards accepted. Must be booked at least a day in advance; closed Christmas and New Year's Day. For E16 per person (shared with others) will take you from the airport to your hotel and vice versa. They also offer a private Mercedes for E38 to perform the same service.*

Rome Ciampino Airport

Bus Link – Buses leave from the airport starting at 6:00am and end at 10:30pm and will take you to the **Anagnina Metro** stop, where you can catch the subway to Termini station. The only other option is taking a taxi or the **Airport Connection Service**.

By Car

To get into Rome you will have to either get on or pass by the **Anulare**, Rome's beltway. If arriving from the north you will be using **Via Cassia** (which can get congested), **Via Flaminia**, **Via Salaria** or the fastest route, the **A1** *(Autostrada del Sole)*, which will dump you onto the Anulare.

If arriving from the south, the fastest route is the **A2**, also referred to as the *Autostrada del Sole*. A more scenic route is along the **Via Appia**.

Sample trip lengths on the main roads:
• **Florence**: 3 1/2 hours
• **Venice**: 6 1/2 hours
• **Naples**: 3 hours
• **Bari**: 13 hours

By Train

When arriving by train, you will be let off at Rome's main train station,

Stazione Termini. From here you can catch a **taxi** at the row of cabs outside the front entrance, walk down to the **Metro** and catch a train close to your destination, or hop on one of the **buses** in the main square (Piazza Cinquecento) just in front of the station.

Termini is a zoo. Packed with people from all over the world, queuing up to buy tickets, trying to cut in line to get information, and in some cases looking for unprotected belongings. So don't leave your bags unattended here or in any train station in Italy. The **Tourist Information** office is located near the train tracks *(Tel. 06/487-1270)*. You can get a good map here and make a hotel reservation. The **Railway Information** office faces the front entrance along with the taxis and buses. If you're planning a trip, you should come here to find out when your train will be leaving. All attendants speak enough English to get by. There is a **baggage storage area** at Termini which is open from 5:15am to 12:20am. For E2.5 you can store an item there for 12 hours. There are also lockers available for E2.5 for 6 hours.

Sample trip lengths and costs for direct *(diretto)* trains:
- **Florence**: 2 1/2 hours, E23
- **Venice**: 5 hours, E33
- **Naples**: 2 hours, E16
- **Bari**: 12 hours, E40

Getting Around Town

By Car

If you are thinking of driving in Rome some people would wonder if you are nuts. Unless you are from Boston and are used to aggressive driving tactics, driving a car to get around Rome is a crazy idea, considering that the public transportation system is so good and that virtually everything is within walking distance. If you want to rent a car for a day trip to the beach at Lido di Ostia or another excursion, that's another story. But even in those circumstances, you can still get to those destinations and most others by train from Stazione Termini.

So think twice about renting a car while in Rome, and if you do rent a car, beware of those automobiles with a big letter "P" taped to the rear windows or trunks. It stands for *Principinate di Patente Fresche*, meaning a newly licensed driver. They are the worst. Also beware of the cars with the words *Scuola Guida* (Driving School) on them.

Remember too that if you rent a car you'll need to buy gas, which besides being expensive can sometimes be inconvenient, because many stations in Italy are unmanned self-service and the pumps only take crisp Euro bills. So if you rent a car, remember to carry crisp bills at all times.

Renting a Car

Cars can be rented at **Fiumicino** or **Ciampino airports**, booked in advance by a travel agent, or rented at many offices in the city, especially at the **Stazione Termini**. Try the following places:

• **Avis**, *Information Tel. 06/41998. Their office at Termini Station is open Monday-Saturday 7:00am-8:00pm, and Sundays from 8:00am-11:00pm (Tel. 06/413-0812). Their office at Fiumicino is open every day from 7:30am-11:00pm (Tel. 06/7934-0195).*
• **Hertz**, *Customer Service 06/5429-4500. Main Office is on the Via Veneto #156. The phone number is 06/821-6881 or 06/321-6834. The office number at Fiumicino it's 06/6501-1448; at Ciampino it's 06/7934-0095. Web: www.hertz.com.*
• **National/Maggiore**, *Car reservations in Italy 1478/67067. Van Reservations in Italy 1478/48844. Web: www.maggiore.it. Fiumicino Tel. 06/65-010-678.*

The fees usually include the costs for towing, minor repairs, and basic insurance, but you should ask just to make sure. Also most firms require a deposit equal to the daily cost of the rental, which is usually between E100 and E150. The minimum age for rental usually is 21 and you must have had a drivers license for at least a year. Rules and regulations will vary according to company, since the concept of standard industry practices hasn't hit Italy yet.

Towed Car?

If your car happens to have been towed, it means you parked in an illegal spot. To find out where your car is call **Vigili Urbani**, *Tel. 06/67691*, and give them the registration number, make of car and place where it was removed. They will tell you where your car has been placed, but you can only pick up your car after you have paid your fine at Via della Consolazione 4. Take your receipt with you when you retrieve your car. On Sundays the office to pay your fine is closed, but the towers are still working – so don't park illegally on Sundays.

Parking Your Car in Rome
If you are just passing through, or you've decided to rent a car to get around Rome, you are going to have to deal with the Byzantine Roman parking system. There are spaces on the street indicated by blue lines where you can park for E1 per hour. This is usually only from 8am – 8pm. The tickets can be purchased at the vending machines along the sidewalks (which use coin only) or at *tabacchi* stores or newsstands. Ask for a *biglietto per parcheggio* (parking ticket). There are also some large public and private parking garages

situated all around the city, where you can leave your car overnight if the hotel you are staying at does not have a garage. These public lots are located at: ParkSi in Villa Borghese, Parking Ludovisi on Via Ludovisi 60, and Parking Termini in front of the main train station.

By Moped

If you are looking for a new experience, a different way to see Rome (or any city in Italy), try renting a moped. Walking, riding a bicycle, driving a car, taking the bus, or riding in a taxi cannot come close to the exhilaration of riding a moped.

A moped gives you freedom. A moped gives you the ability to go from one corner of Rome to another, quickly. Riding a moped makes you feel in tune with the flow of the city. With no plan, no structure, no itinerary, no boundaries, you can go from the tourist areas to a part of Rome tourists rarely see. You can find monuments and markets in Rome you would never have seen if not on a moped. It makes you feel a part of the city, and this familiarity gives you the confidence to widen your explorations.

Now that I've almost convinced you to rent one, I'll counsel you to think hard about not renting one. Traffic in Rome is like nothing you have ever seen, and as such makes riding a moped rather dangerous. Only if you feel extremely confident about your motorcycle driving abilities should you even contemplate renting a moped. This isn't the Bahamas where everyone's polite. The Romans will just as soon run you over as make way for you.

Moped Caution & Rates

If you cannot ride a bicycle, please do not rent a moped. The concept is the same, one vehicle just goes a little faster. Also, start off renting a 50 cc (**cinquanta**), not a 125 cc (**cento venti cinque**). With more than twice the engine capacity, the 125 cc is a big difference, and in the traffic of Rome it's best to start slow. But if you insist on riding two to a moped, then a 125 cc is necessary. It's the law too. (Not that any Italians abide by it). Also you need to be at least sixteen years old to rent a moped, but you don't need a motorcycle license. Just hop on, and ride away ... but don't let Mom and Dad know about it.

A sizable deposit (around E100+) is required for each moped. The deposit will increase based on the size of moped you want to rent. Your deposit can be cash in any currency, travelers checks, or on a credit card. This is standard procedure for all rental companies. Do not worry, you'll get your money back. Daily rates are between E25 and E40. Renting for a more extended period can be a better bargain. Rates should be prominently posted.

Personally, I find a moped to be the most efficient and fun way to get around Rome. They're inexpensive, quick, easy to maneuver, and practical since parking is virtually impossible for a car. But, granted, I have had my accidents. Once, as I was speeding between cars that were stopped at a light, a pedestrian walked in front of me and POW, next thing you know I'm wrapped around a pole. And then there was the time a public bus decided that he had the right of way in a circle and casually knocked me down. Anyway, only if you're *un po pazzo* or very brave should you attempt to rent a moped.

Renting a Moped
• **Bici e Baci**, *Via del Viminale 5, Tel. 06/482-8443. Web: www.romeguide.it/ bicibaci/ bicibaci.html. Open 8:00am-7:00pm. All credit cards accepted.* Extensive selection of bicycles, scooter, and cars. They also organzie guided bike tours or scooter tours in English.
• **Scooters for Rent**, *Via Quattro Novembre 96, Tel. 488-5685. Open 8:30am-8:00pm, seven days a week.* A centrally located moped rental, just off the Piazza Venezia.
• **I Bike Rome di Cortessi Ferruccio**, *Viale Galappatoio, near Via Veneto. Tel. 06/322-5240. Open Monday-Saturday 9:00am-1:00pm and 4:00pm-8:00pm, and Sundays 9:00am-8:00pm.* They rent from the same underground parking garage (connecting the Piazza di Spagna Metro Stop and the Via Veneto) as does Hertz. Maybe that's why you get a 50% discount with a Hertz card.
• **St. Peter's Moto**, *Via di Porto Castello 43, Tel. 06/687-5719. Open Monday-Saturday 9:00am – 1:30pm and 3:30pm-9:30pm.*
• **Scoot-A-Long**, *Via Cavour 302, Tel. 06/678-0206. Open Monday-Saturday 9:00am-7:00pm, Sundays 10:00am-2:00pm and 4:00pm-7:00pm.*
• **Scooter Center**, *Via in Lucina 13/14. Tel. 06/687-6455. Open daily 9:00am-7:30pm. Credit cards accepted. One day E50. Three days E100.*
• **Happy Rent**, *Via Farini 3, Tel & Fax 06/481-8185. Web: www.happyrent.com.* They also have other rental locations by the Colosseum and the Spanish Steps, they rent bicycles, scooters, and cars.

By Bicycle
Bicycles make getting from one spot in Rome to another quicker and easier, but if you haven't been on one in awhile, trying to re-learn on the streets of Rome is not a good idea. And don't even think about having children younger than 14 try and ride around Rome unattended. Not only could they get lost very easily, but the traffic laws are so different they may not be able to adapt very well.

I've seen older teenagers fare very well, especially around the Trevi Fountain, Spanish Steps area. Letting your kids do this gives them a sense of freedom, but reinforce to them how careful they have to be.

Renting a Bicycle

Please refer to the scooter rental place above that I listed as also renting bicycles. The cost for an entire day varies from place to place, and year to year, but the latest price is around E15 per day and E5 per hour, except at the one below, which is only E13 a day and E4 per hour.

• **Bici Pincio**, *Viale di Villa Medici & Viale della Pineta, Tel. 06/678-4374.* A location in the Borghese Gardens and one near the Piazza del Popolo, this company has this side of Rome to themselves and only rents bicycles.

By Taxi

Taxis are the best, but also the most expensive, way to get around Rome. They are everywhere so flagging one down is not a problem. And cab stands are dispersed all over the city too. The strategically placed **cab stands** that will benefit you the most as a tourist are the ones in Piazza del Popolo, Piazza della Repubblica, Piazza Venezia, and at Piazza Sonino just across the bridge in Trastevere.

Since taxis are so expensive I wouldn't rely on them as your main form of transportation. Use them as a last resort, like when you start to get tired from walking. Also have a map handy when a cabby is taking you somewhere. Since they are on a meter, they sometimes decide to take you on a little longer journey than necessary. And also watch out for the fly-by-night operators who don't have a licensed meter. They will really rip you off.

The going rate as of publication was E2 for the first 2/3 of a kilometer or the first minute (which usually comes first during the rush hours), then it's Euro 30 cents every 1/3 of a kilometer or minute. At night you'll also pay a surcharge of E2.5, and Sundays you'll pay E1 extra. If you bring luggage aboard, you'll be charged E1 extra for each bag. In conjunction, if you go from Rome to Fiumicino you will charged E7 extra, Fiumicino to Rome E6, and between Ciampino and Rome you will be charged E5 extra.

Rome also has several radio taxi cooperatives: **La Capitale** *(Tel. 4994),* **Roma Sud** *(Tel. 6645),* **Roma** *(Tel. 3570),* **Cosmos** *(Tel. 88177)* and **RadioTaxi Tevere** *(Tel. 4157).* Be warned that when you call for a taxi the cab's meter starts running when it is summoned, not when it arrives to pick you up, so by the time a cab arrives at your location there will already be a substantial amount on the meter.

By Bus

At each bus stop, called **fermata**, there are signs that list all the buses that stop there. These signs also give the streets that the buses will follow along their route so you can check your map to see if this is the bus for you. Also, on the side of the bus are listed highlights of the route for your convenience. Nighttime routes (since many of them stop at midnight) are indicated by black spaces on newer signs, and are placed at the bottom of the older signs. In conjunction the times listed on the signs indicate when the bus will pass the *fermata* so you can plan accordingly.

Riding the bus during rush hour is like becoming a sardine, complete with the odor, so try to avoid the rush hours of 8:00am to 9:00am, 12:30pm to 1:30pm, 3:30 to 4:30pm, and 7:30pm to 8:30pm. Yes, they have an added rush hour in the middle of the day because of their siesta time in the afternoon.

The bus fare costs Euro 75 cents and lasts for 75 minutes, during which time you can transfer to any other bus, but you can only ride the Metro once. Despite the convenience and extent of the Roman bus system, which helped me get anywhere I wanted to go in Rome for a long time, since the advent of the Metro I recommend taking the underground transport as it is easier, quicker, less crowded, and more understandable.

Never board the metro or a bus without a ticket, which can be bought at any ATAC booth or kiosk and at tobacco shops (*tabacchi*), newsstands (*giornalaio*) and vending machines in the Metro stations. Once on board the bus remember to stamp the ticket at the rear stamp machine. If you do not have a ticket or have one and do not stamp it with the date and time, and an inspector catches you, you face an instantaneous E25 fine. For more information, call **ATAC**, *Tel. 06/4695-4444;* or **ACOTRAL**, *Tel. 06/5912-5551.*

ATAC Bus Tours

If you like the local scene, take the no-frills Giro di Roma tour on the **silver bus #110** offered by **ATAC**, the intra-city bus company *(Tel. 06/469-51)*. This three hour circuit of the city leaves from the information booth in the middle of the **Piazza Cinquecento** in front of the train station daily at 10:30am, 2:00pm, 3:00pm, 5:00pm and 6:00pm, and takes you to over 80 sites of historic and artistic significance, and stops at the most important sights like the Colosseum, Piazza Venezia, St. Peter's, and more.

Cost is only E7.5 and you can pay by credit card. To book a seat on these luxury buses with tour guides and an illustrated guide book call 06/4695-2252 between 9:00am and 7:00pm.

Bus Passes

If you are staying in Rome for a while or need to use the buses frequently, you can buy one of the following bus tickets at most newsstands, *tabacchi*, or ATAC booths by the station, and in the Metro. These tickets are:
• **Daily Ticket** *(B.I.G.): E3 (Valid for unlimited Metro, Bus, Trolley and Train with the Commune di Roma which includes going to Ostia but not Fiumicino Airport or Tivoli)*

• **Weekly Ticket** *(C.I.S.): E12 (Valid for everything under the B.I.G.)*

By Metro

The Roman *Metropolitana* (**Metro**) has two lines (Linea A and Linea B) that intersect in the basement of Termini station. You'll find these and all other stations marked with a prominent white "M" inside a red square up on a sign outside. **Linea A** is probably the most used by the tourists since it starts near St. Peter's, and has Piazza del Popolo, Piazza di Spagna, Piazza Barberini, and Piazza della Repubblica along its route. **Linea B** comes in a close second since it takes you to the Colosseum, the Circus Maximus, and the Piramide.

Buses used to be the way to get around Rome quickly, efficiently, and inexpensively, but now that convenience has been superseded by the Metro. But beware, the Metro can get quite crowded around **Stazione Termini** and during rush hours. Sardine-like is the best way to describe it. Besides the crush of humanity, the rides can be very pleasant. But, always be on the lookout for pickpockets. There are signs (in Italian) in the Metro and on buses warning people about them, so be prepared. The best way to do that is to put your wallet in your front pants pocket. And women, to make sure you are not the recipient of unwanted gropes on your derriere, keep your back to the wall if possible. And if you feel hands on you be sure to push them away and make a scene, otherwise it won't stop.

The Metro runs from 5:30am to 11:30pm.

Metro Lost & Found

If you misplace something on the metro or the bus, you can report the item missing at the office at the main station, *Servizio Movimento delle*

How to Buy a Metro Ticket

Walk down the steps into the subterranean caverns of the Roman Metro, then buy the ticket at the ever-present ticket booths or vending machines in any station. To get to the trains you stamp the ticket in a bright orange machine.

The stamp received marks the start of the 75 minutes you can ride on public transportation, but only once on the Metro. Late at night, the ticket booths are usually closed, so you'll have to use one at the ever-present vending machines in all stations. Simply have Euro 75 cents ready. A touch tone screen awaits your commands. Press the upper left image on the screen to indicate to the machine you want a 75 minute ticket. Then insert your bills or coins as indicated, and presto your ticket and change (if any) will appear.

Ferrovie dello Stato (Tel. 06/4669, ext. 7682). But you probably won't get it back, especially if it is an expensive item.

Take the Metro to the Beach!

If you're interested in going to the beach or visiting the ruins at Ostia Antica, take the Linea B Metro to the Magliana stop and transfer to a train that will take you there. Your metro ticket is valid for the train as well.

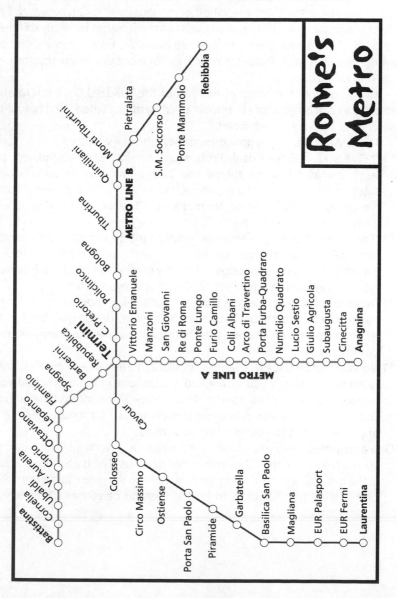

Where To Stay

Hotels in Italy are strictly controlled by a government rating system that categorizes them from "no star" hotels to "four star deluxe" hotels. Each and every hotel must prominently display their official ranking for all visitors to see.

These ratings have little to do with price. They only indicate what types of facilities are available at each hotel, and even then the designation can be ambiguous. Also, the stars do not indicate what level of service you will receive, how clean the hotels are, whether management is surly or sweet. Even in hotels with the same rating, the quality of facilities can be vastly different. The stars only indicate which facilities are available. Listed below is the star ranking (see Chapter 6, *Planning Your Trip*, for more details on accommodations and ratings).

You'll find the stars listed at the end of the italicized basic information section (name of hotel, address, phone, price, cards accepted, etc.) before the review itself begins for each hotel.

This is what the Italian government says the stars mean:

*****Five star, deluxe hotel: Professional service, great restaurant, perfectly immaculate large rooms and bathrooms with air conditioning, satellite TV, mini-bar, room service, laundry service, and every convenience you could imagine to make you feel like a king or queen. Bathrooms in every room.

****Four star hotel: professional service, most probably they have a restaurant, clean rooms not so large, air conditioning, TV (maybe satellite), mini-bar, room service, laundry service and maybe a few more North American-like amenities. Bathrooms in every room.

***Three star hotel: a little less professional service, most probably do not have room service, should have air conditioning, TV and mini bar, but the rooms are mostly small as are their bathrooms. Some rooms may not have bathrooms.

**Two star hotel: Usually a family-run place, some not so clean as higher rated hotels. Mostly you'll only find a telephone in the room, and you'll be lucky to get air conditioning. About 50% of the rooms have either a shower/bath or water closet and sometimes not both together. Hardly any amenities, just a place to lay your head.

*One star hotel: Here you usually get a small room with a bed; sometimes you have to share the room with other travelers. The bathroom is usually in the hall. No air conditioning, no telephone in the room, just a room with bed. These are what used to be the low-end pensiones. Definitely for budget travelers.

Hotels By Map

No Hotel Reservations?
If you get to Rome without a reservation, there is a free hotel finding service located at the end of **track #10** at the train station hat will get you a room. There is no fee, but you usually do have to pay them for the first night's stay up front. The service calls ahead and books your room, gives you a map, and will show you how to get to your hotel. It's a great service for those who have arrived in Rome on a whim. Sometimes the lines are long, so be patient.

Near Termini Station
   1. **IGEA**, *Via Principe Amadeo 97, Tel. 06/446-6913, Fax 06/446-6911. E-mail: Igea@venere.it. Web: www.venere.com/it/roma/igea/Mastercard and Visa accepted. 42 rooms, 21 doubles, 21 singles, all with shower and W/C, air conditioning, and TV. Single E60-90; Double E80-140;. Breakfast included. (Map A)* ***
   The rooms are large, clean, and with full bath facilities, air conditioning and TV in each room. The lobby is large and spacious, completely covered in white marble making it a pleasant place to relax; and the staff is friendly, knowledgeable, and professional. This is a thoroughly modern recently upgraded three star hotel that is 300 meters from the train station. Granted there's not much to do around the station, and the restaurants are better almost anywhere else in the city, but if you want a lot of amenities for a good price, near the station, stay here.
   2. RICHMOND, *Largo Corrado Ricci 36, Tel. 06/6994-1256, Fax 06/6994-4145. E-mail: Richmond@venere.it or romint@flashnet.it. Web: www.venere.com/it/home/roma/richmond/richmond.html. 13 rooms. Single E115-140; Double E270. Breakfast included. (Map D)* ***
   Not really located near the train station, but close enough, this colorful little hotel is simply fantastic. The rooms are large and incredibly accommodating, and all expected three star amenities are included. The main feature is the terrace, which has a stupendous view over the Forum, Victor Emanuel Monument and Colosseum and is the ideal place to relax in the evenings. Somewhat distant from the main tourist area of the Pantheon, Navona and the Spanish Steps, but this helps to make your stay here tranquil. Without any qualms I would highly recommend this hotel for your stay in Rome. Nearby is one of the best enoteca in Rome, *Cavour 313*, and a superb Irish pub, *Shamrock*.
   3. **BRITANNIA**, *Via Napoli 64, Tel. 06/488-3153, Fax 06/488-2343. E-mail: britannia@venere.it. Web: www.venere.com/it/roma/britannia/. 32 rooms all with private baths. Air conditioning. Parking Available. All credit cards accepted. Single E120-210; Double E160-240. Breakfast included. Children up to 10 years old share parent's room for free. (Map A)* ***
   Located just north of the Via Nazionale, down a small side street, this is an efficiently run hotel that offers guests every conceivable attention. The

entrance hall blends into the American-style bar area and the breakfast room. The rooms are all modern with different furnishings in each. All are clean and comfortable and come with a safe, satellite TV and mini-bar. The bathrooms are also modern with hair dryers, sun lamps and courtesy toiletry kits. In the mornings, they have Italian and English language newspapers at your disposal and in the evenings chocolate on your pillow. The service is supremely courteous and professional. Situated near a Metro stop for easy access to all parts of the city.

4. DIANA, *Via Principe Amadeo 4, 00185. Tel. 475-1541, Fax 06/486-998. E-mail: Diana@venere.it. Web: www.skytours.de/diana.htm. 190 rooms all with private baths. All credit cards accepted. Single E160; Double E220. Suites E320. Breakfast included. Lunch or Dinner costs an extra E20. (Map A)* ***

Located near Stazione Termini and the opera, this is a comfortable well run three star hotel on the Principe Amadeo, a street in limbo caught between the old and the new. This is definitely an old and elegant hotel. The lobby and common areas are an eclectic mixture of marble floors and columns with subtle lighting and paintings, with two meeting rooms that can hold 30-40 people. And the restaurant is large enough to hold 300 people and the food is quite good. The room sizes vary greatly but the smallest are still very comfortable even without the mini-bar. But fear not, you still have the satellite TV.

The bathrooms are nothing special (only 30 have hair dryers) but all come with bath and shower. There is an American style bar open all the time with intimate little glass tables that seem straight out of *La Dolce Vita*. This place is comfortable and cozy, a good value for your money, and the service is exquisitely professional. Also, they have special rates for groups of 20 or more that will make your stay very cheap if you're arranging for a group. You need to call or fax for details.

5. GALILEO, *Via Palestro 33, Tel. 06/444-1205/6/7/8, Fax 06/444-1208. E-mail: hgalileo@uni.net. Web: www.travel.it/roma/galileo/galileo.html. Single E60-115; Double E150. All credit cards accepted. 80 rooms all with bath. Breakfast included. (Map A)* ***

There are four beautiful floors in this hidden treasure near the train station. The only drawback is that the entrance is down a driveway that leads to a garage. But once you're inside everything is transformed to cater to all your needs. They have a lovely garden terrace on the first floor where you can have your breakfast or relax at the end of the day. The prices are somewhat low for a three star, I think because of the driveway situation. A good hotel near the train station with accommodating amenities.

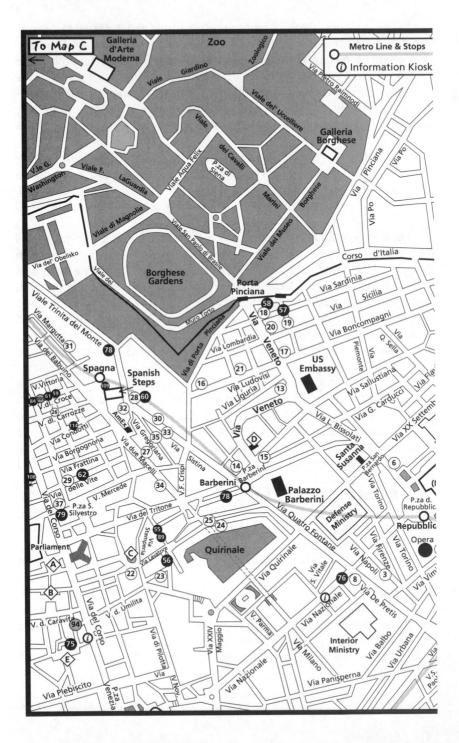

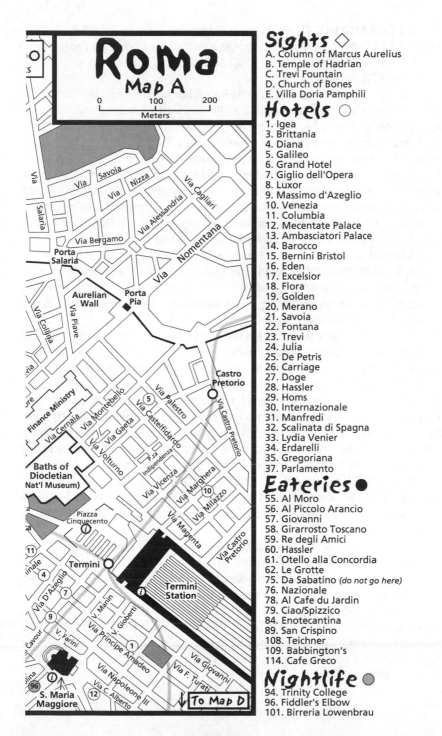

Roma
Map A

0   100   200
Meters

Sights ◇
A. Column of Marcus Aurelius
B. Temple of Hadrian
C. Trevi Fountain
D. Church of Bones
E. Villa Doria Pamphili

Hotels ○
1. Igea
3. Brittania
4. Diana
5. Galileo
6. Grand Hotel
7. Giglio dell'Opera
8. Luxor
9. Massimo d'Azeglio
10. Venezia
11. Columbia
12. Mecentate Palace
13. Ambasciatori Palace
14. Barocco
15. Bernini Bristol
16. Eden
17. Excelsior
18. Flora
19. Golden
20. Merano
21. Savoia
22. Fontana
23. Trevi
24. Julia
25. De Petris
26. Carriage
27. Doge
28. Hassler
29. Homs
30. Internazionale
31. Manfredi
32. Scalinata di Spagna
33. Lydia Venier
34. Erdarelli
35. Gregoriana
37. Parlamento

Eateries ●
55. Al Moro
56. Al Piccolo Arancio
57. Giovanni
58. Girarrosto Toscano
59. Re degli Amici
60. Hassler
61. Otello alla Concordia
62. Le Grotte
75. Da Sabatino *(do not go here)*
76. Nazionale
78. Al Cafe du Jardin
79. Ciao/Spizzico
84. Enotecantina
89. San Crispino
108. Teichner
109. Babbington's
114. Cafe Greco

Nightlife ●
94. Trinity College
96. Fiddler's Elbow
101. Birreria Lowenbrau

6. LE GRAND HOTEL, *Via Vittorio Emanuele Orlando, Tel. 06/4709, Fax 06/474-7307. Web: www.romeguide.it/legrandhotel/legrandhotel.html. Single E195-310; Double E275-450; Suites E950. Extra bed costs E75. Breakfast E20. (Map A)* *****

Located between the Piazza della Repubblica and Piazza San Bernardo, near the American speaking church in Rome, Santa Susanna, this top-class luxury hotel has everything you'd ever need, and the prices to match. There is a hairdresser service, beauty salons, and saunas. The hotel used to be located in one of the most fashionable quarters which has long since lost its chic, but that doesn't detract from the opulent ambiance of the hotel itself. The rooms and suites are palatial, some with 16 to 17 foot ceilings. You'll feel like a prince or princess when they serve you afternoon tea downstairs at 5:00pm. If tea is not your style, there's a very relaxing but expensive American-style bar. A wonderful place to stay if you are part of the world elite.

Selected as one of my *Best Places to Stay* – see Chapter 12.

7. GIGLIO DELL'OPERA, *Via Principe Amadeo 14, 62 rooms all with bath. Tel. 06/484-401 or 488-0219, Fax 06/487-1425. E-mail: Giglio.dell.Opera@venere.it. Web: www.venere.it/it/roma/giglio_dell_opera/ . Single E80-160; Double E100-200. (Map A)* ***

Close to the opera, this hotel is a favorite with some of the performers and their hangers-on. Unfortunately I think they have realized that they attract a chic and fashionable crowd, and as a result their prices have risen proportionately. The rooms are attractive in a neo-classic style, some are more modern but all have a comparable level of comfort. Each bathroom comes with courtesy toiletry kit but is lacking a hair dryer. The lounge area is large and there is a small and intimate area that serves as a bar in the evenings, but you'd better know music to get involved in the conversations. Breakfast is served in a spartan, white, brightly-lit room off the lobby. A fun, eclectic place to stay.

8. LUXOR, *Via A. De Pretis 104, Tel. 06/485-420, Fax 06/481-5571. E-mail: reception@hotel-luxor.it. Web: www.hotel-luxor.it. 27 rooms all with bath. Single E65-120; Double E105-180. Breakfast included. All credit cards accepted. (Map A)* ***

This is a quaint little hotel off the Via Nazionale, situated in three stories of a building built in the last century. The lobby is a little cramped but the proprietor and her husband will do almost anything to make you happy. The hotel has all the amenities of a three star hotel and you'll just love the classic "fin de siecle" beds and armoires. Each room is different from the other and all are quite large and accommodating. The bathrooms are comfortably sized with complimentary toiletry kit and hair dryer. There is a very small roof garden for relaxation. Centrally located, on the best local shopping street, and it is near a Metro.

9. MASSIMO D'AZEGLIO, *Via Cavour 18, Tel. 06/460-646 or 487-0270, Fax 06/482-7386. Toll free in Italy 167/860004. Toll free in the US 800/223-9832. E-mail: hb@bettojahotels.it. Web: www.uni.net/bettoja/. Credit cards accepted. 198 rooms, all with private baths. Single E170; Double E265. (Map A)* ****

Located near Stazione Termini, this hotel first opened in 1875 and maintains its traditional manner which fills the place with old world charm.

My Favorite Hotels in Rome

You'll find plenty of great hotels when in Rome, but for a truly relaxing stay here is a list of my ten best to help make your stay in the Eternal City that much better.

Two star hotels

37. PARLAMENTO, *Via delle Convertite 5, 00186 Roma. Single without bath E65. Single E40-95. Double E50-115.*

20. PENSIONE MERANO, *Via Vittorio Veneto 155, 30 rooms 28 with bath. Single without bath E45-50; Single E55-65; Double without bath E65-70; Double E85-100.*

Three star hotels

38. LOCARNO, *Via della Penna 22, 38 rooms all with bath. Single E120; Double E190-310.*

32. SCALINATA DI SPAGNA, *Piazza Trinita Dei Monte 17, 15 rooms all with baths. Single E150-200; Double E240-290.*

10. VENEZIA, *Via Varese 18, 61 rooms all with bath. Single E180; Double E200.*

2. RICHMOND, *Largo Corrado Ricci 36, 00184 Roma. Tel. 06/6994-1256, Fax 06/6994-4145. 13 rooms. Single E165; Double E170.*

Four star hotels

17. BAROCCO, *Piazza Barberini 9 (entrance on Via della Purificazione 4), 37 rooms all with bath. Single E150-200; Double E240-290.*

26. MECENATE PALACE, *Via Carlo Alberto 3, 62 rooms all with bath. Single E190-240; Double E225-325.*

Five star hotels

16. EDEN, *Via Ludovisi, 49, 100 rooms all with private bath. Single E280-495; Double E460-825.*

28. VILLA HASSLER, *Piazza Trinita Dei Monti 6, 80 rooms all with bath. Single E370-460; Double E500-660.*

They have all the modern amenities of a four-star in Italy, but the look and feel of the place is definitely 1950s in a quaint sort of way. One of the best parts is the Cantina restaurant downstairs that looks like a wine cellar. There are lots of nooks and crannies in which to get lost. A good choice for around the train station and the opera.

10. VENEZIA, *Via Varese 18, Tel. 06/445-7101, Fax 06/495-7687. E-mail: info@hotelvenezia.com. Web: www.hotelvenezia.com. Credit cards accepted. 61 rooms all with bath. Single E180; Double E200. Generous buffet breakfast included. (Map A)* ***

This is definitely the best hotel near the Stazione Termini. For a three star the prices are quite good and the service is excellent. Located on a side street away from all the noise, you would never know that you're a block from the train station. If you are traveling alone ask for one of the single rooms on the fifth floor so you can relax and enjoy the wonderful Roman evenings on the individual balconies. Some rooms have showers to cater to North Americans; others have baths for the Asians. You can select which option you want.

The hotel caters to travelers, business customers, and visiting academics since the University is just around the corner. You'll love the 16th century altar that serves as buffet table for breakfast and bar at night, as well as the huge 16th century table in the conference room. The ever charming and hospitable owner and operator, Patrizia Diletti, will bend over backwards to make your stay pleasant This is a wonderful hotel with some of the most attentive, friendly and multi-lingual service I have encountered in the Eternal City.

11. COLUMBIA, *Via del Viminale 15, Tel. 06/474-4289, Fax 06/474-0209. E-mail: info@hotelcolumbia.com. Web: www.hotelcolumbia.com. 45 rooms all with bath. Single E180; Double E200. (Map A)* ***

Owned by the ever accommodating Patrizia Diletti, who is the proprietor of the excellent hotel Venezia listed above. This hotel has all of the positive features of the Venezia, plus a small roof garden. What makes this hotel and the Venezia stand out is the attentive and friendly service, as well as the clean and comfortable rooms. The lobby is nothing to write home about, but the rooms have all gone through a year and half renovation to fit them with all modern conveniences. And now I can say that the Columbia is a wonderful place to stay. Located by the Opera and the Via Nazionale, you are also close to the train station, and have easy access to the Metro and buses to get you anywhere you want to be when in Rome. An excellent choice.

12. MECENATE PALACE, *Via Carlo Alberto 3, Tel. 06/4470-2024, Fax 06/446-1354. E-mail: info@mecenatepalace.com. Web: www.mecenatepalace.com. All credit cards accepted. 62 rooms all with bath. Single E190-240; Double E225-325. Breakfast included. (Map A)* ****

Attentive service, elegant accommodations, first class dining, and a spectacular view of Rome all add up to a wonderful stay. This hotel is a study in cozy elegance and is new, having only opened in 1995. Conveniently located near the train station, it boasts its own roof garden with a wonderful view of St. Peter's in the distance and Piazza Santa Maria Maggiore nearby. Fast becoming famous for its exceptional service and beautifully appointed, welcoming rooms, the Mecentate is one of Rome's most sophisticated hotels. And what a great restaurant: the Terrazza dei Papi is fast becoming famous, not only because of chef Pasquale D'Anria's specialties, but also as a result of the splendid panorama of the city from its rooftop perch.

Via Veneto Area

13. **AMBASCIATORI PALACE**, *Via Vittorio Veneto 62, Tel. 06/47-493, Fax 06/474-3601. E-mail: ambasciatorirome@diginet.it. Web: www.hotelambasciatori.com. 142 rooms and 8 suites, all with private bath. All credit cards accepted. Single E200-250; Double E250-355; Suite E455. Buffet breakfast included. (Map A) ******

Virtually in the center of the Via Veneto, this hotel deserves its luxury rating since it has impeccable service, palatial rooms, and a top class restaurant La Terrazza to complement its fine ambiance. Your every need can be taken care of here: massage, evening companion, theater reservations, travel arrangements, etc. If you're looking for deluxe treatment at a deluxe price, look no further. A simply marvelous hotel on one of Rome's most fashionable streets.

14. **BAROCCO**, *Piazza Barberini 9 (entrance on Via della Purificazione 4), Tel. 06/487-2001/2/3, 487-2005, Fax 06/485-994. E-mail: hotelbarocco@holelbarocco.it. Web: www.hotelbarocco.com. 37 rooms all with bath. Single E150-200; Double E240-290. Breakfast included. All credit cards accepted. (Map A) *****

If you're looking for an intimate and elegant four-star experience and don't want to get lost in the crowd at a larger hotel, this is the place for you. The entrance hall is tastefully decorated with photos of Roman scenes. Each room is different from the other, some with two levels, others with small terraces; and all come with an electronic safe, TV, A/C and everything else befitting a four star.

Every decoration and piece of furniture is supremely elegant. The bathrooms are a little small but come with hair dryer and courtesy toiletry kit. In the summer, breakfast is served on the roof terrace. A great location for an evening's relaxation. Centrally located with the Trevi Fountain, Spanish Steps, Via Veneto all around the corner. A great place to spend an entire vacation, or simply the last night of a long one. I love this quaint, intimate little place.

Selected as one of my *Best Places to Stay* – see Chapter 12.

15. **BERNINI BRISTOL**, *Piazza Barberini 23, Tel. 06/488-3051, Fax 06/482-4266. E-mail: bbsina@tin.it. Web: http://sinahotels.com/hotels/bristol/. 124 rooms all with private baths. Single E290; Double E450; Suite E650-1,300.. Continental breakfast buffet E22. (Map A)* *****

The hotel is located in the Piazza Barberini at the foot of the Via Veneto facing Bernini's Triton Fountain. This is another hotel that deserves its luxury rating. Established in 1870, this hotel still retains the charm and atmosphere of that era. The entrance salon is beautifully appointed with antique furniture and lamps as well as a crystal chandelier. All rooms are elegantly furnished (each in its own style), well lit, and quite large.

The bathrooms are large and come with a phone and courtesy toiletry kit. They offer every possible convenience and comfort here and are definitely waiting on that fifth star. The suites on the top floor all have wonderful terraces with splendid views. The restaurant where you are served an abundant breakfast has a panoramic view over the rooftops of Rome. Perfectly located for shopping and sightseeing, you can get to the Spanish Steps and Trevi Fountain in minutes.

16. **EDEN**, *Via Ludovisi, 49, Tel. 06/474-3551, Fax 06/482-1584. E-mail: Reservations@hotel-eden.it. Web: www.hotel-eden.it/index_e.html. 100 rooms all with private bath. Single E280-495; Double E450-825, Suites E700. Continental breakfast is E14 extra, buffet breakfast is E20. (Map A)* *****

The best just got more expensive, bt if you can afford it, this place is well worth it. Located west of Via Veneto in the exclusive Ludovisi section, the Eden is a long-established top-ranked, exclusive hotel. One of the *Leading Hotels of The World*, it has a sophisticated level of service and amenities virtually unmatched the world over. Located just off the crowded Via Veneto here you are in the center of it all, but it is supremely quiet too. The terrace restaurant has a spectacular view of the city and the Villa Borghese. Chef Enrico Derflingher is the former personal Chef to the Prince of Wales and Diane, which means you'll receive food fit for royalty. Also available is a complete gym with everything from cardiovascular equipment to free weights. The Eden is truly a paradise on earth.

Selected as one of my *Best Places to Stay* – see Chapter 12.

17. **WESTIN EXCELSIOR**, *Via Vittorio Veneto 125, Tel. 06/4708, Fax 06/482-6205. All 244 doubles, 38 singles, and 45 suites have private baths. Single E180-310; Double E250-500, Suite E700. An extra bed costs E50. Continental breakfast is E15 extra and American breakfast is E25. (Map A)* *****

This superb five star hotel is located on the east side of the Via Veneto not far from the walls that lead to Villa Borghese, and right across the street from the American Embassy. All rooms and common areas are done up with ornate moldings and elegant decorations. A truly palatial experience. They have a world-renowned restaurant, La Cuppola, as well as a piano bar at night. A wonderfully elite hotel, now owned by the Westin chain which only makes it that much more elegant.

18. GRAND HOTEL FLORA, *Via Vittorio Veneto 191, Tel. 06/489-929, Fax 06/482-0359. Web: www. yourhotelfinder.com/marriott_international.shtml. All 8 suites and 155 rooms have private baths. All credit cards accepted. Single E200-220; Double E250-270. Breakfast included. (Map A)* ****

Located immediately at the top of the Via Veneto by the old Roman walls, this old-fashioned hotel has first class traditional service. The public rooms are elaborately decorated with antiques, oriental rugs, and soothingly light color schemes reminiscent of the turn of the century. The rooms are immense and some have wonderful views over the walls into the lush greenery of Villa Borghese. Try and request one of those rooms, since Borghese is beautiful at night. The bathrooms have been recently renovated and come with all modern creature comforts. This hotel offers everything you could want: location, service, and great rooms. Now owned by Marriott which has helped to upgrade the entire facility.

19. RESIDENCE GOLDEN, *Via Marche 84, Tel. 06/482-1659, E-mail: hotel.golden@tin.it. Web: www.venere.com/it/roma/golden/. 12 of the 13 rooms have private baths. All credit cards accepted. Single E60-90; Double E90-140. (Map A)* **

An upscale pensione since it has air-conditioning, TV, phone, and mini-bar in every room. And the prices in the high season reflect the realization that they have good accommodations. The hotel is located on the first floor of an old house, on a quiet street off of the Via Veneto. The stark white breakfast room that serves the mini-buffet in the mornings doubles as the bar/lounge in the evenings. All the amenities of a three star, in a great location at the prices of an upscale two star. Clean, comfortable and well situated.

20. MERANO, *Via Vittorio Veneto 155, Tel. 06/482-1796, Fax 06/482-1810. All credit cards accepted. 30 rooms 28 with bath. Single without bath E45-50; Single E55-65; Double without bath E65-70; Double E85-100. (Map A)* **

Another relatively inexpensive place to stay. Ideally located on the Via Veneto at rock bottom prices. The only reason the prices are so low is that you have to ride an elevator up to the third floor of a building to get to the hotel. The entranceway is dark but the rooms are warm and cozy. Everything is spic and span in the bathrooms, and you don't have to worry about remembering to buy your drinks for the evening, since they sell beer, soda, and water. If you want to enjoy Rome inexpensively, this is one of the best places from which to do it.

21. SAVOIA, *Via Ludovisi 15, Tel. 06/474-141, Fax 06/474-68122. Web: www.venere.com/it/roma/savoy/. 135 all with bath. All credit cards accepted. Single E100-425; Double E150-425; Suite E500. (Map A) ****

Located in the upscale Ludovisi section west of Via Veneto, this is a comfortable and well run hotel that has recently jacked up their prices astronomically. They have an excellent restaurant, offering both a la carte and a superb buffet and a lively but still relaxing bar downstairs. The service is impeccable as it should be and the decor is elaborately expensive. The rooms, even the ones that face the Via Veneto are quiet and comfortable. The location is perfect, especially if you're a spy since the hotel is almost directly across the street from the American Embassy.

Trevi Fountain Area

22. FONTANA, *Piazza di Trevi 96, Tel. 06/678-6113, 06/679-1056. Web: www.venere.com/it/roma/fontana/. 24 rooms all with bath. Single E180; Double E225. A/C costs E15 extra. All credit cards accepted. (Map A) ***

The location of this hotel is great, but is not secluded or tranquil because it is in the same square as one of Rome's most famous monuments, the Trevi Fountain. You can hear the cascading waters and ever-present crowds far into the night. If you're a heavy sleeper this hotel's location is perfect, but if not try elsewhere. The rooms are sparse but comfortable and since this is a converted monastery, some rooms have been made by joining two monk's cells together. There is also a pleasant roof garden from which you can sip a drink and gaze over the rooftops of Rome.

23. TREVI, *Vicolo del Babuccio 20/21, Tel. 06/678-9563, Fax 06/6994-1407. 29 rooms all with bath. All credit cards accepted. Single E85-150; Double E95-180. Breakfast included. (Map A) ***

Located on a quiet side street near the Trevi Fountain, this ideal little three-star is in a wonderful location, in a beautiful palazzo, but down a side street so it is peaceful at night. Each room comes with every conceivable modern convenience. They have a roof garden, which is a great place to relax in the evenings and is where the buffet breakfast is served in good weather. But since they're just around the corner from Dunkin' Donuts you have that choice too. Though only a three-star, the prices here are rather dear, but the location and accommodations warrant them. Very professional service. An elite, upscale hotel.

24. JULIA, *Via Rasella 29, Tel. 06/488-1637, Fax 06/481-7044. E-mail: info@hoteljulia.it. Web: www.hoteljulia.it. 33 rooms all with bath. Single E70-105; Double E125-155. All credit cards accepted. (Map A) ***

In the heart of Rome, on a small, tranquil little side street near the Trevi Fountain, the Julia is a hotel of great comfort and style. The entry way is small, the rooms are adequately sized, the bathrooms are relatively small and come only with showers. The singles are minuscule. The service is excellent but the main selling point is the ideal and tranquil location.

25. DE PETRIS, *Via Rasella 142, Tel. 06/481-9626. Fax 06/482-0733. 45 rooms all with bath. Single E110-140; Double E135-190. All credit cards accepted. Breakfast included. (Map A)* ***

Just across the street from the Julia, this is also in an ideal and tranquil location. Very accommodating and comfortable with all necessary three star amenities. Each room is different from the other in terms of furnishings and layout. The bathrooms are well-appointed. The breakfast is extensive and is served in a quaint room. A good choice in the heart of Rome.

Piazza di Spagna Area

26. CARRIAGE, *Via delle Carrozze 36, Tel. 06/679-3312, Fax 06/678-8279. E-mail: hotelcarriage@alfanet.it. Web: www.hotelcarriage.net. All credit cards accepted. 30 rooms all with bath. Single E100-150; Double E150-205; Suite E330. Breakfast included. (Map A)* ***

Located near the Piazza di Spagna on a pedestrian side street, which makes it blissfully quiet. This elegant little hotel is luxuriously furnished with a variety of antiques and has a courteous and professional staff. They have a lovely roof garden terrace from which you can have your breakfast or an evening drink. There's not much of a view, but just being beyond the street level with the open sky above you has a calming effect. The rooms are not that large but are comfortable and come with every convenience such as TV, mini-bar and phone. The bathrooms are immaculately clean and have hair dryers and courtesy toiletry kit. Request one of the two rooms with tiny balconies that overlook the rooftops. A quaint, comfortable and convenient place to stay.

27. DOGE, *Via Due Macelli 106, Tel 06/678-0038, Fax 06/679-1633. All credit cards accepted. 18 rooms all with bath. Single E55-90; Double E75-125. Breakfast included. (Map A)* **

The accommodations here are clean and spartan as well as comfortable, and you'll notice the prices are pretty good considering this is one block from the Spanish Steps. It's located on the fourth floor of an apartment building that you enter by walking through the entrance/retail show space of a local sports store, which is the reason that the prices are so low. A good value for your money in a prime location which is key since Rome is so large. Only 11 rooms, so reserve far in advance.

28. VILLA HASSLER, *Piazza Trinita Dei Monti 6, Tel. 06/678-2651, Fax 06/678-9991. E-mail: hasslerroma@mclink.it. Web: www.hotelhasslerroma.com/. All credit cards accepted. 80 rooms all with bath. Single E370-460; Double E500-660.. Continental breakfast E23 extra. Buffet breakfast E35 extra. (Map A)* *****

In many travelers' opinions this is the best hotel in Rome. Oil sheiks, movie stars, travel publishers, nouveau riche, and landed gentry all have made the Hassler their home away from home for over a century. Located at the top of the Spanish Steps, with its own garage, a relaxing courtyard restaurant in the summer, and an excellent (but expensive) roof garden restaurant with a great view of the city. Remember to request one of the nicer rooms facing the church belfry and the Spanish Steps because the view will be stupendous. Even if you don't stay here, come to the restaurant, sample the food, and enjoy the superb view. One of the best, most famous, and ideally located hotels in Rome. If you have the means, I recommend it highly.

Selected as one of my *Best Places to Stay* – see Chapter 12.

29. HOMS, *Via Delle Vite 71, Tel. 0/679-2976, Fax 06/678-0482. All credit cards accepted. 50 rooms 49 with bath. Single without bath E40-50; Single E70-85; Double without bath E100-145; Double E150-190. Breakfast included. (Map A)* ***

Located on the same street as the great Tuscan restaurant Da Mario and just across from the Anglo-American bookstore, this hotel is also virtually in between the Trevi Fountain and the Spanish Steps. The hotel has a quaint, pleasant ambiance and decor and has just been upgraded from two star status. Despite the fact that some rooms do not have baths, they made the effort to improve and have been rewarded for it. Since Via Delle Vite is not well traveled here you will be able escape the traffic noise. The lobby area is dark, but the rooms are light and airy (though small) with simple furnishings. The bathrooms are tiny too but do have complimentary toiletry kits. There is also a wonderful terrace with great views of the rooftops of Rome, which, I believe, is the main reason this place gained its three star status.

30. INTERNAZIONALE, *Via Sistina 79, Tel. 06/6994-1823, Fax 06/678-4764. E-mail: internazionale@venere.it. Web: www.venere.it/it/roma/internazionale. All credit cards accepted. 42 rooms all with bath. Single E130-140; Double E190-220; Extra bed E55. Buffet breakfast included. (Map A)* ***

Written up in both *Travel & Leisure* and *Forbes*, this little Roman hideaway offers old-world charm, modern comfort and super rates for its ideal location. A huge breakfast is served in an elegant salon. In all this is a wonderful hotel. Located just a stone's throw away from the top of the Spanish Steps, you can hardly find a better location. The building was erected in first century BCE, and the lobby contains artifacts from that period, which have been unearthed within the walls of the hotel during recent renovations. The rooms are accommodating and comfortable and the staff professional and very atten-tive. The rooms are all different from one another with a wide variety of unique decorations and furnishings, supplied by Andrea Gnecco, owner and archi-tect. Those on the fourth floor have private terraces. The bathrooms have all the amenities of a three star including complimentary toiletry kit.

This family-owned gem is a superb hotel in an ideal location, one of my favorite choices when in Rome. But remember to request a room on a higher floor, or on the inside to avoid traffic noise at night. There is much history here, and if you want to come face to face with it, stay in room A1. A former employee witnessed a spectral monk on a donkey clip-clopping through that room only a few years back, and other eerie encounters have purported to have occurred as well!

31. MANFREDI, *Via Margutta 61, Tel. 06/320-7676, Fax 06/320-7736. Web: www.venere.com/it/roma/manfredi/. Credit cards accepted. 17 rooms all with bath. Single E140-190; Double E160-245; Triple E200. American style breakfast buffet included. (Map A)* ***

This cozy, accommodating hotel is located near the Spanish Steps and has all the charm, service, and amenities of a four-star hotel, but it is on the third floor of a local building so they are a relegated to three star status. They even have VCRs in some rooms as well as movies to rent at the front desk for your convenience. The street they're located on is cute, extremely quiet, and home to some of Rome's best antique stores and art galleries. If you only stay here for the American style buffet breakfast of ham, eggs, cheese, fruit etc., it is worth it. A good place to stay in a great location.

32. SCALINATA DI SPAGNA, *Piazza Trinita Dei Monte 17, Tel. 06/ 679-3006 and 06/679-0896, Fax 06/684-0598. E-mail: info@hotelscalinata.com. Web: www.venere.com/it/roma/scalinata/. All credit cards accepted. 16 rooms all with baths. Single E175-225; Double E200-325. Breakfast included. (Map A)* ***

Just across the piazza from the Hassler at the top of the Spanish Steps, this used to be a moderately priced, quaint little pensione, but once it received its three star rating the prices here have skyrocketed. Nothing much else has changed, but it is still well worth the price because of the view from their large roof terrace. The roof terrace is open in the summer months for breakfast, as well as for your own personal nightcaps in the evening. The rooms are basic, but accommodating and comfortable in three star style. This place has plenty of character and ambiance and you will simply adore the roof terrace. I highly recommend this hotel.

33. LYDIA VENIER, *Via Sistina 42, Tel. 06/679-3815, Fax 06/679-7263. 28 rooms all with bath. Single E40-95; Double E50-145. All credit cards accepted. (Map A)* **

A small, spartan hotel, that offers few amenities except for its excellent location. The furnishings are simple and basic and the bathrooms functional with a limited courtesy toiletry set. The breakfast room is comfortable and accommodating. All in all a good budget hotel in an ideal location, but ask for a room on the inside of the building away from the street. Traffic noise can be disturbing until the wee hours.

34. ERDARELLI, *Via Due Macelli 28, Tel. 06/679-1265, Fax 06/679-0705. Web: www.venere.com/it/roma/erdarelli/. 28 rooms all with bath. All credit cards accepted. Single E90; Double E115. (Map A)* **

Just down from the Piazza di Spagna in a building that looks like it has seen better days on the outside but which is clean and accommodating on the inside. The singles are minuscule and the doubles functional but the real selling point for this budget two-star is its ideal location. You can get A/C for an extra E10 and in August this is a necessity. Nothing grand but clean and comfortable at a good price for Rome.

35. GREGORIANA, *Via Gregoriana 18, Tel. 06/679-4269. Fax 06/678-4258. 20 rooms all with bath. Single E110; Double E190. No credit cards accepted. (Map A)* *******

Situated in a building on a small side street just off the top of the Spanish Steps which used to be a convent, the Gregoriana is a small hotel that is tranquil and comfortable with all possible three star amenities. The rooms are all decorated in Deco style and come with A/C and TV and a few have a small terrace. The bathrooms are small but clean and functional. Breakfast is served in the room except in warm weather when they open their little roof terrace. An intimate and comfortable place to stay while in Rome. But they do not accept credit cards so be prepared to have cash available.

36. MARGUTTA, *Via Laurina 34, Tel. 06/322-3674, Fax 06/320-0395. All credit cards accepted. 24 rooms all with bath. Single E33-95; Double E45-120. Breakfast included. (Map A)* ******

The prices are good for the location and the star rating. And it is only a two star because there is no TV or mini-bar in the room, and no air conditioning, which is a must in August. The hotel has been totally renovated and is as modern as can be. There's a relaxing lounge area and the rooms are spacious and airy. Rooms 50 and 52 share a terrace and are very nice, and #59 is another great place to stay too. The bathrooms are micro, especially those with showers which have rather noisy screen doors. The ones with bathtubs are a little bigger and all come with phone and courtesy toiletry kit. And the location is fantastic, right between the Piazza del Popolo and the Spanish Steps, almost right on the super shopping street Via Del Corso. Who could ask for more? That, coupled with the excellence of the accommodations and the low prices, makes this place a definite rare gem of price/quality considerations.

37. PARLAMENTO, *Via delle Convertite 5, Tel. 06/6992-1000, Fax 06/679-2082. All credit cards accepted. 22 rooms, 19 with bath. Single without bath E65. Single E40-96. Double E50-130. Breakfast included. (Map A)* ******

They have added a small (read micro) elevator so you no longer have to climb the entire three flights of stairs to get to this wonderful two star. A homey atmosphere with simply furnished rooms. There is a view of the rooftops of Rome from their tiny terrace, where in the summer you are served your breakfast. In a completely renovated building, the common rooms are decorated with panoramic frescoes of Roman scenes. The rooms are all decorated differently, some have antique style furniture, and all have TVs and sound-proof windows (but if your room is on the main road, this is Rome, so noise does seep in). The bathrooms are very new and kept immaculate; some even have a phone. Most of the staff speaks English and are more than willing to help you find what you're looking for. A great price/quality option.

38. LOCARNO, *Via della Penna 22, Tel. 06/361-0841, Fax 06/321-5249. E-mail: info@hotellocarno.com. Web: www.hotellocarno.com/. All credit cards accepted. 38 rooms all with bath. Single E207; Double E155-230; Suite E245 and up. Breakfast E12. (Map C) ***

I simply adore this hotel and I have no idea why it is still only a three star. Situated between the Piazza del Popolo and the Tiber River, in a nice neighborhood of stores and galleries, this hotel is wonderfully accommodating and amazingly comfortable. It has a very relaxing American-style bar, spacious common areas, a small side-garden patio, and a roof terrace where breakfast is served in good weather. The rooms are tastefully decorated with all possible three star amenities, and the service is superb and utterly professional. Why they are still a three star is beyond me, because this place is great.

There are excellent restaurants all around, *Da Bolognese* for example, which means you won't have to wander far for your gastronomic pleasures. On a side street, the Locarno offers a respite from the hectic pace of Rome. One of the best three stars Rome has to offer.

39. VALADIER, *Via della Fontanella 15, Tel. 06/361-0592, 361-0559, 361-2344, Fax 06/320-1558. E-mail: info@hotelvaladier.com. Web: www.hotelvaladier.com/. 48 rooms and suites all with bath. Single E110-270; Double E130-360. Suite E200-400. All credit cards accepted. (Map C) ****

The first word that comes to mind concerning this place is opulent. There is black marble everywhere and the effect is doubled by the placement of the many mirrors and shining brass fixtures. But you ain't seen nothing yet. The wood paneling here sparkles, it's so well shined. The rooms are no less ostentatious with lights, mirrors – some on the ceilings for you exotically amorous types – and the ever-present marble. The bathrooms are a little small but accommodating and have every amenity.

If you want to feel like an oil sheik who has money to burn, spend your stay in Rome here. Ideally located between the Piazza del Popolo and the Spanish Steps, you are in walking distance to many sights and shops.

Centro Storico
(Piazza Navona, Pantheon, Campo dei Fiori Area)

40. CAMPO DEI FIORI, *Via del Biscione 6, Tel. 06/687-4886, Fax 06/687-6003. All credit cards accepted. Four singles with shower each E90; Nine doubles with shower each E115, 14 doubles without shower each E190. Breakfast E10. (Map B) **

Here you'll find another great roof terrace in Rome. The hotel is on six floors in a sliver of a building without an elevator that can make this hotel an

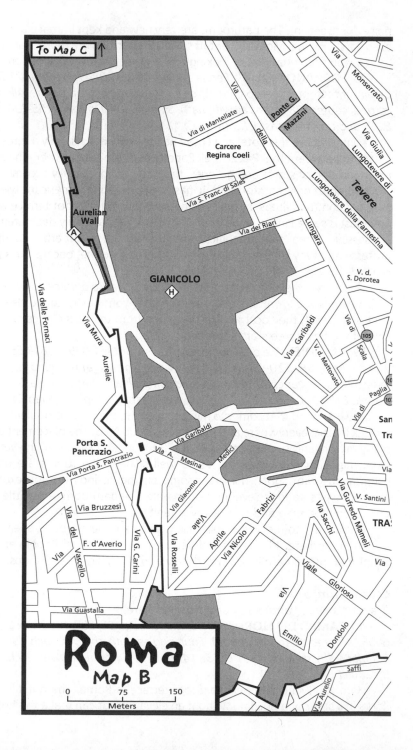

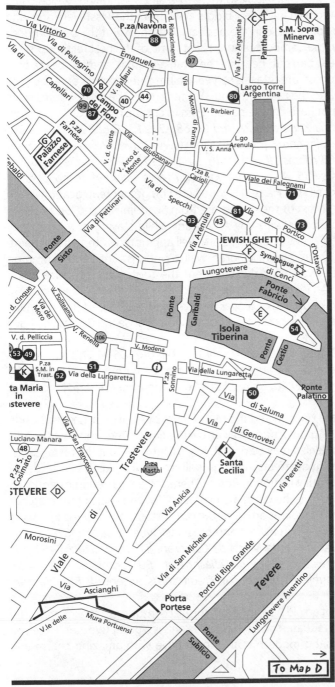

Sights ◇
A. Aurelian Wall
B. Campo dei Fiori
C. Pantheon
D. Trastevere
E. Isola Tiberina
F. Jewish Ghetto
G. Palazzo Farnese
H. Gianicolo
I. SM Sopra Minerva
J. S. Cecilia in Trastevere
K. SM in Trastevere

Hotels ○
40. Campo dei Fiori
43. Arenula
44. Del Sole
48. Trastevere

Eateries ●
49. La Canonica
50. Camparone
51. Gino in Trastevere
52. Sabatini I
53. La Tana de Noantri
54. Sora Lella
70. La Carbonara
71. Hostaria Guilia
73. Vecchia Roma
80. Brek
81. Anacleto Bleve
87. Vineria Reggio
88. Cul de Sac
93. Alberto Pica

Nightlife ●
97. John Bull Pub
99. Drunken Ship
104. Ombre Rosse
105. La Scala
106. Accademia
107. Artu Cafe

ⓘ Information Kiosks

exercise routine in and of itself. Also there's no air conditioning, which could be a problem in August. Only a few blocks away from the Trastevere area and its nightlife, here you are also in the perfect location to visit the best outdoor market in the city, the Campo dei Fiori, eat at some of the best restaurants (La Carbonara), a great bar/pub nearby (The Drunken Ship), and the best sights just around the corner. Breakfast is served in a basement dining area, but you are free to bring it to the roof with you. Ask for one of the inside rooms since the windows do not have double paned glass to cut the noise from the street.

41. **GENIO**, *Via Zanardelli 28, Tel 06/683-2191, 06/683-3781, Fax 06/6830-7246. E-mail: leonardi@travel.it. Web: www.travel.it/roma/ianr. Credit cards accepted. 65 rooms all with bath. Single E125-190; Double E190-250 An extra bed costs E35. A large breakfast buffet is included. (Map C)* ****

Located almost in the Piazza Navona here you get a great location in the Old City of Rome. Most of the guests are from Scandinavia and Germany so you may not rub elbows with any Americans while staying in this recently upgraded four star hotel. The rooms are well-appointed with tasteful paintings, Persian rugs, and cream colored wall coverings. The lobby/common areas seem a little worse for the wear but the roof garden terrace has a spectacular view. An ideal place to be served your breakfast in the morning. A great way to wake up, looking over the river and rooftops of Rome, which is the main reason it is now a four star hotel. If you choose the Genio, you have chosen well.

42. **PORTOGHESI**, *Via dei Portoghesi 1, Tel. 06/686-4231, Fax 06/687-6976. Mastercard and Visa accepted. 27 rooms all with bath. Single E140; Double E195. Jr. Suite E210. Suite E300. Extra bed E25. Breakfast included. (Map C)* ***

Between Piazza Navona and the Mausoleum of Augustus, nestled beside the church of Sant'Antonio, and on a narrow medieval street, this small hotel's central location is ideal. It may be not be near a Metro line but the restaurants, shops, food stores, small streets, and sights all around it make this place ideally suited for a wonderful vacation in Rome. There are a smattering of antiques all over the hotel to give the place a feeling of old world charm that matches its unique location. The rooms are small but comfortable and there is a relaxing roof garden to enjoy. A great bed and breakfast type place to stay.

43. **ARENULA**, *Via Santa Maria de'Calderari, 47, Tel. 06/687-9454, Fax 06/689-6188. E-mail: hotel.arenula@flashnet.it. 50 rooms all with bath. Single E60-90; Double E125-115. All credit cards accepted. Breakfast included. (Map B)* **

On the inside of an old building from the last century, in a quaint area (The Jewish Ghetto) and situated on a small street, this is a great two star. Here you have everything that a modern hotel would have with amazing charm and

Bed & Breakfasts in Rome

To accommodate the massive influx of tourists for the recent Jubilee celebrations, the city of Rome formalized an already existing cadre of top notch apartments, homes and villa which have been housing travelers for years, into the Bed & Breakfast Association of Rome. To find out more information about these places, visit the association's website at *www.bbitalia.com* (E-mail: *info@bbitalia.com*, Tel/Fax 06/687-7348).

One of the best, the **Villa Delros**, is located near where I used to live, about three kilometers outside the 'beltway' around Rome in a bucolic natural setting. This recently opened modern B&B has three excellent rooms to choose from, with air conditioning, a strongbox for your valuables, satellite TV, hairdryer, direct dial phone and mini-bar. They also have a swimming pool and a variety of common areas in which to relax. Excellent meals are prepared upon request and, best of all, the owner, Rosmarie Truninger Diletti, is effervescently friendly and she goes out of her way to make sure your stay is comfortable – without actually getting in the way. Multilingual and with a vibrant zest for life, she really makes your stay pleasant.

Villa Delros, Tel/Fax 06/33678402 or 06/33679837, E-mail: info@hotelvenezia.com (reference the Villa Delros when you E-mail). Closed December 1 to March 1. Minimum stay 3 days. Double E150 including breakfast. Dinner upon request: Large E15 or Small E7.5. Both are well worth it. Credit Cards not accepted. Free pickup from local public train station. Pickup at the airport E60. Pickup at Termini downtown E30.

ambiance. On the first floor is the small entrance, TV lounge, breakfast area and ten of the rooms. On the third floor the rooms come only with shower but all have a small complimentary toiletry set. They also have A/C and TV in the rooms and have recently given each room their own bath. They are bucking for three star status but right now they are a great price/quality place to stay while in Rome.

44. DEL SOLE, *Via del Biscione 76, Tel. 06/6880-6873 or 687-9446, Fax 06/689-3787. E-mail: info@solealbiscione.it. Web: www.solealbiscione.it/. 58 rooms only 24 with bath. Single without E45-67; Single E67-80. Double without E65-95; Double E80-110. No breakfast. No credit cards. (Map B)* **

A wonderful two star in a great location with two relaxing roof garden areas. Supposedly the oldest hotel in Rome, it seems its age as you enter, but the rooms are clean and comfortable. Ten rooms have TV and only 24 with

Stay in a Convent - For Less

Some of the best and least known places to stay, which can reduce the cost of a stay in Rome, are convents. While you may think that convents would only take women pilgrims as guests, most also welcome single men, married couples, and families with children. Couples 'traveling in sin' are usually not welcome, but some well placed pieces of jewelry can usually fool the best nun. All these convents are immaculate (no pun intended) since the nuns take pride in their work.

Suore Teatine, *Salita Monte del Gallo 25, 00165 Roma. Tel. 06/637-4084 or 06/637-4653, Fax 06/3937-9050. E35 per person with full board. E30 with half board. E25 with only breakfast. Not all rooms have private bath. Curfew is 11:00pm.*

Franciscan Sisters of the Atonement, *Via Monte del Gallo 105, 00165 Roma. Tel. 06/630-782, Fax 06/638-6149. E35 per person with full board. E30 with half board. E25 with only breakfast. All rooms have private bath. Curfew is 11:00pm. English spoken. Parking available. Great spacious pine-shaded garden.*

Suore Dorotee, *Via del Gianicolo 4a, 00165 Roma. Tel. 06/6880-3349, Fax 06/6880-3311. E40 full board. E35 half board. Some rooms have private baths. Curfew is 11:00pm. Recommended by the Vatican Tourist Information Bureau.*

Pensione Suore Francescane, *Via Nicolo V 35, 00165 Roma. Tel. 06/3936-6531. E27 per person with breakfast. No private baths. No curfew. Small but lovely roof garden with views of St. Peter's. English spoken. Great location.*

Domus Aurelia-Suore Orsoline, *Via Aurelia 218, 00165 Roma. Tel. 06/636-784, Fax 06/3937-6480. E50 for a double. E37 for a single. E60 for room with three beds. All rooms with private bath. Breakfast extra. 11:30pm curfew.*

Suore Pallotini, *Viale della Mura Aurelie 7b, 00165 Roma. Tel. 06/635-697, Fax 06/635-699. E27 for single with breakfast. E50 for double without private bath. E65 for double with private bath. 10:00pm curfew for first night. Any night after that they give you a key.*

Fraterna Domus, *Via di Monte Brianzo 62, 00186 Roma. Tel. 06/6880-2727, Fax 06/683-2691. E35 per person with full board. E30 with half board. E27 with breakfast only. Single rooms add E9 extra. All rooms with private bath. Curfew is 11:00pm.*

Le Suore Di Lourdes, *Via Sistina 113, 00187 Roma. Tel. 06/474-5324, Fax 06/488-1144. E25 per person without bath. E27 per person with bath and breakfast. Curfew is 10:30pm.*

private bath. Not as nice as the Hotel Campo dei Fiori just up the street, but is still a good place to stay for those on a budget, and the staff is much more accommodating than the Campo dei Fiori. Keep a look out for Cleopatra, the resident cat.

45. MARCUS, *Via del Clementino 94, Tel. 06/6830-0320, Fax 06/6830-0312. Web: www.venere.com/it/roma/marcus/. 18 rooms all with bath. Single E65-95; Double E100-150. All credit cards accepted. (Map C)* **

This small two-star is in an ideal location deep in the heart of the *centro storico* by the Pantheon. The atmosphere here is pleasant and accommodating and filled with the character of a 17th century building. The entryway is beautiful which leads to the second floor lobby. The rooms are very spacious and come with A/C (for E10 extra per day), and double windows to keep out noise. The bathrooms are minuscule and only have showers and some come with hair dryers. If they had a lobby on the ground floor, and added a few more amenities, this would be a three-star; but for now it is a wonderful two-star.

46. SOLE AL PANTHEON, *Piazza dell Rotunda 63, Tel. 06/78-0441, Fax 06/6994-0689. All credit cards accepted. 62 rooms all with bath. E-mail: solealpantheon@italyhotel.com. Web: www.venere.it/roma/solealpantheon/ . Single E210; Double E325; Jr. Suite E375. Breakfast E15. (Map C)* ****

This is a place that used to be a small, well-appointed *pensione* that upgraded its rooms prior to the "star" rating system and voila: we have a fantastic four-star hotel. The clean white walls and delicate furnishings attest to its status as one of Rome's best small hotels. Most of the furniture is of the neo-classic mold leaning towards modern. Some of the rooms have a view over the *Piazza della Rotunda* and the Pantheon, which is a beautiful people watching scene, and come with soundproof windows so it's relatively quiet at night. The building has been around since 1513 so you'll be staying in history while here. The service is exquisite and everything conforms to the highest standards, making this a well-located fine little four-star hotel. For those with the means, a great place to stay.

47. SANTA CHIARA, *Via Santa Chiara 21, 00186 Roma. Tel. 06/687-2979, Fax 06/687-3144. E-mail: stchiara@tin.it. Web: www.albergosantachiara.com/ . All credit cards accepted. 96 rooms all with bath. Single E160-197; Double E175-215.. Suite E215-360. Breakfast included. (Map C)* ***

A three star that should be a four star, and their prices reflect that. This is a supremely elegant hotel in the heart of Rome near the Pantheon. Once you enter the lobby you feel as if you've been whisked away to a palace. Everything is marble, buffed to a high polish, and the ceilings reach to the sky. The rooms are all tastefully decorated and the ones on the top floors get great breezes, if you don't want to use your air conditioning, and some have small balconies. There is also a tranquil inside terrace area, the service is impeccable and the breakfast buffet huge. This place is great. If you want four star accommodations for a three star price, stay here.

Trastevere

48. TRASTEVERE, *Via Luciano Manara 24/25, Tel. 06/58-14-713, Fax 06/ 58-81-016. 30 rooms all with bath. All credit cards accepted. Single E60-80; Double E65-95. (Map B)* **

Located in the heart of Trastevere, one of the city's oldest and most distinctive neighborhoods, here you will be surrounded by locals and far from the thundering herd of tourists. The Roma Trastevere train station is only 700 meters away, which means you should get the local train from the airport and not the one that goes directly to Termini. The rooms are all spacious and accommodating, though simply furnished. If you want to stay in local atmosphere of Trastevere, this is the best option.

Where To Eat

Before I guide you to the wonderful restaurants Rome has awaiting you, below I've prepared an augmented, Rome-specific version of Chapter 11, *Food & Wine*. The list of restaurants by map is on the next page.

Roman Cuisine

"Italian Food" is definitely a misnomer, because each region of Italy has its special dishes, and in most cases so do each province and locality. As a rule, Roman cooking is not elegantly refined and is considered a rustic cuisine. The food is basic, unpretentious , and enjoyable. Gone are the days of the Roman Empire's lavish banquets.

Authentic Roman dishes today are often based on simple ingredients, such as tomatoes, garlic, hot pepper, and parmesan cheese, and the results are magnificent. If you are bold try some of the favorite dishes, like brains, tripe, oxtail, and pig's snout. If not treat yourself to the omnipresent pasta and grilled meats.

Besides these staples, Romans enjoy a harvest of seafood from the shores just 15 miles from their city; and as a result prepare excellent grilled seafood dishes, the famous *spaghetti alla vongole verace* (spicy clam sauce), as well as other pastas brimming with many fruits from the sea. The Roman countryside provides exquisite fresh greens and vegetables, which arrive daily at the city's open air markets. Also in never-ending supply are the local cheeses like *pecorino*, made from sheep's milk, and plump *mozzarella* balls, generally made from the milk of water buffaloes.

The Jewish ghetto has made a lasting impression on Roman cuisine. The most memorable dish to come from there is the *carciofo alla giudia*, a small

List of Restaurants by Map

Map A – see pages 150-151
55. Sora Lella
57. Da Mario
58. Da Olimpico
59. Giovanni
60. Girarrosto Toscano
61. Al Moro
62. Re degli Amici
63. Babington's Tea Rooms
64. Hassler
65. Otello alla Concordia
66. Le Grotte

Map B – see pages 164-165
49. La Canonica
50. Camparone
51. Da Cencia
52. Gino in Trastevere
53. Sabatini I
54. La Tana de Noantri
55. Sora Lella
67. La Carbonara
68. Guilia
70. Vecchia Roma

Map C – see pages 174-175
56. La Capricciosa
69. Orso "80"
71. Da Alfredo all'Angoletto
72. Alfredo alla Scrofa
73. Dal Bolognese
74. Buca di Ripetta
75. La Nuova Compania
76. La Fontanella
77. La Screstia
78. Del Tempo Perso
79. Il Casale
80. Er Cucurucu

artichoke flattened and fried. What I'm trying to say is that it is very difficult not to eat well in any one of Rome's 5,000-plus restaurants. But what I have supplied you with here are some of the best in and around your hotel choices.

In case you didn't know, lunch hour is usually from 12:30pm to 3:00pm, and dinner anywhere from 7:30pm to 10:00pm, but is usually served at 8:30pm. So enjoy your meal and remember to take your time. Meals are supposed to be savored, not rushed through.

Traditional Roman Fare
You don't have to eat all the traditional courses listed below, but in some restaurants it is considered bad form not to. But most Italians accept the difference in our culture, even if they don't understand it, so don't feel embarrassed if all you order is a pasta dish or an entrée with a salad or appetizer.

But if you do want to order the way the Italians do, expect to spend a lot of time over dinner which is the traditional way to spend an evening. Meals consists of an *antipasto* (appetizer) and/or soup and/or pasta and is called **primo**; a main course is **secondo** (usually meat or fish) with separately ordered side dishes of *contorni* (vegetables) or *insalata* (salad) which come either *verdi* (green) or *mista* (mixed); then **dolci** (dessert), which can be cheese, fruit, or *gelato* (ice-cream). After which you then order your coffee and/or after-dinner drink.

Note: Pasta is never served as an accompanying side dish with a secondo and especially never on the same plate. It is always served as a separate course. It is time to forget everything you thought you knew about "Italian" food that was learned at some run-of-the-mill restaurant chain. In Italy it's time to eat well prepared food the proper way!

Antipasto – Appetizer
• **Bruschetta** – Garlic bread brushed with olive oil
• **Antipasto Misto** – Mixed appetizer plate. Differs from restaurant to restaurant
• **Tomate, Mozzarella ed olio** – Tomato and mozzarella slices covered in olive oil with a hint of basil

Primo Piatto – First Course
Pasta
• **Spaghetti alla carbonara** – Spaghetti tossed with bacon, garlic, peppers, grated cheese, and a raw beaten egg
• **Bucatini all'amatriciana** –Thin tubes of pasta with red pepper, bacon, and pecorino cheese
• **Penne all'arrabbiata** – Literally means angry pasta. It is short ribbed pasta tubes with a hot and spicy tomato base, garlic and parsley sauce (this is my favorite, but if your stomach can't handle spicy food, steer clear of this delicacy)
• **Fettucine al burro** – Fettucine with butter and parmesan
• **Spaghetti alla puttanesca** – Literally means whore's spaghetti! So named because the ingredients, peppers, tomato, black olives and garlic are so basic that prostitutes could quickly create a meal between tricks.

Zuppa – Soup
- **Stracciatella** – a light egg–drop soup
- **Pasta e ceci** – a filling pasta and chick pea soup
- **Zuppa di telline** – soup made from tiny clams

Secondo Piatto – Entrée
Carne – Meat
- **Abbacchio** – Milk-fed baby lamb. Can be grilled (*alla griglia*), sautéed in a sauce of rosemary, garlic, onions, tomatoes, and white wine (*alla cacciatore*), or roasted (*al forno*)
- **Saltimbocca alla Romana** – Veal fillets that are covered in sage and prosciutto and cooked in butter and white wine
- **Pollo alla cacciatore** – Same dish as the lamb above but replaced with chicken
- **Pollo alla Romana** – Chicken stewed with yellow and red bell peppers
- **Pollo al diavolo** – So called because the chicken is split open and grilled over an open fire and flattened by a weight placed on top of it. I guess it's what Romans think hell would be like.
- **Fritto misto** – a selection of mixed deep-fried meats and seasonal vegetables
- **Lombata di vitello** – Grilled veal chop
- **Porchetta** – Tender suckling pork roasted with herbs
- **Maile arrosto can patate** – Roasted pork with exquisite roast potatoes

Pesce – Fish
- **Sogliola alla griglia** – Thin sole lightly grilled
- **Ciriole** – Small tender eels dredged from the Tiber

Contorno – Vegetable
- **Carciofi alla giuda** – Jewish-style artichokes, pressed flat and fried. Usually served with an anchovy garlic sauce.
- **Peperonata** – Stewed red and yellow bell peppers
- **Patate arrosto** – Roasted potatoes that usually come with a grilled meats but can be ordered separately.
- **Insalata Mista** – Mixed salad. You have to prepare your own olive oil and vinegar dressing. American's thirst for countless types of salad dressings hasn't hit Italy yet.
  establishments make their own. That's right, Limoncello is mostly made prohibition-style. One place that makes some of the best is La Buca di Ripetta. But they'll only serve it to you if they consider you 'worthy' of such a special drink, lovingly created, and sparingly served.

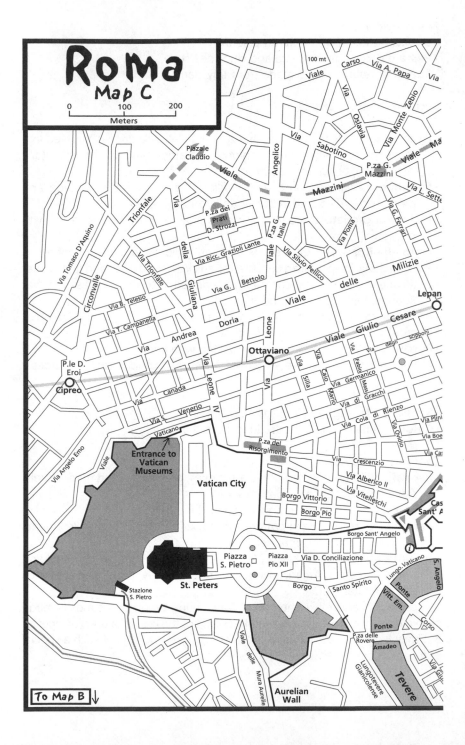

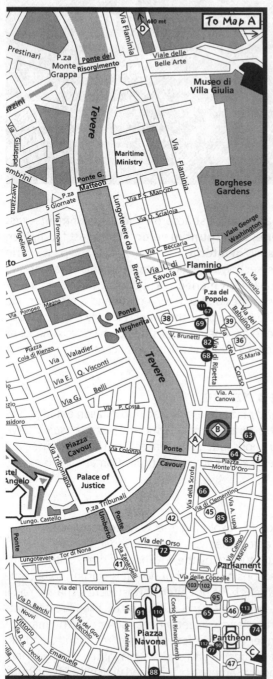

Sights ◇

A. Tomb of Augustus
B. Mausoleum of Augustus
C. Santa Maria Sopra Minerva
D. Ponte Milvio

Hotels ○

36. Margutta
38. Locarno
39. Valadier
41. Genio
42. Portoghesi
45. Markus
46. Sole Al Pantheon
47. Santa Chiara

Eateries ●

63. La Capricciosa
64. Arancio d'Oro
65. Da Alfredo all'Angoletto
66. Alfredo alla Scrofa
67. Dal Bolognese
68. Buca di Ripetta
69. Del Tempo Perso
72. Orso "80"
74. La Sacrestia
77. La Caffetteria
82. Buccone
83. Al Parlamento Achilli
85. Vini e Buffet
88. Cul de Sac
90. Cremeria Monteforte
91. Tre Scalini
110. Dolce Vita
111. Rosati
112. Sant'Eustachio
113. Tazza d'Oro

Nightlife ◉

95. Black Duke
102. Ned Kelly's
103. Oliphant

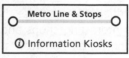

○══════○ Metro Line & Stops

ⓘ Information Kiosks

Where to Get Your Wine to Take Home

The most complete and best located store to buy your duty free wine quota (three liters per person) is **Buccone** *(Via di Ripetta 19-20, Tel/Fax 06/361-2154)* near the Piazza del Popolo. The walls of these two storefronts are lined from floor to ceiling with bottles from every different region in Italy, as well as other countries. Extensive does not do this place justice. The prices here are comparable with duty free at the airport and you get a much better selection. The prices for Sambuca and Limoncello are better at the airport, but get your wine here.

Reviews Explained

The reviews below are arranged first according to establishment – first **ristorante/trattorie/pizzerie**, then **spuntini veloci** (italian fast food), then **enoteche** (wine bars), and finally **gelateria** (ice cream shops) and **pasticcerie** (pastry shops). Within the first section the eating establishments are separated into specific areas in Rome. Each entry mentions a price that reflects dinner for two, if two people order two dishes apiece (i.e., a pasta and a meat for one person and an antipasto and a fish dish for the other, etc.) exclusive of wine. Obviously, if you only choose to eat one dish per sitting, which we Americans are apt to do, the actual price for your meal will be significantly less than what is indicated in this guide.

RISTORANTE, TRATTORIE & PIZZERIE

Ristorante, **trattorie** and **pizzerie** are all traditional italian eateries. The ristorante are more formal, trattorie are more rustic and pizzerie usually serve only pizza's and other baked goods. But all the places listed here will offer you an excellent meal, quality service and an authentically Roman dining experience.

Trastevere

This is the perfect place for exploring the way Romans actually live. **Trastevere** literally means "across the river," and this separation has allowed the area to remain virtually untouched by the advances of time. Until recently it was one of the poorest sections of Rome, but now it is starting to become gentrified, though these changes have not altered Trastevere's charm. You'll find interesting shops and boutiques, and plenty of excellent restaurants among the small narrow streets and *piazzetta* (small squares). The maze of streets is a fun place to wander and wonder where you're going to end up.

This area offers some of the best dining and casual nightlife in town. Here you can sit in a piazza bar, sipping Sambuca or wine and watch the life of Rome pass before your eyes. To accommodate this type of activity, many stores have begun to stay open later.

49. LA CANONICA, *Vicolo dei Piede 13, just off of the Piazza Santa Maria in Trastevere. Closed Mondays. Major credit cards accepted. Tel. 06/580-3845. Dinner for two E40. (Map B)*

In the capital of the Catholic world, what better way to dine than in a deconsecrated chapel transformed into one of Rome's most entrancing restaurants? Located near Rome's only exclusive English language movie theater, Il Pasquino, La Canonica's Baroque facade is delicately covered with vines and flowers. In the summer months tables are set outside. For me, the best place to sit is inside where it is always cool and you can soak in the atmosphere of a renovated chapel that now has meats, kegs, and bottles hanging from the ceiling. If you come to Rome, you have to eat here.

The menu is dominated by seafood and pasta. My recommendations: *spaghetti alla vongole verace* (spicy clam sauce of garlic, basil, oil, and hot peppers) or the *spaghetti alla carbonara* (a light cream sauce, covered with ham, peas, and grated parmesan cheese), or a simply incredible *penne all'arrabiata* (spicy tomato sauce). For the main course, try the light fish dish of *sogliola alla griglia* (grilled sole). The *grigliato misto di pesce* (mixed grilled fish) is also good.

50. CAMPARONE, *Piazza in Piscinula 47. Tel 06/581-6249. Closed Mondays. Credit cards accepted. Dinner for two E38. (Map B)*

This restaurant owns the entire block, starting with the bar/café on the left, the restaurant in the middle, and the pizzeria/birreria on the right. The outside seating at the restaurant is the best place to enjoy a true Trastevere evening. Their food includes an excellent rendition of *ossobuco alla Romana* which they prepare with *fungi* (mushrooms). Mainly known for their grilled meats and some of their pastas. Located off the beaten path near the Tiber River and the Isola Tiberina.

51. GINO IN TRASTEVERE, *Via Della Lungaretta 85, 00153 Roma. Tel. 06/580-3403. 06/580-6226. Closed Wednesdays. Dinner for two E40.*

The spacious and bright interior makes you want to sit outside under their awning on the side or in the front by the main road. Wherever you end up the food will be exceptional. One of the proprietors, Paulo, will greet you at the door and make sure everything is perfect all night long. Since it's popular it tends to get crowded, so get there early (7ish) or late (10ish) otherwise you may be in for a wait. But later is better because then you can watch the parade of people pass by on their way to Piazza Santa Maria and a night on the town in Trastevere.

They have an extensive fish and meat menu: try the *sogliola alla griglia* (grilled sole), or the *saltimbocca alla Romana* (veal shanks in sauce and spices) for seconds. Your primo piatto has to be one of their great Roman pasta dishes like *arrabiatta* (tomato-based with garlic and peppers), or *vongole verace* (clams in a spicy oil, garlic, and basil sauce). Or if the desire for pizza hits you, it's great here.

52. SABATINI I, *Piazza Santa Maria in Trastevere 13, Tel. 06/581-8307 (outside seating) or 06/581-2026 (inside seating with an entrance on side). Closed Wednesdays, and two weeks in August. No credit cards accepted. Very expensive. At least E50 for dinner. (Map B)*

Besides the excellent fish dishes here, you can soak up the Trastevere lifestyle, especially in summer when outside seating is available. At night the floodlights keep the church at the opposite end of the piazza aglow. Try the *spaghetti alle cozze* (mussels), *zuppa di pesce*, the *spiedino misto di pesce al forno* (mixed grilled fish), and the grilled sole (*sogliola alla griglia*). If you want to see the fish grilled go to the very back of the restaurant and there they'll be roasting over an open fire, scales and all. (The waiter will de-bone, de-head and de-tail either at your table or by the fire). The inside is cozy and comfortable and they have singers walking through the tables serenading the customers, which is nice if you like that sort of thing.

53. LA TANA DE NOANTRI, *Via della Paglia 1-2-3, 00158 Roma. Tel. 06/ 580-6404 or 06/589-6575. Credit cards accepted. Closed Tuesdays. Dinner for two E38. (Map B)*

Located past Piazza Santa Maria and past the tables laid out for La Canonica, this superb restaurant has rather boring seating inside, but oh so wonderful places outside in the Piazza di San Egidio at night. Here you can sit under awnings and savor dish after dish of succulently seasoned Roman specialties. Great atmosphere and great food.

Rome's Best Eateries

You'll find plenty of good eateries in Rome, but for a truly great meal every time, here is my list of favorites.

49. LA CANONICA, *Vicolo dei Piedi 13, Dinner for two E40.*

56. AL PICCOLO ARANCIO, *Vicolo Scandberg 112, Dinner for two E45.*

62. LE GROTTE, *Via delle Vite 37, Dinner for two E35.*

68. LA BUCA DI RIPETTA, *Via di Ripetta 36, Dinner for two E35.*

70. LA CARBONARA, *Campo dei Fiori 23, Dinner for two E45.*

73. VECCHIA ROMA, *Piazza di Campitelli 18. Dinner for two E43*

84. ENOTECANTINA, *Via del Croce 76, Meal for two E30.*

85. VINI E BUFFET, *Piazza della Torretta 60, Meal for two E25.*

86. CAVOUR 313, *Via Cavour 313. Meal for two E25.*

88. CUL DE SAC, *Piazza di Pasquino 73, Meal for two E25.*

I've had the *pizza con salsiccia* (with sausage) as a primo, then moved onto the *braccioline di abbacchio* (literally translated it means "little arm of lamb"). My partner had the *tortellini alla crema con funghi* (cheese or meat stuffed tortellini with cream sauce and mushrooms). Even though we were too full to go on, we lingered over a bottle of white wine then ordered some *spaghetti alla carbonara* to close out the night. It was a real feast in a great atmosphere.

54. **SORA LELLA**, *Via di Ponte Quattro Capi 16, Tel. 06/686-1601. Closed Sundays. Credit cards accepted. Dinner for two E60. (Map B)*

A wonderful little local place magically situated on the Isola Tibertina in the middle of the Tiber River, you'll find great local atmosphere and wonderful food. Family-run for generations, they prepare real *cucina romana* (Roman cooking) here. There are only two rooms that can seat maybe 45 people. Try their *gnocchi alla amatriciana* (dumplings in a red pepper, bacon and pecorino cheese sauce) or the *spaghetti al tonno* (with a tuna sauce). For seconds their *abbacchio* (lamb) is some of the best in Rome. It may seem expensive but the food and exclusive atmosphere justifies the cost.

Trevi Fountain Area

The **Trevi Fountain** is the place where you toss a coin at Neptune's feet for a guarantee that you will one day return to Rome. It is an impressive 18th century baroque statue that dominates the square it is in. In fact, it seems too large for so small a space, especially at night when it is lit up by floodlights. All around Trevi are shoe stores and small *pizzerie* and is one of the most popular spots in Rome.

55. **AL MORO**, *Vicolo delle Bollette 13 (off Via del Lavatore), Tel. 06/678-3495. Closed Sundays and the entire month of August. No credit cards accepted. Dinner for two E55. (Map A)*

The food is excellent in the Roman style, the ingredients are all fresh and of the highest quality, but the prices are a little high, and since this a popular eating establishment you'll need to make reservations. I swear the *spaghetti al moro* (a light carbonara sauce with cheese, egg, bacon, and red pepper flakes) is the best pasta dish I have ever tasted. They make an excellent *all'arrabbiata* (hot and spicy sauce) too. I also enjoyed the *scampi alla moro* (broiled shrimp). Other excellent dishes are the *abbacchio romanesco al forno con patate* (roasted lamb with superb roasted potatoes with a sprinkle of rosemary).

The inside front room is dominated by a large picture of Moro himself, long since passed away. The other two rooms have wine bottles surrounding the walls above the tables and are relatively roomy. If you want to sit outside you'll be crowded against a wall on a lightly traveled little *via*. I recommend the inside seating.

56. AL PICCOLO ARANCIO, *Vicolo Scandberg 112, Tel. 06/678-6139. Closed Mondays. Credit cards accepted. Dinner for two E45. (Map A)*
Located on a dark side street near the Trevi fountain you would walk right past if you did not know this place existed. Great food served either at the few tables outside, or in the boisterous inside rooms. Excellent pastas, great meat dishes, wonderful service. An ideal choice when in Rome.

Via Veneto Area
The **Via Veneto** was backdrop for the 1959 film *La Dolce Vita*. It used to be the chic gathering place for international movie stars but now it's simply an expensive place to stay, shop, and eat. Yet is still retains a lot of character. The area is hectic and thoroughly Roman, filled with shopping opportunities, offices, and only a few sights like the **Baths of Diocletian**.
57. GIOVANNI, *Via Marche 64, Tel. 06/482-1834. Closed Saturdays and the entire month of August. Credit cards accepted. Dinner for two E75. (Map A)*
Close to the hustle and bustle of the Via Veneto is this good restaurant with an Adriatic flair. The owners are from Ancona and they serve fresh fish brought in from there. The soups in their restaurant are also very good, so if you've had your fill of pasta, come here and try the seafood and soups. I really like the *calamaretti ai ferri* (small shrimp cooked over an open flame). The house white from the Verdicchio region is quite good.
58. GIRARROSTO TOSCANO, *Via Campania 29, Tel. 06/493-759. Closed Wednesdays. No credit cards accepted. Dinner for two E60. (Map A)*
Located in the cellar of a huge building facing onto the Aurelian Wall, this is a first-class restaurant that accepts orders until 1am. An ideal place to come back to after a night of revelry if you have a lingering hunger. The food is mainly veal and beef grilled on a spit over an open wood fired oven. Prior to the meal you can indulge in melon, *prosciutto di Parma* and *ovoline* (small mozzarella cheeses). The servings are large and so are the prices, and befitting its location near the Via Veneto the service is excellent.
Beside the food you'll enjoy the rustic atmosphere, with hams hanging in the entrance way along with a table filled with fresh produce. In the dining area bottles of wine line the walls above the tables, and the wood paneling adds to the peasant appeal at princely prices.

Piazza di Spagna Area
Around the **Piazza di Spagna** is where it all happens in Rome. You have the best shops, great restaurants, and beautiful buildings. Stately *palazzos* lining the streets look like an ideal place to live, but today much of the housing has been replaced by offices, shops, boutiques, or restaurants. Only the lucky few can afford an apartment in this location.

This area is home to the **Spanish Steps**, which gets its name from the Piazza, which gets its name from the Spanish Embassy to the Holy See that used to sit on the site. The area was adopted by British travelers in the 18th and 19th centuries, because it was not yet a popular location. The British presence is still here in the form of Babbington's Tea Rooms, an expensive but satisfying establishment in the piazza; as well as a plaque commemorating the house where Keats died in 1821. The area used to be called *il ghetto degli Inglesi* – the English ghetto.

At the beginning of Spring, the steps are laden with banks of flowers that make the whole area look like a garden. Even though you are not suppose to sit and relax on the steps anymore (a rule in place since 1996), you'll find others doing it. So sit a spell and watch the world walk by.

59. RE DEGLI AMICI, *Via della Croce 33b, Tel. 06/679-5380 or 678-2555. Credit cards accepted. Closed Mondays and the last three weeks in June. (Map A)*

This *trattoria* close to the Spanish Steps has been serving traditional Roman food for years. If you don't want a full meal their antipasto bar will more than suffice, and after 7:30pm, you can get one of their excellent pizzas. My favorite is the one named after the restaurant, made with sausage, mozzarella, oregano and tomatoes. The pasta dishes here are also something that shouldn't be missed. Try any of the Roman specialties: *carbonara, amatriciana,* or *arrabiata.*

60. HASSLER, *Piazza Trinita dei Monti 6, Tel. 06/678-2651. Credit cards accepted. Open 7 days a week. Dinner for two E60. (Map A)*

If you have the money to spend, the view down the Spanish Steps and over the rooftops of Rome from the glassed-in and air-conditioned terrace is worth every penny. You can pick out the Castel Sant'Angelo, the Jewish Ghetto's synagogue, the Pantheon, and the Quirinale Palace from the terrace. The food used to be passable, but now the Italian and Continental menu has begun to sparkle. The multilingual waiters will tell you that the *abbacchio al forno* is excellent, and I'd agree. There are many fine dishes on the menu, so you can order anything, but remember it's expensive.

61. OTELLO ALLA CONCORDIA, *Via Della Croce 81. Tel. 06/679-1178. No credit cards accepted. Closed Sundays. Dinner for two E40. (Map A)*

This is a family-run, small trattoria set off the main road, Via della Croce. It's location used to render it unnoticed, but now it seems to be crowded all the time. And with good reason – the food is excellent. You enter through a tiny entrance then a small shady garden to get to the restaurant. They have now made the garden eating area enclosed in removable glass, so people can eat out here all year round. In the summer it's especially nice.

On the inside the walls are filled with countless oil paintings, many received as trade for a good meal by a struggling artist. The prices are perfect and the food is simple, basic, and good. I loved the *abbacchio arrosto can patate* (roast lamb with grilled potatoes). The pasta dishes are not that good, which is strange for Rome, but if you stick with the meat dishes and vegetables you'll have a great meal. They open at 7:30pm. Make sure you get here early (or make reservations) or else you'll have a wait. The help is surly, but in a congenial Roman way.

62. LE GROTTE, *Via delle Vite 37. No telephone. Credit cards accepted. Dinner for two E35. (Map A)*

This place has superb atmosphere and exquisite food. They are known for their excellent antipasto bar and superb pizza. I've had the *spaghetti alla vongole verace* (spicy clam sauce) and the *pollo arrosto* (spit roasted chicken) and loved them both. The food is down-to-earth peasant style in the true Roman fashion, and mixes well with the rustic ambiance. While dining here you really do feel as if you are in a series of caves (grotte). When in Rome make sure you eat here not only for the food, but the excellent atmosphere as well.

63. LA CAPRICCIOSA, *Largo dei Lombardi 8 just off of the Via Del Corso. Tel. 06/6794027 & 6794706. Open lunch and dinner (until 1 am). Closed Tuesdays. Credit cards accepted. Dinner for two E38. (Map A)*

Don't be fooled by the name. This is no ordinary pizzeria. It is a large, wonderfully authentic Italian restaurant with over 50 tables inside. At night and on weekends, the restaurant expands outside into the Largo dei Lombardi. The best place to dine is outside, because inside the nickname for this place could be La Cucaracha. In a convenient location directly in the middle of Rome's premier shopping area, Via del Corso, this is a good place to stop in after an evening of shopping. But remember to bring cash, because La Capricciosa doesn't like to accept credit cards.

They have a large selection of antipasto with all sorts of prepared vegetables, ham, salami, and mozzarella. Mainly a pasta and pizza restaurant (pizza served only in the evenings), they also serve great meat and vegetable platters. Their best pizza is the gargantuan *pizza capricciosa*, one with everything, Italian style. They also make all of the Roman pasta staples perfectly: *arrabbiata, amatriciana,* and *vongole*. One pasta dish that is a little different but really good is the *spaghetti al burro con funghi* (with butter and mushrooms). Or try the *mezzo pollo al diavolo* (half chicken cooked on the grill) if you're in the mood for poultry.

64. ARANCIO D'ORO, *Via Monte d'Oro 17, Tel. 06/686-5026. Credit cards accepted. Closed Mondays. Dinner for two E45. (Map C)*

Refine, elegant and not frequented by tourists. This is gem of a restaurant hidden down a small side street, with a small sign and curtains hindering the view inside so people who do not know of it walk right on by. Tuesdays and Thursday are fresh fish days. Excellent food, great service, wonderful atmosphere. Come here when in Rome.

65. **DA ALFREDO ALL'ANGOLETO**, *Piazza Rondanini 51, Tel. 06/686-8019, 06/686-1203. Credit cards accepted. Closed Mondays and August 11-15. Dinner for two E50. (Map C)*

A vibrant and noisy trattoria specializing in fish for many years. Try to resist the lure of the innumerable, mouth-watering *antipasti* or you won't have room for the superbly fresh fish, the enormous Mediterranean prawns, or the still live lobsters in the display case awaiting your cooking instructions. This tentatively can be called the best seafood restaurant in Rome so if you want some come here. Mushrooms are another Alfredo specialty from late summer to late autumn. I recommend you try any of their seafood dishes, roast meats, or pastas.

There is outside seating on the small piazza as well as air-conditioned inside seating. The decor is simple, with wine bottles lining the shelves set above the tables. Come here for great food and wonderful atmosphere.

66. **ALFREDO ALLA SCROFA**, *Via della Scrofa 104, Tel. 06/654-0163. Closed Tuesdays. Credit cards accepted. Dinner for two E55. (Map C)*

There are photographs of the very rich and famous literally papering the walls. The restaurant has been in business for over half a century and was even frequented by Douglas Fairbanks and Mary Pickford which should give you an idea of what the prices are like now. All the pasta dishes are superb, especially *fettucine al triplo burro* (a rich artery clogging concoction made with triple butter sauce). The wine list is excellent and so are their house variations. If you like music with your meal, there is a strolling guitarist inside. One of *the* places to be seen in Rome.

67. **DAL BOLOGNESE**, *Piazza del Popolo 1-2, Tel. 361-1426., 06/322-2799. Closed Mondays and Sunday evenings, and August 9-25. Credit cards accepted. Dinner for two E47. (Map C)*

The cooking is Bolognese in style, which some claim is the best in Italy. Why? Because of the *parmigiano reggiano* cheese and the *prosciutto di parma,* as well as their affinity for pastas that use one or both of these ingredients. They have a menu in English to help you search through their great dishes. The *fritto misto alla bolognese*, which includes fried cheeses, meats and vegetables, is great. The *misto di paste* (mixed pasta and sauces) was filling enough for two. By ordering this dish you get to sample a variety of dishes while only ordering one. They have outside seating, perfect for people watching, but the intimacy of their inside rooms decorated with a fine collection of modern paintings appeals to me more. Also inside, you don't have to breathe exhaust fumes while you eat.

68. **LA BUCA DI RIPETTA**, *Via di Ripetta 36, Tel. 06/678-9528. Closed Mondays and the whole month of August. No credit cards accepted. Dinner for two E35. (Map C)*

This is a very small, friendly local trattoria, where you must arrive early if you have not made a reservation. Immensely popular for its food, reasonable prices, and festive atmosphere. Also, the jovial *padrone* is in constant attendance. The food is basic, straightforward Roman fare. Try the *lasagna al forno, saltimbocca alla romana,* or the *ossobuco di vitello.* They take their food seriously, so if you want to eat the Roman way with course after course, this is the place to do it. The restaurant is only one tiny room, its high walls covered with cooking and farming paraphernalia like enormous bellows, great copper pans, etc. Reservations are needed. When in Rome, you simply must dine here.

69. DEL TEMPO PERSO, *Via dell'Oca 43, Tel. 06/322-4841 or 322-0947. All credit cards accepted. Dinner for two E37. (Map C)*

Great rustic, succulent Roman fare, a stone's throw away from the Piazza del Popolo – and at great prices too. The restaurant has a small outside seating area enclosed by planters in which you can eat your meals on wooden tables. There is also some seating inside, but in the summer, the terrace is the best place to be. This *osteria* is not haute cuisine, but every dish is excellent. They have the largest selection of pastas, pizzas and meat dishes I have seen anywhere in Italy, so if you can't find something you like here, you don't like to eat.

Come here for the Roman specialties such as *spaghetti alla carbonara, penne all'arrabiata,* or *bucatini all'amatriciana;* or really treat yourself and sample the super-fantastic *tagliatelle ai funghi porcini* (with porcini mushrooms) with the most succulent sauce you can find anywhere. For seconds, the *abbacchio arrosto con patate* (lamb with rosemary potatoes) is exquisite as is the *vitello arrosto con patate* (veal with rosemary potatoes). Mimmo, the head waiter, is perfectly attentive, and since he was married to an American he speaks good English. While in Rome, definitely try this place. I did not put it on the top ten list, but it is number ten and a half.

Centro Storico
Piazza Navona, Pantheon and Campo dei Fiori Area

The **centro storico** is the old medieval heart of Rome. Literally translated centro storico means 'historic center' and this is where you will find many of Rome's main sights, as well some of the best nightlife, restaurants and cafes. **Piazza Navona** is the perfect place to explore Rome's tapestry of history. The square itself has a charm that makes you want to come back over and over again. It is like a living architectural gallery, with its baroque churches and buildings lining the square and the immense statues standing majestic in the square itself.

On a hot day, the fountains here are a visitor's oasis, allowing for needed foot soaking refreshment. But before you take your shoes off and relax your sore feet, stroll to the center of the piazza and take note of the magnificence of Bernini's **Fontana Dei Quattro Fiumi** (Fountain of Four Rivers). You'll also find great ice cream, wonderful cafes, good restaurants as well as fire-eaters,

American Pie

If you are looking for an oasis of Americana in Rome, there are now plenty of places to satisfy this craving. **McDonalds**, which only ten years ago was a rarity in the eternal city, now number over twenty. Another bastion of Americana, which I never thought would succeed in Italy, **Dunkin' Donuts**, is flourishing with one store at the Trevi Fountain *(Via S. Vincenzo 1)* and another in the main hall of Termini Station *(Tel. 06/ 785-1987, E-mail: g.cont@iol.it, Web: www.dunkin'donuts.com)*. And if you're looking for something a little more upscale but still completely American, there is now a **Planet Hollywood** *(Via del Tritone 118, Tel. 06/4282-8012)* near the Piazza Barberini, and a **Hard Rock Cafe** *(Via Veneto 62a, Tel. 06/420-3051)* right across the street from the American Embassy. Also available is **T-Bone Station** *(Via F. Crispi 29/31, Tel. 06/6787-650, Web: www.tbone.it)*, which is a quality American-style steakhouse.

painters, jugglers, caricaturists, tourists, rampaging Italian children, and much more.

And from mid-December to mid-January, the square becomes a giant Christmas market with booths and stalls selling stuffed animals, toys, handicrafts, and candy that looks like coal. Since it is the central focus of the holiday season there are also some great toy stores in the piazza which I loved to visit as a kid.

Another focal point of the area is the **Pantheon**, built almost two thousand years ago by Consul Marcus Agrippa as a pantheistic temple, hence its name. The city's population was centered in this area during the Middle Ages, and except for the disappearance of a large fish market, the area has remained virtually unchanged.

The area is completed by the **Campo dei Fiori** (literally translated this means "field of flowers") which has a produce and flower market every morning except Sundays. The entire centro storico is genuinely picturesque and intriguing, with a maze of interconnecting narrow streets and *piazzetta* (small squares); and evokes a feeling of what Rome was once like many eons ago, with the centuries-old buildings and the peddlers, carts, and small stores lining the narrow streets.

70. LA CARBONARA, *Campo dei Fiori 23, Tel. 06/654-783. Credit cards accepted. Closed Tuesdays. Dinner for two E45. (Map B)*

Located in the best piazza for atmosphere, and the food's great as well. As could be expected, *rigatoni alla carbonara* is the house specialty so give that a try here. It is prepared to perfection in a rich peppery sauce of egg, cheese, and bacon. They also make the best *spaghetti alla vongole verace* (spicy clam sauce) I've ever had anywhere. The *fritto misto* (lightly fried mixed vegetables and cheese) is excellent since most of the produce comes in directly from the *mercato* in the square. The market can be a problem at early lunch since there are still discarded veggies on the ground where the tables should be. There's no smell, but the sight isn't too appetizing. As always, I loved the *abbacchio alla griglia* (roast baby lamb) and the roasted potatoes.

A word or warning. Periodically minstrels will play tunes for patrons. Some people find this to be too touristy. So if you do not like music played for you when you eat, do not come here. Or go inside where the minstrels do not enter. Also, you are not required to tip the musicians, but can if you want.

71. GUILIA, *Via della Barchetta 19, Tel. 06/6880-6466. Dinner for two E37. (Map B)*

They have a beautiful arched interior with brown tiled floors that emits all the character of Rome. The dishes are basic but great Roman fare too, like the *penne all'arrabbiata* or the *spaghetti alla vongole*. Besides the pasta they have fresh fish and grilled meats. These guys are off the beaten track and their prices are great. Give them a try if you're in the neighborhood.

72. ORSO "80," *Via dell'Orso 33, Tel. 06/656-4904. Credit cards accepted. Closed Mondays. Dinner for two E43. (Map C)*

This is a fine Roman restaurant, a place to come for some classic pasta dishes, good fresh fish, and juicy meats. They bake their breads on-site in their red-brick pizza oven. Basically this is a restaurant with a little bit of everything for everybody. Pasta, pizza, fish, grilled meats, home-made breads, extensive antipasto, etc. I really like the Roman favorite *spaghetti alla carbonara* as well as the *abbacchio alla griglia* (grilled baby lamb). The place always seems to be crowded even though it's large, so try to get here early. Located near Piazza Navona, Pantheon, and Campo dei Fiori making it ideally situated.

73. VECCHIA ROMA, *Piazza di Campitelli 18, Tel. 06/656-4604. No credit cards accepted. Closed Wednesdays. Dinner for two E43. (Map B)*

The setting of the piazza with its Baroque church and three beautiful palazzos makes your meal worthwhile, even if the buildings are covered in grime. This menu changes constantly, but the basics are the wide variety of antipasto (which could be a meal in itself), as well as *agnello* (lamb) and *capretto* (goat) or their grilled artichokes. You have to try the artichoke, since this is the Jewish ghetto and the dish is a local favorite. One of Rome's best locations. The ambiance is delightful, the service great, and the food *fantastico*.

74. LA SACRESTIA, *Via del Seminario 89, Tel. 06/679-7581. Closed Wednesdays. No credit cards accepted. Dinner for two E43. (Map C)*

Close to the Pantheon, this restaurant has over 200 places for seating, and offers good food at reasonable prices. The decorations leave much to be desired, especially the garish ceiling and fruit-clustered grotto. Come for their pizzas, served both during the day and at night, an unusual offering for an Italian restaurant. They also serve good cuts of grilled meat, and the pasta is typically Roman also, which naturally makes it good.

75. DA SABATINO, *Piazza S. Ignazio 169, Tel. 06/67.97.821. (Map A)*
Do not eat here. Not only have I been rudely received here, but fellow travelers I have conferred with have confirmed that this place despises tourists. I have never, ever experienced such rude, belligerent behavior in my life. And it is not a theme they are trying to present. This is not a game. They honestly do no care for tourists. They will take your money, gladly, but they will give you bad, late, and despicable service.

Sadly, this place is located in one of the most beautiful piazzas in Rome. But do not be swayed by the attractive setting. The waiters' behavior will make your meal and the time you spend here ugly.

SPUNTINI VELOCI

In the middle of a shopping spree or tourist frenzy stop in one of these places for a light meal or a filling snack. Called *Spuntini Veloci*, these are Italian-style fast food places where you can get cold and hot entrees, baked pasta and boiled pasta, excellent meat choices, salads and more. All fast, all good, all at reasonable prices. Come to these places if you want to satisfy your hunger quickly, with authentic Italian food, but do not want to reduce yourself to going to (ugh) McDonalds.

76. NAZIONALE, *Via Nazionale 26/27, Tel. 06/4899-1716. Closed Sundays and in August. Hours 7am–10pm. Meal for two E20. (Map A)*
A classic cafeteria-style food place with all modern flourishes. Plenty of traditional choices here like boiled and baked pastas, as well as appetizing and fast quiches, tarts, sandwiches (*panini* or *tramezzini*). This place is packed for lunch, but all day long locals and tourists drop in to grab a bite since it is very close to *Termini* train station.

77. LA CAFETTERIA, *Piazza di Pietra 65, Tel. 06/679-8147. Closed in August and Sundays in July. Hours 7am-9pm. Meal for two E25. (Map C)*
Near the Pantheon this upscale, regal and traditional little cafeteria serves up scrumptious breakfast, lunch and dinner. You can find some of the best quick and healthy food in the city here, at a good price. Always a little crowded, but if you want quick eats in a relaxing ambiance in the old historic center this is the place to come.

78. CIAMPINI AL CAFÉ DU JARDIN, *Viale Trinita dei Monti, Tel. 06/678-5678. Closed Wednesdays and all of March. Hours 8am-7pm. Summer hours 8am-1am. Meal for two E20. (Map A)*
In a fantastic location near the Villa Borghese, Villa Medici and the top of the Spanish Steps this frenzied and always full local place is perfect for hungry tourists and locals alike. A combination cafeteria, ice cream parlor and

restaurant, here you'll find many choices, both hot and cold, and you can get some excellent ice cream for dessert.

79. CIAO/SPIZZICO, *Via del Corso 181, Tel. 06/678-9135. Hours 7am-midnight. Fridays until 1:30am. Saturdays until 2:00am. Meal for two E20. (Map A)*

Located on the hippest, happiningest shopping street in Rome, almost right next door to the great department store La Rinascente, this place will satisfy your hunger quickly for breakfast, lunch, dinner, as well as a late night snack when you stumble back from the disco. Your choices are many from pastas, to meat, salads, cheese or fruit. Service is fast, and many of the first course pasta dishes are created right in front of your eyes. The portions are large and the ingredients fresh and tasty and the prices are reasonable. This place is an Italian-style food court with all sorts of choices.

80. BREK, *Largo di Torre Argentina 1, Tel. 06/6821-0353. Open 12-3:30pm and 6:30-11:00pm. Meal for two E20. (Map B)*

An Italian-style fast food place, which is all over the country. They have just opened this location in Rome. There is restaurant seating upstairs, café fare downstairs, all quick, all convenient, and all very tasty. Located near the Pantheon, Campo dei Fiori and Navona this is a good place to come and grab a quick bite in the middle of the day.

ENOTECHE

Wine bars (*enoteche*) have existed in Italy since the beginning of grape cultivation, but in the past have usually been dark, dingy affairs populated by older men, playing cards at rickety tables, slurping hearty local vintages from chipped mismatched glasses. Most of those places are gone, and have been replaced with newer, more upscale, ambient, fern-filled establishments such as those listed below. These places offer some excellent vintages from all over the Italian peninsula and the world. Usually open mid-day until the wee hours of the morning, with a break in the afternoon, *enoteche* are an upscale place for Italians to go for lunch, an early meal, a light dinner or just for a quiet evening out. These places offer excellent light food such as salads, sandwiches, crepes, quiches, and salami and cheese plates.

81. ANACLETO BLEVE, *Via S. Maria del Pianto 9a, Tel. 06/686-5970. Meal for two E25. (Map B)*

Located at the entrance to the Jewish quarter, just off the Via Arenula this place has one of the best selections of wines in all of Rome. Lunch is served in the side room and is an exquisite buffet, with hot plates prepared quickly, as well as typical local artesian cheeses and salamis, all accompanied by their superb vintages served by the glass. Wonderfully courteous service. A superb option when near the Campo dei Fiori. It's hard to find especially since their sign is upside down and backwards.

82. BUCCONE, *Via di Ripetta 19, Tel. 06/361-2154. Lunch served everyday, dinner only Thursday-Saturday. Meal for two E25. (Map C)*

A great enotecha in Rome, not only because of the offerings by the glass but also the bottled selection you can choose from. Mentioned in a sidebar in this book as the best place to buy wine to bring home, Buccone also stands on its own as a place to come in and grab a tasty, light and healthy snack and a glass of wine at either their counter serving area or side room. An excellent choice for wine lovers, in a fun local area near the main shopping street of Via Del Corso.

83. AL PARLAMENTO ACHILLI, *Via dei Prefetti 15, Tel. 06/687-3446. (Map C)*

Located in the *centro storico* near the Parlamento, here you can find (if you can find the place) ample supplies of bottles for sale, as well as glasses of their vintages offered at their counter top serving area. You can get some small snacks to go with your glass of wine. There are also cognacs and liqueurs for sale as well as chocolates, candies, jams and other boutique food items. To be complete they need a small seating area, but many locals come in for a quick glass of wine and wander out.

84. ENOTECANTINA, *Via del Croce 76, Tel. 679-0896. Closed Sundays. Meal for two E28. All credit cards accepted. (Map A)*

Opened in 1860, until a few years ago this was an old-fashioned wine store selling local vintages directly from large vats. You would walk past the huge wooden doors and into the cool, dark, and damp store lined with shelf upon shelf of wine and olive oil, and it would seem as if centuries had been erased. Now it's a fern-filled wine bar with wooden stools with ceramic seats, and ample seating. Light meals and snacks of all sorts are served here, and wine by the glass. A great place to stop in a perfect location.

85. VINI E BUFFET, *Piazza della Torretta 60, Tel 06/687-1445. Open 12:30pm-2:30pm and 7:30pm to midnight. Closed Sundays. Meal for two E25. (Map C)*

Set on a tiny side streets, near the Parliament building, just off the Via del Corso, this little wine shop and café is a breath of fresh air. It is a simply fantastic place to grab a light lunch (sandwiches, crepes, salads, etc.) and some great wine. My favorite wine bar in Rome because it evokes an ambiance of time past. The rustic and charming setting is authentically Roman and offers a unique dining experience. This is my favorite enotecha in Rome.

86. CAVOUR 313, *Via Cavour 313, Tel. 06/678-5496. Open 12:30pm-2:30pm and 7:30pm-12:30am. Closed Sundays. Meal for two E25. (Map D)*

Wow. What a great wine bar. Rustic and down-to-earth atmosphere. Superb light and healthy local food, prepared fresh. If you happen by the Colosseum or Forum, you simply must stop here for lunch, an afternoon snack or a light dinner. An excellent menu of local salamis, cheeses, sandwiches, salads and much more, all accompanied by a varied and extensive wine list. My second favorite place to Vini e Buffet above.

87. VINERIA REGGIO, *Campo dei Fiori 15, Tel. 06/6880-3268. Open 12:30pm – 2:30pm and 7:30pm – 2:00am. Closed Sundays. Meal for two E25. (Map B)*

An ideal location, in the same piazza as the bar, The Drunken Ship, and the excellent restaurant La Carbonara, this is a wine bar and late night spot for fun too. The seating outside is great on a warm day, and when it's not, you'll mostly only find places at the bar since seating inside is very limited. An adequate menu and wine list, what really makes this place is their location in the Campo dei Fiori.

88. CUL DE SAC, *Piazza di Pasquino 73, Tel. 06/6880-1094. Open 12:30pm-3:30pm and 7:00pm-12:30am. Closed Mondays for lunch. Meal for two E25. (Map B&C)*

This intimate winebar with outdoor tables set up in nice weather has over 1,400 Italian and foreign vintages for you to sample. This place has been around since the 1970s and serves up hot and cold light meals as well as dessert and ice cream. Quick informal service and a stunning ambiance, especially inside among the bottles lining the walls and at the marble topped tables.

GELATERIE

Gelato, or what we would call ice cream, is a combination of whole milk, eggs, sugar, and natural flavoring – or fresh fruit and sugar in the fruit flavors. It is a less firmly frozen, softer, more intensely flavored and colored creation than what we know as ice cream here in North America. The best fruit *gelato* is made from crushed fresh ripe seasonal fruit. The best milk-based *gelato* is flavored with all-natural ingredients and has a silky consistency. They will all melt faster than ice cream does, so be prepared for that on a hot summer day.

Besides *gelato* there are also three different types of frozen concoctions savored by the Italians:

Semifreddo, which means "half cold," and refers to any of a variety of chilled or partially frozen desserts including cake, whipped ice cream. It vaguely resembles a mousse, which is what the chocolate flavor is called.

Sorbetto is basically a fruit sorbet and has become popular in many Italian restaurants as a separator between the fish and meat courses to act as a palate cleanser. It also makes a wonderful dessert.

Granita is frozen flavored ice water. It usually, but not always, comes in lemon, orange or coffee flavors. Besides homemade varieties, you can find some excellent packaged granitas sold from coolers at most cafes. This is my favorite.

Some gelato shops for you to try include:

89. SAN CRISPINO, *Via della Panetteria 42, Tel. 06/679-3924. Open Noon to 12:30am Mondays, Wednesdays, Thursdays and Sundays; and Noon to 1:30am Fridays and Saturdays. Closed Tuesdays.*

Easily the best *gelateria* in Rome. Located near the Trevi Fountain, here you can find any flavor imaginable, and whether its creamy or fruity, all are made from scratch. All ingredients are natural, without preservative so you cannot choose by color, since the *nocciola* (hazelnut) looks like vanilla, the *pistacchio* looks like chocolate, and the *Stracciatella* (chocolate chip) looks like mud. There are no cones, only cups priced at E1.5, E2 and E3 which are filled to overflowing every time. Or you can get your favorites packed for take-out in styrofoam tubs. You simply must come here when you are in Rome.

90. CREMERIA MONTEFORTE, *Via della Rotonda 22, Tel. 06/686-7720. Closed Mondays.*

The ice cream in this minuscule little local *gelateria* is some of the best in the entire city. Since there's not much room, grab a cone or a cup here and wander out and sit by the Pantheon. All natural ingredients. Great ice cream.

91. TRE SCALINI, *Piazza Navona 28, Tel. 06/6880-1996. Closed Wednesdays.*

A staple in Rome for many years, here you can grab a cone and eat in the piazza, or sit at a table outside and watch the world go by. Very upscale and very pricey, but this is place is world renowned as a great *gelateria* in Rome.

92. PALAZZO DEL FREDDO, *Via Principe Eugenio 65/67, Tel. 06/466-4740, Closed Mondays. Open noon-11pm. Sundays 10am – Midnight.*

A famous, traditional gelateria near the train station that has been in existence since 1924. The ice creams and sorbets are all made with the finest ingredients and maintain a traditional quality and character unfazed by any new trends. You can sample cones and cups of their exquisite ice creams either outside on their patio, inside at the bar or in their own interior courtyard. Rather out of the way. Come here only if you are staying by the train station.

93. ALBERTO PICA, *Via della Segiola 12, Tel. 06/6880-6153. Closed Sunday mornings. Holiday August 15-30. Hours 8am to 2am.*

You will be overwhelmed with the choices here, especially the creative concoctions, and all are made with all natural, organic ingredients. Located just off of the Via Arenula, a stones throw from the Campo dei Fiori, this place is open late to satisfy your ice cream cravings after you have been bar hopping into the wee hours.

Seeing the Sights

For the Jubilee year, Rome introduced nine **tourist information kiosks** run by multilingual staff from 9:00am-6:00pm every day. At the locations below, you can get excellent maps of Rome, wonderful color brochures of the local museums and tons of information about virtually anything to do in Rome. Despite outliving their usefulness for the Jubilee, Rome has realized the importance of these kiosks and will keep them open open, dispensing similar information though not as extensive. They will also act as ticket booths for theatrical performances, museums, special events and sporting events. You should make a point of stopping at one of these kiosks when you first arrive in Rome. The information they dispense is invaluable, and their free maps the best available. On the maps in this book, the location of each kiosk is noted.

Look for these kiosks at:
• **Termini Train Station**, *Tel. 06/4890-6300. Open 8:00am-9:00pm daily*
• **Termini**, *Piazza Cinquecento, Tel. 06/4782-5194*
• **Castel S. Angelo**, *Piazza Pia, Tel. 06/6880-9707*
• **Imperial Forums**, *Piazza Tempio della Pace, Tel. 06/6992-4307*
• **Piazza di Spagna**, *Largo Goldoni, Tel. 06/6813-6061*
• **Piazza Navona**, *Piazza Cinque Lune, Tel. 06/6880-9240*
• **Via Nazionale**, *Palazzo delle Esposizioni, Tel. 06/4782-4525*
• **Trastevere**, *Piazza Sonnino, Tel. 06/5833-3457*
• **San Giovanni**, *Piazza S. Giovanni in Laterano, Tel. 06/7720-3535*

The chief difficulty most visitors find is that there is so much to see in this huge historic city. With even a month's worth of concentrated touring, you'd only scratch the surface. If your time is limited, consider a sightseeing tour or series of tours by bus. This way you can be sure to see at least the greatest sights in Rome and its environs. There are a variety of tours available through **Appian Line,** *Piazza dell'Esquilino 6, Tel. 06/487-861*; **Carrani***Via Vittorio E. Orlando 95, Tel. 06/474-2501*; **Green Line**, *Via Farini 5, Tel. 06/483-787*; and **Vastours**, *Via Pienmonte 34, Tel. 06/481-4309*. One of the best is **Stop 'n' Go Bus Tours**, *Tel. 06/321-7054*, which stops at a number of different sights in Rome and also offers half day trips to Tivoli and Ostia Antica and a full day trip to Cervetri and Tarquinia.

If you want a personalized tour of Rome, by licensed tour guides, that can also be arranged through the following organization: **Centro Guide Roma**, *Via S. Maria delle Fornaci 8, Tel. 06/639-0409, Fax 06/630-601*, **Centro Assistenza Servizi Turistici**, *Via Cavour 184, Tel. 06/482-5698*, **Italian Language and Culture for Foreigners,***Via Tunisi 4, Tel. 06/3975-0984; www.arcodidruso.com; E-mail: cultura@arcodisdruso.com*, or **Walking Tours of Rome**, *Via Varese 39, Tel. 06/44-51-843, Fax 06/44-50-734; www.enjoyrome.com.*

Ten Must-See Sights in Rome

The Vatican Museums alone can take you an entire day to work through, so don't believe that you can do all of these places justice in a few short days. Also, when you visit Piazza Navona, Piazza di Spagna, and Trevi Fountain, you will get a different experience depending on the time of day you go. At night each of these places livens up with Italians of all ages strolling, chatting, sipping wine, strumming guitars, while during the day they may only be swarmed by tourists. Take your time – don't do too much, and don't rush through. Take your time, be Italian and savor the experience. These ten could easily last you a week.

Sistine Chapel – Site of Michelangelo's magnificent frescoed ceiling and walls.

Vatican Museums – Everything you could imagine including Egyptian, Greek & Roman artifacts, as well as the best collection of paintings and sculptures anywhere in the world.

St. Peter's – The world's largest cathedral, exquisitely decorated.

Castel Sant'Angelo – The fortress that used to protect the Vatican, now houses a wonderful armaments museum.

Imperial and Roman Forums – The center of ancient Roman life. A great place for people of all ages to explore.

Capitoline Museum on the Campidoglio – The second best museum in Rome, with many fine sculptures and paintings.

Piazza Navona – In what used to be the place for naval gladiatorial battles is now a lively piazza filled with wonderful fountains, churches, and palazzi as well as good cafés and restaurants.

Piazza di Spagna – Walk to the top and get a great view of the city. Sit by the fountain during siesta and enjoy Rome as it passes you by.

Trevi Fountain – One of the most beautiful fountains in Italy. At night, when lit up it is a magnificent sight.

Saint Paul's Outside the Walls – Location of many buried Saints, some fine sculptures and mosaics. Walls ringed with portraits of all the popes.

A map of Rome (which you can get at any newsstand or the information kiosks listed above), some walking shoes, and a spirit of adventure are all you need to explore the innumerable piazzas, churches, galleries, parks, and fountains of this unique city. If you want the most up to date information about what is happening in Rome, whether a museum exhibit, performing arts festival, or simply what is going on in the local American community, pick up a copy of *Wanted in Rome* (Euro 75 cents) at any newsstand. This is the resource for the ex-pat community to know exactly what's going on in Rome.

List of Sights by Map

Sight	Map	Sight	Map
Imperial Forums	D	Pantheon	C & B
Trajan's Forum		Borghese Gardens	A & C
& Market	D	Galleria Borghese	A
Forum of Caesar	D	Vitt. Eman. Memorial	D
Forum of Augustus	D	Piazza del Popolo	C
Basilica of Maxentius		Via Veneto	A
& Constantine	D	Via Appia Antica	D
Colosseum	D	Trastevere	B
Arch of Constantine	D	Isola Tiberina	B
Roman Forum		Ponte Frabricio	B
& Palatine Hill	D	Jewish Ghetto	B
Baths of Caracalla	D	Palazzo Barberini	A
Baths of Diocletian	D	Palazzo Farnese	B
Campidoglio	D	Gianicolo	B
Circus Maximus	D	St. Paul's Outside	
Catacombs	D	The Walls	D
Altar/Mausoleum		S Maria Sopra Minerva	C & B
of Augustus	C	S Pietro in Vincoli	A
Pyramid	D	SM Maggiore	A & D
Ponte Milvio	C	S Giovanni in Laterano	D
Aurelian Wall	A,B,C,D	S Clemente	D
Column of M. Aurelius	C	S Cecilia in Trastevere	B
Temple of Hadrian	C	SM in Trastevere	B
Castel St. Angelo	C	Capitoline Museum	D
St. Peter's	C	National Museum	A
Vatican City	C	Galleria Borghese	A
Piazza Navona	C	Villa Giulia	C
Piazza di Spagna	A	Vatican Museums	C
Campo dei Fiori	B	Museu della	
Trevi Fountain	A	Civilta Romana	D

Rome maps can be found on the following pages:
Map A: pages 150-151
Map B: pages 165-165
Map C: pages 174-175
Map D: pages 196-197

If you saunter through the narrow streets of old Rome, behind the **Piazza Navona**, for example, or along the **Via Giulia** or near the **Pantheon**, you'll get many unexpected and revealing glimpses of flower hung balconies, inner courtyards, and fountains. Here, perhaps more than in the impressive ruins of antiquity, you will get the feeling of this city where civilizations have been built on the ruins of the previous ones for centuries. Rome is an ancient city whose vitality seems to be renewed perpetually by each new generation.

Ancient Rome

The Imperial Forums
Via IV Novembre 94. Admission E2.5. Tel. 06/679-0048. Open 9:00am-8:00pm and in the summers on Saturday until midnight. Metro-Colosseo.
The **Imperial Forums** were built in the last days of the Republic, when the Roman Forum became inadequate to accommodate the ever-increasing population, and the emperors needed space to celebrate their own magnificence. These forums were used as meeting places for Romans to exchange views, as lively street markets, or as places where official announcements could be proclaimed to the populace. The first was built by Julius Caesar, and those that followed were created by Augustus, Vespasian, Domitian, Trajan, Nerva, and Hadrian.

After the fall of the Roman Empire, these places of great import fell into disrepair; by the time of the Middle Ages and the Renaissance all that was left are the ruins we see today. Gradually, over the centuries, these monumental ruins became covered with soil until they began to be excavated in 1924.

Trajan's Forum
Located well below current street level, this is the most grandiose of the Forums of the imperial age and reflects the emperor's eclectic taste in art and architecture. Here you can see one of the finest monuments in these Imperial Forums, **Trajan's Column**, built to honor the Victories of Trajan in 113 CE. It is over 30 meters high and is covered with a series of spiral reliefs depicting the military exploits of the Emperor against the Dacins in the 1st century CE.

At the summit of this large column is a statue of St. Peter that was placed there by Pope Sixtus V in the 17th century.

Trajan's Market
This is a large and imposing set of buildings attached to Trajan's Forum, where people gathered and goods were sold. In the vast semi-circle is where the merchants displayed their wares.

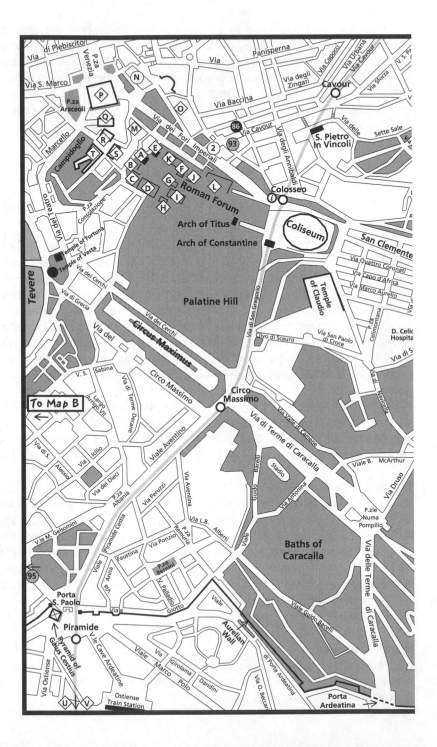

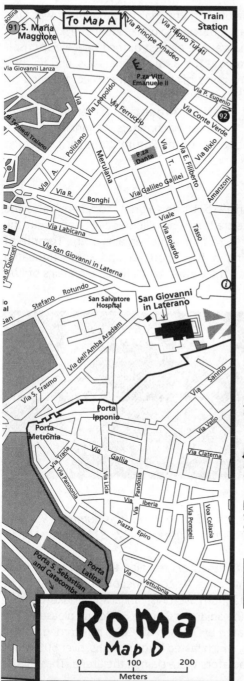

Sights ◇

A. Arch of Septimus Severus
B. Rostra
C. Temple of Saturn
D. Basilica Giulia
E. Curia (Senate House)
F. Temple of Anthony & Foustina
G. Temple of Caesar
H. Temple of Castor & Pollux
I. House of the Vestal Virgins
J. Temple of Romulus
K. Basilica Emilia
L. Basilica of Maxentius
   & Constantine
M. Caesar's Forum
N. Trajan's Fourm/Column/Market
O. Augustus' Forum
P. Vitt. Emanuele II Monument
Q. S.M. d'Araceoli
R. Capitoline Museum
S. Senatorial Palace
T. Conservatorio
U. St Paul's Outside the Walls
   Metro - San Paolo
V. Museo della Civilta Romana
   Metro - EUR Palasport or Fermi

Hotels ○

2. Richmond

Eateries ●

86. Cavour 313
92. Palazzo del Fredo

Nightlife ◐

96. Fiddler's Elbow
98. Shamrock
100. Radio Londra

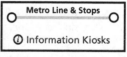

Metro Line & Stops

ⓘ Information Kiosks

Forum of Caesar
Located to the right of the Via dei Fori Imperiali (the road itself was built in 1932 on the site of a far more ancient road to more adequately display the monuments of ancient Rome), this was the earliest of the Imperial Forums. It was begun in 54 BCE to commemorate the Battle of Pharsalus, and finished in 44 BCE. Trajan redesigned many parts of this Forum to meet his needs in 113 CE and celebrate some of his victories.

For example, Trajan added the **Basilica Argentaria** (Silver Basilica) that was a meeting place for bankers and money changers. Originally a bronze statue of Julius Caesar stood in the center of this Forum; currently it is located in the Campidoglio.

Forum of Augustus
Built around the time of Christ's birth, this Forum commemorates the deaths of Brutus and Cassius (the traitors who allied against Caesar) at the Battle of Philippi in 42 BCE. Here you'll find some remains of the **Temple of Mars**, the god of war, including a high podium and some trabeated (horizontal) columns. To the side of the temple you'll find the remains of two triumphal arches and two porticos.

Really Seeing the Sights

If you are interested in seeing the Eternal City from a bird's eye view, **Umbria Fly** offers airborne tours of Rome. You will take home some memorable photos from this tour! Each 20 minute flight offers the best views of Rome for only E50 per adult and E25 per child accompanied by an adult.

For more information on how to get to the Urbe Airport (Via Salaria 825) and times of departures each day, call 06/8864-1441.

THE COLOSSEUM
Piazza del Colosseo. Admission E5. Hours in the summer 9:00am-7:00pm. In the winter 9:00am-5:00pm. Buses 11, 27, 81, 85, 87. Metro-Colosseo.

The **Colosseum** (*Flavian Amphitheater*) remains the most memorable monument surviving from ancient Rome. Its construction began in 72 CE by Vespasian on the site of the Stagnum Neronis, an artificial lake built by Emperor Nero near his house on the adjacent Oppian Hill for his pleasure. The Colosseum was eventually dedicated by Titus in 80 CE. It is recorded that at the building's opening ceremony, which lasted three months, over 500 exotic beasts and many hundreds of gladiators were slain in the arena. These types

of spectacles lasted until 405 CE, when they were abolished. The building was severely damaged by an earthquake in the fifth century CE and since then it has been used as a fortress and as a supply source for construction material for Vatican buildings.

What we see today is nothing compared to what the building used to look like. In its prime it was covered with marble, and each portico was filled with a marble statue of some important Roman.

The Colosseum used to be fully elliptical and could hold over 50,000 people. Each of the three tiers is supported by a different set of columns: Doric for the base, Ionic for the middle and Corinthian for the top. Inside, the first tier of seats was reserved for the knights and tribunes, the second tier for citizens, and the third tier for the lower classes. The Emperor, Senators, Government Officials and Vestal Virgins sat on marble thrones on a raised platform that went around the entire arena.

Inside the arena we can see vestiges of the subterranean passages that were used to transport the wild beasts. Human-powered elevators were employed to get the animals up to the Colosseum floor. At times the arena was flooded to allow for the performance of mock naval battles. Unremarkable architecturally, the Colosseum is still an engineering marvel to admire. A great site for kids to explore.

ARCH OF CONSTANTINE
Piazza Colosseo. Buses 11, 27, 81, 85, 87. Metro-Colosseo.
Located near the Colosseum, this monument was built in 312 CE to commemorate the Emperor's victory over Maxentius at the Ponte Milvio (the oldest standing bridge in Rome) and is comprised of three archways. This is the largest and best preserved triumphal arch in Rome. The attic is not continuous but is broken into three parts corresponding to the placement of the arches.

Even though this is the Arch of Constantine, the attic panels are from a monument to Marcus Aurelius. On one side of the attic the bas-reliefs represent Marcus Aurelius in his battle with the Dacians, and on the opposite side there are episodes of deeds by Marcus Aurelius and Constantine. On the lower areas there are bas-reliefs from earlier arches of Trajan and Hadrian.

THE ROMAN FORUM, PALATINE HILL & NEARBY SIGHTS

Largo Romolo e Remo 1. Tel. 06/699-0110. Admission E6. Open 9:00am-8:00pm and in the summers on Saturday until midnight. Buses 11, 27, 85, 97, 181, 186, 718, and 719. Metro-Colosseo.

The best way to get an overall view of the **Roman Forum** is to descend from the Piazza del Campidoglio by way of the Via del Campidoglio, which is to the right of the Senatorial Palace. You get a clear view of the Forums in the front, with the Colosseum in the background, and the Palatine Hill on the right. The entrance is some distance down the *Via dei Fori Imperiali*. You can also enter from the Via di San Gregario near the Colosseum.

The Roman Forum lies between the Palatine and Quirinale hills and was first a burial ground for the early settlers of both locations. Later the area became the center for the religious, commercial and political activities of the early settlers. The surrounding area was greatly expanded in the Imperial era when Roman emperors began building self-contained *Fora* in their own honor. The entire area has been decimated by war, used as a quarry for other buildings in Rome, and has been haphazardly excavated, but is still a wonder to behold. A great site for kids to explore.

In the Roman Forum you'll find the following sights and more:

Arch of Septimus Severus

Built in 203 CE to celebrate the tenth anniversary of the Emperor Septimus Severus' reign. This triumphal arch is constructed with two lower archways flanking a larger central one and is the one of the finest and most imposing structures remaining from ancient Rome. Over the side arches are bas-reliefs depicting scenes from victorious battles fought by the Emperor over the Parthians and the Mesopotamians.

In 1988, in pure Italian fashion, one half of the arch was cleaned to allow citizens to decide whether the complete structure should be cleaned. By 1998 they decided how they wanted it and were finally getting around to cleaning the other half. In a few years it will be covered in pollution grime again.

Rostra

Located directly to the left of the Arch of Septimus Severus, this building was decorated with the ramrods, rostra, of ships captured by the Romans at Antium in 338 BCE. It was the meeting place for Roman orators. All that remains now is the semi-circular flight of entry stairs. In front of it is the **Column of Phocas**, erected in honor of the Eastern Emperor of the Roman Empire, Nicephorus Phocas, in 608 CE. The column was the last monument to be erected in the Forum.

Temple of Saturn

Built in 497 BCE, it was restored with eight ionic columns in the 42 BC with the bounty from the Syrian wars. In the temple's basement was the Treasury of State. Only the threshold of the door which opens towards the Forum remains.

Basilica Giulia

Started in 54 BCE by Julius Caesar on the site of the destroyed Baslica Sempronmia and completed by Augustus, it was destroyed by fire and restored in 12 BCE, and restored a final time in 416 CE. The Basilica consisted of a huge 2 storied hall with five aisles. It once housed the Roman law courts.

Basilica Emilia

Located to the right of the entrance to the Forum, this is the only remaining Republican Basiclia and was built in 179 BCE. It was restored on several occasions by Gens Aemilia and now bares his name. Because of the ravages of fire, destruction by "barbarian hordes" and neglect, little remains today. The facade consisted of a two story portico and 16 arches. It was one of the largest buildings in Rome and was used by money-changers and other business people.

The Curia

Founded by Tullus Hostilius and initially erected between 80 BCE and 44 BCE, it was completed in 29 BCE by Augustus and restored several times. It was the house of the Senate, the government of Rome in the Republican period, and the puppet government during the empire. It was once covered with exquisite marble but is today a combination of stucco and brick. The structure was rebuilt after a fire in 283 CE, and converted into a church in the seventh century CE. The interior is still a large plain hall, with marble steps that were used as the senator's seats. Take the time to go inside and sit where the Roman Senators sat ages ago.

Temple of Anthony & Faustina

Built by Antonius Pius in honor of his wife Faustina in 141 CE, after his death the temple was dedicated to the emperor as well. The temple was later converted to a church in the 11th century, **San Lorenzo in Miranda**. All that remains of the original Roman temple are the ten monolithic columns that are 17 meters high, and an elegant frieze. The baroque facade is from the 1600s.

Temple of Caesar

Also known as the Temple of the Divine Julius, this temple was built by Augustus on the site where the body of Julius Caesar was cremated and where Marcus Antonius made his famous funeral oration after the assination. It was inaugurated on August 18 29 BCE. The little that now remains includes the round altar where the funeral pyre was most likely erected. Septimus Severus restored the Temple after it has been damaged by by fire.

Temple of Castor & Pollux

Built in 484 BCE and dedicated to the cult of Castor and Pollux, the temple has been restored many times, most notably by Hadrian and Tiberius. The facde once faced the square of the forum adn there were 19 original comuns (only three remain). Inside, the Senate would meet periodically to deal with concerns of weights and measures. At the foot of the podium, money changers, bankers and barbers would set up shop.

House of the Vestal Virgins

This is where the vestal virgins lived who dedicated themselves to maintaining the sacred fires in the nearby **Temple of Vesta**. A portico of two stories adorned with statues of the Vestals surrounded a round open court that was decorated with flower beds and three cisterns. In the court you can still see the remains of some of the statues and the pedestals on which they sat.

Arch of Titus

Erected in 81 CE by Domitian to commemorate the conquering of Jerusalem by Titus. The arch contains bas-reliefs of the Emperor and of soldiers carrying away the spoils of Jerusalem. It is one of the most imposing structures remaining from ancient Rome and a pilgrimage site for every Jewish tourist to the city.

Temple of Romulus

Once considered as a comemorative building for Romulus, son of Maxentius, who died in 309 CE at a very young age. It is now know as the Temple of Jupiter Stator. The brick construction dates back to the Maxentius-Constantine period and consists of a domed, round, central location, preceded by a semi-circular face flanked by two rectangular sections.

Basilica of Maxentius

Built between 306 CE and 312 CE by the Emperor Maxentius and completed by Emperor Constantine. The last remaining column was removed in 1613 and placed in front of the Santa Maria Maggiore to commemorate Christianity's pre-emmenence over paganism. This is the location where the giant statue of Constantine once stood, the head and foot of which are now on display at the Capitoline Museum.

The Palatine Hill

This is one of the seven hills of Rome and was the residence of the Roman emperors during the Golden Age as well as the Imperial Period. It was here, in 754 BCE, that Romulus is said to have founded the city of Rome. But actual records and not just myth have indicated that settlement was actually established in the 9th century BCE. Aristocratic families also resided here, leaving behind wonderful architectural relics most of which have been excavated today, making the Palatine Hill one of the must-see places when you tour the Forum. It is also a wonderful respite from the hectic pace of Rome, filled with lush greenery and plenty of shade; it's a great place to have a picnic or go on a relaxing walk through history.

Here you'll find the baths of Septimus Severus, the Farnese Gardens, the House of Livia, the Flavia Palace, the House of Augustana, and more. Many of the ruins are under excavation and as such are only occasionally accessible for foot traffic, but all can be viewed.

BATHS OF CARACALLA
Via Terme di Caracalla, Tel. 06/575-8626. Admission E4. Hours Monday– Saturday 9:00am until one hour before dark. Mondays and Holidays 9:00am– 1:00pm. Buses 90, 90b, 118. Metro-Circo Massimo.

Built in 217 CE by the Emperor Caracalla, these baths were second in size only to the Baths of Diocletian. They were used until the sixth century when they were destroyed by Gothic invaders, and today it takes quite an imagination to reconstruct the building mentally. The baths were once rich with marble and statues and decorated with stucco and mosaic work. All that is left are the weathered remains of the massive brick structure which offers an insight into the scale of the baths, but doesn't offer a glimpse of their beauty. Today, on cool summer evenings, opera performances are held among the ruins of the **Calidarium**, the circular vapor bath area.

BATHS OF DIOCLETIAN
Viale E de Nicola. Open 9:00am-2:00pm, Holidats only until 1:00pm. Buses 57, 64, 65, 75, 170, 492, and 910. Metro-Repubblica.

These were the most extensive baths of their times in which more than 3,000 bathers could be accommodated at one time. They were built by Maximilian and Diocletian from 196–306 CE. Today the **National Museum** is located within their walls, as is the **Church of Santa Maria Degli Angeli**.

CAMPIDOGLIO
Piazza del Campidoglio 1. Open 9:00am-7:00pm. Closed Mondays. E5. Buses 94, 95, 713, 716. Metro-Colosseo.

The Capitoline Hill is one of the seven hills of Rome. It forms the northwest boundary of the Forum and today is home to the **Capitoline Museum**, **Senatorial Palace**, the **Palace of the Conservatori**, the **Church of Santa Maria D'Aracoeli** (formerly the Temple of Juno Moneta), and the bronze **statue of Marcus Aurelius**. The Palazzo di Senatori (Senatorial Palace) was finished in the beginning of the 14th century; the statue was placed there in 1528, and the piazza along with the other two buildings were completed in 1570. These last three structures as well as the stairs leading up to them were based on a design developed by Michelangelo, who died in 1564 not seeing his plan completed.

The **Capitoline Museums** were founded by the Popes Clement XII and Benedict XIV and-house some exquisite works (see Capitoline Museum in the *Museums* section below).

To ascend the hill, take either the steep stairway that leads to the church, the winding ramp of the Via delle Tre Pile, or from between the two of these by way of the monumental stairs, Cordonate, which were designed by Michelangelo. At the entrance to these stairs you'll find two imposing Egyptian lions and at the top you'll find the statues of Castor and Pollux.

The church of Santa Maria D'Aracoeli was originally a pagan temple then was converted for use as a Christian church. In the 12th century it was given its present form with a colonnade of mismatched ancient columns, stolen from a nearby Roman ruin, and a wide nave. The enormous set of stairs in front are one of the church's main features.

You must visit the museums on this hill, since they are second in magnificence only to the Vatican Museums, and certain exhibits are even better. Also, having your picture taken in front of the large pieces of Constantine's statue is a wonderful memento.

CIRCUS MAXIMUS
Via del Circo Massimo. Buses 15, 90, 90b, 94. Metro-Circo Massimo.

This circus (race-track) was established on the flat lands to the south of the fortified Palatine Hill. It was erected in 309 CE by the Emperor Maxentius in honor of his deified son Romulus, whose temple is nearby. Then in Imperial times it was expanded, destroyed, enlarged and used as a quarry until little is left of the original marble.

But today its shape is clearly visible underneath the contoured grass and earth, and some of the original seats remain at the turning circle of the southwestern end. The slight hump running through the center marks the location of the *spina*, around which the chariots, and at times runners, would race. In its prime the Circo Massimo could hold between 150,000-200,000 spectators, more than most modern stadiums.

CATACOMBS
Saint Callistus (Via Appia Antica 110, Tel. 06/513-6725. Closed Wednesday.)
San Sebastian (Via Appia Antica 132, Tel. 06/788-7035. Closed Thursday.)

Santa Domitilla (Via di Sette Chiese 282, Tel. 06/511-0342. Closed Tuesday.)
Entrance for each E5. Hours for each 8:30am-12:00pm and 2:30pm-5:00pm
Buses 118 and 218.

Located next door to one another on and around the Via Appia Antica south of the city, these tombs were originally an ancient Roman necropolis. They were then used by the early Christians as a meeting place as well as one of worship, and were finally a haven for them from prosecution. Here you can visit the **crypts of the Popes**, the crypt of Saint Cecilia, the crypt of Pope Eusebius, as well as frescoes dating back to the 3rd century CE. All three are an eerie reminder of the time before Christianity dominated the Western world. A time when Christians were actually the ones being persecuted instead of doing the persecuting. A great site for kids to explore.

ALTAR & MAUSOLEUM OF AUGUSTUS

Piazza Augosto Imperatore. Altar open 9:00am-2:00pm. You need to call to gain access to the mausoleum, Tel. 06/6710-3819. Closed Sundays. Buses 81, 90, 119, 926. Metro-Spagna.

The excellently preserved altar was built from 13-9 BCE to celebrate the peace established by Emperor Augustus following his victories in Gaul and Spain. It consists of a simple raised altar enclosed by a four-walled screen with openings at the front and back. Reconstructed and housed in a temporary structure in 1938 by Mussolini to glorify Italy's past, the carved friezes of flowers on the lower walls were created by Greek masons imported to Rome. The upper section displays mythical scenes in the history of Rome as well as scenes form the consecration ceremonies of thre altar itself.

The altar orginally stood in the Campo Marzio. Fragments came to light in the 1568 during reconstruction on the Palazzo Fiano. Additional pieces were excavated in the mid-19th and early 20th centuries. Finally in 1938 a professional excavation and reassembly was undertaken. Currently a more permanent structure is on the verge of being completed to house the altar, which will also contain a small museum.

The mausoleum of Augustus is the circular structure nearby that is overrun with grass and shrubs. It used to be a series of intricate passageways where niches of urns filled with funeral ashes were located, and it used to be topped with a large statue of Augustus. It has been used as a fort, a bull ring, a theater and a concert hall. In 1938 when the altar of Augustus was dedicated, the medieval buildings surrounding the mausoleum were razed and the present piazza was built, creating a rather stagnant, overly modern backdrop to this ancient historic site.

PYRAMID OF GAIUS CESTIUS

Piazzale Ostiense. Buses 13, 23, 57, 95, 716. Metro-Piramide.
Built in 12 BCE as a tomb for the Praetor Gaius Cestius, this structure is a prime example of the influence that Egypt and its religion had on ancient Rome. During early Rome a cult of Egyptology was one of the largest of the pagan religions. Built of brick and rock and covered with limestone, this is one of the more striking structures left from ancient Rome and as such is a great photo op, one that my family has been coming back to since the '50s.

If you are out here in the mornings, other than Sunday, make a point of heading to the **Testaccio market** in Piazza Testaccio. A wonderfully authentic local market. If you're out here at night, or in the evenings, the Testaccio section is the place to be for nightlife. Rome's best discos are located here, and there are number of restaurants from which to choose.

PONTE MILVIO

Via Flaminia/Piazza Cardinale Consalvi. Take the 225 bus to Piazza Mancini and walk to Piazza Cardinale Consalvi, or take the 201 bus from Piazza Mancini.
Located north of the Aurelian and Servian walls, the Ponte Milvio was the first Roman bridge over the Tiber and was built in 109 CE. This bridge was the location of many military campaigns throughout Italian history, including one battle that helped establish Christianity as the world's dominant religion. Here in 312 CE Emperor Constantine defeated forces led by Maxentius. Constantine made a pact that if he won the battle, he would convert to Christianity. If he had not won this battle, pagan worship would more than likely be much more prominent than it is today.

The current bridge has been destroyed and rebuilt countless times but retains its original form. It was last destroyed in 1849 when Garibaldi's troops blew it up to prevent the advance of the French army. In 1985 it was closed to vehicular traffic for restoration and remains a pedestrian bridge today. The is a daily market on the side farthest from the city center which is worth visiting if you are in the area.

AURELIAN WALL

Built from 272-279 CE, this wall is a testament to the faded glory of the Roman Empire. Built to protect Rome from an incursion of Germanic tribes, one of the best places to witness its protective shield is at the top of the Via Veneto at the **Porta Pinciana**. The walls enclosed not only the old city of Rome but also what used to be farmland.

Today the walls extend to the Baths of Caracalla in the south, Piazza del Popolo in the north, Trastevere and Saint Peter's in the west, and the University and Stazione Termini in the East. They have a total length of about 12 miles, and consist of concrete rubble encased in brick almost 12 feet thick and 25 feet high. In some places their height is 50 feet. There is a parapet running across the top and there are 380 square towers interspersed along its length. These towers are a distance of two arrow shots apart, which was one hundred ancient Roman feet or just under 30 meters, which not so coincidentally enough is about 100 modern American feet.

There were 18 main roads over which gates were built. Many have been rebuilt to accommodate different defense strategies throughout the ages; most recently they were adapted for the onslaught of automobile traffic. The ones that are the best preserved with most of their Roman features are the **Porta San Sebastiano** (take bus 188 from San Giovanni in Laterano), **Porta Asinara** (next to Porta San Giovanni) and the **Porta Toscolana** (behind the train station).

COLUMN OF MARCUS AURELIUS
Piazza Colonna. Buses 56, 60, 62, 85. Metro-Barberini.

Carved between 180 and 196 CE, this column is a continuous spiral of sculptures celebrating Marcus Aurelius' military victories. It used to be surrounded by buildings from its own era, but only the ruins of the Temple of Hadrian located in the wall of the *Borsa* remain (see description below). Statues of Marcus Aurelius and his wife used to adorn the top of the column, but they were replaced by St. Paul in the 16th century. Today this piazza has been made into another of Rome's car-free zones, since the citizens of this city, as well as other cities in Europe, are realizing that automobiles may enhance individual transportation possibilities, but they drastically eliminate community livability.

TEMPLE OF HADRIAN
Piazza di Pietra. Buses 56, 60, 62, 85. Metro-Barberini.

Located near Piazza Colonna and the Via del Corso, this is a fantastic example of architectural pastiche, where structures from different eras are molded and blended together into one building. In this case, one wall of the modern Roman Stock Exchange (*Borsa*) has eleven Corinthian columns that remain from the temple dedicated by Antonius Pius to his father Hadrian in 145 CE.

This is a great place for photos of how Rome's ancient past is woven together with the ever-changing present. While here please note the path that runs in front of this sight. It leads to the Trevi Fountain and the Pantheon, and is marked with exhibit signs describing what the significance of this sight is. By building this pathway and erecting these signs, Rome has decided to forgo simply being a museum in spirit and has started to formally make itself into one.

Christian Rome

CASTEL SANT'ANGELO

Lungotevere Castello 50, Tel. 06/687-5036. Admission E5. Open 9:00am–7:00pm. Closed the second and fourth Tuesdays of the month. Last entrance time is 1 hour before closing. Buses 23, 34, 64, 280, 982. Metro-Lepanto.

Also known as the **Mausoleum of Hadrian** since it was built for Hadrian and his successors, for eighty years it was used as a funeral monument where the ashes of the Roman emperors were stored. As the papacy began to establish itself near the tomb of St. Peter's during the Middle Ages, the structure was converted into a fortress for the Popes. During that period the bulky battlements and other military fortifications were added. A covered walkway leads from Saint Peter's to the Castel Sant'Angelo and, because of the volatile political situation in Italy for many centuries, this walkway was used more than once to protect the Pope. Since then it has been used as a residence for popes and princes, as a prison, and as a military barracks.

On the summit of the building is the statue of an angel (hence the name of the castle), and rumor has it that in 590 CE, Gregory the Great saw a vision with an avenging angel sheathing its sword at the summit of the castle. He took this to mean the plague that had ravaged Rome was over. To commemorate this event he placed an angel on top of the building. Today the castle houses a museum with one of the best collections ever assembled of armaments from the Stone Age to the present day. There are also some nondescript art exhibits and luxuriously preserved Papal apartments. A must-see when in Rome. A great site for kids to explore.

SAINT PETER'S

Piazza San Pietro. Hours 8:00am–6:00pm, but only until 5:00pm in the winter. Tel. 06/6988-4466. Buses 19, 62, 64, or 492. Metro-Ottaviano.

Located in the monumental square **Piazza San Pietro**, Saint Peter's is a masterpiece created by **Bernini** between 1655 and 1667, and is the largest church in the world. The square itself is oval and 240 meters at its largest diameter. It is composed of 284 massive marble columns, and 88 pilasters forming three galleries 15 meters wide. Surrounding the square, above the oval structure are 140 statues of saints.

In the center of the square is an obelisk 25.5 meters high with four bronze lions at its base, all of which were brought from Heliopolis during the reign of Caligula (circa 40 CE) and which originally stood in the circus of Nero. It was placed here in 1586. Below the monument you can see the points of the compass and the names of the winds. Around this obelisk during the Christmas season a life-sized crèche is erected, and since 1980 has become a

Proper Attire at Museums & Churches

When you're visiting most museums and monuments in Italy, follow these necessary rules: **Women**: wear either long pants or a long skirt or dress, and a top with sleeves. **Men**: wear long pants and no tank tops. Both men and women will be denied entry to St. Peter's, and to many other sights as well, if you are wearing shorts or short skirts and/or a revealing top!

site that many Italians come to admire during that season. If in Italy during this time, come out and pay a visit, especially at night, when it is all lit up.

Also of interest are two porphyry's (disks) in the ground in St. Peter's Square, located on either side of the obelisk. If you stand on either disk and look at the columns (which run four deep) surrounding the square, it appears as if there is only one column instead of four! People line up to stand on the disks and witness this optical illusion which displays the brilliance of the architects of the structure.

To reach Saint Peter's you must pass the obelisk and walk up a gradual incline. The church rises on the site where Saint Peter is buried. The early Christians erected a small oratory on the site of the tomb, but that was destroyed in 326 when Constantine the Great erected the first Basilica on this site. Over the centuries the church began to expand and became incongruously and lavishly decorated, so that by 1452 Nicholas V decided to make it more uniform. He commissioned Bernardo Rossellino to design a new structure. When the Pope died three years late this work was interrupted, but in 1506 Pope Julius II, with the assistance of Bramante, continued the work on a grander scale.

Bramante died in 1514 before his work could be finished. His successor was Raphael, and when he died four years later, Baldassare Peruzzi and Antonio de Sangallo the Younger took over the responsibility jointly. Work was interrupted by the sack of Rome in 1527, then again in 1536 when Peruzzi died. When Sangallo died in 1546, the project was taken over and modified by the 72-year old **Michelangelo**. Before he died eight years later, he had modified Bramante's plan for the dome and we are blessed with his pointed Florentine version today. After he died, the plans he made for St. Peter's were more or less adhered to by his successors Vignola, Pizzo Ligorio, Giacomo dell Porta, Domenico Fontana, and finally Carlo Maderno, who designed the facade according to his plan. On November 1, 1626, **Urbano VIII** dedicated the Basilica as we know it today.

The Facade

Rounding off, the **facade** is 115 meters long and 45 meters high, and is approached by a gradually sloping grand staircase. At the sides of this staircase are the statues of **Saint Peter** (by De Fabis) and **Saint Paul** (by Adamo Tadolini). On the balustrade, held up by eight Corinthian columns and four pilasters, are the colossal statues of the Savior and St. John the Baptist surrounded by the Apostles, excluding Saint Peter.

There are nine balconies, and from the central one the Pope gives his Christmas and Easter benedictions. There are five doors from which to enter the church, but today only the large central one is used.

The Interior

The church is more than 15,000 square meters in area, 211 meters long and 46 meters high. There are 229 marble columns: 533 of travertine, 16 of bronze, 90 of stucco, and 44 altars. On the floor of the central nave you'll find lines drawn identifying where other churches in the world would fit if placed in Saint Peter's. Kids love to explore this aspect of the basilica.

Also on the floor, near the front entrance, is a disk of red porphyry indicating the spot where **Charlemagne** was crowned Holy Roman Emperor by Leo III on Christmas Day in 800 CE. To the right of this, in the first chapel, is the world famous *Pieta* created by Michelangelo when he was only 24, in the year 1498. In the niches of the pilasters that support the arches are statues of the founders of many religious orders. In the last one on the right you'll find the seated bronze statue of Saint Peter. The statue's foot has been rubbed by so many people for good luck that it has almost disappeared.

Just past the statue is the grand **cupola** created by Michelangelo. One of the most amazing architectural wonders of all times, it is held up by four colossal spires which lead to a number of open chapels. Under the cupola,

Free English-Language Tours of St. Peter's

One of the best ways to see St. Peter's and one of the least known is on an **English-language tour** of the basilica by trained volunteer guides. Available seven days a week, Monday-Saturday at 3:00pm and Sundays at 2:30pm, the tour lasts an hour and a half and offers an in-depth historical and religious perspective of this magnificent church. The tours start at the information desk to the right as you enter the portico of St. Peter's. *For more information, call 06/6972.*

To coordinate your day, go to the Vatican museums in the morning, have a light lunch, get here for the tour about half an hour early, and enjoy a stimulating and fact-filled afternoon.

The Swiss Guards

The world's smallest and perhaps most colorful army, The Swiss Guards were formed in 1506 by Pope Julius II as the papal protectors and remain so today. You can often see them in their trademark blue, red and yellow tunics, purported to have been designed by Michelangelo himself, with a plumed Spanish Conquistadorial helmet sitting jauntily on their heads. For routine work, the guards dress down to their more modern blue uniforms and berets.

This tiny force is all that is left of the papal military corps that medieval popes commanded to exert worldly power over much of the Italian peninsula, a power that has been reduced to the 108 acres of the Vatican City. Most of the guards' work is purely ceremonial, but their main task is much like that of the Secret Service in the U.S., except the Swiss Guards' protectee is the pope, not the president.

New recruits are sworn in annually on May 6, the anniversary of a 1527 battle in Rome in which 147 Swiss Guards were killed defending Pope Clement VIII from troops of the Holy Roman Emperor Charles V. To become a Swiss Guard one must be Roman Catholic of Swiss nationality, be under the age of 30, stand at least 5 feet 8 inches tall and be willing to learn Italian.

above the high altar rises the famous **Baldacchino** (or Grand Canopy) made by Bernini. It's made from bronze taken mainly from the roof of the Pantheon. In front of the altar is the **Chapel of Confessions** made by Maderno, around which are 95 perpetually lit lamps illuminating the **Tomb of Saint Peters**. In front of the shrine is the kneeling **Statue of Pius VI** made by Canova in 1822.

Throughout the rest of the Basilica you'll find a variety of superb statues and monuments (including the magnificent *Pieta* by Michelangelo), many tombs of Popes, and a wealth of chapels, not the least of which is the **Gregorian Chapel** designed by Michelangelo and executed by Giacomo della Porta. It is rich in marbles, stuccos, and mosaics, all put together in the creative Venetian style by Madonna del Soccorso in the 12th century.

If you grow tired of the many beautiful works of art and wish to get a bird's eye view of everything, you can ascend into Michelangelo's Cupola either by stairs (537 of them) or by elevator. If you come to Saint Peter's, you should do this. Kids of all age love it.

VATICAN CITY

Piazza San Pietro. Buses 19, 62, 64, or 492. Metro-Ottaviano. The city is generally inaccessible except for official business, but you can look into gardens from the cupola of St. Peter's.

Vatican City sits on the right bank of the Tiber river, in the foothills of the Monte Mario and Gianicolo section of Rome. In ancient Rome this was the site of the Gardens of Nero and the main circus where thousands of Christians were martyred. Saint Peter met his fate here around 67 CE. Today it is the world center for the Catholic Church, rich in priceless art, antiques, and spiritual guidance.

The Vatican (officially referred to as **The Holy See**) is a completely autonomous state within the Italian Republic and has its own radio station, railway, newspaper, stamps, money, and diplomatic representatives in major capitals. Though it doesn't have an army, the **Swiss Guards**, who are volunteers from the Swiss armed forces, guard the Vatican day and night.

Piazzas, Fountains, Monuments, Palazzi & Gardens

PIAZZA NAVONA
Buses 70, 81, 87, 90.
The piazza is on the site of a stadium built by Domitian in 86 CE that he used for mock naval battles, other gladiatorial contests, as well as horse races. The stadium's north entrance has been excavated and you can see the stone arch of the entrance outside of the Piazza Navona toward the Tiber on the south side of the Piazza di Tor Sanguigna. Located some 20 feet below the current street level, this is an intimate glance at how much sediment has built up in Rome over the past 2,000 years.

After the Roman era the piazza was lined with small squatters' homes which followed the tiers of the stadium, but because of its wide open space it soon became a prime spot for large palazzi. Today the style of the piazza is richly Baroque, featuring works by two great masters, **Bernini** and **Borromini**. Located in the middle of the square is Bernini's fantastic **Fontana Dei Quattro Fiumi** (Fountain of Four Rivers), sculpted from 1647-51. The four figures supporting the large obelisk (a Bernini trademark) represent the four major rivers known at the time: the Danube, the Ganges, the Nile, and the Plata Rivers. The idea behind the representation of the statues is that the Catholic church reigns triumphant over the world.

Besides the statue's obvious beauty and meaning, Bernini has hidden a subtle treasure in this piece. When visiting Rome, notice the figure representing the Nile shielding its eyes. Some historians interpret the position of the figure's hand blocking its view of the facade of the church it is facing, **Santa Agnese in Agone**, as a statement of revulsion. This church was designed by Bernini's rival at the time, Borromini, and Bernini, as the story is told, playfully showed his disdain for his rival's design through the sculpted disgust in his statue. Others claim the revulsion comes from the fact that the church, built as a family chapel for Pope Innocent X's Palazzo Doria Pamphili, is located on the site of an old neighborhood brothel. Maybe both are true?

To the south of the piazza is the **Statue of Il Moro** (actually a replica) created by Bernini from 1652-54. To the north is a basin with a 19th century **Statue of Neptune** struggling with a sea monster.

To savor the artistic and architectural beauty, as well as the vibrant nightlife of the piazza, choose a table at one of the local bars or cafés and sample some excellent Roman *gelato* (ice cream), grab a coffee, or have a meal and watch the people go by. Navona has been one of Rome's many gathering spots for people of all ages since the early 18th century. You'll find local art vendors, caricaturists, hippies selling string bracelets, and much more. This is the place to come for ice cream in Rome, and Tre Scalini is the most famous *gelateria*. The piazza is also home to a fun Christmas fair that lasts from mid-December to mid-January. Filled with booths and performers, it is much like an old fashioned carnival that kids of all age love. Another feature of Navona that kids will love is that it contains two of Rome's best toy stores. This is a place you cannot miss if you come to Rome.

PIAZZA DI SPAGNA & THE SPANISH STEPS

Buses 52, 53, 56, 58, 60, 61, 62, 71, 81. Metro-Spagna.

This is one of the most beautiful and visited spots in Rome. It is named after the old Spanish Embassy to the Holy See that used to stand on the site. The 137 steps are officially called the *Scalinata della Trinita dei Monti*, and are named for the church which they lead to at the top. But most people just call them the **Spanish Steps**. The fountain in the middle of the piazza is known as the **Barcaccia** and was designed in 1628 by Pietro Bernini in commemoration of the big flood of 1598. To the right is the column of the **Immaculate Conception** erected in 1865 by Pius IX. The Spanish Steps were built in the 17th century. Besides being the location of fine works of art and architecture, it is also a favorite meeting spot for Italians of all ages.

GALLERIA DORIA-PAMPHILI

Piazza del Collegio Romano, 2. Tel. 06/679-7323; www.doriapamphilj.it. Open 10am-5pm, closed Thursday, E8 museum, E4 private apartments (these are only open 10:30am to noon).

A private home just off the Via del Corso is also home to a fantastic museum, recently reopened to the general public. Here you can tour their incredible art collection and a number of private apartments dolled up with exquisite furnishings. Audio tour in English narrated by the owner is available and recommended. Works by Caravaggio, Titian, Velasquez, Lippi, and other incredible artists. The family came into prominence when their relative became

Pope Innocent X in the 1600s. This place is unusual because not too many private homes have been opened up to the public for viewing.

CAMPO DEI FIORI
Campo dei Fiori. Buses 46, 62, 64, 65, 70.

This is a typically Roman piazza that hosts a lively flower and food market every morning until 1:00pm. Here you'll find the cries of the vendors blending with the bargaining of the customers. Though there are now some vendors specifically catering to the tacky souvenir needs of tourists, the majority of the stands are for the locals, and the majority of the visitors are the same. A perfect place to see and smell the vibrant local beauty and bounty of Rome.

The campo used to be a square where heretics were burned at the stake and criminals were hanged. The monument in the middle is in memory of Giordano Bruno, a famous philosopher who was burned here in 1600.

The campo is also a great place to come at night, because it is home to a great restaurant, **La Carbonara**, that serves the best *spaghetti alla vongole verace* I've ever had, and a great American-style bar, **The Drunken Ship**. It is also an active local shopping area. So if you're looking for intriguing and original items, or rare antiques, wander through the back streets around this piazza, Piazza Navona and the Pantheon.

TREVI FOUNTAIN
Piazza di Trevi. Buses 52, 53, 56, 58, 60, 61, 62, 71, 81. Metro-Barberini.

Another meeting place for Italians in the evenings. You'll always find an impromptu guitar solo being performed as well as wine being savored by many. A great place to hang out in the evenings and make new friends. This is the largest and most impressive of the famous fountains in Rome and is truly spectacular when it is lit up at night. Commissioned by Clement XII, it was built by Nicola Salvi in 1762 from a design he borrowed from Bernini and takes up an entire wall of the Palazzo Poli built in 1730. In the central niche you see Neptune on his chariot drawn by marine horses preceded by two tritons. In the left niche you see the statue representing Abundance, and to the right Health. The four statues up top depict the seasons and the crest is of the family of Clement XII, Corsini.

There is an ancient custom, legend, or myth, that says that all those who throw a coin into the fountain are destined to return to Rome. So turn your back to the fountain and throw a coin over your left shoulder with your right hand into the fountain and fate will carry you back. That is if you can get close enough. In the summer, and especially at night, this place is packed wall to wall with people. Also, please don't try and recreate Anita Ekberg's scene in the film *La Dolce Vita* when she waded through the fountain to taunt Marcello Mastroiani. It is completely illegal to walk in the fountain, and the authorities enforce this regulation severely. If they didn't, the local kids would all swim in and collect the coins thrown by tourists.

PANTHEON

Piazza della Rotonda. Tel. 06/6830-0230. Open Monday-Saturday 9:00am-6:30pm, Sundays 9:00am-1:00pm. At 10:00am on Sundays is a mass. Tel. 06/6830-0230. Buses 70, 81, 87, 90.

Located in a vibrant piazza, the **Pantheon** is one of the most famous and best preserved monuments of ancient Rome. Besides the architectural beauty, the entrance area to the Pantheon is by far the coolest place in Rome during the heat wave of August. So if you want to relax in cool comfort in the middle of a hot day, park yourself just in front of the entrance under the portico.

First constructed by Agrippa in 27 BCE, it was restored after a fire in 80 CE and returned to its original rotunda shape by the Emperor Hadrian. In 609 CE, it was dedicated as a Christian Church and called Santa Maria Rotunda. In the Middle Ages it served as a fortress. In 1620 the building's bronze ceiling was removed and melted into the cannons for Castel Sant'Angelo and used for Bernini's Baldacchino (Grand Canopy) in Saint Peter's that marks the site of the saint's tomb.

But during all this pillage the Pantheon was never left to ruin. It always remained in use and thoroughly maintained. The building is made up of red and gray Egyptian granite. Each of the sixteen columns is 12.5 meters high and is composed of a single block.

You enter the building by way of the cool and comfortable portal area and the original bronze door. As you enter it is impossible not to feel the perfect symmetry of space and harmony of its architectural lines. This feeling is somewhat lessened by the fact that the Roman authorities have placed a ticket booth inside along with a small souvenir stand each of which detracts from the perfection of the structure. Sad. Nonetheless you will still be awed by the marvelous dome (diameter 43 meters) with the hole in the middle through which rain cascades during moments of inclement weather.

There are three niches in the building, two of which contain tombs: the tomb of **Victor Emmanuel II** (died 1878), one of Italy's few war heroes, and the tombs of **Umberto I** (died 1900) and **Queen Margherita** (died 1926), and in another niche the tomb of renowned artist **Raphael Sanzio** (died 1520).

Around the Pantheon are a number of wonderful and famous cafes, restaurants and shops. It is a meeting place for locals and tourists alike and is a fun area to enjoy any time day or night.

THE BORGHESE GARDENS

Buses 95, 490, 495, 910. Metro-Spagna.

The most picturesque park in Rome, complete with bike and jogging paths (you can rent bikes in the park), a lake where you can rent boats, a wonderful museum – **Galleria Borghese** – lush vegetation, expansive grass fields, the Roman **zoological park**, a large riding ring, and more.

This is the perfect place to come and relax in the middle of a hard day of touring. Sundays fill the park with families, couples and groups of people biking, jogging, walking their dogs, playing soccer, strolling or simply relaxing in Rome's largest green space. Small food stands are interspersed in the park offering refreshments and snacks.

The gardens are a great sanctuary just outside the ancient walls of Rome. If you only want an afternoon's respite from the sights of the city, or you're tired of spending time in your hotel room during the siesta hours, escape to these luscious and spacious gardens.

To get to the gardens is simple enough: either exit the old walls of Rome through the gates at the Piazza del Popolo or at the top of the Via Veneto. From the Piazza del Popolo exit , the gardens will be on your right through the iron gates just across the busy Piazzale Flaminio. Once you enter you will be on the Viale Washington. Anywhere to the left of you, after a few hundred meters, will be prime park land. From the Via Veneto exit, cross the major thoroughfare in front of you and you're in the Borghese. From here stroll to your right and you will instantly find a pleasant area to picnic or take a small nap for the afternoon.

Borghese Gardens is home to Rome's **zoo** (but I would not recommend visiting it since the accommodations for the animals are criminal), several museums (including Galleria Borghese and the Galleria Arte Moderna), playing fields for *calcio*, a small lake, an amphitheater, and many wooded enclaves to have a wonderfully secluded picnic. Make sure you keep an eye for those heated Italian couples if you have kids in tow.

Galleria Borghese

One of Rome's finest museums is in the Borghese Gardens, the **Galleria Borghese**. For those of you who entered the Gardens from Piazza del Popolo, it will be a long hike up the Viale Washington to the lake, and around it to the Viale Dell'Uccelleria (the zoo will be on your left) which leads directly to the Galleria Borghese.

From the Via Veneto it is not quite as long. From where you first entered the gardens, there is a road, Viale Del Museo Borghese, on your right. Take this all the way to the Galleria.

The Galleria Borghese was built by Dutch architect Hans van Santes during the 1820's. It houses a large number of rare masterpieces from many disciplines and countries. There are classical works of Greeks and Romans, along with 16th and 17th century paintings by such notables as Raphael, Titian, Caravaggio, and Antonella da Messina. Sculptures are also featured with works by Lorenzo Bernini, Pietro Bernini, and Houndon. A must see when in Rome.

For more details, see the Galleria Borghese description below under *Museums*.

VITTORIO EMANUELE II MONUMENT
Piazza Vittorio Emanuele. Buses 70, 81, 87, 90.
A monument to the first king of Italy who died in 1878. Work started in 1885 but was not finished until 1910. It is an inflated version of the Temple of Fortune on the hillside at Praenestina. To all in Rome it is affectionately called "The Wedding Cake," since its shape and white marble make it look eerily like a larger version of one. The monument is also home to the tomb of the unknown soldier.

ISOLA TIBERINA
Buses 44, 75, 170, 710, 718, 719.
Halfway across the river going towards Trastevere, this island used to be a dumping ground for dead and sick slaves. At that time, the 3rd century BCE, there was a cult of healing *(aesculapius)* located here. Currently half the island is taken up by a hospital showing that traditions do live on. The church on the island, **San Bartolomeo** was built in the 12th century, and was substantially altered in the seventeenth. One of the bridges to the mainland, **Ponte Fabricio**, is the oldest in Rome. A fun place to explore with wide walkways around the island and along the river. If you have kids, keep them in tow because there are no railings.

PONTE FABRICIO (DEI QUATTRO CAPI)
There is some debate as to whether this is the oldest span in Rome still in use, or the Ponte Milvio. The actual first bridge in Rome the, **Pons Aemilius**, an arch of which is still visible south of the Isola Tiberina, and was washed away in 1598 and never rebuilt. This is a good place to cross the Tiber going towards Trastevere after you've been exploring the Jewish Ghetto and the Sinagoga.

PALAZZO BARBERINI
Via delle Quattro Fontane, 13. Tel. 06/482-4184. Admission E5. Hours 9:00am–9:00pm Tuesday-Friday, until midnight on Saturdays, until 8:00pm on Sundays. Closed Mondays. Buses 95, 490, 495, 910. Metro-Barberini.
Located just off the Piazza Barberini on the Via Quattro Fontane, this baroque palace was started by Carlo Maderno in 1623 with the help of Borromini and was finished in 1633 by Bernini. When the entrance was rearranged to the south from the northeast in 1864, the baroque iron gates were designed, built and installed by Francesco Azzuri.
One wing of the palace is the site of the **Galleria Nazionale d'Arte Antica**. Besides the wonderful architecture which is impossible to miss, the

gallery has many wonderful paintings such as *Marriage of St. Catherine* by Sodoma, *Portrait of a Lady* by Piero di Cossimo, and *Rape of the Sabines* by Sodoma. A wonderful little museum, and a great place to visit in the evenings since it stays open so late.

PALAZZO FARNESE
Piazza Farnese. Buses 23, 65, 70, or 280.

This palace represents one of the high points of Renaissance architecture. It was started in 1514 by Antonio da Sangallo the Younger for Cardinal Alessandro Farnese (later Pope Pius III), and was continued by Michelangelo who added the large window, the molding on the facade, the third floor of the court, and the sides. It was finally finished by Giacomo della Porta. As well as being an architectural wonder, there is a first floor gallery of frescoes depicting mythological subjects by the painters Carracci, Domenichino, and Reni.

The palace became the French Embassy in 1625 and remains so today. As such it is not open to the public unless you get written permission from the French government.

Roman Neighborhoods

PIAZZA DEL POPOLO
Buses 90, 119. Metro-Flaminio.

This impressive piazza is the base of the ascent to the **Pincio**, a relaxing area of Rome where you can get some great views of the city. It was consolidated as a piazza in 1538 during the Renaissance, and today has been made another car-free zone in the city of Rome. Citizens of this city, as well as other cities in Europe, are realizing that automobiles may enhance individual transportation possibilities, but they drastically eliminate livability. In 1589, the **Egyptian Obelisk** which is 24 meters high and came from Egypt during the time of Ramses II in the 8th century BCE, was moved from the Circus Maximus and erected in the middle of the square. The present layout was designed by G. Valadier at the beginning of the 19th century and is decorated on its sides with two semi-cycles of flowers and statues. During this re-design the obelisk was placed in a new fountain with the present sculpted lions.

There are two symmetrical baroque churches at the south end of the piazza flanking the intersection of the Via del Corso. These two churches, **Santa Maria dei Miracoli** (1678) – also called Santa Maria del Popolo – and **Santa Maria in Monesanto** (1675) both have picturesque cupolas that were begun by C. Rainaldi and finished by Bernini and Carlo Fontana respectively.

Eerie Roman Trivia

There is a movie theater directly next to Santa Maria dei Miracoli that played the first-run release of the "Exorcist" when it came out in the 1970's. During the first showing of the film, the cross on the top of the church was somehow dislodged from its perch, and avoiding the rooftops, fell directly in front of the movie theater and shattered. No one was hurt but all of Italy was shocked. This is a true story.

VIA VENETO
Buses 52, 53, 56, 58. Metro-Barberini.
Definitely the most famous and most fashionable street in Rome. It used to be the center of all artistic activities as well as the meeting place for the jet set, but it doesn't quite have the same allure it used to. Nonetheless, it's still a great place to wander since it is flanked by wonderful hotels, stores, and cafés.

At the bottom of the street is the **Piazza Barberini**, where you'll find the graceful **Fontana delle Api** (Fountain of the Bees) as well as the more famous **Fontana del Tritone**, both designed and sculpted by Bernini. Both sculptures were created to celebrate the Barberini family and their new palace just up the Via delle Quattro Fontane. Up the Via Veneto a little ways from the Piazza Barberini is the grandiose **Palazzo Margherita**, built by G. Koch in 1890 and is now the home of the American Embassy. You'll recognize it by the armed guards and the American flag flying out front.

CHURCH OF BONES
Right at the bottom of the Via Veneto you will find the famous 'Church of Bones,' **Santa Maria della Concezione**. In the **Cappucin crypt** of the church there is a macabre arrangement of the bones of over 4,000 skeletons of ancient friars who were exhumed and decoratively placed on the walls. The reason this display exists is that a law was passed many centuries ago which decreed that no graveyards or burial grounds could exist inside the walls of Rome. Rather than part with the remains of their brothers by re-burying them in a cemetery outside the walls, the Cappucin brothers exhumed the fraternal remains and decorated the crypt with them. I guarantee that you'll never see a sight like this anywhere else.

VIA APPIA ANTICA
Buses 118 and 218.
The most celebrated of all Roman roads was begun by Appius Claudius Caecus in 312 BCE. The road has been preserved in its original character as

have the original monuments. At first it was the chief line of communication between Rome and Southern Italy, Greece, and the eastern possessions of the Roman Empire. Now it is a well traveled picturesque road to the country and the famous Roman/Christian **catacombs**.

TRASTEVERE
Buses 44, 75, 170, 710, 718, 719.

This is the perfect place to immerse yourself in Roman life. **Trastevere** literally means "across the river" and this separation has allowed the area to remain virtually untouched by the advances of time. Until recently it was one of the poorest sections of Rome, but now it is starting to become gentrified. Yet these changes have not altered Trastevere's charm. You'll find interesting shops and boutiques, and plenty of excellent restaurants among the small narrow streets and *piazzette* (small squares). The maze of streets is a fun place to wander and wonder where you're going to end up.

During the month of July the *Trasteverini* express their feeling of separation from the rest of Rome with their summertime festival called **Noiantri**, meaning "we the others," in which they mix wine-induced revelry with religious celebration in a party of true bacchanalian proportions. *Trasteverini* cling to their roots of selling clothing and furnishings to make ends meet by continuing to hold the **Porta Portese** flea market on Sundays. The market and event are true Trastevere even though the area has been gentrified for decades.

This area offers some of the best dining and casual nightlife in town. Here you can sit in a piazza bar sipping Sambuca or wine and watch the life of Rome pass before your eyes. To accommodate this type of activity many stores have begun to stay open later. Trastevere is a great place to enjoy for a day or even more, because it is the way Rome used to be.

JEWISH GHETTO
Buses 780, 774, 717.

Long before any Pope reigned in Rome, another religion thrived here: Judaism. The ancient Jewish quarter is a peaceful, tiny riverside neighborhood with narrow curving street and ocher apartment buildings. It looks much like any other section of Rome until closer inspection reveals Kosher food signs, men in skullcaps and spray painted stars of David. Technically the Ghetto ceased to exist in 1846 when its walls were torn down, but the neighborhood that retains its name remains home to Europe's oldest and proudest Jewish community.

The history of the Jews in Rome dates back to 161 BCE when Judas Maccabaeus sent ambassadors to Rome to seek protection against the Syrians. Over time many traders followed these emissaries and a Jewish community sprouted. After Rome colonized and eventually conquered the

Land of Israel culminating in 70 CE with the fall of Jerusalem and the destruction of its Temple (an event etched in stone on the Arch of Titus), over a short time as many 40,000 Jews settled in Rome. They contributed in all aspects of Roman society and they and their religion were accepted as different but equal. But that was before Christianity became the religion of the state, at which point discrimination against the Jews became widespread.

In the 13th century, for instance, the Catholic Church ordered Jews to wear a distinctive sign on their clothing: a yellow circle for men and two blue stripes for women. Anti-Semitism continued to grow to the point where in 1556, Pope Paul IV confined all Jews to this small poor section of the city and closed it in with high walls. This was not the first virtual imprisonment of its kind, because the Venetians did the same thing to its Jewish population four decades earlier. In Venice the Jews were forced to live on the site of an old cannon foundry, or *getto*. The name stuck and has since evolved to mean any section of a city that is composed of one type of activity (e.g., an Office Ghetto), or is inhabited by one group of people, usually underprivileged.

Today there are over 16,000 Jews living in Rome and the Ghetto is still the meeting place. To find out more about this neighborhood stop in the **Jewish Museum** in the **Sinagoga** *(Lungotevere de Cenci, Tel. 06/684-0061, Fax 06/6840-0684; open 9:00am-6:30pm Tuesday-Friday, until 8:00pm on Sundays and also from 9:00pm-midnight on Saturdays in the summer. English tours E7.).* Inside you will find a plan of the original ghetto, as well as artifacts from the 17th century Jewish community.

Besides learning about the history of the ghetto, you can find some of Rome's truly great restaurants here along with many ancient Roman buildings, arches, and columns completely incorporated into modern day buildings. It seems as if a number of structures have been better preserved in this area. Maybe it is because the locals did not have the resources to tear them down and replace them. Whatever the situation, visit the Ghetto and feel history come alive.

GIANICOLO
Piazza Garibaldi. Bus 41.
Offering one of the best panoramas of Rome, the **Gianicolo Hill** is located between Trastevere and the Vatican, across the river from the old city of Rome. At the terrace of the Piazza Garibaldi, you'll find the equestrian statue of Giuseppe Garibaldi, as well as a panoramic photo, with accompanying titles for all the domes and buildings of note, of the scene laid out in front of you This is a perfect photo opportunity. The walk may be a little tiring but the view is calming and serene.

Churches

SAINT PAUL'S OUTSIDE THE WALLS

Via Ostiense. Church open 7:00am–6:00pm. Cloisters Open 9:00am–1:00pm and 3:00pm–6:00pm. Metro-San Paolo.

Located a short distance beyond the Porta Paolo, **St. Paul's Outside the Walls** (San Paolo Fuori le Mura) is the fourth of the patriarchal basilicas in Rome. It is second only in size to St. Peter's and sits above the tomb of St. Paul. It was built by Constantine in 314 CE and then enlarged by Valentinian in 386 CE and later by Theodosius. It was finally completed by Honorius, his son.

In 1823, the church was almost completely destroyed by a terrible fire and many of its great works of art were lost. Immediately afterward, its renovation began and today it seems as magnificent as ever. (So much so that every time my family returns to Rome, whoever is left lines up just inside to the left of the entrance to the *quadroportici* with its 150 granite columns and get our picture taken with the palm trees in the background. We've been doing this since the 1950's and in that time the palms have grown from stubby bushes into gigantic trees.) With the beautiful garden surrounded by the great rows of columns, the palms growing in the center, the gigantic statue of St. Paul, and the facade with mosaics of four prophets (Isaiah, Jeremaih, Ezekial, and Daniel), just getting inside this church is a visual treat.

The interior is 120 meters long and has four rows of columns and five naves. The columns in the central nave are Corinthian that can be identified by their splendidly ornate capitals. The walls contain Medallion Portraits of the Popes from Saint Peter to Pius XI. On the High Altar still sits the ancient Gothic tabernacle of Arnolfo di Cambio (13th century) that was saved from the fire in 1823. Saint Paul rests beneath the altar in the confessional. The mosaic in the apse, with its dominating figure of Christ, was created by artists from the Republic of San Marino in 1220.

To the left of the apse is the **Chapel of St. Stephen**, with the large statue of the saint created by R. Rainaldi, and the **Chapel of the Crucifix** created by Carlo Maderno. This chapel contains the crucifix which is said to have spoken to Saint Bridget in 1370. Also here is St. Ignatius de Loyola, who took the formal vows that established the Jesuits as a religious order. To the right of the apse is the **Chapel of San Lorenzo** and the **Chapel of Saint Benedict** with its 12 columns. One other place of note in the church are the cloisters that contain fragments of ancient inscriptions and sarcophagi from the early Christian era.

SANTA MARIA SOPRA MINERVA

Piazza della Minerva (behind the Pantheon). Hours 7:00am–7:00pm. Buses 70, 81, 87, 90.

Built on the pagan ruins of a temple to Minerva (hence the name) this must-see church was begun in 1280 by the Dominican Order which also commissioned the beautiful Santa Maria Novella in Florence. With their wide Gothic vaulted nave and aisles, the two churches are much alike in design. The facade was created during the Renaissance by Meo del Caprino in 1453.

In this expansive church, you can find many tombs of famous personages of the 15th through the 16th centuries as well as beautiful paintings, sculptures, frescoes and bas relief work. Saint Catherine of Siena, who died in Rome in 1380, rests at the high altar. To the left of the altar is the statue of *Christ Carrying the Cross* created by Michelangelo in 1521. The bronze drapes were added later for modesty. If you compare this work to the one to the right of the altar, *John the Baptist* by Obici, you can easily see why Michelangelo is considered such a master. His statue looks like it could come to life, while Obicis is just carved out of stone.

The Masters in Rome

Listed here are where you can find some of the works of the Masters of Italian art:

Michelangelo — Sistine Chapel, Statue of Moses (San Pietro in Vincoli), Pieta (St. Peter's), Dome of St. Peter's, Christ Carrying the Cross (SM Sopra Minerva), Campidoglio square and steps.

Bernini — The Ecstasy of Santa Teresa (SM della Vittoria, Via XX Settembre 17), Ecstasy of Beata Ludovica Albertoni (S. Francesco a Ripa, P.za S. Fracesco d'Assisi), the Baldacchino (St. Peter's), the Throne (St. Peter's), the Tomb of Pope Alexander VII (St. Peter's) the square and colonade of St. Peter's, Fountain of the Four Rivers (Piazza Navona), San Andrea al Quirinale, Elephant Obelisk (outside of SM Sopra Minerva), Ponte San Angelo.

Caravaggio — Painting of Saints Peter and Paul (SM del Popolo), Madonna dei Pellegrini (SanAgostino, Via della Scrofa 80), The Life of St. Matthew (three paintings in S. Luigi dei Fracesi), and a number of works, including Young Girl with Basket of Fruit, and The Sick Bacchus (which is a self-portrait) in the Borghese Gallery.

Raphael — Numerous works, including Lady of the Unicorn and Deposition in the Borghese Gallery, Chigi Chapel (SM del Popolo), La Fornarina (Palazzo Barberini), Cherub holding a Festoon (Academy of San Luca), Double Portrait (Doria Pamphili Gallery), The Prophet Isaiah (Sant'Agostino), the Loggia di Psiche (Villa Farnesina), and a number of works, including the School of Athens, in the Vatican Museums.

Behind the altar are the tombs of Pope Clement VII and Leo X which were created by the Florentine sculptor Baccio Bandanelli. In the Sacristy is a chapel covered with frescoes by Antoniazzo Romano, brought here in 1637 from the house where Catherine of Siena died.

In front of the church is a wonderful sculpture designed by Bernini and carved by Ercole Ferrata called *Il Pulcino* of an elephant with an obelisk on his back.

SAN PIETRO IN VINCOLI

Piazza di San Pietro in Vincoli. Hours 7:00am–12:30pm and 3:30pm–6:00pm. Metro-Cavour.

Located only a few blocks from the Colosseum, this church was founded in 442 by the Empress Eudoxia as a shrine dedicated to preserving the chains with which Herod bound St. Peter in Jerusalem. These chains are in a crypt under the main altar.

But the reason to come to this church is the tomb of Julius II. Not really the tomb itself, because the great patron of the arts Julius is actually interred in St. Peter's, but come for the unforgettable seated figure of *Moses*. Created by the master himself, Michelangelo, this statue captures the powerful personification of justice and law of the Old Testament.

In fact, Moses appears as if he is ready to leap to his feet and pass judgment on you as you stand there admiring him. You can almost see the cloth covering his legs, or the long beard covering his face move in the breeze. Flanking Moses are equally exquisite statues of *Leah* and *Rachel* also done by Michelangelo. Everything else was carved by his pupils. Because of this one work, this church is definitely worth your time.

SANTA MARIA MAGGIORE

Piazza di Santa Maria Maggiore. Tel. 06/483-195. Hours 8:00am–7:00pm. Buses 4, 9, 16, 27, 714, 715. Metro-Termini.

Like St. Paul's Outside the Walls, St. Peter's, and St. John Lateran, this is one of the four patriarchal basilicas of Rome. Its name derives from the fact that it is the largest church (*maggiore*) in Rome dedicated to the Madonna (*maria*). The facade, originally built in the 12th century, was redone in the 18th century to include the two canon's houses flanking the church. It is a simple two story facade and as such is nothing magnificent to look at, and as result, if you are not going out of your way to come here, many people simply amble on by.

But the interior, in all its 86 meters of splendor, is interesting and inspiring mainly because of the 5th-century mosaics, definitely the best in Rome, its frescoes, and multi-colored marble. On the right wall of the **Papal Altar** is the funeral monument to Sixtus V and on the left wall the monument to Pius V, both created by Fontana with excellent bas-reliefs. Opposite this chapel is the

Borghese Chapel, so called since the sepulchral vaults of the wealthy Borghese family lie beneath it. Here you'll view the beautiful bas-relief monumental tombs to Paul V and Clement VIII on its left and right walls. Towards the west end of the church is the **Sforza Chapel** with its intricately designed vault. Pius VI's eerie crypt is below and in front of the main altar.

SAN GIOVANNI IN LATERANO

Piazza San Giovanni in Laterano 4, Tel. 06/7720-7991. Hours Bapistery: 6:00am–12:30pm and 4:00–7:00pm; Cloisters 9:00am-5:00pm. Buses 16, 85, 87, and 650. Metro-San Giovanni.

Another of the great basilicas of Rome. Most people don't realize that this church is the cathedral of Rome as well as the whole Catholic world, and not St. Peter's. Established on land donated by Constantine in 312 CE, that first building has long been replaced by many reconstructions, fires, sackings and earthquakes over the centuries. Today, the simple and monumental facade of the church, created by Allessandro Galiliei in 1735, is topped by fourteen colossal statues of Christ, the Apostles, and saints. It rises on the site of the ancient palace of Plautinus Lateranus (hence the name), one of the noble families of Rome many eons ago.

To get inside, you must pass through the bronze door that used to be attached to the old Roman Senate house. The interior of the church, laid out in the form of a Latin cross, has five naves filled with historical and artistic objects. In total it is 150 meters long, while the **central nave** is 87 meters long. This central nave is flanked by 12 spires from which appear 12 statues of the Apostles from the 18th century. The wooden ceiling and the marble flooring are from the 15th century.

The most beautiful artistic aspect of the church is the vast transept, which is richly decorated with marbles and frescoes portraying the *Leggenda Aurea* of Constantine. One piece of historical interest is the wooden table, on which it is said that Saint Peter served mass, which you'll find in the **Papal Altar**.

SAN CLEMENTE

Via di San Giovanni Laterano. Admission E2 (to the lower church). Hours to visit the basement 9:00am–1:00pm. Not on Sundays. Catch bus 65. Metro-San Giovanni.

Located between the Colosseum and St. John Lateran is this hidden gem of a church, **San Clemente**. One of the better preserved medieval churches in Rome, it was originally built in the fifth century. The Normans destroyed it in 1084 but it was reconstructed in 1108 by Pachal II. Today when you enter you are in what is called the **Upper Church**, a simple and basic basilica divided by two rows of columns. Above the altar are some intricately inlaid 12th century mosaics.

The thrill of this church is that you can descend a set of stairs to the **Lower Church**, which was discovered in 1857, and immediately you have left the Middle Ages and are now in subterranean passages that housed an early Christian place of worship, from the days when Christians had to practice their religion below ground for fear of persecution.

Even further below that are the remains of a temple dedicated to Mithraic, a religion that practised in the 4th century CE known for their barbaric blood rites. Brought to Rome from Asia Minor in 67 BCE by soldiers of Rome's Legions, this pagan religion became entrenched in the military because of its bonds of violence, fidelity, loyalty and secrecy. Before the Roman Legions adopted it, Mithraic was the religion of Alexander the Great's army.

This is a must see church while in Rome. They also have a bucolic little porticoed garden, where you can relax, with a spritzing fountain in the center.

SANTA CECILIA IN TRASTEVERE

Via Anicia. Hours 10:00am–noon and 4:00pm–6:00pm. Buses 181, 280, 44, 75, 717, 170, 23, 65.

Normally visitors don't go to Trastevere to visit churches. Instead they are attracted by the more secular delights of this part of Rome. But if you're interested in beautiful churches, **Santa Cecilia** is one to visit in Trastevere; the other is Santa Maria.

Santa Cecilia was founded in the fifth century and had a make-over in the ninth century as well as the 16th. A baroque door leads to a picturesque court, beyond which is a baroque facade, with a mosaic frieze above the portico, and a beautiful bell tower erected in the 12th century. There are several important works of art to be found in the church, not the least of which is the expressive statue of Santa Cecilia by Stefano Maderno. It represents the body of the saint in the exact position it was found when the tomb was opened in 1559.

Another place of interest to visit on the church grounds is the Roman house where Santa Cecilia suffered her martyrdom by being exposed to hot vapors. There are two rooms preserved, one of them the bath where she died. It still has the pipes and large bronze cauldron for heating water. A great church to visit, not just for the art, but also for the history.

SANTA MARIA IN TRASTEVERE

Piazza Santa Maria in Trastevere 1. Hours 7:00am–7:00pm. Mass at 9:00am, 10:30am, noon, and 6:00pm. Buses 181, 280, 44, 75, 717, 170, 23, 65.

A small church in Trastevere, in a piazza of the same name that is frequented by many locals and tourists alike, making the church one of the most visited. Around this church are some of the best restaurants and cafés in all of Rome, a popular English language theater, a handsome 17th century fountain where hippies hang out, and the Palace of San Calisto.

This was one of Rome's earliest churches and the first to be dedicated to the Virgin Mary. It was built in the 4th century and remodeled between 1130-1143. It is best known for its prized mosaics, especially the 12th and 13th century representation of the Madonna which adorns the facade of the church. The Romanesque bell-tower was built in the 12th century. The interior is of three naves separated by columns purloined from ancient Roman temples.

On the vault you'll find exquisite mosaics depicting the Cross, emblems of the Evangelists, and Christ and the Madonna enthroned among the Saints (created by Domenichino in 1140). Lower down, the mosaics of Pietro Cavallini done in 1291 portray, in six panels, the life of the Virgin.

Museums

CAPITOLINE MUSEUM
Piazza del Campidoglio 1. Tel. 06/6710-2071, Admission E5. Hours 9:00am-7:00pm. Closed Mondays. Buses 44, 46, 56, 57, 90, 90, 94, 186, 710, 713, 718, 719. Entrance E5.

The **Capitoline Museum** is actually two museums, the **Capitoline** and the **Palazzo dei Conservatori**. The Capitoline Museum is the perfect place to come to see what ancient Romans looked like. Unlike Greek sculpture, which glorified the subject, Roman sculpture captured every realistic characteristic and flaw. There are rooms full of portrait busts dating back to the republic and imperial Rome, where you have many individuals of significance immortalized here, whether they were short, fat, thin, ugly. Here they remain, warts and all. Because of these very real depictions of actual Romans, and many other more famous sculptures, this museum ranks only second in importance to the Vatican collections.

Besides the busts, you'll find a variety of celebrated pieces from antiquity including *Dying Gaul*, *Cupid and Psyche*, the *Faun*, and the nude and voluptuous *Capitoline Venice*. Then in the **Room of the Doves** you'll find two wonderful mosaics that were taken from Hadrian's Villa many centuries ago. One mosaic is of the doves drinking from a basin, and the other is of the masks of comedy and tragedy. Besides these items in the interior, the exterior itself was designed by none other than the master himself, Michelangelo.

The **Palace of the Conservatori** is actually three museums in one, the **Museum of the Conservatori**, the **New Museum**, and the **Pinocoteca Capitolina**. It too was also constructed by a design from Michelangelo. What draws me to them, as well as most people young at heart, are the largest stone head, hand and foot you're ever likely to see. A great place to take a few pictures. These pieces are fragments from a huge seated statue of Constantine.

You could wander here among the many ancient Roman and Greek sculptures and paintings but remember to see the famous *Boy with a Thorn*, a graceful Greek sculpture of a boy pulling a thorn out of his foot, the *She-Wolf of the Capitol*, an Etruscan work of Romulus and Remus being suckled by the mythical wolf of Rome, the death mask bust of Michelangelo, the marble *Medusa* head by Bernini, the celebrated painting *St. Sebastian* by Guido Reni that shows the saint with arrows shot into his body, and the famous Caravaggio work, *St. John the Baptist*.

NATIONAL MUSEUM – MUSEO DELLE TERME

Baths of Diocletian, Viale delle Terme. Admission E1. Hours 9:00am–2:00pm. Holidays until 1:00pm. Closed Mondays. Buses 57, 64, 65, 75, 170, 492, 910. Metro-Repubblica.

If you like ancient sculpture you'll enjoy this collection of classical Greek and Roman works, as well as some early Christian sarcophagi and other bas-relief work. Located in the **Baths of Diocletian**, which are something to see in and of themselves, this museum is easily accessible since it is located near the train station and right across from the Repubblica Metro stop. Since there are so many fine works here, you should spend a good half day perusing the items, but remember to start with the best, which are located in the *Hall of Masterpieces*. Here you'll find the *Pugilist*, a bronze work of a seated boxer, and the *Discobolus*, a partial sculpture of a discus thrower celebrated for its amazing muscle development.

At the turn of the century this collection was graced with the Ludovisi assembled, collected by Cardinal Ludovico Ludovisi and a number of Roman princes. The most inspiring of these many fine works of art is the celebrated *Dying Gaul and His Wife*, a colossal sculpture from Pergamon created in the third century BCE. The collection also contains the famous Ludovisi throne, created in the 5th century BCE and which is adorned with fine Greek bas-reliefs.

Another must-see in the museum is the *Great Cloister*, a perfectly square space surrounded by an arcade of one hundred Doric columns. It is one of the most beautiful architectural spaces in Rome, which is saying something. Rumor has it that it was designed and built by Michelangelo in 1565, which may be the case, but since he was so busy many experts believe that it is actually the work of one of his more famous, and possibly intimate pupils, Jacopo del Duca. Another great museum to see in Rome.

Rome the Museum

For years Rome has been considered a museum in and of itself, but finally the city fathers have made it official. Rome's sights still stand out for all to see, but now Rome has constructed a pathway between many of the major sights in the centro storico area (including Trevi Fountain and the Pantheon) with an official sign, like you would find in an exhibit in a museum, describing the history and significance of each sight – in Italian, English, and Braile.

GALLERIA BORGHESE
Villa Borghese, Piazza dell'Uccelliera 5. Tel. 06/632-8101. Admission E6. Hours 9:00am–9:00pm, until midnight on Saturdays, only until 8:00pm on Sundays. Closed Mondays. Entrance is only available in two-hour increments starting at 9am. Closed Mondays. Buses 95, 490, 495, 910. Metro-Spagna.

Located in the most picturesque public park in Rome, and housed in a beautiful villa constructed in the 17th century, the ground floor contains the sculpture collection, which would be considered without peer if not for the fact that it is located in Rome where there are a number of other superb collections. The sculptures are just the appetizer because the main draw of this museum is the beauty of the gallery of paintings on the first floor.

But before you abandon the sculptures, take note of the reclining *Pauline Borghese*, created by Antonio Canova in 1805. She was the sister of Napoleon, and was married off to one of the wealthiest families in the world at the time to ensure peace and prosperity. She looks quite enticing posing half naked on a lounge chair. Another work not to miss is *David and the Slingshot* by Bernini in 1619. It is a self-portrait of the sculptor. Other works by Bernini are spotlighted and intermixed with ancient Roman statuary.

On the first floor there are many great paintings, especially the *Madonna and Child* by Bellini, *Young Lady with a Unicorn* by Raphael, *Madonna with Saints* by Lotto, and some wonderful works by Caravaggio. If you are in Rome, you have to visit this museum. Advanced booking is suggested from *www.ticketeria.it,* otherwise you may not gain access since there are a limited number of spaces available. There is a gift shop and snack bar in the basement area where you pick up your reserved tickets. You will also have to relinquish your handbags, camera, umbrellas, etc., for safekeeping at the basement baggage area.

MUSEUM OF VILLA GIULIA

Piazza di Villa Giulia 9. Tel. 06/332-6571. Admission E5. Hours 9:00am–6:30pm Tues-Fri, Sundays until 8:00pm and Saturdays in the summer open also from 9:00pm-midnight. Closed Mondays. Buses 19b or 30b. Metro-Flaminio.

Located in the Palazzo di Villa Giulia, built in 1533 by Julius III, and situated amid the Borghese Gardens, this incredible archaeological museum contains 34 rooms of ancient sculptures, sarcophagi, bas-reliefs, and more, mainly focusing on the Etruscan civilization. Items of interest include the statues created in the 5th century BCE of a *Centaur*, and *Man on a Marine Monster*; Etruscan clay sculptures of *Apollo*, *Hercules with a Deer*, and *Goddess with Child*; objects from the Necropoli at Cervetri including a terra-cotta work of *Amazons with Horses* created in the 6th century BCE and a sarcophagus of a "married couple," a masterpiece of Etruscan sculpture from the 6th century BCE.

PALAZZO ALTEMPS

Museo Nazionale Romano, Piazza Sant'Appolinare 44, Tel. 06/683-3759. Open 9:00am-9:00pm Tues-Thurs and until midnight every other day except Monday when it is closed. Admission E5.

A must-see museum while in Rome. Located just outside the Piazza Navona, this little museum has an elegant collection of sculptures and paintings, but best of all it is a respite from the frenetic pace of Rome, and is a peaceful museum that is an architectural curiosity in and of itself. Besides the excellent pieces inside, the building itself offers a glimpse into what life was like many years ago in Rome. The inner courtyard is mesmerizing and the private chapel an oasis of calm. Though it does not have as many pieces as the Vatican or the Campidoglio, you will able to savor each piece without having to fight the crowds at those other places.

Masterpieces Made to Order!

Have you ever wanted to own a Michelangelo, or a Raphael, or a Caravaggio? Well, now's your chance. If you want an exact, painstakingly painted copy, all done perfectly legal, contact **Studio d'Arte** *(Via F Crispi 24a, Tel. 06/4741-644)*. Though copies, these are works of art in and of themselves, and will be expensive. These are not prints. So if you are seriously interested, give them a call, and stop by their showroom to see the paintings they have in stock, or arrange to have your favorite painting — whether it is a scene from Michelangelo's Sistine Chapel or Caravaggio's Drunken Bacchus — re-done just for you.

VATICAN MUSEUMS
Viale Vaticano. Tel. 06/6988-4466. Admission E6.5. From November to the first half of March and the second half of June through August open 8:45am-12:45pm. From the second half of March to the first half of June and September and October open 8:45am to 3:45pm. Closed most Sundays and all major religious holidays like Christmas and Easter. The last Sunday of every month in January, February, April, May, July, Aug., September, October, November and December are open and the entrance is free. Buses 19, 23, 32, 45, 51, 81, 492, 907, and 991. Metro-Ottaviano.

The Vatican Museums keep rather short hours, so make a point of getting here early since the lines are very long. There are a number of self-guided tape cassette tours available that take you through different sections of the Vatican Museums. Touring the museums is almost like an amusement park ride, except the sights you see are amazing works of art. These are the best way to get an insight into the many splendid works you are witnessing.

Pinacoteca Vaticana
A wonderful collection of masterpieces from many periods, covering many styles all the way from primitive to modern paintings. Here you can find paintings by Giotto (who was the great innovator of Italian painting, since prior to his work Italian paintings had been Byzantine in style), many works by Raphael, the famous *Brussels Tapestries* with episodes from the Acts of the Apostles created by Pieter van Aelsten in 1516 from sketches by Raphael, and countless paintings of the Madonna, Virgin, Mother and Child, etc.

Pius Clementine Museum
Known mainly as a sculpture museum, it was founded by Pius VI and Clement XIV. You can also find mosaic work and sarcophagi from the 2nd, 3rd and 4th centuries. One mosaic in particular is worth noting, the *Battle between the Greeks and the Centaurs*, created in the first century CE. The bronze statue of Hercules and the **Hall of the Muses** that contain statues of the Muses and the patrons of the arts are also worth noting. Here you can also find many busts of illustrious Romans including Caracalla, Trajan, Octavian and more.

In the **Octagonal Court** are some of the most important and the beautiful statues in the history of Western art, especially the *Cabinet of the Laocoon*. This statue portrays the revenge of the gods on a Trojan priest, Laocoon, who had invoked the wrath of the gods by warning his countrymen not to admit the Trojan horse. In revenge the gods sent two enormous serpents out of the sea to destroy Laocoon and his two sons.

Chiaramonti Museum
Founded by Pope Pius VII, whose family name was Chiaramonti, this

museum includes a collection of over 5,000 Pagan and Christian works. Here you can find Roman Sarcophagi, *Silenus Nursing the Infant Bacchus*, busts of Caesar, the Statue of Demosthenes, the famous *Statue of the Nile* with the 16 boys representing the 16 cubits of the annual rise of the Nile, as well as a magnificent Roman chariot recreated in marble by the sculptor Franzone in 1788.

Etruscan Museum

If you can't make it to any of the Necropoli around Rome, at least come here and see the relics of a civilization that preceded Ancient Rome. Founded in 1837 by Gregory XVI, it contains objects excavated in the Southern part of Etruria from 1828-1836, as well as pieces from later excavations around Rome. Here you'll find an Etruscan tomb from Cervetri, as well as bronzes, gold objects, glass work, candelabra, necklaces, rings, funeral urns, amphora and much more.

Egyptian Museum

If you can't make it to Cairo to see their splendid exhibit of material excavated from a variety of Egyptian tombs, stop in here. Created by Gregory XVI in 1839, this museum contains a valuable documentary of the art and civilization of ancient Egypt.

There are sarcophagi, reproductions of portraits of famous Egyptian personalities, works by Roman artists who were inspired by Egyptian art, a collection of wooden mummy cases and funeral steles, mummies of animals, a collection of papyri with hieroglyphics, and much more.

Library of the Vatican

Founded through the efforts and collections of many Popes, this museum contains many documents and incunabula. Today the library contains over 500,000 volumes, 60,000 ancient manuscripts, and 7,000 incunabuli. My favorite are the precious manuscripts, especially the *Codex Vaticanus B* or the 4th century Bible in Greek.

Appartamento Borgia

Named after Pope Alexander VI, whose family name was Borgia, since he designed and lived in these lavish surroundings. (What about that vow of poverty?) From the furnishings to the paintings to the frescoes of Isis and Osiris on the ceiling, this little "museum" is worth a look.

Sistine Chapel

This is the private chapel of the popes famous for some of the most wonderful masterpieces ever created, many by **Michelangelo** himself. He started painting the ceiling of the chapel in 1508 and it took him four years to finish it. On the ceiling you'll find scenes from the Bible, among them the *Creation*, where God comes near Adam, who is lying down, and with a simple touch of his hand imparts the magic spark of life. You can also see the *Separation of Light and Darkness*, the *Creation of the Sun and Moon*, *Creation of Trees and Plants*, *Creation of Adam*, *Creation of Eve*, *The Fall and the Expulsion from Paradise*, the *Sacrifice of Noah and his Family* and the *Deluge*.

On the wall behind the altar is the great fresco of the *Last Judgment* by Michelangelo. It occupies the entire area (20 meters by 10 meters) and was commissioned by Clement VII. Michelangelo was past 60 when he started the project in 1535. He completed it seven years later in 1542. Michelangelo painted people he didn't like into situations with evil connotation in this fresco. The figure of Midas, with asses' ears, is the likeness of the Master of Ceremonies of Paul III, who first suggested that other painters cover Michelangelo's nude figures.

This covering was eventually done by order of Pius IV, who had Daniele da Volterra drape the most prominent figures with painted cloth. These changes were left in when the entire chapel underwent its marvelous transformation a few years back, bringing out the vibrant colors of the original frescoes that had been covered by centuries of dirt and soot.

Rooms of Raphael

Initially these rooms were decorated with the works of many artists of the 15th century, but because Pope Julius II loved the work of Raphael so much, he had the other paintings destroyed, and commissioned Raphael to paint the entire room himself. He did so spending the rest of his life in the task. Not nearly as stupendous as the Sistine Chapel work by Michelangelo, but it still is one of the world's masterpieces.

Chapel of Nicholas V

Decorated with frescoes from 1448-1451 by Giovanni da Fiesole. The works represent scenes from the life of Saint Stephan in the upper portion and Saint Lawrence in the lower.

The Loggia of Raphael

Divided into 13 arcades with 48 scenes from the Old and New Testaments, these were executed from the designs of Raphael by his students, Giulo Romano, Perin del Vaga, and F. Penni. The most outstanding to see are the *Creation of the World*, *Creation of Eve*, *The Deluge*, *Jacob's Dream*, *Moses Receiving the Tablets of Law*, *King David*, and the *Birth of Jesus*.

Grotte Vaticano

The Vatican caves seem to be a well-kept secret even though they've been around for some time. I think that's because you need special permission to enter them, and if you haven't made plans prior to your arrival it is quite difficult to gain access at short notice. To gain permission you need to contact the **North American College** in Rome *(Via dell'Umita 30, Tel. 06/672-256 or 678-9184).* The entrance to the Grotte is to the left of the basilica of St. Peter's where the Swiss Guards are posted. The Grotte were dug out of the stratum between the floor of the actual cathedral and the previous Basilica of Constantine. This layer was first excavated during the Renaissance. After passing fragments of inscriptions and mosaic compositions, tombstones, and sarcophagi, you descend a steep staircase to get to the Lower Grottos, also called the **Grotte Vecchie** (the Old Grottos).

Here you'll find pagan and Christian Necropoli dating from the 2nd and 3rd century. The Grotte are divided into three naves separated by massive pilasters that support the floor of St. Peter's above. Along the walls are numerous tombs of popes and altars adorned with mosaics and sculptures. At the altar is the entrance to the **Grotte Nuove** (New Grottos), with their frescoed walls, marble statues, and bas-reliefs.

MUSEO DELLA CIVILTA ROMANA
Piazza G Agnelli 10, Tel. 06/592-6041. Open 9:00am – 7:00pm. Holidays only until 1:30pm. Closed Mondays. Metro-EUR Palasport (Marconi) or Fermi.

If you've always wanted to see a scale model of ancient Rome, you have to visit this museum. In it you'll find a perfect replica of Rome during the height of empire in the 4th century BCE. This piece is an exquisitely detailed plastic model that brings ancient Rome to life. It really helps to bring some sense to the ruins that now litter the center of Rome. Even if you are not a museum person, this exhibit is well worth seeing. Ideal for kids of all ages.

The rest of the museum contains little original material, and is made up of plaster casts of Roman artifacts. The museum is located in the section of Rome called **EUR** (Esposizione Universale di Roma), which was built as an exposition site for an event that was to take place in 1941. It is a perfect example of grandiose fascist architecture and its attempt to intimidate through size. Built with Mussolini's guidance halfway between Rome and its old port of Ostia, it was an attempt to reclaim some of Rome's glory and add to its grandeur. EUR has none of the human feel of the rest of Rome, since it is in essence an urban office park with a connected residential ghetto eerily similar to American suburbs, but with a little more style.

MUSEO TIPOLOGICO NAZIONALE DEL PRESEPIO
Via Tor de' Conti 31a, Tel. 06/679-6146. Open 5:00-8:00pm (weedays) and 10:00am-1:00pm & 5:00-8:00pm holidays. Admission E3.

This museum exhibits creches and individual statuettes for creches (over 3,000) from all over the world, made from all kinds of materials. Each of these nativity scenes and figurines help illuminate for us the way in which Christmas is celebrated worldwide. If you are an afficionado of creches, as is my mother, you simply must make a point of visiting this great little museum.

MUSEO INTERNAZIONALE DEL CINEMA E DELLO SPETTACOLO
Via Bettone 1, Tel. 06/370-0266, Fax 06/3973-3297.
This museum contains film making equipment, costumes used in movies, a film library of over 5,000 mostly rare and unique films, a photographic library with over 2 million photos from 1850 onward, and a comprehensive video cassette library. If you are a videophile you will simply love this museum. But you need to book in advance to get in. There are no regular hours. Call or fax and request a time and date to be introduced to this small but informative museum of film.

'Nero's Golden House' Open Again!

After 15 years of additional excavations, the **Domus Aurea** is once again open to public viewing. Known as Nero's Golden House, the Domus Aurea was Nero's palace that he had built after the great fire of 64 CE destroyed his first abode, not to mention a great deal of Rome. Nero appropriated a huge amount of land in much of central Rome and had the greatest craftsmen of the day work on the structure, and a number of innovations were introduced that played a part in inspiring early Renaissance painters, sculptors, and architects. But Nero only lived in the palace a few short years, after which most of it was abandoned and much of the grounds given back to the people of Rome.

You can view eight rooms today, all underground, and admire the vaulted ceilings, extant pieces of frescoes and stone reliefs, beautiful floor mosaics, and pieces of broken sculpture here and there. It's a magnificent building, and well worth the sight if you are in the neighborhood of the Colosseum and have the time. Be sure and get the audio guide, since you will be accompanied by someone who is only there to show you from room to room . You have to call in advance and make a reservation, since only small groups are allowed at a time.

Directions: same as for the Colosseum – Buses 11, 27, 81, 85, 87. Metro-Colosseo. Hours: 9am to 8pm summer; 9am to 5pm winter; closed on Tuesdays. Admission E6. Tel. 06/399-67700. When you get off the bus or metro, look for the public gardens across the street from the Colosseum (Calle Oppio Gardens). The street entrance is on Viale della Domus Aurea.

PICCOLO MUSEO DELLE ANIME DEL PURGATORIO

Lungotevere Prati 12, inside the Chiesa del Sacro Cuore del Suffragio. Open every day 7:30-11:30am and 4:30-7:30pm.

This has got to be the wierdest museum in Rome. It is the museum for the souls in purgatory and used to be called the Christian Afterlife Museum. There are supposedly records of souls in purgatory expressing their displeasure of where they are by impacting the physical world, such as a burnt handprint that appears on a missal, which suddenly appeared there during mass one day.

MUSEO STORICO NAZIONALE DELL'ARTE SANITARIA

Lungotevere in Sassia, Tel. 06/68351. Open Mon., Wed. & Fri. 9:30am-1:30pm.

Located in the interior of a hospital founded by Pope Innocent III in 1198, the museum holds pieces, surgical instruments, apothecary cases, wax models, apothecary pots, a laboratory and an extensive library that are precious records of the history of medicine and how it has been practised over the ages. If you think doctors are a bunch of quacks today, wait until you see what they worked with and believed years ago.

GALLERIA COMUNALE D'ARTE MODERNA

Via Reggio Emilia 54, Tel. 06/884-4930. Admission E3. Open everyday from 10:00am-9:00pm. Holidays and Sundays 9:00am-2:00pm. E-mail: GalleriaModerna@comune. roma.it. Metro B – Policlinico.

Situated in the old Peroni brewery, whose renovated open spaces make for a perfect backdrop for this superb gallery of modern art. A working museum with laboratories as well as exhibit space, multimedia rooms, bookshops and also displays of the recent history of the building when it used to cater to the more 'spiritual' interests of the citizens of Rome. If you want a change of pace, or simply a taste of something different, stop by this brand new, just opened gallery of modern art in Rome. Nearby, in another section of the Peroni Brewery, is a Coin department store, so you can satisfy some consumer needs while here too.

Literary Rome

For centuries Rome has been luring artists from all over the world to be inspired by its charms. Here you can explore the city with the realization that Virgil, Robert and Elizabeth Browning, Hans Christian Anderson, Henry James, Lord Byron, Mark Twain, Goethe and more all traced the same steps you are taking.

If you are interested in following almost exactly in these famous writers' footsteps, read on, for we are going to trace for you the paths taken, the places stayed and the restaurants/cafés frequented by literati of times gone by. The perfect place to start is the **Piazza di Spagna**. In the 18th and 19th century this piazza was literally (no pun intended) the end of the line for many traveling coaches entering the city. Near the western end of the piazza, the **Via delle Carrozze** (Carriage Road) reminds us that this is where these great coaches tied up at the end of their long journeys. More often than not, travelers would make their homes in and around this area.

At Piazza di Spagna #23, you'll find **Babbington's Tea Rooms** (see above, *Where to Eat*) where Byron, Keats, Shelley, and Tobias Smollett all shared at one time or another some afternoon tea. Across the piazza, at #26, is the **Keats/Shelley Memorial** where Keats spent the three months before his death in 1821 at the age of 25. The memorial contains some of Keats' manuscripts, letters and memorabilia, as well as relics from Shelley and other British writers. Keats and Shelley still reside in Rome, in the **Protestant Cemetery** near the metro stop Piramide. Located at *Via Ciao Cestio 6*, it is open all day, but visitors must ring the bell for admittance. Next, at #66 in the piazza, the grand poet George Gordon (Lord) Byron took lodging in 1817 and performed work on *Child Harolde's Pilgrimage*.

From here, you can explore the **Via Condotti**, Rome's center for high level consumerism. **Caffe Greco**, at #86, is where, in its double row of interconnecting rooms, you could have found Goethe, Hans Christian Anderson or Mark Twain sipping an aperitif and other drinks that were a little stronger than can be found at Babbington's. In 1861, one of the upper rooms was also the lodging for Hans Christian Anderson of *Ugly Duckling* fame. A little further along, at #11 Via Condotti, poet Alfred Lord Tennyson and writer William Thackeray made their home when they visited Rome.

Just off the Via Condotti, at Via Bocca di Leone #14, is the **Hotel d'Inghlitera** where Mark Twain scratched many pages for *Innocents Abroad* in 1867 and where Henry James initially stayed during his forays into the Eternal City. Later on, James would reside at the **Hotel Plaza** at Via del Corso 126 where he began his work *From a Roman Notebook*, which described his exploration of the city, its culture, history, and expatriate social activities.

Further down the Corso, at #20, is where the German poet Goethe made his home from 1786 to 1788. Here he penned his immortal travel diary *Italian Journey*. Goethe's old house now contains a small museum of photographs, prints, journals, books, and other material relating to the poet's travels in Italy.

At Bocca di Leone, #43, you'll see where Robert and Elizabeth Browning lived in 1853. This is where Robert got the inspiration for his epic poem *The Ring and the Book*, a tragic tale of the murder of the Comparini family and their daughter Pompilia (who had lived on the Via Bocca di Leone in 1698), by Pompilia's husband, Count Franchescini.

Another famous writer who resided in Rome was the magnificent Charles Dickens, who wrote part of his *Pictures From Italy* at Via del Babuino #9. If you get a chance, try and read this book, since it brings the Rome of that time to life as vividly as he brought London to life in his many other books.

Nightlife & Entertainment

Rome is filled with many discos, pubs, and *birrerias* (bars) where you can spend your evening hours having wild and raucous times. If that's what you want to do, I've compiled a list of the best places to go. But if you want to do like most of the Romans do for evening and nightly entertainment, seat yourself at a bar/café or restaurant, savor your meal or a few drinks and revel in the beauty that is Rome. Lingering in the evening air while recalling the day's events or planning tomorrow's is a great way to relax, slow down your pace of living, and adapt to the culture.

Anyway, there are a few great places in Rome where you can become part of the culture. The best is in **Trastevere** at one of the little open air cafés where you can either stay all night sipping a few glasses of wine, or visit after you've had your dinner in one of the restaurants around the piazza (see Trastevere, *Where to Eat*). This is definitely *the* best place to go for a night out in Rome.

Another is **Campo dei Fiori**, which also has many cafés and restaurants where you can sit while you watch the life of Rome amble past. Three other great nightspots are the **Piazza Navona**, around the **Pantheon**, and around the **Trevi Fountain** where you can admire the fine sculpture, the beautiful people, and the many different life forms that comprise the streetlife of Rome.

But if this sedate, appreciative, slow-paced lifestyle is not for you, by all means try one of the following. I found them all perfect for letting off some steam.

Map references for the nightlife entries are as follows: numbers 91, 94, and 96 are on map A (pages 150-151); numbers 97, 99, and 104-107 are on map B (pages 164-165); numbers 95, 102 and 103 are on map C (pages 174-175); and numbers 96 (also on Map A), 98 and 100 are on map D (pages 196-197).

Irish-Style Pubs

94. TRINITY COLLEGE IRISH PUB, *Via del Collegio Romano 6, Tel. 06/678-64-72. E-mail: trinity-pub@flashnet.it. Web: www.trinity-rome.com. Open 7:30am to 3:00pm and 8:00pm to 2:00am. Credit cards accepted. (Map A)*

This is more of a place to come for a good meal and a few pints rather than a watering hole in which to drink the night away. The menu comes complete with pub fare such as sandwiches, Shepherd's Pie, salads, hamburgers, hot dogs, french fries and more, as well as an extensive and excellent Roman menu. The atmosphere and ambiance are impeccably upper crust. A great place to come for an intimate meal or some early evening drinks and relax over one of the many complimentary newspapers in a variety of languages. Another plus to this place is that in the summer, the air conditioning is cranked, so it's the perfect spot to escape the heat of Rome. An upscale crowd hangs out here.

95. THE BLACK DUKE, *Via della Maddelena 29, Tel. 06/6830-0381. Open for lunch in the summers. Open until 2:00am all year long, every day. (Map C)*

Located near the Pantheon there is outside seating bordered by large shrubs that separate you from the street. You can also sit inside in the large downstairs dining and bar area that seats 120 people. The air circulation is not that great so non-smokers beware...even in the small area designated for your use, breathing can be quite difficult. Here you can savor a full menu of authentic pub grub in the traditional dark and dinghy (yet clean and comfortable) English/Irish pub setting of dark wood decor and furnishings. More of an upscale crowd.

96. THE FIDDLERS ELBOW, *Via dell'Olmata 43, Tel. 487-2110. Open 7 days a week 5:00pm -1:15am. (Maps A&D)*

Rome's oldest authentic pub, which has knock-offs in Florence and Venice, this place has a slightly run-down feel but that gives it a truly Irish flavor. Located near the Piazza Santa Maria Maggiore, you'll get a taste of home here

When in Rome ... Do as the Irish Do!

When you think of Rome, you picture magnificent monuments, savory food, wonderful wine, flavorful gelato, and most importantly romantic moons hovering over picturesque piazzas stirring long forgotten passions. To that list you can add Irish pubs and cold Guinness on draught, because everywhere you look in the Old City of Rome you'll find quaint, authentic Irish-style pubs, jam packed with customers, the majority of whom are Italian. From Campo dei Fiori, to the Pantheon, to Via del Corso, to Trastevere and beyond, stopping in a local pub for lunch or a pint in the evening has become a facet of daily life in Rome.

Only a few years ago there were but a small number of seedy, vaguely pub-style bars, mainly catering to the foreign population. Today you can find authentic Irish-style pubs everywhere, filled to capacity with Italians enjoying the time honored Anglo-Saxon tradition of bellying up to the bar and throwing down a few pints.

Just as we in the States have adopted coffee bars into our culture, so have the Italians incorporated Irish-style pubs into the fabric of their everyday lives. Cheers.

but no real food. Only snacks like potato chips, peanuts and salami sticks are served. A little off the beaten path, unless you are staying near the Train Station, this is not really a place to go out of your way to visit. Mixed crowd.

97. THE JOHN BULL PUB, *Corso Vittorio Emanuele II 107a, Tel. 06/687-1537. Open 12:00pm to 2:00am. (Map B)*

The English John Bull company's version of what the Irish Guinness is promoting all over the world: authentic pub experience in which to sell their beer. There is wood, brass, glass, and mirrors, and English knickknacks everywhere. Totally British, including the friendly service. Ideally located near Piazza Navona, The Pantheon and Campo dei Fiori on the main street Vittorio Emanuele, this is a fun place to come for a few drinks or their extensive antipasto spread at happy hour. Besides that you can muster up some sandwiches, salads, or other basic pub food for around E2.5.

98. SHAMROCK IRISH PUB, *Via del Colosseo 1/c, Tel. 06/679-1729. Open noon to 2:00am. (Map D)*

A truly authentic Irish pub, complete with two dart boards in the back. The place to play darts in Rome. Located near the Colosseum, the superb small hotel, Hotel Richmond and the great enoteca on Via Cavour, Cavour 313. If you are looking for great pub food, cold beer, a fun crowd, stop in here in the evenings, or in the middle of the day whilst touring.

Bars & Discos

99. THE DRUNKEN SHIP, *Campo dei Fiori 20/21, Tel. 06/683-00-535. Open 1:00pm-2:00am. Some days (the schedule changes ... this is Italy, remember), they don't open until 6:00pm. Happy Hour 6:00-9:00pm. (Map B)*

The best bar in the best location in Rome. American owner Regan Smith has created a wild and raucous American style bar in one of Rome's oldest piazzas. Loud music, rowdy crowd, great drinks, draft beer and bilingual and beautiful waitresses. The crowd is mainly Italian with a sprinkling of foreign students and travelers. All adventurous and fun.

You'll love the Jello shots and adorable English speaking waitresses and bartenders. The decor is dark wood and the whole place has a slight tilt to it befitting, I suppose, a drunken ship. This is the place to come for a pint or two in the early evenings as well as the best place to party the night away. They have specials every night to keep you coming back for more. A younger crowd hangs out here.

100. RADIO LONDRA, *Via di Monte Testaccio, 65B. Tel. 06/575-0044. Open Monday-Friday 9:00pm to 3:00am, and Saturdays until 4:00am. All credit cards accepted. (Map D)*

This place is totally insane, and crowded, and loud, and completely out of this world. You have segments of all parts of society here, making for a complete viewing pleasure. If the goings-on inside the inferno gets too hot, you can always sojourn to one of the tables on the terrace. A great place to meet other single people, not necessarily tourists. The interior is complete with an 18th century vaulted ceiling and 1940s style decor. They offer live music Tuesday through Friday. Food specialties are house pizza and grilled steaks. Located in the recently trendy Testaccio section of town by the Piramide Metro stop, around here you will find most of Rome's dance clubs and hot night spots.

101. BIRRERIA LOWENBRAU MUNCHEN, *Via delle Croce 21, Tel. 06/ 679-5569. Open 11:00am-11:00pm. All credit cards accepted. (Map A)*

You can eat here if the need for Viennese cuisine creeps up on your stomach (you'll find plenty of German tourists here enjoying the staples from their homeland), but I find it's a perfect place to have the best German beer on tap. It's a festive place to throw down a few pints with your travel partners. They serve their large beers in glass boots which adds to the charm of this *birreria*. In conjunction you're in one of the best nighttime areas in Rome, around the Piazza di Spagna, where you can go for a casual stroll before or after your drinking adventure.

102. NED KELLY'S AUSTRALIAN PUB, *Via delle Coppelle 15, Tel. 06/ 685-2220. Open 6:30pm to 2:00am week days and 3:00pm on weekends. Lunch open Monday-Friday 12:30-3:30. (Map C)*

A small hole in the wall place that is the unofficial rugby and darts bar in Rome. One board is to the right as you walk in and there is league play in the winter. There are four owners, two of which do most of the bar work. David, the lone American, helps draw some local foreign students and Tony, the manager of the local rugby club, brings in the Italian rugby community. This mix of fifty-fifty Italian/foreigners makes for a fun place in the evenings. Then at lunch from 12:30pm to 3:00pm, they have one of Rome's best salad bars. Located a stone's throw from the sports bar Oliphant.

103. OLIPHANT TEX MEX RESTAURANT, *Via delle Coppelle 31/32, Tel. 06/686-14-16. Open 11:00am to 2:00pm. Happy hour 6:00-8:00pm. (Map C)*

Besides the Tex Mex menu, this place is also a really great sports bar — if you're into that. TVs are everywhere in the bar area and there's an American flag fluttering in the middle of the restaurant, a crew boat hanging from the wall, a cut-out of Michael Jordan by the bar, surfboards precariously placed everywhere, and other athletic memorabilia thrown in for that authentic sports bar feel. The menu is super-extensive, complete with nachos (E2.5), quesadilla (E7), BBQ back ribs (E13), burgers (E12) and hot dogs (E7.5). A great place to watch the game and escape back into where you came from for a while.

104. OMBRE ROSSE, *Piazza Sant'Egidio 12, Tel. 06/588-4155. Hours 7am-2am. (Map B)*

Wonderful service from morning 'til the wee hours. Strange for a late night place to open so early, but they are, and their breakfasts are excellent. There are all kinds of wines, as well as beer on tap in this oasis of calm in the frenzy of late night Trastevere. Inside or out, here you'll be able to grab a quick bite to eat and a superb glass of wine. One of my favorites.

105. LA SCALA, *Piazza della Scala 60, Tel. 06/580-3763. Closed in August. Hours 7pm-2am. (Map B)*

Divided into five rooms, each with a different theme, this is a great late night place in Trastevere. There are plenty of courses to sample, including the *Vecchia America* (a steak with chili and french fries), the *Mexico e Mexico* (ossobucco, rice, chili and french fries), as well as many pizzas. An excellent late night place with food, music, dancing, and little corners for couples to cuddle in. The patio is a little 'foo-foo' but inside its more fun.

106. ACCADEMIA, *Vicolo della Renella 88/90, Tel. 06/589-6321. Open 6:30pm-2:00am. (Map B)*

With two big rooms and a grand terrace, this place has enough space for everyone. There's live music, great food and fun times. A good place to come for a late night drink or a romantic small dinner in one of the upstairs rooms with a view over the rooftops of Rome.

107. ARTU CAFÉ, *Largo MD Fumasoni Biondi 5, Tel. 06/588-0398. Closed Mondays. Open 6:00pm-2:00am. (Map B)*

Inside you'll find a comfortable entry room with a few tables, a fireplace leading to a cozy bar area, then from there you have a back room where the hip locals hang out. This place has a great feel, an extensive snack menu, an adequate wine list, and friendly wait staff. It's one of my favorite places to come for a late night after dinner drink when I'm in Trastevere.

Cafes/Bars

The cafes and bars of Rome are where the locals gather. These places are the heart and soul of the city, and if you want to grab drink or a snack at some of the most authentic, try any of these listed here. Regular bar hours vary, but most are open early (6am) for breakfast, and close late (around 10pm). Come here for a truly authentic Roman experience.

108. TEICHNER, *Piazza San Lorenzo in Lucina 17, Tel 06/687-1683. Closed Sundays. Open 8am–midnight.*

A classic cafe in a calm and relaxing piazza, generally overlooked by tourists, amid the chaos of Rome. My favorite place to grab a cup of coffee or gelato in Rome. You can get all sorts of snack to nibble on as well as foodstuffs to bring home with you from the small store inside. Just off the main shopping street, Via del Corso, this is a perfect cafe at which to stop for a break. And if the tables are all full, there are also two other cafes to choose from in this, the most relaxing piazza in Rome.

109. BABBINGTON'S TEA ROOMS, *23 Piazza di Spagna, Tel. 06/678-6027. Credit cards accepted. Closed Thursdays.*

A great place to grab a spot of tea. In the mornings when they serve massive breakfasts of scones, shepherd's pie, and other British culinary delights (if there is such a thing). This ancient café, with its heavy furniture, musty decor, and creaky floors has been serving customers for several centuries. The service is out of the 18th century, but the prices are from the 21st. Expect a cup of tea to cost over $5. A required stop on the literary tour of Rome.

110. DOLCE VITA, *Piazza Navona 70a, Tel. 06/6880-6221. Closed Mondays.*

Located in one of the best piazzas in the world, Piazza Navona, whether seated inside, but preferably out, you will have an authentic Italian café experience at this time honored locale. The patio area has a view over the entire piazza, the church by Borromini, and the fountain of the rivers by Bernini; and is the perfect spot to grab a coffee or an after dinner drink and watch the Romans walk by.

111. ROSATI, *Piazza del Popolo 5, Tel. 06/322-5859.*

Since 1922 this historic café has opened its doors on one of the most animated piazzas in Rome, Piazza del Popolo. Since traffic has been lessened in the piazza, sitting outside is not such a noxious affair, and is a great place to watch Romans and tourists alike cavort. Inside the elegant atmosphere remains as hospitable as ever. The breakfast *cornetti* are exquisite, as are many of their pies, pastries, sandwiches and snacks, all made in house.

112. SANT'EUSTACHIO, *Piazza Sant'Eustachio 82, Tel. 06/686-1309. Closed Mondays.*

Opened in 1938 this place has been a favorite since then in the *centro storico* around the Pantheon, especially at night. The attraction has remained the same – great coffee and wonderful ambiance. You can also get all sorts of sweets, snacks and drinks. A perfect spot to take a break from touring and sample an authentic piece of the Roman way of life.

113. LA TAZZA D'ORO, *Via degli Orfani 84, Tel. 06/679-2768. Closed Sundays.*

In an historic location near the Pantheon, and maintaining a bustling ambiance out of the 1940s, this place is perfect for a mid-day or early evening coffee and snack. It's a wonderful slice of another era. Snacks, ice creams, liqueurs, pastries, and other goodies are also served. I recommend at least one cup of coffee here, just to savor the atmosphere. They also make the most amazing *Granita al Cafe* (iced coffee drink). The coffee is frozen and crushed, and served between two layers of whipped cream. The iced coffee was the best I ever had!

114. CAFÉ GRECO, *Via Condotti 86, Tel. 06/678-5474. Closed Sundays. Open 8am to midnight.*
This places has been here since 1740 and has been a stop on the grand tour of Rome since then. A unique and elegant café where you can get all sorts of drinks, snacks and pastries. Expensive, but worth at least one stop just to be a part of the history. Another required stop on the literary tour of Rome.

Opera

If you are in Rome from December to June, the traditional opera season, have the proper attire (suits for men, dresses for women), and a taste for something out of the ordinary, try the spectacle of the opera:
TEATRO DELL'OPERA, *Piazza D. Gigli 1, 00184 Roma. Tel. 06/481-601, Fax 06/488-1253.*

Movies in English

ALCATRAZ, *Via Cardinal Merry del Val, Tel 06/588-0099. Mondays only.*
NUOVO SACHER, *Largo Ascianghi 1, Tel. 06/581-8116. Original language on Mondays only.*
PASQUINO, *Piazza San Egideo 10, Tel. 06/580-3622. Three screens. Daily films in English.*
QUIRINETTA, *Via M. Minghetti 4, Tel. 06/679-0012. Original Language films daily.*

Sports & Recreation

There are many different sporting activities to participate in and around Rome, since the city is only 15 miles from the beach and 65 miles from great skiing country. Below is a list of possible activities:

Amusement Park

There is a permanent amusement park, **Luna Park**, in EUR on the outskirts of Rome and accessible by Metro. To get there take the Metropolitana on Linea B to the EUR stop. EUR stands for *Esposizione Universale Romana*, a grandiose project sponsored by Mussolini as a permanent exhibition to the glory of Rome. The park is to your left as you enter EUR along the Via Cristoforo Colombo. The rides are simple but the atmosphere is fun and rather old style carnival-like.

Bicycling

Reckless Roman drivers can make biking on the city streets dangerous if you're not careful, and especially if you're a young North American used to the defensive drivers in the States and Canada. But if you are interested in riding a bicycle you can rent them at many different locations (see *Getting Around*

Town) and take them for a trip through the **Borghese Gardens** (see *Seeing the Sights*, above) or along the city streets. I find it easy and manageable but I ride a bike a lot back home. So if you don't ride a bicycle normally I would advise against trying to do so here in Rome. This is not the Bahamas.

Boating

Rowboats can be rented at the **Giardino del Lago** in the Villa Borghese. You can also rent dinghies at **Lido di Ostia** (see *Excursions & Day Trips* below). If you are in Italy near the end of April, you may want to try the annual Tiber Descent starting near Peruiga and ending up in Rome. Canoeists travel about 15km a day and lasts for six days. You can join for any or all of the days. For more information visit the descent's website *www.discesadeltevere.org* or contact the organizer Andrea Ricci at *andrearicci@libero.it*.

Bowling

There are two good bowling alleys *(bocciodromi)* in Rome, but unless you have your own car, both of these places are far outside of the old walls of the city and thus rather difficult to get to except by taxi:
• **Bowling Brunswick**, *Lungotevere Aqua Acetosa, Tel. 396-6696*
• **Bowling Roma**, *Viale Regina Margherita 181, Tel. 861-184*

Golf

There are a variety of 18 hole and 9 hole courses all around Rome:
• **L'Eucalyptus Circolo del Golf**, *Via della Cogna 3/5, 04011 Aprilla. Tel. 06/ 926-252, Fax 06/926-8502*. Located 30 km from Rome, this is an 18 hole par 72 course that is 6,372 meters long. It is open all year except on Tuesdays. They also have a small executive course, driving range, pro shop, tennis courts, swimming pool, guest quarters, and a restaurant/ bar.
• **Golf Club Torvalaianica**, *Via Enna 30, 00040 Marina di Ardea. Tel. 06/913-3250, Fax 06/913-3592*. Located 25 km from Rome, this is a 9 hole par 31 course that is 2,208 meters long. It is open all year except Mondays. They have a driving range as well as a restaurant/bar.
• **Golf Club Castel Gandolpho**, *Via Santo Spirito 13, 00040 Castel Gandolpho. Tel. 06/931-2301, Fax 06/931-2244*. This is an 18 hole par 72 course near the Pope's summer residence that is 5,855 meters long. It's open all year except on Mondays. They have a driving range, carts, pro shop, swimming pool, and a restaurant/bar.
• **Circolo del Golf di Fioranello**, *Via della Falcognana 61, 00134 Roma. Tel. 06/713-8080 or 731-2213, Fax 06/713-8212*. Located 17 km from the center of Rome, this is an 18 hole par 70 course that is 5,417 meters long. It is open all year except for Wednesdays. They also have a driving range, pro shop, swimming pool, and a bar/restaurant.

• **Macro Simone Golf Club**, *Via di Marco Simone, 00012 Guidonia. Tel. 0774/ 370-469, Fax 0774/370-476.* Located 17 km from Rome, this is an 18 hole par 72 course that is 6,360 meters long. It is open all year except for Tuesdays. They also have an 18 hole executive course, driving range, pro shop, swimming pool, tennis courts, massage room, sauna, gymnasium, and an excellent restaurant and bar.

• **Golf Club Parco de' Medici**, *Viale Parco de' Medici 20, 00148 Roma. Tel. 06/655-33477, Fax 06/655-3344.* Located 10 km outside of the city center, this is an 18 hole par 72 course that is 5,827 meters long. It is open all year except on Tuesdays. They also have a driving range, swimming pool, tennis courts, and a restaurant/bar. This is the course most accessible and nearest the city center.

• **Circolo del Golf di Roma – Aqua Santa**, *Via Appia Nuova 716 or Via Dell'Aquasanta 3, Roma 00178, Tel. 06/780-3407, Fax 06/7834-6219.* Located 11 km from Rome, this is an 18 hole par 71 course that is 5,825 meters long. It is open all year except on Mondays. They have a driving range, putting green, swimming pool, and a restaurant/bar.

• **Olgiata**, *Largo Olgiata 15, Roma 00123, Tel. 06/378-9141. Fax 06/378-9968.* Located 19 km from the center of Rome, in a housing development similar to many golf courses in the U.S. At Olgiata there is an 18 hole par 72 course that is 6,396 meters long and a 9 hole par 34 course that is 2,968 meters long. The course is open all year except on Mondays. They have a driving range, pro shop, swimming pool and a bar/restaurant.

River Trips

In July and August you can take a river trip through central Rome. The trips are organized by the **Amici del Tevere**. Check the journal *This Week in Rome* for details, a local periodical available in most hotels and at the American Express office.

Swimming

Most public pools in Rome Open in June and close in August. The major outdoor pool in Rome is at the **Foro Italico** (*Tel. 396-3958*), open June to September. An indoor pool at the Foro Italico is open November to May. You can gain entry to private pools at hotels for a fee. Below is a list of those available:

Hotel Parco dei Principi, *Via G. Frescobaldi 5, Tel. 06/854-421. Open 10am-6pm M-F. E25.*

Shangri La, *Viale Algeria 141, Tel. 06/591-6441. Open 9am - 6:30pm M-Sat. E6 half day; E10 full day. Sun E10 half day; E15 full day.*

Cavalieri Hiton, *Via Cadlolo 101, Tel. 06/35-101. Open 9am - 7pm M-F E40, Sat and Sun E50. Under 12 half price.*
Villa Pamphili, *Via della Nocetta 107, Tel. 06/6615-8555. Open 9am - 9pm. E12. Under 12 half price.*
The best nearby beach is at **Lido di Ostia**, less than an hour west-northwest of Rome. The beaches are clean and large, and they have plenty of *cabanas* to rent where you can change your clothes. And you can get there by Metro then public train, all for the price of a subway ticket. There are also some excellent seafood restaurants where you can leisurely eat, sip wine, and enjoy the beautiful Italian summers.

Tennis
The following public courts require reservations and there are hourly fees charged:
• **Circolo Montecitorio**, *Via Campi Sportivi 5, Tel. 06/875-275*
• **EUR**, *Viale dell'Artigianato 2, Tel. 06/592-4693*
• **Foro Italico**, *Tel. 06/361-9021*
• **Tennis Belle Arti**, *Via Flaminia 158, Tel. 06/360-0602*

Shopping

Because the very best of Italian design and craftsmanship are conveniently located all over Rome, this city is one of the finest shopping places in the world. You can find beautiful items made from the very best material, and as such this is not the place to look around for cut-price bargains. Leather and silk goods predominate, but Rome is also an important location for jewelry, antiques and general top of the line *pret-a-porter* (ready to wear) fashion.

The main shopping area is near the Spanish Steps and is a network of small and large streets featuring the famous **Via Condotti**. The shopping area boundaries extend over to **Via della Croce** in the north to **Via Frattina** in the south, and **Via del Corso** in the west to **Piazza di Spagna** in the east.

Romans, like most Italians, prefer to shop in boutiques, and the Via Condotti area has these quaint little shops selling everything from shirts to gloves. This specialization originated from the village craft shops of old, and generally ensures top quality and personal service. In Italy, **department stores** are the exception rather than the rule, but in this shopping area there are some that warrant a look, like **La Rinascente, STANDA, UPIM**, and **Coin** (see sidebar).

To get instant respect, you may have to dress the part here in Italy. It's not like in the malls back home where it doesn't matter how you dress; here in Rome the wealthier you look the better assistance you'll get. Unfortunately as tourists we usually leave our best attire back home, but try the best you can. Shorts and tank tops usually will get you no respect at all, particularly if you're shopping on the Via Condotti and Via Borgognona. This holds true, and I can

Italian Department Stores

It's always fun to go to supermarkets and department stores in other countries to see what the natives enjoy. Even if you don't buy anything, it's still fun to browse. Both STANDA and UPIM are designed for the Italian on a budget, while Rinascente is a little more chic.

STANDA, *Viale di Trastevere 60 and Via Cola di Rienzo 173.*

Italy's largest food market, the perfect place to find that food product to bring back to the States with you. Since most of their stuff is vacuum sealed and pre-packaged you should not have any problems with customs. STANDA also has a large selection of housewares and clothing. This is the combined K Mart and Safeway of Italy, with slightly better quality products.

UPIM, *Via Nazionale 111, Piazza Santa Maria Maggiore and Via del Tritone 172.*

This department store is just like STANDA, except without the food.

LA RINASCENTE, *Piazza Colonna and Piazza Fiume.*

This is much more upscale than the other two and has about the same prices as boutiques. Very chic shopping.

vouch for this personally, if you're shopping on some of the parallel streets like Via Frattina, some of the little cross-streets, and even in Piazza di Spagna or Via del Babuino.

Other shopping districts are less formal, and many of these are worth investigating if you have time, because in these locations is where you'll find some real bargains. **Via del Tritone** and the streets around the **Trevi Fountain**, **Via Cola di Rienzo** across the Tiber and north of the Vatican, **Piazza San Lorenzo** in Lucina and the streets around **Piazza Campo dei Fiori** are all areas where you will find less expensive leather bags and shoes. **Via Veneto** also has more of an international flavor, but boy, is it expensive.

Besides these areas, Rome also has many colorful street markets offering a vast selection of top quality fruit, flowers, vegetables, prosciutto, salami, cheeses, meat and fish, as well as cheap and inexpensive clothes. Because of this proliferation of small shops and markets, and the Italian penchant for shopping in them, there are few large department stores or supermarkets in the city center.

Bargaining is an accepted practice in clothes markets, but elsewhere transactions are conducted in a more roundabout way. At food stalls, cheeses and other weighed items have *prezzi fissi* (fixed prices), and in nearly all clothes shops, you can try asking for a *sconto* (discount). Reasons for meriting a *sconto* may be numerous – buying two articles at once is a good example – but if you are bold you will ask for a *sconto* for no good reason at all, and will usually get one. This practice applies to all but the very grandest of shops. Try it in hotels too.

Surprisingly few shopkeepers speak English, but in the larger shops there is usually one person on hand who understands enough to be able to help you. Try to get your shopping done in the morning hours, when the stores are not so busy. At night, traditionally when Italians shop, it is so crowded it is difficult to get assistance.

Antiques

Today, the typical Roman antique can be either a precious Roman artifact or pieces in the baroque and neoclassical style. There are also many French and English antiques masquerading as Italian. One thing that they all have in common is that they are extremely expensive.

Some good antique shops in Rome can be found in the **Via del Babuino** and the **Via Margutta**. Other shops can be found on the **Via dei Coronari**, and the **Via Giulia**. And don't forget to check out the **Porta Portese** Sunday market *(open 6:30am–2:30pm)*. You'll find some interesting antiques there, but not too many.

But the best area to visit to find antiques is the area of the old city of Rome, the *centro storico* from Piazza Navona to the tip of the peninsula that points towards St. Peter's. There are also some excellent stores on the other side of Via Vittorio Emanuele, around the Campo dei Fiori in that same area.

Outdoor Markets

Many natives buy their vegetables, fruits, flowers, meats and cheeses from one of the many street markets held daily all over the city. Stalls of inexpensive clothing are also available, and I advise you not to miss the

Fantastico Shopping Streets!

Top of the Line Shopping – Via Condotti, Via Borgognona, Via Bocca di Leone

Mid-Range Fashion – Via Nazionale, Via del Corso, Via Cola di Rienzo, Via del Tritone, and Via Giubbonari

Antiques – Via del Babuino, Via Giulia, Via dei Coronari, around Piazza Navona

Inexpensive Shoes – Fontana di Trevi area

Leather Goods and Apparel – Via due Macelli, Via Francesco Crispi

Straw and Wicker Products – Via dei Deiari, Via del Teatro Valle

High Fashion, Exclusive Service
If you're looking for high-end fashion accessories and top of the line service, look no further than Shigeo Amino's two stores in Rome, **Avriga**. You'll find the best of the best, all at duty-free prices. One store is near the Trevi Fountain *(Via del Lavatore 46-47, Tel. 06/678-7875)* and another is almost directly across from the American Catholic Church in Rome, Santa Susanna's *(Via XX Settembre 122, Tel. 06/481-5616).*

opportunity to wander through one in the mornings, since they are usually closed in the afternoons.

Here are some of the better markets, most of which are open from 7:00am and close at 2:00pm, Monday through Saturday:

CAMPO DEI FIORI, *Piazza Campo dei Fiori. Closed afternoons and Mondays.*

Rome's oldest and definitely best market held in the cobblestone square in the center of Rome's old medieval city. You can buy flowers (the name Campo dei Fiori means fields of flowers), fruits and vegetables, all delicately presented under makeshift awnings or giant umbrellas. Also available are hardware products, clothing and more. Surrounding the square are some *Alimentari* and *Panneterie* where you can pick up cold cuts, cheeses, and bread for picnics.

PORTA PORTESE, *Ponte Sublico. Open 6:30am–2:30pm, Sundays only.*

This flea market stretches along the Tiber from Ponte Sublico (where the Porta Portese is) in the north to the Ponte Testaccio in the south. That's roughly south of the center of Trastevere along the river. It is not even on most maps, but tell a cab driver where you're going and he'll know, since it is truly a Roman institution where anything and everything under the sun is sold: from live rabbits to stolen antiques to trendy clothes to kitchen items and all sorts of odds and ends. The clothes and accessories are inexpensive but are not of the highest quality, as befits most flea markets. Not many tourists venture here, but it's safe (though beware of pickpockets), and if you like flea markets, it is a whole lot of fun. A great place to come and get Italian soccer jerseys, hats and scarves. And it goes without saying that you have to bargain.

TESTACCIO, *Piazza Testaccio, Metro – Piramide. Closed Sundays.*

An authentic Roman covered market in the newly gentrified section of Rome. This market is in an old working class section of Rome, which was indelibly transformed into the grid pattern that exists today at the end of the 19th century. This neighborhood is named after the earthenware jugs (*testae*) which were discarded here. Today it is home to one of Rome's best local markets. Come here for the atmosphere and leave with baskets of fruit and vegetables.

PIAZZA VITTORIO EMANUELE, *Metro – Termini. Closed Sundays.*
Located 5 minutes from the south of Termini station is an excellent fresh fruit market which circles the Piazza Vittorio Emanuele. Ideally situated if you are staying by the train station, or want to grab something quick before you get on the train. A wonderfully authentic local market.

ANTIQUES & COLLECTIBLES UNDERGROUND FLEA MARKET, *Via Fr. Crispi, Tel. 06/3600-5345, Admission E2. Open First Saturday (5:00-8:00pm) and Sunday (10:30am-7:30pm) of every month. Saturdays.*
Though technically not an outside market, which means it should not be under this heading, this is a fantastic flea market that should be visited if you are in Rome on the First Saturday and Sunday of every month. Located in an underground parking garage near the Via Veneto and the Spanish Steps, you can find all sorts of interesting knick-knacks here that would be impossible to find anywhere else.

English-Language Bookstores
ANGLO-AMERICAN BOOKSTORE, *Via delle Vite 102. Tel. 06/679-5222. Credit cards accepted. Monday–Friday 9:00am–1:00pm, and 3:30pm–7:30pm. Saturdays 9:00am–1:00pm.*
Located between the Spanish Steps and the Trevi Fountain, this bookstore caters to all manner of bibliophiles and computer nerds too. As well as a full selection of travel books, paperbacks, history books, etc. They have a multimedia computer center too.

THE CORNER BOOKSHOP, *Via del Moro 48, Tel. 06/583-6942. Credit cards accepted. Open Mondays 3:30pm–7:30pm, Tuesday–Sunday 10:00am–1:00pm and 3:30pm–7:30pm.*
Located in Trastevere, just over the Ponte Sisto, this place is owned by the very knowledgeable, helpful, and friendly Claire Hammond,and features English-language titles exclusively. They're stocked with hardbacks, paperbacks in non-fiction, fiction, general interest and more. Also a great place to meet other ex-pats or fellow travelers.

ECONOMY BOOK AND VIDEO CENTER, *Via Torino 136, Tel. 06/474-6877. Web: www.booksitaly.com. Credit cards accepted. Mondays 3:00pm–7:30pm, Tuesday–Saturday 10:00am–1:00pm and 3:30pm–7:30pm.*
This mainstay of the English-speaking community for the past three decades buys and sells secondhand English language paperbacks and have an excellent selection of both new and used books, including everything from fiction to non-fiction, children's, science fiction, best sellers and mysteries. They also carry a complete range of guidebooks on Rome and Italy.

THE ENGLISH BOOKSHOP, *Via di Ripetta 248, Tel. 06/320-3301. Credit cards accepted. Open Mon-Sat 9:00am – 7:00pm.*

The newest English language bookshop in Rome, just off the Piazza del Popolo and parallel to the Via del Corso. In this ideal location, you will find all sorts of great titles.

LIBRERIA 4 FONTANE, *Via Quattro Fontane 20a, Tel. 06/481-4484. Credit cards accepted. Open Mon-Sat 9:00am – 7:00pm.*

All sorts of English and American titles available in this small shop up from the Piazza Barberini.

THE LION BOOKSHOP, *Via dei Gresci 36, Tel. 06/3265-4007. Credit cards accepted. Open Mon-Sat 9:00am – 7:00pm.*

A wide selection of fiction, science fiction and new releases from London and New York in this mainstay of the ex-pat community in Rome.

Newspapers

The *International Herald Tribune* is published jointly by the Washington Post and The New York Times and printed in Bologna for distribution throughout Italy. They have an insert specifically for Italy. You can also find a condensed version of *USA Today*. There used to be the local English-language paper for Rome, *The Daily American*, but that perished years ago. You can also find newspapers from all over the world, in any language, at almost any newsstand.

AUTHENTIC ITALIAN FOOD STORES

As mentioned above in outdoor markets, the best places to get your fresh fruit, cheese, salami, ham, turkey, and bread for a picnic would be at any of the markets mentioned above in the section under *Outdoor Markets*. But if you are looking for something special, listed below are some food stores and shops where you can find some excellent authentic food products and unique gift items.

Alimentari & Gastronomie

Italy is a land of fine food, all made from the best ingredients and crafted with care by local artisans who learned their trade through time-honored traditions of excellence. And the place to find these tasty traditional foodstuffs is in small local *alimentari* and *gastronomie*. Listed below are some of the best, from which you can bring back something tasty to remember Italy. But also these places are great just to stop and savor the sights and smells or Rome. If you cannot make it to one of those listed below, stop in any local food store you run across and you will find many tantalizing gifts or ingredients to take home with you. These places are usually open 9am -12:30pm and 4pm-7pm.

LA CORTE, *Via della Gatta 1, Tel. 06/678-3842. Closed Saturday afternoons.*

Smoked fish, salmon, pate of smoked fish, and all sorts of meats, olives, prepared and packaged food fill up this quaint and colorful little store near the Piazza Venezia and the great chocolate store *Moriando & Gariglio*.

ANTICA SALUMIERIA, *Piazza della Rotonda 4, Tel. 06/687-5989. Closed Thursday afternoons and Saturday afternoons in the summer.*

Located in the same piazza as the Pantheon, the entry display is always tantalizing whether with smoked fish, mushrooms and truffles and an assortment of many different typically Italian food products. Here you can also find all sorts of cheese, salamis, olive oils, and packaged goods.

IL SALUMIERE DI GIUSEPPE CIAVATTA, *Via del Lavatore 31, Tel. 06/ 679-2935. Closed Thursday afternoons and Saturday afternoons in the summer.*

An excellent variety of local, artesian foods as well as local and European cheeses, salamis, pates, wine and olive oil. Located near the Trevi fountain, this small store is easily accessible during your tourist wanderings.

VOLPETTI ALLA SCROFA, *Via della Scrofa 31/32, Tel. 06/686-1940. Closed Sundays and Tuesday afternoons.*

One of the most famous and in my opinion, by far the best *gastronomie* in the center of town. They have an ample supply of cheeses and salamis, as well as local and foreign delicacies like caviar, sauces, salmon, mushrooms and truffles. There is also an excellent *rosticceria* inside with an inviting buffet of quick dishes like *pasta al forno* (baked pasta), *gnocchi* (on Thursdays), *pollo arrosto* (juicy roasted chicken ... you have to try this), and a variety of *verdure* (green veggies) and *contorni* (vegetable side dishes). A great place to come for a quick bite and to load up on gift food items.

ANTICA NORCINERIA, *Via della Scrofa 100, Tel. 06/6880-1074.*

Almost directly across the street from Volpetti this place has a much better selection of salamis, and also carry bread. More of a locals shop because they also serve choice cuts of meat, here you can find all sorts of regional salamis as well as a number of gift items.

LATTICINI, *Via Collina 16, Tel. 06/474-1784. Closed Sundays.*

By far the best cheese store in Rome. They have all kinds of different cheeses to choose from and offer excellent advice, shrink wrapping service (*sotto vuoto*) which will keep your choices fresh if you want to bring them back with you. A little out of the way, but well worth the trip if you are looking for some exotic cheeses and great prices.

F.LLI CARILLI, *Via Torre Argentina 11, Tel. 06/6880-3789.*

Located close to the Pantheon and Campo and Piazza Navona, this place is a wonderful local alimentari run by two brothers. You can find all sorts of pastas, cheeses, meats and more here. Ideally located with friendly service.

SALUMERIA, *Via della Croce 43, Tel. 06/679-1228.*
They are more than their sign suggests since they carry all sorts of cheeses, sauces, pastas, focacci – and not just salami. Well located near the Spanish Steps, this a great local store though a bit pricey because of its location.

Cioccolaterie
Listed below are some artisan chocolate stores where you can get some tasty morsels to snack on or to bring back as gifts. The chocolate is all made in house and all lovingly selected, packed and wrapped while you wait. A wonderful experience and great chocolate at each. Unless otherwise noted, these stores are open regular shop hours, which means 9am -12:30pm and 4pm-7pm.

MORIANDO & GARIGLIO, *Via del Pie di Marmo, Tel. 06/699-0856. Closed Sundays, August, and Saturdays in July.*

A gem of a chocolate store in the ambiance, presentation, flavor and price. This place came to Rome in 1886 bringing with it a grand tradition of chocolate making from the Alps. Still a family business they use nothing but the best chocolates and mix their ingredients in the traditional ways. In all there are 80 varieties of chocolate covered sweets to choose from. Located behind the Pantheon this place is perfectly situated for you to stop in while touring. This is my favorite chocolate store in Rome.

LA BOTTEGA DEL CIOCCOLATO, *Via Leonina 82, Tel. 06/482-1473. Closed Sundays.*

This chocolate store located near the Colosseum needs to be mentioned even though it is a bit out of the way. There are over 50 types of chocolate candies for sale, all made in-house, all made from only the best cacao from Brazil. Here you'll find delicious white chocolate concoctions as well as the sublimely rich *superamaro* 80 percent pure chocolate candies. The owner, Maurizio Proietti is a second generation chocolate artisan, and his creations will make your soul sing.

PUYRICARD, *Via delle Carrozze 26, Tel. 06/6929-1932. Closed Sundays.*

A transplanted French chocolate maker has made its home on one of Rome's best shopping streets near the Spanish Steps. Placed here with the intent of luring in the many female shoppers, they have been successful in doing just that. With 92 varieties to choose from, and many awards for excellence to their name, you can find something to satisfy even the most discerning palate. Whether you want something with Grand Marnier, with nuts, or simply a glob of dark chocolate, Puyricard is the place to come. You can also get items gift wrapped to bring home with you. Everything here is rather pricey, but well worth it.

Pasticcerie

Rome is filled with some incredible pastry shops. Listed below are the best, but stop in any *pasticceria* you pass and you will not be disappointed. The Romans make superb pastries.

VALZANI, *Via del Moro 37b, Tel. 06/580-3792. Closed Tuesday and in Spring also Mondays.*

One of the last truly traditional *pasticcerie Romane* where you can find all sorts of classic pastries. Located in a small fragrant little shop, here you can grab a cup of coffee, select a delectable morsel and be transported to culinary heaven. Located in Trastevere, just across the Ponte Sisto from Campo dei Fiori, this is a superb place to savor an authentic Roman pastry. This is my favorite pastry shop in Rome.

LA DELIZIOSA, *Vicolo Savelli 50, Tel. 06/6880-3155. Closed Tuesdays.*

The name of this place says it all – *Deliziosa* means Delicious. One of the best pastry shops in the city, here you can find all sorts of filled pastries, crumbly, spongy, thick, gooey, heavy, light, some creatively concocted, others made from traditional recipes, but all incredibly delicious. When in Rome, if you're hungering for a pastry, come here.

LA DOLCEROMA, *Via dei Portico d'Ottavia 20b, Tel. 06/689-2196. Closed Sunday afternoons and Mondays.*

Here you will find exquisite Austrian and American style pastries made by Stefano Ceccarelli and which are famous city wide. All sorts of pastries abound in this wonderful little shop including strudels and tarts all covered in rich abundance of chocolate, marzipan, fruit preserves and anything else that is delectable and attractive. You can also find cherry, lemon and pecan pies and chocolate chip cookies, a rarity in Italy. So if you have a craving for them, come here.

IL FORNO DEL GHETTO, *Via del Portico d'Ottavia 2, Tel. 06/687-8637. Closed Saturdays.*

In this small store located in the heart of the Jewish quarter in Rome, you can sample the creations of three generations of pastry makers. Traditional Italian and Jewish-Roman pies and pastries abound, filled with fruit, covered in chocolate and begging to be eaten. My favorite is the tasty cheese cake. In the mornings you can sample their home-made breakfast creations.

L'ANTICO FORNO, *Via della Scrofa 33, Tel. 06/686-5405. Closed Sundays.*

Right next door to Volpetti, the great alimentari mentioned earlier, here you can get all sorts of tasty pastries as well as excellent pizza by the slice. Everything is made in-house in the their extensive back room, so it is all fresh and oh-so-tasty.

INTERESTING LITTLE SHOPS

Rome is filled with all sorts of funky little shops and exotic clothing boutiques, all stuffed with so many different types of products that after shopping here a day at the mall will seem boring. Three of the most interesting little shops where you can find all sorts of interesting gifts or keepsakes are listed below. Unless otherwise noted, these stores are open regular shop hours, which means 9am -12:30pm and 4pm-7pm.

TERECOTTE PERSIANE, *Via Napoli 92, Tel. 06/488-3886, Open 10:00am– 1:30pm and 3:30pm–8:00pm.*

Come here for an eclectic mix of terra cotta figures, tiles, masks, planters and post boxes. Located in a small courtyard just down from the American church in Rome, Santa Susanna's, the place is filled with everything terra-cotta you can imagine. Even if you don't want to buy, come and browse. The prices are rather high, so do not be afraid to bargain.

L'IMPRONTA, *Via del Teatro Valle 53, Tel. 06/686-7821.*

For the most amazing, intricate and colorful prints of the piazzas, monuments, and buildings of Rome, in all shapes and sizes, framed or unframed, visit this wonderful little shop. It's an adventure to find this place since it is tucked away on a tiny side street between the Pantheon and Piazza Navona; but once you get here you will not be disappointed.

AI MONESTARI, *Corso Rinascimento 72, Tel 06/6880-2783. Closed Thursday afternoons. In the summer closed Saturday afternoons.*

Located just outside the Piazza Navona, this tiny shop is filled with soaps, jams, pates, olive oils, wines, all made by men of the cloth. Hence the name of the place – *Ai Monestari* means 'of the monastery.' These monk-made products are all made with the best ingredients, have ever so quaint packaging and make perfect keepsakes or gifts.

CHIMERA, *Via del Seminario 121, Tel. 06/679-2126; open Mon. 3:15pm- 7:30pm, Tuesday-Thursday 10:30am-7:00pm; Friday 10:30am-5:30pm; Mondays and Saturdays 1:00-7:00pm; closed Sundays.*

This consignment shop/antique store specializes in collector's items and objects like paintings, drawings, porcelain, silver, jewelry, art, coins, and much more. A short walk from the Pantheon, located in the basement of a 16th century palazzo, this is where Rome's well-heeled pawn their family heirlooms so they can continue living the life of luxury. An antique shop of the utmost tradition and discretion, this is a fun place to visit when you are around the Pantheon.

FEFE ALDO, *Via della Stelletta 20b, Tel. 06/6880-3585. Open 8:00am – 8:00pm.*

A small store near the Pantheon that is an outlet for handmade stationery crafts, journals, address books, and artisan book binding products. Here you can find all of the same stuff that is in the far more upscale and expensive Il Papiro (see below). The stores a mess, since it is really a small warehouse, but if you take the time to look through what they have you will find some real gems at great prices.

IL PAPIRO, *Via del Pantheon 50, Tel 06/679-5597, Email info@ilpapirofirenze.it, Web: www.ilpapirofirenze.it.*
This is but one store of three surrounding the Pantheon. Here you can get all sorts of unique stationery gift items like journals, pens, blotters, cards, wrapping paper and more. They started in Florence but have now firmly established themselves here in Rome. A great store, but look at Fefe Aldo and Daniela Rosati (see below) for similar items at a lower price.

DANIELA ROSATI, *Via della Stelletta 27, Tel. 06/6880-2053. Open 9am-7pm.*
Just down the street from Fefe Aldo, this place is a quaint little shop that makes boxes, all sorts and sizes of boxes. It is a little cluttered since the shop is really only a small artisan factory. But do come here and price boxes before you go to either Il Papiro or Fefe Aldo. If you like what you see, you'll save a lot of money.

PELLICANO, *Via del Seminario 93, Tel. 06/6994-2199.*
If you have ever wanted a tailormade tie (*cravatta su misura*), this is the place to come. They can usually do it in 10 days, but if you ask they will rush an order for you. A small intimate little store with reams of silk waiting for you. And the prices are the same as Brooks Brothers back home. High quality attentive service at a reasonable price.

BONORA , *Via dei Prefetti, 44, Tel. 06/73593. Closed Sundays. Hours Monday-Saturday 9:30am–1:00pm and 3:30pm–7:30pm. In winter open only Monday afternoons. In summer open only Sat mornings.*
And now that you have your tailormade tie, you can stroll over to this elegantly refined little store by the Parliament building to have a pair of shoes tailormade. Sorry, only men's shoes. And once again the prices are incredibly reasonable. The same as you would pay for a pair of regular shoes at Brooks Brothers.

GUSTO, *Piazza Augusto Imperatore 9, Tel. 06/322-6273.*
This is by far the most extensive and complete kitchenware store I have seen in Rome. It is also an enoteca and restaurant, but I suggest you come here to find that unique gift for the kitchen. Not that the food isn't good here ... but boy is the line long. Gusto is now the hippest place to grab a bite downtown.

POIGNEE, *Via Capo le Case 34, Tel. 06/679-0158, Fax 06/678-9382, E-mail: poignee@surfingontheweb.it, Web: www.poignee.com.*
An incredibly unique urban artifacts store where you can pick up antique brass door handles, shelf handles, locks, and so much more. In this store you can find basically everything you have ever imagined needing to complete that restoration project you have been putting aside so you can find that one special item. Check out their website to see what I mean.

CARTOLERIA PANTHEON, *Via della Rotunda 15, Tel. 06687-5313.*
Here you will find articles of wonderful design and high quality such as note cards, photo albums, stationary, telephone books, schedulers, and many

other items which would be perfect as inexpensive and completely unique gifts.

PINEIDER, *Via Fontanella di Borghese 22, Tel 06/6830-8014. Also located at Via due Macelli 68, Tel. 06/678-9013.*

Two locations for this superb little stationary store that carries much more than that. Here you'll find all sorts of funky pens, schedulers, note cards, notebooks with creative designs, pencil cases, back packs. Another one of my favorites since both are so easily accessible.

GALLERIA SAN CARLO, *Via del Corso 114-116, Tel. 06/679-0571.*

This is a really cool toy store on Rome's best shopping street, the Via del Corso. Here you can find dolls, doll houses, toy cars/buses/planes, models, backgammon boards, chess sets, stuffed animals and a whole lot more. Two slender hallways display the items in glass cases. Find something you like and ask one of the attendants to get it for you. A great place to find gifts for kids of all ages.

CAMPO MARZIO PENNE, *Via Campo Marzio, 41, Tel. 06/688-07877.*

Not far from the Chamber of Deputies, the specialty here are calligraphy pens and sets, leatherbound notebooks, sketch pads, photo albums.

FABRIANO, *Via del Babuino, 13, Tel. 06/326-00361.*

Located between the Spanish Steps and Piazza del Popolo this place has with modern stuff, including photo albums, notebooks, sketch pads, address books, etc.

Excursions & Day Trips

I've planned some fun excursions for you: **Tivoli Gardens**, **Castel Gandolfo**, **Frascati**, **Ostia Antica** and **Cervetri**. And if you've got the time, you can also visit the incredible ancient ruins of **Pompeii** and **Herculaneum** (they are listed in the *Naples and Amalfi Coast* chapter, as is the beautiful **Isle of Capri**, which you can also visit from Rome if you so desire).

TIVOLI GARDENS

Tivoli has about 45,000 inhabitants, and is situated on the **Aniene**, a tributary of the Tiber, overlooking Rome from its place on the **Sabine Hills**. This town is where the wealthy ancient Romans built their magnificent summer villas, and the three main attractions are **Villa Adriana** (Hadrian's Villa), **Villa d'Este**, and **Villa Gregoriana**.

The **Villa Adriana's** main attraction is its huge grounds, where you and lizards can bask in the sun. There are plenty of secluded spots to relax or enjoy a picnic on the grass. The building itself was begun in 125 CE and completed 10 years later, and was at the time the largest and most impressive villa in the Roman Empire. From his travels **Hadrian**, an accomplished architect, found ideas that he recreated in his palace. The idea for the **Poikile**, the massive colonnade through which you enter the villa, came from Athens. And the

---

Exploring Beyond Rome

Whether you wish to explore outside of Rome for a day, a weekend or longer, **Elegant Etruria** is a travel organization to consider. They help find the best accommodations, offer sightseeing tours, and make your travel easier and worry-free. So if you want to explore the best of the little hill towns around Rome and want someone else to make all the arrangements for you, contact Mary Jane Cryan at Elegant Etruria.

Elegant Etruria, *Palazzo Pieri Piatti, Vetralla (VT) 01019 Italia, Tel. 0761/485008, Fax 0761/485002, E-mail: macryan@tin.it, Web: www.dbws.com/Etruria/Home.htm.*

Serapeum and **Canal of Canopus** were based on the Temple of Serapis near Alexandria, Egypt.

The **Villa D'Este's** main draw are its many wonderful fountains. The villa itself was built on the site of a Benedictine convent in the mid-16th century. The **Owl Fountain** and **Organ Fountain** are especially beautiful, as is the secluded pathway of the **Terrace of the Hundred Fountains**. If you make it out to Tivoli, these gardens and their fountains cannot be missed, especially at night during the months of May through September when they are floodlit. They are simply spectacular then.

The **Villa Gregoriana** is known for the **Grande Cascata** (the Great Fall), which is a result of Gregory XVI diverting the river in the last century to avoid flooding. The park around the cascade has smaller ones as well as grottoes. This is the least interesting of the three villas.

The addresses and hours of the three villas are:

- **Villa Adriana,** *Bivio Villa Adriana, 3.5 miles southwest of Tivoli. Open Tuesday–Sunday, 9:30am–1 hour before sunset. Closed Mondays. Small fee required.*
- **Villa d'Este,** *Viale delle Centro Fontane. Open Tuesday–Sunday, 9:30am to 1.5 hours before sunset. May–September also open 9:00pm–11:30pm with the garden floodlit. Closed Mondays. Small fee required. Sundays free.*
- **Villa Gregoriana,** *Largo Sant'Angelo. Open Tuesday–Sunday 9:30am to 1 hour before sunset. Closed Mondays. Small fee required. Sundays free.*

Arrivals & Departures

Tivoli is about 23 miles east of Rome. Take the Via Tiburtina (SS5). The Villa Adriana lies to the right about 3.5 miles before the town. By train from Stazione Termini, the trip takes about 40 minutes.

Where To Eat

Tivoli simply abounds with restaurants, many offering a magnificent panoramic view of Rome. Here are some of my suggestions.

1. ADRIANO, *(near Hadrian's Villa), Via di Villa Adriana 194, Tel. 0774/ 529-174. Closed Sunday nights. All credit cards accepted. Dinner for two E65.*

Basically at the front of the entrance to Hadrian's Villa, this restaurant attached to a hotel has a beautiful garden terrace. They make excellent *crostini di verdure* (fried dough with vegetables inside), *raviolini primavera con ricotta e spinaci* (ravioli with spring vegetables, spinach and fresh ricotta), *tagliata di coniglio alle erbette* (rabbit with herbs) and more. The prices are a little rich for my blood, but the food keeps me coming back for more.

2. LE CINQUE STATUE, *Largo S Angelo 1, Tel. 0774/20366. Closed Fridays. All credit cards accepted. Dinner for two E55.*

In front of the entrance to Villa Gregoriana this place has outside seating where you can enjoy the local cuisine. They make many of their pastas in house

so they're sure to be fresh. They also specialize in meats, like *maialino* (baby pork) and *abbacchio* (lamb) *arrosto* as well as their *verdure fritte* (fried vegetables).

3. **VILLA ESEDERA**, *(near Hadrian's Villa), Via di Villa Adriana 51, Tel. 0774/534-716. Closed Wednesdays. All credit cards accepted. Dinner for two E35.*

You can get some interesting antipasti like the *insalatine di pesce* (small fish salad), then you can move on to their pastas, which are all made in house, and are all superb, especially the *spaghetti all'amatriciana* (with tomatoes, cream and spices) and the *penne all'arrabbiata* (with tomatoes, garlic oil and hot pepper). These and all their pastas are simply amazing. Perfectly Roman and bursting with flavor from the freshest ingredients. Not a fancy place but great food.

CASTEL GANDOLPHO

Located above **Lake Albano**, with a wonderful vista over the valley, **Castel Gandolpho** is the location of the summer residence of the Pope. From up at the Castel Gandolpho, you can enjoy a fabulous view of the wooded slopes that fall swiftly down into the murky waters of a volcanic crater. The one real sight is the **Palazzo Pontificio** (Papal Palace), built in 1624. During the summer months when the Pope is in residence, every Sunday at noon His Eminence gives an address in the courtyard of the palace. No permit is required to enter. First come, first served is the rule.

Arrivals & Departures

Castel Gandolpho is about 15 miles east of Rome. Take the Via Appia Nuova (SS7) for about 30 minutes. By train from Stazione Termini, it's about 35 minutes. From the station you will have to take a local taxi up to the Castel, unless you feel adventurous and want to walk the three kilometers uphill. Just follow the signs on the side of the road.

Where To Eat

ANTICO RISTORANTE PAGNANELLI, *Piazza A Gramsci 4, Tel. 06/936-0004. Closed Tuesdays. All credit cards accepted. Dinner for two E45.*

This restaurant with a nice view of the lake has been in existence since 1882, and they still serve all the traditional dishes created with produce from the local countryside. They make a wonderful *strozzapreti all'amatriciana* (pasta with tomatoes, cream and spices), *risotto al'erbe* (rice dish with herbs), *maialino arrosto* (roast baby pork), *bracciole di cinghiale* (roast boar shanks) and other savory dishes. Rumor has it that the Pope even has stopped in once or twice.

FRASCATI

If wine is what you're looking for, **Frascati** is where you want to be. This town's wine is world famous, and this little town is simply dotted with wine bars where you can sample the vintages. The ambiance of this hill town is magnificent too.

Frascati is a great place to stay while visiting Rome if you can't stand the urban hustle and bustle. Since it's only 35 minutes and $5 away, Frascati's relaxing pace, scenic views, quaint little wine shops, excellent local restaurants, and winding old cobblestone streets should be seriously considered as an alternative to downtown Rome.

Since this is still primarily an excursion, I've listed more restaurants and wine bars than hotels – though I hope some of you will opt to stay here and enjoy Frascati's many charms.

Consider Frascati!

Rome can be a bit overwhelming both for a first-time visitor and the Roman veteran. Yes, it's beautiful and charming and filled with some of the world's best-known sights and prized artistic treasures. But it's also large, congested, noisy, polluted and challenging. Another reason for staying in the countryside is that most prices at most hotels and restaurants seem to have gone through the roof.

So if you are someone who would rather see Rome but not stay in Rome, consider **Frascati**. This quaint, charming, quiet, little hill town is the perfect place to get away from it all while still having access to everything. The town is only 35 minutes away by train (the fare is E3) and the trains run every 45 minutes or so until 10:00pm. Granted if you want to take a nap in the middle of the afternoon, your hotel would be way out here, but that is what the Borghese gardens are for. Bring a picnic lunch and take a little siesta in the shade in one of the prettiest and peaceful gardens in any city in the world.

In Frascati, you'll be able enjoy many good restaurants, sample the fine local wines from quaint little wine stores located all over the city. They serve you glasses or carafes from huge vats. You'll also be able to savor the ambiance of an ancient medieval town, with its cobblestone streets and twisting alleys. Here you'll be able to gaze out your windows and see lush valleys below, instead of looking out onto another building as you would probably do in Rome. And if you come in October, you'll be able to experience a wine festival of bacchanalian proportions.

So if you are used to the calm serenity of country life, but still want to experience the beauty that Rome has to offer, Frascati may be your answer.

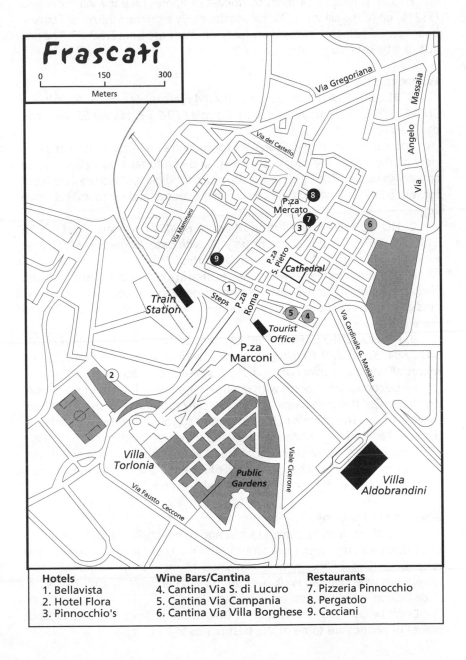

Frascati

0   150   300
Meters

Via Gregoriana

Massaia

Angelo

Via

Via del Castello

Via Mammani

P.za
Mercato 8
7
3
6
9
P.za
S. Pietro
Cathedral
1
Steps
P.za
Roma
Train
Station
5 4
Tourist
Office
Via Cardinale G. Massaia
P.za
Marconi
2
Viale Cicerone
Villa
Torlonia
Public
Gardens
Villa
Aldobrandini
Via Fausto Ceccone

Hotels	Wine Bars/Cantina	Restaurants
1. Bellavista	4. Cantina Via S. di Lucuro	7. Pizzeria Pinnocchio
2. Hotel Flora	5. Cantina Via Campania	8. Pergatolo
3. Pinnocchio's	6. Cantina Via Villa Borghese	9. Cacciani

Arrivals & Departures
Frascati is roughly 14 miles southeast of Rome. Take the Via Tuscolana (SS215) up to the hill town (25 minute drive). By train from Stazione Termini, board a local train that leaves every forty minutes or so from Track 27. The ride lasts a little over 35 minutes. Cost E3.

Where to Stay
1. **BELLAVISTA**, *Piazza Roma 2, 00044 Frascati. Tel. 06/942-1068, Fax 06/942-1068. 13 rooms all with bath. Double E70-80. Breakfast E5. All credit cards accepted.* ***
You have room service, TV in your room, and a hotel bar, as well as a nice view of the valley. The rooms are clean and comfortable as befits a good country three star. The building is quite quaint and old, but restored perfectly for your comfort. I love the high ceilings in the rooms, making them feel much larger.

2. **HOTEL FLORA**, *Via Vittorio Veneto 8 00044 Frascati. Tel. 06/941-5110, Fax 06/942-0198. 33 rooms only 30 with bath. Single E60-65; Double E75-95. Breakfast E6. All credit cards accepted.* ***
An old hotel, decorated with style, located in a central position in Frascati. Similar amenities to the Bellavista, but not as good a view. Located a little ways outside of town, this hotel is set in a wonderfully tranquil environment. A good place to stay.

3. **PINNOCCHIO'S**, *Piazza del Mercata 20, Tel. 06/941-7883, Fax 06/941-7884. Single E30-40 (Double used as a single); Double E50-65. Seven rooms all with bath, mini-bar, and TV. No credit cards accepted.* **
Large comfortable rooms with gigantic bathrooms, located upstairs from a restaurant of the same name, where you can grab yourself a snack until late in the evening. The office is in the restaurant so you'll need to enter there to get your key. Perfectly located on the central market square. The market is a sight you have to see while in Frascati and a great place to get some fruits, vegetables (you can even get fresh bags of mixed salad), meats, and cheeses. The place is alive with bargaining and local greetings.

Where to Eat & Drink
Some of the wine bars are so small and so nonchalant about the tourist trade that they don't even have names. Also many of the places do not have telephones. One of the owners explained to me, *"Why should we have telephones when we can walk over and talk in person?"* That makes sense, since Frascati is such a small intimate little town.
Don't be put off by this casual hill town attitude, since the ones without names or phones are some of the best places to visit. Enjoy.

Wine Bars

4. CANTINA VIA SEPULCRO DI LUCURO, *Via Sepulcro di Lucuro 6. No Telephone.*

Located just off the main road (Via Catone), this place has a small area for seating outside separated from the rest of the world by large planters. The inside is quite cool, like a wine cellar. Just inside the door is an antique wine press that they still use during the pressing season. Inside or out you'll get some of the best wines Frascati has to offer.

5. CANTINA VIA CAMPANIA, *Via Campania 17. No Telephone.*

Just down the road from the wine bar listed above, this place has one and a half of its four inside walls covered with wine vats, and the rest of the space taken up with strange looking tools used in the wine trade, as well as large empty bottles that you only wish you could take home with you ... full. The owner is quite friendly and if it's not too crowded will sit down and chat. Great wine. Wonderful atmosphere.

6. CANTINA VIA VILLA BORGHESE, *Via Villa Borghese 20. No Telephone.*

Small wine store filled with large 1,000,000 liter barrels called *botte*, and 500,000 liter barrels called *mezza botte*. Each cask is numbered and initialed with the vineyard it came from. Not very scenic atmosphere and no tables to sit at, but they will sell you a bottle of their finest for only E1. That's about a dollar for an excellent bottle of Frascati wine.

Restaurants

7. PINNOCCHIO, *Piazza del Mercato 20, Tel. 06/941-6694 or 942-0330. Dinner for two E28.*

A large statue of Pinnocchio advertises this superb restaurant in Frascati's quaintest and most vibrant square (it's actually a triangle). There is outside seating with large planters separating you from the pace of this market-dominated piazza. Inside you'll find tiled floors and wood paneling giving the place a nice rustic flair. They serve great *canneloni ai quattro formaggi* (with four cheeses), as well as great Roman staples such as *amatriciana, carbonara, and vongole.*

For seconds try their *scampi alla griglia* (grilled shrimp) which is reasonably priced at only E8. If you find you've lingered too long over your Sambuca, Pinnocchio's has some wonderful rooms upstairs.

8. PERGATOLO, *Via del Castello 20, Tel. 06/942-04-64. E7-Cold plate with wine and bread; E10-First course of pasta, pizza, or meat, second course of the cold plate with wine and bread.*

Wild and fun atmosphere, a little on the touristy side with singers serenading the diners. You can either enjoy or ignore it in this large and spacious restaurant that has a deli counter displaying all the available meats, cheeses, breads, salamis, etc., that you'll be served. There are roaring fires behind the counter where your meats are all prepared.

If you've come to Frascati for the day or the week, this is one place you have to try, just for the fun of it. Say hi to the beautiful manager Tiziana for me.

9. CACCIANI, *Via Alberto Diaz 13, Tel. 06/942-0378. Closed Mondays. Holidays January 7-15 and 10 days after Ferragosto. All credit cards accepted.Dinner for two E55.*

One of the most famous restaurants in this region. It has a beautiful terrace that offers a tranquil and serene atmosphere. For starters, try the *crostini con verdure* (baked pastry appetizer filled with vegetables). Then try the home-made *fettuccine alla Romana* (made with tomatoes, chicken and spices) or *spaghetti con le vongole verace* (with clams in a hot oil and garlic sauce). For the entrée try the *fritto misto di carne* (mixed fried meats) the *saltimbocca*, or any of their grilled fish.

Seeing the Sights

If you've driven to Frascati, you were able to savor the lovely scenic route along the old **Appia Antica** past the Catacombs and ruined tombs. The town is perched halfway up a hill, and on a clear day you will have splendid views of all of Rome and its scenic countryside.

Besides the great views, the wine, and the chance for some relaxation, Frascati has a wealth of villas and spacious parks that were formerly residences of princes and popes. One of these residences, **Villa Aldobrandini** which sits just above the town, and has a magnificent garden in which you can find solitude. To enter the villa's grounds you need to first get a free pass from the **Aziendo di Soggiorno e Turismo**, in Frascati's Piazza Marconi. *The hours are Monday–Friday 9:00am–1:00pm.*

Besides the beauty of its old villas, many of which were damaged in Allied bombings because the Germans had taken over the town for their headquarters, Frascati's draw is the fine **white wine** that bears its name. All wines seem to lose a special *qualcosa* when they travel, so if you are a wine lover, do not miss out on this chance to drink Frascati's wine directly at the source.

To enjoy this succulent nectar, there are old, dark wine stores, with heavy wooden tables and chairs located all over town. At one of these you can sit and enjoy this unspoiled and inexpensive wine, the way the natives have been doing for centuries. The **Cantina Vanelli**, just off Piazza Fabro Filzi, is a prime example of one such wine store, and a fine traditional location to sample Frascati's produce. Just ask for a *bicchiere di vino* (glass of wine). An alternative to the cramped quarters of these wine stores but with quite a bit less atmosphere would be to sit at one of the sidewalk cafés offering superb views along with great wine.

Frascati is the perfect place to wander through, getting lost in the alleys, side streets, steps leading nowhere, and winding roads (all cobblestoned). If you follow the sporadically placed yellow signs that say *Ferario Pedonale*, you'll be guided through all the major sights and sounds of this hill town. These signs are prominently displayed so that the revelers who come for the wine festival can find their way around even after having a glass or two of the local vintage. One distinguishing feature is that there seem to be more *alimentari* (little food stores) per person than in any other city I've ever seen.

If you are fortunate enough to be in Frascati during the month of October, the town celebrates a **wine festival** of pagan proportions that lasts several days and nights. Come out to witness and partake in the debauchery, but please do not drive back to Rome afterwards – take the train.

CERVETRI

Cervetri used to be the Etruscan capital of Caere, but today Cervetri is not known today for the town of the living, but the towns of the dead the Etruscans built. These **Necropoli** are large circular mounds of tombs laid out in a pattern of a street, like houses in a city.

Today these round roofs are densely covered with grasses and wild flowers. Inside they have been furnished with replicas of household furnishings carved from stone. Most of the original artifacts are in the **Villa Giulia Museum** or **Vatican Museums** in Rome, but the burial sites themselves are eerily significant. *The site is open Tuesday to Sunday 9:00am–4:00pm. Admission E4.*

After viewing the necropolis you can settle down among the mounds and have a picnic lunch, and imagine what life would be like during that time. After sightseeing you can return to the town by taxi, or by car if you have one, and take in the limited sights the little town has to offer. From the crowded main piazza you can climb steps to a **museum** with a lovely medieval courtyard. But the main sights out here are the Necropoli.

Arrivals & Departures

Cervetri is about 28 miles west northwest of Rome. A 45 minute drive up the Via Aurelia (SS1), which will give you a more scenic view, or the Autostrada A12, which connects to the 'beltway' around Rome by route 201. By train from Stazione Termini it takes 1 hour and 10 minutes; from Roma Tiburtina it takes 50 minute to get to Cervetri-Ladispoli. Once in the town, to reach the **Necropolis** you can grab a local taxi, or take the two kilometer walk along a little road. There are signs on the road to guide you where you're going.

Where to Eat
   DA FIORE, *near Procoio di Ceri, Tel. 06/9920-4250. Closed Wednesdays. Dinner for two E30. No credit cards accepted.*
   A simple little local *trattoria* in the open country not far from the ruins and only four kilometers from the Via Aurelia. They make great pastas like *penne al funghi* (with mushrooms) *al ragu* (with tomato and meat sauce) or *con salsiccia* (with sausage). They also have grilled meats and their famous *bruschetta* (garlic bread as an appetizer) and pizza – all cooked in a wood burning oven.

OSTIA ANTICA & LIDO DI OSTIA

   Founded in the fourth century BCE, **Ostia Antica** feels about as far away from Rome as you can get, but is actually only 15 miles southwest of the city, a mere 45 minutes by subway then a short train ride. As with excursions to Pompeii or Herculaneum, you get the sensation that the clock has been turned back nearly 2,000 years. And what most people do not know is that Ostia contains the largest sampling of mosaic floors anywhere in Italy. Some of which are as intricate as tapestries.

   This city was once the bustling seaport of Ancient Rome, but today it is calm and serene respite from the hectic pace of modern Rome. The mosaic tile floors document the great variety of goods and services available in Ostia, documenting how busy the port was at one time. Commodities included furs, wood, grain, beans, melons, oil, fish, wine, mirrors, flowers, ivory, gold, and silk. Among the services offered were caulkers, grain measurers, maintenance men, warehousing, shipwrights, barge men, carpenters, masons, mule drivers, stevedores and divers for sunken cargoes.

   As at Pompeii, the houses are the most interesting part of the city. There were large villas and average sized abodes but the majority of Ostian residences were apartment buildings. There were also many public amenities including a theater, baths, and a fire department. The theater is small but is still put to use today for modern renditions of Greek and Roman plays.

   The city is well preserved despite having been subject to repeated attacks by pirates and hostile navies. The only invasions it undergoes now are from packs of marauding Italian school children on their cultural outings, rampaging through its archaeological excavations – the main reason to come here (see below).

   Ostia was abandoned starting in the 5th century CE. By the late 4th century no new burials had been made in its cemetery and the road to Rome was overgrown with bushes and trees. What led to Ostia's decline was that its two harbors were silting up and were thus of no use to Rome anymore. And today the beach at Ostia (Ostia Lido) is three miles beyond the seawall of the ancient town. Without an identity or commercial base of its own – as Pisa had,

Florence's old port city – archeological records indicate that citizens began leaving the decaying town of Ostia in droves. When Saint Augustine was passing through the city in the 4th century CE, it was already in full decline. By that time the Emperor Constantine had revoked its municipal status and assigned it to be governed by the village of Portus, which had grown up around a 'new,' harbor built by Trajan.

When in Rome, if you are interested in seeing an ancient Roman city being unearthed from its tomb and you do not have the time to get to Pompeii, Ostia Antica is an option which will not disappoint. Also, Ostia Antica is a wonderful respite from the hectic pace of Rome and is great place for kids to wander around.

Arrivals & Departures

Ostia Antica is about 15 miles southwest of Rome. Take the Via del Mare (SS8) for about 25 minutes. By metro and train, take Linea B to the Piramide station, and catch the train to Ostia Antica or continue to Lido di Ostia (the beach). It takes about 45 minutes from Stazione Termini. Your Metro ticket is valid for both trips so it will only cost you Euro 75 cents. Once at Piramide follow the signs for "Lido."

On the way back you may catch a train that goes to the Magliana Metro station instead of Piramide. Don't panic, just follow the signs for "Linea B" and once there get on the train at the track that says "Direz. Termini-Rebibbia." Check the signboard at the Ostia station for the return train. There is a ticket booth in the station but it cannot hurt to have your return ticket already purchased.

Where to Eat

On the way from the train station to the site there are a couple of cafes and a restaurant where you can grab a bite to eat. Inside the archeological site itself you will find a café to grab a bite to eat. None of them are worth writing home about, but they will satisfy your hunger.

Seeing the Sights

Ostia Antica gives an excellent notion of what life in the metropolis was like at the height of the Empire. This city presents to the modern world a picture of Roman life only a shade less vivid than that of Pompeii. The plan of the city is regular but not too regimented. It is scenic, monumental and functional. Its backbone is the major east-west street, the *Decumanus Maximus*, nearly a mile long, which was once colonnaded, and runs from the **Porta Romana** straight to the **Forum**.

You enter the excavations in Ostia at the aforementioned **Porta Romana**. The *Decumanus Maximus*, takes you past the well-preserved old **theater** and the **Piazzale dei Corporazione** (Corporation Square), a tree-lined boulevard once filled with over seventy commercial offices of wine importers, ship owners, oil merchants, or rope makers. All of these shops are worth a visit, but the well-preserved laundry and wine shop are best because these offices are tastefully decorated with more exquisite mosaic tiled floors representing their trades. A must see stop around this area is the site museum which has many of the excavated statues.

Farther down the *Decumanus Maximus* you arrive at the **Capitolium**, a temple dedicated to Jupiter and Minerva, located at the end of the **Forum**. The **insulae** (apartment blocks) are of particular interest since they are often four or five stories high. This is where the regular people and smaller merchants lived. Only the most wealthy of the merchants were able to build themselves separate villas. The *insulae* were well lighted, had running water, and a means for sanitation (i.e., garbage removal and toilets) on each floor.

Two private home of interest that should be visited are the **House of the Cupid and Psyche**, which is west of the Capitolium, and the **House of the Dioscuri**, which is at the southwest end of town.

My favorite way to tour this site as well as most other archeological sites is to go off of the beaten path. Leave the already excavated section and wander through the areas, which have not yet been dug up. This helps to give you an idea as to the amount of labor involved in actually excavating sections, and usually makes for great places to relax. And who knows maybe you'll turn up and ancient artifact or two.

The site is open daily 9:00am–6:00pm in summer, 9:00am–4:00pm in winter. Admission E5. The museum is open one hour less.

Lido di Ostia

Lido di Ostia is the beach about four kilometers from the ruins of Ostia Antica. Take the same route that you took to the ruins but continue on a little farther either by car or by train (see *Arrivals & Departures* above for more details). This is a perfect place to visit after a day of wandering through Ostia Antica.

Treat yourself to a seaside celebration. There are rafts to rent, umbrellas to use, *cabanas* to change and cavort in, restaurants to go to, and hotels to stay at if you get to tired and don't want to get back to Rome. Lido di Ostia is a typical Italian beach and it's close to Rome. But don't go on the weekend unless you like mobs of people.

Try either of these restaurants if you're hungry:

LA CAPANNINA DA PASQUALE, *Lungomare Vespucci 156, Tel. 06/ 567-0143. Closed Mondays. Holidays in November. All credit cards accepted. Dinner for two E55.*

A little expensive but the location is supreme, especially the outside seating right on the sea. They have a superb antipasto table, which could serve as your whole meal if you're not too hungry. Their pastas and rice dishes are also good since many of them have been homemade at the restaurant. Try the *risotto ai frutti di mare* (rice with seafood ladled over the top). They are known for their seafood dishes so try anything *al forno* (cooked over the grill), with their wonderfully grilled potatoes. The service is stupendous, as it should be based on the price.

TRE PULCINI, *Viale della Pineta di Ostia 30, Tel. 06/562-1293. Closed Mondays. All credit cards accepted. Dinner for two E55*

A simple family-run place with mama Antoinetta in the kitchen and Renato in the restaurant. Here you'll experience some true down home Italian cooking. Try their *sauté di cozze e vongole* (sautéed muscles and clams), *zuppa di pesce* (fish soup), or their *fritto misto* (mixed fried seafood). You can also get some homemade *gelato* (ice cream) as dessert, which is made daily by the daughter Cristina. You can enjoy all of this either outside on the balcony or in the air-conditioned comfort of the interior.

RURAL RETREATS AROUND ROME

I've provided a three day escape plan if you want to get outside of Rome. Peace and tranquillity are but a drive away in the hills surrounding the Eternal City. Some of these excursions are mentioned in greater detailed earlier in this chapter.

Day One

The perfect place to start is **Tivoli**, an ancient vacation spot famous for its large villas, lush gardens and picturesque waterfalls. The best way to get out to Tivoli from Rome is to make your way to the Raccordo Annulare, the beltway around the city. Follow this east until you get to the Via Tiburtina exit. This will take you all the way out. If it is easy for you to get directly on the Via Tiburtina downtown do so instead.

Drive first to **Villa d'Este**. Originally built as a Benedictine convent, it was transformed into a sumptuous villa by Cardinal Ippolito II of Este. Here you will be transfixed with the stunning beauty of the lush gardens and beautiful fountains.

After wandering the paths that cut through the vegetation, get back in the car for the short jaunt up to the **Villa Gregoriana**, in the town of Tivoli itself. Walking along the dirt path in the Villa's grounds you pass the Grotta delle Sibille and then are able to witness the panorama of the Grande Cascata with its wonderful waterfall.

After bathing in the beauty of these two villas it's time for some repast before you venture into the third, Hadrian's Villa.

For lunch stop in **Adriano** (*Via di Villa Adriano 194, Tel. 0774/529-174*) located just outside of Hadrian's Villa. Sample some of their *crostini di verdure* (fried dough with vegetables inside), or *raviolini primavera con ricotta e spinaci* (ravioli with spring vegetables, spinach and fresh ricotta).

After lunch venture onto the grounds of Hadrian's Villa. The building itself was begun in 125 CE and completed 10 years later, and was at the time the largest and most impressive villa in the Roman Empire. From his travels Hadrian, an accomplished architect, found ideas that he recreated in his palace.

Once you have satisfied all your architectural voyeurism, it's onto **Frascati** where we will spend the night.

To get to Frascati, take route 636 under the A24 highway, past the Via Prenestina and the Via Casalina. Once there we will check into our quaint old hotel, the **Bellavista** (*Piazza Roma 2, Tel. 06/942-1068*). Evening is the perfect time to spend at an outside café or wine bar in Frascati, savoring the quiet ambiance of this Roman hill town as well as the full bodied white of the region. If you want to be in the center of everything for dinner try **Pizzeria Pinnocchio** (*Piazza del Mercato 20, Tel. 06/941-6694*). If you want a quiet meal overlooking the fields of Frascati, try **Zaraza** (*Viale Regina Margherita 21, Tel. 06/942-2053*).

Day Two

The next day take a leisurely stroll through the thriving gardens of the **Villa Aldobrandini**. Afterwards simply wander the streets of this lovely medieval town, watching the tapestry of daily life unfold around you.

For lunch, let's go to **Pagnanelli** (*Piazza A Gramsci 4, Tel. 06/936-0004*) in **Castel Gandolpho**, only a few minutes drive away. Take route 216 through the town of Marino. There's not much to see here except for the wonderful **Palazzo Pontificio**, the summer residence of the Pope, located in the **Piazza del Plebiscito**. From the piazza and the restaurant you have wonderful views of the lake below. The scene is truly enchanting. After lunch take the car for a spin down to the lake and around the beautiful blue waters.

The afternoon and early evening will be spent getting to **Velletri** and **Anagni** then finally onto **Fiuggi** for the night and their curative baths the next morning. Don't hesitate to stop along the way and take some amazing photos of the picturesque Italian countryside.

To get to **Velletri** from Castel Gandolpho you can either take the less scenic Route 7, or the more pleasant route 217. You can get on Route 7 straight from Castel Gandolfo, but to catch the 217 you need to drive down to the lake and go south around it until the junction for 217. In Velletri we can admire the fourth century **Cattedrale di San Clemente** and walk slowly through the historical center of the town, taking in the small details of everyday life.

Next on our tour is **Anagni**, which we arrive at by taking Route 600 north out of town, which hooks up with Route 6 at Collefore and will take us to Anagni. This is a wonderful medieval town with steep, narrow streets winding around beautiful palazzi. The town's cathedral rises solitary on the highest point in town. Beside this eleventh century monument with its simple facade is the powerful twelfth century bell tower. If you're hungry stop for a small snack at one of the cafés in town, but don't eat too much; in Fiuggi we're going to have a great meal.

To get to **Fiuggi**, only a short drive away, we catch the Route 155r. Fiuggi is famous for its curative waters at the **Fonte di Bonifacio** or the **Fonte Anticolana**. The waters and the tranquillity are always an excuse to linger here for a day. We will spend the night at the **Grand Hotel Palazzo Delle Fonte** (*Via dei Villini 7, Tel. 0775/5081*) a spectacular four star hotel, founded in 1913 with tennis courts, indoor and outdoor swimming pools, luscious gardens and more. If you don't want something so upscale, try **Hotel Fiuggi Terme** (*Via Prenestina 9, Tel. 0775/551-212*), another four star that runs about half the price since it has about half the amenities.

Fiuggi is a city split in two: Fiuggi Fonte where the curative waters are, and Fiuggi Citta with its quaint winding streets. We will be eating dinner in the old city at **La Torre dal 1961** (*Piazza Trento e Trieste 18, Tel. 0775/55382*) so you may want to drive to the restaurant. Eating here at Antonio and Maria Ciminelli's wonderful restaurant is a culinary delight. Everything they serve is exquisite. I especially like the filet of trout (*filetto di trota*) lightly cooked in extra virgin olive oil.

Day Three

Today will be leisurely, spent being 'cured' by the waters, savoring the peace and quiet of the hills, and sampling the fine food and atmosphere of Fiuggi. For lunch try **Villa Hernicus** (*Corso Nuova Italia 30, Tel. 0775/55254*) near the waters. Their *spaghetti con vongole e peperoncini verdi* (with clams and green peppers) is wonderful.

After you've had enough peace and quiet to last a life time ... it's back to Rome. We can get back by taking the Via Prenestina all the way.

Practical Information for Rome
ATM Machines

Called **Bancomat** machines, ATM's are everywhere in Italy, making it convenient for you to withdraw money directly from your checking account. One drawback is that you can withdraw only up to E250 each day. But the advantages of using an ATM over traditional travelers checks are easy to discern.

The ATM gives you excellent, up-to-date exchange rates that are better than most exchange offices. Also, the transaction fee, a fixed rate of around $1.50, is usually lower than the fees charged by currency exchange places. Another advantage is that you are not constrained by bank or business hours. You can access your money anytime.

Despite the advantages of ATMs I would strongly suggest bringing some travelers checks with you. Why? If there is a bank strike (and that could happen at any time in Italy), the ATMs won't be filled up with cash and you'd be left without money. And also have a credit card handy just in case.

Baby-sitters

A list of reliable, English-speaking baby-sitters can be obtained through the **American Women's Association of Rome** (AWAR), *Tel. 06/482-5268.* In addition the American Embassy also has babysitter listings.

Banking & Changing Money

Banks in Italy are open Monday through Friday, 8:30am to 1:30pm and from 2:45pm to 4:00pm, and are closed all day Saturday and Sunday and on national holidays. In some cities the afternoon open hour may not even exist, and in some cities, like Rome, banks may open on Saturday mornings and extend longer on Thursdays. Once again, bank hours, like business hours, vary region to region, and even city to city within the region. Check outside of banks for their posted hours of operation. Even if the bank is closed, most travelers' checks can be exchanged for Italian currency at hotels as well as shops and at the many foreign exchange offices in railway stations and at airports.

Shop around for the best exchange rate. Each bank offers a different rate and exchange fee, as do the **Casa di Cambio**, smaller exchange establishments. Sometimes the rate charged to exchange your money is a set fee, a situation that is best when you change a large amount of money. Other places charge a percentage of the total which is generally more beneficial for smaller amounts.

Besides banks, there are plenty of exchange bureaus (*casa di cambio*) around, some of which actually offer great rates and low service charges. When using these tiny, hole in the wall yet completely reputable places, if you are changing small amounts (i.e. $20) look for ones that offer a low percentage transaction fee (i.e. 1% to 2% of the amount you're exchanging). If you are changing large amounts, find one that has a reasonable set fee (i.e. E1-3). One such exchange place that is open until 9:00pm on weekdays and until 2:00pm on Saturdays, is in the **Stazione Termini**. But use this as a last resort since the lines are always ridiculously long, just like American Express.

If all else is closed, simply change your money at your hotel or any of the four star hotels that line the Via Veneto. You won't get the best rate but at least you'll have money. Some places to change your money are:

• **American Express**, *Piazza di Spagna 38, Tel. 06/67-64-1. Open weekdays 9:00am to 5:30pm, and Saturdays from 9:00am to 12:30pm.* American Express is always a great option, especially if you have their travelers checks. Remember, the lines here are long, but if you're looking for a good rate and a chance to interact with other travelers, these lines are great meeting spots.

• **Banco Nazionale del Lavoro**, *Via Veneto 11, Tel. 06/475-0421. Open 8:30am to 6:00pm Monday through Saturday.*
• **American Service Bank**, *Piazza Mignanelli 15. Open 8:30am to 6:30pm Monday through Saturday.*

Business Hours

Store hours vary all over Italy, but as a rule they are open from Monday through Friday, 9:00am to 1:00pm, then re-open at 3:30 or 4:00pm to 7:30/8:00pm, and Saturdays from 9:00am to 1:00pm. In large towns, of which Rome is one, which mainly to cater to tourists, stores are open on Saturday afternoons and Sundays as well. Most stores everywhere else in Italy are closed on Sundays, and everywhere they are closed on national holidays. Don't expect to find any 24-hour convenience stores just around the corner in Italy. In Italy you need to plan ahead.

Food stores (*alimentari*) keep their own hours but generally follow the regular business hours listed above. *Alimentari* usually close at least one other day of the week besides Sunday. In most cases this day is Thursday (*Giovedi*), but it varies region to region, and even city to city within the region. There is a sign outside each *alimentari* that you can check to see which day they are closed (*chiuso*).

Basically, you must plan on most stores being closed from 1:00pm to 4:00pm, since this is the Italian siesta time. During that time, the only places open are restaurants, and most of those close at 2:30pm or 3:00pm.

Church Ceremonies in English

• **All Saints' Church** (Anglican), *Via del Babuino 153b, Tel.06/3600-2171. E-mail: allsaints_roma@hotmail.com. Sunday Mass 8:30am and 10:30am (sung)*
• **Church of Jesus Christ of Latter Day Saints**, *Piazza Camaro 20, Tel. 06/827-2708.*
• **Methodist Church**, *Via del Banco di Santo Spirito 3, Tel. 06/686-8314. E-mail: iasb.trad@tiscalinet.it. 10:30 Sunday Service.*
• **Rome Baptist Church**, *Piazza San Lorenzo in Lucina 35, Tel. 06/687-6652. E-mail: rombaptist@compuserve.com. 10am Sunday worship.*
• **St. Andrews** (Scottish Presbyterian), *Via XX Settembre 7, Tel. 06/482-7627. E-mail: david.huie@flashnet.it. Sunday Service at 11:00am*
• **St. Patrick's** (English-speaking Catholic), *Via Boncompagni 31, Tel. 06/420-3121. Sunday mass at 10:00am*
• **St. Paul's within the Walls** (American Episcopal), *Via Napoli 58, Tel. 06/488-3339. E-mail: stpaul@mclink.it. Sunday Mass 8:30am and 10:30pm (sung)*
• **San Silvestro** (English-speaking Catholic), *Piazza San Silvestro 1, Tel. 06/679-7775. Sunday Mass at 10:00am and 6:00pm.*

- **Santa Susanna** (American Catholic), *Piazza San Bernardo, Tel. 06/488-2748, Web: www.santasusanna.com. Sunday Mass at 9:00am, and 10:30am. Saturdays and weekdays at 6:00pm. 11am services at Marymount International school out the Via Cassia.*
- **Synagogue,** *(no services in English) Via Lungotevere dei Cenci, Tel. 06/684-0061*

Computers in Rome

If you decide to bring your laptop, remember to carry along a three-pronged adapter so you can plug it into the wall to recharge your batteries. You can get them at most hardware, Circuit City or Radio Shack stores in North America.

If you can't find these devices, you can order them from the **Franzus Company**, (pronounced Francis), *Murtha Industrial Park, PO Box, 142, Beacon Falls, CT 06403, Tel. 203/723-6664, Fax 203/723-6666.* They also have a free brochure, *Foreign Electricity Is No Deep Dark Secret,* which can be mailed or faxed to you.

If you forget to bring your own, most computer stores in Italy carry them too but at a much higher price. You will also need an adapter to plug in your modem cable to access your e-mails. You can get them at the same places mentioned above.

Also, when dialing out you may have to add a prefix "8" to your modem string in the software setup. Most hotels in Italy require an "8" to be dialed for you to access an outside line.

Credit Card Lost?

If you lose your credit card, these numbers will come in handy:
- **American Express,** *Tel. 800/872-000 (travelers checks), Tel. 800/874-333 (credit cards)*
- **Bank Americard,** *Toll free in Italy 167/821-001*
- **Citibank,** *Tel. 06/854-561*
- **Diner's Club,** *Tel. 800/864-064*
- **Mastercard,** *Tel. 800/870-866*
- **Thomas Cook/Mastercard,** *Tel. 800/872-050 (traveler's checks)*
- **VISA,** *Tel. 800/874-155 (traveler's checks), Tel. 800/877-232 (credit cards)*

Doctors & Dentists (English-speaking)

In case of need, the **American Embassy** *(Via Vittorio Veneto 119, Tel. 06/46741)* will gladly supply you with a recommended list of English-speaking doctors and dentists. A hospital where English is spoken is **Salvator Mundi**, *Viale della Mura Gianicolensi 67, Tel. 06/588-961, Website www.smih.pcn.net, E-mail: dg.smih@pcn.net.* I had my tonsils out there and am doing fine today.

Another place is the **Rome American Hospital**, *Via VE Longoni 69, Tel. 06/ 22551, Web: www.rah.it.* They have a physician on call 24 hours a day. An organization that can hook you up with physicians all over the world is **Personal Physician Worldwide**. See Chapter 7, pages 85-86, for contact information. A recommended heart specialist is **Aleardo William Madden**, MD, a Fellow in the American Heart Association. For an appointment, call *06/ 7049-1747 (Via Baldo degli Ubaldi 272.)*

A well-recommended dental clinic is **Bazzucchi Dental Center**, *Via I Vivanti 201, Tel 06/520-0202, E-mail: Bazzucchi@mail.wing.it, Web: www.bazzucchi.it.*

Embassies & Consulates
• **Australia**, *Via Alessandria 205, Tel. 06/852-721*
• **Canadian Embassy**, *Via GB de Rossi 27, Tel. 06/445-981*
• **Great Britain**, *Via XX Settembre 80a, Tel. 06/482-5441, Web: www.grbr.it*
• **Ireland**, *Piazza di Campitelli 3, Tel. 06/697-912*
• **New Zealand**, *Via Zara 28, Tel. 06/441-7171, E-mail: nzemb.roma@flashnet.it*
• **South Africa**, *Via Tanaro 1, Tel. 06/852-541, E-mail: sae@flashnet.it*
• **United States**, *Via Veneto 199, Tel. 06/46741*

Emergencies
The following numbers should be used in case of emergency: **113**- Police; **112** – Caribinieri (military police), **118** – Ambulance (Red Cross), and **115** – Fire. There are police and caribinieri offices in Termini station by the tracks. Other **Caribinieri** stations include: Via Mentana 6 and Piazza Venezia. Other **Polizia** stations include: Via Farini 40, Via S Vitale 15, or Piazza del Collegio Romano.

Festivals in Rome
• **January 1**, Candle-lit processional in the Catacombs of Priscilla to mark the martyrdom of the early Christians.
• **January 5**, Last day of the Epiphany Fair in the Piazza Navona. A carnival celebrates the ending.
• **January 21**, *Festa di Sant'Agnese*. Two lambs are blessed then shorn. Held at Sant'Agnese Fuori le Mura.
• **March 9**, *Festa di Santa Francesca Romana*. Cars are blessed at the Piazzale del Colosseo near the church of Santa Francesca Romana.
• **March 19**, *Festa di San Giuseppe*. The statue of the saint is decorated with lamps and placed in the Trionfale Quarter, north of the Vatican. There are food stalls, sporting events and concerts.

- **April**, *Festa della Primavera* (festival of Spring). The Spanish Steps are festooned with rows upon rows of azaleas.
- **Good Friday**, The Pope leads a candlelit procession at 9:00pm in the Colosseum.
- **Easter Sunday**, Pope gives his annual blessing from his balcony at noon.
- **April 21**, Anniversary of the founding of Rome held in Piazza del Campidoglio with flag waving ceremonies and other pageantry.
- **May 1**, *Festa del Lavoro*. Public Holiday
- **First 10 days of May**, international horse show held in the Villa Borghese at Piazza di Siena.
- **May 6**, Swearing in of the new guards at the Vatican in St. Peter's square. Anniversary of the sacking of Rome in 1527.
- **Mid-May**, Antiques fair along Via dei Coronari
- **First Sunday in June**, *Festa della Repubblica* involving a military parade centered on the Via dei Fori Imperiali. It's like something you'd see in Moscow during the Cold War.
- **June 23-24**, *Festa di San Giovanni*. Held in the Piazza di Porta San Giovanni. Traditional food sold: roast baby pig and snails.
- **June 29**, *Festa di San Pietro*. Festival to Saint Peter. Very important religious ceremony for Romans.
- **July**, *Tevere Expo* involving booths and stalls displaying arts and crafts, with food and wine lined up along the Tiber. At night there are fireworks displays and folk music festivals.
- **July 4**, A picnic organized by the American community outside Rome. Need to contact the American Embassy *(06/46741)* to make reservations for the buses to take you out there.
- **Last 2 weeks in July**, *Festa de Noiantri* involving procession, other festivities, feasting and abundance of wine all in Trastevere.
- **July & August**, Open air opera performances in the Baths of Caracalla.
- **August 15**, *Ferragosto*. Midsummer holiday. Everything closes down.
- **Early September**, *Sagra dell'Uva*. A harvest festival with reduced price grapes and music provided by performers in period costumes held in the Roman Forum.
- **Last week of September**, Crafts show held in Via dell'Orso near Piazza Navona.
- **Early November**, Santa Susanna Church Bazaar. Organized by the church for the Catholic American community to raise money for the church. Great home-made pies and cookies as well as used books and clothes. Auction of more expensive items held also.
- **December 8**, Festa della Madonna Immacolata in Piazza di Spagna. Floral wreaths inlaid around the column of the Madonna and one is laid at the top by firefighters.

• **Mid-December**, Start of the Epiphany Fair in the Piazza Navona. All throughout the piazza a fair filled with food stands, candy stands, toy shops opens to the public. Lasts a week. A must see.
• **December 20-January 10**, Many churches display elaborate nativity scenes.
• **December 24**, Midnight Mass at many churches. I recommend the one at Santa Maria Maggiore.
• **December 25**, Pope gives his blessing at noon from his Balcony at St. Peter's. The entire square is packed with people.
• **December 31**, New Year's Eve. Much revelry. At the strike of midnight people start throwing old furniture out their windows into the streets, so be off the streets by that time, or else your headache from the evening's festivities will be much worse.

Health Clubs
• **Roman Sports Center**, *Via del Galoppatoio 33, Tel. 06/320-1667. Open 9:00am-10:00pm.*
• **Le Club**, *Via Igea 15, Tel. 06/307-1024. Open Monday-Friday 7:30am– 7:00pm, Saturday 4:00pm-6:00pm.*

Internet Access
• **Splashnet**, *Via Varese 33, Tel. 06/4938-2073.* Email your friend and family with Yahoo, Hotmail, AOL and others. No Email address? No problem. They can set you up on hotmail or Yahoo free of charge. A great place to come and stay in touch with folks at home ... and you can do your laundry at the same time. Open in the summers from 9:00am to 1:00pm and Winter from 9:00am to 10:00pm. E2.5 per half hour on line time.
• **Marco's**, *Via Varese 54. Open 10:00am to 2:00am every day.* Just down the street from Splashnet, Via Varese is turning into the Internet access point for travelers in Rome. A grungy bar type atmosphere with video games, pool tables and beverage service. Internet access costs E2 per half hour and E4 per hour.
• **Freedom Traveller**, *Via Gaeta 25, Tel. 06/478-23-862. E-mail: info@freedom-traveller.it. Web: www.freedom-traveller.it.* Also located nearby the other two places listed above, you get access for E2.5 for 30 minutes or less. Student discount for an hour E4.
• **The Netgate**, *Piazza Firenze 25, Tel 06/689-3445, Email roma.pantheon@thenetgate.it. Also at Borgo S. Spirito 17, Tel. 06/6813-4082, E-mail: roma.vaticano@thenetgate.it; Termini Station, Tel. 06/ 8740-6008, E-mail: roma.terminie@thenetgate.it.* Their website is *www.thenetgate.it.* Three locations in Rome for you to use the internet. Rates start at E2 per hour.

Language Study

If you want to travel in Italy and actively pursue learning the language at the same time there are many different schools all over the country. But the best way to do this would be to have everything arranged for you by organizations that specifically connect students with schools in Italy. Two of the best to contact, with quite similar names, are:
• **Language Studies Abroad**, *Tel. 800/424-5522*.
• **Language Study Abroad**, *Tel. 818/242-5263*.

Laundry Service

• **Uondo Blu**, *Principe Amadeo 70, Tel. 06/474-4647*. Coin operated laundry open seven days a week from 8:00am to 10:00pm. If you need clean clothes, this place is inexpensive and convenient to the train station. Wash E3. Dry E3.
• **Aqua & Sapone**, *Via Montebello 66, Tel. 06/488-3209*. Self-service wash and dry E3 each. Open every day from 8:00am to 10:00pm. Also located near the train station but on the other side.
• **Splash LavaService**, *Via Varese 33, Tel. 06/4938-2073*. Self-service laundry with internet access (see Splashnet description below) and satellite TV to keep you occupied while you wait for your laundry. Wash and dry costs E3 each. Open seven days a week from 8:00am to 10:00pm.

Papal Audiences

General audiences with the Pope are usually held once a week (Wednesday at 11:00am) in Vatican City. To participate in a general audience, get information through the **North American College** *(Via dell'Umita 30, Tel. 06/679-0658, Fax 06/679-1448)*, the American seminary in Rome. Catholics are requested to have a letter of introduction from their parish priest. Ticket pickup is the Tuesday before the Wednesday audience.

For attendance at a Papal audience women should dress modestly, with arms and head covered, and dark or subdued colors are requested. Men are asked to wear a tie and a jacket.

At noon every Sunday, the Pope addresses the crowds gathered beneath his window in St. Peter's square. During the latter part of the summer, because of the heat in Rome, and now more so for tradition, the Pope moves to his summer residence at **Castel Gandolpho** in the Alban Hills about sixteen miles southeast of Rome. Audiences are also regularly held there.

Pharmacies

Farmacia are open from 9:00am to 1:00pm and reopen from 3:30pm to 7:30pm. At nights and on Sundays and holidays, one pharmacy in each district remains open on a rotating schedule. For information, dial 192 then 1 through

5 depending on the zone (see phone book for zones) for the location of the pharmacy nearest you. Also a list of open pharmacies for holidays and Sundays is published in the Rome daily, *Il Messagero*.

Police
- **Pubblica Sicurezza**, *Tel. 06/4686* (for theft, lost and found, petty crimes)
- **City Police** (Vigili Urbani), *Tel. 06/67691* (for car towings)
- **Carabinieri**, *Tel. 112* (for emergencies, violent crimes, etc.)
- **Highway Police** (Polizia Stradale), *Tel. 06/557-7905* (for parking tickets, etc.)

Postal Services (Rome & Vatican)
You can buy stamps at local tobacconists (they are marked with a "T" outside) as well as post offices. Mailboxes are colored red, except for the international ones, which are blue. Post offices are open from 8:25am to 1:50pm on weekdays, and 8:25am to 11:50am Saturday. Some, like the one on Via Firenze, near the Economy bookstore are open until 5:00pm, Monday through Saturday. The two exceptions to this rule are: the **Main Post Office** (Piazza San Silvestro), which is open Monday through Friday from 9:00am to 6:00pm, and Saturday from 8:30am to 12:50pm; and the branch at **Stazione Termini** (*Via Terme Diocleziane 30*, near the McDonalds on the Piazza della Repubblica), which is open 8:30am-6:00pm Monday – Friday and Saturdays 8:30am – 2:00pm..

If you want to have your postcards mailed by the Vatican, with their official stamp, go to the **Vatican Post Office** (*Via di Porta Angelica 23*, close to Piaza Risorgimento) which is open 8:30am-6:00pm Monday – Friday and Saturdays 8:30am–11:50am.

Public Restrooms
These are scarcer than flying pigs, but many were established all over Italy recently. When in need, there are always McDonalds, which have sprouted up all over Rome and Italy after they bought out the Italian burger chain *Burghy*. If no McDonalds is evident, try a well-heeled restaurant or hotel. Ask for the *servizio* or *toilette*.

Supermarkets
You can usually find all the food you need at an *alimentari*, but if you want a wider selection, there is a supermarket, **GS Supermarket** (open 9:00am–7:00pm everyday except Sunday) in the tunnel system between the Piazza di Spagna and the Via Veneto which is reached through the Metro. From the Via Veneto simply follow the signs to Spagna. From the Piazza di Spagna follow the signs to Via Veneto and you will find it.

Support Groups
• **Alcoholic Anonymous**, *Tel. 06/474-2913*
• **Narcotics Anonymous**, *Tel. 06/860-4788*
• **Overeaters Anonymous**, *Tel. 06/884-5105*

Tour Companies
Some of the companies that offer you a variety of tourist services and tours are listed below. Most are open Monday through Friday 9:00am-5:30pm, Saturday 9:00am-12:30pm and closed on Sundays. But besides these three, there are a number of alternatives while in Rome.
• **American Express**, *Piazza di Spagna 38, Tel. 06/676-41. For lost travelers checks the toll free in Italy is 800/872-000. For lost/stolen cards 800/874-333*
• **Carrani Tours**, *Vie V.E. Orlando 95, Tel. 06/474-2501, Fax 06/4890-3564*
• **Thomas Cook Travel**, *Piazza Barberini 21A, Tel. 06/482-80-82. Toll free number in Italy 800/004488.*

Tourist Information & Maps
You can buy maps and guide books at most newsstands and bookstores. This may be necessary even though the tourist offices give away free maps for the subway, buses, as well as an extensive map of the streets of Rome. Besides the tourist kiosks (refer to *Seeing the Sights* section), below are some sources for tourist information:
• **American Express**, *Piazza di Spagna 38, Tel. 06/676-41*
• **Rome Provincial Tourist Board** (**EPT**), *Via Parigi 5, Tel. 06/488-3748*
• **EPT Termini**, *between tracks #2 and 3, Tel. 06/487-1270*
• **EPT Fiumicino**, *just outside customs, Tel. 06/601-1255*
• **Italian Government Travel Office** (ENIT), *Via Marghera 2, Tel. 06/49711*
• **Enjoy Rome**, *Via Marghera 2, Tel. 06/446-3379 or 444-1663*
• **Centro Turistico Studentesco e Giovanile**, *66 Via Nazionale, Tel. 06/467-91*

Most of the time, especially in high season, these places will run out of tourist material, and in grand Italian fashion, nothing gets done about it. So newsstands are your only recourse. Also, the maps given out at the tourist offices and kiosks may not be as extensive as is needed when in Rome, especially if you want to use the bus system. There are maps which you can buy at newsstands which not only list the bus routes but also have an index of streets which will help you locate places of interest in Rome. The cost for these maps is anywhere from E3.5-5. A bargain and a great keepsake of your trip to Rome.

Wanted in Rome

An excellent periodical that features classified ads about accommodations, jobs, and more. Also included are the latest performing arts activities in Rome. A great resource for tourists and ex-pats alike. Cost is E75 cents and you can find it at most English language bookstores. Office located at *Via dei Delfini 17, Tel. 06/679-0190, E-mail: wantedinrome@compuserve.com, Web: www.wantedinrome.com.*

Chapter 14

florence & tuscany

A visit to Italy is not complete without a trip to **Firenze** (**Florence**), which is one of the most awe-inspiring cities in all of Europe. The Renaissance reached its full heights of artistic expression here, and it was in Florence that countless master artists, writers, inventors, political theorists and artisans lived and learned their craft, then excelled at filling the world with the glow of their brilliance. Michelangelo and Leonardo da Vinci may be the best known outside of Italy, but I'll wager you've also heard of Dante, Petrarch, Machiavelli, Giotto, Raphael and many other learned and talented Florentines.

Strolling through the cobblestone streets of Florence is like being in an art history book come to life. The sights, smells, and sounds of this wonderful medieval city must be experienced first-hand to appreciate and understand the magical atmosphere. So read on, and I'll guide you through the amazingly lovely city of Florence!

Alive with History – Beautiful Firenze!

Florence started out simply, as the market square for the ancient Etruscan town of **Fiesole**, which is located on a hill about three miles (five kilometers) to the northeast. Farmers displayed their fruits and vegetables on the clearing along the **Arno**, and the Fiesole people came down to buy. About 187 BCE, the Romans built a road through the marketplace, and later a military garrison was established here.

As the Roman roads extended through central and northern Italy, Florence grew and prospered, and it became a trade center for goods brought down from the north. Because of its significance invaders sought its spoils; and in 401 CE a horde of Ostrogoths besieged the city; then in 542 the Goths made an unsuccessful attack. Soon after, the Lombard conquest swept over Florence, and the city became the capital of a Lombard dukedom. In time, the Holy Roman Empire led by Charlemagne drove the Lombards out and in 799 ordered new fortifications built. Charlemagne's death in 814 ended the Holy Roman Empire's hold on Florence, at which time it became an independent city-state.

With its new-found freedom, Florence expanded rapidly. The Florentines became energetic merchants and bankers, expert workmen, brave soldiers, and shrewd statesmen. By the 1100s their guilds were among the most powerful in Europe, and Florentine textiles were sold throughout the continent. Florentine bankers financed enterprises in many countries, and in 1252 the city coined its first gold pieces, called **florins**, which became the accepted currency for all of Europe.

Although Florence was largely self-governing, for a long time the city was the property of German princes. The last to hold it was Countess Matilda of Tuscany. At her death in 1115, the countess bequeathed Florence to the papacy. In the early 1200s, the papal power was supported by a political group called the **Guelfa**, while the claims of the German emperor were backed by another group, the **Ghibellines**. This conflict lasted almost a hundred years and was formally initiated in 1215 when the rival factions each tried to seize control of the city.

Aided by several popes, the Guelfa held power in the city until 1260 when their army was almost wiped out at a battle near Siena. The Ghibellines held the reins for six years, until in 1266, Charles of Anjou, the champion of Pope Clement IV, marched down from France and smashed the forces of the German emperor at the battle of Benevento – at which point the Guelfa exiles were able to return to Florence.

In 1293, the **Ordinances of Justice** were passed. These laws excluded from public office anyone who was a member of a Florentine guild. As a result many powerful people were barred from holding public positions, and the strength of the merchant-nobles was thus reduced for a time. Because of these laws, Florence remained a republic for about 150 years; but the control of the city, however, soon passed back into the hands of the wealthy.

The **Medici** family gradually took possession of Florence, installing their puppets throughout city government. Giovanni de' Medici was the first of this family to gain real wealth and influence. His son Cosimo was the real ruler of Florence for many years; it was he who brought exiled Greek scholars to the city. Under Cosimo's grandson **Lorenzo the Magnificent**, Florence ascended to its greatest heights as a cultural center.

An Incredible Statue, a Fabulous Inn!

If this is your first visit to la bella Italia, you must visit Florence. The small Renaissance streets, the countless art galleries, the friendly people, and the fine food all make this city a joy to visit. But not in high season. Florence in the summer is a zoo of tourists (not quite as bad as Venice, but close) all crammed together or queued for blocks to see the main sights. Florence definitely should be visited in the off-season, not only to save on your hotel bills (hotels drop their rates dramatically in the off-season) but also to make your entire stay more enjoyable and relaxing.

It is one thing to savor the excellence of Michelangelo's **David** virtually alone, and almost believe that you saw it move, but quite another to have to fight your way through a crowd just to get close enough to try and see that majestic statue. But no matter when you visit, if you're looking for some peace and tranquillity, try the unmatched **Torre Di Bellosguardo**, one of my favorite hotels anywhere.

A medieval castle perched prominently above the city, here you'll find some of the best views of Florence. It is a supremely romantic spot filled with gardens, olive trees where horses graze, an open lawn in front, and a pool with a bar all overlooking this magnificent city. But there are only 16 rooms here, so if you want to experience the best accommodations Florence has to offer you must plan far enough in advance.

After Lorenzo died in 1492, the city's excesses brought on a reform movement headed by **Girolamo Savonarola**, a Dominican friar. The Medici family was expelled in 1494 and Savonarola then ruled Florence himself until 1498, when a popular reaction to his rule erupted and he was put to death.

In 1512 *la familgia Medici* were restored to the city, and in 1537 it became part of the Grand Duchy of Tuscany. Upon the death of the last Medici in 1737, Tuscany passed to the Austrian Hapsburgs. In 1861 it was formally annexed to the newly formed Kingdom of Italy, of which Florence was the capital from 1865 to 1870.

In World War II, Florence was a battleground, as was the entire country. Italy entered the war on the German side in 1940, and soon after German troops occupied Florence. When the Allies advanced in 1944, the Germans declared Florence an open city, yet in retreating they destroyed all the bridges except the Ponte Vecchio, and they demolished many medieval dwellings as well. Later the Allied Military Government restored the less seriously damaged structures helping to maintain the old charm the city retains today.

In 1966, Florence's many masterpieces were lost when the Arno River overflowed its banks, rising as high as 20 feet

Rebirth of Art & Science in Florence

Florence, rather than Rome, was the cradle of the Italian **Renaissance**. This rebirth of classical knowledge soon gave way to new creativity in art and literature, and Florentines led the procession. **Dante's** magnificent poetry made the Tuscan dialect the official language of Italy. **Francesco Petrarch** composed his lovely sonnets here, and **Giovanni Boccaccio's** Decameron was penned here as well. **Niccolo Machiavelli**, another Florentine, set down his brilliant, cynical observations on politics based on the intrigue intrinsic to Florentine politics.

Giotto was the first of many immortal Florentine painters and sculptors. **Michelangelo** worked by day on the city's fortifications and by night on his paintings and statues. **Ghiberti** labored almost a lifetime on the doors for the Florentine Baptistery. Many other great artists studied or worked in Florence, among them **Leonardo da Vinci**, **Donatello**, and **Raphael**.

(6 meters) in some places. Many of the more important damaged works have since been restored, but thousands of irreplaceable treasures were lost to ruin brought by the mud and water.

Four Day Itinerary In & Around Florence

DAY ONE

Morning

To begin, let's walk to the **Accademia** and see Michelangelo's *David*. Make sure that you have made reservations already by going to *www.firenze.net* and booking specific entry times. Take in all the other works by the master which are located here.

Lunch

Walk back to the **Piazza San Lorenzo** where there is a daily market. Go to **Nerbone's** in the **Mercato Centrale** for lunch. Try one of their amazing *Panini* (boiled beef or pork) served on a *Panino* bread roll. They'll ask whether you want some juice (*sugo*) placed on the roll. Tell them *si* (yes); it makes it much tastier. Order a beverage and sit at one of the tables directly in front of the quaint little place.

After your meal, wander through the market. Check out all the different cuts of meat the Italians use in their recipes. Upstairs is the vegetable and fruit market. A good place to buy some healthy snacks for later.

Afternoon
After you're done shopping head to the nearby **Piazza Duomo**. Admire the bronze doors on the belfry, the simplicity of the baptistery, and the expanse of the church. Take the time to go all the way up top of the dome.

If needed, take a little siesta. If it's not needed head to the **Piazza della Signoria** and admire the statues in the Loggia. Also go into the **Palazzo della Signoria** and admire the staircase that leads to their museum. This was the residence of the Medici until the Palazzo Pitti was made available. If you're interested go upstairs and pay the fee to see the inside.

Just outside of the Piazza dell Signoria is the **Uffizzi Gallery**, which you'll be going to tomorrow. Remember to have made your reservations well in advance using *www.firenze.net.*

Now make your way to the **Ponte Vecchio** over the river **Arno**. Shop for jewelry in the many little stores if you want, but make sure you stop in the middle of the bridge and take each other's photo with the river as a background. Follow the bridge over to the other side of the Arno.

From here we're going to the **Pitti Palace** and the **Boboli Gardens**. Each museum has beautiful artwork in the building, and the gardens offer peace and tranquillity are filled with many wonderful statues. If you bought some snacks at the **Mercato Centrale** you may want to take the time to have a brief picnic in the gardens. When you leave, check out the store **Firenze Papier Mache** in the piazza across from the palace.

Evening
Return to your room to freshen up and get ready for dinner. Tonight we're going to a wonderful local place called **La Bussola**, *Via Porta Rossa 58, Tel. 055/293-376.* You can either sit at the counter and have a simple meal of pizza or sit in the back and soak up all the ambiance and romance of Florence. Try their *spaghetti alla Bolognese* (with a meat and tomato sauce) or their *tortellini alla panna* (cheese or meat stuffed tortellini in a cream sauce).

After dinner wander over to the Piazza Santa Maria Novella and stop at the **Fiddler's Elbow** for a pint. This place has an authentic Irish Pub atmosphere, great Italian people and fun times. If dancing is your desire, try the **Space Electronic** nearby at *Via Palazzuolo 37, Tel. 055/292-082.*

DAY TWO
Morning
Get to the **Uffizzi Gallery** a half an hour before your reservations indicate you should and pick up your tickets . You'll probably spend all morning wandering around this huge museum.

Lunch

For lunch try a quaint basement restaurant between the **Duomo** and the train station and near Piazza Santa Maria Novella, **Buca Lapi,** *Via del Trebbio 1, Tel. 055/213-768.* There are old travel posters plastered all over the walls and ceiling, and the tables surround the cooking area so you can view quite a display while you wait for your food. Depending on the season, it may be closed for lunch. Try their *cinghiale con patate fritte* (roasted wild boar with fried potatoes) or their *pollo al cacciatore con spinacio* (chicken 'hunter style' which is made with tomatoes, spices and brandy and comes with spinach)

Afternoon

Remember the church in the piazza where the **Fiddler's Elbow** was last night? We're going there now (**Chiesa di Santa Maria Novella**) to check out the overall ambiance and to admire the frescoes painted by Michelangelo. While we're in this area of town, check out the store **Il Tricolore,** *Via della Scala 25,* just off the piazza. This is the official outlet for the police and military in Florence where you can buy a variety of items like pins, hats, shirts, badges, that you can take home as gifts. Some items they won't sell to you, like guns, knives, and uniforms.

Next we're walking slightly across town to get to the place where Michelangelo is buried, **Chiesa di Santa Croce**. Inside the church you will also find many other graves of prominent Florentines including Dante Aligheri. There is a leather shop attached to the church where you can find some of the best hand-made leather goods anywhere. It is also a treat to watch them work the leather. A great place to visit and/or shop.

Late Afternoon

From here, we're going up to the **Piazzale Michelangelo** to watch the sun set. This is really a hike. If you do not want to walk, the cab ride will be quite dear, but the view is worth it. Remember to take your camera and high speed film to catch all the light possible. You'll get some of the best shots of Florence from up here. If you want to splurge on a fantastic meal, try **La Loggia,** *Piazzale Michelangelo 1,* once you get up here. It's very expensive but well worth it. Or, on the way back down the hill into town, stop at **Il Rifrullo,** *Via San Niccolo 55, 055/213-631,* to get a pint of beer or glass of wine. At night this is an isolated and relaxing place to come and savor the Florentine evenings.

From here take the long walk across the river and to the train station to establish your itinerary for tomorrow's adventure. You may have to wait a little while in the information office, but it's worth it so you won't have to do it in the morning.

Evening
For dinner tonight we're going to the **Tredici Gobbi** (which means "13 hunchbacks") located on Via Porcellana. Situated down a small side street near the Arno, here you can enjoy a combination of Italian and Hungarian cuisine. For an after-diner drink wander over to the nearby **Excelsior Hotel** and go up to their roof deck. Enjoy a *sambuca con tre mosce*, literally translated it means "sambuca (a liquorice drink) with three flies," but in actuality the flies are coffee beans. When you bite into the beans as you sip the Sambuca the combination of tastes is phenomenal. Here you have a view over all of Florence as it lines the Arno.

DAY THREE
Since you've now seen virtually everything that a traveler is supposed to see in Florence, let's take a day trip outside of the city to **Pisa** and **Lucca**. We'll first go to Pisa to admire the leaning tower, and its cute little market near the Arno. Next we'll go to Lucca to walk around the romantic walls and see a virtually perfectly preserved old medieval town.

Pisa
Once you arrive in Pisa, stop in the tourist office just outside the station to the left and pick up a map of the city. Then if you're tired take the No. l bus directly to the **Piazza dei Miracoli** which has the church, baptistery and leaning tower. Admire them all and take plenty of pictures. If you decide to walk (it only takes about 15 minutes to get to the Piazza dei Miracoli) you must pass by the colorful market of **Piazza Vettovaglie** near the river and just off of the **Borgo Stretto**, the street with the famous covered sidewalk. It's well worth the visit.
For lunch we'll stop at the **Il Cavallino**, *Via San Lorenzo 66, Tel. 0577/ 432-290*. It's off the beaten tourist path and that's one reason why the food is so great. Try the Roman specialty, *penne all' arrabiata* ('literally translated it means 'angry pasta' and is a tomato-based sauce with garlic, hot peppers, and parsley). Or sample the *sogliola alla griglia* (grilled sole) or the *petto di pollo alla griglia* (grilled chicken breast).

Lucca
Now it's back to the train station and onto Lucca. Once you arrive simply walk out of the station towards the old walls of the city. Follow the path leading to the walls where you will find an entrance into the walls themselves. Follow the stairs inside up to the top. Now you're on the old battlements and ramparts. Walk around them to your left about 400 meters until you get to the **Piazza Verdi/Vecchia Porto San Donato** where the tourist office is located. You'll know you're there by the size of the piazza inside the walls and

the fact that this is where tour buses park. Descend and pick up a map of the city from the tourist office, you'll need it.

Now it's time to go to the **Torre del Guinigio**. This tower has trees and bushes growing on its top. Go up here to get great views of the city and the surrounding area. Use the map to explore the old Roman amphitheater, Puccini's museum, the cathedral, and more. And of course, take some more walks along the romantic tree-lined battlements.

For dinner, we'll be going to **Da Leo Fratelli Buralli**, *Via Tegrini, Tel. 0583/492-236*. This is the best, most authentic restaurant in Lucca. It caters to the locals, the food is stupendous and the atmosphere festive. Try the *fettucine all rucola e gamberi* (pasta with a cheese and shrimp sauce), the *pollo arrosto con patate* (exquisite roasted chicken and potatoes flavored with rosemary and olive oil), or the *pollo fritto e zucchini* (chicken and zucchini fried in olive oil). If you miss the last train back to Florence, which leaves at 9:00pm, get a room at the **Piccolo Hotel Puccini**, *Via di Poggio 9, Tel. 0583/55-421*.

DAY FOUR
Siena

Located about an hour and a half from Florence, Siena is a perfect day trip. Here you have the famous **Campo**, a tower that rises above the city for great photos, quaint medieval streets and plenty of ambiance to spare. The cathedral seems out of place since it is so large in a relatively small square. If the Florentines hadn't conquered the city when they did, the locals would have made the tower almost twice as large. Did you know that in its hey-day Siena was larger than either London or Paris?

Once you arrive at the station you can easily walk up the hill, then descend into the old town. Or take bus number 1 or 8 to get dropped off near the tourist office (ask at the information desk inside which bus takes you to the tourist office; I was told they may be changing).

Despite its past prominence, you can wander around Siena quite easily. In your walking make sure you stop in **Pizzigheria** at *95 Via della Citta* just off the Campo. Here you'll find the most savory aromas emanating from their meats and cheeses hanging haphazardly all over the store. A perfect place to get a snack. You'll recognize the store from afar by the stuffed boar's head hanging outside with sunglasses on.

If you want a sit-down meal on the quaint Campo with actual waiters serving you, try the **Spada Forte**. Their specialty is all types of pizza and the succulent *Cinghiale alle Senese* (wild boar).

If You Miss These Places, You Haven't Been to Florence

After spending all your time and money to come to this Renaissance paradise, there are a few sights that if you don't see you can't really say you've been to Florence. The first of which, the **Duomo** with its campanile and baptistery, is hard to miss. The next, the **Ponte Vecchio**, is a gem of medieval and Renaissance architecture and is filled with gold and jewelry shops. And if you miss Michelangelo's **David** in the Accademia you shouldn't show your face back in your home town. That work of art is as close to sculpted perfection as any artist will ever achieve.

Last but not least is the art collection in the **Uffizzi Gallery**. To actually do this museum justice you may need to spend close to one day wandering through its many rooms. And don't forget to shop at the **San Lorenzo Market** or browse through the local **Mercato Centrale**.

There are countless other wonderful sights to see and places to go in Florence. Walking the streets is like walking through a fairy tale. But if you haven't seen the items above, you haven't been to Florence.

Arrivals & Departures

By Bus

There are many different bus companies in Italy, each serving a different set of cities and sometimes the same ones. Buses should be used only if the train does not go to your destination since traffic is becoming more and more of a problem in Italy.

The most convenient bus company in Florence is located directly next to the train station in **Piazza Adua**, called **Autolinee Lazzi**, *Tel. 055/215-154*. They have over 50 arrivals and departures a day to and from a variety of different locations like Pisa, Lucca, Prato, and Pistoia. Two other bus companies are: **Autolinee Sita**, *Tel. 055/214721 or 284661*, and **Autolinee CAP**, *Tel. 055/218603*.

By Car

If arriving in Florence from the south, for speed you will be on the **A1** **(E35)**. If you were looking for a more scenic adventure, you would be on the **Via Cassia** which you can take all the way from Rome. If arriving from the north in a hurry, you would also take the **A1 (E35)**, but if in no rush you would probably take the **SS 65**.

Sample trip lengths on the main roads:
• **Rome**: 3 1/2 hours

• **Venice**: 4 hours
• **Bologna**: 1 1/2 hours

If you need to rent a car while in Florence, please refer to the *Getting Around Town* section of this chapter, below.

By Train

The station, **Stazione Santa Maria Novella**, is located near the center of town and is easily accessible on foot to and from most hotels. The **tourist information office** in the station, *Tel. 055/278-785*, is open daily from 7:00am to 10:00pm and is your first stop if you don't have a reservation at a hotel. The **railway office**, at the opposite end of the station from the tourist information office, is where you plan your train trip from Florence. To get served you need to take a number and wait your turn, a concept that is still foreign to many Italians.

The wait can be quite long, but it is entertaining watching Italians become completely confused about having to take a number, wait in a queue, and actually do something in an organized fashion. First your average Italian will attempt to assert his Latin ego to an information officer, whether they are serving someone else or not, get rebuffed, attempt to do it again with another information officer, get rebuffed again, finally look at the machine spitting out numbers and the directions associated with it, stare as would a deer trapped in an oncoming car's headlights, turn and glare at the long line formed since they first attempted their folly, then ultimately strut out of the office without getting the information they need. I've seen it happen so many times!

There are **taxis** located just outside the entrance near the tourist information office as well as **buses** that can take you all over the city.

Sample trip lengths and costs for direct *(diretto)* trains:
• **Rome**: 2 1/2 hours, E40
• **Venice**: 3 1/2 hours, E15
• **Bologna**: 1 hour, E10.

Getting Around Town

By Bus

There is no need to go by bus in Florence unless you're going up to Fiesole. But if you need to, first get information from the booth at the **Piazza della Stazione** across the piazza from the station itself. Here they can give you all the information you need to get anywhere you want to go. A ticket costs Euro 75 cents and is reusable within an hour.

At all bus stops, called **fermata**, there are signs that list all the buses that stop there. These signs also give the streets that the buses will follow along its route so you can check your map to see if this is the bus for you. Also, on the side of the bus are listed highlights of the route for your convenience.

Nighttime routes (since many buses stop a midnight) are indicated by black spaces on newer signs, and are placed at the bottom of the older signs. In conjunction, the times listed on the signs indicate when the bus will pass the *fermata* during the night so you can plan accordingly.

Riding the bus during rush is very crowded, so try to avoid the rush hours of 8:00am to 9:00am, 12:30pm to 1:30pm, 3:30 to 4:30pm, and 7:30pm to 8:30pm. They have an added rush hour in the middle of the day because of their siesta time in the afternoon.

The information number for the local bus company, **ATAF - Autobus Urbani** , is *Tel. 055/5650-222.*

By Car

Renting a car is relatively simple, as things go in Italy, but it is somewhat expensive. You can rent a car from a variety of agencies all over Florence. All prices will vary by agency so please call them for an up-to-date quote.

• **Avis**, *Borgo Ognissanti 128r, Tel 055/21-36-29 or 239-8826*
• **Avis**, *Lungarno Torrigiani 32/3, Tel 055/234-66-68 or 234-66-69*
• **Budget**, *Borgo Ognissanti 134r, Tel. 055/29-30-21 or 28-71-61*
• **Euro Dollar**, *Via il Prato 80r, Tel 055/238-24-80, Fax 055/238-24-79*
• **Hertz**, *Via Maso Finiguerra 33, Tel. 055/239-8205, Fax 055/230-2011*
• **Maggiore**, *Via Maso Finiguerra 11r, Tel. 055/21-02-38*

Most companies require a deposit that amounts to the cost of the rental, as well as a 19% VAT added to the final cost, which can be reimbursed once you're home (see Chapter 7, *Basic Information*). A basic rental of a Fiat Panda costs E80 per day, but the biggest expense is gasoline. In Italy it costs more than twice as much per gallon as it does in the States. If you're adventurous enough to think of renting a car, remember that the rates become more advantageous if you rent for more than a week.

By Moped

Since Florence is so small, the areas in Tuscany I'm recommending are quite close together, and the drivers are not quite as crazy as Romans, a moped (50cc) or **vespa** (125cc) is one of the best ways to get around and see the countryside. But this isn't a simple ride in the park. Only if you feel extremely confident about your motorcycle driving abilities should you even contemplate renting a moped.

Rentals for a moped (50cc) are about E30 per day, and for a 125cc (which you'll need to transport two people) about E40 per day. From some companies you can rent even bigger bikes, but I would strongly advise against it. You can also rent the cycles for an hour or any multiples thereof.

• **Firenze Motor**, *Via Guelfa 85r. Tel 055/280-500, Fax 05/211-748. Located in the Centro section to the right of the station and north of the Duomo.*

• **Noleggio dell Fortezza** *(two locations),Corner of Via Strozzi and Via del Pratello, Open 9:00am to 8:00pm, the 15th of March to 31st of October; and Via Faenza 107-109r. Tel. 055/283-448.* **Scooter prices**: *1 hour E5/ half day E10/1 day E20.* **Bicycle prices**: *1 hour E1.5/half day E5/1 day E8.*
• **Motorent**, *Via San Zanobi 9, Tel. 055/490-113, in the Centro area.*
• **Sabra**, *Via Artisti 8, Tel. 055/576-256, in the Oltrarno area.*
• **Free Motor**, *Via Santa Monaca 6-8, Tel. 055/293-102, in the Oltrarno area.*

By Bicycle

Some of the moped rental places listed above also rent bicycles, but by far the best bicycle rental service and definitely the most professional is:
• **Florence By Bike**, *Via San Zanobi 120/122, Tel./Fax 055/488-992; Open from 9:00am-7:30pm every day; Email: ecologica@dada.it; Website: www.florencebybike.it. Credit cards accepted.* Not only do they offer bicycles for rent (1 hour E2; 5 hours E6; Day E10; Weekend E20) at great prices, but they also offer guided city tours as well as countryside tours. Located near Piazza Santa Maria Novella, this is the place to come for good quality bike rentals and fun and informative bike tours.

By Taxi

Florence is a city made for walking, but if you get tired, taxis are good but expensive way to get around. They are everywhere, except on the streets designated for foot traffic so flagging one down is not a problem. But since they are so expensive I wouldn't rely on them as your main form of transportation. Also have a map handy when a cabby is taking you some-where. Since they are on a meter, they sometimes decide to take you on a little longer journey than necessary.

The going rate as of publication was E2.5 for the first 2/3 of a kilometer or the first minute (which usually comes first during the rush hours), then its Euro 50 cents every 1/3 of a kilometer or minute. At night you'll also pay a surcharge of E1.5, and Sundays you'll pay Euro 50 cents extra. If you bring bags aboard, say for example after you've been shopping, you'll be charged Euro 50 cents extra for each bag.

There are strategically placed cab stands all over the city. But if you cannot locate one, here are some radio taxi numbers:
• **Radio Taxi**, *Tel. 055/4242 or 4798 or 4390*
• **Taxi Merci**, *Tel. 055/296230 or 210321 or 371334*
• **Moto Taxi**, *Tel. 055/4386 or 355741 or 359767*

Florence Website
You can book museum tickets, find special events, locate quaint little stores, book hotels, and help plan all aspects of your trip with *www.firenze.net.*

Where To Stay

Centro Storico

The **Centro Storico** is the very heart of Florence. Anywhere you stay, shop, eat, or drink will be relatively expensive, since this is the prime tourist area of Florence. In this area you have the **Duomo** dominated by Brunelleschi's huge dome; the **Baptistery** next door with its beautiful bronze doors; the **Piazza della Signoria** with its copy of Michelangelo's *David,* and under the cobblestones are Bronze age relics proving that Florence is centuries older than anyone ever thought.

There is also the unforgettable collection of art in the **Uffizzi Gallery**; the **Ponte Vecchio**, built in 1345 and once home to butchers, blacksmiths, greengrocers, tanners and leather workers but now filled with gold shops; the **Piazza della Repubblica** that once was the site of a Roman Forum; the **Jewish ghetto**, which was until the end of the 19th century an open air market; the **Mercato Nuovo** or Straw Market with its many fine examples of Tuscan craftsmanship; and the Fifth Avenue of Florence, the **Via Tornabuoni**, where it seems expensive just to window shop.

1. ALDINI, *Via Calzaiuoli 13, Tel 055/214-752, Fax 055/216-410. Web: www.venere.com/it/firenze/aldini/. Mastercard and Visa accepted. 15 rooms all with private bath, telephone, and air conditioning. Single E60-75; Double E105-120. Breakfast Included.* **

This centrally located overpriced two star charges what it does because some of the rooms have views of the Duomo. There are no TVs in the rooms and truly limited ambiance with few amenities. What used to be a bargain is now just trying to suck tourists dry. Avoid at all cost despite the location. If they add more amenities or drop their price back down to a reasonable level I'll recommend this place again. Until then read on.

2. BEACCI-TORNABUONI, *Via Tornabuoni 3, Tel. 055/212-645, Fax 055/283-594. E-mail: info@bthotel.it. Web: www.bthotel.it/. All credit cards accepted. 28 rooms all with private bath. Single E125-190; Double E190-230. Extra bed E30. Buffet breakfast included.* ***

Located on the top three floors of a 14th century palazzo on the world famous and elegant shopping street, Via Tornabuoni. There is a wonderful rooftop garden terrace that will make you fall in love with Florence every evening you spend up there. I preferred the rooms overlooking the garden for the quiet, but the ones on the street make for good people watching. A much better deal with infinitely better atmosphere than La Residenza which is just down the street. This place is coordinated like an old castle, with nooks and crannies everywhere, and plenty of common space besides the terrace to sit and write your postcards home. You'll be surrounded by antiques and will feel as if you've stepped into an Agatha Christie novel.

The breakfast is an abundant buffet which can be served to you in your room at no extra charge. The rooms are all furnished differently but with the finest taste and character. All have double beds. An excellent place to stay.

3. BERNINI PALACE, *P.za di San Firenze 29, Tel. 055/288-621. Fax 055/ 268-272. E-mail: info@firenzealbergo.it. Web: www.firenzealbergho.com. All credit cards accepted. 86 rooms. Single E130-175; Double E215-250. Breakfast included. Parking E25. *****

Centrally located just behind the Palazzo Vecchio, the Bernini is an elegant and refined hotel. The breakfast room is once where the Italian Parliament met when Florence was the capital of the country. An auspicious location for an equally impressive buffet. The rooms are spacious, the windows are sound-proof, and the hotel come complete with all necessary four star amenities. The bathrooms are well appointed and also have phones. A wonderful place to stay in Florence. Professional, high end, attentive service.

4. BRUNELLESCHI, *P.za Sant'Elisabetta 3, Tel. 055/290-311. Fax 055/ 219-653. E-mail: info@hotelbrunelleschi.it. Web: www.hotelbrunelleschi.it. All credit cards accepted. 96 rooms. Single E215; Double E290. Breakfast included. Parking E25. *****

Filled with an antique ambiance, accentuated by the 6th century Byzantine tower and the 12th century medieval church which have been absorbed into the hotel, this place is characterized by a rustic elegance and Tuscan refinement. The furnishings are a mixture of modern and antique, the structure is bathed in history accentuated by a small museum with a few Roman artifacts. The rooms are large and filled with every imaginable comfort, as are the bathrooms with their double sinks, courtesy toiletry kit and hairdryers. The breakfast buffet is abundant. From the terrace you have a wonderful view of the Duomo. Located in a tiny piazza in the heart of Florence, near all the sights, and in the middle of the best shopping in the city, this four star is a great choice.

5. CALZAIUOLI, *Via Calzaiuoli 6, Tel 055/212-456, Fax 055/268-310. Web: www.venere.com/it/firenze/calzaiuoli/. All credit cards accepted. 45 rooms all with private bath, TV, Telephone, mini-bar, and air conditioning. Breakfast included. Double E120-215. Extra bed E35. ****

Located in a recently renovated old palazzo and perfectly situated in the quiet pedestrian zone between the Duomo and Palazzo Vecchio. Some rooms have great views of the Duomo and with that view, its location, and all the amenities it offers this is a good place to stay. The rooms are spacious enough,

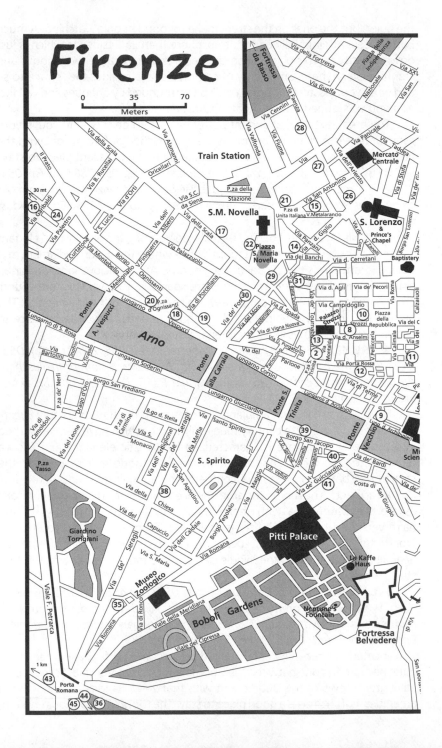

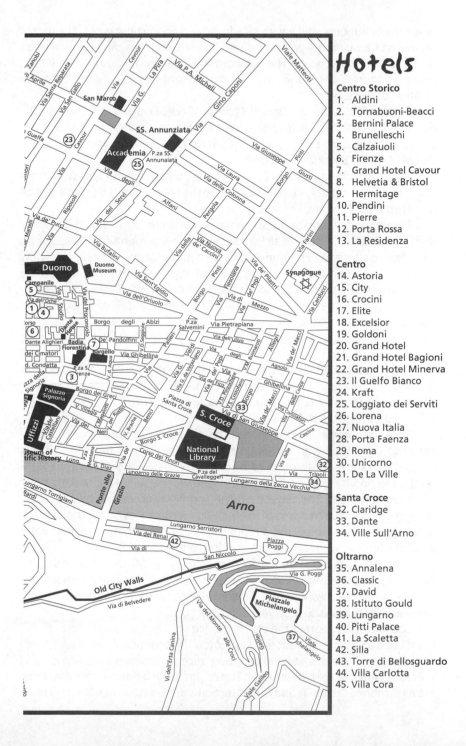

Hotels

Centro Storico
1. Aldini
2. Tornabuoni-Beacci
3. Bernini Palace
4. Brunelleschi
5. Calzaiuoli
6. Firenze
7. Grand Hotel Cavour
8. Helvetia & Bristol
9. Hermitage
10. Pendini
11. Pierre
12. Porta Rossa
13. La Residenza

Centro
14. Astoria
15. City
16. Crocini
17. Elite
18. Excelsior
19. Goldoni
20. Grand Hotel
21. Grand Hotel Bagioni
22. Grand Hotel Minerva
23. Il Guelfo Bianco
24. Kraft
25. Loggiato dei Serviti
26. Lorena
27. Nuova Italia
28. Porta Faenza
29. Roma
30. Unicorno
31. De La Ville

Santa Croce
32. Claridge
33. Dante
34. Ville Sull'Arno

Oltrarno
35. Annalena
36. Classic
37. David
38. Istituto Gould
39. Lungarno
40. Pitti Palace
41. La Scaletta
42. Silla
43. Torre di Bellosguardo
44. Villa Carlotta
45. Villa Cora

as are the bathrooms, and have a nice floral and ribbon print motif. The rooms on the Via Calzaiuoli are perfect for people watching, but can be a little noisy on the weekend evenings. The hallways are small, so if you're there with a group of tourists getting in and out can be arduous. You can't beat the location or the service.

6. FIRENZE, *Piazza dei Donati 4 (off of Via del Corso), Tel. 055/268-301, Fax 055/212-370. No credit cards accepted. 60 rooms, 35 with private bath. Single without bath E27-33; Single E33-38; Double without bath E42-53; Double E47-63. Breakfast included. ***

This is two different hotels. One is new, the other's left in a time warp from the 1950s. My recommendation is based on the new section, so call in advance to get your reservations.

Even though this place doesn't have air conditioning, it should be higher than a one star. The lobby is all three star, as are the rooms in the new wing with their phones and TVs. Room 503 caught my fancy since it has a great view of the Duomo from the bed: when you wake up in the morning there's the most romantically picturesque scene right in front of you. Besides the beauty and comfort of the new wing, the lobby and breakfast area is of a much higher standard than any other one star I've been in. It's beautiful and quite inexpensive. They speak English, so make sure you tell them that you want to stay in the new wing.

7. GRAND HOTEL CAVOUR, *Via del Proconsolo 3, Tel. 055/282-461. Fax 055/218-955. E-mail: info@hotelcavour.com. Web: www.hotelcavour.com. American Express and Visa accepted. 89 rooms. Single E100-115; Double E150-175. Breakfast included. Parking E20. ****

Near the Bargello and the Uffizzi, this old hotel has traditional and regal common areas filled with authentic antiques. The rooms are large and very comfortable and the bathrooms come with all necessary amenities. The rooms on the top floor are the best because of the wonderful views. Make a point of requesting them. The terrace on the top floor, accessible by all guests, though less than quaint in and of itself, has panoramic views over the city. The hotel restaurant, Beatrice, has a refined and elegant atmosphere and serves exquisite food. A wonderful three star in a prime location.

8. HELVETIA & BRISTOL, *Via dei Pescioni 2, Tel. 055/287-814. Fax 055/288-353. E-mail: ppanelli@charminghotels.it. Web: www.holidaycityeurope.com/ helvetia-bristol-florence/index.htm. American Express and Visa accepted. 52 rooms. Single E175; Double 225. Breakfast E20. Parking E23. *****

Located in the heart of the centro storico right by the Palazzo Strozzi, this is a refined and super elegant five star hotel. The common areas are anything but common, the bar is situated in a magnificent garden in the summer, and the restaurant is of the highest level. The rooms, each different from the other, are all furnished tastefully and the bathrooms are awash in marble. This hotel is stupendous, the staff is superb and the services offered sublime, including professional babysitting. A top of the line hotel in Florence.

9. HERMITAGE, *Vicolo Marzio 1 (Piazza del Pesce), Tel. 055/287-216, Fax 055/212-208. E-mail: florence@hermitagehotel.com. Web: www.hermitagehotel.com/. Mastercard and Visa accepted. 16 rooms all with private bath and jacuzzi. All rooms E240. Breakfast included.* ***

Only steps from the Ponte Vecchio but located above the tourist noise, this wonderful little hotel is on the top three floors of an office building and is reached by a private elevator. It has the most beautiful roof terrace, complete with greenery and flowers and a great view of the rooftops of Florence, as well as the Arno and the Ponte Vecchio. They serve breakfast up there in good weather and it is a great place to relax in the evenings.

The rooms are not that large but the ambiance and the location make up for it, as does the spacious terrace and common areas. The staff speaks a variety of languages. For a three star the place is great. Recently updated with jacuzzi style baths in every room so you can luxuriate here at the end of the day. A great hotel in a great location.

10. PENDINI, *Via Strozzi 2, Tel. 055/211-170, Fax 055/-281-807. Email -pendini@dada.it. Web: www.tiac.net/users/pendini/hotel.html. All credit cards accepted. 42 rooms all with private bath. Only 25 with air conditioning. Single E80-110; Double E110-150. Breakfast included. Extra bed costs E30.* ***

Ideally situated in the heart of Florence by the Piazza della Repubblica in a quaint old palazzo. The breakfast room is located in an archway between two buildings. They have twelve rooms that overlook the piazza and all are well appointed and quite large, perfect for family stays. Most bedrooms have brass or wooden beds, pretty floral wallpaper, and soft pastel carpeting. The furnishings are all classic antiques and exceedingly comfortable. The staff is more than accommodating, and they speak perfect English. An ideal central location for your stay in Florence. There are special rates for families.

11. PIERRE, *Viale de' Lamberti 5, Tel. 055/216-218, Fax 055/239-6573. Web: www.venere.com/it/firenze/pierre. All credit cards accepted. 39 rooms. Single E175; Double E235. Breakfast included. Parking E22.* ****

The courtesy, hospitality and professionalism of the staff helps to make a stay here wonderful. The entry hall is adjacent to a spacious bar where many guests congregate in the evenings before and after dinner. The rooms, all rather large by Italian standards, have fine furnishings and colorful carpets to complement the various amenities of this excellent four star hotel. It's located right by the Piazza della Signoria, deep in the heart of Florence's best shopping district. The continental breakfast comes complete with local Tuscan cheeses and salamis and an assortment of breakfast cereal. A good choice for a relaxing stay in Florence.

The Best Hotels in Florence

These are my favorite places to stay in Florence:

One Star

6. FIRENZE, *Piazza dei Donati 4 (off of Via del Corso), Tel. 055/268-301, Fax 055/212-370.*

38. ISTITUTO GOULD, *Via dei Serragli 49, Tel. 055/212-576, Fax 055/280-274.*

Two Star

16. CROCINI, *Corso Italia 28, Tel. 055/212-905, Fax 055/239-8345. E-mail: hotel.crocini@firenze.net. Web: www.hotelcrocini.com.*

41. LA SCALETTA, *Via Guicciardini 13, Tel. 055/283-028, Fax 055/289-562. E-mail: lascaletta@italyhotel.com. Web: www.venere.it/firenze lascaletta.*

Three Star

9. HERMITAGE, *Vicolo Marzio 1 (Piazza del Pesce), Tel. 055/287-216, Fax 055/212-208. E-mail: florence@hermitagehotel.com. Web: www.hermitagehotel.com/.*

36. CLASSIC, *Viale Machiavelli 25, Tel. 055/229-3512, Fax 055/229-353.*

25. LOGGIATO DEI SERVITI, *Piazza SS. Annunziata 3, Tel. 055/289-593/4, Fax 055/289-595. E-mail: info@loggiatodeiservitihotel.it. Web: www.loggiatodeiservitihotel.it/.*

Four Star

43. TORRE DI BELLOSGUARDO, *Via Roti Michelozzi 2, Tel. 055/229-8145, Fax 055/229-008. E-mail: torredibellosguardo@dada.it. Web: www.torrebellosguardo.com/.*

21. GRAND HOTEL BAGLIONI, *P.za dell'Unita Italiana 6, Tel. 055/23-580, Fax 055/235-8895. E-mail: hotel.baglioni@firenzealbergo.it. Web: www.hotelbaglioni.it.*

Five Star

20. GRAND HOTEL, *Piazza Ognissanti 1, Tel. 055/288-781, Fax 055/217-400. Toll free number in America 1-800-221-2340.*

45. VILLA CORA, *Viale Machiavelli 18-20, Tel. 055/229-8451, Fax 055/229-086. Web: www.villacora.com.*

12. PORTA ROSSA, *Via Porta Rossa 19, Tel. 055/287-551, Fax 055/282-179. American Express, Diners Club, Mastercard and Visa accepted. 80 rooms all with private bath. Single E67-85; Double E100-195. ****

Don't even think of staying here. Yes it's quaint, yes the rooms are large, yes the prices are relatively inexpensive, but the place is rather run-down and the staff is so surly and not helpful that it makes even a one night stay unbearable.

If your tour group has booked you here, make the best of it. The rooms are comfortably appointed with Liberty style antiques, and you are in the middle of everything in Florence, so the stay won't be all bad. But if you have a choice, avoid this hotel like the plague.

13. LA RESIDENZA, *Via de' Tournabuoni 8, Tel. 055/218-684, Fax 055/284-197. E-mail: la.residenza@italyhotel.com. Web: www.venere.com/it/firenze/residenza/. All credit cards accepted. 24 rooms. 20 with bath. Single without bath E55-80; Single E85-125; Double without E85-120; Double E140-200. Breakfast included. Parking E15. ****

A small but accommodating hotel in a central location with a clientele that is very international, many who come to have access to the world famous shopping street on which the hotel is located. The roof garden is a great place to relax in the evenings. The bar and restaurant are also located in the roof, and it is also where breakfast is served in the mornings. The rooms, many of which have some grand terraces, are simple yet comfortable, but the bathrooms are quite small. Not the best place to stay in Florence, but as it is included here, it is better than most. I can think of nothing negative, it's just that little seems to stand out about the hotel.

Centro

This section of town is north of the Duomo and west of the Via Tornabuoni, and is home to many reasonably priced hotels, restaurants, and stores. Here you'll find the **Mercato of San Lorenzo**, a huge daily outdoor clothing market, and the **Mercato Generale**, Florence's main food market where you can find everything from swordfish to buffalo-milk mozzarella.

Also located in the Centro is the train station from which you'll be embarking on the terrific excursions I've planned for you to Fiesole, Pisa, Siena, and Lucca.

14. ASTORIA, *Via del Giglio 9, Tel. 055/239-8095, Fax 055/214-632. E-mail: reception@astoria.boscolo.com. Web: www.boscolohotels.com/astoria. All credit cards accepted. 103 rooms. Single E250; Double E315. Breakfast E15. Parking E20. *****

Within walking distance of the train station, down a quaint side street, this is an elegant hotel. The communal area – bar, piano salon, and the in-house restaurant, Palazzo Gaddi - are all pleasantly refined. In the summer the hotel restaurant's garden is a wonderful place for a meal. The hotel encompasses a number of different buildings, including the 16th century structure after which the restaurant is named and where the conference facilities are located. The rooms are all soundproofed against Florence's buzzing traffic and come complete with all necessary four star amenities; and the bathrooms are more than adequate. A well situated four star,which will make your stay in Firenze a pleasant one.

15. CITY, *Via Sant'Antonino 18, Tel. 055/211-543, Fax 055/295-451. E-mail: info@hotelcityflorence.com. Web: www.hotelcityflorence.com. All credit cards accepted. 18 rooms. Single E105-E145; Double E140-180. Breakfast included. Parking E15.* ***

Located within walking distance of the train station and right by the superb San Lorenzo Market, this is a wonderful three star deep in the heart of Florence. In the hands of expert and professional service you will find your stay here more than pleasant. Filled with spacious rooms, soundproofed from Florence's city noise, each filled with wonderful furnishings and well equipped bathrooms. The common areas are nicely decorated in cathedral-like vaulted rooms. Also available is a dry cleaning service and scooter rental. This is a wonderfully intimate three-star. More of a bed and breakfast than a hotel, since there are only 18 rooms.

16. CROCINI, *Corso Italia 28, Tel. 055/212-905, Fax 055/239-8345. E-mail: hotel.crocini@firenze.net. Web: www.hotelcrocini.com. Closed December 18-26. All credit cards accepted. 1 suite, 20 rooms (17 with private bath, 2 with shared bath, 1 with private bath outside of room). Single E90; Double E110. Breakfast E8. Parking E10.* **

Situated in a tranquil residential area outside of the central tourist area, near the Teatro Comunale and the big park Le Cascine, this is a professionally run little two-star that I recommend highly. More than highly. A stay here not only does not drain your bank account, but it also liberates your soul. A member of the Family Hotels consortium, this hotel is located in a wonderful palazzo and the rooms are well, if simply appointed, and come with satellite TV. The breakfast is basic but filling. A good choice for travelers to Florence who want high quality accommodations but do not want to spend too much for it.

17. ELITE, *Via della Scala 12, Tel. and Fax 055/215-395. 10 rooms all with bath or shower. Single E50-60. Double E75. Breakfast E7. All credit cards accepted.* **

A quaint little hotel located on a great street in a perfect area for sightseeing, shopping, or dining. You'll love the wooden staircase that takes you from the lobby and breakfast salon to your quiet and spacious rooms. The prices are good for the location even though there are only a few amenities other than comfort and cleanliness, not to mention accommodating service. More of an inexpensive bed and breakfast than a hotel.

18. **WESTIN EXCELSIOR**, *Piazza Ognissanti 3, Tel. 055/264-201, Fax 055/210-278. Toll free number in America 1-800-221-2340. Web: www.hotelbook.com/static/welcome_05800.html. All credit cards accepted. 200 rooms all with private bath. Single E395; Double E615. Continental breakfast E15. American breakfast E22. ******

Directly across from its sister, The Grand Hotel, the prices here have really gone through the roof. Granted everything here is of the highest standard, especially the roof garden/restaurant where you can have your meal or sip an after-dinner drink, listen to the piano player, and gaze out at the splendor that is Florence, but wow, the prices have more than doubled in the past couple years. You don't have to stay here to enjoy the view; just come for dinner. Great rooms and perfect service. A superb five star luxury hotel. They have everything and more that you could want during your stay. If you can afford it, this is one of the best luxury hotels in Florence.

19. GOLDONI, *Borgo Ognissanti 8, Tel. 055/284-080, Fax 055/282-576. E-mail: info@hotelgoldoni.com. Web: www.hotelgoldoni.com. American Express and Visa accepted. 20 rooms. Single E70-100; Double E125-175. Breakfast E5. Parking E10. ****

In a central but removed location near the Arno river, this small three star hotel is situated on the second floor of an 18th century palazzo. Most of the rooms face onto a quiet courtyard garden, and all are of different size but are comfortably furnished. The bathrooms are basic but come with all three-star amenities. The breakfast buffet is abundant. A quiet, comfortable place to stay, slightly off the beaten path.

20. GRAND HOTEL, *Piazza Ognissanti 1, Tel. 055/288-781, Fax 055/217-400. Toll free number in America 1-800-221-2340. All credit cards accepted. An ITT Sheraton hotel. 106 rooms all with private bath. Single E395; Double E615; Continental breakfast E15. American breakfast E22. ******

Aptly named, this hotel is wonderfully grand. Located in a pale yellow and gray palazzo built in 1571, everything has been superbly restored to offer modern creature comforts while retaining the old world charm. Even though it is on a main thoroughfare, it is extremely quiet. The reception area is classically elegant. Each bedroom has beautiful neo-classic furniture and elegant decorations and frescoes; the bathrooms are a luscious oasis. Your breakfast is served on a small balcony overlooking an internal garden. More pleasant and comfortable than the Excelsior by maybe a whisker as a result of its recent renovation, but remember to go to the Excelsior for their roof-bar restaurant.

21. GRAND HOTEL BAGLIONI, *P.za dell'Unita Italiana 6, Tel. 055/23-580, Fax 055/235-8895. E-mail: hotel.baglioni@firenzealbergo.it. Web: www.hotelbaglioni.it. All credit cards accepted. 195 rooms. Single E140-185; Double E175-225. Breakfast included. Parking E25.* ****

Within walking distance of the train station, set in a piazza off the main road near the San Lorenzo market, this is a hotel of grand tradition situated in an austere palazzo from the 18th century. There is an elegant and spacious entry hall; and roof garden restaurant with panoramic views over the rooftops of Florence with a dramatic presentation of the Duomo. The breakfast buffet is served up here in good weather. The rooms are large and well appointed in four star style, the best of which face the piazza; the bathrooms are simply elegant. A top quality hotel in Florence.

22. GRAND HOTEL MINERVA, *P.za Santa Maria Novella 16, Tel. 055/ 284-555, Fax 055/268-281. E-mail: info@grandhotelminerva.com. Web: www.grandhotelminerva.it/. All credit cards accepted. 99 rooms. Single E155-185; Double E200-250. Breakfast included. Parking E22.* ****

Located in one of the best piazzas in the city, within walking distance of the train station, the Minerva is a comfortable and modern hotel. The entry hall with its garden is elegantly accommodating, off of which you will find the restaurant and breakfast room. All rooms are equipped with the necessary four star amenities and more, including video players. The bathrooms are lavish and some have hydro-massage and sauna. Available to guests for free is a pool and fitness center. And guests also receive free bicycle rentals. This is a great place to stay in a prime location.

23. IL GUELFO BIANCO, *Via Cavour 29, Tel. 055/288-330, Fax 055/295-203. E-mail: info@ilguelfobianco.it. Web: www.ilguelfobianco.it/. American Express, Mastercard and Visa accepted. 29 rooms all with private bath. Single E100; Double E170. Continental breakfast included.* ***

Not in my favorite area of Florence, even though it is close to everything important; but there is something about this hotel that catches my heart. Maybe it's Room 24, with the only terrace located on the inside courtyard. A perfect place to unwind after a day of sightseeing. Or maybe number 27 and 28, two large doubles that are basically suites with living and sleeping space. If you stay here, call well in advance to book either of these rooms. Every room has all necessary modern comforts like a mini-bar, A/C, satellite TV, and are all well appointed and comfortable. The bathrooms are modern, large and brilliantly white. There are many places to sit and relax, like two different courtyards downstairs, and little balconies and terraces strewn everywhere.

From the outside you would think this is just another hotel, but once you enter you are in another, quieter, more relaxing world.

24. KRAFT, *Via Solfernino 2, Tel 055/284-273, Fax 055/239-8267. Web: www.venere.com/it/firenze/kraft. All credit cards accepted. 80 rooms. Single E135-175; Double E205-250. Breakfast included. Parking E20.* ****

This refined hotel is out of the city center in a tranquil area, but close enough for walking access. The roof garden, where breakfast is served, offers exquisite panoramic views along the Arno. The piano bar and restaurant also have views over the rooftops of Florence, making it a wonderful place to end the day. The rooms are spacious and furnished with style and come with every imaginable four star amenity. A wonderful choice for those who want elegance outside of the main tourist area. There is also a terrace with an elongated lap pool for summer cooling and sightseeing of a different sort.

25. LOGGIATO DEI SERVITI, *Piazza SS. Annunziata 3, Tel. 055/289-593/4, Fax 055/289-595. E-mail: info@loggiatodeiservitihotel.it. Web: www.loggiatodeiservitihotel.it/. All credit cards accepted. 29 rooms all with private bath. Single E139; Double E201; Suite E268-382. Breakfast included. E40 for an extra bed.* ***

Located in a 16th century *loggia* that faces the beautiful Piazza della SS Annunziata, this hotel is filled with charm and character. The interior common areas consist of polished terra-cotta floors, gray stone columns and high white ceilings. The rooms are pleasant and comfortable and are filled with elegant antique furnishings. All are designed to make you feel like you just walked into the 17th century, and it works.

But they do have the modern amenities necessary to keep us weary travelers happy, especially the air conditioning in August. Some rooms face what many believe is one of the most beautiful piazzas in Italy (no cars allowed), while the rest face onto a lush interior garden. The bathrooms come with every modern comfort. The service, the accommodations, everything is at the top of the three star category. So, if you want to have a wonderful stay and also to feel as if you've stepped back in time, book a room here.

Selected as one of my *Best Places to Stay* – see Chapter 12.

26. LORENA, *Via Faenza 1, Tel. 055/282-785, Fax 055/288-300. E-mail: hotellorenaalbergo@tin.it. Web: www.florentia2000.com/att_commerciali/hotel_lorena/. 16 rooms, 10 with bath. Single without bath E45-60; Single E60-72; Double E100. All credit cards accepted. Continental Breakfast E4. Hotel closes its doors from 2:00am to 6:00pm.* **

A pleasantly run hotel located just off of the large San Lorenzo market. Perfectly located for shopping and sightseeing. The rooms are nondescript but comfortable and the prices are good. Not many amenities except for location, comfort and cleanliness. They have added A/C and TV in each room as a prelude to moving to three star status. There is still some work to go in that department but for now they are on the higher end of two stars both in quality and price.

27. NUOVA ITALIA, *Via Faenza 26, Tel. 055/287-508, Fax 055/210-941. American Express, Mastercard and Visa accepted. 21 rooms all with private bath. Single E70. Double E105. Extra person E25. Breakfast included.* ******

The fans in every room did a great job except in August. Some rooms have A/C so request those in late summer. Each room is plainly but comfortable furnished. This family-run hotel is ideally located near most of the sights and night spots, and the prices are very good. You'll just love the old Mama as she caters to you during your meals in the breakfast area, which looks just like a country *trattoria*. Not many real amenities, just a pleasant place to lay your head with friendly and accommodating service.

28. PORTA FAENZA, *Via Faenza 77, Tel 055/214-287, Fax 055/210-101. E-mail: info@hotelportafaenza.it. Web: www.hotelportafaenza.it/home.html. All credit cards accepted. 25 rooms. Single E80-150; Double E95-175. Breakfast included. Parking E12.* *******

Situated in a beautiful and completely refurbished old palazzo from the 1700s, this hotel is located near the train station, a bit removed from the centro storico. The Lelli family, including Canadian wife Rose, operates this cute little hotel, which is part of the Family Hotel consortium, and as such is well respected. A recent series of renovations have made visible some older architectural details which lends an air of history to a stay here. The rooms are spaciously spartan and filled with modern but comfortable furnishings and come with all necessary three-star amenities. There is also a babysitter service available and dry cleaning as well. Not in my favorite location in Florence, but overall a good three-star.

29. ROMA, *Piazza Santa Maria Novella 8, Tel. 055/210-366, Fax 055/215-306. E-mail: hotel.roma.fi@dada.it. Web: www.firenzealbergo.it/hotelroma/. American Express, Diners Club, Mastercard and Visa accepted. 60 rooms all with private bath. Single E165; Double E225.* ********

The main draw of this hotel is the roof terrace which overlooks the beautiful Piazza Santa Maria Novella. All the rooms are completely modern and spartan in appearance. The common areas are decoratively appointed with marble, columns, and frescoes with an omnipresent pastel blue shade. Because of the color, when you walk into this hotel you will be instantly relaxed.

Everything about this hotel is classically elegant. The rooms are adequately spacious and are all furnished and decorated in the same style. The bathrooms come with their own phone and every other modern convenience. A good place to stay, but it is best in the off-season because the prices are much better then.

30. UNICORNO, *Via dei Fossi 27, Tel. 055/287-313, Fax 055/268-332. E-mail: hotel.unicorno@usa.net. Web: www.venere.com/it/firenze/unicorno/ . 27 rooms, all with bath. Single E75-100; Double E110-140. All credit cards accepted. Breakfast included. Parking E15. ****

Near Piazza Santa Maria Novella, this hotel is situated in a palazzo from the 1400s. Completed renovated and complete with all modern amenities, this is a wonderfully located and comfortably accomodating three star. The rooms and bathrooms come with all necessary three star features and the staff goes out of its way to make you comfortable. The breakfast buffet is large and filling. Though not spectacular, I would definitely recommend this hotel for a stay in Florence.

31. DE LA VILLE, *P.za Antinori 1, Tel. 055/238-1805/6, Fax 055/238-1809. E-mail: delaville@firenze.net. Web: www.hoteldelaville.it. All credit cards accepted. 69 rooms. Single E155-295; Double E205-265. Breakfast included. Parking E22. *****

An elegant hotel within walking distance of the station, in an optimal location between the Duomo, the Ponte Vecchio and the Piazza Santa Maria Novella. The rooms are very comfortable, soundproof, each uniquely furnished, and have all necessary three star amenities including satellite TV. The bathrooms are well appointed, and come complete with all amenities including a phone. The common areas are charming, especially the terrace, which is great place to relax at the end of the day. Breakfast is excellent and the staff is professional and courteous.

Santa Croce

This is the area of Florence in which Michelangelo played as a child before he was sent to the country to live with a stone carver, from whom he learned the fundamentals for his amazing ability to carve figures from huge blocks of marble. Located to the east of the Centro Storico and the Centro sections of Florence, Santa Croce is more of an authentic, residential, working class neighborhood and seems far from the maddening crowds, even though it's just around the corner from them. The church that gives this area its name, Santa Croce, contains the graves of Michelangelo, Galileo, and other Italian greats; and is the home of an excellent leather school from which you can get great products while watching them produce the wares.

This is also the area in which Florentines come to dine at regular Tuscan restaurants or some of the newer restaurants offering nouvelle cuisine. The area is also home to another food market, the **Mercato Sant'Ambrogio**, located in the Piazza Ghiberti. There is also a prime picnic location, not nearly as nice as the Boboli Gardens but still a respite from the crowds, in the Piazza Massimo d'Azeglio.

32. CLARIDGE, *P.za Piace 3, Tel 055/234-6736, Fax 055/234-1199. All credit cards accepted. 32 rooms. Single E65-90; Double E90-130. Breakfast included. Parking E15.* ***

A comfortable and functional three star hotel that has an ample entrance hall and a covered *cortile* in the center of this elegant villa. The rooms are simply decorated but come with all necessary three star comforts. What sets this hotel apart is its location. Outside of the main tourist center, here you can get away from it all while being only a short walk from everything. The highest floor has wonderful views of Santa Croce. A wonderful three-star for those who want to be in Florence but not surrounded by tourists.

33. DANTE, *Via San Cristofano 2, Tel. 055/241-772, Fax 055/234-5819. Web: www.venere.com/it/firenze/dante/. All credit cards accepted. 14 rooms. Single E75-90; Double E100-135. Breakfast E10. Parking E12.* ***

A small hotel, only 14 rooms, near the picturesque piazza of Santa Croce. The main draw of this bed and breakfast style hotel are the ten rooms with kitchenette. These are very useful for families, as are the spacious and comfortable rooms and bathrooms. The common areas are tiny but overall this is a rather pleasant place to stay in Florence, near enough to everything, but just outside the main tourist center to make your stay here authentically local.

34. VILLE SULL'ARNO, *Lungarno C. Colombo 3, Tel. 055/67-09-71, Fax 055/678-244. E-mail: villesullarno@italyhotel.com. Web: www.villesullarno.it/ . 47 rooms all with bath. Single E150; Double E210-230. Breakfast included. All credit cards accepted.* ****

Located away from the center of things, about ten minutes by bus or car, which makes the hotel very quiet and tranquil. They have a good sized swimming pool and a lovely garden where breakfast is served in the summer. The rooms are large and comfortable with all the amenities of a four star, including air conditioning and cable TV. The ones on the river are wonderfully tranquil as are the others because in this location you are definitely away from the hustle and bustle of Florence. A good choice for those that do not like the pace of city life.

Oltrarno

Oltrarno, literally "the other side of the Arno," is home to many of Florence's artisans, leather workers, etc. It is looked upon as a city unto itself since it wasn't incorporated into the walls of Florence until the 14th century (people remember their history in Europe). Most of the beautiful architecture was destroyed during World War II, not only by the Germans but also by the Allied bombings. Thankfully both sides spared the Ponte Vecchio, The Duomo, and the other great pieces of architecture on the other side of the river.

Also spared was the **Palazzo Vecchio** (also known as the **Medici Palace**) and the **Boboli Gardens**, where Michelangelo first began his serious artistic training with the support of the Medici family. Beyond these sights and the artisans' shops, the only other place to visit is the **Piazza Santo Spirito** that boasts a 15th century church with the unfinished facade by Brunelleschi. The piazza is also home to a small fresh **produce and flower market** every morning.

35. ANNALENA, *Via Romana 34, Tel. 055/222-402, Fax 055/222-403. Email - info@hotelannalena.it. Web: www.hotelannalena.it. American Express, Diners Club, Mastercard and Visa accepted. 20 rooms, 16 doubles, four singles all with bath. Single E95. Double E135. Breakfast included.* ***

This place has at times been a convent, a school for young ladies, a gambling casino, a safe haven for Italian Jews during WWII, and now finally it has become the Hotel Annalena. It takes over the entire floor of a beautiful Florentine palazzo and has all the necessary amenities of a good three star hotel. The lobby area doubles as breakfast room and evening bar space. The rooms are large with high ceilings and seem to be *fresco* (cool) all year round. Located just beyond the Palazzo Pitti and near one of the entrances to the Boboli Gardens, this hotel is a little off the beaten path which makes for a wonderfully relaxing stay. The rooms all have antique style furnishings, terra-cotta floors and come with small terraces overlooking the garden.

36. CLASSIC, *Viale Machiavelli 25, Tel. 055/229-3512, Fax 055/229-353. All credit cards accepted. 20 rooms all with private bath. Single E80; Double E115. Breakfast included.* ***

Located in a quaint little palazzo from the nineteenth century situated outside the old city walls, here you can get a taste of Florentine life without the constant clamoring of mopeds riding past your bedroom window. Piazzale Machiavelli is an exclusive address and this hotel shows it. The lush garden in the rear (there's a glassed-in section for winter guests) is your breakfast location as well as your mid-afternoon slumber spot, and there's a small bar just off the garden for evening drinks.

Your rooms are palatial, with immense ceilings and clean bathrooms. Each room is furnished quite differently. Some have antique furniture, others have newer but sill attractive pieces. The diversity lends a spot of charm. I would recommend this gem to anyone who likes to tour and then escape the hectic pace of the city. One minor note, they do not have air conditioning, but when I was there on a 90 degree day each room was very cool. These old palazzi were built to keep cool in the summer and remain warm in the winter. This place really is a classic and the choice for truly discerning vacationers.

37. DAVID, *Viale Michelangelo 1, Tel. 055/681-1695, Fax 055/680-602. E-mail: david@italyhotel.com or info@davidhotel.com. Web: www.davidhotel.com. All credit cards accepted. 24 rooms. Single E85; Double E160. Breakfast included.* ***

By far one of the more pleasant little hotels in Florence. I recommend it highly. Situated in a small villa from the 19th century, the David has wonderfully accommodating and comfortable common areas. The rooms are all furnished with wonderful antiques along with safes, satellite TVs, and well appointed baths. There is a beautiful garden that is a joy to relax in during good weather. Located near the Statue of David in the Piazzale Michelangelo overlooking Florence, this wonderful hotel is in a serene setting, and is a perfect choice for the price conscious who want to see Florence, but wish to stay outside of the main town.

38. ISTITUTO GOULD, *Via dei Serragli 49, Tel. 055/212-576, Fax 055/280-274. No credit cards accepted. 25 rooms, 20 with private bath. Single E18; Double E32 per person.* (no star)

If you don't have your own bathroom here you're still okay, since you only have to share two toilets and two showers with four other rooms. The office is on the ground floor of a magnificent palazzo that you will enjoy exploring. There are limited office hours (9:00am–1:00pm and 3:00pm–7:00pm) but they do give you your own key so you can go in and out as your please. (A rarity in Florence for one-stars.) The rooms, on the second and third floors scattered all over the palazzo, are quite large. In your search throughout this wonderful building you'll find immense common rooms with comfortable chairs and a quaint little terrace overlooking some rooftops in the rear, which are a great places to relax with a glass of Chianti and a meal of bread, cheese and salami.

Also, they separate the more mature budget travelers from the younger crowd, so the late night adventures of the young'uns don't keep us older and wiser folks awake. This is a fantastic budget hotel in truly ambient surroundings. And the best part of your comfortable stay is that the proceeds benefit a home for boys and girls from eight to 18 who cannot live with their own families.

39. LUNGARNO, *Borgo S Jacopo 14, Tel. 055/264-211, Fax 055/268-437. E-mail: bookings@lungarnohotels.com. Web: www.lungarnohotels.it/lungarno_e.shtm. All credit cards accepted. 66 rooms all with private bath. Single E215-290; Double E340; Suite E510.* ****

An excellent location right on the river, only a few meters from the Ponte Vecchio, and situated down a quaint, Florentine side street with some great restaurants and food shops. Even though most of the hotel is modern, it is a quaint, classic establishment. The lounge just off the lobby offers a relaxing view of the river and the Ponte Vecchio.

An ancient stone tower is part of the hotel, with a great penthouse suite. If you want the atmosphere of the tower, specify this upon making your reservation. Some of the rooms have terraces overlooking the river, which makes for a perfect place to relax after a tough day of sightseeing. You need to specify this too.

A great feature of the hotel is the more than 400 modern paintings that line the walls. Some by Picasso, Cocteau, Sironi, Rosai and more. Another plus is the fact that hotel has bicycles available for guests to use free of charge. This is one of the great hotels in Florence.

40. PITTI PALACE, *Via Barbadori 2, Tel. and Fax 055/239-8711. E-mail: pittipalace@vivahotels.com. Web: www.venere.com/it/firenze/pittipalace/. All credit cards accepted. 73 rooms. Single E215-230; Double E200. Breakfast included. Parking E22.* ***

A comfortable three star only a few paces from the Ponte Vecchio in the Oltrarno. The rooms are all different sizes, all furnished in a chic modern style, and some have balconies. The bathrooms are functional and complete with all necessary amenities. The two terraces on the sixth floor offer incomparable panoramic views over the Boboli gardens, Palazzo Pitti, the Duomo and the rest of the city across the river. The breakfast buffet is abundant. A well-located, nice hotel. A stay here is comfortable, quiet and accommodating.

41. LA SCALETTA, *Via Guicciardini 13, Tel. 055/283-028, Fax 055/289-562. E-mail: lascaletta@italyhotel.com. Web: www.venere.com/it/firenze/lascaletta/. Mastercard and Visa accepted. 12 rooms, 11 with private bath. Single without E75; Single E85-95; Double without E100; Double E110-130. Breakfast included.* **

No ifs, ands, or buts about it, this is the best place to stay in the Oltrarno ... and maybe all of Florence, if you don't want to spend a lot of money. But you have to reserve your rooms well in advance. Let's say at least 4-5 months in advance, to guarantee you'll get a room overlooking the garden! Yes, there's no air conditioning, but it's not needed. This ancient building seems to soak up the cold air in the summer and retain the warm in the winter.

The rooms are large, clean and comfortable. The location is ideal and amazingly quiet and relaxing. And best of all there are two incomparable terraces overlooking all the best sights of Florence. Relaxing on these terraces after a day on the town makes a stay here sublime.

The furnishings are eclectic and simple, but comfortable; and the layout is scattered throughout the building, with everything connected by staircases. The prices are superb but they won't last forever. Management has already put air conditioning in three rooms, and when all are complete, the hotel should get its three star rating. That will send their prices through the roof, just like it did with La Scalinetta di Spagna in Rome. A great place to stay while in Florence.

42. **SILLA**, *Via dei Renai 5, Tel. 055/234-2888, Fax 055/234-1437. E-mail: hotelsilla@tin.it. Web: www.hotelsilla.it/. American Express, Diners Club, Mastercard and Visa accepted. 54 rooms all with private bath. Single E90; Double E90-120.* *******

Located on the first floor of an old palazzo, you enter from a lightly traveled side street just off the Lungarno. The white marble stairs are covered with a red carpet that makes you feel very presidential as you ascend to the lobby. The double rooms are rather large while the singles are quite tiny, but all have high ceilings and come complete with the amenities of a good three star. The large terrace among the flowers and trees is where you have your breakfast and can enjoy a nice view of the Arno. Off the beaten path and boasting a professional staff, which makes the stay here quiet and relaxing.

43. **TORRE DI BELLOSGUARDO**, *Via Roti Michelozzi 2, Tel. 055/229-8145, Fax 055/229-008. E-mail: torredibellosguardo@dada.it. Web: www.torrebellosguardo.com/. 16 room all with bath. Single E195; Double E265; Suites E275-325. All credit cards accepted.* ********

If you have the means, this is the only place to stay while in Florence. Once you walk in the gates you will love it. The ancient towered palazzo that is the hotel will make you feel like you have stepped back to the Renaissance. Besides this completely unique and accommodating building, this wonderful hotel has the best views over Florence. They are stunningly amazing. Also the grounds are filled with gardens and olive trees where horses graze; there is a huge open lawn in front flanked by fir trees; and they have a swimming pool with a bar – all of which overlook the magnificent city of Florence below.

The old palazzo used to be a small English language school, St. Michael's, that catered to 100 students (of which I was one). So you can imagine that currently, with only sixteen luxury rooms, the size of your accommodations are quite impressive. The interior common areas are like something out of a movie script, with vaulted stone ceilings and arches, as well as staircases leading off into hidden passages. You're a short distance outside of the old city walls but here you will find pure romance, complete peace, and soothing tranquillity. In fact the hotel is so magnificent that you have to reserve well in advance, since they are booked solid year round. I can't say enough about the view, it is simply something you have experience. Also, and most importantly, if you aren't already in love, you'll find it or rekindle it in this wonderfully majestic hideaway. This is one of the great, unique places to stay in all of Italy!

Selected as one of my *Best Places to Stay* – see Chapter 12.

44. **VILLA CARLOTTA**, *Via Michele di Lando 3, Tel. 055/233-6134, Fax 055/233-6147. Web: www.venere.com/it/firenze/villacarlotta/. All credit cards accepted. 27 rooms all with private bath. Five more in a gatehouse building. Single E105-160; Double E160-235. Breakfast included. A meal at their fine restaurant costs only E27.* ********

The hotel is like something out of a dream, with its sunlit tea room used for breakfast, its small garden on the side with fish swimming in the fountain, and elegant dining in the magnificent restaurant below. To top it all off you have a real bar with stools from which you can get any type of concoction your heart desires.

The location is perfect for those who like to get away from it all. Off the beaten path in a quiet and calm section of town. The rooms are all pleasantly furnished with all necessary amenities. A truly great place to stay.

45. **VILLA CORA**, *Viale Machiavelli 18-20, Tel. 055/229-8451, Fax 055/ 229-086. E-mail: reservation@villacora.it. Web: www.villacora.com/. All credit cards accepted. 47 rooms all with private bath. ingle E195-270; Double E270- 430; Deluxe Double E335-500; Suite E470-1,300. A full buffet breakfast included.* *****

You'll find this extravagant and ornately decorated hotel (once a nine-teenth century *palazzo*) on a residential street that curves up to the Florentine hills. It is truly magnificent with its chandeliers, statues, bas-relief covered walls, gilded mirrors and staff that will wait on you hand and foot. If you want to stay in the lap of luxury and are willing to pay for it, this is the place for you. There is a pool-side restaurant, Taverna Machiavelli, where you can eat and relax after a hard day's touring. Another important feature is the rooftop terrace garden, offering excellent views of Florence. And the rooms are superb, stupendous, *fantavolosso* – think of any adjective and the rooms will surpass it! A great place to stay if you have the money.

Where To Eat

Before I guide you to the culinary delights you'll encounter in Florence, I've prepared an augmented version of Chapter 11, *Food & Wine*, for you to better enjoy the wonders of Tuscan cuisine. *Buon appetito!*

Tuscan Cuisine

During the Renaissance, Florence and Tuscany experienced a burst of elaborate cuisine, mainly the result of Catherine de Medici importing a brigade of French chefs, but today that type of cuisine has given way to more basic fare. Tuscan cooking has its roots in the frugal peasant cuisine that was the result of the region being agriculturally poor for so many centuries. The food is simple but healthy, with the emphasis on fresh ingredients which accentu-ates the individual tastes of each dish.

Grilled meats are a staple of the Florentine diet, with *bistecca alla Fiorentina* rivaling anything Texas could dream of producing. The Florentines tend to over-salt their vegetables and soups, but you can ask for them to be prepared *senza sale*, without salt, and no one will be insulted at all. You'll also find beans and olive oil prominently used in many dishes, as well as many types of game that populate the hills of Tuscany. And if you like cheese, my favorite is the full flavored *pecorino* made from sheep's milk.

Tuscany is not really known for its pasta dishes, but Tuscans do make an excellent *pasta alla carrettiera*, a pasta dish with a sauce of tomato, garlic, pepper, and parsley. If you want a simple, filling, healthy meal, you'll find one in Tuscany. Just don't expect some extravagant saucy dish. For that go to France.

Suggested Tuscan Cuisine

You don't have to eat all the traditional courses listed below. Our constitution just isn't prepared for such mass consumption, so don't feel bad if all you order is a pasta dish or an entrée with a salad or appetizer.

Antipasto - Appetizer
• **Crostini** – Chicken liver pate spread on hard, crusty bread
• **Pinzimonio** – Raw vegetables to be dipped in rich olive oil
• **Bruschetta** – Sliced crusty bread roasted over a fire covered with olive oil and rubbed with garlic; sometimes comes with crushed tomatoes, or another version has an egg on top (*Aqua Cotta*)

Primo Piatto - First Course
Zuppa – Soup
• **Ribollita** – means reboiled. A hearty mushy vegetable soup with beans, cabbage, carrots, and chunks of boiled bread.
• **Panzanella** – A Tuscan *gazpacho* (cold soup) made with tomatoes, cucumbers, onions, basil, olive oil, and bread.

Pasta
• **Pappardelle alla lepre** – Wide homemade pasta with a wild hare sauce
• **Pasta alla carrettierra** –Pasta with a sauce of tomato, garlic, pepper and parsley
• **Tortelli** – Spinach and ricotta ravioli with either cream sauce or a meat sauce

Secondo Piatto - Entrée
Carne – Meat
• **Bistecca alla Fiorentina** – T-bone steak at least two inches thick cooked over coals charred on the outside and pink in the middle. Welcome to Texas!
• **Fritto misto** –Usually lamb, rabbit or chicken, with peppers, zucchini, artichokes dipped in batter and deep fried
• **Arista di Maiale** – Pork loin chop cooked with rosemary and garlic
• **Spiedini di maiale** – Pork loin cubes and pork liver spiced with fennel and cooked on a skewer over open flames
• **Francesina** – Meat, onions, and tomatoes stewed in red wine

• **Trippa alla Fiorentina** – Tripe mixed with tomato sauce and served with a variety of cheeses

Pesce – Fish
• **Bacca alla Fiorentina** – Salted cod cooked with tomatoes and spices (usually garlic and fennel)
• **Seppie in Zimino** – Cuttlefish simmered with beans

Contorno – Vegetable
• **Fagioli all'ucceletto** – White beans with garlic and tomatoes and sometimes sage
• **Insalata Mista** – mixed salad. You have to prepare your own olive oil and vinegar dressing. American's lust for countless types of salad dressings hasn't hit Italy yet.

Formaggio – Cheese
• **Pecorino** – Cheese made from sheep's milk

Tuscan Wines

Tuscany is known for its full bodied red wines, especially the world famous **Chianti**. A bottle of Chianti has surely graced the table of every Italian home at least once. Robust, full-bodied and zesty, the many reds produced by the Chianti vines in Tuscany have attained worldwide acclaim. To be called Chianti a wine must be made according to certain specifications and the vines must be located in certain areas. Within this production zone seven different subregions are recognized: Chianti Classico, Chianti Colli Aretini, Chianti Colli Fiorentini, Chianti Colli Senesi, Chianti Colline Pisane, Chianti Montalbano and Chianti Rufina.

Produced between Florence and Siena, Chianti Classico is more full-bodied than the others in its family, and comes from the oldest part of the production zone. If the wine is a Chianti Classico you'll find a black rooster label on the neck of the bottle. An austere wine, ideal when aged and served with meat dishes, it is also well suited for tomato-based pasta dishes especially those with meat in them.

Chiantis can be called *vecchio* (old) if the wine has aged two years and is given the respected and coveted *Riserva* label when aged three years and *Superiore* if aged for five years. With Chianti wines you can expect the best, especially if it is a Classico.

From the Chianti region you should try the following red wines: **Castello di Ama**, **Castello di Volpaia**, and **Vecchie Terre di Montefili**. Outside the region try some **Rosso delle Colline Luchesi** from the hills around Lucca, **Morellino di Scansano** from the hills south of Grossetto, and **Elba Rosso**, made on the island of Elba.

The hills of Tuscany are filled with vineyards large and small supplying grapes to make some of the world's best vintages. When in Tuscany you must sample at least a little of this bounty. There are plenty of wine cellars and *enoteche* (wine bars) in every city in this region for you to sample the regional offerings. And you can't forget a glass of wine with your meal. Some Tuscans say that their food is bland so that they can enjoy the wine with their meals more. Whatever the reason, you'll love sampling the different varieties.

Most wines are classified by the type of grape used and the district from which the wines are produced. Some of the best wines come with a **DOC** (*Denominazione di Origine Controllata*) label that indicates the wine comes from a specially defined area and was produced according to specific traditional methods. If the label reads **DOCG** (G stands for *Garantita*) the wine will be of the highest quality, guaranteed.

Some whites you might enjoy are a dry **Montecarlo** from the hills east of Lucca or a dry **Bolgheri** from the coast. The red wines mentioned above also have some excellent white wines to complement them.

Some of these wines may be a bit pricey in restaurants so you may want to buy them at a store and sample them back in your hotel room or on a picnic. At restaurants, in most cases the house wines will be locally produced and of excellent quality, so give them a try too. No need to spend a lot of money on a labeled bottle of wine, when the house wine is better than most that we get back home.

The Best Dining in Florence

11. BUCA LAPI, *Via del Trebbio 1, Tel. 055/213-768.*

3. LA BUSSOLA, *Via Porta Rossa 58, Tel. 055/293-376. Closed Mondays.*

27. LA CASALINGA, *Via dei Michelozzi 9r, Tel. 055/218-624.*

20. IL CIBREO, *Via dei Macci 118r, Tel. 055/234-1100. All credit cards accepted.*

12. COCO LEZZONE, *Via dei Parioncino 26, Tel. 055/287-178. No credit cards accepted.*

32. DEL GALLO NERO, *Via Santo Spirito 6r, Tel. 055/218-898.*

33. LA LOGGIA, *Piazzale Michelangelo 1, Tel. 055/234-2832, Fax 055/234-5288. American Express, Diners Club, Mastercard and Visa accepted.*

15. NERBONE, *Mercato Centrale. No telephone. No credit cards accepted.*

5. OLIVIERO, *Via delle Terme 51r, Tel. 055/287-643. All credit cards accepted.*

19. TREDICI GOBBI, *13 Hunchbacks, Via Porcellana 9R.*

Centro Storico

1. ANTICO FATTORE, *Via Lambertesca 1-3, Tel. 055/261-225. Closed Sundays. Credit cards accepted. Dinner for two E40.*

This wonderful Tuscan restaurant was virtually destroyed when terrorists bombed the Uffizzi Gallery some years ago, and now it has re-opened. A wonderful but somewhat expensive restaurant that is no worse for the wear. Everything is spotlessly clean and they have recreated their Tuscan charm. The food is as good as ever. Try their *tortellini ai funghi porcini* (meat or cheese stuffed tortellini with a savory mushroom sauce). It is exquisite. Then for seconds anything on the grill is great, including the *lombatina di vitello* (veal chop) or the *bistecca di maiale* (pork steak).

2. DA BENVENUTO, *Via della Mosca 16r, Tel. 055/214-833. Closed Sundats and in August. Visa accepted. Dinner for two E35.*

A little off the beaten path, behind the Uffizzi gallery, this place is frequented by locals and tourists alike and is authentically Florentine. Locally know as "da Gabriella" after the hospitable owner, you'll love the atmosphere here as well as the food. Some dishes available are *crostini da fegatini* (baked dough stuffed with beans), *spaghetti alla carrettiera* (with a spicy tomato sauce), and as always meat dishes are plentiful for the main course. Tuscan cooking and character abound here. A wonderful choice while in Florence.

3. LA BUSSOLA, *Via Porta Rossa 58, Tel. 055/293-376. Visa and Mastercard accepted. Closed Mondays. Dinner for two E45.*

My favorite place in Florence. You can get superb pizza in this pizzeria/ristorante as well as pasta. The ambiance is like something out of a movie set, especially in the back. They have a marble counter where you sit and watch the pizza master prepare the evening's fare in the wood heated brick oven. Or, if you're into the formal dining scene, try the back with tablecloths, etc. Wherever you sit the food will be excellent.

For pasta, try the *quattro formaggi* (four cheeses) or the *tortellini alla panna* (cream sauce). You can get any type of pizza you want here and can even ask to mix and match ingredients. The pizza master is more than willing to accommodate.

4. DA GANINO, *Piazza dei Cimatori 4, Tel. 055/214-125. All credit cards accepted. Closed Sundays. Dinner for two E38*

The best place to sit in the summer is at the communal wooden benches outside which are hedged in by flower pots. The two rooms inside are made to look rustic with their wooden paneling, yokes hanging from the walls and marble topped tables. The somewhat pricey food is still great, especially when eaten in the secluded piazza. Try the *petto di pollo alla crema di limone* (chicken breast with cream and lemon sauce) or the *coniglio e verdure fritte* (fried country rabbit and vegetables). You have to try rabbit at least once before you leave Tuscany, it's one of their specialties, so it might as well be here.

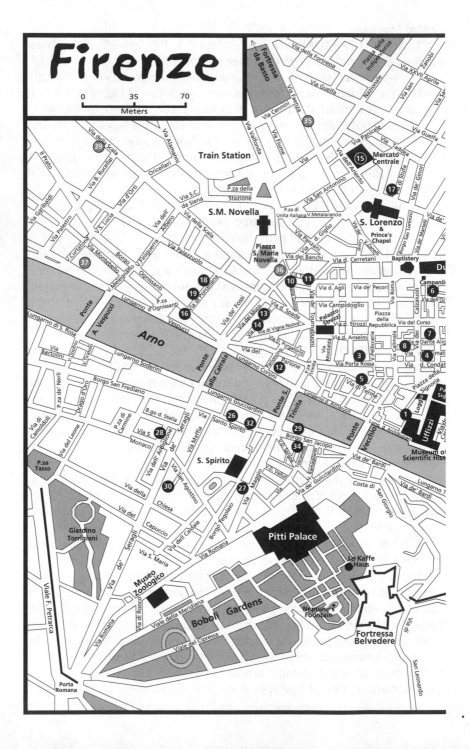

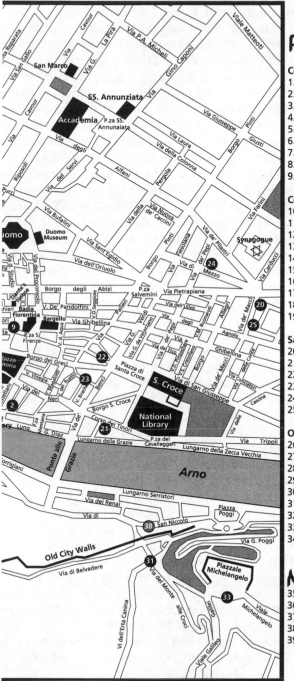

Restaurants ●

Centro Storico
1. Antico Fattore
2. Da Benvenuto
3. La Bussola
4. Da Ganino
5. Oliviero
6. Ottorino
7. Del Pennello
8. Dei Verrazzano
9. Vini Vecchi Sapore

Centro
10. Le Belle Donne
11. Buca Lapi
12. Coco Lezzone
13. Garga
14. Latini
15. Nerbone
16. Il Profeta
17. Serrolo Gozzi
18. Sostanza
19. Tredici Gobbi

Santa Croce
20. Il Cibreo
21. Del Fagioli
22. Leo in Santa Croce
23. Mossacce
24. La Pentola dell'Oro
25. Il Pizzaiuolo

Oltrarno
26. Angiolino
27. La Casalinga
28. Cavalo Nero
29. Cinghiale Bianco
30. Diladdarno
31. Fuori Porta
32. Del Gallo Nero
33. La Loggia
34. Mama Gina

Nightlife ●
35. Dublin Pub
36. Fiddler's Elbow
37. Harry's Bar
38. Il Rifrullo
39. Space Electronic

5. **OLIVIERO**, *Via delle Terme 51r, Tel. 055/287-643. All credit cards accepted. Closed Sundays and August. Dinner for two E60.*
The cuisine here is created with a little flair. The chef Francesco Altomare uses the finest fresh ingredients to prepare excellent meals that are unique every day and are based on what is available at the markets. The *insalata tiepida di polpo* (octopus salad) is exquisite as is the *tegamino di porcini gratinati al parmigiano e rosmarino* (lightly fried grated porcini mushrooms with parmesan and rosemary). I am not too enamored with their pasta dishes, but their fish and meat courses make up for it. A wildly creative *cotoletto di vitello farcite con cacio pecorino e pistacchi* (veal cutlet cooked with pecorino cheese and pistachio) may not sound delectable, but it is. At Oliviero's you will get a wonderful meal, creatively prepared. Dine here for a culinary adventure; skip it if you want something ordinary. This is where the 'in' crowd sups.

6. **OTTORINO**, *Via delle Oche 12-16, Tel. 055/218-747 or 055/215-151. Visa and Mastercard accepted. Closed Sundays. Dinner for two E47.*
One of the city's oldest restaurants, Ottorino is located on the ground floor of a beautiful medieval tower, brightly lit with long pale wooden communal tables. It serves authentic Tuscan cuisine as well as some dishes that are not very Tuscan. One of my favorites is *tagliatelli al coniglio* (light pasta in a rabbit sauce). A place to find a great meal in a comfortable atmopshere.

7. **DEL PENNELLO**, *Via Dante Aligheri 4, Tel. 055/94-848. No credit cards accepted. Closed Sunday for dinner and Mondays. Dinner for two E30.*
The huge antipasto display is the perfect lunch or dinner repast. You can get as much as you want for one low price. But naturally they would rather you not eat them out of house and home. When done grazing, try the *spaghetti alla carbonara* (with cheese ham, peas, and an egg) or *alla bolognese* (tasty bologna meat sauce), followed by the *petti di pollo alla mozzarella* (chicken breasts smothered in mozzarella) or the *bistecca di maiale* (pork steak). A fine restaurant in an excellent location.

8. **DEI VERRAZZANO**, *Via de' Tavolini 18r, Tel. 055/268-590. Closed Sundays. American Express accepted. Dinner for two E25.*
What a wine bar. This place has excellent though simple food, incredibly refined ambiance, and all at a good price, if you can get in the door. Almost always crowded, especially at lunch, you will feel like a rather upscale native if you can get a table here. Don't expect a full menu since this is not a restaurant, but you will get great *panini* filled with tasty salami and cheeses, as well as salads, soups and other light fare. The wines by the glass are local Chianti from the Castello di Verrazzo region (hence the name of the place).

9. **VINI VECCHI SAPORI**, *Via dei Magazzini 3r, Tel. 055/293-045. Closed Mondays. No credit cards accepted. Dinner for two E20.*
A wonderful wine bar deep in the heart of the *centro storico* on a side street near the P.za della Signoria. An extensive wine list accompanies the

simple, light traditional fare including crostini, salami, cheese, salads and soups. For those who are not wine lovers, beer is available, and everything is priced well. The atmosphere is informal, accommodating and comfortable. This place is open from 10am until the city shuts down. Despite its central location, Vini Vecchi Sapori is only lightly touristed since it is just off of the main path between the Ponte Vecchio and Duomo.

Centro

   10. LE BELLE DONNE, *Via delle Belle Donne 16r, Tel. 055/2380-2609. Closed Saturdays, Sundays and in August. No credit cards accepted. Dinner for two E40.*

   A bric-a-brac styled little *trattoria* that is always packed with locals clamoring for the excellent food they prepare here. Pasta is served in all its forms, soups are plentiful, as are the obligatory meat dishes especially the Florentine favorite – tripe. And don't forget the desserts. If you are looking for classical Tuscan cooking this is a great place to have a meal. Centrally located near the Piazza Santa Maria Novella.

   11. BUCA LAPI, *Via del Trebbio 1, Tel. 055/213-768. All credit cards accepted. Closed Sunday for dinner and Mondays. Dinner for two E35.*

   One of the very best restaurants Florence has to offer. On a small street, down in the basement of an old building, Buca Lapi treats you to the food of a lifetime (and the spectacle of one too). There is a small open kitchen surrounded on two sides by tables from which you can see all the food being prepared. The decor is bizarre in a fun way, with travel posters covering the walls and ceiling.

   The tortelli stuffed with ricotta and spinach in a butter and sage sauce was unparalleled. Or try the *spaghetti al sugo di carne e pomodoro* (with meat and tomato sauce) for starters, then try either the *pollo al cacciatore con spinacio* (chicken cooked in tomato-based spicy sauce with spinach) or the *cinghiale con patate fritte* (wild boar with fried potatoes). A superbly intimate restaurant with wonderful culinary and visual experiences.

   12. COCO LEZZONE, *Via dei Parioncino 26, Tel. 055/287-178. No credit cards accepted. Closed Saturdays and Sundays in the Summer and Tuesdays for dinner. In the winter closed Sundays and Tuesdays for dinner. Dinner for two E45.*

   Located in what was once a dairy, Coco Lezzone's long communal tables contrast sharply with the white tiled floors. Despite the strange decor, Florentines and tourists alike pack themselves in to enjoy the authentic Tuscan cuisine and atmosphere. The portions are pleasantly large, the meats are amazingly good, especially the *arista al forno* (roasted pork). Also try the *piccione* (pigeon) cooked over the grill (don't worry, they're farm raised – they don't go out to the piazza and catch them for dinner.) Where else will you be able to eat pigeon? They also have *coniglio arista* (roasted rabbit), a must when in Florence since rabbit is a Tuscan specialty.

13. GARGA, *Via del Moro 9, Tel. 055/298-898. American Express, Diners Club, Visa and Mastercard accepted. Closed Sundays and Mondays. Dinner for two E45.*

If you want to get in on some of the best pasta in Florence, look no further. Try the *pennette al gorgonzola e zucchine*. For seconds, try the *petto di pollo al pomodoro e basilico* (chicken breast with tomato and basil) or the *scaloppina di vitella al limone* (veal with light lemon sauce). The food and the ambiance touch the edge of nouvelle cuisine, so if you're interested in trying something different in a unique atmosphere this place is great.

14. LATINI, *Via Palchetti 6, Tel. 055/210-916. American Express, Mastercard and Visa accepted. Closed Mondays and Tuesdays for lunch. Dinner for two E40.*

The hams hanging from the ceiling and a huge oxen yoke gives this place a wonderfully local flavor. They specialize in meat dishes (which are wonderful) but you can complement that with one of their *insalata mista* (mixed salad). The service is brusque in the Tuscan manner and the location down a little street makes the ambiance perfectly authentic. Try the *spiedini misti* (mixed meat grill) or the *pollo arrosto* (roasted chicken) and you won't be sorry.

15. NERBONE, *Mercato Centrale, 055/219-949. No credit cards accepted. Closed Sundays. Meal for two E12.*

When in Florence, you have to come here. No questions asked. This is a truly authentic Florentine eatery. In operation since 1872, this small food stand in the *Mercato Centrale* serves up the most incredible atmosphere. Though they offer a limited variety of food, what they do have is superb. This place is known for the best boiled meat sandwiches (pork, beef, or veal) for only E3, which are called *panini*. Your only choice of meats is what they have boiling in the big vats that day. The sandwich you get is just the meat, the bread, and some salt, but it is amazingly tasty. The 'chef' takes the boiled meat out of the steaming hot water, slices it right in front of you, ladles it onto the meat, pours a little juice over it for flavor (they usually ask if you want this ... say *si*), sprinkles it with a little salt, and *presto*, the best lunch you'll have in Florence. That is if you are a carnivore.

You can also order pasta, soup, and salads as well. To eat your simple but truly authentic Florentine meal, either stand at the counter and sip a glass of wine or beer, or take your meal to the small seating area just across the aisle.

16. IL PROFETA, *Via Borgognissanti 93, Tel. 055/212-265. American Express, Diners Club, Visa and Mastercard accepted. Closed Sundays and Mondays. Dinner for two E38.*

A cheerful unpretentious place with simple, basic food served to you by friendly waiters. The kitchen is visible at the end of the dining room so the sound of pots and pans clattering adds a rustic touch to your meal. They make good pastas, especially the *penne carrettiera* (garlic, tomatoes and pepper) which is a little like *penne all'arrabbiata* in Rome, and the house special *penne profeta* (with cream, ham, and mushrooms) which is really great. Next, sample the finely cooked *lombatina di vitella* (veal cutlet) or the ever present *bistecca alla Fiorentina*.

17. SERROLO GOZZI, *Piazza San Lorenzo 8, No telephone. No credit cards accepted. Closed Sundays. Dinner for two E22.*

This inexpensive, small, rustic *trattoria* is situated smack dab in the middle of the bustling San Lorenzo market. The seating is at long communal tables that line the walls with benches on one side and chairs on the other. Being just across the street from the food market, Mercato Generale, guarantees you'll have the freshest ingredients. The fare is purely Tuscan. I liked the *arista di maiale al forno* (pork grilled over the fire) and the *vitello arrosto* (roasted veal). Super inexpensive, completely authentic, and very satisfying. The service is brusque and informal. A real working man's place.

18. SOSTANZA, *Via della Porcellana 25, Tel. 055/212-691. No credit cards accepted. Closed Saturdays for dinner and Sundays. Dinner for two E50.*

Aptly named "Sustenance," this down to earth, tiny little restaurant is in itself a piece of Florentine history and is frequented by tourists, bohemian artists, the elite and more. You enter this place by pushing aside the tacky beads that line the entrance, and enter the dining area which is narrow and crowded. All around you are the noises from the kitchen in the back which adds to the charm of this place. The waiters are brusque, but that's part of their shtick; the plates land in front of you with a thud, but everyone has a great time. Try any of their meat dishes made in the perfect Tuscan manner. Other than salads that's what they do well. They have a *mega-bistecca al manzo* (huge beef steak) that would choke a Texan.

Come here for a taste of a non-tourist *trattoria* and a sampling of true Florentine cuisine. Over the years they have become a little pricey, but the meal and the simple, local, rustic atmosphere is worth it.

19. TREDICI GOBBI *(13 Hunchbacks), Via del Porcellana 9R. Tel. 055/ 284-015. Credit cards accepted. Dinner for two E35.*

Mainly Florentine cuisine, with a few Hungarian dishes added for flair. A moderately priced restaurant with some expensive meat dishes, such as the excellent *bistecca Fiorentina*. The pasta is average except for the exquisitely tasty rigatoni with hot sauce. They have menus in a variety of different languages so you'll always know what you ordered.

The atmosphere is simple and rustic and the back room with its brick walls is my favorite spot for dinner. Other fine dishes are the *fusilli* with rabbit sauce. 'Thumper' never tasted so good. For seconds they also serve wild boar and veal. After enjoying your meal, soaking up the delightful atmosphere, it's time for the dessert cart. These well-presented delicacies and a steaming cup of café will round out an excellent meal. Don't miss this place while in Florence.

Santa Croce
     20. IL CIBREO, *Via dei Macci 118r, Tel. 055/234-1100. All credit cards accepted. Closed Sundays, Mondays and August. Dinner for two E65.*
     They serve a combination of traditional and *nouvelle cuisine* and it is excellent. But, if you like pasta don't come here – there's none on the menu. Their mushroom soup is excellent as is the typically Roman buffalo-milk mozzarella. All the ingredients are basic and simple, but everything seems to be prepared in a whole new way. Their *antipasti* are abundant. Try the *crostini di fegatini* (baked dough stuffed with liver). Then for seconds sample the *salsicce e fagioli* (sausage and beans). If you want to try the *cibreo*, the restaurant's namesake, which is a tasty Tuscan chicken stew made from every conceivable part of the bird, you need to order it at least a day in advance while making reservations. If you want the same food for half the price, simply go to the *vineria* on the other side of the kitchen. That's where you'll find me.
     21. DEL FAGIOLI, *Corso dei Tintori 47, Tel. 055/244-285. American Express, Diners Club, and Visa accepted. Closed Sundays. Dinner for two E30.*
     A straightforward Tuscan *trattoria* with great food for a good value. The rustic appearance with the wood paneling and antlers hanging on the walls reflects the peasant cuisine served. The menu is not that extensive but you can get a good *salsicce alla griglia* (grilled sausage) for a dinner and some *fagiole and zucchini* as an appetizer. Since they are a typical Tuscan restaurant their specialty is grilled meats.
     22. LEO IN SANTA CROCE, *Via Torta 7r, Tel. 055/210-829, Fax 055/239-6705. All credit cards accepted. Closed Mondays. Dinner for two E42.*
     A brightly lit, trying-to-be-upscale restaurant near the church of Santa Croce that serves really good food. They prepare dishes from all over Italy so you're not confined to the normal Tuscan peasant fare. You can get the abundant *antipasto di casa* and sample a variety of local produce and meats. Then you can try a good rendition of the Roman favorite *spaghetti all carbonara* (ham, cheese, mixed with an egg). Consider also the *cordon bleu* or the ever tasty *filetto di pepe verde* (beef with green peppers).
     23. MOSSACCE, *Via del Pronconsolo 55, Tel. 055/294-361. No credit cards accepted. Closed Sundays. Dinner for two E37.*
     This was once a place for locals, but now the tourists have taken it over. You can still stop here for great food, but the authenticity of the atmosphere has disappeared along with the locals. The meats are especially exquisite, especially the *ossobuco* (stewed veal knuckle in a tomato sauce). Try some *ribollita* (mixed boiled meats) too. I suggest you sit all the way in the back around the "L" of a dining area so you can enjoy your meal in front of the small

open kitchen and watch the cooks prepare the food. That alone makes this restaurant a lot of fun.

24. LA PENTOLA DELL 'ORA, *Via di Mezzo 24/26r, Tel. 055/241-821. Closed Sundays and August. Only open in the evenings. Visa accepted. Dinner for two E45.*

The atmosphere here is rustic as well as refined, the service is courteous, but what draws people to this lovely local place is the menu. Owner and chef supreme Giuseppe Alessi creates amazing dishes from simple ingredients. He has a number of cook books in print, and creates many notable and palate pleasing *piatti*. Off the beaten path so you won't find many tourists here, unless the secret is already out. An excellent choice while in Florence.

25. IL PIZZAIUOLO, *Via de' Macci 113r, Tel. 055/241171. Closed Sundays and in August. No credit cards accepted. Dinner for two E25.*

If you want a real Florentine experience far away from the thundering herds of tourists, this simple little pizza place is for you. In the area around Santa Croce that is fast becoming known for grand restaurants, this local joint stands out for its traditional authenticity. In some circles the pizza and *calzone* are considered the best in the city. There's also antipasto and salads but the reason to come here is the pizza; and to spend an authentic evening or afternoon in a typical Florentine neighborhood pizza parlor, surrounded by locals. Remember to make reservations since Il Pizzaiuolo is always packed.

Oltrarno

26. ANGIOLINO, *Borgo Santo Spirito 36r. Tel. 055/239-8976. Closed Mondays in summer. All credit cards accepted. Dinner for two E35.*

This is one of the best *trattorie* in Florence with a grand vaulted main room and aromas wafting throughout that will make your mouth water. The service if efficient, and the wine list plentiful with a distinct local flavor, a direction in which the menu also leans. You can find *crostini* (baked dough stuffed with meat and or vegetables), *verdure all griglia* (grilled vegetables), ravioli, and many other traditional Tuscan dishes. My favorites are the *tortellini alla panna* (meat or cheese stuffed pasta in a cream sauce) or the *tagliatelli con funghi* (pasta with mushrooms). The main courses are focused on meat. A wonderful place to grab either lunch or dinner while in Florence.

27. LA CASALINGA, *Via dei Michelozzi 9r, Tel. 055/218-624. Closed Sundays and the first 20 days in August. No credit cards accepted. Dinner for two E25.*

Here in this authentic Oltrarno-style *trattoria* you'll find a few tourists intermingling with the local artisans and residents. The cooking is classic Tuscan that is simple, tasty and filling. The antipasto is a mixed salad with sliced meats and cheeses thrown in. For seconds you'll find some Tuscan favorites like *bolliti misti con salsa verde* (mixed boiled meats in a spicy green sauce), *lo spezzatino* (Tuscan stew), *le salsicce con le rape* (sausage with turnips), and *il baccala alla livornese* (cooked cod Livorno style – salty). Sample away and don't forget to wash it all down with some of the great house wine.

28. CAVALO NERO, *Via dell'Ardiglione 22, Tel. 055/294-744. Closed Sundays, August, Dec 25 and Jan 1. Open only in the evenings. American Express and Via accepted. Dinner for two E65.*

A high end *ristorante* in a local neighborhood, down a small side street, off the beaten tourist path. A mixture of traditional and creative cuisine where you can get many local favorites as well as *cucina nuova* concoctions. A pleasantly simple yet refined atmosphere combined with a robust cuisine makes for an excellent meal at the Cavalo Nero. And don't forget the desserts. They are exemplary. Also be aware of the automatic 10% *coperto* (cover charge) added on, which can act as your tip.

29. DEL CINGHIALE BIANCO, *Borgo San Jacopo 43, Tel. 055/215-706. Mastercard and Visa accepted. Closed Tuesdays and Wednesdays. Dinner for two E40.*

Wild game is the specialty here as befits a place named The White Boar, so get ready to enjoy some fine peasant dishes. I tried the wild boar cold cuts but liked the assorted salamis of Tuscany better. The chicken breast cooked with ham and cheese was not Italian, but it was great. I like the wrought-iron motif that dominates the place, especially the old cooking pot hanging from the ceiling. A simple place with good food and great atmosphere.

30. DILADDARNO, *Via de' Serragli 108r, Tel. 055/225-001. Closed Mondays, Tuesdays, and from July 16 to August 16. No credit cards accepted. Dinner for two E30.*

This *trattoria* offers some of the best and most authentic Florentine dishes. Try the *trippa alla Fiorentina* (boiled tripe), *ossobuco* (stew made with a veal knuckle in a tomato sauce), *ribollita* (boiled meats), *bistecca* (huge grilled steaks of beef), or the *rognoncini* (stewed kidneys). All can be enjoyed with some tasty house wines. There is a tiny garden inside that can be enjoyed in good weather. Off the beaten track, which is why the prices (and food!) are so good.

31. FUORI PORTA, *Via Monte alle Croci 10r, Tel. 055/234-2483. Closed Sundays and August. No credit cards accepted. Dinner for two E30.*

This lovely cantina has a rather extensive menu for a wine bar. You can get pastas – such as the *tagliatelle con astice e zuchine* (with onions and zucchini), *crostini*, soups and salads and some excellent desserts. The wine list is extensive, filled with both Italian and foreign vintages. Lovely atmosphere, with a quaint terrace, definitely off the beaten path, just outside the old walls of Florence at the foot of the hills of the Piazzaale Michelangelo. A good place to stop in for a filling snack and a relaxing glass of wine.

32. DEL GALLO NERO, *Via Santo Spirito 6r, Tel. 055/218-898. Closed Mondays and August. AMEX and Visa accepted. Dinner for two E30.*

Go down the stairs and you'll find yourself in a large vault-like room, which is the *trattoria*. The menu is filled with Tuscan *antipasti* and soups, like the *minestra di pane* (a tasty bread soup); but my favorites are the series of *crostini* (stuffed pastry baked in the oven). You can get the crostini stuffed with mozzarella, *prosciutto* (ham), salami, and all manner of vegetable. They are delicious and filling, especially with a wonderful bottle of Chianti.

Learn to Cook in Florence

Since 1973, Giuliano Bugiali has been teaching Italian cooking to visitors in Florence, and it's all in English. To get information about how to spend an enjoyable culinary experience while soaking up all the glories of this great city, contact **Giuliano Bugiali's Cooking in Florence**, *PO Box 1650, Canal Street Station, New York, NY 10013-0870, Tel. 212/966-5325, Fax 212/226-0601.*

Make sure you order one with the *gallo nero* (black rooster) label on the stem. It's the namesake of the restaurant and indicates that the Chianti is of the finest quality.

33. LA LOGGIA, *Piazzale Michelangelo 1, Tel. 055/234-2832, Fax 055/234-5288. American Express, Diners Club, Mastercard and Visa accepted. Closed Wednesdays. Dinner for two E55.*

Come for the view of Florence, stay for the food, try to escape from the prices. This ideally located restaurant and café has a great panoramic view of Florence, which seems to make your meal that much better, until the bill arrives, then cardiac arrest sets in. Come dressed for success or the other customers will give you the once-over. Try the *pollo al diavolo* (chicken cooked over an open fire) after the *spaghetti al frutti di mare* (with seafood). The taglietelle with bacon and broccoli in olive oil is the single best pasta dish I've ever had, even at twice the price of ordinary restaurants. You can't go wrong eating here.

34. MAMMA GINA, *Borgo S Jacopo 37, Tel. 055/239-6009, Fax 055/213-908. All credit cards accepted. Closed Sundays. Dinner for two E42.*

A large place with great food. I tried their *tortellini all crema* with apprehension since I do not believe that Florentines know how to make good pasta, and was more than pleasantly surprised. But first I had some great *bruschetta* (grilled bread covered with olive oil, garlic and tomatoes). For seconds I had the *petti di pollo alla griglia* (chicken breasts o the grill). You might also try the *penne stracciate alla Fiorentina* (a meat and tomato based pasta) and the *petti di pollo al cognac con funghi* (chicken breast cooked in cognac with mushrooms ... it gives it kind of a cacciatore taste). This is a really great place to get great food in a wonderful atmosphere. If you do not like smoke you have to ask them to seat you away from the people who do ... and most people do.

Seeing the Sights

The sights of Florence are fascinating, incredible – add your own superlatives after you've seen them! Florence is a living breathing museum filled with inspiring open air sights, and some of the best museums in the world. The sights below are numbered and correspond to the *Florence Sights* map on pages 332-333.

1. STATUE OF DAVID AT THE ACCADEMIA

Via Ricasoli 60, Tel. 055/214-375. Open 9:00am–7:00pm Tuesday–Saturday. Sundays 9:00am–1:00pm. Closed Mondays. Admission E6.

The **Accademia** is filled with a wide variety of paintings, sculptures, and plaster molds by artists from the Tuscan school of the 13th and 14th centuries; but the museum's main draw is a must-see for you in Florence. Here you will find a statue that is as close to perfection as can be achieved with a hammer and a chisel, Michelangelo's *David*. This masterpiece was started from a discarded block of marble another sculptor had initially scarred. Michelangelo bought it on his own – no one commissioned this work – since it was less expensive than a new piece of marble, and finished sculpting *David* from its confines at the age of 25 in the year 1504, after four years of labor. It was originally in front of the Palazzo della Signoria, but was replaced with a substitute in 1873 to protect the original from the elements.

Leading up to the *David* are a variety of other works by Michelangelo, most unfinished. These are called *The Prisoners,* since the figures appear to be trapped in stone. These statues were designed to hold the Tomb of Pope Giulio II on their sculpted shoulders, but Michelangelo died before he could bring the figures to life. And now they appear as if they are struggling to be freed from the marble's embrace.

Also included in this wonderful exhibit of Michelangelo's sculptures is the unfinished *Pieta*. Many art critics have spent their entire lives comparing this Pieta with the more famous one in St. Peter's in Rome. This statue looks older, sadder, more realistic, most probably since it was created by Michelangelo at the end of his life. The *Pieta* in Rome appears more vibrant, youthful, optimistic, and alive. Once again, this was probably because he sculpted the *Pieta* in Rome when he was a young man,

Also in the Accademia is the **Sala Dell'Ottocento** (The 19th Century Hall) that is a gallery of plaster model and other works by students and prospective students of the Academy. Despite the medium, plaster, these works are exquisite. The holes you see in the casts are iron markings used as guides so that when carved into marble the figure can be recreated perfectly.

2. PIAZZA & CHURCH OF SS ANNUNZIATA
Tel. 055/210-644. Open 7:00am-7:00pm.

Just around the corner from the Accademia, this piazza is relatively isolated from the hustle and bustle of Florence's tourist center, so that when you enter it you feel as if you walked back into Renaissance Florence. This is how all the piazzas must have looked and felt back then, no cars, only people milling around sharing the Florentine day.

In the center of the square sits the equestrian *Statue of the Grand Duke Ferdinando I* by **Giambologna** and **Pietro Tacca** (1608). The two bronze fountains with figures of sea monsters are also the work of Tacca (1629).

The church, like the piazza, is also a hidden jewel in Florence. Erected in 1250, reconstructed in the middle of the 15th century by **Michelozzo**, was again re-done in the 17th and 18th centuries, and remains today as it was then. Entering hte Basilica you are instantly struck by the magnificence there in, the carved and gilded ceiling, and the profusion of marble and stucco.

The church is particularly famous for a miracle which is thought to have taken place here. A certain painter named Bartlomeo was commissioned to paint a frescoe in 1252 of the Annucniation. When he was about to paint the face of Mary in the painting he fell asleep, only to find the face painted for him, supposedly by angelic hands, after he awoke. The frescoe is located insie the tempietto to the left of the entrance. The frescoe became the heart of the Baslica, which was subsequently dedicated to Our Lady Annuciate. So there you have it!

3. PONTE VECCHIO
Literally meaning *Old Bridge*, the name came about because the bridge has been around since Etruscan times. Not in its present form, of course. The present bridge was rebuilt on the old one in the 14th century by **Neri di Fiorvanti**. Thankfully this beautiful bridge with its shops lining each side of it was spared the Allied and Axis bombardments during World War II. Today the shops on the bridge belong to silversmiths, goldsmiths, and some fine leather stores. In the middle of the bridge are two arched openings that offer wonderful views of the Arno. On the downstream side of the bridge is a bust of **Benvenuto Cellini**, a Renaissance Goldsmith and sculptor, done by Rafaele Romanelli in 1900. At night on the bridge you'll find all sorts of characters hanging out, sipping wine, and strumming guitars.

Take time to notice the **Vasarian Corridor** which spans the Ponte Vecchio and once linked the Uffizzi with the Pitti Palace. It was used as a defense corridor as well as a private passageway. As you walk from the Uffizzi side of the Arno to the Pitti side (the Otrarno) the corridor will be on the left above the shops. The corridor can be visited by appointment Tuesday-Saturday starting at 9:30am. *To book a tour call, Tel. 055/23885 well in advance. Tickest are E6 and also offer entrance to the Uffizi.*

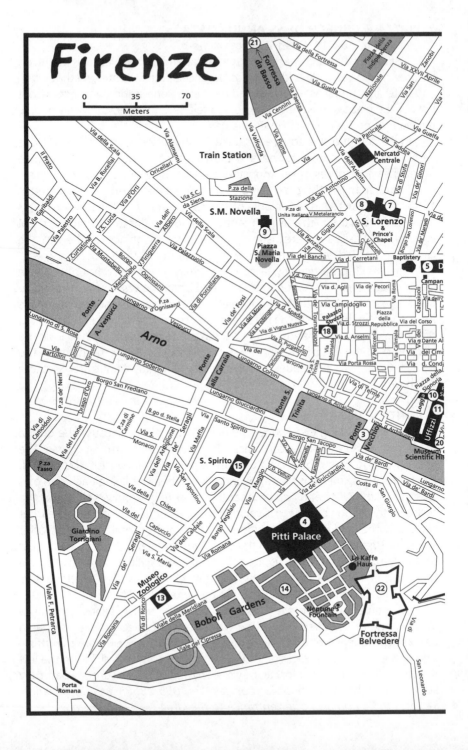

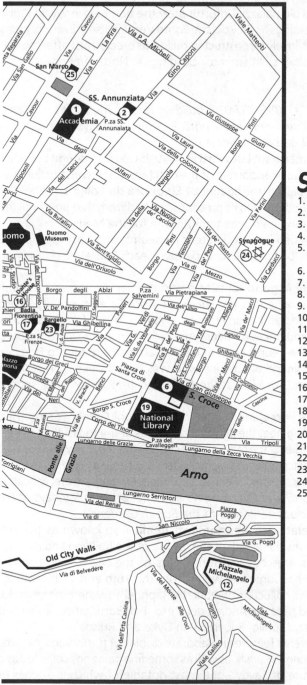

Sights

1. Academia
2. SS. Annunziata
3. Ponte Vecchio
4. Pitti Palace
5. Duomo, Baptistery, Campanile & Museum
6. Santa Croce
7. San Lorenzo
8. Prince's Chapel
9. Santa Maria Novella
10. Palazzo della Signoria
11. Uffizzi Gallery
12. Piazzale Michelangelo
13. Museo Zoologico
14. Boboli Gardens
15. Santo Spirito
16. Dante's House
17. Church of the Badia
18. Palazzo Strozzi
19. National Library
20. Museum of Scientific History
21. Fortressa da Basso
22. Fortressa Belvedere
23. Bargello
24. Tempio Israelico
25. San Marco

On the street from the Ponte Vecchio to the Pitti Palace there used to be a series of wonderful old palazzi. Unfortunately the bombers in World War II didn't avoid these buildings as they did the Ponte Vecchio itself. Even so, today the street is filled with lovely reconstructed buildings erected just after the war which makes them older still than most buildings in North America.

4. PITTI PALACE

Piazza dei Pitti. Tel. 055/287-096. Building hours: Tues. - Sat. 9:00am - 7:00pm. Most museums only open until 2:00pm. Sundays and Holidays 9:00am - 1:00pm. Closed on Mondays.

Built for the rich merchant **Luca Pitti** in 1440, based on a design by Filippo Brunelleschi. Due to the financial ruin of the Pitti family, the construction was interrupted until the palace was bought by **Eleonora da Toledo**, the wife of Cosimo I. It was then enlarged to its present size. And from that time until the end of the 17th century, it was the family home for the Medicis.

Currently it is divided into six different museums; and since the upkeep and security for this building is so expensive, each museum charges an entrance fee:

The **Museo degli Argenti** contains precious objects collected over time by the Medici and Lorraine families. There are works in amber, ivory, silver, crystal, precious woods and enamel work. Located in the former Summer Apartment of the grand dukes of Medici, the collection includes the *Salzburg Treasure* (gold and silver cups, vases and other articles) brought to Florence by the Archduke Ferdinand of Lorraine who was Grand Duke of Tuscany in 1790. (*The 1st, 3rd, and 5th Mondays and 2nd, and 4th Sundays of the month closed. E6.*)

The **Museo delle Porcelane** is situated in the Boboli Gardens and housed in a quaint little building near the Belvedere Fortress at the top of the hill. This porcelain collection reflects the taste of the Medicis and the many families that resided in the Pitti Palace after the Medici's decline. There are pieces made in Capodimonte, Doccia, Sevres, Vienna, and Meissen and all are delicately exquisite. (*The 1st, 3rd, and 5th Mondays and 2nd, and 4th Sundays of the month closed. E2 includes entrance to the Boboli Gardens.*)

The **Galleria Palatina e Apartamenti Reali**. Also known as the Pitti Gallery, this exhibit runs the length of the facade of the building and includes paintings, sculptures, frescoes and furnishings of the Medici and Lorraine families. This gallery has some fine works from the 16th and 17th centuries and the most extensive collection of works by Raphael anywhere in the world. Other artists included here are Andrea del Sarto, Fra' Bartolomeo, Titian and Tintoretto, Velasquez, Murillo, Rubens, Van Dyke and Ruisdal.

The royal apartments feature an elaborate display of furnishings, carpets, wonderful silks covering the walls, as well as some fine paintings collected and displayed by the house of Savoy – the most notable of which is a series of portraits of the family of Louis XV of France. (*E6 includes entrance to the Museo delle Carozze.*)

The **Museo delle Carrozze** houses carriages used by the court of the houses of Lorraine and Savoy when they ruled Florence. This was my favorite museum in Florence when I was a child. The carriages are extremely elaborate and detailed, especially the silver decorated carriage owned by King Ferdinand II of the Two Sicilies.

The **Galleria d'Arte Moderna**. The gallery occupies thirty rooms on the second floor of the palace and offers a thorough look at Italian painting from neo-classicism to modern works covering the years up to 1945. The emphasis is on the art from Tuscany and has some works similar to French impressionists. Organized chronologically and by theme. (*The 1st, 3rd, and 5th Mondays and 2nd, and 4th Sundays of the month closed. E4 includes entrance to the Galleria del Costume.*)

The **Galleria del Costume** contains clothing from the 16th century to modern day. All are exhibited in 13 rooms of the Meridiana Wind. It is an excellent way to discern the changes in fashion from the 18th century to the 1920s. Today, because of television, major fashion changes occur almost every year; but back then it could take generations before any noticeable change occurred. Also included are historical theater costumes created by the workshop of Umberto Tirelli.

5. DUOMO & BAPTISTERY, CAMPANILE, & CATHEDRAL MUSEUM

All located at the Piazza del Duomo. Hours: **Duomo** *– Church open Mon.- Sat. 10:00am–5:00pm, Sun. 1:00pm–5:00pm. Entrance to the dome costs E3.* **The Baptistery** *– Open everyday 2:00pm–5:30pm. Entrance E2.* **The Campanile** *– Open 8:30am–6:50pm (9:00am -4:20pm in off season). Admission E3.* **Cathedral Museum** *(Museo dell'Opera del Duomo) – Closed Sundays. Summer hours - Mon. through Sat. 9:00am - 7:30pm. Until 6pm in off-season. Holidays open 9:00am–1:00pm. Tel. 055/230-2885.*

Duomo

When you're in Florence the one sight you have to visit is the **Duomo**, Florence's cathedral. It was consecrated in 1436 by Pope Eugenio IV as **Santa Maria del Fiore** (Saint Mary of the Flowers), and that is still its official name, but everybody calls it "The Duomo" because of its imposing dome. It was started in 1296 by Arnolfo di Cambio on the spot where the church of Santa Reparata existed. After di Cambio's death in 1301, the famous Giotto took over the direction of the work, but he dedicated most of his attention to the development of the Bell Tower (*Campanile*).

When Giotto died in 1337, Andrea Pisano took over until 1349 (death didn't cause his departure, he just moved on to other projects). By 1421 everything else was finished except for the dome, which **Brunelleschi** had won a competition to design and build. It took 14 years just to construct the gigantic dome. Over the years, slight modifications and changes have been made, and in 1887, the current facade of the Duomo was finished by architect **Emilio de Fabris**.

The interior of the Duomo is 150 meters long and 38 meters wide at the nave and 94 meters at the transept. There are enormous gothic arches, supported by gothic pillars, which gives the interior a majestic quality. The dome is 90 meters high and 45.5 meters in diameter and is decorated with frescoes representing the Last Judgment done by Giorgio Vasari and Federico Zuccari at the end of the 16th century. In the niches of the pillars supporting the dome are statues of the Apostles.

The central chapel is home to the **Sarcophagus of San Zanobius** that contains the saint's relics. The bronze reliefs are the work of Lorenzo Ghiberti (1442). When you've finished wandering through the cathedral and admiring the art and stained glass windows, you can go to the top of the Duomo and get some great views of Florence. The way up is a little tiring, but the magnificent photo opportunities – both inside and out – are fabulous. Don't miss these views!

The Baptistery

Definitely considered one of the most important works in the city, the **Baptistery** was built on the remains of an early Roman structure which was transformed into a paleo-Christian monument. The Baptistery, built in the 10th and 11th centuries was dedicated to Saint John the Baptist, the patron saint of Florence. Up until 1128, it was the cathedral of Florence. This small structure just didn't reflect the growing stature of the city of Florence, so they erected the Duomo.

Its octagonal shape is covered with colored marble. On the pavement by the Baptistery you'll find the signs of the Zodiac. Inside is the tomb of Giovanni XXIII by Donatello and Michelozzo in 1427. Next to the altar, you'll see the *Angel Holding The Candlestick* by Agostino di Jacopo in 1320. To the left between the Roman sarcophagi is the wooden statue *Magdalen* by Donatello in 1560.

But the true masterpieces of the Baptistery are the bronze paneled doors by **Ghoberti** and **Andrea Pisano da Pontedera**. The public entrance is the **Southern Door**, created by Andrea Pisano da Pontedera and is of least interest. The east and north doors are far more beautiful and intricate. Michelangelo described the east door as "the door to paradise." On it you'll find stories of the Old Testament, beginning as follows from the top left hand side:

• Creation of Adam; original sin; expulsion of Adam and Eve from Paradise
• Stories of Noah and the universal deluge (coincidentally some of these panels were almost lost in the flooding of 1966)

• Jacob and Esau; Rachel and Jacob; Isaac blesses Jacob
• Moses receives the Ten Commandments on Mount Sinai
• The battle against the Philistines; David and Goliath.

From the top right hand side:
• Adam works the soil; Cain and Abel at work; Cain kills Abel
• Three angels appear to Abraham; Abraham sacrifices Isaac
• Joseph meets his brothers in Egypt; Stories of Joseph
• Joshua crosses the Jordan River; The conquering of Jericho
• Solomon receives the Queen of Sheba in the Temple.

The Campanile

Giotto died while he was attempting to complete the **Campanile**, but after his death **Andrea Pisano** and **Francesco Talenti** both scrupulously followed his designs until its completion. The only part they left out was the spire that was to go on top, which would have made the Campanile 30 meters higher than its current 84. The tower is covered in colored marble and adorned with bas-reliefs by Andrea Pisano and Luca della Robbia and Andrea Orcagna. Sculptures by Donatello, Nanni di Bartolo, and others used to be in the sixteen niches but are now in the Cathedral Museum.

Cathedral Museum (*Museo dell'Opera del Duomo*)

This is the place where many pieces of artwork that used to be in the Cathedral or the Campanile are now located. Their removal and placement here was mainly done to help preserve them from the environment as well as the onslaught of tourists hordes. Most of the items are statues and bas-relief work. The most famous ones to keep an eye out for are *St. John* by **Donatello**, *Habakkuh* by Donatello, *Virgin with Infant Jesus* by **Arnolfo**, and *Choir Gallery* with many scenes by Donatello.

6. SANTA CROCE

Piazza Santa Croce. Open 10:00am -12:30pm and 2:30pm - 6:30pm (3-5pm in off season). Closed Wednesdays.

The church of **Santa Croce** sits in the Piazza Santa Croce, surrounded by ancient palazzi renowned for the architecture. The one opposite the church is the **Palazzo Serristori** by Baccio D'Agnolo in the 16th century. Facing the church on the right hand side at #23 is the **Palazzo dell'Antella** built by Giulio Parigi in the 17th century. In this piazza, on any night, when all the shops are closed, you will feel as if you've stepped back into the Renaissance.

In the center of the square is a statue of **Dante Aligheri**, he of *Divine Comedy* fame, sculpted by Enrico Pazzi in 1865. This is a wonderfully ornate yet simple church belonging to the Franciscan Order. Construction was begun in 1295 but its modern facade was created in 1863 by Nicolo Matas. The frescoes on the facade were created in only 20 days by 12 painters working non-stop. It has a slim bell tower whose Gothic style doesn't seem to fit with this modern exterior. The interior, on the other hand, fits perfectly with the simple stonework of the bell tower.

Initially, the walls inside had been covered with exquisite frescoes created by Giotto but these were covered up by order of Cosimo I in the 16th century. What remains is a basic monastic church that conveys piety and beauty in its simplicity. Of the many Italian artistic, religious, and political geniuses that lie buried beneath Santa Croce, the most famous has to be that of **Michelangelo** himself. Other prominent Florentines buried here are **Niccolo Machiavelli**, **Galileo Galilei**, **Dante Aligheri** and **Lorenzo Ghiberti**.

Leather School at Santa Croce

Besides the beautiful bas-reliefs, exquisite sculptures, and other works of art in Santa Croce you can find an excellent and relatively inexpensive **leather school** (Scuola del Cuoio). To get there go through the sacristy and you'll end up in the school that was started by the monks more than three decades ago. Here you'll find all kinds of fine leather products for sale but the best part is being able to see them being manufactured right in front of you in what were once cells for the monks.

The prices and selection are good and seeing the artisans at work is something that shouldn't be missed when in Florence (Tel. 244-533, Tuesday–Saturday, 9:00am–12:30pm and 3:00pm–6:00pm. All credit cards accepted.).

7. SAN LORENZO

Piazza San Lorenzo. Tel. 055/213-206. Open Tues - Sat. 9:00am–2:00pm, Sundays and Holidays 9:00am - 1:00pm. Closed Mondays.

One of the oldest basilicas in Florence. The architecture is the work of **Filippo Brunelleschi**, done from 1421-1446, but the church was finished by his pupil **Antonio Manetti** in 1460. The facade was never completed even though Michelangelo himself submitted a variety of designs for its completion.

The interior is made up of three naves with chapels lining the side walls. In the central nave at the far end are two pulpits that are the last two works of **Donatello** who died in 1466 after completing them. You'll find plenty of works by Donatello in this church, including:
• The stucco medallions in the Old Sacristy that represent the Four Evangelists that are Stories of Saint John the Baptist
• The terra-cotta Bust of Saint Lawrence in the Old Sacristy
• The bronze doors with panels representing the Apostles and Fathers of the Church in the Old Sacristy.

8. PRINCES' CHAPEL

Piazza San Lorenzo. Tel. 055/213-206. Open Tues - Sat. 9:00am-2:00pm, Sundays and Holidays 9:00am - 1:00pm. Closed Mondays.

Attached to the church of San Lorenzo, but with the entrance just around the corner to the back of the church, this octagonal building's construction was begun in 1604 on a design by Prince Giovanni dei Medici. It houses the tombs of a variety of Medici princes ... hence the name. It is of interest to many tourists because of the tombs in the New Sacristy which were created by Michelangelo himself. *The Tomb of Lorenzo, Duke of Urbino* (created by Michelangelo) has a statue of the duke seated and absorbed in meditation as well as two reclining figures that represent Dawn and Dusk. On the opposite wall is the *Tomb of Giuliano, Duke of Nemours* (also created by Michelangelo) which shows a seated duke replete in armor, ready for action, as well as two reclining figures that represent night and day. Another Michelangelo work in the New Sacristy is the unfinished *Madonna and Child.*

If you like Michelangelo's brilliant sculptures but want to avoid the crowds that congregate at the museum that houses the David, this is the place to come. And you can get some shopping done in the San Lorenzo market afterwards.

9. SANTA MARIA NOVELLA

Piazza Santa Maria Novella. Open 7:00am-11:30am and 3:30pm-6:00pm Monday-Saturday, and Sundays 3:30pm-5:00pm.

Built in 1278 by two Dominican friars, **Fra Ristoreo** and **Fra Sisto**, the church was created in the Gothic style with green and white marble decorations that are typically Florentine in character. The church was completed in 1470. To the left and right of the facade are tombs of illustrious Florentines all created in the same Gothic style as the church.

The interior of the church is in a "T" shape with the nave and aisles divided by clustered columns that support wide arches. Down the aisles are a variety of altars created by **Vasari** from 1565 to 1571. As a young artist, Michelangelo worked on many of the frescoes as commissioned by his teachers. This is where he got his initial training that helped him create the now famous frescoes in the Sistine Chapel in Rome.

The peaceful and expansive cloister are a rare treat. Come for a serene visit that marks back to the days of Michelangelo. (*Hours: weekdays 9:00am - 2:00pm. Holidays 8:00am -1:00pm. Closed Fridays. Entrance E2.*)

You can spend hours in here admiring these magnificent frescoes created by many Florentine artists including **Domenico Ghirlandaio** (Chapel of High Altar), **Giuliano da San Gallo** (Gondi Chapel), **Giovanni Dosio** (Gaddi Chapel), **Nardo di Cione** (Strozzi Chapel) and more. And if you're tired of sightseeing and need a little break, Florence's best pub, The Fiddler's Elbow, is in the piazza outside the church.

10. PIAZZA, PALAZZO, & LOGGIA DELLA SIGNORIA
Piazza della Signoria
This piazza, with the Palazzo, the Loggia, the fountain, the replica of the statue of David, the cafes and *palazzi* is incomparable in its beauty. Over the centuries great historical and political occurrences, as well as the lives of average Florentines, have all flowed through this piazza.

Today the square is the site of the annual sporting event, **Calcio in Costume** (soccer played in period garb), where the different sections of the city vie for dominance in a game that is a cross between soccer, rugby, martial arts and an all-out war. This annual contest used to be played in the square of Santa Croce but was moved here during modern times. If you are in Florence during June, when the event covers three of the weekends in that month, you definitely have to try and get tickets. The entire piazza is covered with sand, and stadium seats are put up all around the makeshift field, and then the fun begins. The event is a truly memorable experience.

In the small square on the left is **Ammannati's Fountain** with the giant figure of *Neptune*. The statue is commonly called *Biancone* (Whitey) by the locals because of its bland appearance. Giambologna created the equestrian statue representing *Cosimo I dei Medici* on the left of the square.

Palazzo della Signoria – Palazzo Vecchio
Piazza della Signoria. Open Monday–Friday 9:00am–7:00pm, and Sundays 8:00am–1:00pm. Closed on Saturdays. Admission E5 for upstairs galleries.

The most imposing structure in the square is the **Palazzo Signoria**. It is 94 meters past the fortified battlements to the top of **Arnolfo's Tower**. In fact I strongly encourage you to go up to top where the art conservationists work. You can walk along the turreted top, and get some terrific views of the Duomo and other aspects of the city.

The entire structure is rather severe, but at the same time elegant. Its construction began in the late 13th century and took hundreds of years to finish. It was once the home of **Cosimo de Medici** and other members of the Medici family before the Pitti Palace was completed.

In front of the building on the platform at the top of the steps, ancient orators used to harangue the crowds, and for this reason this section of the building is called *Arringhiera* (The Haranguing Area). Located here are several important sculptures including the *Marzocco* (a lion symbolizing the Florentine Republic; a stone copy of the original sits in the National Museum); *Judith and Holofernes* created by Donatello in 1460, which is a record of the victory over the Duke of Athens; the copy of Michelangelo's *David* (the original is in the Accademia), and *Hercules and Cacus* created by Baccio Bandinelli.

Above the main door is a frieze with two lions and a monogram of Christ with the inscription *Rex Regum et Dominus Dominantium* (King of Kings and Lord of Lords), which used to record the time that the Florentine republic elected Christ as their King in 1528. The inscription used to read *Jesus Christus Rex Florentinei Populi S P Decreto Electus* (Jesus Christ elected by the people King of Florence) but was changed in 1851.

The interior is mainly filled with artwork glorifying the Medici family who ruled the Florentine Republic for centuries. So if you need a break from religious art and all those paintings of the Madonna and Child, this is the respite you've been looking for. Everything is elaborate and ornate, as befitting the richest family in the world at that time.

You enter through the courtyard which was designed by Michelozzo in 1453. The elaborate stucco decorations on the columns and frescoes on the arches were added in 1565 on the occasion of the wedding between Francesco dei Medici and Joan of Austria. The fountain in the center, *Graceful Winged Cupid* was done by Verrochio in 1476. From here most of the art to see is upstairs, so either take the staircase up or use the elevator.

What follows is a description of the important works to see in each room:

Hall of the Five Hundred – Salone dei Cinquecento

This is the most splendid and artistic hall in Florence. It was designed for public meetings after the Medicis had been thrown from power. When Cosimo I regained the family's control over Florence, he had the hall enlarged and used it for his private audiences. On the wall opposite the entrance you'll find three large magnificent paintings by Baccio D'Agnolo, Baccio Bandinelli and Giorgio Vassari: *The Conquest of Siena; The Conquest of Porto Ercole; The Battle of Marciano*. On the wall across from this you'll find: *Maximilian Tries to Conquer Livorno; The Battle of Torre San Vincenzo; The Florentines Assault Pisa*. Underneath these painting you'll find sculptures by Vincenzo de Rossi representing *Hercules Labors*.

The ceiling is divided into 39 compartments with paintings by Giorgio Vasari that represent *Stories of Florence and the Medici*. The coup de grace is in the niche of the right wall at the entrance. Here you'll find Michelangelo's unfinished work, *The Genius of Victory*, which was designed for the tomb of Pope Julius II. If you only have a little time, spend it here. This room is magnificent.

Study of Francesco I de Medici

Here you'll find the work of many of Florence's finest artists crammed into as small a space as imaginable. The walls and even the barrel shaped ceiling are covered with paintings, and niches are filled with a variety of bronze statues. Elaborate, ostentatious and overwhelming. It is perpetually roped off, but you are able to view its splendor.

Hall of the Two Hundred – Salone dei Duecento
It is called thus since this is where the Council of two hundred citizens met during the time of the Republic for their important decisions. The walls are adorned with tapestry, the ceiling is ornately decorated, chandeliers hang low, and statues and busts adorn any free spot. The center of the room is occupied by the seating for the Council of 200.

Monumental Quarters – Quartieri Monumentali
These are a series of rooms that get their names from a member of the Medici family. Each are elaborate in their own right, filled with paintings, sculptures, frescoes, and more. From here you'll find many more interesting rooms and paintings as you explore, both on this floor and the one above, but this is the bulk of the beauty in the Palazzo Signoria.

The Loggia della Signoria
In the Piazza, on the right of the Palazzo as you face it, is the expansive and airy **Loggia della Signoria**, a combination of Gothic and Renaissance architecture. It was built by Benci di Cione, Simone Talenti and others during the years 1376–1382. At either end of the steps are two marble lions, one of which is very old, the other made in 1600.

Underneath the arch are some wonderful sculptures: *Persius* by Cellini in 1553 under the left hand arch; *The Rape of the Sabines* by Giambologna in 1583 under the right arch; *Hercules and the Centaur* by Giambologna in 1599 under the right arch also. There is also *Menelaus supporting Patroclus* and a few other less important works. All of them, since they are open to the elements and pollution, have been stained and discolored, but all are excellent studies in human anatomy.

11. UFFIZZI GALLERY
Piazza del Uffizzi. Open Tuesday to Saturday 9:00am–2:00pm, Sundays and Holidays 9:00am–1:00pm. Closed Mondays. Admission E6. Tel. 055/218-341. Web: http://musa.uffizi.firenze.it.

The building housing the **Uffizi Gallery** was begun in 1560 by Giorgio Vasari on the orders of the Grand-Duke Cosimo I. It was originally designed to be government offices, but today holds the most important and impressive display of art in Italy, and some would say the world. The gallery mainly contains paintings of Florentine and Tuscan artists of the 13th and 14th centuries, but you'll also find works from Venice, Emilia, and other Italian art centers as well as Flemish, French, and German studies. In conjunction there is a collection of ancient sculptures.

These fabulous works of art were collected first by the Medici family (Francesco de' Medici started it off in 1581) then later by the Lorraine family. The last of the Medici, the final inheritor of that amassed wealth, Anna Maria

Reservation Service for Uffizzi & Other Museums

It is strongly recommended that you reserve tickets in advance so that you do not have to stand in the incredibly long lines which are common at the Uffizzi, Accademia and other museums, especially in the summer.

Once you have ordered your tickets you will not have to wait in that incredibly long line outside the Uffizzi. Simply walk up to the bookstore to the left side of the entrance, pick up your tickets, and enter at the time designated.

You can also get tickets for the Uffizzi and other museums on the web through **www.firenze.net**. The site is self explanatory and makes life so much easier for people wanting to get into Florence's wonderful museums without having to waste precious hours waiting in line.

Reservations for the Uffizzi can be made for a specific day and a specific time of entry, as long as ticket availibility lasts, by calling 011/ 39/055/294-883, Monday thru Friday 8.30am-6.30pm; Saturday 8.30am-12.30 am. On Saturday and holidays an answering service is operative. Fax 011/39/055/264-406. Charge for reservations by phone - E2. Tickets - E6.

Luisa donated the entire Gallery to the Tuscan state in 1737 so that the rich collection gathered by her ancestors would never leave Florence. Not everything would go as planned, since in the 18th century some pieces were stolen by Napoleon's marauding forces, but most of these were later returned after a ransom was paid. Some items were damaged in the great flood of 1966, and still others were damaged in 1993 when a terrorist car bomb ripped through parts of the Gallery. Even with all these occurrences, the Uffizzi is still one of the finest galleries in the world.

As you enter the Uffizzi, you will find the statues of Cosimo the Elder and Lorenzo the Magnificent, as well as several busts of the rest of the Medici rulers. It is ironic that they are so prominently displayed since when they ruled most Florentines despised their despotic ways. But now they are immortalized in time because of the philanthropic gesture of their last heir.

Anyway, it would be virtually impossible to list all the paintings and sculptures exhibited, so let me make a list of those that you absolutely must see if you visit the gallery. If you want a more complete listing or an audio guided tour, you can get those as you enter. Also, the museum is in the process of preparing for a move from the upper floor to the two lower floors. If that

occurs, the room designations indicated below will no longer be valid.
• *Madonna of the Pomegranate, The Primavera, The Birth of Venus,* and *Annunciation* - Botticelli - Room X (This is the main Botticelli room, but there are Botticelli's strewn from Room X to XIV)
• *Self Portraits of Titian, Michelangelo, Raphael, Rubens, Rembrandt and more* - Third Corridor
• *Madonna of the Goldfinch* - Raphael - Room XXV
• *Holy Family* - Michelangelo - Room XXV
• *Venus of Urbino* - Titian - Room XXVIII
• *Young Bacchus* - Caravaggio - Room XXXVI
• *Portrait of an Old Man* - Rembrandt - Room XXXVII
• *Portrait of Isabelle Brandt* - Peter Paul Rubens - Room XLI

The most recent purchases are concerned with self-protraits of some of the world's masters including Giotto, Maasaccio, Paulo Uccello, Filippo Lipp, Botticelli, Leonardo, Michelnagelo and others. A rare peek into the past to see what these painters really looked like. Another sight to see at the Uffizzi is thye view from the Cafetteria Bartolini, located on the second floor at the very end of the second hall way. The food's not that great, but the view is great for photographs.

12. PIAZZALE MICHELANGELO
From this piazza you have a wonderful view over the city of Florence being dissected by the river Arno. Remember to bring your camera since this is the best public view of the city. The best view, public or private is from the Hotel Torre di Bellosguardo, but if you desire that vista you have to spend the night since they don't allow sightseers on their grounds. At the center of the Piazzalle Michelangelo is a monument to **Michelangelo** dominated by a replica of the statue of *David*. Round the pedestal are four statues that adorn the tombs of famous Medicis which Michelangelo created. If you are up here around dinner time and want to grab something to eat, try the restaurant La Loggia on the opposite side of the piazza from the vista, across the road.

If you don't want to walk up the steep hill to the piazza, take bus number 13 from the station.

13. MUSEO ZOOLOGICO LA SPECOLA
Via Romana 17, Tel. 055/222-451. Closed Wednesdays. Open 9:00am–noon and until 1:00pm on Sundays.
This is an outing for the entire family. They have vast collection of stuffed animals from all over the world, some extinct, as well as bugs, fish, crustaceans, and more. You won't believe the extent of this collection, and that's just the animals. The best part of the exhibit is the collection of over 500 anatomical figures and body parts that were made in very life-like colored wax between

1175 and 1814. Every part of the body has been preserved separately as well as in whole body displays. They even put human hair on the heads of female reproductions to make them look more realistic.

One exhibit you may not want your kids to see is the part on reproduction, which gets pretty graphic. That room is at the end so you can march ahead and steer your impressionable ones into another room if you choose.

The other stuff is very tame. The last room has miniature wax scenes that are completely realistic depictions of the toll taken by the Black Death (the Plague). One particular tiny image of a rat pulling on a dead man's intestine is quite intense. Look at these pieces as art, not the anatomy tools they were used for, and you'll appreciate them immensely. The museum is used by many art students to study anatomy and you will find them discreetly sketching throughout the entire display.

14. THE BOBOLI GARDENS
Located behind the Pitti Palace. Tel. 055/213-370. Open 9:00am - 4:30pm (Nov-Feb), 5:30pm (Mar. & Oct.), 6:30pm (Apr., May & Sept.), 7:30pm (June, July & Aug.). Closed the first and last Mondays of each month. E3 with Museo delle Porcelane.

Hidden behind the Pitti Palace is your respite from the Florentine summer heat and the hordes of tourists. Began in 1549 by Cosimo I and Eleanor of Tudor, the gardens went through many changes, additions, and alterations before they reached their present design. Among its many pathways and well-placed fields, the **Boboli Gardens** are the only true escape from the sun, humidity, and crowds that swarm through Florence in July and August. If you are inclined to walk in a calm, peaceful garden, far from the bustling crowds, or if you wish to enjoy a relaxing picnic, the Boboli is your place.

In the groves and walks of the Boboli you can find many spots to sit and enjoy a picnic lunch, or you can simply enjoy the platoons of statuary lining the walks. Some of the most famous works here include: *Pietro Barbino Riding a Tortoise*, commonly called 'Fat Baby Bacchus Riding a Turtle' (you'll find reproductions of this statue in almost every vendor's stall in Florence); a Roman amphitheater ascending in tiers from the Palazzo Pitti, designed as a miniature Roman circus to hold Medici court spectacles; and *Neptune's Fountain* at the top of the terrace, created in 1565 by Stoldo Lorenzi.

From this fountain a path leads to the adorable **Kaffeehaus**, a boat-like pavilion that offers a fine view of Florence and drinks to quench your thirst. Keep going up until you reach the **Ex Forte di Belvedere**, which offer magnificent views of all of Florence, and **Cypress Alley**, lined with statues of many different origins.

Also in the gardens is the **Museo delle Porcelane** with a delicate porcelain collection from the Medici and Lorraine families.

La Limonaia
Even if you are not looking for it, you can't miss the **Limonaia**, a room 340 feet long and 30 feet wide that became the 'hospital' for all the devastated works of art during the Flood of '66 (see story below). Originally used to house the Boboli Gardens' lemon trees during the winter months, this room, many experts felt, was the savior of the Florentine masterpieces, because of its insulation from the Florentine humidity. Most of the art treasures from the disastrous flood of '66 were brought here to be rehabilitated. I guess you could say that all art lovers can be thankful that the Medicis had a passion for lemons.

Porta Romana
This garden stretches seemingly forever, and it hides some of the best green spaces at its farthest corners, near Florence's **South Gate** (**Porta Romana**). If you exit here and take the big road to your left, Piazzale Michelangelo, you will walk through some incredibly bucolic Florentine neighborhoods.

15. SANTO SPIRITO
Piazza Santo Spirito. Open 8:00am-Noon and 4:00pm-6:00pm. Closed Wednesday afternoons.
Begun in 1444 by Brunelleschi, and continued after his death in 1446 by Antonio Manetti, Giovanni da Gaiole and Salvi d'Andrea. The last of these built the cupola that was based on Brunelleschi's design. It has a simple, plain, seemingly unfinished facade, in contrast to the interior.
Divided into three naves flanked by splendid capped Corinthian columns, this church looks very similar to San Lorenzo. There is a central cupola with two small naves in the wings of the cross that have small chapels just off of them. Lining the walls are some small chapels capped by semi-circular arches are adorned with elaborate carvings. The main altar, created by Giovanni Caccini (1599-1607), is Baroque in style and intricately displayed. In the chapels off the wings of the cross to the right and left of the main altar are many fine works of art to be enjoyed (two of which are *Madonna con Bambino* by Fillipino Lippi and *San Giovanni and Madonna with Baby Jesus and Four Saints* by Masi di Banco).
Many of these works are difficult to see since light does not find its way into this church very well.

16. DANTE'S HOUSE
Via Santa Margherita 1, Tel. 055/219-416. Open 10:00am-6:00pm (until 4:00pm in off season). Closed Tuesdays. E3.
Dante's House and the accompanying museum of his life sits along one of the most medieval streets in Florence, tiny, cramped and evoking the

conditions of his time. The house is quaintly picturesque. It was reconstructed a little haphazardly in the 19th century. The ground floor is a precursor with furnishings from Dante's time period. Upstairs is where the museum is (*entrance at Via S. Margherita 1*). It contains various manuscripts from Dante's time including many different versions of the *Divine Comedy*, Dante's most famous work. Not the greatest site in the world, but if you're a Dante fan this is a must see in Florence.

17. CHURCH OF THE BADIA
Via del Proconsolo. Open 9:00am-7:00pm.

Directly almost directly in front of the Bargello museum, this building was a Benedictine monastery founded in 978. The church is where it is rumored that Dante saw his love Beatrice for the first time. The church and accompanying buildings have gone through many changes over time. In 1285 the facade was built; in the 1400's extensive renovations were done on the cloisters, and in the sixteenth century the church was given a Baroque look and feel by Matteo Segaloni.

From the courtyard of the building you can admire the campanile of the Palazzo Vecchio, one of the characteristic structures in the skyline of Florence.

The interior of the church contains many notable paintings as well as tombs of respected Florentines, including Ugo di Toscana whose mother founded the monastery and Bernardo Giugni. The organ in the church, built by Onofrio Zeffirini da Cortona in 1558, still works and is used at every mass. Through a door on the right side of the church you enter the amazing *Chapel of the Oranges* (closed during mass) created by Bernardo Rossellino from 1432-38.

18. PALAZZO STROZZI
Piazza degli Strozzi. Tel. 055/288342. Hours Mon- Sat. 9:00am-1:00pm. Closed Sundays.

One of the most beautiful Renaissance palazzi in Florence built by and for one of Florence's most powerful families, the Strozzi. Construction was begun August 6th, 1489 because of astrological reasons, was stopped in 1504 for the same reasons, restarted in 1523, and suspended again in 1538 because of the death of Filippo Strozzi il Giovane. In true Italian fashion, work was never totally completed, but constant renovations and reconstructions have occurred.

The proportions of this three story building are exemplary and is something to be viewed for its Renaissance look and feel. It now houses some cultural institutes which are not open to the public, but you are allowed to enter the courtyard and look around at the archways and portals.

19. NATIONAL LIBRARY
Piazza Cavaleggeri1, Tel. 055/249191. Open Mon.-Fri. 10:00am-12.30pm; 3:00pm-6:30pm; Saturdays 10:00am-12.30pm.

The **Biblioteca Nazionale** is one of the most important libraries in Italy, located in the Santa Croce section of Florence in an eclectic building on the Piazza dei Cavaleggeri just off of the Lungarno. It was built between 1911 and 1935. The collection of books was started around 1714 by Angelo Magliabechi and was called at the time Biblioteca Magliabechiana. It was expanded in successive years by incorporating other libraries with the Magliabechi collection; then in 1861 it was renamed the National Library.

Today the library contains over 85 kilometers of shelves, 25,000-plus manuscripts and around 5 million books and 1 million letters. There are many ancient pieces in the library, including *Il Messale* (Catholic Missal) from the 10th century, *Il Codice della Commedia*, the oldest surviving Italian manuscript from before the 10th century, the *Maguntina Bible* from 1462, and *La Commedia* published in Florence in 1481 with comments by Cristoforo Landini and signed by Botticelli. Not your average titles found in libraries elsewhere. If you are a bibliophile make a pilgrimage here.

20. MUSEUM OF SCIENTIFIC HISTORY
Piazza dei Guidici 1, Tel. 055/239-8876. Web: http://galileo.imss.firenze.it/index.html. Hours Mon., Wed., Thurs., Fri. 9:30am - 5:00pm. Tues. & Sat 9:30am-1:00pm. Closed Sundays and most holidays.

Located along the Lungarno and near the Uffizzi is the **Museo di Storia della Scienza**. Situated in the severe Palazzo Castellani which was built in the 14th century, the building was first used as a civil courthouse from 1574 to 1841, and up to 1966 one part of the building was the *Accademia della Crusca*, but the massive flood of that year forced the relocation of that organization.

Since 1930 the Museo di Storia della Scienza has been housed here. The exhibit is mainly a collection of scientific instruments from the 16th and 17th centuries. There are astrolabs, solar clocks, architectural tools and more. Of great interest are the original instruments used by Galileo (rooms IV and V). Also of interest are the map-making materials and ancient geographical tools (room VII). There is also a splendid reconstruction of the map of the world made by Fra Mauro.

On the second floor you will find the precious astronomical clock from the 15th century (room XII) and many instruments created and used in the 17th century, including the amazing mechanical *mano che scrive* (hand that writes) and *l'orologia del moto perpetuo* (clock of perpetual motion). For those interested in scientific discovery, or for those who need a break from art, this is a wonderful museum to visit.

21. FORTRESSA DA BASSO
Viale Filippo Strozzi, 1 Tel. 055/49721. The parks inside are open 24 hours a day..
Take the Via Valfonda to the right of the train station to get here, the Fortress of San Giovanni. Also known as the Fortressa da Basso ("below") as compared to the Fortressa Belvedere ("with a good view"). This is an enormous pentagonal fortification built by the decree of Alessandro de' Medici more to eliminate internal strife through a show of force than for defense of the city. Construction was started under the guidance of Sangallo il Giovane in 1534. The outside walls were originally over 12 meters high and the walls nearest the station and the train tracks are the only ones of that height today. On the inside there is an octagonal building of note, the *corpo di guardia* (guard house).

22. FORTE BELVEDERE
Via S. Leonardo. Tel. 055/234-2425. Open 9:00am-8:00pm. Only the grounds are open to the public.
Also called the Fort of St. George, this fortress was constructed in the 1500s by the decree of the Grand Duke Ferdinand I on a design by Bernardo Buontalenti e Don Giovanni de' Medici. Its battlements were used in the defense of the city for centuries. From the battlements you have an amazing panorama of the city and the valley of the Arno. A great place for photo opportunities.
At the center of the structure is the Palazzina di Belvedere, built between 1560 and 1570, and only open for special exhibits.

23. MUSEO NAZIONALE DEL BARGELLO
Via del Proconsolo, Tel 055/210-801. Open Tuesdays - Saturdays 9:00am-2:00pm and Sundays 9:00am -1:00pm. Holidays 8:30am-1:50pm. Closed Mondays. E4.
Located almost behind the *Palazzo* Signoria in the quaint Piazza S. Firenze, you will find one of the most important collections of art and artifacts in the world. Located in the building that was the first seat of government in Florence, and was in 1574 the seat of the justice department, police, and customs, this is a rather severe, austere palazzo that was restored from 1858 to 1865. After the great flood of 1966 most of the ground floor had to be redone.
You will find great sculptures from the Renaissance. Featured prominently are those created in Tuscany, which are some of the best ever made. After entering into the small area called *Torre Volognana* you are ushered into the *Cortile* (courtyard) area complete with a fountain and six allegorical marble statues by Bartolomeo Ammannati, *Oceano* by Giambologna, *Allegoria di Fiesole* by Tribolo and *Cannone di S. Paolo* by Cosimo Cenni.

Elsewhere in the museum you will find some beautiful works by Michelangelo including *Bacco* (1496-97) *David-Apollo* (1530-32) which is the first large classical sculpture by the artist, and *Bruto* (1530), which means ugly, and is the only bust created by Michelangelo of Lorenzino di Medici. On this floor are also some beautiful bronze statues by a variety of artists.

On the second floor (which you get to by stairs constructed by Neri di Fioravante from 1345-1367) are some interesting bronze animal sculptures including the famous *tacchino* (turkey) made by Giambologna. The other featured artist in the museum is Donatello whose works are displayed in the *Salone del Consiglio Generale*, constructed by the same architect who built the stairs. Here you'll find *S. Giorgio* (1416) accompanied by two statues of *David*, one younger in marble (1408-9) and the other more famous one in bronze (circa 1440). Other works by Donatello include the *Bust of Niccolo of Uzzano* made of multi-colored terra-cotta, *Marzocco* (1418-20), a lion that symbolizes the Florentine Republic, *Atys-Amor*, a wonderful bronze, and the dramatic *Crucifixion*.

There are many other works here, too many to mention, but suffice to say that this is a museum that shouldn't be missed while in Florence, especially if you like sculpture. The Accademia and the Uffizzi get all the press in Florence, but this is one of the best museums of sculpture anywhere in the world.

24. TEMPIO ISRAELICO

Via Luigi Carlo Ferini, Tel. 055/245-252 Open Sun.-Thurs. 10:00am - 1:00pm & 2:00pm-5:00pm. Fridays 10:00am -1:00pm. Closed Saturdays & Jewish Holidays. E3.

Built from 1874 to 1882, this eclectic synagogue with Byzantine/Moorish motifs is definitely worth seeing. There is no need to enter unless you are curious, but the building also contains the *Museo Ebraico di Firenze* (Hebrew Museum of Florence), with some ancient ceremonial objects and a sacred torah. The sight to behold is the unique architecture and facade, quite different than most buildings in Florence. Located a little ways away from everything in the Santa Croce section of town.

25. SAN MARCO

Piazza San Marco, Tel. 055/287-628. E7.

This place is a hidden treasure. Actually this 'place' is the church, the cloisters, the museum next to the church, and the *Biblioteca de Michelozzo*. The church has some incredible works by Fra Bartolemeo and Michelozzo, as well as Donatello's workshop. The museum has what could be the largest collection of Fra (Beato) Angelico paintings anywhere. The library (biblioteccha) is a spartan presentation of some ancient documents.

You can also visit the rooms on the top floor, where Fra Angelico, the accomplished artist and Dominican friar, lived and worked. Other individuals, such as Savonarola stayed for short and long periods in the little monastic cells. At the top of the main set of stairs is a beautiful Fra Angelico fresco, and the frescos in each of the cells are by Fra Angelico or his students.

The Flood of 1966

Standing at the center of the Ponte Vecchio, surveying the incomparable beauty and serenity of the sights of Florence, it seems incredible to imagine this magnificent city virtually blanketed with oily, muddy surging walls of water. But that was reality not long ago, on November 3, 1966, when Florence's last massive flood occurred and devastated many of the city's historic and artistic treasures.

On that day, the normally complacent **Arno** turned into a life threatening, destructive river, coursing through the labyrinth of Florence's many streets. On that night, and the subsequent days, despite the valiant efforts of an army of students from all over the world and the courageous Florentines, the world lost many priceless art treasures, and many irreplaceable documents and manuscripts.

Not the First

But this was not Florence's first experience with a flood's devastation. For many centuries Florentines had been ravaged by the power of nature, a power which had been enhanced by the meddlesome hand of man. What remains of these past floods are the commemorative plaques, all over the city, indicating the high water marks from each of the individual disasters.

How could such calamity occur in one of the world's most historic cities? How could it have been prevented?

Leonardo da Vinci clearly saw the cause of these periodic floods, and even made excellent recommendation for their remedy. He designed projects to develop water impoundments in the hills around Florence, to develop tributaries off the Arno, to develop chambers beneath Florence to hold excess flood waters. In conjunction, a proposal was made to initiate a government-sponsored reforestation plan, first by Gianbattista Vico del Cicerto, and later by many other visionaries.

Centuries of Deforestation

But each and every suggestion went unheeded by those in power. Why? Mainly because the trees around Florence were needed to support the growing population's demand for fuel and construction material. Couple this with the root destruction caused by grazing goats and sheep, which helped support the successful wool trade, and this left the surrounding hills, once thick with impenetrable forests, barren and desolate and open to rain water run-off that helped stimulate the devastating Florentine floods.

Since the massive flood of 1333, moderate floods have occurred in Florence every 24 years, major floods every 26 years, and massive floods (like the one in 1966) every 100 years.

Extensive Damage

The flood in 1966 was a catastrophe. Try and imagine trees and automobiles being hurled down the Arno into the living masterpiece of the **Ponte Vecchio**, destroying the gold shops in its wake. The **Uffizi Gallery**'s cellars, which were the government offices for the Medicis, were completely submerged; and many works of art, in conjunction with the State Archives containing valuable papers of the Medici family and the Florentine governments, were covered in water and fuel oil. This fuel oil was a modern addition to the Florentine floods. It was used as heating for Florentine homes, and was dredged up all over the city by the swirling waters of the Arno.

At the **Biblioteca Nazionale Centrale** the most devastation occurred, when close to one and a half million of nearly three million volumes disappeared from the miles of shelving into the brackish waters. The **Chiesa di Santa Croce** almost lost the bones of Michelangelo, Machiavelli, Galileo, and the composer Rossini to the muddy Arno water. The museum next door had its *Crucifix* by Giovanni Cimabue battered and eventually destroyed by the black tide.

The **Bargello**, a museum with sculptures comparable to the collection in the Accademia, was awash with 14 feet of oily mud and water. Many of Michelangelo's works found here were completely covered with slime, and had to be blanketed with clouds of talcum powder to extract all the potentially damaging oil.

The beautiful bronze doors of the **Baptistery** near the Duomo were almost lost to the flood. The door on the east side, containing magnificent scenes from the Old Testament, had five of its panels pried loose, luckily to be saved by a protective gate that surrounded the door. Almost every museum, library, and residence was affected in some way by the flood of 1966. But now, with better river water management, through the proper use of dams and improved communication between the two major dams above Florence, the effects of centuries of deforestation can be better controlled. And hopefully history in this case will not repeat itself.

Nightlife & Entertainment

Florence is definitely not known for its nightlife. Most Florentines usually only engage in some form of late night eating and drinking at a restaurant that stays open late. Heated dancing and wild debauchery don't seem to part of the Florentine make-up, except for a few places mentioned below.

Here are some places to go if you get that itch to be wild; you'll find each listing on the Florence restaurants map, pages 320-321.

35. DUBLIN PUB, *Via Faenza 27r. Tel. 055/293-049. Closed Mondays. Open from 5:00pm to 2:00am.*

A true Irish pub, dark and dingy and open only at night. They serve Kilkenny, Harp, Guinness for E3.5 a pint and E2 a half pint; as well as some Bulmers Cider. A hopping nightlife spot with true Irish ambiance. I prefer Fiddler's Elbow, but they're close enough together that you can try them both. This one is near the outdoor San Lorenzo Market and the Mercato Centrale.

36. THE FIDDLER'S ELBOW, *Piazza Santa Maria Novella 7R, Tel. 055/ 215-056. Open 3:00pm–1:15pm everyday. Harp, Kilkenny, Guinness, and Inch's Stonehouse Cider on draught. Pint E3.5, half-pint E2.*

If you want to enjoy a true Irish pub outside of Ireland, you've found it. Step into the air conditioned comfort, sit among the hanging musical instruments, belly up to the dark wooden bar, eye yourself in the mirror, and have a pint. For snacks (you have to pay for them), they have peanuts, salami sticks for the Italians, and four types of Highlander Scottish potato chips (they call them crisps): Roast Beef Taste, Cheddar & Onion, Caledonian Tomato, and Sea Salt.

If you want to be a part of the ex-pat community here in Florence, this is one of the places to go. But it is also one of the main nightspots for young Italians in Florence too. If you want to meet people, Italian or otherwise, this is the place to come. Whether it's sitting on the patio or inside at one of the many tables you're bound to have some fun.

There is also a TV in the back room that is usually commandeered for soccer or rugby games. You can also enjoy Fiddler's Elbows in Rome, Venice and Bologna.

37. HARRY'S BAR, *Lungarno a Vespucci 22, 50123 Firenze. Tel. 055/ 239-6700. American Express, Mastercard and Visa accepted. Closed Sundays.*

Based on the famous Harry's Bar in Venice (see the Venice chapter in this book), but with no business connections (Italians obviously have different trademark laws than we do). This is now the place to find the best burgers in Florence. They also mix some strong drinks in the evening, so if you have nothing to do and just want to get out of the hotel room, pop in here.

38. IL RIFRULLO, *Via San Niccolo 55, Tel. 055/213-631. Large beer E2.5, small beer E1.5, Crepe E2.5. Open from 8:00am to midnight.*

Located in the Oltrarno, this is a charming and relaxing place where you can enjoy a drink in the garden in the summer, in front of the fireplace in the winter, or up at the bar whenever you please. The atmosphere in the front room is all pub, in the back room all *taverna*, and in the garden, all party. They have a bar set into ancient struts that hold up the building; the tables are under an overhead canopy. They serve Whitbread Pale Ale, Campbell's Scotch Ale, Stella Artois (Belgian) and Leffe (a Belgian Double Malt on tap), as well as some of the largest and most scrumptious crepes around. Come early; remember that Florence closes down early even on weekends.

39. **SPACE ELECTRONIC**, *Via Palazzuolo 37, 50123 Firenze. Tel. 055/ 292-082, Fax 055/293-457.*

The largest and loudest discotheque in the city. They've had music videos playing here before anybody knew what music videos were (I still remember seeing Mick Jagger crooning the words to Angie); and they continue to be the trendsetters when it comes to club antics. They play all sorts of music, so no one is left out. A fun place with many different levels and dance floors, where you can enjoy the company of your friends, or leave in the company of a newfound one.

Opera

If you are in Florence from December to June, the traditional opera season, and have the proper attire (suits for men, dresses for women) and a taste for something out of the ordinary, try the spectacle of the opera.

• **Teatro Communale**, *Corso Italia 16, 50123 Firenze. Tel. 055/211-158 or 2729236, Fax 055/277-9410*

Movies in English

If you need a little video fix, try **Cinema Astro**, *Piazza San Simone (near Santa Croce), closed July 10–August 31 and Mondays. Tickets cost E4.* There's a student discount on Wednesdays for E3. Films are in English here every night at 7:30pm and 10:00pm. Either call for the schedule or stop by and pick one up.

Sports & Recreation

Balloon Rides in Tuscany

Contact **The Bombard Society**, *6727 Curran Street, McLean VA 22101-3804. Outside Virginia, toll-free Tel. 800/862-8537, Fax 703/883-0985. In Virginia or outside, Tel. 703/448-9407; you can call collect.* Call for current price and information about the most amazing way to view the most spectacular scenery in the world.

Golf

• **Circolo Golf dell'Ugolino**, *Via Chiantigiano 3, 51005 Grassina, Tel. 055/ 320-1009, Fax 055/230-1141.* Located 9 km from Florence this is a par 72, 18 hole course that is 5,728 meters long. Open all year round except on Mondays. They have tennis courts, a swimming pool, a pro shop, a nice bar and a good restaurant.

• **Poggio de Medici Golf & Country Club**, *Via San Gavino 27, 50038 Scarperia. Tel. 055/83-0436/7/8, Fax 055/843-0439.* Located 30 km from Florence this is a 9 hole, par 36 course, that is 3,430 meters long, and is open all year round except for Tuesdays. They have a driving range, putting green and a clubhouse with snacks and drinks.

Pools

If you need a break from touring and want to lounge around a pool for the day, below is a list of places that have pools that you can pay to use. Note that some of them are hotels and are conveniently located near the center of town.

• **Costoli**, *Viale Paoli, Tel. 055/678-012, Open in the summer, 10:00am-6:00pm.*
• **Bellariva**, *Lungarno Colombo, 6, Tel. 055/677-521, Open in the summer.*
• **Le Pavoniere**, *Viale degli Olmi, Tel.055/367-506, Open in the summer.*
• **Hotel Villa Medici**, *Via Il Prato, 42, Tel. 055/238-1331, Open in the summer.*
• **Hotel Villa Cora**, *Viale Macchiavelli, 18, Tel. 055/229-8451, Open in the summer.*
• **Hotel Villa La Massa**, *Candeli, Bagno a Ripoli, Tel. 055/651-0101, Open in the summer.*
• **Hotel Minerva**, *Piazza S.Maria Novella, 16, Tel. 055/284-555, Open in the summer.*
• **Hotel Kraft**, *Via Solferino, 2, Tel. 055/284-273, Open in the summer.*
• **Crest Hotel**, *Viale Europa, 205, Tel. 055/686-841, Open in the summer.*
• **Hotel Villa Le Rondini**, *Via Bolognese Vecchia, 224, Tel. 055/400-081, Open in the summer.*
• **Park Palace Hotel**, *Piazzale Galileo, 5, Tel. 055/222-431, Open in the summer.*
• **Hotel Villa Belvedere**, *Via Senese, 93, Tel. 055/222-501, Open in the summer.*

Tennis

If you have a hankering to serve and volley, here are some tennis clubs in Florence where you can rent a court.

• **Circolo Tennis alle Cascine**, *Viale Visarno, 1, Tel. 055/354-326*
• **Fiesole Tennis**, *Via Pian di Mugnone, Fiesole, Tel. 055/554-1237*
• **Circolo Tennis S. Quirichino**, *Via S. Quirichino, 8, Tel. 055/225-687*
• **Tennis Michelangelo**, *V.le Michelangelo, 61, Tel. 055/681-1880*
• **Tennis Club Rifredi**, *Via Facibeni, Tel. 055/432-552*

• **Novantanove**, *Via dei Brozzi, 99, Tel. 055/375-631*
• **Circolo di Tennis**, *Via Scandicci Alto, Tel. 055/252-696*

Shopping

Antiques

Many of the better known antique stores have been located in the **Via dei Fossi** and **Via Maggio** for years, but there are some interesting little shops in the **Borgo San Jacopo** and the **Via San Spirito**, all located in the **Oltrarno** section of Florence across the river.

When shopping for antiques in Florence, there is one important thing to remember: the Florentines are excellent crafts people and as such have taken to the art of antique fabrication and reproduction. In fact under Italian law, furniture made from old wood is considered an antique, even if it was carved yesterday. These products can be sold as antiques and usually have a price tag to match. But in terms of American understandings, they are not antiques. They only look like it.. If you find a 'real' antique by American standards, it is usually designated by a stamp indicating that it is a national treasure and as such cannot be taken out of the country.

Artisans

If you want to see some of this excellent antique fabrication and reproduction work, as well as genuine restoration in progress, you need venture no further than across the river to the Oltrarno section. In these narrow streets you'll find small workshops alive with the sounds of hammers and saws, intermingled with the odors of wood, tanning leather, and glue. When I lived in Florence this was my favorite area to come to. Watching someone creating something out of nothing has always been a relaxing adventure, and besides, not many tourists even venture into these tiny alcoves of Florentine culture.

Some of the best known shops are located in the **Via Santo Spirito**, **Viale Europa**, **Via Vellutini**, **Via Maggio** and the **Via dello Studio**. Strangely enough, on these same streets are your real antique shops. How convenient to have the fabricators and reproducers next door to the 'legitimate' antique dealers. In other words, inspect your goods carefully.

Books & Newspapers in English

BM Bookshop, *Borgo Ognissanti 4r, Tel 055/294-575. Open Winter: Mondays 3:30pm-7:30pm, Tuesday-Saturday 9:00am-1:00pm and 3:30pm-7:30pm. Open Summer: 9:30am-1:00pm and 3:30pm-7:30pm daily.*

An extensive collection of English language books in both hardcover and paperback. This is also one of the meeting places for the English-speaking community in Florence. Located in the Centro area.

English Bookstore Paperback Exchange, *Via Fiesolana 31r, Tel 247-8154. Open Monday-Saturday 9:00am-1:00pm and 3:30pm-7:30pm. Closed in August. Closed Mondays November–February.*

The unofficial English-speaking bibliophile meeting place, this store has the largest and best priced selection of new and used English-language paperbacks in Florence. If you want to exchange a book you have already read they are very generous with trade-ins. The only stipulation is that the book you select as your trade-in has to be used. Located in the Santa Croce section of Florence, just around the corner from **Sbigoli Terrecotte**, which is an excellent pottery shop.

Libreria Internazionale Seeber, *Via Tornabuoni 68r, Tel. 055/215-697. Open regular business hours.*

This is an extensive and old fashioned bookstore that's been around since the 1860s to serve the expatriate community. An entire room is devoted to foreign books, not all of which are in English. Even if you can't find what you want, this is a fun place to browse.

The Papier Mache Store

One store you simply cannot miss is the small studio/gallery of the artist Bijan, **Firenze of Papier Mache**, *Piazza Pitti 10, 50125 Firenze, Tel. 055/230-2978, Fax 055/365-768.* He makes beautiful masks covered with intricate sketchings of famous paintings, as well as beautiful anatomical forms, all from papiermache. Even if you don't buy anything, simply browse and savor the beauty of his work. Since the shop is near the Palazzo Pitti, one of your 'must see' destinations while in Florence, there's no reason why you shouldn't take a peak in here.

Cartolerie - Stationary Stores

L'INDICE SCRIVE, *Via della Vigna Nuova 82r. Tel. 055/215-165. Mastercard and Visa accepted.*

A wide variety of stationary products and unique pens are featured in this store. Most of the items are hand-made, including the diaries, ledgers, guest books, desk sets. etc. A great place to get a gift for someone back home.

IL PAPIRO, *Piazza Duomo 24r, Tel. 055/215-262. Credit cards accepted. E-mail info@ilpapirofirenze.it, Web: www.ilpapirofirenze.it.*

If you like marbleized paper products, this is the store for you. You can get boxes, notebooks, picture frames, pencil holders, basically anything you could imagine. The prices are a little high but that's because of the great location and high quality products. They also have three locations in Rome, all around the Pantheon.

IL TORCHIO, *Via de Bardi 17, Tel. 055/234-2862.*
A much less expensive store than **Il Papiro**, with similar stuff, and they make it in front of you while you shop. Located 2 blocks east of the Ponte Vecchio (as you cross the bridge turn left), this place off the beaten tourist path, but well worth the slight detour.

Ceramics

If you are interested in the famous painted ceramics from Tuscany and Umbria, you don't have to go to the small towns where they are manufactured – there is a great store behind the stalls in the San Lorenzo market called **Florentina** (*Via dell'Ariento 81r, 50123 Firenze, Tel. 055/239-6523*). Owned by a stereotypical friendly Irish woman and her Italian husband, this store has everything you could want at prices similar to what you would get if you traveled to Deruta in Umbria or Cortona in Tuscany.

Another ceramics store is located near Santa Croce around the corner from the English Bookstore Paperback Exchange. The **Sbigoli Terrecotte** (*Via S. Egidio 4r, 50122 Firenze, Tel/Fax 055/247-9713*) has works from Deruta priced virtually the same as if you were in that town. This store also has a laboratory of its own where they make, bake and hand paint their own ceramics.

Markets

The markets in Florence are all hustle and bustle, especially in the high tourist season. But despite the crowds you can have a great time browsing and shopping. And of course, the prices are sometimes close to half what they are in stores. Remember to bargain because usually the starting price is rather high. The best bet when bargaining is to make a counter offer at half of the initial price. Then let the games begin. Bargaining is half the fun of buying something in an Italian market.

MERCATO CENTRALE, *immediately north of Piazza San Lorenzo, near the Duomo, open Monday–Friday, 7:00am–2:00pm and 4:00pm–8:00pm, Saturday 7:00am-12:15pm and 1:00pm-5:00pm. Sunday 3:00pm-5:00pm.*

This is Florence's main food market for wholesale and retail fish, fresh meat, vegetables, cheeses, oils, breads, and many other delicacies. The meat and fish section is on the ground floor, with a few vegetable stands thrown in, but if you're into healthy food, make your way upstairs to their fruit and vegetable market. The aroma is enough to make you want to come back every day you're in Florence. Try to find some *caciotta* (sheep's milk cheese) and *finocchiona* (salami flavored with fennel) because they are an exquisite local delicacy. This is the best place to shop for your picnic supplies as well as a must see while in Florence. The market itself is surrounded by the large clothing market of San Lorenzo.

When you visit the Mercato Centrale, don't think of leaving without getting a sandwich at **Nerbone's** (see review above in *Where to Eat*). In operation since 1872, this small food stand serves the absolutely best boiled pork, beef, or veal sandwiches, for only E3. They're simply called *panini* and your only choice of meat is what they have boiled for the day. The sandwich is just the meat, the bread, and some salt, but it is amazing. You can stand at the counter and sip a glass of wine or beer, or take your meal to the small seating area just across the aisle.

MERCATO DI SAN LORENZO, *located near the Duomo, everyday from 8:00am-dark. Closed Sundays in the winter.*

This is the largest and most frequented street market in Florence, and it completely dominates the church of San Lorenzo and its piazza, as well as spilling into most adjacent streets. You can find everything from shoes to pants, T-shirts, belts, and much more, most at prices close to half of what you would pay in a store. Both Florentines and tourists come here looking for bargains. Again, remember to bargain, because once a merchant marks you as a tourist the price quoted is usually higher than that quoted to Italians.

MERCATO NUOVO, *located in the Logge del Mercato Nuovo off the Via Por San Maria near the Piazza del Signoria, open daily 9:00am–5:00pm.*

This is the famous Straw Market. They sell traditional products made from straw but also exquisite leather products, ceramics, linens (like table clothes and napkins), statues, and other hand-made Florentine crafts.

MERCATO DELL PULCI, *located in the Piazza dei Compi about four blocks north of the church of Santa Croce, open Tuesday–Saturday, 8:00am–1:00pm, 3:30pm–7:00pm, and the first Sunday of each month from 9:00am–:007pm.*

This is Florence's famous flea market. If you want antiques and junk at obviously trumped up prices, come here. They think tourists will pay anything for a true Italian antique – so remember to bargain. The next market, Mercato di Sant'Ambrogio, is located just to the east of this market.

MERCATO DI SANTO SPIRITO, *Located in the piazza in front of Santo Spirito. Open the second Sunday of every month from 8:00am-7:00pm.*

A great market filled with antiques, junk, clothes, imported figures from Africa, military surplus, and much more. A great place to people watch, grab a great boiled meat sandwich, pick up some cashews to snack on or buy a gift to bring home. In my book, one of the best in Florence. Come here if you happen to be in the city the second Sunday of the month. In conjunction, the only *alimentari* in the city open on that Sunday is in the piazza.

Picnic & Food Supplies

If you can't make it to the **Mercato Centrale** or the **Mercato di Sant'Ambrogio** for your Boboli Garden or day trip picnic supplies, here's a small list of food stores from which you can get almost everything you want.

The perfect amount of meat for a sandwich would be *mezzo etto* (about 1/8th of a pound) and the same goes for your cheese. Also, at most bars you can order a sandwich to go if you're too lazy to make your own, and you can also get some *vino* or *birra* to take with you.

VERA, *Piazza Frescobaldi 3r, Tel. 055/215-465. No credit cards accepted.*

Located in the Oltrarno section of Florence, this store is a food connoisseur's delight. It is indisputably Florence's best stocked food store, conveniently located close to the Boboli Gardens. It has the best fresh cheeses, salamis, hams, roasted meats, freshly baked breads, olive oil, soups and salads. If you want fresh fruit you're also in luck – but not here, you have to go to the store across the street.

VINO E OLIO, *Via dei Serragli 29r, Tel. 055298-708. No credit cards accepted.*

You can find any type of wine or olive oil you could dream of in this store. Since it is slightly expensive you may not want to get your wine for the picnic here, but it is a great place to buy gifts for friends at home. If you don't want to carry them with you on the rest of your trip, the owner will arrange to have them shipped to wherever you choose.

ALESSI PARIDE, *Via delle Oche 27-29r, Tel. 055/214-966. Credit cards accepted.*

This store is a wine lovers paradise. They have wines from every region of Italy and there's one room entirely dedicated to Chianti. This store may also be a little expensive for picnic supplies, but you can get any manner of wine imaginable here, as well as selected liquors, chocolates, marmalades, and honeys.

Superb Little Shops

OFFICINA PROFUMO-Farmaceutica di Santa Maria Novella, *Via della Scala 16 n, Tel. 055/230-2883 or 2649, Fax 055/288-658.*

A beautiful centuries-old establishment with the most refined soaps, shampoos, creams, bath and other personal hygiene products. The goods were originally made from the monastery of Santa Maria Novella. Store is located nearby the same church.

ALICE'S MASKS ART STUDIO, *Via Faenza 72r, Tel. 055/287-370.*

Here you can find some great papiermache masks and other wonderful stuff.

BETTY FLORENCE, *Piazza Madonna Aldobrandini 9/10r, Tel. 055/216-548.*

This place has great and reasonably-priced leather wallets, bags, belts, etc. Directly across the street from the entrance to the Cappelle Medici.

G. VENEZIANO, *Via dei Fossi, 53r, Tel. 055/287-925.*

A lovely store with particularly nice things for the home and kitchen.

Excursions & Day Trips

If you have the time, there are a number of great day trips and longer excursions in the region. For many, a trip to Italy is not complete without visiting one of the most famous sights in the world – the **Leaning Tower of Pisa**, located, you guessed it, in Pisa!

There's also the charming walled city of Lucca with its romantic walkway on the ramparts of the old walls; the winding medieval streets and expansive Campo of **Siena**, with one of the most impressive clock towers in Italy; and the ancient town of **Fiesole**, once the Roman Empire's dominant town in Tuscany.

PISA

Located 56 miles west of Florence, with a population of a little over 100,000 people, **Pisa** is mainly known for its leaning tower; but it is alive with history and filled with many beautiful architectural landmarks that are decorated with intricate ornamentation.

The famous **Campo dei Miracoli** is in the northwestern part of the city. In this square are the **baptistery**, a circular church building used for baptisms; the **cathedral**, built from 1063 to 1160; and the marble bell tower, known to the world as the **Leaning Tower of Pisa**. It is thought that in the cathedral the astronomer **Galileo** first made the observation that later became known as the principle of the motion of a pendulum. But the bell tower is why people come to Pisa.

At 179 feet (55 meters) high and 50 feet (15 meters) wide, it was built on unstable ground and as a result it began to tip during its construction and is now 15 feet (4.6 meters) out of perpendicular. Other monuments include a cemetery, the Church of Santa Caterina, several museums, and many libraries. The city suffered considerable damage during World War II, but its art treasures and architectural purity still attract a large number of tourists from all over the world.

A naval base under Roman control, Pisa became a Roman colony after 180 BCE. The town had a Christian bishop by 313 CE. Pisa's greatest time was back in the 12th century, when its population was greater than 300,000. Pisa was considered a city of marvels because its merchants and its strong navy had traveled all over the Mediterranean, bringing back not only new products but new ideas and styles in art. The famous **Pisan Romanesque** architecture, with its stripes and blind arcades, had its origins in the Moorish architecture of Andalucia in Spain, whose ideas and styles were brought back by Pisa's world travelers.

During this successful time, the **Duomo** was built and the Baptistery and Campanile were begun. But these weren't the only glory of Pisa. It has been described as being a city of ten thousand towers, most of which do not exist today. How unfortunate that the one which has survived is about to fall. Most of the other Pisan monuments no longer with us today were destroyed in the bombings at the end of World War II.

Pisa historically aligned itself with the rulers of Tuscany, mainly in Florence, if only for expediency. Their navy was vast and fierce and they were constantly at war somewhere in the Mediterranean, usually against the Muslim world, even if they did adapt their science and architecture to their own uses.

Pisa's decline began in 1284, when the mercantile port of Genoa devastated the Pisan navy at the **Battle of Meloria** near Livorno. But the final blow to Pisa's Mediterranean dominance was delivered by nature. The silt from the Arno gradually filled in the Pisan port and the cost of dredging was too great for the city to bear. From that point on Pisa became a pawn that the other Italian city states traded back and forth. Eventually coming under the control of Florence, the Medici dukes gave Pisa a lasting gift, Florence's own university. This institution helped Pisa stay alive and vital, and in touch with the changes going on in the world.

For more information about Pisa, check out their well organized web site at *www.pisaonline.it.*

Arrivals & Departures

By car, take the A11 directly to Pisa from Florence. Trains from Florence arrive at the Stazione Centrale, which is a pleasant 10-15 minute walk to the leaning tower and the other tourist sights. Or if you are a little tired, take the No. 1 bus from the station to the sights.

Where to Stay

I'm suggesting that you take a day trip up this way from Florence, spend the day, see the sights, explore the old city by the Arno, have lunch and maybe dinner, then catch one of the frequent trains home. But if you happen to tarry a little longer than expected, here's a concise list of hotels in a variety of price ranges that are worthy of your attention.

1. ARISTON, *Via Cardinale Maffi 42, Tel. 050/561-834, Fax 050/561-891. Web: www.pisaonline.it/hotelariston/. 35 rooms all with bath and radio. Single E26-44; Double E35-57. Breakfast E5. All credit cards accepted.* ***
Located right by the Leaning Tower and the other main sights in Pisa. You'll have the tower to keep you company, but this is so far away from the real center of the city located around the river. But even so, this is a good inexpensive option for a short stay in Pisa.

2. JOLLY CAVALIERI, *Piazza della Stazione 2, 56125 Pisa. Tel. 050/43290, Fax 050/502-242. Toll free in Italy 167-017703. Toll free in US and NYC 800/221-2626. Toll free in NY State 800/247-1277. 100 rooms*

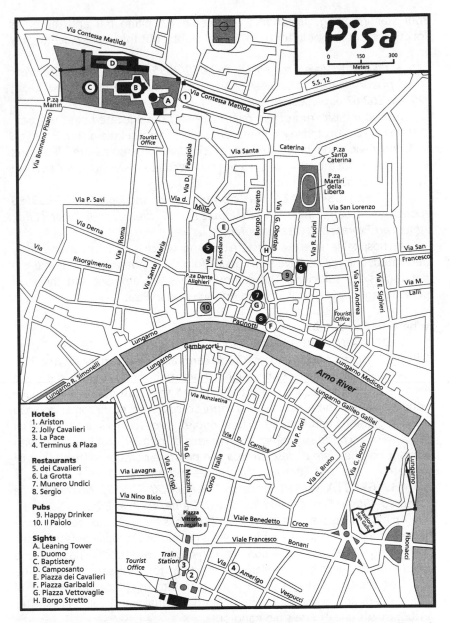

Pisa

0   150   300
Meters

Via Contessa Matilda
Via Contessa Matilda
S.S. 12

P.za Manin

Via Bomano Pisano

Tourist Office

Via Santa   Caterina

P.za Santa Caterina

P.za Martiri della Liberta

Via P. Savi

Via d. Mille

Via San Lorenzo

Via Derna

Via Roma

Via Santa Maria

Via

Risorgimento

Via D. Faggiola

Borgo Stretto

G. Oberdan

Via R. Fucini

Via San Francesco

Via San Andrea

Via E. Sighieri

Via M. Lalli

P.za Dante Alighieri

S. Frediano

Tourist Office

Pacinotti

Lungarno

Gambacorti

Lungarno

Lungarno R. Simonelli

Lungarno Mediceo

Arno River

Lungarno Galileo Galilei

Via Nunziatina

Via P. Gori

Via G.

Bovio

Lungarno

Hotels
1. Ariston
2. Jolly Cavalieri
3. La Pace
4. Terminus & Plaza

Restaurants
5. dei Cavalieri
6. La Grotta
7. Munero Undici
8. Sergio

Pubs
9. Happy Drinker
10. Il Paiolo

Sights
A. Leaning Tower
B. Duomo
C. Baptistery
D. Camposanto
E. Piazza dei Cavalieri
F. Piazza Garibaldi
G. Piazza Vettovaglie
H. Borgo Stretto

Via Lavagna

Via F. Crispi

Via G. Mazzini

Corso Italia

Via D. Carmine

Via G. Bruno

Via Nino Bixio

Piazza Vittorio Emanuelle II

Viale Benedetto   Croce

Viale Francesco   Bonani

Bastione San Gallo

Fibonacci

Tourist Office

Train Station

Via   Amerigo

Vespucci

all with bath. Single E75-145; Double E95-195. Breakfast extra. All credit cards accepted. ****

Located near the train station and away from the main sights, this could be an option if you've lingered too long over dinner and don't want to take the train back to Florence or have missed the last one. All the amenities of a four star including air conditioning, cable TV, piano bar and more. Its location is not so hot in terms of tourist sights, but this is the place to stay in Pisa.

3. LA PACE, *Viale Gramsci 14, Tel. 050/29351. Fax 050/502266. Web: www.pisaonline.it/HotelLaPace/. 70 rooms all with bath. Single E40-50; Double E62-67. Breakfast included. All credit cards accepted.* ***

Just your basic, run of the mill, three star hotel located near the train station in Pisa. Located in a commercial gallery that is a little bland. Here you will find peace and quiet but not much else. The rooms are clean and comfortable, but the atmosphere is not too electric. Let's be honest. Pisa is not known as a hot bed for hotels.

4. TERMINUS & PLAZA, *Via Colombo 45, Tel. and Fax 050/500-303. 55 rooms all with bath. Single E55-60; Double E70-82. Breakfast E6. Diner's Club, American Express and Visa accepted.*

An hospitable hotel in an austere building, which is well kept up and finely decorated. The rooms have functionally furnished, nothing special, and the bathrooms are sufficient. The common areas are ambiant and the staff personal and professional. A good option while in Pisa.

Where to Eat & Pubs

5. DEI CAVALIERI, *Via San Frediano 16, Pisa. Tel. 050/49-008. Closed Saturdays for lunch and Sundays. Credit cards accepted. Dinner for two E32.*

A small place near a public high school (right around lunch the place empties out to the sounds of excited kids and their motorbikes). They have good pasta dishes here, such as *con funghi porcini* (with mushrooms), *coniglio e asparagi* (rabbit and asparagus) or *vongole verace* (clams in a garlic and oil sauce). For *secondo*, try either the *coniglio al origano* (rabbit made with oregano) or the *fileto di pesce fresco can patate e pomodoro* (fresh fillet of the catch of the day with roasted potatoes and tomatoes).

6. LA GROTTA, *Via San Francesco 103, Tel. 050/578-105. No credit cards accepted. Closed Sundays and in August. Dinner for two E35.*

An old Pisan restaurant built in 1947 that has the look and feel of a cave, hence the name. As such the atmosphere is unique and compliments the rustic Pisan cuisine. Try the *risotto ai fiori di zucchini* (rice with zucchini flowers), the *spaghetti alla vongole* (with clam sauce), then for later sample either the *coniglio* (rabbit) or the *vitello* (veal). If you're up late, this place stays open until 1 or 2:00am and becomes a wine bar serving drinks and cold plates after 11:00pm. It's one of Pisa's hip hang outs.

7. NUMERO UNDICI, *Via Cavalca 11. Tel. 050/544-294. No credit cards accepted. Closed Saturdays at dinner and Sundays. Dinner for two E23.*

A small, down to earth, local place situated by the University that has a nice outside patio. Located near the old market in Pisa this is the perfect place to sample Pisan home cooking. They make great *lasagnas*, *crepes*, and *foccace* (a crepe-like concoction with meats, cheeses, and vegetables baked inside the crisp doughy exterior), but my favorite was a dish of assorted salamis. Centrally located, good atmosphere and great food.

8. SERGIO AMERICAN BAR, *Lungarno Pacinotti 1 Tel. 050/48-245. American Express, Diners Club, Visa and Mastercard accepted. Closed Sundays and Mondays for lunch. An expensive place. Dinner for two E75.*

Why this place is called an American Bar I will never understand since they serve traditional Pisan fare. Great fresh food prepared in exquisite Pisan style in an environment that looks like something out of an old castle. They have large keys and porcelain dishes hanging on the walls interspersed among the haphazardly placed paintings. If you try any of the *antipasti* that can be enough for a meal. Two such dishes are the *salumi tipici toscani con crostini* (Tuscan salami with crostini) or the *pesce spada con insalata di stagione* (swordfish with salad). If you sample any of their meats or seafood dishes your price will easily meet the anticipated E75, if not your bill will be dramatically less.

9. HAPPY DRINKER, *Vicolo del Poshi 5-7. Open from 4:00pm to 12 midnight.*

An authentic Irish atmosphere serving up great pints of Guinness, Harp, or Caffreys for E3. On a side street off the main Borgo Stretto. Inside seating only but what a wonderful place it is. Frequented by locals and tourists alike.

10. IL PAIOLO, *Via Cortatone e Montanara 9. Open for lunch and dinner.*

The interior has the look and feel of a German beer garden complete with the communal wooden tables. Outside it's just another café on a quiet street. They serve the German beer Weininger for E3 a pint. They also have a limited *trattoria* type menu for those desiring to have some food with their ale. A wonderfully rustic, medieval atmosphere.

Seeing the Sights

Much of the main tourist area centers around the **Campo dei Miracoli** (Square of Miracles) and its famous **Leaning Tower**, but Pisa has other attractions that you should explore as well. The sights below are lettered and correspond to the letters on the map of Pisa.

PIAZZA DEL MIRACOLI

It is called the **Square of Miracles** because of the stupendous architectural masterpieces filling the square. These are living testimony to the greatness that the city of Pisa reached at the height of its glory. The square is surrounded by imposing walls begun in 1154, which in turn are surrounded by countless vendors selling a wide variety of trinkets for the tourists.

The following sights are on display in the piazza:

A. THE CAMPANILE, OR THE LEANING TOWER

Tickets E15. You will need to make reservations in advance at www.duomo.pisa.it.

It's open once more. You can climb the leaning tower of Pisa again. So get ye to Pisa. The 293 steps of the tower can once again be traversed.

The most unique tower in the world because of the fact that it leans, and the degree to which it does. There are other towers in Italy, but none has the beauty and charm of this one, nor are any others on the verge of falling over as is this one.

The lean in the tower was not planned, but it was noticed when the tower reached a height of 11 meters. The builders continued to build even though they realized that the foundation was unstable. The tower was begun in 1174 by Bonanno Pisano and finished in 1350 by Tomaso Pisano, so the family spent many years trying to discover ways to eliminate the list, unsuccessfully. The tower is 55 meters, 22 centimeters high, and its steepest angle is almost 5 meters. This angle has been increasing at almost a millimeter a year.

It was getting so bad that serious measures were undertaken to reduce the list of the tower. Cables were attached around the outside to keep the tower from leaning any further. And a drilling rig removed soil from underneath the side of the foundation opposite the list. Pressure was exerted on the cable to pull the tower into the space vacated by the drilled soil, and the tower's lean has been corrected one-half a degree, or about 16 inches. The authorities could have corrected the entire lop-sided structure, but that would eliminate it as a unique tourist attraction, now wouldn't it?

Graveyard of Ancient Ships

Just a short stroll from the Leaning Tower, archaeologists are unearthing at least ten Roman ships, many complete with cargoes, that sank some 2,000 years ago in a recently rediscovered harbor in Pisa. Merchant vessels, a warship, and a ceremonial boat are all being excavated, along with boxes and boxes of artifacts, from coins and lamps to amphorae that are still full. These artifacts, and the boats themselves, are being readied for removal to the nearby Arsenali Mediciei, a large warehouse structure which is being transformed into a temporary laboratory and museum where the final phases of restoration will occur.

This important find will be open to the public soon, but if you want a sneak preview , visit their website at **www.navipisa.it**. When in Pisa, take some time to visit this historic find.

Anyway, during its useful days the tower was employed by **Galileo Galilei** when he conducted experiments with the laws of gravity. Today the tower, with its six galleries each surrounded by arches and columns, as well as the bell cell located at the top, is only used for drawing the tourist trade to Pisa.

B. THE DUOMO

Open 8:00am–12:30pm and 3:00pm–6:30pm. In January only open until 4:30pm.

Started in 1063 by Buschetto, it was finally consecrated in 1118 after Rainaldo finished the work. The bronze doors are reproductions, by 16th century Florentine artists, of the originals that were lost in the fire of 1569. The facade is covered with many columns and arches as was the Pisan style at the time.

The interior contains numerous sculptures and mosaics, among which is the famous mosaic *Christ and the Madonna* started by Francesco of Pisa and continued by Cimabue. The celebrated pulpit is the work of Giovanni Pisano, of the same family that built the Campanile. There is also the famous lamp that hangs in the center of the nave that was created by Stolto Lorenzi. It is called the **Lamp of Galileo**, who, as rumor has it, discovered through observation and experimentation the oscillation of pendulum movements. Last but not least is the statuette in ivory by Giovanni Pisano of the *Madonna and Child*.

C. BAPTISTERY

Open 9:00am–1:00pm and 3:00pm–6:30pm. In January only open until 4:30pm.

Begun in 1153 by the architect Diotisalvi, it is circular in form with a conical covering. Later the facade was adapted by Nicola Pisan and his son Giovanni to fit the other works in the square. The interior has five baptismal fonts created by Guido Bigarelli of Como in 1246 and the masterpiece of a pulpit created by Nicola Pisano in 1260.

D. CAMPOSANTO

Open 8:00am–6:30pm. In January open from 9:00am–4:30pm. Admission E3.

A rather serene and unpretentious cemetery, very unlike the foreboding "city of the dead" found in Genoa. This one was started in 1278 by Giovanni di Simone. It was enlarged in the 14th century and stands today like an open air basilica with three aisles. The center soil is rumored to have been brought from the Holy Land. The corridor around the earth is formed by 62 arches in a Gothic style of white and blue marble.

You'll also find some beautiful frescoes along the walls and floors that were partially destroyed during World War II but have since been restored.

E. PIAZZA DEI CAVALIERI

This is the most harmonious piazza in the city after the famous Piazza dei Miracoli with its leaning tower. Literally translated the name means square of the knights, and it is named for the Knights of St. Stephen, an order established by Cosimo I de Medici to defend Florence and her holdings from pirates. The statue above the fountain by Francavilla in 1596 that is opposite the **Palazzo dei Cavalieri** (Knights Palace) is dedicated to this order. On its facade you'll find floral displays, symbols, coats of arms as well as sacred and profane images which are described as graffito style decorations. In niches above the second row of windows you'll find six busts of Tuscan grand dukes, from Cosimo I to Cosimo III de Medici.

The other buildings in this irregularly shaped piazza were built in the 16th and 17th centuries and include the **Church of St. Stephen's**, next to the Palazzo dei Cavalieri on the eastern side. On the western sides is the **Palazzo del Collegio Puteano** built in 1605. The southern side is occupied by the **Palazzo del Consiglio** (Council Chambers) of the order of the Knights of St. Stephen. On the northern side is the **Palazzo dell'Orologio** (Clock Palace). In the same piazza, next to the Palazzo dell'Orologio, the infamous **Muda Tower** (Tower of Hunger) used to sit. This was where Count Ugolino della Gherardesca was imprisoned with his sons and nephews in 1288 and left to starve to death. This situation was recorded for all to remember in Dante's *Inferno*.

If you're walking from the train station to the Leaning Tower walk through this piazza. It's a nice place to sit and watch Pisan life pass you by.

F. PIAZZA GARIBALDI

This piazza is at the end of the Borgo Stretto with its covered walkways, and is brimming with real Pisan life – not the tourist trap situation like at the Piazza dei Miracoli. From here you are mere meters away from the Piazza Vettovaglie with its outdoor market, and are near the Ponte de Mezzo, from which you can see the beautiful palazzi lining the Arno as it meanders towards the sea. If you are walking from the train station you will most probably pass over this bridge and through this piazza to get to the Piazza dei Miracoli. The area around the Piazza Garibaldi will give you a genuine feel for the real life in Pisa.

G. PIAZZA VETTOVAGLIE

There's a market in this square every morning from 7:00am to 1:30pm. Just off the Via Stretto, here you'll find the hustle and bustle of a small Italian market, with vendors hawking their wares rather vocally. You'll find everything from produce to used clothes in the stalls and around the piazza are little shops that compliment the food being sold outdoors. There are butchers, *alimentari*, and bakers so that the Pisan housewife can get all she needs here to make her family's daily meals.

The market spills out onto the Via Domenico Cavalca and around the corner. Great sights, sounds, and smells to remember Pisa by. Also, the street just mentioned has a variety of different little restaurants to sample if the market's wares have tempted your appetite.

H. BORGO STRETTO

If you can't get to Bologna to see their famous covered streets, this little street has a taste of it for you. The sidewalks are covered so this street is always filled with people whatever the weather. Just look out for the motor scooters and bicycles that find their way up on the sidewalk at those times. You'll also find street performers and mimes entertaining the bustling crowds. You can either people-watch or shop at the many delightful stores. The market in the Piazza Vettoglie is just off this street.

Practical Information
Car Rental
• **Avis**, *Airport, Tel. 050/42028*
• **Hertz**, *Airport, Tel. 050/49187*

Tourist Information
• **Piazza Duomo**, *to the right of the Camposanto, Tel. 050/560-464.*
• **Piazza Stazione**, *Tel. 050/42-291.* Just as you exit the doors of the station the office is located directly on the left. They can give you a map to guide your way through the streets to the sights.

LUCCA

Try not to miss this city. Instead of making this a one-day adventure, I highly recommend staying at least one or two days to savor its beauty and charm. Located 46 miles west of Florence and 14 miles northeast of Pisa, **Lucca** is closer to Pisa than to Florence and it is still one of the least visited cities in Tuscany, but we guidebook writers are starting to change that.

Most motorists coming from the north drive past in their haste to get to Pisa, and most people arriving from Florence fail to take the hour ride further north because Lucca doesn't have an architectural anomaly like the Leaning Tower of Pisa. But what Lucca has, even with a slowly growing tourist trade, is charm, and lots of it.

Lucca's Walls

Lucca is surrounded by walled fortifications, which were designed to keep marauding Florentines at bay, and which are now the site of a flowering greenbelt around the city. A tree-lined garden boulevard on top of the walls and encompassing the ramparts of the old fortifications extends clear around the city and is perfect for a *passegiatta* (slow stroll). A peaceful and enchanting activity any time of the day. The garden walkway has a thin sliver of asphalt which bicyclists and roller bladers share with strolling pedestrians. But on either side of the walkway is grass, countless trees and shrubs that make this city a wonderfully romantic paradise.

At the battlements, of which there are 10, each coincidentally shaped like a heart, there are plenty of places to cuddle with your loved one, or sit at a wooden table and have a calming afternoon picnic. If you're with a family, the kids can roam free, exploring the nooks and crannies of the walls, while you and your spouse enjoy brief interludes of intimacy.

Besides the walls, which with Ferrarra's are the best preserved in Italy, Lucca offers a tight grid road system, a remnant of its Roman occupation, which now gives it the feel of a compact Renaissance town. I love exploring the many tiny little streets and reveling in the enjoyment of making new discoveries in the maze. In this labyrinth of a city is **San Michel in Foro**, which is located on what used to be Lucca's Forum. Every column on this church is different, some are intertwined like corkscrews, some doubled, and some carved with medieval looking monsters.

Often confused with San Michel is Lucca's **Cathedral**. The Duomo rests at the end of the Via Duomo in Piazza San Martino. This structure is perhaps the most outstanding example of the Pisan style of architecture outside of Pisa. Its porch with three arches, and three levels of colonnades, give it an unusual facade, but typically Pisan.

Explore Lucca!

Besides these sights, Lucca is a city to explore. You can walk its labyrinth of tiny streets and feel a part of the Renaissance. Through your exploration you will find the busy shopping area around Via Fillungo, the 12th century church of **San Frediano**, the Roman **amphitheater** (a must-see so you can compare the different centuries and cultures combined into modern day life), the **Torre Giungi**, which is the tower that overlooks the city. It has one special feature, a garden complete with full-grown trees on the top. Here you can take fine panoramic pictures of the area. Besides these there are plenty of other discoveries waiting for you in Lucca.

Arrivals & Departures

Car is quickest, about one hour away from Florence on the A11 past Prato and Pistoia, two excellent destinations on their own. So if you stop at them, the trip will take somehwat longer. When driving in Italy always remember *Fare il Pieno* (fill 'er up) whenever you stop for gas, because sometimes gas stations are few and far between.

Trains from Florence take between an hour and an hour and a half depending on how many stops the train has to make. As of press time the

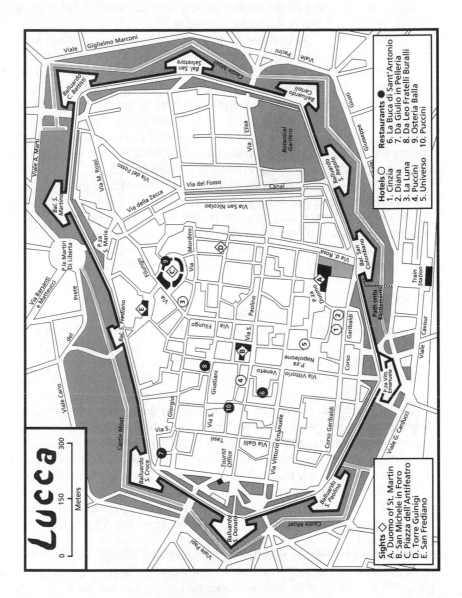

Lucca

0   150   300
Meters

Sights ◇
A. Duomo of St. Martin
B. San Michele in Foro
C. Piazza dell'Antifeatro
D. Torre Guinigi
E. San Frediano

Hotels ○
1. Cinzia
2. Diana
3. La Luna
4. Puccini
5. Universo

Restaurants ●
6. La Buca di Sant'Antonio
7. Da Giulio in Pelleria
8. Da Leo Fratelli Buralli
9. Osteria Balla
10. Puccini

trains that depart Florence for Lucca are at 9:42am, 1:42pm, 3:42pm, 4:42pm, 5:13pm, 5:42pm, 6:45pm, and 8:35pm. Returning to Florence you'll find many trains in the evening, also usually leaving every two hours: 3:00pm, 5:00pm, 7:00pm, and 9:00pm. Make sure you check all this information prior to your departure if you're going for a one-day adventure.

To get inside the city walls when you arrive by train you can either take the adventurous/native route or the more mundane. The native route from the station is to walk straight out of the station and keep going straight on the left hand side of the Piazza Ricasoli. Cross the road avoiding the maniacal drivers and follow the path to a passageway that leads into the walls. At night it's very well lit and safe. When you enter the stairs inside the ancient walls, if you can ignore the graffiti covering them, you'll feel as if you've walked back into the Middle Ages. Follow the stairs up to the wooded walkways on top of the walls. The perfect way to introduce yourself to the city, up on the picturesque and romantic walkway of the old walls. From here descend to the walled city below and you're on your way to exploring.

The more mundane way to enter the city would be to go through the elaborate and imposing **Porta San Pietro**, which was built around 1566, just a short distance left down the main road from the station. The gate still has Lucca's proud motto of independence, *Libertas*, etched over the top.

Where to Stay

The hotels listed here are inside the walls of the old city. If you come to Lucca there is no point in staying anywhere else since all the flavor, ambiance, and romance is inside the old city walls.

1. **CINZIA**, *Via della Dogana 9, 55100 Lucca. Tel. 0583/491-323. No credit cards accepted. 12 rooms, 3 with bath. Single E12-16; Double E20-30.* *

On a quaint little street that has ivy covering the sign on the door, the Cinzia is a good budget hotel where you'll find quality inexpensive lodging. Everything is spic and span but there are not too many amenities. A clean and comfortable place to lay your head, but expect little else. Despite all that it lacks, this hotel is usually booked well in advance, so make reservations.

2. **DIANA**, *Via del Moinetto 11, 55100 Lucca. Tel. 0583/492-202, Fax 0583/ 47-795. E-mail: info@albergodiana.com. Web: www.albergodiana.com/. Credit cards accepted. 9 rooms, 8 with bath. Single without bath E45-50; Single E48-52; Double E65-70.* **

A nice small hotel in a great location down a cute side street deep in the heart of Medieval Lucca. If you want to stay inside the walls of Lucca at this place, it's best to book in advance, because with its location and relatively inexpensive prices, this hotel is in great demand.

3. **LA LUNA**, *Via Fillungo, Corte Compagni 12, 55100 Lucca. Tel. 0583/ 493-634, Fax 0583/490-021. E-mail: laluna@onenet.it. Web:*

www.hotellaluna.com/. American Express, Diners Club, Mastercard, an Visa accepted. 30 rooms all with bath. Single E45-55; Double E70-80. ***
This is a professionally run small hotel with beautiful rooms done up in antiques and a comfortable lobby bar area in which to relax. This hotel and the Puccini are the two best places to stay inside the old city walls. The restraurant in the tiny square, Pizzeria Italia, though not written up here, is worthy of a visit.

4. PUCCINI, *Via di Poggio 9, 55100 Lucca. Tel. 0583/55421 or 53487, Fax 0583/53487. Web: www.hotelpuccini.com/index0.html. E-mail: hotelpucciniluc@onenet.it. 14 rooms all with bath. Single E55; Double E77. Credit cards accepted.* ***
Located right up from the *Piazza San Michelle*, this is a beautifully appointed little three star hotel that has all necessary amenities.The lobby is small but the accommodations are intimate, comfortable and cozy. The Puccini playing in the lobby is a soothing addition. This is the place to stay in Lucca despite the condescending attitude of the staff.

5. UNIVERSO, *Piazza del Giglio 1 (next to the Piazza Napoleone), 55100 Lucca. Tel. 0583/493-678, Fax 0583/954-854. Web: www.hotels-venice.com/ lucca_hotels.html. Credit cards Accepted. 72 rooms. Single E60-85; Double E120-130.* ***
Established in the 11th century and wonderfully located on the Piazza del Giglio, this is a good option while in Lucca. The rooms are not that large but have all the amenities of a good three star. It's ideally located near the station and the Duomo but its prices are a little too expensive for my taste. They have a wonderful little bar with seating on the square. A larger, less intimate place than most of the other hotels in Lucca. A close third behind Puccini and La Luna.

Where to Eat
6. LA BUCA DI SANT'ANTONIO, *Via della Cervia 1/3, Tel. 0583/55881. Closed Sunday evenings, Mondays, and in July. All credit cards accepted. Dinner for two E50.*
This is an exceptional restaurant, the most classic and traditional of all places in Lucca. In a splendid location directly behind Piazza San Michele, the atmosphere in here is 19th centruy opulence. The cooking is all local with many meat dishes to choose from, as well as tasty grilled vegetables. And the dessert cart is not to be missed. Make reservations here, and dress well when dining. Appearance is important here.

7. DA GIULIO IN PELLERIA, *Via delle Conce 45, Tel. 0583/55948. Closed Sundays and Mondays, and in August. American Expres and Visa accepted. Dinner for two E40.*
A quaint and colorful local trattoria whose menu has not changed for at least 25 years. All sorts of meat and vegetable dishes abound, as well as rustic pies that combine both ingredients. The prices have risen in the past few years

Best Eats in Lucca

When in Lucca there is really only one place to eat: **Da Leo Fratelli Burelli**. It has great atmosphere and is boisterously local with friends calling to each other across the crowded dining space inside. Don't sit outside at the narrow strip of terrace; only tourists bother to eat there. Inside is where the action and ambiance are. As you enter you'll pass by their kitchen where you can see two or three female chefs slaving over hot stoves preparing their scrumptious meals. Seeing how hard they work makes you appreciate even more the fantastic food they prepare. When in Lucca, don't miss this place.

because of this places popularity, but they are still reasonable. Come here for fine local cooking in a rustic, authentic atmosphere.

8. DA LEO FRATELLI BURALLI, *Via Tegrimi 1, 55100 Lucca. Tel. 0583/ 492-236. Closed Sundays. No credit cards accepted. Dinner for two E30.*

This place is perfect. If you're going to have one meal (or two, or three) have it here, but not outside in the thin sliver of seating area on a small side street. You have to come inside and truly the enjoy the vibrancy of this Luccan staple. The energy inside is electric with friends calling to each other across the room, and the food clattering down in front of you as it is served.

From the open kitchen you pass by on your way you can see the frenzied female cooks preparing the food for hundreds of people each evening. This place is the best in Lucca and the prices are inexpensive too. Try the *fettucine all rucola e gamberi* (with cheese and shrimp) or the *pasta al pomodoro e ragu* (with tomato and meat sauce). For seconds sample the *pollo arrosto con patate* (roasted chicken with potatoes), a cold dish of *prosciutto e mozzarella* (ham and mozzarella), or some *pollo fritto e zucchini* (fried chicken and zucchini).

9. OSTERIA BARALLA, *Via Anfiteatro 5, Tel. 0583/44-0240. Closed Sundays and in August. No credit cards accepted. Dinner for two E30.*

After ten years this place has re-opened to rave reviews, and has re-immersed itself into the social life of Lucca. A true local, hosteria that has been pain stakingly restored to offer a colorful ambiance. And under the titelage of chef Alessandro Carmassi, the food is exquisite and traditional. An excellent choice for a meal while in Lucca.

10. PUCCINI, *Corte San Lorenzo 1, 55100 Lucca. Tel. 0583/316-116, Fax 0583/316-031. Web: speweb.monrif.net/prodotti/ristorantepuccini/. Dinner for two E55.*

An expensive but pleasant restaurant that has a somewhat modern ambiance. Try the *antipasto di mare* (seafood antipasto) or the *penne agli scampi* (pasta with shrimp). For seconds, I recommend the *grigliata mista* (mixed grilled meats from Tuscany). A definitely high class eatery that requires proper attire.

Seeing the Sights

Lucca is a small walled city that has a few memorable sights to see, but the most important is the entire package itself. Lucca is like a medieval town come to life, with its tiny twisting streets and its converted walls and battlements. It is a great place to explore. You'll get lost without a map for sure, but since the walled city is so small you'll eventually find something you recognize, especially the walls.

If you come to Lucca, stroll and picnic along these glorious tree-lined promenades. It will be a romantic and memorable experience.

A. THE DUOMO OF ST. MARTIN
Open 7:00am–7:00pm.

This is perhaps the most outstanding example of Pisan style outside of Pisa. It was begun in the 11th century and completed in the 15th. The facade has three levels of colonnades with three different sized arches. Behind and on the arches are beautiful 12th and 13th century bas-reliefs and sculptures. If you look hard enough you can find a column carved with the tree of life with Adam and Eve crouched at the bottom and Christ at the top, as well as a variety of hunting scenes with real and fantastic animals, dancing dragons, and more, all created by anonymous artists.

The dark interior is a showcase for Lucca's most famous artist, **Matteo Civitali** whose work has not escaped beyond the walls of Lucca. Rumor has it that until his mid-thirties, a ripe old age for some at that time, he was a barber, when he then decided he'd rather be a sculptor. His most famous work is the octagonal *Tempietto* done in 1489. It is a marble tabernacle in the middle of the left aisle. It contains a cedar crucifix, The *Volto Santo* (Holy Image) which is said to have the true portrait of Jesus sculpted on it by Nicodemus, an eyewitness to the crucifixion. Every September 13th the image is removed to join a candlelight procession around town.

Further up the left aisle you can find Fra Bartolomeo's *Virgin and Child Enthroned* as well as the *Tomb of Ilaria del Caretto*, a magnificent work by the Siennese artist Jacopo della Quercia. You will

---

Explore Lucca By Bike!

Cicli Barbetti, *Via Anfiteatro 23, Tel. 0583/854-444*, is located near the amphitheater, and is the only place to find bicycles to rent in the city. There really isn't a need to rent one, since the city is so small, but if you like to ride, this is the place rent a bike.

also find the Madonna *Enthroned with Saints* by Domenico Ghirlandaio and a strange *Last Supper* with a nursing mother in the foreground and what looks like cherubs floating above Christ's head.

B. SAN MICHELE IN FORO
Open 7:00am – 7:00pm.
This church is so grand that most people mistake it for Lucca's cathedral. It is located in the old Roman Forum and is a masterpiece of Pisan Gothic architecture. The huge facade rises above the level of the roof, making the church look even larger and grander. You'll notice that every column in the five levels of Pisan-style arcading is different. Some will be twisting, some doubling, some carved with relief monsters and more.

While the entire facade is quite ornate and elaborate, the interior is more austere. It is best known for the place where Puccini started his musical career as a choirboy. As a reminder of this, just down the small road directly in front of the church is a wonderfully intimate place to hang your hat, the Piccolo Hotel Puccini. Besides the memory of Puccini, the interior of San Michelle in Foro contains a glazed terra-cotta *Madonna and Child*, a 13th-century *Crucifixion* hanging over the high altar, and a memorable painting of saints that lived during the plague years.

C. PIAZZA DELL'ANFITEATRO
A remarkable relic dating from Lucca's ancient Roman past is the **Roman Amphitheater**. Today it is lined with modern shops and medieval houses, and only the barest of outlines of the ancient arches can still be seen. Any marble that was once here was used to build the Cathedral and San Michele.

This place seems like an oasis from the past filled with modern comforts where you can lounge at a café and watch the Italian children playing their never ending game of *calcio*.

D. TORRE GUINIGIO
Open 9:00am–7:00pm in the summer and 10:00am–4:00pm in the winter. Admission E3.
A tower rising above a neighborhood that has scarcely changed in 500 years. Here the medieval ancestors of the **Guinigi** family had their stronghold with the tower as their lookout. One of Lucca's landmarks, it is also one of the most elaborate medieval family fortresses.

From the top you have the greatest views over all of Lucca. It's just a short walk up the 230-plus steps to reach the lush garden on the top, complete with trees sprouting from the ramparts. Remember to bring your camera and take some great pictures.

E. SAN FREDIANO
Open 7:00am-7:00pm.
A rather tall church with an even taller *campanile (bell tower)*, both built in the 12th century and completed with colorful mosaics in the 13th century. The interior contains a magnificent baptismal font which is covered with bas-reliefs. The chapels around the central nave are elaborately decorated.

Also inside is the **mummy of St. Zita**, patroness of domestic servants. She was canonized in 1696, long after her birth in 1218. She put in many years of service as a servant for a rich family in Lucca with whom she stayed until her death. She is revered for her selfless acts of charity towards the poor, and now she is pickled in a coffin in Lucca.

Practical Information
For car rentals:
• **Avis**, *Viale Luporini 1411, Tel. 0583/51-36-14*
• **Hertz**, *Via Catalani 59, Tel. 0583/58585*

For tourist information:
• **APT**, *Vecchia Porta San Donato/Piazzale Verdi. Tel 0583/419-689. Hours 9:00am-7:00pm.* You can get a map, a list of hotels, or better yet, they can actually help you find the hotel you want and point you in the right direction. Very helpful, very professional (by Italian standards), and ideally located for people arriving by bus or car. For those of you arriving by train, it's a short walk from the station.

SIENA
Siena is generally described as the feminine counterpart to the masculine Florence, and even its nickname, **City of the Virgin**, belies this feminine quality. Located 42 miles south of Florence, this picturesque walled city is known for its many quality buildings, narrow streets, immense churches, and quaint little restaurants; but the two reasons why I love Siena are that cars are banned from the center of the city, making for a pleasant automobile-less environment (similar to Venice but without the water); and also for the biannual event called the **Palio**.

The well-preserved walls with towers and bulwarks of Siena are seven kilometers long and were built from the 13th to the 15th centuries. The ramparts on the outskirts are now used as public gardens. They are beautiful but not nearly as romantic or inviting as those from Lucca.

Siena was once a prosperous, stable, and artistic city in its own right even before she was absorbed into the Grand Duchy of Tuscany in 1559, which was ruled by Florence, after years of siege by Cosimo de Medici. Once it became a part of Florence, Siena was not allowed to continue to pursue its previously prosperous banking activities, nor were they allowed to continue their flourishing wool trade. Because of these actions, and the general despotic rule of Florence, Siena fell into a long period of decline. But today, as other Italian cities have also, Siena has learned how to succeed by marketing its ancient charm.

For tourist information in Siena, head to the tourist office, *Piazza San Domenico, Tel 0577/940-809; open 9:00am to 7:00pm*. You can get maps and hotel reservations if needed.

Arrivals & Departures
By Car
Either take the Florence-Siena Superstrada or the slower but more scenic Route 22 that runs through the heart of the Chianti wine region. From Rome take the A1 to the Via di Chiana exit, then head west on route 326 into Siena. You'll have to leave your car at one of the many parking lots on the outskirts of the city center, since no automobiles are allowed into the city.

By Train
From Florence there are over a dozen trains a day. The trip takes 1 1/2 hours. The train station is located one mile from the center of the city, but do not fear. Just exit the station, stand on the curb and catch either bus 15, 2, or 6 and they will all take you to a dropping off point near the information desk in the center of town, from which you can get a map (Euro 50 cents) and hotel reservations if needed. Everything else from that point on is walking distance.

If, or should I say when, the blue bus ticket machine in the lobby of the train station is out of order, simply go to the train ticket window and purchase a bus ticket for Euro 75 cents. It's good for an hour once you punch it in the machine on the bus. I recommend buying your return fare in advance if you're not going to stay the night, so you don't have to worry about that detail on your return to the station in the evening. If you don't want to catch the bus, the old town is a short walk up the hill.

Renting a Car
If you're staying in Siena for a while and want to view the magnificent countryside, you can always rent a car, van, or moped. There's one place just outside the walled city where you can do this:
• **General Cars**, *Viale Toselli 20/26, Tel. 0577/40-518, Fax 0577/47-984*

Where to Stay

1. **CANON D'ORO**, *Via Montanini 28, 53100 Siena. Tel. 0577/44-321, Fax 0577/28-08-68. Credit cards accepted. 32 rooms all with bath. Single E20-40; Double E30-50. Breakfast E5.* ******

The oldest hotel in the city, located down a small white walled entrance way. Situated in two stories of a 12th century palazzo, this hotel has the feel of a three star but with better prices. The rooms are quiet since the hotel is located in part of the *zona pedonale* (walking area). Definitely the best inexpensive place to stay while in Siena. But you have to book well in advance for the comfort of these accommodations.

2. **ANTICA TORRE**, *Via di Fieravecchia 7, 53100 Siena. Tel. 0577/222-255, Fax the same. Web: www.karenbrown.com/italyinns/ hotelanticatorre.html. 8 rooms all with bath. Single E60; Double E80. Amex, Mastercard and Visa Accepted. Breakfast E8.* *******

This small hotel is located on a discrete and quiet street near Santa Maria de' Servi. The hotel itself is a tower built in the 1500s which makes the

Highlights of Siena

Siena is a beautifully quaint little town with winding medieval streets and charming old buildings. There's really not too much to do here except absorb the atmosphere and ambiance, and find a place to settle down for a good meal, which is enough in and of itself. Two of the best places to eat here are:

8. **SPADA FORTE**, *Piazza del Campo 12. Credit cards accepted.*

9. **DA VASCO**, *Via del Capitano 6/8. Tel. 0577/288-094. No credit cards accepted.*

Obviously if you can get to Siena while the **Palio** is in session, you simply must do it. The pageantry, the horse race, the costumes, the intensity all evoke a time long gone and will sweep you back through the centuries. Held biannually on July 2 and August 16, plan well in advance to get a place to stay and a ticket to the horse race that is held in the **Campo**.

If you only have a little while in Siena the **Campo** is where to head since it is the gathering place for the locals, young and old alike. Notice the sloped stone surface that seems to float down to the **Palazzo Pubblico**, a building regal in bearing and boasting one of the most imposing clock towers in Italy. This tower, the **Torre del Mangia**, must be scaled while you're in Siena. If you're fit enough, the 112 meters and more than 400 small confined steps can be taken easily. Once at the top you will be treated to the most amazing panoramic view over the town and the surrounding countryside.

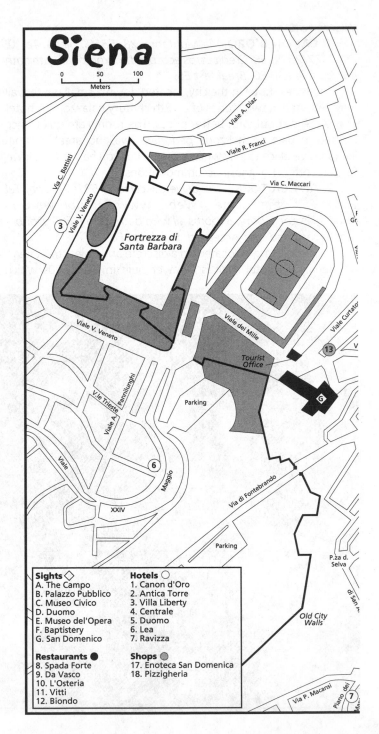

Siena

0   50   100
Meters

Viale A. Diaz

Viale R. Franci

Via C. Maccari

Via C. Battisti

Viale V. Veneto

③

**Fortrezza di
Santa Barbara**

Viale V. Veneto

Viale dei Mille

Viale Curtato

⑬

Tourist
Office

V.le Trieste

V/le Pannilunghi

Viale A.

Parking

G

Viale

⑥

Maggio

XXIV

Via di Fontebrando

Parking

P.za d.
Selva

di San

Old City
Walls

Sights ◇
A. The Campo
B. Palazzo Pubblico
C. Museo Civico
D. Duomo
E. Museo del'Opera
F. Baptistery
G. San Domenico

Hotels ○
1. Canon d'Oro
2. Antica Torre
3. Villa Liberty
4. Centrale
5. Duomo
6. Lea
7. Ravizza

Restaurants ●
8. Spada Forte
9. Da Vasco
10. L'Osteria
11. Vitti
12. Biondo

Shops ◉
17. Enoteca San Domenica
18. Pizzigheria

Via P. Macansi

Piano dei

⑦

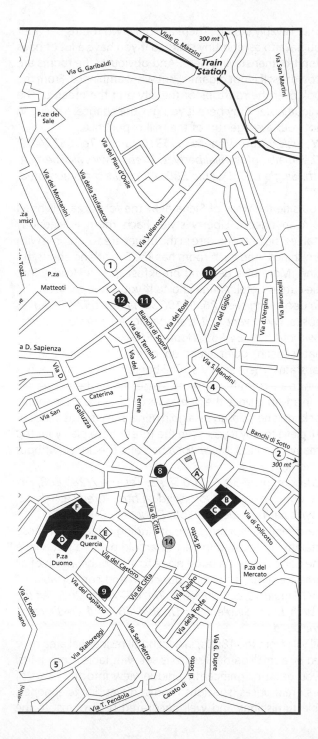

atmosphere here so unbelievably quaint. There are only two rooms per floor and to get to them you have to ascend tiny stairs so if you have a lot of bags or need an elevator don't bother staying here. And obviously the rooms are not that big since the tower itself is not gigantic, but what ambiance. From the top rooms you can look over the rooftops of the city and the green of the countryside. A very unique hotel. Stay here if you get the chance. Staying in a medieval tower is not your average run of the mill experience.

3. VILLA LIBERTY, *Viale Vittorio Veneto 11, 53100 Siena. Tel. 0577/449-666, Fax 0577/44770. E-mail: info@villaliberty.it. Web: www.villaliberty.it. 12 rooms all with bath. Single E50. Double E80. All credit cards accepted. Breakfast included.* ***

Just a little ways outside the walls of Siena near the *fortrezza* this hotel has been renovated in an eclectic Liberty style. Each room is elegantly furnished and comfortable. The best ones are in the upper area and come with more modern style furnishings. And each room has TV. Everything about this place is accommodating. More of a bed and breakfast than a Holiday Inn. Definitely not a 'cookie-cutter' hotel. A fine choice if you some to Siena.

4. CENTRALE, *Via Cecco Angiolieri 26, 53100 Siena. Tel. 0577/280-379, Fax 0577/42-152. Website: www.venere.it/toscana/siena/centrale. 7 rooms, 6 with bath. Double without bath E43-60. Double E55-75.* **

A small place that is clean, quiet, kept up nicely and is bucking for promotion to three star status. There are TV's, mini-bars and direct dial phones in each room, two of which are cute little terraces. To get a room here you have to book many months in advance since the location is excellent and the rooms are few. The proprietor knows he's sitting on a gold mine, but is still as pleasant as can be. A wonderful place to stay if you have the foresight to plan your trip well in advance. Not many amenities. More like a bed and breakfast (without the breakfast) than a hotel.

5. DUOMO, *Via Stalloreggi 34-38, 53100 Siena. Tel. 0577/289-088, Fax 0577/43-043. Web: www.sienaol.it/hduomo/indexi.htm. Credit cards accepted. 25 rooms all with bath. Single E45-E65; Double E60-100.* ***

Comes with all the amenities of a three star, including cable TV for those in need of such entertainment. Located in part of an old palazzo just a little distance away from the Campo, this is a good place to stay within reach of all major sights. The rooms are simply furnished but clean and comfortable.

6. LEA, *Viale XXIV Maggio 10, 53100 Siena. Tel. 0577/283-207, Fax the same. 12 rooms all with bath. Single E35; Double E67. All credit cards accepted. Breakfast included.* **

Situated in a small villa from the 1800s, in a tranquil residential area near the center, surrounded by a small garden which is set with tables and chairs. From the top floors you get a magnificently unique view into the heart of Siena. This hotel offers great prices, spacious rooms, direct dial telephones, simple but comfortable furnishings and well decorated bathrooms. In the morning breakfast is a basic continental fare served in the same room that accommodates the bar and reception area. A great two star in Siena. A budget travelers paradise.

7. PALAZZO RAVIZZA, *Pian dei Mantellini 34, Tel. 0577/280-462, Fax 0577/221-597. Web: www.emmeti.it/Welcome/Toscana/Senese/Siena/ Alberghi/Ravizza/ravizza2.uk.html. 30 rooms all with bath. Single E60-122. Double E90-165. Breakfast E9. All credit cards accepted.* ***

A quality place to stay in Siena, right in the middle of things, this is a quaint little bed and breakfast type hotel in business since 1929. The building the hotel is located in has been owned by the same family for about two hundred years. Situated in a tranquil spot in the centro storico with good views over the city and the surrounding countryside, the furnishings are antique and the atmosphere wonderful. Buffet breakfast is served in their garden area and they are known to make a picnic lunch for you if asked. The evenings can be spent in the large tavern room.

There is a public parking area just down the Via P. Mascagni and off of Via dei Laterino near a quaint little old cemetery if you come by car. Truly a great three star in Siena and the prices show it.

Where to Eat

Since Siena is a university town, snack and fast food places abound, but there are also some excellent restaurants. Siena specialties include *cioccina* (a special variation on pizza) *pici* (thick Tuscan spaghetti with a sauce from ground pork), and *pancetta* (sausages and chicken breast added to tomatoes and cooked with red wine).

Siena is also known for its different varieties of salamis that you can buy at any *alimentari*. I recommend the alimentari **Morbidi**, *Via Banchi di Sotto 27*. Local food specialties include:

Soppressata, either sweet or hot, is an excellent boiled salami made from a mixture of rind and gristle with black peppercorns added. Don't let this description fool you. The sweet *soppressata* is the best.

Buristo is a cooked salami made from the blood and fatty leftovers of sausages. It is heavily spiced.

Finocchiona is a salami made of peppered sausage meat seasoned with fennel seeds. And *Salsiccioli secchi* are made from lean crusts of pork or boar, spiced with garlic and black or red pepper.

8. SPADA FORTE, *Piazza del Campo 12. Credit cards accepted. Dinner for two E32.*

If you're at the top of the Campo looking down at the Palazzo Pubblico, this place is on your right at the end of the wall. They have scenic outside tables from which you can watch the goings-on in the Campo, as well as inside seating in a typically spartan Sienese restaurant environment. There is a huge antipasto menu which should satisfy you for lunch. If not, try one of their pizzas.

The *barrocciaia* (tomatoes, sausage and garlic), and the *salsiccia* (tomato, mozzarella and sausages) are both good. If you're into meats, try the *cinghiale alle senese* (wild boar cooked over the open flame) or the *agnello* arro*sto* (roasted lamb). A really good restaurant.

9. DA VASCO, *Via del Capitano 6/8. Tel. 0577/288-094. No credit cards accepted. Dinner for two E22.*

Small quaint little place just down from the Duomo. The atmosphere is typically austere with brick ceiling and whitewashed walls. The food is good and inexpensive. Try the *penne all'arrabbiata* (with a tomato, garlic, pepper sauce), the *spaghetti alla carbonara* (with cheese, ham, and egg), or the *ravioli all quattro formaggi* (thick sauce with four cheeses). For secondo, try the *bistecca di maiale* (pork steak) or the *omelette al formaggio* (cheese omelet).

10. L'OSTERIA, *Via dei Rossi 79/81. Tel. 0577/287-592. No credit cards accepted. Dinner for two E25.*

Literally translated it's "The Restaurant" and it seems to be very popular with the locals. Located down a side street past two other more touristy places making it a little ways away from the thundering crowds. Squeeze through the worn hanging beads and cram yourself in here to enjoy a wonderfully local atmosphere with superbly prepared food. Try the *penne con melanzane e peperoni* (eggplant and pepperoni salami) for primo, and either the *pollo ai peperoni* (chicken with pepperoni), the *bistecca di vitello* (veal steak), or the *bistecca di maiale* (pork steak) for secondi. You won't be disappointed.

11. VITTI, *Via Monatanini 14-16, Tel. 0577/28-92-91. No credit cards accepted. Dinner for two E22-30.*

Tranquil outside seating off the main road as well as in the *zona pedonale* (walking zone). Your food is passed through a window from the kitchen to the waiter. The inside is uncomfortably small with only a counter and standing room only, but the Sienese seem to enjoy the food so much they cram themselves in for lunch, leaving the outside seating to tourists. In the window of the place are some dishes that are not on the menu, so if one of them catches your eye ask to order something from the *finestra* (window). From the menu try some of their pasta, particularly the *tortellini alla panna* (cheese stuffed pasta in a rich cream sauce) or the *lasagna al forno* (oven baked lasagna) for primo. For secondo try the *petto di tacchino arrosto* (roasted turkey breast).

12. IL BIONDO, *Via del Rustichetto 10, Tel. and Fax 0577/280-739. Closed Wednesdays. Dinner for two E40.*

Another place you should think of trying, since the ambiance at the outside seating is so peaceful and colorfully local and the food is great. You can get a good seat inside in a plain whitewashed Sienese-style restaurant, but try the outside. They make some good pasta here including *spaghetti alla vongole* (with clam sauce) and *penne alla puttanesca* (literally translated it means whore's pasta, made with tomatoes, garlic, black olives, olive oil and meat). For seconds, try the *saltimbocca alla Romana* (veal shank stewed in tomatoes and spices) or the *bistecca alla griglia* (beef steak cooked on the grill that would make a Texan proud).

Seeing the Sights
The Palio Race

The best time to visit because of the pageantry, and the worst time to visit because of the crowds, is during the biannual **Palio**, held on July 2 and August 16. The Palio is a festive time awash in colorful banners, historic pageantry, and a wild bareback horse race that runs three times around the **Piazza del Campo**. The race lasts all of 90 seconds but will leave you with memories to last a lifetime.

A *palio* literally is an embroidered banner, the prize offered for winning the race. The first official Palio was run in 1283, though many say the custom dates back farther than that. During the Middle Ages, besides the horse races, there were violent games of primeval rugby (which you can see in Florence twice a year during their *Calcio in Costume* festival) and even bullfights to settle neighborhood bragging rights.

The contestants in the horse race itself are jockeys from the seventeen neighborhood parishes or *contrade* in Siena. During a Palio ten horses ride in the first race and seven horses ride in the next since the square is not big enough to accommodate all the horses at once. The jockeys willingly risk life and limb for the pride of their small area of the city. At two places in the Piazza del Campo there are right angles at which the horses have to turn, and usually at these points you'll have at least one jockey lose his seat or a horse its footing.

But this is more than a horse race. It is really a sanctioned community-wide regression into the Middle Ages, with the coats-of-arms that represented each *contrade* at that time being displayed prominently by members of that neighborhood. The *contrade* used to be military companies, but these became outdated when the Spanish and Florentines laid siege to Siena and conquered it. At that time there were 59 *contrade*, but plagues and wars decimated the population until by the early 18th century there were only 23 left. Today only seventeen remain and the coats-of-arms for each *contrade* is as follows: *Aquila* (eagle), *Bruco* (caterpillar), *Chiocciola* (snail), *Civetta* (owl), *Drago* (dragon), *Giraffa* (giraffe), *Istrice* (porcupine), *Leocorno* (unicorn), *Lupa* (she-wolf), *Nicchio* (shell), *Oca* (goose), *Onda* (wave), *Pantera* (panther), *Selva* (wood), *Tartuca* (turtle), *Torre* (tower), and *Valdimontone* (ram).

Prior to the race there is a good two hour display of flag throwing by the *alferi* of each *contrada*, while the medieval *carroccio* (carriage), drawn by a white oxen, circles the Campo bearing the prized *palio* each neighborhood wants to claim as its own.

To witness this event, however, you have to plan way in advance since at both times of year the Palio is jam-packed. You can see the Palio in one of three ways: in the center of the Piazza where people are packed like sardines on a first come first serve basis; in the viewing stands which cost anywhere from E100 to E175; or in one of the offices or apartments that line the piazza. To get a seat in the viewing stand you'll need to plan at least 6-9 months in advance and get your tickets through your travel agent. To view the spectacle from an office or apartment you'll need to have connections. Maybe the company you work for has dealings with the banks and other companies whose offices line the square. However you witness this blast from Siena's medieval past, you will have memories for a lifetime.

A. THE CAMPO

Eleven streets lead into the square where, in the past, the people of Siena used to assemble at the sound of the **Sunto bell** to learn the latest news. Today it still is the gathering place for all the locals and tourists. You will see at most times of the day the young lounging on the stones and their elders congregating at cafés. The piazza is concave and irregular with a ring of rather austere buildings surrounding it, but even so it is a marvel of architectural harmony. On the curved side of the Campo sits the **Fonte Gaia** (Gay Fountain) made by Jacopo della Quercia. The water from this fountain comes here from 30 km away through a series of pipes and aqueducts from the 13th century. A feat of ancient engineering.

On the map the Campo looks flat, but it's actually a gradually sloping surface with bricks that seem to float down to the **Palazzo Pubblico**. A great place to grab a bite to eat at one of the many restaurants, sip a drink at one of the cafés, or to simply rest your tired tourist feet by relaxing on the cobblestone slope.

B. PALAZZO PUBBLICO

At the Campo. Tower open 10:00am–dusk. In the winter open only until 1:30pm. Admission E3.

One of the most attractive and imposing Gothic buildings in all of Tuscany. Most of it was built between 1297 and 1340, with the top story being raised in 1639. This building reflected the wealth and success of Siena, which was almost the same size as London and Paris during the fourteenth century. The little chapel underneath the tower was dedicated by the town to the Virgin Mary when the terrible plague known ever since as the *Morte Nera* (Black Death) came to an end. In Siena alone 65,000 people died of the plague in the summer of 1348. That was over half of their population. The intricate wrought-iron gate that covers the entrance was made in 1445.

The best part of this building is the **Torre del Mangia**. It offers the greatest sights in all of Siena. Unfortunately you have to climb up 400 small confined steps to top of the bell tower. It's 112 meters high, was built in 1334, and is still in amazing shape. The clock was made in 1360 and the huge bell was raised to its present position in 1666. Imagine having to haul a bell that weighs 6,764 kilos up a pulley system to the top of the tower? Remember to bring your camera because the views of the countryside and the city are stupendous. You can see past the old walls, look over the terra-cotta tiles of the city roofs, lush fields, and forests for as far as the eye can see. A definite must-see when in Siena.

C. MUSEO CIVICO
At the Campo. Open 9:30am–7:30pm Monday–Saturday. Open Sunday 9:30am–1:30pm.
Inside the Palazzo Pubblico is the **Museo Civico**, which is filled with many wonderful paintings, frescoes, mosaics, and tapestries. Upstairs is the famous **Sala del Mappamondo** (Hall of the Map of the World). From its large windows you can look out onto the market square. The other three walls are frescoed with scenes of the religious and civil life of the Siena Republic. In this museum you'll find many examples of the some of the finest Sienese art anywhere.

D. THE DUOMO
Piazza del Duomo. 7:30am–1:30pm and 3:00pm to dusk from December to March. From March to November open 9:00am–7:30pm. Admission E3.
The combination of Gothic and Romanesque architectural elements in the Cathedral of Siena is a result of the large amount of time spent completing it. Nonetheless it doesn't appear as if the two styles contrast too much with each other. Despite being incredibly elaborate the facade seems quite harmonious and attractive. The side walls and steeple are striped black and white like the *Balzana* that is the standard of the town. It was started in 1200 and finished in the 1400s.
Inside the cathedral there are even more elaborate and rich decorations. It has three naves and is 90 meters long and 51 meters high, and the walls are covered with the white and black *Balzana* stripes also. All around the nave you'll see a row of 172 busts of Popes, from Christ to Lucius III, all made in 1400. Beneath them are 36 busts of Roman Emperors. The graffito and inlaid floor is a succession of scenes from the Old Testament, which took from 1372 to 1551 to complete. The earlier ones are done in black and white, and the later scenes have a touch of gray and red in them.
You can't miss the intricate and elaborate pulpit which was made by **Nicola Pisano** from 1265 to 1268. It is of white marble and supported by nine columns resting on nine lions. There are 300 human figures and 70 animal figures decorating this delightful work. Besides the pulpit there are countless

remarkable paintings, sculptures, reliefs, and stone coffins all attributed to famous Italian masters. The statues on the Piccolo altar have been attributed to **Michelangelo**. In the **Piccolomini Library** you'll find beautiful frescoes of the life of Pope Pius II made by the master Pinturicchio. As you leave the library you'll see the monument to Archbishop Bandini's nephews made in 1570 by Michelangelo.

There were plans to have made this cathedral a small part of a much larger place of worship; but those plans were stunted for a variety of reasons, including the plague and the eventual Florentine conquest of the city. Today only a few pillars and walls remain from the plans for that grandiose church.

E. MUSEO DELL'OPERA DEL DUOMO
Piazza del Duomo. 7:30am-1:30pm and 3:00pm to dusk from December to March. From March to November open 9:00am-7:30pm. Admission E3.

In the **museum of the cathedral** is a valuable collection of the treasure of paintings, statues, and fragments the cathedral once displayed. One of the best paintings is Duccio di Buoninsegna's *Maestra* (1308-1311) that was originally on the high altar. You'll find a group of three sculptures, the *Three Graces*, which are Greek works of the 2nd century BCE that were once in the Piccolomini Library. And you can't miss the exquisitely beautiful goldsmith's work, *Rosa d'Oro* (Golden Rose) that was given to the city of Siena by Alessandro VIII in 1658. Another work of interest is the plan of the unfinished facade of the Baptistery by Giacomo di Mino del Pelliciaio.

F. BAPTISTERY OF SAN GIOVANNI
Piazza del Duomo. Open 9:00am-1:00pm and 3:00pm-5:00pm year round. In the summer open until 7:00pm.

This is really the **crypt** of the Cathedral. Here you can find the **baptismal fonts** by Jacopo della Quercia, the bronze bas-relief of Bishop Pecci by Donatello, and many bronze reliefs of the Old and New Testament. The Baptistery was begun in 1315, but its facade has never been finished.

G. CHURCH OF SAN DOMENICO & THE SANCTUARY OF SANTA CATERINA
Costa San Antonio. Church is open from 9:00am-6:00pm. The Sanctuary is closed 12:30pm-3:30pm Monday-Saturday and all day Sundays.

The Basilica is indelibly linked with the cloistered life of the local saint. It rises monumental and solitary overlooking the surrounding landscape and city. Its simple brick architecture of the 13th century was modified in the 14th and 15th centuries but still remains more like the walls of a convent than a church. You can't miss the **chapel of St. Caterina** inside where the saint's head is preserved today in the silver reliquary. In the other chapels of the church you'll find paintings by Sienese artists of the 14th through 16th centuries.

The house where St. Caterina used to live is now **Caterina Sanctuary**. The rooms she lived in as a youth have been frescoed by artists of all times with scenes from her life. It is a simple home but it is of cultural significance, since St. Caterina is one of the patron saints of Italy.

Shopping

There a a series of arts and crafts stores all over Siena, as well as the usualy internationally known boutiques. But to me, some of the best memories to take back with you are culinary in nature. As such, listed below are two stores where you can buy food products.

13. **Enoteca San Domenica**, *Via del Paradiso 56. Tel. 05/77-27-11-81.*

Right near where the bus lets you off from the station you can buy gifts of great Chianti wine for only E4. They also have other wonderful gifts of local products. There are a number of these little shops all over Siena, but this one is the best and the best located.

14. **Pizzigheria**, 95 *Via della Citta.*

There is a boar's head outside with a pair of glasses resting on his snout. Enter here and enjoy some of the most succulent food aromas. A good place to buy any picnic supplies you may need, but there's a less expensive place up the road. Just stop here for the sight and smell of the sweet salamis hanging.

Practical Information

For car rentals:
- **Avis**, *Via Simone Martini 36, Tel. 0577/27-03-05*
- **Hertz**, *Hotel Lea, Via XXIV Maggio, Tel. 0577/45085*

For tourist information:
- **Piazza San Domenico**, *Tel 0577/940-809. Place to get maps and hotel reservations if needed. Open 9:00am to 7:00pm.*

FIESOLE

Fiesole is five miles east of Florence on a hill overlooking the city. Well before Florence existed, Fiesole dominated this part of the Arno valley. Fiesole was one of the 12 important towns of ancient **Roman Etruria** from 80 BCE on, and later was named the capital city of Roman Etruria. But in 1125 CE all this dominance came to an end, when Florence sacked and began its control of Fiesole and all of Tuscany. After the takeover, Fiesole was used by many of the Medici family as a refuge from the toil of governing, and the heat of the summer.

Even today Fiesole is a great respite from the heat or the hectic pace of Florence. Remember to bring a jacket because it is quite a bit cooler up in the hills. This is the place to stay if you want to get away from everything after you've finished your touring. It's only a 20 minute bus ride away (the buses leave from the station every 15 minutes). This is a tranquil location for a family vacation that offers access to Florence quickly and easily. If you're bothered by traffic noise or a hectic pace, I would seriously suggest staying up here and commuting to Florence every day.

Besides being a refuge, Fiesole's archaeological excavations offers visitors a small glimpse into the ancient past. There are also many fine churches and vistas to enjoy. You'll really feel above it all here, since almost every road offers a perfect panorama of Florence below.

Arrivals & Departures
By Bus or Taxi

The easiest and least expensive way to get to Fiesole from Florence is to take the #7 bus from the Piazza della Stazione. The ride takes only 20 minutes (with a soundless but still intrusive advertising video playing on a TV the whole time). If you take a taxi it'll cost you about $25. Both rides will offer you glimpses of fine villas and gardens as you weave through the winding road up to Fiesole. Remember to pack yourself a picnic lunch which you can create from the ingredients you buy at one of the street markets or the *alimentari* listed in this section of the book. If you forgot, there are a number of bars, cafés, and restaurants to choose from. When in Fiesole look out for little starlings that imagine themselves cars as they sweep two feet above the road pavement on the hills surrounding the town. A beautiful sight to see.

You catch the bus at the side of the train station in Florence under the awnings. Tickets are sold at the *Giornalaio* inside the station or at the ticket office catty-corner to the bus stop outside. Tickets cost E2.

Where to Stay

1. VILLA SAN MICHELLE, *Via Doccia 4, 50014 Fiesole. Tel. 055/59-451, Fax 055/598-734. 36 rooms all with bath. American Express, Diners Club, Mastercard and Visa accepted. Single E350; Double E500-650. Jr. Suite E950-1,000. Suite E1,200. Breakfast included.* *****

Located in a converted monastery that has a facade attributed to Michelangelo. If nothing else this hotel will allow you to bring stories of beautiful views, ancient habitations, and opulent surroundings back home. The reception area of the hotel is an old chapel, and in the dining room, the bar is made from an ancient Etruscan sarcophagus (imagine if a bar in Washington, DC was made from the coffin of a Civil War soldier ... ah, the Italian culture is so laid back).

Each room has a four poster bed and everything else is rustically luxurious. The best rooms overlook the gardens that surround the hotel. This is *the* hotel for those of you with plenty of disposable income. Here you can enjoy an

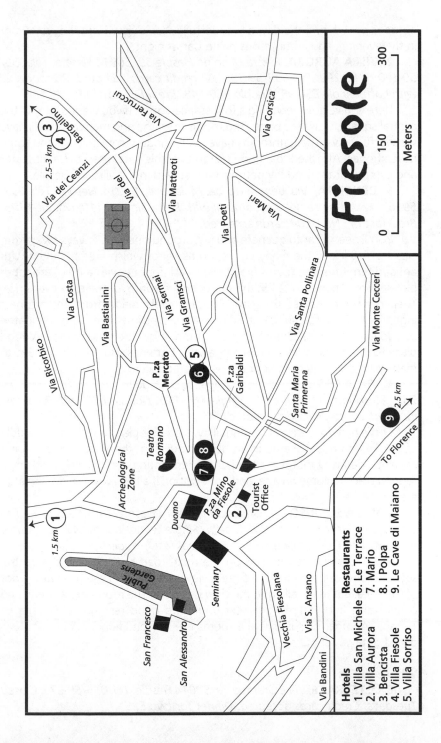

Fiesole

0   150   300

Meters

Hotels
1. Villa San Michele
2. Villa Aurora
3. Bencista
4. Villa Fiesole
5. Villa Sorriso

Restaurants
6. Le Terrace
7. Mario
8. I Polpa
9. Le Cave di Maiano

Via Ferrucci

Via Corsica

Via Matteoti

Via del

Via Poeti

Via Mari

Via dei Ceanzi

Bargellino

2.5-3 km

Via Costa

Via Ricorbico

Via Bastianini

Via Sermai

Via Gramsci

P.za Mercato

P.za Garibaldi

Santa Maria Primerana

Via Santa Pollinara

Via Monte Cecceri

2.5 km

To Florence

Teatro Romano

Archeological Zone

Duomo

P.za Mino da Fiesole

Tourist Office

1.5 km

Public Gardens

San Francesco

San Alessandro

Seminary

Vecchia Fiesolana

Via S. Ansano

Via Bandini

outdoor pool during the day, a wonderfully scenic view from the restaurant in the evening, and a boisterous piano bar at night.

2. **VILLA AURORA,** *Piazza Mino de Fiesole 39, 50014 Fiesole. Tel. 055/ 59-100 or 59-292, Fax 055/59-587. All credit cards accepted. 26 rooms all with bath. Single E50-95; Double E80-148. Breakfast costs E9.* ****

Here you've got everything a four star can offer. If you want to stay in the central square, this is the place. The rooms are large and modern and all have wonderful views. The bathrooms have every modern convenience and some have phones. Attached to a good restaurant, this hotel used to be a theater and *osteria* for the wealthy patrons who stayed in the villas of Fiesole.

3. **BENCISTA,** *Via Benedetto da Maiano 4, 50014 Fiesole. Tel. 055/ 59163, Fax is the same. 42 rooms all with bath. Single E110; Double E125. Breakfast E7. No credit cards accepted.* ***

You'll need a car to get here and get around since it is a ways away from Fiesole. You'll love the many public rooms, all of which are appointed with antique furniture. The rooms (you have to ask for one with a view) are sober but elegant. Opened in 1925, this has been a favorite for travelers ever since. Their restaurant serves up great Tuscan meals made from the freshest ingredients. Breakfast, lunch, and dinner are served in a large room dominated by two large columns. Breakfast in the summer is out on the terrace. A good place to come and relax and recharge your batteries. No TV so you have to make your own entertainment in this isolated location.

4. **VILLA FIESOLE,** *Via Beato Angelico 35, 50014 Fiesole. Tel. 055/597-252. 28 rooms, all with bath. Single E65-110; Double E80-160. Breakfast included. All credit cards accepted.* ***

Come here for peace and tranquillity, since this place is truly in the middle of the Tuscan hills. Located in an historic building, the Villa Fiesole is great romantic getaway that has a pool, a garden setting and relaxing ambiance. A good place to come on a second honeymoon if all you want to do is lounge around.

5. **VILLA SORRISO,** *Via Gramsci 21, 50014 Fiesole. Tel. 055/590-27, Fax is the same. Seven rooms, 6 with bath. Single without bath E17-30; Double without bath E35-45; Double E40-55. Breakfast included.* *

A wonderful little one star on the main road just up from the central square. Some of the rooms have great views overlooking a nearby valley, not of Florence. But that's all right, the view is superb. The rooms are all clean and comfortable and you're right next door to a good restaurant, Pizzeria Le Terrace. Another plus is that the rooms are air conditioned. A perfect low-priced getaway spot.

Where to Eat

6. **LE TERRACE,** *Viale Gramsci 19, 50014 Fiesole. Tel. 055/59-272. Closed Tuesdays. Credit cards accepted. Dinner for two E25.*

This is a huge place with both indoor and somewhat cramped outdoor seating, but with stupendous views of a lush green valley below. Ignore the tacky wooden life-sized waiter at the entrance and come for the view and the inexpensive food. As you enter you'll pass by the brick wood-burning oven where they make a wide variety of pizzas that will please even the most discerning eater. Besides pizza they make good pastas. Some recommendations: *tortellini alla panna e prosciutto* (with cream and ham), and *tagliatelli della casa* (house favorite made with onions, sausage, saffron in a thick cream sauce). If you're interested in meat dishes, try their *pollo fritto* (chicken fried in olive oil), or the *coniglio fritto* (rabbit fried in olive oil) and compare whether rabbit really does taste like chicken.

7. MARIO, *Piazza Mino #9, 50014 Fiesole. Credit cards accepted. Dinner for two E37.*

They have two different menus rolled into one. A traditional menu and one they call a *cucina creativa* (creative cooking) menu. Both are rather sparse, so check them out in the window before you stop here to see if you want anything. They have outside seating on the main square, as well as a few tables inside. Some of the more creative dishes are the *ravioline salmone e vongole* (little ravioli with a salmon and clam sauce), and the *filetto o coniglio alle mele* (thin slices of rabbit served with apples).

8. I POLPA, *Piazza Mino #21/22, 50014 Fiesole. Tel. 055/59133. Credit cards accepted. Dinner for two E30.*

Try their country style *bruschetta*. They brush the coarse toasted garlic bread with succulent olive oil and cover it with fresh tomatoes. Then sample their *pennette all fiesolana* (with cream sauce and ham). If the meat bug hits you try the *scaloppini ai funghi porcini* (veal with porcini mushrooms). Reservations on the weekends are recommended.

9. LE CAVE DI MAIANO, *Via delle Cave 16, 50014 Fiesole. Tel. 055/59133. Closed Thursday and Sunday nights. All credit cards accepted. Dinner for two E50.*

One of the most popular restaurants for Florentines escaping their hectic, tourist-jammed city during the summer time. You'll need a car or will have to grab a cab from Fiesole, to get here, since it is about 3-4 kilometers outside of the town of Fiesole proper. You'll be served typical Tuscan food in a truly rustic atmosphere. The restaurant is blessed with a perfect garden environment. They specialize in all types of grilled, roasted, and fried meats. A great place to try if you've come up to Fiesole and want something a little different and out of the way.

Seeing the Sights

CATHEDRAL OF SAN ROMULUS, *in the Piazza della Cattedrale (also Piazza Mino di Fiesole). Open daily 7:30am–noon and 4:00pm–7:00pm.*

Built in the 11th century, the best part of this church is the bell tower whose chimes toll the half hour and the hour. You can hear it all over the countryside informing you of your place in the universe.

THE ARCHEOLOGICAL ZONE, *Open Winter 9:00am–6:00pm, Summer 9:00am–7:00pm. Closed on Tuesdays.*

The museum itself houses epics from prehistoric, Etruscan, Roman and medieval times; but the best part of this place is the **Roman Theater**, partially restored, that dates back to the 1st century BCE. It's like a mini-Pompeii or Roman Forum.

The steep five minute climb (if you're fit) from the west end of **Piazza Mino** up to the **Church of San Francesco** will give you wonderful views of Florence and the Arno valley, especially from the benches near the **Church of San Alessandro** *(open daily 7:30am–noon and 4:00pm–7:00pm.)* Remember to bring your camera. The Church of San Francesca itself is relatively nondescript, but the cloisters are worth seeing as is the small museum that has a few Etruscan remains and relics collected by Franciscan missionaries in the Orient many years ago. Below the church you can see the public gardens and the **Basilica of S Alessandro**, which is on the site of the ancient **Roman temple of Bacchus** *Gardens open 7:00am – 7:00pm; Basilica open same hours).* Cheers.

You can see everything there is to see in Fiesole in less than a day, so you can spend the rest of your time soaking up the great panoramic views, eating wonderful food, and celebrating the tranquillity with some Chianti. But remember, you are only 20 minutes away from the center of Florence by a bus that leaves at least twice an hour. So let me reiterate: if you like the splendor of Florence but can't seem to be able to stomach the noise and congestion, stay here in Fiesole. It will make your tour that much more pleasant and rewarding.

Practical Information for Florence

Airports
• **Aereoporto A.Vespucci- Firenze**, *Tel. 055/373-498*
• **Aereoporto G.Galilei -Pisa**, *Tel. 050/40132*

Church & Synagogue Ceremonies in English
• **St. James**, American Episcopal Church, *Via Rucellai 9, Tel. 055/294-417.* Located in the Centro section of Florence.
• **St. Marks**, Church of England, *Via Maggio 16, Tel. 055/294-764.* Located in the Oltrarno section of Florence.
• **Synagogue**, *Via L.C. Farini 4, Tel. 055/245-251/2.* Located in the Santa Croce section of Florence.

Consulates
• **British Consulate**, *Lungarno Corsini 2, Florence, Tel. 055/284-133*

• **United States Consulate**, *Lungarno Amerigo Vespucci 38, Florence, Tel. (055) 239-8276*
If you are Canadian, Irish, or another nationality, you'll need to contact your embassy in Rome (see the *Rome* chapter, Practical Information section).

Emergencies
These are the rapid response numbers for the police, caribineiri and fire.
• **Polizia Soccorso Pubbblico** (police), *Tel. 113*
• **Carabinieri Pronto Intervento**, *Tel. 112*
• **Vigili del Fuoco** (fire), *Tel. 115*

Local Festivals & Holidays
• **January 1**, New Year's Day
• **April 25**, Liberation Day
• **Ascension Day**
• **May 1**, Labor Day
• **Month of May**, Iris Festivals
• **Cricket Festival**, Sunday of the Ascension, usually in May, with floats and many little (mehcanical) crickets sold in cages. Live crickets were once sold, but animal rights activists convinced the city to switch to electronic crickets.
• **May and June**, *Maggio Musicale Fiorentino*
• **Mid-June to August**, *Estate Fiesolana*. Music, cinema, ballet and theater
• **Three Weekends in June**, *Calcio in Costume*
• **June 24**, St. John the Baptist's Day celebrated with fireworks
• **August 15**, *Ferragosto*
• **First Sunday in September**, Lantern Festival
• **November 1**, All Saints Day *(Ognissanti)*
• **December 8**, Conception of the Virgin Mary *(Immacolata)*
• **December 25 & 26**, Christmas

Laundry
After you're on the road for a few days, and especially if you're going to be on the road for quite a while, you're definitely going to need to do some laundry, quickly, easily, and inexpensively. If you're staying at a four star hotel don't bother reading this because you've already sent your clothes down to be starched and pressed by the in-house staff.

For the rest of us, we need to find a good coin operated laundry, and in Florence they have just the thing.
• **Wash & Dry**, *four different location, all open seven days a week from 8:00am to 10:00pm. Last wash allowed in at 9:00pm. General number*

055/436-1650. E3 for wash, E3 for dry, E3 for detergent. E6 for large. Located at: Via dei Serragli 87/R (in the Oltrarno); Via della Scala 52/54R (by the train station and Piazza Santa Maria Novella) – has air conditioning; Via dei Servi 105/R (by the Duomo) – has air conditioning; Via Ghibellina 143r (near the Duomo).
- **Laundrette**, *Via del Guelfa 33. Open seven days a week from 8:00am to 10:00pm. Wash E3, Dry E2, Detergent E3.*
- **Tintoria La Serena**, *Via della Scala 30r, Tel. 055/218-183. Open seven days a week from 8:00am - 10:00pm. Total of E7 for washing and drying one load.*

On-Line Access
    Internet Land, *Via degli Alfani 43r, 50121 Firenze. Tel./Fax 055/263-8220. Web Site: www.internetland.it.*
    The place in Florence to come to surf the web, scan a document, get one typed and printed, fax a letter home, or e-mail your friends.

Postal Services
    The **central post office** in Florence, *Via Pietrapiana 53-55,* is in the Santa Croce section of town; but stamps can be bought at any tobacconist (store indicated by a **T** sign outside), and mailed at any mailbox, which are red and marked with the word *Poste* or *Lettere.* You can send duty free gift packages (need to be marked "gift enclosed") home to friends or relatives as long as the cost of the gift(s) in the package does not exceed $50. You will need to box them in official boxes or envelopes which can be bought at *cartolerie* (stationery stores).
    If you need to mail a package of material which you brought with you on you trip, you need to mark the package "American goods returned." Rules, rules, rules.

Tourist Information & Maps
- **Information Office**, *Via Manzoni 16, Tel. 055/247-8141.* Located in the Santa Croce area of Florence. Provides city maps, up-to-date information about Florence and the province of Florence, which includes museum hours, events, and bus and train schedules.
- **Information Office** at the Train Station, *Via Stazione 59r. Open 7:00am to 10:00pm. Tel. 055/282-893/283-500.* They can book hotel rooms for you here; but you do have to pay the first night's stay in advance plus a fee of E5 for a deluxe hotel, E4 for a four-star, E3 for a three-star, E2 for a two star, and E1.5 for a one star. There's a form that you need to fill out prior to getting to an attendant that indicates the specific requirements you want in your room, i.e. whether there is a private bath, double bed, and how much you want to spend.

• **American Express**, *Lungarno Guicciardini 49, Tel. 055/288-751.* Located in the *Oltrarno* section of Florence. *Via Dante Alighieri 22r, Tel. 055/50981.* Located in the Centro Storico section of Florence. They offer a full complement of tourist information.

Tour Operators

• **American Express**, *Lungarno Guicciardini 49, Tel. 055/288-751.* Located in the *Oltrarno* section of Florence. *Via Dante Alighieri 22r, Tel. 055/50981.* Located in the Centro Storico section of Florence. They offer a full range of tours.

• **Wagon-Lit**, *Via del Giglio 27r, Tel 055/21-88-51.* Located in the Centro section of Florence. They offer your basic bus tours of Florence and Tuscany.

• **World Vision Travel**, *Via Cavour 154/158r. Tel 055/57-71-85, Fax 055/582-664; and Lungarno Acciadi 4. Tel. 055/29.52.71, Fax 055/215-666.* They offer your basic bus tours of Florence and Tuscany.

• **CIT**, *Via Cavour 56-59, Tel. 055/294-306.* Located in the Centro section of Florence. They offer your basic bus tours of Florence and Tuscany.

• **Walking Tours of Florence**, *Tel. 055/580-430. Email: holitaly@dada.it.* One of the best ways to learn all about the Roman, medieval and Renaissance history, and the architecture, people and events of Florence. Every Tuesday, Thursday, and Saturday at 10:00am and Wednesday evening at 6:00pm. Cost is only E20 per person.

Chapter 15

Umbria

Called the "Green Heart of Italy," Umbria is a beautiful slice of mother nature's paradise, filled with stunningly beautiful fairy-tale like medieval towns. Covered with lush green forest and manicured fields, Umbria is located in the center of Italy and is bordered by Tuscany and Lazio, the provinces that are home to Florence and Rome. Umbria is one of the smallest regions of Italy at only 8,500 square kilometers, but what it lacks in size it makes up for in art, architecture, natural settings, outdoor sporting activities, delicious cuisine, intricate arts & crafts, welcoming people and a passionate way of life.

Even though it is one of only a few Italian provinces not bordered by the sea, Umbria's mountains offer plenty of scenic splendor. Besides the natural beauty of the rolling hills and lush valleys, Umbria is filled with stunningly beautiful medieval towns like the capital, **Perugia**. Spreading majestically over the tops of a series of hills, Perugia is interlaced with winding cobblestones streets, an aqueduct turned walkway, ancient *palazzi*, Etruscan and Roman arches, and picturesque piazzas. Besides Perugia, the main towns of interest in Umbria include, **Spoleto**, **Todi**, **Gubbio**, **Orvieto**, and **Assisi**; each of which are rewarding destinations in and of themselves. Besides all the natural scenic beauty and fairy tale-like medieval towns, one of the main attractions here is that Umbria is very lightly touristed (except for Assisi which is a major pilgrimage sight) and an incredibly inexpensive alternative to the crowding your find in the more well-known areas of Italy.

Set in the mountains, spring and fall are the best times to visit, not only because of the welcoming weather but also for the abundance of local produce turning every meal into a memory. In the summer it can be hot and muggy, and in winter cold and wet – but Umbria should not be missed because of its stunning scenic beauty.

One main attraction that this province has to offer for seasoned Italophiles is that despite being between the main tourist attractions of Rome and Florence, Umbria is off of those crowded tourist corridors. At most times of the year, when the rest of Italy is swarming with hordes of tourists, you can venture into Umbria and have it almost all to yourself. The locals still outnumber the tourists in Umbria.

In Umbria's exotic urban settings you will find some wonderful Etruscan, Roman, Romanesque and Renaissance works of art and architecture. **Perugia** has the imposing and historically significant Etruscan Arch and Roman aqueduct turned walkway. **Orvieto** has its extensive Etruscan Necropolises and an awe inspiring cathedral. In **Gubbio** there are excellent examples of an ancient Roman temple, mausoleum, and theater just outside of an incredibly beautifully, well preserved and scenic medieval hill town. **Todi** as a whole is an inspiration and a wonderful respite from the hectic pace of modern life.

Umbria - Land of Truffles

Truffles (tartufi) have been described by epicureans as the ultimate indulgence, and if you have ever tasted a dish flavored with them you will realize that this is not only true, but is an incredible understatement. The **tartufo nero** (black truffle) is the more abundant and has a heartier flavor of the two varieties found in Umbria. The **tartufo bianco** (white truffle) is more subtle but found in less quantities. Gathered fresh from late September through December, you would be remiss not to savor any dish flavored with these tasty tubers if you venture to Umbria during that time.

Truffles grow wild and are discovered by trained dogs whose keen sense of smell allow them to locate these aromatic morsels despite the fact that the truffles develop over a foot underground. Most truffles are not very large, and weigh very little, but are incredibly expensive. Recently a New York City restaurant bought the largest ever found, though it weighed a little under 16 oz, and paid more than $300 per ounce for it

The aroma of tartufi, or as the more upscale say, 'perfume', is indescribably luscious. The best description could be that they are pungently aromatic, since the smell is overpowering but tantalizingly delicious. Walk into any alimentari or salumeria where they are sold when in season, and the sapore (aroma) will overwhelm you.

But **Spoleto** is the jewel of the region. Second only to Todi in quality of medieval character, this ambient hill town is home to some of the best restaurants in Italy, a direct result of the fact that this town hosts the world-renowned **Spoleto Festival** every summer. But what sets Spoleto apart, not only from towns in Umbria, but from every place I have visited on the planet, is its immediate proximity to pristine, untouched, verdant natural settings. Just across the Ponte delle Torre — a medieval aqueduct located only a few meters from the centro storico — which spans a deep gorge over to the hillside of Monte Luco, you will find an extensive array of hiking trails through deep forest, with scenic views and the peace and calm that only untouched natural settings can offer. Spoleto is a combination of quaint and colorful medieval setting, complete with cosmopolitan shopping and eating establishments, immediately next door to the purity of nature. A situation unique anywhere else in the world.

The Romanesque style is evident in many of the cathedrals in the region, as is the Gothic style, which is particularly exemplified by the cathedral in Orvieto. The Renaissance also flourished and spread throughout the region which has also left us with some stunning architectural wonders. Umbria also boasts some of the Renaissance period's major artists, including the most famous from the Umbrian school, **Pietro Vannucci** (better known as **Perugino**) whose works are exhibited in the National Gallery of Umbria and the Collegio del Cambio in Perugia.

The medieval towns in Umbria are so well preserved, and are as yet relatively undiscovered, that a visit to the region is truly like walking back in time. Located in every town are prime examples of floating architecture, or *casa pensili* (hanging houses) – archways connecting rooms of buildings located far above the level of the street. Something you never see in North America. So if you want to taste all the flavor of medieval Italy without the congestion of tourists, be a true traveler and come to Umbria.

Perugia

The capital city of Umbria and of the province named after it, the charming old medieval city of **Perugia** is a stunning place to visit. Besides being the seat of some major cultural institutions like the National Gallery of Umbria in the Prior's Palace, and the home to a number of universities including one specifically for foreigners, Perugia also has the vitality and ambiance of true Italian city.

Stretching over hilly ridges, Perugia has been the home of human development since prehistoric times. The seven bronze **Eugubine tablets** – located in Gubbio – which date from the 3rd century BCE to the 1st century BCE, give indisputable proof that the Umbrian people had their own language before they were under the dominion of the Etruscans. During the 3rd century BCE, Perugia became one of the twelve key cities of the Etruscan federation. After the Etruscans were defeated by Rome, the city was absorbed into the Roman Republic as a colony. Then when the Roman Civil War was won by Octavian, Perugia was razed because of its allegiance to Mark Anthony. Some years later it was rebuilt by Octavian, then Emperor Augustus who gave the city its name (Augustus Perusia).

Once Christianity became the religion of the Empire, Perugia followed suit and started its own diocese in the 5th century CE. Around this time the city was ruled by the Byzantine Empire since the Roman Empire had dissolved and split, until it came under ecclesiastical rule in the 8th century. From the 11th century onward Perugia became a 'free' commune (meaning the nobles ruled and the serfs served, but the city wasn't under anyone else's yoke but their own). During the 12th and 13th centuries Perugia fought a series of battles for the control of the region with Chiusi, Cortona, Assisi, Todi and Foligno; and eventually ended up victorious after defeating Assisi in 1202, allowing the city to extend its reach over much of the surrounding area.

Despite dominating the region, internally Perugia was in turmoil. Different factions of nobles fought over the right to govern, never reaching a conclusion, until finally, caught up in their own power struggles, the entire social and economic fabric of the city became frayed. Because of this weakness, in 1540, the city was conquered by the forces of Pope Farnese and came under the rule of the Papal States for three centuries.

Around 1840, a brief flirtation with freedom resulted in Napoleon's forays into the region, at which time the citizens took great pleasure in destroying the Rocca Paolina fortress (an oppressive symbol of papal control of the city) and threw the Swiss Guard out of the city. Twenty years later, on September 14, 1860, the city became part of the kingdom of Italy.

Perugia retains a quaint medieval charm with stunning old palazzi, winding streets climbing up and down the hills, with archways and buildings traversing the passageways. The main street, Corso Vannucci, and main square, Piazza IV Novembre, are the perfect place for a walk any time day or night, and is where you will find the majority of the population every night strolling along, munching on ice cream, socializing, before and after dinner. Most of the best shops are located in this area and in the evenings the area is filled with locals taking their evening stroll. A great sense of community thrives in Perugia making the city a fun and lively place to visit when you come to Umbria. Since it is located near many of the cities of note in the region, Perugia is a perfect place from which to take day trips to the other towns mentioned in this chapter.

Arrivals & Departures

The reason that Perugia still retains much of its medieval charm is that even though it is in close proximity geographically to Rome and Florence, Italy's two main tourist centers, train schedules are not strategically coordinated between those locations. Whether coming from Florence or Rome, you will have to change trains in **Castiglione del Lago**, and most of the trains which come here are milk runs which tend to stop at every little town along the way.

If you don't rent a car – which I recommend when visiting Umbria – once here, moving around the region can be cumbersome by either bus or train. Renting a car will be more expensive, but it will also allow you to visit tiny little hill towns quickly and easily. To visit Orvieto, Todi and Gubbio from Perugia a car is best, though Gubbio can be easily accessed by bus. To visit Assisi both train and bus are good options. To visit Spoleto from Perugia the train is a good option. A bus schedule (*orario*) for the local line, **Autolinee Regionali**, and a train schedule (*Orari Ferroviari*) is available at the local tourist office in Piazza IV Novembre.

Orientation

Perugia's *centro storico* sits on top of the crests of five hills and looks somewhat like the claw of the city's mascot, the Griffin. At the base of the main hill surrounding the train station are more modern urban developments, which though unsightly will not detract from your visit to the quaint, colorful and character-filled old town. The *centro storico* is bisected by the **Corso Vanucci**, which runs from the cathedral to the **Piazza Italia**, which is where the buses from the main train station let you off. It is also where the escalator arrives – snaking through the **Papal Fortress** (*Rocca Paolina*) – from the **Piazza Partigiani**, where the inter-regional bus terminal is located.

Umbria Websites

For up to date information about events and activities in Perugia visit *www.perugia.com*, the official web site for the city. This site also has links for *Assisi.com*, *Gubbio.com*, *Spoleto.com*, *Todi.com* among others. Granted they are in Italian, but even so they will help you plan your trip.

Getting Around Town

Break out your hiking shoes, get a bottle of water and get ready to do some hiking. The only way to explore Perugia is on foot and since it is located on a series of hills, you are going to do some stair- and hill-climbing while here. Aware of this, the Perugini have placed escalators in key locations throughout the town making the longer climbs more manageable now, while still retaining the charm of this stunning medieval town.

One of the most interesting escalators is the one that comes from the main parking and bus area, **Piazza dei Partigiani**. These *scala mobili* (literally meaning moving stairs) are underground and surrounded first by modern concrete walls. But these walls turn to ancient brick and you find yourself in the remnants of a 16th century underground fortress with vaulted passages, parts of old rooms, pieces of ancient passageways and an odd feeling that you suddenly went back in time. This place is the **Rocca Paolina** (see **A** on map), a fortress built by Pope Paul III in 1540 on the ruins of the Palazzo Baglioni, which was destroyed when the Papal States conquered Perugia. Then when the Papal States were expelled from Perugia, the fortress the popes built was partially destroyed. This paved the way for this stunning set of *scala mobili* to be built, making an introduction to Perugia very much like an amusement park ride with one defining difference – this is real.

Interwoven with these escalators are small roads, even smaller stairways, Etruscan and Roman archways, and a pedestrian aqueduct, all of which make Perugia a perambulating paradise. At the same time much of the central core

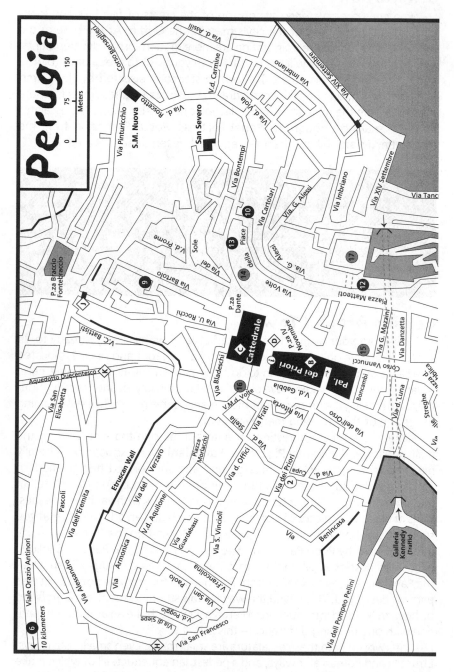

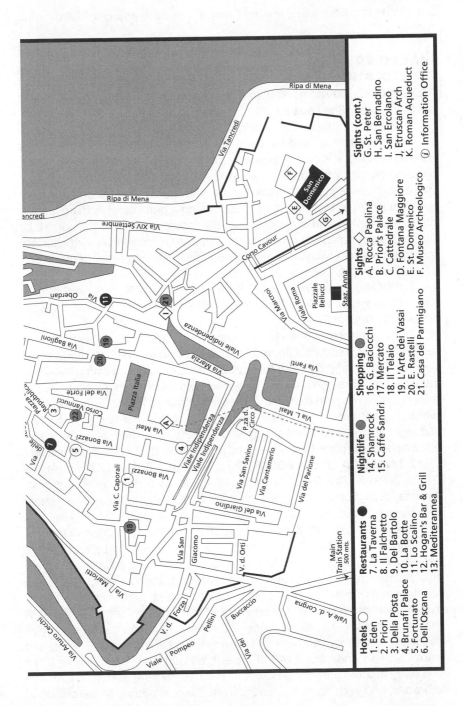

Sights ◇
A. Rocca Paolina
B. Prior's Palace
C. Cattedrale
D. Fontana Maggiore
E. St. Domenico
F. Museo Archeologico

Sights (cont.)
G. St. Peter
H. San Bernadino
I. San Ercolano
J. Etruscan Arch
K. Roman Aqueduct
(i) Information Office

Shopping ●
16. G. Baciocchi
17. Mercato
18. Il Telaio
19. L'Arte dei Vasai
20. E. Rastelli
21. Casa del Parmigiano

Nightlife ○
14. Shamrock
15. Caffe Sandri

Restaurants ●
7. La Taverna
8. Il Falchetto
9. Del Bartolo
10. La Botte
11. Lo Scalino
12. Hogan's Bar & Grill
13. Mediterannea

Hotels ○
1. Eden
2. Priori
3. Della Posta
4. Brunafi Palace
5. Fortunato
6. Dell'Oscana

is off limits to automobiles, making Perugia a relaxing and peaceful vacation spot.

Where to Stay

1. EDEN, *Via Cesare Caporali 9, 06123 Perugia. Tel. 075/572-8102, Fax 075/572-0342. 50 rooms all with bath. Single E45. Double E60. All credit cards accepted. Breakfast E3.* **

A wonderful little two star just off the Piazza Italia where the buses from the train station stop, and the escalator from the bus depot empties. This hotel's main lobby is on the third and fourth floor of an old building, which probably explains why they are only a two star even though and the rooms are spacious, clean and comfortable, come with televisions, and some have spectacular views. Even the rooms overlooking a quiet courtyard are great. I prefer the comfort and spaciousness of the rooms on the fourth floor. Make sure to request them. The bathrooms come with blow dryer and courtesy toiletry set. A great two star hotel, with wonderful service, in a superb location at excellent prices.

2. PRIORI, *Via del Priori, 06123 Perugia. Tel 075/572-3378, Fax 075/572-3213. 50 rooms all with bath. No credit cards accepted. Breakfast included. Single E50; Double E70.* **

Right in the center of town the decor here is 'old Umbrian' with antique furnishings, terra cotta tile floors and flowered drapes. The bathrooms come with blow dryer and courtesy toiletry set and are accommodating though a little cramped. The hotel has a large terrace with nice views. A great place to relax in the evenings. In the summer the terrace is used for the buffet breakfast which includes juice, fruit, cereal, pastries and coffee and tea. A quaint two star right in the middle of things with all the amenities of a three star elsewhere. Great place to stay at a good price. By far the best two star in town.

3. LOCANDA DELLA POSTA, *Corso Vannucci 97f, 06123 Perugia. Tel 075/572-8925, Fax 075/572-2413. Web: www.venere.com/it/perugia/locanda_della_posta/. 40 rooms all with bath. All credit cards accepted. Breakfast included. Single E105; Double E155. Suite E200.* ****

This is the best hotel on the best street in Perugia, Corso Vannucci, surrounded by traditional cafés, cute little shops, and old palazzi like the beautiful Priori Palace nearby. Corso Vannucci is the main promenade where all of Perugia comes out at night to parade around, young and old alike joined together in a community ritual of togetherness. Here you are ideally situated in the middle of everything. The hotel is a 17th century palazzo that once was the old post office, hence the name of the hotel. Over the centuries they've had many a celebrity stay here, including Frederick II of Prussia, Goethe, and Hans Christian Andersen. In 1990 the entire hotel was completely restored and every modern amenity was added. The hotel retains all of its charm and character, and each room is different from the next adding to the old world ambiance. The bathrooms are large and refined with all modern conveniences. By far the best place to stay in Perugia.

4. BRUNAFI PALACE, *Piazza Italia 12, 06123 Perugia. Tel. 075/573-2541, Fax 075/572-0210. Toll free in Italy 167/273-226. Toll free fax (USA) 1-888/661-0219. Email - sina@italyhotel.com. Web: www.italyhotel.com/sina. 93 rooms all with bath. All credit cards accepted. Breakfast included. Single E245; Double E300.* *******

In the centro storico right next to the Rocca Paolina, this is an over-priced yet extremely elegant and attentive hotel. Recently the Palace Hotel Bellavista has been absorbed in the Brunafi, which resulted in the word 'Palace' being added to the name of the hotel. The ancient palazzo has been completely restored with all modern amenities while retaining its charm, elegance and ambiance. The entrance hall instantly transports you back in time with its elegant tapestries and antique furnishings. The rooms are all differently furnished and are all clean and comfortable. The bathrooms unfortunately are not all that big, but do have all modern necessities. A wonderful place to stay, though it is a little expensive for my taste.

5. HOTEL FORTUNA, *Via Bonazzi 19, 06123 Perugia. Tel 075/572-2845, Fax 075/573-5040. Web: www.venere.com/it/perugia/fortuna/. All credit cards accepted. Single E75-90; Double E95-110.* *****

Situated in the *centro storico*, just off of the Corso Vanucci, this place was completely restored in 1992 with air-conditioning added in 1999. Despite all the changes this hotel has maintained it charms and comes with all three star amenities. The second floor houses the breakfast room and evening bar area. The third floor has a nice sitting room with a fire place and there is a big terrace on the fifth floor overlooking the rooftops of Perugia. Wonderful little three star in an ideal location.

6. CATELLO DELL'OSCANA, *06134 Locanda Cenerente, Perugia. 075/690-125, Fax 075/690-666. Email - info@oscano-castle.com. Web: www.oscano-castle.com. 100 rooms all with bath. All credit cards accepted. Breakfast included.* **Castle***: Suite or jr-suite on the top floor of the castle is E200. 3 rooms elsewhere in the castle E160.* **Villa Ada***: Double E110 per room per night.* **La Macina***: Weekly rates E300 to 625. Buffet breakfast included and is served in the dining room of the Castle.*

Stunning. Incredibly beautiful. Amazing. Like something out of a fairy tale. Simply unbelievable. By far the best place to stay in all of Umbria. If you have a car, and you have the means, stay here. Near Perugia, but set deep in the surrounding verdant, forested hills, this amazing medieval castle presents an atmosphere of unparalleled charm and ambiance. There are three locations to choose from: the Castle (a medieval structure complete with towers and turrets that is simply but elegantly decorated and equipped with every comfort), the Villa Ada (a 19th century residence adjoining the castle that is more modern but no less accommodating), and La Macina (a country house down the hill from the other two structures, and comes with complete apartments and has an adjacent pool).

All three offer the setting for an ideal vacation, but the castle is the place to stay because of its unique, one of a kind medieval setting. A perfect place to spend a honeymoon or simply have the vacation of a lifetime. Dinner is served nightly in the castle and the menu varies daily based on what is available in the local markets.

Where to Eat

7. LA TAVERNA, *Via delle Streghe 8. Tel. 075/572-4128. Closed Mondays, January 7-21 and all of July. All credit cards accepted. Dinner for two E60.*

Not to be missed. Excellent atmosphere (just getting here is like a walk back in time, located just off of the Corso Vanucci) with its vaulted ceilings and arched doorways, simply superb food, and the most attentive service. Come prepared to have a great meal in authentically medieval surroundings. Everything here is excellent and the waiter will be more than willing to help translate if need be. They make a tasty *tagliatelle al ragu di anatra* (pasta with duck sauce), *linguini con pecorino e olio* (pasta with pecorino cheese and oil), and *crostini al tartufo nero* (baked dough with black truffles). In fact if you come here in truffle season sample anything they make with them. Granted, most any dish with truffles will be the most expensive dish on the menu – as well as the most mouth-wateringly delicious – so be prepared for that.

This is an upper echelon restaurant – make sure you dress for the occasion – and most cognoscenti believe it the best in town. I concur.

8. IL FALCHETTO, *Via Bartolo 20, Tel 075/573-1775. Closed Mondays. Open 12:30-2:30pm and 7:30 - 10:00pm. All credit cards accepted. Dinner for two E40.*

Pink tablecloths, vaulted brick ceilings, soothing music, oil lamps on every table, and attentive service all set the scene for a serene meal. In back is where the locals congregate and is a little more boisterous, but both front and rear receive tasty local recipes made with exquisite care and presented with a slight flair. The grilled vegetable antipasto is perfect to start with and the *tagliatelle ai porcini* (with mushrooms) or *al tartufo nero* (with black truffles) are both tasty pasta dishes. For seconds they have a number of tasty grilled and oven baked meats and fish.

9. OSTERIA DEL BARTOLO, *Via Bartolo 30. Tel. 075/573-1561. Closed Sundays and January 7-25. All credit cards accepted. Dinner for two E75.*

An elegant but small place run by the effervescent and attentive Walter Passeri. They bake their bread in-house which makes it a wonderful complement to the meal. The pastas and desserts are also all made in-house. And as befits a restaurant in Perugia they too create quality truffle dishes. The menu here changes constantly, but be assured you will receive a superb gastronomical extravaganza. You need to make reservations and you must dress well. This is a very nice place, and if you are into that type of ambiance, as well as creatively prepared food at upscale prices, this is the place for you.

10. LA BOTTE, *Via Volte Della Pace 33. Tel. 075/572-2679. Open 12:30-2:30pm and 7:30-10:00pm. Credit cards accepted. Dinner for two E25.*

This is a small, simple, down-to-earth trattoria, off the beaten path, down in the basement of a medieval building down a small side street, that serves a vast array and tasty pasta and meat dishes at incredibly good prices. Locals and travelers alike flock to this little hole in the wall because of the tasty food and accommodating, relaxing family atmosphere. The entryway looks like a bar or café, but in the back under the while walls and vaulted brick ceilings you'll get some wonderful food, including *penne alla vodka* (with tomatoes, cream, meat and a touch of vodka), *spaghetti alla carbonara* (egg, cheese, bacon and peas), or my favorite, *penne al panna e funghi* (with a creamy mushroom sauce).

11. PIZZERIA LO SCALINO, *Via S. Ercolano 8. Tel. 075/5722-5372. Open 12:00-3:00pm and 7:00-10:00pm. Closed Friday afternoons. Dinner for two E20.*

A tiny local place whose entrance is located on the steps to the church of San Ercolano. A little cramped but comfortable, and frequented by the locals not only for the great pizza, but the warm and accommodating atmosphere. The pizza chefs prepare your pies in a small space in the dining area. Only a few varieties of pizza are available, a few salads, a couple of meat dishes, an excellent bruschetta for appetizer, but what the menu lacks in quantity, the food and local atmosphere makes up for in quality.

12. HOGANS BAR & GRILL, *Piazza Matteoti 20. Tel. 075/572-7647. Open 12:00-3:30pm and 7:00pm-2:30am every day. Dinner for two E20.*

This is a hopping place, packed every night, that serves American and Southwest style food such as burgers, steaks, burritos, sandwiches, baked potatoes, salads and appetizers of all kinds, as well as real American-style desserts like cheesecake and chocolate brownies. Inside you will find bits and pieces of Americana covering the walls such as license plates, photos of Michael Jordan, gas station signs and the like. For a fun time and taste of home, away from home, come here.

13. PIZZERIA MEDITERANNEA, *Piazza Piccinino 11/12, Tel 075/572-1322. Closed Tuesdays. Open 12:30-2:30pm and 7:30pm - midnight. Dinner for two E25.*

All they serve is pizza and it is so good and the atmosphere so electric that people line up to get it. Opening onto a small piazza just past the Duomo sits this festive little pizzeria. A small place with only two rooms, one of which has the pizza oven, this is the favorite hangout for the younger set at night. They only serve pizza, so if you are in the mood for it, give this place a try. If you do not show up early you will definitely have to wait. To get on the list of diners, flag down a waitress and she will give you a number. If you do not want to wait, La Botte is just around the corner.

Seeing The Sights

A. ROCCA PAOLINA
Piazza Italia.

A fortress built by Sangallo the Younger by the order of Pius III as the Papal States emphatic display of dominance over the city of Perugia. An entire medieval neighborhood, as well as the Baglioni Palazzi were covered over to create this ostentatious display of papal authority which even today makes Perugini leery of the influence of the Pope. In 1860 the fortress was destroyed and what remains underground is now used as a totally unique exhibition space, and a conduit for the escalators from Piazza Partigiani.

B. PRIOR'S PALACE,
Corso Vannucci. Tel. 075/574-1247. Closed the first Monday of the month. Open 9-7, holidays 9-1.

Home to the **National Gallery of Umbria** on the third floor, the Prior's Palace is also known as the Town Hall and is an outstanding example of medieval architecture. As such is considered one of the most elegant and famous in all of Italy. Begun in 1293, it was completed in 1443 after the building was consolidated with other homes and pre-existing towers all under one huge roof.

The entrance on Corso Vannucci is through a round portal, almost underneath an imposing tower and guarded by two Griffins – the symbols of the city – sinking their claws into two calves. The entire facade on the Corso is quite imposing and rather fortress-like. Before entering, take some time to check out the ornamental entrance with its friezes, twisted columns, sculptures and ornamental foliage. The Atrium is inside the entrance off of Corso Vanucci and is a covered courtyard with pillars and vaults.

The entrance on the Piazza IV Novembre is just to the left of the tourist information office up a flight of stairs and through a pointed portal. Above the portal are bronze statues of a Griffin and a Lion – the symbol of an old ruling family, the Guelphs. Through the portal is the Sala dei Notari (Lawyer's Room), an impressive hall that has some exquisite frescoes and grandiose arches. The frescoes are some scenes from the Bible and Aesop's fables. Other rooms in the building include the Sala del Consignio Comunale (City Council Hall), which contains a fresco by Pinturicchio, and the Sala Rossa (Red Hall) containing a mural by Dono Doni.

The National Gallery is the third floor and is a must-see in Perugia. It contains masterly examples of the paintings from the Umbrian school, which date from the 13 century CE to the 19th. Perugia's most famous artist, Perugino, is featured in rooms 12-14 with his *Adoration of the Magi* (room 12),

Miracles of San Bernardino (room 13) and *The Dead Christ* (room 14). Also accessible off of the Corso Vanucci is the **Collegio del Cambio**. To the left of the facade of the Palazzo dei Priori, beyond the archway to the Via dei Priori are three portals, through which you can enter the fresco-laden room containing major works by the cities most famous artist, Perugino.

C. CATHEDRAL OF SAINT LAWRENCE
Piazza IV Novembre.
The steps on the left side of the building facing the Piazza IV Novembre is *the* place to hang out, whether it's sunny or not. You'll have to fight for space with the natives and locals alike, as well as some rather bold pigeons, but this is where you can sit and watch the life of Perugia pass by.

The building itself is an imposing Gothic church constructed between the 14th and 15th centuries CE. It still has an incomplete facade but nonetheless is beautiful. The main entrance is between Piazza Dante and Piazza IV Novembre and has a coarse stone facade with a massive Baroque portal and a large circular window above that. The left side of the building is decorated with ornamental masks by Scalza flanking the plain portal with its ancient wooden doors. Above the portal is the votive Crucifix placed here in 1539. To the right side of the portal is the 15th century pulpit of San Bernardino. To the left of the portal is the *Statue of Pope Julius III*, an intricate bronze by Danti from the 16th century.

The interior is divided by octagonal columns into one nave and two aisles. The Chapel of San Bernardino – to the right as you enter – which is enclosed by beautiful wrought iron railings, contains a stunning fresco by Federico Barocci. In the Chapel of the Holy Ring, enclosed by 15th century wrought iron railings – to the left as you enter – is a silver and gold plated copper tabernacle which contains the onyx wedding ring purported to have been worn by the Virgin Mary. Hmmm? A poor carpenter able to afford an expensive onyx ring? You be the judge of its authenticity.

Also please note the 16th century multi-colored stained glass windows by Arrigo Fiammingo and the 16th century carved choir seats. In the right transept are the tombs of Pope Martino IV, Pope Urbano IV and Pope Innocenzo III as well as the marble sculpture of Pope Leo XIII.

D. FONTANA MAGGIORE
Piazza IV Novembre.
The **Great Fountain** (*Fontana Maggiore*) is the monumental heart of medieval Perugia, built between 1275 and 1278 with the decorative sculptures created by Nicola and Giovanni Pisano. Topped by a bronze basin, the fountain has an upper stone basin held up by slender columns topped with a variety of capitals.

This basin consists of 24 red marble panels separating some of the Pisano brother's statues which depict scenes from the Bible, historical and mythological figures, and some saints. The lower basin has 50 panels on which are depicted the months of the year, the signs of the Zodiac, scenes from the Old Testament, the founding of Rome and Aesop's fables.

E. BASILICA OF SAINT DOMENICO,
Via Cavour. Open 7:00am-noon & 4:00-7:00pm.

An imposing Gothic church built in the 14th century then rebuilt in the 17th with a huge campanile (bell tower) and separate attached cloisters (not open to the public). On the bare facade is the elegant 16th century portal above a double flight of stairs. The interior is enormous and plain, a simplicity that gives it a peaceful and rather calming effect on the soul. Some elegant pieces include the 18th century organ and the splendid tomb of Pope Benedict XI. The apse is lit by a large, 23 meter high 15th century window. Most of the frescoes that adorn the walls have not survived the test of time. In every chapel there are exquisite paintings depicting a variety of religious themes, as well as a number of crypts containing personages of importance in Perugia.

F. MUSEO ARCHEOLOGICO NAZIONALE DELL'UMBRIA,
Via Cavour. Open 9:00am-5:00pm. Holidays 9:00am-1:00pm. E2.

To get to this museum go through the archway to the left of San Domenico, into the internal courtyard, go down the right portico to the entrance upstairs. The museum wraps around the 1st floor of the courtyard and contains many interesting archaeological relics culled from the many excavations in Umbria. You will find Etruscan, Roman and more recent artifacts. A simple, little museum that is worth a short visit.

G. BASILICA OF SAINT PETER
Borgo XX Giugno. Open 7:00am-noon & 4:00-7:00pm.

Located quite a ways from the centro storico through a rustic working class neighborhood, down the Corso Cavour past St. Domenico, through the Porta San Pietro and along the Borgo XX Giugno. The Basilica of San Pietro was built in the 10th century on the site of an even older cathedral. The church is dominated by a beautiful 15th century campanile. You enter the church through a rather run-down but at the same time elegant porticoed courtyard. Oddly enough there is a bar/café just off of the courtyard where you can grab a refreshment after your long walk over here.

The dark interior contains a single nave with two aisles divided by 18 Roman columns. This church, in contrast to San Domenico, is elaborate in its decoration — very much like San Ercolano — and has a wealth of art work, most of which is rather difficult to see without night vision glasses since the lighting is so poor even on the brightest day. Give your eyes time to adjust and take the time to view magnificent frescoes and paintings adorning virtually every inch of space on the walls. The sacristy contains some works by Caravaggio and Perugino, and the Chapel of the Sacrament has a *Pieta* by Perugino.

Behind the altar, through the intricately carved 17th century choir is a small terrace at the back of the church overlooking an incredibly panoramic view of the surrounding countryside. Take the time to get back here and admire the view, and savor the wood carved choir and doors that lead here.

H. ORATORY OF SAN BERNADINO
Piazza San Francesco. Open 7:00am-noon & 4:00-7:00pm.

The date this building was completed (1461) can be seen on the facade in roman numerals (MCCCCLXI). Masterly crafted by the Florentine Agostino di Antonio di Duccio, the facade is a wonderful series of sculptures of saints in the Perugia-Renaissance style. The 15th century Gothic interior contains the Tomb of Beato Egidio and an ancient 4th century CE Roman-era Christian sarcophagus. In an adjacent building entered through the annex of the Oratory of St. Andrew you get to the Baldeschi Chapel, which houses the Tomb of Bartolo da Sassoferrato, an important 14th century Perugian leader, teacher and lawyer.

I. CHURCH OF SAN ERCOLANO
Via Marzia. Open 7:00am-noon & 4:00-7:00pm.

Dedicated to the patron saint of Perugia, San Ercolano, this church stands on the exact spot where he was martyred when the Goths seized the city in 547 CE. This 13th and 14th century Gothic church is a small octagonal structure with large pointed arches going around it. The interior is accessed through a beautiful double staircase built in 1607. Though more intricate in detail than the original structure, the staircase is the first initiation into the exceptional beauty of this medieval church. At the high altar is a noteworthy Roman-era Christian sarcophagus that contain the remains of San Ercolano. Around the dome are some exquisite frescoes dating to the 16th century which depict a number of scenes from the Bible. Every inch of these walls are covered with frescoes and bas-relief work.

J. THE ETRUSCAN ARCH
Piazza Fortebraccio.

Also known as the **Arch of Augustus**, the original structure was built in the 3rd and 2nd century BCE. Later there were Roman-era additions as well as some during the 16th century. This huge and imposing structure is bordered by some of the old walls of Perugia, clearly indicating the lengths attackers would have to go through to sack the city. Comprised of two powerful Etruscan towers, the right one lowered by an invasion, while the one on the left has an enticing patio on the top and a Roman fountain on the bottom. Above the gate is a sentinel arch, so named because that is where the guards for the city would keep watch. It has since been walled up and now is part of the structure to the left.

K. ROMAN AQUEDUCT
Via di Aquedotto.
What used to be a functioning aqueduct is now a pedestrian street. This may be your only chance to walk along an ancient aqueduct, so take it while you have it. Lining the aqueduct are quaint little homes. Also from this height you get to look down onto other streets and passageways, offering an interesting perspective of this mountain city.

Nightlife & Entertainment
The nightlife and entertainment in Perugia mainly consists of congregating in and around the **Corso Vannucci**, going for a stroll, grabbing an ice cream cone — the preferred social lubricant in Perugia — and meeting with friends at one of the many cafés that line the Corso. This lasts from before dinner through the meal hour and well into the evening, and is especially crowded on Saturday nights when everybody and their grandmother is out for a walk. It is beautiful to see every slice of life coming together for an informal community gathering. You will find young and old, well-off and beggars, wild and conservative, families and singles, all connecting despite their differences. You don't see this too often anymore in the US.

There was a time when the Perugini allowed cars to drive on the Corso Vannucci; but back in the '70s, realizing the detrimental effect it was having on their community, they put a stop to that practice by closing the street to traffic. Italians have not become overdependent on the automobile or let it dominate their lives. In fact on September 22, 1999, every major city in Italy joined other European cities in closing off additional sections of their cities to automobile traffic to show people how less frenetic life can be without cars cluttering up our lives.

Because of this understanding and appreciation for community, places like the Corso Vannucci thrive all over Italy. Along this street there are plenty of restaurants, cafés, and pubs in which to stop if refreshment is needed. Two that we recommend are listed below.

14. SHAMROCK, *Piazza Danti 18. Tel. 075/573-6625. Open 7:00pm - 2:00am.*
Great Irish atmosphere. Medieval vaulted ceilings coupled with dark wood furnishings, brass accents, and authentic Irish knickknacks gives this place a true feel of the Blarney. Definitely the best pub atmosphere in Perugia. Located down a dark medieval alleyway in the basement of one of the oldest buildings in the city, just across from the main entrance to the Cathedral. They

serve a full complement of ales and have a good bar menu as well as snacks like chips, pretzels and peanuts – which you have to pay for. In the early evening, the music selection is contemporary but light. Later, the selection gets a little more techno and loud. They really don't open until around 7:00pm, so this would be a place to come before an 8:00pm dinner for a quick drink or afterward to see how the Italians like to celebrate life.

15. CAFFÉ SANDRI, *Corso Vannucci 32. Tel. 075/61012. Open 7:00am - 11:00pm daily.*

The perfect place to grab a cappuccino or a bite to eat on the Corso Vannucci. You may miss the place even though their window displays are tantalizingly spectacular with fruit tarts, cheeses and other delicacies enticing you inside. Sandri is Perugia's landmark café and, judging from the crowd, it is a local favorite.

The frescoed ceilings remain intact and the proprietors come from the same Swiss family, the Schucan's, who founded the café over 130 years ago, making it feel as if you've stepped back into a 19th century café. When in Perugia, you have to at least stop in for a look. And if this café doesn't appeal to you, fear not, there are plenty of others nearby.

Shopping

The main pedestrian street **Corso Vannucci** is also the best shopping street in Perugia. Along its route and around its periphery — mainly the parallel streets of **Via Baglioni** and **Via G. Oberdan** — you will find traditional little shops offering a wide variety native arts and crafts as well as local and international fashions.

16. I LEGNI DI GIUSEPPE BACIOCCHI, *Via Maeste delle Volte 8. Tel. 075/57-26-080.*

This artists' shop is located to the left of the Cathedral (as you face it from the Piazza IV Novembre) down the little passageway Via Maeste delle Volte, in the basement of a medieval building. Carved wooden figures are his stock in trade and they are simply wonderful. A perfect place to pick up some small gifts for friends, or buy one of his larger magnificent carvings.

Virtually right next to this store is **Talmone**, an excellent candy shop where you can get great gifts to bring home, or something to snack on later in the room. Inside this store are Etruscan walls dating to the 3rd century BCE, and the ruins of a Roman street from the 1st century BCE. Feel free to stop in and sight see or shop for candy.

17. COVERED MARKET, *Open 7:00am-1pm Monday-Saturday.*

Located off of the Piazza Matteoti and through the Palazzo Capitano del Popolo is the covered market of Perugia, which offers dry goods of leather and other crafts in the upstairs section, and fruits, vegetables and other foods on the downstairs.

18. IL TELAIO, *Via Bruschi 2B. Tel. 075/572-6603. Closed Monday mornings. Open 9:30am-1:00pm and 4:00-8:00pm. All credit cards accepted.*

This is a quaint little shop, off the beaten path, which sells local hand-crafted linens, pillow cases, sheets, tablecloths and everything associated with fabrics and textiles. Located past the Hotel Eden, and next to the church of San Angelo di Porta Eburnea, this is a wonderful shop to find unique products from Umbria.

19. L'ARTE DEI VASAI, *Via Baglioni 32. Tel. 075/572-3108. Open 9:30am-1:00pm and 3:45-8:00pm. Closed Sundays. All credit cards accepted.*

If you don't want to venture all the way to Deruta to find ceramics, this store has by far the best selection available in Perugia. The perfect place to find hand-crafted, distinctively hand-painted ceramics, bowls, mugs, cups, plates and more.

20. MAGAZZINI DI EGIDIO RASTELLI, *Via Baglioni 17-29. Tel. 075/57-29-050. Open 9:00am-1:00pm and 4:00-7:50pm. Closed Mondays.*

Large cartoleria with all sorts of distinctly unique Italian notebooks, pens, calendars, day planners, sketch pads, and everything else for office, home or school. Italian stationery is world-renowned for its creative individuality and this store has everything you could want.

21. CASA DEL PARMIGIANO REGGIANO, *Via San Ercolano 36. Tel. 075/573-1233. All credit cards accepted. Open 7:30am-1:30pm & 4:30-8:00pm.*

This is the best place in Perugia to find those exquisitely tasty, pungently aromatic, uniquely Umbrian culinary delight, *tartufi*, not only because of their excellent price but also because they vacuum seal *(sotto vuoto)* them for you so that they stays fresh, if you ask, at no extra charge. You can also get all types of salamis and meats for sandwiches as the product that they are known for, *Parmigiano Reggiano*. You can get this hard cheese used for grating over pasta in the States, but what you probably did not know is that what we receive over there is not the top quality. The Italians keep the best for themselves, and the only way to get some is to buy it here and bring it back with you.

Books in English

22. LIBRERIA C BETTI, *Via del Sette 1. Open 10:00am-1:00pm and 4:00pm-8:00pm.*

This tiny bookstore is located just off of the Piazza della Repubblica. It carries a small selection of English language books to the right just as you enter. Guidebooks are near the back, not that you will need another since you have this one.

Excursions & Day Trips

In actuality, the other towns listed in this chapter (Orvieto, Todi, Gubbio, Assisi and Spoleto) can all be considered day trips from Perugia, but at the same time, each of these places could be destinations in and of themselves. But Deruta is such a small location, and is so much closer to Perugia, that it is the only true day trip.

DERUTA

Located 15 kilometers outside of Perugia, **Deruta** is the generally considered the ceramics capital of Italy — something nearby Cortona over the border in Tuscany would dispute heartily. Let's just say that they're both good. Deruta is a quaint old town situated on a hill overlooking the valley of the Tiber. Unfortunately the new part of the town — which is parallel to and along the Via Tiberina — is a slip-shod, unplanned eye sore. But above from that is a beautiful little hill town filled with the largest selection of **fine ceramic pottery** anywhere.

The prices for the pottery created here is no less expensive than for pieces made here but sold in Florence or Rome, so don't come expecting any bargains. All you will get here is a large selection, not great prices. But what a selection it is. If you want to return home with some fine ceramic pottery, the best in Italy, and dare I say it — the world — come to the source, come to Deruta.

Not really a place to spend much time, except for pottery shopping. The best way to visit is to come and explore the little hill town first, see all the small family-run pottery businesses nestled in the winding cobblestone streets, maybe visit the small **ceramic museum**, buy your pottery, then head back to Perugia.

Getting There: By bus is the only way, other than by car, to get to Deruta. Pick up the bus schedule at the information office in Perugia. Buses are infrequent and as a result you need to plan to ensure that you can get there, have time to look around, then be able to catch a bus back.

Practical Information for Perugia

Festivals
- **Good Friday procession** – La Desolata
- **Mid–July Rock Music festival** – Rockin' Umbria
- **First two weeks of September** – Sagra Musicale Umbria (musical recitals in Perugia's churches)
- **End of October/Beginning November** – Jewel And Antique show
- **2–5 November** – All Souls Fair

Laundry

Le Bolle, *Corso G. Garibaldi 43. Open every day 8:00am-10:00pm. Attendant on duty from 2:00-4:00pm & 7:00-10:00pm.*
Self-service laundromat that is computerized and fully automated. Wash cost: E3 for 8kg (15lbs), E5 for 16kg. Wash takes 25 minutes. Drying cost: E3 for 8kg and E5 for 10kg. Free detergent. If the attendant is not present, call *075/41644* and she will pop down and give you some.

Onda Blu, *Via Pinturicchio 102. Open 8:00am-10:00pm every day.*
Self-service laundromat located near Porta Pesa that is fully automated. Wash cost: E3 for 6.5 kg. Takes 30 minutes. Drying cost: E3 and takes 20 minutes. Detergent costs E3.

Money & Banking

There is only one money exchange shop in Perugia and it is in the Piazza IV Novembre but holds very erratic hours. The best bet to change money is at banks but they are only open 9:00am-3:00pm Monday through Friday. If you need to change money, but not travelers checks, on a Saturday go to the main post office, *Via Mazzini 24, from 9:00am-5:30pm.*

Tourist Information

The **tourist information office** is located in the Piazza IV Novembre next to the stairs leading up to the Prior's Palace. *Open from 9:00am to 1:00pm and 3:00pm to 6:00pm, Tel. 075/573-6458 or 572/-3327.* They have useful maps, and all the information you need for buses, trains, walking tours, etc.

Spoleto

Spoleto is by far the most stunning destination I have ever been to on this planet, and I have visited every continent except for Australia and Antarctica. What makes Spoleto so unique is a combination of different attributes, most of which would entice travelers by themselves, except that Spoleto has them all in one place: medievel charm, natural setting, excellent restaurants, cosmopolitan shops and art galleries, few tourists, and incredibly friendly and accomodating locals.

The ancient medieval town itself, with its winding streets, old buildings is like something out of a fairy tale. But even though this is one of the better preserved medieval towns in all of Italy, Spoleto is still only lightly touristed. During the world-famous **Spoleto Festival** held in June every year, tens of thousands of tourists descend here to savor a two week extravaganza of performing arts. When that is over, it seems that tourists leave the city alone, until the next festival. Spoleto has some of the best restaurants in all of Italy, quaint little artisans' shops selling exquisitely created local crafts, and little galleries and studios filled with locally produced painting and sculpture that is of top quality. But that's not all. Besides the fact that Spoleto is a serene medieval town filled with cosmopolitan distractions, the main distinguishing feature about Spoleto is that it offers instant access to inspiring natural settings.

Just across the **Ponte delle Torre**, an old medieval aqueduct turned walkway, from the centro storico and you are in untouched, pristine nature, laced with hiking trails that snake around the surrounding mountains, and through small local hill towns. Nowhere else in the world can you go from a quaint medieval town, filled with cosmopolitan amenities, to untouched natural settings after a five minute walk. Surrounded by lush, verdant hills, and dominated by the **Rocca fortress**, Spoleto also boasts a prolific artistic and cultural presence.

Situated on green hillside near the lower border of the Umbra Valley, Spoleto was founded by the original Umbrian people, Later it came under Etruscan influence and eventually was absorbed into the Roman Empire around the 3rd century BCE. Its claim to fame during that period came during the second Punic War, where it played a major role in repelling Hannibal's attacks. After the fall of the Roman Empire, Spoleto was a flourishing Lombard capital, then fell under papal influence and became one of the Pope's summer residences. During the rise of Perugia's power it came under that city's jurisdiction; and with Perugia and Todi in the 14th century it rose up against the excessive and abusive powers of the popes. During Napoleon's sojourn in Italy, Spoleto became one of his local capitals and eventually was absorbed into the newly formed state of Italy on September 17, 1860.

Arrivals & Departures

Spoleto has retained its wonderful medieval charm and preserved its raw natural beauty because it is not easily accessible from Florence or Rome, which means that the hordes of tourists that would come from those locations usually do not make their way here. From Perugia the train leaves every hour and takes an hour to get here. From Rome, the schedule is more erratic and the trip takes a little over an hour and a half. Check with your local information office for specific schedules.

Orientation

Spoleto is spread up a hillside with the defining structures being the spire of the **cathedral** and the imposing **Rocca** behind it. To the east up the hill is the **Duomo** whose **piazza** is a central focus of the town. The town's tiny roads twist and turn around the undulation of the hillside, so it's best to use a map or have a compass available to keep yourself on the right track.

Getting Around Town

Spoleto is made for walking, with twisting and turning cobblestone streets and winding staircases leading through quaint medieval passageways. Be prepared to hike up and down hills, but the effort will be worth it since the surroundings will instantly transport you back to a simpler place and time.

Where to Stay

1. CHARLESTON, *Piazza Collicola 10. Tel. 0743/223-235, Fax 0743/222-010. Web: www.spoletohotels.com/charleston.htm. 18 rooms. Single E50; Double E65. All credit cards accepted. Breakfast E6.* ***

In the centro storico of Spoleto, this 17th century palazzo represents a classic blending of the old and new. The common areas are very large and simply furnished and the rooms are comfortably sized with modern 'antique' furnishings. You will also have all three star amenities including TV, VCR, air-conditioning, heat, radio, phone and mini-bar. The bathrooms are small but come with hairdryer and complimentary toiletry kit. Buffet breakfast is served in two small rooms and consists of croissant, yogurt, juice and coffee or tea. In the summer this classical continental fare is served on a small terrace area.

Apart from the private garage, guests also have at their disposal a sauna, two bars, and a reading room. The hotel also offers hiking and biking excursions for those that request it at an extra charge. A great place to stay in Spoleto. And if you are wondering about the name of the hotel, Charleston SC hosts a Spoleto festival every year. The hotel's name comes from that connection.

2. CLITUNNO, *Piazza Sordini. Tel. 0743/223-340. Fax 0743/222-663. Web: www.spoletohotels.com/clitunno.htm. 38 rooms all with bath. Single E50; Double E75. All credit cards accepted. Breakfast included.* ***

Located near the Teatro Romano and recently renovated (1994), the Clitunno offers a pleasant mix of the old and new. The best rooms are furnished with the 'faux' antiques with tiled floors and oriental rugs covering them. These rooms make for quite an ambient stay. The others are accommodatingly comfortable with more modern furnishings. The bathrooms are small but well appointed with all manner of amenities, including a phone. A good hotel in a good location.

3. AURORA, *Via Appolinare 3. Tel 0743/220-315, Fax 0743/221-885. Email - hotelaurora@virgilio.it. Web: www.umbria.org/hotel/aurora/ita/default.html. 40 rooms all with bath. Single E40-50; Double E50-75.* **

A great two star right next to the Teatro Romana and just down from the Piazza del Mercato, the heart of the centro storico. This hotel is very obviously bucking for three star status and as such they are a superb two star, with clean and comfortable rooms and excellent service in an ideal location. The bathrooms are a little small and will need to be upgraded if they want to achieve that extra star, but in terms of price/quality this is a great find.

4. GATTAPONE, *Via del Ponte 6, 06049 Spoleto. Tel. 0743/223-447, Fax 0743/223-448. E-mail: gattapone@mail.caribusiness.it. Web: www.caribusiness.it/gattapone. 14 rooms all with bath. Standard Single E85-95; Superior Single E112-125; Standard Double E95-135; Superior Double E155-180. Breakfast E12. *****

This hotel is set in a magical location overlooking the green valley and the medieval aqueduct that traverses it. All the bedrooms overlook this picturesque scene and is the reason to stay here. The standard rooms are a little on

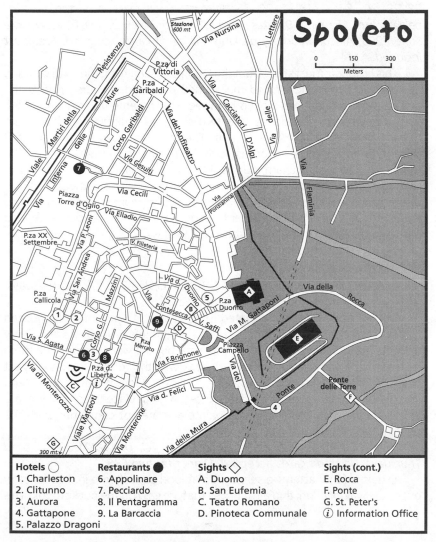

Hotels ○	Restaurants ●	Sights ◇	Sights (cont.)
1. Charleston	6. Appolinare	A. Duomo	E. Rocca
2. Clitunno	7. Pecciardo	B. San Eufemia	F. Ponte
3. Aurora	8. Il Pentagramma	C. Teatro Romano	G. St. Peter's
4. Gattapone	9. La Barcaccia	D. Pinoteca Communale	ⓘ Information Office
5. Palazzo Dragoni			

the small side, but are comfortable and come with baths and showers so you can luxuriate in the tub after a long day of hiking through the mountains. I would suggest springing for the Superior rooms, which are located in the modern extension and offer more space. There are two comfortable bar areas (for guests and anyone who shows up and wants a drink while savoring the view — which is lit up at night), as well as two terraces below where sheep sometimes wander. A quaint rustic touch. This hotel, in its pristine natural setting, is only a short walk to the centro storico. If you are inspired and have the means, without a question, this is *the* place to stay in Spoleto.

5. PALAZZO DRAGONI, *Via del Duomo, 13, 06049 Spoleto. Tel. 0743/ 22 22 20, Fax 0743/22 22 25. Web: www.initaly.com/hisres/palazzo/ palazzo.htm. 15 rooms, 9 suites. Double E125; Superior Double E150; Double Suite E265. Air-conditioning, parking. All credit cards accepted. Breakfast included.* ****

This historic inn just steps from the Duomo, dating from the 14th century, has been lovingly restored and maintained through the years. In fact, the original stone foundations that you can see in the basement date from before 1000 CE, when the residence was two separate structures, with a street running between them! Ask to see it. The common room features vaulted ceilings, as do a number of rooms, with lovely rugs and a medieval feel. The rooms are spacious and charming, and the view from most rooms is incredible, looking out over the rooftops of historic Spoleto. You can see the spire of the Duomo and the walls of the Rocca from the lovely breakfast room on the top floor. Service is friendly and efficient. If you want to feel like you've stepped back into medieval times, this is the place to stay.

Where to Eat

6. APOLLINARE, *Via S. Agata 14. Tel. 0743/223-256. Closed Tuesdays. All credit cards accepted. Dinner for two E60.*

In the heart of Spoleto situated in what was at one time a Franciscan convent, in a short period of time this place has garnered a measure of culinary respect. The ingredients they use are all local but the way they prepare them is in the *cucina nuova* style. They get creative with their dishes so don't expect anything simple and traditional here. Do expect great atmosphere and imaginative food, though at elevated prices. A great place to come if you are into exploring the pleasures of the palate and are not concerned with the effect it has on your wallet.

7. PECCIARDA, *Vicolo San Giovanni 1. Tel. 0743/221-009. Closed Thursdays. No credit cards accepted. Dinner for two E35.*

Exquisite food, attentive service, great local atmosphere in a completely out of the way location, and all at prices that are easy on the pocketbook. This place is fantastic. A real slice of Spoleto. You have to come here if you are in town. Some of the simple but tasty dishes they serve include *gnocchi ripiena* (ricotta cheese dumplings), *stragozzi ai funghi* (local home made pasta with a spicy mushroom sauce) *pollo "alla Pecciarda"* (chicken stuffed with succulent herbs and spices), or a superb *arrosto misto* (mixed grilled meats). You'll come for the food and stay for the out of the way, off the beaten path, local atmosphere.

8. IL PENTAGRAMMA, *Via T. Martani 4/6/8. Tel. 0743/223-141. Closed Mondays and January 15-31. All credit cards accepted except American Express. Dinner for two E40.*

With a new owner and a new cook this place is going through a rebirth, not that it was bad to begin with. It's just that now it's fantastic. Located near the Teatro Romano this place has great local food and a serene musical atmosphere, at good prices. Try some of their *frascarelli con pomodoro e basilica* (pasta with tomatoes and basil) or *tagliatelle ai funghi porcini* (pasta with porcini mushrooms). For seconds the *petto di tacchino e purea di fave* (turkey breast with pureed fava beans) is rather tasty. They also make some great lamb dishes. To try a little of everything they have an abundant sampler menu for E25 per person, which gives you antipasto, pasta, main course and dessert. This is one of Spoleto's best restaurants.

9. LA BARCACCIA, *Piazza F.lli Bardier 3. Tel. 0743/221-171. Website: www.caribusiness.barcaccia. Closed Tuesdays. Credit cards accepted. Dinner for two E35.*

Located just off of the Piazza del Mercato, the heart of the centro storico, in an isolated piazza of its own, this restaurant offers typical local dishes at good prices. They specialize in cooking with truffles and grilling a wide variety of meats, especially veal. Everything they serve is stupendous and the ambiance is rustic and charming. For primo, try the *tortellini al tartufo* (meat filled pasta with truffle sauce), the *tortellini panna e funghi* (meat filled pasta with cream and mushrooms) or the *spaghetti alla carbonara* (with bacon egg, parmesan and pecorino). A great place to eat while in Spoleto.

Seeing the Sights

A. DUOMO

Rising up from the picturesque main square, the spire on the bell tower next to the Duomo acts as a beacon. The bell tower was constructed in the 12th century, with stone material removed from ancient Roman ruins. The Romanesque Duomo, built at the same time, has an imposing facade that is preceded by a portico built at the turn of the 16th century. The facade has five Rosetta windows and a mosaic created by Solsterno from 1207 above which are three more Rosetta windows.

The interior *(open November-February 8:00am-1:00pm & 3:00-5:30pm; March-October 8:00am-1:00pm & 3:00-6:30pm)* is simple with a nave and two aisles. You will find a variety of religious art including some magnificent works by Pinturicchio in the Chapel of Bishop Eroli.

B. SAN EUFEMIA

Located near the Duomo, this is one of the finest examples of simple Umbrian-Romanesque architecture. Constructed in the first half of the 12th century, the facade is basic but inspiring, with a portal window and a sweep of arches on the crown. The interior is white, austere and stark and is divided into three parts – one of which being the women's section above the main floor where women had to sit so as not to distract the men during services. Devoid of much finery, this church is a wonderful example of the piety and beauty of simplicity.

C. TEATRO ROMANO

A well preserved first century CE construction, located just off of the Piazza della Liberta and surrounded on one side by the stables of the 17th century Palazzo Ancaiani. The **church of Santa Agata** occupies what once was the stage area. Also included with the price of entry (E2) is access to the **Museo Archeologico Nazionale** *(Via S. Agata, 9:00am-7:00pm; holidays 9:00am-1:00pm)* which has a few interesting pieces, including artifacts from a warrior's tomb, jewelry, pottery and other material from the Bronze Age through the Middle Ages.

Outside, the Teatro Romano is a wonderful example of how architecture from different eras has been intertwined into the pastiche of daily life in Spoleto. Another example of that is the **Arco di Druso Minore** and **Arco Romano** nearby. These are two Roman-era arches have been completely incorporated into the surrounding buildings.

D. PINOTECA COMMUNALE

Up the Via del Municipio from the Piazza del Mercato – which used to be a Roman Forum – is the Palazzo Communale with its tall tower, small piazza and large flag out front. Begun in the 13th century and renovated in the 18th, this palazzo is now home to the Pinoteca Communale *(admission E2.5, open 10:00am-1:00pm & 3:00-6:00pm, closed Tuesdays)* which contains a small but captivating local museum. My favorite part is the display of old mint pieces that were used to make coins. As you enter, prior to going up to the museum, take a little time to admire the frescoes in the entrance way. Across from the palazzo are some delightful medieval houses set among winding little streets, which should be wandered if you are here.

Included in the price of entry is also access to the remains of an old Roman House, which I found infinitely more interesting than the little museum upstairs. Located to the left of the building, on the Via Visiale, is an excavated Roman home purported to be the home of the mother of Emperor Vespasian.

Also included in the price of admission is access to the **Galleria Communale d'Arte Moderna** *(Piazza Sordini 5, 10:00am-1:00pm & 4:00-7:00pm, closed Mondays)* with a limited but interesting display of local modern art pieces.

E. ROCCA

This fortress stronghold dominates the view over Spoleto. Finished in the second half of the 14th century, from here you can get wonderful panoramic photos of the town and valley. Once a residence of the popes and other aristocracy, it has since been used as an army base and was a prison until 1982. In 1983 the process of restoring back to its former splendor began. Today you can go on brief guided tours *(admission E5, open 3:00-6:00pm Monday-Friday, 10:00am-noon & 3:00-6:00pm Saturday and Sunday)*. The Rocca is being prepared to house a museum relating to the medieval duchy of Spoleto. The guided tour is well worth the price despite the limited material available.

F. PONTE DELLE TORRE

Past the Rocca is one of the most incredible sights I have ever seen in Italy, a medieval aqueduct spanning a gorge and leading to a pristine, verdant hill covered with hiking trails. This 13th century span connects two hillsides and is 230 meters long and 76 meters high and has towering piers and narrow arcades, which cast incredible shadows over the valley in the late afternoon light. It no longer carries water but serves as a foot bridge over the valley. Because of this sight and where it leads, it makes Spoleto a must-see destination when in Italy.

On the Via della Ponte on the way to the aqueduct, is a little bar, **La Portella**, that has tables set out on an overlooking with views of St Peter's. This is a good spot at which to relax anytime day or night.

G. ST. PETER'S

Located just outside of the old walled city, and visible from the Ponte delle Terme, is this fine church built between the 12th and 13th centuries. The beautiful but simple facade is embellished with numerous ornamental bas-relief decorations. There are three portals in the lower level, the center one surrounded by most of the ornamentation. The interior of the church is divided into three parts and was renovated and updated in 1669. This church, though plain, is one of the most important monuments in the region.

Other churches of interest inside the city walls are San Nicolo, San Filippo, and San Domenico.

Shopping

Spoleto does not have many international boutiques – yet – but what they do have are wonderful little shops selling typical works by local artisans. There are unique stores selling ceramics, fabrics, antiques, handmade notebooks as well as shops catering to the needs of the locals like alimentari, salumerie and more. There are also numerous galleries and artists' studios filled with a diverse array of paintings and sculptures. The best shopping is along the **Corso G. Garibaldi**, up the **Via Salaria Vecchia**, and all around the **Piazza del Mercato**.

Practical Information

Festivals
Spoleto Festival, *Mid-June to mid-July. Website: www.spoletofestival.net. Email: tickets@spoletofestival.net.*

A world-renowned festival filled with music, dance, cinematography, theater, art exhibits and more, that goes on every day for a month. An arts extravaganza that has no equal.

Other festivals include:
• **February and March** – Carnival of Spoleto
• **Week After Easter** – Week of the High Middle Ages
• **September** – Experimental Season of Lyrical Opera
• **December 14, 15, 16 and January 1** – Nativity and the Living Crib

Tourist Information
To arrange day trips, find out about bus tours, find train or bus information, get maps, or detailed walking tour information, book a hotel or simply get general information about Spoleto, the **tourist office**, *Piazza della Liberta 7, Tel. 0743/49890, Fax 0743/46241*, is the place to visit.

Gubbio

Gubbio is an ancient medieval town that majestically spreads out along the wind-swept ridges of **Mount Ingino**, with the **Torrente Camignano** river flowing through the town. This incredibly beautiful little town was founded by the ancient Umbrian people and eventually taken over by the Etruscans, as chronicled to in the **Eugubine Tablets** – the Rosetta Stone for ancient central Italian languages, culture and history – which are located here in Gubbio.

These seven bronze tablets give illuminating insight into how the city was run between the 3rd century and 1st century BCE, and are partially written in the Umbrian language – which is a derivation of Etruscan – and simultaneously in a rudimentary form of Latin.

In 295 BCE, Roman rule began and the town remained safe and secure until the end of the empire, like many of the towns in the region. Then it was destroyed during the Gothic wars of the 5th century CE and eventually came under Lombard control in the 8th century CE. By the 11th century the town was a free, independent commune and as such began to grow in power and importance. This situation instantly led to conflicts with Perugia, another strong city-state in the region, which conquered Gubbio handily in the 12th century. Then the city fell under papal control, which was not as benevolent as one might imagine – it was actually quite despotic. The Dukes of Urbino grabbed control for two centuries, then the Papal States reaffirmed their dominance in 1624 until the city was annexed into the new Italian state in the 1860s.

The layout of the town is very Roman with its structured grid pattern and is quite medieval with its ancient buildings, old city walls, and winding streets and steps flowing up and down the mountain. Also added onto this atmosphere are plenty of more 'modern' Renaissance towers and palazzi mingling with Gothic churches, making Gubbio a stunningly beautiful, 'can't miss' town if you are in Umbria.

The main handicrafts in Gubbio are ceramics as well as wrought iron work, carpentry, and copperware. The main flourish in the cuisine comes from the pungently aromatic white truffle that graces the local dishes mainly in autumn and winter. Gubbio loves a party and has a number of fun medieval festivals to enjoy, especially the **Corsa dei Ceri-Candle Tower Race** held on May 15th, replete with costumes and contests. This festival is on par with the best festivals in Italy. In this reenactment of an ancient tradition, separate sections of the city carry enormous wooden towers topped with wax statues of saints (Ubaldo, George, Anthony and Abbot) on their shoulders through the town, then up to the Basilica of San Ubaldo on Mount Ingino. Despite the Christian trappings, the festival is rooted in pagan rituals celebrating the coming of spring and each saint represents ancient pagan gods of fertility.

Another festival of note, this one on the last Sunday in May, is the **Palio della Balestra** – a crossbow competition. In this festival, archers dressed in period garb vie for an accuracy title. Complete with exciting pageantry, this is a fun festival to witness. Also, from July to mid-August, classical plays are performed in the Roman Theater outside of the main city walls.

Arrivals & Departures

Gubbio can only be reached by car or bus. There is no train service. The bus schedule from Perugia is not only infrequent, but erratic. Despite that, Gubbio is a great destination in and of itself, and can also be a quick day trip from Perugia. Listed below is the bus schedule from and to Perugia:

Perugia to:	Gubbio	Gubbio to:	Perugia
7:50	9:00	6:40	7:50
11:05	12:15	7:00	8:10
13:05	14:15	8:00	9:15
13:45	14:55	12:45	13:55
14:10	15:20	13:40	14:50
16:05	17:15	16:00	17:10
17:50 (Sunday)	19:00	18:15	19:25
18:40	19:50	19:15	20:25
19:40	20:50		

Orientation

Gubbio is 40 kilometers north-northwest of Perugia. It is separated into two different sections, upper and lower. In the lower section life revolves around the circular **Piazza Quaranta Martiri**. The upper town is centered on the **Piazza Grande**. Surrounding this piazza are most of the main sights of the city.

Getting Around Town

The best way to get around Gubbio, like most Umbrian towns, is by walking. Inside the old city walls the tiny medieval streets lend themselves to exploration by foot. But since it is nestled along a hillside, you should be prepared for some arduous climbs while you explore.

Where to Stay

1. GATTAPONE, *Via Ansidei 6. Tel. 075/927-2489, Fax 075/927-1269. Web: www.itwg.com/itw02045.asp. Closed January. 28 rooms, all with bath. Single E60-67; Double E80-90. All credit cards accepted. Breakfast E3.* ***

In an ancient building in the center of Gubbio, close to the Piazza Grande and the Palazzo dei Consoli, this old and respected hotel has recently been granted another star rating, and deservedly so. The general impression of the entire hotel is one of cleanliness, and every room is accommodatingly comfortable and come with air-conditioning, heat, mini-bars, telephones and TVs. Breakfast is either served in your room or at a nearby restaurant, Il Taverna del Lupo (see restaurant section below) that is owned by the same family, Mencarelli. The excellent hotel offers an additional asset for English- and French-speaking visitors, Beverly Goodwin. A transplant from the Caribbean island of Antigua, Beverly is helpful, knowledgeable and friendly. She can help you with all aspects of your travel plans in and around Gubbio, which can help make your stay that much more rewarding and memorable.

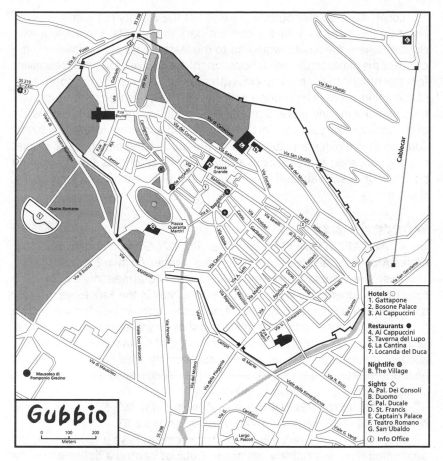

Gubbio

Hotels ○
1. Gattapone
2. Bosone Palace
3. Ai Cappuccini

Restaurants ●
4. Ai Cappuccini
5. Taverna del Lupo
6. La Cantina
7. Locanda del Duca

Nightlife ◉
8. The Village

Sights ◇
A. Pal. Dei Consoli
B. Duomo
C. Pal. Ducale
D. St. Francis
E. Captain's Palace
F. Teatro Romano
G. San Ubaldo
ⓘ Info Office

0   100   200
Meters

2. BOSONE PALACE, *Via XX Settembre 22. Tel. 075/922-0688, Fax 075/922-0552. 35 rooms all with bath. Single E70; Double E100. All credit cards accepted. Breakfast included.* ***

Located in a 16th century building, this hotel is also run by the Mencarelli family. Like the Gattapone above, this hotel maintains an old world charm and ambiance while offering all modern amenities. The entrance is elegant with the aristocratic red divans and a stairway leading up to the guest rooms. Spacious and comfortable, the rooms are decorated with antique furniture and parquet floors covered with oriental rugs. Though on the small side, the bathrooms all have showers and come with a complimentary toiletry kit and hair dryer. An elegant hotel right in the middle of the old city.

3. AI CAPPUCCINI, *Via Tifernate. Tel. 075/9234, Fax 075/661-109. Web: www.venere.com/umbria/gubbio/aicappuccini/. 100 rooms all with bath. Single E150; Double E185-240. All credit cards accepted. Breakfast included.* ****

Located a kilometer outside the walls of the old city but within walking distance, this hotel was once a convent back in the 1600's, complete with cloisters where the monks would go to meditate. While still maintaining the charm of the old structure, the renovations of 1990 have brought this excellent four star hotel into the modern era, with satellite TV (i.e. CNN and sports), air-conditioning, modern bathrooms with all amenities, updated telecommunications equipment, and more. Some of the rooms are the old cells the monks used, updated for your comfort of course, and some are located in a new addition to the older structure. Rooms are around the periphery of a quiet relaxing park area; all are spacious and perfect for relaxing, as is the swimming pool, sun deck and sauna. If you want to stay in the lap of luxury in Gubbio, stay here.

Where to Eat

4. AI CAPPUCCINI, *Via Tifernate. Tel. 075/9234, Fax 075/661-109. Closed Mondays. All credit cards accepted. Dinner for two E75.*

This is the restaurant of the excellent four star hotel mentioned above. The food here is superb so if you cannot afford to stay in the Park Hotel, at least come here for a meal. The cuisine is traditional Umbrian which means you'll find truffles, cheese and meats in most dishes. Try their *maniche ripiene di ricotta zucchine peperoni e pomodoro* (cylinders of pasta stuffed with cheese, zucchini, peppers and tomatoes). For seconds try their succulent *petto di anatra tartufato* (breast of duck with truffles). A charming atmosphere with seating inside and outside in the park terrace.

5. IL TAVERNA DEL LUPO, *Via G. Ansidei 6. Tel. 075/927-4368. Closed Mondays. All credit cards accepted. Dinner for two E70.*

Also run by the Mencarelli group that seems to have a firm grip on the accommodation and culinary options in Gubbio, beyond a doubt this is the best food and most welcoming atmosphere in Gubbio. I recommend trying the menu sampler at E35 per person since you'll get a full meal complete with antipasto, pasta, main course and dessert. The menu changes daily but each option is excellent. If you don't want the fixed menu you can also order a la carte and sample the staples of traditional Umbrian cuisine: pasta, truffles and meat. The ambiance is charming, romantic, and upscale. Come dressed appropriately and be prepared to pay for the privilege.

6. LA CANTINA, *Via Piccotti 3. Tel. 075/922-0583. Website: www.gubbio.com/lacantina. All credit cards accepted. Dinner for two E35.*

Great atmosphere and wonderful food. This place seems to be crowded all the time and for good reason – it is an excellent restaurant. There are some tiny tables set up just before the entrance in their own little cortile, but the place to be is inside in their expansive and rustic dining hall. Try some tasty *tagliatelle al funghi porcini* (with mushrooms) or *al tartufo* (with truffles). For seconds they have meats of all sorts, especially veal, as well as great pizza. A down-to-earth, fun place to eat.

7. LOCANDA DEL DUCA, *Via Picardi 1. Tel. 075/927-7753. All credit cards accepted. Dinner for two E25.*

This is a friendly and irreverent restaurant in a quaint old neighborhood, which serves tasty pastas and meats, but they are really known for their exquisite pizzas. The interior is rustic, set with a wood beamed ceiling; there's a small garden terrace overlooking the small river that flows through Gubbio. A good choice, a little off of the beaten path, and they are open until midnight if you need a late night snack. Even if you don't eat here, pass by and savor the ambiance of the location.

Seeing the Sights

A. PALAZZO DEI CONSOLI

Looking out over the town this imposing structure sits at the east end of the Piazza Grande and is the architectural and monumental core of the city. Ringed with some Renaissance *palazzi*, one of which is the **Palazzo Pretorio**, from this piazza you can get some stunning panoramic views.

The Palazzo dei Consoli is really two 14th century buildings, architecturally associated but clearly distinct. Simple and elegant, the palace is graced with a magnificent Gothic portal, in front of which are a set of steps that face out onto the piazza. The facade is divided by vertical pilaster strips, topped with turrets over which looks a small bell tower.

Also known as the Palazzo dei Popolo, the building now houses the **Picture Gallery** which has some paintings from Gubbio dating from the 14th and 16th centuries; and the **Archaeological Museum**, which houses the seven historically significant **Eugubine Tablets**, the Rosetta Stone for Central Italy. These tablets have a corresponding Umbrian language text, which evolved alongside the Etruscan, and a rudimentary form of Latin. There are also some interesting ancient archaeological finds like stone ceramics and coins. Not laid out and catalogued like the Smithsonian, but interesting and educational nonetheless.

B. DUOMO

A simple austere brick cathedral built in the 12th century, located up the hill from the older Roman town. The facade is graced with a plain circular window above a pointed portal. The interior is in a Latin cross plan and has one nave and many pointed arches supporting the ceiling. Simple and plain inside, except for the paintings and frescoes of the 16th century Umbrian artists along the walls, the church also has an incredibly detailed altar space, organ and choir. This cathedral is a wonderful example of austere medieval beauty.

C. PALAZZO DUCALE

Located directly across from the Duomo, this is a prime example of Renaissance architecture. Built in 1470 on the site of an older Lombard palace, this building contains a splendid internal courtyard surrounded by porticos. In the basement there is an archaeological excavation of the alterations made atop the building during the Renaissance. The palace's foundation can be seen as can segments of the original plumbing. Fragments of medieval ceramics found during the excavations are also on display. The rest of the museum, upstairs, is really just a set of whitewashed walls, scattered antique furnishings, restored pieces from local churches, and an occasional modern art exhibit to fill up the space. Save the E2 cost of entry and buy a drink at The Village instead (see below under *Nightlife*), unless of course you are keenly interested in medieval plumbing.

D. CHURCH OF ST. FRANCIS

Located on the large Piazza Quaranta Martiri, this church was built in the 13th century with a bare facade, a Gothic portal and a small rose window. There is an octagonal campanile at the right side of the church.

The interior has one nave and two aisles. When the sun streams in through the large pointed windows along the sides and the colored windows in the apse, this church simply glows. The attached cloisters evoke images of times past and should be visited if open. Other churches of possible interest to visit in the town, though much simpler in ornamentation, are San Secondo, San Giovanni, and San Pietro.

E. CAPTAIN OF THE PEOPLE'S PALACE

Located on Via dell Capitano del Popolo #6, near the outskirts of this small town, this 13th century building is rather plain, but what's inside is memorable. Home to the **Museum of Torture Instruments**, you can just imagine the displays. They are educational, enlightening and a refreshing reality check concerning the relative safety of modern life.

F. ROMAN THEATER

Located just outside the old city walls, this ancient theater is considered to be one of the largest and best preserved in Italy. Now converted to a verdant park, this old theater is also home to live productions through July and mid-August. Separated into four wedge-shaped sections by flights of stairs with many of the ruins rebuilt and solidified, you really feel as if you've walked back in time.

G. BASILICA OF SAN UBALDO

At the summit of Mount Ingino lies the terminus for the traditional Corsa dei Ceri, the ancient tower up the hill. It can be reached by cable car from the station through the Porta Romana (an immense tower construction evoking a definite medieval feel) or by walking the length of the Corsa dei Ceri through the Porta San Ubaldo. I suggest that route only for the most fit.

Built in the 1514, worthy of note is the engraved marble altar and the glass coffin containing the well preserved body of St. Ubaldo. The three wooden towers used in the Corso dei Ceri festival are on display here year round. On the hillside above the church are the remains of the 12th century Rocca.

Nightlife & Entertainment

8. THE VILLAGE, *Piazza 40 Martiri #29. Tel. 075/922-2296.*

Art, history, architecture and the surrounding natural setting, coupled with a warm, friendly atmosphere make The Village is the place to come for late night festivities in Gubbio. Located in a renovated old church, I can't think of a better place to come with friends or to meet new ones. They serve Bass and Tenents on tap at E4 a pint and serve some basic Italian-style pub food.

Practical Information

Tourist Information

To arrange day trips, find out about bus tours, find train or bus information, get maps, or detailed walking tour information, book a hotel or simply get general information about Gubbio, the **tourist office** is the place to go, *Piazza Oderisi 6, Tel. 075/922-0693 or 922-0790, Fax 075/927-3409.*

Todi

An ancient and stunningly beautiful city surrounded by medieval walls, and filled with quaint winding streets, **Todi** rises up among green hills above where the Naia flows into the Tiber. This little town is a must see destination when in Umbria. Founded by the Tutere, an ancient Umbrian people, and heavily influenced by the Etruscans who settled along the banks of the Tiber, Todi eventually fell under Rome's control during the 4th century BCE and became known as Tuder. When the Roman Empire collapsed, the city underwent its share of destruction from the Goths and Byzantine Empire.

Beginning in the year 1000 it became an independent commune, during which time it extended its domain as far as Amelia and Terni in the 13th century. But then it became part of other empires again in the 14th century, eventually ending up in the hands of the Papal States. When Napoleon was in control of the Italian peninsula, Todi was an important government seat. After Napoleon it once again came under papal jurisdiction.

Todi is now mostly enclosed within the perimeter of the old town walls in a roughly triangular layout. Wonderfully apart from the advance of time, Todi has yet to succumb to the invading hordes of tourists. There is only one hotel in the centro storico, and a small bed and breakfast which means that the residents of the city still far outnumber the tourists, a situation you will find true all over Umbria, but especially so in Todi.

Todi, like all of Umbria, is not a place to pursue frantic sightseeing forays. Todi has a refreshingly gentle feel to it, and is still untainted by the hustle and bustle of frenetic tour groups trying to suck up the Italian experience as if it were a giant Slurpee. Todi is a town where you can fit right into the flow of real Italian life, wander unobtrusively among the friendly locals, sit with them in the parks as their children play, or smile with them in the piazzas as they pantomime one of the scenes in life's play. This is a place to undertake casual meandering, not only around the hilly cobblestone streets lined with medieval homes – some set into old Roman and Etruscan walls. Todi is also a place to rest and be rejuvenated in a fairy tale setting.

Arrivals & Departures

Todi is difficult to get to because the train and bus schedules are erratic. Also, the train station is a ways out of town (take the bus "C" from Piazza Jacapone) and is on a small regional line, which means the trains move much slower and stop at every town along the way. Check with the information office for schedules.

If you are taking the train into Perugia, be aware that Perugia has three different train stations. Trains from Todi stop first at Porta S. Giovanni station in Perugia, then go onto an even smaller station called **Perugia Santa Ana** (which is where you get off, since it is near the escalators up to the center), but they do not stop at the main train station in Perugia.

Orientation

Located 45 kilometers from Perugia, Todi is a small triangular shaped town sprawled along the crest of a hill. The skyline is dominated by Santa Maria della Consolazione in the lower part of town and the Chiesa di San Fortunato in the upper part. The Piazza del Popolo is definitely the central focus of the town around which are situated most of the major sights.

Getting Around Town

The only way to get around town is by walking. The town is small but even so, getting from the lower part of town to the upper can seem longer than it is because of the steep uphill grade. Be prepared to hike while here.

Where to Stay

1. RESIDENZA SAN LORENZO TRE, *Via San Lorenzo 3, Six rooms, four with bath. Tel. & Fax 075/894-4555. E-mail: is@todi.net. Web: www.todi.net/ lorenzo/. Holiday Jan. 15 – Feb 28. Single E50-70; Double without bath E60-65; Double E85-90. Breakfast included. No credit cards accepted.*

Located on the upper floor of a quaint palazzo just off of the Piazza del Popolo, this is definitely the place to stay in Todi. If you simply must have a four star stay, go to the Fonte Cesia below, but you will be missing out on this amazing little residenza. Though not technically a hotel, I would categorize this bed and breakfast-style residence as a three star, despite the lack of mini-bar and TV in the rooms. What this place lacks in unnecessary modern amenities is more than made up for with its charm, ambiance and incredibly scenic panoramic views. There are two rooms that open onto the most breathtaking vistas you can imagine. Each room is furnished with antique furnishings, which adds to the ambiance, but make sure you specifically

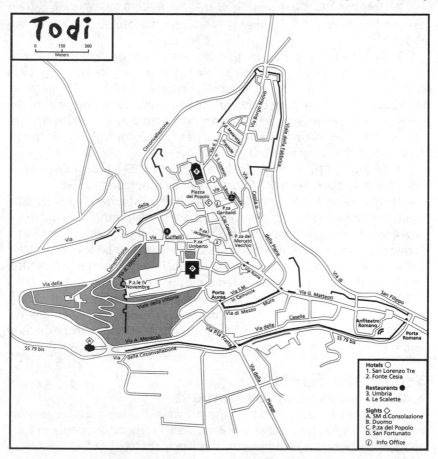

request one of the two rooms with a view and your stay here will be *stupenda* (stupendous).

2. FONTE CESIA, *Via Lorenzo Leony 3, Tel. 075/894-3737, Fax 075/894-4677. E-mail: ontecesia@tagweb.it. Web: www.fontecesia.it/. 37 rooms all with bath. Single E70-95; Double E110-145. All credit cards accepted. Breakfast included. ****

Situated in a noble and antique building in the center of Todi a few paces from the Piazza del Popolo and the Piazza Umberto, this is an excellent small town four star hotel. Opened in 1994, they have made the decor antique to add a touch of old world character. The rooms are spacious, very comfortable and come with every necessary modern comfort, though the bathrooms are minuscule. Their sundeck is a great place to relax as are the downstairs common areas. A good place to stay in Todi.

Where to Eat

3. UMBRIA, *Via San Bonaventura 13. Tel. 075/894-2390. Closed Tuesdays and at the end of December. All credit cards accepted. Dinner for two E55.*

This place has improved in the past few years. Where before the food was average, now it is really good. And before where the service was surly it has come to be professional. Now the atmosphere is local with a little pretense. I think you'll like the *tagliatelle ai funghi* (pasta with local mushrooms) or the *spaghetti agli 'strioli'* (spaghetti with an tasty herb only grown locally). For seconds the *salami di cinghiale* (wild boar) is a succulently tasty local sausage. An excellent choice while in Todi.

4. LE SCALETTE, *Via delle Scalette 1. Tel. 075/894-4422. Closed Mondays. Open 12:00-2:30pm & 7:00pm-1:00am. Dinner for two E35.*

This is a menu that has something for everyone, whether it's pizza, pasta, meats or vegetarian servings. They have terrace seating with some panoramic views, as well as a quaint medieval interior to add to this place's rustic charm. Located just past San Fortunato and Piazza Umberto I, at Le Scalette you will authentic local atmosphere, excellent regional cooking, attentive service, which will all translate into a wonderful meal.

Try their *cappollini al tartufo nero* (stuffed pasta with truffle cream sauce). It is the house specialty and is incredibly delicious. The pizza's overflow the plate and can be considered a meal in themselves. Not as formal or expensive as the Umbria, which — in my opinion — makes this a better place to eat.

Seeing the Sights

A. SANTA MARIA DELLA CONSOLAZIONE

Located a little ways outside of the city walls, this is a must see location when in Todi. A delightful example of Renaissance architecture, begun in 1508 and finished almost a century later, this lovely church, like San Fortunato, stands out from the diminutive skyline of the town. In the shape of a Greek Cross with a large central dome there are four apses each crowned with its own half dome.

B. DUOMO

This church dominates the Piazza Vittorio Emanuele II (also known as the Piazza del Popolo). The rectangular facade with three Rosetta windows and the same number of Gothic portals is simple yet refined. Flanking this facade is the robust bell tower that was once used as a military watchtower.

The interior is divided into three sections. In the left aisle is an interesting bronze of San Martino by Fiorenzo Bacci. The counter facade has a 16th century fresco of the *Last Judgment* by Faenzone. Unfortunately it has not been well preserved but is still powerful. Please also take note of the wooden choir behind the altar, as well as the two paintings portraying *St. Peter* and *St. Paul*, to the left and right of the altar, done by Spagna. For E7.5 you can get a ticket to see the crypt which is a rather non-descript underground area but interesting for medieval history buffs.

C. PIAZZA VITTORIO EMANUELE II (PIAZZA DEL POPOLO)

Besides the aforementioned Duomo, also located in the extensive Piazza Vittorio Emanuele II (more commonly known as the Piazza del Popolo) are the Palazzo dei Priori, Palazzo del Popolo, and Palazzo del Capitano. An extensive piazza that is the heart of this small town, it is located on the site of an ancient Roman Forum and is one the most beautiful medieval squares in all of Europe. Dominated by the Duomo and surrounded by numerous monumental palaces. it transports you back in time.

Across from the Duomo is the turreted **Palazzo dei Priori**, built in the 14th century then joined together with some pre-existing buildings. The trapezoidal shaped tower was originally much higher, but through wars and erosion it remains in its truncated form today. The bronze eagle, the symbol of Todi, that stands out above the second order of windows was made by Giovanni di Gigliaccio in 1339.

The Palazzo del Capitano is a 13th century construction with a set of stairs leading to the second story entrance. The building is the site of the **Roman-Etruscan Museum and Civic Picture Gallery**. There are a number of Roman and Etruscan artifacts that have come from the surrounding area with terracotta and bronze work. In the Picture Gallery you will find fine paintings by many Umbrian and Tuscan artists, as well as gold and ceramic work.

D. SAN FORTUNATO

Rising up above the town this Gothic church *(hours: winter 9:30am-12:30pm & 3:00-5:00pm; summer 8:30am-12:30pm & 3:00-7:00pm)* was built between the 13th and 15th centuries. The half-completed facade overlooks the top of a scenic but fatiguing series of steps and their accompanying green space. There are three portals, the middle one richly decorated with a variety of colonnades, and is flanked by two statues of *Gabriel* and *Virgin Mary*. The other two are smaller versions of the middle.

The interior can be described as majestic but plain, with its three grandiose naves and the cross vaulting, and stark white walls. The wooden choir behind the altar is as extensive as in the Duomo but it is more accessible and visible here. Unfortunately some the fine frescoes are only in fragments now, as preservation work was not started until this century. But even if the interior art work is a little decayed, the serenity of the space is spiritually invigorating.

E. PARCO DELLA ROCCA

Near San Fortunato is the Parco della Rocca, where you have nice panoramic views, peace and quiet — when there aren't any kids running around — a place to picnic and cuddle, a rose garden to stimulate your nose, all of which make you feel as if you are on top of the world. The peaceful sense of continuity and permanence that Todi evokes is personified by this little park and the residents who frequent it.

Practical Information

Festivals & Fairs
• **March-April** – Antiquarian Exhibition of Italy
• **June-July** – National Antique Fair
• **September 8** – Festa di S. Maria della Consolazione
• **September** – Todi festival
• **October 14** – Festa di San Fortunato (Patron saint of Todi)
• **November 11** – Fair of St. Martin

Tourist Information
To arrange day trips, find out about bus tours, find train or bus information, get maps, or detailed walking tour information, book a hotel or simply get general information about Todi, go to the **tourist office**, *Piazza del Popolo 39, Tel. 075/894-2526.*

Orvieto

Umbria is Tuscany's understated cousin, quietly regal, unassuming, yet just as charming, and **Orvieto** is one of Umbria's best cities to visit. Umbria is a region of contrasts, where seemingly impenetrable, thick forests give way to sweeping, fertile valleys, where lush mountains and tranquil hills, dazzling waterfalls and still lakes mingle in a palette greener than any other corner of

Italy. And just over the border with Lazio, the province that Rome is in, the stunning city of Orvieto rests picturesquely on the top of a hill bordered by protective cliffs, waiting for you to arrive on a day trip from Rome.

Orvieto was a favorite refuge of the popes because of this defensible situation. One of the most beautiful towns in all of Italy, Orvieto has a rich array of winding medieval streets and stunning architecture. Its first inhabitants were Etruscan, after which the city became a protectorate of the Roman Empire.

With the empire's decline, Orvieto underwent the inevitable spate of barbarian invasion. It then became a free commune in the 12th century CE and enjoyed a period of artistic and political advancement, until the Papal States suppressed it into their fold in the 14th century. When Napoleon Buonaparte conquered it, he made it an essential center of his dominion until Orvieto was absorbed into the Kingdom of Italy in 1860.

Known not only for its architecture and natural beauty, the town is also famous for the wonderful Orvieto wine that flows from the local vines, as well as the tasty olive oil from the nearby olive groves. Besides its culinary pursuits, the town also is a ceramic center. Local artisans, especially the immensely talented Michelangeli, also create intricate wood carvings as well as delicate lace.

Arrivals & Departures

Orvieto is accessible from Rome by a train which runs every two hours, starting at 6:12am and ending at 8:30pm, and takes an hour and twenty minutes or less depending on the number of stops along the way. Returns start at 9:00am and end at 10:30am. Once at the train station you then take the funiculare (cable car) up the hill, through an avenue of trees before tunneling under the Fortrezza to the Piazzale Cahen. By the funiculare station is where St. Patricks Well is located so stop there before you head up into town if you so wish.

From the station catch the bus 'A' — which should be waiting for you as you exit the funiculare since the bus is timed to its arrival — to the Piazza Duomo and the information office. From the Duomo you can get to all sights, hotels, and restaurants.

Orientation

Located on the top of a hill surrounded by cliffs, the **Corso Cavour** divides the city east to west. On the east is the **Piazzale Cahen** and the **Fortrezza** — built in 1364 and now a pleasant public garden with fine views over the surrounding valley — where the *funiculare* arrives, and at the west is the **Porta Maggiore**.

Getting Around Town

This town is easy to walk since being on the top of a bluff it is mainly flat. Once you take the *funiculare* up from the station there won't be many more serious hills to traverse.

Where to Stay

1. ITALIA, *Via di Piazza del Popolo. Tel 0763/42065, Fax the same. 42 rooms all with bath. Single E65; Double E85. American Express and Visa accepted. Breakfast E7.5.* ***

This 18th century palazzo in the centro storico of Orvieto offers you a pleasant stay right in the heart of things, adjacent to the Piazza del Popolo and just off of the Corso Cavour. The spacious rooms and relaxing common areas are furnished in a classic but comfortable style, with antiques and a floral theme throughout. The best rooms are those facing the small courtyard (*cortile*), but all come with every three star amenity. The only real drawback other than that is the minuscule bathrooms . But besides that, this is a wonderful place to stay in Orvieto.

2. MAITANI, *Via Lorenzo Maitani. Tel 0763/42011, Fax 0763/660-209. Web: www.argoweb.it/hotel_maitani/maitani.uk.html. Closed January 6-26. 40 rooms all with bath. Single E80; Double E130. Suite E150-180. All credit cards accepted. Breakfast E10.* ****

If you want a serene atmosphere you'll find it here in this antique palazzo in the centro storico, only a few steps from the magnificent Duomo of Orvieto. The rooms are all different from one another but are furnished for comfort and style. The bathrooms are all modern, though a wee bit tiny compared to North American standards, and come with a complete complimentary toiletry kit. There is ample public space downstairs in the lounge/bar area, where you can put your feet up at the end of the day. A wonderful place to stay while in Orvieto, in an ideal setting.

3. LA BADIA, *1a Cat., 05019 Orvieto. Tel 0763/301-959 or 305-455, Fax 0763/305-396. All credit cards accepted. Single E125; Double E300.* ****

An unbelievably beautiful 12th century abbey at the foot of Orvieto is home to this incredible hotel that has only recently opened for business. You will be treated to one of the most unique and memorable experiences in the entire world. In the 15th century the abbey became a holiday resort for Cardinals, and today, through painstakingly detailed renovations, an ancient and noble Umbrian family, Count Fiumi di Sterpeto, plays host in this awe-inspiring environment.

The rooms are immense, the accommodations exemplary, the service impeccable, the atmosphere like something out of the Middle Ages. For a fairy tale vacation stay here, and make sure that you eat at least once at their soon to be world-renowned restaurant offering refined local dishes — many

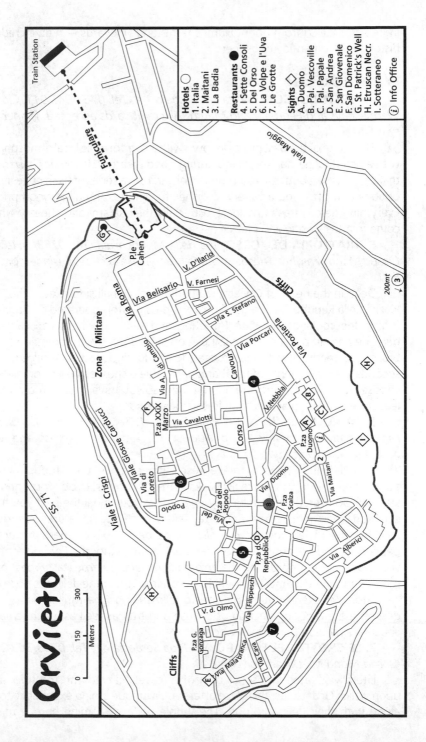

Orvieto

Meters
0   150   300

Hotels ○
1. Italia
2. Maitani
3. La Badia

Restaurants ●
4. I Sette Consoli
5. Del Orso
6. La Volpe e l'Uva
7. Le Grotte

Sights ◇
A. Duomo
B. Pal. Vescoville
C. Pal. Papale
D. San Andrea
E. San Giovenale
F. San Domenico
G. St. Patrick's Well
H. Etruscan Necr.
I. Sotterraneo
ⓘ Info Office

ingredients culled from Count Fiumi's farms and vineyards — in an incredibly historic and romantic atmosphere.

Where to Eat

4. I SETTE CONSOLI, *Piazza San Angelo 1/a. Tel. 0763/343-911. Closed Wednesdays and February and March. All credit cards accepted. Dinner for two E40.*

This is one of the best places in town with a comfortable local atmosphere, with a beautiful garden for dining during good weather. If you don't want to make a decision about the food you can order from a series of fixed price menu options that offer you a variety of dishes to sample, and all at good prices. Everything here is fresh and local, especially their salami and cheese, which come in a tasty antipasto platter.

5. TRATTORIA DEL ORSO, *Via della Misericordia. Tel. 0763/341-642. Closed Monday nights, Tuesdays and February. Visa accepted. Dinner for two E40.*

Deep in the heart of Orvieto, nestled down a small side street off of the Piazza della Repubblica, is a small trattoria passionately operated by Gabrielle (doing the cooking) and Cirò (greeting and seating) where you can find genuine and simple Umbrian cuisine. You should start with the magnificent bruschetta (garlic bread) and proceed to the luscious fettucine alfredo. For seconds there are plenty of meat and vegetable dishes, as well as omelets to choose from. The desserts are home made, so you have to save room for at least one. A great place to sample the local flavor.

6. LA VOLPE E L'UVA, *Via Ripa Corsica 1. Tel. 0763/341-612. Closed Mondays and From July 15 to August 15. American Express and Visa accepted. Dinner for two E35.*

You definitely have to make reservations, since their food, friendly atmosphere and low prices really packs in the customers. Lucio Sforza and his staff will do everything in their power to make your meal the best you have ever had. Their antipasto salami plate (*salumi misti locali*) features all sorts of local favorites. The *gnochetti con olio pepe e pecorino* is a superb mixture of pepper, oil and pecorino cheese over small potato gnocchi. For your entrée you should consider ordering the *arrosto di maiale alle erbe* (tasty roast pork marinated in herbs) that literally melts in your mouth, or the delicious *pollo alla cacciatore* (chicken hunter style) or *agnello sulla griglia* (grilled lamb). For dessert there is good selection of cheese and fruit as well as a rich, creamy chocolate mousse (*mousse di cioccolato*).

7. LE GROTTE DEL FUNARO, *Via Ripa Serancia 41. Tel. 0763/343-276. Closed Mondays. Dinner for two E40.*

Literally situated in a series of grotte (caves) carved into the tufo layer upon which Orvieto sits, this place offers you a unique dining experience to go along with their delicious food. The whole point of coming here is to eat downstairs in the caves, so avoid the terrace. The have a well rounded menu, but in truffle season that aromatic tuber is featured prominently and any dish seasoned with it should be sampled if you are here from October to December. Try Le Grotte when in Orvieto. You will not be disappointed.

Seeing the Sights
A. DUOMO

Stunning! Elegant! Mesmerizing! No words can really describe this amazing cathedral, located in the Piazza del Duomo, whose facade is covered with bas-reliefs, colorful mosaics, and radiating frescoes. The pointed portals on the facade literally jump out at you, and the rose window — flanked by figures of the Prophets and Apostles — is a treasure to behold. Bring binoculars to admire all the intricate detail, since the facade is an entire museum in and of itself.

Most of its ornamentation was created between the 14th and 16th centuries. The bronze doors are contemporary works by Emilio Greco (1964). A museum featuring more of his art is situated on the ground floor of the Palazzo Papale to the right of the Duomo. Above and beside the doors are the Bronze Symbols of the Evangelists. The exterior side walls are alternating horizontal layers of black basalt and pale limestone in the distinctive Pisan style. This same style is translated into the interior, covering both the walls, and the columns which divide the church into a nave and two aisles. The christening font is the work of several artists and is stunning in its intricacies. The apse is lit by 14th century stained glass windows by Bonino and contains frescoes by Ugolino di Prete Ilario.

In the right transept behind an artistic 16th century wrought iron railing is the beautiful Capella Nuova, which contains Luca Signorelli's superlative Last Judgment. It is purported to be the inspiration for Michelangelo's Last Judgment in the Sistine Chapel. A must see, since it is also considered one of the greatest frescoes in Italian art. The chapel also contains frescoed medallions depicting poets and philosophers ranging from Homer to Dante.

B. PALAZZO VESCOVILLE

Located to the right and at the rear of the Duomo, restored in the 1960s, it now houses the **Archaeological Museum** (*open 9:00am – 7:00pm, Holidays 9:00am-1:00pm; admission E2*), which has a collection of material excavated from the Etruscan Necropoli that are located nearby the city. A simple, basic introduction to the history of the region.

C. PALAZZO PAPALE

Situated to the right of the Duomo, this was once the residence of a long line of popes when they came to visit the city. This building dates back to the 8th century and is also known as the **Palace of Bonifacio VIII**. On the ground floor you can find the **Museum of Emilio Greco** (*open 10:30am-1:00pm and 2:00-6:00pm in winter and 3:00-7:00pm in summer*) exhibiting numerous works by this fine sculptor from Catania. On the first floor is the **Cathedral Museum**, which displays miscellaneous works of art, mostly from the Duomo or about the Duomo.

D. SAN ANDREA
On the edge of the Piazza della Repubblica, this plain church is best known for its dodecagonal campanile, a twelve-sided bell-tower. This masterful architectural complement to the church has three orders of windows and a turreted top section. Built between the 6th and 14th centuries on the site of a pre-existing early Christian church, the interior is a single nave with two aisles, a raised transept and cross vaults. The wooden altar by Scalza is worthy of note, as is the pulpit. Situated below the church and accessible by appointment are some ancient ruins dating from the Iron Age up to the medieval period.

E. SAN GIOVENALE
Originally a Romanesque building San Giovenale was reconstructed in the 13th century with Lombard features. The massive square bell tower dwarfs this plain and sturdy looking church. The interior is a simple design with one single nave and two aisles. Note the Romanesque high altar intricately decorated with bas-reliefs as well as the frescoed walls of the Orvieto school from the 13th to the 16th century. This part of town is the ideal location to take relaxing walks, filled with stunning panoramic vistas.

F. SAN DOMENICO
Set back from the Via Arnolfo di Cambio in a less inspiring part of town, this church is famous because St. Thomas Aquinas taught here, and the desk at which he performed his lectures is still inside. You should also take note of the 13th century Tomb of Cardinal de Bray by Arnolfo di Cambio, as well as the Petrucci Chapel built by Michele Sanmicheli, which is below the main church and entered from the a door on the south wall.

G. ST. PATRICK'S WELL
Open daily from 9:00am to 6:00pm, this well, **Orvieto Sotteraneo**, and the **Duomo** are the most famous sights in Orvieto. Built by Antonio Sangallo the Younger for Pope Clement VII, the well served as a reservoir for the nearby fortress if the city was ever put under siege. Hence it is also known as the Fortress Well. Its ingenious cylindrical cavity design was completed in the beginning of the 16th century. Going to a depth of 62 meters, there are two parallel concentric staircases (each with 248 steps ... go on and count them if you want). The water carriers with their donkeys used one spiral staircase

for going up and the other for going down. Each staircase has a separate entrance and is ringed by large arched windows. In the public gardens above the well are the overgrown remains of an Etruscan temple.

H. ETRUSCAN NECROPOLISES

Located on either side of the city the foot of the *tufa* cliffs, the **Necropolis of the Tufa Crucifix** is to the north and the **Necropolis of Cannicella** is to the south. Each date from around the sixth century BCE. Well preserved but ransacked and looted a long time ago, these tombs nonetheless are something to visit while in Orvieto. It's not often that you can come face to face with something that was created almost 2,500 years ago. Inquire at the information office about the ways and means to visit them.

I. ORVIETO SOTTERANEO

If you do nothing else while here, make sure that you sign up to go on one of the guided tours of the subterranean passages that snake underneath the entire city. Guided tours are held every day starting at 11am and go until 6pm, and cost E5. Inquire at the information about the times for the tours in English. At last inquiry they were at 12:15 and 5:15pm. Recently excavated and opened for tourists, the tours of these caves under the city take you on a journey through history, including Etruscan wells, a 17th century oil mill, a medieval quarry, ancient pigeon coops and much more, all thoroughly narrated by well-trained guides. These tours are an extraordinary trip back in time and shouldn't be missed.

Shopping

In general there is great shopping in Orvieto, but without the same run-of-the-mill, cookie cutter, international name brand stores you find in most tourist locations. There are many small artisans' shops, unique boutiques, ceramics re-sellers, all of which add to the rich local flavor that Orvieto cultivates. One store in particular you simply must visit is:

8. Michelangeli, *Via Gualverio Michelangeli 3B, 05018 Orvieto. Tel. 0763/342-660, Fax 0763/342-461. All credit cards accepted.*

An incredible store filled with intricately carved wooden sculptures, toys, figurines, and murals of the most amazing and appealing designs. A perfect store to find the perfect gift or keepsake. Michelangeli's work is slowly becoming recognized around the world. It is rustic but refined, and the very least you should stop in the store, check out the displays, take a look through his portfolios and treat the experience as you would a museum. A great store and a rewarding experience.

Practical Information
Tourist Information

To arrange day trips, find out about bus tours, find train or bus information, get maps, detailed walking tour information, book a hotel, get general information about Orvieto, or book a guided tour for Orvieto Sotteraneo, the **tourist office**, *Piazza Duomo 4, Tel. 0763/301-507 or 301-508, Fax 0763/344-433*, is the place to go.

Assisi

Dramatically situated on a verdant hill highlighted by olive groves and cypress trees reaching right up to the city walls, the beautiful medieval city of **Assisi** stretches majestically along the slopes of Mount Subasio. The home of **St. Francis**, Assisi is an original Umbrian settlement, after which it became a part of the Etruscan federation, and later was incorporated into the Roman Empire. In the 3rd century CE it became a Christian town, then after the fall of the Roman Empire it was destroyed by the Goths in 545 CE, conquered by the Byzantine Empire and eventually fell into hands of the Lombards.

Incorporated into the Duchy of Spoleto, it became an independent commune in the 11th century and achieved great success in the 13th century. During this period of freedom and economic success, St. Francis was born here in 1182 and **St. Clare** in 1193 (a daughter of a rich family, and a contemporary and disciple of St Francis of Assisi, she founded the order of Poor Clares. She died in Assisi in the convent she founded in 1253).

After the 13th century the city became part of the Papal States, then Perugia, then Milan, and finally fell under the control of the powerful Sforza family. And eventually, as a result of internal strife, Assisi was re-incorporated into the Papal States in the 16th century until it became a part of the new state of Italy in the 19th century.

Today Assisi still bears the mark of a robust little medieval town, at least that part which is still encompassed by the old city walls. This stunningly beautiful little Umbrian hill town is a center for art and culture, a major religious pilgrimage site, and a heavily touristed location. As a result, be prepared for crowded streets, something that is unusual in the otherwise lightly touristed region of Umbria. Some of the town's charm was instantaneously leveled when an earthquake struck in 1997, causing severe damage to the city's structures, especially the Basilica of St. Francis. Many of Giotto's fine frescoes were destroyed in this natural catastrophe. An extensive renovation of the church has just been completed as of going to press. Assisi is a wonderful destination, but you may still find scaffolding and supports in place to secure certain structures of historic significance.

Arrivals & Departures

Assisi can be somewhat difficult to get to by train or bus, so if you don't rent a car, which is recommended so you can take in all the splendor of Umbria, expect at least a two hour train trip from Rome, or an hour and a half train or bus trip from Perugia. Buses and trains leave every hour and half to two hours from Perugia and are infrequent from Rome. Contact the local tourist office in Perugia for a more detailed schedule.

Orientation

Assisi is directly between Perugia and Foligno, about 13 kilometers from the former. The town is dominated by the **Basilica of San Francesco** on the northwest end. The core of the city surrounds the **Piazza del Comune** with many major sights in an around the square. All streets in the town seem to lead to this piazza, so it is almost impossible to get lost while in Assisi.

Getting Around Town

Assisi, like most Umbrian towns, is made for walking. Many or the smaller streets and the winding staircases are off-limits to cars, but you do have to contend with hills. So bring your walking shoes.

Where to Stay

1. **SAN FRANCESCO**, *Via San Francesco 48. Tel 075/812-281, Fax the same. 44 rooms all with bath. Single E70; Double E140. All credit cards accepted. Breakfast included.* ***

Located near the cathedral, this classic little three star hotel is right in the center of things. Some of the rooms have grand views of the cathedral. If you want one you need to request it with your reservation. All rooms have plenty of space and are comfortably furnished with a mixture of antiques and more modern furnishings. The bathrooms are minuscule but come with a complete complimentary toiletry kit. This is a good small town three star, a little on the rustic side, with an intimate terrace overlooking the cathedral, a quaint bar area, and a rather well respected restaurant.

2. **FONTEBELLA**, *Via Fontebella 25. Tel. 075/816-456, Fax 075/812-941. Web: www.venere.com/it/assisi/fontebella/. 43 rooms all with bath. Single E70-100; Double E125-210. All credit cards accepted. Breakfast E9.* ****

Almost in the center of Assisi with great views over the valley, this is a very nice four star that won the Premium Hotel Award in Italy for 1998. The common areas are spacious and accommodating. The bathrooms are not too big but do come with all modern amenities and a complimentary toilet kit. The rooms are relatively spacious and comfortable and are designed with a regal yellow and black color scheme. The breakfast buffet, served outside on the terrace in good weather, is quite a spread and is worth the extra money. A fine hotel with all the accoutrements of four star quality – plus their restaurant, Il Frantoio, is pretty good too.

3. SUBIASO, *Via Frate Elia 2. 075/812-206, Fax 075/816-691. Toll free in Italy 167/015070. 61 rooms all with bath. Single E115; Double E185. All credit cards accepted. Breakfast included.* ****

This is the place to stay in Assisi. Almost right at the foot of the Basilica di San Francesco this hotel has some breathtakingly panoramic views over the valley from the balconies of some of the rooms, as well as the sun terrace and garden terrace areas. All rooms are uniquely furnished with attractive antiques and are spacious and comfortable. There are a number of common rooms where you can relax and unwind, and the garden terrace, which houses the restaurant in the summer, is a perfect spot to grab a quiet meal.

4. IL PALAZZO, *Via San Francesco 8, 06081 Assisi. Tel. 075/816-841. Web: www.perugiaonline.com/ilpalazzo/. 40 rooms all with bath. All credit cards accepted. Single E50-60; Double E80-100.* **

The Palazzo Bindangoli-Bartocci – in which the hotel resides – was built in the 1500s and still retains its quaint medieval charm. It is perfectly situated between the Basilica of St. Francis and the main square, Piazza del Commune. The foundation of the building is a mixture of stables, storehouses, and inns that were in use in the 12th century. Each room is different in size, shape and antique furnishings but all are decorative and comfortable. In some rooms you have the original oak and beams for ceiling supports. The third floor rooms enjoy a view over the Spoletana valley. Without a doubt this is the best two star in town, and is pressing hard for three star status.

Where to Eat

There are a large number of restaurants to choose from in this city since it is such a tourist destination and pilgrimage site. Listed below are what I consider to be the two best:

5. LA FORTREZZA, *Piazza del Comune. Tel. 075/812-418. Closed Thursdays and in February. All credit cards accepted. Dinner for two E40.*

In an ideal location right up a small side street from the main piazza, this is a superb local restaurant attached to a two star hotel of the same name (a good, inexpensive option while in Assisi). It has kept up its high traditional culinary standards. For appetizers, their *prosciutto crudo con bruschetta* (ham with garlic bread) is superb. For the pasta dish try the succulently rich *ravioli alla ricotta e tartufo nero* (ravioli with cheese and black truffles) or the tasty *pappardelle alla ragu di agnello* (pasta with lamb sauce). For the main course its tough to decide between their succulent meat dishes like *filetto di vitellone al mosto cotto* (veal), *petto di faraone in crosta* (breaded wild chicken breast), the *coniglio* (rabbit) or *piccione* (pigeon). A great atmosphere with a wide variety of superb food at more than acceptable prices.

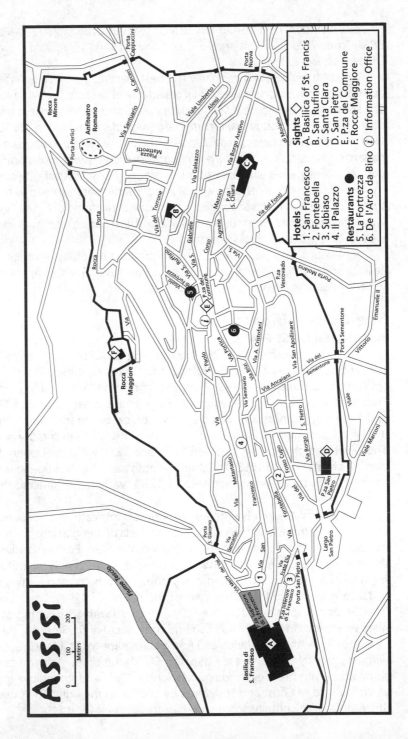

Assisi

0 100 200
Meters

Basilica di S. Francesco

Fiume Tescio

Rocca Minore

Anfiteatro Romano

Piazza Matteotti

Rocca Maggiore

Largo San Pietro

Sights ◇
A. Basilica of St. Francis
B. San Rufino
C. Santa Clara
D. San Pietro
E. P.za del Commune
F. Rocca Maggiore
ⓘ Information Office

Hotels ◯
1. San Francesco
2. Fontebella
3. Subiaso
4. Il Palazzo

Restaurants ●
5. La Fortrezza
6. De l'Arco da Bino

6. TAVERNA DE L'ARCO DA BINO, *Via San Gregorio 8. Tel 075/812-383. Closed Tuesdays, January 8-31, and July 5-15. All credit cards accepted. Dinner for two E55.*

One of the oldest and definitely the best place to eat while in Assisi, and because it is down a small side street it is also one of the least visited by tourists. The specialty of the house is veal and lots of it. And they make it in a variety of different ways, including *al tartufo nero* (with black truffles), *al gorgonzola* (with gorgonzola cheese), *alla brace* (roasted), *all'aceto balsamico* (with balsamic vinegar), *con funghi parmigiano e rucola* (with mushrooms and parmesan), as well as a number of other preparations. To start off your meal try their *bruschetta al tartufo nero di Assisi* (garlic bread spread with black truffles). They also make an excellent *fettucine al profumo di bosco (*smoked wood-flavored pasta with mushrooms and truffles), which was my favorite, as well as other succulently tasty pastas.

A pleasant, upscale, local place with great atmosphere — vaulted brick ceilings and woodsy wrought iron decor — as well as simply scrumptious food. When in Assisi you have to eat here at least once.

Seeing the Sights
A. BASILICA OF ST FRANCIS

Majestic and picturesque, the basilica and its accompanying cloistered convent have graced this rural landscape for many centuries. The basilica is split into two levels; the lowest is reached from the Piazza Inferiore di San Francesco which is currently being held up — after the earthquake of 1997 — with unsightly but necessary wood and iron brackets and scaffolding. In itself it is an enchanting open space, with a series of quaint 15th century arcades. The lower Church was built between 1228 and 1230 while the Upper Church was built from 1230 to 1253. The church is dominated by the huge square bell tower built in four layers, completed in 1239, with arches gracing the top section.

The **Lower Church** is entered through an intricate double portal surmounted with three rose windows. Inside consists of a single nave divided into five bays with a boule transept and a semi-circular apse. Even in the dim light the star-spangled blue vaults between the arches is stunningly beautiful. The remains of St. Francis are located in a stone urn in the crypt, which is down a staircase located in the middle part of the nave.

The side chapels are all wonderfully decorated with 13th century stained glass windows. On the right you can find the Chapel of St. Stephen, then the Chapel of St. Anthony of Padua and finally the Chapel of St. Mary Magdalene with frescoes by Giotto. In the Chapel of St. Martin on the left you can find some significant frescoes, including *Madonna, Child and Angels* by Cimabue as well as *Life of Christ and St. Francis* by Giotto on the right. The Chapel of St. Nicholas also contains some stunning frescoes by Giotto.

The **Upper Church** is reached — since the earthquake in 1997 it has been off-limits but may have reopened — by steps leading from the lower piazza. The facade faces the town of Assisi and looks over the wide lawn of the Piazza Superiore di San Francesco and has a pure linear Gothic look. The one embellishment is the large rose window staring out at the town. The interior of this level is bright and airy, in contrast to the lower section. It consists of one nave with a transept and a polygonal arch, with stunningly colorful frescoes by Cimabue decorating the walls of the apse as well as the transept.

The inlaid wood choir by the altar is a fantastic piece to admire. It was created between 1491 and 1501 by local artist Domenico Individi. The upper part of the nave is adorned with 13th century stained glass windows. Under the gallery, the walls were covered with some of the most magnificent examples of Giotto's work until the earthquake shook them loose and disintegrated them to powder. Sadly, this whole church is being pieced together, but work may well be complete by the time you visit — and these fantastic frescoes will be available for viewing once again.

B. CATHEDRAL OF SAN RUFFINO

Commonly known as the **Duomo**, the beautiful Romanesque facade is divided into three sections. The uppermost is triangular with a pointed Gothic arch; the middle is divided vertically by pilasters and is decorated with three fine rose windows and myriad carvings; and the lower section has three portals, the left of which is used to enter the church. To the side of the Duomo is the massive bell tower adorned with small arches at the top and an off-set clock on the same level as the top layer of the church.

The interior was renovated in the 16th century and consists of a nave and two aisles. The baptismal font in the right aisle was used to baptize St. Francis, St. Clare, St. Agnes, and St. Gabriel. Assisi definitely is a hotbed of sainthood. The apse contains an outstanding 16th century wood choir. The crypt is a must see. Situated underneath the cathedral, and once part of an earlier church, you can find a Roman sarcophagus which used to contain the remains of San Ruffino. Just down the road from here past Piazza Matteoti is a Roman amphitheater worthy of a short visit.

C. BASILICA OF SANTA CLARA

Simply, serenely, and classically Gothic, this 13th century church dominates the piazza of the same name. Attached to the left side of the building are three large flying buttresses with a slender bell tower rising up from the apse. The facade is decorated with two closed horizontal bands, is divided into three levels, and has a wonderful rose window and a plain portal flanked by two lions.

The interior is in the form of a Latin cross with a single nave and is as simple and bare as the outside. A good place to come for soul-enriching peacefulness.

The crypt, reached by a flight of steps, contains the remains of St. Clare in a glass coffin. In the chapel of St. George is the painted cross which supposedly spoke to St. Francis when it was located in the Church of St. Domain. Located here beyond a lattice window are the remains of St. Clare.

D. CHURCH OF SAN PIETRO
Located just inside the city walls, near the Basilica of St. Francesco, this Romanesque-Gothic 13th century church is built on the site of a previous Catholic place of worship. The facade is rectangular with two orders and beautiful in a simple way. The upper level has three rose windows, and the lower has three portals. The interior contains one nave and two aisles, and has some 14th century frescoes and the ruins of some tombs of the same century. For simple beauty and peaceful serenity this is a fine church to visit.

E. PIAZZA DEL COMMUNE
Located in the heart of the old town, built on the site of an old Roman forum and in the midst of some ancient medieval buildings, is the center of Assisi, the Piazza del Commune. The 14th century **Prior's Palace** houses the town council offices, the **Municipal Picture Gallery** contains Byzantine, Umbrian and Sienese frescoes, the turreted 13th century **Palazzo del Capitano del Popolo** has the 14th century **Municipal Tower** rising out from it.

Next to that is the **Church of Santa Maria Sopra Minerva**, built in the first half of the 16th century over the ancient Temple of Minerva. The facade is all ancient Rome from the Augustan period of the first century BCE, while the rest of the building is medieval.

F. CASTLE OF THE ROCCA MAGGIORE
Pass by the Roman Amphitheater as you go out the Perlici Gate to begin the climb up to this imposing fortress, which once served as protector over the city of Assisi. Built after the Lombard occupation, the fortress with its imposing ramparts and towers completely dominates the town below. A perfect place for kids of all ages to explore a medieval fortress.

Practical Information
Festivals
• **3rd and 4th of October** – Festival of St. Francis, Patron Saint of Italy
• **May Day celebration** – Calendimaggio
• **June 22nd** – Festival of the Vows
• **1st and 2nd of August** – Festival of the Pardon

Tourist Information

To arrange day trips, find out about bus tours, find train or bus information, get maps, or detailed walking tour information, book a hotel or simply get general information about Assisi, go to the **tourist office**, *Piazza del Comune 27, Tel. 075/812-450, Fax 075/813-727.*

Chapter 16

Venice

City of Canals & Bridges

Venice is one of the great cultural centers of Europe, and as such attracts tens of thousands of tourists each year. It serves as the capital of the province of Venice (**Venezia**) and the **Veneto region**, which includes the towns of **Padua**, **Verona**, and **Vicenza**.

The historic center of Venice that everyone comes to see is built on a group of small islands and mud banks in the middle of **Laguna Veneta**, a crescent-shaped lagoon separated from the **Adriatic Sea** by a barrier of narrow strips of islands and peninsulas. The modern city covers the whole 90 mile (145 km) perimeter of the lagoon and includes ten principal islands, in addition to those of the mother city and two industrial boroughs of **Mestre** and **Marghera** on the mainland.

The main core of Venice is made up of the islands of **La Giudecca** with its floating cafés and restaurants; **San Giorgio Maggiore**, with its famous 16th century church of the same name; and **San Michele** with its famous cemetery. Other islands include the **Lido**, a resort built in the 19th century with casinos, hotels, and beaches; **Murano**, noted for its glassworks; colorful **Burano**, famous for its lace; and **Torcello**, site of the remains of the **Santa Maria Assunta** cathedral. Even though Venice is separated from the sea by natural and artificial breakwaters, flooding is common from November through March of each year, so if you visit then, remember to bring some galoshes. It only takes a small rainfall for the water level in Venice to rise.

Venice is world-renowned as a city of canals and bridges which have an indescribable beauty and charm that draws a swarm of visitors each year. Chief among the waterways is the **Grand Canal** which starts at the railway station at **Piazza Roma** and ends at **Piazza San Marco** (**St. Mark's Square**). Altogether there are more than 200 canals, which are the main thoroughfares of Venice; and crossing the waterways there are about 400 bridges, the most famous of which is the **Rialto** with its many shops. Other well-known bridges include the **Scalzi**, the **Accademia**, and the infamous **Bridge of Sighs**, which leads from the upper story of the **Doges' Palace** to the republic's prison. It is so named because centuries ago prisoners went over it sighing in trepidation of their torture and death they were to receive on the other side.

Within the Venetian islands, canals, and lagoons, commodities move by barges and tugs, while passenger movement is primarily by *vaporetti* (water buses) or water taxi. The world-famous black *gondolas*, propelled by professional gondoliers, are narrow with high prows and sterns and are used by tourists mainly for short canal passages. Before the modern era gondolas were the main form of transportation for all Venetians who had the means to afford the use of one. Water buses and water taxis have almost completely replaced these elegant and attractive vessels today.

The Early Years

As competing history books will tell you, Venice was either founded on fear and cowardice, or brilliant necessity and creative ingenuity. With the fall of the Roman Empire, the "barbarian" hordes – Goths and Ostrogoths – swept over Italy in the 5th and 6th centuries CE. Instead of facing this onslaught, the people of the Veneto region found shelter on the scores of offshore islets in the lagoons off the coast, which had previously been inhabited by small settlements of fishermen. Here the future Venetians built their houses on pilings on the partially flooded islands and learned to move about by poling in shallow boats, which evolved into *gondolas*.

The "barbarians" were good horsemen but bad boatmen, so they continued to wreak havoc on shore, leaving the lagoons to the Venetians. Because of their intimacy with the water, over the centuries Venice grew into a great maritime power. This success developed because of the astuteness of its merchants and rulers, as well as its centuries-old political, military, and commercial ties with the Byzantium world in Constinantinople, now Istanbul.

Early Venice was a society ruled by its **Doges**, who were first elected in 727 CE. They were chosen by the **Council of Ten**, who were elected by the nobles and rich merchants who accounted for only six percent of the population. The city-state's chief maritime competitors were Genoa and the Amalfi Coast towns south of Naples, but Venice had the advantage of easier access through low Alpine passes to the heart of Western and Central Europe. This easy access and the ability to put aside moral issues and profit from any venture sent its way, helped make Venice a power to be reckoned with in the Mediterranean.

The Venetians' duplicity is shown in their ability to play two sides against each other. For example, the Doges made money off the Crusades by outfitting ships bound for the Holy Land, and at the same time they were paid by their Muslim friends for warnings of the impending arrivals. They also worked to help the Crusaders. In 1204 the Venetians supported the Crusaders in their attack and destruction of Constantinople, their erstwhile Muslim partners in trade. This led to a great increase in Venice's profitability since they had cut out the middle man in their trading.

During this time, one of their main rivals for trade was Genoa. After years of bitter conflict between the two city states, Genoa was defeated in 1381. The Venetians trapped the Genoan fleet inside the Chioggia lagoons south of the city and forced its surrender. At the height of the republic's power, Venice controlled Corfu, Crete, and the Peloponnesus in what is today Greece. On the mainland it acquired the land westward almost to Milan and eastward down the coast of Yugoslavia. Also, because of the defeat of Constantinople, the Black Sea and the eastern Mediterranean were now open for Venetian vessels.

A variety of problems however, contributed to a sharp decline in the republic's stature from the 16th century on. One of the main problems was the situation on the lagoon. What earlier had assisted them would now bring about their decline. Because of its location on sedentary water, the population of Venice was decimated over three centuries by outbreaks of plague. In one, from 1347 to 1349, three-fifths of its inhabitants died. Noticing this weakness, the **Turks**, who had captured Constantinople in 1453, began to take over Venice's Greek lands and possessions.

In 1508 Venice was defeated by the **League of Cambria** but then temporarily regained its maritime power. This dominion over trade with the East ended when the Portuguese opened the Cape Route around Africa, which meant that now the Portuguese had direct access to the spices the Venetians were trading. This precipitated a gradual decline in Venice's influence, affluence and power.

In 1797, the city was conquered by **Napoleon** and later ceded to Austria. In 1848 there was an unsuccessful revolt against the Austrians, and in 1866 Venice finally became part of a unified Italy. Then with the opening of the Suez Canal in 1869, the city regained a direct route to the East, but it never fully recovered its commercial supremacy. Today Venice's glory is all in the past, but we are the welcome beneficiaries of this glory. All that remains of Venice's past renown are the ancient palazzi and attractive vistas of canal and bridge which make the city such a stunning vacation site today. Venice is by far the most romantic and scenic vacation spot in the world. Enjoy your stay.

Arrival & Departures

By Bus

When arriving by bus you have to disembark at **Piazza Roma**, then either walk or catch some form of water transport to your destination. The main local bus service is **ACTV**, *Tel. 041/528-7886*. They have a tourist office in Piazza Roma where you can get maps, tourist information about Venice, and reserve bus seats to a variety of different cities in the region including Mestre, Padua, Mira and Treviso. Once you arrive, you can either walk to your destination or hop on the *vaporetto* at the Piazza Roma *vaporetto* stop on the canal. You will also be able to catch water taxis or gondolas from this location which can be much more expensive.

By Car

If you arrive in Venice by car, be prepared for long waits near **Piazza Roma** before you can deposit your automobile for the duration of your stay. One of the most welcoming aspects of Venice is that it is automobile free. The only way to get to Venice by car is through the mainland town of **Mestre**, then over the bridge (made by Mussolini) to the parking lots around the Piazza Roma. Once you get rid of your car, you can either walk to your destination or hop on the *vaporetto* at the Piazza Roma *vaporetto* stop on the canal. You will also be able to catch water taxis or gondolas from this location which can be much more expensive.

Sample trip lengths on main roads:
- **Padua**: 50 minutes
- **Bologna**: 2 hours
- **Florence**: 4 hours
- **Rome**: 6 hours.

If you want to rent a car, try **Avis**, *Piazza Roma 496/H, Tel. 041/522-5825* or **Hertz**, *Piazza Roma, 496/E, Tel. 041/528-4091.*

By Train

Arriving by train is the most convenient way to get to Venice. The **Stazione di Santa Lucia** is located on the northwestern edge of the city. From here you'll need to either walk to your hotel through the maze of medieval streets, take a *vaporetto* (a water bus), hire a water taxi, or go in style (and expense) in a gondola. All of these transportation services are located on the canal directly in front of the train station.

The **tourist information office**, *Tel. 041/719-078*, on the left, and **hotel information**, *Tel. 041/715-016* on the right, are located side by side near the front entrance of the station. If you need a hotel reservation get in the right line. If you just want information about upcoming events in Venice, a map, etc., get in the left line.

When standing in line you will be confronted with individuals trying to convince you to stay at their hotels. These are all legitimate agents for hotels that do not get that much business. If you do not want to be pestered simply say *No grazie* (no thank you). But if you take the time to listen to these agents you will discover that you can sometimes get a three star hotel at two star prices.

Sample trip lengths and costs for direct *(diretto)* trains:
• **Padua**: 45 minutes, E10
• **Bologna**: 1 1/2 hours, E15
• **Florence**: 3 1/2 hours, E40
• **Rome**: 5 hours, E70.

Orientation

Venice is conveniently separated into six sestieri, or sections, and the houses are numbered consecutively from a point in the center of each section, spiraling out, making finding specific locations an adventure in and of itself. The six *sestieri* are:
• **Cannaregio**, where the Jewish Ghetto is located; not too many tourists here.
• **Santa Croce**, along with San Polo is still considered the 'other side of the canal,' even though the Rialto bridge was built back in 1588 to connect this section of Venice with the more influential San Marco section.
• **San Polo**, site of the famous food market near the foot of the Rialto bridge that is open every morning except Sunday and Monday.
• **San Marco**, which is the cultural and commercial center of Venice and the location that most tourists never leave.
• **Dorsoduro**, where you can have a relaxing meal on the **Zattere**, the series of quays facing the island of **La Guidecca**, and watch the sun go down.
• **Castello**, the location of the **Arsenale**, where many of Venice's ships have been built.

This map of Venice shows the different sections of the city. Each separate subsequent map you'll find later in this chapter shows more detail and lists hotels, restaurants, and sights.

An Insight Into Venice

Venice was the late **Walt Disney's favorite city**. With its scenic canals, ornate bridges, and grandiose palazzi and piazze, it easy to see why Venice grabbed his heart. The whole city is so stunningly beautiful that it has an amusement park feel to it. It's almost as if what you're seeing is too magnificent, too stunning to be real. But it is.

But if you're here in high season you will encounter hordes of tourists; and as you shoulder your way through the crowds some of the luster may start to wear off. To escape from the hordes you may choose to escape into one of the stores that seem to take up every doorway, every building front, every available space on every little street. This rampant commercialism makes parts of Walt Disney's favorite city seem like the ugly strip malls that have grown around his theme parks.

Because of the crowds in the high season, Venice is definitely a place to visit in the off-season. Also because of this tourist influx and the commercialism it creates in the San Marco area, it is advised to stay away from this central area, which is around Piazza San Marco.

In the off-season and in the local areas you will share the city almost completely with Venetians. Also in the off-season hotels virtually cut their rates in half allowing you to upgrade your accomodations without any impact on your wallet. Another plus about the off-season is that you will be able to avoid the aroma that can seep its way from the canals during the heat of July and August.

Yet another plus, is that by coming during the winter you may be lucky enough to be in Venice during one of the rare snow storms that blanket the city with a powdery decoration, almost like fairy dust, turning an already gorgeous area into a magical one. All griping aside, even with the tourist hordes and rampant commercialism, Venice is still a vacationer's paradise and it is easy to see Walt's affection for it.

Getting Around Town
By Vaporetti – Water Buses

The least expensive way to travel around Venice and the most efficient is by vaporetti. If you're staying longer than a week you may want to invest in a Carta Venezia pass, which enables you to take the *vaporetti* for one-third the regular fare. You can buy these at most tobacconists. Some of the *vaporetti* may be quite crowded so be prepared to act like a sardine during the morning and evening rush hour.

The main lines are as follows:

• **Accelerato No. 1** – Stops at every landing spot on the **Grand Canal**.

Obviously this one takes a little time and is a great way to see the whole canal.

• **Diretto No**. **82** – Fastest way to get from the **train station** and **Piazzale Roma** to **Rialto, Accademia**, and **San Marco** stops. Often very crowded and as their name suggests, *diretto* indicates a direct trip.

• **Diretto No**. **4** – Summer time *vaporetto* that basically follows the same path as the No. 1.

• **Motoscafo No**. **52** – The circle line that travels in both directions around the periphery of Venice and to the smaller islands around Venice, **Isola San Michele** and **Murano** (see *Excursions & Day Trips* section of this chapter for more details). A great ride in and of itself for you to see the peripheral areas of Venice from the water.

• **Vaporetto No**. **12** – Goes to **Murano, Burano**, and **Torcello**, all smaller islands around Venice (see *Excursions & Day Trips* section of this chapter for more details); departs from the **Fondamenta Nuove** stop just across from the Isola San Michele.

• **Vaporetti 6** – Goes to the resort of **Lido** and leaves from the **Riva Degli Schiavoni** stop to the east of Piazza San Marco.

By Traghetti – Gondola Ferries

At many points along the Grand Canal, basically near many of the regular *vaporetti* stops, you can cross by using the inexpensive public gondola ferries called traghetti that are rowed by pairs of gondoliers. The times vary for each departure based on whether the gondoliers have enough passengers. In these boats there is standing room only, which causes you to unlearn everything you've ever been taught about boat etiquette. You'll be packed in with crowds of locals, workmen, business people with their briefcases, art students, and others while you're poled along.

By Gondola

Gondolas are privately operated boats operated by professional gondoliers. This is the most delightful way to admire Venice at a leisurely pace. Granted they are expensive (a half hour ride costs over $50) but they're still fun and romantic if you're so inclined. There are only a little over 400 licensed gondoliers in Venice and the licenses, though theoretically open to everyone, are in practice restricted to the sons (not the daughters) of gondoliers.

If you are going to hire a gondola, take one with a specific destination in mind, like going to a specific restaurant or specific site instead of just asking the gondolier to pole you around for a while. Even though gondoliers are trained to take you to the prettiest places for your money, by bringing you to a specific destination you and gondolier become part of the Venice of old, because in the not so distant past gondolas were the main form of transportation for all the elite Venetians when they went out to dinner or the opera.

You can also hire a gondola for *serenate* (group rides in which the gondolas feature an accordionist and a singer) at night. These rides can be very expensive, but if it's your honeymoon or a special occasion, who cares?

Remember to bargain with the gondolier for each ride, whether it's a regular trip or a *serenate*. Their prices are not set in stone and it is the accepted custom to bargain.

By Water Taxi

There are plenty of water taxis, but they too are extremely expensive. If you don't want to be part of the maddening crowds, however, this is the quickest way to get from point A to point B. If you want to get picked up at a certain place at a certain time, call *041/523-2326 or 522-2303.*

By Foot

Let's be serious. Venice is comparable in size to New York City's Central Park, so it's possible for you to walk anywhere you want, as long as you're not in a hurry or worried about getting lost. I've done that plenty of times when I forgot to bring my map with me, but I usually found some out-of-the way shop or café to enjoy on my journeys.

The true beauty of this city is the absence of cars or buses. The streets are designed for walking, the way they should be. This fact alone makes life in Venice seem calmer and more serene than anywhere else. Many Venetians are proud of the fact that throughout their entire lives they have never owned an automobile. Not having owned one for more than a decade now, I can understand their pride.

Buy a Map in Venice

In Venice you need a map. This city is one big interconnecting alleyway with little to no address organization or structure. Sometimes street names are repeated in different districts of Venice and many times there are no street signs on the walls. Venice is confusing to get around and the only way I was able to before I figured out the city was to buy a map. I recommend the **F.M.B. Piante di Citta** with its 'less than attractive' orange/yellow cover for E4 which you can buy at any giornalaio (newsstand).

Three Day Itinerary In & Around Venice

If you want to stay in an inexpensive quality hotel, deep in the heart of the Venice where the locals live, away from the hordes of tourists that descend on this city in the summer, stay at the **Campiello**. Located near the wonderful

Campo Santa Margherita, which comes alive each day with the locals going about their daily lives, it is also situated on a canal where barges serve as a daily produce market.

DAY ONE
Morning

To get started, have a seat at any of the cafés that are in the **Campo Santa Margherita** for a coffee and light breakfast. Spend some time savoring the sights and sounds of the real Venice. Later compare the different pace here to what you experience in the tourist sections.

After breakfast, go to the newsstand in the Campo and buy a map of Venice. You are going to need it. Before starting out, map out your route. Then begin walking through the maze of the streets and make your way to **Piazza San Marco**.

Take your time. Much of the beauty of Venice is simply wandering through its ancient lanes and alleys. By the time you arrive in the square it will probably be around lunch time.

Lunch

For lunch we can go one of two different directions. Option one is to spend a lot of money for little more than the ambiance of sitting at one of the cafés in the Piazza San Marco and admiring the beauty of the surrounding buildings. The most famous spot is definitely **Café Quadri**. This is a rite of passage in Venice, so you might want to do it now.

If you want a truly authentic Venetian experience without as much of a dent put into your wallet, go behind the left side of the church of San Marco and follow the road to **Alla Rivetta**, at Ponte S Provolo. At the first bridge look to your right and admire the **Bridge of Sighs** over the canal a little further down. This restaurant is a gondolier hangout when they are not out ferrying tourists around the canals, and the food and ambiance is great.

Afternoon

After lunch, take the time to look through the **Church of San Marco** and the **Palazzo Ducale**. Then admire the **Bell Tower** and the **Clock Tower** in the piazza. This should take all afternoon. On the way back to your hotel, take a different route. Stop in any church or public building you pass. They are all magnificent. Remember to take your time.

Dinner

For dinner we have two options. If you want to spend the money and savor an incredibly romantic environment go to the terrace restaurant in the world-famous hotel **Danielle**. You will have great views and wonderful food, but it will be super-expensive. If you want good views at better prices and a slightly less romantic setting, try the **Ristorante Al Buso** at Ponte di Rialto. Located right beside the **Rialto** bridge down on the water by the Grand Canal. It only has a few tables set outside for the great canal-side views, but it's worth the wait.

On the way back to your hotel stop in the **Campo San Polo** for an after-dinner drink of dessert and savor the life of another truly authentic local piazza.

DAY TWO
Morning

We will start off this by going back to the Rialto bridge area where you had dinner last night. Right on the other side from where your restaurant was last night is the most wonderful daily market (except Sundays) of fruit, vegetable and fish. Here you can grab some fruit to eat for breakfast, stop in a café for some coffee and wander through the stalls where all of Venice's housewives and restaurants buy their food for the day. You will have some great photo opportunities, sometimes of huge swordfish being dissected, so don't forget your camera.

When done with the market, go back to the Rialto bridge for some more shopping and more great picture taking.

Lunch

Make your way across a large portion of Venice either on foot or by vaporetto to **Pizzeria alle Zattere**, *Zattere ai Gesuati 795*. Why am I making you walk so much? Because this is the best way to get to know Venice. Anyway, this a favorite local pizzeria near the Accademia, known not only for its many varieties of pizza but also for the excellent view of Guidecca island from the pizzeria's tables on the Zattere's floating rafts.

Afternoon

After lunch make you way to the famous museum **Accademia**, *Campo della Carita, Dorsoduro*. Here you will find five hundred years of unequaled Venetian art on display. You can easily spend an entire afternoon in here. If you wish to, please do so, but if you want a change of pace try the **Guggenheim Museum** not far away (*Calle Cristoforo, Dorsoduro*). The museum boasts a magnificent 20th century art collection developed by the intriguing American heiress and art aficionado Peggy Guggenheim. There are works by Dali, Chagall, Klee, Moore, Picasso, Pollock and many others. The place to come if modern art is your thing.

Dinner

For dinner we are going back to the *pescheria* fish market area. Huddled in the corner of this vast market, and located near the old post office, is the

Poste Vecchie. To get here, follow a private wooden bridge from the market that leads to this old converted inn with its low ceilings and dark wooden beams. This restaurant is known for its perfectly prepared fish, especially the grilled variety, and its bountiful *antipasto* table. In the summer you can dine in their splendidly relaxing garden that has vines and leaves hanging overhead.

DAY THREE
Morning
After a simple breakfast either at the hotel or at a café, we are going to take a vaporetto ride on the **Accelerato No. 1** around the entire Grand Canal. This water bus stops at all the landings on the Canal – the perfect way to get a great overview of the city.

Lunch
For lunch, get off the vaporetto at the Riva di Biasio landing and make your way to the Campo San Giacomo del'Orio and La Zucca. Here you'll find exquisite food in a local restaurant near a beautiful piazza, completely off the beaten path. There is no better way to see how the real Venetians live.

Afternoon & Evening
After lunch we are going on more vaporetto rides. I hope you don't get sea sick. We'll start off by making our way to the *vaporetto* stop Fondamenta Nuove, where we are going to catch the *vaporetto* No. 12 and travel to the islands of **Murano**, **Burano** and **Torcello**.

On the island of **Murano**, we are going to go to one of the glass factories and see how the intricate glass pieces are created. The best one to try is **Mazzega SRL**, located at the base of the Ponte Longa, where you can occasionally find young boys flinging themselves into the canal below. After the factory tour wander around and enjoy the peace and tranquillity of this tiny island.

On the island of **Burano**, the brightly colored houses here give it the air of an Italian opera set – a perfect background for some excellent photographs. Stop here for a brief walking tour and some gelato at any of the many little cafés. Spend as much time as necessary savoring the incredible back drop of the colorful homes.

On the island of **Torcello**, once a flourishing center of commerce and culture whose greatness dimmed as that of Venice grew, Torcello is now just a solitary village on a lonely island. Today it is remembered for the fact that Hemingway loved its peace and tranquillity so much. Let's stop here for dinner at either the **Locanda Cipriani** or the **Osteria Al Ponte del Diavolo**. Both places are rather expensive but well worth it because of the great food and ambiance.

Venice Website

For up to date information about events, weather or whatever, in Venice make sure you check out the *www.ciaovenezia.com* website. A must visit site if you are on your way to the most romantic city in the world.

Don't miss the last *vaporetto* back. If you do you'll have to pay an arm and a leg to one of the private water taxis.

Evening

To end your stay in Venice, stop back at the **Piazza San Marco**, have a drink or dessert at one of their outside cafés and soak up the beauty and wonder that is Venice.

Where To Stay

If you are unable to make suitable reservations prior to arriving in Venice, you should stop by the train station and consult with their friendly, multi-lingual hotel finders service, *Santa Lucia Train Station, Tel. 041/715-016.* They'll book you a room based on your specifications: all you need to tell them is what price you want to pay and what types of amenities you want (i.e. private bath, TV in room, etc.) and they will find hotels that match your needs if they can. During the summer high season you may not have much of a choice, but at least you'll get a room. In the same office space, but not the same entrance is the general information office for tourists *(Tel. 041/522-6356)*, where you can get maps, directions, and all sorts of necessary information if you're in a bind.

Venice is very popular as a tourist destination, so if you have a specific hotel in mind, please reserve at least six months or more in advance. But even if you cannot get your first choice, there is no hotel in Venice that is in a bad location. Everywhere is wonderful in this fairy tale city.

San Marco

Directly in the center of Venice, San Marco is the commercial and tourist center of the city. Most people who visit Venice hardly ever leave this section and for good reason. If you only have a little time, even the most seasoned travelers will be able to find everything they desire right here. And at the center of this stage is the Piazza San Marco where people vie with pigeons for space.

The most frequently followed path in this section of Venice is from this piazza along the busy main tourist shopping streets to the Rialto Bridge. You

List of Venice Hotels by Map

Map A – see pages 468-469
1. Ala
2. Bel Sito
3. Bonvecchiati
4. Concordia
5. Do Pozzi
6. Flora
7. Gallini
8. Gritti Palace
9. Kette
10. Santa Marina
11. Santo Stefano
12. Campiello
13. Danieli
14. Gabrielli Sandwirth
17. Locanda Sturion
25. Abbazia
27. Bernardi-Semenzato

Map B – see pages 476-477
1. Ala
2. Bel Sito
8. Gritti Palace
11. Santo Stefano
15. Al Sole
16. Falier
17. Locanda Sturion
18. San Cassiano
19. Agli Alboreti
20. Antico Capon
21. Calcina
23. Pensione Seguso
24. Villa Maravege
26. Amadeus
28. Continental

Map C – see page 486
26. Amadeus
28. Continental

Map D – see page 495
19. Agli Alboreti
21. Calcina
22. Cipriani
23. Pensione Seguso
65. San Trovaso

can find everything you'll need right here: history, architecture, restaurants, cafés, shops, sights, fun, and many people.

For each hotel below, I've listed the *vaporetto* stop and map reference.

1. ALA, *Campo Santa Maria dei Giglio 2494, Venezia. Tel. 041/520-5333, Fax 041/520-3690. E-mail: info@hotelala.it. Web: www.hotelala.it. American Express, Diners Club, Mastercard and Visa accepted. 85 rooms all with bath. Single E100-150; Double E160-240. Breakfast included. Vaporetto Stop – Santa Maria del Giglio. Maps – A & B.* ***

This hotel's location is exclusive, and with its own dock on the adjacent canal and an elegant interior decor, the entire establishment is quite good. The rooms are large with TVs, air conditioning, mini-bars, and direct dial phones; and the bathrooms are as modern as you'll find anywhere and even have their own phones. The setting along the canal is what makes this hotel so beautiful and romantic, as well as a good deal for its location. You'll especially enjoy the beautiful room along the canal where you are served your breakfast. They also have daily Italian and foreign newspapers available for your perusal. A good place to stay while in Venice.

2. BEL SITO, *Campo Santa Maria del Giglio 2517, Venezia. Tel. 041/522-3365, Fax 041/520-4083. E-mail: hbelsito@mbox.vol.it. American Express, Diners Club, Mastercard and Visa accepted. 38 rooms, 34 with bath. Single E80-120; Double E120-170. Vaporetto Stop – Santa Maria del Giglio. Maps – A & B.* ***

Handsomely furnished, centrally located, but still well-situated slightly off the beaten path so you can get away from the crowds. Professionally managed with impeccable service. The hotel has a quiet micro outdoor café to enjoy at breakfast and to relax at during the day. The rooms are a little on the small side and all but 15 of them overlook the intimate church of Santa Maria del Giglia in the local piazza. Furnished in antique Venetian style, despite the refinement the hotel is pet friendly.

3. BONVECCHIATI, *Piazza S. Marco 4488, 30124 Venezia. Tel. 041/528-5017, Fax 041/528-5230. E-mail: bonvecchiati@italyhotel.com. Web: www.holidaycityeurope.com/bonvecchiati-venice/index.htm. American Express, Diners Club, Mastercard and Visa accepted. 86 rooms, 80 with bath. Single E145-225; Double E130-290. Vaporetto Stop – San Marco. Map – A.* ***

An elegantly refined hotel in a wonderfully central location with ideal for access to everything. They have their own canal access for direct arrival by water taxi and gondolas. A nice touch. Try to get a room facing the canal. It makes for a peaceful stay. They also have 24-hour concierge service, room service, direct dial telephone, minibar, satellite color TV and laundry service. You also receive special discount at Do Forni restaurant on St. Mark's Square. The rooms are all furnished in a unique color scheme and are large and comfortable.

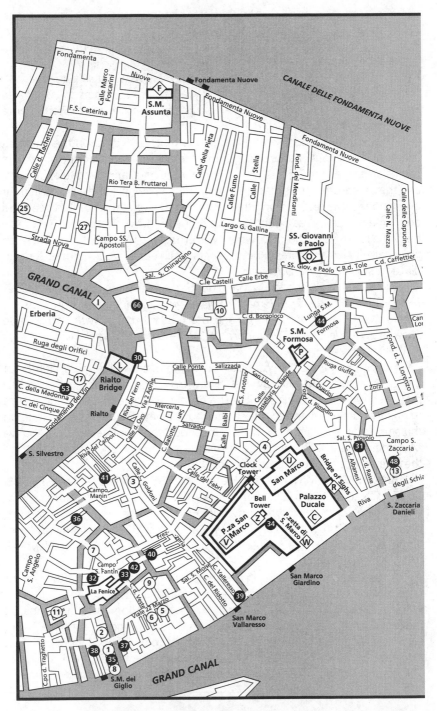

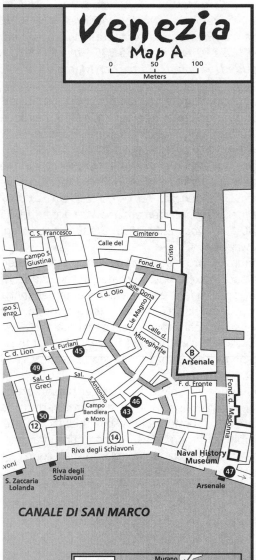

Venezia
Map A

0   50   100

Meters

Hotels ○

1. Ala
2. Bel Sito
3. Bovecchiati
4. Concordia
5. Do Pozzi
6. Flora
7. Gallini
8. Gritti Palace
9. Kette
10. Santa Marina
11. Santo Stefano
12. Campiello
13. Danieli
14. Gabrielli Sandwirth
17. Locanda Sturion
25. Abbazzia
27. Bernardi-Semenzato

Restaurants ●

30. Al Buso
31. Alla Rivetta
32. Al Teatro
33. Antico Martini
34. Cafe Quadri
35. Club del Doge
36. Da Arturo
37. Da Raffaele
38. Giglio
39. Harry's Bar
40. La Colomba
41. Leon Bianco
42. Vino Vino
43. Al Covo
44. Al Mascaron
45. Archimboldo
46. Corte Sconta
47. Da Franz
48. Danieli Terrace
49. Da Remigio
50. Malamocco
53. Alla Madonna
66. Fiaschetteria Toscana

Sights ◇

B. Arsenale
C. Palazzo Ducale
F. Santa Maria Assunta
I. Grand Canal
L. Rialto Bridge
O. Santi Giovanni e Paolo
P. Santa Maria Formosa
R. The Bridge of Sighs
U. Basilica di San Marco
V. Piazza San Marco
W. Piazzetta di San Marco
X. Clock Tower
z. Bell Tower

4. **CONCORDIA**, *Calle Larga San Marco 367, Venezia. Tel. 041/520-6866, Fax 041/520-6775. E-mail: VeniceItaly@hotelconcordia.com. Web: www.hotelconcordia.com. American Express, Mastercard and Visa accepted. 57 rooms all with bath. Single E105-210; Double E155-345. Suite E175-380. Abundant buffet breakfast included. Vaporetto Stop – San Marco. Map – A.* ****

The hotel has 20 rooms that overlook the Piazzetta dei Leoni which is part of the Piazza San Marco. Decor is a mixture of modern and elegant antique with a yellow color scheme throughout. The rooms are all wonderfully attractive, especially the ones with a view over the piazzetta. If you to stay in the most exclusive area in Venice and don't mind a little crowd noise in the evenings, you will like this place. A truly refined hotel in the perfect location.

5. **DO POZZI**, *Via XXII Marzo 2373, Venezia. Tel. 041/520-7855, Fax 041/522-9413. American Express, Diners Club, Mastercard and Visa accepted. 35 rooms all with bath. Single E80-110; Double 115-150. Breakfast included. Vaporetto Stop – San Marco. Map – A.* ***

Don't get put off by the samurai sword in a display case right as you enter. This is actually a very peaceful and relaxing hotel. Located in the middle of everything but set off on its own small side street. They have a garden in the tiny piazza where you can enjoy your breakfast or drinks in the afternoon. You also have air conditioning, phones, mini-bars, room service for breakfast, TVs, and a laundry service, everything a first class hotel can give you – but these aren't first class prices. The reason for that is that all the rooms are small and the bathrooms minuscule.

You can also get lunch or dinner for only E15 more per person at the nearby restaurant Da Raphaele, which is a steal. The rooms are spartan and clean with little ambiance, but are quite comfortable despite their lack of size. The ambiance was left in the lobby common areas. A good price in a great location. Hint: even if you don't stay here, come and relax in their courtyard during the day. It's a nice respite from the thundering herds.

6. **FLORA**, *Calle Larga XXII Marzo 2283A, Venezia. Tel. 041/520-5844, Fax 041/522-8217. E-mail: info@hotelflora.it. Web: hotelflora.it. All credit cards accepted. 44 rooms, 43 with bath. Single E150; Double E200. Breakfast included. Closed November through January. Vaporetto Stop – San Marco. Map – A.* ***

The quaint garden setting, where breakfast and afternoon drinks are served in the summer, is dominated by an old well and old pieces of statuary. This area, the breakfast room service, and the general ambiance lend an old fashioned sense of hospitality to this hotel. A great place in the thick of things where you can still feel you've gotten away from it all. To get to the rooms, some of which are very small, you go up a painted stairway that is something to behold. As a three star they have minibars, phones, and televisions in the rooms. The best rooms are those that overlook the serene garden.

7. GALLINI, *Calle della Verona 3673, Venezia. Tel. 041/520-4515, Fax 520-9103. Mastercard and Visa accepted. 50 rooms, 35 with bath. Single without bath E50-70; Single E70-100; Double without bath E60-90; Double E90-130. Breakfast included. Closed November 15 through March 1. Vaporetto Stop – San Marco. Map – A.* **

The hotel has been in the owner's family for over 50 years, and they make sure everything is as perfect as it can be. There's not much they can do since the hotel has little charm in and of itself; but even so the place is immaculately clean and your stay here will be in a perfect location for a good price, especially in the low season, which is really the best time to come to Venice. The only real amenities in the rooms are A/C. And there is a small bar in the common area in which to relax. An adequate two star.

Eight of the Best Hotels in Venice

One star

20. ANTICO CAPON, *Campo Santa Margherita 3004B, Venezia. Tel. 041/528-5292.*

Two star

12. CAMPIELLO, *Campiello del Vin 4647, Venezia. Tel. 041/520-5764, Fax 041/520-5798.*

23. PENSIONE SEGUSO, *Zattere dei Gesuati 779, Venezia. Tel. 041/528-6858, Fax 041/522-2340.*

Three star

6. FLORA, *Calle Larga 22 Marzo 2283A, Venezia. Tel. 041/520-5844, Fax 041/522-8217.*

11. SANTO STEFANO, *Campo Santo Stefano 2957, Venezia. Tel. 041/520-0166, Fax 041/522-4460.*

24. VILLA MARAVEGIE, *Fondamenta Bollani/Maravegie 1058, Venezia. Tel. 041/521-0188, Fax 041/523-9152.*

Four star

22. CIPRIANI, *Fondamenta San Giovanni 10, La Guidecca, Venezia. Tel. 041/520-7744, Fax 041/520-3930.*

Five star

13. DANIELI HOTEL, *Riva degli Schiavoni 4196, Venezia. Tel. 041/522-6480, Fax 041/520-0208.*

8. **GRITTI PALACE**, *Campo Santa Maria del Giglio, Venezia. Tel. 041/ 794-611, Fax 041/520-0942. American Express, Diners Club, Mastercard and Visa accepted. 96 rooms all with bath. Single E287-330; Double E440-650. Vaporetto Stop – Santa Maria del Giglio. Maps – A & B.* *****

Definitely a top-notch, high-class, deluxe hotel, with lots of local charm. Situated directly on the Grand Canal this early 16th century palace of the Doge Gritti is now one of the world's most celebrated hotels. Here you are treated like royalty, since many of their guests actually are. This *palazzo* that still looks and feels like a private residence, where you'll find Murano chandeliers everywhere as well as Burano lace table linens. There's really no words to describe the splendor of this place. Enjoy a night here if you're not worried about spending the equivalent of a monthly car or mortgage payment. Or if you only want to feel like royalty for a little while, simply have a drink at their bar on the canal or enjoy a fine dinner at their lovely adjacent terrace restaurant. If you want romance, this is one place for it in Venice. You also have access to a swimming pool, tennis courts and the beach at their own facility on the island of Lido.

9. **KETTE**, *Piscine San Moise 2053, Venezia. Tel. 041/520-7766, Fax 041/ 522-8964. American Express, Diners Club, Mastercard and Visa accepted. 69 rooms, all with bath. Single E80-125; Double E115-175. Breakfast included. Vaporetto Stop – Santa Maria del Giglio. Map – A.* ***

If you want luxury for less, this is the place to stay. You have air conditioning, satellite TV, mini-bars, a direct dial phone in the room, a picturesque landing on the canal for gondolas and water taxis, and friendly and efficient service like you'd expect in North America. It's also somewhat off the beaten path so you can enjoy a peaceful night's rest. The public area is filled with comfortable chairs and international magazines where you can relax outside of the comfort of your room, get a little down time or mingle with the other guests. The rooms are all tastefully decorated, and each has different furnishings. Unfortunately, some rooms face onto close walls from adjacent buildings, but except for this the place is great. Near enough to everything but still far enough away. They are also pet friendly and have babysitting service.

10. **SANTA MARINA**, *Campo Santa Marina 6068, Venezia. Tel. 041/ 523-9202, Fax 041/520-0907. E-mail: info@hotelsantamarina.it. Web: www.hotelsantamarina.it. 19 rooms all with bath. Single E125-200; Double E170-250. Vaporetto Stop – Rialto. Map – A.* ***

Located in a small square, on three floors of an old *palazzo*, you get a combination of local flavor and tourist amenities in this location. Here you're in the middle of everything tourists want to see, but still far enough away to be a part of the true life of Venice. The staff is amazingly helpful and your room, though small, is comfortable and quiet. The first floor's color scheme is blue, the second beige, and the third red. There's a verandah that overlooks the Campo with chairs and tables where you can read and relax. Each room is decorated in its own style, which makes every stay here different. Many of the rooms overlook the piazza, which is a perfect situation for people watching. Only open for a few years, the Santa Marina has every modern convenience and is a wonderful place to stay. They are pet friendly and also offer babysitting services.

11. SANTO STEFANO, *Campo Santo Stefano 2957, Venezia. Tel. 041/ 520-0166, Fax 041/522-4460. Mastercard and Visa accepted. 11 rooms and with bath. Single E110-145; Double E145-175. Breakfast included. Vaporetto Stop – SM del Giglio. Maps – A & B.* ***

This charming and ambiant hotel is located on the colorful local Campo Santa Stefano close to the Accademia and Piazza San Marco. A great place to stay in Venice. Many rooms have a view onto the square, but if you're a light sleeper don't ask for one of these since it can get a little noisy at night. The *Campi* in Venice are where the locals' gather in the evenings, which helps to make your stay more colorful. There is also a charming little garden patio for unwinding after a day of being a tourist.

The service is professional and courteous. The rooms are a little on the small side but are comfortable and well furnished with antiques and glassware from Murano. There are TVs in every room, as well as phones, hairdryers, and air conditioning available. The hotel is also pet friendly and has babysitting service.

Castello

This part of town offers the perfect chance to escape from the tourist hordes and discover the real Venice. There are plenty of quiet residential neighborhoods here, where old Italian ladies chat with each other from windows overhead while putting out their laundry to dry. If you're looking to shop this isn't the section of Venice for you, but there are some excellent and relatively inexpensive restaurants. Avoid the Riva degli Schiavoni to find the best prices for restaurants.

Castello is home to the **Arsenale** (where many of Venice's boats have been made) and the **Giardini Publici** (Public Gardens), which are a great place to come and relax.

12. CAMPIELLO, *Campiello del Vin 4647, Venezia. Tel. 041/520-5764, Fax 041/520-5798. American Express, Diners Club, Mastercard and Visa accepted. 16 rooms all with bath. Single E45-80; Double E80-130. Vaporetto Stop – San Zaccaria. Map – A.* **

A friendly, quiet, and clean hotel located just behind the Riva degli Schiavoni. Consider this hotel if you like luxury on a budget. It is inexpensive, near everything, yet still on a quiet little canal. The rooms are clean and quiet and the assistance you get from the owners is stupendous. A good place for a budget traveler with friendly owners and attentive service.

13. **DANIELI**, *Riva degli Schiavoni 4196, Venezia. Tel. 041/522-6480, Fax 041/520-0208. Email: reso72danieli@ittsheraton.com. American Express, Diners Club, Mastercard and Visa accepted. 235 rooms all with bath. Single E235-247; Double E365-435. Breakfast E33. Vaporetto Stop – San Zaccaria. Map – A.* *****

First opened in 1882 with only 16 rooms, the Danieli has expanded to encompass many surrounding buildings. The magnificent lobby, which is built around a Gothic courtyard, with its intertwining staircases and columns, is truly spectacular. You feel as if you're in an ancient medieval castle. The largest and possibly best hotel in Venice as well as the most romantic. They also have access to a pool, tennis courts and private beach on Lido. On top of all that, the perfect place for any meal in all of Venice is their rooftop dining room which has an exquisite view of the Lagoon. If you can't afford to stay here, at least romance yourselves with a dinner or light lunch. You will not be disappointed with either the restaurant or the hotel.

14. **GABRIELLI SANDWIRTH**, *Riva degli Schiavoni 4110, Venezia. Tel. 041/523-1580, Fax 041/520-9455. American Express, Diners Club, Mastercard and Visa accepted. 100 rooms all with bath. Single E80-190; Double E130-300. Closed mid-November to mid-March. Breakfast included. Vaporetto Stop – San Zaccaria. Map – A.* ****

Located in a Gothic palace built in the 13th century, with a beautiful rose garden in its center where you can take a drink from the bar, this is a wonderful place to stay. You can also roast in the sun on the roof terrace overlooking the lagoon, also with its own bar. One of the best, if not the best views in all of Venice. This is one place to come for luxury on the lagoon. The best rooms overlook the water. You don't have to worry about noise, since this is a bit off the main tourist track. All the rooms are tastefully decorated with antiques, chandeliers, and the ever-present roses. A less expensive option for luxury travel. One small minus is that the bathrooms, though clean and accommodating, have not been modernized for some time and are somewhat small. But that also adds to the charm.

Santa Croce & San Polo

For purposes of clarity we have combined these two geographically connected sections of Venice into one. Still considered to be "the other side of the canal," even though the Rialto bridge was built back in 1588 to connect these two sections with the more influential San Marco. Beyond the area around the Rialto, you can find small little pizzerias that serve great good for an excellent price.

There are also plenty of tiny artisan's shops along with your regular touristy stores. **Campo San Polo** is the second largest in Venice and is a center for social life in these two neighborhoods. This is a great area just to roam through the back streets and discover the secrets of Venice.

15. AL SOLE, *Santa Croce 136. Tel. 041/523-2144, Fax 041/719-061. 80 rooms all with bath. All Credit cards accepted. Single E80-120; Double E130-195. Breakfast included. Vaporetto Stop – Ferrovia Bar Roma or San Toma. Map – B.* ***

A little off the beaten path, in one of the older sections of Venice near the church of Tolentini, this is a quaint and comfortable three star at good prices. Situated in the Palazzo Marcello built in the 14th century, the hotel is filled with antiques and features marble columns as a backdrop. The entrance hall, which is just off the breakfast room where you receive an abundant buffet each morning, is large and luminous. The rooms and accompanying bathrooms are different sizes, so when reserving make sure you request one of the larger ones. They all come with every conceivable amenity for three stars such as TV, radio, air conditioning, hair dryers, etc. In the off-season you can get some great discounts but you need to request a discount to receive it.

16. FALIER, *Salizzada San Pantalon 130, Venezia. Tel. 041/522-8882, Fax 041/520-6554. E-mail: falier@italyhotel.com. Mastercard and Visa accepted. 19 rooms all with bath. Single E50-100; Double E70-120. Breakfast included. Vaporetto Stop – San Toma. Map – B.* **

Near the Campo dei Frari and the Frari church, this hotel has good prices and accommodations for a two star. The rooms are furnished with modern amenities and have plenty of space for you, and for your clothes in the armoires. One of the best aspects of the hotel is that the area is not touristy. Instead it is filled with real Venetian shops, cafés, and restaurants that make you feel like you are part of the life here. The wood beamed breakfast room is quite quaint as is the checkerboard entryway. The hotel is off the beaten path and as such is tough to find, but that adds to the charm.

17. LOCANDA STURION, *San Polo 679. Tel. 041/523-6243, Fax 041/522-8378. E-mail: sturion@tin.it. 11 rooms all with bath. Single E50-110; Double E110-180. All credit cards accepted. Breakfast included. Vaporetto Stop – Rialto. Maps – A&B.* ***

One of the wonderful little 'Family Hotels' that are all over Italy. Run by the family that owns the hotel, this little place is quaint, comfortable and accommodating – not to mention ideally located. This place has been in business since the 13th century and is only a few paces from the Rialto bridge and the morning fruit, vegetable and fish market (a must-see while in Venice). Two rooms face out onto the Grand Canal, so if you want the perfect romantic setting for your vacation make sure you request one of these two. The rooms and bathrooms are all different sizes but come with every possible three star amenity: TV, A/C, radio, hair dryer, etc. The breakfast room looks out over the Grand Canal and there is also a small library filled with books about Venice.

Hotels ○
1. Ala
2. Bel Sito
7. Gallini
8. Gritti Palace
11. Santo Stefano
15. Al Sole
16. Falier
17. Locanda Sturion
18. San Cassiano
19. Agli Alboretti
20. Antico Capon
21. Calcina
23. Pensione Seguso
24. Villa Maravegie
26. Amadeus
28. Continental

Restaurants ●
29. Al Bacareto
32. Al Teatro
35. Club del Doge
36. Da Arturo
38. Giglio
41. Leon Bianco
51. Ae Oche
52. Al Giardinetto
53. Alla Madonna
54. Antico Capon
55. Da Fiore
56. Da Ignazio
57. La Zucca
58. Poste Vecchie
59. San Toma
60. Al Gondolieri
61. Alle Zattere
65. San Trovaso

Nightlife ○
69. The Green Pub
70. Margaret DuChamp
71. El Souk

Sights ◇
A. Accademia
D. Frari
E. Santa Maria del Rosario
I. Grand Canal
L. Rialto Bridge
Q. Guggenheim Museum
S. Ponte del Accademia
T. Ponte degli Scalzi

Venezia
Map B

0   50   100
Meters

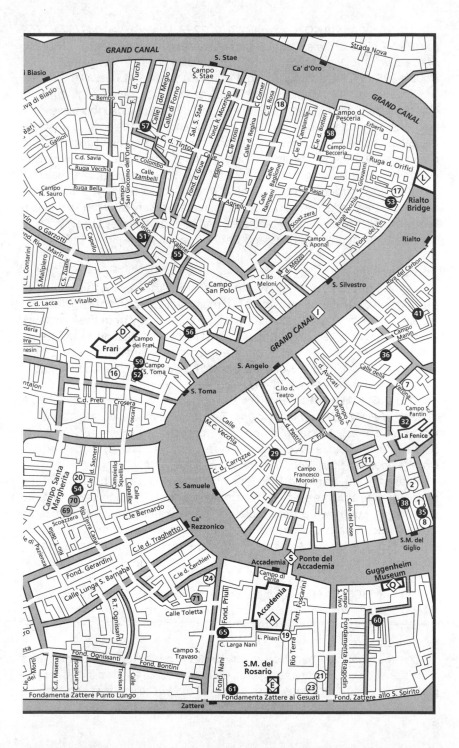

18. SAN CASSIANO, *Calle della Rosa 2232, Venezia. Tel. 041/524-1768 Fax 041/721-033. E-mail: sancassiano@sancassiano.it. American Express, Mastercard and Visa accepted. 35 rooms all with bath. Single E65-135; Double E95-185. Breakfast included. Vaporetto Stop – San Stae. Map – B.* ***

Located in a 16th century Gothic *palazzo* on the Grand Canal, it has its own dock from which you can arrive or depart by water taxi. At this same dock area they have a few tables where you can sit and enjoy the passing boats on the canal and feel completely free of the thundering herds of tourists. The rooms are all elegantly furnished with antiques, and there are chandeliers everywhere. The building is suitably quaint and romantic, except for the stark white breakfast room. The brightness does help to wake you up in the mornings. They have foreign newspapers available every morning so you can keep abreast of news at home. A quaint and comfortable place to stay. Try to get one of the rooms on the Grand Canal. The vista is inspiring.

Dorsoduro

If you want to try and get away from it all while in Venice, this section of the city is great. There are few stores but many real Venetian sights. You'll find artisans, locals buying fruit from a boat that comes daily from the mainland, as well as ritzy hotels and museums. The best place in this section is the Zattere, "rafts" that are home to a variety of different and excellent restaurants. Eating on the water, looking out over the island of La Guidecca, you will be amazed at the beautiful sunsets over the island.

19. AGLI ALBORETI, *Rio Terra Antonia Foscarini, Accademia 884, Venezia. Tel. 041/523-0058, Fax 041/521-0128. E-mail: alboretti@gpnet.it. American Express, Mastercard and Visa accepted. 20 rooms all with bath. Single E72-80; Double E100-125. Breakfast included. Lunch or dinner E22 extra. Vaporetto Stop – Accademia. Maps – B&D.* **

I love the little garden off the lobby where you can have breakfast in the mornings or relax in the evenings for dinner or drinks. The rooms are not quite so spacious, but they're comfortable and come with A/C and heat. Located in the shadows of the Accademia, you are a bridge away from all the major sights, but still have the comfort of a tranquil setting. A comfortable, accommodating and relatively inexpensive two star hotel. One of the best budget places to stay in Venice.

20. ANTICO CAPON, *Campo Santa Margherita 3004B, Venezia. Tel. 041/528-5292. No credit cards accepted. 7 rooms, 6 with bath. Single without bath E25-35; Single E30-65; Double E35-65. Vaporetto Stop – Ca' Rezzonico. Map – B.* *

A super deal in the best local area in Venice. The Campo Santa Margherita and its environs have everything you'll need to feel like a native in this tourist-plagued city. Most mornings there is a small market selling fruit, vegetables, and fresh fish in the piazza. You'll also find places for pizza, pastries, a supermarket, an Irish Pub, a laundry, and more. The hotel is directly in the middle of all this Venetian life, and three of the rooms face this hustle and bustle while the other four face the uninspiring rear. The rooms are large but the bathrooms are quite small. In fact the shower is located above the toilet.

If you've been to Venice before and disliked the crowds, this is the place for you to stay. It is truly a respite from insanity. The perfect antidote for the crowds of Venice.

21. **CALCINA**, *Fondamenta Zattere dei Gesuati 780, Venezia. Tel. 041/ 520-6466, Fax 041/522-7045. American Express, Diners Club, Mastercard and Visa accepted. 30 rooms, 23 with bath. Single E55-E85; Double E95-150. Vaporetto Stop – Zattere. Maps – B&D.* ***

The hotel has views over the large canal in front, a side canal, and the boring rear. Try to get a great view in the front overlooking La Guidecca island because the sunsets are spectacular. They also have a floating terrace out front from which you can enjoy breakfast or an afternoon cocktail. The rooms are clean and comfortable without any true distinguishing feature, except for the tranquillity and calm. The only real amenities are televisions in the rooms and a babysitting service. A great location for joggers.

22. **CIPRIANI**, *Fondamenta San Giovanni 10, La Guidecca, Venezia. Tel. 041/520-7744, Fax 041/520-3930. E-mail: Cipriani@gpnet.it. American Express, Diners Club, Mastercard and Visa accepted. 98 rooms all with bath. Single E375-550; Double E500-800. Vaporetto Stop – Zitelle. Map – D.* ****

This exquisite hotel occupies three beautiful acres at the east end of La Isola del Guidecca. There is a swimming pool, tennis court, saunas, jacuzzis, a private harbor for yachts, a private launch to ferry guests back and forth, an American-style bar with every drink imaginable, and two superb restaurants. Sixty rooms overlook the lagoon, while many others look out over the pool.

This hotel is probably as close to heaven on earth as you'll find in Venice, which makes it unusual for them to have been relegated to four-star status. But its ranking does nothing to alter the exquisite ambiance. There are even private suites that can be rented by the week which have their own butler assigned to them. If you can't afford to stay here, simply come out and enjoy a drink by the pool and see how the other half lives. You'll be amazed.

23. **PENSIONE SEGUSO**, *Zattere dei Gesuati 779, Venezia. Tel. 041/528-6858, Fax 041/522-2340. American Express, Mastercard and Visa accepted. 36 rooms, 18 with bath. Single E125-150; Double E175-200. Breakfast included. In high season your room comes with either lunch or dinner. Vaporetto Stop – Zattere. Maps – B&D.* **

Only a two star but what great atmosphere. The view of the Canal and Guidecca island is especially beautiful when the sun is setting. Recently upgraded, some of the rooms that overlook the now have their own baths. Prices are creeping up fast because this place is bucking for three star status. All the rooms are decorated in a simple fashion and the atmosphere is very much like a bed and breakfast. A great location for peace and quiet, and if you're a jogger you're in a perfect spot to churn out a few miles along the uncrowded canal in the morning. Slightly expensive for a two star, but the view is great as is the tranquil setting.

24. VILLA MARAVEGE, *Fondamenta Bollani 1058, Venezia. Tel. 041/ 521-0188, Fax 041/523-9152. American Express, Diners Club, Mastercard and Visa accepted. 27 rooms. Single E65-92; Double E100-170. Breakfast included. Vaporetto Stop – Accademia. Map – B.* ***

A perfect spot for post-touring relaxation. This impressive 17th century villa, formerly the Russian consulate, is surrounded by beautiful gardens and is just off the Grand Canal. There is a patio with chairs and tables and many plants on one side of the villa facing the Grand Canal.

The inside is simply beautiful with an upstairs tea room as well as a breakfast room that overlooks a flower garden. All the rooms are large, save number 8 which is a tiny single. Each are furnished in a different manner but are comfortable. You can get served in your room from the bar until 11:00pm and that service is stupendous. Basically this place is *meraviglia* (marvelous). Because of the location, ambiance and comfort, reservations are sometimes necessary over a year in advance!

Cannaregio

This section in the north of the main island is where the Jewish ghetto is located. This was the first place in Europe where Jews were isolated from the rest of the population This area was once a cannon foundry, which in Italian is *getto*. Ever since the Jews were forced into this area in Venice, their enclaves have been known by that name. Three of the synagogues in the main square of the tiny island (which comprised the first ghetto) are worth seeing. You'll find some of the tallest buildings in Venice, because once the Jewish population started to increase, the only place they could find more space was to build up.

Compared to the rest of Venice the place looks a little run down, but it is alive with local shoppers buying their supplies for the day, with beautiful side streets and canals that are located away from it all.

25. ABBAZIA, *Calle Priuli 68, Venezia. Tel. 041/717-333, Fax 041/717-949. American Express, Diners Club, Mastercard and Visa accepted. 31 rooms all with bath. Double E75-165. Breakfast included. Vaporetto Stop – Ca' d'Oro. Map – A.* ***

The hotel used to be part of a monastery until about 30 years ago when the monks sold this section of their property. Once inside, you'll be amazed at the beautiful but simple decor. I desperately want one of the wooden abbey benches that line the perimeter of the lobby. The space in the rooms is amazing compared to most other inexpensive hotels. This used to be more affordable but inflation and ego has increased the cost. The rooms come with A/C and TV and there is a wonderful little garden setting in which to relax.

26. AMADEUS, *Cannaregio 227. Tel. 041/715-300, Fax 041/524-0841. 63 rooms all with bath. Single E125-165; Double E150-235. All credit cards accepted. Breakfast included. Vaporetto Stop – Ferrovia Bar Roma. Maps – B & C.* ****

Located near the train station in an antique palazzo that has been completely restored for your comfort, this is an elegant and distinguished hotel. You'll find faux antique furniture, lace from Murano, and other elegant touches welcoming you. The front rooms are all done up with faux antique furniture while the ones in the rear that face the garden (quieter place to stay) have more modern furnishings. Some of those in the rear also have balconies with seating which creates a pleasant relaxing setting. Each type of room is clean and comfortable and comes with every modern convenience. The bathrooms are ample. Breakfast and lunch are served in the hotel's bright restaurant La Veranda, near the garden; dinner is served in their second restaurant La Papageno.

27. BERNARDI-SEMENZATO, *Calle del Oca, SS. Apostoli 4363-4366, Venezia. Tel. 041/522-7257. 041/522-242. Credit cards accepted. 15 rooms all with bath. Single E45-80; Double E60-95. Breakfast E4 extra. Vaporetto Stop – Ca' d'Oro. Map – A.* **

This place has changed quite a bit in the last few years. It's now a renovated, extremely clean, and wonderful little two star in a great location. They even have a roof terrace that overlooks Venetian rooftops for you sun worshippers, or those of you who wish to grab a quiet drink at the end of the evening. Getting up there is kind of rough, but it's still a roof garden. This used to be a budget traveler's paradise but now they're charging a little for about the same amenities. They've put in air conditioning and are in the process of installing TVs in hopes of getting upgraded to a three star by 2002. It used to be a better value but it is still a good place to stay.

28. CONTINENTAL, *Lista di Spagna 166. Tel. 041/715-122, Fax 041/524-2432. E-mail: Continental@ve.nettuno.it. 93 rooms all with bath. Single E60-150; Double E80-200. Breakfast included. All credit cards accepted. Vaporetto Stop – Ferrovia Bar Roma. Maps – B&C.* ***

Located near the train station, the old building housing the hotel is a tranquil and romantic setting, and their restaurant has a wonderful view of the Grand Canal. All the amenities you'd want to find in a three star. There is a large terrace that overlooks the nearby piazza, and a smaller one where you receive your breakfast in the summer months. The rooms are spacious but simply furnished, with some on the Grand Canal. Average prices in he high season but in the low season a really great price for the amenities.

Where To Eat

When applicable, each restaurant reviewed below also lists the closest water taxi *(vaporetto)* stop and map reference.

Venetian Cuisine

Venice is not generally known for its cuisine, especially reasonably priced dining, but they do know how to prepare great seafood dishes, which usually comes placed over a bed of *risotto* (a kind of rice). Even though pasta is not used as often here as in other regions of Italy, the Venetians make very good *spaghetti alla vongole* (clams) or *alla cozze* (mussels). Another favorite is the *zuppa di pesce* (fish soup), that mixes together every kind of fish that could be found at the market. You can't go wrong with fish here, except maybe on Sundays and Mondays when the *pescheria*, the seafood market at the Rialto, isn't open, which means your fish won't be fresh – but, (gasp) horrors, refrigerated for a day. Compared to the frozen seafood we have grown accustomed to, however, everything here is super fresh.

Eating most anywhere in Venice you won't get the bang for your buck that you'd get somewhere else in Italy, since many of the restaurants have been created to cater specifically to the tourists and as such they charge ridiculously high prices. Even the natives go to the mainland to find themselves a good inexpensive meal. But with that word of warning, you can also find some wonderful little pizzeria that caters to the local population and offers tasty and inexpensive offerings. I'll list some later in this section.

Suggested Venetian Cuisine

Traditional Venetian fare is listed below and every course is usually ordered at a full meal. Our constitution just isn't prepared for such mass consumption, however, so don't feel embarrassed if all you order is a pasta dish or an entrée with a salad or appetizer.

Antipasto - Appetizer
• **Insalata di mare** – Seafood salad of shrimp, squid, and clams in a zesty oil, vinegar and herbs sauce.
• **Antipasto misto di mare** – Seafood appetizers taken from a buffet

Primo Piatto - First Course
• **Zuppa di pesce** – Seafood soup with any fish you can imagine cooked into it.
• **Spaghetti alla vongole verace** –Spaghetti with an olive oil, garlic and clam sauce
• **Risotto con cozze** – A rice and mussels dish pumped with a variety of spices

List of Restaurants by Map

Secondo Piatto - Entrée
Pesce (Fish)
• **Grigliata mista di mare** – An assortment of grilled seafood based on whatever the seasonal catch is.
• **Bisato anguilla alla veneziana** – Eel cooked with onion, oil, vinegar, garlic and a little bay leaves
• **Coda di rospa** – Monkfish either broiled or grilled.
• **Fritto misto** – Assorted deep fried seafood

Carne (Meat)
• **Fegato alla veneziana** – Calf's liver sautéed with onions
• **Torresani** – Tiny pigeons served grilled on a spit

Formaggio (Cheese)
• **Asiago** – A dry, sharp cheese from the Veneto mainland

Regional Wines
You'll probably recognize many of the white wines from this region, especially the Friuli wines, such as Pinot Grigio and Pinot Bianco, and the incomparable Soave's which can be found in many stores at home. The reds are not so recognizable except for the Cabernet, and they're not nearly as good as the reds from the Chianti region around Florence. But then again, not many reds can compare to a Chianti.

San Marco
29. **AL BACARETO**, *Calle Crosera 3447, Venezia. Tel. 041/89-336. American Express, Mastercard and Visa accepted. Closed Saturdays for dinner and Sundays. Dinner for two E38. Vaporetto Stop – San Samuele. Map – B.*
Located on the corner of Salizzada San Samuele, this authentic neighborhood *trattoria* serves excellent Venetian dishes. There are a few tables outside from which you can not only enjoy your meal but revel in the sights and sounds of the local neighborhood. The seating inside is warm and comfortable, with a dark wooden beamed ceiling. The inside is where you'll notice many local customers indulging in their favorite meal. If you're adventurous sample their specialty *fegato alla veneziana* (calf's liver sautéed with onions) or any of their great seafood dishes for seconds. For starters try their *risotto pesce* (rice mixed with seafood) or the *zuppa di pesce* (fish soup).
30. **AL BUSO**, *Ponte di Rialto 5338, Tel. 041/528-9078. Credit cards accepted. Dinner for two E32. Vaporetto Stop – Rialto. Map – A.*
Located right beside the Rialto bridge down on the water by the Grand Canal. There are few tables set outside that come with the great canal-side views. It's worth the wait to get one of these tables. Your red jacketed waiters

will serve you a variety of appetizing meals. Their pizza and pasta are both good and inexpensive. To be Venetian for the night, try their *pizza ai frutta di mare* (seafood pizza) or the *spaghetti con pesce* (with seafood). Then for *doppo* (seconds), try the *sogliola alla griglia* (grilled sole), a wonderful finish to any meal.

31. ALLA RIVETTA, *Ponte S. Provolo 4625, Venezia. Tel. 041/528-7302. American Express, Mastercard and Visa accepted. Closed Mondays. Dinner for two E32. Vaporetto Stop – San Zaccaria. Map – A.*

Tucked away at the foot of the Ponte San Provolo behind the Chiesa di San Marco this place is largely overlooked by tourists since many people don't bother to look down as they cross the canal. A hangout for some of the gondoliers as a drinking hole (they have a bar that faces onto the small canal where the gondoliers park their craft) and for many of the locals because of the food, location, and prices.

Their menu is in four languages so you'll be able to know what you are ordering, but here are some suggestions: *antipasto di pesce* (seafood antipasto), then the *spaghetti alla bolognese* (with veal, cream and tomatoes), and finally either the *fritto misti di mare* (mixed fried seafood) or the *cotolette alla milanese* (breaded veal cutlet). The atmosphere is all Venetian and the menu is from all over Italy. Enjoy both together. My favorite place in Venice.

32 AL TEATRO, *Campo San Fantin 1916, Venezia. Tel. 041/522-1052. American Express, Mastercard and Visa accepted. Closed Mondays and in November. Last orders can be placed at midnight. Dinner for E43. Vaporetto Stop – Santa Maria del Giglio. Maps – A &B.*

Al Teatro stays open late to cater to the exiting theater customers (hence the name). It's actually a ristorante, pizzeria, and bar all rolled into one, with great local ambiance. They have seating outside under canopies in the piazza

The Best Restaurants in Venice
29. AL BACARETO, *Calle Crosera 3447. Dinner for two E38.*
31. ALLA RIVETTA, *Ponte S Provolo 4625, Dinner for two E32.*
44. AL MASCARON, *Calle Lunga Santa Maria Formosa 5225, Dinner for two E35.*
47. DA FRANZ, *Fondamenta San Isepo 754, Dinner for two E90.*
54. ANTICO CAPON, *Piazza Santa Margherita 3004, Dinner for two E25.*
58. POSTE VECCHIE, *Pescheria 1608, Dinner for two E50.*
62. ALTANELLA, *Guidecca Calle delle Erbe 270, Dinner for two E45.*
65. SAN TROVASO, *Fondamenta Priuli 1016, Dinner for two E33.*

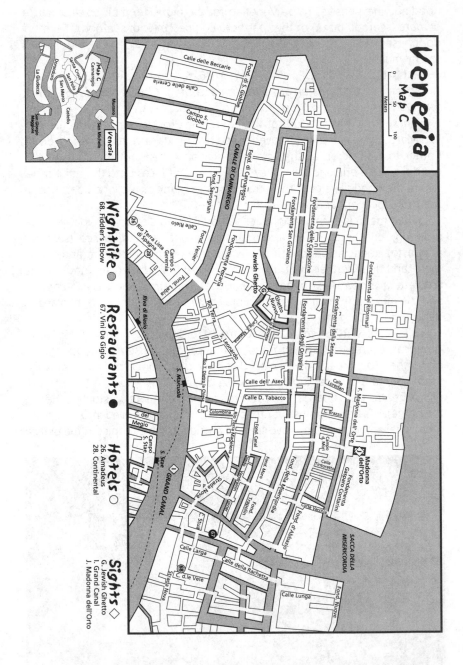

Venezia
Map C

0   50   100
Meters

Calle delle Beccarie

Fond. di S. Globbe

Calle delle Cereria

Campo S. Globbe

CANALE DI CANNAREGIO

Fond. di Cannaregio

Fond. Savorgnan

Calle Rielo

Fondamenta San Girolamo

Fondamenta delle Cappucine

Rio Terra Lista di Spagna

Fond. Venier

Fond. Labbia

Fondamenta Pescaria

Campo S. Geremia

Jewish Ghetto

Ghetto Nuovo

Fondamenta degli Ormesini

Fondamenta della Sensa

Fondamenta dei Riformati

Rio Terra S. Leonardo

Riva di Biasio

S. Marcuola

Calle dell' Aseo

Calle D. Tabacco

Calle Loredan

F. Madonna dell' Orte

C. Brazzo

C. del Megio

C.le Colombina

Campo S. Stae

Fond. Canal

Fond. Moro

Campo 4. Mori

Calle Tintoretto

Madonna dell'Orto

Fondamenta Gasparo Contarini

S. Stae

GRAND CANAL

Strada Nova

Fond. della Misericordia

Fond. Trapolin

Fond. d'Abbazio

Corte Vecchia

SACCA DELLA MISERICORDIA

Calle Larga

Calle della Rachetta

C. Stua

Strada Nova

C. d.le Vele

Calle Lunga

Fond. Nuove

(Map C)
Cannaregio
Santa Croce
San Polo
Dorsoduro
San Marco
La Giudecca
Castello
San Giorgio Maggiore

Venezia
San Michele
Murano

San Giorgio Maggiore

Nightlife ●
68. Fiddler's Elbow

Restaurants ●
67. Vini Da Gigio

Hotels ○
26. Amadeus
28. Continental

Sights ◇
G. Jewish Ghetto
I. Grand Canal
J. Madonna dell'Orto

and plenty of seating inside, but in good weather I believe the atmosphere is best outside. Try the *spaghetti alla vongole* (with a spicy olive oil-based clam sauce or the *risotto di pesce* (seafood rice dish). Then grab some *scampi e calamari fritti* (fried squid and shrimp for seconds).

33. ANTICO MARTINI, *Campo San Fantin 1983, Venezia. Tel. 041/522-4121. All credit cards accepted. Closed Tuesdays and Wednesdays for lunch. Dinner for two E105. Vaporetto Stop – Santa Maria Del Giglio. Maps – A.*

Snuggled onto a back street of Venice, this is an excellent and world-renowned restaurant; but it is quite expensive, so save coming here for a special occasion or if you have money to blow. Not only can you order Italian and Venetian dishes, but the menu is in four languages, making it easy to read and a clear sign they cater to tourists. You can be seated in the piazza out front or surrounded by the local decor inside. They make a good *risotto al mare* (seafood rice dish), a tasty *scampi alla provenzale* (shrimp Provencal), and an excellent *branzino alla griglia* (grilled seas bass). Or you can get *tagliata di Angus* (beef steak) or *fegatto alla veneziana* (tasty liver). After your meal ask for the *formaggio* (cheese tray) and sample some of their delicious cheeses. This place is a staple in Venice.

34. CAFÉ QUADRI, *Piazza San Marco 120-124, Venezia. Tel. 041/22-105. Credit cards accepted. Closed Mondays. Vaporetto Stop – San Marco. Map – A.*

This is a landmark in Venice, along with the other competing cafés in the Piazza San Marco, such as the Florian or the Gran Café Chioggia. You've heard of dueling banjos? Well in San Marco you have dueling cafes, each complete with its own set of musicians competing to lure you in and sample their exorbitantly priced offerings. Expensive, but if you want to say you've been here, have a drink and enjoy the music and the additional ambiance it offers.

35. CLUB DEL DOGE, *Campo Santa Maria del Giglio 2467, Venezia. Tel. 041/794-611. All credit cards accepted. Dinner for two E150. Vaporetto Stop – Santa Maria Del Giglio. Maps – A &B.*

You don't have to stay at the Gritti Palace Hotel to enjoy their restaurant, so if you have some money left over from your trip and want to share a romantic meal with your significant other, this is the place to come. The Gritti's open air terrace is directly on the Canale della Guidecca which offers a great view of the sunset. Their classic Italian cuisine is superb. Even though the menu changes almost daily based on what is available at the market, they'll always have succulent meats, perfectly grilled or fried fresh fish and delicious pastas. Their *antipasto* of *caviale o salmone affumicato* (smoked caviar or salmon) is exquisite, as is their *risotto con code di scampi e zucchine* (rice dish with shrimp and zucchini). After dinner, linger here over a Sambuca Molinari, or a glass of wine and watch the sunset. If you want to go to a high class restaurant, choose this place, not the faux chic Harry's Bar.

36. DA "ARTURO," *Calle degli Assassini 3656A. Tel. 041/528-6974. Credit cards accepted. Dinner for two E50. Vaporetto Stop – Rialto. Maps – A & B.*

An expensive place catering to tourists, thus the hamburger on the menu. Nonetheless it is a quaint little *trattoria* on a small side street that has plenty of local charm and ambiance despite the high prices. The dark wood paneling only enhances the charm. So settle down and enjoy some good Italian, not necessarily Venetian food, like *spaghetti alla carbonara* (with ham, cheese, and eggs) or a *scaloppini al porto* (veal cutlet cooked in port wine) which is stupendous.

37. DA RAFFAELE, *Fondamenta delle Ostreghe 2347, Venezia. Tel. 041/ 523-2317. American Express, Mastercard and Visa accepted. Closed Thursdays and January to mid-February. Dinner for two E48. Vaporetto Stop – San Maria del Giglio. Map – A.*

Even though your first impression is of a haven for tourists since the menu is in four languages, the food here is actually very good. Actually, the Venetians frequent this restaurant but they choose to sit inside, where it's endowed with marble and much cooler, leaving the terrace for the tourists, which is a beautiful place to enjoy a meal. Try the *risotto Raphaele* (made with clams and other seafood) which is for two people. Then later try the assorted fried fish or the grilled sole.

38. GIGLIO, *Campo Santa Maria dei Giglio 2477 (next to the Hotel Ala). Tel. 041/523-2368. Dinner for two E40. Vaporetto Stop – Santa Maria del Giglio. Maps – A & B.*

There is enclosed piazza seating for any kind of weather, and they have a menu in English for easy ordering. Try the *risotto* with seafood, which is served for two people. Then make sure you try the curried chicken with rice pilaf which is stupendous. For later, go to Haig's Grill, the restaurant's attached bar/café, for a drink outside under the stars in this isolated piazza.

39. HARRY'S BAR, *Calle Vallaresso 1323, Venezia. Tel. 528-5777, Fax 041/520-8822. All credit cards accepted. Closed Mondays. 10:30am to 11:00pm (you can order up to 11:00pm). Dinner for two E120. Vaporetto Stop – San Marco. Map – A.*

Harry's has been a place to come for *i cognoscenti* (those in the know) since before Hemingway was killing brain cells here. The downstairs bar is for drinking (if you've money for $6 drinks) and people watching. Try the *Bellini* for which Harry's is famous, made with fresh peach juice and white wine. The restaurant upstairs is very expensive and has a pseudo-sophisticated air and is a hangout for the James Bond wannabee set. No offense to my father who loved this place.

Despite the nouveau-riche atmosphere the food is excellent and there is a wide selection to choose from, especially in the grilled meat and fish department. Their *risotto di scampi* (shrimp and rice dish) is good as is the *risotto all sbiraglia* (rice with chicken and vegetables). I also enjoyed the *scampi fruity con salsa tartara* (friend shrimp with tartar sauce). Remember to bring your credit card because the prices are out of this world.

40. **LA COLOMBA**, *Piscina di Frezzeria 1665, Venezia. Tel. 041/522-1175. All credit cards accepted. Closed Tuesdays. E115. Vaporetto Stop – San Marco. Map – A.*

Mainly known for its fish dishes and fine decorations, La Colomba also has a wide variety of grilled, baked, or fried meats and fish. Sitting on a quiet street with some outdoor tables, this is a good place to come and relax until late into the evening (orders still taken up to 11:00pm). You might want to try the succulent *scampi al curry* with rice pilaf, not originally a Venetian specialty until the city began having vast dealings with the Far East many centuries ago. And yes, be prepared to spend a little money here; it's very expensive. They also make some good pastas, like *spaghetti alla carbonara* (with ham, butter, cheese, and egg) and a great *risotto ai frutti di mare* (with seafood) and a tasty *fresco gazpacho* (cold veggie soup from Spain).

41. **LEON BIANCO**, *Salizzada San Luca 4153, Venezia. Tel. 041/522-1180. No credit cards accepted. Closed Sundays. Open Monday - Saturday 9:00am -1:00pm and 4:00pm to 9:00pm. Meal for two E18. Vaporetto Stop – Rialto. Maps – A & B.*

A surprising inexpensive little wine bar in Venice's most expensive area, San Marco. There's a wide variety of *tramezzini* sandwich filled with a variety of meats, cheeses and vegetables to go along with your wine selections. My favorites are *prosciutto e formaggio* (ham and cheese), *prosciutto e funghi* (ham and mushrooms), and *prosciutto e uovo* (ham and egg, a great breakfast). But basically you can request your own combinations, as long as you speak a little Italian. The perfect place to come for a midday snack and a good glass of wine or an ice cold draft beer, as well as for a light dinner.

42. **VINO VINO**, *Calle Veste 2007A, Venezia. Tel. 041/522-4121. American Express, Mastercard and Visa accepted. Closed Tuesdays. Open 10:00am - 2:30pm and 5:00pm to 1:00am. Meal for two E20. Vaporetto Stop – Santa Maria del Giglio. Map – A.*

A late night wine bar opened by the owners of the Antico Martini (see number 32 above) to cater mainly to the late night theater crowd and others just leaving their restaurant when it closes at 10:00pm. They serve salads, sandwiches, as well as meat dishes like chicken and lamb all prepared by the kitchen at the Antico Martini and for a much better price (about one quarter as expensive). These two places are bookends for another Martini special, a piano bar that serves late night drinks and entertainment.

Castello

43. **AL COVO**, *Campiello della Pescaria 3968, Venezia. Tel. 041/522-3812. American Express, Mastercard and Visa accepted. Closed Wednesdays and Thursdays and 15 days in August. Dinner for two E70. Vaporetto Stop – Riva Degli Schiavoni. Map – A.*

The perfect place to eat is on their patio while sampling the seafood splendor they prepare. The service is quite attentive and the food prepared perfectly. Located near San Giovanni in Bragora, this is true Venetian cuisine with wonderful atmosphere. Try the *spaghetti al nero di seppia* (with octopus ink), or the *verdure fritte* (fried vegetables) for seconds. The *zuppa di pesce* (seafood soup) is also good, as is the *ravioli di branzino* (sea bass ravioli). They also make great grilled meats or fish. Al Covo has also started a lunch menu with even better prices.

44. AL MASCARON, *Calle Lunga Santa Maria Formosa 5225, Venezia. Tel. 041/522-5995. No credit cards accepted. Closed Sundays and mid-December to mid-January and 15 days in August. Dinner for two E35. Vaporetto Stop – Rialto. Map – A.*

Located near Santa Maria Formosa and SS Giovanni e Paolo, this is a plain *bar/trattoria* with a truly rustic atmosphere that serves great food. You can get great boiled or roasted vegetables as an appetizer or a side dish. If you don't mind a wait, order the *penne al pesce spada* (small noodles with a sauce of swordfish), then for seconds any of their fish on the grill, like *branzini* (sea bass) or *sogliola* (sole) which are both excellent.

45. ARCIMBOLDO, *Calle dei Furlani 3219, Venezia. Tel. 041/86-569. No credit cards accepted. Closed Tuesdays. Dinner for two E30. Vaporetto Stop – Riva Degli Schiavoni. Map – A.*

Located on a small canal, off the beaten path near the Scuola di San Giorgio degli Schiavoni. You'll love the local flavor and quiet ambiance of the outside seating. There'll be hardly a tourist around, except for yourself. Try their exquisite *scampi al curry* with rice pilaf and any of their grilled meats. A wonderful place to get away from it all. But bring your map – this is a tough one to find.

46. CORTE SCONTA, *Calle del Pestrin 3886, Venezia. Tel. 041/522-7024. American Express, Mastercard and Visa accepted. Closed Sundays and Mondays. Dinner for two E35. Vaporetto Stop – Arsenale. Map – A.*

Located near the Piazza San Giovanni in Bragora, this restaurant is always full. Despite its plain decor this place is popular because of its food. And being always filled with locals, makes this a boisterous and authenitc night out in Venice. Their menu changes with the tide - i.e. whatever the catch is that day - but they always seem to have a well stocked but diverse *fritture mista di mare* (mixed fried seafood). Since this is a very popular, high end local restaurant, reservations are required. I would definitely recommend this place for a quality night out in Venice.

47. DA FRANZ, Fondamenta San Isepo 754, Venezia. Tel. 041/522-0861 or 522-7505. American Express, Mastercard and Visa accepted. Closed Tuesdays and in January. Dinner for two E90. Vaporetto Stop – Giardini. Map – A.

Located in a tranquil neighborhood area of Venice, way off the beaten path, this is a fantastic culinary adventure away from the tourist hordes. Owned by Gianfranco Gasperini, the menu offers many Venetian dishes, especially seafood like antipasto ai crostacei (crustacean antipasto) and gamberetti con salsa al curry (baby shrimps in a curry sauce). Their rice dishes are also exquisite. Try either the risotto di pesce (rice with fish) or ai frutti di mare (with mixed seafood). For seconds your mouth will water anticipating the grilled fish, the delicately fried shrimp or mixed seafood dish. Expensive but world-renowned. Take a water taxi here and back since it is quite a hike.

48. DANIELI TERRACE, Riva degli Schiavoni 4196, Venezia. Tel. 041/26-480. American Express, Mastercard and Visa accepted. Open 7 days a week. Dinner for two E80. Vaporetto Stop – Riva Degli Schiavoni or Daniele (their private pier if coming by taxi). Map – A.

Located in the gigantic (by Venetian standards) and eclectic Danieli hotel. To get to the restaurant you pass through the magnificent hotel courtyard and lobby and go up to the roof. From the restaurant you can get a great view of the sunset over the Lagoon.

This is a first class restaurant all the way, from their table settings to the wait service. The menu features international favorites but the Venetian cuisine here is excellent. The house specialty, fettucine alla buranella (fettucine with sole and shrimp in a cream sauce), is out of this world. For dessert, many people order flaming crepes. It's a great show. But be prepared to pay dearly for the food, but what wonderfully romantic atmosphere.

49. DA REMIGIO, Salizzada dei Greci, Venezia. Tel. 041/523-0089. Credit cards accepted. Closed Monday dinners and Tuesdays. Dinner for two E60. Vaporetto Stop – Riva del Schiavoni. Map – A.

A true family style Venetian trattoria that is frequented mainly by Venetians. The food is not spectacular, but it is tasty and filling and the atmosphere is rustic and down to earth. As in most Venetian restaurants the specialty is fish. Their mixed seafood grill is scrumptious as are their grilled fish.

50. MALAMOCCO, Campiello del Vin 4650, Venezia. Tel. 041/27-438. American Express, Mastercard and Visa accepted. Closed Thursdays and in January. Dinner for two E45. Vaporetto Stop – Zaccaria. Map – A.

Located just off of the Riva Schiavoni, this pleasant little restaurant is set in a quiet, tiny piazza with its own enclosed seating area outside. Enjoy the weather, the local flavor, and the superb seafood and meat dishes. Try the sogliola al burro (butter fried sole), the medaglioni di vitello con crema e funghi (veal medallion in a cream and mushrooms sauce ... exquisite), or the scampi all'indiana (shrimp with a curry sauce).

Santa Croce/San Polo
51. AE OCHE, *Calle del Tintor 1552A, Venezia. Tel. 041/524-1161. American Express, Mastercard and Visa accepted. Closed Mondays. Dinner for two E23. Vaporetto Stop – San Stae. Map – B.*

Located near the Campo San Giacomo del'Orio in Santa Croce, this is another inexpensive pizzeria frequented by many young Venetians who seem to appreciate the seemingly countless varieties of pizza, and I agree with them. My favorite is the *pizza mangia fuoco* (literally meaning 'eat fire,' a spicy pizza with salami and hot peppers). For other spicy pizzas, go for the *Diavolo* or *Inferno*. As always the best seating is outside where you can watch the Venetians go by. The booths inside are also comfortable, but not quite so scenic. Besides pizza, you can get an *omelet a piacere* (made any way you want). Too bad they're not open for breakfast.

52. AL GIARDINETTO, *Rio della Frescada 2910. Tel. 041/522-4100. Credit cards accepted. Dinner for two E33. Vaporetto Stop – San Toma. Map – B.*

Located just off a quaint little canal under a blanket of vines in their little garden (hence the name). If you have to sit inside, admire the framed painted dinner plates they have on display and enjoy a variety of pizzas that will make you ache for more. Try the *prosciutto e funghi* pizza (ham and mushrooms) and ask for extra mozzarella (*doppia mozzarella*) and you will be very satisfied. A wonderful little place.

53. ALLA MADONNA, *Calle dell Madonna 594, Venezia. Tel. 041/522-3824. All credit cards accepted. Closed Wednesdays, January and seven days in August. Dinner for E55. Vaporetto Stop – Rialto. Maps – A &B.*

Located near the Rialto bridge, you get a good mix of locals and tourists here for both lunch and dinner. It is a simple but superb *trattoria* where you can pick out your own fish from the refrigerated display of the catch bought at the morning market nearby. If you don't want any fish they have a variety of grilled and roast meats based on availability. I like the *maialino arrosto* (baby roast pork). Besides the excellent food, the atmosphere is loud and boisterous which tends to make the meal fun and authentically Venetian. They also have excellent *risotto ai frutti di mare* (rice with seafood) and a superb *fritto misto di mare* (mixed fried seafood). You can also enjoy *spaghetti alla vongole* (with clam sauce), *risotto ai frutti di mare* (seafood rice dish) or *pasta e fagioli* (pasta and beans).

54. ANTICO CAPON, *Piazza Santa Margherita 3004, Venezia. Tel. 041/528-525. Credit cards accepted. Dinner for two E25. Vaporetto Stop – Ca' Rezzonico. Map – B.*

Located right next to and below the one star hotel of the same name, this is a perfect place to enjoy the life of a Venetian piazza. Sit under the awnings or in the sun, but enjoy some good pizza or *crostine* (sandwiches). The *crostino con funghi, prosciutto, e mozzarella* (with mushrooms, ham, and mozzarella) is great, as is the *crostino al inferno* (literally translated it means hell's sandwich; it has tomatoes, mozzarella, hot salami, mushrooms, and *pepperoncini* and is quite tasty, if a little spicy).

55. DA FIORE, *Calle del Scaleter 2202, Venezia. Tel. 041/721-308. All credit cards accepted. Closed Sundays and Mondays, and during August and Christmas. Dinner for two E80. Vaporetto Stop – San Silvestro or San Toma. Map – B.*

This is an elegant but at the same time simple old Venetian *trattoria* that offers great fresh seafood. You'll find some *cucina nuova* (nouvelle cuisine) influence here since they have a different menu every day and try to make each meal a magical journey. One of their staples is *risotto di scampi e funghi porcini* (rice with shrimp and mushrooms) that serves two people. After you've digested this, try their *frittura mista al'Adriatico* (mixed seafood from the Adriatic). It's not meant for two, but after the rice dish, it should suffice.

56. DA IGNAZIO, *Calle Saoneri, San Polo 2749, Venezia. Tel. 523-4852. American Express, Mastercard and Visa accepted. Closed Saturdays and 2 weeks in March and July. Dinner for two E50. Vaporetto Stop – San Toma. Map – B.*

Located near San Polo and the Frari, this is a basic Venetian fish restaurant with great character. Along with the beautiful central garden and the charming rooms with wood beam ceilings, you'll get quality fried or grilled seafood and meats at a reasonable price. They display some of the fish in the window to entice you to come in. Try the *zuppa di pesce* (fish soup) or *spaghetti alla vongole* (with clams) for starters. Then indulge yourself in the *fritto misto al'Adriatico* (mixed fried seafood from the Adriatic) for seconds. They also make a great *ossobuco alla veneziana* (roast veal shank in a spicy tomato sauce).

57. LA ZUCCA, *Calle del Megio 1762, Venezia. Tel. 041/524-1570. Credit cards accepted. Closed Sundays. Dinner for two E25. Vaporetto Stop – San Stae. Map – B.*

A great local place to eat. Zucca means pumpkin, and you guessed it, their specialty pasta in the fall and winter is pumpkin pasta. It is extremely delicious, especially with a cream sauce. They also have fresh fish, chicken, and salads but not too much red meats. So if you're a dedicated carnivore, this healthy menu will discourage you. The owners and staff all have this radiant glow, which is what eating healthy food will do to you. Enjoy a small table outside or one of their inside tables with views of the canal. Some of my favorite dishes were *maiale al curry con riso pilaf* (curried pork with rice pilaf) or the *pollo ai ferri con tzatziki* (grilled chicken with a tasty yogurt sauce). A great place in Venice. Stop here if you get the chance.

58. POSTE VECCHIE, *Pescheria 1608, Venezia. Tel. 041/721-822. American Express, Mastercard and Visa accepted. Closed Tuesdays. Dinner for two E50. Vaporetto Stop – Rialto. Map – B.*

Huddled in the corner of the vast *pescheria* fish market (hence the address), and located near the old post office (hence the name). To get here you follow a private wooden bridge that leads to this old converted inn with its low ceilings and dark wooden beams. This restaurant is known for its perfectly prepared fish, especially the grilled variety, and its bountiful antipasto table. In the summer you can dine in the splendid garden that has vines and leaves hanging overhead. Try their *risotto di pesce* (rice with seafood for two people), then move onto the exquisite *sogliola ai ferri* (grilled sole).

59. SAN TOMA, *Campo San Toma, San Polo 2864A, Venezia. Tel. 041/ 523-8819. American Express, Mastercard and Visa accepted. Closed Tuesdays. Dinner for two E30. Vaporetto Stop – San Toma. Map – B.*

Pizza is their specialty, so try a great *pizza rustica* (with mozzarella, tomatoes, salami, and egg). Or indulge yourself in a staple of Venetian cuisine, *risotto di pesce* (rice with seafood, and kind of *paella*-like concoction). The outside seating is best on this out of the way little piazza. You can enjoy your meal and *vino* under the stars or inside in their rustic, wood paneled environment. With the absence of automobiles, the terrace is best.

Dorsoduro

60. AI GONDOLIERI, *Dorsoduro 366. Tel. 041/528-6396. Closed Tuesdays. All credit cards accepted. Dinner for two E70. Vaporetto Stop – Santa Maria Della Salute. Map – D.*

The menu mainly consists of meats and cheeses, complemented by seasonal vegetables. My favorite is the exotic *filetto di struzzo alle erbe* (ostrich filet). For the adventurous try the *trippa alla parmigiana* (tripe). Other dishes include *filetto d'Angus al tartufo nero* (beef steak with black truffles) or with *Barolo e porcini* (steak in a red wine and mushroom sauce). And for dessert try something from their extensive cake cart like a *strudel di mele* (apple strudel) or *torte alla frutta* (fruit pies). A fine restaurant located near the Peggy Guggenheim Museum.

61. ALLE ZATTERE, *Zattere ai Gesuati 795, Venezia. Tel. 041/520-4224. Credit cards accepted. Closed Tuesdays. Pizza for two E20. Vaporetto Stop – Zattere. Maps – B &D.*

This a favorite local pizzeria near the Campo San Agnese, known not only for its many varieties of pizza but also for its excellent view of Guidecca island from the pizzeria's tables on the Zattere's floating rafts. A perfect place to eat when the sun sets. You can get almost any type pizza here, including *margherita* (with sauce and cheese) and *verdure* (with grilled vegetables). They oblige you by putting extra cheese, salami (they didn't have pepperoni

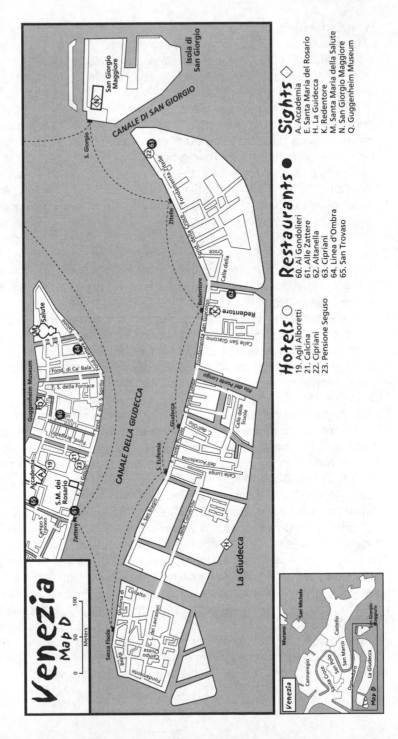

Venezia
Map D

0   50   100
Meters

Sights ◇
A. Accademia
E. Santa Maria del Rosario
H. La Guidecca
K. Redentore
M. Santa Maria della Salute
N. San Giorgio Maggiore
Q. Guggenheim Museum

Restaurants ●
60. Ai Gondolieri
61. Alle Zattere
62. Altanella
63. Cipriani
64. Linea d'Ombra
65. San Trovaso

Hotels ○
19. Agli Alboretti
21. Calcina
22. Cipriani
23. Pensione Seguso

when I last visited), and a sprinkle of oregano if you like. There are also seafood salads and seafood pastas from which to choose.

62. ALTANELLA, *Guidecca Calle delle Erbe 270. Tel. 041/522-7780. No credit cards accepted. Closed Mondays and Tuesdays as well as 15 days in August. Dinner for two E45. Vaporetto Stop – Guidecca. Map – D.*

Located just off the main waterfront walkway, Fondamenta del Ponte Longo, you'll find a tranquil setting and wonderful food. Getting here is an adventure since you have to take the ferry and wind through local streets to find this neighborhood spot. There's peaceful outside seating, but the inside is as pretty and more fun with all the locals bantering about. This is a typical Venetian restaurant with seafood and pasta and both intermixed. You can't go wrong with any of their grilled and fried fish, or any pasta mixed with seafood like *spaghetti alla vongole verace* (with clams in a spicy sauce) or *risotto di pesce* (seafood rice dish), or a fine *zuppa di pesce* (seafood soup). The house wine is really good. A wonderfully authentic and rustic location.

63. CIPRIANI, *Fondamenta San Giovanni 10, La Guidecca, Venezia. Tel. 041/707-744. All credit cards accepted. Dinner for two E200. Vaporetto Stop – Zitelle. Map – D.*

Super-expensive and extremely elegant, this restaurant is part of the magnificent Cipriani Hotel. You can have a restful poolside lunch with bountiful *antipasti* and your basic but tasty club sandwich. Dinner is served in the elegant dining room and the menu contains everything you could possibly desire. They make a great *blinis alla russa con salmone scozzese* (Russian blini with smoked Scottish salmon) for an appetizer and an excellent *pennette con salsa d'agnello al rosmarino* (pasta in a lamb and rosemary sauce). For the entrée, their *fritto di scampi e calamari* (fried shrimp and squid) is excellent. If you are late for dinner, have a drink on the terrace or spend some time in their intimate piano bar. Just coming here for a drink is well worth the trip.

64. LINEA D'OMBRA, *Punta della Dogana-Zattere 19. Tel. 041/528-5259. All credit cards accepted. Closed Sunday nights and Wednesdays. Dinner for two E90. Vaporetto Stop – Santa Maria Della Salute. Map – D.*

Extremely romantic. This is a traditional Venetian restaurant, which means they serve lots of fish dishes, and they also try to be creative with their cooking. Inside is where all the locals sit, but outside on their terrace you get great views of the Canal looking towards La Guidecca. A great place to watch the sun set. You'll find a tasty *salmone alla crema* (light cream sauce with salmon), and their seafood pasta dishes depend on what the market has available that day. Most times you can get *spaghetti con gamberi* (with shrimp) *e zucchine*, or *tagliolini neri con pesce spada* (black thin pasta with sword fish). You'll also find a mixed fried seafood extravaganza if you can't make up your mind. Come for the food, stay for the view. Wonderfully romantic.

65. **SAN TROVASO**, *Fondamenta Priuli 1016, Venezia. Tel. 041/520-3703. American Express, Mastercard and Visa accepted. Closed Mondays. Air conditioned. Dinner for two E33. Vaporetto Stop – Accademia or Zattere. Maps – B &D.*

If they seat you in the side room or upstairs with the locals, you feel as if you entered a heated discussion since everyone seems to know each other and to be talking at once. Couple this with the clatter of pans and the occasional dropped glass or plate from the kitchen and this place has a great local feel to it. And the food is great, otherwise the locals wouldn't come. Try either the *spaghetti newburg* (with shrimp, tomatoes sauce and cream) or the *spaghetti alla carbonara* (with ham, cream and egg). For *secondo* they have plenty of reasonably priced meats and fish. Take your pick, they're all good.

Cannaregio

66. FIASCHETTERIA TOSCANA, *Calle Giovanni Cristomo 5719, Tel. 041/528-5281. Closed Tuesdays and July. Credit cards accepted. Dinner for two E75. Vaporetto Stop – Rialto. Map – A.*

Located near the church of San Giovanni Cristomo this place has pleasant outside seating just across the street in a piazza. But it's only used during the high season. Inside seating is elegant and bright, with the best seats by the window so you can watch the parade pass by. They specialize in seafood here, and if you've been to the Rialto seafood and vegetable market you'll understand why many restaurants in Venice do. They also have international offerings, like sandwiches and such. My favorite though is their *spaghetti alla vongole verace* (with a spicy oil & clam sauce) and then their *fritto misto al mare* (mixed fried seafood). But if you're sick of seafood, try their filets of beef.

67. **VINI DA GIGIO**, *Cannaregio San Felice 3628/a. Tel. 041/528-5140. Closed Mondays and 15 days in January. All credit cards accepted. Dinner for two E60. Vaporetto Stop – Ca' d'Oro. Map – C.*

Located a little off the tourist path, this is a simple local wine bar and *trattoria*. They offer more than 300 different wine choices with your meal of typical Venetian cuisine. Sample their *antipasto di frutti di mare* (antipasto of sea food), then some *tagliatelle nere con sugo di scampi* (dark pasta with shrimp sauce), or *spaghetti alla vongole verace* (with spicy clam sauce), then a *fritto misto di mare and verdure* (mixed fried seafood and vegetables). If you're tired of seafood there is also an extensive menu of grilled meats.

Seeing the Sights

Some people say that Venice is really only a living museum and not a real city any longer, but that's what makes it perfect for tourists. Everywhere you look you see something so beautiful, so awe inspiring that Venice at times seems out of this world. I guess that is probably why this was Walt Disney's favorite city.

Medieval in layout and design, this city built on pilings in a marshy lagoon has everything you could imagine for a vacation, except, during high season, reasonable prices. You can find exquisite churches, beautiful synagogues, pristine *palazzi*, spacious *piazze*, magnificent museums, deserted islands only a *vaporetto* ride away, skilled crafts people blowing glass or making masks right in front of you, superb restaurants, relaxing hotels, and so much more.

The sights are spread across the main maps for this chapter: map A (pages 468-469); map B (pages 476-477); map C (page 486) and map C (page 495).

The Quiet Side of Venice

During the summer months Venice is literally crammed with tourists, and at some point you'll need to take a break from them. If you're in need of a little solitude, basically anywhere away from Piazza San Marco, the Piazzale Roma, and the Rialto Bridge you can find a more serene Venetian experience.

And as you're walking (or taking the *vaporetto* then walking) to these isolated areas, don't be afraid of getting lost. Venice is perfectly safe and since it is so small you'll always find your way back. By wandering around you'll inevitably also find some charming piazza or café that will seem as if it hasn't been touched by a single tourist. So strap on your walking shoes and get going.

Cannaregio – This section in the north of the main island is where the Jewish ghetto is located. Three of the synagogues in the main square of the tiny island that makes up the ghetto are worth seeing. Here you'll find some of the most eclectic buildings in Venice, because once the Jewish population started to increase, the only place they could find more space was to build on top of each other. As a result everything looks a little haphazard but the neighborhood is alive with local shoppers buying their supplies for the day, and beautiful side streets and canals away from the big crowds.

Castello – There's not much to see or do in this section of Venice, but they do have some of the best restaurants. In and around the **Arsenale** you'll find real Venetian neighborhoods, with grandmas chatting at each other from window sills above the canals, children playing in the narrow streets, and life peacefully devoid of the rumble of tourist crowds.

Dorsoduro – By simply walking from the Accademia to the Piazzale Roma in a meandering fashion you'll wander through some of the best neighborhoods that offer a vibrant taste of local color. You'll find artisan's shops, lovely houses, and of course narrow medieval streets and calm canals. And for food, wine, and a calming atmosphere, you can sit for hours on the *Zattere*. Literally

Suggested Rules of Conduct In Venice

Since Venice experiences a massive influx of tourists every year, it is the only Italian city I know of that prints up an official pamphlet advising tourists how to behave while visiting. These rules help travelers from many different cultures remain in harmony with each other and the locals, allowing for daily life of Venice to continue unhindered.

Here are the suggestions Venetians wish tourists to be aware of:

1. When walking on the tiny streets keep to the right, one person behind the other so others coming from the opposite direction may pass.

2. When you stop to admire the view remember to leave space for others to pass; please avoid sitting at any time on the steps of bridges since this will dramatically impede traffic.

3. Always remove backpacks when traveling on the water transport, otherwise you are bound to bump into someone. Remember to have bought a ticket before boarding.

4. No one, men included, can go bare-chested in Venice; and no one can wear beach attire in the city. This means bikini bottoms for both men and women and bra bathing suit tops or sports bras for women. They also frown on tank tops for both men and women. If you are on Lido near the beach ignore this rule.

5. Remember to dispose of trash in public waste bins and not the streets or canals.

6. It is forbidden to have a picnic lunch in Venice. Seriously. This restriction dramatically cuts down on vagrancy. No worries, there are plenty of great restaurants and cafés. So if you bought lunch supplies save them for later in your room.

If you try to follow these simple rules of living, your stay in Venice will be that much more pleasant for everyone involved.

meaning rafts, these open air restaurants are anchored off the eastern edge of the Dorsoduro and face the Isola della Guidecca. Try one of these restaurants for a real treat. It is an experience you'll cherish, especially if you stay long enough to see the sun go down. The glow is magnificent.

Isola la Guidecca – This a thriving neighborhood where everybody seems to know everyone else. If you're interested in gondolas, here you'll find the main gondola repair shop on the Rio del Ponte Lungo. This is a great island just to walk, watch, and listen.

A. ACCADEMIA

Located in Campo della Carita, Dorsoduro. Tel. 041/522-2247. Open Monday–Saturday 9:00am–7:00pm in the summer and 9:00am–4:00pm in winter. Sundays and holidays 9:00am–1:00pm. Vaporetto – Accademia. Maps – B & D.

Five hundred years of unequaled Venetian art are on display at the **Accademia**. The collection began in 1750 when the Republic of St. Mark's decided to endow the city with an academy to feature local painters and sculptors (Accademica di Pittori e Scultori). The original academy occupied the current Port Authority building located by the gardens of the royal palace overlooking the harbor of St. Mark's.

During the French occupation of 1807, the collection was moved to the School and Church of the Carita (in Campo della Carita) which was also the former monastery of the Lateran Canons. Since then it has grown and expanded immensely and is a must-see for anyone visiting Venice who is interested in art.

There are far too many excellent paintings and sculptures to list them all, but these are the ones you should not miss:
• St. George – Montegna (Room 4)
• The Madonna degli Alberelli (Madonna among the little trees) – Giovanni Bellini (Room 5)
• The Tempest – Giorgione (Room 5)
• The Miracle of the Slave – Jacopo Tintoretto (Room 10)
• Banquet in the House of Levi – Veronese (Room 10)
• The Pieta – Titian (Room 10). The last work of this amazing artist.
• Legend of St. Ursula – Vittore Carpaccio (Room 21)
• Detail of the Arrival of The Ambassadors – Vittore Carpaccio (Room 21)
• Presentation at the Temple – Titian (Room 24)

B. ARSENALE

Open 9:00am–noon and 3:00pm–7:00pm Monday–Saturday. Vaporetto – Arsenale. Map – A.

The **Arsenale** is an imposing group of buildings, landing stages, workshops, shipyards and more from which the Venetian Navy was built. Begun in 1100, it has been continually enlarged over the years. Surrounded by towers and walls, the Arsenale has an imposing Renaissance entrance created by Giambello in 1460. In the front of the entrance is a terrace with statues that symbolize the victory of the Battle of Lepanto. At the sides are four lions, the symbol of the Venetian city state.

Inside you'll find the **Naval History Museum** with its collection of relics and trophies of the Italian Navy as well as that of Venice, which has had a much more auspicious and lengthy existence. There is a wonderfully detailed model of the last Bucintoro, the vessel in which the Doge of Venice celebrated the

"Wedding of the Sea" between Venice and the sea by throwing a ring into the Adriatic.

This is a great museum, not only because you have to trek through real Venetian neighborhoods to find it, but also as a result of its impressive collection of armaments, models, relics of modern craft used in World Wars I and II. Kids of all ages love this place.

C. DOGES PALACE – PALAZZO DUCALE

Located in St. Mark's Square (Piazzetta San Marco), San Marco. Tel. 041/ 522-4951. Open Monday–Sunday 8:30am–7:00pm in the summer and 8:30am–2:00pm in the winter. Vaporetto – San Marco. Map – A.

Another must-see while in Venice. To view it all will take the better part of a day if you perform a thorough inspection. Finished in the 1400s after being started in the 9th century by the Doges Angelo and Giustiniano Partecipazio, this was the seat of the government and the residence of the **Doge**, Venice's supreme head of state. The flamboyant Gothic style was mainly created by a family of skilled Venetian marble craftsmen, the **Bons**. It is still a joy to behold despite the devastation by fire in 1577 of one of the building's wings. Since then it has been rebuilt in its original form. It has a double tier of arcading and pink and white patterned walls which gives the building a delicate open air feeling.

Everywhere you roam in this building you will be amazed by the combination of styles and the ornate care in which they were prepared. As you enter you will pass through the **Porta della Carta**, created by the Bon family, with its extravagant Gothic style. Here you'll see the statue of *Doge Frascari* as he is kneeling before the winged lion and the statue of a woman seated at the tallest spire that represents Justice. After passing through you'll enter the courtyard of the Palace, which has a pair of imposing bronze wells in the middle. The one closer to the Poscari Portal is by Alfonso Alberberghetti (from 1559) and the other is by Niccolo del Conti in 1556. Stand here a moment and soak in the typically blended Venetian style of architecture, where they combine Gothic with Renaissance. Also enjoy the countless archways, the exquisite sculptures, and inspiring staircases.

One such staircase is *The Staircase of the Giants*, so named because of the two colossal statues of Mars and Neptune on either side of the landing made by Sansovino and his pupils. Each new Doge of the Republic of Venice was officially crowned on the landing at the top of the stairs.

You will also find some of the most beautiful plaster relief ceilings, marble relief fireplaces, paintings, sculptures, tapestries, medieval weapons rooms and ancient dungeons anywhere in Europe. Keep your eye out for the medieval chastity belt on display in the pistol room. I guarantee it is like nothing you've ever seen before. It really makes you cringe imagining someone having to wear it.

D. FRARI – SANTA MARIA GLORIOSA DE FRARI

Campo dei Frari, San Polo. Tel. 041/522-2637. Open Monday-Saturday 9:30am-noon and 2:30pm-6:00pm. Sun open 2:30pm-6:00pm. Vaporetto – San Toma. Map – B.

This Romanesque-Gothic style Franciscan church contains tombs of many famous Venetian persons. The church was begun by Franciscan monks in 1250 from a design by Nicola Pisano and was later made a little more ornate by Scipione Bon, a member of the famous Venetian family of sculptors, in 1338. It was finally finished in 1443.

Today the unadorned facade is not much to look at but is beautiful in its simplicity. It is divided into three sections by pilaster strips surmounted by pinnacles. Over the central portal are statues attributed to Alessandro Vittorio in 1581. There is a Romanesque bell tower that is the second largest in Venice after that of St. Mark's.

The interior is as simple and as equally beautiful as the exterior. It is laid out in a Latin cross with single aisles set off by twelve huge columns. The main draw for this simple church is the **tomb of Titian**, the grand master of painting who died of plague in 1576. There are two works by Titian featured inside, *Assumption of the Virgin* done in 1518 hanging over the main altar, and *Pesaro Altarpiece* done in 1526, depicting the Virgin with members of the Pesaro family over the second altar. Another work to note is the statue of *St. John the Baptist* by **Donatello** in the altar of the first chapel.

E. GESUATI – SANTA MARIA DEL ROSARIO

Fondamenta delle Zattere, Dorsoduro. Vaporetto – Accademia or Zattere. Maps – B & D.

This church was erected between 1726 and 1743 for the Dominican friars, and was built over a 14th century monastery. The exterior is simple and tasteful in the basic Classical style. This elliptical shaped church has no aisle, making it seem larger than it really is, and contains superb frescoes on the ceiling of the dome by GB Tiepolo.

The first altar contains the *Virgin in Glory with Three Saints,* a masterpiece done in 1747 by Tiepolo. The second altar has a work by GB Piazzetta, *St. Dominic,* done in 1739. The third altar has the *Crucifixion* created by Tintoretto in 1741.

F. GESUITI – SANTA MARIA ASSUNTA

Campo dei Gesuiti, Cannaregio. Vaporetto – Fondamenta Nuova. Map – A.

Built in the 12th century, this grandiose church was given to the Jesuits (Gesuiti) in 1656. It was remodeled between 1715 and 1730 with a Baroque facade designed by Fattoretto. It contains the statues of the 12 Apostles by Penso, the Groppellio brothers, and Baratta.

This is a single-aisled church laid out in a Latin Cross Style and is decorated with a variety of colored marble inlays. The main draw to this church are two outstanding paintings: the *Assumption of the Virgin* by **Tintoretto** and the *Martyrdom of St. Lawrence* by **Titian**.

G. JEWISH GHETTO

Near the train station, Cannaregio. Guided tours of the synagogues available every hour on the hour from 10:00am–4:00pm, and Sunday 10:00am–noon. Tours not available Saturday and holidays. Vaporetto – San Marcuola. Map – C.

This was the first Jewish Ghetto in Europe. The word itself, ghetto, originated here in Venice. This area was once a cannon foundry, which in Venetian was called a *getto*. Ever since the Jews were forced into this area in Venice, their enclaves have been known by that name. The location was established by Ducal decree in 1516 and remained an enforced enclave for the Jews in Venice until 1797, ending with Napoleon's victory over the Republic. The Jews were moved here originally from the section of the city known as La Guidecca (see below) so the government could better keep an eye on them.

Here you'll find five synagogues, three of which are open to the public: **Sinagoga Grande Tedesca**, **Sinagoga Spagnole**, and **Levantina**. The small museum, **Museo Ebraica** *(Campo del Nuovo Ghetto 2902, Tel. 71-53-59, open 10:00am - 4:30pm, closed Saturdays and Jewish holidays. E6 includes a guided tour of three of the synagogues. E3 for the museum only.)*, contains information about the five centuries of Jewish presence in Venice.

H. LA GUIDECCA

Vaporetto – Guidecca. Map – D.

This populous suburb was once the neighborhood set aside for the Jews of Venice prior to their move to the Jewish Ghetto in 1516 – hence its name, which roughly means *The Jewish Area*. A brief excursion here is a wonderful respite from the hectic pace of tourist Venice. You'll find real Venetian neighborhoods, top-of-the-line hotels along the **Fondamenta Zitelle**, abandoned factories, and more. There are not many sights to see, but you can take a relaxing stroll without running into hardly any tourists.

I. GRAND CANAL

Maps – A, B & C.

The **Grand Canal** is shaped like a large upside down "S" bisecting the city. It is almost 2 1/2 miles long, 15 feet deep, and ranges anywhere from 100 to 150 feet across. Usually calm and serene, the canal has become more and more menacing and rough since the introduction of huge ocean liners docking close by.

Lining this wonderful waterway are tremendous old buildings, palaces, and homes dating from every time period and epitomizing every architectural style. You'll also see small canals thrusting off into the darkness, and beautiful gateways and entrances blackened by and beginning to be covered by the water. The best way to see the canal is to take the *vaporetto* around a few times and simply enjoy the view.

J. MADONNA DELL'ORTO

Campo Madonna dell'Orto, Cannaregio. Open 9:00am–5:00pm. Vaporetto – Madonna dell'Orto. Map – C.

This is a simple little church that contains the remains of **Jacopo Robusti**, known as **Tintoretto**, who was buried here in 1594. There are also some exquisite works by the grand master himself, **Titian**. These paintings are in the choir: *Last Judgment, Adoration of the Golden Calf, Moses Receiving the Tablets of the Law*. The tomb of Tintoretto is marked by a simple stone plaque and is just to the right of the choir.

K. REDENTORE

Campo Redentore. Open 9:00am–5:00pm. Vaporetto – Redentore. Map – D.

Built between 1577 and 1592 by Andrea Palladio and Antonio Da Ponte, as part of a thanksgiving for the end of another of the many plague epidemics that struck Venice. Across Europe more than a third of the population died because of the plagues.

A huge staircase leads up to the facade and the entrance to the church. Inside you'll find the same simple harmony as the outside as well as a magnificent Baroque altar adorned with bronzes by Campagna. In the sacristy you'll find *Virgin and Child* by Alvise Vivarini, *Baptism of Christ* by Veronese, *Virgin and Child with Saints* by Palma the Younger, and a variety of works by Bassaro.

L. RIALTO BRIDGE

Vaporetto – Rialto. Maps – A & B.

One of the best places to view the traffic along the **Grand Canal** and all its charm. This is the oldest of the three bridges spanning the canal and was originally made of wood. It collapsed in 1440 and was rebuilt in wood but still remained rather unstable, so in the 16th century the Doges decided to build a more stable bridge. Michelangelo himself submitted a design for the bridge but a local boy, Antonio Da Ponte, was awarded the contract to design and build it, and it was finished in 1592. The Rialto spans 90 feet and is 24 feet high. There are 24 shops lining the bridge separated by a double arcade from which you can walk out onto the terraces and get those superb views for which it is richly famous.

Every morning, except Sunday, on the San Polo side of the Rialto, the **Erberia** (Vegetable Market) and the **Pesceria** (Fish Market) are held. A sight that should not be missed while in Venice, especially the Pesceria.

M. SALUTE – SANTA MARIA DELLA SALUTE

Campo delle Salute. Open 9:00am–5:00pm. Vaporetto – Salute. Map – D.

One of the sights you'll see from St. Mark's Square across the canal is this truly magnificent church. Adorned with many statues sitting atop simple flying buttresses, this octagonal church is crowned with a large dome, and a smaller one directly above it. It was erected as thanksgiving for the cessation of a plague that struck Venice in 1630. During its construction it had a variety of mishaps like the foundation sinking, and the walls being unable to support the dome.

Inside are six chapels all ornately adorned. On the main altar you'll find a sculpture by Giusto Le Court that represents *The Plague Fleeing The Virgin*. The church is replete with Titian's work, including *The Pentecost* to the left of the third altar, *Death of Abel* on the sacristy ceiling, *Sacrifice of Abraham* in the sacristy, *David and Goliath* on the sacristy ceiling, and an early work *St. Mark and The Other Saints* over the altar in the sacristy.

N. SAN GIORGIO MAGGIORE

Isola San Giorgio Maggiore. Open 9:00am–12:30pm and 2:30pm–6:30pm. Vaporetto – San Giorgio. Map – D.

On an island just off the tip of La Guidecca, this magnificent church by Palladio can be seen and admired from St. Mark's Square, but you should go out and visit because the view of the lagoon and the city from its bell tower are priceless and unforgettable.

The church's white facade makes it stand out wonderfully from the ochre and brown colored monastery buildings surrounding it. It was finished in 1610 by Scamozzi from the plans of the master Palladio whose main work is located in the city of Vicenza. The facade is distinctly his, with its three sections divided by four Corinthian columns. In two niches between the columns are statues of *Sts. George* and *Stephen,* and on either side are busts of *Doges Tribuno Mommo* and *P Zini* all by Giulio Moro. The bell tower we mentioned earlier was erected by Benedetto Buratti from Bologna (a city known at the time for its many towers) in 1791 to replace an older one that collapsed in 1773.

The interior is simple yet majestic. It has a single aisle and is shaped like an inverted Latin cross. Three works to admire are: *Crucifix* by **Michelozzo** in the second altar on the right, and *Last Supper* and *Shower of Mana* by **Tintoretto** at the main altar.

O. SANTI GIOVANNI E PAOLO – SAN ZANIPOLO
Campo Santi Giovanni e Paolo, Castello. Open 9:00am–5:00pm. Vaporetto – Rialto or Fondamenta Nuova. Map – A.

Started by the Dominican monks in 1246, **Santi Giovanni e Paolo** was not finished until 1430, probably due to lack of funds just like their Franciscan counterparts when they were building Santa Maria Gloriosa dei Frari. Like that church, it contains the tombs of many well-known Venetian citizens. The church's style is known as Venetian Gothic with its combination of Gothic and Renaissance styles. Unfortunately, the facade was never finished, but it is still beautiful in its simplicity.

The inside is filled with monuments, sculptures, and paintings depicting a large number of Doges and their families. Don't miss the magnificent 15th century Gothic window by Bartolomeo Vivarini.

P. SANTA MARIA FORMOSA
Campo Santa Maria Formosa, Castello. Open 9:00am–5:00pm. Vaporetto – Rialto or San Zaccaria. Map – A.

This church was initially rebuilt in 1492, and has two 16th century facades and a 17th century belfry. It is in the shape of a Latin cross and has no aisles. The walls are covered with wonderful works by such artists as Vivarini and Palma the Elder. A simple, small church that sits in a part of Venice that most tourists never find. The piazza is filled with the sights and sounds of true modern day Venetian life.

Q. GUGGENHEIM MUSEUM
Palazzo Venier dei Leoni, Dorsoduro 701, Calle Cristoforo. Tel. 041/520-6288. Open 11:00am-6:00pm every day except Tuesdays and December 25. Admission E6. Students E4. Vaporetto – Accademia. Maps - B & D.

This is a magnificent 20th century art collection developed by the intriguing American heiress and art aficionado Peggy Guggenheim. It is exhibited in Ms. Guggenheim's old home, where she lived until her death in 1979. Here you'll find all the 20th century movements including cubism, surrealism, futurism, expressionism, and abstract art. There are works by Dali, Chagall, Klee, Moore, Picasso, Pollock and many others. If you love modern art you have to come here.

R. THE BRIDGE OF SIGHS
Vaporetto – San Marco. Map – A.

From the canal side of Ponte della Paglia you can look directly at this covered bridge connecting the Doges Palace and Prigione Nuovo (New Prison). It was built in the 17th century to transport convicts from the palace to the prison to face their punishment. The name presumably derives from the sighs of prisoners as they crossed the bridge.

When on a tour of the Palazzo Ducale you get the opportunity to walk through the bridge to the prison cells where prisoners were kept.

S. PONTE DELLA ACCADEMIA
Vaporetto - Accademia. Map - B.
The least attractive and most modern bridge in Venice, it is one of only three that traverse the Grand Canal. It is a metal and wood construction that seems to fit, but not quite, with the fairy tale images all around it. It's as if an industrial age bridge was placed in error among scenes from Snow White. Nothing magnificent to see but convenient to use to go from San Marco to the Accademia.

T. PONTE DEGLI SCALZI
Vaporetto - Ferrovia Bar Roma. Map - B.
Also known as the **station bridge** since it is right near the station, this is the first bridge you'll cross if you're walking from the station to St. Mark's. A simple, single span bridge made of white Istrian stone, it was erected in 1934 to replace a metal bridge built in 1858. The bridge is approximately 130 feet long and 23 feet above water level.

U. BASILICA DI SAN MARCO
Piazza San Marco. Open 9:30am–5:30pm. Vaporetto – San Marco. Map – A.
The church is large, magnificent and seemingly covered in gold leaf. It was built to house the remains of the republic's patron saint, **St. Mark**, as well as to glorify the strength of Venice's sea power. The structure was begun in 829, a year after St. Mark's remains were brought back from Egypt. By 832 the church had all its main structures and by 883 it was fully decorated. Its beauty was slightly marred in 976 from a fire that was set in the Doge's Palace. Then in 1000 the church was demolished because it was not grand enough. The church we know and love today was started in 1063 and was originally a Byzantine plan. It was finished in 1073 and then for centuries it was adorned with superb mosaics, precious marbles, and war spoils brought back by merchants, travelers, and soldiers, so that today the church is a mix of Byzantine, Gothic, Islamic and Renaissance materials.

As such it is garishly and eclectically magnificent inside and out. A description of all the art and architecture in this incredible place would fill another book, so you might want to hire a local tour guide or purchase one of the local guide books inside the church specifically for the Basilica.

V. PIAZZA SAN MARCO
Vaporetto – San Marco. Map – A.
When the Basilica of St. Mark and the Doge's Palace were being erected,

the grassy field in front of them was filled in and paved (between 1172-1178). On either side of the pavement, elegant houses were built with arcades running the length of them. Many were taken over by government magistrates, called *Procurati*, which gives these buildings their name today, *Procuratie*. In 1264 the square was re-paved with bricks in a herringbone pattern. Then in 1723 it was paved again with gray trachyte and white marble.

The square is 569 feet long, 266 feet at the side of St. Mark's, and 185 feet long at the side facing St. Mark's. The piazza is alive with orchestra music being played by competing cafés and is a wonderful place to stroll and people watch. You won't find many Venetians here, unless it's the off-season since it gets really crowded with tourists during high season.

W. PIAZZETTA DI SAN MARCO
Vaporetto – San Marco. Map – A.

Directly in front of the Doge's Palace, this little piazza blends into the larger Piazza San Marco and is sometimes lumped together with it. Originally it was a market place for foodstuffs, but in 1536 the Doge mandated that it remain clear for public executions. The two columns at the dock (one with the *Lion of St. Mark* atop and the other with a statue of *St. Theodore*) were brought back from the Orient in 1125 and erected in 1172. Here you'll find some peaceful but expensive outside cafés.

X. CLOCK TOWER
Piazza San Marco. Tel. 041/523-1879. Admission E3. Vaporetto – San Marco. Map – A.

Facing St. Mark's, the **Clock Tower** is directly on your left. The clock tower is not the tall brick structure in the middle of the piazza; that's the Bell Tower. The clock tower was built between 1496 and 1499, and the wings were added from 1550-1506. Above the tower is an open terrace upon which stands a bell with two male figures on either side that hammer the bell to indicate the time. These figures have been performing their faithful service for over 500 years and as a result have taken on a dark weather-beaten appearance. Because of this, they are called the Moors.

Beneath the terrace that houses these figures is the symbol of Venice, a golden winged lion. Below the lion is a niche that contains a statue of the Virgin and Child that has been attributed to Alessandro Leopardi sometime in the early 1500s. The clock, just below this, in addition to just telling the time, also indicates the changing of the seasons, the movements of the sun, as well as the phases of the moon.

Z. BELL TOWER
Piazza San Marco. Tel. 522-4064. Open 9:30am–10pm. Admission E3. Vaporetto – San Marco. Map – A.

Built over old Roman fortifications, the **Bell Tower** has been added to off and on since 888. It has withstood floods and earthquakes, but it finally gave in to less than perfect craftsmanship. On July 14, 1902, it collapsed but was reconstructed and re-opened to the public in 1912. It is the most convenient place to get a bird's-eye view of the city and the lagoon. (The next best place is the bell tower of the church of *San Giorgio Maggiore.*) An elevator can take you to the top where there are five bells that toll on special occasions.

In the distant past a cage used to jut from the wall on the piazza side that sometimes would contain criminals to be exposed to the elements as punishment. This practice was abolished in the 16th century. Another tradition, but one designed for pleasure of the people not punishment of prisoners, was to stretch a rope between the tower and the Doge's Palace and have an acrobat walk the span.

Nightlife & Entertainment

Do not come to Venice for wild and wooly nightlife. You simply will not find it here. This city shuts down early and any nightlife up to that point is either held in restaurants which are open late, or in the few pubs and bars that a beginning to emerge on the landscape. Listed below are some of the best.

68. THE FIDDLER'S ELBOW, *3847 Cannaregio (near Ca' d'Oro Vaporetto stop). Tel. 041/523-9930. Open from 5:00pm - 1:30am. Pint E4 half pint E3. Closed Wednesdays but not in the summer. Map - C.*

Come here for a taste of old Ireland. You'll find Harp, Guinness, and Kilkenny on tap, as well as almost any other drink you can imagine. The Irish lads and lassies behind the bar will serve you up proper, so enjoy a pint or two for the homeland (well, their homeland anyway). The premier meeting place for Anglos as well as Italians in Venice. Fiddler's also has pubs in Rome, Florence and Bologna. They are just off the Strada Nuova tucked away in a small *campiello*. A fun place in an ideal location.

69. THE GREEN PUB, *Campo San Margherita 3053A, Tel. 041/520-1993. Pints inside: E4. Pints outside: E5. Map - B*

Small outside seating area on the most perfect piazza in Venice. Not really much ambiance inside, but you can get a tasty brew here. They also have small snacks like sandwiches and *tramezzini*. The Margaret Duchamp a few steps away is a much better place to spend your time and their hours are much better too.

70. MARGARET DUCHAMP, *Campo Santa Margherita 3019, 31023 Venezia. Tel. 041/52-86-255. Open 8:00am to 2:00pm. Pint E4 half pint E3. Closed Sundays. Map - B*

Wonderful patio seating and intimate areas inside. Superb atmosphere, excellent bar snacks such as sandwiches, and salads as well as some basic pasta dishes. There is a wide variety of draught beer on tap like Devil's Kiss (Scotland), Tetley's (England), Elephant (Denmark), Carlsberg (Denmark) and Castlemaine (Australia). They also have fine house wine. The service is superb and the music lively and entertaining (they do enjoy their Bob Marley here). One of the best places to come to experience authentically relaxed Venetian nightlife.

71. EL SOUK PUB, *Accademia 1056A. Tel. 041/520-0371. Pint of Tennents E3. Map -B.*

A real nightclub/harem atmosphere, with a small dance floor where you can work up a thirst. Located right near the Accademia (take the Accademia's *vaporetto* stop). To get here, start at the *vaporetto* stop and go down the road to your right. Take your first right and El Souk will be on the right hand side after a few paces. It's not really a pub. It's more of a disco, so if you want a pint and a conversation, go to one of the pubs above. But if you want dancing and flirting, this is your place.

Opera

If you are in Venice from December to June, the traditional opera season, have brought the proper attire (suits for men, dresses for women), and have a taste for something out of the ordinary, try the spectacle of an opera.

• **Teatro La Fenice**, *Campo S. Fantin 1977, 30124 Venezia. Tel. 041/786-562 or 786-569, Fax 041/786-580.*

Sports & Recreation

In terms of sporting activities, there really is not much to do in Venice proper except jog along the Grand Canal in the early mornings when the crowds aren't around. For recreation you'll have to go to the island of Lido, where you'll find golf, bicycling, horseback riding, tennis and of course, swimming.

But I am averse to mentioning Lido, since it really doesn't seem to into the whole atmosphere of Venice. Why? Lido was built only recently so the architecture has nothing in common with the beauty of Venice, and most importantly on Lido they allow cars and buses, so that tranquil feeling you get while in Venice evaporates instantly when you arrive on Lido. But if you're in need of some sporting fun, Lido beckons. To get there, take *vaporetto* no. 6 or no. 11.

Bicycling

Having a leisurely bicycle ride on Sundays is a favorite pastime of the people on Lido. To rent a bike, tandem, or tricycle, go to Giorgio Barbieri, *Via Zara 5, Lido. No phone number.*

Golfing
• **Circolo Golf Venezia**, *Via del Forte, 30011 Alberoni. Tel. 041/731-1333/ 731-015, Fax 041/731-339.* Located 10 km from Venice proper on the island of Lido, this is an 18 hole, par 72, 6,199 meters long course. It's open year round except on Mondays. They have a driving range, pro shop, bar and restaurant.
• **Ca' Amata Golf Club**, *Via Postioma di Salvarosa 44, 31033 Castelfranco Veneto. Tel. 0432/721-833, Fax 0432/721-842.* Located 30 km from both Venice and Padua, this is a nine hole, par 36 course that is 3,311 meters long. Open from February to December and closed Mondays. This place has a driving range, pro shop, putting green, restaurant and swimming pool.
• **Ca' Della Nave Golf Club**, *Piazza della Vittoria 14, 30030 Martellago. Tel. 041/540-1555, Fax 041/540-1926.* Located 12 km from Venice on the mainland, this is an 18 hole par 72 course that is a challenging 6,380 meters long. It is open year round except on Tuesdays. They have a putting green, pro shop, tennis courts, restaurant and bar.

Horseback Riding
If you want to go riding, you'll have to pay a king's ransom to rent a horse from the **Venice Riding Club** at *Ca'Bianca on the Lido, Tel. 765-162.* They have an indoor riding school and paddock with fixed and competitive fences and a variety of competition horses for hire.

Swimming
Your choices are the pools at the **Excelsior Hotel** and the **Hotel des Bains** where you can purchase very expensive daily or seasonal tickets; and the public beaches are at **San Nicolo** and **Alberoni** at both the north and the south ends of **Lido**. The rest of the beaches are private and attached to hotels for the use of their guests.

Tennis
There are tennis courts for rent at the **Lido Tennis Club** *(Via San Gallo 16, Tel. 041/760-954)*, and from the **Tennis Union** *(Via Fausta, Tel. 041/968-134)*. Court time is expensive and packed in the high season.

Shopping
Books & Newspapers in English
Most newsstands in Venice will carry a variety of different international newspapers and magazines. The most current newspaper will most probably be *The International Herald Tribune*, which is a joint venture between The Washington Post and The New York Times and is printed all over Europe. If you can't seem to find a paper, simply go into one of the better hotels and they

should have some available for sale. Or if they don't have any, they can surely tell you where to find one. As for books, listed below are a few bookstores that have English language titles available.

Libreria Pio X, *Studium Veneziano, Calle di Canonica 337, San Marco. Tel. 041/522-2382. Credit cards accepted.*

A religious as well as a general bookstore near the Ponte della Canonica that also is well stocked with English language books. In conjunction they have many books about Venetian history, architecture, and literature so if you want to bone up on your knowledge of Venice, this bookstore can be of assistance.

Libreria Internazionale San Giorgio, *Calle Large XXII Marzo 2087, San Marco. Tel. 041/38-451. Credit cards accepted.*

There is an excellent selection of travel and information books about Venice and other parts of Italy. You'll also find a selection on art, architecture, and history, but only a small section of paperback literature. There are also some interesting posters and postcards.

Glass Products

Venice has been making glass products for more than 1,000 years. The glass blowing furnaces were moved in 1292, for fire safety reasons, to the five islands of **Murano** (see *Excursions & Day Trips* below) which are five minutes north of Venice by *vaporetto*. To make sure you're not getting a reproduction or something of inferior quality, always check to see if the letters **VM** are stamped on the bottom of the glasswork. The VM *(Vetro Murano)* is the mark for quality Venetian glass.

All over Venice you'll find these cute glass animals and figurines and I bet your kids go ga-ga over them, but on Murano you can see them being made which will thrill the kids even more. Two of the five major manufacturers on Murano have shops in Venice (**Salviati** and **Venini**) but the rest sell only from the island of Murano. Here's the place not only to see glass objects being made but also to get some fine glass pieces at great prices.

Lace Products

The small island of **Burano** (see *Excursions & Day Trips* below) has been producing intricate hand-made lace work for centuries. Mary Tudor of England got her wedding gown made on the island. Since that time the style has been widely copied and some say the French make a better lace now, but an excursion to the island to see how the stuff is made is a fun trip.

Masks

Venice is home to one of the world's best carnivals (*Carnevale* in Italian), designed for everyone to sow their wild oats before the fasting begins for Lent. The merriment generally begins in February or March and lasts for several weeks before it culminates on Shrove Tuesday (Mardi Gras), the day before

Lent begins on Ash Wednesday. During Carnevale the Venetians in times past used to wear masks all the time, allowing men to court and cavort with impunity and women to be able to walk around unchaperoned and meet their secret lovers or find new ones undetected. Since masks are part of their history, Venetians have become quite adept at creating them.

There are all sorts of traditional masks, many taken from the 16th century *Commedia dell'Arte*, and any of these masks would make for a great wall ornament or Halloween costume. The craftsmen carve wooden molds from which they make plaster casts – basically negative images of the mask – which are then layered with papiermache to shape the masks. Then this covering is either left blank for you to paint or is intricately decorated for you. There are plenty of stores where you can watch the mask makers at work.

Paper Products

Venice has been popular for their decorative paper goods for centuries, specifically the marbling effect they produce for the cover of books, desk blotters, pencils, pens, and many other items. When wandering around the back streets of Venice you will surely stumble upon a small shop making and selling their own versions of marbleized paper products.

Shoes

As you would imagine shoes are popular in a city that does not have any cars. Because the Venetians have to walk everywhere, they use up the most shoes per capita than any other city in the world. Even though Florence, Rome, and Milan all have great shoes, most of the prices in Venice are slightly less expensive. Most of the designs here are functional rather than frivolous.

Markets

Erberia (Vegetable Market) and **Pesceria** (Fish Market). *Vegetable market is open Monday through Saturday 8:00am to 1:00pm; the fish market is open Tuesday through Saturday 8:00am through 1:00pm.*

The natives and the restaurants of Venice find their daily produce, cheese, fish, meats, and breads in the large Campo and the adjoining streets near the Chiesa di San Giacomo di Rialto and at the base of the Rialto bridge. It is a bustling, crowded, fun adventure just to go there to buy something. By actually going to market with the Venetians you feel almost a part of them since you're sharing one of their truly unique daily experiences.

Look for the *Pescheria* on your map, since is a great place to visit. Sometimes you'll see a six foot swordfish sliced to perfection for restaurants and home buyers. You can also witness a young Venetian peel shrimp faster than you could eat them. Also most stands sell snails where you can see how the persistent buggers attach themselves to the sides of the ladle when the proprietor scoops them out to be weighed. They are only delaying the inevitable transformation into a delectable butter and garlic *antipasto*. But you have to admire their persistence.

Campo San Barnaba, Dorsoduro. *Open Mondays and Tuesdays, and Thursday through Saturday 9:00am to 1:00pm and 3:30pm to 7:30pm, and Wednesdays 9:00am to 1:00pm.*

Located right off the Piazza Santa Margherita, this is a quaint open air floating market where you can mainly buy fresh vegetables.

Campo San Margherita, Dorsoduro. *Open Mondays, Tuesdays, and Thursday through Saturday from 9:00am to 1:00pm and 3:30pm to 7:30pm.*

A few stalls inter-dispersed around the piazza sell fruits, vegetables, and fish. Not nearly as grand as the Rialto market but one to enjoy nonetheless. This square has to be the best example of true Venetian life there is. Besides the market, come for the mothers playing with their children, the small local shops, and relaxing seating on some of the benches in the square. Don't miss this market.

Calle Regina 2328A. A local pastry factory. Walk by and savor the tantalizing smells that emanate from their open door. You can't go in, but you can watch from the doorway as they prepare the pastries for the shops on the island. But the smell is what brings me back here time after time.

Picnic Supplies

The best place to get picnic supplies is at the **Erberia** (Vegetable Market) and the **Pesceria** (Fish Market) at the base of the bridge on the San Polo section side, which is held every morning except Sundays and Mondays (see *Markets* above).

Excursions & Day Trips

The first three islands mentioned below can all be seen in a four to five hour period. To get to any of them, buy a round-trip ticket for E4 at vaporetto booth #12 at the Fondamenta Nuova. After you have finished your lunch or dinner at one of the fine restaurants on **Torcello** (your last stop) simply stamp your ticket in the yellow machine before boarding the *vaporetto* and you'll be on your way back to Venice.

If you start in the morning around 9:00am and go first to **Murano**, then **Burano**, and then **Torcello**, you will have worked up a powerful hunger. The same goes if you start the trek at 2:00pm or so, after your lunch in Venice. By the time you get to Torcello, you'll be dying to sample their excellent food in a restaurant with wonderful outdoor seating.

To go to just one of the islands, simply purchase a single ticket for E2, and stamp it as you leave and again on your return.

MURANO

Located 3/4 of a mile northeast of Venice, Murano is a lagoon town that is spread among five little islands. It has a relatively quiet and uncrowded feel to it, especially around dinner time, when all the tourists have returned to the crowds of Venice. Since there are no hotels in the island it has remained relatively tourist free, especially at night and in the evenings.

Murano today is what Venice must have been like fifty years ago before international tourism really took off. In Venice every door and building front has been turned into a shop, café, or restaurant for tourists. Here it's more like one out of every four. There are small cafés and restaurants dotting the canal, so if you're in the need for a drink, some coffee, a little ice cream or any type of snack, you'll have it. The island group is roughly divided in half by a relatively large canal that is spanned by one bridge, the Ponte Longo, from which local kids like to jump off of into the water.

Arrivals & Departures

Take *Vaporetto* 52 or 12 from the Fondamenta Nuove. It takes about ten minutes.

Seeing the Sights

Murano is the perfect place to just stroll around and explore. You feel as if you've entered a time warp as you go down certain streets. Make sure you go off the beaten path and really explore. And don't worry about getting lost, the town is small enough that it's impossible for you not to find your way back again. This island chain is world-renowned for its **glass blowing** industry, which dates back to 1291 when the furnaces were banned from Venice as a precaution against fire and industrial espionage. At its height in the 16th century, Murano had 37 glass factories and a population of 30,000. Today the population is only a little under 8,000.

What used to be the closely guarded secret of glass blowing is today common knowledge, but Murano glass is still in demand all over the world because of the skilled artisans that spend their life preparing the fine works of art. And that's what we've come to Murano to see, a glass blowing exhibition. There are a number of small factories dotting the island group, but the one listed below is the most interesting:

• **Civam**, *Viale Garibaldi 24, 30141 Venezia/Murano, Tel. 041/739-323, Fax 041/739-323.* Located where the boat lets you off from Venice. You will get an extensive exhibit of glass blowing technique in their factory shop.

Other recommended sights include:
• **Museo dell'Arte Vetraria**, *Fondamenta Giustiniano and Fondamenta Manin. Tel. 041/739-586. Open Mondays, Tuesdays, Thursdays and*

Saturdays 10:00am–4:00pm, Sundays 9:00am–12:30pm. Closed Wednesdays. This is the Glass Museum.
• **Santi Maria e Donato**, *Campo San Donato. Open 8:00am - noon, 4:00pm - 7:00pm.*

Also check out the **glass factories** on *Fondamenta dei Vetrai*, three of which offer glass blowing exhibitions. And if you get hungry or thirsty there are plenty of cafés and restaurants located all around this quaint little island.

BURANO

Located 5 1/2 miles northeast of Venice, Burano occupies four tiny islands that are inhabited mainly by fishermen and lace seamstresses. It was first settled in the 5th and 6th centuries by refugees from Altinum fleeing Attila's Huns. Mainly known for the traditional art of lace making, which the women

of the town have been handing down to their daughters for centuries, Burano is also a great place to unwind from the hectic pace of Venice.

The brightly colored houses on the island give it the air of an Italian opera set, which also makes it a perfect background for some excellent photographs. There is also plenty of green space in which to relax. Burano and Torcello (our next destination) have more grass than all of the island chain of Venice proper combined. So for those of you who get tired of looking at concrete and marble, coming here for a needed respite.

There are also plenty of little cafés, *gelaterie*, and *trattoria* to quench a hunger or thirst.

Arrivals & Departures

Take Vaporetto number 12 from Fondamenta Nuove. It takes about 35 minutes. You'll first stop at Burano.

Where to Eat

1. **TRATTORIA AI PESCATORI**, *Via Galuppi 371. Tel. 041/730650. Closed Wednesdays and January. All credit cards accepted. Dinner for two E70.*

Come here for great lagoon cooking, which means of course seafood. Located in the center of the island with a terrace you can enjoy in the summer, this is a nice but expensive local place. Try any of their pasta with fish, like *spaghetti ai frutti di mare* (with the fruits of the sea) and any of their grilled or fried fish. The name of the place means Fisherman's Trattoria, so fish is the best here.

Seeing the Sights

Take a look at the lace school and satisfy your curiosity about the inner workings of the lace business. The school is **Consorzio dei Merletti**, *located in the Palazzo del Podesta in the Piazza B. Galuppi. Tel. 041/730-034. Open Monday–Saturday 9:00am–6:00pm, and Sundays 9:00am–4:00pm.*

One other interesting sight on Burano is the **Church of San Martino**, *Piazza B. Galuppi,* with its leaning tower. It's no Pisa, but still intriguing nonetheless.

A store that cannot be missed is **Artistico Bombon**, *Tel. 041/735-551, San Martino 1002 (see #2 on map).* This quaint little shop, on a romantic canal, surrounded by colorfully painted buildings serves up the best glass candies I have ever seen. Despite the fact that the owner has misspelled the French word for candy on the name of his store, everything here is made with exquisite care and tantalizingly tasty detail. The little candies make perfect gifts and are wonderful conversation pieces when placed in bowls at home.

Each little wrapped candy is so perfectly crafted that they will tempt even the most discerning guest into believing they're real. Truly whimsical works of art.

TORCELLO

Located six and a half miles northeast of Venice, Torcello is one of the most fascinating spots in the Venetian Lagoon. The island was settled between the 5th and 7th centuries by the first wave of refugees from the barbarian hordes. It got its name from the tower (*Torcello* means little tower) from which the bishop of Altinum saw his vision of how to make his people safe.

Now just a solitary village on a lonely island, it was once a flourishing center of commerce and culture whose greatness dimmed as that of Venice grew. Since the 18th century, Torcello has been nearly deserted, with a population today of only about 100 people. All that remains of this long ago splendor is a group of monuments that face out onto the scenic but grassy central piazza.

Most of the land that remains has either been abandoned or has been cultivated, mainly for wine. After you've seen the few sights and walked the few hundred meters of town, the only thing left to do is satisfy your hunger at one of the exquisite outdoor restaurants. Eating, drinking, and making idle conversation is the main activity here. That's why Hemingway liked it so much.

Arrivals & Departures

Take *Vaporetto* 12 from Fondamenta Nuove. It takes about 45 minutes. You'll stop at Murano, Mazzorbe, and Burano first. After you get off the boat you'll have a little walk beside a canal that has no shops, stores, houses, restaurants or cafés (how amazing to find an area in Venice devoid of commercialism).

Where to Eat

If you make it to Torcello, you really should try at least a small meal at one of these places:

LOCANDA CIPRIANI, *Tel. 041/730-150 or 73-54-33. American Express accepted. Open mid-March–October. Closed Mondays and Tuesdays. Dinner for two E80.*

An offshoot of Harry's Bar with the same high prices. This used to be a haunt of Hemingway's too. The place serves traditional dishes like grilled meats and fish. The atmosphere is pleasant, especially the seating in the terrace garden area.

OSTERIA AL PONTE DEL DIAVOLO, *Via Chiesa 10/11. Tel. 041/730-401 or 041/730-441. American Express and Visa accepted. Open for lunch only. Closed on Thursdays and in January. Dinner for two E70.*

This restaurant has a relaxing outdoor seating area and serves Venetian specialties like *Tagliatelli con gli scampetti* (tagliatelli pasta with little shrimps). They also make exquisite grilled fish and meats. A high end restaurant that serves great food in a peaceful and calm environment.

Seeing the Sights
• **Cathedral**, *Santa Maria Assunta. Tel. 041/730-084. Open 10:00am–12:30pm and 2:00pm–6:30pm. Closes 2 hours earlier in the winter.*
• **Museo dell'Estuario**, *Santa Maria Assunta. Tel. 041/730-761. Open Tuesday–Sunday 10:30am–12:30pm and 2:00pm–4:00pm. Closed Mondays.*

SAN MICHELE

If you like cemeteries, you should come here to visit the graves of Ezra Pound, Igor Stravinsky, and Frederick Rolfe. Otherwise, you may want to skip this stop altogether. The island is located half a mile north of Venice.

This is the strangest cemetery you'll ever see. Why? You can't bury anybody below the surface since the surface is water, so all they do is stack them one on top of each other and place them in long rows. The island actually is quite scenic and very peaceful, with its organized paths and beautiful tall trees. Not quite the place to have a picnic, but a place to go that I guarantee you not many tourists visit frequently. It's nothing like the cemetery in Genoa that resembles a little town, but it is still quite an experience.

To get here, take *Vaporetto* 52 from Fondamenta Nuove (5 minutes) or Piazza Roma (15 minutes).

PADUA

A city of 242,000 people just 23 miles west of Venice, **Padua** (**Padova**) was a rich trading center even before Roman times. The city was an ally of the Romans in the wars against the Gauls but retained its independence. Throughout the Roman period the city was an important cultural and economic center, and was known for its woolen textile industry.

After the Lombard invasions, Padua, like other neighboring towns, became less prosperous because of the financial and social demands placed on the populations. By 1163, Padua was already a part of the **Veneto to Verona League**, a union of smaller towns created as protection against invading armies. In 1406, the Venetians occupied Padua amicably after the ruler of Padua, Francesco II of Carara, and all his family were killed under mysterious circumstances. The city remained under Venetian rule until 1797, when the city was occupied by the French led by Napoleon. From that point on they were ceded to Austria, became part of the Italian Kingdom, were taken over by the Hapsburg Empire, and finally in 1866 became part of modern day Italy.

Today, Padua may be best known as a university city. The **university** was founded in 1222, and is the second oldest in Italy to Bologna's. Padua became the city where the wealthy Venetians studied law and medicine. By the 15th century it also was the creative outlet for artistic expression and intellectual innovation that was not allowed in the more conservative Venice.

Padua is now also an active commercial center in addition to being a highly respected university city. It was severely damaged during bombing raids during World War II but the town still maintains much of its distinctive character. This is a small city, making it easy to get around, and you can see all the sights in one day. If you're on a day trip from Venice, have no fear about catching your train back. If you've come to stay, I've listed some good hotels in the **Centro Storico** area for you to enjoy.

Padua on the Fly

Gran Caffe Pedrichi is not only a place to get a drink or small bite to eat, but is a fun sight in itself. When it opened in 1831 it was the largest café in Europe, and it still retains its majestic charm. Whatever you get here will cost you an arm and a leg, but the history and ambiance make the money well spent.

If you're looking for something less expensive and filled with local flavor, the **Trattoria Al Santo** is for you. Don't let its spartan appearance fool you – the food is fantastic. You'll need reservations, since the locals already know this is the place to go.

Just down the road from the Trattoria Al Santo is the **Piazza del Santo**, a beautiful open garden in the center of the city that boasts 78 statues of famous Paduans and others that attended the University. Closer to the train station are two interesting sights. The first is the market that is on the ground floor of the **Palazzo della Ragione** and that spills out into the **Piazza delle Erbe** and **Piazza della Frutta**. Come here for great sights, sounds, and smells of a truly authentic Italian market offering fruit, meat, vegetables, clothing and more. The other sight is the **Scrovegni Chapel**, where you'll find some of the best fresco work that the Master **Giotto** created.

Arrivals & Departures
By Car
    Take the Autostrada A4 just after Mestre all the way to Padua. If you have time, drive along the Brenta Canal on route #11 all the way to Padua.

By Train
    There is a frequent service (about every half-hour) from Venice's train station that takes 30 minutes each way. The return is the same: a train leaves from Padua for Venice every half-hour or less.
    Once you leave the train station in Padua you can take bus #8 (buy a ticket for Euro 75 cents at the ticket counter just before you leave the station on the right) to the Piazza Santo. Around this square is where most of the hotels and restaurants are located.

By Water
    The Burchiello water bus leaves Venice on Tuesdays, Thursdays and Saturdays, May through September, at 9:20am from Ponti Giardinetta near Piazza San Marco. The boat arrives in Padua in early afternoon. This may be the best way to get to Padua if you have a little time on your hands. The boat meanders through the waterways and past Palladian villas that line the Brenta Canal. You return to Venice by bus. A wonderful unique way to explore the countryside.

Where to Stay
    I really don't recommend that you stay in Padua, unless you're an experienced traveler and want to stay in a city that is a little off the beaten path. The city has great charm and moves at a slower pace than most other Italian cities. If you choose it can be a good place to stay for a day or two, but in most cases it can be savored as a day trip from Venice. If you do choose to stay, here are some of the best places in the **Centro Storico** I found for you.
    1. AL FAGIANO, *Via Locatelli 45, Tel. 049/875-3396, Fax 049/875-0073. 29 rooms all with bath. Single E55; Double E65. Credit cards accepted. Breakfast E5.* **
    A quaint little two star that is not far from the Basilica del Santo. The rooms are clean, comfortable and spacious, and you even have air conditioning, a must in the summer, as well as television. The floors are tile and the furnishings are basic, but here you can stay for not a lot of money while in Padua. Nothing to rave about, but a good place at a good price.
    2. LEON BIANCO, *Piazzetta Pedrocchi 12, Tel. 049/875-0814, Fax 049/ 875-6184. E-mail: leonbianco@writeme.com. 22 rooms all with bath. All credit cards accepted. Single E80; Double E90. Breakfast E8.* ***
    Simple little hotel with a pleasnat atmosphere in the *centro storico* in a pedestrian zone nearby the famous caffe Pedrocchi. The rooms come with all

three star amenities as do the bathrooms. A great feature of this place is its terrace overlooking the town where you have your breakfast in the mornings. A great small town three star.

3. MAJESTIC TOSCANELLI, *Via dell'Arco 2, Tel. 049/663-244, Fax 049/ 876-0025. E-mail: majestic@writeme.com. 32 rooms all with bath. All credit cards accepted. Single E90-125; Double E112-185. Breakfast included.*

Without a doubt the best place to stay in the *centro storico* area. This is a well-known prestigious hotel in a 15th century palazzo in the heart of the old ghetto. The entrance is dominated by persian rugs and plants. The rooms are filled with wonderful antiques as well as every possible amenity including a video rental service with over 500 titles. Small bathrooms with box style showers or bathtubs, not both. And for a touch of uniqueness, their in-house restaurant serves Brazilian food.

Where to Eat

4. L'ANFORA, *Via del Soncin 13, Tel. 049/656-629. Closed Sundays. No credit cards accepted. Dinner for two E35.*

An informal, lively, local atmosphere. The cuisine is simple, rustic and good. Created with care by Alberto Grinzato and his assistants, you'll find great food, excellent wine, and wonderful prices. One of the more traditional restaurants in Padova. A place to come to sample the local food. They make a great *bruschetta* for appetizer, and are known for an excellent pesto sauce over *trofiette* pasta. For seconds they have a wide array of meat and vegetable offerings. The desserts are made in house and are tantalizingly tasty.

5. DAL CAPO, *Via degli Obizzi 2, Tel. 049/663-105. Closed Sundays and in August. All credit cards accepted. Dinner for two E40.*

By far the best place to eat in Padua. Great food at honest prices and ample portions. The atmopshere is like a bistro from Paris, but don't let that fool you, they make great local food here. Try their *tagliatelle alle erbe aromatiche* (pasta with aromatic herbs), then the *filetto di trota* (trout filet) for seconds. The service is great, the food stupendous, the atmosphere inviting. A wonderful place to eat.

6. PAGO PAGO, *Via Galilei 59, Tel. 049/665-558. Closed Saturday and in July. All credit cards accepted. Dinner for two E35.*

Run by two Neapolitan brothers, this is the place to come for pizza in Padua. They make it every which way, from classic creations like *Margherita* to creative concoctions that include every imaginable ingredient. They also serve great pasta dishes and desserts, both of which are made in-house daily. A fun, irreverent place with all sorts of excellent food, but come here especially for their pizzas. The desserts are made in house. This place is great.

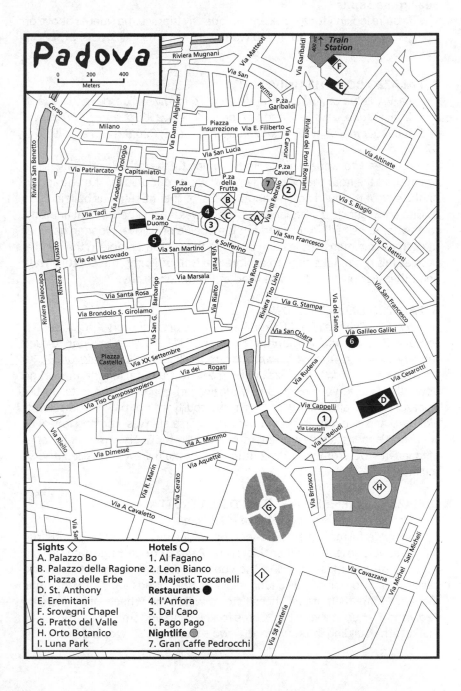

Padova

0   200   400
Meters

Train Station

Riviera Mugnani
Via Matteotti
Via Garibaldi
Via San
Ferruo
P.za Garibaldi
F
E

Corso
Milano
Piazza Insurrezione   Via E. Filiberto
Via San Lucia
Via Dante Alighieri
Via Cavour
Riviera dei Ponti Romani
Via Altinate

Riviera San Benetto
Via Patriarcato
Capitaniato
Via Academia
Orologio
P.za Signori
P.za della Frutta
P.za Cavour
B
7
2
Via VIII Febbraio
Via S. Biagio

Riviera A. Mussato
Via Tadi
P.za Duomo
4
3
C
A
Via San Francesco
Via C. Battisti

5
Via San Martino
e Solferino
Via Prati
Via Roma
Via del Vescovado
Via Marsala
Via Rialto
Riviera Tito Livio
Via del Santo
Via San Francesco

Via Santa Rosa
Barbarigo
Via G. Stampa
Via San G.
Via Brondolo S. Girolamo
Via San Chiara
Via Galileo Galilei
6

Riviera Paleocapa
Piazza Castello
Via XX Settembre
Via dei   Rogati
Via Rudena
Via Cesarotti

Via Tiso Camposampiero
Via Cappelli
D
Via Rielli
Via Dimesse
Via A. Memmo
Via Locatelli
1
Via L. Beludi

Via R. Marin
Via Cerato
Via Aquette
Via Brisosco
H

Via A. Cavaletto
G
Via San
Via Cavazzana
Via Michel San Micheli

I
Via SB Fanteria

Sights ◇
A. Palazzo Bo
B. Palazzo della Ragione
C. Piazza delle Erbe
D. St. Anthony
E. Eremitani
F. Srovegni Chapel
G. Pratto del Valle
H. Orto Botanico
I. Luna Park

Hotels ○
1. Al Fagano
2. Leon Bianco
3. Majestic Toscanelli
Restaurants ●
4. l'Anfora
5. Dal Capo
6. Pago Pago
Nightlife ◉
7. Gran Caffe Pedrocchi

Seeing the Sights
If you're looking for a quick and unique day trip, see the sidebar above on *Doing Padua on the Fly*. But if you want the run of the mill style sightseeing, here it is:

A. PALAZZO BO – THE UNIVERSITY
Via VIII Febraio. Anatomical Theater: Tours given Tuesdays 9, 10, and 11:00am. Wednesdays 3, 4, and 5:00pm. Thursdays 9, 10, and 11:00am and 3, 4, and 5:00pm. Fridays 3, 4, and 5:00pm. Tel. 049/820-97-11; Fax 049/820-97-26.

You need to appear five minutes prior to the scheduled tour, since promptly at the hour the guide leaves and you're out of luck. The entrance is on the side of the building on Canon del Gallo. The theater was built in 1594 by Girolamo Fabricio d' Acquapendente and was the first permanent anatomical theater to be built in the world. It is made up of six oval wooden galleries of decreasing dimensions leading down to the operating table in the middle. Besides this room, take time to explore the **Hall of Forty**, the **Lecture Hall**, and other well preserved rooms used at the old university.

B. PALAZZO DELLA RAGIONE
Piazza delle Erbe. Tel. 661–377 ext. 423. Open February 1–October 31, 9:00am–7:00pm and November 1–January 31, 9:00am–6:00pm. Closed January 1, May 1, August 15, and December 25, and 26. Admission E4.

Don't enter from the Piazza delle Erbe – if you're facing the market go down the road to your right, take your first left and enter the gates of the Palazzo Municipiale. Take the stairs in the courtyard up, pay the ridiculously high fee and see the imposing wooden horse. It was commissioned by Annibale Capodilista for a jousting tournament in 1466. Also inside are a series of faded frescoes from the 13th century, but the main draw is the sizable horse sculpture.

C. PIAZZA DELLE ERBA & PIAZZA DELLA FRUTTA
Market open every day 7:00am – 1:30pm.

A wonderful market environment, one of the best in all of Italy, with fruit and vegetable sellers on either side of the **Palazzo della Ragione** building, with cheese and meat sellers in the cool environment inside. At the back, besides fruit you'll also find vendors selling leather goods and clothing. Inside there are some memorable cheese stores with huge wheels of *Parmigiano Regianno* piled up to the ceiling. Come for the sights and smells of a true Italian market. The building in between the two squares is also worth a look.

D. BASILICA OF ST. ANTHONY
Piazza del Santo. Tel. 663-944. October-April open 6:30am-7:00pm and May-September open 6:30am-7:45pm.

The basilica is dedicated to St. Anthony of Padua, who was born in Lisbon in 1195. He only lived and worked in Padua for two years but he was so popular that when he died in 1231 the Paduans wanted to keep him as their own. And besides, the city didn't have a patron saint yet, and they were pretty sure the Pope was going to canonize him, so they wouldn't let him go. Pope Gregory IX made him a saint as predicted on the 3rd of May 1232, and this basilica was started immediately afterward.

It was completed between 1256 and 1263 as a single nave church. The other two naves and eight cupolas were added later. The facade has four arches and three bronze doors by Camillo Boito. In the niche above the entrance sits a sculpture of St. Anthony created by Napoleon Martinuzzi in 1940, a copy of the original which is kept in the Anthonian Museum. Above this is a loggia with 17 columns.

Inside – remember to dress appropriately or you won't get in, i.e. no shorts or tank tops for men, the same for women as well as short skirts – you'll find the walls covered with countless old and new frescoes, and any free space is taken up by bas-reliefs and sculptures. The big attraction is the main altar that has seven sculptures accredited to **Donatello**, and St. Anthony's tomb and his chapel which are filled with many sculptures and bas-reliefs depicting the saint's life and miracles.

E. EREMITANI
Piazza Eremitani 8. Open summer 9:00am-7:00pm; winter 9:00am-5:30pm. Closed Mondays. Admission is E4 which also gains you entrance to the Scrovegni Chapel.

This is the **Civic Museum of Padua**, founded in the nineteenth century. Here you'll find many Pre-Roman, Roman, Greek, Egyptian and Etruscan antiquities. There is not too much to see as compared to a Smithsonian exhibit, but what they have is laid out in an appealing, interesting, and educational manner.

F. SCROVEGNI CHAPEL
Open summer 9:00am-7:00pm; winter 9:00am-6:00pm. Entrance to the chapel is through the Civic Museum accessed from the Piazza Eremitani 8.

The chapel stands in the Arena gardens and takes its name from Enrico Scrovegni, who built it beside his family home between 1301 and 1303. It is a small simple building that fits a chapel. Inside you'll find a single nave filled with stunning frescoes by **Giotto**, which are the best preserved of the Florentine master.

G. PIAZZA DEL SANTO, PRATTO DEL VALLE

In the **Piazza del Santo** sits the **Pratto del Valle**, an open garden in the center of the city that has 78 statues of famous Paduans and people that attended the University. These figures were selected by the members of the families that contributed to the construction cost of the Pratto. It was once the site of an old Roman amphitheater where pagan rituals were held. Begun in 1775, the center island (Memmia Island) used to have small shops surrounding it, but these were demolished to accommodate the small trees.

There is little shade since the park is wide open, with only a fountain in the center to offer some solace from the sun. Nonetheless it is one of the best sights in Padua. You can get great pictures with statues in the foreground and churches in the rear. If you have kids, you can create a game for them to race around checking up on who's who among the many statues.

H. ORTO BOTANICO

Open April–October, 9:00am–1:00pm and 3:00pm–6:00pm everyday.

The oldest **botanical gardens** in Europe. They were founded in 1545 and extend over an area nearly 21,000 square meters. You'll find many exotic and rare plant species, such as the Palm of Goethe, which was planted in the sixteenth century. A pleasant walk if it wasn't for the E4 charge just to enter.

I. LUNA PARK

Open from May 1 to June 13 every year, and from 4:00pm until midnight every day during that time.

If you or your kids are getting bored in Venice, or you're in Padua and can't think of what to do next, go to **Luna Park**. It's a tiny amusement park with bumper cars, a Ferris wheel, shooting contests, and many other rides as well as your typical food and drink. It's a lot like a county fair in the States. It's hidden away behind a large building past the Pratto della Valle so you have to look to find it.

Nightlife & Entertainment

14. **GRAN CAFFE PEDROCHI**, *Via VIII Febraio. Credit cards accepted. Drinks/Coffee/Pastries all around E5 each.*

When it opened in 1831, this was the largest café in Europe and it still seems that way now. Housed in a neo-classic building near Piazza Garibaldi, this place is *elegantissimo* with its immense ceilings, marble columns and floors, and tuxedoed waiters at your beck and call. You can eat at the overpriced dining rooms or enjoy some pastries and coffee for a little less in the bar/cafe area. You can either sit inside or have a table outside, in the front or back. If you come to Padua you have to at least stop here and enjoy a drink or coffee.

Practical Information
Car Rental
• **Avis**, Piazza Stazione 1, Tel. 049/66-41-98
• **Hertz**, Best Travel, Piazza Stazione, Tel. 049/875-2202

Tourist Information
• **Train Station**, Tel. 049/875-2077
• **Museo di Santo**, *Tel. 049/875-3087*
• **Museo Civico Eretani**, *Tel. 049/875-0655*

Each of these tourist offices will supply you with a not-so-good map, but the center city of Padua is not that large and you may not even need it. These places can help you get a hotel room too if you need it.

English Language Bookstore
• **Feltrinelli International**, *Via S. Francesco 14, Tel. 049/875-0792.*

VERONA
Located 71 miles west of Venice, Verona is home to approximately 270,000 people. It is one the most beautiful and romantic of all northern Italian cities. Its presence is dominated by the fast-flowing Adige River that curves dramatically through the city. Since Verona was a flourishing Roman city from the first century BCE, the city's monuments span over 2,100 years.

Besides its monuments, Verona is also a beautiful city in which to walk because the center is now largely traffic-free, and there are many picturesque "Juliet" balconies overlooking the animated streets filled with shops and people. (Did you know that the play *Romeo and Juliet* was actually first written by an Italian from Vicenza, Luigi da Porto, and was only modified by Shakespeare?)

After a brief period of communal government rule in the 12th century, Verona was controlled by the Della Scala family from 1262 to 1387, under whose rule most of Verona's monuments were built. During this time, **Dante Aligheri**, the man who wrote *The Divine Comedy* (*The Inferno*, *Purgatorio*, and *Paradiso*), visited Verona while exiled from Florence. There is a statue commemorating his stay in the Piazza Dei Signori.

Then in 1404, at the same time as nearby Vicenza, Verona became a part of the Venetian Empire until they were conquered by Napoleon's forces some centuries later. Today, Verona is one of the most prosperous cities in Europe because of its central location, which elicited all those pesky unwanted invasions in the past.

There is so much to see and do while in Verona that it may be a good idea to spend at least two days here if you can.

Verona on the Fly

Let's get down to business – food. **Trattoria Imperio** and **Ristorante Dante** are located in the same square, **Piazza dei Signori**. The former is down to earth and serves inexpensive but very tasty pizzas in a colorful and playful setting, and the other caters to your every culinary desire while surrounding you with ambiance, charm, and character; these are two restaurants you have to try while in Verona.

Just a short distance away from this quaint little piazza with its Baroque buildings is the sight to see in Verona, the **Piazza Bra** and the ancient Roman **Arena**. Despite the age of the Arena, opera and other arts are performed in this ancient structure to this day. This helps to maintain the arena's entertainment lineage that dates back to when gladiators were hacked to death inside its walls. After this you must visit the imposing structure of the **Castelvecchio**, the old castle, and its magnificent three-arched bridge along the river Everything else in the city is window dressing – nice, but not essential sights.

Arrivals & Departures
By Train

From Venice you can catch trains approximately every one and a half hours, and the trip itself takes just that length of time. Once on the ground, the city is within walking distance from the **Porta Nuova Station**. Simply take a right out of the station until you get to the imposing Porta Nuova, then take a left down the Corsa Porta Nuova until you get to the gate with a clock on the imposing arena. From there you have access to everything.

If you want to take the bus from the train station and eliminate the ten minute walk, take either the #1, 11, or 12 bus from **Mariapiedi A** (the bus stop) directly in front of the station. You have to buy a ticket first, so spend your Euro 75 cents for a one-way fare at the *Tabacchi* in the station. The bus will drop you off at the Arena square.

By Car

Take the Autostrada A4 located just after Marghera. You will have to take one of two exits for Verona which are clearly marked. For a more scenic route take the #11 from Mestre and wind your way through the beautiful scenery in these parts. This will take you directly into the city.

Where to Stay
1. **AURORA**, *Piazza delle Erbe 2, Tel. 045/594-717, Fax 045/801-0860. 19 rooms, all with bath. Single E75-100; Double E85-125. All credit cards accepted. Breakfast included.* ******

The best budget hotel in the city. Located in a great piazza, where the bustling market is, this hotel is in an ancient palazzo, with a terrace that has beautiful panoramic views. This is where breakfast is served in warm weather. The best rooms are the ones that face out onto the piazza. All rooms are sufficiently comfortable though not anything special. A great location, a good hotel at an adequate price. You even get TV in your room. Not bad for a two star.

2. BOLOGNA, *Via A Mario 18, Tel. 045/800-6830, Fax 045/801-0602. E-mail: hotelbologna@tin.it. 32 rooms. Single E100-140; Double E125-150. All credit cards accepted. Breakfast included.* *******

Not too far from the Arena, this is a comfortable and hospitable little hotel in an old palazzo. The entry hall has splendid Murano lamps. The rooms are all great, but the two best, in my opinion, are numbers 230 and 232. These two have extra special views and more accommodating spaces. You won't go wrong with a stay here. And the hotel restaurant, Rubbiano, is a favorite in the city.

3. COLUMBA D'ORO, *Via C. Cattaneo 10, Tel. 045/595-300, Fax 045/594-974, E-mail: colombhotel@easynet.it. 49 rooms. Single E100-150; Double E175-225. All credit cards accepted. Breakfast E12.* ********

A hotel with unbeatable atmosphere and charm. Located in an old palazzo, the furnishings are all refined and elegant, and the rooms are *elegantissimo*. The rooms on the second floor have beds that date back to the 18th century, which adds an historical flair to your stay. The bathrooms are covered in marble and come with all necessary four star amenities.

4. DUE TORRI BAGLIONI, *Piazza S Anastasia 4, 37100 Verona. Tel. 045/595-0444, Fax 045/800-4130. 96 rooms all with bath. Single E150-300; Double E225-375. Breakfast included. Credit cards accepted.* *********

Located in the city center, this is a truly elegant hotel furnished in period antiques. And since it has been recently renovated it now has all the modern amenities to make your stay wonderful. This place has all the characteristic charm of a deluxe hotel in a smaller market. Probably the best hotel in Verona. Recently upgraded from a four star but still head and shoulders above the rest of the five stars in Verona.

5. GIULETTA E ROMEO, *Vicolo Tre Marchetti 3, 31700 Verona. Tel. 045/800-3554, Fax 045/801-0862. Web: www.venere.it/veneto/verona/giuliettaeromeo. 30 rooms all with bath. Single E65-125; Double E80-150. Breakfast included. Credit cards accepted.* *******

Situated just off the Arena down a small side street and close to the shopping street Via Mazzini, this is in a quiet and tranquil location in the *zona pedonale* (no cars). It is a clean and comfortable three star, with its professional staff doing everything they can to make your stay pleasant. Every necessary amenity including an accommodating bar/breakfast area downstairs where you relax in the evenings and start your days.

6. MARTINI & PICCOLO, *Via G. Camuzzoni 3, Tel. 045/569-400, Fax 045/577-620, Email: notturno@notturno.it. 81 rooms. Single E90-130; Double E125-175. All credit cards accepted. Breakfast included.* ***

This place consists of two edifices, ergo the two names for the hotel. They share a reception hall, but after getting your key, you will either go one way or the other to find your room. Personally I prefer the Martini, because it has plenty of refinement with ample and pleasant communal spaces, as well as elegant rooms filled with modern furnishings. The Piccolo has also been renovated completely and comes with all necessary three star amenities, as does the Martini. You won't go wrong in either wing of this dual hotel.

7. MASTINO, *Corso Porta Nuova 16, 31700 Verona. Tel. 045/595-388, Fax 045/597-718. 33 rooms all with bath. All credit cards accepted. Single E60-125; Double E100-150. Breakfast included.* ***

Located a few steps from Piazza Bra and the Arena, some of the rooms even have pleasant views of the piazza and the ancient amphitheater. Situated in a historic building, which helps give your stay more cultural significance. The rooms are small but clean, and despite its location the rooms are quiet so you can count on a good night's sleep. A good price for accommodations similar to some four stars in the city.

Where to Eat

There are a number of pizzerias and restaurants on the left side of the Arena which have seating outside: the perfect location to enjoy the pleasant evenings. You'll also find good restaurants along the Via Mazzini or off side streets from this main shopping avenue.

8. LE ARCHE, *Via Arche Scaligere. Tel. 045/800-7415. Closed Sundays and Mondays for dinner, as well as the first three weeks of January. Dinner for two E100. Formal dress required.*

The owner, Giancarlo Gioco, is like a host of an Italian restaurant out of the movies. He's especially attentive to the women, giving them gifts of dessert, drinks, and sample dishes. He can do all that because his prices are so damned high, an average of $120 for two! Come here if you like fish – fried, boiled, baked, roasted, grilled, whatever. You can order your food in a variety of different portion sizes so you can sample a variety of seafood. This is a pleasant place to dine, with excellent food, but only if you're willing to pay the price.

9. DANTE, *Piazza dei Signori, Tel. 045/595-249. Closed Sundays. Credit cards accepted. Dinner for two E45.*

This place was born over 110 years ago as a café, and it has evolved into

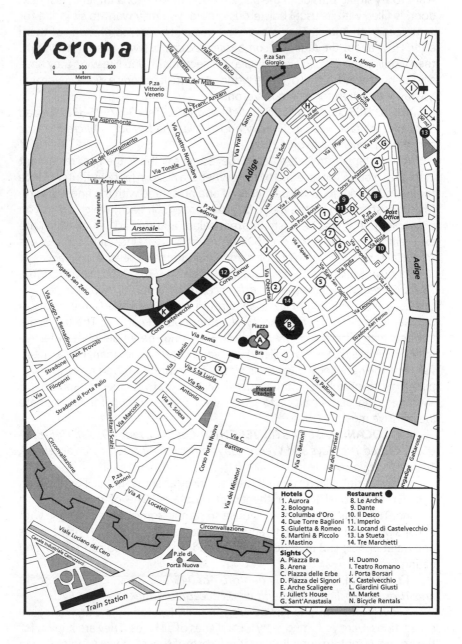

Verona

0 300 600
Meters

Via Rovereto
Viale Nino Bixio
P.za San Giorgio
Via S. Alessio
P.za Vittorio Veneto
Via dei Mille
Via Franc. Anzani
Via Aspromonte
Via Quattro Novembre
Via del Risorgimento
Via Tonale
Via Aresenale
Via Aresenale
Via Prato Santo
Via Sole
Adige
H
P.za del Duomo
Via Brolio
Via Ponte
G
Via Pigna
4
Corso S. Anastasia
E
8
Via F. Emilei
9
D
11
1
C
Via Porta Borsari
Corso Porta Borsari
P.za Viviani
Post Office
P.zle Cadorna
Arsenale
Via Euferna
Via Spade
7
7
6
F
10
Via Nizza
Via Cappello
Via Stella
J
Via della San Cosimo
Rigaste San Zeno
Via Lungo S. Bernardino
Corso Cavour
12
Via Oberdan
5
Via Leoncino
Via Leoni
Stradone San Fermo
Adige
3
2
14
Corso Castelvecchio
K
B
A
Piazza Bra
Via Roma
Via Marin
Ant. Provolo
Stradone
Filopanti
Via
Stradone di Porta Palio
Via S.ta Lucia
Via San Antonio
Via A. Sciesa
7
Via Pallone
Piazza Citadella
Via Marconi
Carmelitani Scalzi
Circonvallazione
Corso Porta Nuova
Via C. Battisti
Via dei Minatori
Via G. Bertoni
Via del Portiere
Gattarosa
Lungadige Gattarosa
P.za R. Simoni
Via A.
Locatelli
Circonvallazione
Viale Luciano del Cero
Canale Industriale Camuzzoni
P.zle di Porta Nuova
Train Station

Hotels ○	Restaurant ●
1. Aurora	8. Le Arche
2. Bologna	9. Dante
3. Columba d'Oro	10. Il Desco
4. Due Torre Baglioni	11. Imperio
5. Giuletta & Romeo	12. Locand di Castelvecchio
6. Martini & Piccolo	13. La Stueta
7. Mastino	14. Tre Marchetti

Sights ◇	
A. Piazza Bra	H. Duomo
B. Arena	I. Teatro Romano
C. Piazza delle Erbe	J. Porta Borsari
D. Piazza dei Signori	K. Castelvecchio
E. Arche Scaligere	L. Giardini Giusti
F. Juliet's House	M. Market
G. Sant'Anastasia	N. Bicycle Rentals

a fine restaurant, somber and sophisticated, just like its namesake. You may want to try sitting outside in the piazza, but if the Trattoria Imperio, just next door, is filled with its usual boisterous crowd, you may want to sit inside for some peace and quiet. They make their pasta in-house, so give any of them a try. How about the *tagliolini con basilico e scampi* (with basil and shrimp), then a grilled sole (*sogliola alla griglia*) for seconds? If you like wine they have a list of hundreds from all over the world. An excellent choice while in Verona. My favorite piazza for dining in Verona.

10. IL DESCO, *Via Dietro S. Sebastiano 7. Tel. 045/595-358. Closed Sundays, the first week in January and the last half of July. All credit cards accepted. Dinner for two E125.*

A few steps from Piazza delle Erbe, some say this is the best restaurant in the city. You will be received by the owner Elia Rizzo in his beautiful entrance room, and all your food will be prepared and presented with the finest of care. My suggestion is to try the *menu degustazione* (E50 each) which offers you a sampling of antipasto, pasta, entrée, salad, and dessert, all of which are excellent. The wine list has over 500 different options, including some wines from California. Make a night of it and soak up the expensive ambiance.

11. IMPERIO, *Piazza dei Signori 8, Tel. 045/803-0160, Fax 045/800-7328. Closed Mondays. Credit cards accepted. Dinner for two E25.*

Located in the large Piazza dei Signori along with the Dante, this is a popular local place. There is plenty of seating outside and in. The tables are covered with different colored tablecloths giving the whole place a festive aura. They have dishes that will make anyone happy: vegetarian, pasta, meat, fish, but they are known for their pizza. There are 32 different varieties of pizza; my favorite here is the *salsiccia* (with tomatoes, cheese, and lots of sausage). The perfect place to come with a large group for an intimate inexpensive meal.

12. LOCANDA DI CASTELVECCHIO, *Corso Cavour 49, Tel. 045/803-0097. Closed Tuesdays and Wednesdays at lunch. All credit cards accepted. Dinner for two E60.*

A wonderful local restaurant, not as pricey as some, but still on the high end. Great regional food, authentic atmosphere. One of my favorites in Verona. They make their pasta in-house so sample some of their *taglialle* with either a pomodoro (tomato) or ragu (meat) sauce. They also serve great soups and meat dishes; and their desserts are made in house. You can't go wrong eating here.

13. LA STUETA, *Via del Redentore 4b, 045/803-2462. Closed Mondays and Tuesday for lunch. All credit cards accepted. Dinner for two E40.*

A lovely little trattoria just across the river, located by the archeological excavations. Here you'll find tasty local dishes of all kinds. They are known for their *gnocchi* (potato dumplings) with all sorts of suaces, pasta e fagioli (pasta and beans), coniglio (rabbit) and miale(pork). A popular and relatively inexpensive place, and as such it is necessary to make reservations.

14. TRE MARCHETTI, *V.lo Tre Marchetti 19b, Tel. 045/803-0463. Closed Sundays, from July to September also closed Mondays., and on holiday in December. All credit cards accepted. Dinner for two E80.*

Another middle of the road place in Verona, which seems to be populated with high priced eateries. They call themselves a *trattoria*, but they are really a *ristorante*. Everything here is refined and elegant, and of the highest level. Service is professional and the dishes are classics., a mixture of local and Italian favorites. My favorite is the *fettucine con porcini e tartufo* (with porcini mushrooms and truffles) but that is a dish only available in truffle season during the Fall. They have some excellent meat and fish dishes as well.

Seeing the Sights

The highlights can be hit rather quickly (see sidebar above, *Verona On The Fly*), or you can take your time and explore one of the prettiest of small cities in northern Italy. Filled with Roman ruins, medieval castles, cobblestone side streets and piazzas, Renaissance palazzi and friendly people, Verona is a perfectly picturesque town to wander through.

A. PIAZZA BRA

The **Forum Boarium** of medieval days of yore is now **Piazza Bra**. The piazza is bounded by the ancient **Roman Arena** to the north, the line of palazzi with their cafés to the west, the 17th century **Gran Guardia** building in the south, and the neo-classic town hall to the east, and in the middle there is a quaint fountain with a park. It is the central meeting place for Veronese.

Enjoy a drink or bite to eat at one of the cafés that line the west side of the piazza and soak up the sights and sounds of the city.

B. ARENA

Piazza Bra. Tel. 800–3204. Tuesdays-Sunday 8:00am-6:30pm in the summer, 8:00am-1:00pm in the winter. Admission E3.

Originally built during the Roman Republican era, the **Arena** must have been completed about 30 CE, judging from mosaics found in an old Roman house in Verona indicating three scenes of gladiators fighting in the arena. These are now in the archaeological museum.

After 325 CE, when the emperor Constantine forbade gladiatorial performances, the arena was used less frequently. That's the official line, but historians tell us that gladiators fought all over the Roman empire as magistrates disregarded Rome's orders, until the emperor Honorius violently put an end to this insubordination in the 5th century. During the Middle Ages the arena was used for capital punishment and trial by combat (sounds a little like gladiators, doesn't it?). By the 16th and 17th centuries, the arena was used for less violent activities like fairs and tournaments, and a variety of performing arts activities. This tradition lives on today.

The arena went through a variety of expansions and today measures 152 by 122 meters. The ancient structure is formed with four concentric rings, with the outermost only retaining four of its original arches. This outer ring used to encircle the entire arena and had 72 arches. Today the second ring is the outer boundary of the arena.

Despite its age, the arena is still used to today for music and theater festivals. Little has had to been done to it to make it more modern, except that the inner space of the arena was modified between 1569 and 1680 by the Venetian Republic. Even its old drainage system still works perfectly. A testament to the Roman Empire's engineering skills.

C. PIAZZA DELLE ERBE
Open 8:00am–1:30pm.

This used to be the Forum of the old Roman city, whose ruins lie a few meters beneath the current piazza. Today the only Roman feature about the square is the *Verona Madonna* statue in the center, placed atop a large marble basin taken from the Roman baths. Today the square is used during the day as an open air market where you can buy fresh fruits, vegetables, and sundries. Don't miss this place while in Verona.

D. PIAZZA DEI SIGNORI

Locally it is known as **Piazza Dante**, because of the statue erected in 1865. It is bounded on the side nearest Piazza Erbe by the **Domus Nova**, a Baroque building of the 17th century. On the opposite side is the **Loggia del Consiglio**, built at the beginning of Veronese Renaissance. This is the second favorite meeting spot in the evenings for Veronese, because of the wide open spaces and the two well-loved restaurants that lay their seating out in the piazza: the **Trattoria Imperio** is a fun-filled local place that is loud and boisterous, whereas **Ristorante Dante** is as somber and sophisticated as its namesake. They compliment each other perfectly.

E. ARCHE SCALIGERE

Just outside of the Piazza Signori, surrounded by the Scalinger palaces, is the **Chiesa di Santa Maria Antica** and the **cemetery of the Della Scala family** which is known to tourists as the **Arche Scaligere**. Here you will find many elaborate shrines, tombs, and sarcophagi. Take some time to wander through and appreciate the beauty of these death monuments.

F. JULIET'S HOUSE
Via Capello 23, Tel. 803–4303. Open 8:00am–6:30pm Closed Mondays. Admission E3.

The Shakespearean story of *Romeo and Juliet* was actually 'borrowed' from a work by a Vicenza author named **Luigi da Porto**, who wrote of the vicissitudes of two unhappy lovers named Romeo Montecchi and Juliet Capuleti. We know for sure that these two families did exist. Dante witnessed and wrote about their quarrels when he sojourned here between 1299 and 1304. Besides these facts, we do not know if Romeo and Juliet were actual people and actually fell in love, and so on.

But no matter – poetry has triumphed and today we can visit **Juliet's House** in Verona and see the balcony from which she sealed her tryst with Romeo and eventually their demise. A bronze statue, made by Nereo Costantini, of fair Juliet has been placed in the courtyard in front of the house. Inside the house looks like it would have in the 14th century. If you've ever had romance in your heart, stop in here.

G. SANT'ANASTASIA

Corso San Anastasia. Open 9:00am–5:00pm.

Also a Dominican church, **Sant'Anastasia** is quite similar to *SS Giovanni e Paolo* in Venice. The facade is simple and plain, but what is of interest is inside. The first two columns are flanked by hunchback figures *(gobbi)* holding holy water bowls on their backs. These two figures are quite unique. Like nothing I've never seen in all my travels throughout Italy.

The nave is subdivided by columns of red Veronese marble and connected by arches. The walls of the aisles on either side of the columns contain the large circular windows that let light into the church. Everywhere inside you'll find ornate frescoes, bas-relief altars, and sculptures. The **Miniscalchi Altar**, also known as the Altar of the Holy Spirit, is especially exquisite. This work has been attributed to the Venetian master Agnolo.

H. DUOMO

Piazza del Duomo. Open 7:00am–noon and 3:00pm–7:00pm.

The **Duomo** is a composite of varying styles, since the original Romanesque building underwent Gothic modifications in the 15th century. The **bell tower**, with its Romanesque base, should have been finished in the 16th century but was only completed in this century. This church is not nearly as interesting and elaborate as Sant'Anastasia but it does have a beautiful work by Titian, *The Assumption of the Virgin*, dating back to 1535-40.

Since this church is near the river and the **Ponte Pietra**, it is a perfect launching place to visit the **archeological zone** and the **Roman Theater** (see next page).

I. TEATRO ROMANO
Tel. 045/800-0360. Open Tuesday-Sunday 8:00am-6:30pm off-season. Performance days 8:00am-1:30pm. Admission E3.

This ancient theater was excavated between 1834 and 1914. It abuts the slope of Colle di San Pietro and has a relatively modern church, SS Siro e Libera, on its steps as a reminder that here in Italy the past, present, and future all fit perfectly together. The orchestra's diameter is almost 30 meters and the two galleries reach a height of 27 meters.

The theater's construction has been carbon-dated to the last quarter of the 1st century BCE. If you're interested in archaeology, this is a fun place to roam for a little while.

J. PORTA BORSARI
This is the best preserved of the five **Roman gates** in Verona, and is the easiest to find. It was named **Borsari** in medieval times because of the toll tax *(Bursarii)* that were levied here on goods in transit. It is of interest because the entire facade has remained intact. It is assumed that this gate was built during the reign of emperor Claudius (41-54 CE), because of the similarity between it and the Porta Aurea in Ravenna which was made in 43 CE.

The openings on the bottom are 3.5 meters wide and a little more than 4 meters high and are framed by Corinthian columns, which support the rest of the construction. The entire complex rises to a height of 13 meters and is made of white Veronese marble. What is of real interest is that this ancient arch has been completely incorporated into the life of the modern city, as have most Roman ruins in Italy – even going so far as being a part of the modern buildings on either side of it.

K. CASTELVECCHIO
Corso Castelvecchio 2, Tel. 045/594-734. Open Tuesday–Sunday 8:00am–6:30pm. Admission E3.

This structure was the final residence of the Della Scala family and was built over a period of twenty years from 1354 to 1375. The magnificent three-arched bridge was built for the private use of the residents of the castle. The building itself has served as an army garrison, a military storeroom, and most recently as a museum with an exquisite collection of paintings, sculptures, tapestries, ancient jewelry, frescoes and more. Most of the works are religious in nature, so if you haven't had your fill of the Madonna and Child, there's more here.

A relatively unknown Italian artist, G. Francesco Caroto (1480-1555) has many works featured here. He studied under Liberale, Mantegna, and was influenced by Leonardo and Raphael and his works show it. One particular painting, though simple in nature, seems to come alive. It is his *Young Boy*

With a Drawing. You can almost feel the boy's joy at creating the stick figure on the paper he holds in his hand.

L. GIARDINI GIUSTI
Via Giardini Giusti 2, Tel. 045/803-4029. Open 9:00am to dusk in summer and 9:00am–8:00pm in winter. Admission E3.

You'll find the lush garden spaces of the **Palazzo Giusti** on the same side of the river as the Roman Theater, outside the ancient walls. The gardens are well tended and are punctuated by a variety of different statues, fountains, and a fish pond. The gardens also feature a labyrinth, citrus grove, and an aviary to protect birds in danger of extinction.

Sometimes these gardens are the backdrop for summer productions of the **Theater of Verona**. They are a lovely place to come, relax, and recharge your batteries if you've had too much of cities.

Nightlife & Entertainment
Opera
If you are in Verona from December to June, the traditional opera season, have the proper attire (suits for men, dresses for women), and would like to see an opera at the opera house, you won't be disappointed. During July and August they offer special productions outside at the Arena in Piazza Bra.
* **Arena di Verona**, *Piazza Bra 28, 37121 Verona. Tel. 045/590-109 or 800-5151, Fax 045/801-1566 or 801-3287*

Discos
* **Alter Ego Club**, *9 Via Torricelle, Tel. 045/91-51-30*
* **Excalibur Club**, *24 Stradone Provolo, Tel. 045/59-41-95*

Pubs
* **Andy Capp Pub**, *13v Nievo, Tel. 045/834-80-82*
* **Double A**, *1/a VC Stell, Tel. 045/803-22-23*

Practical Information
Bike Rental
In Piazza Bra, you'll find a fellow who works out of a van renting bicycles. He is located to the left of the Gran Guardia building as you face it. *Hours:*

Opera & Theater in Verona
In July and August, **operas** are performed at the Arena. For information contact **Entre Lirico**, *Arena di Verona, Piazza Bra 28, 37100 Verona, Tel. 045/800-3204*. The ticket office is in the sixth arch of the Arena.

In July and August there is also a **drama festival**, with an emphasis on Shakespeare's plays, in the **Teatro Romano**, *Tel. 045/800-0360*.

9:00am to 7:00pm. Rates: 1 hour E4; 2 hours E5; 4 hours E8; 1 day E10; 1 week E4/day; 2 weeks E3/day; 1 month E2/day.

Car Rentals
• **Avis**, *Stazione Ponte Nuova, Tel. 045/800-66-36*
• **Hertz**, *Best Travel, Stazione Ponte Nuova, Tel. 045/800-0882*
• **Maggiore**, *Stazione Ponte Nuova, Tel. 045/800-4808*

English Language Bookstores
• **The Bookshop**, *3a Interrato Aqua Morta, Tel. 045/800-76-14*

Flower & Fruit Markets
A small local market is in the **Piazza Arditi**, *open 8:00am to 1:30pm every day*. A large market is open in **Piazza delle Erbe**, *from 8:00am to 1:30pm daily*.

Supermarket
If you're going to be in Verona for a day or a week, it's always important to know here you can get fresh supplies of water, fruit, soda, wine, and beer to stick in your room. In Verona, unlike many Italian cities, there is a large supermarket directly in the center of town. You can get everything your heart desires at the **PAM** supermarket, *Via dei Mutilati #3*, just outside the Piazza Bra through the old Roman gate.

Tourist Information
The **tourist office** has branches at:
• *Porta Nuova Station, Tel. 045/800-0861. Open all year long from 8:30am–7:30pm*
• *Piazza Erbe 42, Tel. 045/803-0086. Open all summer from 9:00am–12:30pm and from 2:30pm–7:00pm*
• *Via Leoncino 61, Tel. 045/592-828, Fax 045/800-3638. Summer 8:00am–8:00pm; Winter 8:00am–7:00pm*

You can get any type of information about Verona at these offices, as well as tourist maps that really are not that good but basic enough that you won't get lost. There's also a **Hotel Booking Office**, *Via Patuzzi 5, Tel. 045/800-9844, open 9:00am–7:00pm, closed Sundays.* They can make hotel reservations for you if you have none. They are a private group that represents about three-quarters of the better hotels in Verona.

All the representatives at the office speak a variety of languages, and use Macintosh as their computer system, so you know you'll get what you want quickly.

Travel Agencies
• **American Express**, *Corsa Ponte Nuova 11, Tel. 045/800-90-40*

Practical Information for Venice
• **American Express**, *Salizzada San Moise 1471, San Marco, Tel. 520-0844. Hours 8:00am to 8:00pm.*

Consulates
• **United Kingdom**, *Dorsoduro 1051, near the Accademia, Tel. 041/522-72-07*
• **United States**, Largo *Donegani 1, Milan, Tel. 01/652-841*
• **Canada**, *Via Vito Pisani 19, Milan, Tel. 01/669-74-51. For emergencies 01/66-98-06-00*
• **Australia**, *Via Borgogna 2 , Milan, Tel. 01/76-01-33-30*

Note that for US, Canadian, and Australian citizens, the closest consulate is in Milan. Some of you from other countries may need to contact your embassy in Rome (see the *Rome* chapter, Practical Information section).

Mail
The main post office is located at *Salizada del Fontegho dei Tedeschi 5554, near the Rialto. Tel. 041/271-7111.* Open Monday–Saturday 8:15am–6:45:00pm. Stamps (*francobolli*) are sold at *tabacchi* all over town.
Venice's **postal code** is *30124.*

Laundry Services
• **Lavaget**, *Cannaregio 1269, Tel. 041/71-59-76, Fondamenta Pescaria.* Located near the station. E8 for three kilos of clothes, soap and dry included. Open Monday–Friday 8:30am–12:30pm and 3:00pm–7:00pm. Drop off clothes and pick up later in the day.

Local Festivals & Holidays
• **January 1**, *Primo dell'Anno* (New Year's Day)
• **April 25**, *Festa Del Liberazione* (Liberation Day)
• **February**, the two weeks before Lent is **Carnevale**, a time of riotous celebration where costumes are worn both day and night, and grand balls and celebrations occur frequently.
• **March**, First Sunday after Ascension day; anybody piloting an oar-powered craft can take part in *La Vogalonga*, the "long row." Participants set off at 9:30am from the Bacino di San Marco and follow a marathon-like course around Venice and its islands. Rowers usually return between 11:00am and 3:00pm.

- **May 1**, *Festa del Lavoro* (Labor Day)
- **August 15**, *Ferragosto* (Assumption Day)
- **September**, First Sunday in September is the **Regata Storica**, the historic regatta. The races are preceded by a magnificent procession on the Grand Canal of period boats manned by Venetians in historic costumes. A spectacle to behold. On par with the Palio in Siena.
- **November 1**, *Ognissanti* (All Saints Day)
- **November 21**, *Festa della Madonna della Salute*, which originated as a time of thanks for being spared from the Plague which at one point had decimated more than 60% of Venice's population. Celebrated on two floating bridges built across the Grand Canal from the Giglio to the Dogana.
- **December 8**, *Festa dell Madonna Immacolata* (Immaculate Conception)
- **December 25**, *Natale* (Christmas)
- **December 26**, *Santo Stefano* (Saint Stephen's Day)

Most stores in Venice take a one or two month vacation in or around Christmas time.

Tourist Information & Maps
- **Ente Provinciale per il Turismo** (three different locations): *Piazza San Marco 71C, Tel. 041/522-6356; Piazzale Roma, Tel. 041/522-7402; Sant Lucia Train Station, Tel. 041/715-016.* They also have an excellent hotel finders service here that comes in real handy if you don't have reservations when you arrive.
- **American Express Travel Service**, *San Marco 1471, Tel. 041/520-0844.* You don't have to be a card member to get assistance here. As always a great private travel service.

Tour Operators
- **American Express Travel Service**, *San Marco 1471, Tel. 041/520-0844.* Same as above. Ask for details on various Venice and area tours, since they change periodically.
- **CIT**, *San Marco 4850, Tel. 041/528-5480*
- **Wagons-Lit/Cook Travel**, *San Marco 289, Piazzetta Leoncini, Tel. 041/ 522-3405*

Chapter 17

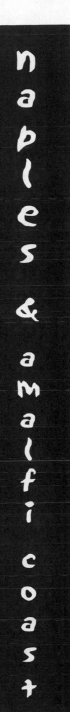

The area around **Naples** has got to be one of the most stunningly beautiful in the world. Napoli is a large port city teeming with passion and adventure, and in the surrounding area you can find exotic, out-of-the-way islands, and pleasantly peaceful little coastal towns. People from all over the world come to this area of Italy to bathe in the pristine paradise of the islands of **Ischia**, **Procida** and **Capri** and to visit the picturesque towns along the **Amalfi Coast**. **Positano** is one of these towns, and once you witness the majesty of the buildings of this stunning village perched precariously on the slope overlooking the water, you will never want to leave.

Naples

Naples is a welcoming if chaotic city, crammed with churches and architectural wonders while also being notorious for crime and corruption. Among all of this somehow the beauty of the city flourishes. In many neighborhoods, life is still lived in the gritty labyrinth of the streets, where old and young participate in the cohesive '*piazza* culture' that makes all of Italy so enjoyable. Out in the streets or in the bustling piazzas the day's or evening's entertainment is right in front of you, whether it's a family quarrel or two lovers in a corner immersed in their cuddling ignoring onlookers. As Dickens wrote, "Neapolitans don't just live their lives, they enact them." To people here, life is a performance and as such it must be lived with gusto. You'll see this quality all over Naples, especially in **Spaccanapoli** (the historic old town of Naples), and this vibrant zest for life is what makes Naples so irresistibly Italian.

Naples is a city that has been conquered, destroyed by wars, and leveled by earthquakes, but it still keeps on ticking. As a port city, Naples is filled with every sort of character from all over the world, as well as some great seafood. Though Naples is not really known for its cuisine, you can find some good restaurants and pizzerias. Naples claims that it is the birthplace of the pizza so you'll have to try at least one while here.

There is much to see in Naples - Italy's third largest city with 1.2 million inhabitants - if you can get used to the chaos. The streets function as outdoor living rooms and are the chaose theory brought to life. The city has an intimacy, tension, a craziness about it that is like an intensely devoted family. Inter-mingled among this passionate human presence you can find the **Teatro San Carlo**, one of the greatest opera houses in the world; the treasures of **Pompeii** grace the **National Museum** (which is a must see if you like archelogical treasures); and curving along the coast of the Bay of Naples are ornate palaces, gardens, churches, Roman ruins, castles and works of art. All of this is tied together with a warm climate and amazing natural scenery making Naples a wonderful vacation option.

Brief History

Naples was originally a Greek settlement and in the 8th century BCE it was called Parthenope, having been settled by people from Rhodes. Near this site, Ionian settlers founded the 'old town' in 7th century BCE, which they called Palaipolis. In the 5th century BCE, the 'new town' of **Neapolis** was founded by newcomers from Chalcis, and the name, only with slight changes, remains today.

These three settlements interacted freely but did not merge until 326 BCE when they became allies of Rome. Though faithful to the alliance, Naples still retained its strong Greek traditions and characteristics until late into the

Be Alert, Be Aware in Naples

During your travels in Naples, the best advice is this: be alert and prepared. For all its charm and vibrancy, Naples at night can be unsafe if you do not stay aware. That being said, it is still 100 times safer than any American city. But as a port city, such as Genoa, Naples attracts people from all over the world, some of whom are sometimes rather unsvaory. So be aware, be alert, and make sure you perform all necessary safety precautions, such as, staying on well traveled streets, not going down dark alleys, and if it is late at night, take a cab.

Roman Imperial period. The town itself became a favorite of many wealthy Roman merchants and magistrates because of its beautiful scenery, the backdrop of Mount Vesuvius and the artistic flair of the population that remains today.

But the peace that Rome brought was not to last. In 543 CE, the town fell into the hands of the Goths. Ten years later it was returned to the rule of the Byzantine Empire. After that it began to assert its independence and was free until 1139, when it was conquered by the Normans and incorporated into the Kingdom of Sicily by Roger II. Frederick the I, Roger II's grandson, founded the **University of Naples** that still exists today. Only forty years later, the capital of the Kingdom of Sicily was moved to Naples.

Still, peace was not to last. Spain gained control of the kingdom from 1503 to 1707, and in 1713 the territory passed to the Hapsburgs. Then in 1748 the Bourbons gained control, and kept control until 1860, when the territory was incorporated into the united Italy we have today.

Arrivals & Departures

The best ways to get to Naples from Rome is by car or train. Bus service is slow, out of the way, and inconvenient from Rome. Bus service to and from Naples is mainly used for getting into remote villages inaccessible by train. The only time you would take a bus to Naples from a major city would be if you're on a tour.

By Car

Located 217 kilometers from Rome, the easiest way to get to Naples by car is via the A2 (Autostrada #2). If you are looking for a more scenic route, the coast road from Ostia Antica will move you past many scenic seaside resorts, including Anzio and Gaeta. But this will take you six hours or more because the roads are small, sometimes only two lanes, and wind endlessly along the coast through little seaside towns. If you have the time, take this route because the sights are wonderful. From Rome directly down the A2 should take four hours at most.

By Train

The train station, Stazione Centrale FS, is located at the eastern end of the city. The **tourist information office** in the station, *Tel. 081/268-779*, can help you locate a hotel if all those in this guide are booked up. Getting from Rome to Naples by train takes four hours. If you catch a *rapido* you can shave an hour off that time.

Getting Around Town
By Bus

Buses can take forever to get you where you want to go, especially at rush hour, but there are times you'll need to take them; for example, when you want to get up to Campodimonte and the National Gallery. The buses congregate at the Piazza Garibaldi outside the train station and each route is posted on the signs at all bus stops for ease of use. You can also get a convenient map from the tourist office that details the main map routes, or you can buy an even better one from a newsstand that lists all the bus routes.

To use the map simply find where you are and where you want to go. Then match up the black numbers (which are the numbers of the bus routes) where you are with those located at where you want to go. For example, if you're at Piazza Garibaldi which is marked number 8 on the map, and you want to go to Piazza Municipio which is also marked number 8 on the map, that means the bus number 8 goes from Piazza Garibaldi to Piazza Municipio.

Riding the bus during rush hour is very tight, so try to avoid the hours of 8:00am to 9:00am, 12:30pm to 1:30pm, 3:30 to 4:30pm, and 7:30pm to 8:30pm. They have an added rush hour in the middle of the day because of their siesta time in the afternoon when the stores close and people go home.

By Foot

You'll obviously need to combine the use of one of the above modes of transport with walking. You'll love the strolls through the *centro storico* and university area, but always be alert. Don't walk at night, especially alone. Remember, this is a port city. During the day, don't go down alleys that are empty of people. Just play it smart.

By Funicular

These hillside trams connect the lower city of Naples to the hills of Vomero, where you can see the Castel San Elmo and the Certosa di San Martino. There are three funiculars that can assist in your ascent, the **Centrale** that leaves from Via Toledo, the **Montesanto** that leaves from Piazza Montesanto, and the **Chiai** that leaves from Piazza Amadeo. A one way ticket costs Euro 75 cents.

By Metro

You can take the metro almost anywhere you want to go in Naples for only Euro 75 cents a trip each way. It's fast, inexpensive, and safe, but always keep a lookout for pickpockets. They flourish here in Naples.

By Taxi

Naples is a very congested city, and as such it will cost you an arm and a leg whenever you choose to transport yourself by taxi, especially during rush hour. But if you want to spend the equivalent of a meal at a good restaurant just to get from point A to point B, by all means.

The going rate as of publication was E2.5 for the first 2/3 of a kilometer or the first minute (which usually comes first during the rush hours), then its Euro 50 cents every 1/3 of a kilometer or minute. At night you'll also pay a surcharge of E1.5, and Sundays you'll pay Euro 75 cents extra. If you bring bags aboard you'll be charged Euro 50 cents extra for each bag.

Besides having to rely on flagging down a cab, there are strategically placed cab stands all over the city.

Where to Stay

1. CONTINENTAL, *Via Partenope 44, 80121 Napoli Tel. 081/764-4636, Fax 081/764-4661. 166 rooms all with bath. Single E115-150; Double E165-205. Credit cards accepted. *****

Located within walking distance to all the sights, but outside of the *centro storico* and directly on the Bay of Naples. A tranquil place with its own swimming pool. Besides a good restaurant, they also have a separate American style bar and a piano bar for your evening's entertainment. This street is a beautiful one to stay on, with a panoramic view of the bay – all hotels on it are superb – but this one, along with Santa Lucia and Vesuvio, stand out from the crowd.

2. CAVOUR, *Piazza Garibaldi 32, 80142 Naples. Tel. 081/283-122, Fax 081/287-488. Email: cavour@italyhotel.com. Web: www.venere.com/it/napoli/cavour/. 98 rooms, 40 with bath, 58 with shower. Single E70-100; Double E105-140. Lunch or dinner E15. Breakfast included. ****

Elegant and accommodating. Situated in a renovated historic building in the busy Piazza Garibaldi. To keep out the trafic noise they have double paned glass. The staff is professional and courteous and do everything to make up for the location. You have air conditioning upon request for an extra E25 per night and satellite TV. The main restaurant is run by Signora Tea who prepares some excellent local dishes. A good three star in an ideal location.

3. EXECUTIVE, *Via del Cerriglio 10, 80134 Naples. Tel./Fax 081/552-0611. Web: www.venere.com/it/napoli/executive/. 19 rooms all with bath. Single E105. Double E145. Credit cards accepted. ****

Located in the *centro storico* in a renovated old convent, this place has a small gym, sauna, and sun deck. The rooms are all comfortable and accomodating. This is a good alternative to the larger hotels in Naples since here you are made to feel special. The rooms are clean and comfortable and have air conditioning, TV, mini-bar and more. Breakfast is served on the sun deck in good weather. More of a bed and breakfast than a hotel. A good choice while in Naples.

4. MERCURE ANGIOINO, *Via Depretis 123, 80121 Naples. Tel. 081/552-9500, Fax 081/552-5909. Email: angioino@tecnet.it. 85 rooms all with bath. Single E100-125; Double E120-150. All credit cards accepted. Breakfast included.* ****

Optimum location in the *centro storico*, near the business district and the Beverello pier where the ferries leave for the islands in the Bay of Naples. Owned by the French chain Mercure, you will receive lavish Gaulish attention. The breakfast room on the first floor is filled to overflowing with the buffet each morning. All the rooms have soundproofed windows so as to block out the noise that makes its way in from the streets below – a necessity in this ideal location. The rooms are all decorated in delicate colors and some are expressly reserved for non-smokers, a rarity in French hotels. The bathrooms are accommodating and have all amenities necessary. The downstairs bar is a great place to relax in the afternoons, or you can order room service from there without a surcharge. A good place to stay.

5. NUOVO REBECCHINO, *Corso Garibaldi 356, 80121 Naples. Tel. 081/553-5327, Fax 081/268-026. Web: www.venere.com/it/napoli/rebecchino/. 58 rooms all with bath. Single E80-100; Double E115-145. All credit cards accepted. Breakfast included.* ***

Convenient location for travelers, right by the station and near the entrance to the Autostrada it also comes with affordable prices. Established in 1890, renovated in 1990. The common rooms are diverse and one is a nice old-fashioned billiard room. Ask for a room on the fourth floor for the best accommodations. All are furnished in style and elegance, but some don't have sound-proofed windows so request that too. The bathrooms are clean and comfortable and decorated in soft ceramic colors. A good three star in a central location.

6. PALACE, *Piazza Garibaldi 9, 80142 Napoli. Tel. 081/267-044, Fax 081/264-306. Web: www.venere.com/it/napoli/palacehotel/. 102 rooms, 52 with bath, 50 with shower. Single E75-100; Double E100-125. All credit Cards accepted. Breakfast included.* ***

In the busy Piazza Garibaldi, this place has many amenities but they can't make up for the intruding chaos of Naples. The rooms are clean, small, and comfortable but come without A/C, a must in the summer months. You also have TVs in the rooms. The restaurant serves international and local cuisine. A good option for the price, but with few amenities. A better bet is the Executive.

7. PARKER'S, *Corso Vittorio Emanuele, 80121 Napoli. Tel. 081/761-2474, Fax 081/663-527. Email: cmbosco@tin.it. 83 rooms, 47 with bath, 36 with shower. Single E175-200; Double E200-225. All credit cards accepted. Breakfast included. Kids stay for 10% extra.* ****

In a renovated historic building, this is a romantic spot with great panoramic views of the harbor and Mt. Vesuvius, especially on the top floor. You can get

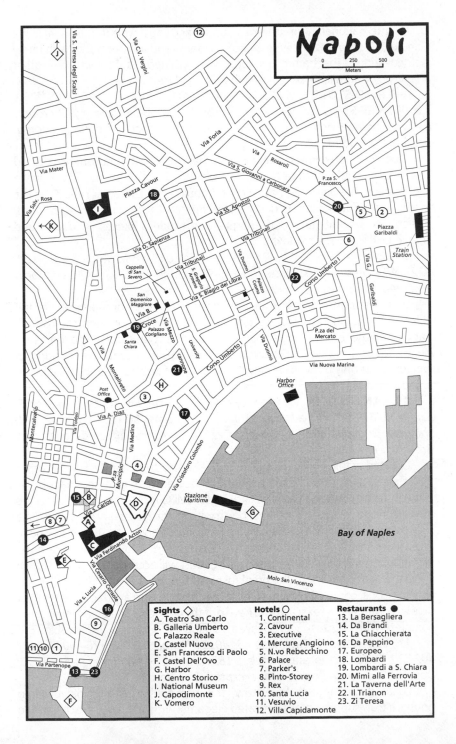

Napoli

0 250 500
Meters

Sights ◇
A. Teatro San Carlo
B. Galleria Umberto
C. Palazzo Reale
D. Castel Nuovo
E. San Francesco di Paolo
F. Castel Del'Ovo
G. Harbor
H. Centro Storico
I. National Museum
J. Capodimonte
K. Vomero

Hotels ○
1. Continental
2. Cavour
3. Executive
4. Mercure Angioino
5. N.vo Rebecchino
6. Palace
7. Parker's
8. Pinto-Storey
9. Rex
10. Santa Lucia
11. Vesuvio
12. Villa Capidamonte

Restaurants ●
13. La Bersagliera
14. Da Brandi
15. La Chiacchierata
16. Da Peppino
17. Europeo
18. Lombardi
19. Lombardi a S. Chiara
20. Mimi alla Ferrovia
21. La Taverna dell'Arte
22. Il Trianon
23. Zi Teresa

local or international cuisine in the restaurant, and you have entertainment in the piano bar. The rooms are large and comfortable and are decorated with lovely wall coverings. The bathrooms come with whirlpool tubs and every other amenity. A tranquil, relaxing accommodating place to stay.

8. PINTO-STOREY, *Via G Martucci 72, 80121 Napoli. Tel. 081/681-260, Fax 081/667-536. Web: www.venere.com/it/napoli/pintostorey/. 25 rooms all with bath. Single E95. Double E110-140. All credit cards accepted. Breakfast included.* ***

This clean and comfortable three star has quite a bit atmopshere. Located in a relatively quiet area of Naples just below the Villa Floridiana, it is only a short walk to the bay. They have air conditioning (for E10 a day) and TV in the rooms. Adequate accommodations with different furnishings in each room, sometimes a combination of antique and modern pieces. A quaint and character filled place to stay.

9. REX, *Via Palepoli 12, 80139 Napoli. Tel. 081/764-9389, Fax 081/764-9227. 40 rooms all with bath. Single E75-95; Double E105-130. All credit cards accepted. Breakfast included.* ***

In a sweet position, near the lungomare, this hotel occupies part of the Palazzo Coppedé. The Liberty style furnishings in the common rooms hark back to another era, lending a quaint charming air to this place. The rooms are clean and comfortable with colorful bed coverings. All rooms have soundproof windows but only a few have views of the Bay of Naples. A great location at a good price.

10. SANTA LUCIA, *Via Partenope 46, 80121 Naples. Tel. 081/764-0666, Fax 081/764-8580. Email: slucia@tin.it. 102 rooms, 90 with bath, 12 with shower. Single E150-200; Double E225-250. All credit cards accepted. Breakfast included.* ****

Located within walking distance of the *centro storico* as well as the other major sites, this tranquil romantic hotel is located with a perfect panoramic view of the bay, Mount Vesuvius and Castel dell'Ovo. Like its brethren on the Via Partenope, this is an excellent choice with all the necessary amenities. The only thing it doesn't have is a swimming pool. Opened in 1922, it has been recently renovated and offers complete attention to all details. The hotel restaurant is only open in the evenings, but they will accomodate you for lunch if you make a reservation. The breakfast buffet is overflowing. The rooms are very spacious, come with every imaginable comfort, and are decorated in light blue to continue the seascape you have out the window. The bathrooms come complete with courtesy sets of toiletries. And the service is impeccable.

11. VESUVIO, *Via Partenope 45, 80121 Napoli. Tel. 081/764-0044. 081/407-520. Email: info@prestigehotels.it. 183 rooms all with bath. Single E150-210; Double E210-260. All credit cards accepted. Breakfast included.* ****

Located on the elite hotel row, this beautifully restored old building houses a truly superb hotel. Decorated elegantly with antiques, the charm and character is reflected in their refinement. You will be offered the most attentive service while staying here. The restaurant, Caruso, on the top floor, offers a stunning panoramic view of the Bay of Naples. For over 100 years this seaside hotel has been the address for many illustrious guests. The rooms are extremely comfortable, decorated with wonderful antiques and colorful wall coverings. The bathrooms are immaculate and also come with every imaginable amenity. If you're driving, they have an underground garage since parking on the street is impossible.

12. VILLA CAPIDAMONTE, *Via Moiariello, 80121 Napoli. Tel. 081/459-000, Fax 081/229-344. Web: www.venere.com/it/napoli/villacapodimonte/. 60 rooms all with bath. Single E95-125; Double E130-180. Breakfast included. All credit cards accepted.* ****

Situated above the city near the magnificent tranquillity of the park Capidamonte (hence the name), a few minutes from the airport and near the Autostrada, this place is a gem. If you want peace and quiet away from the hectic pace of Neapolitan life, this is the place. Virtually brand new, the hotel was opened in 1995 and as such it comes with every imaginable creature comfort. You can wind down in the garden, the terrace, the salons, the library or in your comfortable room. Decorated in soft colors to enhance the peaceful tones, most rooms also offer lovely panoramic views. There are also tennis facilities for you to work on your game. The prices are lower than other four stars because it is so out of the way.

Where to Eat

13. LA BERSAGLIERA, *Borgo Marinaro Sant Lucia, Tel. 081/764-6016. Closed Tuesdays and August. Credit cards accepted. Dinner for two E70.*

The best thing about this place is its location with a view of the Castel dell'Ovo, especially on their terrace overlooking the water. The food is definitely better than Pizza Hut, but the prices are a little high. Though if you do want romantic atmosphere, come here. Try their *spaghetti con vongole* (with clams) or their *linguine agli scampi* (with shrimp). For seconds try their fried or grilled fish.

14. DA BRANDI, *Salita San Anna di Palazzo 1, Tel. 081/416-928. Closed Mondays and one week in August. Credit cards accepted. Dinner for two E30.*

As you know Neapolitans claim to have made the first pizza, and this place claims to have made the first *Pizza Margherita* (simple pizza with fresh tomato sauce, oil, and mozzarella cheese). This place is famous throughout Naples not only for their *Margherita* but also for their *Pizza Biancha* (dough and olive oil only) which is superb. Located in the Spanish Quarter, it's a little walk from the *centro storico* but well worth the time. If in Naples, you have to try this place.

15. LA CHIACCHIERATA, *Piazzetta M Serano 37, Tel. 081/411-465. Closed Sundays and August. American Express Cards accepted. Dinner for two E30.*

A small *trattoria* with only a few tables at the end of the Via Toledo near the Palazzo Reale. They use a lot of vegetables here, especially on their pizza on which they pile mozzarella and provolone. You can also get some *pasta e fagioli* (pasta and beans), some good *pesce arrosto* (grilled fish), and a superb *capretto al forno* (baked 'kid'). The food here is great.

16. DA PEPPINO, *Via Palepoli 6a/b, Tel. 081/764-9582. Closed Sundays. American Express card accepted. Dinner for two E40.*

In the Santa Lucia area near the Castel dell'Ovo this place is open late for night owls, of which there are many in Naples. Here you not only can get great pizza, but a tasty seafood appetizer, superb *bruschetta* (garlic bread with oil and tomatoes), some *linguine alla putanesca* (whore's pasta made with tomatoes, oil, garlic and tuna), and great grilled or fried fish. A fun place to come any time of day or night.

17. EUROPEO, *Via Marchese Campodisola 4/8, Tel. 081/552-1323. Closed Sundays and two weeks in August. Only open for lunch on Friday and Saturday. American Express and Visa accepted. Dinner for two E40.*

This is a small local *trattoria* that is frequented by academics, since it is near the University, as well as manual laborers. Eating here gives you an insight into the cross section of people that make up the community of Naples. They serve a tasty *ostriche e frutti di mare* (oysters and other seafood) appetizer. Then try their *Pizza Margherita* (simple pizza with fresh tomato sauce, oil and mozzarella cheese) or have them put some great sausage on the pizza as well. Or try their superb *spaghetti alla vongole verace* (with spicy clam sauce). For seconds they make a great *frittura di pesce* (fried fish dish).

18. LOMBARDI, *Via Foria 12, Tel. 081/456-220. Closed Mondays. All credit cards accepted. Dinner for two E28.*

Located near the Museo Archeologico Nazionale, this place definitely has the best *Pizza Napoletana* anywhere. Covered in ricotta, mozzarella, vegetables, and almost everything imaginable, this is the tastiest pizza around. If this is a little complicated for you, look over their extensive list of other excellent pizzas. You can order anything from the basic *Margherita* to a pizza with wurstel sausage, with local sausage and more. Also, even with no smoking signs on the walls, nobody adheres to them, so if smoke bothers you ... don't come here.

19. LOMBARDI A SANTA CHIARA, *Via B Croce 59, Tel. 081/522-0780. Closed Sundays and three weeks in August. Credit cards accepted. Dinner for two E33.*

The sister pizzeria to Lombardi's. This place is located in the heart of the *centro storico* right next to the *chiesa di Santa Chiara* and their beautiful cloisters. Here you will find great pizzas of all kinds. For an appetizer try their *mozzarella di bufalo* (buffalo mozzarella) *peperoni*, *melanzane* (eggplant), and *zucchine* plate. A perfectly situated place to stop for a bite to eat in the middle of a day of wandering around the backstreets of Naples. The food is excellent and inexpensive, and the atmosphere is authentically local.

20. MIMI ALLA FERROVIA, *Via A d'Aragona 21, Tel. 081/553-8525. Closed Sundays and a week in August. Credit cards accepted. Dinner for two E60.*

Choose either the terrace or inside in which to dine. At both you will be more than happy. Start with their appetizer of *mozzarella di bufalo, peperoni* or *assagi di paste povere* (a tasty sampling of their pasta dishes). For pasta try their *linguine alla Mimi* (which comes with a great shrimp sauce), then move onto their *frutti di mare e pomodorini* (mixed seafood and small tomatoes). The *calamaretti fritti* (fried calamari) is also good.

21. LA TAVERNA DELL'ARTE, *Rampa S. Giovanni Maggiore 1a, Tel. 081/552-7558. Closed Sundays and August. No credit cards accepted. Dinner for two E40.*

A small local place situated in the heart of the *centro storico* near the University. The service is excellent, either on the terrace or inside. Try the traditional appetizer of *pizze rustiche* (literally country pizza, with a variety of toppings), *salumi artigianali* (literally craftsmen salami – great local salami), *mozzarella fresche* (fresh mozzarella) and *sformato di cipolle* (baked onions). This will definitely fill you up so move directly to a great main course of *maiale in agrodolce* (a sweet and sour pork dish).

22. IL TRIANON, *Via P Colletta 46, Tel. 081/553-9426. Closed Sundays and for lunch, New Years Eve and Christmas. No credit cards accepted. Dinner for two E25.*

Located in the *centro storico*, this is the best pizza in Naples, and that's saying a lot. Besides the many varieties of pizza that come out of their wood burning brick oven, you'll love the high ceilings, slate-yellow walls, tacky print motifs that they call decoration, and the long communal tables. Mainly frequented by University students this place has a fun-filled crowd. Try their filling pizza/lasagna that is loaded with sauce, cheese and meat if a pizza sounds too boring to you, but do not miss this place when in Naples. Great food, local atmosphere.

23. ZI TERESA, *Via Partenope 1, Tel. 081/764-2565. Closed Sunday nights and Saturdays as well as two weeks in August. Credit cards accepted. Dinner for two E65.*

Located across from the Castel dell'Ovo on the water, this is a famous and popular eating spot, and because of that it's rather expensive. It's also surrounded by some of the best hotels in the city, like the Excelsior and the Continental which doesn't help keep prices down. Their terrace is a perfectly romantic spot to have lunch or dinner, but remember to reserve well in advance. Start off with their *antipasto di mare* (seafood antipasto), then move on to their *spaghetti alla vongole* (with clam sauce), then if you're still hungry savor any of their grilled fish.

Seeing the Sights

Naples has plenty to offer, from high culture like opera, museums, and centuries-old castles and palaces, to the simple pleasures of just strolling along the harbor. But always remember that Naples is a port city so use common sense when walking around, and you'll find Naples is a fun place to visit.

A. TEATRO SAN CARLO

Via San Carlo 98f, 80132 Napoli. Tel. 081/797-2331 Or 797-2412, Fax 081/797-2306. Ticket office open Tuesday – Sunday 10:00am–1:00pm and 4:30pm–6:00pm.

This is the most distinguished opera in house in Italy after La Scala in Milan. Naples has a vibrant musical history and this is reflected in the prestige offered its opera house. For centuries Naples was considered the apex of European music and the Teatro San Carlo was the premier opera house of that period. Its neoclassic facade dates from its rebuilding in 1816. The season runs from October to June. Most tickets are always sold out, but you can check at the ticket office between 10:00am and 1:00pm and 4:30pm to 6:00pm Sunday through Tuesday during the season.

B. GALLERIA UMBERTO

Between Via San Carlo and Via Toledo. Open 24 hours.

Modeled after the Galleria Emanuele in Milan, this arcaded shopping area with its glass ceilings is also laid out in a cross pattern. The blending of iron and glass gives it an almost futuristic appeal. A place to visit even if you're going to Milan, just to compare the two structures. And if you like to shop, this should be one of your stops.

C. PALAZZO REALE

Via Ferdinando Acton. Open 9:00am–noon and 3:00pm–5:30pm.

The former **Royal Palace** was begun in 1600 by Domenico Fontana and was restored between 1837 and 1841. You'll see statues of eight former kings who ruled Naples on the facade. This extensive palace contains a magnificent marble staircase built in 1651, 17 heavily decorated apartments, and the **Biblioteca Nazionale** that contains over 1,500,000 volumes as well as many ancient manuscripts and relics. You should come to the Royal Palace just to see the National Library, because it is like nothing you can find in North America.

D. CASTEL NUOVO
Via Ferdinando Acton. Open 9:00am–noon and 3:00pm–5:30pm.

Behind the palace is the magnificent, five-towered **Castel Nuovo**, also referred to as **Maschio Angionino**. This was once the residence of kings and viceroys who ruled the Kingdom of Naples. Built between 1279 and 1283, it pre-dated the Palazzo Reale and was constantly being upgraded. Surrounded by park land, it seems as if it is an oasis in the sea of Neapolitan chaos. An imposing structure that adults and children alike love to explore. Other gardens you can explore are those located next to the Palazzo Reale by the water. A great place to get away from the chaos of Naples for a few hours.

E. CHURCH OF SAN FRANCESCO DI PAOLO
Piazza del Plebiscito. Open 7:00am–noon and 4:00pm–5:30pm.

The **Church of San Francesco di Paolo** was built between 1818 and 1831, and is a fine imitation of the Pantheon in Rome. Solid and stoic it offers an oasis of calm and serenity in the chaos of Naples.

F. CASTEL DELL'OVO
Borgo Marinaro. Open 9:00am–noon and 3:00pm–5:30pm.

If your kids like exploring castles, there is another one near the Castel Nuovo and the Palazzo Reale. The **Castel dell'Ovo** is located off a causeway from the Via Partenope and sits on a small rocky islet. It was begun in the 12th century and completed in the 16th century. It was used as a lighthouse and the first line of defense for the harbor.

G. THE HARBOR
Always a bustle of activity since Naples is one of Italy's biggest ports. You can get more information about the history of the location at the **Marine Station** on Molo Angionino just past the heliport. From this heliport you can take regular helicopter service to the islands of Capri and Ischia as well as the Airport. This is the same location from which you would catch a ferry or hydrofoil over to these two islands.

Napoli Porte Aperte - 'Open Door Naples'
Be aware that at infrequent times and in true Italian fashion, unannounced, the city opens all of its churches, monuments, and gardens for free. Ask at the tourist office or your concierge whether this rare event will occur during your stay.

H. HISTORIC NAPLES – CENTRO STORICO

Located just north of the harbor, this part of Naples is the most fun to walk, since it has winding streets dotted with small churches and quaint old buildings. A fun place to explore in the day (be careful at night), especially along the old main street through the center.

The old main street is a combination of all the streets, from the Via Toledo, the Via Maddaloni, moving to the Via D. Capatelli, and ending at the **Piazza Nolana** with the Via Nolana. This old main street, as well as the small streets and alleys that are offshoots, is lined with shops of traditional artisans like the **Palace of Strumenti Musical**, *Vico San Domenico Maggiore #9*, in front of the church of the same name. Up the stairs to the first floor you'll find guitars and other instruments being crafted by hand.

A unique shop is the **L'Ospedale delle Bambole (The Doll Hospital)**, located on Via S Biagio dei Librai in the *centro storico*. This is the world famous shop where you'll find ancient dolls and puppets hanging everywhere or just lying around. Walk in and have a look around, the proprietor is very friendly and it's not often you find a store that caters to doll repair. Another can't-miss street in the *centro storico* is the **Via San Gregorio Aremeno**, which is commonly known as the Nativity scene street since they sell figurines for crèches year round.

Via Toledo

Formerly Via Roma, this street runs through the heart of the *centro storico*. Sometimes referred to in other guidebooks or on other maps as Via Roma, the natives refer to the street by both names. Officially it is Via Toledo, since it was built by and named after Don Pedro de Toledo. One of Naples main causeways filled with shops, people and congested traffic. A place to walk to mingle with the Neapolitans.

Montecalvario

On the left of this street is the **Montecalvario** section that rises steeply to the **Via Vittorio Emanuele**. Many of these 'streets' are actually steps. An interesting place to walk.

Church of Santa Anna del Lombardi

Piazza Monteoliveto, Open daily 7:15am–1:00pm.

This church, in the **Piazza Monteoliveto** just off the Piazza della Carita, is a great collection of Renaissance sculpture. The church was built in 1411 and later continued in the Renaissance style. Here you'll find the *Pieta*, created in 1492 by Guido Mazzoni. You'll also find some wonderful terra-cotta statues as well as a beautiful 16th century choir stall.

Church of Santa Chiara & Gesu Nuovo
Piazza del Gesu Nuovo. Santa Chiara open daily 8:00am-12:30pm and 4:30pm-7:30pm. Gesu Nuovo open daily 7:15am-1:00pm and 4:00pm-7:15:00pm.

Try to see these two churches. The Jesuit **Gesu Nuovo** was erected between 1585 and 1600 and still maintains its triangular grid-like facade. There are also some beautiful cloisters here. The place is full of roses and cats. It's a great place to relax among the Mediterranean-style tiles covered with bucolic scenes of Naples. There are benches on which to sit where you can enjoy the aroma of the roses and escape from the hectic pace of Naples, at least for a few minutes.

The **Santa Chiara** is one of medieval Naples' main monuments. It was built in 1310 and was recreated in the Gothic style after being bombed during World War II. Inside you'll find many medieval tombs and sarcophagi that belong to the house of Anjou. And don't miss the Nun's choir that sits behind the High Altar, where secluded nuns could watch mass without being seen. This church has a wonderful courtyard that seems to always be empty. There are beautiful frescoes and a lazy palm leaning in the center. The church also has some great art work on its ceiling. They have thoughtfully placed slanted mirrors for you to see the ceiling without having to crane your neck.

Church of San Domenico Maggiore
Piazza San Domenico Maggiore. Open daily 8:00am-12:30pm and 4:30pm-7:00pm.

From the two churches above, go east down the Benedetto Croce to the next piazza on the left to the church of **San Domenico Maggiore**. Built around 1300, with a Gothic facade added in the 19th century, this is one of the most interesting churches in Naples. It has early Renaissance art as well as over 40 sarcophagi of the Anjou family. Here you'll find a combination of Gothic and Baroque architecture.

Capella di San Severo
Via F de Sanctis. Open Mondays and Wednesday-Saturday 10:00am-5:00pm, Tuesdays and Sundays 10:00am-1:30pm. Admission E3.

The **Chapel of San Severo** is a short distance east of the church of San Domenico Maggiore, hidden down the small side street of Via F de Sanctis. Built in 1590 as a burial chamber for the Sangro family, it was embellished with the Baroque style in the 18th century. Now a private museum, the chapel is filled with many fine statues including an eerie *Christ in a Winding Sheet* by Sammartino. You can also find two grisly corpses located downstairs. They are leftovers from the experiments of the Prince Raimondo.

Palazzo Corigliano
Piazza San Domenico Maggiore. Open daily 9:00am-7:00pm.
In the 4th floor library of the **Palazzo Corigliano** (currently a university building dating from the 18th century), located in the Piazza San Domenico Maggiore, you'll find a place to leisurely read a periodical or book and escape the pace of Naples. You can also see the remains of Greek walls in the basement.

Cloisters of San Gregorio Armeno
Between Via Tribunali and Via S. Baglio S. Librai. Hardly ever open. You need to go there and request entrance.
Often closed, you have to ask the nuns if you can enter. If you do gain access you'll adore the beauty of the flowering plants, the splashing fountain, and the comfortable benches. There's a place where you can enter the choir chamber which is all made of wood and peer through the wrought iron grating down onto the church itself. This was where the cloistered nuns celebrated mass, but themselves could not be seen.
Most often they'll only allow women in and usually only on special Sundays, but it doesn't hurt to try. Here you'll be able to see what the life of a cloistered nun is like.

Palazzo Cuomo
Via Duomo, on the corner of the Via Duomo and the Via San Biago ai Librai. Open 9:00am-2:00pm.
The beautiful Renaissance **Palazzo Cuomo**, built from 1464 to 1490, now houses the **Museo Filangieri** featuring arms, armor, porcelain and pictures.

Duomo
Via Duomo. Open daily 8:00am-12:30pm and 5:00-7:00pm.
Up the Via Duomo from the Palazzo Cuomo is the **Cathedral**. It is dedicated to San Gennaro, the patron saint of Naples. Built over the 4th century ruins of a paleo-Christian basilica, this church was erected between 1295 and 1324 in the French Gothic style. After an earthquake destroyed part of it in 1456 it was rebuilt, restored, and altered. It was further updated in the 19th century when part of the facade was replaced, but the church retains its original doors.
On the main altar you'll find a silver bust of **San Gennaro** that contains his skull. In the tabernacle are two vials of dried blood from the saint, which in an event of miraculous proportions, liquifies annually. Believers sigh a breath of relief because the liquification indicates that the saint will continue to protect Naples for the year from Vesuvius' wrath, or whatever might threaten the city. To find the saint's tomb, look under the high altar.

Gite Sotteranea – The Underground City

This is one cool sight. You can go on underground tours of two different **catacombs**, as well as **aqueducts**, **cisterns**, and **Roman** and **Greek cities** that lie below modern Naples. You'll be given candles to help guide you through the slim passages and damp darkness.

One trip starts from the Caffe Gambrinus (there are only a few accessible entrances to the underground city; another entrance is from the Piazza San Gaetano in the *centro storico*). You'll find aqueducts, caves, quarries, Greek markets, medieval houses, Greek tombs, catacombs. There are also special tours that start from the Chiesa di S. Lorenzo. You need to ask a priest to guide you through the courtyard and underground to the location where they are still excavating the jumbled layers of Greek, Roman, and medieval streets, houses, and markets. You have to do a little talking in Italian to get where you want to go but it's worth the trip.

Go to the tourist office in the Piazza del Gesu Nuovo for more complete times, locations, and information about touring the underground city.

I. NATIONAL MUSEUM

Piazza Cavour. Tel. 440-166. Open daily 9:00am-7:00pm. Open September-May, Monday-Saturday 9:00am-2:00pm, Sunday 9:00am-1:00pm. Admission E5.

On the northwestern outskirts of the *centro storico* just off of Piazza Cavour is the **National Museum**, which boasts one of the world's finest collections of antiquities. The building was originally erected as troop barracks in 1586, then was the home of the University from 1616 to 1790. During this time the University began to house the art treasures of the kings of Naples, the Farnese collections from Rome, and material from Pompeii, Herculaneum, and Cumae. A great collection of historical artifacts is housed here.

J. CAPODIMONTE

Park open daily 7:30am-8:00pm. In off-season open 7:30am-5:00pm. Museum open Tuesday-Saturday 9:00am-2:00pm, Sundays 9:00am-1:00pm. Admission E5. Take bus 110 or 127 from the train station or 22 or 23 from Piazza del Plebiscito. If walking, take the Corso Amadeo di Savoia about two kilometers north up the hill from the National Museum to arrive at the park of Capodimonte and the Catacombs of San Gennaro.

The **Catacombs** are only open Saturday and Sunday mornings and like their Roman counterparts, these contain a maze of passageways and tomb chambers. But these are slightly better preserved and have much more artistic representation.

Just across the Piazza Tondo di Capodimonte is the entrance to the park. This 297-acre park commands some wonderful panoramic views of Naples. It is a peaceful respite from the hectic pace of Naples. If you don't get to Vomero you must try and get here. Also located at the park is the **Capodimonte Museum** of arms, armor, porcelain, and pictures. In particular, there are some great works by **Titian**.

K. VOMERO & THE SURROUNDING HILLS

Certosa di San Martino, museum Tel. 578-1769. Open Tuesday-Sunday 9:00am-2:00pm. Admission E4. **Castel Sant'Elmo,** *Open Tuesday-Saturday 9:00am-2:00pm, and Sundays 9:00am-1:00pm.*

If you want to get away from the smog and congestion of Naples just hop on one of the *funiculars* and enter a calm antidote in a residential district high above the city. The district was built from 1885 onwards. You can also get here by climbing the streets in the Montecalvario section.

The Villa Floridiana public park in the southern part of Vomero has a terrace with a wonderful view overlooking the **Bay of Naples**. You'll also find a small museum, **Duca di Martina Museum**, with paintings, porcelain, ivory, china, and pottery here.

Of great interest is the **Certosa di San Martino**, an old monastery erected in the 14th century and remodeled during the Renaissance and Baroque periods. You should take the time to the see the cloisters because they give you a glimpse into the monastic life of the times. Their museum contains some interesting nativity scenes (crèches).

Just north of the monastery is the **Castel Sant'Elmo** that was built in 1329 and added to between the 15th and 17th centuries. When the Austrian Empire controlled this region briefly, Peter the Great's son Alexis fled to this castle to escape his father's wrath. Eventually discovered he was returned to Russia. Come here for the view from the ramparts, as well a chance to explore the many passageways that were used for the defense of the harbor.

Nightlife & Entertainment

RIOT, *in an old building at Via S Biagio dei Librai 26 in the centro storico. Open from 9:00pm-3:00am. No phone.*

To enter come through a wooden door, cross an open courtyard, climb a staircase, and on the right is the secret garden that is the club. It consists of a few rooms in an old building from the 18th century with tall French windows opening out onto a lush terrace of palm trees, pebble paths, and tables at which to sit and enjoy a drink or a smoke.

During the summer they have art exhibits and late night bands, mostly American blues and jazz. The waitresses here are all hip and have a definite attitude. Even so they will serve you drinks and sandwiches outside. It's a bit expensive but the crowd is fun and the atmosphere is like nothing you'll find in the States. I mean how many nightclubs do you know that are in 18th century *palazzi*? It's like something out of an Anne Rice vampire novel. And they are so hip they don't have a phone.

Opera
If you are in Naples from December to June, the traditional opera season, have the proper attire (suits for men, dresses for women), and have a taste for something out of the ordinary, try :
• **Teatro San Carlo**, *Via San Carlo 98f, 80132 Napoli, Tel. 081/797-2331 or 797-2412, Fax 081/797-2306*

Sports & Recreation
Golf
• **Circolo Golf Napoli**, *Via Campiglione 11, 80072 Arco Felice. Tel. 081/526-4296.* Located only 5 km from Naples, this is a 9 hole, par 35, course that is 2,601 meters long. It is open year round except Mondays and Tuesdays. They also have a driving range, pull carts, and a bar/restaurant. A good place to come if you're going through golf withdrawal.

Shopping
The main shopping streets with fancy shops are the **Corso Umberto**, **Via Toledo**, and **Via Chiaia**. Along these streets you'll find your international style, upscale, expensive stores. For additional shopping suggestions, see *Seeing the Sights: Historic Naples* above.

English Language Bookstores
• **Feltrinelli**, *Via San T. d'Aquino 70. Open Monday through Friday 9:00am to 8:00pm, Saturdays 9:00am to 1:00pm.* They have an extensive selection of English language travel guides as well as some paperback novels.
• **Universal Books**, *Rione Sirignano.* This store has books in many different languages and only a small selection of paperbacks in English.

Excursions & Day Trips
If you have any free time while in Naples, try to visit the two ancient cities of **Pompeii** and **Herculaneum**. They are truly a major wonder of the world: two cities trapped in time by a devastating volcanic eruption. What more could you ask for? You can also take day trips from Naples to the beautiful isles of Capri, Ischia or Procida, but these destinations are treated as separate destinations in their own right following this section.

POMPEII & HERCULANEUM

Thousands of people died and many more lost their homes when Vesuvius erupted in 79 CE, submerging Pompeii, Herculaneum, and Stabiae with lava and/or volcanic ash. The lava and ash created an almost perfect time capsule, sealing in an important cross-section of an ancient civilization. If you want to take a trip back in time come to one of these ancient towns. You will find nothing even remotely similar to this anywhere in the world, so if you have a free day, grab a tour bus, rent a car, hop on a train, but make your way to these cities buried in time.

Arrivals & Departures

By car from Rome, take the A2 south, past Naples, connect to the A3 and exit at Pompeii Scavi. Total time elapsed each way, 3 1/2 to 4 hours.

By train, first arrive at **Napoli Centrale**. Go one floor below the Central Station to the **Circumvesuviana** station for a local high-speed train to **Ercolano** (Herculaneum) or **Pompeii Scavi** (4 hours total journey).

The best way to get to either Pompeii or Herculaneum in a day (granted a rather long day) is by tour bus. This way you do not have to worry about driving or catching the right trains. You will leave early in the morning and arrive back in Rome late at night. See information on Tour Companies.

Pompeii

Before the city was buried in time, Pompeii was Rome's main seaport linking it to the rest of the Empire, and as such was an established city with a multicultural population of about 25,000. Because of successive waves of colonization Pompeii was home to Greeks, Egyptians, Gauls, Iberians and every other nationality in the Roman Empire. By 80 BCE, it was also a favorite resort of wealthy Romans.

Shaken by an earthquake in 62 CE, Pompeii recovered, but on August 24, 79 CE Pompeii's days were over. Mt. Vesuvius erupted, spewing ash and pumice pebbles which covered the city, preserving it and some of its unfortunate residents in time. For over 1,500 years Pompeii rested undisturbed, then was discovered in 1711 when a peasant was digging a well on his property. After which two centuries passed, during which time Pompeii and Herculaneum served almost entirely as a quarry for works of art, as a plaything for the various dynasties which misruled Naples, and as a romantic stop on the Grand Tour of Europe for elite European society.

Although rudimentary excavations began in 1763, systematic excavations did not get under way until 1911 and have been progressing slowly ever since. And now only about three-fifths of the site has been freed from the death grip of the volcanic ash. Herculaneum has suffered a less severe intrusion from amateurs interested in unearthing its treasures since on the afternoon of the eruption, rain turned the volcanic ash to mud, which solidified, burying the town thirty to forty feet deep. Electric drills and mechanical shovels are needed to dig here, so progress has been slow, but the town has been better preserved.

Despite this difference, Pompeii still offers the most fascinating introduction into ancient history. Strolling through this dead city is quite ominous. In places there are human forms and family pets forever preserved having died in the embrace of the volcanic ash. Along with these macabre scenes, you can easily imagine life going on here since many pieces of every day existence remain. You can see where people planted gardens, shops where they bought food, and walls are still covered with ancient graffiti. These range from erotic drawings advertising the world's oldest profession, to boasts by one of practitioners to having had over 1,300 men, to drawings of oral sex, to political slogans extolling the virtues of one candidate over another. It seems that a local election was taking place when the eruption occurred.

There are also abundant frescoes depicting mythological scenes in the wealthier homes, as well as frescoes indicating how the owners of the house made a living. The streets have characteristic deep ruts made by wheels of carts – the trucks of antiquity – and are bridged by massive stepping stones, which acted as both a conduit for pedestrians, and also as a traffic calmer.

Some of the best homes to see are the **House of the Faun** and the **House of the Vettii**, both in the residential area north of the **Forum**. Other homes of interest are the **House of the Melander** (located to the east of the Forum), the **Villa of the Mysteries** (located to the west of the main town), and the **House of Pansa** (located to the north of the Forum) that also included rented apartments. Also in evidence in the remains are symbols of the Greek cult of Dionysis, one of many that flourished in the city. **The Temple of Isis** (to the east of the Forum) testifies to the strong following that the Egyptian goddess had here. The public **Amphitheater**, in the east of the city, should not be missed because of its scale and level of preservation. There are locations on the stage area that if a whisper is spoken, even a person standing at the top-most part of the seating area can hear it clearly.

Pompeii is as a whole 160 acres, large enough for a population of between fifteen and twenty thousand souls. The city is surrounded by a wall, which was built in four phases. The earliest dates from the fifth century CE, the latest from just before the reign of Augustus and was allowed to fall in disrepair, evidence of the security of the peace of that era. Latin, Greek and another dead language Oscan were the tongues of choice in Pompeii. Latin because of the Roman influence, Greek because the area around Naples had originally been settled by Greeks and they kept their culture, and Oscan which was a hold over from ancient Italian tribes.

The city was well supplied with public amenities. Lead water pipes found everywhere show that all but the very humblest of houses were supplied with running water. There are all sorts of different housing in Pompeii including apartments and expansive villas. But it's not just the homes and their treasures that Pompeii reveals to us. Ancient tradesmen, their lives, works, and tastes about which literature tells us almost nothing, become more real for us here than anywhere else in the ancient world except for the abandoned port of Rome, Ostia Antica. Most houses either doubled as workshops, or had small workshops in them since the ancient world's slave economy did not foster the development of the factory system.

Pompeii has also enriched our knowledge of ancient Romans relations to their gods. Naturally the Imperial cult whereby Emperors were decreed to be gods, was adhered to, though generally only with lip service. Graffiti backs up this blasphemous stance. One such wall scribbling states "Augustus Caesar's mother was only a woman." The Egyptian sect of Isis was well represented, as was the Roman warrior sect of Mithras, and family cults flourished. This is evidenced by the fact that most houses and workshops had private shrines usually housing busts of ancestors. But the true god of Pompeii was, as with other cities ancient and modern, was the God of Gain. Money, the pursuit of wealth, and the accumulation of possessions were worshipped above all else.

Ironically, going back for their hoards of silver and gold spelled death for many of the residents of Pompeii. Under the hail of pumice stone and ashes many were asphyxiated or engulfed. A particularly disturbing cluster of victims, with their children and burdensome possessions is preserved near the **Nocera Gate**. But most of the remnants of the Pompeiian consumer society – the best-preserved artifacts – are not in Pompeii anymore, they are in the National Museum in Naples. So if you can, make a point of visiting there too. After many years of mismanagement, Pompeii is slowly re-emerging to be a true world wonder. An organization called World Monuments Watch has declared Pompeii one of the world's most imperiled cultural sites, but the good news is that they are helping to restore the ancient city to the wonder it once was. Pompeii is unique anywhere in the world, and is a must-see stop when in Italy.

Gates to the site open year round 9:00am to 1 hour before sunset. Admission E8. The best way to get here and back to Rome in a day, while also receiving the best that Pompeii can offer, is via tour bus. See information on Tour companies.

Herculaneum

Seventeen miles northeast of Pompeii is the smaller town of Herculaneum. Most tour companies will combine a trip to one, with a visit to the other. At the time of the eruption Herculaneum had only 5,000 inhabitants, compared to the 25,000 in Pompeii, had virtually no commerce, and its industry was solely based on fishing. The volcanic mud that flowed through every building and street in Herculaneum was a different covering from that which buried

Pompeii. This steaming hot lava-like substance settled eventually to a depth of 30-40 feet and set rock-hard, sealing and preserving everything it came in contact with. Dinner was left on tables, wine shops abandoned in mid-purchase, sacrifices left at the moment of offering, funerals never finished, prisoners left in stocks, and watchdogs perished on their chains.

Fortunately for the residents, but not for archeologists, the absence of the hail of hot ash that rained down on Pompeii, which smashed the buildings of that city and trapped many residents of that town, meant that many of the inhabitants of Herculaneum were able to get away in time. Despite the absence of preserved remains, Herculaneum offers complete houses, with their woodwork, household goods, and furniture well preserved.

Although Herculaneum was a relatively unimportant town compared with Pompeii, many of the houses that have been excavated were from the wealthy class. It is speculated that perhaps the town was like a retirement village, populated by prosperous Romans seeking to pass their retirement years in the calm of a small seaside town. This idea is bolstered by the fact that the few craft shops that have been discovered were solely for the manufacture of luxury goods. Archaeologists speculate that the most desirable residential area was in the southwest part of town, which overlooked the ocean in many different housing terraces. Here you will find the **House of the Stags**, famous for its beautiful frescoes, sculpted stags, and a drunken figure of Hercules. Farther north you can find the marvelously preserved **House of the Wooden Partition**. It is one of the most complete examples of a private residence in either Pompeii or Herculaneum. Near this house to the north are the **Baths**, an elaborate complex incorporating a gymnasium and assorted men's and women's baths.

Important to remember as you compare Herculaneum with Pompeii is that this town was only recently excavated since more modern tools were needed for the job, allowing for more advanced preservation efforts. But both sites are well worth visiting and are highly recommended by the author. Gates to the site open year round 9:00am to 1 hour before sunset. Admission E5.

Practical Information for Naples

Car Rental
• **Avis**, *Piazza Garibaldi 1, Tel. 081/28-74-69, Via Piedigrotta 44, Tel. 081/761-1365, or Airport, Tel. 081/780-5790.*
• **Hertz**, *Piazza Garibaldi 91, Tel. 081/206-228 or Airport 081/780-2971.*

Consulates
• **United States**, *Piazza della Repubblica, Naples, Tel. 081/583-8111*

Postal Services
You can buy stamps at local tobacconists (they are marked with a "T"

outside) as well as post offices. Mail boxes are colored red. Post offices are open from 8:00am to 2:00pm on weekdays. The two exceptions to this rule are the **main post office** (**Palazzo delle Poste**) at Piazza Matteoti and the office at the Stazione Centrale, both of which are open Monday through Friday from 8:00am to 7:30pm, and Saturdays from 8:00am to noon.

Tourist Information & Maps

The **EPT**, *Tel. 081/268-779*, has an extensive office at the Stazione Centrale, where you can get some pretty good maps, as well information on ferries, reservations for hotels, and pick up a copy of the necessary *Qui Napoli* publication that tells you what's going on around the city.

Capri

The stunningly beautiful island of **Capri** exists today to generate tourist dollars. In the summer the population of Capri increases dramatically, perhaps more than any other island on the globe. Tourists from all over the world, and temporary residents who summer on the island flock to the stunning vistas, relaxed pace, great food, and the beauty of the **Blue Grotto** as well as other amazing sights.

In winter, life reverts to the dreamy pace that has been so characteristic of Capri over the centuries. So if you want to see a relatively pristine part of paradise unsoiled by rampant tourism, try to visit in the winter months. Many tourist stores and restaurants will be closed, but you'll have the island almost to yourself.

But in the summer, despite the crowds, you will be charmed and delighted with its ambiance and character. Capri used to be a residence of some of the emperors of Rome, and it still maintains that regal appearance even today.

Arrivals & Departures

By Ferry or Hydrofoil

Head over to the ferry or hydrofoil docks (they only run in the summer). Go to the Mole Beverello in Naples to catch the ferry or hydrofoil (tourist's cars are not allowed on the island, so you'll have to leave yours in Naples).

Where to Stay

1. CERTOSELLA, *Via Tragara 13, 80071 Capri. Tel. 081/837-0713, Fax 081/837-6113. Email: certosella@infinito.it. Web: www.emmeti.it/Welcome/ Campania/Capri/Alberghi/Certosella/index.it.html. Closed November and Easter. 12 rooms all with bath. Single E70-225. Double E140-175. All credit cards accepted. Breakfast included.* ***

On the way to the Belvedere Tragara in a central but tranquil location.

Operated by the proprietor of the restaurant Canzone del Mare listed below, the food here in their small restaurant, for obvious reasons is superb. The accommodations are pleasant and comfortable with simple furnishings. Some rooms have terraces which are a great place on which to relax in the evenings. The bathrooms are of medium size and come with hair dryers. They have an ample swimming pool for your use too. All the amenities of a three star. A great little hotel.

2. **QUISISANA**, *Via Camerelle 2, 80073 Capri, Tel. 081/837-0788, Fax 081/837-6080. Email: info@quisi.com. Web: www.quisi.com. 150 rooms, 15 suites all with bath. All credit cards accepted. Single E175-200; Double E225-450. Closed November 1 to March 31.* *******

One of the more famous hotels in the entire world. An ultra-luxurious hotel with an indoor and outdoor swimming pool, health club, tennis courts, sauna, a great restaurant, as well as excellent views of the whole island. Here you'd be staying in the lap of luxury in one of the more famous hotels in the world. The rooms are large and comfortable and have all the amenities you could expect: mini-bar, TV, air conditioning, room service, hairdryers and even a safe for your valuables. If you have the means, this is *the* place to stay.

3. **LA RESIDENZA**, *Via F Serena 22, 80073 Capri. Tel. 081/837-0833, Fax 081/837-7564.   Email: info@hotellaresidenza.com.   Web: www.hotellaresidenza.com. 114 rooms all with bath. All credit cards accepted. Single E125-150; Double E150-300.* ******

The second largest hotel on the island (the Quisisana is larger), you'll find everything you could want for your stay on Capri: a good restaurant with a great view, a pool with scenic views and relaxing garden setting, a hotel bar, location on the sea, clean and comfortable rooms, transport around the island, and more. But if you want the romantic intimacy of a smaller hotel, this is not the place to stay. It's so large that guests can get lost in the crowd. But if you want anonymity for you and your special friend, this is a good choice.

4. **SAN MICHELE**, *Via G Orlandi 3, 80071 Capri. Tel. 081/837-1427, Fax 081/837-1420. Email: info@capri-palace.com. Web: www.capri-palace.com/ farm/en/loc2.html. 100 rooms all with bath. Single E65-90; Double E115-150. Breakfast extra. All credit cards accepted.* *****

Oh my, what a view. Located in Anacapri on the edge of a cliff overlooking the water, almost all the rooms have the most spectacular view you could find anywhere. The excellent restaurant and swimming pool share the same scenery. It doesn't have the intimacy of a smaller hotel, but it has worlds of ambiance, character and charm. The rooms are large and comfortable and bathrooms are immaculate.

5. **LA SCALINATELLA**, *Via Tragara 10, 80073 Capri. Tel. 081/837-0633, Fax 081/837-8291. Email: casamorgana@capri.it. 30 rooms all with bath. Single E175-275. Double E250-450. All credit cards accepted. Closed November to March.* ******

Located on the sea, this small intimate hotel offers you the charm you're looking for when you think of Capri. Run by the same family that operates the Quisisana, here they can give you much more personal attention since there are only 30 rooms compared to 150. The hotel also has a pool by which you can get your meals served in a lush garden setting; or you can go to the restaurant that offers perfect views for an intimate dining experience. The rooms are ample, many with great views. They are clean, wonderfully decorated with antiques, and comfortable. This is definitely the most romantic place to stay in Capri.

6. VILLA KRUPP, *Via Matteoti 12, 00871 Capri. Tel. 081/837-0362, Fax 081/837-6489. Closed January. 12 rooms all with bath. Single E55-75; Double E100-140. Visa accepted. Breakfast included.* **

This place is bucking for three star status but they have a little ways to go. But that doesn't mean that a stay here is not pleasant. Located in a wonderful little villa that was once the home of the writer Massimo Gorky who was in love with Capri. Also nearby the gardens of Augustus and close to center of Capri but far enough away from all the confusion. The atmosphere is pleasant and welcoming like a good bed and breakfast. There is a large terrace with good panoramic views, a TV room and small bar area downstairs. The rooms are clean, comfortable and accommodating; the bathrooms come with all amenities. TVs also in the room. A good place to stay at a good price in Capri.

7. VILLA SARAH, *Via Tiberio 3, 80071 Capri. Tel. 081/837-0689, Fax 081/837-7215. Email: demgiu@mbox.caprinet.it. Closed from the end of October until Easter. 20 rooms all with bath. Single E65-E97; Double E100-195. American Express, Mastercard and Visa accepted. Breakfast included.* ***

A villa with a garden located in a tranquil setting away from the bustling crowds along the road that takes you to the Villa Tiberio. The rooms are ample, bright, come with small terraces, are clean and comfortable and are filled with peace and quiet. The bathrooms are also accommodating and come with all necessary amenities. A great place to stay while in Capri.

Where to Eat

8. ADD' O' RICCIO, *Locanda Gradola, Via Grotta Azzurra 4, Tel. 081/837-1380. Open all week. Closed for holidays November 10 - March 15. All credit cards accepted. Dinner for two E55.*

Come here for the food as well as the beautiful terrace overlooking the water, the rocks, and the Grotta Azzurra (Blue Grotto). They make a superb *risotto al mare* (seafood rice dish) and grilled or baked fish. Good atmosphere, great ambiance and location.

9. BUCA DI BACCO DA SERAFINA, *Via Longano 35, Tel. 081/837-0723. Closed Wednesdays and November. All credit cards accepted. Dinner for two E40.*

This is a small *pizzeria/trattoria* with the wood-burning oven the center

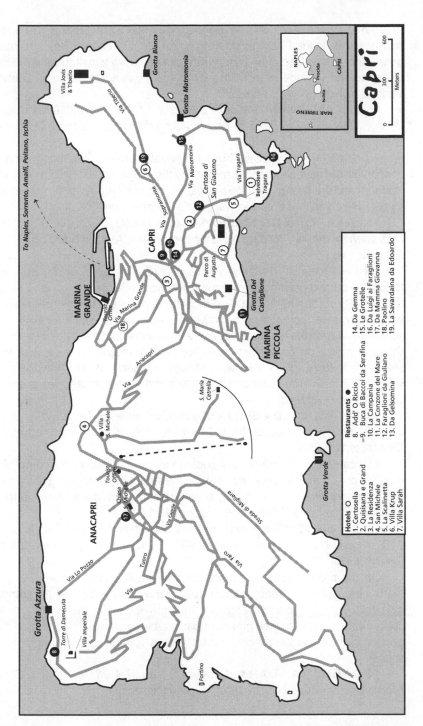

Capri

NAPLES

MAR TIRRENO

Ischia
Procida
CAPRI

0 300 600
Meters

Hotels ○
1. Certosella
2. Quisisana e Grand
3. La Residenza
4. San Michele
5. La Scalinetta
6. Villa Krup
7. Villa Sarah

Restaurants ●
8. Add' O Riccio
9. Buca di Baccoi da Serafina
10. La Campania
11. La Conzone del Mare
12. Faraglioni da Giuliano
13. Da Gelsomina
14. Da Gemma
15. Le Grotelle
16. Da Luigi ai Faraglioni
17. Da Mamma Giovanna
18. Paolino
19. La Savardaina da Edoardo

CAPRI

ANACAPRI

MARINA GRANDE

MARINA PICCOLA

To Naples, Sorrento, Amalfi, Poitano, Ischia

Grotta Bianca
Grotta Matromonia
Villa Jovis & Tiberio
Via Tiberio
Via Matromonia
Certosa di San Giacomo
Via Tragara
Belvedere Tragara
Via Sopramonte
Via Marina Grande
Tourist Office
Parco di Augusto
Grotta Del Castiglione
Via Anacapri
Via
S. Maria Cetrella
Villa S. Michele
Tourist Office
Chiesa S. Michele
Via Cenile
Strada di Migliara
Via Lo Pozzo
Tuoro
Via
Via Faro
Grotta Verde
Grotta Azzura
Torre di Damecuta
Villa Imperiale
Fortino
Grotta Azzura

of attention in the place. As you guessed, they make great pizzas. Try one of their specials, loaded with mozzarella and ricotta cheeses. They also make great pasta dishes, including a *pennette alla peperoni* (small tubular pasta in a tomato and sausage sauce). Since this is Capri, they also serve a variety of seafood dishes for good prices.

10. LA CAMPANINA, *Via delle Botteghe 12, Tel. 081/837-0732. Closed Wednesdays and November to Easter. All credit cards accepted. Dinner for two E70.*

A fine family run, upscale, but rustic establishment. You'll enjoy the air conditioning in the heat of the summer. Try their *linguine ai frutti di mare* (with seafood) and their *conniglio "alla tiberiana"* (rabbit stewed with tomatoes and spices). Here you'll get peasant fare for a princely sum.

11. LA CANZONE DEL MARE, *Via Marina Piccola 93, Tel. 081/837-0104. Only open for dinner. Holidays November to March. All credit cards accepted. Meal for two E55.*

Located at the small marina with a beautiful terrace overlooking everything. The perfect place to enjoy a meal and watch the people go by. You can get a variety of food here, including *bruschetta* (toasted Italian bread) loaded with mozzarella, tomatoes and olive oil, as well as a scrumptious club sandwich. Any of their *antipasti di mare* (seafood appetizers) are superb. Try their *spaghetti con pomodoro e basilico* (with tomatoes and basil) or their *spaghetti ai frutti di mare* (with seafood). For seconds they have a great selection of fresh fish, either grilled, cooked in the oven, or *all'aqua pazza* (in crazy water, i.e. boiled).

12. FARAGLIONI DA GIULIANO, *Via Camarelle 75, Tel. 081/837-0320. Closed Mondays and November 15 to March 15. All credit cards accepted. Dinner for two E55.*

You can enjoy the traditional cooking either in air conditioned comfort inside or out on their terrace overlooking the street. They make a good *risotto alla pescatore* (rice with seafood), *spaghetti ai frutti di mare* (with seafood) and any of their grilled fish dishes, especially the sole.

13. DA GELSOMINA *(Anacapri) Via Belvedere Migliari, Tel. 081/837-1499. Closed Tuesdays and January 20-31. All credit cards accepted. Dinner for two E35.*

Off the beaten path, and quite a hike from Anacapri or Capri, but it's worth the journey. Great peasant food served on a beautiful verandah overlooking the ocean and the lights from Capri below. Try their *spaghetti alla cozze* (with mussels) or their great antipasto table for primo. Then sample their great *conniglio alla cacciatore* (rabbit with a tomato, brandy, and mixed spices).

14. DA GEMMA, *Via Madre Serafina 6, Capri, Tel. 081/837-0461. Closed Mondays and November. All credit cards accepted. Dinner for two E25.*

In the hot summer months, come here to enjoy the cool air-conditioned comfort and great food. Even though Gemma is no longer around to run the place, her family continues the tradition of classic Italian food with just enough flair to make them unique and interesting. They are famous for their *spaghetti alla vongole* (with clam sauce) and the *"fritto alla Gemma"* (fried mozzarella and zucchini and other vegetables).

15. LE GROTELLE, *Via Arco Naturale 5, Tel. 081/837-5719. Closed Thursdays and December 1 - January 3. All credit cards accepted. Dinner for E50.*

Out in the middle of a virtual nature preserve, from the terrace you have a spectacular view of the sea, the stars, and nature. Here you get typical local fare like *pasta e fagioli* (pasta and beans), *ravioli alla caprese* (ravioli with seafood made Capri-style), and fish either fried or grilled. If you sit inside, these delicious smells permeate the rooms making your meal all the more enjoyable.

16. DA LUIGI AI FARAGLIONI, *Strade dei Faraglioni, Tel. 081/837-0591. Open only for dinner. All credit cards accepted. Dinner for two E60.*

The best terrace in Capri. Out on a small peninsula, you can try some wonderfully prepared seafood dishes like *sauté di vongole* (sautéed clams), or *pomodoro "alla Luigi"* (with mozzarella and basil) or *pizza "Monacone"* (filled with vegetables). Come for the romantic view (remember to reserve a spot) and stay for the food.

17. DA MAMMA GIOVANNA *(Anacapri) Via Boffe 3/5, Tel. 081/837-2057. Closed Mondays and the ten days after Christmas. All credit cards accepted. Dinner for two E40.*

Located in the heart of Anacapri, this is a small, quaint, local *trattoria* that makes great pizzas as well as grilled or oven cooked meats and fish. They have a terrace from which you can watch the night pass as you sip your dry house wine and enjoy the food. A great location ins Anacapri. The place to come in this part of the island.

18. PAOLINO, *Via Palazzo a Mare 11, Tel. 081/837-6102. Closed Mondays and January 15 to Easter. All credit cards accepted. Dinner for two E60.*

They've got old stoves and other cooking devices supporting the tables, which lends the place a nice down to earth touch that seems to go well with their sky high prices. Try their *ravioli alla caprese* (ravioli with seafood made Capri-style), *spaghetti con pomodoro (with spicy herbed tomatoes)*, or *rucola e gamberi* (pasta with shrimp) for primo. For seconds try any of their seafood on the grill.

19. LA SAVARDINA DA EDOARDO, *Via Lo Capo Tiberio 8, Tel. 081/837-6300. Closed November to March. All credit cards accepted. Dinner for two E38.*

You can only get here on foot, but it's worth the hike. Some of the best food on the island as well as some of the best prices. The terraces look out over lemon and other fruit trees making the meal a visual and well as aromatic experience. They make great *fiori di zucchine fritte* (fried zucchini flowers) and *conniglio alla cacciatore* (succulent rabbit cooked in tomatoes, brandy, and spices). A nice place to come for a change of pace.

Seeing the Sights

To get to the town of Capri after you've made it to the **Marina Grande**, the main harbor on the island, take the funicular (kind of like a trolley rising up the mountain). Once you reach the Piazza Umberto I, you can enjoy the memorable view out onto the Bay of Naples. This is the perfect piazza to have a seat on any one of the number of cafés and watch the world go by. Granted you'll pay a king's ransom for a coffee but the ambiance and character of the square need to be savored slowly, while seated.

From here you can walk – granted it's a long way – northeast to the **Palace of Tiberius**, the biggest, best preserved Imperial villa on the island. You won't find elaborate mosaic floors or statues in place here, and at first glance the site might seem disappointing, but what makes this place special is the sheer extent of the ruins located in such a superb setting. Built in the first century, the villa was initially 12 stories high but only partial remains of three remain. But the beehive of passageways leading to many small rooms make it evident that this villa functioned as a mini-city, with baths, store rooms and servants' quarters.

The Palace is perched on an imposing hilltop called **Il Salto** (The Leap) from which the Emperor is said to have thrown his enemies (and if you've read any Roman history this is probably true). *Open daily 9:00am until 1 hour before sunset. Admission E3.*

On the south edge of town is the **Certosa di San Giacomo**, a 14th century Carthusian monastery that was founded in 1371, destroyed in 1553 and rebuilt soon after. It was used as a prison and a hospice in the 1800s and today houses a secondary school and a library. The cloisters and the dark Gothic church are open to the public. The frescoes in the church are interesting to view but those cloisters can be missed, especially the **Museo Deifenbach** with its dark and crusty oil paintings.

From the monastery walk along the Via di Certosa to the **Parco Augusto**. From the terrace here you will find some fine views to the south of the island over the **Marina Piccola** (small harbor) and the **Faraglioni** rock formations. Bring your camera. From here you can follow a road that leads to the Marina Piccola and see the private yachts and fishing boats close up.

My favorite part of the island is the town of **Anacapri**. You get here either by bus or taxi from Capri. Anacapri is more relaxed and down-to-earth as compared to the faster-paced, pretentious nature of Capri. Perched high up on a rocky plateau, its flat-roofed whitewashed buildings are obviously Moorish in style. Here you can find the 18th century **Church of San Michele** (*open daily 7:00am-7:00pm*) with its sober Baroque design and intricate frescoed floors. Also in Anacapri is the **Villa San Michele**, which is known for its beautiful gardens and vast collection of classical sculpture (*open summer 9:00am-6:00pm, winter 10:00am-3:00pm; admission E6).* From these gardens are some of the most spectacular views. If you want to go higher, from Anacapri you can walk or take a chair lift up to **Monte Solaro**, which has amazing views over all of Capri. You catch the chair lift from Piazza Vittoria and the trip up here is equally as spectacular as the trip to the Blue Grotto below. Here you will find one of the world's premier picnic spots, so come prepared. But bring a sweater or jacket even on sunny days since the wind tends to cool things down slightly.

Finally, onto the famous **Grotta Azzura** or **Blue Grotto**. You can walk or take a bus down the Via Grotta Azzura from Anacapri. once at the bottom you can hire a boat to take you into the grotto. Or you can come from Marina Grande by motorboat with a number of other people, then transfer to rowboats to enter the grotto. You will have to sit on the floor of the row-boat as the captain (on his back) leads the boat in by pulling hand over hand on a length of fixed chain. The silver-blue light inside is close to indescribable. Suffice to say it is magnificent. The color of the water is caused by refraction of light entering the grotto beneath the surface. Don't foolishly deny yourself the joy of this excursion for fear of being labeled a tourist. The Blue Grotto really is worth seeing no matter how cheesy it appears. *Open 24 hours. Boat trips from Marina Grande go from 9:00am-6:00pm. Cost E5.*

Walking is by far the best way of getting about the island, but horse-drawn carriages, buses and taxis operate, linking Capri and Anacapri. The island seems bigger than its ten square kilometers suggest, due to an undulating landscape resting upon sheer limestone cliffs. If you are walking during the summer months, remember to rest frequently because the hills are very steep, especially in Capri. Anacapri is easier to walk since it rests on a plateau. Also remember to bring along some water to prevent dehydration even in the cooler, off-season months.

Procida

Located in the Bay of Naples, **Procida's** beauty has achieved worldwide acclaim as a result of the Oscar-winning Italian movie, *Il Postino*, partially set on the island. The movie was able to capture the quaint, picturesque quality of this magnificent little island. The island's tiny towns are strewn with houses of fading pink, blue and yellow all thrown together in a Byzantine labyrinth of cobblestone streets.

Originally a volcano that now has five inactive craters, Procida is awash with vineyards and citrus plantations overlooking a spectacular sea dotted with small fishing boats of green, orange, navy and white collecting the day's catch for the local restaurants and households.

Arrivals & Departures

Take the ferry to the island from Molo Beverello in Naples harbor. The trip takes about an hour and the ferries run almost every hour.

Where to Stay

There are not many upscale places to stay on Procida, but with its new-found popularity this might change. For the most part, people come for a day trip, then go back to Naples, Capri, or Ischia. But if you want a little peace and quiet, here are two comfortable options.

1. CRESCENZO, *Via Marina Chiaiolella 33, 80079 Procida. Tel. 081/896-7255, Fax 081/810-1260. 10 rooms all with bath. Double E50-113. Credit cards accepted. Full board E35-55.* ***

The best of the few options available on Procida. An adequate three star with air conditioning and TV in the room. This is like an intimate bed and breakfast in the middle of the Mediterranean. Relaxing, clean and comfortable and near everything of importance.

2. RIVIERA, *Via G. da Procida 36, 80079 Procida. Tel. 081/896-7197. 26 rooms all with bath. Single E25-30; Double E40-50; No credit cards accepted. Full board E35-50.* **

A cute little two star with hardly any amenities. There's a TV and phone in the spartan rooms, and a quaint little garden area in which you can relax, but other than that, this place is bare bones. But there are limited options on the island, and this is one of the best. Procida is rustic but you came here to get away from it all.

Where to Eat

3. GORGONIA, *Marina Corricella 50, Tel. 081/810-1060. Never closed in the summer and only open on the weekends and holidays in the winter. Credit cards accepted. Dinner for two E40.*

In the summer you can enjoy a meal outside on the terrace overlooking the sea. A truly relaxing and romantic way to dine. A *gorgonia* is a local sea plant and that maritime theme is played out in the menu. I really like the *linguini al pescatore* ('fishermen's linguine,' meaning it is covered in seafood). And for seconds, any and all grilled fish are superb.

4. SCARABEO, *Via Saleto 10, Tel. 081/896-9918. Never closed in the summer and only open on the weekends and holidays in the winter. Closed November. No credit cards accepted. Dinner for two E35.*

Located in a splendid little garden, this *trattoria* is as traditional as you can get. Large and boisterous atmosphere filled with locals and tourists alike – and the food doesn't disappoint either. The *antipasto* is overflowing, and the pastas superb. I especially like the *linguine con broccoli e cozze* (pasta with broccoli and mussels). For seconds, the fresh fish just out of the bay is fantastic, as is the succulent *conniglio alla cacciatore* (rabbit stewed in a tomato, spices and wine sauce).

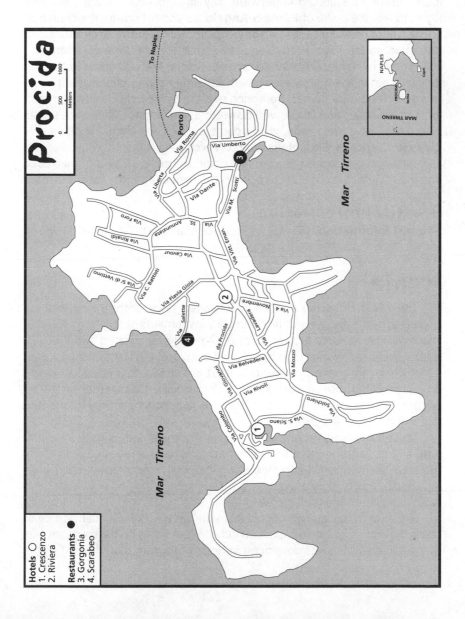

Seeing the Sights

The island is a celebration of natural beauty and uncontaminated locations. Even though it is a popular tourist attraction, Procida has designated a large segment of its mass, the peninsula of **Vivara**, as a nature preserve. Besides nature walks, Procida offers all sorts of water sports, including wind surfing, water skiing, snorkeling, and more. Especially popular is diving to the local reefs and a stunning underwater city. In conjunction there are a few sights to see: the castle of **Punta S Angelo**, an ancient prison; the church of **Santa Maria della Pieta**, the **Abbey of Saint Michael the Archangel** that dates back to the 13th century, and the monastery of **Punta del Monaci**.

Procida is the ideal location to come to witness the way life used to be in Italy (but not in the high season), with fishermen plying their trade, housewives and restaurant owners clamoring over the daily catch, locals congregating in the piazzas, and life slowed down to a human pace. There are scores of amazing vistas on Procida, wide open seascapes and enchanting towns – **Ciraccio, Corricella, Chiaiolella, Pozzo Vecchio** – all bursting with color and alive with activity. Procida has a definite emotional pull with its unhurried pace and friendly attitude. As such, Procida is the perfect antidote for civilization.

Practical Information

• **Tourist Information**, *Via Roma (Stazione Maritima), Tel. 081/810-968*

Ischia

The island of **Ischia** has been inhabited since prehistoric times, as evidenced by the discovery of flint and glass instruments dating from 300 BCE inland, as well as some Bronze and Iron Age objects. Located in the Bay of Naples, the island was formed by volcanic eruptions, the last of which was in 1301, which caused the inhabitants to flee the island for four years. Today the only remnant of those days are the curative thermal baths that make Ischia so popular. But not with Americans for some reason. Ischia is mainly frequented by Europeans; the Americans go to Capri.

These baths have become the gold mine of the island. In the 1950s and '60s, a hotel boom erupted to capitalize on this natural resource, and today there are many thermal complexes for the public and many private ones attached to hotels. They are open from early April to the end of October and cater to an international clientele.

The tourism 'dollars' generated from the baths is Ischia's main source of revenue. Farming is also an important industry (especially on the southern part of the island which is less developed in terms of tourism than the rest of the island), and strangely fishing comes in a distant third. It could be that most of the fish have been culled from the local waters many centuries ago.

Arrivals & Departures

Take the ferry to the island from Molo Beverello in Naples harbor. The trip takes about an hour and the ferries run almost every hour.

Where to Stay

There are so many hotels to choose from on Ischia, most of them attached to a spa/thermal bath. Many are excellent and high priced in response to that excellence. These are the best three, regardless of star rating or price.

1. DELLA BAIA, *Via San Montano, Commune di Forio, 80075 Ischia. Tel. 081/986-398, Fax 081/986-342. Closed October through April. 20 rooms all with bath. Double E90-110. Credit cards accepted. Breakfast included. Full board E75-90. ****

Located on the splendid bay of San Montano far from all the hubbub of the tourists but right by the sea, this hotel is in a splendid position. You can get a massage, practice windsurfing or simply relax in their garden setting or by the sea. The rooms are spacious: each one has its own little garden, TV, mini-fridge and phone. The bathrooms are a little small. Overall, an excellent place to stay.

2. GRAND HOTEL EXCELSIOR, *Via Emanuele Gianturco 19, 80077 Ischia. Tel. 081/991-522, Fax 081/984-100. Email: excelsior@leohotels.it. Web: www.excelsiorischia.it/. 72 rooms all with bath. Single E155-210; Double E220-260. See viewe an extra E26. Credit cards accepted. Breakfast included. Full board E120-165. ******

A superbly luxurious hotel with every conceivable amenity your little heart could desire. Indoor and outdoor pools, tennis courts, mud baths, saunas, fitness center, massage, and an excellent restaurant with a stunning view that serves fine local cuisine. There's also a private beach, water sports equipment rentals, day care, shuttle bus service and so much more. All of this in a quaint old building filled with the finest furnishings money could buy. The service is impeccable, the ambiance unbeatable ... but all for a very high price. And they make you pay extra if your room has a view of the water.

3. VILLA ANGELICA, *Via 4 Novembre 28, Lacco Ameno. Tel. 081/994-524, Fax 081/980-184. Email: angelica@pointel.it. Closed November 1 to April 15. 21 rooms all with bath. Single E40-50; Double E75-90. American Express and Visa card accepted. Full board E60. ****

Located in a tranquil side street in Lacco Ameno, you have quiet terraces on which to sunbathe, a swimming pool filled with a spring of naturally heated water, a fine restaurant serving local dishes and some great views over the water. The rooms are somewhat small but all have balconies on which to relax.

The bathrooms are no larger but are kept spotless. An inexpensive place to stay, away from all the clamor, with a taste of luxury.

Where to Eat

4. DAMIANO, *Ischia Porto on SS270, Tel. 081/983-032. Only open in the evenings. Closed Nov. 15 to March 30. No credit cards accepted. Dinner for two E60.*

Located in a panoramic position above Ischia Porto, this place has wonderful local food and a great atmosphere. They make a great *frutti di mare al gratin* (seafood au gratin), *linguine all'aragosta* (with lobster sauce), *spaghetti alla Maria* (with tomatoes, olive oil and capers), *risotto al pescatore* (seafood rice dish), *calamari ripieni* (stuffed shrimp). The entire menu is superb. They truly take pride in the preparation and presentation of their food.

5. IL FOCOLARE, *Terme via Cretaio 36, Tel. 081/980-604. Open only in the evenings on Saturday and Sunday. Closed Wednesdays (not in summer) and October 31 to December 31. No credit cards accepted. Dinner for two E40.*

A fantastic local place situated in the country above Casamicciola, whose menu changes based on the seasonal produce and other food items available. In January when the pigs go to slaughter, the restaurant's main dishes are *maiale* (pork). In Spring, vegetables take over. In September, pumpkin plays a large part in the ingredients and October sees the introduction of locally grown mushrooms. Another specialty, whenever they can catch enough, is *conniglio al schiano* (rabbit in a *cacciatore* style sauce with tomatoes, wine and spices). You can also get a fine cut of Angus beef. My favorite desserts are *torte alla frutta* (fruit tarts) or *sorbetto al limone* or *al sambuca* (crushed ice dessert of lemon or the liqueur sambuca). The wines are all locally grown, some produced by the family vines.

6. O PORTICCIUL, *Via Porto 42, Tel. 081/993-222. Closed Mondays (not in summer) and November. From January 31 to August 31 only open Saturday and Sunday evenings. Credit cards accepted. Dinner for two E70.*

An expensive option, but with great vistas and equally great food. Feast on classic local cuisine like *antipasto di pesce* (mixed antipasto of fish), *insalata di aragosta* (lobster salad), *frutti di mare a sauté* (sautéed seafood), *zuppa di pesce* (fish soup), *spaghetti alla vongole* (with clam sauce), *bucatini con cozze e pecorini* (pasta with mussels and pecorino cheese), *pesce alla griglia or all'aqua pazza* (grilled or boiled fish). In autumn, the succulent mushrooms are harvested locally and incorporated into the menu. A great place to dine.

7. LA TAVERNETTA, *Via Sant'Angelo 77, Tel. 081/999-251. Closed Wednesdays (not from July 1 to August 31) and October 30 to February 28 (but are open during Christmas season). No credit cards. Dinner for two E30.*

For forty years they've been here, on the jetty of Porto Sant'Angelo serving up inexpensive traditional cuisine to locals and tourists alike. Eat on their terrace for a perfect place to have a meal by the sea. Come here if you're on the island, whether it's for a drink, meal, or a light snack because this is the place to be. Seafood is the staple and it's great, whether grilled, boiled, fried, baked, spread over pasta or served as an antipasto. The menu depends on the season and the catch of the day.

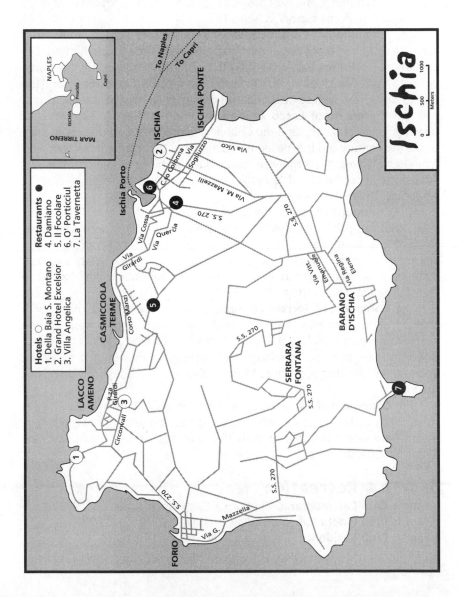

Seeing the Sights

Besides scenic vistas all along the coast, quaint little towns, all manner of water sports, the thermal baths, excellent restaurants and nightlife, Ischia also offers a wide variety of options for sightseeing, since each separate community on Ischia takes pride in its own piece of history.

The **Commune of Ischia** has its 17th century Cathedral with paintings and sculptures from the period, the church of Santo Spirito with some magnificent paintings, the Argonese Castle, and the centuries-old wine cellar and modern perfume factory in Ischia Port.

The **Commune of Casamicciola** is famous for its thermal baths and is about to complete a commercial port to rival and compete with Ischia Port. The sights here include the Piazza Marina with its statue of Emanuele II, the church of Santa Maria Maddelena with a high altar constructed in the 1600s, and the Chiesa della Pieta with some wonderful paintings by Andrea Vaccaro.

The **Commune of Lacco Ameno** is famous for its Greek tombs, its beaches, mineral waters, and the Church of Santa Restituta that dates back to the 4th century and the museum attached to it that contains many objects from Ischia's past; the Argonese tower built in the 15th century, the Villa Arbusto built on the site of Neolithic and Bronze Age settlements, and the Negombo Thermal Gardens.

The **Commune of Forio** is the largest borough on the island and contains many churches rich in frescoes and neoclassic domes, 10 ancient watchtowers, and towns with narrow streets and winding alleys. The best churches to see are the Church of Soccorso and the Brotherhood of Saint Mary the Poor. Another interesting sight is La Mortella, a stone quarry that has been transformed into an exotic and luxuriant botanical garden.

The **Commune of Serrara Fontana** is the least populated, mainly with farmers, and is predominantly hilly. The village of Sant' Angelo is a jewel you simply must see if on Ischia. The Piazza Serrara in the town of the same name is worth a see, as is the Hermitage of San Nicolo at the very top of Mount Epomeo and the church of Santa Maria la Sacra, the oldest parish church on the island.

The **Commune of Barano** is predominantly arable farmland but also has many areas dedicated to tourism, including beaches and thermal spas. The Piazza Barano is worth a visit with the churches of San Rocco and San Sebastian on either side.

Sports & Recreation

• **Tennis Club Cartaromana**, *Via Nuova Cartaromana, Tel. 081/993-622*
• **Tennis Club Pineta**, *Corso Vittoria Colonna, Tel. 081/993-300*
• **Tennis Club Residence**, *Via dello Stadio, Tel. 081/981-246*

- **Tennis Communale**, *Via Cristoforo Colombo, Tel. 081/993-416*
- **Boat Rental**, *Porto di Ischia, Tel. 081/992-383*
- **Ischia Diving Center**, *Via Iasolini 106, Tel. 081/985-008*

Practical Information
Car Rental
- **Center**, *Via Michele Mazzella 109, Tel. 081/992-451*
- **Ischia**, *Via Alfredo de Luca 61/a, Tel. 081/993-259*

Laundry
- **Lavanderia Aurora**, *Via A. DeLuca 91/a, Tel. 081/991-886*. Laundry and dry cleaning services available.

Tourist Information
- **Tourist Information Office**, *Corso Colonna 16, Tel. 081/991-146*

The Amalfi Coast

The steep slopes and rugged beauty of the **Amalfi Coast** have enchanted visitors for centuries. **Mount Vesuvius** reigns majestically in the distance, dominating the scenery as it once controlled the lives of the area's inhabitants with its eruptions. Dotted with little hillside towns, the only way to get to and from them is by car or bus. Neither option is too swift an alternative during the peak summer months, since the serpentine road connecting the towns is bumper to bumper traffic. In the off-season the traffic decreases considerably, but then so does the temperature, and bathing in the sea is one of the attractions of this coastline.

The road, dug almost entirely out of the rock, curves incessantly, but every turn offers coastal panoramic views of unparalleled proportions – which means that sometimes sitting in traffic can be candy for the eyes since you would have flown past the vista if the road was otherwise empty. Each town along the road has its own character but they are all blessed, or some would say cursed, with narrow curving streets and stairs that seem never to end.

The Amalfi Coast is the playground for people of all nationalities because of its unrivaled beauty and holiday options. Filled with high class hotels, excellent restaurants, countless nightlife options, ancient medieval streets and passageways, cultural sights and fun-loving effervescent locals, this area is one you will want to return to time and time again.

Another option for moving between each little town is to take a ferry then walk up the hills to each town.

Amalfi Coast Website
The place to find out about festivals, restaurants, shops, ferry information and more is thre Amalfi Coast website: **www.amalfi.it/**. A great resource to help you plan your trip.

Positano

Situated on a hill overlooking ten pristine beaches, **Positano** has been a part of this beautiful landscape for almost a thousand years. When Emperor Tiberius moved to Capri to escape the intrigue and serious threat of poisoning in Rome, he had his flour brought in from a mill in Positano, a mill that is still working today. In the 10th century Positano was one of the most important commercial centers on the Italian peninsula in active trade competition with Venice, Pisa and Genoa. In the 16th and 17th centuries, Positano was incredibly rich from all their trading activities and it was at this time that many of the beautiful Baroque homes scattered on the hills of the town were built.

Because of its timeless beauty, Positano has been the playground of the rich and famous for centuries. Writers, musicians, nobles, aristocrats – all have come here to bathe in the azure waters and relax in the lush green hillsides. Today it is no different. Filled with excellent restaurants, world class hotels, and all manner of water sports, Positano is a perfect holiday destination.

Arrivals & Departures

You can get to Positano by car via the coast road around the tip of the peninsula or the cross peninsula road. If you go by bus from Naples, catch a SITA bus from Piazza Municipio *(Tel. 081/55-22-176)*. From Salerno you catch the bus along Via SS Martiri Salernitani *(Tel. 089/22-66-04)*. You can also get here by ferry from Sorrento, Capri or Naples.

Where to Stay

1. **CASA ALBERTINA**, *Via della Tavolozza 3, 84017 Positano. Tel. 089/875-143, Fax 089/811-540. Email: alcaal@starnet.it. Web: www.casalbertina.it/. 20 rooms all with bath. Single E90-125; Double E125-155. Credit cards accepted. Breakfast included. Full board E60-85. ***

The hotel is located in quite a tranquil area, but it is also close to the beach, only some 300 steps down to the water. If you don't want to walk back up they have a small shuttle bus to carry you home after your swim. There is a terrace and a solarium for your relaxing pleasure. The rooms are large and well isolated from each other and come in a blue or red color scheme, some of which have nice views over the water. The bathrooms are a little tight but they do have all the modern amenities. Breakfast is a memorable experience filled with meats, cheeses, breads and more, which you can enjoy either in your room or on their little terrace.

The restaurant is superb, with food prepared by Aunt Albertina of the family Cinque that runs the hotel. A true family affair designed to make your stay as relaxing as possible.

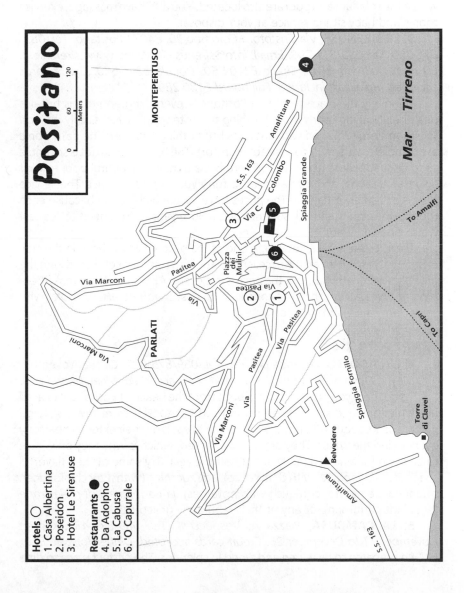

2. POSEIDON, *Via Pasitea 148, 84071 Positano. Tel. 089/811-111, Fax 089/875-833. Email: poseidon@starnet.it. Web: www.starnet.it/poseidon/. 48 rooms all with bath. Double E190-280. Credit cards accepted. Breakfast included.* ****

Located in the heart of Positano and run by the Aono family, this a fine four star hotel. Each room has a nice view from their little balconies where you can have your breakfast served. The furnishings are all antique but still comfortable. The restaurant in the summer is located in a quiet garden setting, where the solarium and pool are also located. You also have massage, exercise rooms and baby-sitting service at your disposal.

3. LE SIRENUSE, *Via Cristoforo Colombo 30, 84071 Positano. Tel. 089/ 875-066, Fax 089/811-798. Email: info@sirenuse.it. Web: www.sirenuse.it. 60 rooms all with bath. Single E210-550. Double E240-650. Credit cards accepted. Breakfast included. Full board E180-280.* *****

Definitely the place to stay in Positano – everything about this hotel is beautiful. Nothing overly fancy, nothing too ostentatious, just simply radiant. The rooms are furnished with antiques but nothing too frilly. The bathrooms are complete with every conceivable comfort. The breakfast buffet is so ample as to dissuade most from lunch. There is a stunningly beautiful pool at your disposal, a sauna, and a small boat to ferry you along the coast. The service here is extremely attentive. The prices have such a wide range because each room comes in a standard, superior and deluxe variety. You need to request which one you want.

Their restaurant, La Sponda, is one of the best, if not the best, in the city. Expensive, yes, but when the excellent Neapolitan cuisine is combined with the great views from the terrace, the price is irrelevant. All the food they make here is great, but I believe the chef concocts the best *spaghetti alla vongole* (with spicy clam sauce) in Positano.

Where to Eat

4. DA ADOLFO, *Locanda Laurito, Tel. 089/875-022. Closed November 1 to May 1. Open only for lunch. No credit cards accepted. Meal for two E30.*

To get here you need to catch a boat from the beach at Positano. Located in a truly romantic and isolated setting but not too far from town. A large place, it seats about 100, but the best place to eat is on their extensive balcony overlooking the water. They are usually packed, which is why they only have to be open for lunch and only about half the year. Try some of their flavorful *spaghetti alla vongole* (with clam sauce), *agli zucchine* (with a zucchini sauce), *totani con le patate* (cuttlefish with potatoes), *la parmigiana di melanzane* (eggplant parmesan), or any of their fabulously grilled fish.

5. LA CAMBUSA, *Piazza A. Vespucci 4, Tel. 089/875-432. Closed November 11 to December 20. Credit cards accepted. Dinner for two E70.*

Be prepared to be wined and dined in splendor. The perfect place to dine is on the terrace facing the beach. If you don't want to order from the menu they have a daily buffet that features many different plates. They are known for their great seafood, like *insalata di pesce* (seafood salad) or *di gamberetti* (small prawns). For *primo* try their *linguini con scampi* (with shrimp), *con frutti di mare* (with seafood), or the *zuppa di pesce* (seafood soup). For seconds you must try any of their grilled fish, served with roasted potatoes. A little expensive, but the food and ambiance are worth the price.

6. **'O CAPURALE**, *Via Regina Giovanna 12, Tel. 089/811-188. Closed Tuesdays (not in summer) and January. Credit cards accepted. Dinner for two E35.*

This place has been in the family for over one hundred years and is part of the life of Positano. You can still find some of the older residents of the town playing cards at some of the tables. People come here for the friendly local atmosphere as well as the fine food. Start off with some *linguine all'astice* (with lobster), *agli scampi* (with shrimp), or *bucatini alla 'caporalessa'* (with mozzarella, tomatoes, eggplant, olives, and capers); then move onto *zuppa di pesce* (seafood soup) and *pesce al aqua pazza* (boiled fish).

Seeing the Sights

Positano snakes its way up from the **Harbor** (Marina Grande) where ferries dock coming from Sorrento, Capri and Naples. Along the beach by the harbor are many chic boutiques that you can find in any holiday resort. For more historic sights, try the **Santa Maria Assunta**, a 12th century church that dominates the Positano hillside. The ancient floor is a Byzantine mosaic and on the main altar is a relief of the Madonna and Child in black marble. An hour hike up the hill is **Montepertuso** (Hole in the Mountain), where there is a large cliff pierced by a hole. Legend has it that the devil challenged the Madonna to make a hole in the mountain. He failed in ten attempts, while the Virgin Mother's finger easily created the hole and at the same time pushed the devil into the mountain below the hole. Anyway, enough local mythology ... from here your vantage point is perfect and the little village quaint. If you don't want to walk you can catch a bus at the harbor piazza (Piazza dei Mulini).

A short hike away from Montepertuso is **Nocelle**, another tiny village with great views and a quiet unassuming life. If you are here on New Year's Day, more specifically at dawn of the New Year, you will stumble onto a huge bonfire and banquet that welcomes in, through copious amounts of revelry, all the possibilities of the future.

Amalfi

Clinging to the rocky coats of the Sorrento peninsula is one of the most beautiful little holiday resorts in Italy, **Amalfi**. Legend has it that the town was established by Constantine the Great as a respite from the intrigue of Rome. By the Middle Ages it had a population of 50,000, but today it is only around 7,000 (when all the tourists leave). During the 16th and 17th centuries it was joined with the other little towns on the Amalfi Coast in competition with the other seafaring states of Venice, Genoa and Pisa.

As a tourist resort, Amalfi offers everything you could need to make your stay pleasant: fine restaurants, wonderful hotels, nightlife, shopping, water sports and sightseeing.

Arrivals & Departures

You can get to Amalfi by car via the coast road or the cross peninsula road. If you go by bus from Naples, catch a SITA bus from Piazza Municipio (*Tel. 081/ 55-22-176*). From Salerno you catch the bus along Via SS Martiri Salernitani (*Tel. 089/22-66-04*). You can also get here by ferry from Sorrento, Capri or Naples.

Where to Stay

1. LA BUSSOLA, *Lungomare dei Cavalieri 16, 84011 Amalfi. Tel. 089/ 871-533, Fax 089/871-369. Email: labussola@amalficoast.it. Web: www.labussolahotel.it/. 63 rooms all with bath. Single E65-75; Double E100-125. Dinner E65 per person. Credit cards accepted. Breakfast included. Full Board E55-75.* ***

La Bussola is strategically placed directly on the walkway along the sea, where they have a private beach. This hotel is located in an old mill and a pasta factory and has been in the hotel business since 1962. The rooms are well decorated and all have balconies. The bathrooms are normal with all necessary modern conveniences. The restaurant is large and has a nice view of the water. On the top floor is a quiet roof garden where you can relax soaking up the wonderful views over the water and the town. A fine three star hotel. A great place to stay in Amalfi.

2. CAPPUCCINI CONVENTO, *Via Annunziatella 46, 84011 Amalfi. Tel. 089/871-877, Fax 089/871-886. Email: cappuccini@amalfinet.it. Web: www.hotelcappuccini.it/. 42 rooms all with bath. Single E90-115; Double E150-190. Credit cards accepted. Breakfast E10. Full board E85-110.* ****

From the hotel's terrace you have your own slice of the Amalfi Coast to enjoy all to yourself. This ex-monastery, built in the 1200s, is so beautiful, so quaint, so filled with character that many couples have their weddings set here. The rooms are what once were the cells for the monks that lived here, all updated with modern conveniences of course. They have a baby-sitting service and a fine restaurant. A peaceful place to stay. A wonderful four star hotel.

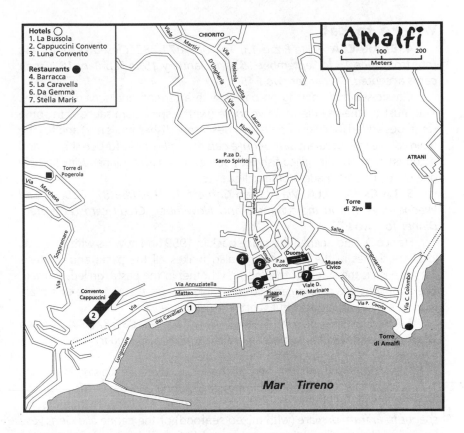

3. **LUNA CONVENTO,** *Via Comite 33, 84011 Amalfi. Tel. 089/871-002, Fax 089/871-333. Email: luna@amalficoast.it. Web: www.lunahotel.it. 45 rooms all with bath. Single E100-130; Double E125-165. Credit cards accepted. Breakfast included. Full board E90-105.* ****

Located in a convent founded by St. Francis of Assisi in 1222, this place is filled with charm. The library is the old cloisters where you can enjoy a quiet read amongst the white columns and archways. There are two restaurants to choose from, each with its own magnificent view of the water and the hotel's private beach area. There is also an outdoor pool in a garden setting to enjoy. The rooms are large and all furnished differently with pieces made by local artisans, and each has its own little terrace with a view of the water.

There are fifteen internal cells turned into rooms that do not have a view. The bathrooms were modernized in 1994 so they have all modern amenities. The staff is professional and courteous. A wonderful place to stay in Amalfi.

Where to Eat

4. **BARRACCA**, *Salita Pizzo 13, Tel. 089/871-285. Closed Wednesdays (not from June 15 to September 15) and January 15 to February 15. Credit cards accepted. Dinner for two E45.*

Classic seafood cooking prepared with attention and served perfectly. You must try the *spaghetti alla vongole* (with a spicy clam sauce with some tomatoes added for color), *risotto alla pescatore* (fisherman's rice) and for the main course the succulent *gamberini e calamari alla griglia* (grilled shrimp and octopus) or any of the grilled fish they serve. For an after-dinner drink sample one of their home made aromatic liqueurs.

5. **LA CARAVELLA**, *Via Matteo Camera 12, Tel. 089/871-029. Closed Wednesdays (not in the summer) and November. Credit cards accepted. Dinner for two E75.*

Franco Di Pino opened this place back in 1959 and now his wife concocts local specialties in the kitchen. She also makes all the pasta and desserts herself. Fish is the staple of this menu, whether in the pasta, grilled, or fried. The atmosphere is relaxing and comfortable despite the presence of a main road nearby. A little pricey but worth the expense.

6. **DA GEMMA**, *Via Fra' Gerardo Sasso 10, Tel. 089/871-345. Closed Wednesdays (not in the summer) and November and January. Credit cards accepted. Dinner for two E55.*

This place represents the best of the local, traditional cuisine in Amalfi. Their *antipasto di mare* (seafood appetizer), *zuppa di pesce* (seafood soup), *linguine all'aragosta* (with lobster sauce), *spaghetti alla cozze* (with mussels), *spaghetti ai frutti di mare* (with mixed seafood) or the *penne alla Genovese* (macaroni-like noodles with a pesto sauce of olive oil, basil and garlic) are all fantastic. And of course their fish, whether boiled, fried or grilled is all fresh and flavorful. Their terrace is a wonderful place to enjoy your meal. For the most part their wine list contains only whites, but that is sensible since they serve mainly fish.

7. **STELLA MARIS**, *Viale delle Regioni 2, Tel. 089/872-463. Closed Thursdays (not at Easter). American Express and Visa accepted. Dinner for two E45.*

Right on the sea, in the heart of Amalfi, this is a great *trattoria* with great food. The first impression you get is that this is a tourist restaurant that only has a superb view of the water and a great terrace, but they also serve great food. Their *spaghetti alla vongole* (with clam sauce), and *sogliola alla griglia* (grilled sole) are the perfect meal. Seafood is also the mainstay of this place. Great atmosphere. Great food.

Seeing the Sights

Some of the sights you can see are the **Duomo of Sant'Andrea** built in the Lombard Romanesque style in 1203. Its fine portico with pointed arches was totally rebuilt in 1865. On the west side is a bronze door that was cast in Constinantinople in 1066. In the crypt you will find the remains of the Apostle, Saint Andrew. How they verify these things I will never know. I guess you have to rely on faith?

Near the Duomo is the tiny **Museo Civico** that does its best to offer a history of the town. If you have nothing else to do you may want to try here. High above the town, reachable by a steady hike, is the **Capuccinni Monastery** that offers fine views of the city. Now a hotel, some areas will be off limits to visitors who are not guests of the hotel.

A 15 minute boat ride away is the **Grotta di Amalfi**, an ancient stalactite cave on the coast. The boat ride itself offers fine vistas, so don't forget your camera. One kilometer away along the coast road is the tiny little village of Atrani, picturesquely sitting along the mouth of a rocky gorge. In the main piazza is the 10th century **church of San Salvatore**, complete with Byzantine bronze doors cast in Constinantinople in 1087.

Ravello

About five kilometers from Amalfi is **Ravello**, a superb little hill town in one of the most enchanting spots in the world. Perched on a 350-foot high cliff overlooking the azure sea of the Amalfi Coast, Ravello has preserved its historical monuments through the ages and incorporated them into everyday life. Stunning.

Arrivals & Departures

You can get to Ravello by car via the coast road or the cross peninsula road. If you go by bus from Naples, catch a SITA bus from Piazza Municipio *(Tel. 081/55-22-176)*. From Salerno, catch the bus along Via SS Martiri Salernitani *(Tel. 089/22-66-04)*. From Amalfi, buses leave from Piazza Flavio Gioia *(Tel. 089/87-10-09)*.

Where to Stay

CARUSO BELVEDERE, *Via San Giovanni del Toro 52, 84010 Ravello. Tel. 089/857-111, Fax 089/857-372. 24 rooms all with bath. Single E65-80; Double E80-250. Credit cards accepted. Breakfast included. Full board. E75-118.* ****

In a truly historic building, this hotel has been open for 102 years but has every modern convenience possible. The rooms may be sparsely furnished but they are wonderfully comfortable. From their stunning garden you have amazing vistas of the water and surrounding area. Everything about this place is designed to relax, from the view of the coast from the restaurant (which is quite good), to the lush garden, to the study room with daily newspapers from around the world.

VILLA MARIA, *Via Santa Chiara 2, 84010 Ravello. Tel. 089/857-255, Fax 089/857-071. Email: villamaria@villamaria.it. Web: www.villamaria.it. 18 rooms all with bath. Single E140-160; Double E160-210. Credit cards accepted. Breakfast included. Full board E53-97.* ***

This is a four star masquerading as a three star. They have a heated pool, a garden terrace area for relaxing, rooms filled with antique furnishings, bathrooms with every modern convenience, beautiful balconies (Room Number 3's is huge), professional service, and a relaxing atmosphere like a bed and breakfast. You can eat inside or out on the terrace with its stunning views over the sea. You also have access to tennis courts only 100 meters down the road.

Where to Eat

CUMPA COSIMO, *Via Roma 44, Tel. 089/857-156. Closed Mondays (not in Spring and Summer). Credit cards accepted. Dinner for two E40.*

On the walls are photographs of the many personalities who have enjoyed the simple local cooking and the hospitality of the Bottone family. For *primo* try the *pasta al pesto* (home made pasta with garlic, oil and basil sauce), or *agli zucchine* (with zucchini sauce), or *ai peperoni* (with peppers). For seconds the *agnello, salsicce* and other grilled meats (lamb, sausage, etc., all supplied by the butcher shop run by the same family) are fantastic. You should also try the fresh fish caught daily right in the Bay. For dessert you might want to try some of their *torte* (cakes) and *sorbetti* (Italian ices) made from locally grown oranges. A great little *trattoria*.

Seeing the Sights

One of the most important monuments is the **Cathedral**, founded in 1086. Here you can admire the Byzantine mosaic work on the pulpit, the bronze doors, and the civic museum located in the crypt. **Villa Rudolph** is another sight to behold, especially in July when the views are complimented with music at the Wagner Festival. **Villa Cimbrone** also contains lush gardens and is known for its breathtaking views, which have been described by many as the best in the world.

Other sights to see while in Ravello are: the church of **San Giovanni del Toro** with its mosaic pulpit; the **Villa Episcopio** where King Vittorio Emanuele abdicated the throne; the cloister of the 13th century **convent of St. Francesco** with its amazing library; and the scenic **Piazza Fontana Moresca**.

Salerno

At the north end of the Gulf of Salerno sits the town of the same name. An industrial center, **Salerno** still has an old town that merits a look because of its winding medieval streets and steps, but mainly it is just another southern Italian port city, devoid of charm. Near the old town, off of the Piazza Amendola, are the public gardens, on the west side of which is the **Teatro Verdi** where many operas are performed. In the middle of the maze of the old town is the **Duomo** built in 1086, restored in 1768 and then in 1945 after allied bombing took its toll on the facade. Inside a flight of steps leads up to an atrium that has 28 ancient columns and 14 sarcophagi purloined from Paestum. The magnificent bronze doors were cast in Constanantinople in 1099.

A little ways north in the Largo Plebiscito is the **Museo Duomo** that contains many relics from Salerno's past. West along Via San Michele is the **Museo Provinciale** with many antiquities, including a huge bronze head of Apollo cast in the 1st century BCE.

Arrivals & Departures

You can get to Salerno by train from Naples in under an hour, or you can take the Autostrada A3 from Naples. There are also ferries from Capri and Naples that will bring you here.

Where to Stay

1. JOLLY HOTEL DELLE PALME, *Lungomare Trieste 1, 84100 Salerno. Tel. 089/225-222, Fax 089/237-571. Web: www.jollyhotels.it. 104 rooms all with bath. Single E110-125; Double E120-145. Credit cards accepted. Breakfast included. Full board E95-148.* ****

The best hotel in Salerno, which says a lot about the types of hotels in the city. Located at the end of the Lungomare along a busy thoroughfare. The rooms have pastel colored curtains to contrast with the white furniture. The double windows are needed to block out the sounds of the street below. The bathrooms are ample with large windows and every modern convenience. All Jolly hotels have professional service, as well as stale North American-style hotel lack of ambiance.

2. PLAZA, *Piazza Via Veneto 42, 84100 Salerno. Tel. 089/224-477, Fax 089/237-311. Email: plaza@speednet.org. Web: www.plazasalerno.it. 42 rooms all with bath. Single E55; Double E65. Credit cards accepted. Breakfast E5.* ***

A simple basic three star located near the station. The accommodations in Salerno are not that upscale, and this is the best three star in town. Located in a building built in the 1800s, you can also see some ancient architectural features that the structure was built around. In an ideal location at the beginning of the walking street area (*zona pedonale*) where you can head out for your evening stroll. The common areas are pleasant enough with plants and flowers as adornment. The rooms are simple with modern furnishings and are comfortable with satellite TV, air conditioning and minibar.

Where to Eat

3. ANTICA PIZZERIA DEL VICOLO DELLA NEVE, *Vicolo della Neve 24, Tel. 089/225-705. Closed Wednesdays, two weeks in August and Christmas. Open only in the evenings. American Express accepted. Dinner for two E35.*

In one of the areas with the most character and ambiance in the city, this rustic little locale is an ideal place to have typical Salernese food at honest prices. Some dishes to try are: *verdure al forno* (grilled vegetables), *funghi al forno* (grilled mushrooms), *melanzane alla parmigiana* (eggplant parmesan), *calzone* and all manner of pizzas. A really local environment with rustic cuisine.

4. AL CENACOLO, *Piazza Alfano I 4/6, Tel. 089/238-818. Closed Sunday evenings and Mondays, as well as August 8-22 and December 25 to February 1. Credit cards accepted. Dinner for two E45.*

Basically right in front of the Duomo, this local favorite owned by Pietro Rispoli is a sure thing when it comes to finding fine food and good atmosphere. They have a fixed menu for E23 that comes with antipasto, first, second, and dessert. If you want to order on your own try some of these dishes: *alici marinate* (marinated anchovies), *gamberi in salsa di limone e zucchine* (shrimp in a lemon/zucchini sauce), *ravioli di pesce con vongole e zucchine* (fish stuffed ravioli in a clam/zucchini sauce), or *cannelloni con le melanzane* (cannelloni with eggplant). For seconds they grill a variety of meats and fish. For dessert, their *mousse al cioccolato* (chocolate mousse) is simply sinful. But if you go with the fixed price menu you will be served some great food too.

Sorrento

This is the jewel on the Bay of Naples. A gem of a little town. Fun and colorful, here you can relax on the beach, shop for the world-famous Sorrentine ceramics, eat at wonderful restaurants, and generally have a peaceful time. The perfect jumping-off point for day trips to the islands in the bay, Pompeii and Herculaneum, the Amalfi Coast and even to venture into Naples. Seasoned travelers who chafe at the chaos of Naples stay here and commute in during the day to enjoy the museums and other sights there. This allows them to escape back to Sorrento for a restful evening.

Sights to see include the churches of **San Francesco**, **San Anonino** and the local **Cathedral**. The **Museo Correale** is not that extensive, but it can be an educational diversion from lazing about at the beach or by the pool. To get a head start on what there is to do in Sorrento, check out their official website, *www.sorrentoinfo.com*.

Arrivals & Departures

You can get to Sorrento by train from Naples easily in around an hour. There are also ferries from the islands and Naples that will bring you here.

Where to Stay

BELLEVUE SYRENE, *Piazza della Vittoria 5, Tel/081/878-1024, Fax 081/878-3963. Email: info@bellevuesyrene.it. Web: www.sorrentopalace.it/bellevue/. Single E150-200; Double E175-300. All credit cards accepted. Breakfast included.* ****

In a tranquil location right by the sea, they also have a nice flowered garden where you can rest peacefully. There is an elevator that takes you from the garden down to the sea. The rooms either overlook the sea or the garden.

Sea views cost a little more. But all rooms are spacious and comfortable and have all necessary four star amenities. A sister hotel to the Sorrento Palace, which is another great hotel in the area, guests of the Syrene can use the pool and tennis facilities at that location.

DEL CORSO, *Corso Italia 134, Tel. 081/807-1016. Fax 081/807-3157. Email: info@hoteldelcorso.com. Web: www.sorrentoaccommodation.com/ hoteldelcorso/. 25 rooms. Single E80; Double E100-115. Breakfast included. All credit catds accepted. ***

If you're coming to Sorrento on a budget this is a good place to stay. The amenities here are rather good for a two star. TVs and A/C in everyroom Some four stars don't have that. Located on the second floor of an 18th century building on a main road, close by everything, and within walking distance to the train station, this hotel may not be luxurious but it is comfortable and accommodating. They also have a sun deck on the roof and a garden patio where breakfast is served. In all a good place to stay in Sorrento.

EXCELSIOR VITTORIA, *Piazza Tasso 34, Tel. 081/807-1044, Fax 081/877-1206. Email: exvitt@exvitt.it. Web: www.exvitt.it. 106 rooms. Single E200-225; Double E250-265. All credit cards accepted. Breakfast included. *****

By far the best hotel in Sorrento. It may not have the highest star rating, but it beats the rest hands down. Still a little pricey but it is worth it. Located in a beautiful villa from the 18th century, this place is an elegant and refined hotel that has hosted many a famous person over the years. The rooms are all spacious and comfortable with beautiful views, antique furnishings, and bathrooms done up in marble. The common areas arebeautiful and all face the sea. There is a park and pool on the hotel grounds where you can relax for hours.

RIVAGE, *Via Capo 11, Tel 081/878-1873, Fax 081/807-1253. Email: info@hotelrivage.com. Web: www.hotelrivage.com/. 48 rooms. Single E80-90; Double E95-125. ****

A recently built hotel with every conceivable modern amenity including AC and TV, roof garden, terrace with panoramic views, and sun deck. A little walk from the center of town, just off of a main road, the Rivage first appears to be a restaurant, but once you descend a set of stairs you are at the reception area. The rooms are all spacious and elegantly furnished, and your stay here will definitely be comfortable. If you are looking for charm and ambiance, you'll need to look elsewhere. But in terms of the price/quality ratio, the Rivage is a good three star.

Where to Eat

ANTICA TRATTORIA, *Via P. Reginaldo Giuliani 33, Tel. 081/807-1082. Closed Mondays (not in summer) and from January to February. All credit cards accepted. Dinner for two E60.*

A super local place with Sorrentine ceramics strewn around everywhere and communcal tables in some locations. An ample menu, filled with all sorts of local flavor, especially seafood and pasta. You cannot go wrong by haviong a meal here. And you'll find you want to come back again and again for the lively atmopshere and superb food.

CARUSO, *Via S. Antonino 12, Tel 081/807-3156. Closed Mondays and in January. All credit cards accepted. Dinner for two E75.*

A refined and elegant place, a lot less boisterous than the Antica Trattoria. Also specializing in seafood and other local favorites, but Senore Caruso throws it all together with his own particular flair. Atmospheric and tranquil, you will have a lovely meal here surrounded by others who share you taste for culinary excellence.

Chapter 18

genoa & the riviera

The seaside splendor of the Ligurian region of Italy is separated into three distinct parts: **The Italian Riviera** to the west of Genoa; **Genoa** and its environs; and the **Gulf of Tigullio**, including the **Cinque Terre** to the southeast of Genoa. Though different in appearance and possibilities they all hold their own special charm. The Italian Riviera is akin to the French Riviera; Genoa is a wonderfully scenic medieval port town; along the Gulf of Tigullio are wonderful resort beach towns hemmed into the sea by picturesque hills; and the Cinque Terre are five wonderful little hill towns that are relics from the past.

Genoa

Genoa (*Genova*) is a gritty seaport city that is known for its excellent restaurants that serve the omnipresent pesto sauce as well as fresh and tasty seafood concoctions. A bustling and vibrant port city Genoa is still quite walkable. The old town is completely closed off to traffic, and with it's winding Medieval streets it is a wonderful place to walk ... during the day.

Genoa's white houses are built on the mountain slopes of the **Ligurian Appenines** above a sheltered harbor at the head of the **Gulf of Genoa**. Among the houses stand medieval churches and Renaissance palaces that illustrate the city's historic greatness. Crowded shipping in the harbor and skyscrapers rising in the business district indicate the city's present prosperity as Italy's chief port.

As well as being a shipping center, Genoa's main industry is **shipbuilding**. The port of Genoa leads all other Italian ports in volume of passengers and freight traffic, and is the main source of city income. It handles fuels and raw materials for the factories of Switzerland and southern Germany and is the chief outlet for the products of northern Italy and much of central Europe – mainly cotton and silk textiles, olive oil, and wine. Genoa has been an important port since the Middle Ages. Venice used to be its main rival, but when that city's trade with the Orient dwindled as result of the Portuguese discovery of a way around Africa, focus shifted westward to the Atlantic, and Genoa's location on the west coast of Italy became a great advantage.

Because of its location, tucked between the mountains and the sea, Genoa has had to be creative with its resources when expanding. One such situation was in the 1950s when the city began reclaiming 250 acres from the sea at Sestri Ponente, four miles to the west, to create the **Cristoforo Colombo International Airport**. Genoa is connected by railroads and highways with the major cities of Western Europe, but this has only been possible through the creation of extensive tunnels and viaducts through the mountains surrounding the city.

Insight Into Genoa

Genoa is a city of contrasts, a melting pot of people, a provincial port city that is bursting with energy and nationalities. The food here, especially the **pesto sauce**, placed over a variety of different types of pastas, and the assortment of seafood available, is delicious.

The main attraction in Genoa is its **centro storico**, a small section of the city with tiny, winding, cobblestone streets that evoke an image of a bustling seafaring medieval town. Tourism is only vaguely apparent on the **Via XX Settembre**, a long, arcaded, upscale shopping street complete with international stores like Gucci, Fendi, and more. What makes Genoa run is business. That's why the good hotels lower their rates dramatically on the weekends, because occupancy drops precipitously. So try and get here on a weekend, stay in a four star hotel, and pay great rates.

If you do come here you can see all that there is to see in a day or two. My favorite sight is the magnificent **Staglieno cemetery** a bus ride away, where you can find a virtual city of the dead compete with scaled down chapels, houses, crypts, roads, alleys and more. You'll find exquisite examples of architecture and sculpture throughout this exquisite cemetery.

If this is your first time in Italy you might prefer the main tourist cities of Rome, Florence, and Venice. Maybe on a subsequent trip you can explore the mysteries of Genoa. But if you have a little time, you'll have fun here!

Genoa is noted for its medieval, Renaissance, Baroque, and Gothic architecture. The **University of Genoa**, which was founded in 1471, is an important center of higher learning for northern Italy. The city also has several commercial colleges and a school of navigation.

As you can probably imagine, Genoa is rich in history. Both the Lombards and the Franks once ran the show here, but when Charlemagne's empire broke up, it became an independent city. Genoa also fought a long series of wars with its southern seafaring neighbor Pisa, which was eventually crushed by Genoa in 1284.

Genoa's foreign trade and maritime power increased greatly during the Crusades. Young knights and their entourages needed convenient locations from which to begin their voyages of salvation, and Genoa was perfectly located. During this time the city began to develop colonies in Spain and North Africa conquered from the Saracens; and trading posts and fortresses were established in the eastern Mediterranean and along the Black Sea. Throughout its entire nautical history there were countless commercial wars with Venice, but these ended when Genoa was defeated by Venice at Chioggia in 1380.

Genoa regained her independence but was eventually conquered by Austria in 1746. Then it was ruled by France in the early 19th century. Its neighbor Sardinia-Piedmont acquired the city in 1814. Finally it became part of the kingdom of Italy in 1861. By the early 20th century, Genoa was the major seaport of Italy, and its tunnels, railway system, and industrial development had extended into the **Po Valley**.

Bombing of the city in World War II damaged both the harbor and industrial plants, but the city remains today as if transfixed in time, especially in the *centro storico* with its winding, narrow medieval streets.

Genoa's Environs

Then once you've seen the quaint old world charm of Genoa, which should take a couple days to explore, it'll be time to really see some sides of Italy not many people experience. Our first stop will be the **Staglieno Cemetery**, which is a veritable city of the dead covering 160 hectares and is so large that it even has its own bus system.

You'll find miniature cathedrals, Romanesque chapels, Egyptian temples, *palazzi*, statues, and more. It's not morbid or macabre but a series of monuments erected to celebrate life. You are helping to remember these people by appreciating the stone images left behind to memorialize them. I'm confident all members of the family will enjoy visiting here.

Next, we'll take a train ride down to the **Cinque Terre** *(the five lands)* that are comfortably removed from both automobile and train access. Each are connected to the other by a small hiking path, which is the main form of transport. These fishing and farming towns, because of their remoteness, are one of Italy's hidden treasures. What you'll find here is peace, tranquillity, great food, wonderful, introspective people, beautiful scenery, and memories for a lifetime.

Other highlights in the Genoa area include the postcard-perfect seaside village of **Portofino** and the fun Riviera resort town of **Nervi** very close to Genoa.

Arrivals & Departures

The best and quickest way to get in and out of Genoa is by train. The city's two main train stations are **Stazione Porta Principe** and **Stazione Brignole**. Porta Principe, not too far from the *centro storico* is the main station.

Getting Around Town

By Bus

The only time you'll really ever need to use the bus is if you go to the seaside resort of Nervi, if you have to get to the small station for the ride on the small electric train into the mountain, or if you want to visit the Staglieno Cemetery. Other than that, all the sights and local flavor are within walking distance between the railway stations, Stazione Porta Principe and Stazione Brignole, and around the *centro storico*.

By Car

Don't even try to drive in Genoa. The city is small and congested with busy traffic circles, small streets, and traffic like you've never seen. Also the city is small enough to walk everywhere, or you can take convenient buses and funiculars. But if you do want to drive, here are a few places where you can rent a car:
• **Avis**, *Piazza Aquaverde (Stazione Principe). Tel. 010/25-55-98*
• **Hertz**, *Via Casaregia 78/a. Tel. 010/570-26-25.*
• **Maggiore**, *Piazza Aquaverde (Stazione Principe). Tel. 010/570-26-25*

By Taxi

To get a radio cab in Genoa, call *010/26-96*. You can hail a cab on the street or grab one of the many **taxi stands** situated around Genoa. Some of the more prominent ones and their telephone numbers are:
• **Piazza Caricamento**, *Tel. 010/20-46-32*
• **Piazza Aquaverde** *(Stazione Principe), Tel. 010/26-12-46*
• **Piazza Nunziata**, *Tel. 010/29-82-32*
• **Nervi**, *Tel. 010/32-15-10.*
• **Via Torino** *(Stazione Brignole), Tel. 010/56-40-07*
• **Piazza Dane**, *Tel. 010/58-65-24*

Where To Stay

Genoa, like Milan, has either high-end three star, four star, and deluxe hotels, or the flea bag one star variety. It's a great city for the budget traveler if you can get a room in one of the few good two stars that are available. In a two star in Genoa you'll get most of the amenities of a three star for the price of a one star in a bigger city like Rome.

The best places to find inexpensive hotels is by the main train station, **Stazione Principe**. The area around the other station, Stazione Brignole, also has hotels, though not as many, but it is in a quieter more residential neighborhood. The best place to get a hotel is just on the edge of Genoa's *centro storico*, the old city, with its countless winding narrow streets filled with shops, cafés, bars, and a few restaurants.

1. AGNELLO D'ORO, *Via Monachette 6, 16126 Genoa. Tel. 010/246-20-84. fax 010/246-23-27. 29 rooms all with bath. Single E45-65; Double E50-75. ****

A pleasant, inexpensive three star hotel down a side street just off the station. The rooms are clean and comfortable if a little small. The prices are good for a three star, but that may be because next door is the best three star in the city, Hotel Europa, and they know they cannot compete. One plus is that if you are traveling with your pet they are accommodating.

2. BEL SOGGIORNO, *Via XX Settembre 19/2, 16124 Genoa. Tel. 010/542-880, Fax 010/581-418. 18 rooms, 17 with bath. Single without bath E33-39; Single E45-65; Double without bath E43-49; Double E50-75. ***

Their prices are outrageously high for a two star since they are located on the ritzy shopping street Via XX Settembre. They have everything but a street entrance and air conditioning, which will permanently keep them at a two star in Liguria. The rooms are clean and comfortable but the prices are ridiculous. Good accommodations in a wonderful and safe location but you can get better prices elsewhere.

3. BRISTOL PALACE, *Via XX Settembre 35, 16121. Tel. 010/59-25-41, Fax 010/56-17-56. E-mail: info@hotelbristolpalace.com. Web:www.hotelbristolpalace.com. 133 rooms all with bath. Single E75-180; Double E93-180; Suite E250. Single weekends E75; Double weekends E95. Buffet breakfast included. *****

Located on Genoa's premier shopping street, you'll be in the middle of everything here. The rates go down dramatically on the weekends, as with the Moderno Verdi. So this is the best time to come and stay in the lap of luxury of a four star hotel. All the amenities of a good four star including a very respectable restaurant. They are pet friendly and offer baby-sitting service too.

4. CARIOLI, *Via Carioli 14/4, 16124 Genoa. Tel. and Fax 010/206-531 and 280-041. 14 rooms, 11 with bath. 1 bathroom in the hall for the other three. 3 singles, the rest doubles. Single without bath E30-40; Single E35-50. Double E50-75. Continental breakfast E4. ***

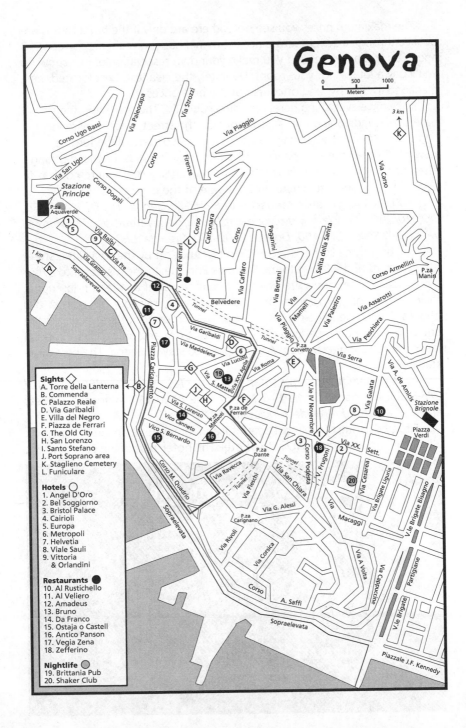

Genova

0 500 1000
Meters

3 km

Sights ◇
A. Torre della Lanterna
B. Commenda
C. Palazzo Reale
D. Via Garibaldi
E. Villa del Negro
F. Piazza de Ferrari
G. The Old City
H. San Lorenzo
I. Santo Stefano
J. Port Soprano area
K. Staglieno Cemetery
L. Funiculare

Hotels ○
1. Angel D'Oro
2. Bel Soggiorno
3. Bristol Palace
4. Cairioli
5. Europa
6. Metropoli
7. Helvetia
8. Viale Sauli
9. Vittoria
   & Orlandini

Restaurants ●
10. Al Rustichello
11. Al Veliero
12. Amadeus
13. Bruno
14. Da Franco
15. Ostaja o Castell
16. Antico Panson
17. Vegia Zena
18. Zefferino

Nightlife ○
19. Brittania Pub
20. Shaker Club

The maximum prices you see noted here are only if the hotel rooms are booked through a travel agent, since the owner has to give them between E13 and E18 for that privilege. If you make your own reservation or just show up you'll pay a lot less for your room. Definitely the cleanest, best located, best managed in the city, and of course at the best prices.

They have everything here, including cable TV. The only thing they don't have is air conditioning and an entrance on the street, since they're located on the third floor of a building. But they have a wonderful little terrace. Your view isn't great but the peace and tranquillity it offers in the mornings, afternoons, and evenings is wonderful. All I can say is, if you're coming to Genoa on a budget, stay here, but, beware of the blind cat.

5. EUROPA, *Via delle Monachette 8, 15126 Genoa. Tel. 010/256-955, Fax 010/261-047. Web: www.venere.it/liguria/genova/europa. 37 rooms all with bath. Single E70-100; Double E100-160. Breakfast E8.* ***

The best three star in the city. Don't get put off by the small little street it's on just off of the Piazza to the Stazione Principe. Inside it's closer to a four star in luxury. The rooms are quiet and comfortable if a little nondescript in their furnishings. All rooms come with A/C, TV, mini-bar and direct dial phones. They have large common areas and a roof deck that overlooks the entire city. They have parking on-site for E11 extra and an excellent cocktail lounge for evening relaxation. A great place to stay in Genoa. The best three star in town.

6. METROPOLI, *Piazza Fontane Marose, Tel. 010/246-8888, Fax 010/ 246-8686. 47 rooms. Single E75-115; Double E100-150. American Express and Visa accepted. Breakfast included.* ***

Situated in one of the most beautiful and romantic *palazzi* in the city, you will find peace and tranquility in this hotel. This hotel, part of the Best Western

The Best Hotels in Genoa
Two star
4. CARIOLI, *Via Carioli 14/4, 16124 Genoa. Tel. and Fax 010/206-531 and 280-041.*

Three Star
5. EUROPA, *Via delle Monachette 8, 15126 Genoa. Tel. 010/256-955, Fax 010/261-047.*

Four star
3. BRISTOL PALACE, *Via XX Settembre 35, 16121. Tel. 010/59-25-41, Fax 010/56-17-56. E-mail: info@hotelbristolpalace.com. Web: www.hotelbristolpalace.com.*

chain, offers comfortable rooms and well equipped bathrooms. The service is professional and attentive. This is an excellent place to stay in Genoa.

7. RIO, *Via Ponte Calvi 5, 16126 Genoa. Tel. 010/29-05-51, Fax 010/29-05-54. 47 rooms, 44 with bath. Single E45; Double E67. Credit cards accepted.* ***

Located deep in the *centro storico* on a relatively wide road, this is a thoroughly modern three star hotel whose prices are so low because of their location. It's safe here during the day, but it is definitely not a place that even I would walk alone in late at night. But what's great about the location is that it is quiet, clean, and comfortable, and you have one of Genoa's best local yet upscale restaurants just across the street. The rooms come with all three star amenities except for A/C.

8. VIALE SAULI, *Viale Sauli 5, Tel. 010/561-397, Fax 010/590-092. 56 rooms. Single E67-100; Double E75-120. American Express and Visa accepted. Breakfast included.* ***

This hotel offers great comfort at great prices. Located in a local area, near the Brignole station, here you will find comfortable communal areas, well appointed rooms, completely soundproofed to the traffic outside. You will find every three star comfort here including AC, TV and more. The service is attentive, and a stay here would definitely be pleasant.

9. VITTORIA & ORLANDINI, *Via Balbi 33, Tel. 010/261-923, Fax 010/246-2656. Email: vittorin@mbox.vol.it. Web: www.venere.it/it/genova/vittoriaandorlandini. 48 rooms. Single E65-75; Double E85-100. American Express and Visa accepted. Breakfast E3.* ***

Located on the main drag from the main train station, this hotel is a labyrinth inside but well furnished and appointed with objets d'art. They offer a few rooms with access to a peaceful garden. These need to be requested. Also, the north facing rooms have an extra little room for relaxing. All rooms are clean and comfortable as are the bathrooms, and come with every three star amenity. The breakfast room is huge and has a nice view over the old section of town down by the water.

Where To Eat

Genovese Cuisine

Genovese cuisine is dominated by the omnipresent **pesto sauce**, a basil, garlic, pine nuts, and olive oil concoction that they put on everything from lasagna noodles to spaghetti to meat and seafood. Also since they're a port city the "fruits of the sea" (i.e., seafood) are also a big part of any menu you'll find. Essentially the indigenous cuisine reflects the austere tastes and tight budgets of the local fishermen and farmers, so you'll find many creative crêpe-type dishes along with pasta and seafood.

Suggested Genovese Cuisine
If you're up for it, try some of these delicious Genovese specialties.

Antipasto - Appetizer
• **Farinata** – a giant crépe made from chickpea flour sprinkled with olive oil and rosemary and then cooked in a wood–burning stove
• **Focaccio** – Crunchy flat bread covered in olive oil
• **Focaccio al formaggio** – the local flat bread with cheese, which is not melted on top but baked inside the pouch of the focaccio
• **Pansotti** – thick chickpea soup

Primo Piatto - First Course
Pasta
• **Pansotti** – Small ravioli stuffed with either mushrooms or spinach, or both, covered with a light walnut sauce
• **Pasta con pesto** – Any type of pasta that is served with the famous light Genovese pesto sauce, which is made from basil, olive oil, and garlic; usually tossed with thin noodles called trenette
• **Gnocchi al pesto** – Semolina dumplings with pesto sauce

Secondo piatto - Entrée
Carne (Meat)
• **Cima all Genovese** – Breast of veal filled with vegetables and hard boiled eggs

Pesce – Fish
• **Fritto misto di mare** – mixed fried seafood
• **Branzino all griglia** – Grilled slab of sea bass
• **Pesce spada con funghi** – Swordfish with mushrooms

Contorno – Vegetable
• **Torta pasqualina** – Vegetables and hard boiled eggs egg rolled in a delicate pastry
• **Insalata mista** – mixed salad. You have to prepare your own olive oil and vinegar dressing. Americans' lust for countless types of salad dressings hasn't hit Italy yet.

10. AL RUSTICHELLO, *Via San Vincenzo 59r. Tel. 010/588-556. Credit cards accepted. Dinner for two E35.*
A small quaint local place that also caters to tourists which is advertised by the sign out front that indicates they speak English and French. I love the brick walls and arched whitewashed ceilings as well as their pasta, pizza, meat

The Best Places to Eat in Genoa

11. AL VELIERO, *Via Ponte Calvi 10/12. Tel. 010/291-829. Credit cards accepted. Dinner for two E35.*

13. BRUNO, *Vico della Casana 9. Tel. 010/208.505. Credit cards accepted. Closed Saturdays. Dinner for two E35.*

16. PANSON, *Piazza delle Erbe 5r. Tel. 010/294-903. Credit cards accepted. Dinner for two E40.*

18. ZEFFERINO, *Via XX Settembre 20. Tel. 010/59-19-90, Fax 010/58-64-64. Credit cards accepted. Closed Wednesdays. Dinner for two E75.*

and fish. They say they specialize in Genovese cuisine but they have pasta from all over Italy. So if you're a pasta nut like I am, come here for some. They also have a good *cotolette alla Milanese* (lightly breaded veal fried in butter).

11. AL VELIERO, *Via Ponte Calvi 10/12. Tel. 010/291-829. Credit cards accepted. Dinner for two E35.*

A small, upscale local place that is tucked on a small side street just off the harbor area. The interior is stark white with archways all over the place. It's tiny so get there early or make reservations. They serve great *spaghetti al pesto* (with a garlic, oil, and basil sauce) and *sogliola ai ferri* (sole cooked over an open fire). There are other seafood dishes, of which there are plenty around E15 each, so if you try any of those besides the *sogliola* your price to eat here will go up. But those in the know in Genoa don't care. This is one place to go if you make it to this beautiful city.

12. AMADEUS, *Via PE Bensa 40r (in the Piazza Nunziata). Tel. 010 247-1039. Dinner for two E20.*

A popular local pizza place especially for the university students, since they serve huge 16 inch pizzas for great prices. The decor is simple and basic, and the only truly interesting feature is the red and white tiled wood burning oven in the room on the right. Here you can watch all the pizza being prepared. The food comes super quick since the pizza chef is a maestro, and if you want to linger over a bottle of wine they have no qualms about that. To get pizza American-style ask them to put on extra mozzarella.

13. BRUNO, *Vico della Casana 9. Tel. 010/208-505. Credit cards accepted. Closed Saturdays. Dinner for two E35.*

Located on the first floor of an old *palazzo*, the dining environment with their tall ceilings is terrific. You feel as if you are outside, this place is so big. Try their *penne ai frutti di mare* (with mixed seafood) or their *ravioli al salmone* (with salmon) for primo. Then move onto either a *filetto ai ferri* (grilled filet of steak) of the *pesce spada ai ferri* (grilled swordfish).

14. DA FRANCO, *Archivolto Mongiardino 2. Closed Sundays and Mondays. No telephone number. Credit cards accepted. Dinner for two E33.*

If you like lobster, this is the place for you. Small and local, down a difficult-to-find side street, you have to have a good map to locate this excellent lobster and champagne restaurant. Their menu has other dishes, but this is what they do best, serve up succulent lobster so you can wash it down with sparkling wine. Can you think of a better way to spend the evening?

15. OSTAJA O CASTELL, *Salita Santa Maria di Castello. Tel. 010/298-980. No credit cards accepted. Dinner for two ... hard to say since the menu changes daily.*

This is a small, local, and irreverent place. They make great food and they have fun preparing it and serving it. The menu is a dead giveaway to their attitude. It has snide remarks written on it. For example: *"Antipasto*: we have it/*Primo*: Whatever we have/*Frutta*: costs too much/*Dolce*: right before the check/*Digestivo*: right after the check/*Vino*: It's good" – and so on and so on. The menu changes daily but if you want a fun, intimate atmosphere in a completely local section of town, and you're a little adventurous, come and give it a try.

16. PANSON, *Piazza delle Erbe 5r. Tel. 010/294-903. Credit cards accepted. Dinner for two E40.*

An upscale restaurant in a rustic locale. They've grown huge plants to protect you from the sights in the lively local piazza but the sound still drifts in if you sit on the terrace. Inside seating is better because you can get the true feel of an upscale restaurant in Genoa. Try some of their *risotto di crostacei* (rice with crustaceans) or any of their pasta with *pesto*. They specialize in both seafood and pesto. For seconds the *fritto misto del golfo* (mixed seafood from the gulf) and the *pesce spada* (grilled swordfish) are both excellent.

17. VEGIA ZENA, *Vico del Serragli 15. Tel. 010/299-891. Closed Sundays and Monday nights. Credit cards accepted. Dinner for two E35.*

Great local seafood place with excellent atmosphere, great service, and a truly wild and crazy owner. They serve a superb *grigliatta mista* (mixed grilled fish for two) as well as almost any other seafood pasta or fish you can imagine. Located in the *centro storico*, this is a place to have dinner from about 7:30pm to 9:30pm, since the area gets dark and deserted after ten in the summer. In the winter only come here for lunch.

18. ZEFFERINO, *Via XX Settembre 20. Tel. 010/59-19-90, Fax 010/58-64-64. Credit cards accepted. Closed Wednesdays. Dinner for two E75.*

They call themselves the ambassadors for Italian cuisine, and if you're willing to pay their prices the food will not disappoint. The restaurant is filled with brass nautical and kitchen objects, wine bottles, and pastoral pictures which gives the entire place a rustic ambiance. With their exquisite service and excellent food this is a perfect place for a romantic dinner. Their *pesto* sauce (garlic, oil and basil) on home-made *fazzoletti* is superb. As are all of their seafood dishes, including the *frittura del golfo* (mixed fried seafood from the gulf of Genoa) and the *Gamberi all Carbone* (succulent shrimp cooked over an open fire).

Seeing the Sights

Genoa's best sights, in my humble opinion, lie outside of town, but inside this port city there are some beautiful palaces, churches, squares, and wonderful old streets that have been alive with people and shops for almost two thousand years.

A. TORRE DELLA LANTERNA

Located near the Stazione Principe, down the Via Andrea Doria.

This is a medieval **lighthouse** last restored in 1543 that stands 117 meters high. Before the advent of electricity, a huge fire would be lit on top of the structure to guide ships into the harbor. If you're into lighthouses, you'll like this one.

B. COMMENDA

Via San Giovanni. Open 7:00am–7:00pm.

Located near the Stazione Maritima, this is the home of the **canons of San Sepolcro of Jerusalem**. A rough church with definite Gothic influences, despite construction having begun in the 12th century.

C. PALAZZO REALE

Located at number 10 Via Balbi. Tel. 010/247-0640. Open Tuesdays, Thursdays, Saturdays and Sundays 9:00am-1:00pm.

This is a 12th century *palazzo* which was greatly modified in the 17th century. It has beautiful hanging gardens overlooking the harbor. Here you'll also find a rich collection of Ligurian paintings with works by Tintoretto, Van Dyke, Strozzi, and others.

D. VIA GARIBALDI

Genoa's most famous street, laid out in 1558. Many *palazzi* have been converted to banks and offices. **Palazzo Bianchi** *(No. 11, open Tuesday– Saturday 9 am–1:00pm and 3:00pm-6:00pm, Sundays 9:00am–noon, admission fee)*, **Palazzo Rosso** *(no. 18, same hours)* are of interest. In **Palazzo Tursi** is now Genoa's **Municipio** which has a beautiful courtyard. Paganini's violin is in the Sala delle Giunta, and three letters from Columbus in the Sala del Sindaco.

E. VILLA DEL NEGRO

Piazza Corveto. Open Tuesday–Saturday 9:00am–7:00pm and Sundays 9:00am–12:30pm. Admission E3.

This is an urban oasis that has streams, cascades, grottoes, and walkways all leading to the **Museo d'Arte Orientale** (**Museum of Oriental Art**), featuring samurai swords and helmets and much more. The botanical gardens were created by Ippolito Durazzo.

Take a Boat Cruise in Genoa

If you want to try something different and enjoy the beauty of Genoa's harbor at night, try a boat cruise that goes until midnight. Affectionately called a booze cruise by some, they also have karaoke and other entertainment. Call **Calata Zingari**, *Tel. 010/256-775 or 010/255-975.*

F. PIAZZA DE FERRARI & PALAZZO DUCALE

Open Tuesday–Saturday 9:00am–7:00pm and Sundays 9:00am–12:30pm. Admission E3.

This piazza is the heart of modern Genoa. It is surrounded by many important civic buildings and was dedicated to the Duke De Ferrari, an outstanding 19th century Genoan who assisted in the creation of a wide range of urban housing in the city. Carlo Barbarini is the architect of the square. The palazzo dates back to medieval times and was once the headquarters of the Genovese Doge.

One of its sections is the remains of the 13th century **Palazzo del Commune** and the 14th century **Torre del Popolo**. Inside you can admire the lovely frescoes and the **Salone dei Gran Consiglio** (**Grand Council Chamber**). The *palazzo* has over 3,500 square yards of displays of precious art, archives, libraries, as well as conference rooms and offices.

G. THE OLD CITY

Just around the corner from the Piazza De Ferrari is the pretty **Piazza San Matteo**. Go south from here and you enter the **old city** of Genoa. Your best route is down Via Dante to Piazza Dante and the **Porta Soprano**, the twin-towered gateway from 1155, where Columbus's father was supposedly gatekeeper.

This is a place for exploring (but not at night or alone, especially if you are a woman). Take the Via Ravecca down from Porta Soprano to the 13th century gothic **Church of Sant'Agostino** and its **Museum of Ligurian Sculpture and Architecture** *(Tuesday–Saturday 9:00am–1:00pm and 3:00pm-6:00pm, Sundays 9:00am–12:45:00pm, admission E3).*

From Sant'Agostino take the Strada di Sant'Agostino to the 12th century **San Donato** *(open 9:00am–dusk)* with its lovely octagonal *campanile* (bell tower). Also near here is the **Santa Maria in Castello** *(open 9:00am–dusk)* which was used by the Crusaders as a hostel. It was rebuilt in the 13th century. Today it has a Romanesque facade. The inside has been adorned with chapels representing the noblest Genovese families. The **Convent** with its three cloisters should also be visited. They also have a small museum with paintings by Brea and some beautiful frescoes from the 15th century.

H. CATHEDRAL OF SAN LORENZO
Via San Lorenzo, Open 9:00am–dusk.
The most elegant and important example of medieval design in and around Genoa. It is beautiful, characterized by its pronounced Roman Gothic style. Over the centuries the cathedral has undergone many reconstructions. In the 13th century the facade was destroyed and replaced by the current black and white striped Gothic styled one we see today. The bell tower was left without a top when constructed in 1427. It eventually got one two centuries later, and it is apparent that it just doesn't quite fit with the rest of the church.

The majestic interior is divided into a nave and two aisles. Remember to visit the **chapel of Saint John the Baptist**. It is one of the greatest works of the Renaissance even though it shows persistent influence of Gothic art in its bas-reliefs. And you have to admire the refined mosaic beauty of the stained glass Rose window. A perfect place to be in early morning as the sun shines through.

I. CHURCH OF SANTO STEFANO
Via XX Settembre. Open 8:00am–7:00pm.
Set in a small *piazza*, the church was used as a Benedictine monastery until the 10th century. The facade is plain and simple and looks like a monastery would. Inside, on the right is a painting of the *Martirio di Santo Stefano* (The Martyring of St. Stephen) by Giulio Romano in 1524. Next to it is the statue of *Mary and Jesus* made in the 17th century. You can gain access to the bell tower from the presbytery on the left. The baptismal font was made in 1676. Notice the relief work of *San Michele Defeating the Devil* done in 1453.

J. BETWEEN VIA SAN LORENZO & VIA GARIBALDI
Built up during the Renaissance, this area's authenticity has survived better than the area around Porta Soprano and the Stazione Principe. Picturesque, old, winding streets containing colorfully local shops, superb traditional restaurants, out of the way pubs, and plenty of interesting people milling about ... at least during daylight hours. Think twice about coming here at night.

There is a quaint, delightful medieval square, **Campetto**; a couple of centuries-old coffee houses in **Piazza Soziglia (Kainguti** at #98r and

Romanegro at #74r); and the sights and sounds of an ancient seafaring city along the twisting cobblestoned paths. For a scenic route that meanders through the center of this section of the *centro storico*, take a series of streets from **Piazza Bianchi** near the water. First in line is the Via Bianchi, which turns into Via degli Orefici to Via Soziglia to Via Luccoli and eventually to the modern **Piazza delle Fontane Marose**. You can take side streets off this main drag of sorts and really grasp the heart of Genoa.

Note: To fully enjoy this section and the entire *centro storico*, I highly recommend purchasing an orange-covered *F.M.B Pianta di Citta* (map of Genoa). Along with the regular map of the entire city, this map also includes a detailed street map of the *centro storico* on the back. The E4 you spend will not only make your exploration that much more enjoyable, but will be a good memento.

K. STAGLIENO CEMETERY
Via Piacenza. Open 8:00am–5:00pm, October 24th–November 4th from 7:30am–5:00pm, Christmas Day 8:00am –noon.

To get to this fascinating cemetery, take bus 34 from Piazza Aquaverde or Piazza Corvetto. The trip takes fifteen minutes and will set you back Euro 75 cents for the bus ticket. On the way back, if you took more than an hour walking through the cemetery - and to do it any real justice you will have to spend more than that amount of time - you will have to buy another ticket at the *giornalaio* near the bus stop.

When you get off the bus at the cemetery, go to your left and around the corner, and the entrance gate is right there. You pass by flower stalls on your way in, so if you want to place a flower on someone's grave, by all means indulge yourself. The best way to start your tour of the cemetery, after you've entered the main gates, is to go past the flower stands and enter the small archway to your right. Walk through the small gravestones, some with tiny pictures on them, until you get to a square of cleared area between the gravestone. On your left is a set of stairs leading up to the interesting stuff. Once up, go to your right and then begin the process of weaving through this magnificent collection of art and celebration of life.

This is a veritable city of the dead covering 160 hectares and is so large it has its own bus system There are centuries-old miniature cathedrals, Romanesque chapels, Egyptian crypts, palaces, statues, all laid out in a haphazard fashion that is representative of the *centro storico*. You'll be amazed at the beauty and sadness of the sculptures, some in bronze, others made from marble. Vines and undergrowth twist everywhere, obscuring some of the smaller paths up the hills between the crypts. A perfect place to spend a few hours wandering around. But remember that this is a cemetery, so be respectful when you visit.

When you enter there will be numbered marble crypts on the walls and on the floors (Oscar Wilde is buried in the Protestant section). From here go to the center with its small plots. Take a left and go up the stairs to the monuments and chapels. Remember to try and act as serious as possible, especially when you pass other people, which is infrequent. This is a cemetery, even if it does look like a miniature city or a museum.

Despite this restriction, Staglieno is definitely one of the best sights to see in Genoa, and really one of the most interesting cemeteries in all of Italy.

L. FUNICULARE ZECCHI RIGHI
Largo Zecca. Open 6:00am–10:00pm. Costs the same as a bus ticket.

Take the **Funiculare Zecchi Righi** up to an overlook above the city. Here you can get some great shots of the city itself and other vistas. You can also walk a little way and explore the dilapidated ruins of the **Forts of Begato, Puin, Sperone**. They are up a small winding road that has cars buzzing around it, so if you're with kids make sure they stick to the sides as you walk. The forts are a little distance away from the funicular, but just follow the signs and you'll make it there. The walk is through dense woods that lends a semblance of tranquillity after the hectic pace of Genoa.

Nightlife & Entertainment
19. BRITANNIA PUB, *Vico della Casana 76A. Tel. 010/294-878. Credit cards accepted. Pints E3-4.*

In a perfect rendition of an English pub, you can enjoy a few pints of Kilkenny (a great Irish beer), Elephant (a superb beer from Denmark), or Dab (an excellent beer from Holland); as well as satisfy your hunger with sandwiches, hamburgers, hot dogs, salads, or simple Italian appetizers like mozzarella and tomatoes. A place to come for lunch, dinner, or late night for drinks on a romantic interlude.

20. SHAKER CLUB, *Via Cesarea 45r. Tel. 010-570-5784. Credit cards accepted. Drinks E4-5.*

You better be dressed well when you come in here, otherwise you'll get the once-over. A piano bar late at night, they also serve drinks and light snacks in the early evenings. There's a bar you can curl up with or small intimate booths in which you can snuggle with your loved one and trade sweet nothings.

Sports & Recreation
Golf
• **Golf Club Arenzano**, *Piazza del Golf 3, 16011 Arenzano. Tel. 010/911-1817, Fax 010/911-1270.* Located 20 km from Genoa, this is a 9 hole par 36, 2,770 meters course. Open year round except in October and on

Tuesdays. They have a putting green, tennis courts, a quaint bar, and a nice restaurant.

• **Circolo Golf & Tennis Rapallo**, *Via Mameli 377, 16035 Rapallo. Tel. 0185/ 261-777, Fax 0185/261-779.* Located 25 km from Genoa in the quaint town of Rapallo, this is an 18 hole, par 70, 5,694 meters course that is open year round. Closed on Tuesdays. They have a good restaurant, pro shop, bar, 6 tennis courts, and driving range.

Swimming
Bathing in the sea around here could be a hair-raising or a skin-discoloring (because of the pollution) situation, so maybe you should try the municipal pools at **Lido d'Albara** on the east side of town. Or better yet, go to **Nervi** just outside of town (see below).

Excursions & Day Trips
The Genoa area includes some beautiful towns, like the fun Riviera resort town of **Nervi**, discussed in this section. Other towns and regions discussed below are given their own section in this chapter.

A little further afield are the seaside towns of the **Golfo di Tigullio** (see section of the same name), which includes **Portofino** – now one of the most photographed and frequented seaside towns anywhere in Europe – as well the quaint towns of the **Cinque Terre** (see section of the same name), five isolated hillside villages hidden from most tourists that are among my favorite destinations in Italy. There are also some wonderful seaside resort towns located on the **Riviera delle Palme** (see section of the same name) to the east of Genoa that include picturesque towns like **Borgio Verezzi** and **Savona**.

NERVI
One of the oldest resorts on the Riviera, today **Nervi** has been incorporated into the city of Genoa but it still has a life of its own. The town is comprised of green parks and gardens that are nestled among the rocks that lead down to the water. There is a scenic and picturesque cliff walk that is entirely carved out of these beautiful rocks.

The beaches are not really sandy, just rocky, kind of like those found halfway up the coast in Maine. Nonetheless, it is a peaceful respite from the hectic pace of Genoa. Once you arrive in Nervi, you won't want to leave, so maybe you should simply stay here and commute the 30-40 minute bus or train ride into Genoa to see the sights, sounds, and smells of the big city.

As a seaside resort you'll find all sorts of bars and cafés, ice cream shops, stores, vendors, and restaurants. But the best parts of Nervi are the seemingly inaccessible swimming areas and the pristine park grounds that surround the beach area.

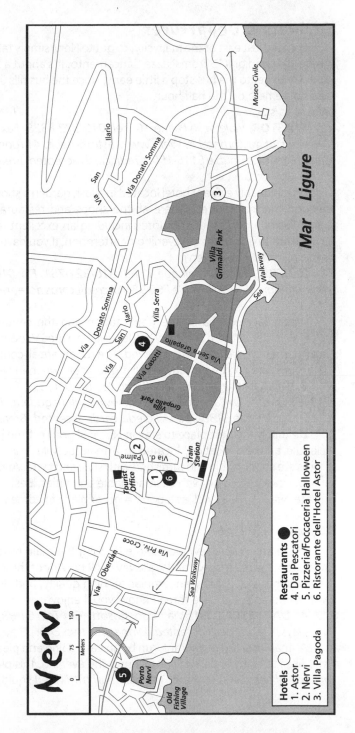

Nervi

0   75   150
Meters

Porto
Nervi

Old
Fishing
Village

Via Oberdan

Via Priv. Croce

Via Palme

Via d.

Tourist
Office

Train
Station

Villa
Grapallo Park

Via Casotti

Via Serra Grapallo

Villa Serra

Via Donato Somma

San Ilario

Via

Via San Ilario

Villa
Grimaldi Park

Via Donato Somma

San Ilario

Via

Sea Walkway

Sea Walkway

Museo Civile

Mar Ligure

Hotels ○
1. Astor
2. Nervi
3. Villa Pagoda

Restaurants ●
4. Dai Pescatori
5. Pizzeria/Foccaceria Halloween
6. Ristorante dell'Hotel Astor

Arrivals & Departures

Located just east of the main city, to get to Nervi simply take bus #17 from Piazza di Ferrari or #15 from Piazza Caricamento. It's about a 30 to 40 minute ride. Try to get to the bus stop a little early, since the bus fills up rapidly. Trains also come here on the half-hour.

Where to stay

1. ASTOR, *Viale delle Palme 16. Tel. 010/372-8325, Fax 010/372-8486. E-mail: astor@astorhotel.it. Web: www.astorhotel.it. 41 rooms all with bath. Single E80-140; Double E115-150. Credit cards accepted. Breakfast E20 extra.* ****

A fashionably elegant hotel located in a lush garden a short walk from the sea and the main street, where all the shops and restaurants are. All the amenities of a good four star hotel, including an excellent restaurant if you choose not to go out for the evening or afternoon. If you have the money, this is *the* place to stay in Nervi.

2. NERVI, *Piazza Pittalunga 1, Tel. 010/322-751. Fax 010/372-8022. 38 rooms. Single E50-75; Double E60-95. All credit cards accepted. Breakfast E5.* ***

Ideally located nearby the train station and the center of town, in a colorful garden setting. The entry hall leads upt to the TV room, restaurant and small garden where breakfast is served. The rooms are all comfortable but the bathrooms are somewhat tiny. In all a good stay when in Nervi.

3. VILLA PAGODA, *Via Capolungo 15, Tel. 010/372-6161. Fax 010/321-218. E-mail: info@villapagoda.it. Web: www.villapagoda.it. 18 rooms. Single E110-150; Double E130-200. All credit cards accepted. Breakfast E12.* ****

Definitely the best place to stay in Nervi. Slightly off the beaten path in a splendid arboreal location, located in a majestic villa from the 1800s. The rooms are comfortable and furnished with style and taste. And the bathrooms are spacious and come with all imaginable amenities. Best of all you have a private beach here as well as a pool. A great place to come for any occasion.

Where to Eat

There are quite a few places to eat along the main road parallel to but away from the main beach and walkway of Nervi. Any of these will satisfy your basic hunger, but if you want ambiance, high quality, and slightly out of the way restaurants, here are three I know you'll enjoy.

4. DAI PESCATORI, *Via Aldo Casotti 6r. Tel. 010/326-168. Closed Mondays. Credit cards accepted. Dinner for two E40.*

A small local fish restaurant, run by an easy-going and pleasant proprietor who likes to enjoy a glass of wine during the evening, this place offers great *gnocchi al pesto* and seafood. The *calamari fritti* (fried squid) as an entrée is superb. As you enter, you'll pass the local bar/café and open kitchen to head to your table. Enjoy the wonderful ambiance and great food of a tremendous seafood restaurant.

5. HALLOWEEN, *Via Caboto. Tel. 010/372-6154. Closed Wednesdays. Dinner for two E40.*

Situated in the center of the old small fishing village of Nervi, here you can sit out on the terrace with a vista of the fishing boats and the harbor. The best place to soak up the past as well as their great pizzas and *focacci* (pizza-like dish with a light crust and ingredients baked in the middle). The best place to go in Nervi because of the quaint harbor view and the incredibly delicious food. Don't let the name fool you into thinking it's a tourist trap. It's a great local place.

6. ASTOR, *Viale delle Palme 16. Tel. 010/372-8325. All credit cards accepted. Dinner for two E55. Open all year round.*

In the summer, you can eat your meal in their beautiful tranquil garden setting. Here you can sample the excellent traditional dishes from Liguria, like *tortellone al pesto* (large tortellini with pesto sauce) as well as any manner of fish prepared in a wide variety of ways (grilled, fried, baked, etc.). For dessert try any of their specialties. These delicacies are home-made on the premises. Superb dining experience.

Practical Information for Genoa

Car Rental
• **Avis**, *Airport, Tel. 010/650-7280 or Via delle Casacce 3, Tel. 010/56-44-12*
• **Hertz**, *Airport, Tel. 010/651-2422 or Via Casaregi 76, Tel. 010/570-2625*

Consulates
• **United Kingdom**, *Via XII Ottobre 2, Genoa Tel. 010/56-48-33*

Laundry
• **"No Name,"** *Via Pre #34, no phone.* Drop off your garments in the morning and pick them up in the afternoon, all for the small cost of E8 per machine (washer and dryer). Run by a multilingual Senegalese with the greatest disposition and smile you'll find in Genoa. He'll write down how many articles of clothing you brought in as a receipt. If you don't want your underthings flashed around the store, remember to count them beforehand. Ideally situated for almost all travelers.

Local Festivals & Holidays
• **January–April**, Genoa Opera Company performances in the *Teatro Margherita* at *Via XX Settembre 16a*
• **Summer**, Ballet Festival in Nervi's park

Postal Services
There is a post office in the Stazione Principe, and another one located just off the *piazza* that houses the train station. It's down a small side street on the right hand side across the piazza (*Salita di San Giovanni #7*).

Tourist Information & Maps
• **EPT**, *Via Roma 11. Tel. 010/581-407*
• **Information Offices** *in both train stations, Stazione Principe and Brignole.* They can call hotels for you to see if there are rooms, but they cannot book these rooms for you. This service saves you the hassle of walking around the city trying to find the hotel of your choice. The office also will give you a simple map that is useful everywhere but in the *centro storico*, since there are so many small winding streets. To navigate successfully in here, buy one of the maps you can get at a newsstand for E4.

Golfo Tigullio & The Cinque Terre

Once known as the Bay of Rapallo, this section of Italy was recently renamed the **Gulf of Tigullio** after the Tigullian people who first settled this area. These ancient people were descendants of the Paicini, Illuati, and Velleiati who lived here during pre-Roman times. Tigullio is also known as the **Riviera di Levante** because of the famous town at its other end. In this area saddled with an identity crisis you will find relaxing resort activities, quaint seaside towns, entertaining water sports, breathtaking views and more. The Gulf of Tigullio is an enormous curve along the Ligurian coast that is enclosed by rocky foothills. The curve starts with **Portofino** and ends with the town of **Sestri Levante**.

The area's main attraction is the sea, in which you will find a complete sampling of Mediterranean nautical vegetation and sea life. Everything from red coral blooms to brilliantly colored sea sponges are accessible for your snorkeling pleasure; and there are lobsters and all manner of seafood to grace your meals. Sailing is another favorite activity since it is the easiest way to get from one town to the next. In the summer the roads get crowded with cars, especially in August when all of Italy shuts down and it seems like everyone heads to the seashore.

Also a part of the Tigullian region is rich vegetation that includes orchids, olive groves, vineyards, alpine pines, chestnut and hazelnut trees, and the rare carnivorous plant, the Roundleaf Sundrew. Don't try to pick that one. Besides the olive oil, excellent wine, and ground chestnut used to make cakes and bread, Tigullio is also world-renowned for its black slate and red and green marble. And crafts are a main part of life here. Everything from wood furniture, lace, velvet fabric, boats and more are still manufactured in the traditional manner all along the coast.

But most of all, the Gulf of Tigullio, and especially the **Cinque Terre**, are places to come to get away from it all and relax. The pace here is slower and much more peaceful. The area is reminiscent of centuries past.

Portofino

The secluded and protected little fishing village of **Portofino** was discovered many years ago by the super-rich and famous and became one of their favorite playgrounds. Accented by the deep blue of the water and the lush green of the nature preserve hillsides, the colorful buildings of Portofino stand out like a fairy tale set. This beauty has now turned the quiet little town into a haven for the not-so-rich-or-famous, but it still retains its charm and character

Today, cafés and boutiques line the quaint little streets, and what used to be an exclusive vacation spot is a traffic jam of humanity during the peak summer tourist months. Nonetheless, Portofino will stun you with her beauty despite the summer crowds. And then, after all the ferries and buses have left for the day, the real romance of Portofino begins. If you choose to stay in town, you will have the beauty virtually all to yourself late at night since there are not many hotels in the town itself.

Arrivals & Departures

Located 36 kilometers from Genoa, trains do not come directly to Portofino, which used to give it some of its exclusivity. You can either come by **car** down the A12 Autostrada, exit at Rapallo, and follow the coast road to Portofino, which will entail long traffic jams in the summer months; or you can come by **ferry** from Genoa, which is probably the easiest and least stressful way to get here. Contact one of these numbers for ferry information and reservations: *Tel. 010/265-712 or 0336/688-732.* The ferries leave from the **Aquarium dock** in Genoa.

Another less expensive but far more arduous way to get here is to take the **train** to **Santa Margherita Ligure**, then catch a bus in Piazza Vittorio Veneto, a short walk towards the water from the station, to get to Portofino. The whole trip will take about three hours, however. This will be a little less expensive than a ferry, but is much longer and much more of a hassle.

Where to Stay

NAZIONALE, *Via Roma 8, 16024 Portofino. Tel. 0185/269-575, Fax 0185/269-578. 13 rooms all with bath. Single E125-200; Double E130-250. Visa accepted.* ★★★★

All you get here is a perfect location a few paces away from the seaside *piazza*, a romantic old building, great views, clean and comfortable rooms with TV, mini-bar, and direct dial phone – but not much else. If you come to Portofino, this is a quaint place to stay and enjoy the ambiance of this tiny little village. But you'll need to make reservations about a year in advance, especially for weekend stays.

PICCOLO HOTEL, *Via Duca degli Abruzzi 31, 16024 Portofino. Tel. 0185/ 269-015, Fax 0185/269621. 22 rooms all with bath. Credit cards accepted. Single E65-115; Double E90-180.* ★★★★

Established in 1926 and renovated in 1991, this quaint 'little" (Piccolo) hotel has its own private beach, serene garden, excellent restaurant, day care services, relaxing bar and all the other amenities of a four star hotel. The service is friendly and the rooms are quiet, comfortable and clean. I prefer it to the Nazionale because of the relaxing common areas.

SPLENDIDO, *Viale Baratta 13, 16034 Portofino. Tel. 0185/269-551, Fax 0185/269-614. 86 rooms all with bath. Credit cards accepted. Single E160-325; Double E325-650.* ★★★★

This is truly splendid. Definitely the place to stay while visiting Portofino. Renovations were made in 1990 that enhanced the already stupendous atmosphere and amenities. Opened in 1901, Hotel Splendido has a well deserved reputation for excellence. Besides the usual amenities of a four star they have tennis courts, an outdoor swimming pool, a quiet garden, an excellent but expensive restaurant, baby-sitting service, and professional attentiveness.

EDEN, *Vico Dritto 18, 16034 Portofino. Tel. 0185/269-091, Fax 0185/ 269-047. 8 rooms all with bath. Credit cards accepted. Single E80-100; Double E90-140.* ★★

Only a two star, but boy is it expensive. Location is everything and this is in the center of the little fishing village. Only eight rooms, so reserve well in advance. They have basically the same amenities as the Nazionale or the Piccolo, even a few more, like TVs in the rooms and a sun deck, but their rooms are not quite as clean or as comfortable. But if you want the beauty and romance of Portofino at more reasonable prices, stay here. They'll eventually be a three or four star if they get their act in gear – leaving budget travelers out in the street in this expensive and elitist town.

Where to Eat

IL PITOSFORO, *Via Molo Umberto I 8. Tel. 0185/269-020. Closed Tuesdays and November. All credit cards accepted. Dinner for two E120.*

Eating here is not going to be inexpensive, so be prepared. You will pay, not only for the food, but also for the magnificent view of the harbor and its *piazza*. Obviously a place designed to fleece the tourists with 130 available seats, but if you're in Portofino come here for a bite. If you only get a pasta dish and a half carafe of wine, that should minimize the damage to your wallet. Try their *linguine all'aragosta* (pasta with lobster sauce), *risotto di mare* (rice covered with seafood), or any of their other tasty, basic, traditional local dishes. Despite all my whining about price it really is a good place to eat.

PUNY, *Piazza Martiri Olivetta 5. Tel. 0185/269-037. Closed Thursdays and January 15 to March 15. No credit cards accepted. Dinner for two E85.*

The most famous restaurant in Portofino, located directly in the main port square with a wonderful terrace overlooking the *piazza* and the port. The green awning shades you from the summer's heat and the baskets of red flowers accent the outside appearance. Inside this has the look of just another local place but it serves superb seafood, pasta, and fresh vegetables. The prices are high because people will pay them, but you can't go wrong here – except if you forget to bring cash. They don't take credit cards.

Seeing the Sights

Leaving the *piazzetta* and its pier lined with fishing nets drying in the sun you can amble up the hill to the **C**hiesa and **Castello di San Giorgio** (*both open 9:00am–5:00pm, admission to the Castle is E3*). Here you will find the remains of the famous St. George, the dragon slayer. From this vantage point you can walk through lush gardens and have superb scenic views over the town and the water on both sides of the peninsula.

Going in the other direction from town you can hike up to a spot with wonderful views of the area, the **Belvedere**. Portofino is the perfect day trip from Genoa, or a quaint romantic getaway on the coast for a few days.

Practical Information

• **Tourist Information Office**, *Via Roma 35. Tel. 0185/77-10-66*

Santa Margherita Ligure

Santa Margherita is one of the more classic, beautiful, elegant and fashionable places in Tigullio, and for that matter in all of Italy. This tiny town has been a glamorous night spot for over 60 years and a fashionable resort since the 19th century. Today it is a representative of true Italian seaside beauty.

Arrivals & Departures

Located 31 kilometers from Genoa, you can either come by **car** down the A12 Autostrada, exit at Rapallo, and follow the coast road to Santa Margherita, which will entail long traffic jams in the summer months; you can come by **ferry** from Genoa, which is probably the easiest and most scenic way to get here; or you can take the **train**. For ferry information and reservations, contact one of these numbers: *Tel. 010/265-712 or 0336/688-732.* The ferries leave from the **Aquarium Dock** in Genoa.

Where To Stay

1. FASCE, *Via L. Bozzo 3. Tel. 0185/286-435, Fax 0185/283-580. E-mail: hotelfasce@hotelfasce.it. Web: www.hotelfasce.it. 12 rooms, 10 with bath. Credit cards accepted. Single E80; Double E90. Breakfast included. Full board E35-40.* **

Located above the center of town a short walk to the Lungomare, this hotel is a member of the prestigious organization of family hotels, and is operated by Jane, the ever-present British proprietress and her Italian husband. Your rooms are large enough with plenty of space to store your clothes in the white formica units with red trim. There are TVs in the rooms but no air conditioning. You can also get quick four hour laundry service by the hospitable Jane. There is a garden terrace area for relaxing with lounge chairs. If requested, you can get an English-style breakfast with cold cuts and cheese along with the regular continental fare. They also have free bicycles for your use, a roof deck and garden area. A quality inexpensive place to stay in Santa Margherita.

2. GRAND HOTEL MIRAMARE, *Via Milite Ignoto 30. Tel. 0185/287-013, Fax 0185/284-651. E-mail: miramare@grandhotelmiramare.it. Web: www.grandhotelmiramare.it. 83 rooms all with bath. Credit cards accepted. Single E110-135. Double E180-210. Breakfast included. Full board E125-187.* ****

Arguably the second best hotel in the city but definitely the most historic. Gugliemo Marconi sent the first radio signals from the terrace of this hotel in 1933. Today that same terrace contains the hotel's pool and a wonderful breakfast buffet in the summer. The common areas are large and well lit. The rooms are spacious and comfortable, though all are furnished in a different style. Established in 1904 and modernized in 1994, this is a wonderful place to stay while in Santa Margherita. They also have a private beach, tennis courts, and an excellent restaurant, as well as all the other amenities for a great four star hotel.

3. IMPERIALE PALACE, *Via Pagana 19. Tel. 0185/288-991, Fax 0185/284-223. E-mail: info@hotelimperiale.com. Web: www.hotelimperiale.com. 102 rooms all with bath. Closed from Dec. 1 to March 1. Single E160-220. Double E260-420. Credit cards accepted. Breakfast included. Full board E200-250.* ****

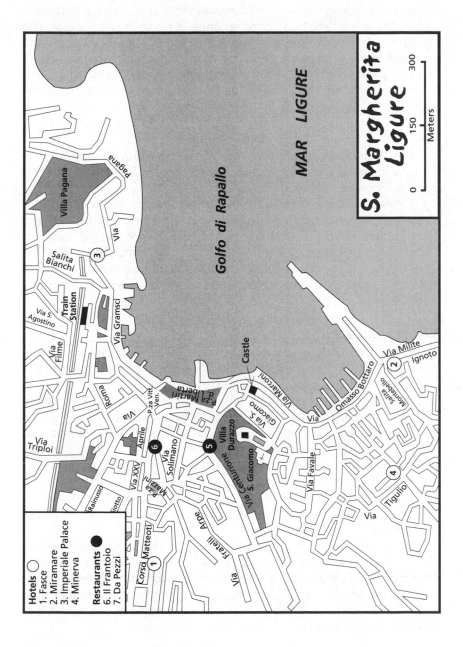

S. Margherita Ligure

MAR LIGURE

Golfo di Rapallo

Villa Pagana

Via Pagana

Salita Bianchi

Via S. Agostino

Train Station

Via Gramsci

Via Filme

Via Roma

Via Triploi

Via XXV Aprile

Via Solimano

P.za Martiri della Libertà

P.za Vitt. Ven.

Castle

Via Marconi

Via S. Giacomo

Villa Durazzo

Via Centurione

Via S. Giacomo

Via Milite

Ignoto

Salita Montebello

Omasso Bottaro

Via Favale

Tigulio

Via

Fratelli Arpe

Corso Matteotti

P.za Mazzini

0   150   300
Meters

Hotels
1. Fasce
2. Miramare
3. Imperiale Palace
4. Minerva

Restaurants
6. Il Frantoio
7. Da Pezzi

Built in 1889, this is the most historic hotel in Santa Margherita which has housed all sorts of royalty and celebrities over the past century. The hotel, with its terraces, balconies and columns, dominates the coastline on this part of the harbor. The entrance hall is a perfect example of elegance with antiques and crystal chandeliers everywhere. In the bar area you will find a piano that is put into use in the evenings, filling the hotel with gentle tunes. The rooms are large and wonderfully appointed with antiques, period pieces and tapestries. The bathrooms are all modern, since the hotel was refurbished in 1992. They come with phones and hairdryers and shower supplies for your convenience. Everything about this hotel is wonderful, including the private beach, swimming pool, tranquil garden and fine restaurant.

4. MINERVA, *Via Maragliano 34/C. Tel. 0185/286-073, Fax 0185/281-697. 28 rooms all with bath. Single E50-65. Double E75-95. Credit cards accepted. Breakfast included. Full board E47-75.* ***

Located in town, they are only a short walk to the port and the Lungomare. They have a peaceful garden area and a terrace with a nice view of the harbor. Their bright entrance hall is filled with Bordeaux-style seats. The rooms have quaint antique furnishings and are quite comfortable with all the amenities of a three star with TV, air conditioning, minibar and room service. The bathrooms are clean and modern with phone and hairdryer. This is a good three star.

Where To Eat

5. IL FRANTOIO, *Via del Giunchetto 23/a. Tel. 0185/286-667. Credit cards accepted. Parking available. Closed Tuesdays (except from July 1 to August 31) and November 7-30. Dinner for two E45.*

This is a wonderful restaurant with an ample wine list, fast courteous service and wonderful food, but if you're looking for pizza they don't serve it here. They do make a wonderful *taglierini con scampi* (pasta with shrimp) and *linguini con gamberi* (with prawns) and make exquisite fish dishes. The catch of the day determines that part of the menu. Il Frantoio offers quality meals and fantastic atmosphere.

6. DA PEZZI, *Via Cavour 21. Tel. 0185/285-303. No credit cards accepted. Air conditioned. Closed Saturdays and Dec. 20 to Jan. 20. Dinner for two E25.*

In a simple, basic atmosphere, the Pezzi family caters to a varied and loyal clientele that comes here for the great traditional local dishes prepared to perfection: ravioli, pasta with a delicious pesto sauce, tasty fresh vegetables stuffed or made into pies, *rustiche crostate* (dough stuffed with veggies, fish and/or meat then baked). Everything is served with their good quality house wine and loads of courteous service. A great local place.

Seeing the Sights

The city is guarded by an imposing **castle** built by the Genovese when they controlled this port city. Today it houses the local **Museo Storico**. The central core of the town is referred to as **Pescino**, named for the fishing industry that for centuries was the town's main form of commerce. The harbor is lined with fashionable boutiques, cafés and restaurants, and is filled with a lively atmosphere of commerce. You can still see the fishing boats returning, where their catch is gobbled up by the buyers for the local restaurants, as well some housewives looking for bargains.

Besides wining and dining, you can visit the **Villa Durazzo** and its gardens dating back to 1560. Inside the villa is the **Museo G. Rossi**, dedicated to the famous local journalist and novelist. You should also check out the church of **San Giacomo di Corte**. Located near Villa Durazzo and located on a panoramic hill overlooking the port, it is adorned with precious marbles and frescoes. Besides the beauty of the church, you can get some great photos of the bay and town from this vantage point.

Practical Information

• **Tourist Information Office**, *Via XXV Aprile 28. Tel. 0185/287-486*

Rapallo

The port town of **Rapallo** is the largest community in Tigullio and is a popular resort town in both the summer and winter because of its mild climate. An amphitheater of hills protects Rapallo from cold northern winds, and as a result the climate is temperate year round. Rapallo is bisected by two streams that empty into its large bay, along which you will find a tree-lined promenade and tiny shops, restaurants and cafés.

Arrivals & Departures

Located 30 kilometers from Genoa, you can either come by **car** down the A12 Autostrada, and take the exit at Rapallo; you can come by **ferry** from Genoa, which is probably the easiest and most scenic way to get here; or you can take the **train**. For ferry information and reservations contact one of these numbers: *Tel. 010/265-712 or 0336/688-732*. The ferries leave from the **Aquarium Dock** in Genoa.

Where To Stay

1. EUROPA, *Via Milite Ignoto 2. Tel. 0185/64692. Fax 0185/669-847. E-mail: info@hoteleuropa-rapallo.com. Web: www.hoteleuropa-rapallo.com. 62 rooms all with bath. Credit cards accepted. Single E75-E95; Double E100-140. Breakfast included. Full board E120-155.* ****

Located in a building built in the 1600s, this place is packed with history. Renovated in 1994 so you have all the necessary amenities for a four star hotel including air conditioning, TV, mini-bar, room service and more. They have a health club, a sauna, relaxing garden area and a good restaurant too. A good four star in the center of everything.

2. MINERVA, *Corso Cristoforo Colombo. Tel. 0185/230-388, Fax 0185/67078. American Express and Visa accepted. 35 rooms all with bath. Single E50-80; Double E80-110. Breakfast included. Full board E50-90. Closed Nov. 27 to Dec. 27.* ***

One street removed from the Lungomare with all its ambiance and life, these two yellow *palazzi* make up a wonderful three star hotel. The entrance hall is bright and airy with some grayish-blue sofas for seating. The rooms are comfortable and clean with cushy double beds. There are all the amenities of a good three star: TV, mini-bar, room service but no air conditioning. The bathrooms are modern but without a phone (seemingly a necessity in this part of the world) but you can get one by asking at the front desk. They also have a lovely garden terrace.

3. RIVIERA, *Piazza IV Novembre 2. Tel. 0185/50248, Fax 0185/65668. E-mail: info@hotel-riviera.it. Web: www.hotel-riviera.it. American Express and Visa accepted. 20 rooms all with bath. Double E110-140. Suite E150. Breakfast included. Full board available. Closed Oct. 30 to Dec. 23.* ***

Ideally situated in the heart of the Lungomare where everyone goes to see and be seen. This is a nice hotel that underwent renovations a few years ago so it is now superb. Some rooms have parquet floors but the best have the wonderful mosaic pavement. These are usually the rooms with balconies that overlook the port. Ask for one of these since the views are tremendous. The bathrooms are clean and modern with hairdryers and shower supplies available. Breakfast is an abundant buffet display of fruits, veggies, rolls and more. The hotel restaurant is also a frequent dining location for the locals since the food is so good and the prices reasonable. This is the place to stay in Rapallo.

4. VILLA MAROSA, *Via Rosselli 10. Tel. 0185/50668/9. No fax. No credit cards accepted. 12 rooms all with bath. Single E40-50; Double E53-70. Breakfast included. Full board available.* **

A small two star located along the river, a short stroll from the Lungomare. Quaint and comfortable, this little hotel has clean and comfortable rooms with TVs and telephones but not much else. There is a peaceful

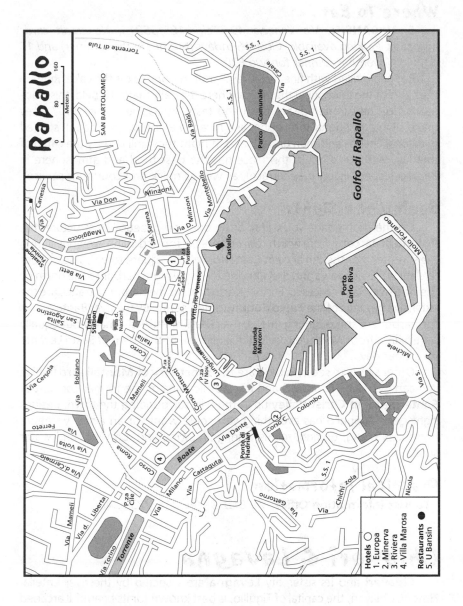

Rapallo

Torrente di Tula

SAN BARTOLOMEO

S.S. 1

S.S. 1

S.S. 1

Casale

Via

Parco Comunale

Golfo di Rapallo

0 80 160
Meters

Canessa

Via Don Minzoni

Via D. Minzoni

Via Montebello

Via Balsi

Via Maggiocco

Sal. Serena

Via

Via Betti

Castello

Molo Foraneo

1

P.za Pastene

P.za Garibaldi

Stazione Funivia

Salita San Agostino

Train Station

P.za d. Nazioni

5

Corso Italia

Vittorio Veneto

Porto Carlo Riva

Via Michele

Via S.

Via Cerçola

Via Bolzano

Via

Mameli

P.za Cavour

Corso Matteotti

Lungomare

P.za 23 Nov.

Rotundia Marconi

3

Via Ferreto

Via Volta

Via d. Carmelo

Corso Roma

Boate

4

Corso

Via Milano

Via Castaguta

Via Dante

Ponte di Hadrian

2

Corso C.

Colombo

Via Gattorno

Via

Chichi zola

Nicola

S.S. 1

Via

Mameli

Via d. Liberta

P.za Cile

Via

Via Torino

Torrente

Hotels
1. Europa
2. Minerva
3. Riviera
4. Villa Marosa

Restaurants
5. U Bansin

garden area to relax in the evenings. If you are in Rapallo on a budget, this is good place to stay.

Where To Eat

5. U BANSIN, Via Venezia 49. Tel. 0185/55913. No credit cards accepted. Parking available. Closed Sundays (but not in the summer) and 15 days in November. Dinner for two E30.

Rapallo is filled with fine restaurants, but this one takes the cake. Right in the heart of the town, near the piazza where the daily market is held, this place serves up fine Ligurian dishes fresh and tasty. In business since 1907, they make all the traditional local dishes like focaccia al formaggio (dough stuffed with local cheese and then baked), and at night they grill and fry the catch of the day. Without a doubt this place has the best food and atmosphere in Rapallo (especially on their terrace), as well as quick and courteous service.

Seeing the Sights

On the promenade you will find the open air gazebo-like structure, the **Rotunda Marconi**, from which concerts are performed in the evenings during the summer months. An ancient **Castello**, with its square tower, sloping roof of slate, little windows and draw bridge, overlooks the harbor to the north by the little river San Francesco. Further north around the harbor entrance are the extensive gardens of the **Parco Communale Casale**. By the river Baote across the harbor are some other gardens, the **Giardini Publici**, smaller but equally as relaxing, from which you can catch a glimpse of the town of Sestri Levante on a clear day.

Other sights to see in Rapallo are the **Sanctuary of Montallegro** (which you can get to by Funicular) and the Gothic ruins of the former convent of **Santa Maria in Christ Valley** up in the hills surrounding the town. Besides sightseeing, Rapallo has everything you could want for an active vacation: horseback riding, golfing, tennis, mini-golf, swimming, bowling, and water sports.

Practical Information

• **Tourist Information Office**, Via Diaz 9. Tel. 0185/230-346

Chiavari & Lavagna

Chiavari and its sister city **Lavagna** are bisected by the river Entella. Historic Chiavari, the capital of Tigullio, is best known for its beautiful arcaded medieval streets. Besides its beauty, the Romans as well as the Genovese in medieval times considered Chiavari to be of strategic importance. And the restaurants here are some of the best in Tigullio.

Arrivals & Departures

Located 42 kilometers from Genoa, you can either come by **car** down the A12 Autostrada and get off at the Chiavari exit; you can come by **ferry** from Genoa, which is probably the easiest and most scenic way to get here; or you can take the **train**. For ferry information and reservations contact one of these numbers: *Tel. 010/265-712 or 0336/688-732.* The ferries leave from the **Aquarium Dock** in Genoa.

Where To Stay

1. BRISTOL, *Corso Mazzini 23, Lavagna. Tel. 0185/395-600, Fax the same. Web: www.venere.it/it/liguria/lavagna/bristol. Credit cards accepted. 27 rooms all with bath. Single E45-65; Double E65-85. Breakfast included. Full board available.* ***

Located near the station and the *centro storico* and only a short walk from the beach, this hotel is simple, basic and comfortable. The rooms are filled with modern furnishings and the bathrooms are small with tiny showers. There are TVs in the rooms but no mini-bars. The main positive point about this place is the restaurant, which serves up wonderful food. An inexpensive place to stay, ideally located.

2. FIESCHI, *Via Rezza 12, Lavagna. Tel. 0185/313-809, Fax 0185/304-400. E-mail: info@hotelvillafieschi.it. Web: www.hotelvillafieschi.it. Credit cards accepted. 13 rooms all with bath. Single E60-100; Double E95-125. Breakfast included. Full board available.* ***

A little difficult to locate, but the isolation makes for a serene setting. The entrance is beautiful and everything is well appointed with traditional Ligurian ornamentation. There are two common rooms: the left room is used for small reunions, the right for the restaurant and breakfast buffet. The food here is stupendous and served in large quantities. The rooms are large and completely renovated so they are modern, clean and comfortable, as are the bathrooms. This is the place to stay in Lavagna.

3. TORINO, *Corso Cristoforo Colombo 151, Chiavari. Tel. 0185/312-231, Fax 0185/312-233. E-mail: hotel.torino@tigullio.net. Web: www.tigullio.net/hoteltorino. Credit cards accepted. 32 rooms 30 with bath. Single without E40-60; Single E45-75; Double without E60-80; Double E65-90. Breakfast included.* ***

Located near the public beaches and community swimming pool, this is a newly renovated hotel on the water. The buffet breakfast is served on the garden verandah and it is also where you can relax in the evenings. The rooms, one group of which are on the ground floor and the rest on the first floor, are all clean, comfortable and spacious. The furnishings are all simple and stylish and the bathrooms are clean and modern. You have TVs in the rooms as well as a radios and mini-bar. A quaint and comfortable three star.

4. **ZIA PIERA**, *Corso Valparaiso 52, Chiavari. Tel. 0185/307-686, Fax 0185/314-139. E-mail: ziapiera@yahoo.com. Web: www.angelfire.com/ok/ziapiera. Credit cards accepted. 27 rooms all with bath. Single E40; Double 75. Breakfast included. Full board available.* ******

A small, simple hotel, comfortable and clean. Located on the walking street by the sea, the terrace on the first floor offers a wonderful view of the sparkling water. The restaurant is located on the ground floor and serves some wonderful fish dishes. In all, a great two star for a good price but with few amenities except for the stunning location in the colorful town of Chiavari.

Where To Eat

5. **ANTICA OSTERIA DA U DRIA**, *Via Costaguta 27, Chiavari. Tel. 0185/323-699. All credit cards accepted except for American Express. Closed Mondays and Sunday nights in the winter. Dinner for two E45.*

Located right by the Villa Rocca, this is an historic local restaurant that has recently undergone some modern culinary changes. The ambiance is enhanced by various pieces of ancient origin hanging on the walls. The menu changes weekly and tends towards the creative side, with the core being fish and meat dishes with a variety of sauces. Their pastas are also very good and you might want to try the *tagliatelle con scampi e asparagi* (pasta with shrimp and asparagus). Their wine list is decent and the service is speedy and courteous. The best place to sit is on the terrace.

6. **BELVEDERE**, *Via alla Chiesa 7, Lavagna. Tel. 0185/390-552. No credit cards accepted. Closed Tuesdays (except in the summer) and January through March. Open only evenings. Dinner for two E40.*

Right beside the large church Santa Giulia, this place is famous for their wonderful garden terrace and the stunning views. You can savor many splendid dishes like *verdure ripiene* (stuffed veggies), *ravioli al ragu* (in an exquisite meat and tomato sauce), and *pasta al pesto con zucchine* (pesto sauce with zucchini over pasta). They also make some great meat dishes as well as fresh fish prepared any way you like. My favorite is the *fritto misto all'italiana* (mixed fried seafood, meat and vegetables ... kind of a surf, turf and garden). My favorite in Lavagna.

7. **IL BOTTEGONE**, *Via Milite Ignoto 3, Lavagna. Tel. 0185/390-079. No credit cards accepted. Closed Wednesdays and October. Only open in the evenings. Dinner for two E30.*

Traditional cooking in a rustic atmosphere at great prices. To start, try their *focaccio al formaggio* (dough stuffed with cheese then baked) or their *torte di verdure* (vegetable pie). For seconds their fish is prepared perfectly at only a little above the price you would pay for it in the market. For authentic local atmosphere you have to try this place if in Lavagna.

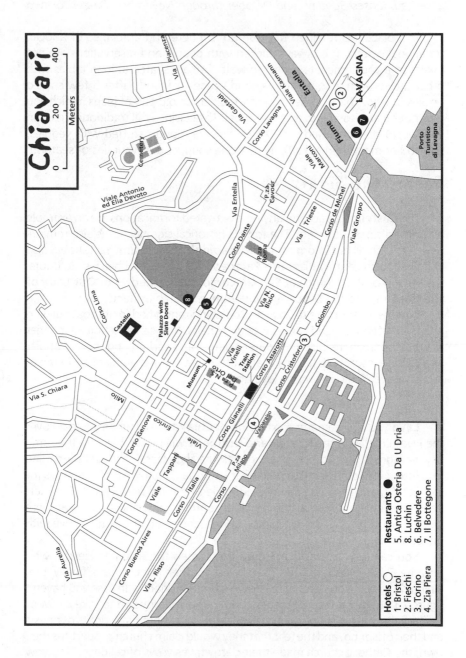

Chiavari

Meters
0 200 400

Via Piacenza
Via Gassaldi
Viale Kasmann
Emella
Fiume
LAVAGNA
① ②
⑥ ⑦
Porto Turistico di Levagna

Corso Lavagna
Viale Marconi

Cemetery

Viale Antonio ed Elia Devoto
Via Entella
Corso Dante
P.za Cavour
Via Trieste
Corso de Michel
Viale Groppo

P.za Roma
Via N. Bixio
Colombo

Corso Lima
Castello
Palazzo with Slate Doors
⑧ ⑤
Via Vinelli
Train Station
Corso Assarotti
Corso Cristoforo ③

Via S. Chiara
Milio
Museum
P.za N. 3 del Orto
Corso Genova
Enrico Millo
Viale
Corso Gianelli
Valpraigo
④

Viale Tapparri
Corso Italia
P.za Milano

Via Aurelia
Corso Buenos Aires
Via L. Risso

Hotels ○
1. Bristol
2. Fieschi
3. Torino
4. Zia Piera

Restaurants ●
5. Antica Osteria Da U Dria
8. Luchin
6. Belvedere
7. Il Bottegone

8. LUCHIN, *Via Brighenti 53, Chiavari. Tel. 0185/301-063. No credit cards accepted. Closed Sundays and October through November. Dinner for two E35.*

This place has retained the true atmosphere and ambiance of a local, traditional *osteria*. It is always packed with people and reservations are not taken, so if you come late expect to wait. You are seated at long tables with other guests with whom you may end up being friends after a few shared bottles of *vino*. This place is as comfortable as an old pair of jeans, which you may not be able to fit into after the meal. The cuisine is all traditional Ligurian with *pesto* pasta, stuffed vegetables, *crostini* (dough stuffed with veggies, seafood or meat then baked), minestrone soup, and all varieties of seafood.

Seeing the Sights
Chiavari

The **Castello** and accompanying ivy-covered fortifications are an example of Chiavari's past notoriety. The town's historical significance is also remembered in its small but informative **Archaeological Museum**. You should also visit the fourth century **Pizzorno Palace** with its beautiful black slate doors, the second century church of **San Giacomo**, the **Cathedral of Our Lady of the Garden**, and the **Diocesan Museum** of church artifacts.

But there is still more to Chiavari. It is world-renowned for its boat building and the crafting of hand carved wooden chairs. You can also find all manner of water sports here including water skiing, wind surfing and more. Popular as a seaside resort with Italians, it also offers the culture, ambiance, character and style we Anglo-Saxons so love about Italy.

Lavagna

Lavagna is like a natural extension of **Chiavari**, and when you pass over the River Entella on the **Maddelena bridge**, it will be like being in the same city. Lavagna's significance is tied in with the slate trade. The first slate mine was found in Mount San Giacomo near Lavagna. The town is also famous for the Fieschi family which centuries ago ruled here for many years. They left behind many monumental architectural contributions, and as a result were judged by Dante Aligheri, the famous Florentine poet, as being "in love with material things."

You can see the **Basilica Sinibaldo**, named for Sinibaldo Fieschi, who became Pope Innocenzo IV. There was another pope in the family too, Sinibaldo's grandson Ottobono, known as Pope Adriani V. In case you haven't figured it out by now, only recently have Catholic clergy had to take a vow of celibacy. Because of some conflicts concerning the hereditary rights of priests and their offspring, and the fear that they would claim church property as their own, the Catholic church made their clergy takes vows of celibacy. That vow has nothing to do with Christ's teaching at all. Other sights to see are the

Santa Giulia church, the **Oratory of N.S. del Carmine**, and the **Santo Stefano Collegiate** church.

A fun time to be here would be August 14th, when the festival **La Torta dei Fieschi** (Fieschi's cake) is celebrated. It commemorates the marriage between Opizzo Fieschi and the Siennese countess Biancha dei Bianchi in 1230 when a cake was shared with all townspeople present. Today revelers get dressed in period garb and play in mock medieval tournaments.

Near Lavagna is the large beach of **Cavi**, perfect for sunbathing and people watching.

Practical Information

Tourist Information Offices
- *Corso Assarotti 1, Chiavari. Tel. 0185/325-198*
- *Piazza della Liberta, Lavaga. Tel. 0185/395-070*

Sestri Levante

Located on the extreme southwest end of the Gulf of Tigullio, the town of **Sestri Levante** is stunningly beautiful. One of its two inlets, the Gulf of Ponente, was renamed the **Baia delle Favole** (Bay of Fables) by Hans Christian Andersen because of its fairy tale beauty. On the other side of the 'island' is the **Baia del Silenzio**, so named for its peace and quiet.

The 'island' really is a peninsula upon which the **Toretta Marconi** (Marconi's Tower) sits watching over the town. The peninsula on which the tower sits at one time was an actual island, but around the 11th century silt had built up from the Gromolo stream between it and the shore. Despite that, it is still known as the 'island' today (things move slower in Italy.)

Sestri Levante is a quaint, quiet little town, perfect for a romantic weekend adventure any time of the year.

Arrivals & Departures

Located 51 kilometers from Genoa, you can either come by car down the A12 Autostrada and get off at the Sestri Levante exit; you can come by **ferry** from Genoa, which is probably the easiest and most scenic way to get here; or you can take the **train**. For ferry information and reservations contact one of these numbers: *Tel. 010/265-712 or 0336/688-732*. The ferries leave from the **Aquarium Dock** in Genoa.

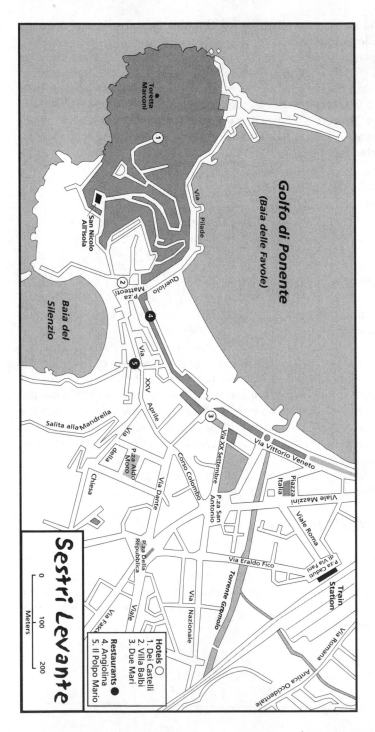

Sestri Levante

Hotels ○
1. Dei Castelli
2. Villa Balbi
3. Due Mari

Restaurants ●
4. Angiolina
5. Il Polpo Mario

0 100 200
Meters

Golfo di Ponente
(Baia delle Favole)

Baia del Silenzio

Toretta Marconi

San Nicolo All'Isola

Via Pilade

P.za Matteotti

Via Queriolo

Via XXV Aprile

Salita alla Mandrella

Via

Chiesa

P.za Aldo Moro

Via Dante

Corso Colombo

Via XX Settembre

P.za San Antonio

Via Vittorio Veneto

Piazza Italia

Viale Mazzini

P.za Della Repubblica

Via Eraldo Fico

Via

Viale

Via Facci

Via Nazionale

Torrente Gramolo

Viale Roma

P.za Caduti di Via Fam.

Train Station

Via Romana

Antica Occidentale

Where To Stay

1. **DEI CASTELLI**, *Via Penisola 26. Tel. 0185/487-220, Fax 0185/44767. E-mail: htl.castelli@rainbownet.it. Web: www.rainbownet.it/htl.castelli. 30 rooms all with bath. Credit cards accepted. Single E85-150; Double E150-175. Breakfast included.* ****

Immersed in a park like setting on the peninsula at Sestri Levante, this wonderful hotel is housed in a castle dating back to the 1100s. In the main part of the castle is the central core of the hotel with the salons and common rooms as well as some of the guest rooms. In the tower, separated from the main building but connected by an underground passage, is the restaurant and bar area. All around the hotel are terraces from which you can enjoy stunning views of Sestri and the Gulf of Tigullio. The rooms are all different in size, shape, architectural touches and furnishing, but all are more than amply spacious. The bathrooms are rather large also, some with mosaic tile and all with every modern convenience. Along with the incredibly romantic ambiance, the hotel also has its own private beach, a swimming pool and pristine garden terrace. A wonderful place to stay with all possible four star amenities.

2. **DUE MARI**, *Vico del Caro 18. Tel. 0185/42695, Fax 0185/42698. 26 rooms all with bath. Credit cards accepted. Single E35-70; Double E45-80; Breakfast included. Full board E40-65.* ***

Built in the 1600s, this attractive old building was turned into a hotel in 1963 and renovated in 1993 to perfection and is an ideal location for a tranquil stay in the heart of Sestri. Situated between the Baia del Favole and the Baia del Silenzio, the common areas are well lit and filled with antique furnishings. The breakfast room turns into a quaint reading area in the afternoons. The traditional restaurant, which specializes in fish dishes and other healthy fare, is located in the internal garden area. Every room has a view of one of the bays or the internal courtyard. Only the rooms on the third floor have air conditioning, which is a must in August. The room furnishings are basic but everything is clean and comfortable. The bathrooms are small but have all necessary conveniences.

3. **VILLA BALBI**, *Viale Rimembranze 1. Tel. 0185/42941, Fax 0185/482-459. Web: www.initaly.com/hisres/balbi/balbi.htm. 96 rooms all with bath. Credit cards accepted. E200-250. Breakfast included.* ****

An old historical building constructed by a noble family from Genoa in the 1600s, it was converted into a hotel in 1947 and is a wonderful place to stay. Everything here is pure elegance with wonderful furnishings and architectural displays. The rooms themselves are filled with ambiance and atmosphere and are quite large with furnishings that are quasi-'antique' but comfortable. The bathrooms are large and complete with all necessary modern conveniences. They have a wonderful terrace garden that also houses an outdoor pool that is heated during the cooler months. Also, on their private beach you can place your order from their good restaurant and be served as you sun yourself. A hotel of the highest caliber.

Where To Eat
4. ANGIOLINA, *Viale Rimembranze 49. Tel. 0185/41198. Closed Tuesdays and from November through December. Credit cards accepted. Dinner for two E70.*

A fine restaurant that serves many traditional dishes, like *zuppa di pesce* (fish soup) and *fritto misto e grigliate* (either fried or grilled mixed seafood), but they also get slightly creative with some dishes like the *insalata di polpo e patate* (mixed salad with octopus and potatoes), *triglie al basilico* (mullet with basil sauce) *spaghetti di frutti di mare* (with fruit of the sea, i.e. a variety of sea food) or *seppie ripiene* (stuffed cuttlefish). The portions are extremely generous, the service quick and hospitable, and the atmosphere good, especially in the terrace area, which all makes for a fine meal.

5. IL POLPO MARIO, *Via XXV Aprile 163. Tel. 0185/48-203. Closed Mondays. Credit cards accepted. Dinner for two E80.*

This is a legendary restaurant in Sestri which specializes in seafood. An old traditional *osteria* that has finally been returned to its former glory, the menu is mainly based on the catch of the day straight out of the *Golfo di Tigullio*. The following dishes merit some mention: *Il grande misto di mare all'antica* (all manner of roasted fish with potatoes, tomatoes and other veggies) and *le frittelle con gamberi* (fried fritters and shrimp). Inside it's quaint and comfortable and the terrace seating is splendid too.

Seeing the Sights
Marconi's Tower on the 'island' was where Gugliemo Marconi began his experimentation with short wave radio signals. Without Marconi's efforts from this tower, who knows when radio would have been invented? Also on the peninsula is the rustic little **Church of San Nicolo of the Island**, built around 1511.

A short distance north of the town are the abandoned copper mines in **Libiola**. Active all the way back to Roman times, the mines are now used for archaeological research as well as an eco-museum.

Practical Information
• **Tourist Information Office**, *Via XX Settembre 33. Tel. 0185/497-011*

Cinque Terre
If you're searching for something off the beaten path, look no further. These five villages are essentially off limits to cars, and to even find them you

have to make five separate detours off the main road far away from the coast since the villages are not linked by any road on which an automobile can travel. Because of this remoteness, these villages have preserved their old world charm and have escaped the onslaught of tourism.

The **Cinque Terre** (the five lands) are the five villages of **Monterosso al Mare, Vernazza, Comiglia, Manarola** and **Riomaggiore**. Each is set beautifully in the coastal cliffs and sloping vineyards of Liguria and are connected to each other by a narrow winding country path. Whenever there is a flood, some of the path is usually washed away but still remains traversable on foot – which is the best way to see the Cinque Terre. Settle yourself into a nice hotel in either Monterosso al Mare or Riomaggiore, or a small but nice *pensione* in Vernazza, and walk to the rest. The other two smaller inside villages don't have official hotels or *pensiones* yet. If you get tired and can't walk back, there's always the local train to pick you up and return you to your 'home' village.

The Cinque Terre were situated high up above on the cliffs for protection from marauding pirates. No one knows where these original inhabitants came from since their highland settlements are no longer in existence, but as a result of the high incidence of red hair and light coloring among the residents of Cinque Terre, experts have speculated that they share a Celtic or Nordic background. When the danger of pirates passed, around 1000 CE, the villages resettled themselves closer to the water's edge to take advantage of the bounty from the sea.

Today most of the permanent residents of each village is either a fisherman or a farmer, but some are turning into hoteliers or restaurateurs. The same rugged terrain that protected them long ago from ocean invaders used to also protect them from the modern invasion of mass tourism. But their defenses have started to crumble. In the two border towns, tourism is flourishing and in Vernazza, more and more homes are opening themselves up to become *pensione*. Soon, I fear, the last of Italy's true beauties is going to succumb to the influences of the rest of the world.

Even with more tourists, the sights, scenery, and tranquillity here are still extraordinary. Make the trip and you won't be disappointed, especially from October to April, when you'll have the place virtually to yourself and the approximately 6,500 residents of all five villages. There won't be much to do here, except hike from village to village, then casually lunch or dine at a different *trattoria* in a different village each day, and let the cares of the world pass from your mind for a little while.

If you want to swim, **Monterosso al Mare** has the best sandy beach among the Cinque Terre.

Arrivals & Departures

By Boat

You can come by boat, which will take you three hours. The train is an hour quicker. But if you're just going for the day, the boat may well be what you're looking for: the trip is designed as a boat cruise, then a three hour stay in Vernazza (the best of the villages), then the return trip.

If you're going to stay a day or two, the trip to Vernazza will cost you E17 round-trip or E9 one way. Contact this number for information and reservations: *Tel. 010/265-712 or 0336/688-732.*

The boat's hours of operation are:

- **July 1–August 26**, *Saturdays, leave from the Aquarium dock in Genoa at 9:40am*
- **July 2–September 3**, *Sundays, leave from the Aquarium dock in Genoa at 8:40am*

By Train

Take one of the local trains from Genoa and it will stop in each of the Cinque Terre. A train leaves from Genoa every two hours or so, and the trip takes about two hours.

Where to Stay

If you want first class hotels, stay in either **Monterosso al Mare** or **Riomaggiore**. From these towns you can either hike or take the local train to the other villages. If you don't mind small, intimate, rustic accommodations far off the beaten path, then stay at one of the *pensione* listed in the other three inner villages of the Cinque Terre.

Usually only the most hardy souls will venture to stay in the inner three villages, giving you even more solitude if that is what you're after. If you're looking for a truly Italian holiday adventure, stay in one of the three smaller villages.

Monterosso al Mare

PORTO ROCA, *Via Corone 1, in Corone, 19016 Monterosso al Mare. Tel. 0187/817-502, Fax 010/817-692. 43 rooms all with bath. Credit cards accepted. Single E90-110; Double E120-150.* ****

Built into a cliff above the village, this beautiful romantic setting is perfect for lovers or honeymoons. You have your own private beach, a quaint little restaurant, and great service. There is a shuttle bus that will run you down to the village since it is quite a hike. If you want to stay in luxury in the Cinque Terre but don't want to be a part of the touristy crowd in Monterosso, stay here.

PALME, *Via IV Novembre 18, 19016 Monterosso al Mare. Tel. 0187/817-541, Fax 0187/818-265. 49 rooms all with bath. Single E75-90; Double E90-120. All credit cards accepted.* ****

Located near the beach but still in a tranquil setting, the hotel is small, clean, and comfortable, except when it gets deathly hot in August. I don't understand how it has four stars without air conditioning. A good place to stay if you want access to the beach as well as instant access to town.

JOLLIE, *Via Gioberti 1, 19016 Monterosso al Mare. Tel. 0187/817-539, Fax 0187/817-273. 31 rooms all with shower. Credit cards accepted. Single E60-85; Double E90-145. Breakfast E10 extra.* ***

Located 150 meters from the beach directly in the center of town, here you'll have the best of both worlds. Despite its location, it is well insulated from the sounds of the city. There is an excellent in-house restaurant and a solarium if you don't want to hit the beach for a tan. A clean, quiet, and comfortable three star hotel.

VILLA ADRIANA, *Via IV Novembre 23, 19016 Monterosso al Mare. Tel. 0187/818-109, Fax is the same. No credit cards accepted. 54 rooms all with bath. Single E35-45; Double E70-80.* **

A two star with its own private beach, a good restaurant, with small, comfortable clean rooms. It's located a little on the outskirts of the town, but they have a shuttle bus you can use to get back and forth. The summer months are not so pleasant since they don't have air conditioning, but the rest of the year this is a great place to stay.

BAIA, *Via Fegina 88, 19016 Monterosso al Mare. Tel. 0187/817-512, Fax 0187/818-322. 29 rooms all with bath. Credit cards accepted. Single E65; Double E60-75.* *

A one star on the rise. Located a little outside of town, they have their own private beach, accommodating staff, a good restaurant, and clean, comfortable quiet rooms. The only thing missing is air conditioning, but they're looking into that in the future. There is no shuttle bus to get you back and forth like the better hotels but this is a great place to stay.

Vernazza

BARBARA, *Piazza Marconi 10, Vernazza 19018. Tel. 0187/812-201. Nine rooms none with bath. Three bathrooms in the hall way. No credit cards accepted. Single E30-40; Double E50-60. Full board E50 per person.* *

A small rustic place with an equally small restaurant and bar situated in a converted family room. The only real amenity is heat in the winter, but if you're going to stay in Vernazza you didn't come for amenities, you came for the old Italian way of life. Here you can enjoy peaceful evenings secluded from the rest of society and take in the experience of time standing still. The rooms are small but clean and comfortable in a countryside sort of way. To pick up your keys you need to go to the Trattoria del Capitano (see *Where to Eat* below).

SORRISO, *Via Gavino 4, Vernazza 19018. Tel. 0187/812-224. 11 rooms 1 double with bath. No credit cards accepted. Single E35; Double E50. Full board E45. *

Set back from the harbor just outside the little town, this is a perfect place to come for reflection and peace, especially in the small garden setting. A truly rustic place. The only amenity is heat in the winter. They have their own restaurant and small bar. Pets are welcome guests too.

Capitalizing on the growing tourist trade swarming through the Cinque Terre, the owners opened another Sorriso located just down the street. They have six rooms at the 'new' location (a renovated home), the prices are the same and they share the phone. Both are like rustic bed and breakfasts.

Riomaggiore
CA' D'ANDREAN, *Via Discovolo 25, Riomaggiore 19010. Tel. 0187/920-040. 10 rooms all with bath. Single E32-40; Double E50-60. Breakfast E5. No credit cards accepted. ***

Located outside of the village of Riomaggiore near Manarola, you'll be completely isolated here. The only real amenities in the simply furnished rooms are heat and a phone; but they are clean and comfortable if you do not expect too much. There is a small bar area downstairs, just off the tiny entrance way, as well as a beautiful internal garden terrace area complete with lemon trees. A perfect place in which to relax.

MARINA PICCOLA, *Via Discovolo 192, Riomaggiore 19010. Tel. 0187/920-103. All credit cards accepted. 7 rooms all with bath. Single E45-55; Double E55-65. Breakfast E5. Full board E60-65. ***

Located outside of the little village, thankfully this place has its own restaurant, of the same name, so you don't have to trek out in the night to find food, as you have to do at the Ca' d'Andrean above. Located on the same street as that hotel too, but a little farther out, this is a pleasant place to stay. The rooms are small but clean and comfortable and most have a view of the sea. The bathrooms also are small but clean. The hotel at *Via Discovolo 202* has three more rooms, all with terraces that overlook the sea. A peaceful place to sit in the evenings.

VILLA ARGENTINA, *Via de Gaspari 37, Riomaggiore 19010. Tel. 0187/920-213. 15 rooms all with bath. Single E40-50; Double E60. Breakfast included. American Express and Visa accepted. ***

The biggest place around, which isn't saying much since it only has 15 rooms. Located outside of the village in a tranquil country setting near the town's famous castle. The rooms are small and clean with heat, a phone in the rooms, and are pet-friendly. There is a small bar area where your breakfast buffet is served. A good rustic two star.

Where to Eat

Seafood and *pesto* are the specialties of the Cinque Terre, as they are all over Liguria. There are plenty of restaurants in **Monterosso al Mare**, but only a few in the smaller villages (Vernazza, Comiglia, Manarola, Riomaggiore). In addition to the restaurants attached to the hotels listed above, most restaurants here are fairly simple affairs.

Vernazza

TRATTORIA DEL CAPITANO, *Tel. 0187/812-224. Dinner for two E60. No credit cards accepted.*

This is the best place for a meal in Cinque Terre. You'll have a great view of the sea as it crashes on the rocks below. *Pesto* and seafood are the specialties. There's a good *zuppa del mare* (seafood soup) for starters. Follow it with a *pasta con pesto* dish, and finish up with any variety of grilled fish that are pulled from the waters below.

Practical Information

Tourist Information

If you want any tourist information about the Cinque Terre, you need to pick it up in Genoa, buy a local guide book, or contact the offices in **La Spezia**, *Viale Mazzini 45, Tel. 0187/770-900.* There are no formal tourist operations in any of the villages.

The Italian Riviera

To the west of Genoa, along the **Riviera delle Palme** (The Palm Riviera), you will find wonderful beaches, pristine natural surroundings, all manner of water sports, quaint little towns filled with character and ambiance, a variety of superb culinary delights and hospitable locals. All of this is set against the vibrant blue of the Mediterranean with intense greens of the Maritime hills as the backdrop. Since the climate is mild year round, the Riviera delle Palme makes for an excellent vacation spot at any time. There are plenty of small towns and villages to choose from, as well as larger ports of call, but in all you will find everything you need to have a fantastic seaside holiday.

Further west, closer to the French border and the French Riviera, is the **Riviera dei Fiori** (The Flower Riviera), known for its abundant flower and plant life, as well as excellent seaside resorts. Popularized at the turn of the century by visiting nobles, aristocrats, artists and more, the Riviera del Fiori has been a holiday playground for many generations. You'll find lots of water sports available, amazing restaurants, scenic nature trails, wonderful museums, stunning architecture, and vibrant small town life.

Varazze

Varazze boasts an excellent tourist port where you can conveniently dock your boat, as well as a renowned shipyard where you could, if you had the means, buy yourself a boat to travel the Mediterranean. Having been a resort for many centuries, Varazze is bursting with hospitality. Once you set foot on the local beaches and venture onto the many panoramic walks you will see why Varazze has been so popular for years. When here, take the time to admire the complex of the ancient **medieval city walls**, relish the beauty of the Romanesque church of **Sant'Ambrogio**, and venture over to see the striking beauty of the 17th century convent **Il Deserto** outside of town.

Besides sightseeing and sunbathing, there are all sorts of water sports available to enjoy, many fine restaurants to savor, and the must-see event of the year: "**Varazze, la Citta delle Donne**" **festival** in May. The festival is in honor of the contributions women have made to society in sport, entertainment, culture, style, the arts and more. It features parades, games, entertainment and is a lot of fun.

Arrivals & Departures

Located 11 kilometers from Savona and 12 kilometers from Genoa, you can either come by car on the A10 Autostrada or Route 1 that motors along the sea. Route 1 can get a little crowded in the summer months. You can also arrive by train quickly and easily.

Where to Stay

1. CLARI, *Via Sardi 9, 17109 Varazze. Tel. 019/98977, Fax 019/934-833. 25 rooms all with bath. Single E30-45; Double E40-60. Credit cards accepted. Full board E30-55.* ******

This place is due for three star status, no doubt about it, and they know it too. That's why their prices are higher than a normal two star. Only 150 meters from the sea, near the Coccodrillo, this hotel is a tranquil oasis. The entrance is pleasant with antique furniture as is the restaurant area. In the summer you can dine in their garden, which makes for a pleasant meal. The rooms were modernized in 1993 and are all comfortably appointed with light green furnishings. And from most of the rooms you get a wonderful view of the sea, since the hotel is located up the hill overlooking the water. An excellent choice.

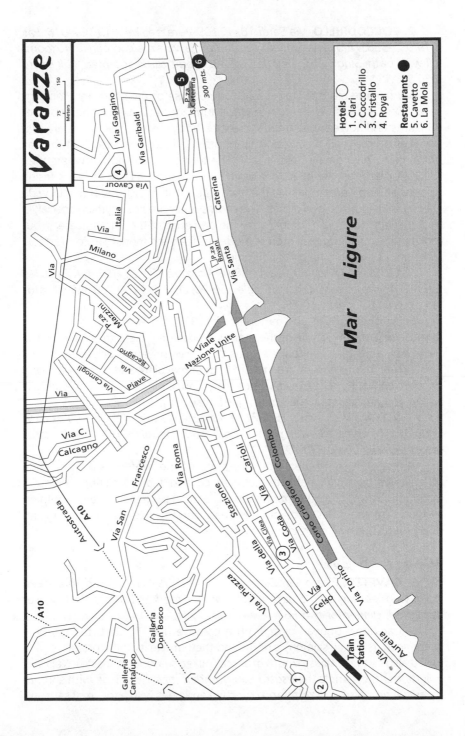

Varazze

Meters
0   75   150

Hotels
1. Clari
2. Coccodrillo
3. Cristallo
4. Royal

Restaurants
5. Cavetto
6. La Mola

Mar Ligure

Via Gaggino
Via Garibaldi
Via Cavour
Via Italia
Via Milano
P.za Mazzini
Via Recagno
Via Camogli
Via Piave
Via C. Calcagno
Via San Francesco
Via Roma
Via Stazione
Via Carioli
Via Coda
Via delle Cilea
Via L. Piazza
Via Celsa
Via Torino
Via Aurelia
Corso Cristoforo Colombo
Viale Nazione Unite
Via Santa Caterina
Caterina
P.za Is. Caterina
P.za Bovani
300 mts.

Autostrada A10
A10

Galleria Don Bosco
Galleria Cantalupo

Train Station

2. COCCODRILLO, *Via Sardi 16, 17109 Varazze. Tel. 019/932-015, Fax 019/932-588. Web: www.venere.com/it/liguria/varazze/coccodrillo. 40 rooms all with bath. Single E55; Double E80-90. Credit cards accepted. Full board E30-55.* ***

My favorite place to stay in Varazze because of the character, comfort, cleanliness and cost. The entrance way is luminous and filled with all number of plants and flowers that helps to create a bucolic ambiance. There are two terraces off the main area that at times are used to grill the catch of the day for dinner. The aroma is magnificent. The terrace on the right is where their pool is located, large enough for a swim and surrounded by deck chairs. Inside there is also a billiards room and the restaurant, from which you can get a wide variety of delectable local dishes. The rooms really are not anything special; in fact they are quite plain compared to the opulence of the common areas, but since the remodeling, each room is modern, clean and more than comfortable enough. But there is no air conditioning.

3. CRISTALLO, *Via F. Cilea 4, 17109 Varazze. Tel. 019/97264, Fax 019/96392. 45 rooms all with bath. Single E60-90; Double E100-120. Credit cards accepted. Full board E50-75.* ****

Established in 1961 and remodeled in 1990, this is a quaint four star on a quiet side street just off of the main seaside road. Here they have all the necessary amenities of a four star plus their own private beach a short stroll away. Their rooms and bathrooms are kept immaculate and come with every modern convenience The restaurant is a pleasant dining experience, especially when you are seated in their plush garden setting.

4. ROYAL, *Via Cavour 25, 17109 Varazze. Tel. 019/931-166, Fax 019/96664. 31 rooms all with bath. Single E60; Double E105. Credit cards accepted. Full board E38-70.* ****

A wonderful renovated little four star, off the beaten path. They pride themselves on traditional attentive service and feature all the necessary amenities as well as a quiet garden dining and relaxing area. There is nothing extravagant about this place, but it is clean, comfortable and welcoming and filled with charming character and ambiance.

Where to Eat

5. CAVETTO, *Piazza San Caterina 7. Tel. 019/97311. Closed Thursdays, 15 days in February and 15 days in November. American Express and Discover accepted. Dinner for two E60.*

A traditional Ligurian place with a creative flair. To start, the *salmone affumicato* (smoked salmon) is great and they smoke it on the premises. You could also try the *antipasto misto di pesce* (mixed seafood antipasto). Next you might want to sample the *risotto con gamberi* (rice dish made with shrimp) or *zucchine e pisselli di zafferano* (zucchini and peas with a touch of saffron).

For seconds, the *fritto misto di mare* (mixed fried seafood) is unbeatable. A quaint, comfortable little place with a terrace overlooking the water.

6. LA MOLA, *Via Marconi 17a. Tel. 019/932-469. Closed Mondays and Nov. 15 to Dec. 15. Credit cards accepted. Dinner for two E55.*

Typical Mediterranean cuisine can be found in this pleasant little local establishment a few paces from the water. *Insalata di mare* (seafood salad), *zuppetta di mollusche* (mollusk soup), *ravioline alla Mola* (small ravioli with prawns), *gnocchi con scampi e zucchine* (gnocchi with shrimp and zucchini) and the *pesce al forno* (grilled fish) are all excellent options. And the service is fast and cordial. The best place to sit is on their terrace overlooking the water.

Practical Information

• **Tourist Information Office**, *Viale Nazione Unite-Palazzo Comunale. Tel. 019/934-609*

Albisola Marina

Ceramics have helped make **Albisola** famous for centuries, and the craft is still practiced today. Many different kinds of ceramic goods can be purchased in the local shops which make for wonderful gifts or keepsakes. There are remains of an ancient **Roman farm complex** here as well as farms, villas and palaces from noble and wealthy families. The **Gavotti** and **Faraggiana villas** house some magnificent furniture and works of art from local potters.

The famous **promenade** between the street and the beach is paved with mosaic tile works by local, famous and obscure artists. So beside the sights and sounds surrounding you as you take your *passegiatta* (walk), you can also admire many fine works of art underfoot. While here you must visit the **Ceramics Museum** and take a romantic stroll through the *centro storico*.

Arrivals & Departures

Located four kilometers from Savona and 19 kilometers from Genoa, you can either come by car on the A10 Autostrada or Route 1 that motors along the sea. Route 1 can get a little crowded in the summer months. You can also arrive by train quickly and easily.

Where to Stay

GARDEN, *Viale Faraggiana 6, 17102 Albisola Marina. Tel. 019/485-253, Fax 109/485-255. 34 rooms all with bath. Single E60-70; Double E80-100. Credit cards accepted. Full board E50-60.* ****

The only four star in town that has all the amenities you need including a fitness center, sauna, swimming pool and air conditioning. Established in

1994, this is a modern hotel and as such may not have as much charm and ambiance as you want. Because of the great local dishes, the restaurant is worth a meal or two. There is a rustic garden setting where you can relax after a tough day walking the *centro storico* or lounging on the beach. The rooms are well appointed with modern furnishings and the bathrooms are sparkling with every possible amenity.

VILLA CHIARA, *Faraggiana 5, 17102 Albisola Marina. Tel. 019/485-253, Fax 109/485-255. 24 rooms all with bath. Single E50-60; Double E60-70. Credit cards accepted. Full board E40-57. ****

Right next to the Garden Hotel, this place is run by the same family. They operate the best four star and three star operations in town. This hotel has a little more character since it was established in 1928 and only recently renovated in 1988. The Garden and Villa Chiara really corner the market on comfort in town. The Villa Chiara has no air conditioning or pool, sauna and fitness center. But the staff is courteous and the rooms are clean and comfortable.

Where to Eat

LA FAMILIARE, *Piazza del Popolo 8. Tel. 019/489-480. Closed Mondays and Jan. 10 to Feb. 10. All credit cards accepted. Dinner for two E45.*

A few paces from the Lungomare, the Vassallo family prepares authentic Ligurian cuisine, simple and succulent for your pleasure. You'll find classic antipasto with *torte di verdure* (vegetable pies), cheeses, and fried vegetables; as well as great pastas like *ravioli di verdure* or *di pesce* (ravioli stuffed with veggies or fish); and wonderful fried and grilled fish and meat. My favorite, though, is oven baked *coniglio alla Ligure* (rabbit in a Ligurian pesto style sauce). Their terrace has a great atmosphere and it is a smoke-free zone.

Practical Information

• **Tourist Information Office**, *Piazza Sisto IV. Tel. 019/481-648*

Savona

An outstanding port of call for the rich and famous as well as a resort town for the rest of us. **Savona** boasts Renaissance palaces and villas magnificently decorated, museums filled with works by the Grand Masters, a theater of impeccable tradition, a medieval *centro storico*, as well as a bustling modern street life surrounded by numerous stores for your shopping pleasure.

The **Priamar Palace** has been restored to house the museums and exhibits that record Savona's rich history. It is a pleasure to wander through and soak up the historic pageantry of the region. In the medieval *centro storico* you'll find the **Leon Pancarda** and **Brandale Towers** overlooking this ancient city center as well as the port.

Savona is one of the major cities along the **Riviera delle Palme** and as such it has all the amenities of larger cities, but is also able to maintain somewhat of a quaint and quiet character. If you're looking for a small, sleepy little port, Savona is not for you. But if you want wonderful sights, great nightlife, excellent restaurants and a wild, uniquely Italian vacation, Savona hits the spot.

Arrivals & Departures

Located 33 kilometers from Genoa, you can either come by car on the A10 Autostrada or Route 1 that motors along the sea. Route 1 can get a little crowded in the summer months. You can also arrive by train without having to worry about traffic.

Where to Stay

1. MARE HOTEL, *Via Nizza 89/r, 17100 Savona. Tel. 019/264-065 and 805-633, Fax 019/263-277. 65 rooms all with bath. Single E50-75; Double E60-110. Credit cards accepted. *****

This *palazzo* by the sea, about 1.5 kilometers from the center of Savona, offers instant access to the clear blue Mediterranean, as well as intimate privacy on your own beachfront area. The entrance has a modern feel with light gray and bright blue tones everywhere. The restaurant is just as stimulating with giant tanks of fish and lobsters for your viewing and dining pleasure. The rooms are nice, quite ample and furnished in a simple but comfortable style. The bathrooms are large and filled with every modern convenience. Near the sea they have a garden setting with palm and banana trees as well as countless flowers, where you can savor an evening cocktail. A great place to stay.

2. RIVIERA SUISSE, *Via Paleocapa 24, 17100 Savona. Tel. 019/850-853, Fax 019/853-435. E-mail:g.monti@rivierasuissehotel.it. Web:www.rivierasuissehotel.it. 73 rooms, 70 with bath. Single E50-70; Double Double E75-95 Credit cards accepted. ****

Centrally located between the train station and the port, this is an old establishment, opened in 1880 but recently renovated in 1990. The ambiance and simple, pleasant character of this place are its strong points. The bar and restaurant have a grand piano strategically gracing the area. The rooms are all furnished differently. Some are basic with modest bathrooms, but there are fourteen that are more modern and quite a bit more comfortable. Ask for one of these if you stay here.

Where to Eat

3. IN BARBA AL TIRANNO, *Via Cimarosa 4r. Tel. 019/803-029. Closed Mondays (not in summer), two weeks in February and one in October. Credit cards accepted. Dinner for two E70.*

The cuisine here is Ligurian-influenced with a creative flair. You'll find traditional dishes (like *pesto*) alongside wildly imaginative concoctions (like marinated salmon in pear sauce). A fun and tasty dish is the *lasagnette di pesce con zenzero* (fish lasagna with a ginger sauce). They also grill wonderful meats and fish if you want to keep it simple. If you don't want to have to choose, they offer a gourmet menu course for only E28 where you can sample a *primo*, *secondo* and a dessert. For all the creative flair the ambiance is simple, almost like being at home.

4. OSTERIA BACCO, *Via Quadra 17/19r. Tel. 019/833-5350. Closed Sundays, Easter, August and Christmas. Credit cards accepted. Dinner for E45.*

In a festive local atmosphere, Bacco offers up genuine and tasty seafood dishes. All imaginable seafood is prepared here: tuna, swordfish, octopus and more. I really love their fried octopus and potatoes with a sprinkling of rosemary (*fritelle di rosmarino e polpo con patate*). Their *ravioli di pesce*

(seafood ravioli) and *spaghetti ai frutti di mare* are also exquisite. Grilled or fried fish is the staple for seconds. The house wine is local, robust and wonderful.

5. VINO E FARINATA, *Via Pia 15/r. No telephone. Closed September. No credit cards. Dinner for two E30.*

In two nondescript rooms with seating for about 120, this place is always packed with locals. The food is great, simple, inexpensive and authentic Ligurian and Savonese dishes. You'll only find regional bottled wine here, and a full bodied house wine offering as well. For real local atmosphere and cooking, this is the place to come. The *pesto* is perfect, the fish grilled delectably, and the service is attentive. You shouldn't miss this place for an authentic evening out.

Practical Information
• **Tourist Information Office,** *Via Paleocapa 23/6. Tel. 019/820-522*

Borgio Verezzi

The dual village of **Borgio Verezzi** sits at the foot of a mountain that helps to protect it from the gusts of the north winds. This is really two towns: **Borgio**, down by the beach, is the local resort with all manner of water sports and the scenic **Grotte di Valdemino** with their wonderful display of stalactites thousands of years old; and the upper hamlet of **Verezzi**, which has a more quaint and ancient feel to it, with its Saracen stone buildings and quiet life compared to its brother village below. You can find the impressive bell tower of **Santo Stefano** near here.

In August this little town is taken over by theater attendees from all over the world who flock to the famous **Festival Teatrale**. If you are looking for a beach resort, with its accompanying hustle and bustle, as well as a medieval town setting, this village with an identity crisis is for you.

Arrivals & Departures

Located 28 kilometers from Savona, you can either come by car on the A10 Autostrada or Route 1 that motors along the sea. Route 1 can get a little crowded in the summer months. You can also arrive by train without having to worry about traffic.

Where to Stay

VILLA DELLE ROSE, *Via Sauro 1, 17022 Borgio Verezzi. Tel. 019/610-461, Fax the same. 44 rooms all with bath. Single E40-50; Double E55-80. Credit cards accepted. Full board E30-50.* ***

One of the oldest hotels in town, and their prices reflect that seniority.

Filled with character and charm that harks back to yesteryear. Still a little rough around the edges, despite the renovation in 1994, but that adds character. You can get some fine food served at their restaurant, a bucolic garden setting, and clean and comfortable rooms with eclectic antique furnishings. They also have TVs in the rooms, but no air conditioning.

VILLA GLORIA, *Via XXV Aprile 58, 17022 Borgio Verezzi. Tel. 019/610-571, Fax 019/611-908. 31 rooms all with bath, Single E30; Double E45. Credit cards accepted. Full board E40-45. ***

No air conditioning here either, but they do have a private beach where you can relax after using their fitness facilities. A small three star with clean and comfortable rooms that are a little plain. This town is so small that these two options are the cream of the crop. Definitely not the Excelsior in Rome, but you will have a pleasant and comfortable stay with either option.

Where to Eat

DA CASETTA, *Piazza San Pietro 12. Tel. 019/610-166. Closed Tuesdays (but not from June through August) and November. Credit cards accepted. Dinner for two E45.*

The Bianchi family owns this restaurant, which offers perfectly authentic Ligurian cuisine with tastes and smells that will tantalize you throughout your meal. The *antipasto* is so abundant that a meal may not be necessary after you have the stuffed vegetables, grilled chicken, pasta salads, marinated olives, cold cuts and more. This is the perfect place to try some *picagge* (Ligurian fettucine) *al pesto* (in a basil, garlic, olive oil sauce) and *fiori di zucca ripieni* (stuffed pumpkin flower). The brick interior is a perfect compliment to the rustic and traditional cooking.

Practical Information

• **Tourist Information Office**, *Via Mateotti. Tel. 019/610-412*

Albenga

Developed in the 1st century BCE by the Romans and named Albingaunum, the town of **Albenga** was the local capital. In the 5th century BCE, it was the seat of the Roman Catholic Diocese. A beautiful town, part resort, part history lesson, Albenga is an enjoyable vacation spot and a rewarding place to visit.

Arrivals & Departures

Located 44 kilometers from Savona, you can either come by car on the A10 Autostrada or Route 1 that motors along the sea. Route 1 can get a little crowded in the summer months. You can also arrive by train without having to worry about traffic.

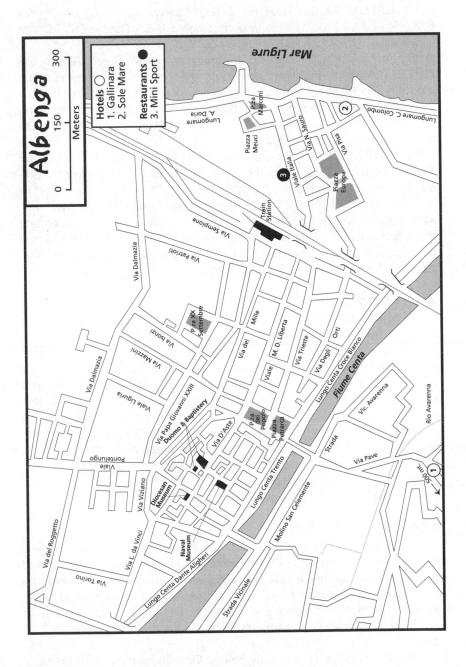

Where to Stay

1. GALLINARA, *Via Piave 66, 17031 Albenga. Tel. 0182/53086, Fax 0182/541-280. 25 rooms all with bath. Single E45-65; Double E65-75. Visa accepted. Full board E30-50. Breakfast E5.* ***

Located a little ways outside of the main town on the way to Alassio, this place is situated in a modern building with a discrete facade. The rooms are modestly appointed, all of which - except those on the ground floor - have cute little balconies. The bathrooms with shower are clean and modern. Everything about this place is simple and basic but comfortable. There are TVs in the rooms but no air conditioning.

2. SOLE MARE, *Lungomare Colombo 15, 17031 Albenga. Tel. 0182/ 51817, Fax 0182/52752. 22 rooms, 20 with bath. Single E50-70; Double E70-80. No credit cards accepted. Full board E60-70.* ***

Located along the sea, this place is a basic, simple hotel with few amenities, except the proximity to the water. They do have an adequate restaurant and rooms that were modernized in 1993 to include TVs and new bath furnishings. A little distance from the main town, just past the train station, here you'll have a nice seaside stay.

Where to Eat

3. MINISPORT, *Viale Italia 35. Tel. 0182/555-118. Closed Wednesdays and Oct. 1-15. Credit cards accepted. Dinner for two E60.*

Inside a game park, the Minisport serves up typical Ligurian fish dishes made the traditional way. The *antipasto* is extensive enough for an entire meal with fish, vegetables, meats, and pasta salads. Their *spaghetti alla marinara* (sea food) or *alla vongole* (clams) are both great, as is their *riso alla marinara* (rice seafood dish). For seconds they grill a superb fish and prepare a succulent *fritto misto* (mixed fried fish dish). And just like the *antipasto* all the portions are more than generous. You can also get a gourmet meal for only E28 if you don't want to order from the menu. The wine list is not that extensive, but is in the process of being upgraded once they build a bigger wine cellar. A good place for a perfect local meal whether inside or on their terrace.

Seeing the Sights

The historic town center is part Roman, medieval, Renaissance and Baroque and loaded with character and ambiance. The cathedral and baptistery, both built in the 5th century BCE, are amazing sights to behold. The **baptistery** has its colorful mosaics and sculptures, and the **cathedral** has its Romanesque-Gothic influence and impressive bell tower. There are the 12 imposing 12th-14th century **towers** to be seen and photographed all over town.

A must-see is the 16th century **Peloso Cepolla** palace with its medieval tower that houses the **Roman Naval Museum**, with remains of amphorae from a 1st century BCE Roman freighter that was resurrected just off the coast of Albenga. Another interesting visit is the **Diocesan Museum**, which houses late medieval sculptures, frescoes, jewels and valuable canvases.

Practical Information
• **Tourist Information Office**, *Via B. Ricci. Tel. 019/554-752*

Andora

On the hill behind the town, the ruins of the **ancient castle** lie watching over the historic town of **Andora** and its famous seaside resort. Considered one of the most characteristic resorts on the Riviera delle Palme, Andora has charm, grace, character, and style. Besides the obvious sunbathing, swimming, sailing and other water sports, you can also view the Gothic **church of Saints James and Philip** and a stunning ten arched **medieval bridge**. Small and serene, Andora will soothe you into a peaceful stay.

Arrivals & Departures

Located 60 kilometers from Savona, you can either come by car on the A10 Autostrada or Route 1 that motors along the sea. Route 1 can get a little crowded in the summer months. You can also arrive by train without having to worry about traffic.

Where to Stay

ARISTON, *Via Aurelia 75, 17020 Andora. Tel. 0182/6101, Fax 0182/ 85008. 16 rooms all with bath. Single and Double E60-90. Credit cards accepted. Full board E60-90.* ****

The place to stay in Andora. Swimming pool, private beach, sauna, fitness center, fine food, shuttle bus service, along with air conditioning and TV in the rooms all add up to a comfortable stay. Small and intimate - like a bed and breakfast - but with clean, comfortable and modern amenities, this is a wonderful place to stay while in Andora.

TRIESTE, *Via Aurelia 87, 17020 Andora. Tel. 0182/85041, Fax 0182/684-419. 24 rooms all with bath. Single and Double E45-65. Credit cards accepted. Full board E35-50.* ***

A simple little place with a private beach as the only real amenity – that and a shuttle bus service. In a peaceful and calm setting near the Ariston above, the Trieste was established in 1953 and renovated in 1982, so it may appear a little worn around the edges, but your rooms and bathrooms are kept comfortable and clean. An inexpensive option while in Andora.

Where to Eat

LA CASA DEL PRIORE, *Via Castello 34. Tel. 0184/87330. Closed Mondays (not in the summer) and Jan. 2 through Feb. 10. Credit cards accepted. Dinner for two E90.*

The cuisine is Ligurian with a touch of creativity thrown in. Next to the restaurant is a piano bar you can enjoy after your meals – but don't miss the meal. It will be great. You can get a gourmet fixed price meal for E40, for which you'll get two *antipasti*, two pasta, one second course and a dessert. Perfect for two people. If you order *a la carte* it will be a little more expensive. To whet your appetite, the house offers free Spumante and small appetizers. The pastas are wonderful, especially the *ravioli neri ripieni di pesce lama al pomodoro* (black ravioli stuffed with swordfish in a tomato sauce) as well as the *tagliatelli al ragu di polpo e zucca* (pasta in a sauce of octopus and pumpkin).

For seconds you can't go wrong with the surf or the turf. They grill an amazing sole and white fish, and make a succulent *filetto di Angus* (Angus beef filet). And if you are into desserts, this restaurant supplies an army of options.

Practical Information

• **Tourist Information Office**, *Via San Daminao 1. Tel. 019/85796*

San Remo

The historic resort town of **San Remo** is in the center of the tiny **Riviera dei Fiori** (Riviera of Flowers), close to the French border. Even though there are over 2,000 varieties of flowers in agricultural cultivation in and around San Remo, still the most characteristic plant is the palm. Besides the local flora, San Remo is awash with sumptuous villas in which you will find some of the most amazing art. It is also home to a gloriously romantic medieval section of town (**La Pigna**), with winding cobblestone streets meeting together in small squares and exiting down covered passageways. San Remo contains wonderful hotels built at the turn of the century, is home to exquisite restaurants with some of the most scintillating Ligurian food, boasts an excellent 18-hole golf course, and has all imaginable water sports available. San Remo has it all.

San Remo was popularized in part by the Czarina Maria Alexandrovna who brought the nobles from her country to this small little Ligurian town around the turn of the century. As a sleepy little village in existence for over 1,000 years, San Remo was doing quite fine, thank you very much, but from 1874 to 1906, more than 190 villas and 25 hotels were built to accommodate the influx of nobility from all over the world who were attracted by the

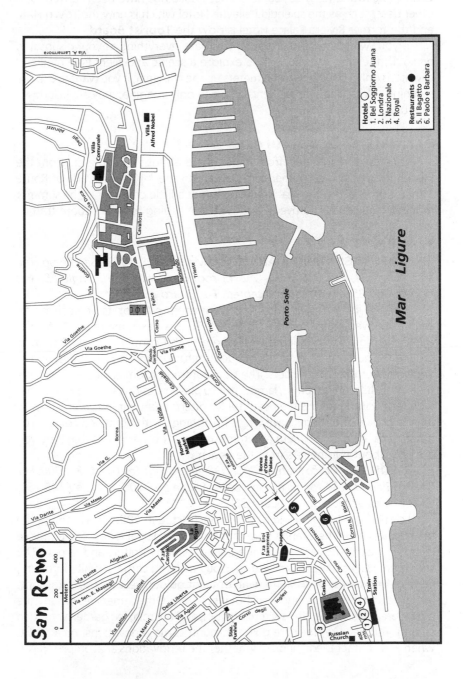

San Remo

Mar Ligure

Porto Sole

Hotels ◯
1. Bel Soggiorno Juana
2. Londra
3. Nazionale
4. Royal
Restaurants ●
5. Il Bagatto
6. Paolo e Barbara

Czarina's patronage. Today some of these buildings have been converted to other uses, such as the splendid Bellevue Hotel which is now the **Town Hall**, and the former Riviera Palace Hotel is now the **Tourist Board**.

If you want to be a beach bum, you have everything at your disposal to do so. If, the next day you wish to explore a scenic and silent little medieval town, it is only a couple hundred meters up the hill. Next, if you want to explore stunning villas, filled with opulence you can only imagine, they are just down the road.

Arrivals & Departures

Located 26 kilometers from Imperia and about 20 kilometers from the French border, you can either come by car on the A10 Autostrada or Route 1 that motors along the sea. Route 1 can get a little crowded in the summer months. You can also arrive by train without having to worry about traffic.

Where to Stay

1. BEL SOGGIORNO JUANA, *Corso Matuzia 41, 18038 San Remo. Tel. 0184/667-631, Fax 0184/667-471. 43 rooms all with bath. Single E50-65; Double E65-85. Credit cards accepted. Full board E50-70.* ***

Opened in 1910, this hotel has maintained much of its original charm, even if its overall glamour is a bit faded. That is easily made up for by the numerous flowers and plants everywhere in the common areas. Displayed around the hotel you'll also find antique furniture from the turn of the century and well worn Persian carpets. The best common room is where they serve meals with its many columns, lamps, stucco plaster designs and more. Another wonderful sitting area is the beautiful Mediterranean garden verandah with lounge chairs. The rooms have white furnishings with floral bed covers. The bathrooms are a little old but accommodating. Another plus is that here you are only about two meters from the beach.

2. LONDRA, *Corso Matuzia 2, 18038 San Remo. Tel. 0184/668-000, Fax 0184/668-073. 134 rooms all with bath. Single E85-100; Double E125-150. Credit cards accepted. Full board E125-150.* ****

Located in a beautiful old *palazzo* constructed in 1850, this is one of the great hotels from the Czarina's era that is still wonderful today. The entrance is impressive with its size and arrangement of period furniture and carpets. The rooms are just as magnificent and spacious with red carpets, white furniture, curtains and bed spreads that are an opulent golden yellow. The bathrooms are large and the fixtures modern, but just barely. Other amenities include the ample breakfast buffet, the swimming pool, and the relaxing garden verandah setting. But beware, they are going through some renovations. As a result, when you contact them, find out whether the renovations are completed yet.

3. NAZIONALE, *Corso Matteotti 3, 18038 San Remo. Tel. 0184/577-577, Fax 0184/541-535. E-mail:nazionale.im@bestwestern.it. 78 rooms all with bath. Single E75-100; Double E105-120. Credit cards accepted. Full board E110-120. *****

The last remaining grand hotel situated near the casino, this wonderful old *palazzo* underwent a perfect reconstruction in 1993 to bring it into the modern world. The doors are now opened by magnetic strip cards and not the quaint keys they used to have, but the renovations couldn't snuff out the ambiance and personal attention that made this hotel one of the best since 1904. The rooms are all well appointed with period pieces and accented with floral curtains and bedcovers. The bathrooms were given the most modern of makeovers in the reconstruction and now have all amenities. One of the last great hotels left.

4. ROYAL HOTEL, *Corso Imperatrice 80, 18038 San Remo. Tel. 0184/5391. E-mail:royal@royalhotelsanremo.com. Web:www.royalhotelsanremo.com. 202 rooms all with bath. Single E105-200; Double E180-310. Credit cards accepted. Full board E118-195. ******

Another of the all-time great places to stay. This is a fantastic five star filled with every luxury you could imagine. It is opulent in every detail. There are tennis courts, a swimming pool, sauna, shuttle bus service, beautiful garden verandah, an excellent but expensive restaurant, private beach, child care services and more. This is the place to stay in San Remo if you have the means. Every need you have will be catered to.

Where to Eat

5. IL BAGATTO, *Via Matteotti 145. Tel. 0184/531-925. Closed Sundays and from June 15 to July 15. Credit cards accepted. Dinner for two E70.*

Situated in an old *palazzo*, this place has refined cuisine at a reasonable price. If you don't want to order from the menu, there is a fixed price option for E20 and another for E30 per person. If you go *a la carte* you have to try their *risotto alla marinara* (seafood rice dish). Also all their grilled or oven baked fish dishes are superb. Their wine list is quite extensive with over 400 labels from Italy, the rest of Europe, California and South Africa. Great food, wonderful atmosphere and perfect service. The air conditioning comes in handy in summer too.

6. PAOLO E BARBARA, *Via Roma 47. Tel. 0184/531-653. Closed Wednesdays and in Summer also Thursdays at lunch. Credit cards accepted. Dinner for two E80.*

Only about 30 seats are available here in this elegant restaurant. Barbara is always bustling around making sure everyone is happy, and Paolo is in the kitchen ensuring the food quality is perfect. The staples of the menu are fish from the sea and vegetables from the mountains, all creatively cooked together to develop a culinary symphony in your mouth. Or in layman's terms, scrumptious with an original twist. You can't go wrong here, but you will need to order an entire Italian meal if you're really hungry since the portions are a little small. *Buon Appetito!*

Seeing the Sights

Some of the most refined and elegant **villas** are on the Corso degli Inglesi, which runs from the Casino out of the west side of town. They are not open to the public, but just taking a stroll and soaking up the exquisite gardens and architectural refinement is a treat. This *passegiatta* is akin to, but much better than, a walk through some of the old neighborhoods in New Orleans.

Next, along the eastern part of town on the Corso Felice Cavallotti, are other stunning villas, two of which you can enter and browse through. The first, **Villa Nobel**, was the property of the Swedish scientist who invented TNT, but not wanting to be remembered for such a calamitous invention, devised the concept of and funded the Nobel Prize. In the villa is a permanent collection of Nobel relics and a gallery of Italian Nobel Prize winners. The second, **Villa Ormond**, has incredibly rich and lush gardens accented by spewing fountains and the ever-present palm trees.

Other sights to see are the **Russian Orthodox church** built by Czarina Maria Alexandrovna, the **Borea d'Olmo Palace** that houses the informative **Civic Museum** with its beautifully frescoed vaults in the hallway, and the **San Siro Duomo** and its baptistery. Last but not least, the town does have a magnificent casino, where you can not only gamble but revel in the opulence of yesteryear.

Practical Information

• **Tourist Information Office**, *Largo Nuovalini 1. Tel. 0184/571-571/2/3*

Bordighera

On the Riviera dei Fiori almost at the French border, **Bordighera** is an elegant seaside holiday resort known for its mild climate, stunning beauty and lush vegetation. The old town sits on a hill with a commanding view over the sea. Originally a fishing village – the steep slopes provided protection from marauding pirates – the town started to develop along the coastal plains in the late 1800s to accommodate the influx of tourists. In the 'modern' town below are some exquisite hotels that stand among beautiful flowering gardens and tree-lined avenues. Bordighera has been a favorite of cosmopolitan travelers for over a century.

At the turn of the century it hosted illustrious artists, scholars, nobles, and other aristocrats. Included in this group was the famous artist Claude Monet, who so loved the vibrant colors in the area that he featured them in many of his paintings.

Arrivals & Departures

Located 37 kilometers from Imperia and about 10 kilometers from the French border, you can either come by car on the A10 Autostrada or Route 1 that motors along the sea. Route 1 can get a little crowded in the summer months. You can also arrive by train without having to worry about traffic.

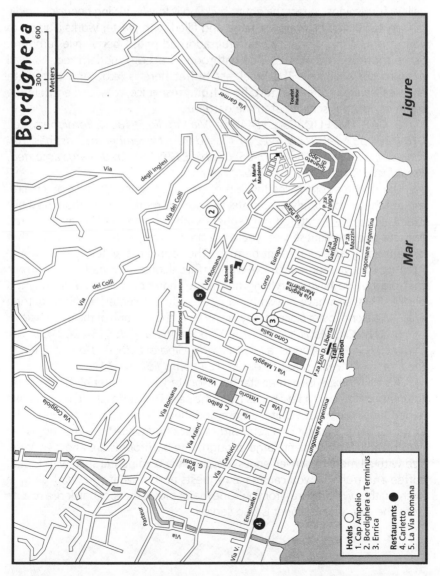

Where to Stay

1. BORDIGHERA E TERMINUS, *Corso Italia 21, 18012 Bordighera. Tel. 0184/260-561, Fax 0184/265-727. E-mail:info@bordigheraterminus.com. Web:www.bordigheraterminus.com. Closed in November. 28 rooms all with bath. Single E16; Double E35-60. Minimum three nights. Credit cards accepted. Breakfast included. Full Board E45-50.* ***

In the center of the 'modern' town the hotel has lush garden setting where the restaurant is located. The entrance hall is elegant with its golden yellow furnishings. In fact the entire building is lovely, having been splendidly built in 1850. The hallways are large and filled with plaster works leading to your rooms, which are very beautiful, adorned with Liberty style furniture. Some rooms have balconies. The bathrooms, recently modernized, have all modern conveniences. The breakfast buffet here is large and tasty with cheeses, salamis, cereal, yogurt, fresh fruit, fresh juice, rolls, and eggs. In the summer, lunch is served out in the garden.

2. CAP AMPELIO, *Conca D'Africa, Via Virgilio 5, 18012 Bordighera. Tel. 0184/264-333, Fax 0184/244-244. Closed from November to Christmas. 104 rooms all with bath. Single E75-85; Double E120-140. Credit cards accepted. Breakfast E5. Full board E90-120.* ****

Located in a zone called the 'basin (*conca*) of Africa' because of a micro-climate that is constantly temperate, the hotel is more modern than most but is able to create a cultured atmosphere with the fine furnishings, flowered terraces and excellent service. There is a circular bar just off the main hall that is manned by an ever-present barman. The rooms are all fully carpeted and furnished in style. Some also have wonderful balconies. The bathrooms are not that big but do have everything and more than you will need, including a phone. They also have a swimming pool, a fitness center, and lush garden area. A relaxing, quiet place to stay, away from the hubbub of the town below.

3. ENRICA, *Via Novaro 1, 18012 Bordighera. Tel. 0184/263-436, Fax 0184/261-344. 22 rooms all with bath. Single E40-50; Double E50-70. Breakfast E3. Credit cards accepted. Full board E50-60.* ***

A small, inexpensive three star hotel located in the center of the 'modern' town as well as only a few paces from the sea. The atmosphere is not unlike a bed and breakfast. Quite accommodating, familial, and friendly. The entrance hall is a quaint checkerboard of black and white tiles. The rooms are comfortably furnished and large enough. The bathrooms are about average size with all modern conveniences. Breakfast is continental style with bread, coffee and fruit, but you can make requests and, if what you want is in the kitchen, they will prepare it for you. One major plus is the roof garden, a respite from the day, where dinner is also served.

Where to Eat

4. CARLETTO, *Via Vittorio Emanuele 339. Tel. 0184/261-725. Closed Wednesdays, June 27 to July 15, and November 8 to December 22. Credit cards accepted. Dinner for two E90.*

The Pessina brothers offer up some wonderful food here in a quaint and comfortable environment with an emphasis on fish dishes. The servings are ample and if you don't want to order *a la carte* you can get a gourmet meal for only E33 per person. I love their *zuppetta di vongole verace* (soup of spicy clams) and the *pesce spada affumicato* (smoked swordfish). The desserts are sinful, especially the *piatto misto di dessert* (mixed dessert plate) that gives you a sample of everything. The wine list is amazing and can really only be appreciated by those with the most refined palate, i.e., not me.

5. LA VIA ROMANA, *Via Romana 57. Tel. 0184/266-681. Closed Wednesdays and Thursdays at lunch. Credit cards accepted. Dinner for two E90.*

Located on one of the most beautiful streets in the Italian Riviera, this restaurant is housed in one of the buildings from the 'belle époque,' built at the turn of the century and filled with Liberty style furnishings. The menu is naturally dominated by seafood and you can get some of the best tastes of Mediterranean cuisine here. For *antipasto* try the delicious *cus-cus con pesce bianco* (Arab-style pasta with white fish), *la zuppetta di vongole e gamberi rossi* (soup with clams and red prawns), or the ever tasty *bruschetta al peperoncini* (garlic bread with hot peppers).

Most of the pasta dishes are typical Ligurian with *pesto* as the base. Delicious. For seconds you cannot go wrong with any of the grilled or fried fish offerings. They also offer five different set menu options with interesting combinations of different dishes for a set price. A great way to sample the local cuisine.

Seeing the Sights

Of touring interest are the winding streets of the **old town**, especially the 17th century **Santa Maria Madelena**; the **Marabutto**, an ancient stone battery surrounded by lush pines; the **tourist harbor** with some remaining local fishing boats; the **Bicknell Museum** that houses local historical and archaeological information; and the **International Civic Museum**, which contains the second largest collection of English language books in Italy. A leisurely stroll through Bordighera's quaint and charming streets is a great way to spend a day.

Practical Information

• **Tourist Information Office**, *Via Roberto 1. Tel. 0184/262-322*

Chapter 19

Milan

Milan is Italy's chief industrial, financial, and commercial center. Left untouched during the "war to end all wars," 60 percent of the city was destroyed by bombings during World War II, but within a decade the industrious people of Milan had rebuilt their city. Unfortunately the 60 percent that was destroyed was some of the finest architecture in Italy.

Today Milan is where Italy gets down to business. Image is everything is this frenetic trendy town; but beautiful is not the first word that springs to mind when describing Milan. Known around the world as the capital of high fashion and slick design, Milan is the mecca of elegance and taste. Yet the actual physical presence of Milan is oddly unappealing. The buildings are fundamentally bland and the city seems devoid of vibrant *piazze* and other places for the locals to gather.

As someone who grew up in Rome, each time I visit Milan I search for hints of those items that are purely Italian – a baroque church facade on a small side street, a *palazzo* the warming color of ocher, or a *piazza* with a Bernini fountain teeming with families at play – but am always left disappointed. The quiet provincial capital that used to have such features no longer exists. Milan has been swallowed up by commercialism. The *piazza* culture found everywhere else in the country has been erased in Milan along with the human face of the city. As a result, Milanese feel themselves to be, both in physical and spiritual terms, closer to Zurich than to Rome, and more European than Italian.

Even with a lack of overall beauty, the city's Gothic **cathedral** is one of the largest and most attractive churches in the world, rising like a brilliant white crown in the heart of the city. Another great church is that of **Sant' Ambrogio**, built in the 4th century, where St. Ambrose baptized St. Augustine, and many emperors were crowned with the "iron crown" of Lombardy. Nearby stands the former convent of **Santa Maria delle Grazie**, where Leonardo da Vinci's famous but oddly disappointing *The Last Supper* is painted on the refectory wall. If you come to Milan you have to see this.

Brera Palace is the home of the **Academy of Fine Arts and Science**. Its galleries contain works by the great Italian masters and other artists. **La Scala**, Milan's opera house, is world-renowned. The city has two famous libraries, three universities, a school of commerce and agriculture, an academy of music, and a celebrated archaeological museum.

As Italy's greatest railway center, Milan sits at the junction of lines crossing the Alps via the **Simplon Tunnel** and **St. Gotthard passes**. Other lines lead east to Venice and south to Genoa and peninsular Italy. The road network converging upon Milan carries a constant flow of foreign and national tourists.

Insight Into Milan

Milan is a thoroughly modern city steeped in commerce and high fashion. The hectic pace, where meals are rushed, is so unlike any other Italian city that it will seem as if you are in another country. The regular Italian piazza culture that helps create community all over Italy does not exist here. The only way people have a collective experience anymore is by watching the same show or soccer game on the TV. The fast pace, the lack of a sense of community, and the fact that the city is geared around big business all make Milan less Italian and increasingly more European.

Hotels in Milan mainly cater to businessmen who are attending some convention or another. Tourists are basically an afterthought here. And the sights, save for the imposing Gothic Cathedral and Da Vinci's Last Supper, are few and far between, because Milan was virtually razed during World War II and rebuilt soon after. But if you are an opera fan, **La Scala**, the most famous opera house in the world, beckons. And if you want to see the most exquisite selection of foods anywhere in the known world, come here to shop and eat at the many **Peck's** stores. Other than that, Milan can easily be missed.

But if you do come to Milan you ought to see **The Last Supper**, go up on the observation deck of the Cathedral, visit the **Leonardo Da Vinci Museum of Science and Technology**, and go to the **Fiera Sinigallia market** at Porta Ticinese, which is held every Saturday. Otherwise you haven't been to Milan.

Milan is also the starting point for the famous Italian scenic route called the **Autostrada del Sole** (Highway of the Sun).

Milan is the largest of the industrial cities of northern Italy, where most of the country's manufacturing is done, of which the textile, printing and publishing, chemical, and machinery industries are the most important. Electricity from Alpine waterfalls furnishes power for this industrial production. Among the products of Milan and its suburbs are airplanes, automobiles, locomotives and railway cars, refrigerators, elevators, bicycles and motorcycles, tires, precision instruments, chemicals and drugs, furniture, and food products. Skilled artisans also create fine jewelry and art wares. The annual **Milan Fair** attracts buyers from all over the world since Italian design is revered internationally. Milan also is home to the largest stock market in Italy.

Brief History
Because of its location Milan has a long history of raids and invasions. The city started as Mediolanum, a Gallic town, and was taken over by the Romans in 222 BCE. It was burned a number of times – once by the Huns, twice by the Goths, and again by the German, Frederick Barbarossa in 1162.

After a period of civil strife, the house of **Visconti** gained control of this powerful city-state. When the last Visconti duke died in 1447, three years later the rule of the **Sforzas** began, and continued until 1535. Most of the ancient beauty of the city was created by the heads of these two great houses. When the Sforza line died out, Spain seized Milan and held it until 1706. Then the city fell to Austria, which governed it until Napoleon created his short-lived Kingdom of Italy and made Milan its capital. After Napoleon's fall, Milan was restored to Austria. Then finally in 1859 it was included in the new united kingdom of Italy.

Milan's industry, trade, and population swelled in the period between the two world wars. Currently the population hovers around 1.5 million people. The construction boom after World War II included numerous skyscrapers and factories of modern design, and the streets were widened, eliminating what once was a quaint medieval feel to the city, and turning Milan into a city that accommodates the automobile better than it does human beings.

Arrivals & Departures
By Air
When coming to Milan you will either arrive at **Malpensa**, which handles all incoming flights from North America, Australia, and the United Kingdom, or **Linate**, which handles most of the domestic and other European air traffic. Transportation from Milan's airports is not as sophisticated as is it from Rome's Leonardo da Vinci. From Linate there is **bus service** to the Milan Central Train Station leaving every 20 minutes, and **ATM** Municipal Bus Service #73 from

Piazza San Babila (corner of Corso Europa) every 15 minutes. Duration for both is 30 minutes. From Malpensa, there is a bus that leaves for the Milan Central Train Station every 30 minutes.

Once at the train station you have access to Milan's extensive Metro system, which takes you virtually everywhere you want to go. If you're in more of a hurry or in need of more comfort, take a taxi from in front of the station.

Directly from the airport into town, the quickest but the most expensive way is to take a taxi. The fare starts at E2 and rises rapidly. Be prepared to pay the cost of a night's hotel room for your ride from the airport.

By Bus

Getting in and out of Milan is best done by train – driving is the worst option and bus is almost as bad. Traffic in and around this region is bumper to bumper. The only saving grace for the bus is that you don't actually have to drive. The only time to use a bus around Milan (if you don't have a car) is if the train doesn't go where you're heading.

All inter-city buses leave from the **Piazza Castello** (at the Cairioli metro stop). Each company has its own office located here.

By Car

Driving in Milan is worse than any other city in Italy, if you can imagine that. It's not the drivers who are so bad, but it's that there are so many cars and the city is so large and spread out. Also, as the center of Italian commerce, Milan can be reached by a variety of different avenues from many different locations, making everything completely confusing.

From the east and west the **E64** Autostrada bisects the top part of the city. Arriving from the south you would use the **A1** (**E35**) or the **A7** (**E62**). From the north you can get to Milan on the **A9** (**E35**) and **A8** as well as on countless other smaller thoroughfares. That old saying about how all roads lead to Rome should actually refer to Milan.

If you want to rent a car while in Milan you can do so at both airports and at the locations given in the *Renting a Car* section of this chapter.

Sample trip lengths on main roads:
• **Rome**: 6 hours
• **Venice**: 4 1/2 hours
• **Florence**: 4 hours.

By Train

The **Stazione Centrale** is Milan's primary railway station and it's like a chaotic mini-mall inside. There are all sorts of shops, eateries, a supermarket, two different levels to get lost in, travel agencies, pickpockets, hustlers, and your trusty **tourist office**, *Tel. 02/669-0532*. This station connects Milan with all other major cities in Italy as well as elsewhere in Europe. The other stations

(**Stazione Nord**, **Porta Genova**, and **Porta Garibaldi**) connect Milan to smaller municipalities like Como and Asti.

A word of advice for first timers to Milan: if you can avoid it stay somewhere else other than around the train station. Located north of the center of Milan, the area around the station is away from all the sights and is not in the best neighborhood. It's safe but the ambiance is not as nice as downtown. You will find the best deals here, but as a first time visitor, it's best to hop on the Metro and stay downtown near the Cathedral.

Sample trip lengths and costs for direct *(diretto)* trains:
• **Rome**: 5 hours, E30
• **Venice**: 3 hours, E20
• **Florence**: 3 hours, E25.

Getting Around Town
By Bicycle
They can be rented from **Vittorio Comizzoli**, *Via Washington 60, Tel. 02/ 498-4694*. I would advise against renting a bike, however, since Milan is such a large city, and is definitely not as picturesque as Rome or Florence, so renting a bike would only put you in harm's way and make your visit less than pleasant.

By Foot
Unlike Florence and Venice, and similar to Rome, Milan is a large city that is not the best walking town. That's why they have a huge Metro system. You can walk the city. It's safe. But to get from point A to point B, why not just take the Metro? It only costs Euro 75 cents one way, which is about 70¢. And if the Metro is too much work for you, there's always the ever-present taxis.

By Metro
Find the big red signs with a black "M" which indicate that the **Metropolitana Milanese** is just below. Be prepared for a quick, safe, and efficient ride. The metro was built in the 1960s and is kept immaculate. There are three lines: **red** (#1), **green** (#2), and **yellow** (#3). Since the lines are all color coded, they can be followed quickly and easily. The Metro information number is *02/875-495*.

There are maps everywhere inside and outside the trains, so it is easy to find which train to board. This is a simple, easy, intuitive metro system to use. Parts of it are still under construction, since they have to stop periodically and excavate some ancient Roman ruins they uncover.

Tickets cost Euro 75 cents and are sold at local newsstands in the stations, at tobacconist's shops (the ones marked with a blue "T" sign), at each metro stop, or can be bought from machines in the stations. The lines at station ticket counters are invariably long so buy tickets in advance. Also most of the ticket machines only take coins, and the machines that do take bills are usually out of order. Welcome to the chaos that is Italy (and this is their most modern city). All the machines have easy to use and understandable directions in English, French, Italian, and German but even so the Milanese do not seem to have a grasp of how to use them. I had to show a few Milanese how to use the machines. The Italian culture is so high-touch (i.e., they like to interact with people) that machines scare them, whereas we North Americans have incorporated machines into our daily lives and can figure them out easily.

You can get a map of the Metro system from the FS information counter at the Stazione Centrale. You can bring bikes on the metro with a special pass.

If you know you're going to be taking the Metro frequently while you're staying in Milan, here are a number of options that can save you money. You can get the following types of tickets at the **Stazione Centrale ATM office**, *Tel. 2/669-70-47*, or the **Duomo office**, *Tel. 0/89-01-97*:

• **One day ticket** (24 hours after you stamp it) for E2.5. If you're going to take five trips or more in a two hour period this will save you money. All you need to do is stamp it once then keep it with you in case an inspector hops on the train. You enter through the gates near the central conductor's booth in every station. If the conductor is around you'll need to show him/her the ticket at this point too.

• **Two day ticket** (48 hours after you first stamp it). Same concept and rules as the 1 day (24 hours) ticket. E5.

By Taxi

As in most Italian cities, taxis are everywhere. If you can't locate one on the street, there are plenty of taxi stands all over the city where the taxis line up and wait for fares. Here is a brief list of where some of these taxi stands are located: Piazza del Duomo, Piazza Scala, Piazza Cinque Giornate, Largo San Babila, Largo Treves, Piazzale Baraca and Piazza XIV Maggio.

Here are some radio taxi numbers that may come in handy if you're caught in the rain somewhere. But remember that when you call a taxi to come get you, your fare starts when the taxi leaves for your location, not when the taxi picks you up, like it does most everywhere else.

• **AAAAAAA**, *S Ambrogio, Tel. 02/53-53. Open 24 hours.*
• **La Martesana**, *Tel. 02/52-51*
• **Cooperitiva Esparia**, *Tel. 02/832-12-13*

Renting a Car

I don't recommend renting a car unless you want to take a day trip to a place that cannot be reached by train. Driving in Milan is worse than virtually any city in Italy. But if you have the need to be behind the wheel, here are some rental car agencies you can call.

• **Avis**, *Piazza Duomo 6, Tel. 02/86-343-94/89-01-06-45; or Stazione Centrale, Tel. 02/669-02-90/670-16-54*
• **Hertz**, *Viale Marelli 314, Tel. 02/26-22-33-99*
• **Maggiore**, *Stazione Centrale, Tel. 02/669-0934*

Where To Stay

Milan is not the best city for low-budget tourists, unless you want to stay well off the beaten path, that is, nowhere near a Metro line. In the center of the city, the best location, you only have a few three star hotels and very few two stars. The budget one stars have been relegated to the outskirts, and most are not even near a Metro line. We've listed the best and least expensive three stars we could find, as well as few excellent two stars and all the good four stars.

Another problem with staying in Milan is that it's mainly a convention city, which means that most of the hotels are usually booked for some business convention, mainly dealing with fashion or industry. So remember to reserve well in advance.

1. AMBROSIANO, *Via S. Sofia 9, 20122 Milano. Tel. 02/58-30-60-44, Fax 02/58-30-50-67. Web: www.hotelinformation.com/html/italy/milan/ambrosiano. Closed for Christmas. 40 rooms all with bath. Single E95; Double E140. All credit cards accepted. Breakfast included.* ***

A modern professional hotel in a quiet residential neighborhood. Characteristic of a North American styling and comfort, but with limited charm. They have a small workout room where you can exercise and unwind after your day. Besides the comfort of the rooms, they offer a beautiful garden where you relax and write your postcards after a tough day of touring. Well priced with good amenities.

2. ANTICA LOCANDA SOLFERINO, *Via Castefidardo 2, Tel. 02/656-905. Closed in August. 11 rooms all with bath. Single E90; Double E110. All credit cards accepted. Breakfast included.* **

In a charming neighborhood with an excellent restaurant literally surrounding the hotel, this place has more character than charm. Meaning, the rooms are somewhat clean, comfortable and well priced, but the proprietress leaves me cold. Also the entrance is located next to the restaurant of the same name which stays open until 1-2am, and the rooms are located above it. This does not make for a good night's rest. Try someplace else unless you are a night owl and like surly service.

3. ARIOSTO, *Via Ariosto 22, Tel. 02/481-7844, Fax 02/498-0516. Web: http://brerahotels.com/ariosto. Closed in August. 38 rooms all with bath. Single E140; Double E180. All credit cards accepted. Breakfast included.* ***

A clean, upper-middle class hotel that is plain, plastic, ultra-hygienic ... but it's located in the middle of nowhere. If you want to get away from it all, this

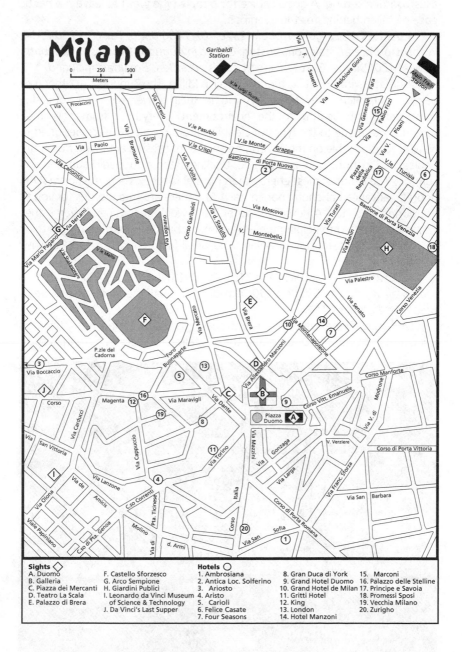

Sights ◇
A. Duomo
B. Galleria
C. Piazza dei Mercanti
D. Teatro La Scala
E. Palazzo di Brera

F. Castello Sforzesco
G. Arco Sempione
H. Giardini Publici
I. Leonardo da Vinci Museum
  of Science & Technology
J. Da Vinci's Last Supper

Hotels ○
1. Ambrosiana
2. Antica Loc. Solferino
3. Ariosto
4. Aristo
5. Carioli
6. Felice Casate
7. Four Seasons

8. Gran Duca di York
9. Grand Hotel Duomo
10. Grand Hotel de Milan
11. Gritti Hotel
12. King
13. London
14. Hotel Manzoni

15. Marconi
16. Palazzo delle Stelline
17. Principe e Savoia
18. Promessi Sposi
19. Vecchia Milano
20. Zurigho

is the place to come. They have all the amenities of a good three star including a lush garden setting. A good choice for people who want to leave the hectic pace of Milan behind for the evenings.

4. ARISTON, *Largo Carrobbio 2. Tel. 02/7200-0556, Fax 02/7200-0914. Web: http://brerahotels.com/ariston. Closed in August. 48 rooms all with bath. Single E120; Double E170. All credit cards accepted. Breakfast included.* ***

A great environmentally friendly hotel in Milan. The Zurigho is another (see below, #20). Here they do everything in their power to make your stay comfortable and healthy to the environment. Everything from how their furniture was made to the types of cleaning products they use are designed to be as safe as possible on the environment. The mattresses are made from pure unbleached cotton, and are double thickness for orthopedic support and comfort. The lamps use less energy than normal fixtures. There is a no smoking floor, an advanced phenomenon in Italy. And there are free bicycles for you to use during your stay. An excellent hotel that I would recommend even if they weren't committed to helping the environment, but because of that I can think of no better place to stay in Milan. The breakfast consists of tasty organic products.

5. CAIROLI, *Via Porlezza 4. Tel. 02/801371, Fax 02/7200-2243. 38 rooms all with bath. Single E100; Double E150. All credit cards accepted. Breakfast included.* ***

Managed by the ever vigilant Andrea Magistradi, this priceless little hotel is located between the Duomo and the Castello Sforzecca in a tranquil spot.

Milan's Top Hotels

Five Star
7. THE FOUR SEASONS, *Via Gesu 8, 20120 Milano. Tel. 02/77088, Fax 02/7708-5000, Toll free number in Italy 167/801-203. Web: www.fourseasons.com/milan/index.html.*

Four Star
9. GRAND HOTEL DUOMO, *Via San Raffaele 1. Tel. 02/8833, Fax 02/8646-2027. Web: www.grandhotelduomo.com.*

Three Star
4. ARISTON, *Largo Carrobbio 2. Tel. 02/7200-0556, Fax 02/7200-0914. Web: http://brerahotels.com/ariston.*

Two Star
19. VECCHIA MILANO, *Via Borromei 4, Tel. 02/875-042 and 02/875-971, Fax 02/8645-4292.*

Located on a small side street, they have a sauna and sunning area for relaxing. Also near the Carioli metro stop, they are ideally located away from but accessible to all sights. A good choice when in Milan.

6. FELICE CASATI, *Via Casati 18. Tel. 02/2940-4208, Fax 02/2940-4618. Web: www.venere.com/it/milano/felicecasati. Closed in August. 50 rooms all with bath. Single E80-135; Double E120-190; All credit cards accepted. Breakfast included.* ***

Basically between the central station and Porta Venezia this place has clean and spacious rooms. Another family-run hotel which virtually guarantees a good stay. Recently renovated, all the furnishings come in calming pastels now. The bathrooms are distinguished by a high level of cleanliness. Breakfast is a little disorganized and is served in a small room which doesn't make for much comfort. If you want it served in your room it comes at a higher price. Metro is within walking distance. A good place to stay in Milan even without A/C.

7. FOUR SEASONS, *Via Gesu 8, 20120 Milano. Tel. 02/77088, Fax 02/ 7708-5000, Toll free number in Italy 167/801-203. Web: www.fourseasons.com/milan/index.html. 98 rooms all with bath. Single E500; Double E650. All credit cards accepted. Breakfast E25.* *****

You will be staying in the lap of luxury in this one of a kind hotel. Situated in a dramatically reborn 15th century ex-convent in the center of Milan, and decorated with delicate antiques, the Four Seasons is a stupendous place to stay, just a tiny step below that of the Principe e Savoia. There are splendid frescoes in the entrance hall, the rooms are ample and comfortable, each uniquely furnished, but all come with video players to accompany the satellite TVs as well as fax machines. The bathrooms are refined and elegant with marble counters and brass fixtures, and come complete with every imaginable accessory. There are two restaurants: La Veranda where you are served breakfast and a quick lunch or dinner, and Al Teatro which has much better atmosphere and is only open for dinners.

The hotel also has conference facilities for the business traveler and a fitness center for health buffs. And besides all these amenities, the service is exquisitely professional, and the entire atmosphere *elegantissimo* – in keeping with the refined reputation for Four Seasons hotels worldwide.

8. GRAND DUCA DI YORK, *Via Moneta 1a. Tel. 02/87-48-63, Fax 02/ 869-03-44. Closed in August. 33 rooms all with bath. Single E110; Double E140. All credit cards accepted. Breakfast E6.* ***

Located in the heart of the historic center, only five minutes from the Cathedral and with easy access to a Metro stop, this is good place to stay. They try to give it a castle-like appearance in the common areas; the rooms are plainly furnished but comfortable. Located in an historic building it has all the necessary amenities of a three star and is in a golden location. They are pet friendly, have a serene garden setting and offer parking services.

9. **GRAND HOTEL DUOMO**, *Via San Raffaele 1. Tel. 02/8833, Fax 02/ 8646-2027. Web: www.grandhotelduomo.com. 153 rooms all with bath. Single E200-300; Double E250-350; Suite E400-550. Breakfast included. All credit cards accepted.* ********

Situated right in the *centro storico* a stone's throw from the cathedral. If you want location this is the place to stay. The hotel is in an old building, and has great views of the Cathedral from some rooms and the dining room, making a stay here a scenic adventure. This would be my recommendation for anyone who is staying in Milan for the first time, since it is ideally located around all the main shopping and sights. They have a good restaurant where a simple continental breakfast is served but they do offer baby-sitting service and are pet friendly.

10. **GRAND HOTEL ET DE MILAN**, *Via Manzoni 29 (at the corner of Via Montenapoleone. Tel. 02/723-141, Fax 02/8646-0861. Web: www.grandhoteletdemilan.it/. 50 rooms. Superior E300-400; Deluxe E400-500; Suites E500-600. All credit cards accepted. Breakfast E15.* *********

In a great location, especially for avid shoppers, with all the extra amenities to make this a deluxe hotel. Their suites are all dedicated to famous personages that have graced their hotel including Verdi, Puccini and the Duke and Duchess of Windsor. There is a convenient reading room with many international newspapers on reading rods like you used to have in school libraries. If that's too sedate for you, the hotel bar attracts a rousing crowd of locals as wells as tourists, so there's always something happening there. If you want to stay in the lap of refined elegance, at an address that is central to the heart of Milan, and have the money to spend, stay here.

11. **GRITTI**, *Piazza SM Beltrade 4. Tel. 02/80-10-56, Fax 02/89-01-09-99. 40 rooms all with bath. Single E80-150; Double E170-250. All credit cards accepted. Breakfast included.* *******

Located at the start of Via Torino, this is a nice hotel. The entrance hall is decorated with antique furnishings, and the bar is where you can relax and strike up a conversation in the evenings. The rooms are all decorated differently but are clean and comfortable and filled with every three star amenity. The bathrooms are a little small, but are new, with red and grey color patterns and come with bath and shower, hair dryer and complimentary toiletry kit. Parking is available and the hotel is pet friendly.

12. **KING**, *Corso Magenta 18. Tel. 02/874-432, Fax 02/8901-0798. Web: www.venere.com/it/milano/king/. 35 rooms all with bath. Single E70-150; Double E100-210. All credit cards accepted. Breakfast included.* *******

Ideally located with clean and comfortable rooms. They have recently completed renovations, which have upgraded their facilities making them a quite nice three star. The rooms are a little tiny, some come with great views over the rooftops, but all have the necessary amenities for a three star like TV, phone, air conditioning, mini-bar, etc. This is an adequately functional hotel in an ideal location.

13. LONDON, *Via Rovello. Tel. 02/7202-0166, Fax 02/805-7037. Closed in August. 29 rooms, 22 with bath. Single without bath E60; Single E70; Double without bath E80; Double E90. All credit cards accepted. Breakfast E6.* ******

This place is nice, but it is definitely overpriced. It's only a two-star, granted in a great location, but not all the rooms have bath. Their prices are the same as the Giulio Cesare, a three star across the street and they don't have nearly as many amenities. There is character and charm here, but not enough for these prices.

14. MANZONI, *Via Santo Spirito 20. Tel. 02/7600-5700, Fax 02/784-212. 35 rooms all with bath. Single E140; Double E180; Suite E200. All credit cards accepted. Breakfast included.* *******

Located on a quiet street within walking distance of the Duomo and La Scala. This is a completely modern hotel in a high rent district. The rooms are tranquil, clean and comfortable, but there are precious few amenities. If you've come to Milan for shopping, this could be your place of residence since they are ideally located for consumer forays.

15. MARCONI, *Via F. Filzi 3. Tel. 02/6698-5561, Fax 02/669-0738. Web: www.venere.com/it/milano/marconi/. Closed August 6-18. 69 rooms all with bath. Single E100; Double E140. All credit cards accepted. Breakfast included.* *******

Located near the central station this is a great family-run hotel. The Groppellis will do anything in their power to make your stay more pleasant. The rooms are spacious and newly renovated with comfortable furnishings and satellite TV. The bathrooms are clean, elegant and functional and come with hair dryer and a complete complimentary toiletry kit. The breakfast is abundant and is served in a small but accommodating ground floor room. In good weather it is served in a quaint inside courtyard garden area. Mainly a businessperson's hotel, it is also a wonderful place to stay as a tourist.

16. PALAZZO DELLE STELLINE, *Corso Magenta 61. Tel. 02/481-8431, Fax 02/8520-7540. E-mail: hotelpalazzostelline@tin.it. Web: www.hotelpalazzostelline.it/. Closed in August. 108 rooms all with bath. Single E110; Double E150. All credit cards accepted. Breakfast included.* *******

In a unique location outside of the main area of Milan but still with good access by Metro, this is an excellent choice when in Milan. The entrance hall is large and well lit with modern design furnishings that contrast well with the history of the *palazzo*. The rooms are filled with modern, pastel colored furniture. Many have balconies with views over the rooftops of Milan. The bathrooms all come with hydro massage bath as well as shower, have a rich complimentary toiletry kit available and hair dryer for your use. As befits a three star there is also satellite TV for your viewing pleasure.

17. PRINCIPE DI SAVOIA, *Piazza della Repubblica 17 (near the Giardini Publici), Tel. 02/62-301, Fax 02/659-5838. Web: www.paradigma.it/hoprinsav.html. All credit cards accepted. 285 rooms all with bath. Single E320-380; Double E380-550. All credit cards accepted. Breakfast E15.* *****

This is one of the most elegant and prestigious hotels in of all Italy. Expensive, ritzy, filled with every amenity imaginable, the service is impeccable. Situated in a neoclassic *palazzo* that evokes a feeling of refined elegance, this hotel has an historic tradition of accomodating the most discerning travelers. Recently absorbed into the ITT Sheraton chain, an amazing transformation has been made. While the Principe has always been elegant, Sheraton's influence has dusted off its hidden charm, and polished the ambiance so the true beauty of this hotel can shine through. The rooms are enormous and delicately furnished with beautiful antiques, with marble bathrooms and modern conveniences. The hotel comes with two restaurants, a fitness center with a lap pool and sauna, and a beauty center. Courtesy limousine service to the center is provided.

18. PROMESSI SPOSI, *Piazza Oberdan 12. Tel. 02/29-51-36-61, Fax 02/2940-4182. Web: www.venere.com/it/milano/promessisposi. Closed in August. 40 rooms all with bath. Single E80. Double E110. All credit cards accepted. Breakfast included.* ***

Located in a residential part of Milan just away from the center, but still on a Metro line, this is a quiet modern hotel that usually caters to business people arriving for Milan's many trade exhibits. The rooms are spartan in character and the simplicity is accentuated with the bamboo furniture. The rooms are all comfortable and quite spacious and the bathrooms come with shower and hair dryer.

19. VECCHIA MILANO, *Via Borromei 4, Tel. 02/875-042 and 02/875-971, Fax 02/8645-4292. 27 rooms all with bath. Single E65; Double E90. Extra person E30. American Express and Visa Accepted. Breakfast Included.* **

Though the rooms are clean and comfortable, they are a little spartan, and in some cases the walls are paper thin. The bathrooms are microscopic and there is no A/C which is a must in some of the summer. It's off the beaten path enough that your stay will be quiet and tranquil in the evenings. This is *the* place to stay in Milan for budget travelers. And when I say budget, I mean do not expect any amenities, save satellite television. Milan has very few low priced hotels. This is one of them, and relative to the rest in the city, it is a great place to stay.

20. ZURIGO, *Corso Italia 11a, 20120 Milano. Tel. 02/7202-2260, Fax 02/7200-0013. Web: http://brerahotels.com/zurigo. Closed December 23 to January 9. 41 rooms all with bath. Single E120; Double E170. All credit cards accepted. Breakfast E5.* ***

Like the Ariston this is an environmentally friendly hotel. The bicycle in the foyer lets you know that bicycles are available for use by the guests free of charge. There is a teeny elevator to bring you up to your rooms which have a jungle feel to them because of the African-style bed covers. The bathrooms are not very big but do have hairdryers and complimentary toiletry kit. A good place to stay with clean and comfortable, if not large, rooms. Just as ecologically conscious as the Ariston since these two places are part of the same chain.

Where To Eat
Milanese Cuisine
Milanese cuisine is a melting pot not only of Italy but also of neighboring nations, particularly France. Even so, there still remains a distinct Milanese style of cooking that uses butter, cheese, milk and cream in what is usually categorized as **Northern Italian** cooking. One item that is used frequently in Milanese cuisine is rice, which comes from the multitude of rice paddies on the outskirts of town. One of the staples is *risotto al salto*, leftover rice fried like a pancake.

You'll notice that many restaurants in Milan subscribe to the concept of *cucina nuova*, an elegant approach to food preparation. For Milan this type of cuisine is a perfect match, since they push the envelope of traditionalism in so many different industries (fashion, jewelry, furnishings, etc.), but as a die-hard Italophile I prefer the traditional style of food preparation.

Another change you might sense in Milan is that it is no longer considered "bad form" to eat a rushed lunch of a *panino* (sandwich) which you can get from a myriad of *paninoteca* (sandwich bars), or to eat a pizza that takes ten minutes to prepare. This trend is exemplified by the growing numbers of *pizzerie*. And for both of these items you can request any number or type of ingredients. So we tourists can order our sandwiches and pizzas prepared any way we want them, instead of being constrained to the set ingredients for both *panini* and pizza as you are in most other Italian cities.

Suggested Milanese Cuisine
Below are the typical offerings of Milanese cuisine.

Antipasto - Appetizer
• **Antipasto misto** – a variety of different food such as cheese, prosciutto, olives, etc., from a buffet

Primo Piatto - First Course
• **Risotto alla Milanese** – a creamy rice dish made with saffron and marrow and is usually bright yellow in color
• **Risotto** (with a variety of ingredients) – The same creamy sauce as the Milanese risotto but with any number of ingredients such as vegetables, fish, cheese and/or meat

• **Risotto al salto** – Leftover rice fried like a pancake with the consistency of the fried potatoes you usually get for breakfast in the States

Secondo Piatto - Entrée
Pesce – Fish
You can get any type of seafood you want, since many restaurants have fresh fish sent in daily from the coast on ice; as always when you eat fish in a land-locked city, you'll find the prices to be quite astronomical
Carne – Meat
• **Cotoletta alla Milanese** – Breaded thin cutlet of veal sautéed in butter, served crisp on the outside but succulent on the inside
• **Ossobuco** – Usually served with the *risotto alla Milanese*, this is a veal shank cooked with tomatoes and wine then sprinkled with garlic, parsley and a touch of lemon
• **Rostin Negra** – Pork or veal slowly cooked in a pot-roast with a variety of herbs, wine and butter; a truly typical Milanese dish

Formaggio – Cheese
• **Gorgonzola** – a sharp, pungent, pale and delicious local cheese usually mistaken for the French Roquefort, but this is made with cow's milk, not ewe's milk; takes its name from the small town ten miles outside of Milan where it was originally produced

21. ALFIO, *Via Seneto 31, Tel. 02/7600-0633. American Express, Visa and Mastercard accepted. Closed Saturdays and Sundays at Lunch. Dinner for two E90.*
Fish is the flavor here and a great place to savor it is in their inside garden seating area. You can get pasta with seafood such as the *spaghetti alle vongole* (with clams in either a red or white sauce) or *con polpa di granchio* (crab meat). You can also get fresh fish grilled as well as prime cuts of meat, so this is the place to come to satisfy any palate. The clientele here is definitely as refined as is the decor. Remember to dress appropriately.

22. AL PORTO, *Piazzale Generale Contore, Tel. 02/8940-7425. No credit cards accepted. Closed Sundays and Mondays for lunch. Dinner for two E60.*
What used to be an old canal toll-house is now a great seafood restaurant. You'll feel like you're at sea with all the maritime decorations of fishing nets, ropes, wheels and more. The menu depends greatly on what fish they are able to purchase from the coast, but they'll always have the freshest and most reasonably priced plates in Milan. You can always find an excellent *risotto* or pasta made with fresh seafood. The best place to enjoy your meal is out on the terrace. I suggest the *scampi alla griglia*, but then I'm partial to any type of shrimp.

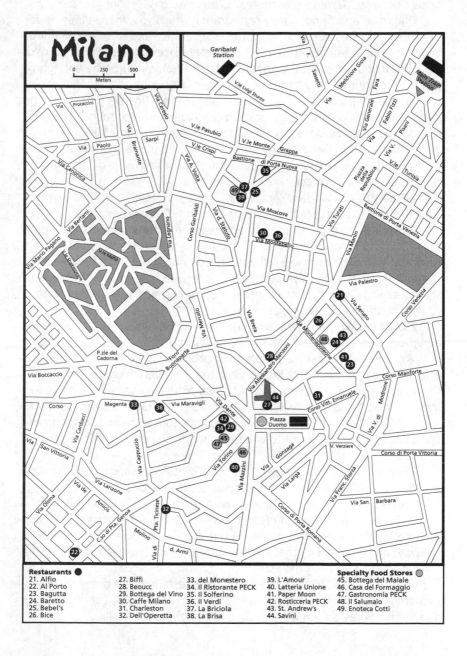

Milano

0 250 500
Meters

Restaurants ●
21. Alfio
22. Al Porto
23. Bagutta
24. Baretto
25. Bebel's
26. Bice
27. Biffi
28. Beoucc
29. Bottega del Vino
30. Caffe Milano
31. Charleston
32. Dell'Operetta
33. del Monestero
34. Il Ristorante PECK
35. Il Solferino
36. Il Verdi
37. La Briciola
38. La Brisa
39. L'Amour
40. Latteria Unione
41. Paper Moon
42. Rosticceria PECK
43. St. Andrew's
44. Savini

Specialty Food Stores ○
45. Bottega del Maiale
46. Casa del Formaggio
47. Gastronomia PECK
48. Il Salumaio
49. Enoteca Cotti

23. BAGUTTA, *Via Bagutta 14-16, Tel. 02/7600-2767. American Express, Visa and Mastercard accepted. Closed Sundays. Dinner for two E45.*

One of Milan's famous artsy restaurants, which you will instantly notice since the walls are covered with murals, caricatures, and pictures of famous and some not so famous artists. This is a great place to try food from all over Italy, but if you just want the *antipasto* table, that will surely be enough to satisfy your hunger. They have Roman dishes like *penne all'arrabbiata* (spicy tomato based pasta with garlic, oil, parsley, and hot peppers) and the *saltimbocca alla Romana* (veal shank in a zesty tomato-based sauce). They also have *tagliatelli alla bolognese* (with light veal, tomato and cream sauce) as well as *trenette al pesto Genovese* (pasta with a superb pureed garlic, basil, olive oil, pine nuts sauce). If fish is your desire, try their *fritto misto di mare* (mixed fried seafood)– it's perfect.

24. BARETTO, *Via Sant' Andrea 3, Tel. 02/781-255. American Express, Visa and Mastercard accepted. Closed Sundays. Dinner for two E75.*

This is a small, expensive restaurant near the Montenapoleone shopping area. The dark wood paneling gives the feel of Germanic influence but the food is all Italian. They have excellent *risotto* dishes here, and if you want to overload on seafood try the superb *salmone can salsa di gamberi* (salmon with shrimp sauce). To get here you enter through an archway and a pleasant courtyard off one of the shopping streets.

25. BEBEL'S, *Via San Marco 38, Tel. 02/657-1658. All credit cards accepted. Closed Wednesdays. and Saturday mornings. Dinner for two E45.*

You can order great pizza from their prominently placed wood-burning brick oven, or you can try the buffet table that has everything you could want for an entire meal. You can also get fresh fish (they sometimes have live lobsters on ice) and grilled meats. They make great Italian staples like *filetto alla griglia* (grilled veal) and *sogliola alla griglia* (grilled sole). Located in the Brera section, you may want to cab back and forth between this restaurant and your hotel.

26. BICE, *Via Borgospesso 12, Tel. 02/702-572. American Express, Visa and Mastercard accepted. Closed Mondays. Dinner for two E60.*

An expensive restaurant that serves great food from all over Italy, especially their superb cuts of meat, for example the *cotoletta alla Milanese* (breaded veal cutlet lightly pan fried in butter); as well as fish, which in Milan is always a dead giveaway that the restaurant will be expensive. If you're in a fish mood you have to try their *scamponi giganti alla griglia* (giant shrimps on the grill). They now have branches of their restaurant all over the world, including New York, Chicago, Palm Beach, San Diego, Paris, London, Tokyo, and Buenos Aires, so you know how trés chic this place really is.

27. BIFFI, *Galleria Vittorio Emanuele, Tel. 02/805-7961. American Express, Visa and Mastercard accepted. Closed Sundays. Dinner for two E60.*
Located in the Galleria, this is the perfect place to see or be seen. You can get a buffet of cold and hot antipasti, pasta, salad, fish and meat; and you can couple that with a small drink or a cappuccino. They have "outside seating" in the Galleria where you can watch the people walk by, or dine or drink inside in a modern environment. If you come to Milan you should try this place for an afternoon *aperitivo*, or try the Savini (below) for a ritzy dinner.

28. BOEUCCI, *Piazza Belgioioso 2, Tel. 02/7602-0224. American Express accepted. Closed Saturdays and Sundays for lunch as well as the whole month of August. Dinner for two E80.*
This formal but not really stuffy restaurant is frequented by businessmen and locals alike. The service is perfect and the food is good. Try the veal *scaloppini con porcini* (veal with mushrooms) and *risotto alla Milanese* (rice with meat and tomatoes). Even though *coperto* (seating charge) was supposed to be done away with, they still hang onto that fleecing tradition here.

29. BOTTEGA DEL VINO (PECK), *Via Victor Hugo 4, Tel. 02/861-040. American Express, Visa and Mastercard accepted. Dinner for two E30.*
Not just a wine bar and store, this is also a gourmet "fast-food" establishment. At lunch time it is packed with Milanese satisfying their need for excellent cuisine. They have red painted tractor seats set on stools for seating around deli-like counter areas made of beautiful light wood. To wash down all the great food they have in excess of 150 vintages from all over Italy for you to sample by the glass, or you can test the beer on tap.

30. CAFFE MILANO, *Via San Fermo 1, Tel. 02/2900-3300. All credit cards accepted. Closed Mondays. Dinner for two E75.*
The place to come for a Sunday brunch in Milan. They even advertise an "American Brunch" but it's not up to speed with all the greasy, fatty, meaty foods we are used to eating. They serve plenty of fresh fruit, luscious breads, juices, coffee, omelets, and only a little *prosciutto* (ham). Nonetheless, you will love the hearty atmosphere and healthy foods. Also a respected nightlife location because of its artistic flair and after-theater specials. The section of town that the restaurant is in, Brera, is known for its late night dining adventures.

31. CHARLESTON, *Piazza Liberty 8, Tel. 02/798-631, Fax 02/7600-1154. American Express, Visa and Mastercard accepted. Closed Mondays and Saturdays for lunch. Dinner for two E30.*
An inexpensive pizzeria that serves some of the best pizza in town. You can also have *antipasto* which is laid out on a vast "L" shaped table just as you walk in. They have succulent meats, great pasta as well as seafood, but I recommend the pizza. Their namesake pizza, the Charleston, is covered with sauce, mozzarella, mushrooms, ham, and hard boiled egg and is exquisite.

This brightly lit modern restaurant is organized on different levels, with the roaring wood burning pizza oven in the back, all of which gives the impression of much more space. If you're in the mood for outside seating they have it too. Another plus to the place is that it stays open until 1:00am, so you can spend many hours of eating and drinking here with your friends in the tranquillity of a small *piazza* in the center of town.

32. DELL'OPERETTA, *Corso di Porta Ticinese 70, Tel. 02/837-5120. American Express, Visa and Mastercard accepted. Closed Sundays. Dinner for two E45.*

This places is a local nightlife favorite with a central bar where patrons can stop for a drink up until 2:00am, or you can sit down for *trattoria* dining. I love the *tagliatelline* with a cream of mushroom sauce. The menu changes weekly to keep things lively. Weekend evenings you can sometimes find live jazz or blues bands playing.

33. DEL MONESTERO, *Corso Magenta 29, Tel. 02/869-3069. All credit cards accepted. Air conditioned dining room. Dinner for two E35.*

A small local place that specializes in seafood. Try the *spaghetti ai calamari alla marinara* (with squid and spicy tomato sauce) then the *misto fritto di gamberini e calamari* (mixed fried shrimp and squid). The atmosphere is intimate and friendly and the food is great.

34. IL RISTORANTE (PECK), *Via Victor Hugo 4, Tel. 02/876-774. American Express, Visa and Mastercard accepted. Dinner for two E90.*

This is the place to come and sample everything that the Peck food stores have to offer. Located downstairs from the Bottega del Vino, the setting is relaxing even without windows, the service is excellent and, of course, the food is sublime. The amount of potential choices is far beyond human comprehension, so even if you or your travel partner is the pickiest of eaters you are bound to find something to like.

35. IL SOLFERINO, *Via Castelfidardo 2, Tel. 02/659-9886. All credit cards accepted. Closed Saturdays at lunch and Sundays. Dinner for two E60.*

Next door to the Locanda Solferino inn, the atmosphere is cozy, romantic, and fashionable but not fancy. Most of the food is made in a simple way without much garnish or presentation but it is excellent. The *cotoletta alla Milanese* (breaded thin cutlet of veal sautéed in butter, served crisp on the outside but succulent on the inside) is excellent here, as is the *piccantina di vitello ai funghi porcini* (veal with mushrooms) The menu includes fresh pastas and homemade patés. La Briciola and L'Amour are right across the street.

36. IL VERDI, *Piazza Mirabello 5, Tel. 02/651-412. American Express, Visa and Mastercard accepted. Closed Saturdays at lunch and Sundays. Dinner for two E60.*

This is the place to come for salads or meat or fish or whatever strikes your fancy. But all the food is prepared in a light healthy fashion and this concept for the meals is reflected in the clean, well-lit, modern decor. You'd better make reservations since if you arrive after 8:30pm without one you'll be waiting for hours. They are known for their many varieties of salads, so if you're in a healthy mood stop here to graze.

37. LA BRICIOLA, *Corner of Via Solferino and Via Marsala, Tel. 02/655-1012. All credit cards accepted. Closed Sundays and Mondays. Dinner for two E45.*

This place, like its brother L'Amour and the II Solferino across the street, gathers a rather eclectic crowd in the evenings. Not only does it cater to the theater crowd but the Brera section where the restaurant is located is known as the "artist" section of Milan. Served in an environment of a wood floor, glass and pink tablecloths, the food here is of local persuasion, with prices to match the upscale clientele but not the peasant fare. You can get the Milanese favorite here, *cotoletta alla Milanese* (lightly breaded veal fried in butter) as well as many other options.

38. LA BRISA, *Via Brisa 15, Tel. 02/872-001. American Express, Visa and Mastercard accepted. Closed Sundays at lunch and Saturdays. Dinner for two E45.*

Just before you enter you can glimpse some Roman ruins that were dug up during a building construction. The restaurant is a plain and simple local place that serves basic but great food, except for the curried rice called *risotto al' Indiana*. At first I thought, how do people from Indiana make rice that is so good, then I realized they meant from India. A quaint little place especially in their terrace garden. You can get great fish and meats and as well as pastas that are all made in-house. If you're in the area, give it a try.

39. L'AMOUR, *Via Solferino 25, Tel. 02/659-0176. Open only in the evenings from 7:30pm - 1:00am. All credit cards accepted. Closed Mondays. Dinner for two E50.*

The brother restaurant of La Briciola around the corner, these two share a kitchen which helps to make their food quite similar. A quaint local atmosphere in a restaurant that caters to the late night theater crowd. You can get a wide variety of dishes, including the local favorite *cotoletta alla Milanese* (veal cutlet lightly breaded and fried in butter).

40. LATTERIA UNIONE, *Via dell Unione 6, Tel. 02/874-401. No credit cards accepted. Open for lunch only. Closed Sundays. Lunch for two E30.*

This is actually a *latteria*, or dairy store, which supplies the neighborhood shoppers with cheese, yogurt, butter, milk, eggs, etc., but it also is a fine vegetarian restaurant. It is so popular with the local office workers that it is jam-packed for lunch time, so if you want to try their food get there a little before noon or just after 2:00pm. They stop serving at 3:00pm, and don't serve on the weekend. It is basically a business lunch crowd place but the food is great. Their menu includes thick minestrone soup, omelets, stuffed tomatoes and peppers, and *risotti* with a variety of vegetable combinations.

Pizza in a Hurry!

If you're in a hotel around the train station, call **Pizza Oggi**, *Tel. 02/ 6900-1330*, and they'll get you a pizza in 30 minutes or less. They serve the train station area since that is also the university area. They're open from 6:30-9:30pm every day. They have two different sizes, **Super** (1 person) and **Mega** (2 people). The best order in my opinion is a **Margherita Mega** (E7), which is a plain tomato and cheese pizza, then pile on the toppings at E1.5 extra. First get extra cheese (mozzarella), then try either salami, wurstel (sausage), pepperoni, funghi (mushrooms), verdure fresche (mixed fresh vegetables) or salame piccante (spicy salami).

41. PAPER MOON, *Via Bagutta 1, Tel. 02/792-297. American Express, Visa and Mastercard accepted. Closed Sundays. Dinner for two E40.*

This pizzeria serves great light crust pies that come with almost every topping imaginable (if you can't find one you like ask them to put on the toppings you want) as well as pastas, and a strange concoction called *la Bomba* (the bomb). It's a puffed up *calzone* with a *prosciutto* and *formaggio* (ham and cheese) filling. A great local place with fun decor and tasty food.

42. ROSTICCERIA PECK, *Via Cantu 3, Tel. 02/869-3017. American Express, Visa and Mastercard accepted. Meal for two E25.*

Primarily a takeout place for roasted meats, you can also use their stand-up counter to sample their delicacies. You can get spit roasted chicken as well as pork, beef, and even vegetables all prepared with excellence. They also have perfectly prepared pasta dishes, either hot or cold, that make my mouth water even now. Your meal will be quick, but it will be satisfying.

43. ST. ANDREW'S, *Via Sant'Andrea 23, Tel. 02/7602-3132, Fax 02/798-565. American Express, Visa and Mastercard accepted. Closed Sundays. Dinner for two E45.*

Despite the name nothing about this place is British, except for some decor and the Beef Wellington, but I guess they think this is what a British place is supposed to look like. They serve excellent typical Milanese rice and pasta dishes, as well as *Cotoletta alla Milanese*. Ask the manager, Piero Vezzulli, for his suggestions and you'll have a fine meal. Needless to say it's expensive since it's around the ritzy Via Montenapoleone shopping street.

44. SAVINI, *Galleria Vittorio Emanuele, Tel. 02/805-8343. American Express, Visa and Mastercard accepted. Closed Sundays. Dinner for two E100.*

Also located in the Galleria, this place is a little more expensive than Biffi, but if you want to impress your friends, or at least someone who knows Milan, dine here so you can tell them you did. Everything about the place spells upper crust, from the crystal chandeliers to the impressive wine list to the multilingual waiters. The food, surprisingly enough, is just as good, but very, very expensive. They have an enclosed "outside seating" area in the Galleria where you can enjoy the parade of Milanese as you eat you meal. PS: They won't allow you in shorts or any other inappropriate attire.

Seeing the Sights

Not nearly as scenic as other cities in Italy – chiefly a result of the devastating bombing during World War II – Milan still has some excellent sights to see, including the beautiful Gothic **Duomo**, the world-famous **La Scala** opera house, the **Galleria**, and Da Vinci's *Last Supper*. But most people don't come here to sightsee, they come to do business.

See the map on page 665 for sights references.

A. DUOMO

Piazza del Duomo. Open 7:00am–7:00pm. October–May 9:00am–4:30pm. Access to the top of the cathedral costs E2. By elevator E3.

If you want Gothic, here you have Gothic at its best. This ornately decorative church was begun in 1386 and is the work of countless architects, artists, and artisans who labored here for centuries, and it is still unfinished today since it is undergoing continuous reconstruction, maintenance, and restoration work. This massive structure is crowned by 135 spires with statues and relief work interspersed everywhere. At night the spires are lit which makes an excellent scene, especially from the dining room at the Hotel Duomo. One of the best ways to get a bird's eye view of the square is to ascend to the outside viewing area above the facade of the cathedral.

The interior, like the exterior, is covered in statues, relief work, and many other decorations. The stained glass windows are of particular interest especially on a bright sunny day. The statue you see in the square is of Vittorio Emanuele II, done in 1896 by Ercole Rosa.

B. VITTORIO EMANUELE GALLERIA

Many buildings and houses were demolished to make this huge arcade which was dedicated to Vittorio Emanuele II. Started on March 7th, 1865, it was finally finished in 1877 – and so was the architect Mengoni. The day before the opening ceremony the architect plunged to his death from the scaffolding.

Created in the form of a cross, the major wing is 195 meters long and the minor wing is 105 meters long. In the center of the cross you'll find a dome that rises 50 meters above the floor. The inside of the gallery is known as the glass sky since it completely covers all people who enter. It's the perfect place to be in a rainstorm.

Inside you'll find shops and restaurants catering to your every need. It is the central meeting place for business people, artists, opera singers, fashion models and tourists alike. It is really the heart and soul of Milan. Devastated in the bombings during World War II, it has been lovingly re-created to its original form.

C. PIAZZA DEI MERCANTI

The **Piazza dei Mercanti** (Merchant's Square) is a small, quaint old square that is not really a part of the modern city of Milan. It is bounded by the **Palazzo della Ragione** (Palace of Reason), built in 1233, and the **Loggia of the Osii**, built in 1316, on the north and south; and the **Palatine Schools** and the **Panigalaros house** on the east and west.

In the niches of the Loggia of the Osii, you can find the statues of the Milanese saints. But besides the sculptures and ancient architecture, this is a place to come and get away from the pace ofmodern Milan.

D. TEATRO LA SCALA

Via Dei Filodrammatici 2, 20121 Milano. Tel 02/861-781 or 861-772, Fax 02/861-778. Open Monday-Saturday 9:00am-noon and 2:00-6:00pm. Sundays 9:30am-12:30pm and 2:30pm-6:00pm. Admission E5.

If you are an opera fan you've come to Milan to catch a performance at **La Scala**, the most famous and prestigious of all opera houses in the world. Built between 1776 and 1778 on the old site of the church of Santa Maria alla Scala, it is the work of the architect Giusseppe Piermarini. Developed in the neoclassical style, the facade has a covered portico and gable with a relief work depicting Apollo's Chariot. The building suffered bomb damage during World War II but was rebuilt and renovated as perfectly as could be possible, and re-opened in 1946.

If you can't catch a performance here, just come to visit their museum which offers a variety of operatic costumes, all the way from Ancient Grecian times to the present. There are also many objects that trace the evolution of the theater, as well as 40,000 books that deal with opera and the theater, and records that have over 600 different opera singers recorded.

E. PALAZZO DI BRERA

Via Brera 28, Tel. 862-634. Open Tuesday-Saturday 9:00am-2:00pm and Sundays 9:00am-1:00pm. Admission E4.

Built in 1170 by an order of religious men called the Umiliati as a monastery and place of worship. Then in the 13th century the **Church of St. Mary of Brera** was added onto the building and it has been so named ever since. In 1772 the building began its new life as an institute of artistic preservation as commissioned by Mary Teresa of Austria. The first part of the collection was donated by the Abbot Giusseppe Bianconi in return for his appointment as secretary to the new museum. Many of its current works were donations from religious orders by decree of Napoleon himself. In the nineteenth century the collection was enriched by many private donations.

All the works were moved for safekeeping during World War II because of the bombings of the city, then on June 9th, 1950, the collection opened for viewing again. Today you can find works from the 14th century up to present times. Among the most noteworthy are Moccirolo's *Oratorio*, Raphael's well-known *Sposalizio delle Vergine*, Mantegna's *Cristo Morto* and Bramante's *Cristo alla Colonna*.

F. CASTELLO SFORZESCO

Foro Buonaparte. Metro – Carioli. Open Tuesday–Sunday 9:30am–5:30pm.

What you see today is only a smaller scale of the original citadel. In the beginning it consisted of many forts all enclosed in a great star-shaped fortress with imposing ramparts. Despite its reduction in size it is still Italy's largest castle.

The current fortress was built in 1450 over the ruins of a viscount's fort, which itself had been built over the ruins of the **Porta Giovia Castle**. Under the rule of Lodovico Sforza in 1495, the castle started to take on many artistic accents with works by such masters as Leonardo da Vinci and Bramante. During the Spanish, French, and Austrian control of the area, this beautiful castle was used as a military barracks and was treated so poorly that after a while it could only be considered a ruin. Finally in 1890, when the Austrian troops were forced to leave, the Italians decided to restore it and in 1893 the work began. But in 1943 parts of the building and its museums were damaged in the WWII bombings, but these too were reconstructed.

Today you should visit the castle not only to see its immense towers and walls and stroll through the beautiful park inside, but also to see their extensive art collection, underground archaeological museum and Historic Document Archives. In the **Ancient Arts Museum**, you'll find a wide variety of artistic works, including fabulous gems by Michelangelo and Leonardo da Vinci, Italy's greatest artists. Look for the *Pieta Rondanini*, Michelangelo's last and unfinished work as well as a hall dedicated to ancient arms such as axes, shields, spiked clubs, spears and more. In the **Historic Document Archives**, started in 1902, there are preserved documents, some of which date back to 1385. Any bibliophile will love this collection.

G. ARCO SEMPIONE

Piazza Sempione.

This monument is also called the **arch of peace**. Construction began in 1807 to celebrate Napoleon's victories in war. It consists of three barrel vaults supported by Corinthian columns on pedestals and needs to be seen if you can't make it to Paris and see the Arc de Triomphe. The reclining figures near the top represent the four main rivers in Italy.

H. GIARDINI PUBLICI
Located halfway between the main train station and the Duomo. Open 6:00am–dusk.

These gardens are a fine place to come and get away from the hectic pace of Milan. If you're so inclined there is also a small **zoo** to enjoy. Walk along wooded paths and escape it all.

I. LEONARDO DA VINCI MUSEUM OF SCIENCE & TECHNOLOGY
Via San Vittore 21, Tel. 4801-0040. Metro San Ambrogio. Open Tuesday–Sunday 9:00am–5:00pm. Admission E5 – Adults; E3 kids under 18.

Inaugurated in 1953 for the fifth centenary of Leonardo's birth, this unique museum is a must-see while in Milan. Located on the site of the Olivetano Monastery, this museum now houses a collection of material that gives a complete synthesis of Leonardo da Vinci's work and experiments in many fields. Here you'll find reproductions of his designs and mechanical models of his inventions, some of which you (and the kid inside you) can actually test out. There are also copies of pages from the *Gates Codex* (used to be called the *Codex Hammer* until software billionaire Bill Gates bought it) on display.

If you've had enough of Leonardo's inventions and the Codex you can walk through other wonderful exhibits all related to science and technology. There's one about the history of aviation, one dealing solely with typewriters, one about land transportation, one dedicated to clocks. Besides all of this there is also an excellent reproduction of Leonardo's *Last Supper* painted by Giovanni Mauro Dellarovere at the end of the 16th century. So if you don't want to brave the line and see the real one come here instead.

J. DA VINCI'S "THE LAST SUPPER"
Piazza Santa Maria delle Grazie. Tel. 498-7588. Metro-Carioli. Open Tuesday–Sunday 8:30am–1:30pm. Admission E3.

To the left of the church of Santa Maria delle Grazie is the refectory of the Dominican convent that houses the most famous of Leonardo's work, *The Last Supper*. Painted between 1495 and 1497, the painting is not standing up to the test of time and man. The humidity in the room doesn't help maintain the fresco and a doorway was built underneath it cutting off one of Christ's legs that was visible under the table. Also restoration work that was done in 1726 and 1770 actually increased the painting's deterioration. Efforts are underway now, using modern techniques, to save the invaluable work, but if I were you I'd see it sooner rather than later since it may not be around for long.

Nightlife & Entertainment

The nightlife in Milan centers around the theater, then a light dinner and wine afterwards. Most restaurants stay open after midnight, making this your best outlet for subtle entertainment.

There are a variety of theaters in Milan. Contact your travel agent in North America or your hotel while in Milan about getting tickets. If you want to go to La Scala to see some opera you should plan at least six months in advance (see above under *Seeing the Sights* for La Scala's phone and fax). If theater and a late dinner are not to your liking, here's a small list of pubs that may be more up your alley.

NAVY PUB/VICTORY, *Via Borgogna 5, Milano. Tel. 02/76-02-07-18. Half pints E3. Pints E4.*

Great atmosphere inside and out. Their terrace is fenced in by beer barrels and pseudo-fish nets and the inside has an English-style wooden bar at which to stand as well as red velvet booths at which to sit. You can enjoy a Guinness, Harp, or Kilkeny on draft. A popular place.

HOBBIT PUB, *Via dei Missaglia 59a, Tel. 02/89-30-03-66.*

They serve bottle beers from all over the world and stay open until 2:00am for your entertainment pleasure. The atmosphere is definitely English-pub style coupled with fun music. If you get hungry they have sandwiches, chips, peanuts, etc., to munch on. More of a younger crowd.

BIRROTECA WOODSTOCK, *Via Lodovico II Moro 3, Tel. 02/89-12-04-79.*

Open until 3:00am, this place also serves beers from around the world. As you can guess by the name, this bar draws a little more eclectic crowd. If you get hungry they have your basic pub fare like sandwiches, chips, and peanuts.

Sports & Recreation
Golf
• **Golf Club Bergamo Ol'Albenza**, *Via Congoni 12, 24030 Bergamo. Tel. 035/640-707, Fax 035/640-028.* Located 50 kilometers from Milan and only 13 kilometers from Bergamo, this is the home course of the famous Italian golfer Constantino Rocca who came in second to John Daly in the 1995 British Open. The main course is an 18 hole, par 72 that is 6190 meters long. The small course is 9 holes, par 36, and 2462 meters long. Open year round except from December 22nd to January 5th and Mondays. They have a restaurant, bar, driving range, and electric carts.
• **Golf Club Carimate**, *Via Airldi 2, 22060 Carimate. Tel. 031/790-226, Fax 031/790-226.* Located 27km from Milan and 15 km from Como this is an 18 hole, par 71 course that is 5,982 meters long. It is open year round except on Mondays. They have a driving range, tennis course, and a fine bar and restaurant.

- **La Pinetta Golf Club**, *Via al Golf 4, 22070 Appiano Gentile. Tel. 031/933-202, Fax 031/890-342.* Located 25km from Milan and 12 km from Como this is an 18 hole, par 71 course that is 6,035 meters long. It is open year round except Tuesdays. They have a driving range, pro shop, swimming pool, tennis course, pro shop, and a bar and restaurant. A great place to come for a family outing while you go play golf.
- **Golf Club Milano**, *Viale Mulini S Giorgio 7, 20052 Parco di Monza. Tel. 039/303-081/2/3, Fax 039/304-427.* Located 20 km from Milan, this is an 18 hole, par 71 course that is 6,083 meters long. Open year round except for Mondays. They have a driving range, pro shop, swimming pool, and restaurant/bar.
- **Molinetto Country Club A.S.**, *SS Padana Superiore 11, 20063 Cenusco sul Naviglio (in Milan). Tel. 02/9210-5128, Fax 02/9210-6635.* Located 10 km from the center of Milan, this is an 18 hole par 71 course that is 6,1025 meters long. Open year round except Mondays. They have a driving range, pool, and bar/restaurant.
- **Golf Le Roverdine**, *Via K Marx, 20090 Noverasco di Opera (in Milan). Tel. 02/5760-2730, Fax 02/5760-6405.* Located only 4 km from the city center, this is an 18 hole, par 72 course that is 6,322 meters long. It is open year round except on Mondays. They have a driving range, carts, pro shop and a great nineteenth hole bar. This is the closest place to play. Enjoy.
- **Circolo di Campagna Zoate Golf Club**, *Via Verdi 6, 20067 Zoate di Tribiano. Tel. 02/9063-2183, Fax 02/9063-1861.* Located 18 km from Milan, this is an 18 hole par 72 course that is 6,122 meters long. It is open year round except Mondays. They have a pro shop, swimming pool, restaurant and a bar.
- **Barlassina Country Club**, *Via Privata 42, 20030 Birago di Camnago. Tel. 0362/560-621, Fax 0362/560-934.* Located 20 km from Milan this is an 18 hole par 72 course that is 6,184 meters in length. It is open year round except Mondays. They have a driving range, pro shop, swimming pool, tennis course, guest house, bar, and a restaurant.

Shopping

The best and most expensive shopping streets in Milan are the **Via Montenapoleone** and **Via della Spiga**, and all the little alleys surrounding these two parallel streets. Be prepared to spend through the nose here, but at the same time you will get the best service and quality of product available. Taking a stroll down these streets you'll witness the opulence and splendor of Milan's stores and the beauty of these elegant streets.

There are so many great stores in Milan that to do them justice would require a separate book – and in fact one excellent resource exists for both

Milan and elsewhere in Italy, which I'm pleased to recommend: *Made in Italy* by Anne Brody and Patricia Shultz.

The *salumiere*, where you can get delicious picnic and specialty food supplies, are numbered for you to locate on the map of Milan.

Fashion & Accessories

Milan is the seat of Italian fashion, and plays a close second to Paris in world fashion. There are plenty of small designer's shops that feature dresses that have either been on the runways during the 'Fashion Week' of spring or fall, or they have deliberately 'copied' these new fashions – or should I say modified them with their own creative direction. Whatever the case, most of these designer outfits will cost you an arm and a leg, but if it's fashion you want, it's fashion Milan has.

If you're looking for leather accessories Milan definitely has the greatest diversity in price and styles than any other city in Italy. Many of their products are made locally and many others come from the many factories that surround Bologna. Wherever the finished leather comes from you'll notice that the selection is gargantuan. The Milanese thrive on taking risks and employing novel new designs. In essence, you'll never have a problem finding something new and different in Milan. What you may have trouble finding is something in your price range, but if you're here to shop, that doesn't mean you actually have to buy, does it? Go ahead, you're on vacation.

Home & Office Furnishings

In most everything the Milanese are willing to try any new approach as long as it's aesthetically appealing and has practical application. This is probably best expressed in their home furnishings industry. The city thrives on a culture of modernism and its industry allows this creativity to flow through the production into your home or office.

There are a myriad of showrooms and/or retail stores all over Milan in which you can admire and buy the latest and greatest designs in home and office furniture, lighting fixtures, housewares, and accessories for the office and home. Some of them can be much more fun than going to a museum because it seems as if these pieces are alive.

Bookstores (English-Language)

Milan has become the publishing capital of Italy, for magazines, newspapers, and books; and many of Milan's publishers have established their own well-stocked, large bookstores. Many of these bookstores contain English-language titles, but even if they didn't I'd suggest that you visit them anyway. Just wandering around the stacks of books in a foreign bookstore helps to give you a feel for what makes the people tick. Listed below are some bookstores and newsstands with English-language titles:

RIZZOLI, *Galleria Vittorio Emanuele 79, Tel. 02/807-348. American Express, Mastercard and Visa accepted.*

The Rizzoli company was founded in 1909 and is currently one of the top publishers in Italy. This is a large two story store, with a small English language book section along with guidebooks located on the ground floor. But if you're a bibliophile that shouldn't stop you from browsing through the rest of the bookstore.

AMERICAN BOOKSTORE, *Via Camperio 16, Tel. 02/878-920, Fax 02/7202-0030. American Express, Mastercard and Visa accepted.*

As you guessed, this is exclusively an English-language bookstore. You can find everything from best-sellers to travel books. The best place to replenish your stock of novels for the rest of your trip; and since it's open for lunch (as are most bookstores) you can browse here after a light lunch and wait for the museums and stores to open again. There is only a small selection of used books which are priced from E3-4. The new novels are priced between E7-8. A great place not only to browse but to hear your native language spoken, and possibly hook up with some ex-pats or tourists for a night out on the town.

MONDADORI, *Corso Vittorio Emanuele 34, Tel. 02/705-832. American Express, Mastercard and Visa accepted.*

One of the most respected publishers in Europe and Italy's largest, it is still under the management of the Mondadori family. This store has three floors dedicated mainly to Italian titles, but there is also a fine section of English-language books, including Italian books translated into English.

MARCO, *Galleria Passarella 2, Tel. 02/795-866. American Express, Mastercard and Visa accepted. Open on weekdays until 10:30pm.*

Basically a newsstand on hormones, this place has newspapers and magazines from all over Europe, but unfortunately not many English titles. They advertise themselves as a "supermarket of information" and this is obviously the case. They also feature best-selling books in Italian and a few in English. But still the best place for English-language titles is over at the American Bookstore.

L'ARCHIVOLTO, *Via Marsala 2, Tel. 02/659-0842. American Express, Mastercard and Visa accepted.*

Even though this store is not affiliated with one of the giants of Milanese and Italian publishing, it's still a fun place to browse. If you like old and antique architectural drawings this is the place for you. Mainly a bookstore for architecture, city planning, and design enthusiasts, it can still be enjoyable for the average Joe like me.

Salumiere (Picnic Supplies)

When the fashion is put aside, the food comes to the front. The Milanese are well-known for their love of good food, whether in a restaurant or to take home. Milan's *salumiere* are part of the culture of the city, and if you visit Milan try to visit at least one to get a taste of the local life. You'll find mountains of cheeses, salamis, prosciutto, patés, homemade pastas, pastries and more. Each of the stores listed below is a perfect place to find a culinary reminder of your voyage to bring back to the States.

There are many other *salumiere* or *alimentari* in Milan, but you'll not find a better selection, more superior service, or the memories of shopping at Peck's (see below). A must-see.

The Peck Stores

There are now five Peck stores that serve carry-out gastronomic excellence and one, **Il Ristorante**, that offers creative cuisine consisting of the many ingredients found in their stores. Peck is the place to go for all forms of prepared foods, salamis, cheeses, fruit, vegetables and wine. They have everything you'll need to create your own picnic or full course meal. Even if you're not in the mood to sample their wares, Peck is a great visual experience. When in Milan you simply have to come and enjoy the visual feast. They make Dean and Deluca, the famous New York-based food specialty store, pale in comparison. Each store, all located within a stone's throw from one another near the Duomo, carry a variety of different products, designed in this way so you'll have to frequent almost all of them to get the ingredients you need for that special soirée.

Peck was founded by a Czech immigrant who brought his salami making skills with him to Milan in 1883. Now the chain is owned and operated by a quartet of Italian brothers named Stoppani, who have continued the excellence, and expanded it to become the undisputed gourmet delicatessen chain in the world.

Since the choices seem endless, and you may not know what to get, ask for a sample of something before you buy. They will be more than happy to oblige in all of the shops. See map on page 673 for locations.

45. BOTTEGA DEL MAIALE, *Via Victor Hugo 3, Tel. 02/805-3528.*

Just across the street from Gastronomia Peck, this store offers everything possible created from its namesake, *Il Maiale* (The Pig). You'll find snouts, ears, feet (for *Ossobuco*) as well as salamis, sausages, and cutlets. The hams hanging precariously from the ceiling compete with the salt-cured pork for your attention. Try an *etto* (about 1/4 of a pound) of *salami Milanese* – in my opinion the best salami in Italy.

29. BOTTEGA DEL VINO, *Via Victor Hugo 4, Tel. 02/861-040.*

Not just a wine bar and store, this is also a gourmet "fast-food" establishment. See review above in *Where to Eat, #29.*

46. CASA DEL FORMAGGIO, *Via Speronari 3, Tel. 02/800-858.*

This aptly name "House of Cheese" is a cheese lover's fantasy with over 300 varieties from all over Italy. You can get the best mozzarella made with buffalo's milk outside of Rome. They also have cheeses made with olives, spices, and nuts. If you missed out on a visit to Parma or Bologna, try a small cut of their *parmigiano reggiano*. Made from the curds of the cheese making process this dry, brittle cheese simply melts in your mouth.

If you've never seen a skinned rabbit before, look in the window of the *Supermercato* just across the street, they always have a few of them lying there waiting to be bought, heads, tails, eyes and all.

47. GASTRONOMIA PECK, *Via Spadari 9, Tel. 02/871-737.*

This is the main deli that offers everything you could ever imagine wanting. The shelves are packed full of platters of prepared foods, fresh pastas, smoked meats, and vegetables and fruits to go. Why the servers wear polka-dotted bow ties I can't tell you, but everything else in here is a self-explanatory food lover's dream.

42. ROSTICCERIA, *Via Cantu 3, Tel. 02/869-3017.*

This is a meat takeout palace. You can get spit roasted chicken as well as pork, beef, and even vegetables all prepared with excellence for a quiet picnic in the park. See review above in *Where to Eat, #42.*

Another place of interest for gourmet food supplies is not Peck-affiliated but is still good:

48. IL SALUMAIO DI MONTENAPOLEONE, *Via Montenapoleone 12, Tel. 02/701-123. No credit cards accepted. Closed Sundays.*

This place has everything to prepare a five-course gourmet meal, and salami too. Dozens of varieties. You can find home-made pasta, rice, salads, pies, vegetables, barrels of pickles, vats of olives, roasted and cured meats (some of which hang from the ceiling), and cheese. Tons of it. The cheeses here outnumber the salamis. In the center you can find your dessert. But be prepared to pay for the right to eat these delicacies. Since it's located in this ritzy neighborhood the prices here are quite a bit more than at Peck's. But if you can't get downtown to enjoy the splendor of the Peck stores, you can find all the gifts and supplies you could imagine here.

Markets

Milan definitely has more flea markets and street markets than any other Italian city. Remember, as we've said earlier in the book, always bargain. Don't just accept the first price given. Since you might be pegged as a tourist the price will usually be close to twice as much as offered to Italians. Also, if you're looking for interesting items and you want to avoid the crowds you have to get to each market early.

FIERA SINIGALLIA, *Porta Ticinese. All day Saturdays.*

There are countless peddlers and regular stall holders selling everything from tapes to antiques, as well as books, clothing (new and used) and a variety of curiosities. Definitely the best selection of all the markets. It has grown so big that it merges with the next market on the list below.

MERCATO PAPINIANO, *Viale Papiniano (Porta Ticinese section). Tuesday Mornings and all day Saturdays.*

A good variety of goods, including clothes (new and used), housewares, food, and flowers. The main selection here is food and lots of it. Basically this market and the Sinigallia are one and the same. They stretch from the Porta Ticinese past the Porta Genova and encompass the Piazza San Agostino and beyond. These two combined are quite a sight when you're in Milan on a Saturday. You can spend all day here.

Wine

49. ENOTECA COTTI, *Via Solferino 42, Tel. 02/2900-1096, Fax 02/2900-1222.*

A large wine shop and liquor store with all kinds of wines from all over Italy and Europe. A great place to find a nice bottle to bring home with you. Located in the Brera section, this might be a little out of the way for some, but it is worth the trip.

Excursions & Day Trips

The three nearby towns I'd recommend for day trips or brief excursions are **Bergamo**, **Pavia**, and **Certosa**. Rich in Renaissance history, these towns offer a relaxing escape from the pace of Milan.

BERGAMO

Situated picturesquely at the foot of the **Bergamo Alps**, this is really two distinctly different towns. The older **Citta Alta** (Upper City) consists of narrow winding streets with battlements surrounding them that were built between 1561 and 1592; and then you have the modern **Citta Basso** (Lower City) resting on the plain below. The lower city is modern and has limited appeal. What we're here for is wandering through and enjoying the tiny medieval streets and buildings of the older Citta Alta.

Bergamo was originally a Gaelic settlement and is first recorded in history in 200 BCE as the Roman settlement *Municipium Bergamum*. Bergamo remained relatively unimportant until it joined the Lombard League of towns in 1167. The next big political event was when the Kingdom of Milan took control in 1264. As Venice flexed its muscles, it came under Venetian control from 1428 to 1797. Then France took it over and eventually joined the unified Italy.

Though Bergamo's past doesn't seem too exciting, it has left us with a scenic old town to wander through on our day trip. Since cars are not allowed in Citta Alta, the town's seven hills can sometimes feel like seventy. But strolling through the streets lined with fourteenth and fifteenth century buildings and *palazzi* really takes your mind off the climb. Besides the architecture, Bergamo offers you scenic vistas of the valley and up into the Alps.

Bergamo is the perfect little town to visit when the hectic pace of Milan has begun to grate on you. It's the best place to come to and recharge your batteries, and to give yourself memories that will last a lifetime. This little town is a perfect place to stay and savor the sights, sounds, and smells of intimate Italian life. If you're staying in Milan and are tired of the brusque manner in which you may be treated, come here for a few days and appreciate the sense of care and community you are given. You'll not want to go back to Milan, this place is so enchanting.

Bergamo - A Charming Hill Town

If you are in this area of Italy, come and visit **Bergamo Alto**. The cobblestone narrow streets, medieval buildings, and squares create an ambiance that is charming, romantic, and out of this world. Stay a day or more and soak up the beauty of Italy in this fantastic hill town.

Arrivals & Departures

By Train

A train leaves from Milan virtually every hour on the quarter hour and takes an hour to get to Bergamo. Once off the train you're in the Citta Basso (the lower city). Where you're going is the Citta Alta (the upper city).To begin the last part of our journey buy a bus ticket at the *giornalaio* just on the left before you leave the station. Before you get on bus #1 which goes from the station to the *funiculare*, which will take you up the hill to the old city and back, first stop at the **tourist office**, *located outside of the station on the Viale Papa Giovanni XXIII, #106, Tel. 035/242-226.* To get there just go up the road in front of the station, past the first road. Before the first light on the left hand side in the large building with Banco di Roma is the tourist office. They have excellent maps and information.

Now armed with all necessities, either go back to the station and board bus #1 or cross the road and wait at the bus stop for the #1. Once on board punch your ticket like a good Italian and sit back for the short five minute ride. The bus pulls up in front of the *funiculare* which will take you up the hill. Your bus ticket is also good for the ride up; just show it to the conductor who is waiting by the gate to check. The *funiculare* takes all of five minutes.

Where to Stay

In Bergamo the best place to stay is in the Citta Alta. There are a number of hotels in the lower town, but if you want to stay in a real medieval town, complete with ambiance and charm, check out the hotels listed below.

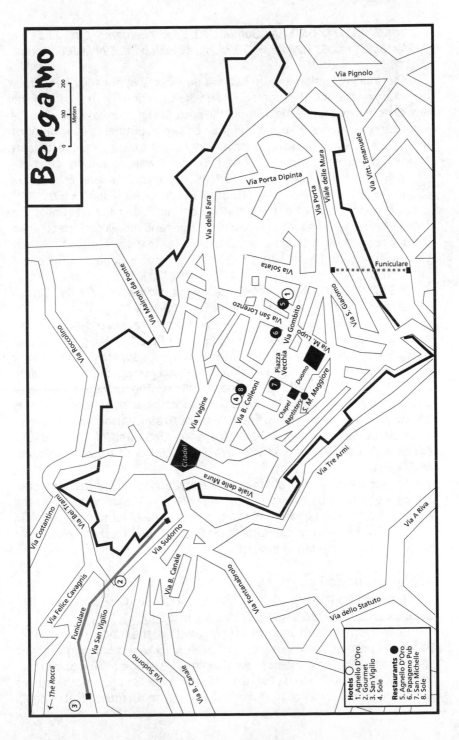

Bergamo

Via Pignolo

Via Vitt. Emanuele

Via Porta Dipinta

Via della Fara

Viale delle Mura

Via Porta

Via S. Giacomo

Funiculare

Via Solata

Via M. Lupo

Via San Lorenzo

Via Gombito

1
5
6

Piazza Vecchia

7
Duomo

Chapel
Baptistery
S. M. Maggiore

4 8
Via B. Colleoni

Via Vagine

Citadel

Viale delle Mura

Via Tre Armi

Via A Riva

Via Rocolino

Via Maiforni da ponte

Via Felice Cavagnis

Via Costantino

Via Bel Trami

Funiculare

Via San Vigilio

The Rocca

2

3

Via Sudorno

Via Sudorno

Via B. Canale

Via B. Canale

Via Fontanabolo

Via dello Statuto

0 100 200
Meters

Hotels
1. Agnello D'Oro
2. Gourmet
3. San Vigilio
4. Sole

Restaurants
5. Agnello D'Oro
6. Papageno Pub
7. San Michelle
8. Sole

1. AGNELLO D'ORO, *Via Gombito 22, 24129 Bergamo, Citta Alta. Tel. 035/249-883, Fax 035/235-612. 20 rooms all with bath. Single E60; Double E90.* ******

The small reception area is also the entrance way for their beautifully decorated restaurant. The rooms are all on the small side but they have all the amenities of a three star hotel without the price. Staying here you'll be virtually in the center of things, if such a thing can be said about the calm environs of the Citta Alta. A great place to stay. They have a quaint, small restaurant attached where you can enjoy meals if you don't want to wander out.

2. GOURMET, *Via San Vigilio 1, 24129 Bergamo, Citta Alta. Tel. and Fax 035/437-3004. 11 rooms. 1 Single E50, 9 Doubles E90; 1 suite E160.* *******

This place is located in the Citta Alta but outside of the walls near the second *funiculare*. Their rooms are a little larger and more comfortable than the ones downtown but you pay a little extra for that comfort. In all a great place to stay. Eating here is another story: their food is good, but the prices are sky high.

3. SAN VIGILIO, *Via San Vigilio 15, Bergamo, Citta Alta. Tel. 035/25-31-79, Fax 035/40-20-81. 7 rooms, all doubles, E90-120.* *******

Located above the Citta Alta. The views from up here over the Citta Bassa and the Citta Alta are stupendous. You reach here by taking the second *funiculare* all the way to the top. Their restaurant is superb so don't worry about going down to the Citta Alta for dinner and missing the last *funiculare* at 10:00pm (on weekends the last one is 1:00pm). The rooms are Italian-size but comfortable, and I have to say it again, the restaurant is great and empties out into a nice garden setting. The best place to stay. Bucolic and relaxing.

4. SOLE, *Via B Colleoni 1, 24129 Bergamo, Citta Alta. Tel. 035/218-238, Fax 035/240-011. 10 rooms all with bath. Single E60 (double used as a single); Double E80.* ******

The rooms are all small but they have everything you'd find in a three star: TV, phone, private bath, etc. The atmosphere is not quite as stuffy as the Agnello and their restaurant is better too. This is the place to stay for less in Bergamo in the heart of the Citta Alta. Great central location. Perfect for touring and just wandering around.

Where to Eat

5. AGNELLO D'ORO, *Via Gombito 22, 24129 Bergamo, Citta Alta. Tel. 035/249-883, Fax 035/235-612. Dinner for two E40.*

I love the haphazard decor of this place with all the copper pots, ceramic plates and pitchers, as well as plenty of other knickknacks hanging from the ceiling and walls. These intimate surroundings boast some fairly good food, like their *tortellini alla panna* (pasta stuffed with cheese and smothered in a rich cream sauce) as well as their *filetto di bue alla griglia* (grilled filet of beef).

I think the Ristorante Sole (see next entry) has a better atmosphere but that may be because of their beautiful patio.

6. **PAPAGENO PUB**, *Via Gombito, Bergamo, Citta Alta. Tel. 035/236-624. Open 1:00am - 2:00am. Closed Tuesdays. Meal for two E20.*

The ambiance of an English pub here in a small Italian town. They serve Guinness and three German beers on tap for E5 a pint. No food is served except in the mornings when they offer coffee and danish to the students who wander in. This is the after hours place to go in Bergamo to enjoy a few pints and try to be a part of the life of the town. Since the Citta Alta houses a local university, many restaurants stay open at night to cater to the nocturnal yearnings of the younger set. This is the best place to go to be a part of such adventures.

7. **SAN MICHELLE**, *Piazza Vecchia, 24129 Bergamo, Citta Alta. Tel. 035/225-335. Dinner for two E40.*

Located on the central square with plenty of seating from which to enjoy the spectacle of this small medieval town, you will also get a good meal. They make excellent pastas like their *Tortellini della casa* (home-made) *con ricotta ed erbetta* (pasta stuffed with ricotta cheese and made with garlic, and other herbs and spices). For seconds try their *misto formaggi alla griglia* (mixed grilled cheese). There are two other restaurants on the *piazza* also with outside seating, which will not disappoint if this one is full. They also have a tourist menu for only E20 which serves up the best they have to offer, as well as 1/4 liter of wine and 1/2 liter of mineral water. That may be your best bet.

8. **SOLE**, *Via B Colleoni 1, 24129 Bergamo, Citta Alta. Tel. 035/218-238, Fax 035/240-011. Tourist menu E20; Gastronomes menu E40.*

Simply a great restaurant, with the best seating located in the splendid garden area. The place has a festive atmosphere generated by the white walls, red chairs, and pink tablecloths. You can order individual dishes from the menu if you so desire, but the best deal is their tourist menu which offers you a choice of pasta, then meat, as well as a dessert. If you're really a hearty eater, and expect to spend some time here in the evenings (always a good idea), their larger menu *gastronomica* comes with the same offerings as the tourist menu, as well as an *antipasto*, fish or meat, wine, dessert, and Irish coffee to finish up the meal. You have to have at least one meal here while in the Citta Alta.

Seeing the Sights

Let's start off at the **Piazza Vecchia**, which holds a number of the town's beautiful sights.

PIAZZA VECCHIA

Several outdoor cafés ring this square which is the heart of the old town. In the middle of the square is the **Fontana di Alvise Contarini**, named after the Venetian mayor that gave the fountain to the town in 1780. The buildings that line the square are of 11th and 12th century origin. On the south side is the **Palazzo della Ragione** (Palace of Reason). Fires destroyed the ground floor in the second half of the 15th century and the building was restored with arcades instead of walls which I think adds to its character.

Next to this building is the **Torre Civica** where the bells toll every evening at 10:00pm 100 times (a tradition dating back to an ancient curfew). On the west side is the **Palazzo del Podesta** and was the home of the Venetian mayors that ran the town many centuries ago. The building is now the seat of the faculty of modern languages and literature for the University. To the north is the **Biblioteca Civica** (the Civic Library) that was started in 1604; the facade was only completed at the beginning of this century. You will find well-preserved parchments, scrolls, and other documents inside.

Through an arched passageway under the Palazzo della Ragione you can enter the **Piazzetta del Duomo**. In this little piazza you'll find the Cathedral, the Baptistery, the Colleoni Chapel, and also the Church of Santa Maria Maggiore:

Duomo
Piazza Duomo. Tel. 035/217-317. Open 8:00am-noon and 3:00pm-6:00pm.

Started in 1459 and continued in 1699, it was finally completed in the middle of the 19th century. It is a small cathedral but then Bergamo is a small little hillside town. Inside you'll find the *Madonna and Child* by BG Moroni and a painting by GD Tiepolo, *The Martyrdom of St. John.*

Baptistery
Open by reservations only. Tel. 035/217-317.

Built in 1340 by Giovanni da Campione, originally it was located at another site and was moved here in 1898. The upper part has refined columns and eight 14th century statues that represent the saintly virtues. Inside you'll find bas-reliefs of Christ's life and the baptismal font built by Giovanni da Campione.

Colleoni Chapel
Piazza Duomo. March-October open 9:00am-noon and 2:00pm-6:00pm. November-February open 9:00am-noon and 2:30pm-4:30pm. Closed Mondays.

This chapel, created in 1472, is considered one of the earliest works of Renaissance art in northern Italy, even though the exterior shows definite signs of the flowery Gothic style.

Basilica of Santa Maria Maggiore
Piazza Duomo, Tel. 035/246-855. November-March open 8:00am-noon and 3:00pm-6:00pm, and open April-October 8:00am-noon and 5:00pm-7:00pm.
    Built in 1137, this Romanesque church was once used as a sort of safety deposit box by the rich families of Bergamo. They would store their jewels and documents here. In the *loggia* of the entrance you'll find a statue of St. Alexander, the patron saint of the town.

CITADEL
Piazza della Citadella, Tel. 035/242-839. Open 9:00am-12:30pm and 2:30pm-6:00pm. Closed Mondays and holidays.
    Now the **Natural Science and Archaeological Museum**, this building was built in 1300 and was once part of larger fortresses of that time. An imposing and impressive structure which houses an interesting, though limited, museum.

VIALE DELLE MURA
    This road leads around the walls and offers scenic views of the lower city and of the Alps. The walls were built by the Venetians in 1561 to protect this strategically located hill town. From the rampart of San Grata, you can admire the rolling hills at the back of the town. When you come to Bergamo you should spend an afternoon strolling around the walls.

THE ROCCA
Via Rocca, Tel. 035/262-566. Open October-March, Saturdays and Sundays 10:00am-noon and 2:00pm-6:00pm. Open April-September every day from 10:00am-noon and 3:00pm-7:00pm.
    Located high above the town you can find the remains of a Viscount's castle from the fourteenth century. All that remains today is the circular dungeon. The fortress itself was built in 1331. Outside you'll find the peaceful **Parco delle Rimembranze**. Inside you'll find the **Risorgimento Museum** and great views of the town from the windows in the dungeon.

Practical Information
• **Tourist Information**, *Viale Papa Giovanni XXIII, #106, Bergamo, Citta Basso. Tel. 035/242-226.* They can give you maps and hotel information but are unable to do the booking for you. The map is very good for both the Citta Alta and the Citta Bassa.

Pavia & Certosa

Pavia is an interesting city, especially in the area around the University and Duomo, since that is where the old medieval core is located. But **Certosa** is the prize here: **La Certosa di Pavia** (the charterhouse of Pavia; see "F" under *Seeing the Sights* below) is a gem that you should definitely check out if you're visiting Milan. It has a beautiful marble facade that is the work of Amadeo and Montgegazza, and the portal is covered with reliefs that celebrate the history of Certosa. In the **Old Sacristy**, you'll find the hippopotamus tooth triptych created by Baldassare degli Embriachi. It is the oldest sculpture in the Certosa, containing 64 ivory molds that feature stories from both the Old and New Testaments. But my favorite part is the **Cloister**, a small building next to the church that contains 24 cells that were used by the Cathusian monks, each with its own garden.

The **Duomo** in Pavia pales in comparison. It is a simple brick structure that looks like it was part of the dark ages, while the Certosa evokes the beauty of the Renaissance.

Arrivals & Departures

By Train

There are trains every half hour leaving from Milan to **Pavia**. Once in Pavia, leave the station, pass the first street, and turn left at the second street, Via Trieste. About fifty feet down is the bus station. Here you can get a round trip ticket to **Certosa** for E2. The buses leave every half hour and take about 10 minutes to get to the church.

By Car

The easiest way to get here is by car.

Tourist Information

The Pavia and Certosa **information office** is located on *Via Filzi 12, Tel. 0382/22-156.* They offer first-rate information about the city and the church as well as an excellent map you can use to make your way around.

To get to the information office, leave the station, go past the first street, then take a left on Via Trieste. Go past the bus station to the first corner and take a right. The information office will be on the right hand side in the middle of the street.

Where to Stay

Pavia

I have always considered Pavia a place to pass through on the way to Certosa. You may be enamored with it, though, and if you are, here is a list of places to stay:

1. ARISTON, *Via Scopoli 10D, Tel. 0382/34-334, Fax 0382/25-667. Web: www.aristonparty.com/lite/ariston.html. 60 rooms all with bath. Single E80; Double E100. Breakfast E7 extra. All credit cards accepted.* ****

Deep in the heart of Pavia, you can explore and enjoy the university and old town much better here than at the other places. But then again you're farther away from the train station. You'll have all the amenities of a four star including a decent restaurant. The rooms are small but clean.

2. EXCELSIOR, *Piazzale Stazione 25. Tel. 0382/28-596, Fax 0382/26-030. 20 rooms all with bath. Single E60; Double E90. Breakfast E4 extra. All credit cards accepted.* ***

Located only 50 meters from the train station, this is a good clean hotel managed by Luigi Bricchi. The only drawback would be in the summer since they do not have air conditioning. The price is right for a brief stay but so is the four star Moderno or Ariston above. The extra money you spend on them will be well worth it.

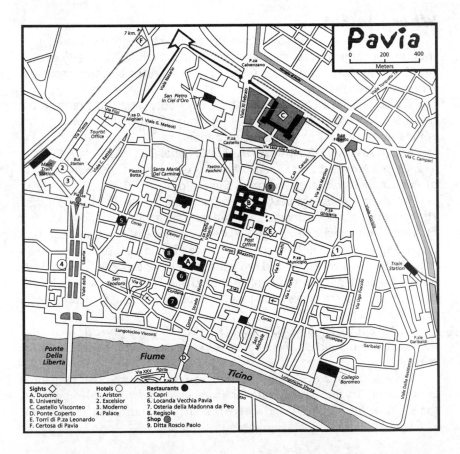

Pavia

Sights ◇	Hotels ○	Restaurants ●
A. Duomo	1. Ariston	5. Capri
B. University	2. Excelsior	6. Locanda Vecchia Pavia
C. Castello Visconteo	3. Moderno	7. Osteria della Madonna da Peo
D. Ponte Coperto	4. Palace	8. Regisole
E. Torri di P.za Leonardo		**Shop** ●
F. Certosa di Pavia		9. Ditta Roscio Paolo

3. MODERNO, *Viale Vittorio Emanuele II 41, Tel. 0382/303401, Fax 0382/25-225. 54 rooms all with bath. Single E90; Double E130. Breakfast E7 extra. All credit cards accepted.* ****

Located near the train station, you'll find all the amenities ofa four star in a small city for a very reasonable price. Even though it's in the center of town you won't notice any noise since it is completely soundproofed. Established in 1913, this old inn has rooms that are clean, modern, and comfortable. A good and convenient place to stay at a good price.

4. PALACE, *Viale Liberta 89. Tel. 0382/27441/2/3/4, Fax 0382/27441. 52 rooms all with bath. Single E90; Double E130. All credit cards accepted.* ****

Located on a busy thoroughfare, this is a quaint Italian hotel with all the four star amenities (such as TV, mini-bar, air conditioning, room service, etc.) at small city prices. You can get full board for only E110 a person from their more than adequate restaurant. The rooms are clean, somewhat tiny, but comfortable.

Where to Eat

There are not many restaurants in this city, which is a good indication that they do not get many tourists. But the ones they do have are pretty good.

5. CAPRI, *Corso Cavour 32. Closed Tuesdays. All credit cards accepted. Dinner for two E30.*

A plain little local place on one of the city's busy shopping streets, you'll find plenty here to satisfy your hunger, including *pizza al frutta di mare* (pizza with seafood), as well as grilled meats and fish.

6. LOCANDA VECCHIA PAVIA, *Via Cardinal Riboldi 2, Tel. 0382/304-132. Closed Mondays and Sunday nights as well the first of January and all of August. All credit cards accepted. Dinner for two E90.*

Some consider this the best restaurant in Pavia. It certainly is the most chic. Their motto is "We love tradition and we recreate it with a passion" and this fits well with their *cucina nuova*. Located near the cathedral, you can find unique but appetizing dishes such as *piccione alla marinata di verdure e vino rosso* (pigeon in a vegetable and red wine sauce), or *pasta fresca alla scampi e zucchine* (fresh pasta with shrimp and zucchini). The atmosphere is elegant but cramped and the prices are a little high, but for a creative meal in Pavia, come here.

7. OSTERIA DELLA MADONNA DA PEO, *Via Dei Liguri 28, Tel. 0382/302-833. Closed Sundays and August. All credit cards accepted. Dinner for two E60.*

In a small room down a tiny side street you can get some great traditional local cooking. Try their salami plate for an appetizer (*salumi tipici*), move onto the *pasta a fagioli* (pasta and beans), and then finish with a succulent

Ossobuco (ham bone cooked in tasty tomato based sauce with wine). An authentic local *osteria* but at really high prices.

8. REGISOLE, *Piazza Duomo 1. Closed Mondays. All credit cards accepted. Dinner for two E30.*

Known for their varieties of pizza they also have plenty of pasta dishes, including *carbonara* (with cheese, ham, and egg), *vongole* (spicy tomato based clam sauce), and *alla panna* (with a thick cream sauce); and meats and fish. The seating outside facing the Duomo is the best when the weather permits.

Seeing the Sights

Even though I've raved about Certosa, there are some fine examples of Renaissance art and architecture in Pavia. I especially like the University buildings. But the real prize, again, is the charterhouse which is described at the end of this section.

A. THE DUOMO
Piazza del Duomo. Open 7:00am–7:00pm.

A notable example of the Lombardy Renaissance period, this structure is the work of Rocchi, Amadeo, and Bramante (1488). It is the shape of a Greek cross surmounted by an immense dome, the third largest in Italy, built in the 19th century by the architect Maciachini. It is an unfinished work since there has been no attempt to put a face or sides of marble over the plain brick exterior.

B. THE UNIVERSITY
Strada Nuova 65. Tel. 0382/24764.

This is one of Italy's finest universities. Built from 1400 to 1500, the imposing set of structures were developed under the Viscontis and later restructured with a design by Piermarini and Pollach. The northern courtyards retain Pessina's 16th century plan with its Doric columns. Scattered throughout the maze of buildings are monuments to Allessandro Voloto, Antonio Bordoni, Bartolomeo Panizza, and Camillo Golgi. The best way to explore is to simply wander around and soak up the beauty of the ancient buildings.

C. CASTELLO VISCONTEO
Tel. 0382/308-774. Open Tuesday through Saturdays 9:00am to 1:30pm and Sundays 9:00am to 1:00pm. Closed Mondays.

Built between 1360 and 1365, this was an important non-military building during the Lombardy period of the 1300s. The building is surrounded by a deep ditch and protected by drawbridges. It originally was a complete square with four towers, but only two of the towers remain today.

You'll find the **Civic Museum** inside as well as a large unkempt grassy courtyard.

The Civic Museum has a fine archaeological collection that includes specimens of Roman glass as well as a Romanesque section with an exceptional collection of floors and mosaics.

D. PONTE COPERTO

The covered bridge over the **Ticino** is a 1951 reconstruction of a 13th century bridge destroyed during the bombings of the Second World War. Unlike the Ponte Vecchio in Florence, this famous bridge is only used for traffic and not commerce.

E. TORI DI PIAZZA LEONARDO

These are two of what used to be many towers that dotted the city. The towers reach a height of 60 meters. The clock face on one tells the time and the phases of the moon.

F. CERTOSA DI PAVIA

Certosa. Tel. 0382/925-613. Open 9:00am–11:30pm and 2:30pm–6:00pm in the summer, and only until 4:30pm in the winter. For March, April, September, and October, only open until 5:30pm. Closed Mondays.

The **Charterhouse of Pavia** is a wonderful example of 15th century Lombard art. It was originally built as a family mausoleum but is now a series of buildings built in different periods. The church is an ornate marble structure whose portal is covered with bas-reliefs celebrating the history of Certosa. The interior of the church is in three naves with chapels overflowing with rich works of art, such as Perugino's *Eternal Father* and Bergognone's *Saint Ambrose*. The **Old Sacristy**, made in the early 1400s, holds the hippopotamus tooth triptych created by Baldassare degli Embriachi, the oldest sculpture in Certosa. It contains 64 ivory molds featuring stories from the Old and New Testament as well as the *Legend of the Three Wise Men*. On the sides and at the base are 94 statuettes of Saints.

The **Cloister**, a small building annexed to the church, is the most interesting architecturally. Here you'll find 24 cells of the Carthusian monks, each with its own garden, that offer us insight into the domestic religious life of the 15th century. This is a place you cannot miss if you visit Milan or Pavia.

Shopping

The main shopping streets are the ones that bisect the city into quarters: the **Strada Nuova** from north to south and the **Via Cavour** and **Via Mazzini** from east to west. You'll find all sorts of local and international shops here.

One shop not on the main thoroughfares I think you'll like, which I've listed on the map, is:

9. DITTA ROSCIO PAOLO, *Corso Carlo Alberto 32, Tel. 0382/22-185.*
Located north of the university just outside its walls, this small brass shop features inexpensive old cane handles, pots, pans, trays, pitchers, and more. If you like brass or antique brass objects, this is a great store to visit and get some nice gifts.

Practical Information for Milan

Car Rental
• **Avis**, *Linate Airport, Tel. 02/71-51-23, Malpensa Airport 02/4009-9375, plus 10 locations dowtown.*
• **Hertz**, *Linate Airport, Tel. 02/7020-0297, Malpensa Airport 02/4009-9010, plus 5 locations downtown.*

Consulates
• **US Consulate**, *Via Principe Amadeo 4, Tel. 02/29-00-18-41*
• **Canadian Consulate**, *Via Vittor Pisani 19, Tel. 02/669-74-51. For emergencies 01/66-98-06-00*
• **United Kingdom Consulate**, *Via S. Paolo, Tel. 02/869-34-42*
• **Australian Consulate**, *Via Borgogna 2, Tel. 02/76-01-33-30*

Local Festivals & Holidays
• **First Sunday in June**, *Festa dei Navigli.* Located along the Navigli (canals) in the Ticinese section this is a folklore celebration with music and a festival. And even though it is a Sunday most of the stores will be open to accommodate the increased business.
• **December 7**, St. Ambrose day, patron saint of Milan. Features an open-air market surrounding the Basilica of Sant'Ambrogio commonly referred to as "O Bej O Bej."

Postal Services
• **Main Post Office**, *Via Cordusio 4, Tel. 02/869-20-69.* Located near the Duomo, between it and the castle. *Open Monday - Friday 8:45am to 7:30am and Saturdays 8:45am to 5:00pm.*

Supermarkets
There are not many near the center of town, so when you're in the need of food in your room and when all the stores are closed during the day and on Sundays, the places listed below will come in handy. They are open from 7:00am until 7:00pm every day.
• **Il Mercato**, *in the train station, lower level.* Open seven days a week featuring all sorts of necessary foods for the traveler and other items that only locals could need. Ideally located for the traveler in need of anything.

- **STANDA**, *Via Sarpi 33/Via Paila 2/Via Betrami 2*
- **Unese**, *Viale Bianca Maria 28*
- **SMA**, *Via L Mancin 2/4*
- **Natura Si**, *Via Fara 31*. An environmentalist's dream. Everything in here is natural, biodegradable, recycled, recyclable, organically grown, etc.

Tourist Information & Maps
- **EPT Office**, *in Central Station, Tel. 02/744-065, or at Linate Airport, Tel. 02/ 80-545*. They have maps of the city that are really no help if what you're looking for is down a side street. In conjunction they have information about hotels and can book them for you if you arrive in Milan without a room.

Tour Operators
- **American Express**, *Via Brera 3, Tel. 02/7200-3694*
- **Wagon-Lit**, *Corso Venezia 53, Tel. 02/7600-4133, Fax 02/7600-4980*

Chapter 20

the lake region

The northern lake region of Italy has been a preferred spot for vacationers and settlers for centuries. The most important visitor was probably **Julius Caesar**, whose legions left a lasting impression on the landscape with the remains of the forts and cities they built many years ago.

The quaint medieval charm of the lake towns, many of which were founded by the Romans, with their terraced gardens and terra-cotta roofed villas – though stunningly beautiful – pale in comparison to the natural splendor of the breathtaking scenery. This natural beauty has turned what used to be a relatively tourist-free region that could be enjoyed in calm serenity, into a heavily visited area during many times of the year. If you visit in July, August, or early September, the traditional time for Europeans to take their vacations, you will feel as if you're immersed in downtown rush hour instead of the pleasant environs of **Lago Maggiore** or **Lago di Como**.

But even during those hectic months, when most of Italy is swamped with tourists, you can still find some small lakeside town to escape from it all. Or you can hike up into the mountains for some revitalizing fresh air, or grab a ride on a ferry boat and float on the tranquil waters of the lakes on your way to a remote villa or garden. The Lake region is splendid even during the peak months, and if you are a lover of all things Italian, you would be remiss not to visit this region at least once.

Even though I counsel being car-less in Italy through most of the rest of the book, sometimes a car comes in handy in this region. Without the use of an automobile, you may have to restrict yourself to exploring just one lake by ferry or local bus service that moves along the *lungolago*, the lakeshore drive. With a car you'll have the freedom to explore all the lakes at will, and be able to take excursions to wonderful hill towns like Bergamo's Citta Alta, or experience the romantic beauty of Verona or Venice.

When to Go

Most hotels, restaurants, and shops close during the winter, and ferry service is cut back dramatically, but that time of year is also serenely peaceful. The time to really avoid is July through September, when it seems as if all of Europe has descended on the lakes.

The best time to come is during the Spring months (March to early June) or the Fall months (late September through October). During these periods the ferries operate on a slightly curtailed schedule and some hotels and restaurants are closed, but you will usually have the lakes virtually all to yourself. During these months you may encounter a mist or haze settling over the lakes and periodically obscuring the mountains, but that sometimes can add to the medieval, mystical charm of this wonderful region.

Touring the Lakes

The best way to tour each individual lake is by **ferry**, whether it is a **car ferry** *(traghetto auto)* or a **passenger-only ferry** *(traghetto)*. The ferries take longer than driving a car around the *lungolago* road, but on the water you will be blessed with far superior views of obscure villas and gardens, and best of all you will avoid the maddening traffic that descends during the peak months and even on the weekends in the off-season. The ferries go to all the main towns on each respective lake, so you can enjoy a complete lake experience only by utilizing them. But don't expect to be able to see everything quickly. The ferries take time, and you can't do everything in a day.

To save time, consider packing a sandwich and eating on the ferry as it skims the calm waters of the lake. You can also take **hydrofoils** both ways or

Hotel Meal Plans on the Lakes

Most hotels on the Northern Lakes require you to purchase a **full board meal plan**, *which could effectively double the cost of your stay. In some places this is a blessing, since there is not much around, but in places like* **Riva del Garda** *or* **Desenzano** *it really isn't necessary. Unfortunately, you may have to live with it. Inquire about the meal plan prior to arrival. It's better not to get it if you have the option, because if you decide you would like full board after you've settled in, you can simply purchase it on-site.*

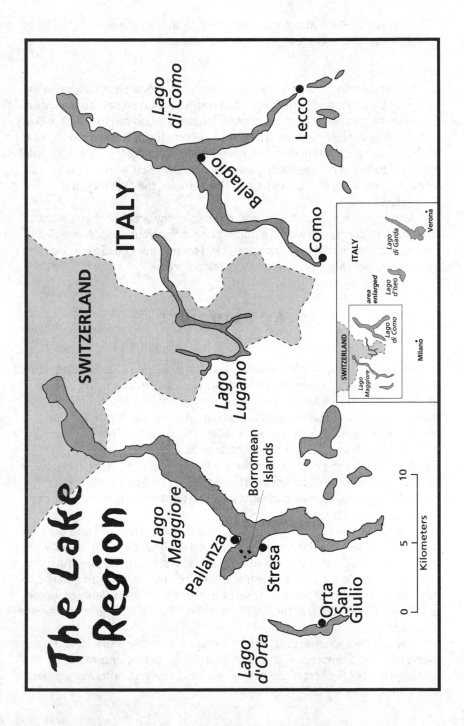

in one direction. But hydrofoils do not go to all the destinations on the lakes and they cost about twice as much as the ferries.

What to Do
Besides bathing in the spectacular scenery, and sometimes bathing in the waters of Lake Orta and Lake Garda – but not in Lake Como or Lake Maggiore; pollution has invaded even these pristine locations – you can try your hand at water skiing, wind surfing, jet skiing, and sailing. These water sports, hiking in the mountains surrounding the lakes, and exploring the charming little medieval towns is my idea of a great travel experience – but not from July through September if you can help it! Remember, the lake region is rather congested then.

Also, there are a number of golf courses in the area. So if you want to combine a relaxing holiday with a golfing one, bring your clubs. A short list of the golf courses in the area includes:Piandisolae, Alpino di Stresa, Des Iles Borromees, Dei Laghji, Varese, and Castelconturbia.

Lake Maggiore

The second largest of the Alpine lakes after Garda is **Lake Maggiore** (**Lago Maggiore** in Italian, and it's also known as **Verbano**). The lake was formed during the Ice Age from the slow movement of glaciers coming down from the Alps. This is evidenced by the U-shaped shoreline, its extended length, and the wide inlets advancing into the valley. The majority of the lake is in Italy, but a small section extends into Switzerland in its northern reaches. The lake has been inhabited since around the ninth century BCE. There have been recent archaeological discoveries that indicate an Iron Age people lived on the lake, who are now referred to as **Golasecca**, after the site of one of their most important burial mounds.

The climate on Lago Maggiore is splendidly mild, which not only assisted human settlement but also a stable agricultural life. These ancient visitors were in all likelihood attracted to the stunning northern scenery, the plentiful game and rich soil, and the beautiful, pristine waters teeming with an abundance of fish. Since the arrival of these early settlers, there have been plenty of visitors to Lago Maggiore, many of them quite famous – Byron, Goethe, and Wagner among them.

It would take volumes to list all of the magnificent towns to visit, with their medieval streets, impressive churches, imposing castles, and more, so I've compiled a list of the best of the best. Once here, use your hotel as a jumping-off point for area sights.

Lakeside Attractions

Visit the **Villa Taranto**, a house built in 1875 and located on the Castagnola between the towns of Intra and Pallanza. (These two towns are so close together it is almost as if they are one.) At the villa you'll find over 20,000 species of plants flourishing on over 20 hectares of land. The botanical gardens are quite splendid. Take a relaxing stroll through terraces, lawns, and fountains that make up the grounds. If you're here at the end of April through the beginning of May, you will have stumbled upon the magnificent **Tulip Week**.

If architecture is your pleasure, see the fabulous **Santa Caterina del Sasso**, located between Reno and Cerro on the water. The best way to approach is by boat, where you can get the perfect view of the buildings hewn out of the rock walls of the **Sasso Ballaro**. This monastery was built in the 13th century and added onto over the centuries. Seeing it perched on the cliff walls is mesmerizing.

Another building of architectural interest is the fortified palace on the **Rocca** in Angera. Built by the Visconti family in 1350 on the ruins of an earlier fortress, this place is worth a visit because of the vaulted ceilings and its medieval charm. I also love the tiny village set at the palace's feet that looks as if it hasn't changed in centuries.

Another architectural and historical sight are the remains of the **Vitaliano Castle**, built by Count Ludovico Borromeo between 1519 and 1526 that now rests on one of the three islands that are between Canero and Cannobio. The ferry doesn't stop here (it's really just a speck of an island with a fortified castle on it) but does get close enough for pictures to be taken. Truly magnificent.

Looking for something to bring back home, either for yourself or a friend? Don't miss the **Wednesday Market** at **Luino**, where you can get crafts, food, local clothing, and more. At the same time you can enjoy the sights and sounds of a boisterous local market.

Stresa

For those of you who insist on the best hotels with all the amenities, like swimming pools, saunas, tennis courts, and more, then you'll want to come to **Stresa**. Called the Pearl of Verbano, Stresa sits below the green slopes of **Mottarone** and offers a cool climate in the summer and mild temperatures in the winter, as well as picturesque beaches, beautiful landscaped gardens, fine restaurants, and much more. Stresa is the perfect place from which you can explore the rest of Lago Maggiore.

Arrivals & Departures

Located 80 miles northwest of Milan, there are a number of daily trains from Milan. If you're driving, take the E 62 to the SS 33, which brings you into town.

Where to Stay

GRAND HOTEL DES ILES BORROMEES, *Corso Umberto I 67, 28049 Stresa. Tel. 0323/30431, Fax 0323/32405. E-mail: borromees@stresa.net. Web: www.stresa.net/hotel/borromees. 182 rooms all with bath. Single E200; Double E350. All credit cards accepted.* *****

This is Stresa's best five star deluxe hotel. Located in a picturesque, romantic old building, this fine hotel is superbly situated on the town's main street as well as the lake's edge. They have their own indoor and outdoor swimming pool, tennis courts, health club, sauna, massage parlor, sun room, private beach, and snorkeling equipment for rent. On top of all that there is a piano bar, a restaurant with a scenic view over the lake, a lovely and relaxing garden, and everything else you can imagine that comes with a deluxe hotel. The rooms have high ceilings, antique furniture, and magnificent views, either of the lake or the mountains.

REGINA PALACE HOTEL, *Corso Umberto I, 28049 Stresa. Tel. 0323/933-777, Fax 0323/933-776. E-mail: h.regina@stresa.net. Web: www.stresa.net/hotel/regina. 166 rooms all with bath. Double E200-250; Suite E350. Breakfast included. All credit cards accepted.* ****

Another superb hotel situated in an historic and romantic building. Overlooking the lake, this place has its own private beach, a pretty garden area for relaxing, outdoor swimming pool, tennis and squash courts, gymnasium, sun room, sauna, snorkeling equipment, day care, discounts on golf at local courses, and more. The restaurant has perfect views of the lake and the Borromean Islands, and the piano bar offers relaxation in the evening. Since they are only a four star they seem to try harder than the five star deluxe, and offer a better price. The only real difference is that the Grand Hotel above has an indoor pool, a plus in the winter time. The rooms here have high ceilings, quaint antique furnishings, and spectacular views of the lake and/or the mountains.

LA PALMA, *Corso Umberto I 33, 28049 Stresa. Tel. 0323/32401, Fax 0323/933-930. E-mail: h.lapalma@stresa.net. Web: www.stresa.net/hotel/lapalma. 126 rooms all with bath. Single E150; Double E175. Breakfast E10. All credit cards accepted.* ****

Located on the main street and on the water's edge, this hotel also has its own private beach and a swimming pool. Situated in a more modern building than the Regina Palace and Grand Hotel, it is not nearly as charming and romantic in comparison, but it is still a grand hotel. Its location is perfect and the views over the water and the islands are just as good, especially from the restaurant, the swimming pool, and the tranquil garden area. They have a health club, sauna, sun room, and snorkeling equipment, plus a quiet lounge for a drink in the evening.

HOTEL DU PARC, *Via Gignous 1, 28049 Stresa. Tel. 0323/30335, Fax 0323/33596. E-mail: duparc@internetpiu.com. Web: www.stresa.net/hotel/ duparc. Closed October 15 to March 15. 22 rooms, all with bath. Single E100; Double E150. Breakfast E8. All credit cards accepted. ****

Nestled in a verdant setting, nearby the local tourist information office, this hotel is set a short distance back from the main street and the shoreline in the upper part of Stresa. Situated in a romantic little villa with panoramic views, this is the perfect choice for those travelers wanting a nice place to stay for not a lot of money. The only real amenities are a small restaurant that serves good food, room service, cable TV and air conditioning, as well as a tranquil garden area in which to relax. The rooms seem a little small compared with the four and five stars but your stay here will be wonderful A charming place to stay.

LA FONTANA, *Via Sempione Nord 1, 280949 Stresa. Tel. 0323/32707, Fax 0323/32708. Closed in November. 19 rooms all with bath. Double E110. Matercard and Visa accepted. Breakfast E6. ****

A tranquil little hotel that has a beautiful internal garden with a fountain. A short way from the center of town but still accessible. This place started off as a private villa built in the 30's and still has many of the original architectural features. From the third floor you can get good views over the lake. All the rooms on the first floor and three on the second have balconies. A cute little place with clean comfortable rooms for not a lot of money; the price is low because they have very few amenities except for cleanliness and comfort.

SEMPIONE, *Corso Italia 46, 28049 Stresa. 0323/30463. No fax. 17 rooms, 6 with bath, 11 with shower. Single E30-45; Double E50-65. No credit cards accepted. ***

A good two star with clean and comfortable rooms. The ones with shower have tiny bathrooms, but the facilities are more modern. They have their own restaurant service, but I suggest eating out, especially at L'Emiliano almost next door (see *Where to Eat*). This hotel is a great budget traveler's option.

Where to Eat

L'EMILIANO, *Corso Italia 50, Tel. 0323/31396. Closed Tuesdays, Wednesdays for lunch, and January and February. All credit cards accepted. Dinner for two E80.*

The atmosphere is functional and the food is fabulous. If you want to save some money, order their *menu degustazione* for E28 per person that gives you a first and second course. Their menu is a twist between traditional and *cucina nuova* and mainly consists of fish from the lake. Try their *ravioli di pesce con bisque di crostacei* (ravioli stuffed with fish and served with a crustacean sauce) or *their spaghetti freddi con cozze ed erba cipollina* (cold spaghetti with a sauce of mussels and baby onions). If meat is what you crave, try their *costoletta d'agnello profumate al rosmarino* (lamb cutlets cooked with a touch of rosemary), a succulently exquisite alternative to seafood.

PIEMONTESE, *Via Mazzini 25, Tel. 0323/30235. Closed Mondays and holidays. Credit cards accepted. Dinner for two E60.*

Located in the center of Stresa away from the water, the restaurant of the brothers Bellossi specializes in seafood and fish from the lake. In this elegant environment, try some of the *taglierini con vongole verace* (thin spaghetti-like pasta with a spicy oil-based clam sauce) or the tasty *involtini di sogliola e salmone* (rolled filets of sole and salmon). They also offer meat dishes like *costoletta d'agnello al timo con patate arrosto* (lamb cutlet cooked with thyme and served with roast potatoes).

Practical Information
• **Tourist Information Office**, *Piazzale Europe 3, Tel. 0323/31050-30416*

Borromean Islands

Just offshore from Stresa, the three enchanting little **Borromean Islands** will make you feel like you've stepped back in time. The **Isola dei Pescatori** has an ancient and picturesque little fishing village and that's about it, but it is a great place to escape for a while. The **Isola Bella** has its imposing **Palazzo Borromeo**, complete with a spectacular terraced garden. A tour through the palace brings you in contact with the wealth of the Borromeo family, furnished with Venetian chandeliers and mirrors, puppets, and more. If you come to this island, take the guided tour (*Tel. 30556; open April–November 9:00am–noon and 1:30pm–5:30pm. Admission E6*).

The **Isola Madre** is world-famous for its **villa** and landscaped **gardens** featuring a wide variety of exotic birds (*open April–November 9:00am–noon and 1:30pm–5:30pm; admission E6*). Inside the villa you'll find a cute little collection of dolls and puppets dating from the 16th to the 19th centuries. All the islands are just a short ferry ride or small personal boat taxi ride away from Stresa, and are so close that you can visit them all in less than a day. If you want to stay overnight, here are my recommendations:

Where to Stay

VERBANO, *Via Ugo Ara 2, Isola dei Pescatori. Tel. 0323/30408, Fax 0323/33129. E-mail: hotelverbano@tin.it. Web: www.verbanohotel.it. 12 rooms, 8 with bath, 4 with shower. Double E140. Breakfast Included. Full board E120. All credit cards accepted.* ***

A truly magical place to stay. Only a short private boat ride away from Stresa, you'll have peace and quiet in the evenings and get the opposite view from the tourists on the mainland, allowing you to savor at the lights of the small town of Stresa reflecting off of the lake. Located in a romantic old building, the hotel has its own private beach – but that's about it. Take them up on the full board meal option, since there are few places to eat on the island. When you come to this place you feel like you're getting away from it all.

ELVEZIA, *Lungolago Vittorio Emanuele 18, Isola Bella. Tel. 0323/30043. E-mail: info@elveziahotel.com. Web: www.elveziahotel.com. 9 rooms, none with bath. Three bathrooms in the hallway. Single without shower E35-45; Double without shower E50-60. Double E55-70. Full board E50. Credit cards accepted.* *

Only for the budget traveler extraordinaire. Though rustic it is s pleasant, and best of all, inexpensive, place to stay on this truly magical island. Some of the rooms are mere closets and no room has a private bath. Take the full board, since their restaurant is the best place to eat on the island (see below, *Where to Eat*) and full board is less than the price of a meal ordered *a la carte*.

Where to Eat

ELVEZIA, *Lungolago Vittorio Emanuele 18, Isola Bella, Tel. 0323/30043. Open only in the evenings by reservation only. Closed Mondays and November and March. All credit cards accepted. Dinner for two E45.*

This place has been in the Rossi family for generations. Even though it is large, about 140 seats available, and caters mainly to tourists, they still offer personal attentive service and great food. It's best to find a seat on the verandah porch area overlooking the water. Try their *antipasto di pesce all'isolana* (fish appetizer made island-style), or *le lasagnette alle verdure* (small vegetable lasagna). For seconds any of their fish dishes are superb.

Pallanza

Pallanza is a tiny resort town, more commonly known as **Verbania** to Italians, that has the luck of not having the main *lungolago*, SS 33, run right through the center of town. The main draw here, as mentioned earlier, is the **Villa Taranto**, a house built in 1875 and located two kilometers north of town, where you'll find over 20,000 species of plants flourishing on over 20 hectares of land. Besides the lovely botanical gardens, there are quaint grounds in which you can take relaxing strolls through terraces, lawns, and fountains (*Open April–October 8:30am–7:30pm. Admission E6.*)

Arrivals & Departures

Located on the north shore of Lago Maggiore across from Stresa. You can arive by ferry from Stresa; by car take the SS 33 to the SS 34 around the lake to Pallanza.

Where to Stay

You'll find that many of the hotels require you to also purchase a full-board meal plan. Inquire about this when making your reservation.

GRAND HOTEL MAJESTIC, *Via Vittorio Veneto 32, 28048 Verbania Pallanza. Tel. 0323/504-305, Fax 0323/556-379. E-mail: reception@grandhotelmajestic.it. Web: www.grandhotelmajestic.it. 119 rooms 56 with bath, 63 with shower. Single E130; Double E175; Suite E260. Breakfast included.* ****

Located directly on the lake shore and situated in a romantic old building complete with private beach, indoor swimming pool, private gardens, tennis courts, health club, piano bar, sunbathing terrace, and two restaurants with scenic views over the water. The rooms are expansive, comfortable and come with simple yet elegant furniture, as well as every conceivable amenity. Definitely the place to stay in Pallanza.

IL CHIOSTRO, *Via del Ceretti 11, 28048 Verbania Intra. Tel. 0323/ 53151, Fax 0323/401-231. 49 rooms, only 40 with shower. Single E70; Double E100. Credit cards accepted. Breakfast included.* ***

Located in Pallanza's sister town of Intra, this beautiful, quaint, charismatic, romantic hotel is located in a 17th century monastery. The second best place to stay while in Verbania in terms of amenities, but the best in terms of character, ambiance and uniqueness. You'll be up the slope of the mountain here, with a stunningly beautiful inner garden courtyard surrounded by arcaded walkways where you can sit and relax. Similar in style to colonial Spanish architecture, you'll find peace and tranquillity as well as a good restaurant, room service, lobby bar, tennis courts and more. The rooms have been completely refitted to contain every modern comfort. If only the monks had it so good when they lived here.

CASTAGNOLA, *Via al Collegio 18, Verbania Pallanza. Tel. 0323/503-414, Fax 0323/556-341. 107 rooms, 3 with bath, 104 with shower. Single E65; Double E90. Visa and Diners Club accepted.* **

What a two star! Located on the mountain overlooking the water and the sister cities of Pallanza and Intra, here you'll find yourself in a tranquil, romantic environment complete with tennis courts, ample park lands for *bocce* or *calcio*, a gymnasium, an excellent restaurant and more. The hotel has huge ceilings, creating the feeling of immense space in your rooms. The bathrooms have been modernized with showers, but are quite small. A great place to stay for the budget traveler and anyone else.

Where to Eat

MILANO, *Corso Zanitello 2, Tel. 0323/556-816. Closed Tuesdays, January 10-February 10 and the first 10 days of August. All credit cards accepted. Dinner for two E50.*

Located on the shoreline and next to the information office, this is the best place to eat in Pallanza, especially on their lakeside terrace with the view of the water and the little island of San Giovanni. Situated in an old villa with beautiful gardens and elegant dining rooms, you can't go wrong with the setting or the food. The chef/owner Egidio Sala makes sure of that. Some of his dishes are a little exotic, like the appetizer *trota alla menta e aceta rossa* (trout with a mint and red vinegar sauce) and the pasta dish *tagliolini agli scampi e zafferano* (thin spaghetti-like pasta with shrimp and saffron) but they all taste fantastic. For seconds their meats are superbly and simply prepared, as are their fish dishes.

LA CAVE, *Viale delle Magnolie 16, Tel. 0323/503-346. Closed Wednesdays and the first two weeks of November. All credit cards accepted. Dinner for two E45.*

Located along the lake shore, the atmosphere here is comfortable and relaxing. Couple that with fantastic service and superb food, and you have a great place to eat. They present their dishes at your table in a covered cart so you can get an idea of what you're going to get. Try any of their fish and seafood *antipasti*. For *primo*, sample the exquisite *tagliolini all'astice* (pasta with lobster). For seconds you have a wide variety of options from seafood to meat, many of them roasted over an open flame. The second best place to try after the Milano.

Practical Information
• **Tourist Information Office**, *Corso Zanitello 8, Tel. 0323/503-249*

Lake Orta

Lake Orta is less populated, less touristed, more attractive, and exceedingly more romantic than Lago Maggiore. Only half a mile across and eight miles long, it has an almost spiritual air about it that perhaps emanates from the chapels and monasteries and churches surrounding its shores; or maybe these structures were placed here because the lake has a gentle, tranquil, and almost indescribable beauty.

Besides the village of **Orta San Giulio** and its accompanying island, the only other real attractions around the lake is the **Sacro Monte** complex above the town with twenty chapels dedicated to St. Francis, and the **Sanctuary of Madonna del Sasso** that sits perched on a rocky outcrop near Boletta and the lake. For up to date information about Lake Orta, check out their new website, *www.orta.net*.

Orta San Giulio

This small medieval town with its twisting cobblestone streets and Baroque buildings is the perfect place to stay and use as an embarkation point to explore the lake. The main square, closed to traffic, with its cafés and quaint **Palazzetto della Communita**, is the meeting place of the town and has a calm demeanor about it. While here, visit the island of **San Giulio** only a short boat ride away.

Life on the island moves at a relaxed and slow pace. From the cloistered **convent** of the Closed Benedictine nuns to the **San Giulio Basilica**, you will feel transported back to medieval Europe. There's not much to do here but take it easy, eat, and poke around.

Arrivals & Departures

Orta San Giulio is located 75 km northwest of Milan. You can either take the train, or drive; by car, take the E 62 past Lago Maggiore to SS 229. Take this north to Orta San Giulio.

Where to Stay

HOTEL SAN ROCCO, *Via Gippini 11, 28016 Orta San Giulio. Tel. 0322/ 911-977, Fax 0322/911-964. Web: www.hotelsanrocco.it. 74 rooms, 61 with bath, 13 with shower. Single E95-140; Double E145-210; Full board E60. Breakfast included. Credit cards accepted.* ****

Seventy percent of the rooms here have views of the lake, which are stunning, so make sure you request one of these. This is a beautiful, quaint, old building with a swimming pool, sauna, private beach, health club, sun room and great views. Just outside the main town, you'll find tranquillity galore, as well as a fine restaurant and relaxing piano bar. The rooms are large, with high ceilings and all imaginable modern amenities. Without a doubt, the place to stay on Lake Orta.

LEON D'ORO, *Piazza Motta 43, 28016 Orta San Giulio. Tel. 0322/911-991, Fax 0322/90303. E-mail: leondoro@lycosmail.com. Web: www.orta.net/ leondoro. 37 rooms, 5 with bath, 32 with shower. Single E75; Double E90. Full board E80. Credit cards accepted.* ***

Located in the center of town and on the water. A great combination. This place offers location, a private beach, a lobby bar, and a great restaurant with a superb view over the lake. The rooms are clean and comfortable. A good three star for budget travelers.

ORTA, *Piazza Motta 1, 28016 Orta San Giulio. Tel. 0322/90253, Fax 0322/905-646. E-mail: hotelorta@ortasangiulio.net. Web: www.orta.net/ hotelorta. 35 rooms 13 with bath, 23 with shower. Rooms E60-80. Full Board E80Credit cards accepted.* ***

Another inexpensive and great place to stay. In the same square as the Leon D'Oro, this place is in a quaint old building, with larger rooms and modern amenities, such as TV, room service, laundry service, etc. They also have a good restaurant with wonderful panoramic views over the lake.

Where to Eat
VILLA CRESPI, *Via G. Fava 18, Tel. 0322/911-902. Closed Mondays in the summer. Credit cards accepted. Dinner for two E60.*

Near the gates of the town, this is a magical restaurant. Great ambiance and delicious food, which is mostly local dishes influenced by fish from the lake and game from the mountains. If you want an alternative to *a la carte* ordering, try one of their *menu degustazione* where you can sample a variety of their dishes

Practical Information
• **Tourist Information Office**, *Via Olina 9/11, Tel. 0322/90355*

Lake Como

This lake is a European tourist paradise – or purgatory - depending on when you visit. Over the centuries **Lake Como** has become the destination for royalty – and most recently for the nouveaux riche glitterati – as a result of its intense landscapes and scenery. You can find every imaginable activity around Lake Como including swimming (in pools, not the lake), sailing, canoeing, water skiing, sailing, fishing, golf, hunting, tennis, hiking, rock climbing and much more. If you're not into active vacations and prefer the more sedate pursuits like sightseeing, Como will not disappoint. There are vast parks, exotic gardens, lush villas, picturesque villages, and ancient castles, basilicas, art galleries and museums scattered along the lake.

In this way, it is a tourist paradise since there is so much to do, but as with the rest of the lakes in Northern Italy, if you visit between July and September it will be a tourist hell, since the shoreline and tiny villages will be packed with many, many vacationers.

Como

Como produces almost one-fifth of the world's silk supply. Ancient merchants stole the secret of the silk worm from the Chinese many centuries ago, and began production of the seductive cloth along the banks of Lake

Como and on the outskirts of the city. As such, you can find many bargains on silk in Como. If shopping is of little interest, you should visit the neo-classic **Villa Olmo** also on the outskirts of town. It is currently the seat of the local government, but the magnificent gardens are open to the public year round *(9:00am–noon and 1:30pm–6:00pm)*.

Como is the perfect jumping-off point from which to explore the lake and its many little towns either by ferry or car. You can also hop on the *funiculare*, located on the north edge of the city, and go up to the **Brunate** section of Como that is dotted with exquisite mansions and gardens. A short way outside of town (5 km) is the village of **Cernobbio**, where you can find the princely **Villa d'Este** with its lush gardens and enormous grounds. The villa is now the area's best five star deluxe hotel, but you can still wander through the grounds even if you're not staying there.

Arrivals & Departures

Located 70 kilometers north of Milan, you can either take the train from there (four times a day) or drive up the Autostrada A9 straight to the city.

Where to Stay

GRAND HOTEL VILLA D'ESTE, *Via Regina 40, Cernobbio 22012. Tel. 031/511-471, Fax 031/512-027. Web: www.villadeste.com. 113 rooms, 45 suites all with bath. Singles E260-430. Doubles/Suites E430-1,775. All credit cards accepted.* *****

What grandeur. If you stay here just for the building, the 10 acres of gardens, and the romantic atmosphere, it is well worth it. Besides the natural beauty you have an indoor swimming pool, tennis courts, sauna, private beach, glorious views over the water and the most attentive staff this side of Buckingham Palace. The rooms come with antique furnishing, marble bathrooms, jacuzzi, and every other imaginable amenity. Other services provided include: room service, limousine service, private helipad, hair and beauty parlor, baby-sitting service, laundry & dry cleaning, and gift & jewelry boutique.

METROPOLE E SUISSE, *Piazza Cavour 19. Tel. 031/269-4444, Fax 031/ 300-808. Web: www.hotelmetropolesuisse.com/index_ita_tot.htm. Closed December 20-January 10. 71 rooms all with bath. Single E90-120; Double E110-165. All credit cards accepted. Breakfast E12.* ****

Facing the Piazza Cavour as well as the lake, this is one of the oldest hotels in the town. The rooms are spacious each with a different style of furnishings. Some come with antiques from the '30's, others are done in the elaborate Venetian style, and some have more modern assemblies. The bathrooms are accommodating and come with a small complimentary toiletry kit. Each floor has its own sauna for your use. All the amenities of a four star hotel.

TERMINUS, *Lungo Lario Trieste 14. Tel. 031/329-111, Fax 031/302-550. Web: www.albergoterminus.com. 38 rooms all with bath. Single E110-140; Double E140-200. All credit cards accepted. Breakfast E15.* ***

Renovated to have all modern facilities this charming hotel has also maintained the ambiance of its 19th century roots. The common areas are filled with epochal pieces, tiled and mosaic floors which all helps to give the place character and charm. Each room is different in terms of dimensions and decor. In the small tower there is one room that covers two floors. A splendid place to stay.

HOTEL CONTINENTAL, *Via Innocenzo XI 15, 22100 Como. Tel. 031/ 260-485, Fax 031/273-343. Web: www.continental-hotel.net. 65 rooms all with shower. Single E80; Double E120. All credit cards accepted. Breakfast included.* ***

Now a Best Western, this charming hotel is located in a renovated old building closer to the train station than the lake. It is definitely a nice place to stay, especially since the rooms were completely renovated in 1994 and the common areas were renovated in 1997. It's quiet and peaceful and has a nice restaurant so you don't need to go out at night. They have all the facilities for you to engage in water sports, for a price. The rooms are clean and comfortable if a little crowded, with TV, mini-bar, radio, and phone which are necessities for a three star hotel.

FIRENZE, *Piazza Volta 16. Tel. 031-300-333, Fax 031/300-101. E-mail: info@albergofirenze.it. Web: www.albergofirenze.it. 40 rooms all with bath. Single E75; Double E105. All credit cards accepted. Breakfast included.* ***

In a central location, five minutes from the Duomo, Piazza Cavour or the lake this hotel is located in a beautiful building. Going upstairs to the first floor you are confronted with a brightly lit mirrored hall which blends into the bar/ breakfast area. The rooms are spacious and accommodating with green doors, parquet floors, cute little lamps on the wall, and beautiful furnishings. Only thirteen rooms so far have A/C so if you come in the summer ask for one of those. The bathrooms with their black and white motif are clean and accommodating. Hair dryers available on request. A good hotel at a good price.

QUARCINO, *Salita Quarcino 4. Tel. 031/303-944, Fax 031/304-678. E-mail: info@hotelquarcino.it. Web: www.hotelquarcino.it. 13 rooms only 3 with bath. Single E65; Double E85. Mastercard and Visa accepted. Breakfast included.* **

Located near the *funiculare* up to Brunate about 10 minutes from the center of Como in a tranquil and lush setting. A favorite of budget travelers. The rooms are spartan but dignified and the bathrooms are kept clean.

Where to Eat

· **DA ANGELA**, *Via Foscolo 16, Tel. 031/304-656. Closed Sundays and August. All credit cards accepted. Dinner for two E75.*

Local food at luxury prices. Located near the Stazione F.N. Lago (not the main train station), this is a popular place in Como. An elegant but rustic atmosphere, try their *coniglio alle olive* (rabbit with olives) or their fantastic *gnocchetti al sugo di salsicce e pomodoro* (little gnocchi in a sauce of tomatoes and sausage).

IMBARCADERO, *Via Cavour 20, Tel. 031/277-341. Closed the first ten days in January. Credit cards accepted. Dinner for E60.*

Located a few meters from the water's edge, this relaxed place offers great traditional dishes, simple in preparation but bursting with flavor. In the summer they open up their terrace so you can enjoy a great meal and the sounds, sights, and smells of the lake. An inexpensive and quite satisfying alternative to ordering a la carte is their *menu del giorno,* which offers a different primo and secondo each day for only E25 per person. Fish, soup, pasta, and meat all find their place onto this menu.

Practical Information

· **Tourist Information Office**, *Piazza Cavour 17, Tel. 031/274-064*

Bellagio

The location of this village is utterly divine. Surrounded by the lake on three sides, you have fantastic views over the water as well as the east and west shores of the lake. And while here you can enjoy strolls through the winding medieval streets or engage in any number of water sports. Down on the eastern shore of the peninsula is the quiet port of **Pescallo** with its many boats. The most famous sights here are the Villa Melzi and the Villa Serbelloni.

The **Villa Melzi**, *Lungolario Marconi, open 10:30am-4:00pm,* is known for its gardens ornately strewn with monuments and a small little pond of its own covered with lily pads and flowers. The **Villa Serbelloni** is now a five star hotel whose gardens are only open to non-guests from *10:30am to 4:00pm, closed Mondays.* Also known for its intricate gardens, the only way to truly appreciate them is by staying there – but the price is rather high.

Arrivals & Departures

Located 80 kilometers north of Milan, you can drive here by taking the Autostrada A9 to Como, go through town to the north end near the *funicular.* Here the *lungolago* road turns into the SS 583, which will lead you along the Lake to Bellagio. You can also take the train to Como, and simply take a ferry from there to Bellagio.

Where to Stay

GRAND HOTEL VILLA SERBELLONI, *Via Roma 1, 22021 Bellagio. Tel. 031/950-216, Fax 031/951-529. E-mail: inforequest@villaserbelloni.com. Web: www.villaserbelloni.it. Closed October 30 & April 10. 66 rooms, 28 suites all with bath. Single E200-245; Double E300-600. Credit cards accepted. Breakfast included. ******

This is an incredible place – supreme grandeur overlooking the town of Bellagio and Lake Como. You'll find everything you could imagine in a hotel, including pool, tennis courts, bus service, private beach down at the lake, water sports equipment, day care, a piano bar, an excellent restaurant, room service, laundry service and more. And all presented in a gorgeous old romantic mansion that will make your heart soar. The Kennedys stayed here as did the Rothschilds, which gives you an idea of the level of service. The rooms are all diverse in dimension and furnishings but all are of the highest level of comfort and accommodation. This is the place to stay in Bellaggio.

SPLENDIDE EXCELSIOR, *Lungolario Marconi 26, 22021 Bellagio. Closed September 20 & March 15. Tel. 031/950-225, Fax 031/951-224. Web: splendide.interfree.it. 47 rooms, 13 with bath, 34 with shower. Single E80; Double E110. American Express and Visa accepted. Breakfast included. ****

Located along the lakeside road, this hotel is situated in a romantic old *palazzo* built in 1912. The common areas are in the turn of the century style while rooms have been transported from the '70's. Some rooms on the first floor have tiny balconies overlooking the lake. The bathrooms are dated but accommodating. There is a heated indoor swimming pool, a garden area for relaxing, and a good restaurant with a scenic view over the lake as well as a piano bar for entertainment at night. They actually feature a small orchestra with three and sometimes four pieces. A great place to stay for the price.

HOTEL FIRENZE, *Piazza Mazzini, 46 22021 Bellagio. Tel. 031/950-342, Fax 031/951-722. E-mail: hotflore@tin.it. Web: www.bellagio.co.nz/florence. Closed November and March. 34 rooms, all but one single with bath. Single E110-130; Double E160-200. American Express, Mastercard and Visa accepted. Breakfast included. ****

In the center of town, this hotel occupies two romantic old buildings, one built in 1720, the other from the past century. The entry hall is like something out of the middle ages, very elegant. The rooms are all different sizes and come with a variety of different furnishings but all are comfortable and spacious. The bathrooms are ample and come with hair dryer and complete complimentary toiletry kit. They have a beautiful garden area as well as a really good restaurant and lobby bar that features American jazz in the high season.

Where to Eat

SILVIO, *Fraz Loppia Via Carcano 12, Tel. 031/950-322. Closed January and February. Master card and Visa accepted. Dinner for two E40.*

A family-run place near the Villa Melzi. Mom's in the kitchen, and her son and husband are serving and greeting in the dining room. All you'll find here is whatever they caught on the lake in the morning or during the day. They fry, grill, or bake the fish to perfection and also mix it with *risotto* (rice) or ladle it over pasta. They have a relaxing terrace area that should be enjoyed in the summer. The best place to eat while in Bellagio.

Practical Information

• **Tourist Information Office**, *Lungolario A. Marconi, Tel. 031/950-204*

Lake Garda

At 32 miles long and 10 miles across at its widest point, **Lake Garda** is the biggest Northern Italian lake. It is also the mildest in climate, causing the waters to teem with all sorts of fish and unfortunately, water craft; and the shoreline abounds with all sorts of produce, vegetation, and tourists. As Italy's most visited lake, over the years the hotel and restaurant service has become first-class. You can get from town to town by ferry, hydrofoil, or the **Gardesana highways** which pass along the shore and through any mountains that get in the way.

Besides scenic natural beauty and your fellow tourists, you'll be able to enjoy some of the most impressive and well-preserved medieval architecture in the region, especially the **Torre San Marco** at **Gardone Riviera**, as well as the remains of an ancient Roman villa near **Sirmione**. There are smaller villages along the shore of the lake that warrant exploring as well.

One of the best ways to do this is during market day. So on Mondays visit the market at **Manerba**, Tuesdays it's **Desenzano** and **Limone**, Wednesdays try **Gargnano**, Thursdays stop at **Lonato** and **Toscolano**, Fridays is the market day of rest, Saturdays enjoy **Salo's** market as well as the one at **Sirmione**, and on Sundays visit **Padenghe**. You'll be able to find all sorts of arts, crafts, local produce, cheese, meats, bread, and more at each of these colorful markets. If you're in the area on the first weekend of the month, head to Desenzano for their small antiques market.

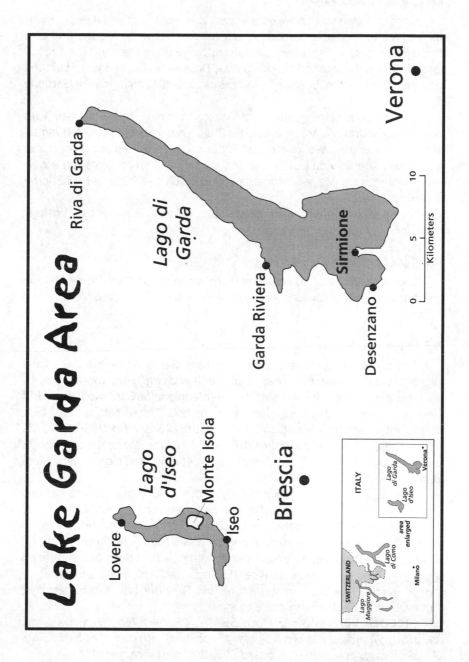

Desenzano

From this town you'll have easy access to any of the other lakeside towns by ferry or the Gardesana road, which follows the water's edge and cuts through a variety of mountainous outcroppings along the way. The second largest city on the lake to Riva del Garda, Desenzano lies in a wide gulf and has some fine beaches, but is not nearly as picturesque as Sirmione or Gardone Riviera.

This is a good starting point from which to explore the lake. Their 16th century **cathedral**, *Via Mazzini, open 9:00am–noon and 3:30pm–5:00pm,* is virtually nondescript save for the *Last Supper* painted by Tiepolo. There is also a luxurious **Roman villa** built in the 2nd century CE that contains some well-preserved mosaics, *Via Villa Romana, open 9:30am–1:30pm and 3:30pm–6:00pm.*

For up-to-date information, check out the Lake Garda website: *http://gardalake.de/.*

Arrivals & Departures

Located only about 30 km away from Verona and 90 km from Milan on the Autostrada A4. You can also get here by train from both Verona and Milan.

Where to Stay

This is not the best place to stay on Lake Garda, since it is one of the biggest towns, but even so it has character and charm. For a more romantic and scenic adventure, try and stay in either Sirmione or Gardone Riviera. But if you do choose to stay here, check into the hotels listed below:

PARK, *Lungolago C. Battisti 17. Tel. 030/914-3495, Fax 030/914-2280. Web: http://gardalake.it/park-hotel. Closed 15 days in December. 50 rooms all with bath. Single E75-90; Double E95-140. All credit cards accepted. Breakfast included.* ****

Opened in 1879 and known initially as Due Colombo, this place has had the honor of accommodating Kafka among other personages of note. Today the name has changed but the ambiance and charm of the old hotel remain. There are grand ballrooms surrounded by pillars filled with classic furniture. The rooms and bathrooms are decorated in a style best described as refined elegance. They come with satellite TV, frigo bar, A/C, heat, etc. Basically everything that makes a four star a four star. The hotel has seen better days, but even so it is a charming place to stay.

PICCOLA VELA, *Via dal Molin 36. Tel. 030/991-4666, Fax the same. Web: http://gardalake.it/piccola-vela. 43 rooms all with bath. Double E75-80. All credit cards accepted. Full board E95. Breakfast included.* ***

In the heart of Desenzano, this building is surrounded by olive groves and umbrella laden tables. The staff here is professional and courteous and the atmosphere elegant and refined. The piano bar is a great place to relax in evenings and strike up conversation. The rooms on the third floor have all been remodeled to include modern furnishings and spacious bathrooms with hairdryers and complete complimentary toiletry kit. The rooms on the other floors are not quite as alluring and have much smaller bathrooms. But from each room you have a nice view of the lake., and there is a pool to enjoy as well. The breakfast buffet is a continental feast with warm croissants, yogurt, fresh fruit, coffee, tea, milk, and juice. A fine place to stay in Desenzano that comes with a pool surrounded with a relaxing garden and has access to a private beach.

Where to Eat

CAVALLINO, *Via Murachette 9, Tel. 030/912-0217. Closed Sunday nights and Tuesdays at lunch. All credit cards accepted. Dinner for two E80.*

A wonderful little restaurant that serves everything from game to fish to pasta. Their terrace in the summer is an ideal place to savor the *anatra e coniglio in salsa al pepe* (duck and rabbit in a pepper sauce) or *trenette all'astice* (long flat noodle in a lobster sauce), definitely their most tasty dish. A great place to sample the food from the region.

ESPLANADE, *Via Lario 10, Tel. 030/914-3361. Closed Wednesdays. Credit cards accepted. Dinner for two E75.*

About 500 meters outside of town along the shore road to the south, this is an elegant place with a nice terrace in the summer from which you can have a romantic view of the area. Mainly a menu of fish from the sea and the lake, they also serve local specialties like rabbit and duck.

Practical Information

• **Tourist Information Office**, *Piazza Mateoti, Tel. 030/914-1510*

Sirmione

On the south side of the lake extending out into the water on a slender peninsula, **Sirmione** is a truly romantic and historic town to spend a few beautiful days. An impressive sight is the **Rocca Scaligera** fortress in the center of town, built in the 12th century to guard the lake. This massive construction with towers and battlements extending out into the water to create a safe harbor is still imposing today (*Piazza Carducci. Open 9:00am–12:30pm and 2:00–6:00pm in summer. and 9:00am–1:00pm in winter. Closed Mondays. Admission E3*).

Out on the tip of the peninsula is the **Grotte di Catullo**, a grandiose Roman villa complex with rooms, corridors, and underground areas still very well preserved *(Via Catullo. Open 9:00am–6:00pm in summer and only until 4:00pm in winter. Closed Monday.)* Other features of the town are the well-known **thermal baths** and the enchanting, winding medieval streets.

Arrivals & Departures

From Verona, only about 30 km away, take either train or bus. By car, take the Autostrada A4 and then the SS 11 at Pescheria del Garda to Sirmione.

From Milan, about 90 km away, take either train or bus. By car, take the Autostrada A4 to Desenzano, then take the SS 572 just over six km to the lone road that branches left to Sirmione and its peninsula.

Where to Stay

VILLA CORTINE PALACE HOTEL, *Via Grotte di Catullo 6, 25019 Sirmione. Tel. 030/990-5890, Fax 030/916-390. Web: www.hotelvillacortine.com. 55 rooms all with bath. Double E320-700. Suote E470-800. Credit cards accepted.* *******

What a beautiful old building, located out near the ruins of the ancient Roman villa. Here you'll have peace and quiet as well as a private beach, swimming pool, and tennis courts. They also have a nice restaurant, relaxing bar, garden area, room service, TV and superb service. The rooms have large ceilings and come with every possible amenity. Luxury at the lake is what this is. Stay here if you have the means.

HOTEL CONTINENTAL, *Via Punta Staffalo 1/9, 25019 Sirmione. Tel. 030/990-5711, Fax 030/916-278. 53 rooms all with bath. Single E100-130; Double E150-190. Breakfast E8 extra.* ******

A modern hotel with a balcony in every room. Located on the lakeside, they have a private beach, swimming pool, water sports equipment, and good restaurant. A step down from the ambiance of the Villa Cortine but still a perfect place to relax. The rooms are modern, with great views, are clean, and comfortable and come with satellite TV, air conditioning, and mini-bar.

CATULLO, *Piazza Flaminia 7. Tel. 030/990-5811, Fax 030/916-444. Web: www.hotelcatullo.it. Closed January 10 and March 15. 57 rooms all with bath. Double E100-115. All credit cards accepted. Full board E85. Breakfast included.* *****

A few paces from the *terme* (baths) by the lakeside, this place has its own small little private beach. Marble floors cover the main common rooms helping to cool the place in the summer. For relaxing moments there is a small intimate little bar arranged with teeny tables. Or you can sojourn out to the covered terrace with views of the lake. The rooms are spacious and comfortable and all come with tiny balconies. The bathrooms are normal sized but with all necessities. An excellent choice.

SPERANZA, *Via Casello 6. Tel. 030916-116, Fax 030/916-403. Closed November 25 and February 25. 13 rooms all with bath. Single E75; Double E90. Visa and Mastercard accepted. Breakfast included.* ******

A tiny two star with honest prices, personable owners, and a pleasant atmosphere. Not only is this hotel gracious, clean and comfortable and in the historic old section of Sirmione but it makes you feel as if you are at home. Run by two generations of the Sacchella family with Franco greeting you at the reception with his wonderful mother, Elisa; and Aunt Liliana in the kitchen preparing your breakfast. The rooms are modern, well-lit and comfortable. Some on the *piazza* have their own little balconies. The bathrooms are clean, not very big and come with a box shower stall. A great two star. Perfect place for budget travelers or above.

Where to Eat

VECCHIA LUGANA, *Piazzale Vecchia Lugana 1, Tel. 030/919-012. Closed Sunday nights and Tuesdays. All credit cards accepted. Dinner for two E80.*

An expensive place that has recently started to serve superb food. The dishes are prepared with the best ingredients, presented well, and taste exquisite. One of their best pastas is *ravioli di pesce al profumo d'erba cipollina* (seafood ravioli with a baby onion sauce). You can also get a buffet of vegetables or fish as a meal or appetizer. They also make great meats and fish on the grill. You can savor the succulent taste of the food either in the elegance of the inside dining or outside on their terrace facing the water.

LA RUCOLA, *Via Strentelle 7, Tel. 030/916-326. Closed Thursdays and January. All credit cards accepted. Dinner for two E75.*

An elegant local restaurant, some of their dishes seem a little odd to me. It's as if they're just mixing things together to be creative and get a reputation. The smells were good, the tastes the same but the ingredients ... I don't know. One of the strangest dishes is their *astice freddo con patate calde* (cold lobster with hot roasted potatoes). For a different – and delicious – meal, come here.

Practical Information

• **Tourist Information Office**, *Viale Marconi 2. Tel. 030/916-114*

Gardone Riviera

Gardone Riviera is a place of beauty and tranquillity when not being swarmed by zillions of invading tourists. As you enter the town, the majestic **Torre San Marco** rises from the water to greet you. The tower is a beautiful medieval and Renaissance lighthouse and has a private harbor area (*Open*

9:00am–1:00pm and 3:00pm–6:00pm; open only until 4:00pm in the winter).

Other features of the town are its splendid mansions, particularly the **Villa Turati** that contains one of Europe's most entertaining and extensive botanical gardens, with plants from the Mediterranean, Africa, and the Alpine regions (*Via Roma, open 10:00am–noon and 2:00pm–6:00pm and only until 4:00pm in the winter).* **Villa Cargnacco**, also known as **Il Vittoriale**, is also worth visiting, with its amphitheater where the plays of Gabriele d'Annunzio are performed in July and August (*open 8:30am–12:30pm and 2:00–6:00pm, only until 5:00pm in winter; closed Mondays; admission E3).*

Besides the villas and the tower at Gardone Riviera, you can take quiet, relaxing walks through the lush mountain trails, and appreciate the majestic beauty all around you. A great place to relax. Don't forget to bring your clubs since there is a golf course almost right on the lake.

Arrivals & Departures

By car, make your way to Desenzano (see above). Once at Desenzano take the SS 572 along the lake shore to the town. Alternatively, take the ferry from Desenzano, Sirmione, or Riva del Garda.

Where to Stay

GRAND HOTEL FASANO, *Corso Zanardelli 160. Tel. 0365/290-220, Fax 0365/290-221. E-mail: fasano@italyhotel.com. Web: www.grand-hotel-fasano.it. Closed September 31 and February 29. 84 rooms all with bath. Single E150-220; Double E230-290. No credit cards accepted. Breakfast included.* ****

During the second half of the 18th century, the precursor to this place was the summer residence for the imperial court of Austria, and today it retains much of that charm and ambiance. Nothing is left out, everything is elegant and refined. Situated directly on the lake, there is a large terrace where you get served an abundant buffet breakfast in the summer. The rooms are all very spacious and arranged with furnishings from the 18th century. Some rooms come with ample balconies from which the views of the lake are stupendous ... you will need to specifically request one of these. Marble bathrooms with double sinks add to the refinement. They also have a small private beach where you have boats at your disposal. The pool is heated if the lake water hasn't warmed yet. They also have tennis courts and a lush private park for your enjoyment. Definitely the best place to stay in Gardone Riviera.

MONTEFIORI, *Via dei Lauri 8, 25083 Gardone Riviera. Tel. 0365/290-235, Fax 0365/25083. E-mail: hotelmontefiori@gardainforma.com. Web: www.gardainforma.com/montefiori. 31 rooms all with bath. Single E70-100; Double E160-200. Credit cards accepted.* ***

Set off in a park above the lake, this nice hotel radiates peace and tranquillity. Located in a small old *palazzo* with tennis courts, swimming pool, and great views over the area. The rooms are spacious and accommodating with TVs if the grandeur of the lake becomes too boring. A great relatively inexpensive place to stay.

Where to Eat

VILLA FIORDALISO, *Corso Zanardelli 132, Tel. 0365/20158. Closed Mondays and the 10th of January through the 25th of February. Dinner for two E90.*

Super elegant dining, whether on the terrace in the garden during summer or in the rooms decorated in the intricate Liberty style. The food is excellent and the presentation is refined, but the portions are minuscule. Many of their dishes are made from the day's catch from the lake or the Adriatic.

Try their *tagliolini con calamaretti e asparagi* (with small calamari and asparagus) and then some *filetto di pesce persico e menta* (perch with a light mint sauce). They also have a *menu degustazione* for E30 per person which is good, just as non-filling, and a lot less expensive.

Practical Information

• **Tourist Information Office**, *Corso Repubblica 35, Tel. 0365/20347*

Riva del Garda

At the northernmost end of Lake Garda, **Riva del Garda** has plenty of winding medieval streets to keep you entranced and occupied while exploring. On the west side of town are short cliffs, and on the east side is a small pebble-strewn beach. Surrounding the city beach (there is another beach just further west) are gardens that make for a pleasant picnic, stroll, or just a lazy afternoon doing nothing at all.

In the middle of both of these is the imposing 12th century **Rocca Fortress** with a vast moat. Now a local **museum**, Roman artifacts and other goodies from the past are on display (*Piazza Battisti, open 9:00am–1:00pm and 3–5:00pm, only until 4:00pm in the winter; closed Mondays.*)

Arrivals & Departures

All the way at the north end of this expansive lake, Riva del Garda is one of the two largest towns (the other is Desenzano) and can be reached by ferry from any other town on the lake with ferry service. Or you can get yourself stuck in traffic following the lake road around Lago Garda.

Where to Stay

HOTEL DU LAC ET DU PARC, *Viale Rovereto 44, 38066 Riva del Garda, Tel. 0464/551-500, Fax 0464/555-200. Web: www.garda.com/dulac. 170 rooms, 135 with bath, 35 with shower. Also available are 32 private bungalows. Double E130-240; Bungalow E160-260. Breakfast E8 extra. Credit cards accepted.* ****

This very nice modern hotel is not too far outside of town, and is situated in the middle of lush green gardens and lawns. An old building filled with character, stay here for a holiday paradise, complete with indoor and outdoor pool, tennis courts, gymnasium, health spa, sauna, sun room, piano bar, several restaurants, water sports equipment and more.

EUROPA, *Piazza Catena 9. Tel. 0464/55-433, Fax 0464/521-777. Web: www.rivadelgarda.com/europa. Closed in December. 63 rooms all with bath. Single E70-80; Double E110-130. All credit cards accepted. Breakfast included.* ***

A Best Western hotel deep in the heart of the *centro storico*, dominating the small *piazza* on which it sits with its wonderful 18th century facade. The interior, completely renovated about 15 years ago, presents a modern style. The restaurant has a terrace overlooking the lake that makes a wonderful setting for a meal. The rooms are spacious as are the bathrooms. These come in a light red marble and have a complimentary toiletry kit available. The sun terrace is on the roof surrounded by lush potted plants. A good three star in an excellent location.

LUISE, *Viale Rovereto 9. Tel. 0464/552-796, Fax 0464/554-250. Web: www.hotelluise.com. Closed from November to Easter. 57 rooms all with bath. Double E90-150. All credit cards accepted. Breakfast included.* ***

A little ways outside of Riva in a more modern building erected in the '60's. The inconvenience of being situated here is counteracted by the lush greenery surrounding the garden terrace and tennis courts making the road seem non-existent. The common areas are ample and modern and have satellite TV, frigo bar and everything else a three star needs. The bathrooms are modern and functional and come with hair dryer and courtesy toiletry kit. A popular hotel with bicycle enthusiasts.

Where to Eat

VECCHIA RIVA, *Via Bastione 3, Tel. 0464/555-061. Closed Tuesdays (not in high season) and January. All credit cards accepted. Dinner for two E65.*

A super elegant restaurant that takes classic dishes and explores the possibilities with them. They have a terrace that is perfect for summer dining. They make great *crepes al caviale* (with caviar) served with a yogurt sauce. Most of the second courses are based on the fresh catch of the day from the lake, many of which are covered in a creative sauce in an attempt to enhance the fish's flavor. If you like culinary adventure, come here.

RESTEL DEL FER, *Via Restel del Fer 10. Tel. 0464/553-481. Closed Tuesdays and in November. all credit cards accepted. Dinner for two E55.*

Located out of town by the Luise and Hotel du Lac et du Parc, this place is known for its succulent fish dishes (embellished with *funghi* – mushrooms – when in season). Their pasta is made in-house so it is incredibly fresh and tasty, and they also make their own olive oil which is also amazing. This is a traditional restaurant, which means they also offer great meat dishes; I especially like the *costolette di agnello* (lamb cutlets).

Practical Information

• **Tourist Information Office**, *Giardino di Porta Orientale, Tel. 0464/554-444*

Chapter 21

alpine italy

Why go the Rockies, or any other North American winter resort, when you can afford to go to the Alps? The scenery is better in the Alps, the skiing is better, and off the slopes the community life in the villages is much better by far.

Alpine Italy is a land in and of itself, culturally separate and distinct, but still very much a part of the heart and soul of Italy. Alpine Italy spans a number of different Italian provinces starting in and snaking west to east through Piemonte, Val d'Aosta, Lombardia, Trentino Alto-Adige, and eventually culminating in Friuli Venezia Giulia. Since Alpine Italy extends from France, passing by Switzerland and Austria and ending at Eastern Europe, it encompasses all manner of natural settings, and entails a wide variety of cultural influences, that to really do this area justice would entail an entire book. Without that luxury I'll do my best to capture the area's essence in this one small chapter, and few choice destinations.

Alpine Italy's diversity is expressed through its varied cuisine. Italian favorites abound but you can also find *strudel* and *snitzel*, and beer is as plentiful as the wine. Sausage is as plentiful on the table as pasta.

The scenery is varied as well. You can find cows lounging around with bells around their necks as you would in Switzerland. There are mountain chalets as you would find in Austria. Spotting an old timer in the traditional attire of *Leiderhausen* is not unheard of. In all, anywhere you go in Alpine Italy will be a change of pace from a regular Italian vacation. Whether it is for skiing in the winter, hiking in the summer, or just exploring all year round, Alpine Italy is a perfect place to come to get away from it all, and to find something you would never expect to see while on a trip to Italy.

A prime example of this is the "Ice Man," a prehistoric traveler who was frozen in the Alps, and who now resides in a museum in **Bolzano**. This rare, one of a kind, glimpse into humanity's past is a rare treasure, and is a must see if you come to Alpine Italy.

Since Alpine Italy is so extensive, we are only going to cover what would be considered some of the major locations. But from these places there are innumerable day trips to scenic little towns, stunning nature preserves, pristine mountain refuges and more. Featured here are the towns of **Aosta** and **Courmayeur** in Val d'Aosta, **Bolzano** and **Merano** in Trentino Alto Adige; and **Bormio** in Lombardia. These are the gems of the region, but there are plenty of other places to explore in Alpine Italy, and so much to do.

Aosta

If you're interested in Roman ruins with a backdrop of snow-capped mountains, complete with medieval churches, buildings, and towers as a foreground, this unique scene can be yours in **Aosta**. Sitting in the flat lands of the nearby mountains of **Monte Emilius** (3,600 meters) and **Becca di Nona** (3,200 meters) this town was built as a Roman fort and the gateway through the **Great** and **Little St. Bernard** passes.

The Roman fort was erected in 25 BCE and was then called Augustus Praetoria Salassorum, and today an arch dedicated to Augustus remains in the city. The plan of the town still retains the simple structured layout of its Roman origins and the old town is surrounded by the walls erected at that time. These walls form a rectangle 725 meters by 572 meters that contains twenty lookout towers. The city is the capital of the autonomous region known as **Val d'Aosta** and is a prime location for skiing in winter and kayaking, rafting and hiking in the summer. Aosta is a good jumping-off point for any of these activities.

Arrivals & Departures

Aosta is 98 kilometers from Turin, from which three trains leave daily: one in the early am, one at 1:00pm, and one in the late evening. The trip takes about an hour each way. If you don't want to rush, stay the night.

Where to Stay

1. HOLIDAY INN AOSTA, *Corso Battaglione 30, 1100 Aosta, Tel. 0165/23-63-56, Fax 0165/23-68-37. 50 rooms all with bath. Single E100-130; Double E130-170. Breakfast E15 extra. Credit cards accepted.* ****

Located in the heart of the city in a building that was renovated in 1994.

The rooms are what you would expect in a high class hotel: clean, comfortable, and quiet. There are fitness and sauna facilities available as well as an excellent restaurant, La Taverne Provencale, and a nice bar that makes for a cozy retreat in the evenings.

2. **EUROPA**, *Piazza Narbone 8, 11100 Aosta, Tel. 0165/236-363, Fax 0165/40-566. 71 rooms, all with bath. Single E100-160; Double E130-200. Credit cards accepted.* ****

Located in the heart of the city, this is an exceptional hotel complete with elegant furnishings, a fitness center, piano bar, two-tiered restaurant that serves local and international food. The rooms are perfect with everything you could want, even a video cassette player for rent.

3. **CECCHIN**, *Via Ponte Romano 27, 11100 Aosta, Tel. 0165/45262, Fax 0165/31736. Web: www.adava.vao.it/Alberghi/aosta/cecchin.htm. 10 rooms all with bath. Single E70; Double E120. Breakfast E8 extra. Mastercard and Visa accepted. Closed in November.* ***

Located right by the ancient Roman bridge, this is a quiet, simple bed and breakfast style hotel with only 10 rooms. Do not be put off by the entrance, which is through a trattoria, this is an informal family run place. The furnishings and accommodations are rustic but comfortable. The bathrooms are basic but have everything you need. There is no air conditioning but it is hardly needed even in the summer.

4. **ROMA**, *Via Torino 7, 11100 Aosta, Tel. 0165/40821, Fax 0165/32404. E-mail: hroma@libero.it. Web: www.adava.vao.it/Alberghi/roma/roma.htm. 33 rooms, 3 with bath, 30 with shower. Single E70-85; Double E120-130. Credit cards accepted.* ***

Located near the Arch of Augustus, this is a hospitable, clean and comfortable three star housed in a renovated older building. One of the oldest hotels in town, the renovations have given a more modern look and feel to the place. Their restaurant creates some wonderfully appetizing local dishes and their downstairs bar is a place to relax after a tough day. Some of the rooms have just recently got TVs but with the stunning vistas out your window, there's no need to sedate yourself with media *soma*.

5. **TORINO**, *Via Torino 14, 11100 Aosta, Tel. 016544593, Fax 0165/361-377. Web: www.hotelturin.it/. 50 room only 45 with bath. Single without bath E40-60. Single E55-70; Double E80-90. Breakfast E8 extra. Credit cards accepted.* ***

Same type of amenities as the Hotel Roma, which is just down and across the street from this location, except they have TVs in every room. The hotel restaurant is not as good, but is quite tasty. The rooms are clean, quiet, and comfortable. A good option when in Aosta.

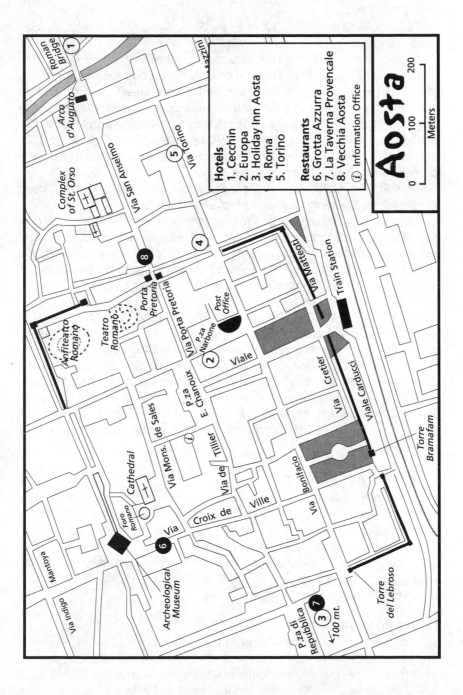

Aosta

0   100   200
Meters

Hotels
1. Cecchin
2. Europa
3. Holiday Inn Aosta
4. Roma
5. Torino

Restaurants
6. Grotta Azzurra
7. La Taverna Provencale
8. Vecchia Aosta
(i) Information Office

Where to Eat

6. LA TAVERNA PROVENCALE, *Via Guido Saba 1, Tel. 0165/236-356. Credit cards accepted. Dinner for two E45.*

A two-tiered brightly lit hotel restaurant attached to the Holiday Inn. They serve the local favorites here all made perfectly. Try the *bouillabaisse* for *primo*, after a fine plate of *grigliata di verdure* (grilled vegetables) for starters. Then you can either move onto a fine fish dish like *pesce persico alle verdure di stagione* (filets of perch cooked with seasonal vegetables) or a great meat dish like *tagliata di manzo ai petali di carciofi* (beef steak with artichoke leaves). Or if you want to save a little money and still get two courses plus dessert, try one of their four fixed price menus from E20-30.

7. GROTTA AZZURRA, *Via Croix de Ville 97, Tel. 0165/262-474. Closed Wednesdays. No credit cards accepted. Dinner for two E40.*

A great little pizzeria, and, as the name suggests – the *grotta azzurra* is the famous grotto under the Isle of Capri in the Bay of Naples – it serves fine fish dishes. Try their *insalata di mare* (seafood salad) and their *spaghetti alla vongole verace* (with a spicy clam sauce), or a fine *zuppa di mare* (seafood soup). And if you can't choose between the fish options, you can always select a pizza made with mounds of cheese.

8. VECCHIA AOSTA, *Piazza Porte Pretoriane 2, Tel. 0165/361-186. Closed Tuesday Nights and Wednesdays, two weeks in July and two weeks in October. Credit cards accepted. Dinner for two E45.*

A nice internal ambiance with an ancient Roman feel and look about it. You can be served outside on their terrace also. Here they make some fine local specialties like *ravioli al sugo di arrosto* (roasted ravioli) as well as some great fondues. You can also get a tourist menu for E15 per person, as well as a gastronomic menu for E18. A great place to come and relax and eat simple hearty food.

Seeing the Sights

Take in the Roman ruins and the extant Roman structures, or wander around the medieval and Gothic churches gracing this pleasing town. These are the sights in the town, but outside you will find many too: those of the natural bent. Hiking, skiing, kayaking and other outdoor pursuits can be found in the mountains surrounding Aosta. For more information contact the **tourist office**, *Piazza Chanoux 8, Tel. 0165/23-66-27 or 35655, Fax 0165/34667, 9:00am-noon and 3:00pm-8:00pm.*

PONTE ROMANO

Located over the **Butheir River** at the eastern part of the city, this is an ancient Roman bridge still in use (after centuries of renovations, of course) even though the course of the Butheir river changed during the Middle Ages and didn't flow underneath the bridge. The humpbacked span is 6 meters wide and 17 meters long and was built in the time of Augustus, at the end of the first century BCE.

ARCO D'AUGUSTO
Piazza Arco d'Augusto.

Not grand or imposing by comparison to those found in Rome, but this **arch** is astounding in that it was built in 25 BCE in homage to Augustus and to commemorate the victory by the Romans over a local tribe called Salassi. This monument, which is perfectly aligned with the Praetorian gate, is 11.5 meters high and represents a combination of Doric and Corinthian styles. The arch used to be adorned with statues, bas-reliefs, and trophies but these were removed during the many "Barbarian" invasions of the Roman Empire. The crucifix that is under the vault was placed there in 1542.

TEATRO ROMANO
Via Bailage. Open Winter 9:30am–noon and 2:00pm–4:30pm. Summer open 9:00am–7:00pm.

This was once a covered **theater** that was used so that shows could be performed in inclement weather. Its construction was begun after the city was erected and sits over private residences that had already been in place. What remains of this theater is the facade (which is 22 meters high), the *cavea* (which was used to help cover the theater), the stage, and the side portico. All are very well preserved.

ANFITEATRO ROMANO
Via dell'Anfiteatro. Contact the Sisters of San Giuseppe in advance to arrange for a visit, Tel. 0165/262-149.

Built in the middle of the first century CE, this **amphitheater** used to measure 86 meters by 76 meters and had 60 arches on each of its two floors. It could hold over 2,000 spectators (double the number of inhabitants in the city at the time). It is a little worse for wear, and all that remains today are eight arches that have been incorporated into the **Convent of the Sisters of San Giuseppe**. This could be a more interesting ruin if the city would bother to take the time and money to excavate it properly.

PORTA PRAETORIA
Located between via Sant'Anselmo and Via Porte Pretoriane.

This once was the eastern entrance to the town and dates back to 25 BCE, when the city was founded. It is made of parallel double stone walls and is open at the bottom by three arches. The external wall is 4.5 meters thick and the internal wall is about 3.5 meters. The space between the walls was used as a weapons storeroom. Today over three meters of the gate and wall lie under the ground, due to the periodic flooding of the Dora over the years. The tower next to the gate was built in the 12th century as a residence for the lords of the city. Today the ground floor is used as an exhibit space featuring local artists.

CATTEDRALE
Piazza Cattedrale. Open 7:00am–7:00pm.
Built on the sight of the Roman forum that dates from the fourth century CE, this Romanesque **cathedral** was constructed from 994 to 1026. It was altered many times over the centuries, with addition of the cloister, a neo-classic facade, and cross vaults inside. On a bright sunny day you will really appreciate the spectacle of the sun streaming through the 23 stained glass windows.

COMPLEX OF SAINT ORSO
Via and Piazzetta dell'Orso. Tel. 0165/262–026. Winter 9:30am–noon and 2:00pm–5:30pm. Summer 9:00am–7:00pm.
This Romanesque and Gothic complex includes the church of Saints Peter and Orso, the bell tower clock, the crypt, the Museum of Treasure, the cloister of Saint Orso, the buildings of the Priorate, and the ancient cemetery. Everything about this complex gives us an insight into the religious day to day life from the fifth century to the fifteenth century.

Sports & Recreation
Hiking
The best time to hike in this area is July, August, and the first two weeks of September. Otherwise it can be a little chilly. Contact the tourist office in Aosta listed above, and request a free list of campgrounds, trails, and alpine refuges *(rifugi alpini)* for rent along the many twisting trails of the surrounding peaks. For more detailed information, contact the **Club Alpino Italiano**, *Tel. 0165/40194, Fax 0165/36-32-44*, located above the tourist office in Aosta.

Skiing
High season is November through March, and as such can be very crowded. It is best to make reservations well in advance. Contact the local **tourist office**, *Piazza Chanoux 8, Tel. 0165/23-66-27 or 35655, Fax 0165/ 34667, 9:00am-noon and 3:00pm-8:00pm*, for a free pamphlet they distribute called *Winter Season, Aosta Valley*. The pamphlet contains up-to-date information about skiing, hotels, events, and more. Courmayeur is the best known ski resort in the area and is Italy's oldest (see below).
Aosta has a *funiculare* to carry skiers up **Mount Emilius**. It is located just behind the train station away from the historic part of town. In the winter,

Aosta fills up with skiers from all over the world – not only to sample her slopes but to also bathe in her beauty and charm.

Courmayeur

Courmayeur and its sister city five kilometers away, **Entreve**, are located at the base of **Mont Blanc**, the highest peak in the Alps. Entreve is at the entrance to the Mont Blanc Tunnel which offers easy access to France. Both towns serve up some of the best skiing in Italy. The economies of Courmayeur and Entreve are completely geared towards winter sporting activities, and to a lesser but not insignificant degree summer relaxation and hiking, since many hotels stay open year round. In fact there is summer skiing, horse back riding, hang gliding, canoeing and over 280 km of mountain hiking trails in the vicinity.

Courmayeur is Italy's oldest Alpine resort and as such is able to offer skiers of all levels everything they need to have the time of their lives. There are over 140 km of downhill and cross-country skiing runs. Just a few hundred meters from the main square, **Piazzale Monte Bianco**, is the **Funivia Courmayeur**, which transports skiers and sightseers up the first leg of the mountain to reach the choicest slopes this area has to offer. In Entreve there are two more such *funivie* running up Mont Blanc for your skiing pleasure. In the summer the *funivie* carry hikers and nature lovers up into the mountains to explore the area's natural beauty. Courmayeur and Entreve are year round paradises.

Arrivals & Departures

If you're driving from Aosta, take the E 25 straight into Courmayeur. Be aware that during most times of the year there will be a lot of traffic, since this road leads to the **Mont Blanc Tunnel** that cuts through the mountain into France and the ski center of Chamonix.

The only other way to get here is by bus. You'll find the **tourist office** in the bus terminal, *Piazza Monte Bianco, Tel. 0165/842-060*. Here you can get up to date information about skiing, hiking, alpine huts, hotel availability, etc. They also supply superb maps.

Where to Stay

Wherever you stay, you're going to pay through the nose. This is another of those places that was created by the rich and famous many years ago for their pleasure, then left for the not-so-rich-and-famous to enjoy later. But the prices stayed the same.

I strongly recommend making reservations at least six months in advance, summer or winter (in June virtually everything shuts down so shopkeepers, restaurateurs, and hoteliers can take their vacations), especially if you want to stay on a weekend.

GALLIA GRAN BAITA, *Strada Larzy, 11013 Courmayeur. Tel. 0165/844-040, Fax 0165/844-805 (US & Canada Tel. 402/398-3200, Fax 402/398-5484; Australia Toll Free 800/810-862; England Tel. 071/413-8886, Fax 071/413-8883). E-mail: info@HotelGallia.it. Web: www.hotelgallia.it/. 50 rooms and 3 junior suites all with bath. Single E130-230; Double E220-400; Breakfast E15 extra. Credit cards accepted.* ***

Located on the edge of town on the way to Entreve, you don't have to worry about the location since the hotel has a free shuttle bus to pick you up and drop you off wherever and whenever you choose. Wood and stone is the motif inside giving this place a truly rustic Alpine appeal. There's a relaxing bar to return to after a day of skiing with an adjacent fireplace. Or you can take a dip in their heated indoor pool, relax in the sauna, sun room or garden, or tone a few more muscles in the gym. If any of this doesn't grab you they have their own spa that offers everything from being wrapped in seaweed to getting a wax treatment. They also have baby-sitting services. A truly great place to stay despite the fact that they were recently demoted from four star status to three. Everything is as excellent as it was before.

PALACE BRON, *Via Plan Gorret 41, 11013 Courmayeur. Tel. 0165/846-742, Fax 0165/844-015. 27 rooms, 1 junior suite all with bath. Single E150-200; Double E250-370. Breakfast E15 extra. Credit cards accepted.* ****

Located above the town of Courmayeur, here you can get away from all the hustle and bustle of the ski town and besides the view from the restaurant, lounge, and piano bar is breathtaking. Windows are everywhere to make sure you don't miss the snow-capped beauty. Whitewashed walls, wood paneling and fireplaces dominate the decor downstairs and the rooms come with floral patterned bed spreads, curtains and chairs. Not quite as down to earth and wonderfully all encompassing as the Gran Baita, but here you have a tranquil upscale B&B type setting. You can enjoy the spectacular garden in the summer as well as utilize a shuttle bus to take guests to and from various locations all year round.

PAVILLON, *Strada Regionale 62, 11013 Courmayeur. Tel. 0165/846-120, Fax 0165/8460-122. E-mail: info@pavillon.it. Web: www.pavillon.it. 50 rooms, 10 of which are junior suites, all with bath. Single E150-260; Double E200-420. Credit cards accepted.* ****

Near the *funivia* that takes skiers up the mountain, this is one of the largest places in town, and it only has 50 rooms. The exterior with its stone, dark wood, yellow awnings and cascading red flowers is quite impressive. The lobby and the rooms are finished with light wood and earth tones, creating a calming effect. Their restaurant, Le Bistroquet, has magnificent views of the mountains and serves superb food. Other than that they have an indoor swimming pool, sauna, sun deck, weight rooms, and shuttle bus to cart guests back and forth to their destinations. Right in the middle of things. Basically in stumbling distance from many watering holes. A great choice in Courmayeur.

DEL VIALE, *Viale Monte Bianco 74, 11013 Courmayeur. Tel. 0165/846-712, Fax 0165/844-513. E-mail: info@hoteldelviale.com. Web: www.hoteldelviale.com/. 23 rooms, 12 with bath, 11 with shower. Single E90-150; Double E100-260. Credit cards accepted.* ***

Located on the way to Entreve and near the Gran Baita, this is a rustic looking typical little guest house/hotel with great interior decor. The restaurant is a wonderful spot, with its open kitchen separated by only a thick wooden table for the dining area, and with the roaring flame in the fireplace oven. All the ambiance seems to have been used up in the common areas, for the rooms are whitewashed and the furniture is basic Italian modern; though they are comfortable and come with every three star amenity.

CHALET PLAN GORRET, *Via Plan Gorret 45, 11013 Courmayeur. Tel. 0165/844-832, Fax 0165/844-842. Web: www.emmeti.it/Welcome/ Valdaosta/Valdigne/Courmayeur/Alberghi/Gorret/gorret2.uk.html. 6 rooms all with shower. Double E150-175. No credit cards accepted.* ***

Do you want to stay in a real alpine chalet? This is the place. If you are thinking about staying someplace that is quaint and filled with character and ambiance, you've got the Chalet Plan Gorret. It is so intimate and romantic you'll fall in love all over again just by staying here. No upscale amenities except for privacy (you're up a hill from the main town near the Palace Bron), along with great views, a small bar area, and good hearty food served with the meal plan. And last but not least, the atmosphere kindles romance. If you like staying in country inns or Bed and Breakfasts, this is the place for you.

Where to Eat

Many of the hotels will require you to purchase a half meal plan depending on the season, which means you get to eat breakfast and one other meal of the day at the hotel. With your other meal here are two restaurants I know you'll love. If these don't please your palate, there are plenty more around.

PIERRE ALEXIS 1877, *Via Marconi 54, Tel. 0165/843-517. Closed Mondays. Visa Accepted. Dinner for two E45.*

An authentic rustic place that serves excellent local salami as an appetizer. The soups and most other offerings have a strong base of cheese in them, and then you get to the fish and meat dishes and the cook goes wild. Maybe it's some sort of French influence, but they have a great *trota in salsa delicata al pepe rosa* (trout in a delicate red pepper sauce) and other interesting dishes. There are also plenty of hearty meat dishes for you Alpine food lovers.

LE RELAIS DU MONT BLANC, *S.S. 26 #18, Tel. 0165/846-777. Closed Tuesdays and Wednesdays for lunch as well as all of June as well as October 15 through November 30. All credit cards accepted. Dinner for two E50.*

A large place, over 100 people can be seated at one time. The restaurant features exquisite fondues. Anything to do with cheese this place does great: *minestra di formaggi* (mixed cheese soup), *maccheroni ai formaggi alpini* (macaroni and alpine cheese). Besides the cheeses, the chef seems to roast the meats to perfection too. You can't go wrong here.

Sports & Recreation

Funivia Ticket Prices
- **1 day pass**, *E30*
- **2 day pass**, *E50*
- **3 day pass**, *E80*
- **4 day pass**, *E110*

- **5 day pass**, *E130*
- **6 day pass**, *E160*
- **7 day pass**, *E180*
- **8 day pass**, *E210*

Ski Guides

You can hire **alpine ski guides** to take you on guided skiing through the mountains. You need a group of at least two and no more than eight including the guide. Cost per person (excluding the guide, of course) is E38. You get to ski or hike from Italy to France or vice-versa, then take a bus in the other direction. Loads of fun but exhausting.

Ski School Rates Per Hour
- **1-2 People**, *E30*
- **3 People**, *E40*
- **4 People**, *E50*

Bolzano

Charming buildings and character-laden streets, filled with friendly people, great food, and wonderful attractions, make **Bolzano** a great place to visit. This city is the center of commerce and tourism in the north of Italy, and is on the route of the main artery through the Alps into Austria, **The Brenner Pass**. And now with the addition of the one of a kind "**Ötzi**," the '**Ice Man**,' a mummified man found by two hikers in 1991, Bolzano is now a must-visit location.

With only about 100,000 people, Bolzano has a small town feel but contains all manner of big city amenities. Great shopping, wonderful art galleries, excellent museums, superb restaurants, and world-class hotels make Bolzano an excellent vacation spot. Couple that with its location deep in the heart of the Alps, and Bolzano can be a jumping-off point for all sorts of winter sporting activities, or summer hiking, mountain biking or rafting adventures. Bolzano can be a one or two day vacation in and of itself, or it can be the place from which you start to explore the rest of the Trentino-Alto Adige region.

One of the major advantages here is that you will be hard pressed to find an English-speaking tourist. Mainly Austrians come to see the region of their country that was annexed by Italy only a few decades ago. Many Austrians still consider this region of South Tyrol only temporarily in Italy's hands. Despite this situation, Bolzano, from any perspective, is a great place to visit.

For more information about Bolzano, visit *www.bolzano.net/*; *E-mail: info@bolzano-bozen.it.*

Arrivals & Departures

Opened in 1999, Bolzano now has a small **airport** that has flights from Frankfurt and Rome. (*Airport Bolzano Dolomiti, Tel. 0471/251-681, E-mail: info@abd-airport.it, Web: www.abd-airport.it.*) By taxi from the airport you are only 25 minutes away from the center of town.

Bolzano can also be reached by train, bus or car. This ease of access makes it a welcoming destination for all travelers. Train from the closest major Italian cities, Venice or Milan, will take about 3-4 hours, depending on the type of train you catch. The Autostrada 22 from the south brings you just outside of town. Travel time by car is slightly less than by train since you have less stops and detours to make.

Getting Around Town

The public transportation of South Tyrol, where Bolzano and Merano are located, is connected through an integrated transport system which allows you to use bus, train and tram with the same ticket (**travelcard**). These cards cost E6, E13 and E25. **Weekly travelcards** are convenient for tourists E13 and are available from news agents as well as official ticket booths and tourist offices. For more information contact *www.sii.bz.it/en/benvenuti.php.*

Orientation

Set along the confluence of two rivers, the Isarco running along the southern boundary of the town and the Talvera bisecting the city from the north, Bolzano is set in a natural bowl between stunning mountain peaks. The train station is the starting point for most visitors. To get to the center of town from here simply walk out the station, across the Via Garibaldi, through the piazza in front of the station and up the Viale Stazione. This will lead to the main piazza of the town, the **Piazza Walther**. This is where the Duomo is located. Just as you get to the piazza, on the right hand, at the end of the Viale Stazione is the **information office**. Stop in here for a map. Though Bolzano is laid out on a simple plan, it cannot hurt to have some navigational guidance as you wander around.

Where to Stay

CITTA STADT, *Piazza Walther 21, Tel. 0471/975-221, Fax 0471/976-688. E-mail: hotelcitta@interbusiness.it. 102 rooms. Single E55-80; Double E80-110. All credit cards accepted. Breakfast included.* ***

A quaint traditional old hotel situated in a Liberty style building from 1912 that almost directly faces the Duomo. The entry hall is pleasant, and the rooms are comfortably adorned with warm wooden floors and functional furnishings. The bathrooms are more than ample with all necessary 3-star amenities. Well located. A nice place to stay in Bolzano.

PARKHOTEL LAURIN, *Via Laurin 4, Tel. 0471/311-000; Fax 0471/311-148. E-mail: info@laurin.it. 96 rooms. Single E110-160; Double E160-230. All credit cards accepted. Breakfast included.* ****

Definitely the best place to stay inside the city walls of Bolzano. Situated in an historic building surrounding a pleasant garden, a playground for kids, a small pool, and a bar that seems never to close, the Parkhotel is a treat. The tiled rooms are all styled differently but come with all 4-star amenities. The bathrooms are resplendent with marble. The ideal place to stay in Bolzano.

Where to Eat

South Tyrol is not only a fantastic holiday destination, but it also offers many great food products: Speck, wine, apples, dairy products, bread, honey, berries, and grappa are all true delights for your palate.

That may be the case, but I am sure you are wondering ... what the heck is speck? **Speck** is a lightly smoked raw ham seasoned for a minimum of 22 weeks. It has a milder, more delicate and better-balanced flavor than strongly smoked raw hams from Northern Europe, which are only seasoned for a short time. Also it has a more distinctive flavor than cured Mediterranean hams, what is called *prosciutto crudo* further south. However you describe it, a trip to Tyrol isn't complete without sampling some Speck. But do not try and take it home. Customs will not let it through. So enjoy it while you are here.

One product you can take home is **honey**. Genuine South Tyrolean honey is a natural product without any additives and which is rich in natural and wholesome organic substances. It is a pleasure you will be able to enjoy for some time after you return from your vacation here.

South Tyrol is also known for its **fruity wines**, both white and red, which have been distilled since pre-Roman times. They go well with the local cheeses and the distinctive bread products available, such as the famous *Vinschgerl* and the popular *Schüttelbrot* And though the growing season is short, you can find a vast array of fruits and vegetables. Especially flavorful are the strawberries, blackberries, currants and apples.

And no meal is complete without a taste of **grappa** afterwards. It certainly is an acquired taste, but once you acquire it, it is something you will savor for life.

CAVALLINO BIANCO, *Via Bottai 6, Tel. 0471/973-267. Closed Saturday nights and Sundays. No credit cards accepted. Dinner for two E40.*

One of the most characteristic *trattorie* in Bolzano, and the food is great. As a result it is always packed, with tourists and locals alike. Finding a free table is not easy, but it is worth the effort. When here sample anything and everything you can. From soups to sausage, the food is filling and good. But bring cash. No credit cards are accepted.

GUMMER, *Via Weggenstein 36, Tel. 0471/970-280. Closed Saturday nights and Sundays. No credit cards accepted. Dinner for two E35.*

A great combination of *osteria*, cafe and restaurant. As such the ambiance is a little confusing, but that does not detract from its popularity. The food here is exquisite in the traditional, filling sense. The goulash is great, as is the wurstel sausage, and all forms of roast vegetables are delectable. You cannot go wrong with a meal here, but bring cash. They do not accept credit cards.

HOPFEN & CO, *Piazza delle Erbe 17, Tel. 0471/303387. Closed Sundays. All credit cards accepted. Dinner for two E40.*

Another traditional place, this one more of the beer garden variety with communal tables and massive steins of amber ale. Situated on three floors, as well as an outside area in good weather, here you will find a great meal with tons of character. Also open for breakfast, this is a frequent stop for locals in the mornings. Not fine dining by any stretch of the imagination, but I do recommend this place highly.

Seeing the Sights

CASTEL MARECCIO

Via Claudia de' Medici, Tel. 0471/976615, Fax 0471/300746.

Now used mainly as an exhibition hall, this old castle and set of cloisters is a picturesque example of the architectural beauty of the region. Located only a few paces outside of the main town, set in a lush surrounding, this place is like something out of a fairy tale.

CHIESA DEI DOMENICANI

Built in 1272, this is a simple, plain structure on the outside, but filled with the glory of God on the inside. Inside you will find some incredible frescoes by Giotto, but to me its main draw is its quiet rustic charm.

DUOMO

Piazza Walther.

The Duomo is a striking focal point for visitors and resident alike. Of ancient construction, begun in 1180, but over time pieces were added, others removed, and finally we are left with this glorious adornment to a magical city. The interior is Gothic with three naves and is filled with stunning art created by a variety of artists including Konrad Erlin, Friedrich Pacher, and Karl Hernici. If you are wondering why the names are not Italian, but seem Germanic, it is because South Tyrol, where Bolzano is located, was until very recently part of Austria, not Italy.

MUSEO ACHEOLOGICO DI ALTO ADIGE

Via Museo 43, Tel. 0471/982-098, Fax 0471/980-648, Web: museo@iceman.it, E-mail: www.iceman.it. Open 10am - 6pm.

This is the place you most likely have come here to see. The one, the only, the home of **"Ötzi,"** the **'Ice Man.'** Now world famous for this one exhibit, the museum can also stand on its own without Ötzi. The mummy's discovery nearby in 1991 set the world's imagination ablaze, since he is so well-preserved for a guy laying about in glacial ice for 5,200 years! Researchers have learned a lot about prehistoric life in this part of Europe from Ötzi.

Though the Ice Man does tie in well with the other exhibits that document the entirety of the region's history, from the Old Stone Age to more modern times.

MUSEO CIVICO,

Via Cassa di Risparmio 14, Tel. 0471/974-625, Fax 0471/980-144. E-mail: museo.civico@comune.bolzano.it, Web: www.comune.bolzano.it.

The **Municipal Museum** (Museo Civico) contains the most extensive collections of art and cultural history of its kind in South Tyrol. There are exquisite artifacts from the Middle Ages to the 20th Century, Romanesque Madonnas and crucifixes, winged Gothic altars as well as entire Gothic rooms, festival masks and local costumes.

MUSEO DI SCIENZA NATURALI

Via Bottai 1 - Bindergasse 1, Tel. 0471/412-960 , Fax 0471/412-979, E-mail: naturmuseum@provinz.bz.it, Websites - www.naturmuseum.it or www.museonatura.it.

South Tyrol's **Museum of Natural History** is located in the building that at one time held the administrative offices of Archduke Maximilian. It now offers the visitor an overview of the various typical landscapes of South Tyrol. The principal attraction is its salt-water aquarium.

PIAZZA WALTHER

With the creation of a large subterranean parking structure in town, freeing this expanse from the invasion of the automobile, this piazza has regained its character and charm. Surrounded by elegant buildings, many of which are now hotels, stores and banks this is a wonderful piazza within which to take a stroll. Truly the heart of the city.

Practical Information

Tourist information
Piazza Walther 8, Tel. 0471/307000, Fax 0471/980128, E-mail: info@bolzano-bozen.it

Merano

Set in a valley among picturesque mountains, **Merano** is located deep in the heart of the Alps, and is a jumping-off point for many outdoor activities in Northern Italy. A small town of around 30,000 people, Merano is a place to come to relax as well as to be active. Merano also offers scenic natural beauty and a quaint character-filled medieval townscape.

Besides the obvious skiing all year round (yes, all year round), in the summer you can access golf courses, hiking trails, rafting adventures, hang gliding, and other outdoor activities. Merano is also a spa town, but with a twist. The Grape Cure has been a popular Merano tradition for the last 120 years. The sweet, dark Merano grapes are an ideal natural purifying agent and are recommended in the cure of all sorts of gastrointestinal problems; and is known to have a very beneficial effect on the body as a whole. Guests from all over Europe come to the town to regain top-form every year in September and October by following the famous Merano grape cure. Maybe you will too?

But whether you take the plunge into the Grape Cure or not, Merano is famous throughout Europe as being a center for outdoor activities. It is a place where you can have fun with the whole family.

Arrivals & Departures

Located 24 kilometers from Bolzano, 330 km from Milan, and only 150 km from Innsbruck, Merano can be reached by train, bus and car. The Autostrada 38 skirts the town from the south. Frequent train service is offered from points south, including Bolzano, and points north including Austria.

Though train is incredibly efficient in getting you from one large destination to another, in Merano it is always best to have a car since much of what there is to do and see is outside of town in the beauty of the Alps. Some things to do, such as rafting, will also entail transportation to and from your activity, so not everything will require a car. But there will be activities where a car may be necessary. See Car Rental section below.

Getting Around Town

The public transportation of South Tyrol, where Bolzano and Merano are located, is connected through an integrated transport system that allows you to use bus, train and tram with the same ticket (**travelcard**). These cards cost E6, E13 and E25 Lira. **Weekly travelcards** are convenient for tourists E13 and are available from news agents as well as official ticket booths and tourist offices. For more information, contact *www.sii.bz.it/en/benvenuti.php*.

Orientation

Bisected by the River Passirio, the main part of town is on the north shore with the train station on the west and the Duomo to the East. The Corso Liberta which runs from the Piazza Mazzini in the West to the Piazza d. Rena in the East is the city's main street. Along this boulevard is where the tourist office is located.

Where to Stay

CASTEL RUNDEGG, *Via Scena 2, Tel. 0473/234-100, Fax 0473/237-200. E-mail: sinnjul@pass.dnet.it. 30 rooms. Single E100-120; Double E160-260. All credit cards accepted. Breakfast included. *****

Located a little more than a kilometer outside of town, this hotel sits in a beautiful park setting. The communal areas are magical and rooms are comfortable and tranquil. This hotel is a place to come to relax. They also have a well appointed workout room with stationary bicycles, stepmaster and weights, along with a swimming pool. A great place to stay just outside of Merano.

PALACE & SCHLOSS MAUR, *Via Cavour 2, Tel. & Fax 0473/271-000. E-mail: hotel.palace@dnet.it. 130 rooms. Single E120-150; Double E180-300. All credit cards accepted. Breakfast included. ******

Far and away the best place to stay in and around Merano. This is a hotel of long and grand tradition in an historic building that is furnished with exquisite pieces. The rooms are spacious, comfortable and come complete with every imaginable amenity. You also have prompt laundry service at your disposal, a bar with live music, a wonderful hotel restaurant, a covered pool, as well as spa services. If you have the means, this is definitely a great place to stay.

WESTEND, *Via Speckbacher 9, Tel. 0473/447-654, Fax 0473/222-726. E-mail: westend@cenida.it. 22 rooms. Single E50-70; Double E75-100. All credit cards accepted. Breakfast included. ****

A three star of the highest level. Situated in a building from the 1800s, in a lush garden setting right by the river, this is a well run hotel owned operated by the Strohmer family. The rooms are well lit, of ample size, and wonderfully comfortable and accommodating. The bathrooms are spacious and come with all necessary amenities, including a phone. The common areas are quaint and comfortable. There are bicycles available for guests, which is one of my favorite touches. A classic place to stay in Merano. Filled with ambiance and charm.

Where to Eat

SISSI, *Via Galilei 44, Tel. 0473/231-062. Closed Mondays. Some credit cards accepted. Dinner for two E65.*

Located near the base of the *funiculare*, this is an excellent restaurant of the highest quality. Simple yet refined, the food here is exquisite and the ambiance comfortable. Andrea Fenoglio and his wife Sabrina have made this into the restaurant of choice in Merano. All manner of dishes abound. You cannot go wrong with a meal here.

Seeing the Sights

CORSO DELLA LIBERTA

The heart and soul of Merano, a grand boulevard that through its architecture evokes the elegance of times past. Along this street you will find the **Puccini Theater** as well as the **Kurhaus**, both mentioned below. Across the Ponte del Teatro, along the Via Piave are the thermal baths which have helped to make Merano famous.

KURHAUS

Corso della Liberta

This truly magnificent building, designed by Vienna architect Friedrich Ohmann in 1914, is, without doubt, the loveliest example of Liberty-style architecture in the entire Alpine region. The great hall holds over 1,000 people and is equipped to host international congresses, conferences, exhibitions and concerts.

MUSEO CIVICO

Via delle Corse 42, Tel. 0473/236-015. Tues to Sat 10am to 5pm. Sundays and public holidays - 10am to 1pm (August 4pm to 7pm)

Created in 1900, this small museum contains items of interest associated with the history of Merano and the region. A variety of different pieces of art, sculpture, artifacts, and more fill the space. An interesting way to spend an hour or two in Merano.

PRINCES' CASTLE

Via Galilei, Tel. 0473/230-102. Tues to Sat 10am to 5pm. Sundays and public holidays 10am to 1pm. Closed on Mondays.

Residence of the Counts of Tyrol starting in 1470 when Merano was the capital of Austrian province of Tyrol. It is now one of the most complete and well-preserved castles in the Alto Adige province with antique furniture and a rich collection of old arms, weapons and musical instruments.

PONTE DELLA POSTA

This elegant bridge with its wonderfully ornate Liberty-style golden railings was built in 1906 and recently tastefully restored in 1993.

PUCCINI THEATER

Corso della Liberta

The civic theatre, dedicated to the famous composer Puccini, was designed in 1900 by Martin Düfler, the most imaginative proponent of German Liberty-style architecture. It is an attractive construction with classical elements and floral decorations.

THE TAPPEINER WALK

A delightful promenade, 380 meters above the town along the side of Monte St. Benedetto. Here you will find 4 km of exotic vegetation and glorious views, all laid out by local doctor Franz Tappeiner (1816-1902) who later gave it to the town. A great place to take a relaxing and invigorating stroll.

Sports & Recreation

Bicycling

Free-of-charge bike rental from the Health Spa Center parking lot (*Via Piave 9*), and at the main Railway Station from the end of May to the end of September. You can get the use of a free bike simply by putting down a refundable deposit. Credit cards accepted.

Golf

The **Passiria Valley Golf Club** is a 9-hole, wide open course, that sits on a somewhat challenging undulating terrain. If you need a golf fix, its the only game in town. (*Tel. 0473/641-488, Web: www.golfpasseier.com. Open from March 1 to November 30*).

Ice Skating

The new ice-rink at the **Meranarena** is open for skating from October to March. Located at Via Palade 74, across the river from the main town, near the Maia Race Course. (*Tel. 0473/236982*).

Mini-Golf

If you want to hit around a little ball in a farcical setting you can also play putt putt in Merano. Located in the Marconi Park, near Hotel Palace, open April to end October.

Mountain Biking Tours

Organized by the **Mountaineering School** from April to October. (*Tel. 0473/235-223 or 0473/563-845 in winter, or portable phone 0348/260-0813*).

Orchestra in The Park

Free daily concerts are available in the Parco Marconi from April to early June and August. Activities such as these help to make Merano a tourist destination all year round.

Rafting

Day trips are available to raft rivers in streams in the area. Information available from the **Mountaineering School**, the **Merano Tourist Offices**, or the Rinner family at **Laces Camping Site**, *Tel. 0473/623217.*

Spa Health Center

A place to pamper yourself in a sauna, with a massage, mud bath and more. (*Via Piave 9, Tel. 0473/237-724.*)

Skiing Year Round

The **Merano 2000** ski area, at over 2,000 meters above sea level, has a total of 40 kms of ski runs and can accommodate up to 7,000 skiers an hour. Served by a cable-car, five chair lifts and one ski lift this place is a great ski area. Further information is available from the Merano Tourist Offices. The website for Merano 2000 is *www.meran2000.net.*

Wine Tasting

The **Cantina Sociale di Merano** offers guided visit and tasting session Fridays at 14.30 for E7 per person. Must make reservation. Tour lasts approx. 1 hour. (*Via S. Marco, Tel. 0473/235-544*)

The **Rametz Castle Wine Cellar** offers guided tours and tasting sessions from Monday to Friday at 16.30. Winter months from November to end of March tours only offered on Thursdays at 16.30. E6 per person. (*Via Labers 4, Tel. 0473/211-011*)

Shopping

Markets

Tuesdays: fruit-and-vegetable market, 8am to 1pm, near the main Railway Station.

Fridays - extensive general market, 8am to 1pm, near the main Railway Station.

Saturdays - Farmers' Market, 8am to 1pm, behind the main parish church. Flea Market - last Saturday in month, 8am to 4pm, in the old Steinach square.

Practical Information

Car Rental
• **Gotsch Rover Garage**, *Via Kuperion 28/30 , Maia Bassa, Industrial Zone, tel. 0473/210-567*

Tourist Information
Corso Libertà 35, Tel. 0473/272-000, Web: www.meraninfo.it.

Bormio

You haven't heard of **Bormio**? Well, that is part of its charm. This little town at the foot of a series of mountains where the small river Frodolfo streams through, is one of the most important winter and summer sporting centers of the entire Alpine region.

Bormio serves as a base for ski vacations in the winter and hiking adventures into the **Stelvio National Park** in the summers. Stelvio is home to glaciers, trails and alpine refuges, a nature lovers paradise. The town of Bormio itself was famous in ancient times for its nine hot springs, and became a way-station in the 15th and 16th centuries for travelers between the Duchy of Milan or the Republic of Venice into Northern Europe. Today Bormio is a popular ski resort for Italians, but its fame and fun have evaded the radar of North America, until now.

During the week you will find the town virtually empty, but on the weekends, the skiers of Italy arrive. Whether empty or full, in the old historic center, around the twisting and turning little roads, you are awash in charm and character. Even the more modern development on the out skirts cannot negate the beauty that radiates from this adorable little town. Bormio is one of THE places to visit in the entire Alps for all sorts of outdoor as well as leisure activities. If you want to breathe in the crisp Alpine air, luxuriate in thermal baths, ski yourself silly, eat at great restaurants, soak up the charm of a tiny medieval town, or party until dawn, Bormio is the town for you.

Arrivals & Departures

Bormio is located on the edge of the Stelvio National Park with the only way to get here being by road. The closest larger town is Sondrio at 69 kilometers away. The closest Italian airport is Milan, from which it is best to rent a car and drive here. The road in from Milan is the SS38. Two roads out are either the SS 301 going west or the SS300 going east. Get a map of the region from the **Touring Club Italiano** (*Via Marsala 8, 00185, Roma. Tel. 06/49 98 99*) or the **Italian Government Tourist Offices** (*Web: www.italiantourism.com*).

Another option for getting here if you do not want to be burdened with the expense or hassle of car, and which most people do if they are only going to be heading to Bormio and nowhere else, is to arrange for a bus/van to pick them up at the airport. These can be arranged through your hotel. Most hotels in Bormio work together to have guests picked up at Milan airport and ferried to Bormio. The bus takes about 3 1/2 to 4 hours, and will usually include a stop in Como for a bite to eat. Remember Bormio is really remote, but is well worth the extra effort getting here.

Orientation

Situated at the meeting point of the SS310 from the west, the SS38 form the south and the SS300 form the east, the small town/ski resort of Bormio is nestled into a valley just on the edge of the Stelvio National Park in the Italian Province of Lombardia.

SS301 turns into Via della Vitttoria and meets SS300 at the Piazza Cavour, the center of town. Radiating from this piazza almost in the form of a trident are the Via Roma to the south, Via de Simoni in the middle and Via Al Forte to the north.

The Via Roma turns into the Via Milano which is where two of the hotels listed are located: Baita Clementi and Palace. South of the Via Roma is the Frodolfo River, across which are the *funiculare* (cable cars) up to the ski areas. The two main roads across the river are the Via Coltura and the Via Funivia where the Genzianella and the Larice Bianco hotels are located.

Where to Stay

If these are booked, which is more than likely since Bormio really is a hot spot, you can find other hotels at the local website, *www.hotels.valtline.it/hotel_bormio.htm*.

BAITA CLEMENTI, *Via Milano 46, Tel. 0342/904-473, Fax 0342/903-649. E-mail: baita.clementi@novanet.it. Web: www.baitaclementi.com/. Closed April 15 - June 20 and Sept. 15 - Dec 12. 41 rooms. Single E70-105. Double E105-170. All credit cards accepted. Breakfast included.* ***

Located just outside the main small town, the style here is rustic but refined with beautiful terra-cotta tile floors. The common areas are accommodating and comfortable. The rooms (12 of which are apartment style and can be rented by groups of people) are elegant with beautiful furnishings. Also available are squash courts, sauna, sun room, massage room, and ping pong. My favorite three star in Bormio.

GENZIANELLA, *Via Funivia 6, Tel 0342/904485, Fax 0342-904158. E-mail: genzia@valtline.it. Web: www.genzianella.com/. Closed ion May and November. 40 rooms. Single E45-70; Double E90-140. Visa accepted. Breakfast and lunch included.* ***

Recently upgraded from a two star, this place is in an excellent spot located right near the lifts. Despite this ideal winter sport location, this hotel is a tranquil and comfortable. They offer wonderful accommodations, great prices and attentive service. The common areas are simple though well appointed. The rooms are the same, and most have small balconies to enjoy. The bathrooms are smallish but have all necessary amenities. A great place to stay.

LARICE BIANCO, *Via Funivia 10, Tel 0342/904-693, Fax 0342/904-614. E-mail: larice@valtline.it. Web: www.larice.bormio.it/. Open all year. 45 rooms. Single E60-70; Double E95-120. All credit cards accepted. Breakfast E10.* ***

Located near the Genzianella, by the lifts for skiing, and near the bus station. Another good three star, this one a little less expensive. The common areas are spacious and well furnished. The bar area is graced with a piano which is usually played in the evenings. A comforting addition. The rooms are clean and comfortable though unspectacular. Everything here is very simple, rustic, yet refined in an Alpine sort of way.

PALACE, *Via Milano 54, Tel. 0342/903-131, Fax 0342/903-366. E-mail: info@palacebormio.it. Web: www.palacebormio.it/. Open all year. 80 rooms. Single E90-130; Double E120-180. All credit cards accepted. Breakfast E10.* ****

The best four star in town, and one that is reasonably priced as well. An incredibly comfortable located in a park setting a short walking distance outside of the main small town of Bormio. The common areas are wonderful. Excellent places to relax and meet others. There is also a large covered pool, tennis courts, gym, jacuzzi, massage service as well as a sun room. The rooms come with every imaginable comfort, most with balconies. A truly wonderful place to stay. My favorite in Bormio.

Where to Eat

TAULA, *Via Dante 6, Tel 0342/904-771. Closed Wednesdays for lunch and Thursdays. Holidays May 1 - July 1 and November 1 to December 1. All credit cards accepted. Dinner for two E65.*

This is an upscale place. The ambiance is elegant, the service professional and enthusiastic and the food spectacular. All local favorites are served here, some of which you'll need Open Road's *Eating & Drinking in Italy* to decipher what they actually are! Despite their obscure names, they will all tantalize. The desserts are also exquisite. One red mark is that the wine list is limited, featuring mainly local favorites. But overall, this is the best place to eat in Bormio. Located between the Via de Simoni and the Via Roma at the end furthest away from the Piazza Cavour.

Seeing the Sights

In the Piazza Cavour is the **Collegiata dei Ss. Gervasio e Protasio** built in the 11th century and renovated during the Baroque period. Along the Via

d. Vittoria, located in the Palazzo de Simoni, is the **Museo Civico**, a series of exhibits commemorating the history of the town. Bormio is not really a town filled with traditional sights. It is a ski town and the focus of the people here is on just that activity.

Sports & Recreation

Skiing
BORMIO SKI AREA, *Tel. 0342/901-451, Fax 0342/904-305, E-mail: sib2000@valtline.it, Web: www.sib.bormio.it/piste.htm.*

Bormio is filled with all levels of different slopes, from red to blue to the highest difficulty, black. As a ski resort Bormio can accommodate rank beginners and outright experts. And snowboarding is welcome here as well. All sorts of ski schools abound, all with different prices, but the average is about E30 for a private one on one lesson. A 7-day ski pass cost only between E130 in low season to E150 in high season.

Summer Activities
Hiking, mountain biking and rafting are but some of the activities available in Bormio, and all of the Alps, in the summer months. The ski slopes are open to rampaging mountain bikers, other trails become accessible for hikers, who go out for day trips or spend the nights in mountain refuges (*rifugi*). These are small cabins in the Alps that are well maintained and used by hikers and bikers alike. These places are very different from what we have grown to expect in America, say for example along the Appalachian trail. These mountain refuges are palaces in comparison. Completely enclosed, with simple facilities, they are insulated from the elements. They can get crowded during peak summer months, but they are still a welcome respite from the wind, rain, and cold.

All information associated with these activities is available from the tourist office, or an Italian language website, *www.alpinia.net/*.

Thermal Baths
BORMIO THERME, *Via Stelvio, Tel 0342/901-325, Web: www.bormioterme.it/, E-mail: info@bormioterme.it. Hours 9am-10pm.*

Prices range from E12 for a thermal bath to E25 for a thermal bath and massage. Also available is aromatherapy, sauna, swimming and all sorts of other spa-like activities, all in a public center located in a modern building in the town of Bormio. Also in this spa is an extensive fitness center you can use for only E12 a day.

Practical Information
Tourist Office, *Via Roma, 87, Tel. 0342/903-594, E-mail: info@bormio.com, Web: www.bormio.com/.*

Chapter 22

**b
o
l
o
g
n
a**

Bologna is called "the Fat, Learned, and Turreted." This fair city is considered fat because its food is the best in Italy. This cultured Italian city is considered learned because it houses the oldest university in Europe. And finally Bologna is considered turreted because it has many beautiful churches, *palazzi*, two leaning towers, and once had the most towers of any city in Italy.

Bologna earns all these nicknames, and has many more points of interest, but even then tourists seem to avoid this beautiful city located just 60 miles north of Florence and about 100 miles southwest of Venice. But then, the loss is theirs. We'll keep the capital of Italy's cuisine, the seat of Europe's oldest university, and the best preserved historic center all to ourselves.

No Italian city has achieved a better balance between progress and preservation as has Bologna. Much of the city center still looks the same way it did centuries ago. In conjunction, Bologna possesses none of the noisy congestion or chaos of Rome or Florence. Instead it offers a glimpse into the lives of real Italians as they go about their business, and it invites you to enjoy life along with them. Just don't expect the romantic ambiance of Lucca, or the Renaissance splendor of Florence, or the bucolic charm of Venice – except of course for the miles upon miles of covered (arcaded) sidewalks. This is a real, living, breathing Italian city, virtually free of tourists, where you can enjoy the sights and sounds, and food and drink as they do.

Brief History

Started as an Etruscan settlement of **Felsina**, the town was captured by marauding Gauls, renamed **Bononia**, and kept this name when it became a Roman colony in 139 BCE. As you'll notice by the map, the city center today is still dissected in an orderly fashion along the lines of an ancient Roman camp.

After the Roman Empire dissolved, Ravenna was the stronger of the two cities in the region, but in the 11th century Bologna broke away from its clutches. Bologna then became an independent commune of the **Lombard League** during the 12th and 13th centuries. In 1278, Bologna became part of the Papal States but was ruled by a succession of local "first citizens."

Bologna's high point, besides being home to the oldest university in Europe (founded in the 5th century CE as the **Imperial School of Bologna**; it later became a university in the 13th century CE), was probably when **Charles V** was crowned emperor in Bologna in 1530 instead of in Rome. That period marked the end of the Renaissance and the beginning of four and a half centuries of foreign rule. In 1796 the town was incorporated into Napoleon's empire. Then in 1815 it reverted back to Papal rule, and eventually became part of the new Italian state in 1860.

Now Bologna is known for its food and its sights, and as the birthplace of **Guglielmo Marconi**, the inventor who gave us the wireless radio.

Arrivals & Departures
By car, take the A1 directly from Florence to Bologna (or any number of smaller more scenic routes). The trip from Florence lasts 2 1/2 hours. By train from Florence, you'll arrive at the station on the outskirts of the old city. The walk to most hotels will take 10 minutes, but a cab is recommended. Train trips from Florence last 2 hours.

Getting Around Town
By Foot
The center of Bologna is very small, is specifically designed for pedestrian traffic, and in fact in certain areas no private cars are allowed. Walking is really the only mode of transport you'll need. Now if you want to explore farther afield and see what the outskirts of town look like, you'll need a car or a cab, but otherwise Bologna is made for walking.

By Taxi
If you're a long way from your hotel and need a cab, simply flag one down, or call one of these numbers to have one sent to you: *Tel. 051/53-41-41* or *051/37-27-27*. When you get off the train a taxi stand is on the right outside of the station. Most places suggested in here will be a short taxi ride away, unless you feel like lugging your bags a mile. The fare shouldn't be any more than E5 unless you've got loads of luggage.

Renting a Car
If you want to visit the countryside but don't want to take the train, here a few agents that will rent you a car:
• **Avis**, *Via Marco Polo 91A, Tel. 051/634-1623, Fax 051/634-6420*
• **Hertz**, *Via Amendola 17/22 B, Tel. 051/25-37-43*
• **Maggiore**, *Via Carioli 4, Tel. 051/25-25-25*

Orientation

Bologna, for the purposes of this guide, has been divided into easy to understand quadrants. If you use **Via Ugo Bassi**, **Via Rizzoli**, and **Strada Maggiore** as the line that dissects the city in half horizontally, and **Via M D'Azeglio** and **Via dell'Indipendenza** as the line that dissects the city vertically, you can easily see the northwest, northeast, southwest, and southeast quadrants.

At the center of this delineation are the **Piazza Maggiore** and **Nettuno**, the cultural and social centers of downtown Bologna.

Where to Stay

1. AL CAPPELLO ROSSO, *Via de Fusari 9. Tel. 051/261-891, Fax 051/ 227-179. E-mail: info@alcappellorosso.it. Web: www.alcappellorosso.it. 33 rooms all with bath. Single E140-210; Double E190-310. All credit cards accepted. Breakfast E13. ****

A hundred meters from the Piazza Maggiore you are presented with a sublimely refined entrance hall which sets the tone for this fine four star. The rooms are furnished with well-appointed antiques which help to make your comfort assured. The bathrooms are nicely accessorized with hairdryers and a complete complimentary toiletry kit. Breakfast is a Bolognese original with local cakes, donuts, rolls and other sweets.

2. CENTRALE, *Via della Zucca 2, 40121 Bologna. Tel. 051/225-114, Fax 051/223-162. 20 rooms 17 with bath. Single without bath E45-60; Single E50-70; Double without bath E55-75; Double E65-85. Credit cards accepted. ***

As the name indicates, this hotel is located in the center of Bologna with shopping and sightseeing all around. On the third floor of a building, you need to catch the lift up to your clean but spartan rooms, some of which have nice views over the rooftops of Bologna. Most rooms face the Via Ugo Bassi and can be noisy in the morning if you have your windows open. In the heat of summer that is necessary because not all the rooms have air conditioning. Make sure you request one that does have air conditioning as well as a private bath and your stay in Bologna will be pleasant and comfortable.

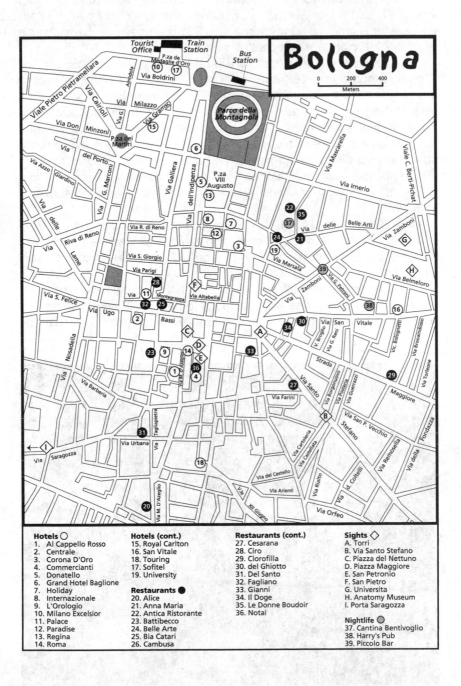

Hotels ○
1. Al Cappello Rosso
2. Centrale
3. Corona D'Oro
4. Commercianti
5. Donatello
6. Grand Hotel Baglione
7. Holiday
8. Internazionale
9. L'Orologio
10. Milano Excelsior
11. Palace
12. Paradise
13. Regina
14. Roma

Hotels (cont.)
15. Royal Carlton
16. San Vitale
17. Sofitel
18. Touring
19. University

Restaurants ●
20. Alice
21. Anna Maria
22. Antica Ristorante
23. Battibecco
24. Belle Arte
25. Bia Catari
26. Cambusa

Restaurants (cont.)
27. Cesarana
28. Ciro
29. Clorofilla
30. del Ghiotto
31. Del Santo
32. Fagliano
33. Gianni
34. Il Doge
35. Le Donne Boudoir
36. Notai

Sights ◇
A. Torri
B. Via Santo Stefano
C. Piazza del Nettuno
D. Piazza Maggiore
E. San Petronio
F. San Pietro
G. Universita
H. Anatomy Museum
I. Porta Saragozza

Nightlife ○
37. Cantina Bentivoglio
38. Harry's Pub
39. Piccolo Bar

3. CORONA D'ORO, *Via Oberdan 12, 40126 Bologna. Tel. 051/236-456, Fax 051/262-679. E-mail: corona.d.oro@italyhotel.com. Web: www.venere.com/it/bologna/coronadoro/. 35 rooms all with bath. Double E180 - 290. Credit cards accepted. Breakfast included.* ****

The crown prince of the small chain that includes the Orologio and the Commercianti. I think a better value for your money is the Hotel Tre Vecchi, but even so this hotel has everything you could want in a first class place. The elegant design conserves architectural elements from various periods, which makes the ambiance luxurious. Mainly a businessperson's hotel, since Bologna has few tourists. But even so, you will find the rooms spacious and comfortable. There's an airy lobby with a skylighted atrium, colorful tile floors, frescoes and an abundance of fresh flowers. Most rooms have small balconies, and if you're up high enough you can overlook the rooftops, towers, and domes of Bologna.

4. DEI COMMERCIANTI, *Via De' Pignattari 11, 40124 Bologna. Tel. 051/ 233-052, Fax 051/224-733. E-mail: commercianti@italyhotel.com. Web: www.venere.com/it/bologna/commercianti/. 31 rooms all with bath. Double E120-190. Credit cards accepted.* ***

Virtually the same location as its sister hotel, L'Orologio, with the same professional manner and service that caters to traveling business persons. All your needs will be taken care of by the helpful desk staff (more so than at the

The Best Hotels in Bologna
Three star

4. DEI COMMERCIANTI, *Via De' Pignattari 11, 40124 Bologna. Tel. 051/233-052, Fax 051/224-733. E-mail: commercianti@italyhotel.com. Web: www.venere.com/it/bologna/commercianti/.*

13. REGINA, *Via dell'Indipendenza 51, 40121 Bologna. Tel. 051/248-952, Fax 051/224-143. E-mail: regina@bolognahotels.com. Web: http://bolognahotels.com/regina/index.htm.*

Four star

6. GRAND HOTEL BAGLIONI, *Via dell'Indipendenza 8, 40121 Bologna. Tel. 051/225-4454, Fax 051/234-840. E-mail: ghb.bologna@baglionihotels.com. Web: http://bolognahotels.com/grandhotelbaglioni/.*

15. ROYAL CARLTON, *Via Montebello 8. Tel. 051/249-361, Fax 051/249-724. Web: http://bolognahotels.com/royalhotelcarlton/index.htm*

L'Orologio). Great location for shopping and sightseeing. All the amenities and professional service you'd expect from a North American hotel except that the rooms are a little smaller. Ideally located too in the center of Bologna.

5. DONATELLO, *Via dell'Indipendenza 65, 40121 Bologna. Tel. 051/24-81-74, Fax 051/24-81-74. E-mail: hoteldonatello@digibank.it. Web: www.hoteldonatello.com/direzione.htm. 39 rooms all with bath. Single E100; Double E140. Credit cards accepted.* ***

An older hotel run by the Ravaglia family whose lobby looks like it's barely hanging onto its former glory. Upstairs the mood is more upbeat with slightly modern appointments, making your stay here comfortable. The rooms are spartan with hardly any amenities except for cleanliness and comfort. There are soundproof windows and walls, satellite TV in every room, air conditioning and mini-fridge in each room too. The main draw of this place is location. A good choice for simplicity and price.

6. GRAND HOTEL BAGLIONI, *Via dell'Indipendenza 8, 40121 Bologna. Tel. 051/225-4454, Fax 051/234-840. E-mail: ghb.bologna@baglionihotels.com. Web: http://bolognahotels.com/grandhotelbaglioni/. 140 rooms all with bath. Single E150-200; Double E200-350. All credit cards accepted. Breakfast included.* ****

A former 16th century seminary, this is Bologna's most splendid hotel. The color scheme is of salmon, beige, and light blue, giving the whole place a relaxing feel. A strange feature of the hotel is that it has several yards of early Roman roads on display in the basement, so it can also even be considered a small museum. The hotel restaurant, I Carracci, is expensive but exquisite. This is *the* place to stay in Bologna if you have the means. Attentive, personal service with every modern comfort imaginable.

7. HOLIDAY, *Via Bertiera 13, 40126 Bologna. Tel. and Fax 051/235-326. Web: www.venere.it/it/bologna/holiday/. 36 rooms all with bath. Single E160; Double E180. Breakfast included. Credit cards accepted.* ***

Clean, modern, professional hotel in the Golden Group Hotel chain that includes the Paradise and University. Here they bring out the best in everything despite the limited space they have. The rooms are medium sized and the bathrooms are so small they can only accommodate a box shower. But they do have phones in the bathrooms and a very rich courtesy toiletry kit. They also rent bicycles for only E2 per day. A great way to stay in Bologna.

8. INTERNAZIONALE, *Via dell'Indipendenza 60. Tel. 051/245-544, Fax 051/249-544. E-mail: internazionale@bolognahotels.com. Web: http://bolognahotels.com/internazionale/index.htm. 120 rooms. Single E90-190; Double E160-300. All credit cards accepted. Breakfast included.* ****

After going through a complete renovation in facilities and service, this is once again a fine hotel in Bologna. The rooms are colorfully decorated with red, green, beige, or yellow accessories. The bathrooms are richly appointed with marble floors and come with phones, hairdryers, and a complimentary toiletry kit. In a good location on the main *passeggiata* street with all the stores and cafés. A good place to stay.

9. L'OROLOGIO, *Via IV Novembre 10, 40100 Bologna. Tel. 051/231-253, Fax 051/260-552. E-mail: orologio@italyhotel.com. Web: www.venere.com/it/bologna/orologio/. 29 rooms all with bath. Double E120-190. Credit cards accepted.* ***

A professional hotel that caters mainly to businessmen, but they do have all the amenities and service you'd expect from a North American hotel. They take their work seriously, unlike a lot of hotels in Italy, where it's just a way to make money. Part of a group of hotels in the city that also includes the Hotel Corona d'Oro (four star) and the Hotel Commercianti. They all offer shuttle service to the train station at a small charge, free bicycles for your use and all the necessary amenities for their star rating. The rooms here are smaller than the others but then so are the prices.

10. MILANO EXCELSIOR, *Viale Pietramellara 51. Tel. 051/246-178, Fax 051/249-448. Toll free in Italy 167/860-200. 70 rooms all with bath. Single E200-250; Double E250-300. All credit cards accepted. Breakfast included.* ****

Right in front of the train station, which can be a little hectic at times. They have recently completed a total renovation making everything on the inside stupendous. They accommodate pets here and have designated one floor for non-smokers, a rarity in Italy. The rooms are clean and comfortable, are furnished with a modern flair and have the obligatory satellite TV. The bathrooms have all modern accessories including hairdryers. A great place to stay if only it wasn't in such a location devoid of character and charm.

11. PALACE, *Via Montegrappa, 40120 Bologna. Tel. 051/237-442, Fax 051/231-603. 113 rooms all with bath. Single E80-90; Double E105-115. Credit cards accepted.* ***

One of the oldest hotels in Bologna and it looks it. They've attempted modernization in most of the rooms but you'll still feel as if you've stepped back into the 1950s, which gives the place a little charm. Located on a relatively quiet little street, here you are located in the prime shopping and sightseeing areas of Bologna. But don't expect personal service, this place is big, sterile, and businesslike.

12. PARADISE, *Viccolo Cattani 7, 40126 Bologna. Tel. 051/231-1792, Fax 051/234-591. Web: www.venere.com/it/bologna/paradise/. 18 rooms all with bath. Single E80-130; Double E120-200. Credit cards accepted. Breakfast included.* ***

Clean, modern, professional hotel in the Golden Group Hotel chain that includes the Holiday and University. Though this hotel is definitely the runt of the litter it is still a good place to stay. All done up in a calming purple and green decor, these hotels are the place to stay if you expect professional, courteous service all the time. The rooms are somewhat small but they usually cater to the traveling businessperson who doesn't need to spread out so much.

13. REGINA, *Via dell'Indipendenza 51, 40121 Bologna. Tel. 051/248-952, Fax 051/224-143. E-mail: regina@bolognahotels.com. Web: http:// bolognahotels.com/regina/index.htm. 61 rooms all with bath. Single E75-120; Double E120-160. Credit cards accepted.* ***

This hotel is itching to become a four star. The decorations, the service, the amenities all point to this becoming reality soon, so grab the prices while you can. The rooms here are a little smaller and the furnishings not as ornate, but you'll still have plenty of money left over if you stay here instead of at a luxurious four star. They also have a pleasant bar and dining area. Great location too.

14. ROMA, *Via d'Azeglio 9. Tel. 051/226-322, Fax 051/239-909. 90 rooms all with bath. Single E110-140; Double E130-190. All credit cards accepted. Breakfast E9.* ***

Located in an old building in the *centro storico* this is a friendly accommodating place that guests return to time and time again. The plentiful breakfast helps to start the day off on the right foot. Some of the rooms have small terraces with views over the rooftops of Bologna. You need to specifically request one of these. The rooms are spacious but the suites are gigantic. The bathrooms come with all modern conveniences. A great, comfortable, accommodating, clean, friendly, professional hotel.

15. ROYAL CARLTON, *Via Montebello 8. Tel. 051/249-361, Fax 051/ 249-724. Web: http://bolognahotels.com/royalhotelcarlton/index.htm 251 rooms all with bath. Single E150-180; Double E180-220. All credit cards accepted. Breakfast included.* ****

Only a few paces from the main train station, the Carlton welcomes you with an immense reception hall containing gigantic carpets and with antique furnishings nicely arranged. The double rooms contain both shower and bath while the singles only have showers. But all come with telephones, hairdryers and every other imaginable convenience. The rooms are large, comfortable and have the prerequisite TV, mini-bar, A/C, etc. that are standard in four stars. The American-style bar is a great place to relax and the restaurant is quite respectable. Breakfast is a mix of Continental and American since they offer eggs made any way you want them, as well as salamis cheeses, fruit, yogurt, cereal, juice, rolls and coffee and tea. A comfortable and accommodating hotel.

16. SAN VITALE, *Via San Vitale 94, 40125 Bologna. Tel. 051/225-966, Fax 051/239-396. Credit cards accepted. 15 rooms all with bath. Single E60-75; Double E75-80.* *

A tranquil little hotel with a small garden in back in which to relax and have a drink from the bar. The rooms are all on the first and second floors with no elevator, but all are clean and very comfortable. And the bespectacled proprietress is very helpful with all your touring interests. A great inexpensive place to stay, in a quiet area off the beaten path.

17. SOFITEL, *Viale Pietramellara 59. Tel. 051/248-248, Fax 051/249-421. Web: www.yourhotelfinder.com/sofitel.shtml. 244 rooms all with bath. Single E200; Double E300. All credit cards accepted. Breakfast included.* ****

Another good four star in Bologna with one exception: its location. Situated directly in front of the train station this place offers comfort and class, most of all in the rooms, some of which are reserved for non-smokers. A busy businessperson's hotel I would only recommend staying here as a last resort or if you want to save money on the weekends. During those days their prices drop dramatically to fill up the rooms. The restaurant serves good Bolognese and international cuisine and everything about this place is nice, except for the location and the size. It's too big to be personal.

18. TOURING, *Via de' Mattuiani 1/2, 20124 Bologna. Tel. 051/584-305, Fax 051/334-763. E-mail: hoteltouring@hoteltouring.it. Web: www.hoteltouring.it/. 40 rooms.. Single E70-110; Double E90-190. Credit cards accepted.* ***

Recently renovated in 2001, this place is much better than it has been in the past. They have a terrace on the road that doesn't offer the greatest views, but at least it's a place to relax other than your room. This is a simple, plain yet elegant hotel with upgraded atmosphere, and the prices are reasonable. I am very impressed with the improvements they have made. Touing is now more than a place to lay your head. Check out their website to see what I mean.

19. UNIVERSITY, *Via Mentana 7, 40126 Bologna. Tel. and Fax 051/229-713. Web: www.venere.com/it/bologna/university/. 21 rooms all with bath. Single E160; Double E180. Credit cards accepted. Breakfast included.* ***

This is a clean, modern hotel in the Golden Group Hotel chain that includes the Holiday and Paradise. The entrance hall is not that big and is just off of the breakfast room where you are served a buffet of classic Bolognese breakfast cakes, rolls, fruit, juice, coffee and tea. The rooms and bathrooms are not that large but are comfortably accommodating. There are a number of business services available (photocopying, fax, telex, e-mail) that comes in handy if you are on business. Good location.

Where to Eat
Cucina Bolognese

Bologna has many nicknames, but the one that fits the most is *Bologna La Grassa* – Bologna the Fat. The reason for this moniker is that this city has arguably the best all-round cuisine in Italy and the citizens of this fair city enjoy it wholeheartedly. The main local dishes are based on pasta, pork, cream, cheese, and ham; and pasta is so revered here that the city government has a giant golden tagliatelli noodle enshrined in its Chamber of Commerce offices.

The cuisine is so good in Bologna because cooks are able to draw on the freshest and best ingredients from the surrounding area. They can get the best *prosciutto* and *formaggio* from Parma (see *Excursions & Day Trips* section), which is world-renowned for its excellence. They get the freshest fruits and vegetables from the local farms, and the most succulent pork, salami, and other sausage as well. If you came to Bologna and want to remain on a diet, you came to the wrong place.

For restaurant locations, refer to the map on page 757. Below is a mini-guide to Bolognese cuisine:

Antipasto
- **Prosciutto di Parma con melone** – Local ham with melon
- **Salsicce misto** – Plate of grilled local sausages, usually pork

Primo Piatti
- **Tortellini alla panna** – Cheese- or mea- filled pasta made with a thick, rich cream sauce, covered with the local parmigiano cheese; basically any type of tortellini is a local favorite
- **Risotto alla parmigiana** – Rice cooked with an abundance of the local cheese, Parmigiano Reggiano
- **Tortellone alla Bolognese** – Large tortellini with ground veal, milk and fresh tomato sauce; tortellone are also local favorites
- **Tagliatelli alla Bolognese** – Pasta with a delicate ground veal, milk and fresh tomato sauce

Secondo Piatti
- **Griglia Mista** –Mixed grill with local pork, beef, vegetables, sometimes fruit
- **Cotoletta alla Bolognese** – Veal cutlet smothered in delicate milk and tomato sauce

- **Maiale arrosto** – Roast pork – basically any type of pork in Bologna is good since that's where the excellent local ham comes from too

Cheese
- **Parmigiano Reggiano** – Local parmesan cheese that is served in chunks; cut off a piece and just let it melt in your mouth

Wines
- **Sforza** – A light local carbonated white wine served as the house wine at many local restaurants

The Best Restaurants in Bologna

21. ANNA MARIA, *Via Belle Arti 17/a, Tel. 051/266-894. Closed Mondays, six days in January and 15 days in August. All credit cards accepted. Dinner for two E45.*

28. CIRO, *5B Via de Gessi. Closed Wednesdays. Credit cards accepted. Dinner for two E35.*

32. FAGLIANO, *Calca Vinazzi de Gessi. Credit cards accepted. Closed Thursdays. Dinner for two E38.*

34. IL DOGE, *Via Caldarese 5a. Tel. 051/22-79-80. Closed Mondays. Credit cards accepted. Dinner for two (only pizza) E20.*

37. CANTINA BENTIVOGLIO, *Via Mascarella 4B. Closed Mondays. Open 8:00pm - 2:00am. Snacks and wine for two E28.*

20. ALICE, *65a Via D'Azeglio, Tel. 051/583-359. Closed Wednesdays. Credit cards accepted. Dinner for two E30.*

This is a classic, intimate dining establishment a little off the beaten path from the historic center. A great place to come if you're staying out this way. Enjoy their *risotto al pesce e carne* (rice with fish and meat) or the *risotto alla medici* (cheese and ham). For seconds they make a great *vegetariana con formaggio alla griglia* (vegetarian dish with grilled cheese).

21. ANNA MARIA, *Via Belle Arti 17/a, Tel. 051/266-894. Closed Mondays, six days in January and 15 days in August. All credit cards accepted. Dinner for two E45.*

Anna Maria Monari does everything here, from preparing the ragu sauce to turning the roast to tabulating the check – and she does them all well. You'll find plenty of traditional dishes, including either *tagliatelle, tortellini, tortellone, tagliolini or quadreti in brodo* (different types of pasta in soup); as well as *pasta e fagioli* (pasta and beans) or *trippa coi fagioli* (tripe with beans). They have a great *zuppa di verdure* (vegetable soup), *maiale al forno* (grilled pork) *verdure al forno* (grilled vegetables) or *frittura* (fried). Dining is either inside or outside on their terrace. A wonderful place in Bologna.

22. ANTICA RISTORANTE, *San Lobbe 3d. Credit cards accepted. Closed Sundays. Dinner for two E38.*

Down a twisting alley that is between the Via del Inferno and the Via Oberdan, here you can enjoy a relatively inexpensive meal in quiet and comfortable surroundings. (Bring a map to find it). They serve Bolognese specials like *Tagliatelle Bolognese* (with veal, milk and tomato sauce) and *tortellini al Basilico e pomodoro* (cheese or meat stuffed pasta with a basil and tomato sauce). For secondo they have *castrate* (lamb) and *grigliata mista* (mixed grill with lamb, pork and beef).

23. BATTIBECCO, *Via Battibecco 4/b, Tel. 051/223-298. Closed Sundays and Holidays as well as August. All credit cards accepted. Dinner for two E70.*

Somewhat of an upper crust locale, with many excellent regional and international dishes. You'll find that *Prosciutto di Parma, Parmigiano Reggiano*, and local salamis are featured in almost all the appetizers, soups, and pastas. For seconds try some of their seafood concoctions like *antipasti di gamberetti e calamari* (*antipasta* of small shrimp and squid), or their fresh vegetables either cooked in oven or grilled (*verdure al forno or grigliatta*) or their *scampi reali al whisky* (large shrimp cooked in a whisky sauce). You can also find cold roast beef, which is excellent.

24. BELLE ARTE, *Via Belle Arti 6, Tel. 051/126-76-48. Closed Sundays. No credit cards accepted. Dinner for two E30.*

Set on a side street with outside seating under an awning, and a larger area inside of plain brick with whitewashed walls festooned with pictures, this is a good place to come for a relaxing meal. Try the *tagliatelle ragu bolognese* or the *tortellini alla panna*. They also have some Roman favorites like *amatriciana* and *arrabbiata*. If you're in search of meat try the *braciola di maiale* (arm of pork) or the *grigliatta misto* (mixed grill with pork, lamb and beef).

25. BIA CATARI, *Via Montegrappa 7/8, Tel. 051/22-48-71. Closed Mondays. Credit cards accepted. Dinner for two E38.*

If you want some seafood, this place specializes in it. They only have inside seating but the space is large, light and comfortable. Try the *antipasto di mare freddo* (cold mixed seafood) or the *cocktail di gamberi* (shrimp cocktail). Skip the pasta altogether and head right to the *fritto misto di mare* (fried mixed seafood) or the *grigliatta mista* (grilled mixed seafood). A great atmosphere with fine service, even for tourists.

26. CAMBUSA, *Via Mascarella 8, Tel. 051/266-645. Closed Mondays and August. All credit cards accepted. Dinner for two E40.*

If you like fish come here, but that's basically all they have. Everything from sardines to crustaceans baked in the oven, cooked over the grill, or lightly fried in a succulent batter. And they prepare the fish perfectly. But since, as you probably realize, Bologna is land-locked, this really isn't an authentic Bolognese restaurant, but it has great atmosphere and wonderful food. For dessert try their excellent *cannoli*.

27. CESARINA, *Via Santo Stefano 19/b, Tel. 051/232-037. Closed Mondays and Tuesdays at Dinner. All credit cards accepted. Dinner for two E70.*

Enjoy the beauty of Piazza Santo Stefano from the terrace of this restaurant or savor the smells from the kitchen if you sit inside. This place is rather upscale even though they serve many traditional local peasant dishes. Their *fritto misto* (mixed fried vegetables) is simply great and their *tortellini in brodo* (tortellini in soup) is perfect. They also make an excellent *spaghetti alla vongole verace* (with a spicy clam and oil-based sauce), *risotto alla pescatore* (rice with fish), or *scampi alla griglia* (grilled shrimp).

28. **CIRO**, *5B Via de Gessi. Credit cards accepted. Closed Wednesdays. Dinner for two E35.*

Here you can have a peaceful dinner on a private terrace on a small side street away from all the hustle and bustle of Bologna. If you want to watch the pizza chef at work, sit inside around the tile-covered oven. Besides pizza they serve great pastas, especially the *spaghetti alla carbonara* (with cheese, ham, and egg) or the *tortellini al piacere* (tortellini made any way you want them). For seconds try any of their pizzas. Knowing that most people in this city like their cheese, they have an option to double the cheese for an extra E1. This makes the pizza very much like a North American concoction.

29. **CLOROFILLA**, *Strada Maggiore 64c, Tel. 051/235-343. Closed Sundays. Credit cards accepted. Meal for two E20.*

Specializes in vegetarian meals with a large menu. They also have wines and beers that were prepared ecologically. You can get fruit salads, regular salads, soybean burgers, *cous cous*, a variety of cheeses, veggie sandwiches, and much more. Even though Italian food itself is fresh and healthy, if you don't even want to see meat on the menu, come here and enjoy an ecologically friendly meal in air conditioned comfort.

30. **DEL GHIOTTO**, *Via San Vitale 9B, Tel. 051/26-68-51. Closed Sundays. Credit cards accepted. Dinner for two E30.*

As you enter you'll see a small bar with a marble counter in front of a beautiful wood frame of large mirrors, and to your right are a few tables in this cute little ristorante. The whitewashed walls really set off both the mirrors and the dark wood beamed ceiling. A friendly local place, try the *tagliatelli al ragu* (with meat sauce) or the *risotto alla parmigiana* (rice with a rich parmesan sauce) for *primo*. For *secondo* they have *arrosti misti* (great mixed roasted meats) or *fritto misto* (mixed deep fried meats and veggies).

31. **DEL SANTO**, *Via Urbana #7F. Credit cards accepted. Dinner for two E35.*

Real Bolognese cooking at an authentic local *trattoria*. You can sit outside under the arcaded sidewalk and a canopy on a busy road and breathe exhaust fumes, or sit inside in a plainly furnished place. Try any of their *tortellini* or *tortellone* dishes, especially the *alla panna* (with a thick rich cream sauce that you cover with parmesan). For seconds try the *cotoletta alla bolognese* (veal cutlet covered with milk and tomato sauce) or the *scaloppine alla pizzaiolo* (veal covered with melted cheese and tomato sauce).

32. **FAGLIANO**, *Calca Vinazzi de Gessi. Credit cards accepted. Closed Thursdays. Dinner for two E38.*

Located on a little side street just off the main road, Via Ugo Bassi, they have outside seating under an awning as well as a large inside seating area covered in wood and marble. They make great pastas, especially the local favorites *tortellini alla panna* (with cream sauce) and *tagliatelli alla Bolognese* (with veal, milk and tomato sauce.) They also make a dish that is similar to *penne all'arrabbiata* from Rome, called *penne all'diavolo* (devil's pasta, meaning it's hot and spicy with garlic and hot peppers in a tomato and olive oil base). They also serve pizza for lunch and dinner, as well as some wonderful dishes cooked over the grill. Try the *formaggi alla griglia* (grilled cheeses) or the *grigliatta vegetale* (grilled vegetables).

33. GIANNI, *Via Clavature 18. Tel. 051/22-94-34. Credit cards accepted. Closed Mondays. Dinner for two E38.*

Down a little alley off of the Via Clavature, you can get a taste of real Bologna here. Both in the decor, which is simple brick walls with pictures of the city interspersed, as well as the menu, which changes daily based on the produce available. The staples you'll find are the *tortellini* or *tortelloni* pasta dishes (small and large cheese stuffed pasta with a variety of sauces) as well as an antipasto of *prosciutto di Parma* and any form of *maiale* (pork) or *vitello* (veal). A great experience for dining because of its hidden location and great food.

34. IL DOGE, *Via Caldarese 5a. Tel. 051/22-79-80. Closed Mondays. Credit cards accepted. Dinner for two (only pizza) E20.*

A large place on a side street off the Via San Vitale that has a great atmosphere created by wood paneling and stained glass windows and the superb service. As you sit down they bring you a small *bruschetta* (hard garlic bread covered in olive oil and tomatoes). Anything you try here will be good, especially the pizza that they make in the centrally located pizza oven. Each pizza is large, at least 12 inches and they're generous with their toppings – maybe not like in North America, but still a good amount. They also have a good selection of meat and fish dishes.

35. LE DONNE BOUDOIR, *Via Mascarella 5a, Tel. 051/23-54-24. No credit cards accepted. Closed Mondays. Open 7:00pm - 4:00am. Dinner for two E45.*

An eclectic decorative touch with posters of old, and some dead, American film stars. After getting past the café/bar entrance, you enter the cramped surroundings that serves as the dining room. If you're over 5'8" tall, you need to sit at one of the booths against the wall so you can stretch your legs. The food is great, especially any of the *tortellini* or *tortelloni* dishes, and the *mozzarelle fritte* (fried balls of mozzarella) and *verdure fritte* (fried vegetables) are delicious. Beware of the waitresses, they are not the most pleasant (to foreigners), but ignore their surliness and enjoy a fabulous meal.

36. NOTAI, *Via De' Pignattari, Tel. 051/228-694, Fax 051/265-872. Closed Sundays. Dinner for two E45.*

Upper crust dining with a hint of *cucina nuova* thrown in. Start off with an appetizer of the *prosciutto di Parma* (local ham) or the *salsicce in olio d'olivo* (local pork sausages in olive oil). Next try the *tortellini alla bolognese* (cheese stuffed pasta covered in a delicate veal, milk and tomato sauce) or the *spaghetti al pomodoro e salsicce fresca* (with tomato sauce and fresh sausages). That should fill you up, but if you're still hungry try their *filetto al tartuffo* (steak covered with savory truffles).

Late Night Cafes & Restaurants

Calm by day, Bologna, in large part due to the presence of tens of thousands of students, comes alive at night, especially in the small neighborhood *osteria*. You will find them open late all over town, mainly on the weekends to cater to a late night eating and drinking crowd. Most of these places, as you might expect, are around the university.

37. CANTINA BENTIVOGLIO, *Via Mascarella 4B. Closed Mondays. Open 8:00pm–2:00am.*

Enter, walk through an entrance corridor, and descend the stairs to a vast renovated wine cellar. On most nights the place will be packed by 9:30pm, not only to hear the tantalizing live music but also to enjoy the *vino*, plates of pasta and *crostini* (sandwiches, like their *pizzaiolo* with mozzarella, tomatoes and oregano) or the *prosciutto* (with mozzarella and ham). If you want a true late night adventure, Bologna-Style, try this place.

38. HARRY'S PUB/OSTERIA, *Via Vinazzetti 5. Closed Sundays. No credit cards accepted. Open 8:00pm–3:00am.*

A dark, rustic wooden decor, definitely not of the same kind we have come to know and love (hate?) in Venice, Florence and Rome. This is a down-to-earth place serving drinks and small snacks, like pasta, sandwiches and salads, as well as desserts and ice cream. Drinks are around E5 and the pints are E3.

39. PICCOLO BAR, *Piazza Giusseppe Verdi 4, Tel. 051/227-147. Open 8:30am–3:00am.*

Hip little café/bar that's open until the wee hours for beer (Bass on tap; pint costs E3), wine, drinks, and a few snack foods like small pizza or *crostini* (sandwiches) made to order. Deep in the heart of the student section this is where Bologna's version of P.I.B.s (people in black) hang out. Try to shed the colorful tourist clothing and put on subtler colors prior to coming here. Also, if you're generally frightened of people with tattoos and long hair, this isn't the place for you. Enjoy the ambiance of the evening and the parade of counterculture locals while sitting at the tables on the piazza. If they're all full, and they usually are, settle next to the bar or at one of the small tables inside. Besides drinks they also serve coffee to keep you going until closing. A fun place at night and a relaxing place during the day. Rumor has it that this is a 'druggie' hangout, but I noticed no such activity while I was there. Just good clean alcohol and cigarettes.

Seeing the Sights

Bologna is literally made for walking and sightseeing. There are over 20 miles of arcaded sidewalks that make a brief *passegiatta* a veritable stroll into history. Some of these arcades, or *portici,* date back to the 12th century when the *comune* (the government of Bologna) faced a housing shortage as a result of massive enrollment in the University, so they ordered housing to be built onto existing buildings over the sidewalks. As it turned out, the Bolognese grew attached to these *portici,* not only for their beauty, but also for the protection they offer from the elements.

The best part of Bologna as a walking paradise is that a large part of the historical city center is off-limits to private automobiles, giving you the freedom to move. Bologna is so well preserved that you can walk down medieval streets and witness, side by side, countless historically sacred living exhibitions of northern Italian architecture from the 12th through the 18th centuries.

For locations of these sights, refer to the map on page 757.

A. TORRI GARISENDA & ASINELLI, PIAZZA DI PORTA RAVEGNANA

Torre degli Asinelli is open daily from 9:00am–6:00pm. In the winter only until 5:00pm. Admission E3.

Known as the **Due Torre** (two towers), these structures were erected in the 12th century as military observation posts. Eventually towers became the fashionable structure to erect as a symbol of your family's wealth (that's why one of Bologna's names is "The Turreted"), as well as a wise military investment for the city. Today only a small handful of them remain, the largest of which is the **Asinelli Tower**, which rises over 320 feet and has a wonderful observation deck from which you can see all of Bologna.

The **Garisenda Tower** right next to it leans a little and appears as if it is trying to affectionately touch the Asinelli Tower. From where the towers are located, five ancient avenues branch off and lead to a gate on the old city walls. The best of these streets to take is the **Via Santo Stefano**.

B. VIA SANTO STEFANO

This is a terrific street to wander along. Stop at the **Piazza del Mercanzi**, which is dominated by the **Merchant's Palace**, an ornate Gothic building that served as the center of Bologna's trade in the 14th century and today houses the chamber of commerce. Inside you will find a gold plated replica of a pasta noodle.

As you proceed down Via Santo Stefano, it's like walking back in time. With each building you pass, the centuries seem to drop away. You'll pass rows of graceful *palazzi* built by the powerful families of Bologna. Numbers 9 through 11 are interesting because of their sculpted terra-cotta facades.

One of the best places along this street is at a small triangular square with a grouping of seven little churches known collectively as **Le Sette Chiese**. You can explore each of their tiny ancient chapels and cloisters of these interconnected buildings and feel as if you are the only one who knows about this humble and hushed place.

C. PIAZZA DEL NETTUNO

In this piazza you're confronted by a startling nude, hugely muscled statue of *Neptune*, trident in hand, attended by four sirens squirting water from their nipples. If you stare at the fountain enough it seems to come to life. Besides the statue you'll find plenty of Bolognese hanging out and communing. A great *piazza* in which to relax, one that merges into the large Piazza Maggiore.

D. PIAZZA MAGGIORE

This *piazza* is one of the most theatrical public spaces in Italy. This vast, raised square is bordered by Gothic and Romanesque facades and the large basilica of **San Petronio**. It is the place to come and socialize for Bolognese. Just off this piazza is a little neighborhood of streets named after the wares they have sold since the Middle Ages where you can find some great stores.

For example, try the **Paolo Atti & Pigli** on Via Caprarie that sells a wide array of fresh breads and pastas. A few doors down is the **Pescheria Brunelli** that sells mountains of fresh fish daily. At the corner of the Via Drapperie and Via Caprarie you'll find a great gourmet store, **Tamburini**, which has anything and everything culinary you could imagine. You'll find hams, salamis, sausages, cheeses, olive oil, bread, pastas, and the best sight is an immense pig, impaled on a large spit being turned ever so slowly over an open fire. The smell is so tantalizing that you can't help but buy something.

E. SAN PETRONIO

Piazza Maggiore, Tel. 051/220-637. Open 7:30am-7:00pm.

Located on the south side of the Piazza Maggiore, this Gothic basilica is the largest church in Bologna and is dedicated to the city's patron saint. It was begun in 1390 but it was never completed according to plan. In fact, construction stopped abruptly in 1650 and never continued. The sculpture on the main doorway of the facade is by Jacopo della Quercia. The interior nave is 117 meters long, 48 meters wide and just over 40 meters high, and the decorations are purely Gothic. A majestic church.

F. SAN PIETRO

Via dell'Indipendenza. Open 7:00am-7:00pm.

If you exit Piazza Maggiore and go up Via dell'Indipendenza towards the train station, you'll run into the Cathedral on the right hand side of the street.

It was founded in 910 and has a choir created by Tibaldi in 1575, and a Baroque nave created in 1605 which has been added to periodically through time. Even though smaller in scale than San Petronio, I found this church to be filled with much more interesting pieces of artwork.

G. UNIVERSITA
Via Zamboni 33, Tel. 051/259-021.
The **University**, founded in 1088, is the oldest such institution in Europe. By the 13th century it had attracted more than 10,000 students from all over Europe. Its alumni include Dante Aligheri, Petrarch, Thomas a Becket, and more recently Federico Fellini.

The campus, being in the center of a city, contains both old and new buildings on both sides of the **Via Zamboni**. To see real Italian university life, all you need to do is stroll through the maze of streets that encompass the school. The walls are covered with graffiti and posters and there are many coffeehouses or *trattoria* catering to the students.

H. ANATOMY MUSEUM OF DOMESTIC ANIMALS
Via Belmeloro 8, Tel. 051/354-243. Open Monday-Saturday 9:00am– 1:00pm and on Wednesday also open 3-5:00pm.
You need to call ahead for an appointment to see these samples of dissected pets. A lesson in anatomy that should not be approached on a full stomach or if you're even a wee bit queasy.

I. PORTA SARAGOZZA & GUARDIA HILL
Through the Porta Saragozza and up the Guardia Hill stands the sanctuary of the **Madonna di San Luca**. As you stroll up the hill, even if it is raining, you will stay completely dry. All thanks to an arcade formed of no fewer than 666 arches. This same walk has been traversed every May since the 15th century as part of a religious procession in which a revered Byzantine image of the Madonna is carried to the sanctuary. Besides this sacred image, from here you can see the vast carpet of red brick of Bologna, reposing quietly below.

Nightlife & Entertainment
Nightclubs
If you're into the nightclub scene, the clubs in Bologna are a little different. They are more like upscale bars for dancing and drinking and can get loud, so if you're not into the noise scene, these places will not be right for you.
• **Penny**, *Via delle Moline 18D Tel. 051/235-050. Closed Sundays. Open 10:30pm - 5:00am.*
• **La Dolce Vita**, *Via Porta di Castello, 2/II, Tel. 051/22-35-20. Closed Mondays. Open 10:00pm - 5:00am.*

Pubs
Being a university town, there seems to be an affinity for the Irish/English-style pub atmosphere. The drinking is definitely not as heavy, but the ambiance is true to form. Here are a few places you should try if you crave a pint of ale and rustic pub atmopshere.
- **The Irish Times Pub**, *Via Paradiso 1D, Tel. 051/261-648. Happy Hour 7:30pm - 8:30pm from Tuesday - Friday; 6:30pm - 8:30pm Saturday and Sunday. Closed Mondays.* Serves Guinness, Harp and Kilkenny for E3 a pint.
- **Il Druido**, *Via Mascarella 26B, Tel. 051/22-67-57.* Serves drinks, wine, and pints of Guinness, Harp, and Kilkenny for E3 a pint.
- **King's Road Pub**, *Via Saragozza 15, Tel. 051/644-8426.* Serves food since they are also a restaurant and Labatts for E3 a pint.

Opera
If you are in Bologna from December to June, the traditional opera season, have the proper attire (suits for men, dresses for women), and have a taste for something out of the ordinary, try the truly amazing spectacle of the opera:
- **Teatro Comunale**, *Largo Respighi 1, 41026 Bologna. Tel. 051/529-011 or 529-999, Fax 051/529-934*

Sports & Recreation
Golf
- **Golf Club Bologna**, *Via Sabbatini 69, 40050 Monte San Pietro. Tel. 051/ 969-100, Fax 051/672-0017.* Located 18 km from Bologna, this is a relatively short par 72, 18 hole course. It tops out at 6,171 meters in length and is open year round except on Mondays. They have a driving range, pro shop, good restaurant, nice bar, and a refreshing pool.
- **Castenaso Golf & Country Club**, *Via Ca Belfiore 8, 40055 Castenaso. Tel. 051/788-126, Fax 051/789-006.* Located 10 km from Bologna, this is only a nine hole course, 2560 meters in length, and is a par 33. It's open from September to July and is closed Monday mornings. They have a driving range and a putting green.
- **Golf Club Centro**, *Via Dei Tigli 4, 44042 Cento. Tel. 051/683-0504, Fax 051/ 683-5287.* Located 30 km from Bologna, this is also a nine hole course. It is shorter, only 2,486 meters and is a par 27. The course is open year round except on Mondays. They have a club house, driving range, practice green, and a good practice bunker.
- **Golf Club Molino Del Pero**, *Via Molino del Pero 323, 40036 Monzuno. Tel. 051/677-0506.* Located 25 km from Bologna, this is a par 35, nine hole course that is 2,610 meters long. The course is open year long

except on Mondays. The facilities available are a driving range, bar, and a pro shop.
- **Argenta Golf Club**, *Via Poderi 2A - SS16, km 100, 44011 Argenta. Tel. 0532/852-545.* Located 45 km from Bologna, 40km from Ravenna, and 32km from Ferrara, this is a par 71, 18 hole course that is 6,400 meters in length. It's closed from January 5th to February 21st and Tuesdays the rest of the year. They have a restaurant, bar, driving range and putting green.

Tennis
- **Giardini Margherita**, *Viale R Cristiani 2*
- **Bocciodromo Primavera**, *Via G Bertini*

Shopping
Since Bologna has over 20 miles of arcaded sidewalks and most of the historic city center is free from automobile traffic, it is definitely made for walking and window shopping. All around the **Piazza Maggiore** and **Nettuno**, in the modern **Galleria** just off the **Via Cavour**, and all along the **Via dell' Indipendenza** and **Marconi** are located the small specialized shops that make shopping in Italy so much fun.

Leather goods for many of Italy's most famous designers are manufactured in and around Bologna, which makes all types of shoes, belts, briefcases, wallets, purses, etc., with or without the famous name label, an extremely good value. You'll find many of these shops on the major streets listed above. Lately there has been an encroachment of the Bennetons, the McDonalds, and other worldwide chains, but the majority are still homegrown little Italian stores.

Books & Newspapers in English
- **Fetrinelli International**, *Via Zamboni 7b, Tel. 051/26-80-70.* Located near the University, they have a small section of books in English.

Department Stores
- **STANDA**, *Via Rizzoli 7*
- **Rinascente**, *Via Ugo Bassi 21*
- **COIN**, *Via dei Mille/Piazza Martiri*

Markets
- **Piazza Otto Agosto**, *Fridays and Saturdays from 8:00am–7:00pm.* Food, clothing, shoes, watches, flea market stuff, antiques. Come to browse or get a good bargain.
- **Piazza San Francesco**, *Wednesdays from 8:00am–6:00pm.* Flowers and plants.

- **Piazza Aldrovandi**, *Every day from 7:00am to 1:00pm and from 4:00pm to 7:30pm*. Great selection of cheese, meat, fruit, and vegetables.
- **Piazza di Porta San Mamolo**, *Every day from 7:00am–1:00pm*. Food products, and a variety of clothing, shoes, belts, etc.
- **Via Ugo Bassi**, *Open all day, every day*. This is actually a covered market that sells food products, a variety of goods like clothing shoes, etc.

Supermarkets
- **COOP Emilia Veneto**, *Via Montebello 2/3*
- **Conad**, *Via Finelli 8*
- **PAM**, *Via Guglielmo Marconi 28/A*
- **Conad**, *Via Santo Isaia 67*

Excursions & Day Trips

In this section, I'll lead you to **Parma** and **Ferrara**, both charming old towns with tons of character and ambiance. Each can be a day trip from Bologna or a full length excursion with you ending up spending the night.

PARMA

With a population of approximately 180,000, **Parma** is the provincial capital and a well-known Italian university town. Back in 183 BCE, Parma started off as an isolated Roman outpost and colony, then after the fall of the Roman Empire, Parma was controlled by a variety of rulers. First they passed from Milan's control (1346 to 1512) to Papal control (1512 to 1542). Then in 1542, Pope Paul III gave the duchies of Parma and Piacenza to his son, Pier Luigi Farnese. In case you hadn't figured it out yet, only recently has the Catholic church made sexual abstinence a requirement for the priesthood.

After the Farnese male line died out in 1731, the duchies were transferred to the Bourbons. Then in 1807, Parma came under the control of the French, and eventually were given to Napoleon's wife, Maria Louise. But then the Italian movement for their own country took hold, the people of Parma expelled the French in 1859 and Parma was incorporated into the new Italian state.

Parma – that warm, medieval city of domes, spires, and bell towers, a city rich in history - is mainly known for its food products: *Prosciutto di Parma*, and especially its famous cheese called *Parmigiano Reggiano*. Cows in Parma are imported and bred specifically for the richness and quantity of their milk, the milk that will eventually become the king of cheeses. Cheese making in Parma is considered an art form as well as a respected career, one that is passed down from father to son and sometimes, but very rarely, from mother to daughter. The whey, which is the byproduct of the cheese making process, becomes the diet of the huge Parma pigs, those that provide the succulent *Prosciutto di Parma*.

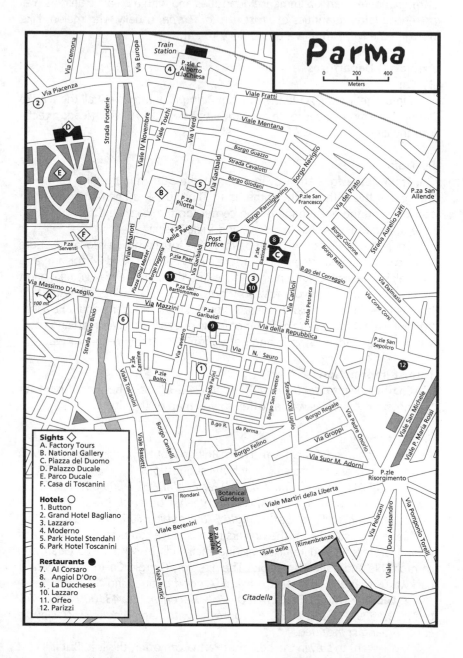

Parma

0   200   400
Meters

Sights ◇
A. Factory Tours
B. National Gallery
C. Piazza del Duomo
D. Palazzo Ducale
E. Parco Ducale
F. Casa di Toscanini

Hotels ○
1. Button
2. Grand Hotel Bagliano
3. Lazzaro
4. Moderno
5. Park Hotel Stendahl
6. Park Hotel Toscanini

Restaurants ●
7. Al Corsaro
8. Angiol D'Oro
9. La Duccheses
10. Lazzaro
11. Orfeo
12. Parizzi

As you'll notice when you go to any restaurant in Parma, they all use *Parmigiano Reggiano* in immense quantities and with a creative flair, as well as serving large quantities of *Prosciutto di Parma*, usually with melon. Like Bologna the Fat, Parma is a great place to eat.

Arrivals & Departures
By Car
Simply get on the A1 highway from Bologna and follow it all the way to Parma. For a more scenic route, take the smaller road SS 9 which leads directly into the city.

By Train
Trains leave for Parma every hour at the 38th minute, and return to Bologna at the 25th minute of the hour. The trip takes one hour. The **train station** is on the north edge of the center, on the Piazzale C. Alberto della Chiesa, and at the end of Via Verdi and Viale Toschi.

To get to the Piazza del Duomo where the **tourist office** is located – here you'll pick up a great free map ... there's no need to spend E4 for one at a Giornalaio – leave the station and go straight through the *piazza*, take a left on Viale Boteggo, then your first right onto the Via Garibaldi. Follow that for five minutes on the left hand side until you get to Via Pisacane and take a left. You'll see the Duomo from here. Once in the piazza look to your left and you'll see the tourist office. Stop in and get your map and you're on our way.

Tourist Information
• **IAT Office**, *Piazza del Duomo 5, Tel. 0521/234-735*. They can book your hotel from here as well as offering you map of the city.

Where to Stay
Parma is a good a one day trip from Bologna, but if you like it here or wish to stay a night or two, here are my hotel suggestions.

1. BUTTON, *Borgo Salina 7, 43100 Parma. Tel. 0521/208-039, Fax 0521/ 238-783. Web: www.parmaitaly.com/hotel-button.html. Credit Cards ac-cepted. 41 rooms all with bath. Single E70; Double E105. Breakfast E6.* ***

Centrally located near the university, this place caters to the budgets of visiting professors and families visiting their kids at school. It's clean and comfortable and quite affordable. The director, Giorgio Cortesi, bends over backwards to make your stay pleasant. A good budget choice.

2. GRAND HOTEL BAGLIANO, *Viale Piacenza 12c, 43100 Parma. Tel. 0521/292-929, Fax 292-828. 169 rooms all with bath. Single E150; Double E200. Breakfast included.* ****

If you want to stay in the best that Parma can offer, this is it. But it'll cost you. They have everything from a piano bar to saunas to barbers and hair stylists, as well as a first class restaurant. First class, top notch, A-number-one. The best in Parma.

3. LAZZARO, *Via XX Marzo 14, 43100 Parma. Tel. 0521/208-944. 8 rooms, 3 doubles with bath, 5 singles, only two with bath. Single without bath E30; Single E40; Double E50.* *

If you missed the last train back to Bologna, which is not really possible unless you stumbled into the station around midnight, this is a wonderfully inexpensive place to stay. Couple that with their fine restaurant and you have a great combo. The rooms are small but clean and comfortable. I would even suggest staying here if you want to spend some more time in the city, since they are located a stone's throw from the Duomo on a quiet little side street. And you can't beat the price.

4. MODERNO, *Via A Cecchi 4, 43100 Parma. Tel. 0521/772-647. 46 rooms, 37 with bath. Single without bath E30; Single E35; Double without bath E40; Double E50.* **

A typical hotel near the train station in a town that doesn't get many tourists. It's run-down, the service is non-existent, and the ambiance is nil. Even though this is a two star and the Lazzaro is a one star, go there first. Use this only as a second-to-last resort.

5. PARK HOTEL STENDHAL, *Via Boboni 3, 43100 Parma. Tel. 0521/208-057, Fax 0521/285-655. E-mail: stendhal.pr@bestwestern.it. Web: www.bestwestern.it/stendhal_pr/. Credit cards accepted. 60 rooms all with bath. Single E110-150; Double E130-180. Suite E190. Breakfast E10 extra.* ****

Located in an old palace near the center of town and the train station, this is mainly a businessman's hotel but they have all the amenities for a fine tourist stay, including a great restaurant. Now a Best Western, you fill find excellent accommodations here. The rooms are elegant and immaculate. Renovated in 1997, this hotel offers every possible four star amenity.

6. PARK HOTEL TOSCANINI, *Viale A Toscanini 4, 43100 Parma. Tel. 0521/289-141, Fax 0521/283-143. Credit cards accepted. 48 rooms all with bath. Single E140; Double E170. Breakfast E8.* ****

Located near the Toscanini museum, this hotel is the perfect place to stay for you music lovers since they have a piano bar. A good four star that caters mainly to the Italian businessman traveling to Parma. Nonetheless you'll find the lodgings clean, accommodating and comfortable. Though functional it also has a bit of charm.

Where to Eat

7. AL CORSARO, *Via Cavour 37, Tel. 0521/235-402 or 221-311. Dinner for two E30.*

You have to look inside if you've seated yourself on their outdoor patio, especially if you have kids, since their bar is half of a twenty foot boat. This is a

Neapolitan restaurant, ergo the nautical theme. Try any of their special pastas (*carbonara, arrabiata or amatriciana*) and save yourself for the pizza of the house, the *Napoli* (with tomatoes, mozzarella, oregano and anchovies).

8. ANGIOL D'OR, *Vicolo Scutellari 1, Tel. 0521/282-632. Closed Sundays. All credit cards accepted. Dinner for two E65.*

An elegant but simple dining experience. The chef is superb and makes the best of the local ingredients when they are fresh. For this reason, the menu here changes dramatically every three months. I've had some good *tortelli di patate con porcini* (potato tortelli with porcini mushrooms) and *petto di pollo con salsa di vino rosso* (breast of chicken cooked in red wine sauce). You can either choose to sit inside or outside on their quiet terrace.

9. LA DUCCHESE, *Piazza Garibaldi 1, Tel. 0521/235-962. Credit cards accepted. Closed Mondays. Dinner for two E30.*

You have to go with a pasta first course and a pizza second course here. They are both great. Try the local pizza, *Parmigiana* (with tomatoes, mozzarella, ham and cooked egg) or the *prosciutto fungi* (ham and mushrooms) if you're not in the adventurous mood. For pasta they make an excellent *capelleti alla parmigiana* (pasta shaped like little hats with ricotta, spinach, grated cheese and butter) as well as a *carbonara* (with egg, butter and ham).

10. LAZZARO, *Via XX Marzo 14, Tel. 0521/208-944. No credit cards accepted. Dinner for two E30.*

If you've ever wanted to try filet of horse (*fileto di cavallo*) look no further. It's really quite good, and no, it doesn't taste like chicken or beef. It's tender and succulent and a true culinary experience, definitely one you can tell your friends about. If that doesn't grab you, try their *costine di agnello* (lamb chop). For *primo* sample some of their truly native pasta dishes like the *tortelli dei erbetta* (pasta stuffed with ricotta and made with butter and covered in *parmigiano*). A great atmosphere with good food just off the Piazza del Duomo.

11. ORFEO, *Via Carducci 5, Tel. 0521/285-483. Credit cards accepted. Dinner for two E25.*

A fun local place with over 120 seats in four different rooms. This place gets packed on the weekends and is loud and boisterous. Simple decor except in the *cantina vecchia* in the basement with its arched brick ceilings. The pizzas are great. If you're in the front room you can enjoy the spectacle of the pizzas being prepared. Try any of their offerings and you'll be satisfied, especially with the German beer they offer on tap.

12. PARIZZI, *Strada Repubblica 71. Tel. 0521/285-952. Credit cards accepted. Closed Mondays and in the summer also Sundays. Dinner for two E48.*

A large, friendly place set in an elegant dining environment, that is after you get past the rather shabby covered walkway you have to use to get to the entrance. Everything here is great, especially the local dishes. For primo try the *tortelli d'erbetta alla parmigiana* (pasta stuffed with ricotta in butter and covered with *parmigiana*). Then be adventurous with the *trippa alla parmigiana* (tripe made in local fashion smothered in cheese). For a healthier diet try the *teste di funghi ai ferri* (grilled heads of mushrooms).

Seeing the Sights

In the town where cheese and ham are king, start your visit with a factory tour, but there are other charms besides culinary to this wonderful old city.

A. FACTORY TOURS

If you're interested in going on a tour of a ham or cheese factory and store, first contact the **Consortio dei Parmigiana**, *Via Gramsci 26a, Tel. 051/29-70-00* or the **Consortio di Prosciutto**, *Via M. Dell'Arpa 8b, Tel. 0521/24-39-87. Tours available 9:00am–5:00pm Monday–Saturday.* You get a guided tour of their facilities and may even get some free samples at the end. An eye-opening experience to the refined creation of artisan foods.

B. NATIONAL GALLERY

Palazzo della Pilotta. Open 9:00am–1:45:00pm. Admission E3.

In the Palazzo della Pilotta, you'll find *La Scapigliata* here, Leonardo da Vinci's sketch of a young girl, as well as other fine works of art. To enter the gallery you must first pass through the **Farnese Theater**, built in 1615.

C. PIAZZA DEL DUOMO

Baptistry, *Tel. 235-886. Open 9:00am–12:30pm and 5:00pm–6:00pm. Admission E2.* **Cathedral**, *Tel. 235-886. Open 9:00am–noon and 3:00pm–7:00pm.*

Baptistry

A pink marble octagonal building, begun in the Romanesque style by Beneddetto Antelami and completed in the Gothic style between 1256 and 1270. Main attractions are the 13th century bas-reliefs and frescoes inside.

Cathedral

Covered in pillars, this Romanesque basilica dates from the late 12th century. The expansive facade joins together with the *campanile* (bell tower) on the right, which is 63 meters high and was built between 1284 and 1294. Inside the church you'll find the amazing fresco of the *Assumption of the Virgin of Correggio* made between 1526 and 1530, as well as the relief work done by Beneddetto Antelami in 1178, *Descent from the Cross*. Look also for the Roman mosaics in the crypt.

D. PALAZZO E PARCO DUCALE
Palazzo is open from Mon.-Sat 8:00am-noon. Tel. 0521/230-023. Parco is open Dec/Jan 7:00am-5:30pm; Nov/Feb 7:00am-6:00pm; Oct/Mar/ Apr 6:30am-7:00pm; May/June/July/Aug 6:00am-midnight.

If you need a respite from the city, come here to these extensive Baroque gardens. The building is off-limits since it is currently a military academy, but you can still enjoy the peace and quiet of the gardens.

E. CASA DI TOSCANINI
Borgo Rodolfo Tanzi, Tel. 285-499. Open Tuesday-Sunday 10:00am-1:00pm. Tuesday and Thursday also open from 3:00pm-6:00pm. Free. Need to make reservations.

Just south of the park on the Borgo Rodolfo Tanzi is the birthplace of **Arturo Toscanini**, the magnificent musical conductor. The house now contains a small museum of memorabilia from the maestro's life, which should be visited if you are a classical music buff.

Shopping
The main streets of the town are **Via della Repubblica**, **Via Mazzini**, and **Via Garibaldi**, where the citizens gather to shop and stroll, especially in the early evening hours before their dinner meal. The main square for hanging out and planning which shops to hit is the **Piazza Garibaldi**. With its cafés offering outside seating, this piazza is the meeting area for the citizens of Parma.

Cheese
If you're looking for cheese, look no further than **Formaggeria Del Re**, *Via Garibaldi 46E*, featuring wheels of *parmigiana*. At **Formaggeria**, *Via Borgo Del Gallo 8A* you won't find huge wheels of *parmigiana* but you will find mounds of different types of cheese.

Food Stores & Markets
• **Salumeria**, *Via Garibaldi 42F*
• **Salumeria**, *Via della Repubblica 54a*
• **Market**, *Piazza Ghiaia.* A great source of picnic supplies if you're off to relax in the **Parco Ducale**. They have cheeses, meats, breads, fruits, veggies, as well as clothes and household items. The market atmosphere stretches onto surrounding streets.

FERRARA
Ferrara is a small walled city with a population of only 155,000, with many tiny cobblestone streets that seem right out of the Middle Ages, as well

as wide streets and sumptuous palaces that are reminiscent of the Renaissance. Ferrara started off as an independent community, but from 1208 to 1598 was controlled by the **Este family** who, history shows, were particularly cruel and despotic, even though they were tolerant of different religions as well as great patrons of the arts. After 1598, Ferrara became a papal state, then it was taken over by Napoleon and was ruled by France until it was eventually incorporated into the new Italian state in the nineteenth century.

One of the things I find most appealing about Ferrara is the fact that it is small enough and flat enough, and many of the streets are closed to automobile traffic, that residents will commute to work on bicycles. At rush hour it's fun to sit in a café and watch the swarms pedal on by. You can join them if you like, since Ferrara has plenty of bicycles by the municipal government.

But one of the best things to do in Ferrara is take a stroll around her walls. Second only in romance to those of Lucca, the walls were the creation of the Renaissance. Here you can see trees and undergrowth covering what once were part of a formidable military defense system.

You can also stroll through the old ghetto where by papal decree the Jews were housed beginning in 1627. Prior to the church's control, Ferrara was an open and tolerant city. When the Jews were expelled from Spain in 1492, because of their valuable skills, the ruler at the time, Ercole d'Este invited as many as could come to stay in Ferrara. Even after their internment in the ghetto, they were still relatively free to roam the city. Today you can admire the **synagogues** on Via Mazzini as well as the **Jewish Museum** amongst them.

And if you can, try and come here on the last Sunday in May, since Ferrara celebrates its famous **Palio**. Filled with pageantry and life, this is a spectacle second only to the Palio of Siena.

Arrivals & Departures
By Car
Take the A13 highway or a more scenic route (the smaller road 64) straight up to Ferrara. The drive takes between 30 and 40 minutes.

By Train
Morning trains are: 8:35, 10:26, 10:42, 11:42, 12:26. The return times in the afternoon are spaced about the same, roughly every 45 minutes to an hour, so you can spend a good day of sightseeing then head back to Bologna. Remember to check with the train information to verify times. The trip takes about half an hour from Bologna.

You can get into the walled town from the train station by walking for fifteen minutes or catching either bus #9 or #1. Once you see the castle with its moat on the right hand side, ring the bell for the bus to stop. It will continue past the castle and stop about fifty feet away. Now you're just past and across the street from the tourist office, where you can rent bicycles and get maps and information about the city.

Tourist Information
• **Ufficio Informazioni e Accoglienza Turistica**, *Corso Giovecca 21-23, Tel. 0532/209-370, Fax 0532/212-266. or Via Kennedy 8, Tel. 0532/765-728, Fax 0532/760-225. Open Monday through Saturday 8:00am to 5:00pm.* To get to the main office at Corso Giovecca, just past the Castello Estense take bus number 1 or 9 from the station. This is where you can rent bicycles and pick up maps and all sorts of tourist information.

Getting around Town
By Bicycle
At the **Ufficio Informazioni Turistica**, *Corso Giovecca 21-23, Tel. 0532/ 209-370, Fax 0532/212-266,* you can get all sorts of tourist information and you can rent bicycles. The rates are E3 per hour; E6 per 3 hours; E10 per 6 hours; and E15 all day long. The bikes are all in good shape and are relatively inexpensive to rent.

By Foot
Ferrara is a walker's city. Small and compact. Perfect for short strolls. If you start to get tired, just stop at one of the many cafés and have a pick-me-up and be off again. Along the way you'll be able to soak in the sights and sounds of a magnificent Renaissance capital.

Where to Stay
1. ANNUNZIATA, *Piazza Repubblica 5, 44100 Ferrara. Tel. 0532/201-111, Fax 0532/203-233. Web: www.annunziata.it/. 26 rooms, all with shower or bath. Credit cards accepted. Single E125; Double E180; Suite E200. Breakfast included.* ****
This used to be a run-down little one star until someone decided that with a little renovation and some private baths it could make a small town listing as a four star. And so in 1990 it was renovated and *voila*, magically you have a really good hotel with all the necessary amenities. Located in an historic building and set in a tranquil environment you'll find all the necessary amenities for a four star. The rooms are relatively tiny but comfortable.
2. ASTRA/BEST WESTERN, *Viale Cavour 55, 44100 Ferrara. Tel. 0532/ 206-088, Fax 0532/247-002. Web: www.astrahotel.com/. American Express, Mastercard and Visa accepted. 69 rooms all with bath. Single E130; Double E190. Breakfast included.* ****
On the main street from the station set in a quiet *piazza*, they will take care

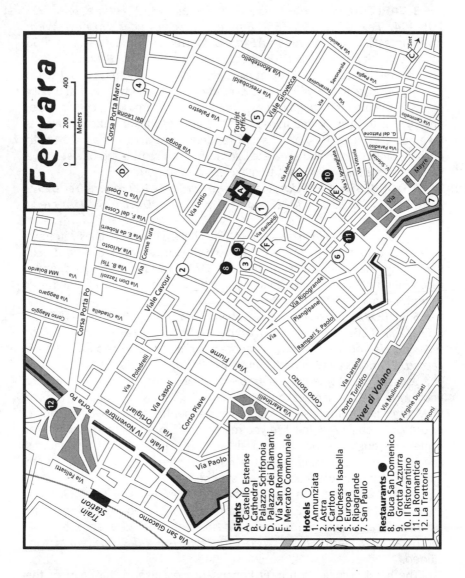

Ferrara

Meters
0 200 400

Sights ◇
A. Castello Estense
B. Cathedral
C. Palazzo Schifonoia
D. Palazzo dei Diamanti
E. Via San Romano
F. Mercato Communale

Hotels ○
1. Annunziata
2. Astra
3. Carlton
4. Duchessa Isabella
5. Europa
6. Ripagrande
7. San Paulo

Restaurants ●
8. Buca San Domenico
9. Grotta Azzurra
10. Il Ristorantino
11. La Romantica
12. La Trattoria

of your every need here. Catering mainly to business travelers, the Astra has air conditioning, a restaurant, room service, bar, mini-bar, TV, air conditioning and more. Located 200 meters from the castle and other sights, it is perfectly situated for both business and pleasure.

3. CARLTON, *Via Garibaldi 93 (Piazza Sacrati), 44100 Ferrara. Tel. 0532/ 205-904, Fax 0532/205-766. E-mail: info@hotelcarlton.net. Web: www.hotelcarlton.net/. American Express, Mastercard and Visa accepted. 58 rooms all with bath. Single E100; Double E150. Breakfast E8 extra.* ***

Located in a pristine and quiet *piazza* just off the beaten track but still in walking distance to everything. This is a thoroughly modern hotel that usually caters to the discriminating businessman. The rooms are clean, comfortable, and cozy with their TV and mini-bar. It has little character but everything is taken care of here. They also have a residence just across the piazza with kitchen, dining room, and separate bedroom if you're thinking of a stay of a week or more and really want to make yourself at home.

4. DUCHESSA ISABELLA, *Via Palestro 68/70, 44100 Ferrara. Tel. 0532/ 202-121, Fax 0532/202-638. 28 rooms all with bath. Double E210. All credit cards accepted.* ****

A quaint four star on a quiet street. They have all the amenities you crave as well as a tranquil garden setting in which you can relax after a day of wandering the side streets of the city. Their restaurant is good and I recommend it, but if you crave variety, the hotel is centrally located to many other fine eating establishments.

5. EUROPA, *Corso Giovecca 49, 44100 Ferrara. Tel. 0532/205-456, Fax 0532/212-120. E-mail: info@hoteleuropaferrara.com. Web: www.hoteleuropaferrara.com/. American Express, Mastercard and Visa accepted. 42 rooms all with bath. Single E100; Double E150.* ***

Located in a 17th century *palazzo* with views of the Castello Estense, here you'll have all the amenities of a three star with a splash of antiquity thrown in. Most of the rooms have 16-foot ceilings either frescoed or wood beamed or both, so you'll really feel like you're in a *palazzo*. The sitting room is like something out of a Victorian novel: antique chairs and table, beautiful couches, mirrors and paintings on the wall and more. For a pleasant stay with a touch of class at reasonable prices, stay here.

6. RIPAGRANDE, *Via Ripagrande 21, 44100 Ferrara. Tel. 0532/765-250, Fax. 0532/764-377. E-mail: ripahotel@4net.it. Web: www.4net.com/ business/ripa/. American Express, Mastercard and Visa accepted. 40 rooms all with bath. Single E120-140; Double E300-320. Breakfast included.* ****

The hotel occupies a former Renaissance *palazzo* in the heart of the historic district. The forty rooms upstairs are all equipped with TVs and air conditioning, and twenty have sitting rooms as well as kitchenettes. There is also a pleasant courtyard in the back with a wonderful restaurant facing out onto it. A truly romantic hotel that offers motorboat tours of the surrounding rivers on the weekends as well as bicycle rentals. They are kid friendly with baby-sitting and a playroom. They do it all.

7. SAN PAULO, *Via Baluardi 9, 44100 Ferrara. Tel. 0532/768-333, Fax 0532/762-040. No credit cards accepted. 20 rooms 17 with bath. Single without bath E40; Single E45; Double without bath E48; Double E55.* ******

Located in the historic ghetto district, the rooms here are simply furnished, and because of the location are quiet. The bathrooms are functional with box showers that can be rather confining for someone of larger size, like myself for example. The common areas are rustic with terra-cotta tile floors. This is also a good place to stay for budget travelers. Fido is also welcome here.

Where to Eat

8. BUCA SAN DOMENICO, *26b Piazza Sacrati. Pizzas cost E8. Credit cards accepted. Dinner for two E20.*

Rustic decor with wooden booths and tables. You can have some really good pizza here. Try their *alla salsiccia or ai funghi* (with sausage or with mushroom). If pizza is not to your liking they have a great *spaghetti con pomodoro e basilico* (with tomatoes and basil). Or try the *zuppa di verdure* (vegetable soup) or their *mozzarella e pomodoro* (mozzarella with tomatoes and olive oil) for something lighter.

9. GROTTA AZZURRA, *Piazza Sacrati 43, 0532/209-152, Fax 0532/210-950. Credit cards accepted. Dinner for two E45.*

A high-end restaurant and as the name indicates, this is a seafood place. The decor is maritime and Neapolitan with chandeliers, mirrors, white walls and memorabilia. Try the *antipasto di mare* (seafood antipasto) or the *cocktail di gamberi* (shrimp cocktail) for appetizer. Then try some of their grilled or fried fish such as *grigliatta mista* (mixed grill) or the *fritto di gamberetti* (fried shrimp). If seafood is not to your liking they also have many meat and pasta dishes.

10. IL RISTORANTINO, *Vicolo M, Aguchie 15, Tel. 0532/25-922. Closed Sundays. Credit cards accepted. Dinner for two E35.*

A great little place, hence the name (*ristorantino* means small restaurant), with a friendly simple decor. Try their *spaghetti all'amatriciana, tagliatelle alla bolognese* (with meat sauce), or their *penne all'arrabbiata* (with a spicy tomato based sauce) for *primo*. Then for *secondo* try the *salamina di Ferrara* (salamis of Ferrara) or the wonderful *scaloppina ai funghi porcini* (veal covered with a mushroom sauce).

11. LA ROMANTICA, *Via Ripogrande 36, Tel. 0532/765-975. Credit cards accepted. Dinner for two E35.*

The dark wooden chairs and beams on the ceiling contrast well with the stark white walls and few plants interspersed around the restaurant. For starters try either their *salumi tipici* (local salamis) or the *patate al forno* (roast potatoes). For seconds either try a great *penne all'arrabbiata* (a hot and spicy tomato-based pasta dish) or the *costoletto di agnello allo sherry* (lamb cutlet cooked in a sherry sauce).

12. LA TRATTORIA, *Viale Po 13/17, Tel. 0532/55-103. Closed Tuesdays. Credit cards accepted. Dinner for two E35.*

Located near the station and the Porta Po, this is a simple place with a wood beamed ceiling, white washed walls, paintings and ferns hanging haphazardly for color. Their antipasto table seems sparse but it certainly can be filling, especially the sampling of local salamis. They serve excellent grilled meats and make wonderful *tortellini* with cream sauce.

Seeing the Sights

Ferrara is a stunningly beautiful city with a definite medieval feel to it. The main sights include the castle, the cathedral, the city walls and the many beautiful *palazzi*; but what you'll remember most about Ferrara is the tranquil pace and historic feel.

A. CASTELLO ESTENSE – ESTE CASTLE

Piazza Castello. Tel. 299-279. Open Tues-Sun 9:30am-1:30pm and 2:30pm-5:30pm. Admission E3.

Built in 1385 as protection for the Este family, this castle is the embodiment of a medieval fortress and comes complete with a moat around its perimeter. The castle was upgraded with marble balconies and tower *loggias* during the 16th century when the building became the local ducal palace. These are still in evidence today. Inside you'll find magnificent frescoes from the Fillippi school of the 16th century.

B. CATHEDRAL

Piazza Cattedrale. Tel. 202-392. Open Monday-Saturday 7:30am-noon and 3:00pm-6:30pm. Sunday 7:30am-1:00pm and 4:00pm-7:30pm.

Built in the 12th century, this large cathedral shows signs of Romanesque, Baroque, and Gothic influences. You should spend some time admiring the marble facade with its many arches, stained glass windows, bas-reliefs, and columns all showing signs of different artistic influences. On the right hand side of the church as you face it you'll find small stores built into the walls and foundations. A unique sight if there ever was one. It's not often you see the blatant merging of commerce and Catholicism. Inside the church there are many tapestries, paintings, sculptures, frescoes and more to admire.

C. PALAZZO SCHIFONAIO

Via Scandiana 23, Tel. 64178. Open 9:00am-7:00pm. Admission E3.

This palace was built for the rest and relaxation of the ducal family,

Schifonaio. It contains some of the greatest masterpieces of the Renaissance period, including the **Room of the Months** filled with exquisite frescoes and the **Room of the Stuccoes** with its shining golden roof. All throughout you'll find a vast art collection that spans many centuries. This is Ferrara's main claim to artistic fame.

D. PALAZZO DEI DIAMANTI – PALACE OF DIAMONDS

Corso Ercole I d'Este, Tel. 205–844. Open Tuesday–Saturday 9:00am–2:00pm, and Sundays 9:00am–1:00pm. Admission E3.

When you first see this palace you'll know why it was given its name. The walls appear to be covered with carved stones in the shape of diamonds. When the early morning sun, as well as that at the end of the day, reflects off these many diamonds the sight is magnificent. On the first floor you'll find the many beautiful paintings of the **Picture Gallery** and on the ground floor you'll find many works of modern art.

Shopping

On the **Via San Romano** you'll find narrow curved pedestrian streets graced with elegant old arches and fine small shops. If you took away the neon and modern signs, this small street would make you feel as if you stepped back into the Renaissance. Here you can sense and feel the market atmosphere. At the end of the street you'll find the Cathedral with shops built into the foundation and wall.

F. Mercato Communale

Located on the corner of Via Santo Stefano and the Via del Mercato, you'll find a quaint little enclosed market bustling with business here every day from 7:00am to 1:00pm. Only on Fridays is it open in the afternoon from 4:30pm to 7:30pm. You can find fruits, vegetables, cheeses, garden supplies, pet supplies, clothes, basically everything an Italian shopper could need or a tourist could want for picnic supplies or a gift for someone at home.

Practical Information for Bologna

Car Rental
• **Avis**, *Via Marco Polo 91, Tel. 051/634-1632*
• **Hertz**, *Airport, Tel. 051/647-2015 or Via Amendola 051/254-830*

Laundries
• **Laundry**, *Via Todaro 4. Tel. 051/24-07-40. Open Monday to Friday, 8:00am–7:00pm, Saturdays 8:30am–1:00pm. Not open Sundays. Self service.*
• **Saragozza**, *Via Saragozza 41, Tel. 051/33-10-62. Open Monday to Friday 8:00am–7:00pm, Saturdays 8:30am–1:00pm. Not open Sundays. Self service.*

• **Bolle i Sapone di Masetti Giovanni**, *Via Petroni 22B, Tel. 051/22-17-79. Open Monday to Friday, 8:00am-7:00pm. Saturdays 8:30am-1:00pm. Not open Sundays. Self service.*

Postal Services
The post office is located at *Via Guerrazzi #10*, open Monday to Friday, 8:00am-6:00pm. You can also buy stamps at local tabacconist stores and mail letters and post cards at the ever present red mailboxes.

Tourist Information & Maps
• **IAT Office**, *Piazza Medaglio d'Oro, Stazione Ferroviara, 40121 Bologna. Tel. 051/246-541. Open Monday to Saturday, 9:00am-7:00pm.* This is the hotel reservations and information office at the station that can book rooms for you if you have none. They offer a free, excellent tourist map.
• **Informazione Ferrovie**, *Stazione Ferroviara, Tel. 051/264-490. Open 8:00am-8:00pm.* This is where you get train scheduling information. You need to take a number and wait for it to be called. The service representatives are behind glass doors that only open when they've finished with another customer. Be prepared and quick. They close the doors and change the numbers very fast. Italians are completely baffled by such an orderly system. They are not used to waiting in lines. After trying to cut in line, they'll stand there amazed that they are being rebuffed. Some will storm off in a huff, others will meekly succumb to the system and take a ticket. The beauty of Italy is that everything functions despite all this chaos.

Tour Operators
• **Big Tours**, *Via Indipendenza 12, 40121 Bologna, Tel. 051/23-84-11, Fax 051/265-771*
• **Conray**, *Via Andrea Costa 3a, 40134 Bologna. Tel. 051/43-02-06, Fax 051/61-45-252*
• **Wagon-Lit Travel**, *Piazza Azzarita 1L. Tel. 051/52-01-06*

Chapter 23

Turin

Situated 78 miles southwest of Milan, with a population just topping one million people, **Turin** (**Torino**) is the major city in the western Alps. The city lies on the banks of the **Po River** near the foot of the Alps in northwestern Italy. There is enough of interest to justify a one night stay, and maybe a little more.

Because it is the home of automobile makers **Fiat** and **Lancia**, Turin has been called the Detroit of Italy, but despite the industrial presence Torino retain the intimacy and pace of a much smaller city. Besides automobiles, it is also a major industrial center for ball bearings, rubber and tires, clothing, textiles, leather goods, paper, chemicals, and food products.

Torino is really a rare gem of a city and has lately been making itself more accessible, inviting and navigable for tourists. A walk through Torino will take you down and through tree-lined avenues and boulevards, tranquil Baroque *piazze* and arcaded streets. There are over 20 miles of arcaded sidewalks that make a brief *passegiatta* a veritable stroll into history. Some of these arcades, or *portici*, date back to the 12th century.

Every street offers at least one stylish shop or stunning Baroque vista; the museums are excellent; the buildings have maintained their ornate turn-of-the-century facades; the cafes are intimate and plentiful; the food – which includes cheese, wine, pastries and chocolates – is among Italy's best. When you visit you will encounter very few tourists but many friendly natives.

Turin has also been a center of learning and religion for many years. The **University of Turin** was founded in

1404, and the **Cathedral of St. John the Baptist** was built from 1491 to 1498. This marvelous church houses the chapel of the **Holy Shroud** and contains a holy relic, the **Shroud of Turin**. Despite the fact that modern carbon dating and other investigative techniques have disproved the robes' authenticity, this cloth is still believed to have been used to wrap the body of Jesus after his crucifixion.

Torino's name comes from the **Taurini Gauls**, who inhabited this location in pre-Roman times. During the reign of Augustus, the Romans rebuilt and walled the city and gave it the grid pattern that still exists today. In 570 CE, it fell to the Lombards, and under Charlemagne it was assigned to the margraves of Susa. Linked to the House of Savoy in 1046 by a noble marriage, it served as the capital of the Piedmont for several centuries. In 1720 it became the capital of the Kingdom of Sardinia, and in the years 1861 to 1865 it was the capital of a newly united Italy. The city was heavily bombed by Allied air raids during World War II because of its industrial nature, but by 1959 its industries and landmarks had been restored.

The main excursion is the lovely town of **Asti**, with its magical, medieval charms.

Arrivals & Departures

Your best bet for arrival and departure is the train. Turin is not far from Milan, and travel time by train from Milan or its airport, Malpensa, should be about no more than an hour and a half. From Rome, the train trip should take about six hours.

Touring Torino

Torino is made for walking, especially down the arcaded Via Roma. Everywhere you go you'll find exquisitely maintained Baroque and Renaissance architecture. When not promenading, visit the **Royal Armory** (excellent ancient arms and armor), the **Cathedral of St. John the Baptist** (home of the Holy Shroud), the **Palatine Gate** (built by Emperor Augustus), the **Valentino Castle and Park**, **Palazzo Madama** (which houses the **Museum of Ancient Art**), the **Automobile Museum** (with one of the world's best collection of antique cars, some models dating back to 1893), and you simply cannot miss the **Egyptian Museum** and the **Galleria Sabauda** (collection of Masters art), Torino's two must-see museums. And every Saturday there is a magnificent **flea market** located by the marvelous cast-iron-and-glass food markets.

Getting Around Town

By Bicycle

You can rent a bicycle at a stand in the beautiful and tranquil **Parco Valentino**. The "shop" is located on the Viale Matteoli and is open from 9:30am–12:30pm and 3:00pm–7:00pm, Tuesday through Sunday. You can rent the bikes for E6 per day or E2 per hour. You need to leave a picture ID and E3 cash as a deposit.

By Bus

This is a large bustling city, but the bus system, as in all Italian cities, is excellent so you can get around easily. At a cost of only E1 per trip, you can go anywhere in the city quickly and efficiently from 6:00am to 12:30am.

Tickets must be bought at a *Tabacchi* prior to boarding the buses, and convenient maps are available at most main bus terminals and at the APT tourist office on Via Roma.

By Taxi

I wouldn't recommend using your car in this big congested city. You can find taxis all over the streets and at conveniently located taxi stands, but if you want to call one from your hotel try one of these three companies:

• **Central Taxi**, *Tel. 011/33-99*
• **Pronto Taxi**, *Tel. 011/57-37*
• **Radio Taxi Torino**, *Tel. 011/57-30*

Where To Stay

Turin's hotels are functional as befits a businesslike town, but several have something approaching charm. One item to note is that the city's hotels are virtually empty on the weekends because Torino has not yet been discovered by tourism. Therefore most of these hotels are more than willing to offer amazing discounts if you stay over the weekend. All you have to do is ask prior to arriving.

1. AMADEUS E TEATRO, *Via Principe Amadeo 41, 10122 Torino, Tel. 011/817-4951, Fax 011/817-4953. 26 rooms all with bath. Single E100; Double E140. Closed in August. Credit cards accepted. Breakfast included.* ***

A small boutique hotel that is well located and at a good price. Recently some rooms and common areas were renovated, bringing this place into the 20th century. The entrance is elegant with blue and white ceramic tile. There is a quaint little *cortile* in the center with a lone palm tree blooming. This is a good three star after its recent renovations. I would recommend it warmly. The rooms have every necessary amenity and are clean, comfortable and spacious.

2. BEST WESTERN GENIO, *Corso Vittorio Emanuele II 47, 10121 Torino, Tel. 011/650-5771, Fax 011/650-8264. E-mail: genio.to@bestwestern.it. Web: www.bestwestern.it/. 120 rooms all with bath. Single E60-100; Double E95-130. Breakfast included. All credit cards accepted.* ***

Right in front of the train station in a quaint old building, with a grand entrance below the porticos between Via Nizza and Via Saluzzo. The entrance hall is large and comfortable with an area to relax directly to the left. Each room, though different in decoration, layout and size, are all clean and comfortable. The Genio is a hotel with a long and storied tradition in Torino, and the staff make a point of attending to your every detail. A great place to stay. They are trying to move up a star and it shows.

3. BEST WESTERN GENOVA E STAZIONE, *Via Sacchi 14b, 10122 Torino, Tel. 011/562-9400, Fax 011/562-9896. E-mail: genova.to@bestwestern.it. Web: www.bestwestern.it/. 59 rooms all with bath. Single E60-100; Double E95-130. All credit cards accepted. Breakfast included.* ***

Another Best Western, this one is right next to the main train station. The atmosphere is best in the rooms and hallways and not in the reception area. This is a good hotel, with a staff that caters to your every need. In an old building, many rooms have cathedral-style windows that definitely adds a touch of class. Each room is a little different than the rest. Some are larger, some smaller, some lavishly decorated, others are simple, but all are clean and comfortable – but only 30 have air conditioning. The bathrooms are perfectly appointed with all necessary amenities. A good place to stay but not in the heat of summer.

4. BEST WESTERN GRAN MOGOL, *Corso Novara 16, 10122 Torino, Tel. 011/561-2120, Fax 011/562-3160. E-mail: granmogol.to@bestwestern.it. Web: www.bestwestern.com. 45 rooms. Single E60-100; Double E95-130. All credit cards accepted. Breakfast included.* ***

And yet another Best Western, not quite as good as the Genio or Genova e Stazione but on par with the Piemontese. Also situated near the station, this is a comfortable and tranquil hotel. The facade is modern and everything has the look and feel of the recent renovations. All the rooms have similar, standard, basic furnishings a la North America, which means they are kept clean, are comfortable and ample in size and the bathrooms have every necessary amenity. There is air conditioning, satellite TV, room service, etc., that you expect from any three star. The staff here is courteous and work hard to keep your business.

5. BEST WESTERN PIEMONTESE, *Via Berthollet 21, 10125 Torino, Tel. 011/669-8101, Fax 011/669-0571. E-mail: info@hotelpiemontese.it. Web: www.hotelpiemontese.it/. 33 rooms, 2 with bath, 31 with shower. Single E60-100; Double E95-130. Credit cards accepted.* ***

Located in a quiet street near the station and town center, you will find all the amenities of a good three star with excellent attention to detail. They

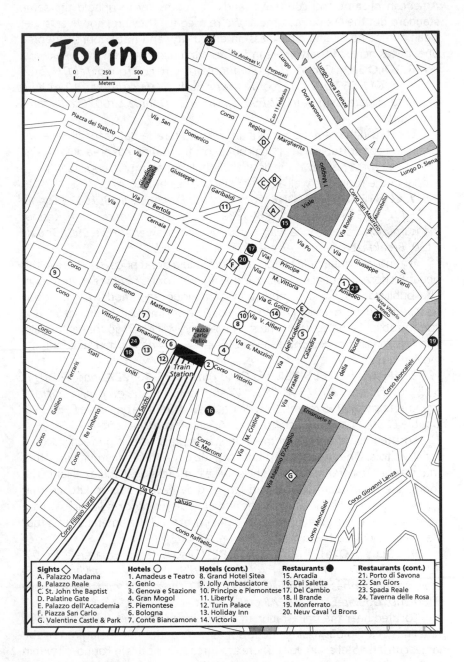

Torino

0 250 500
Meters

Sights ◇
A. Palazzo Madama
B. Palazzo Reale
C. St. John the Baptist
D. Palatine Gate
E. Palazzo dell'Accademia
F. Piazza San Carlo
G. Valentine Castle & Park

Hotels ○
1. Amadeus e Teatro
2. Genio
3. Genova e Stazione
4. Gran Mogol
5. Piemontese
6. Bologna
7. Conte Biancamone

Hotels (cont.)
8. Grand Hotel Sitea
9. Jolly Ambasciatore
10. Principe e Piemontese
11. Liberty
12. Turin Palace
13. Holiday Inn
14. Victoria

Restaurants ●
15. Arcadia
16. Dai Saletta
17. Del Cambio
18. Il Brande
19. Monferrato
20. Neuv Caval 'd Brons

Restaurants (cont.)
21. Porto di Savona
22. San Giors
23. Spada Reale
24. Taverna delle Rosa

have room service, laundry service, and are pet friendly. The service is North American prompt and courteous, and the rooms try to uphold the same standard but they're not as large as we're used to. They are, however, super clean and comfy. Being a business oritented city, and not a tourist oriented one, prices here, as everywhere in Torino are much lower on the weekends.

6. BOLOGNA, *Corso Vittorio Emanuele II 60, 10122 Torino, Tel. 011/562-0190, Fax 011/562-0193. 47 rooms, 4 with bath, 33 with shower, 10 without anything. Single with bathout E50; Single E70; Double E100. Credit cards accepted. ***

Located in the center city, this is an inexpensive alternative for all travelers. Clean and comfortable with a small but accommodating bar area downstairs. They also have a person at the desk all night long, a rarity in two stars. There are TV in the rooms as well as direct dial phones but no A/C.

7. CONTE BIANCAMONE, *Corso Vittorio Emanuele II 73, 10122 Torino, Tel. 011/562-3281, Fax 011/562-3789. Web: www.venere.com/it/torino/biancamano/. 25 rooms, 2 with bath, 23 with shower. Single E90; Double E120. Breakfast included. All credit cards accepted. ****

If you want quaint old restored buildings at a great price, stay here in this beautiful hotel in a peaceful and tranquil area of Torino near the train station. The public areas are a combination of antique and modern with lovely frescoed and high ceilings with reliefs. The rooms are large, clean and comfortable, if a bit spartan. The staff is always willing to go that extra mile. The only missing ingredient is air conditioning. Stay here when air conditioning is not needed.

8. GRAND HOTEL SITEA, *Via Carlo Alberto 35, 10122 Torino, Tel. 011/517-1071, Fax 011/548-090. Web: www.venere.com/it/torino/grandhotelsitea/. 119 rooms, 92 with bath, 27 with shower. Single E180-190; Double E230-240. Breakfast included. All credit cards accepted. *****

Located near the front of the train station, this hotel is perfectly located for all visitors. One of the largest hotels in the city, it rivals anything any other four star has to offer in the city. The service is professional and excellent. The rooms are clean, comfortable and large. They have a superb kitchen that specializes in local Piemontese cuisine as well as dietetic cooking which you can have brought up to your room to enjoy in private. All the amenities of a four star. A lovely place to stay.

9. JOLLY HOTEL AMBASCIATORI, *Corso Vittorio Emanuele II 104, 10122 Torino, Tel. 011/5752, Fax 011/544-978. Web: www.jollyhotels.it. E-mail: torino_ambasciatori@jollyhotels.it. 199 rooms all with bath. Single E180-200; Double E200-250. All credit cards accepted. *****

Located near the train station in a completely restored old building, this hotel has been in business for quite some years and is now being run by the largest Italian hotel chain, Jolly. There are three Jolly Hotels in Torino, all within walking distance of one another and all offering the same four star amenities.

This is the second best. The decor is a little overbearing but their rooms are clean and comfortable. In this hotel you can enjoy evenings in their piano bar, as well as movie rentals that cost an extra E8.

10. JOLLY HOTEL PRINCIPI DI PIEMONTE, *Via P. Gobetti 15, 10122 Torino, Tel. 011/562-9693, Fax 011/562-0270. Web: www.jollyhotels.it. E-mail: torino_principidipiemonte@jollyhotels.it. 107 rooms all with bath. Single E180-200; Double E200-250. All credit cards accepted.* ****

How jolly, another Jolly. This is the best of the three in Torino and it is located right in the heart of the city, close to the station, just off of Via Roma, and ideally situated near the few tourist sights and some good cafés and theaters. The eight floors of this rather severe building hide some rather pleasant accommodations. Each floor inside is decorated in a different color, each appealing in its own manner. The top floors offer a great view of the city. The rooms are large and comfortable, and furnished with every amenity. The buffet breakfast is huge and their restaurant I Gentilom offers some superb *cucina piemontese* as well as some international favorites. A truly grand hotel.

11. LIBERTY, *Via Pietro Micca 15, 10121 Torino, Tel. 011/562-8801, Fax 011/562-8163. Web: www.venere.com/it/torino/liberty/. 35 rooms all with shower. Single E70-100; Double E90-130. Breakfast E8. Lunch or Dinner E25. Credit cards accepted.* ***

Located on the first floor of a Liberty-style older building in the Parisian and Viennese style of the *fin du siècle*, here you have charm, character and superb furnishing taste all rolled into one. In business since the 1800s, this family-operated hotel provides meticulous clothes cleaning services, hot and cold buffet breakfast and a local, home-cooking style restaurant. If you like antiques and comfort stay here. Besides the style they also have air condition-ing, TV, radios, and direct dial phones in the rooms, as well as prompt room service. This is the best place to stay in Torino if you're tired of cookie-cutter hotels.

12. TURIN PALACE, *Via Sacchi 8, 10122 Torino, Tel. 011/562-5511, Fax 011/561-2187. Web: www.venere.com/it/torino/turinpalace/. 125 rooms all with bath. All credit cards accepted. Single E100-130; Double E140-220. Breakfast included.* *****

The Turin Palace is in an old building that was turned into a hotel in 1872 when the train station was built across the street. For more than a century this hotel has been the hotel of choice for those in the know. Everyone from rock stars to ambassadors have been lodged in this quaint and comfortable hotel, which has been renovated and modernized and now offers every creature comfort you could want. Some of the downstairs public rooms have wonder-fully preserved 1930's furnishings, and the bar is a curious amalgamation of Asian antiques. The rooms are magnificently appointed, clean, roomy and comfortable and come with air conditioning, satellite TV and more.

13. HOLIDAY INN TURIN CITY CENTER, *Via Assietta 3, 10122 Torino, Tel. 011/516-7111, Fax 011/516-699. 57 rooms, 12 with bath, 45 with shower. Single E170; Double E220. Breakfast included. All credit cards accepted.* ****

Located on one side of the train station in a beautiful park-like site, this charming old hotel has been completely modernized by the management of the Holiday Inn. They have an excellent restaurant that you should try even if you do not get the full board option. The rooms are perfectly clean and comfortable, and if you don't want to stay in them the hotel has a quaint little bar area. Another relaxing feature is the availability of a refreshing sauna. And to top it off pets are welcome too. Remember, we're in Italy. This is not your typical Holiday Inn. This place has style and character.

14. VICTORIA, *Via Nino Costa 4, 10122 Torino. Tel. 011/561-1909, Fax 011/561-1806. Web: www.hotelvictoria-torino.com/. 92 rooms all with bath. Single E100; Double E140. All credit cards accepted. Breakfast included.* ***

A wonderful three star establishment that could easily be one star higher. Alittle soft around the edges since the decorations are so delicate, but an ideal place to stay for business or pleasure. Located on a tranquil street a few minutes from the train station and right in the center of town. The decor, service and attitude will remind you more of France than of Italy, but it is accommodating nonetheless. In the entry way you will be greeted with bouquets of flowers adorning the classic furniture. Also downstairs are magazines, newspapers and books available for guests. In the rooms you'll find antiques, each furnished different than the next. Air conditioning has not arrived in all the rooms yet, but once it does this place should easily be a four star. The bathrooms are clean and come with all amenities. On a quality/price ratio, this is the place to stay in Torino.

Where To Eat

Besides being known for its industry, the **Piedmont** region and Torino should also be known for their simple cuisine and their tasty wine. The food is a blend of Northern Italian peasant staples mixed in with some elegant French flair. You'll find more butter than olive oil in cooking, a blasphemy in the south, and cheese, mushrooms and truffles are used instead of the abundant tomatoes and peppers down south.

During carnival, they have a special dish called *Tofeja* which is prepared with beans that are soaked for 12 hours, then cooked with minced pork like the skin, ears, and snout (which really doesn't sound appetizing but it is). These are all spiced with parsley and garlic, then rolled up in a light dough mixture (the *Tofeja*), then cooked over night. When not served at carnival it can be found as an hors-d'oeuvre in many restaurants. They also have another appetizer called *capunet* that is boiled cabbage leaves stuffed with minced meat and a variety of spices, as well as a *fresse*, which is a mixture of minced liver, raisins, salt, pepper and cinnamon roasted in the oven with a sauce of red wine, tomato, and brown sugar. A great pasta dish is *agnolotti*, which is a ravioli-like pasta stuffed with boiled cabbage and roasted lamb.

You can also get some tasty cheeses in this region. There is the *toma* which is aged perfectly for three months and used as a snack between dishes but not in cooking. There is also the *tomini*, which is cow and goat milk combined and sold only after 2 or 3 days of production. It's soft, succulent and ever so tasty. My favorite is the *savignon*, which is a combination of buttermilk curds, salt, pepper, and spices that is typical of the village of **Settimo Vittone**. There's nothing like spiced cheese curds.

This region of Italy is also know for its desserts, which are usually tarts filled with fresh fruits like peaches, and sweetened with sugar and cocoa, and sometimes almonds.

The **wines** of the region can be bubbly and sweet, like those from **Asti**. Offered in both a sparkling (*spumante*) and regular version (*Carema* or *Erbaluce*), they have been produced since the Middle Ages. Both were particularly sweet back then since the only preservation method for wine at the time was the application of sugar. Today the wines are light and dry, with a distinct character that can hold its own against the best the world has to offer.

Restaurant locations can be found on page 793.

15. ARCADIA, *Galleria dell'Industria Subalpina 16, Tel. 011/532-029. Closed Sundays and August. All credit cards accepted. Dinner for two E45.*

Right in the center of Torino this place is swamped for lunch with the business crowd. They serve a local Piemontese-style menu, including a wonderful mixed vegetable dish made local-style (*misto di verdure alla piemontese*) and an assortment of beef dishes like *filetto alla monferrina* (fillet fried in flour). The dessert tray is piled high with local favorites and the waiters are always attentive and alert.

16. DAI SALETTA, *Via Belfiore 37, Tel. 011/668-7867. Closed Sundays and August. Dinner for two E40. Visa accepted.*

Run by the Saletta cousins, this place only has seven small tables from which to enjoy their magnificent pasta dishes, most of which are smothered in creamy cheese sauces. You must sample the local *toma* cheese here, the perfect snack between dishes. All of their braised or roasted meats are excellent, but not for the diet conscious. This is another great local place where you can have some perfect Piemontese food and atmosphere. You will need reservations.

17. DEL CAMBIO, *Piazza Carignamo 2, Tel. 011/546-690. Closed Sundays, the first week in January and all of August. Dinner for two E100. All credit cards accepted.*

A super elegant restaurant with over 200 years experience in fine food preparation. Each room is finer than the next and each is a perfect spot for a romantic evening. In this fine environment the service is impeccable and the food exquisite. Their menu changes frequently but you can usually count on getting: *La tartra di verdurine all'antica con fonduta di Castelmagno* (a plate of vegetables chopped for you to dip in a succulent fondue of Castelmagno cheese); *tartufo con fiori zucca* (truffles cooked with pumpkin flowers); or the superb *filetto di vitello con funghi e scalogno* (veal filet with mushrooms and scallions).

18. IL BRANDÉ, *Via Massena 5, Tel. 011/537-279. Closed Sundays and Mondays and August. No credit cards accepted. Dinner for two E45.*

Reservations are definitely necessary to eat at this wonderful little *trattoria* since they only have eight tables. Two cousins by the last name of Mottura run the place and offer a set menu, as well as a series of different dishes with mainly a Normandy (French) influence. Try some of their rabbit dishes or their *gnocchi alle erbe* (small dumplings made of flour covered in herbs and spices) and wash it all down with some excellent *Barolo* wine from Piedmont.

19. MONFERRATO, *Via Monferrato 6, Tel. 011/819-0061. Closed Saturdays and Sundays as well as August. Dinner for two E50. All credit cards accepted.*

This well-lit, modern restaurant is across the Po River from the center of town. The cuisine is perfect in preparation, presentation, and taste. Try some of their braised, boiled, and exquisitely prepared lamb dishes. I especially like the *agnello con funghi* (lamb with mushrooms). They also have a good set of warm appetizers.

20. NEUV CAVAL 'D BRONS, *Piazza San Carlo 157, Tel. 011/562-7483. Closed Sundays. Dinner for two E90. All credit cards accepted.*

What started out as a beer hall in 1947 became known as the Pub Lancia and Steakhouse, and now has given itself a more refined name. There are three rooms with a few tables and many decorations which lends a refined atmosphere. The menu includes everything from seafood to pasta to meat. Try their *gamberini stufato all'Arneis e zafferano* (shrimp stuffed with cheese and saffron) or the *filetto di trota in pan brioche can salsa di sidro* (trout pan-fried in cider). They also have a vegetarian menu, featuring such dishes as a delicious *ravioli di zucchine e porri* (ravioli made with zucchini and leeks) and the *sformata di spinaci con fonduta* (soufflé/fondue of spinach and cheese). If you're in the mood for cheese, go for the *flan di Castelmagno in salsa* (molded cheese soaked in a great sauce).

21. PORTO DI SAVONA, *Piazza Via Veneto 2, Tel. 011/817-3500. Closed Mondays, Tuesdays for dinner and all of July. Dinner for two E35. No credit cards accepted.*

The clientele of this place includes actors, authors, businessmen and students. It is a local favorite. The *cucina piemontese* served here is superb, all the way from antipasto to dessert. Try anything on the menu, especially their braised or boiled mixed meats or some of their *gnocchi* with different cheese sauces. An inexpensive and delightfully tasty insight into the heart and soul of Torino.

22. SAN GIORS, *Via Borgo Dora 3, Tel. 011/521-1256. Never closes. Dinner for two E45. Visa accepted.*

Not a place for those in search of a quiet meal. Located in the midst of the Mercato di Porta Palazzo, this place is loud and boisterous, especially at lunch. If you want a taste of the local flavor come here and sample their *carrello di bolliti misti* (plate of boiled meats which is big enough for two) and soak up the atmosphere.

23. SPADA REALE, *Principe Amadeo 53, Tel. 011/832-835. Closed Sundays. Dinner for two E50. All credit cards accepted.*

One of the most frequented restaurants in the city, thanks mainly to the great food and hospitality of the owner Adriano Stefanini. It is open late and caters to actors from the theater, professional athletes, and a wide variety of locals. The cuisine is creative, to say the least, and changes constantly. Mint and curry seem to be the spice staples in many of the dishes. Come here for out of the ordinary cuisine.

24. TAVERNA DELLE ROSE, *Via Massena 24, Tel. 011/538-345. Closed Saturdays at Dinner, Sundays, and August. Dinner for two E60. All credit cards accepted.*

A small three room popular local place. The owner and cook Neri Barbieri prepares an excellent antipasto offering, some great pasta dishes like *spaghetti all'aragosta* (with lobster) and *papardelle ai funghi* (large strips of pasta in a mushroom sauce), and superb grilled and roasted meats. A place for a good down home Piemontese meal but at a somewhat high price.

Seeing the Sights

The real sights of Torino are the 11 miles of arcaded sidewalks, stunning Baroque buildings and beautiful and accommodating city layout and design. In terms of museums, the best (see "E" below) houses the Egyptian collection and the Galleria Sabuada. Those seeking spiritual experience will no doubt head to the Cathedral of St. John the Baptist to take in the Holy Shroud.

A. PALAZZO MADAMA

Piazza Castello, Tel. 011/436-1455. Open Tuesdays and Thursdays 2:30pm–7:30pm, Wednesdays, Fridays, and Saturdays 9:00am–2:00pm. Admission E4.

Located in the central heart of the old town of Torino, at one end of the Via Roma, is the **Piazza Castello** which contains the massive **Palazzo Madama** that houses the **Museum of Ancient Art**. The core of this building was built in the 13th century on the remains of the Roman east gate to the garrison city. Stark and medieval on one side and a Baroque glass-fronted palace on the other, the Palazzo Madama was enlarged in both the 15th and

16th centuries, with the Baroque west front and the magnificent double staircase. It is a sumptuous reminder of the wealth of the family of Savoy. The museum is on the ground and second floors and has a valuable collection of sculptures, stained glass, paintings and other works.

B. PALAZZO REALE

Piazza Castello, Tel. 011/436-1455. Open Tuesday–Saturday 9:00am–5:00pm. Admission E6. Gardens free.

On the north side of the Piazza Castello is the **Palazzo Reale** (**Royal Palace**), an austere apricot colored, plain brick building built between 1646 and 1658 for Carlo Emanuele II. It contains 26 sumptuously decorated apartments *(Reali Apartamenti)* with gilded walls and an eclectic collection of treasures. Especially noteworthy is the **Apartamento di Madama Felicita**. In the right wing is the **Royal Armory** with a vast collection of arms and armor dating from the 15th to the 17th centuries which is believed to be the best in Europe. To the east of the palace are the **Royal Gardens**, developed by the creator of the gardens at the Palace of Versailles, Louis le Notre in 1697.

C. CATHEDRAL OF ST. JOHN THE BAPTIST

Piazza San Giovanni, Tel. 011/436-6101. Chapel open Tuesday–Saturday 9:00am–noon and 3:00–5:30pm. Church open everyday 7:00am–noon and 3–5:30pm.

Located west of the Palazzo Reale off Via XX Settembre is the home of the **Holy Shroud of Turin**. This church was built between 1492 and 1498, and the bell tower was added in 1720. The Holy Shroud was purported to have been the linen cloth in which the body of Christ was wrapped after his descent from the cross. Despite the fact that its origin has been carbon dated to the 13th or 14th century, the faithful still believe in its authenticity. The shroud is located in the **Capella della Santa Sindone** (chapel of the Holy Shroud) which is topped with a honeycomb black marble dome. Above the doors is Luigi Ganga's copy of Leonardo da Vinci's *Last Supper*, which is considered the best copy of that fresco ever done.

D. PALATINE GATE

Located northwest of the Cathedral, the arch was built by Emperor Augustus and was the north gate of the old Roman town. It is a simple structure which has two brick towers, but really is a prime example of how history in Italy all blends together into the present.

E. PALAZZO DELL'ACCADEMIA DELLE SCIENZE

Via Accademia delle Scienze 6, Tel. 011/61-7776. Open Tuesday–Saturday 9:00am–2:00pm and 3:00pm-7:00pm. Admission E6.

This palace was initially built as a Jesuit college in 1679 and was converted to the **Academy of Sciences** in 1757. Today it houses the **Museum of Antiquities**, with Greco-Roman and Etruscan material mainly from the Piemontese and Ligurian regions; the **Egyptian Museum** (**Museo Egizio**), one of the finest collections of Egyptian antiquities in the world, including a wonderfully evocative statue of Ramses II; and the **Galleria Sabauda**, with its fine collection of canvases by Italian and Flemish masters including Fra Angelico, Mantegna, Bellini and Van Eyck.

Aside from the Shroud, the Egyptian Museum is Torino's chief tourist draw. Any native will tell you that after Cairo, Torino has the finest Egyptian collection in existence.

F. PIAZZA SAN CARLO

This symmetrical square was laid out in 1638. Here you'll find the **Church of Santa Cristina** built in 1637 with a facade by Juvara in 1718; and the **Church of San Carlo** built in 1836. In the center of the piazza stands the equestrian statue of Duke Filiberto Emanuele sculpted in 1838. Running through this beautiful Baroque *piazza* is Turin's main shopping street, **Via Roma**. This street is a perfect place for a *passegiatta* (stroll) as well as window shopping or people watching.

Located a few blocks from the *piazza* is Torino's most beautiful building, the **Palazzo Carignano**, *Via Accademia della Scienza 5*. Built in the late 17th century, it is a Baroque marvel of undulating lines and red brick ornament, including motifs of native North American headdresses to commemorate Piemontese participation in a French victory over the tribes of Quebec. Today it houses a wonderful museum about the unification of Italy, **Museo Nazionale del Risorgimento Italiano**, *(9:30am-6:30pm Tues-Sat and 9:00am-12:30pm Sundays, Entrance E5, free on Sundays)* since it was the birthplace of Carlo Alberto and Victor Emmanuel, two great Italian patriots. It was also the seat of the Italian Parliament from 1861 to 1864 when the government was here in Torino before it moved to Florence and then Rome. A walk in any direction from this *palazzo* will take you down and through tree-lined avenues and boulevards, tranquil Baroque *piazze* and arcaded streets.

G. VALENTINO CASTLE & PARK

Via Massimo d'Azeglio, Tel. 011/669-9372. Open Tuesday-Saturday 9:00am-6:00pm and Sundays 10:30am-6:00pm.

A tranquil respite from the pace of a large city, this park also contains the **Botanical Gardens**, which were established in 1729, and the magnificent **Castello del**, a Disney-like medieval castle created for an exhibition in 1884, which is a great place for kids to visit.

Another great place for kids of all ages is the **Palazzo delle Esposizioni**, which houses the popular and world famous **Museo dell'Automobile** *(Tuesday-Sunday 9:30am-12:30pm and 3:00pm-7:00pm)* featuring car models dating back to 1893. If you're a car buff, and even if you're not, you have to come see this excellent museum.

Nightlife & Entertainment

VINCENZO NEBIOLO, *Via Priocca 10, Tel. 011/436-4558. Closed Sundays and August.*

A quaint little wine bar open from 6:00am to 10:00pm right in the heart of the Mercato di Porta Palazzo. They serve many different wines, most local at E3 per liter, as well as superb *Panini* sandwiches with a variety of cheese and salami fillers.

BRITANNIA PUB, *Via Carlo Alberto 34, Tel. 011/54-33-92. Open from 6:00pm until 2:00am. Pints E4.*

Your traditional English-style pub with Guinness, Harp and Kilkenny on tap. They also serve simple *Panini* and other warm and cold snacks.

DUKE OF WELLINGTON, *Via Caboto 26, Tel. 011/59-99-41. Open from 6:00pm until 2:00am. Pints E4.*

Another English-style pub with a variety of bottled beer and typical English and German offerings on tap. They also serve simple sandwich and *Panini* type food.

LONDON PUB, *Via Tripoli 38, Tel. 011/39-99-86. Open from 6:00pm to 2:00am. Pints E4.*

Yet another English-style pub. These establishments are definitely catching on in style with the Italians. Ten years ago you would have found just one in most cities. Guinness, Harp and Kilkenny on tap.

Opera

If you are in Torino from December to June, the traditional opera season, have the proper attire (suits for men, dresses for women), and have a taste for something out of the ordinary, try the spectacle of the opera.

• **Teatro Reggio do Torino**, *Piazza Castello 215, 10124 Torino. Tel 011/88151, Fax 011/881-5214*

Sports & Recreation

Golf

• **A.S. Golf Club Le Fronde**, *Via S Agostino 68, 10051 Avigiliano, Tel. 011/938-053, Fax 011/930-928.* Located 25 kilometers from Torino, this is an 18 hole, par 72, 6000 meter course that is open from February to December except on Mondays. They have a driving range, carts, pull-carts, a pro shop, bar & restaurant, and a pool (for your companion to lounge around while you hit the links).

• **Golf Club La Margherita**, *Strada Pralormo 29, 10002 Carmagnola, Tel. 011/979-5113, Fax 011/979-5204.* Located 25 kilometers from Torino, this is an 18 hole, par 72, 6278 meter course that is open from March to

December except on Tuesdays. They have a driving range, pool, pro shop, and restaurant/bar.
- **Golf Club Margara**, *Via Tenuta Margara 5, 15043 Fubine, Tel. 0131/778-555, Fax 0131/778-772*. Located 65 kilometers from Torino, this is an 18 hole, par 72, 6043 meter course that is open from February to December except for Mondays. They have two tennis courts, an Olympic size swimming pool, guest house, pro shop, restaurant and bar. Conceivably you and your family could spend a few enjoyable days playing tennis, golf, swimming, and dining here.
- **Golf Club Associazione Sportiva I Roveri**, *Rotta Cerbiatta 24, 10070 Fiano, Tel. 011/923-5667, Fax 011/923-5669*. Located 20 kilometers from Torino, you can either play the 18 hole, par 72, 6218 meter course or the 9 hole, par 36, 3306 meter course. They are open from March to November except on Mondays. There's a driving range, gymnasium, putting green, pro shop and restaurant/bar.
- **Circolo Golf Stupinigi**, *Corso Unione Sovietica 506 A, 10135 Torino, Tel. 011/347-2640, Fax 011/397-8038*. Located only 4 kilometers from Torino, this is a 9 hole, par 33, smallish 2170 meter course. They are open year round except August and Mondays. They have a driving range and a restaurant/bar. Good for day trips and short rounds of golf.
- **Vinovo Golf**, *Via Stupinigi 182, 10048 Vinovo, Tel. 011/965-3880, Fax 011/962-3748*. Located 3 kilometers from Torino, this is a 9 hole, par 32, short 2082 meter course that is open from January 10th to December 20th except for Mondays. They have a driving range, restaurant, and pro shop. Perfect for day trips and short rounds of golf.
- **AS Golf Club Cherasco**, *Loc. Fraschetta Cascina Roma, 12062 Cherasco, Tel. 0172/489-772, Fax 0172/488-304*. Located 50 kilometers from Torino and 40 kilometers from Asti, this is an 18 hole, par 72, 5987 meter course that is open from March through November except on Tuesdays. They have a driving range, tennis courts, pro shop, and restaurant.

Shopping

Torino is a shopper's paradise and the best place for that is the elegant **Via Roma** where you can find all sorts of unique purchases, including shoe stores, tailors, *alimentari*, cafés, restaurants, jewelers, department stores, furriers, and much more. Even if you don't spend any money, Via Roma still is a fun place to window shop and people watch.

Books & Newspapers in English
- **Libreria International Luxembourg**, *Via Accademia dell Scienze 3, Tel. 011/561-38-96. Mondays 3:00am to 7:30pm. Tuesday through Friday 8:00am to 7:30pm. Closed Sundays*. There's a good selection of travel

books, fiction, and non-fiction works as well as books relating to science and industry.

Excursions & Day Trips

The excursions below will be a definite change from the size and scope of Torino. From Torino you can get to medieval **Asti**. This town is the perfect place to find an escape from the hectic pace of Torino.

ASTI

Asti hit the big time back in 89 BCE, when it became a Roman garrison town, and over time it emerged as one of the most powerful city republics in Italy during the Middle Ages. Bologna was known as the city of towers in its day, but Asti should be known as the city of towers today. Despite the many wars that were fought for its control during the Middle Ages and after, more than one hundred 13th century towers still remain intact for tourists to admire. Today the city and its region are best known not for these incredible towers, but rather for their renowned bubbly, *Asti Spumante*, and views that can be savored while sipping it. To see a little more of Asti check out the official site for the city at *www.axt.it/inglese/home.htm*.

Arrivals & Departures

There are trains from Turin every half hour that cost E4. The trip takes a little under 40 minutes. You will disembark at the station in **Piazza Marconi**,which is only a short walk, via a series of twists and turns down some medieval streets, to the triangle-shaped **Piazza Vittorio Alfieri**. You'll need to take this five minute walk to get to the tourist office so you can pick up a map of the city and get help with hotel reservations if needed. **Autolinee Giachino**, *Tel. 0141/937-155,* runs bus service into many of the small hill towns surrounding Asti.

Where to Stay

1. **CAVOUR**, *Piazza Marconi 18, 14100 Asti, Tel. 0141/530-222. 19 rooms only 16 with shower. Single without bath E30; Single E50; Double without bath E40; Double E60. Breakfast E6 extra.* ******

Located in the *piazza* of the train station, this is the best inexpensive alternative available. Situated in an historic old building that has been beautifully renovated, they have good amenities for a two star like TVs, direct dial phones, a night porter, room service, a bar, parking and more. But they don't have air conditioning, so if it's hot stay elsewhere. A step up for the budget traveler.

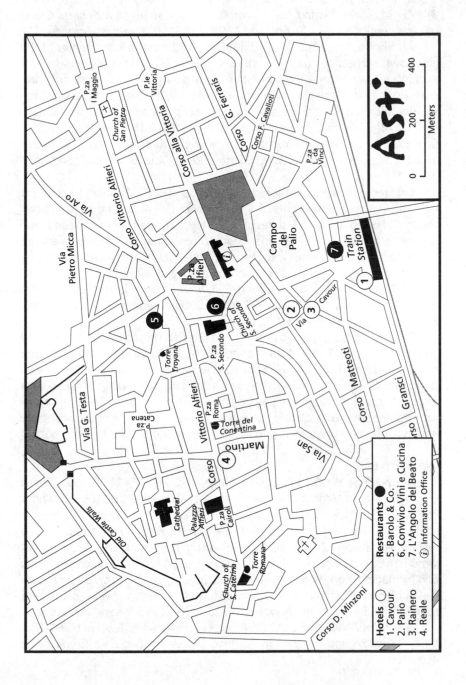

Asti

0 200 400

Meters

Hotels ○
1. Cavour
2. Palio
3. Rainero
4. Reale

Restaurants ●
5. Barolo & Co.
6. Convivio Vini e Cucina
7. L'Angolo del Beato
ⓘ Information Office

2. PALIO, *Via Cavour 106, 14100 Asti, Tel. 0141/34371, Fax 0141/ 34373. 34 rooms, 1 with bath, 33 with shower. 4 suites all with bath. Credit cards accepted. Single E80; Double E120; Suite E150. Breakfast included.* ***

Also housed in a renovated old building and located in the center of the city down some small medieval streets, this hotel is perfectly situated for exploring. They have all the amenities for a pleasant stay, including hydro-massage tubs in all the rooms. No restaurant here, but there are plenty within walking distance. The rooms are large, spotlessly clean, and comfortable.

3. RAINERO, *Via Cavour 65, 14100 Asti, Tel. 0141/353-866, Fax 0141/594-985. Web: www.hotelrainero.com/. E-mail: info@hotelrainero.com. 54 rooms all with bath. Credit cards accepted. Single E50-60; Double E75-85. Breakfast E8 extra.* ***

Located in the center of the old city, in a quaint old building on a nice street near the station and the sights of the old town. Not all the rooms have been modernized and renovated, so request to stay in the *zona verde* (green zone) on the ground floor to get the best accommodations. If you want air conditioning in the summer you need to request it and it will cost an extra E6 per night. A good place to stay based on a price/quality ratio.

4. REALE, *Piazza Alfieri 6, 14100 Asti, Tel. 0141/530-240, Fax 0141/ 34357. 25 rooms all with bath. All credit cards accepted. E90-100; Double E125-160. Breakfast included.* ****

This historic hotel opened in 1793 and has been host to many famous and infamous people. Today it has been renovated making it modern and comfortable; but it has been able to retain its old charm and has recently been upgraded to four star status. The rooms are large and well furnished with adequate space for working if you've come here on business. The bathrooms too are spacious with double sinks and come with every other necessary amenity. The best place to stay in Asti in terms of the bang for your buck.

Where to Eat

5. BAROLO & CO., *Via Cesare Battisti 14, Tel. 0141/592-059. Closed Sunday nights and Mondays as well as the last three weeks of August. Dinner for two E45. Credit cards accepted.*

Located near the Torre Troyana, the tallest tower in Asti, this place is a restaurant on top and a wine bar on the bottom floor. You can get some great *lardo* (smoked pork fat which is surprisingly tasty) local salami, *crostini caldi con formaggio* (baked dough with cheese inside), *insalatina di funghi freschi* (salad of fresh mushrooms) and a scrumptious *stracotto al vino rosso* (beef stew with red wine sauce). A wonderful local place in taste and atmosphere.

6. IL CONVIVIO VINI E CUCINA, *Via GB Giuliani 4/6, Tel. 0141/594-188. Closed Sundays and ten days in August. Dinner for two E50. Credit cards accepted.*

Located in the *centro storico* of Asti, this place is a cantina in the early afternoons that offers some great Italian wines, and at night it is a restaurant that features local, traditional, simple peasant fare like chicken, rabbit, *gnocchi* and more. There's usually an afternoon wine sampling you don't want to miss that comes complete with tasty tapas-like snacks.

7. L'ANGOLO DEL BEATO, *Via Gattuati 12, Tel. 0141/531-668. Closed Sundays, the first ten days of February, and the first twenty days of August. Dinner for two E50. All credit cards accepted.*

The food here is superb with a nice ambiance despite the fact that the restaurant is located near the train station. The *gallina bollita* (broiled chicken) is perfectly cooked and spiced and comes with an excellent array of freshly cooked vegetables. Since you're in the mountains now, they also serve an excellent variety of *coniglio* (rabbit), so maybe this is the time to try some.

Seeing the Sights

The main attraction are the towers dotting the city, but if you like wine tasting, there are some great nearby vineyards. Other pleasures include skiing in the winter and hiking in the summer. For more information about sights contact the local **tourist office**, *Piazza Alfieri, Tel. 53-03-57, open Monday through Friday 9:30am-12:30pm and 3:30pm–6:00pm, and Saturday 9:30am-12:30pm.*

THE TOWERS OF ASTI

Torre Troyana is located in the Piazza Medici; Torre Rossa is in Corso Vittorio Alfieri; and Torre dei Conentina in Corso Vittorio Alfieri.

In Asti not only can you can find over one hundred medieval towers, but you can also locate the highest tower in the Piedmont region, the **Torre de Troyana**. Built in the 13th century, it is accompanied by other of its brethren, including the **Torre Rossa**, a sixteen-sided structure which is Asti's oldest, and where it is purported that the patron saint of the town, San Secondo, was imprisoned and beheaded. Another interesting tower to look for is the **Torre dei Conentina**.

PALIO OF ASTI

Held on the third Sunday in September every year, this festival recreates the city's liberation in 1200. In period garb, townspeople and horses parade the streets to the triangular **Piazza Alfieri** where they re-enact the oldest known horse race in Italy. A great sight to see if you're in Asti at the time. About as good as the Palio of Siena, which means it is splendid. Make reservations at hotels well in advance.

CAMPO DI PALIO

Every Monday and Wednesday from 8:30am to 1:30pm vendors sell fruits and vegetables from this location. A wonderfully typical local setting that shouldn't be missed if you're in town at that time.

CATHEDRAL
Piazza Cattedrale. Open 7:30am–noon and 3:00–7:00pm.
Built between 1309 and 1348 on the site of an earlier church, this simple church with its brick facade is decorated with statues and has many Baroque frescoes covering the walls inside. Notice the mosaics decorating the floor of the main altar.

CHURCH OF SAN PIETRO
Corso Vittorio Alfieri. Open Tues–Sat 9:00am–noon and 3–6:00pm. Sun 10:00am–noon.
This 15th century church is better known for its 12th century octagonal baptistery. The church itself contains many fine terra-cotta works as well as a cloister that brings you back in time. The baptistery usually contains exhibits of local artists.

VINEYARD & CASTLE TOURS
*You can get information about the wine tours from the **tourist office** at Piazza Alfieri, Tel. 53-03-57, open Monday through Friday 9:30am-12:30pm and 3:30pm–6:00pm, and Saturday 9:30am-12:30pm.*
Surrounding the city are many vineyards, some of which still have ancient castles on their grounds. The tours last for 2 to 3 hours and are offered year round. At the tourist office you can also find information about visiting Asti's extensive **wine cellar**.

Practical Information for Torino
Car Rental
• **Avis**, *Airport, Tel. 011/470-1528 or Stazione Portanuova, Tel. 011/669-9800.*
• **Hertz**, *Airport Tel. 011/567-8166 or Via Magellano 12, Tel. 011/502-080*

Laundry Services
• **Lavanderia Vizzini**, *Via San Secondo 30, Tel. 011/54-58-82. Open Monday–Friday 8:00am to 12:30pm, and 3:30pm to 6:30pm.* Bring in your wash in the morning and pick it up at night. Cost for 4 kilos is E8; 6 kilos is E12.

Postal Services
• **Central Post Office**, *Via Alfieri 10 and Via Arsenale 13, Tel. 011/54-70-97. Open Monday through Friday 8:30am-5pm, Saturdays 9am-12 noon.*

Tourist Information & Maps

Both of these offices will supply you with a workable map of the city and help you find a room if you've arrived without one. In conjunction you can pick up the latest information on what's happening during your stay *(Un Ospite a Torino)* in town and throughout the province.

• **APT Office**, *Via Roma 226, Tel. 011/53-59-01*
• **Information Office**, *Porta Nuova Train Station, Tel. 011/53-13-27. Web: www.turismotorino.org*

Tour Operators

• **AviaTour**, *Via Pomba 29, Tel. 011/557-6066*
• **Comitours**, *Via Carlo Alberto 29, Tel. 011/55-471*
• **Wagons-Lit Turismo**, *Piazza San Carlo 132, Tel. 011/548-456 and Largo Orbassano 62, Tel. 011/318-1933*

Travel Advisory

The local government travel organization strongly suggests that tourists, especially women walking alone, avoid Via Nizza next to the train station at night. But as always, in comparison to most American cities, you should be more than safe in Torino.

Chapter 24

trieste

A crossroads between Central Europe and the Mediterranean worlds, **Trieste** has always been an active commercial center. Situated at the eastern edge of Italy, and bordering on Austria and Yugoslavia, Trieste has also been a melting pot of different cultures. This is evident in the local foods where apple strudel, a quintessential Austrian dessert, is as common as *spaghetti alla vongole*; and Roman ruins mix together with Art Nouveau buildings and Greek Orthodox churches. You can also find traces of Venetian, French and Austrian influences in the local dialect. Because of all this Trieste remains a center for cross-cultural awareness and is filled with art galleries, museums, neoclassic architecture, and a scaled-down version of the Milan opera house La Scala, plus much more.

Different areas of the city reflect different architectural influences. The *centro storico* is a jumble of small streets befitting the medieval influence that created it. The majority of the rest of the city is set in the neoclassic style thrust upon the city in the 18th century when the medieval city walls were torn down and a construction boom occurred to accommodate the growing commercial influence. Many of these buildings, once used by local traders as offices, residences and warehouses, are still in use today.

Since it is tucked away bordering Slovenia and only 25 miles from Croatia, Trieste has been largely overlooked by most tourists visiting Italy. Sequestered geographically, and influenced by so many different cultures, the city itself is a little different than most Italian cities. On top of that, Trieste never has been and never will be a tourist town. Its lifeblood is commerce, like shipping and insurance, and education (they have an excellent university). Trieste is a place to come if you've been overloaded with the Renaissance splendor of the rest of Italy. The charm of Trieste is its easy pace and friendly if often serious citizens.

The food here, like the culture, is a synthesis of many influences. The main gastronomic establishment, the 'buffet' (deli-like eateries) reflect this. They serve sandwiches made with many different types of salami, prosciutto and cheese; as well as the famous boiled pork succulently served on rolls with spicy mustard as an accompaniment. These buffets are the heart and soul of the city's neighborhoods.

Though Italian, Triestans have little of the animated flair we associate with Italy. Stoic, serious, and austere in nature, you will find Triestans more similar to their Austrian or Balkan cousins than their Italian brothers and sisters. But in their own quiet way they are friendly and fiercely proud of their unique city.

In my opinion it would be much more rewarding to visit Austria and Eastern Europe, which would give you a true taste of these cultures, rather than venture almost to Slovenia for a watered-down version of both of them. Granted, if you do take the time and effort to visit you will find Trieste accommodating, comfortable and virtually devoid of tourists. But if getting away from tourists is your main goal, that can more easily be done in the quaint and charming little hill towns of Umbria or Tuscany, which are only a few hours from either Rome or Florence.

Brief History

Trieste has been a center of commerce and culture since the beginning of recorded history and before. Unmistakable evidence shows that Upper Paleolithic societies dwelled in the region, and that trade began to develop with Phoenician assistance. Soon after this, the city was integrated into the Roman world and prospered along with it. With the collapse of the empire, barbarian raids swept down from Eastern Europe putting the city in a state of siege.

From that point on into modern times, Trieste, like the rest of Italy, was gobbled up by one empire after another, from the Franks to the Byzantine domination to Venetian government, to a brief period of Spanish control, and on to the Hapsburgs and the Austrian Empire. Then, on November 3, 1918, Trieste was joined with the Italian Peninsula as a result of the success of the **Risorgimento**, which helped unite all of Italy under one flag. But after World War II, Trieste and the Venezia Giulia region were torn from Italy and became an autonomous province under the administration of the United Nations Command. Finally, on October 26th, 1954, Trieste returned to the *azzurri* fold. All this outside influence has developed Trieste into the mixture of cultures it is today. One moment truly Italian, the next Germanic, and with a dash of Eastern European thrown in for flavor. A truly dynamic city.

Arrivals & Departures

Trieste can be reached from Venice by train in 2 1/2 hours. It takes about the same amount of time by car depending on traffic and weather conditions. As you approach Trieste, both the road and railway tracks snake along the hillside overlooking the water, a stunning vista with which to be introduced to the city.

Getting Around Town

By Bus

Buses criss-cross the city and run from 5:00am to midnight. Tickets per trip are Euro 75 cents and can be purchased at any *Tabacchi*.
• **City and Provincial Routes**, *ACT, Via d'Alviano 15, Tel. 1670/16675*

By Foot

Trieste is an easy walking city. With only 227,000 citizens, it is not very large. But if you don't want to walk there is always a bus available or a taxi.

By Taxi
• **Radio Taxi**, *24-hour service, Tel. 040/307-730*

Renting a Car
• **Avis**, *Piazza della Liberta, Tel. 040/451-521. Airport Tel. 0481/777-085*
• **Hertz**, *Piazza della Liberta, Tel. 040/422-122. Airport, Tel. 0481/777-025*
• **Maggiore**, *Viale Miramare 2 (railway station), Tel. 040/421-323*

Where to Stay

1. **ABBAZIA**, *Via della Geppa 20, 34100 Trieste. Tel. 040/369-464, Fax 089/369-769. Web: www.arsenal.it/hotelwrl/hotel.htm. 21 rooms all with bath. Single E95; Double E150. Credit cards accepted. Breakfast included.*
***

A few paces from the railway station in the heart of the commercial district. Despite the location this is an accommodating hotel. The owners abandoned a farming life to become hoteliers and they work hard to make your stay pleasant. The rooms are comfortable and clean with only a TV and mini-bar to keep you company. The common areas are off-limits to smokers. A clean hospitable place to stay, but without many amenities.

2. **AL TEATRO**, *Capo di Piazza G. Bartoli 1, 34100 Trieste. Tel. 040/366-220, Fax 089/366-560. 45 rooms all with bath. Single E70; Double E100. Credit cards accepted. Breakfast included.* **

A great one star hotel almost in the Piazza Unita d'Italia and close to the Opera. Musicians frequent this establishment and you can hear them practicing their instruments or tuning their voices most days. In a building built in

1780, surrounded by the Palazzo Communale and the Palazzo Modello, this hotel is perfect if you want to stay in the heart of the city without paying an arm and leg. The rooms are amazingly spacious, with teak furnishings seemingly leftover from the '70s. Some rooms have great views of the Piazza Unita d'Italia. A great pace to stay in Trieste at a good price.

3. COLUMBIA, *Via della Geppa 18, 34100 Trieste. Tel. 040/369-333, Fax 089/369-644. 40 rooms all with bath. Single E100; Double E150. Credit cards accepted. Breakfast included.* ***

Located right next door to the Abbazia, this place is quite a bit better. Everyone who works here takes pride in their hotel. They know it's good and

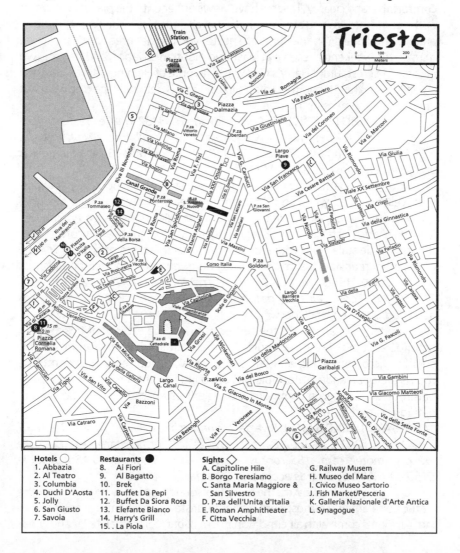

Hotels ○	Restaurants ●	Sights ◇	
1. Abbazia	8. Ai Fiori	A. Capitoline Hile	G. Railway Musem
2. Al Teatro	9. Al Bagatto	B. Borgo Teresiamo	H. Museo del Mare
3. Columbia	10. Brek	C. Santa Maria Maggiore &	I. Civico Museo Sartorio
4. Duchi D'Aosta	11. Buffet Da Pepi	San Silvestro	J. Fish Market/Pesceria
5. Jolly	12. Buffet Da Siora Rosa	D. P.za dell'Unita d'Italia	K. Galleria Nazionale d'Arte Antica
6. San Giusto	13. Elefante Bianco	E. Roman Amphitheater	L. Synagogue
7. Savoia	14. Harry's Grill	F. Citta Vecchia	
	15. . La Piola		

they want to make sure you have a wonderful stay. They have air conditioning, though it's not really needed too much in the summer. The rooms are clean and comfortable and all are furnished differently, but all are beautifully appointed. The bathrooms are clean and modern. There is a large salon room for breakfast and afternoon tea. The best three star in the city.

4. DUCHI D'AOSTA, *Piazza dell'Unita d'Italia 2, 34100 Trieste. Tel. 040/ 7351, Fax 089/366-092. Web: www.grandhotelduchidaosta.com/. 52 rooms all with bath. Single E180; Double E240; Suite E480. Credit cards accepted. Breakfast included.* ****

A real gem. Definitely the best place to stay in Trieste: refined, quiet, comfortable and clean. All rooms have views either onto the *piazza*, the water or the *centro storico* and are furnished with antiques from the grande époque era. Situated directly in the heart of Trieste, you can get great deals if you are here on the weekends, reserve at least two nights in advance, and stay for two nights. Their restaurant Harry's Grill was a favorite of Hemingway (is there any bar in Europe that Hemingway didn't love?) and is definitely the most elegant dining establishment in the city.

5. JOLLY HOTEL TRIESTE, *Corso Cavour 7, 34132 Trieste. Tel. 040/760-0055, Fax 040/362-699. Web: www.jollyhotels.it. E-mail: trieste@jollyhotels.it. 174 rooms all with bath. Single E135-340; Double E180-420. All credit cards accepted. Breakfast included.* ****

Another modern Jolly hotel near the train station. All rooms are spacious and well furnished with room to work and relax. The windows are sound-proofed and there is air conditioning, mini-bar, television and everything you expect in a four star in Italy. Everything about Jolly hotels is professional, though a little stale – but your stay will be perfectly accommodating. Try one of the other four stars first but if you stay here you will be more than satisfied.

6. SAN GIUSTO, *Via Belli 3, 34100 Trieste. Tel. 040/764-824, Fax 089/ 762-661. 62 rooms all with bath. Single E90; Double E140. Credit cards accepted. Breakfast included.* ***

Situated a distance from the center of town. The exterior of this modern hotel doesn't look like it has much to offer, but inside everything is bright, colorful, accommodating and large. The breakfast buffet is abundant. The rooms are clean and comfortable but are a little on the small side, as are the bathrooms. Definitely a commercial traveler's establishment, but accommodating for tourists too.

7. SAVOIA EXCELSIOR, *Riva del Mandracchio 4, 34124 Trieste. Tel. 040/ 77941, Fax 040/638-260. E-mail: savoiaexcelsior.ts@starhotels.it. Web: www.starhotels.com. 155 rooms all with bath. Single E120-180; Double E150-240. All credit cards accepted. Breakfast included.* ****

On the main road by the harbor, the soundproofed windows keep the traffic noise out and atmosphere makes your stay pleasant and accommodating. All rooms come with air conditioning, mini-bar, color satellite TV and other four star amenities, with modern furnishings and appliances in the bathrooms. Their bar stays open until midnight, which is good because the rest of the city goes to bed well before then. Their restaurant is passable and serves local dishes as well as international favorites. If you want four star comfort, this is an option in Trieste.

Where to Eat
Cucina Triestina

Cooking in Trieste is a combination of Italian, German, Austrian, and Eastern European all blended together with the best of each. If you can't find something you like in Trieste, it's safe to say that you don't like food.

A great traditional Triestan snack that you can find at one of the many 'buffets' that dot the city is the *rebechin,* which consists of hot *porzina* (pork) with mustard, sausages, hot ham from Prague, goulash and other meats thrown together; it is definitely Austrian in nature but prepared and presented with Italian flair. You can also find many confectioners that offer typical Central European concoctions, like *strudel* and *krapfen,* as well as *sacher* cake that originated in Austria and the *dobnos* and *rigojanci* of Hungarian origin. And all the while you can also get some fantastic pasta dishes that are truly Italian.

8. AI FIORI, *Piazza Hortis 7, Tel. 040/300-633. Closed Sundays, Mondays, and July. Credit cards accepted. Dinner for two E50.*

A family affair with Fulvio Rimini greeting you and Arturo Rimini cooking for you. Set in a seafaring atmosphere with a lobster tank, wood ceiling beams that look like the ribs of a ship, and fishnets in the window. The *polpo con sedani* (octopus with celery) is exquisite, as is the *zuppa di frutti mare* (mixed seafood soup) for starters. Next indulge in their fresh seafood preparations like the *aragosto ai funghi* (lobster with mushroom sauce). And do not miss their desserts: *strudel di mele* (apple strudel), *mousse di melone nella sua salsa* (melon mousse in its own juice) or the *sorbetto di stagione* (seasonal sorbet). The wine list is extensive and your choices are served with a flourish. If you don't want to order from the menu they have a fixed price offering that covers all the bases. Situated in a quaint little *piazza.*

9. BREK, *Via San Francesco D'Assissi 10B. Open from March 1 to December 31 everyday 11:30am-3:00pm and 4:30pm-10:00pm. American Express accepted. Dinner for two E15.*

A large, modern, rustic cafeteria-style buffet/pizzeria/self-service restaurant with tile floors and wooden tables and chairs. An inexpensive place to come for lunch or dinner where you can get hamburgers, *petto di pollo* (chicken breast), *patate fritte* (french fries), pasta, salads and other simple fare. They are also family friendly and have a children's menu. Right around the corner from the Synagogue.

10. BUFFET DA PEPI, *Via Cassa di Risparmio 3, Tel. 040/366-858. Closed Sundays. No credit cards accepted. Dinner for two E19.*

Frequented by people from all walks of life who are enamored with the typical, traditional, and flavorful fare, as well as the rustic atmosphere. Wonderfully inexpensive and exquisitely tasty, the simple offerings (there is no menu) vary almost daily; but you can always find some *salsicce di Vienna* (Vienna Sausage), *porchetta* (roast baby pork), *prosciutto* (ham), a variety of vegetables and simple side dishes, as well as the fantastic boiled meat sandwiches with or without mustard. All can be accompanied by beer on tap or local wines. One of the many buffets in town, this is by far the best. The food is tremendous, the service fast and friendly and the local atmosphere enjoyable. It gets packed at lunch, standing room only and most evenings too.

11. BUFFET DA SIORA ROSA, *Piazza A. Hortis 3, Tel. 040/301-460. Closed Saturday nights and Sundays. No credit cards accepted. Dinner for two E20.*

Also called 'Mama Rosa,' this simple local place offers a clean ambiance, friendly service, and traditional dishes all at great prices. You will love the classic *porchetta* (roast baby pork) and *salsicce di maiale* (spicy pork sausage) all accompanied by loads of local bread to sop up the succulent juices. They make great *gnocchi di patate al pomodoro* (potato dumpling with tomato sauce) or *ai formaggi* (or with cheese sauce), *gnocchi di pane al ragu* (flour dumpling with a meat and tomato sauce). They also have a tasty *zuppa di verdure* (vegetable soup), and *pasta e fagioli* (pasta and beans). But the menu changes based on what is seasonably available. The front room can get a little crowded but the back room is quite spacious. The second best buffet in town on a quaint little *piazza*.

12. ELEFANTE BIANCO, *Riva III Novembre 3, Tel. 040/362-603. Closed Saturdays for dinner and Sundays. Credit cards accepted. Dinner for two E45.*

A refined, elegant local restaurant that is open late into the night to cater to the theater crowds. Start off with the *insalata di pollo* (chicken salad) and move to the *filletto alla brace* (grilled beef filet), the *stracciata di vitello* (veal strips), the *rombo al forno con patate* (turbot fish cooked in the oven with potatoes), or the *sogliola ripiena al pomodoro* (stuffed sole in a tomato sauce). They also have great pasta dishes, especially the spaghetti with tomatoes, garlic, hot red peppers and basil. There's air conditioning inside, but the best place to dine is on the patio/terrace.

13. HARRY'S GRILL, *Piazza dell'Unita d'Italia. Tel. 040/760-0011. All credit cards accepted. Dinner for two E65.*

Definitely the restaurant that truly represents Trieste. Harry's Grill has been the place to come in Trieste for many years because of its ideal location, refined elegance and excellent food. All kinds of local dishes and international favorites are served here, from seafood to steak, sandwiches to salami, and pasta to prosciutto. The wine list is excellent, the ambiance enchanting, the service exemplary ... everything about Harry's Grill is wonderful. When in Trieste, eat at least one meal here. It's located on the ground floor of the best hotel in the city, Duchi d'Aosta.

14. LA PIOLA, *Via San Nicolo 1b, Tel. 040/366-354. Closed Sundays. Credit cards accepted. Dinner for two E35.*

A mixed and varied offering in a local, artsy, friendly atmosphere near the port and around the *centro storico*. The menu changes daily but you can usually sample *linguini al basilico* (pasta with basil sauce), *tagliatelle alla pugliese* (pasta with tomatoes and a rich southern Italian cheese), *ravioli al ricotta e spinaci* (pasta with ricotta cheese and spinach), *gnocchi di patate ripiene* (stuffed potato dumplings), *lasagna al forno* (baked lasagna) all types of salads, *porcini grigliati* (grilled succulent baby pork), *Angus al piacere* (Angus beef made anyway you want), and much more. A great place to come that offers something for everyone.

Seeing the Sights
A. CAPITOLINE HILL
Located high above the city, the Capitoline Hill is home to the **church of San Giusto**. Two basilicas were erected between the ninth and eleventh centuries that were combined in the fourteenth century to become this extremely simple church with its asymmetrical facade. It is elegantly enriched by the Gothic rose-style stained glass window. At the same time the two basilicas were combined, an impressive bell tower was erected at the entrance to the new church.

Also on the hill is the **Memorial to the Fallen Soldiers of World War I**. In the gardens leading up to this monument are small remembrance stones adorned with flowers scattered in the grass and among the trees that are personal monuments to those who died. Near the memorial are the remains of the **Roman Forum** with its two rows of columns. Also in the ancient castle is the **Civic Museum** (*Armeria*), where old weapons and furnishings are on display, a little boy's paradise. If you have an archaeological or military bent this museum will stimulate your interest (*Open 9:00am-1:00pm everyday. Closed Mondays, Jan. 1&6, Easter, April 25, May 1, August 25 and December 25 & 26*).

From the ramparts of the castle you can get a complete view of the city, the hills around it beautifully covered with trees and scenic homes, and the surrounding sea. Also on the hill is the **Orto Lapidario** located in the **Castello do San Giusto**, which contains Roman and medieval relics found in Trieste and its environs (*Piazza Cattedrale. Open January to Mach. 9:00am-5:00pm; August & September 9:00am-7:00pm; October to December 9:00am-5:00pm. Closed Jan. 1 & 6, December 25 & 26. Entrance E6.*)

B. BORGO TERESIANO

A neighborhood of eighteenth century buildings created in the neoclassic style. The homes belonged to the traders of the time where they maintained their warehouses, showrooms, and residences. Some notable buildings to see are the **Palazzo Carciotti**, which overlooks the sea and is currently the Harbor Office; the **church of San Antonio Taumaturgo**; and the **Tergesteo** located in the Piazza della Borsa, that contains a cross-vaulted arcade filled with cafés that is one of the most popular meeting places for the locals (a must-see when in Trieste).

C. SANTA MARIA MAGGIORE & SAN SILVESTRO CHURCHES

Santa Maria Maggiore, open summer 7:00am-noon and 3:30pm-7:00pm/ Winter 7:00am-noon and 4:00pm-8:00pm. San Silvestro open Thursday-Saturday 10:00am-noon.

Santa Maria Maggiore is an example of a Baroque church, which was begun in 1627 by the Jesuit Giacomo Briana (that's why the church is also called *dei Gesuiti*) and was completed in 1682. The second church, located next to the first, is the oldest completely preserved house of worship in Trieste. It is built in a simple linear Romanesque style. Both simple churches are set in the old city high on the hill near the Roman Amphitheater. Be prepared to hike to get to them.

D. PIAZZA DELL'UNITA D'ITALIA

Created in the 19th century at the expense of some fine medieval neighborhoods, this *piazza* is the central focus of Trieste. It is a vast rectangle overlooking the sea with the Town Hall at the far end and other 19th century buildings lining the other two sides of the *piazza*. These include the **Palazzo Modello**, the **Casa Stratti** (which houses the **Caffé degli Specchi**, a famous café), the **Palazzo del Governo**, the **Lloyd Triestino palace**, the enchanting **Hotel Duchi d'Aosta**, and the most famous Baroque building in Trieste, the **Palazzo Pitteri**. Opposite this last building is **Mazzoleni fountain**, which represents the four continents known at the time. Next to it is Charles VI's Baroque column.

E. ROMAN AMPHITHEATER

Built between the first and second centuries CE, the ruins of an ancient Roman Amphitheater are located in the center of the city permanently on display. Professionally excavated in 1938, the theater lies on a slope of the Capitoline Hill, and when in use was able to hold 6,000 spectators. The statues that were placed in a semi-circle along the top are maintained in the **Museo Civico** on the top of the hill. Located near the amphitheater is the **Tor Cuchera**, the best preserved tower from the 14th century. Also nearby is an ancient display of a necropolis that pre-dates the Roman era.

F. CITTA VECCHIA

The old town is a series of medieval alleyways that should not be missed, but to get there you need to traverse an incredibly steep climb. The old town also contains the **Arco di Riccardo**, located in the Piazzetta Barbacan, an Augustan gate of the old Roman walls erected in 33 BCE. Nearby, just outside the old city area is the **Rotunda Panzera**, an interesting neoclassic style building.

G. RAILWAY MUSEUM

Stazione di Campo Marzio 1/Via G. Cesare 1. Tel. 379-4185. Open 8:30am-1:30pm. Closed Mondays. Entrance E5.

Located in the old railway station, this museum consists mainly of a collection of electric and steam powered locomotives. This station used to be the heart of Trieste, and these locomotives connected the town with Central and Eastern Europe. A railway lover's delight. You can take a ride on either an electric or steam train. The electric train travels around the city and its environs *(Linea Transalpina, a three-hour run from 10:00am to 1:00pm)*. The steam train is more of a day-long excursion that travels through Friuli-Venezia Giulia and occasionally into areas of Slovenia, Croatia and Austria *(7:20am to 9:30pm)*. For more information about reserving seats, call *040/379-4185* and ask about historical train excursions.

H. MUSEO DEL MARE

Via Campo Marzio 1. Open 8:30am-1:30pm. Closed Mondays and Holidays. Entrance E6.

Located in the restored *palazzo* of Lazzaretto di San Carlo, here you can find a fine collection of ancient models of ships, bas-reliefs with a maritime theme, ship documents, seafaring instruments, and charts from the 19th century, as well as relics of Giusseppe Ressel, the inventor of the propeller. If you've ever built a model you will simply love the models of ships they have on display.

I. CIVICO MUSEO SARTORIO

Largo Papa Giovanni XXIII 1. Open 9:00am-1:00pm. Closed Mondays, January 1, Easter, April 25, May 1, August 8, and December 25.

Originally this was a 19th century private residence of the upper class. Today it retains this refined flavor with a collection of *objet d'art*, a rich library, a collection of drawings, a marvelous oil painting by Tiepolo, and an intact set of rooms upstairs with the original furnishings and decorations from the period.

J. FISH MARKET & AQUARIUM

Aquarium - Open April to October 9:00am-7:00pm, November to March

9:00am to 1:00pm. Closed Mondays and Holidays. **Fish Market** *- Riva N. Sauro 1. Open 8:00am-2:00pm everyday except holidays.*

The **Pesceria Centrale** (Central Fish Market) is an old red brick building dominated by a small bell tower. Savor the sights, sounds and smells of an authentic fish market selling every imaginable type of seafood available. A great place to visit when in Trieste. Located right next to the local **aquarium**.

K. GALLERIA NAZIONALE D'ARTE ANTICA

Open 9:00am-1:00pm and 3:00pm-7:00pm. Closed Mondays, Jan. 1&6, Easter, April 25, May 1, August 25 and December 25& 26.

Located in the Palazzo Economo in Piazza Liberta, this museum has a large number of works from the Venetian and Lombard schools. There are works by Crespi, Guardi, Bernini, and Canaletto.

L. SYNAGOGUE

Via San Francesco d'Assisi 19. Open 9:00am-12:30pm, not on Saturdays and Jewish holidays.

Besides Byzantine, Gothic and Greek Orthodox-style churches, Trieste is home to one of the most important Jewish temples in Europe. Located on the Via San Francesco, this massive temple was completed in 1912 and is based on Syrian architecture. Also of Jewish interest is the **Risiera in San Saba** just outside town. This is a building that was used for rice husking up to 1913, then was turned into the only Nazi extermination camp located inside the current Italian borders. It was dedicated as a national monument in 1965.

Nightlife & Entertainment

Walking Street

Viale XX Settembre, a tree-lined pedestrian street, is where Triestans go for their evening *passegiatta*. Here you'll find authentic local shops, and with the cafés and shops, it seems as if you have been transported to Vienna or Paris. The feel is comfortable and accommodating and there is nary an American chain store to be found. You'll find candy stores, jewelers, toy stores, shoe stores, cafés, cleaners, *gelateria* (ice cream stores), bookstores, *profumerie* and more.

Historical Cafés

These establishments have been around for centuries serving up coffee, tea and pastries to their patrons. They are filled with ambiance and atmosphere and can be rather pricey, but are a wonderful place to relax and soak up the feel of Trieste.

- **Antico Caffé Tommaseo**, *Riva 3 Novembre 5, Tel. 040/366-765*
- **San Marco**, *Via Battisti 18, Tel. 040/371-373*
- **Pasticceria/Pirona**, *Largo Barriera Vecchia 12, Tel. 040/636-046*

Discos & Piano Bars
- **Machiavelli**, *Viale Miramare 285, Tel. 04044104*
- **Salomé**, *Via S. Michele 11, Tel. 040/307-414*
- **Tor Cucherna**, *Via Chiauchiara 7, Tel. 040/368-874*

Shopping

Shops are open from 9:00am to 1:00pm and then they reopen at 3:30pm and stay open until 8:00pm.

Trieste comes complete with all kinds of shops, many of which are local vendors selling traditional and local products. Most of the shops do not cater to tourists and are meant for the locals, which means they have housewares, furniture, kitchen stuff, and more, making Trieste a truly local shopping experience. Every other city in Italy seems like an American mall compared to the intimacy and regionality of shopping here. There is also a program designed to encourage tourist shopping, **Weekend a Trieste "T for You,"** which offers discounts to non-residents at stores bearing the appropriate sign. A great way to save money while you spend.

Markets

Old City Antique Market – on display the third Sunday of every month. About 60 shops and dealers display their wares.

Annual Antique Market – located in the exhibition center during the first week of November is the area's largest antique fair with dealers from Italy, Austria and Eastern Europe.

Mercato di Piazza della Liberta – Flea market style. Closed Sundays, Mondays and holidays.

Mercato di Piazza Ponterosso – Fish, fruit, vegetable, and flower market. Closed Sundays, Mondays and holidays.

Mercato Ittico di Riva N. Sauro – Fish, fruit, vegetable, and flower market. Closed Sundays, Mondays and holidays.

Mercato Coperto di Via Carducci – A covered market consisting of a variety of foods and dry good. Closed Sundays, Mondays and holidays.

Excursions & Day Trips

Excursions include **Muggia**, **Colla di Gretta**, **Castello di Duino**, **Grotta Gigante**, and **Palmanova**. With the exception of Palmanova (which is worth an overnight), I've planned each as a day trip from Trieste, so there are no hotel selections.

MUGGIA

Muggia is a small Venetian-style town overlooking the gulf of the same name. Its historical center, enclosed by medieval walls, is incredibly charming. The **castle**, erected in 1375, still keeps watch over the town, but since it

Take a Tram to Opicina

The tram departs every 22 minutes from Piazza Oberdan. The only funiculare railway operating in Europe (railway is the operative word since there are funiculars in operation in Genoa and other cities but are not as long); it was built in 1902 and expanded in 1928 and links the city with the Carso plain, destination **Opicina**. A scenic and fun way to spend part of the day. There's not much to see or do in Opicina. The whole reason to come out here is the trip itself.

is now private property it is not open to the public. A perfect little town where you can stroll through the narrow streets, with quaint *piazzettas* and get lost in the medieval ambiance and character. The harbor is always filled with small fishing boats and pleasure craft of all different colors, shapes and sizes. In the **Piazza Marconi**, the main square, you can find the Gothic-Venetian style **Duomo** built in the 13th century. The Gothic rose stained glass window is impressive. You can find the **Basilica dell'Assunta** on Mount San Michele in the old town overlooking the whole bay. Built in the 10th century, it is well preserved and should be visited not only for the view but for the bas-reliefs and frescoes.

Arrivals & Departures

Located only 12 kilometers from Trieste, Muggia can easily be reached by local bus service or by car.

Where to Eat

ALL' ARCHIDUCA, *Strade per Chiampore 46, Tel. 040/271-019. Closed Sunday nights, Thursdays, and January 1-16. Credit cards accepted. Dinner for two E60.*

A small place located on the outskirts of the town, their terrace is where you should dine in the summer. All dishes are prepared in a traditional yet creative manner with fresh ingredients from the sea and local farms. There are many dishes to choose from. Some of the best pasta dishes are *bucatini al raguttino di pesce* (pasta in a tomato and fish sauce), *risotto alla vongole* (rice with clam sauce), *risotto agli scampi* (rice with shrimp sauce), *tagliatelle ai calamaretti con erbe del carso* (pasta with small squid and herbs from local farms). For seconds try the *filetto di branzino agli asparagi* (bass filet with asparagus). It is superb.

LA RISORTA, *Riva de Amicis 1/a, Tel. 040/271-219. Closed Sunday nights and Mondays. Credit cards accepted. Dinner for two E90.*

A family-run restaurant with top-level cooking. Some dishes to try: *scampi fritti con verdurini agrodolci* (fried shrimp with vegetables with a bitter sweat sauce), *tagliatelle nere ai frutti di mare e zucchine* (black pasta with seafood and zucchini), *filetto di branzino in pasta filo con salsa di basilico* (bass filet on a bed of thin pasta in a basil sauce). They also grill and fry all manner of fish and seafood. The wine list mainly consists of white since the majority of dishes served here are seafood. An expensive place with refined food and a lovely terrace on which to dine.

COLLA DI GRETTA

Just north of Trieste is **Gretta Hill**, which features the impressive 70-meter high **Faro della Vittoria** (Victory Lighthouse), and the **Riviera di Barcola** which is one of the favorite beach areas around Trieste. A great place to come for fun in the sun during summer. The lighthouse can be seen from miles away and was made by Giovanni Mayer and features a scaled dome on which a bronzed winged victory stands.

At the end of the Riviera di Barcola is the stunningly impressive **Castello di Miramare**. Snow white and surrounded by the sea, with waves that break just beneath it, the castle was built between 1856 and 1860 and was the 'love nest' of Maximillian of Hapsburg and Charlotte of Belgium before they became the monarchs of Mexico. The castle is now a museum that features the ostentatious furnishings, monuments, and paintings of the elite society from the 19th century. Surrounding the castle are some plush parks, with ponds, statues, flowers, and staircases for you to enjoy. A perfect place to relax and get away from it all. All along the way out here there are public beaches, which are packed on summer weekends with sunbathers.

Arrivals & Departures

Public bus 36 operates along Route 14 from the main train station in Trieste to the Castle, but it is easier to go by car. If you want to walk it is about 40 minutes to an hour away, but most of the way you are walking along the ocean which makes for a pleasant *passegiatta*.

Where to Eat

TAVERNETTA AL MOLO, *Riva Massimiliano e Carlotta 11, Grignano, Tel. 040/224-275. Open 7 days a week. Credit cards accepted. Dinner for two E55.*

Known for its wonderful seafood dishes, great views, and live melodic symphony music on the weekends. The *antipasto al Molo* (a combination of shellfish and a variety of other seafood boiled and served tepid) is great as are the *calamari ripieno* (stuffed octopus). For pasta try the *gnocchetti alla marinara con salsa di molluschi* (small dumplings in a seafood and clam sauce), or the succulent *ravioli di pesce al ragu di scampi* (seafood ravioli in a shrimp sauce). For seconds the *fritto misto* (mixed fried fish) is great, as is any of the fresh fish. The restaurant is known to have some of the best choices of seafood and fish in the region.

CASTELLO DI DUINO

If you want to see landscapes of unsurpassed beauty come out to **Duino**. Only 16 kilometers from Trieste along the coast road and inland, getting here you will be blessed with wonderful scenery. Unfortunately you will only be able to view the **Castello di Duino** as it protrudes out from the rocks over the sea. Since it is the home of the United World College, gaining access is not possible. But the scene itself and the photographs you can take are wonderful. An especially great view is from the ruins of the ancient stronghold, **Dama Bianca** (White Lady) believed to have been built in the 12th century. Frame the castle in one of the ruined archways for a stunning photographic memory.

From the Dama Bianca you can savor the view and nature by taking a hike along the **Sentiero Rilke**, a path that runs along the ridge that is named after the German poet of Austrian origin. The path runs from Duino to Sistiana among woods and rocks and has landscapes of rare beauty. A nature lover's dream.

Arrivals & Departures

Take the train from Trieste, or drive on Route 14 from Trieste along the seaside until Sistiana. From here the road snakes inland back to the coast at Duino.

Where to Eat

ALLA DAMA BIANCA, *Fraz. Duino 61c, Tel. 040/208-137. Closed Wednesdays (not in the summer). Credit cards accepted. Dinner for two E48.*

Branka Miladinovic runs this place with bubbly enthusiasm. It is a simple little local place that specializes in fresh seafood dishes. You know it's fresh since Branka's husband is the fisherman who catches the meals for the day. I really like the antipasto of *pesciolini fritti* (small fried fish), the *ravioli aperto ripieno di pesce con ragu di scampi* (large open ravioli stuffed with fish in a shrimp sauce) and the *risotti marinari* (seafood rice dish), any of the freshly caught fish cooked just the way you want it grilled, (*grigliata*) fried (*fritto*), boiled (*bolitto*), baked (*al forno*), whatever ... all you have to do is ask. A wonderful place to dine, especially on summer nights when you can be seated on their terrace only a few paces from the sea.

GROTTA GIGANTE

Grotta Gigante is the world's largest cave open to the general public, or so says the Guinness Book of Records. The gigantic hall is large enough to allow St. Peter's in Rome fit easily inside. The height is 107 meters, 280 meters long and 65 meters wide. A nature lover's dream with a dizzying array of stalagmites in the shape of palm trees (one of which, the Ruggero column, is 12 meters high) and many tunnels leading deep into the mountain. The "Upper Entrance" leads visitors through a tunnel that was inhabited from early times into the Roman period. Outside the grotta is a museum of speleology and paleontology where one of the entrances to the cave is located.

The guided tours through the caves are an experience not to be missed while in the Trieste area. Phone and hours are: *Tel. 040/327-312, Fax 040/368-550. Tours from November to February start at 10:00am, 11:00am, noon, 2:30pm, 3:30pm and 4:30pm; in March and October they're at 9:00am, 10:00am, 11:00am, noon and 2:00pm, 3:00pm, 4:00pm and 5:00pm; from April to September they are every half hour starting at 9:00am but not from 12:30pm to 1:30pm. Closed January 1 and December 25, Mondays and the 2nd week of July to the 2nd week in September.*

Arrivals & Departures

It's only a short day trip by car. Take Route 58 to Opicina, then get on Route 202 to the Sgonico exit (follow the signs once you exit). Or contact the tourist office in Trieste to arrange for a guided bus tour.

Where to Eat

RISTORANTE MILIC, *Borgo Grotta Gigante 10, Tel. 040/327-330. Closed Mondays. Meal for two E48.*

If you get hungry after walking through the cave, right nearby is the Ristorante Milic, run by the family of the same name serving traditional local cooking in rustic country ambiance. The brick archways, wooden chairs, oxen yokes made into hanging lights, black wood beamed ceilings, and the red and white checkerboard tablecloths give this place a down to earth feel. And the food is pretty good too. Known for their hearty meat and vegetable dishes.

PALMANOVA

Just off the Autostrada from Trieste and Venice, **Palmanova** is one of the most unique towns anywhere in Europe. Only about 5,500 inhabitants live in this star-shaped defensive fortress town built in 1593. The design worked so well that it was never conquered in battle, only through negotiation. The town was initially called 'Palma,' but the 'Nova' was added in 1807, the year that the outside battlements were built during the Napoleonic era.

Palmanova is perfectly symmetrical with only three entrances. At the center of the star is the six-sided **Piazza Grande** surrounded with statues of the past Venetian rulers of the town. On one side of the *piazza* is the **Duomo** that had its facade created between 1615 and 1636 by Vincenzo Scamozzi. Inside at the second altar to the left is a fine piece by Alessandro Padovanino, *Pala delle Milizie* (1641). To the left of the altar is the *Madonna* by Domenico da Tolmezzo.

The **Historical Museum** – where a description of the fortress's use over time is displayed – and the **Information Office** are nearby just around the piazza. Down the Borgo Cividale is the **Museo Storico Militare** with many military uniforms and arms on display. They also have great views from the battlements.

Full of charm and history, Palmanova is a spot to visit when going or coming from Trieste. If you don't visit, you will regret it.

Arrivals & Departures

It's a day trip by car from Trieste. Take A4 to the Palmanova exit and follow the signs to the town; or take the train. Expect about an hour trip by either conveyance.

Where to Stay

If you want to spend the night and had a little too much *vino* at Al Convento (see below under *Where to Eat*), there are not many hotels here and no three or four stars, so below is the best two star in town.

HOTEL COMMERCIO, *Borgo Cividale 17, 33057 Palmanova. Tel. 0432/928-200, Fax 0432/923-568. 34 rooms all with bath. Single E65-75. Double E75-95. All credit cards accepted.* ***

A small place that needs to be accessed by an elevator. The rooms are smallish as are the bathrooms, but they are clean and comfortable. Located inside the old fortress walls near the Museo Storico Militare, you have TVs in the rooms as well as mini-bar, air conditioning, and phone. They also have a restaurant that makes good pizza. Nothing fancy but clean, comfortable and accommodating.

Where to Eat

AL CONVENTO, *Borgo Aquileia 10. Tel. 0432/923-042. Closed Wednes-days. All credit cards accepted. Dinner for two E45.*

Al Convento makes a lot of wild and creative dishes but all are tasty. The combinations they put in their soups are amazing. Try the *cozze e curry* (muscles with curry) or a specialty of the house, *strudel di verdure* (vegetable pie). The *ravioli con tartuffo* (with truffles – not the chocolate kind) is excellent, as is any dish with this aromatic and delicious fungus. Or sample the *ravioli con pesce e asparagi* (with fish and asparagus).

They also import their steak from the US, so if you have a hankerin' for beef Tex, this is your place. They also have bison from the US, which is a little gamey but good. I had to come to Palmanova to try American Bison – how incongruous.

Practical Information for Trieste

Car Rental
- **Avis**, *Airport, Tel. 0481/777-025 or Stazione, Tel. 040/422-122*
- **Hertz**, *Piazza della Libeta, 040/42-15-21*

Consulates
- **United States**, *Via Roma 15*
- **Great Britain**, *Vicolo delle Ville 16*
- **South Africa**, *Strada dal Friuli 109/3*

Emergency Numbers
- **Carabinieri**, *Tel. 112*
- **Municipal Police**, *Tel. 366-111*
- **Ambulance**, *Tel. 118*
- **Hospitals**, *Tel. 399-1111*

Laundry
- **Laundromat**, *Via Ginnastica 36, Tel. 040/367-414*

Postal Services
The central post office is located at *Piazza Vittorio Veneto 1, Tel. 040/367-198*. But stamps can be purchase at any *Tabacchi*.

Public Holidays
- January 1, Easter Monday, 26th April, May 1st, August 15th, November 1st, November 3rd, December 8th, December 25th and 26th.

Tourist Information & Maps
- **Tourist Office**, *Via San Nicolo 20, Tel. 040/679-6111. Train Station, Tel. 040/420-182.* Both locations have a hotel reservations and information center that can make reservations for you if you have none, and you can get a free, excellent tourist map. You can also get guided tours out of this office for an extra fee.

Chapter 25

Southern Italy

Southern Italy is still a land of immigrants waiting to move, but today instead of moving to America like their great grandfathers or grandmothers would have, they move to industrial northern Italian cities like Milan or Turin. Without many jobs in the south, Southern Italians are forced to move even if they know they will be cursed because of their accents and their place of birth.

The main work for people in the south is still in small-scale agriculture, local fishing endeavors, and small-scale crafts manufacturing, with a smattering of limited industrial activities. Despite its poverty, Southern Italy can be a wonderful place to visit for an experienced traveler. The sights to see, many of which have a definite Middle Eastern or Moorish influence, are few and far between; but when you do stumble on some isolated Norman castle or recently excavated Greek ruin the effect is powerful.

In essence, if you've never been to Italy, or still haven't seen all there is to see in Rome, Florence, Venice and other cities, Southern Italy would not be the best vacation for you. Southern Italy is only for the hardiest and most experienced travelers. The poverty in the South makes some people desperate, and inexperienced tourists make for easy marks. But even with that being said ... Southern Italy is safer than the lawlessness that reigns in virtually every American inner city.

Bari

Bari is known in Italy as the 'gateway to the East' because as a port city it is heavily involved in trade with the

Eastern Mediterranean. Bari also is the chief embarkation point for passenger ships to Greece and beyond, as it was an embarkation point centuries before for many of the Crusades.

Because of its location and port, Bari became the cornerstone of several ancient empires and was a major stronghold of Byzantine power. The old city still has some remnants of the look and feel of many centuries ago and should be explored. But like Naples, this is a port city, so it is best to explore during the day, not at night.

As the capital of **Apulia**, Bari also is the seat of an archbishop, a major university, and a naval college. Besides shipping, the city's other industries include shipbuilding, petrochemical refinement, and tourism. Bari also is the site of Italy's first atomic power station.

Not far away from Bari are two other attractions: the **Castellana Grottoes**, limestone caves that are 48 km (30 miles) south, and the Apulian **Trulli dwellings** – rock houses built in a spiral design, thought to have an ancient Middle Eastern influence. These are located in **Alberobello**, just a few miles farther south of Castellana. On your way to Bari, look out the car or train window for a sight of some of these Trulli dwellings. They look like something from another planet. Other regional sights you'll see on your way to Bari are fields upon fields of olive trees.

In all, Bari is a good place to stay and explore the region and its local flavor. It's also a perfect place to stop over on your way to points east. Again, a word of warning: this is a port city like Genoa and Naples and as such you need to be aware of your surroundings. The crime that comes with a port city is doubled since this is the country's poorest region. Don't wear flashy jewelry, make sure you carry your handbag away from the road, and always walk down streets that are populated. And women, please do not walk alone in the *centro storico* at any time. The most important rule you can follow is do not go into the Old City after dark, ever. They don't call Bari *scippoladdri* (the land of petty thieves) for nothing.

If you are not planning to catch a ferry to Greece or the Balkans, Bari may not be high on your list of destinations anyway. But if you do stop here, and despite my warnings to be alert, you will find some interesting sights and enjoy a general ambiance of warmth and welcome.

Bari's Santa Claus

Have you ever wanted to see Santa? In Italy he is the patron saint of seafarers, prisoners, and children. **Saint Nicholas of Bari** is buried in the **Church of San Nicola**. Better known to us as Saint Nick or Santa Claus, here's your chance to finally see that portly, paramount, patriarchal provider of presents.

Arrivals & Departures

Bari is 262 km from Naples and 458 km from Rome. The main form of transport into and out of the city is still train or car. Since the journey is long and tedious, the train is the fastest, most efficient means of getting here. By train from Rome, which usually comes through Naples,it's seven or eight hours. From Naples it would only be four hours. Bari is blessed with a number of railway stations all in the same vicinity. On the map I indicate only one in the Piazza Aldo Moro but in actuality it is three in one: **Apulo Lucane Station** (local), **Bari Nord Station** (points north) and the **Main Railway Station** (arrivals from all locations). One hundred meters down the Via Giusseppe Capruzzi, behind these three towards the water, is the **Sud-Est Railway Station** for destinations to the south.

If you decide to come by car from the north, the Autostrada A14 lets you off on the outskirts of the city. If you're coming from Barletta or Trani, the coast highway 16, which runs parallel to the Autostrada, would be the path to follow. Coming by car takes about the same amount of time as the train.

Ferries to Greece

One of the main reasons people come to Bari is to use the **ferry** and **hydrofoil** service to get to Greece. Your Eurorail or Interrail pass does not give you a discount on the fares, but most ferry lines offer discounts for students as well as for round-trip tickets. Just like everything in Italy, you have to ask for these discounts since they don't automatically offer them to you. For information about prices and schedules, go to the **Stazione Maritima** on Molo San Vito in the port (not the Stazione Maritima for trains on the Corso Vittorio Veneto) and check with the different ferry lines. Below is a list of the main offices' ferry lines. They also have a ticket window at the Stazione Maritima.

"Stop Over in Bari"

The city has a program by just that name (Stop Over In Bari), which is in place from June to September and assists all travelers under 30 who are not residents of the region in finding inexpensive lodging or camp sites. You can also get information about food stores, restaurants, laundromats, and more when you arrive in Bari. You can get all this at the **Information Office** in the train station at the **Stazione Maritima** or at their main office (*Via Dante Aligheri 111, Tel. 080/521-45-38*).

This program is designed to encourage travelers to stay a few extra nights in Bari and it seems to be working. During the summer, Bari has become a backpackers' heaven and is a great place to find a party and a companion.

• **Marlines**, *Car Ferry Terminal Box 3-4, Tel. 080/521-76-99*
• **Poseidon**, *Corso de Tullio 40, Tel. 080/521-0022*

• **Ventours Ferries**, *Corso de Tullio 16, Tel. 080/521-05-56*
• **Yasco**, *Corso de Tullio 40, Tel. 080/521-0022*

Taking the hydrofoil is much quicker than the ferry. While the ferries take most of a 24-hour day to reach their destinations, the hydrofoils get you there in five hours. They cost twice as much, but if you're in a hurry they're perfect.

Where to Stay

1. **BOSTON**, *Via Piccinni 155, 70122 Bari. Tel. 080/521-6633, Fax 080/ 524-6802. Web: www.inmedia.it/boston/. 70 rooms, 20 with bath, 50 with shower. E75-100; Double E100-130. Breakfast included. Credit cards accepted. ****

Situated in a modern building with all necessary three star amenities. The location suits both business and pleasure travelers. The rooms are adequately sized with modern furnishings. Buffet breakfast is continental and comes with cereal, fruit, cheese, yogurt, rolls, butter and jam and is served in the small room near the entrance. You can also rent videos at the front desk. Not really for family stays in one room since their size is not that large, but they are perfect for couples or singles.

2. **JOLLY HOTEL BARI**, *Via G. Petroni 15, 70122 Bari. Tel. 080/536-4366, Fax 080/536-5219. Web: www.jollyhotels.it. 164 rooms all with shower. Single E100-130; Double E130-160. Credit cards accepted. *****

Jolly hotels are everywhere in Italy, and most are close to the train station and this one is no exception. A modern hotel, preferred by traveling businessmen because of the convenience and service. The rooms are clean, comfortable, filled with modern furnishings, and come with air conditioning, satellite TV and room service but are not as large as we are used to in North America. The hotel restaurant is good enough to sample since they make some tasty local dishes. The ever present manager Gabriele Delli Passeri really makes an effort to ensure your stay is pleasant.

3. **PALACE**, *Via Lombardi 13, 70122 Bari. Tel. 080/521-6551, Fax 080/ 521-1499. E-mail: palaceh@tin.it. Web: www.palacehotelbari.it/. 197 rooms all with bath. Single E90-100; Double E100-130. All credit cards accepted. Breakfast included. *****

The Palace is a prestigious hotel in Bari. It is elegant, refined, and filled with antique furnishings and decorations. Each room is designed differently but despite all this finery they are quite comfortable and accommodating. Where the rooms are all different, the bathrooms are all the same with courtesy toiletry sets that come with everything, including face cream for the lady and slippers for the man. Breakfast is a buffet feast and is served in an exquisitely elegant salon. Situated between the *centro storico* and the business district, you could not find a better location. But despite being in the midst of it all, you'll not be disturbed by the traffic or nightlife, since each room's windows are double paned. The Palace and the Villa Romanazzi Carducci are the places to stay in Bari.

4. PENSIONE GIULIA, *Via Crisanzio 12, 70122 Bari. Tel. 080/521-6630, Fax 080/521-8271. 14 rooms only 10 with shower. Single without bath E45; Single E55; Double without bath E60; Double E70. Breakfast included. Credit cards accepted.* **

This is definitely the best budget traveler's alternative in Bari. Its location a few blocks up and over from the train station is a safe and quiet neighborhood and the prices are good. You don't have air conditioning and need to make reservations for the rooms with bath, but this is a good place to stay. The rooms are clean if a little worn, and they're comfortable. There is also a little sitting room and bar area.

5. VILLA ROMANAZZI CARDUCCI, *Via G. Capruzzi, 70057 Bari. Tel. 080/522-7400, Fax 080/556-0297. Web: www.villaromanazzi.com/. 89 rooms all with bath. Single E120-160; Double E180-200. All credit cards accepted. Breakfast included.* ****

An elegant and refined hotel, located on a tranquil site. It's the only one in Bari that is surrounded by a sea of green vegetation with a pool in which to relax. Besides that, the hotel is located in a building filled with character that was built in 1850, and the restaurant is located in the old stables. The ambiance is wonderful. The rooms are large and comfortably appointed with wonderful marble floors. The entrance hall itself is quite elegant with carpets, divan seats and a sculpture in the center. The bar is well-stocked and is located in the park area around the hotel. Your abundant buffet breakfast is served in the refined elegance of an interior salon, and the private garage is ideal for automotive travelers.

6. VISA EXECUTIVE, *Corso Vittorio Emanuele 201, 70122 Bari. Tel. 080/521-6810, Fax 080/524-5178. E-mail: executive.bari@italyhotel.com. 21 rooms all with shower. Single E80-90; Double E100-130. Breakfast included. Credit cards accepted.* ***

Located in a renovated older building near the Municipio (Town Hall), this is mainly a businessman's hotel. The Executive offers professional and hospital service which makes for a very comfortable stay in an exclusive and refined atmosphere. All rooms have double paned glass to eliminate traffic noise and are quickly transformable into elegant and well-equipped offices. If you want a double bed you need to ask for it since most are singles that pull down like a murphy bed from a wall unit. There are direct dial phones, air conditioning, TV, room service, and a downstairs bar. For the price it is a good place to stay.

Where to Eat

7. AI DUE GHIOTTONI, *Via Putignani 11, Tel. 080/523-2240. Closed Sundays and two weeks in August. All credit cards accepted. Dinner for two E65.*

What a perfect name for this simply excellent restaurant: The Two Gluttons. You had better come ready to eat since their portions are large. Heck, you wouldn't even be able to finish your antipasto if it was your main meal. They make excellent pasta dishes, as well as a variety of fish plates. When in Bari, eat at least one meal here.

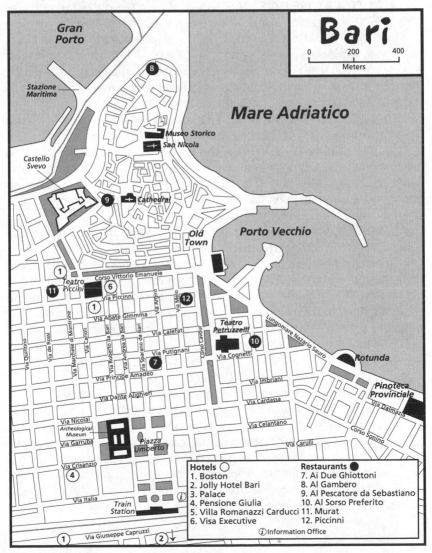

Hotels ○
1. Boston
2. Jolly Hotel Bari
3. Palace
4. Pensione Giulia
5. Villa Romanazzi Carducci
6. Visa Executive

Restaurants ●
7. Ai Due Ghiottoni
8. Al Gambero
9. Al Pescatore da Sebastiano
10. Al Sorso Preferito
11. Murat
12. Piccinni

ⓘInformation Office

8. AL GAMBERO, *Corso de Tullio 8, Tel. 080/521-6018. Closed Sundays, Christmas and August. No credit cards accepted. Meal for two E48.*

Located deep in the heart of the old city, I recommend you eat lunch here, not dinner, but eat here you must. Their terrace has a wonderful view of the port area and they make superb *spaghetti alla cozze* (with mussels), *alla vongole verace* (with a spicy clam sauce) and *al frutti di mare* (with a variety of sea food). They always have a fire burning outside where they cook the specialty of the region, grilled fish. In the winter they still cook outside, but mainly meats like *vitello* (veal).

9. AL PESCATORE DA SEBASTIANO, *Via Frederico II di Svevia 6, Tel. 080/523-7039. Closed Mondays. All credit cards accepted. Meal for two E65.*

Located in the old town right by the castle, this is a place to come for lunch, not dinner. A good upscale restaurant that cooks mainly fish and seafood over an open fire, but they also specialize in some great home-made pasta dishes. The best place to sit in the summer is outside on their terrace where you can gaze at the majestic Castle across the *piazza*.

10. AL SORSO PREFERITO, *Via de Nicolo 46, Tel. 080/523-5747. Closed Sundays and 15 days in August. Credit cards accepted. Dinner for two E55.*

Located near the Porto Vecchio, this is a well-respected and frequented local place that serves both local and national dishes. They feature a wide variety of pasta dishes as well as a great *bistecca alla fiorentina alla brace* (steak cooked over an open flame), and my favorite *agnello al forno* (lamb cooked over a fire pit). The food is superb.

9. MURAT, *Via Lombardy 13, Tel. 080/521-6551. Closed Sundays and August. All credit cards accepted. Dinner for two E65.*

One of the finer restaurants in Bari. This place is refined and elegant both on the terrace and inside. They have a great gourmet menu with wine for E30 per person that includes native dishes and some simple *cucina nuova* creations. Try some of their *minestra di verdure* (vegetable soup), *stracceti di pasta alla cozze* (pasta with mussels), *filetto di spigola gratinato con mozzarella* (sea bass au gratin with mozzarella).

12. PICCINNI, *Via Piccinni 28, Tel. 080/521-1227. Closed Sundays and August. All credit cards accepted. Dinner for two E75.*

The ambiance here is refined, elegant, and discreet, especially in their inside garden seating area. One of the higher-end restaurants in Bari. Here you'll find many of the magistrates from the town hall just down the road. The menu consists of a variety of local, national, creative and international dishes. Sample dishes include *filetto di Angus al pepe verde* (filet of Scottish Angus beef with pepper), *spaghetti con fiori di zucchine* (with zucchini flowers), and *pappardelle con radicchio e gamberi* (wide strips of pasta with radish and shrimp). There's something for everyone here, but you'll pay the price.

Seeing the Sights

Bari is an easy town to walk around in and is the best way to enjoy the town's castles, churches, and harborfront area. In Bari there is a new town and an old town. Most of the interesting sights are located in the **old town** and around the **Porto Vecchio** (Old Port).

NEW TOWN

The main feature of the new town is the palm-shaded **Piazza Umberto I**, located two blocks in front of the train station. Another sight to see in the new town is the **Teatro Piccinni** (*Tel. 521-3717; concert season is in the spring; the rest of the year the theater is closed)*, which is located in the **Town Hall** (**Municipio**) in the **Piazza della Liberta** and on the Corso Vittorio Emanuele. This is the city's busiest street and it conveniently divides the new town from the old town. Another theater to see is the **Teatro Petruzzelli** which is located on the Corso Cavour (*Concert season is in the spring; the rest of the year the theater is closed)*.

Behind the theater is the **Lungomare Nazario**, a beautiful seafront promenade that runs past the old harbor. If you go in the other direction you'll find the **Pinoteca Provinciale** in its gray and white towered building, about a kilometer down the promenade. This is the home of the provincial picture gallery with works by Tintoretto, Bellini, Vivarini, and Veronese (*Lungomare Nazario Saura, Tel. 392-421; open Tuesday-Saturday, 9:00am-1:00pm and 4:00pm-7:00pm, Sundays 9:00am-1:00pm.)*

LEVANT FAIR

Fair takes place in the fairground by the municipal stadium, off of Lungomare Starita.

This is the annual fair that runs for 10 days in mid-September, located about 2.5 kilometers from the center of town. This is the largest fair in southern Italy and goods from all over the world, especially Eastern Europe, are exhibited and sold here. A festive atmosphere. Don't miss it if you're in Bari while it's being held.

OLD TOWN

Around the old city is a peaceful seaside promenade. Strolling here is the perfect way to get a feel for Bari as it used to be. To the left of the old city is the **Gran Porto** (Grand Harbor), where the big liners and ferries dock. To the right of the old city is the **Porto Vecchio** (Old Port) that evokes a definite nautical feel.

CATHEDRAL

Piazza Duomo. Open daily 8:00am-noon and 4:00pm-7:00pm.

This 12th century church with a Romanesque facade and Baroque influences resides in the center of the old city. In the crypt you can find an ornate painting of the Virgin from Constinantinople, and the church's archives contain many large scripture rolls from the 11th century. Also notice the Romanesque architecture characteristic of the choir and chapel protruding ever so perfectly from the nave.

CHURCH OF SAN NICOLA
Via Palazzo Citta. Open daily 8:00am–noon and 4:00pm–7:00pm.
This is a large church built over an ancient Byzantine castle that once occupied the site. The funding came from Crusader and pilgrim donations in 1087, but it sat incomplete until the late 13th century. Besides being one of the finest achievements of Romanesque architecture in the region, the church contains the remains of **Saint Nicholas of Bari**. This patron saint of seamen, prisoners, and children, better known to us as **Saint Nick** or **Santa Claus** (ignore those northern European claims to Sinter Klaas, Father Christmas, and all their other Santa Claus allegations – this is the real deal, or so my Bari sources tell me!) So if you or the kids really want to see Santa, bring them to San Nicola here in Bari.

The first weekend in May is the **Festival of St. Nicholas** and it is quite a spectacle. On the Saturday of the festival a sea of people in ancient Norman attire swarm out of the Swabian Castle and head for the Basilica of San Nicola where they re-enact the delivery of the bones of the saint. The next day a statue of the saint is taken by procession to the sea where it is greeted by a flotilla of boats that make their way along the coast.

CASTELLO SVEVO
Piazza Federico II di Svevia. Museum open daily 9:00am–1:30pm and 3:30pm–7:00pm. Admission E3.
The **Castle** is located on the outskirts of the old town, almost directly in front of the Cathedral. Begun by Frederick II in 1233 and converted into a palace by Bona Sforza, the wife of Sigismund II of Poland and the last duchess of Bari in the 16th century (her remains are located in San Nicola). It was later used as a prison and a light house/signal station. Recently a **Roman city** was discovered on the site. There is also a small **museum** containing copies of Apulo-Norman sculpture.

Practical Information
English Language Bookstores
• **Feltrinelli**, *Via Dante Aligheri 91. Open Monday through Friday 9:00am to 8:00pm, Saturday 9:00am to 1:00pm.* They have an extensive selection of English language travel guides as well as some paperback novels. Located a half block away from **Stop Over in Bari's** main office.

Postal Services
You can buy stamps at local tobacconists (they are marked with a "T" outside) as well as post offices. Mail boxes are colored red. Post offices are open from 8:00am to 2:00pm on weekdays. The one exception to this rule is the main post office, **Palazzo delle Poste**, *located behind the university at Piazza Cesare Batista, Tel. 080/521-0381, open Monday through Friday from 8:00am to 7:30pm, and Saturdays from 8:00am to noon.*

Tourist Information & Maps
• **Stop Over in Bari**, *Via Dante Aligheri 111, Tel. 080521-4538. Open Monday through Saturday 9:00am-8:00pm and Sundays 10:00am to 5:00pm.* They also have offices in the *Stazione Centrale* and *Stazione Maritima.* They can supply you with all the information you need to know.
• **EPT**, *Piazza Aldo Moro 33A, Tel. 080/524-2244.* Located just to the right as you leave the station. In perfect Italian disorganization, the government is sponsoring two different agencies to give out virtually the same information. If you don't get everything you need from **Stop Over in Bari**, try here.

Barletta

Barletta is small compact town and is one of the principal ports in the region. It has a few sights of interest and can be easily walked. The best time to come is on the last Sunday in July when the annual **Disfida di Barletta** festival occurs. One of Italy's most famous medieval pageants, the Disfida reenacts a duel between Italian and French knights that occurred on February 13, 1503, to determine who would maintain control of the town. The Italians won.

Arrivals & Departures

Barletta is 40 minutes from Bari by train (E4) or 50 minutes by car, taking the coastal highway 16.

Where to Stay

1. **ARTU**, *Piazza Castello 67, 70051 Barletta. Tel. 0883/332-121, Fax 0883/332-214. 32 rooms, 8 with bath, 24 with shower. Single E65-80; Double E100-130. Breakfast included. Credit cards accepted.* ****

Located right in the center of all the sights that Barletta has to offer, you are also close to the beach at this hotel. This is a renovated old building that is perfect for a romantic weekend. All the amenities are here, including a restaurant that features local and international cuisine as well as great pizzas, and a piano bar for nightly entertainment. The rooms are super clean and very comfortable.

2. ROYAL, *Via L. De Nittis 13, 70051 Barletta. Tel. 0883/531-139, Fax 0883/531-466. 34 rooms all with bath. Single E50-60; Double E60-90. All credit cards accepted. Breakfast included.* ***

Located in the center of Barletta in an older building, the rooms are all different and all face into an inner atrium which makes them quiet and relaxing. Furnished with modern pieces, the rooms are comfortable but lack character. The bathrooms come with a courtesy set of toiletries and are clean and ample. A good place to stay when in Barletta.

Where to Eat

3. ANTICA CUCINA, *Via Milano 73, Tel. 0883/521-718. Closed Sunday nights and Mondays as well as the last week in January and the month of July. Credit cards accepted. Dinner for two E75.*

This place has sort of a rustic sophisticated charm with its antiques hanging on the wall and tables laid out for an elegant dinner. Open for a little over ten years, this is one of Apulia's best restaurants. Their traditional dishes

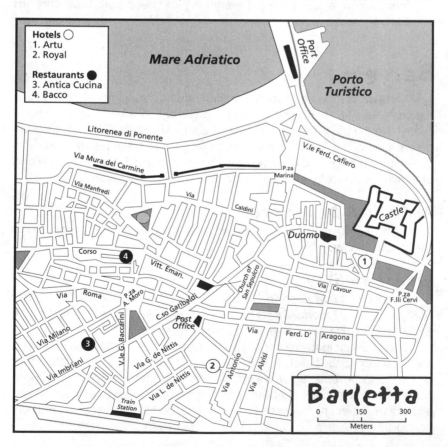

made with local ingredients are an expression of the region. If you like anchovies try their *alici marinate in olio e aceto* (anchovies marinated in oil and vinegar) or the *melanzane arrosto con polpa di granchio e merluzzo* (roasted eggplant covered with crab meat and pulped cod meat). Their *spaghetti con fiori di zucchine al profumo d'aglio* (with zucchine flowers and garlic) is also good, as is the *frittura alla barlettana* (local fried seafood: calamari, octopus, mullet, and whatever else is caught that day).

4. BACCO, *Via Sipontina 10, Tel. 0883/571-000. Closed Sunday nights and Mondays, as well as August. Credit cards accepted. Dinner for two E85.*

Another great restaurant in the city, as well as the region. The owner, Franco Ricatti, recently opened a second Bacco in Rome, so business must be good. The atmosphere is always friendly and the menu includes two different gastronomic options, so you can sample a wide variety of food at a lower cost. They make traditional dishes as well as creative ones. Their *zuppetta di fagioli e cozze* (soup of beans and muscles) is particularly good as is the *fusilli al ragu di scorfano* (twisted pasta with a ragu sauce of scorpion fish).

Seeing the Sights

From the train station, walk straight ahead down the Viale Giannone to the second street on the right, Corso Garibaldi. Take a right and walk a couple hundred meters to the **Church of San Sepolcro** on the left hand side (*Corso Vittorio Emanuele, open summer Monday–Saturday 10:00am–noon and 6:30pm–8:30pm; open winter 10:00am–noon and 5:30pm–8:00pm*). This is a 12th century Gothic church whose facade is a little worse for wear. You'll know it is the right church by the five meter tall **Colosso** next to the church towers. This is a 4th century bronze statue which represents a Byzantine emperor holding the cross and globe, the symbols of his two realms of power. Inside the church the only ornate item left is the large baptismal font.

Go back to the Corso Garibaldi and follow it to the **Duomo** (*Piazza Duomo; open 7:00am–noon and 4:00pm–7:00pm daily*). As you walk, the street name changes to the Via Duomo and curves to the right. Also known as the church of **Santa Maria Maggiore**, this is part Romanesque and part Gothic. The west end and *campanile*, built between 1147 and 1193, are Romanesque; the nave and choir inside, built in the 14th century, are Gothic. Some items to admire are the fine pulpit and tabernacle built in the 13th century.

From the Piazza del Duomo you can see the enormous **castle** (*Via del Duomo, Tel. 31114; open October–April, Tuesday–Sunday 9:30am–1:00pm and 4:00pm–6:30pm*). This was first a Saracen and Moor outpost, then it was enlarged by the Hohenstaufens (Normans) in the 13th century, and finally the four bastions were added in 1537 by Carl V. The castle is now home to a **museum** and **picture gallery**.

After you've explored the twisting streets of this beautiful medieval town, take a walk east of the harbor and go to their **public bathing beach** for a dip in the Adriatic.

If you have a car, take the time to drive 30 km south down route 170 to **Castel del Monte** *(on Route 170, open Tuesday–Sunday 10:00am–12:30pm and 4:00pm–7:00pm)*. This is the most amazing Norman castle in Italy. It was built circa 1241 to be a hunting lodge for Frederick II. This early Gothic structure is a perfect octagon, ringed by eight towers with eight rooms of the same size on each floor. The rooms on the upper floor, with their particularly fine windows, are believed to have been Frederick II's apartments. The structure was also the final prison for Frederick II's grandsons.

Trani

Known for its scenic old city and peaceful gardens at the **Villa Comunale**, this is a seaport city seemingly trapped in time. You'll just adore the quaint little harbor with the old city surrounding it. But as in all port cities, no matter how small, especially if they are in the south of Italy, always be alert.

Arrivals & Departures

Trani is between Barletta and Bari. You can take a train from Bari and get here in 30 minutes, or a train from Barletta and get here in 10 minutes. Also if you drive on **highway 16** along the coast between Barletta and Bari, you'll pass through Trani.

Where to Stay

1. ROYAL, *Via de Robertis 29, 70059 Trani. Tel. 0883/588-777, Fax 0883/582-224. 46 rooms all with shower. Single E50-75; Double E75-100. Breakfast included. All credit cards accepted.* ****

This was the first Jolly hotel built in the south, then it converted to a Holiday Inn and now it is a Royal hotel. Located in the center of town near the train station, when you enter through the private tunnel you instantly get the impression that this is a good hotel. There is a quaint gazebo in which you are served your breakfast buffet. The rooms are comfortable and tranquil, and modern since all were renovated in 1990. Even so, the original antique style and charm was saved. Really the only nice place to stay in Trani.

Where to Eat

2. TORRENTE ANTICO, *Via E Fusco, Tel. 0883/47911. Closed Sunday nights and Mondays, as well as the second week in January and the last two weeks of July. Credit cards accepted. Dinner for two E70.*

The only thing wrong with this place is that it is a little pricey. Other than that, the atmosphere is pleasant, the food is prepared and presented perfectly, and its taste is superb. All thanks to the great chef here, Savino Pasquadibisceglie (say that three times fast). Try their *filetto di spigola con zucchine* (filet of sea bass with zucchini) or the wonderful *salmone gratinato con erba cipollina* (salmon au gratin with herbs and small onions). Also try their *spaghetti alla vongole verace* (with a spicy clam sauce) or their *pennette alla marinara* (small macaroni with a tomato meat sauce) or their *tagliatelli ai porcini* (pasta with a mushroom sauce sautéed in butter). They also serve all varieties of seafood and fish for seconds.

3. **OSTERIA CACCIAINFERNO**, *Via San Nicola 9, Tel. 0883/585-978. Closed Mondays and the last week in September. No credit cards accepted. Dinner for two E30.*

A great local place in one of the best spots in the city right by the cathedral. There are two rooms and in the summer you can enjoy your meal in the small

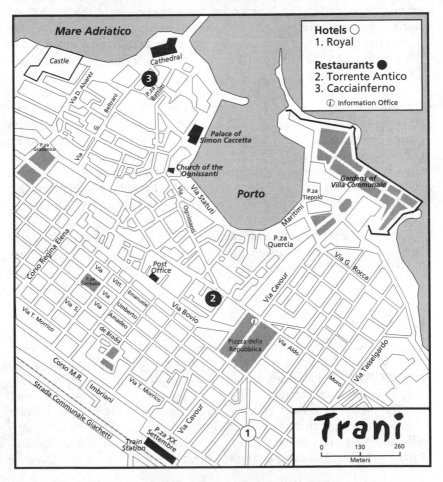

nearby *piazzetta*. The clientele are mainly young since the prices here are quite low and the food is good. Try some of their *bruschetta* (garlic bread) to start accompanied by some of their *zuppa di frutta di mare* (seafood soup). Their specialty is grilled meats of all kinds. A real rustic place that I know you will enjoy. The service is informal and relaxed.

Seeing the Sights

From the train station, take Via Cavour (if you want to, as you walk down Via Cavour, stop at the **tourist office** in the Piazza della Repubblica and pick up a map and some information about other sights) for about half a mile to the **Piazza Plebiscito** and the **Villa Comunale gardens**. Here you can enjoy a relaxing picnic, a scenic view out over the Adriatic, or a panoramic sight of the old city and its cathedral across the harbor.

To get to the cathedral, walk around the harbor. You'll pass the **Church of the Ognissanti** (*Via Ognissanti; open 8:00am–noon and 4:00pm–7:00pm*) with its deep porch and beautiful Romanesque carvings above the door. Keep going around the harbor and take a left into the **Piazza Trieste**. In this *piazza* is the **Palace of Simone Caccetta** built in the 15th century (*open 9:00am–1:00pm and 4:00pm–7:00pm.*)

Go through this *piazza* and into an open area facing the sea. The **cathedral** sits in this area almost on the water's edge (*Piazza Duomo, open 9:00am–1:00pm and 4:00pm–7:00pm*). Built between 1150 and 1250, this church and bell tower dominate this small town. You'll find beautiful bronze doors made in 1160 and a stone doorway carved in the 13th century. The interior is magnificent with its double columns, the only example of such a construction in Apulia. Inside is the **Crypt of St. Nicholas the Pilgrim** (died 1094) under the transept and the **Crypt of St. Leucius** (died 670) under the nave.

One last sight to see is the **castle** to the west of the cathedral. Built between 1233 and 1249 by Frederick II, it is no longer open to the public since it is now a prison but is quite a sight to see.

Lecce

Situated halfway along the Salentine peninsula (the heel of the Italian boot), **Lecce** is the capital of its province and is one of the most interesting towns in Southern Italy. Virtually untouristed, Lecce boasts an array of 17th century Baroque architecture.

The palaces, buildings, churches, and arches are covered with intricate swirls and designs that characterize *barocco leccese*. Even though many different conquerors swept through this area – Greeks, Cretans, Romans, Saracens, Moors, Swabians, and more – as you'll see from the architecture the main influence was the Spanish Hapsburgs during the 16th and 17th centuries. It's almost as if everything else was discarded outright and the Spanish remade this town and others in their own image. Some people call the city the Athens of Apulia because of its beauty.

Besides viewing Lecce's architecture, the city is the perfect jumping-off point to explore the Salentine peninsula, which is dotted with medieval fortresses and castles. You'll also see countless olive tree groves and hill towns. Exploring the base of Italy's heel is like going back in time, but it is an adventure not to be undertaken except by the most experienced travelers. Lecce and this area is only for those travelers who know Italy and have at least a decent command of the language.

Arrivals & Departures

Located about 100 km from Bari, there are three trains a day that go between the two cities. The trip takes about an hour and a half to two hours depending on the number of stops the train makes.

To get into town from the train station, you can either walk for 10-15 minutes straight out of the station down the Viale Oronzo Quarta into the centro storico, or you can take bus #1, 2, 3, or 15 from the station to the area around the Piazza Sant' Oronzo in the center. You need to buy a ticket at the newsstand in the station first. The cost is Euro 50 cents one way.

Where to Stay

1. PRESIDENT, *Via Salandra 6, 73100 Lecce. Tel. 0832/311-881, Fax 0832/372-283. 154 rooms all with bath. Single E80-100; Double E110-150. All credit cards accepted. Breakfast included.* ★★★★

One of the finest hotels in the Puglia region, this place offers professional hospitality and comfortable lodgings. Located in the center of the city in a new building with large rooms and functional modern furnishings. The bathrooms are also large and have all necessary four star amenities including courtesy toiletries. The common areas are also large and accommodating and furnished with refinement and comfort in mind. A wonderful place to stay when in Lecce.

2. RISORGIMENTO, *Via Augusto Imperatore 19, 73100 Lecce, Tel. 0832/242-125, Fax 0832/245-571. 57 rooms. Single E70; Double E110. All credit cards accepted. Breakfast E8.* ★★★

This was the first hotel in Lecce situated in an old and historic building. An elegant structure with quiet and comfortable rooms and arranged with antique furnishings. The best rooms are 208 and those between 301 and 306, since they also have private terraces. The entrance hall is elegant, as is the restaurant and party room. The pavement is a wonderfully decorated extravaganza in a style all its own. There is room service, TV and air conditioning and

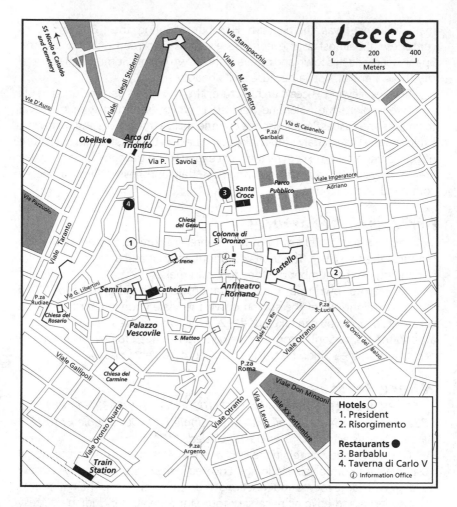

Lecce

0   200   400
Meters

Hotels ○
1. President
2. Risorgimento

Restaurants ●
3. Barbablu
4. Taverna di Carlo V

ⓘ Information Office

the place is really great, but the breakfast is Italian style, meaning coffee, tea and a roll or two.

Where to Eat

3. **BARBABLU**, *Via Umberto I #7, Tel. 0832/241183. Closed Mondays, the last week in June, and the first week in September. Credit cards accepted. Dinner for two E50.*

Located in an old building in the *centro storico*, this place has great atmosphere both inside and out on the terrace; the food is superb. The antipasto table is overflowing with goodies like eggplant, pepperoni, local sausage, zucchini, cheeses, and more. For your first course, try the *spaghetti alla vongole verace* (with a spicy clam sauce), it's excellent in these parts. For seconds, they make great fish or meat dishes, so try either. I like the *saltimbocca alla leccese* (ham shank cooked in tomatoes and spices).

4. TAVERNA DI CARLO V, *Via G Palmieri 46, Tel. 0832/248-818. Closed Sunday nights and Mondays. In the summer also closed Saturdays. In Winter Saturday for lunch. Closed all of August. Visa accepted. Dinner for two E35.*

A classic atmosphere of an old tavern, this place is located on the bottom floor of a building that dates to 500 CE and is located in the *centro storico* of Lecce. You can also sit outside on the terrace and watch Lecce go by as you eat. They make many traditional Lecce dishes here, including *zuppa di farro con ceci o fagioli* (soup made with flour and chickpeas or beans), *zuppa di lenticchie* (lentil soup) and a thick and tasty *stufato di verdure fresche* (fresh vegetable stew). For seconds try some local favorites like the *pezzetti di cavallo alla griglia* (small pieces of grilled horse meat) or *involtini di trippa con patate* (rolled tripe with potatoes). They also have a plentiful supply of fish dishes.

Seeing the Sights

The old town of Lecce is a maze of small winding streets which are a joy to wander. Start in the center of town at the **Piazza San Oronzo** where the information office is. In the center of the *piazza* is the **Colonna di San Oronzo**, with a statue of the saint on top, which once stood, without the statue, in Brindisi to mark the end of the Appian Way. Also in the *piazza* is a partially excavated **Anfiteatro Romano** that dates from the 2nd century.

North of the *piazza* in the **Piazza della Profettura** is the best church to see in Lecce, **Church of Santa Croce**, built between 1549 and 1697 (*open 9:00am-1:00pm and 5:30pm-7:30pm*). It has an ornately decorated facade and a beautiful exterior. The interior is only two simple rows of columns supporting bare white walls. Behind the church are the peaceful **Giardini Publici** where you can relax with a picnic lunch.

East of the Piazza San Oronzo is the imposing trapezoid **Castello**, built from 1539 to 1548 during the reign of Charles V (*not open to public*). To the west of this sight is the **Arco di Trionfo**, erected in 1548 in honor of Charles V. If you're interested in cemeteries, go up the Viale San Nicolo to the church of **SS Nicolo e Cataldo**, founded in 1180, and the cemetery it tends to. The **cemetery** is filled with small mausoleums of every imaginable style and shape all clustered together on tiny paths (*Viale San Nicolo, open 8:00am-1:00pm and 4:00pm-7:00pm; cemetery is open 9:00am-6:00pm. Sundays 9:00am-1:00pm*).

Back in the center of the city is the **Piazza del Duomo** (*open 8:00am-11am and 4:30pm-7:30pm*). This is an entire complex of buildings that stand out because of their white facades. First you have the looming **Cathedral of Sant'Oronzo** and *campanile* built from 1658 to 1670 that stands 70 meters high. The interior is mainly from the 18th century. To the right of the cathedral is the **Palazzo Vescovile**, the Bishop's Palace, which was constructed in 1652 (*Piazza del Duomo, not open to public*). Further right is the **seminary** built in 1709, with its richly decorated facade and courtyard containing a beautiful fountain (*not open to public*).

If you're interested in more churches Lecce has the **Chiesa del Gesu** *(Piazza Gastromediano, open 8:00am–11am and 3:30pm–5:30pm)*, **San Irene** *(Via Vittorio Emanuele, open 8:30am–noon and 3:00pm–6:00pm)*, **Santa Chiara** Chiara *(Piazza Santa Chiara, open 8:00am–11am and 4:00pm–7:00pm)*, **San Matteo** *(Via San Matteo, open 8:00am–noon and 4:00pm–6:00pm)*, **Chiesa del Carmine***(Piazza Tancredi, open 8:00am–11am and 4–7:00pm)*, and the large **Chiesa Rosario** *(Via G. Libertini, open 8:00am–11am and 3:30pm–5:30pm)*.

Practical Information

Postal Services
You can buy stamps at local tobacconists (they are marked with a "T" outside) as well as post offices. Mail boxes are colored red. Post offices are open from 8:00am to 2:00pm on weekdays. The one exception to this rule is the **main post office (Palazzo delle Poste)** located in Piazza Libertini *(Tel. 0832/303-000)* which is open Monday through Friday from 8:00am to 7:30pm, and Saturdays from 8:00am to noon. You can't miss it, it's basically in the shadow of the castle.

Tourist Information & Maps
• **EPT tourist office**, in the center of town in the *Piazza San Oronzo* between the Duomo and castle. *Tel. 0832/316-461*. Here they can supply you with maps of Lecce as well as Gallipoli. If you want to charter a bus to take you to the sights, contact the travel office of **CTS**, *Via Palmieri 91, Tel. 0832/301-862*.

Gallipoli

Located on the edge of the Gulf of Taranto and the Ionian Sea, this little port town is situated on a rocky island connected to the more modern city by an ancient bridge, the **Ponte Citta Vecchia**. The beautiful **old town**, with its narrow winding streets, evokes images of centuries past. This is a fun place for a day or two.

Arrivals & Departures
There is a train from Lecce every two hours. The trip takes 45 minutes and costs E3. If you go by car, simply take highway 101 straight to Gallipoli. You'll

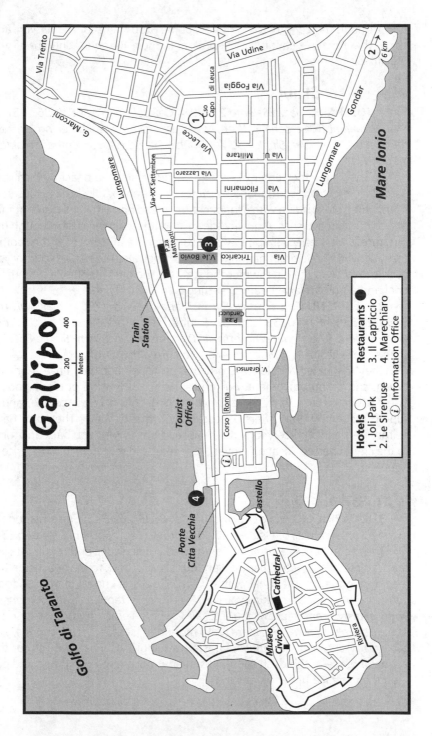

Gallipoli

Golfo di Taranto

Mare Ionio

0 200 400
Meters

Via Trento
Via Udine
2 → 6 km
di Leuca
Via Foggia
G. Marconi
C.so Capo
1
Via Lecce
Gondar
Via ù Militare
Via Lazzaro
Lungomare
Via Filomarini
Via-XX Settembre
Lungomare
P.za Matteotti
3
V.le Bovio
Via Tricarico
Via
Train Station
P.za Carducci
V. Gramsci
Corso Roma
Tourist Office
i
4
Ponte Citta Vecchia
Castello
Cathedral
Museo Civico
Riviera

Hotels ○ **Restaurants** ●
1. Joli Park   3. Il Capriccio
2. Le Sirenuse 4. Marechiaro
                ⓘ Information Office

pass through the country town of Galapone. Stop there for a brief visit and enjoy the town's beautiful cathedral and their Baroque Church of the Crucifixion.

Where to Stay

1. JOLI PARK, *Piazza Salento 2, 73014 Gallipoli. Tel/Fax 0833/263-321. E-mail: joliparkhotel@esperia.it. Web: www.esperia.it/joliparkhoteleng.htm. 87 rooms all with shower. Single E60-70; Double E80-95. Visa accepted. Breakfast included.* *******

Located near the center of modern Gallipoli and the beach, which isn't hard since the city is surrounded by water, this is an ex-Jolly hotel. Housed in a renovated old building with a lot of charm, it also has a good restaurant that makes traditional dishes. A quality, clean, comfortable place even though the furniture is a bit eclectic. You have air conditioning and TV in all the rooms, many of which have great panoramic views. They also have a bus to ferry you back and forth to the old town or the station. And did I mention a swimming pool and a quiet relaxing garden setting?

2. LE SIRENUSE, *Litoranea Santa Maria di Leuca, 73014 Gallipoli. Tel. 0833/22536, Fax 0833/22539. E-mail: lesirenuse@esperia.it. Web: www.esperia.it/lesirenuseeng.htm. 120 rooms all with bath. Single E60-70; Double E80-120. All credit cards accepted. Breakfast included.* *******

They're located a little ways out from Gallipoli but they have a private beach, snorkeling equipment, horseback riding, tennis, an outdoor pool, a disco, a piano bar – wait, there's more – mini-golf, a bocce course, and a superb restaurant that offers a beautifully romantic view. They also have hairdressers and a nursery for kids as well as a bus to take you back and forth to the city. A perfect location. Private, peaceful and relaxing. And the price is right too.

Where to Eat

3. IL CAPRICCIO, *Viale G. Bovio 14, Tel. 0833/261-545. Closed Mondays in the summer and all of October. Credit cards accepted. Dinner for two E60.*

The menu here is a combination of traditional dishes and regular Italian fare. A direct result of the many Italian tourists who flock to the beaches in the area during the summer (mainly in August). So if you know your Italian food you can always find something you like. For example: *tagliatelle alla bolognese* (with a tasty meat sauce) *spaghetti all vongole verace* (with a spicy clam sauce), *spaghetti ai frutti di mare* (with mounds of seafood). For seconds, you can't go wrong with the *grigliata mista* (mixed grill of meat and fish) or the *zuppa di pesce* (a thick fish soup). Pleasant atmosphere both inside and out – on their terrace under an awning.

4. MARECHIARO, *Lungomare G Marconi, 0833/266-143. Closed Tuesdays. Credit cards accepted. Dinner for E60.*
Located just before the Ponte Citta Vecchia, this place used to be a dump frequented by local fishermen, but it has slowly upgraded its decor. The food is as filling and robust as before. Enjoy their many fish dishes either inside with the rustic decor or outside where you can gaze at the sea. It's a large place, over 200 seats, but reservations would be advised in the high season. For firsts, try the *zuppa di pesce alla gallipolina* (fish soup made Gallipoli-style with mounds of seafood) which is so filling it can take the place of a pasta. For seconds try any of the many fish they make roasted over an open flame and you'll come away satisfied.

Seeing the Sights

An old road, the **Riviera**, runs all the way around this small town and offers views of both the **Gulf of Taranto** and the **Ionian Sea**. Visit the **Castello** (*Piazza Imbiani, ipen 9:00am–1:00pm and 4–7:00pm*), built from the 13th century to the 17th century just over the bridge on the left. You can get some great views from the ramparts.

The **cathedral** is located down the Via Antoinette de Pace in front of the castle (*open 8:00am–11am and 3:30pm–5:30pm*). Built between 1629 and 1696, there are some beautiful choir stalls here. Beyond the cathedral on the same road is the **Museo Civico**, (*Via Antoinette de Pace, open 9:00am–1:30pm and 4:00pm–7:00pm Tuesday–Sunday*) which contains many artifacts, sculptures, and paintings of the region's past. If you arrive in the morning, don't miss the **fruit and vegetable market** in front of the castle in the Piazza Imbriani.

After you've visited this scenic, beautiful, and unique little town head up the coast on the Gulf of Taranto side to some wonderful beaches and resorts. During the *Ferragosto* holidays in August, this seaside town of 20,000 people swells with Italian vacationers. For more information about the town and the surrounding area, stop at the **information office** just across the bridge from the old town, *Corso Roma 225, Tel. 0863/476-202.*

Otranto

A little fishing village situated panoramically on a beautiful bay, **Otranto** was founded in the 6th century BCE by the Greeks (Hydrus). The small port then came under Roman rule (Hydruntum) and later became the capital of Byzantine Apulia. It was razed to the ground in 1480 by the Ottoman Turks and all its citizens were slaughtered. There are some ancient churches here, and a castle with a terrific view where you can gaze across at the Republic of Albania.

Arrivals & Departures

There are two trains a day from Lecce to Otranto. The trip takes 45 minutes and costs E3. By car from Lecce, go through the seaside resort of San Cataldo with its lighthouse, and take the scenic coast road. The trip will take about 45 minutes.

Once you arrive, to get to the tourist office from the train station go around the right side of the circle and bear left down the hill on Via Pantaleone. There will be signs indicating that you should go right. Follow them and you'll have a much longer walk. Instead, go through the stoplight and go to the Lungomare d'Otranto, which runs along the beach. Go three blocks to the right and you'll hit the Piazza de Donno. Bear to the left down Via Vittorio Emanuele II and you'll enter the old town in a few blocks.

Turn right on Via Basilica to get to the local **tourist office** and the cathedral. Pick up a map here and begin your exploration into the byways of this charming seaside escape.

Where to Stay

GRAND HOTEL DANIELA, *Litoranea San Cataldo, 73028 Otranto. Tel. 0836/806-648, Fax 0836/806-667. E-mail: ghdaniela@esperia.it. Web: www.esperia.it/ghdanielaeng.htm. 146 rooms all with shower. Single E70-120; Double E120-220. Credit cards accepted.* ****

Ooo-la-la – what luxury! Great views, a private beach, snorkeling equipment, sauna, gymnasium, bocce courts, tennis courts, horseback riding, swimming pool, nursery for the kids, hairdressers, piano bar and much more. This is the place to stay to have all the luxuries of the world at your fingertips when you're in the middle of nowhere. Located outside of town, they also have a shuttle bus to take you from the train station and back.

BELLAVISTA, *Via Vittorio Emanuele 19, 73028 Otranto. Tel. 0836/801-058. 22 rooms, 2 with bath, 20 with shower. Single E45-55; Double E55-65. No credit cards accepted.* **

The best budget choice in the area in terms of cost, and you get air conditioning, which is imperative in the summertime down here. They have their own restaurant attached to the hotel which serves great local food. There's a full board option for only E45 per person.

Where to Eat

TRATTORIA DA SERGIO, *Corso Garibaldi 9. Tel. 0836/801-408. Closed Wednesdays in Winter, February and November. American Express accepted. Dinner for two E60.*

Exclusively a local-style seafood restaurant. Some great dishes here are *frutti di mare con linguini or risotto* (linguini or rice with mounds of fresh seafood), *gamberoni alla griglia* (large grilled shrimp) or some great *pesce spada alla griglia* (grilled swordfish). You can enjoy both inside and outside seating.

TRATTORIA VECCHIA OTRANTO, *Corso Garibaldi 96, Tel. 0836/801-575. Closed Mondays in Winter and November. Credit cards accepted. Dinner for two E50.*

Opened in 1981, this rustic restaurant on Otranto's main street is a well-respected local place that serves traditional dishes like *tonnarelli alla polpa di ricci e peperoni* (wide strips of pasta with sea urchins and pepperoni) or *zuppa di pesce all'otrantina* (special local seafood soup). They have inside and outside seating. I'd recommend the local flavor inside.

Seeing the Sights

The **cathedral of Santissima Annunziata**, begun in 1080, is the last home for the remains of those slaughtered by the Ottomans. The church contains ancient columns that have had 12th century capitals placed on them. You'll also find some unique well-preserved 12th century mosaic tile floors that depict the passing of the months and of battles won in the area (*Piazza Duomo, open 8:00am–noon and 3:00pm–5:00pm).*

A smaller church, **San Pietro**, of 19th century origin sits on a side street in the upper part of town with its Byzantine dome and frescoes. Next visit the **Castello di Aragonese** (*Via Castello, currently under reconstruction; open 9:00am–1:00pm and 4:00pm–7:00pm; admission E3).* The castle affords wonderful views, on clear days, across the **Straits of Otranto**. The straits are 75 kilometers wide, and you can see across to the mountains of Albania – a country once ruled by Italy.

For more information about Otranto, and to get a map of the city and surrounding area, contact the local **tourist office**, *Via Basilica 8, Tel. 0836/801-436*, which rests at the foot of the cathedral.

Chapter 26

Sicily (**Sicilia**) is a large, mountainous, fertile island at the center of the Mediterranean. It is a geological extension of the Apennine Mountains, separated from the toe of the mainland by the **Straits of Messina**. About the size of Vermont Sicily has always been someone else's prize. It was first overrun by the Siculi and Sicans. The Greeks arrived in the 8th century BCE and left behind the ruins of temples and theaters. The Romans made the island their first province. The Arabs contributed a flourishing legacy of crops including oranges, lemons, melons and pistachios which all are part of the vibrant agricultural economy today. The Normans left behind their castles, cathedrals and fair skinned, blue eye genes. And the centuries of Spanish and Austrian control from afar help make Sicily vulnerable to its latest ruler, unofficially of course, the Mafia. Today, some claim that the Mafia remains the island's most profitable industry, with an estimated annual income of between $4 and 6 billion.

Besides the Mafia, which you can study by going on officially sanctioned tours of local Mafia sights, the extensive historical sites related to the other former powers are part of the island's attraction. Among the ancient Greek ruins on the island are the Greek **Taormina theater** and **San Domenico Monastery** near **Messina**, the Greek theater in **Syracuse**, and the 5th-century BCE **Temple of Concord** in **Agrigento**. It's also a fun adventure to visit the **Isole Eolie**, off the north shore by Messina.

Early Settlements

Before invaders came to Sicily, we know, based on excavations at **Realmonte** near Agrigento, that man's

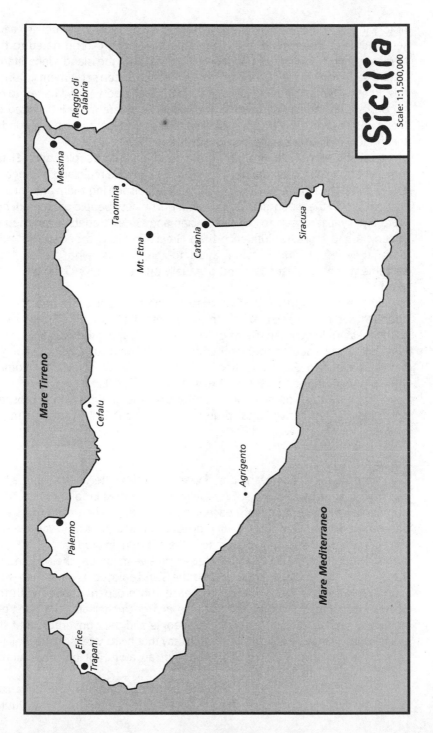

Sicilia
Scale: 1:1,500,000

Reggio di Calabria

Messina

Taormina

Mt. Etna

Catania

Siracusa

Mare Tirreno

Cefalu

Agrigento

Palermo

Mare Mediterraneo

Erice
Trapani

history in Sicily dates back to the early Paleolithic period. There are also early settlements at **Stentinello** and **Lipari** that have been carbon dated to the Neolithic period. During the Copper and Bronze ages, the island's inhabitants traded with many of the other developing Mediterranean settlements. During this time the **Isole Eolie** and its capital Lipari rose in power and began to go off on its own tangent separate from Sicily. They were more influenced by Malta and the western Peloponnesian culture, while Sicily came mainly under the influence of **Greece** and the **Phoenicians**.

Near the end of the Bronze Age, a contingent of people called **Siculi** (which helps explain the island's name) came from the mainland and began to dominate the small settlements of the island, dispersing them and forcing them inland to the mountains for protection. The new people prospered, but were mainly just vassals to the Phoenician and Greek traders. Even though Phoenicia had a greater influence than Greece in Sicily, especially the port cities, they left the main colonization to the Greeks, who started their settlements on the east coast and gradually pushed the Siculi people westward.

By the fifth century BCE, **Syracuse** on the east coast had become the strongest settlement and had helennized almost all of Sicily. The Siculi looked to the western Phoenician towns of Marsala and Trapani for assistance; they were holding fast against the Greek colonization. As a result a war was fought between the two Sicilian factions, which had to be settled by Roman intervention with the two **Punic Wars** of 264–212 BCE.

With the Roman domination, the interior of the island began to prosper. Splendid villas and fertile fields sprung up throughout Sicily, providing much of Rome's produce.

Foreign Invasions

After the fall of Rome, the island was invaded by the Vandals in the 5th century CE, then by the Goths. Eventually the Byzantine Empire took control and almost three centuries of peace lasted until 826. Then the Moors and Saracens took control of Sicily. Their biggest change to the island was to move the capital from Syracuse to **Palermo**, where it remains today.

In 1061, the Norman conquest began (five years before their successful invasion of another island, England) and the island enjoyed its most successful period in history. In 1302, the era of peace and prosperity ended with the Spanish domination. This period saw the rich get richer and the poor get poorer, creating a division between the people and their governors that still exists today. It may be an exaggeration to say that history passed the Sicilians by for the next five hundred years, but not an awful lot of consequence occurred during this long period.

Then on May 11, 1860, **Garibaldi** landed at Marsala and began to dismantle the Kingdom of Sicily and merge it with the Kingdom of Italy. During this time the people were greatly oppressed, which gave rise to the beginnings of what we know today as the **Mafia**. At the beginning of the twentieth century, a massive emigration began, mainly to America and Australia, spreading the Sicilian culture all over the world.

Sicily Today

Sicily has since to recover economically and remains a poverty-stricken island off the coast of Italy, still basically controlled by the Mafia. Everything from the government to industry bends to their will, making it even more difficult for the island to recover. But the Sicilians are fiercely independent people, and most are working hard to combat organized crime and overcome their poor economic situation.

Besides its rich ancient history, there are many other reasons to visit Sicily: water sports, beaches of rock and sand (including black sand), natural beauty, great food and friendly people (for the most part). For touring, the island can be roughly divided into the north shore and south shore areas. The **north shore** has reefs, olive groves, secluded coves and countless seaside resorts, including **Cefalu**, a gorgeous Arab-Norman city with good beaches.

In the center of the north coast is **Palermo**, the ancient and current capital and the island's largest city with a population of approximately 801,000. Be sure to visit the central market and 12th-century **Monreale Cathedral**, which has impressive biblical mosaics. About 80 km west of Palermo lies the ancient village of **Erice**, atop a mountain, where you can still find the remains of a temple dedicated to Venus.

The **southern coast** has an even milder climate than the North, which means you can enjoy swimming most of the year, although between November and March it can get quite chilly. Among the areas not to be missed are **Agrigento** (to see the **Valley of the Temples**) and **Mt**. **Etna**, an active volcano just topping 3,200 meters on the east coast. The last time the volcano erupted was in January 1992. The time previous to that was in March 1987, when two people were killed. Although scientists say it can erupt at any time, if you play it safe you shouldn't be in any danger. There is also good winter skiing around Mt. Etna that offers great ocean views.

Arrivals & Departures
By Air

As of press time, there were no direct flights from North America or Australia to either Catania in the east or Palermo in the west. You will have to fly through Milan or Rome first, then transfer to **Alitalia** to get to Sicily. Fares today are changing very rapidly, but expect to pay about $300 for a round-trip between Rome and Palermo, and about $302 for a round-trip between Rome and Catania. It may be slightly cheaper if you purchase your tickets in Italy, but it might also be more expensive ... go figure.

You can get direct flights from London to both Palermo and Catania, so this could be an option for you when traveling from North America or Australia. There are also direct flights from Dublin to both Palermo and Catania. In conjunction, you can catch a flight from all major Italian cities directly to Palermo or Catania, so if you're already in Italy and have the urge to see Sicily it is easy, but not inexpensive, to get to the island.

By Car
The drive down to Sicily through southern Italy is beautifully scenic, especially down the coast, but it takes quite a while. From Rome it will take over 14 hours just to get to Messina. But if you have the time, the scenery is wonderful, and if you don't have the money to fly you can drive, take the train, the ferry, or the hydrofoil.

By Ferry
There are over twenty ferries a day from **Reggio di Calabria** to **Messina** (cost is E5), as well as a hydrofoil service that is faster (E4) but doesn't allow cars. You can also catch ferries from the cities listed below as well as others in Italy:
• **Genoa to Palermo**, 23 hours
• **Naples to Palermo**, 11 hours
• **Naples to Catania to Syracuse**, 15 hours/19 hours
• **Naples to the Aeolian Islands to Milazzo**, 7 hours/8 hours
• **Cagliari Sardinia to Palermo**, 14 hours
• **Cagliari to Trapani**, 11 hours
• **Livorno to Palermo**, 19 hours

So if you are in one of these cities, have time to spare, and don't get seasick too easily, try the ferry option.

By Hydrofoil
For a faster alternative to ferries from Naples, try the hydrofoil. It'll cost a little more but the ride will be smoother and it will be over sooner.
• **Naples to Palermo**, 5 hours and 30 minutes
• **Naples to the Aeolian Islands to Milazzo**, 4-6 hours

By Train
If you like long train rides you can enjoy the southern Italian scenery and take the train from any place in Italy to Sicily. From Rome it will take over 14 hours just to get to Messina. But if you have the time, the scenery is wonderful, and if you don't have the money to fly this is a nice, scenic option.
The train fare from Rome is E50. The ferry ride from Reggio di Calabria is included in the train fare.

Climate & Weather

The climate of Sicily varies throughout the entire island. To the north, along the coast, you can expect hot summers and mild winters making it perfectly Mediterranean. The temperatures along the southern coast and inland are much higher and you can have more drastic temperature fluctuations. Rain is rare but it does increase with altitude. This makes Sicily, strangely enough, a great place to ski in the winter, since the mountains above 1,600 meters get covered with snow.

In the summer expect to experience the hot and humid *Scirocco* winds that blow in from the Sahara, bringing with it discomfort and clouds of reddish dust.

When to Go

Sicilians will tell you that anytime is a good time to travel to Sicily, and they aren't kidding. The climate doesn't vary greatly, making Sicily a pleasant trip any time of year – although the summers can get unbearably hot at times. The northern coast's climate is more stable than that of the southern coast and inland. If you want to try the beach from November to March, it's not a good idea, since it will be like autumn back in the US.

So the best time to go to Sicily and enjoy good warm weather is September through the first week in November. To enjoy good skiing, go between December and March.

Public Holidays & Festivals

Offices and shops in Sicily are closed on the following dates, so prepare for the eventuality of having virtually everything closed. This is your cue to stock up on picnic snacks, soda, whatever, because in most cities and towns there is no such thing as a 24-hour 7-11.
- **January 1**, New Year's Day
- **January 6**, Epiphany
- **April 25**, Liberation Day (1945)
- **Easter Monday**
- **May 1**, Labor Day
- **August 15**, *Ferragosto* and Assumption of the Blessed Virgin (climax of Italian family holiday season. Hardly anything stays open in the big cities through the month of August)
- **November 1**, All Saints Day
- **December 8**, Immaculate Conception
- **December 25/26**, Christmas

Local Events & Festivals
- **Agrigento**, *Sagra del Mandorlo in Fiore*, 1st to 2nd Sunday in February
- **Catania**, *Festa di San Agata*, February 3-5

- **Acireale**, *Carnevale Acese*, Sunday and Shrove Tuesday
- **Sciacca**, *Carnevale*, Sunday and Shrove Tuesday
- **Trapani**, *Processione del misteri*, Good Friday and Easter Sunday
- **Marsala**, *Sacra rappresentazione*, Holy Thursday
- **Acata**, *Festa di San Vincenzo*, 3rd Sunday after Easter
- **Pergusa**, *Sagra del Lago*, 1st Sunday in May
- **Naro**, *Festa di San Calogero*, June 18
- **Palermo**, *Festa di U Fistinu*, July 11-15
- **Marsala**, *Sagra del Vino Marsala*, 3rd Sunday in July
- **Messina**, *Passeggiata dei giganti*, August 14
- **Siracusa**, *Festa di San Lucia*, December 13

Getting Around Sicily

Sicily is connected by an extensive highway system, a superb train system, and naturally, since Sicily is an island, a complete shipping service involving ferries, hydrofoils, and liners. Your mode of transport will depend on how long you're staying in Sicily and what you want to see.

If you're only visiting coastal towns, it might be fun to take a ferry between them. If you are going to rural, off the beaten path locations, you'll need a car, because even if the train did go to where you're going, the *Locale* would take forever since it stops at every town on its tracks.

By Train

You can get most anywhere in Sicily by train, much the same as on the mainland. There are more extensive rail systems on the east of the island to accommodate the flow of trains from the mainland. Here you should expect delays since the trains may have had trouble getting across on the ferry.

There are some small towns that the trains do not go to, but you should avoid these anyway. You never know when you're going to stumble onto something better left unseen in one of the mountain villages.

By Car

The expressways, called **Autostrada**, are superhighways and toll roads. They connect all major Sicilian cities and have contributed to the tremendous increase in tourist travel. By car is the best way to see Sicily since you don't have to wait for the trains, which are inevitably delayed, something that rarely happens on the mainland.

Driving is the perfect way to see the entire variety of Sicily's towns, villages, seascapes, landscapes, and monuments. The Sicilian drivers may be a little *pazzo* (crazy), but if you drive confidently you'll be fine. A word of caution, again: Sicily is best explored along its coastline and a little inland. Once you start roaming through the mountain towns, unless you know what you're doing, anything could happen.

Car Rental in Sicily

You have all the major international and national players in the car rental business here in Sicily. Below please find a list of their addresses and phones numbers separated by city.

CATANIA
- **Avis**, *Via V. Giufridda 19/21, Tel. 095/9544-5536*
- **Hertz**, *Airport, Tel. 095/341-595*

MESSINA
- **Avis**, *Via Vittorio Emanuele 35, Tel. 090/66-26-79*
- **Hertz**, *Via Vittorio Emanuele 113, Tel. 090/363-740*

PALERMO
- **Avis**, *Via Principe di Scordia 12, Tel. 091/586-940; Aeroporto di Punta Raisi, Tel. 091/591-684*
- **Hertz**, *Via Messina 7, Tel. 091/381-688; Aeroporto di Punta Raisi, Tel. 091/213-112-682*

SYRACUSE
- **Avis**, *Via Savoia 13, Tel. 0931/61125*

TAORMINA
- **Avis**, *Via S. Pancrazio 6, Tel. 0942/23041*
- **Hertz**, *Via Don Bosco 10, Tel. 0942/23282*

Basic Information

Banking Hours

Banks in Sicily are open Monday through Friday 8:30am to 1:30pm and from 3:00pm to 4:00pm, and are closed Saturdays, Sundays and national holidays. In some cities the afternoon open hour may not even exist. Even if the bank is closed, most travelers checks can be exchanged for Italian lire at most hotels and shops and at the many foreign exchange offices in railway stations and at airports.

Business Hours

Store hours are usually Monday through Friday 9:00am to 1:00pm, 3:30/4:00pm to 7:30/8:00pm, and Saturdays 9:00am to 1:00pm. Most stores are closed on Sundays and on national holidays. Don't expect to find any 24-hour convenience stores just around the corner. If you want to have some soda in your room after a long day of touring you need to plan ahead.

Also, you must plan on most stores not being open from 1:00pm to 4:00pm. This is Sicily's siesta time. Don't expect to get a lot done except find a nice restaurant and enjoy the pleasant afternoons.

Consulates
• **United States**, *Via GB Vaccarini 1, Palermo. Tel. 091/302-590*

Safety & Precautions
Sicilian cities are definitely much safer than any equivalent American city. You can walk most anywhere without fear of harm, but that doesn't mean you shouldn't play it safe. Listed below are some simple rules to follow to ensure that nothing bad occurs:
• At night, make sure the streets you are walking on have plenty of other people. Like I said, most cities are safe, but at night in certain areas the rules change.
• Always have your knapsack or purse flung over the shoulder that is not directly next to the road. Why? There have been cases of Italians on motorbike snatching purses off old ladies and in some cases dragging them a few blocks.
• Better yet, have your companion walk on the street side, while you walk on the inside of the sidewalk with the knapsack or purse.
• Better still is to buy one of those tummy wallets that goes under your shirt so no one can even be tempted to purse-snatch you. That's really all you should need, but always follow basic common sense; if you feel threatened, scared, alone, retrace your steps back to a place where there are other people.
• Be especially on guard against street thieves and pickpockets in Palermo and other large towns.

Sports & Recreation

Sicily is an island, thus the water sports at their beach resorts are prevalent. But they are also a mountainous island, so their skiing is actually quite good too, despite the fact that they are close to Africa. Sicily is a prime vacation spot for both winter and summer sports, so if you're in the mood for either while on the island you can find what you want.

Food & Wine
Food
Most Sicilian food is cooked with fresh ingredients raised or caught a short distance from the restaurant, making their dishes healthy, fresh, and satisfying. There are many restaurants in Sicily of international renown, but you

shouldn't limit yourself only to the upper echelon. In most cases you can find as good a meal at a fraction the cost at any *trattoria*. Also, many of the upper echelon restaurants you read about are only in business because they cater to the tourist trade. Their food is good, but the atmosphere is a little hokey.

The traditional Sicilian meal has been influenced by the Middle East, Greece, France, and Spain as a result of the island's past conquests. Other influences include the sea (what better place to find a meal) and the fact that the island's climate is perfect for growing all sorts of herbs and spices, and vegetables and fruits.

Suggested Sicilian Cuisine

As I've said in other chapters, you don't have to eat all the traditional courses listed below. Our constitution just isn't prepared for such mass consumption.

Antipasto - Appetizer
- **Arancine di Riso** – Rice balls filled with meat sauce and peas; very Middle Eastern
- **Antipasto Di Mare** – Mixed seafood appetizer plate; differs from restaurant to restaurant
- **Tomate, Mozzarella ed olio** – Tomato and mozzarella slices covered in olive oil with a hint of basil
- **Minestre di pesce** – Fish soup; varies by region and restaurant

Primo Piatto - First Course
Pasta
- **Pasta con le sarde** – Made with sardines, raisins, pine nuts, onions, tomatoes, fennel and saffron
- **Spaghetti alla Norma** – Made with tomato, fried eggplant and ricotta cheese; typical of Eastern Sicily
- **Penne alla Paola** – Short ribbed pasta tubes made with broccoli, pine nuts and raisins
- **CousCous** – Made with fish, chicken, beans or broccoli; Middle Eastern

Zuppa – Soup
- **Minestre di pesce** – Fish soup; varies by region and restaurant

Secondo Piatto – Entrée
Carne – Meat
- **Involtini** – Meat stuffed with cheese and onions
- **Falsomagro** – Meat stuffed with salami, hard–boiled eggs and cheese
- **Coniglio alla cacciatore** – Rabbit cooked with red wine, tomatoes and spices

Pesce – Fish
- **Tonno alla cipollata** – Tuna made with onions
- **Pesce spada alla ghiotta** – Swordfish made with tomatoes, olives and capers
- **Pesce spada alla griglia** – Grilled swordfish

Contorno – Vegetable
- **Caponata** – Eggplant, tomatoes, spices, capers, olives, tuna eggs and shrimps cooked together
- **Fritella** – tomatoes, onions, artichokes, beans and peas all stewed together

Formaggio – Cheese
- **Pecorino** – Sheep's cheese
- **Piacentino** – Pecorino flavored with peppercorns and saffron

Dolce - Dessert
- **Cassata** – Sponge cakes made with ricotta, almond paste, chocolate and candied fruits
- **Cannoli** – fried pastry with a mixture like the Cassata

Wine
Sicily's best wines are **Etna** (red and white, wide variety) from the Catania area and **Marsala** (white, dry or sweet) from the Trapani province. You should also try some **Casteldaccio**, a dry white from around Palermo, and if you like sweet wine, an **Eloro** from around Syracuse should suffice. If you're on the Eolie Islands, try their unique red and white **Malvasia**.

Messina

Ninety percent of **Messina** was destroyed in the earthquake of 1908, after which the city was rebuilt with wide avenues intersecting at right angles, making her an entirely modern looking city. Some of the most famous buildings were painstakingly reconstructed, but they too met their demise during the Allied bombings during World War II. But prior to all this destruction the city was so quaint and charming that William Shakespeare used it as the setting for his play *Much Ado About Nothing* (see sidebar on *Shakespeare's Italy* in Chapter 10).

Messina is your main point of entry into Sicily from the mainland, so you will most probably have to pass through this unimpressive city. This is a place to stay only if you're so exhausted from your journey down to Sicily that you cannot make it any further. Otherwise continue on with your journey.

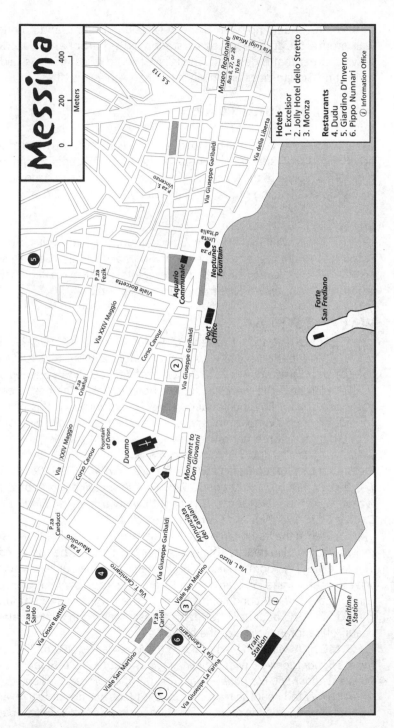

Messina

0 200 400
Meters

S.S. 113

P.za S. Vincenzo

Via Luigi Micali

Museo Regionale
Bus 8, 27, or 28
10 km

Via della Liberta

Via Giuseppe Garibaldi

P.za d'Italia

Neptune's Fountain

Aquario Communale

P.za Fezik

Viale Boccetta

Via XXIV Maggio

Corso Cavour

Port Office

Via Giuseppe Garibaldi

Forte San Frediano

Fountain of Orion

Via XXIV Maggio

Corso Cavour

Duomo

Monument to Don Giovanni

Annunziata dei Catalani

P.za Cristuli

P.za Carducci

P.za Maurolico

Via T. Cannizzaro

Via Giuseppe Garibaldi

Via L. Rizzo

P.za Lo Sardo

Via Cesare Battisti

Viale San Martino

Via T. Cannizzaro

P.za Carioli

Viale San Martino

Viale San Martino

Via Giuseppe La Farina

Train Station

Maritime Station

Hotels
1. Excelsior
2. Jolly Hotel dello Stretto
3. Monza

Restaurants
4. Dudu
5. Giardino D'Inverno
6. Pippo Nunnari

ⓘ Information Office

Women should not walk alone in Messina at night, and no one should walk around the area near the train station or the harbor after dark. Never go down a street that is deserted. This is just a word of caution. As said before, Italian and Sicilian cities are much safer than American cities.

Getting Around Town

By Bus

If you want to catch the bus to save your weary feet, you need to purchase tickets from any *Tabacchi* or newsstand for Eurto 75 cents, or get an all-day pass for E3. To get to the Museo Regionale, you need to catch the northbound yellow buses traveling on the Via Garibaldi numbered 8, 27, or 28.

By Foot

The city is walkable from the train station, the hydrofoil station, or the Stazione Maritima to any of the sights and each other. The only sight not accessible from the main disembarkation points is the Museo Regionale, which is about 45 minutes on foot from the train station.

Where To Stay

1. **EXCELSIOR**, *Via Maddalena 32, 98100 Messina. Tel. 090/293-8721. 44 rooms, 7 with bath, only 22 with shower. Single without E20-40; Single with E50-60; Double without E40-55; Double with E60-80. Visa accepted. *****

Located near the train station, this hotel is not in the best area but the prices are cheap. But then again so are the amenities in this place: no air conditioning, no TV, no room service, not all the rooms have bath or shower. How did it get a three star rating? If you're a budget traveler, this is the least expensive place to stay with any star rating.

2. **JOLLY HOTEL DELLO STRETTO**, *Via Garibaldi 126, 98100 Messina, Tel. 090/363-860, Fax 090/590-2526. E-mail: messina@jollyhotels.it. Web: www.jollyhotels.it. 96 rooms, 48 with bath, 48 with shower. Single E100-110; Double E120-140. No credit cards accepted. ******

Located in the harbor area off the main street Via Garibaldi, this is the only really good hotel in the city. They have their own private beach, air conditioning, satellite TV, room service, laundry service, a passable restaurant that serves local cuisine and an inviting bar. The rooms are kept clean and comfortable (the air conditioning helps in the summer) and bathrooms are immaculate. The abundant buffet breakfast is served in a large salon with a beautiful panoramic vista of the harbor.

3. **MONZA**, *Viale San Martino 63, 98100 Messina. Tel. 090/673-755, Fax is the same. 58 rooms only 36 with shower. Single without E20-30; Single with E40-50; Double without E50-60; Double with E60-70. No credit cards accepted. ****

Also located near the train station, this place has absolutely no amenities except for phones in the room — that have to go through a switchboard — and only passable heat in the winter. Only stay here as a last resort, or if you can't afford anything else.

Where to Eat

4. DUDU, *Via C Battisti 122, Tel. 090/674-393. Closed Mondays and the last week in September. American Express accepted. Dinner for two E38.*

Located between the train station and the Duomo, this is a small place with seating for only 30 patrons. Dudu serves wonderful local dishes and has a down home rustic atmosphere. The specialty of the house is the *stoccafisso "alla ghiotta,"* a pungent and tasty ensemble of stock fish made with tomatoes, capers, olives and onions. For dessert try their *torta di limone* (lemon pie). Seating outside available.

5. GIARDINO D'INVERNO NINO LIBRO, *Viale Boccetta 381, Tel. 090/ 362-413. Closed Mondays and 15 days in August. Credit cards accepted. Dinner for two E50.*

Located a small distance from the harbor and the center of the city. You'll need to take a cab here and back. They make local, traditional favorites as well as creating new and different dishes. They have the local *pesce stocco "alla ghiotta"* (stock fish made with tomatoes, capers, olives and onions) as well as *crespelle ai profumi di Sicilia* (pasta pancakes stuffed with tomatoes, basil, eggplant, and beef or horse meat).

6. PIPPO NUNNARI, *Via Ugo Bassi 157, Tel. 090/293-8584. Closed Mondays and August. Credit cards accepted. Dinner for two E50.*

A classic and elegant environment. Remember to dress appropriately for a meal here. The food is simple but satisfying. Open with an antipasto of marinated fish or the basic *insalata di mare* (seafood salad). For the next course you have to try the *fettucine alla "Nunnari"* which is pasta with eggplant, ham, tomatoes and mozzarella. For the final dish try any of their fish *alla brace* (cooked over open flames) especially the *pesce spada* (swordfish), which was probably caught that morning.

Seeing the Sights

Really the only place to visit when in Messina is the **Museo Regionale** (*Via della Liberta 465; open Monday–Saturday 9:00am–1:30pm and 3:00pm– 5:30pm, Sundays 9:00am–12;30pm; admission E3; take bus 8, 27, or 28*). You'll find many paintings and sculptures, such as works by **Caravaggio**, including the *Adoration of the Shepherds* and the *Resurrection of Lazarus*. You can also find Sicilian hand-crafted works including embroidery, silver, and fabric work.

Another point of interest is the **Duomo** (*Piazza Duomo; open 8:00am– noon and 4:00pm–7:00pm*). Originally built by Roger II, this **cathedral** has undergone many reconstructions and the only original parts that remain are her basilica-style floor plan with three aisles. Destroyed by two earthquakes and engulfed in flames, all the precious mosaics and frescoes perished years ago. Today it's a rather bland example of what it used to be. The best sight to see here is the **Fontana di Orione** in the middle of the square. Designed in 1547 by Florentine artist Montorosoli, a pupil of Michelangelo, this statue depicts several reclining nudes.

Across the piazza from the Duomo is the smaller **Chiesa Annunziata dei Catalani** (*Via Giuseppe Garibaldi; open 8:30am–noon and 3:30pm–6:30pm*) built in the same period. Another bland church, but one that is a little more interesting architecturally than the Duomo. In the Piazzetta dei Catalani near the church is the 16th century **Monument to Don Giovanni d'Austria**.

A final sight of interest is the **Aquario Comunale** (*Via Mazzini, Tel. 48897; open 9:00am–2:00pm; admission E3*) which is a relaxing place to come when everything else is closed. Here you can enjoy the colorful fish as they float in their tranquil world.

Practical Information
Local Festivals & Holidays
The **Ferragosto Messinese** is held on August 13th and 14th every year where the mythical giants of Mata and Grifone are paraded through the streets of the town. The festival ends with the feast of the Assumption on August 15th, a religious procession headed by a statue of Mary atop a pole surrounded by *angeli*. A wonderful example of a blending of pre-Christian and Christian celebrations.

Postal Services
The **central post office**, *in the Piazza Antonello (Tel. 090/77-41-90)*, is near the Duomo. *Open Monday through Friday 8:30am–5:00pm, Saturdays 9:00am–12 noon*. But if you're in a hurry, stamps can be bought at any tobacconist (stores indicated by a **T** sign outside), and mailed at any mailbox, which are red and marked with the word *Poste* or *Lettere*.

Tourist Information & Maps
There is a **tourist office** outside of the train station to the right *in Piazza della Repubblica, Tel. 090/674-236, and another in Piazza Carioli, Tel. 090/ 293-5292, both of which are only open from 8:30am to 1:00pm, Monday through Saturday.*

Both places will give you tourist information about the surrounding areas and useful city and area maps.

Cefalu

Cefalu is a small port of exquisite beauty located on the north shore of Sicily. Once a quiet little fishing village, today it is one of Sicily's main tourist attractions, and as a result Cefalu has lost little of its charm and character. It's a great place to spend a couple of days exploring the winding streets surrounded by Norman, Arab and medieval architecture.

You can walk along the Vittorio Emanuele and escape back in time as you see fishermen mending ageless nets in the high vaulted boathouses that line the water. On the same street is a relic from the Saracen occupation, the **lavatoio**, an ancient bath house and laundromat (*Via Vittorio Emanuele, open 8:00am–1:00pm and 3:30pm–7:00pm*). You can also enjoy the pristine beaches that surround the city. From the train station to the south and into the *centro storico* of Cefalu, everything is within easy walking distance.

Palermo is only an hour away by train, so conceivably you could venture here as a day trip from the capital. If you haven't done so yet, you can also get to the **Lipari Islands** from here by taking a hydrofoil.

Where To Stay

Most of the hotels in the area are outside of the old city and near the spectacular beaches, none of which is a four star. I have listed here the best three hotels near the *centro storico* and the best beachside resort near the city at the Beach Mezzaforno.

1. BAIA DEL CAPITANO, *Spiaggia Mazzaforno, 90015 Cefalu. Tel. 0921/20005, Fax 0921/21063. Web: www.cefalu.it/dove_alloggiare.htm. 39 rooms, 9 with bath, 30 with shower. Single E60-70; Double E80-110. Full board E90 per person. All credit cards accepted. Breakfast included. ****

Located a short distance out of town on one of the two best beaches around, this is the one of the best hotels in the area. They have their own private beach, snorkeling equipment for rent, water skiing, beautiful views, a swimming pool, tennis courts, sauna, day care for little kids and a wonderful restaurant. The hotel is small which helps make the service extra attentive. They also have a shuttle bus to pick you up at the train station and to transport you back and forth into town. The rooms are tiny but are comfortable. They have their own little terraces with panoramic views.

2. KALURA, *Via V. Cavallero 13, 90015 Cefalu. Tel. 0921/21354, Fax 0921/22501. 80 rooms all with bath. Single E80. Double E130. All credit cards accepted. Breakfast included. *****

A little ways out of town and completely immersed in Mediterranean vegetation, this place offers a uniquely beautiful panoramic view. The building itself is not new and definitely shows its age, but is well maintained. The rooms are clean, comfortable and spacious, and each has its own terrace (to get a sea view will cost E15 extra). Your meals are served on a terrace. There is a pool

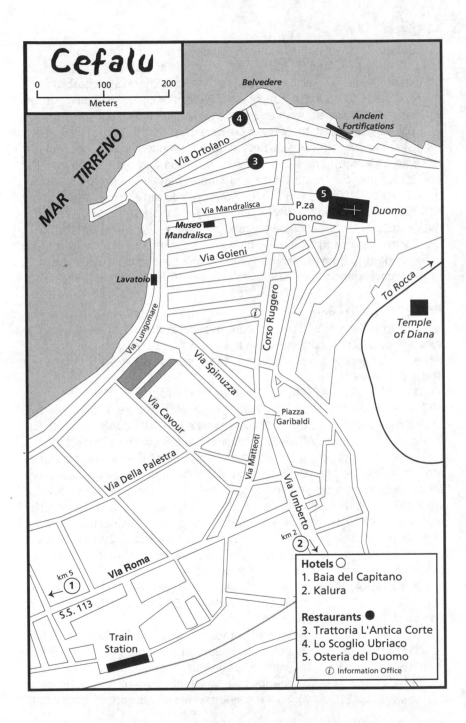

Cefalu

0   100   200
Meters

MAR TIRRENO

Belvedere

Ancient Fortifications

Via Ortolano

Via Mandralisca

Museo Mandralisca

Via Goieni

Lavatoio

Via Lungomare

Corso Ruggero

P.za Duomo

Duomo

To Rocca

Temple of Diana

Via Spinuzza

Via Cavour

Piazza Garibaldi

Via Della Palestra

Via Matteoti

Via Umberto

km 2

km 5

Via Roma

S.S. 113

Train Station

Hotels ○
1. Baia del Capitano
2. Kalura

Restaurants ●
3. Trattoria L'Antica Corte
4. Lo Scoglio Ubriaco
5. Osteria del Duomo
ⓘ Information Office

for adults and one for kids and a lovely park to play in. On top of all that the hotel organizes trips and walks for all guests.

Where To Eat

There are many little restaurants and *trattorie* that have sprouted up because of the tourist trade. These are three of the best:

3. L'ANTICA CORTE, *Cortille Pepe 7, Tel. 0921/23228. Closed Thursdays and all of November and December. Credit cards accepted. Dinner for two E35.*

Located in a small courtyard that exudes ambiance, here you can feel as if you walked back in time while also enjoying fantastic food. Their terrace in the small courtyard is the best place to enjoy your meal. You'll have plenty of options since their menu is super extensive. Try any of their pastas, especially a local favorite *taglierine all'anchova e mollica* (pasta with anchovies, bread crumbs and oil) or *spaghetti al ragu* (with a super tasty meat and tomato sauce). Most of the ingredients come from the area so everything is fresh. They even make their own pasta.

4. LO SCOGLIO UBRIACO, *Via CO di Bordonaro 24, Tel. 0921/23370. Closed Tuesdays, but not in summer, and November. Credit cards accepted. Dinner for two E38.*

Sit at their beautiful terrace by the sea that offers magnificent panoramic views. In the high season reserve well in advance to get a good table outside. The atmosphere is peaceful, the service professional, and the food perfect. Try some of their *spaghetti al cartoccio* (with a spicy tomato-based sauce and a variety of seafood) or *spaghetti alla barcola* (with a subtle tomato-based sauce and swordfish). For seconds, sample the exquisite *fritti misti* (fried calamari and shrimp) and you'll leave truly satisfied.

5. OSTERIA DEL DUOMO, *Via Seminario 5, Tel. 0921/21838. Closed Mondays and December. Credit cards accepted. Dinner for two E40.*

The ambiance here, with the cathedral so close you can almost touch it, is historically exciting, especially out on their terrace. The owner Enzo Barranco will greet you at the door and is as hospitable as can be, even if his English is not that good. Try the amazing and incredible *penne in barca* (tubular pasta in a tasty clam and oil sauce). Try any of their grilled fish, whose smell permeates the inside of the place.

Seeing the Sights

The views from the mountain are especially rewarding, so try and get up it. It's a great walk. Besides the natural beauty surrounding this lovely town, take time to visit the **Duomo** (*open 9:00am–noon and 3:30–7:00pm*), an austere 12th century Norman cathedral built during the reign of Roger II. The scene of the fortress-like Duomo located at the base of the **Rocca**, the large head-shaped hillock that dominates the town is quite impressive. Inside you'll find 16 columns supporting beautiful Saracen-style horseshoe arches, and some of the most impressive mosaics left in Sicily. These mosaics stand out even more since the rest of the interior is quite bland. To enter you need to be wearing proper dress. No shorts, short skirts, thin-strapped dresses, tank tops, etc., allowed.

Situated on Via Mandralisca, which connects with the Piazza Duomo, is the **Museo Mandralisca** (*Tel. 21547; open 9:00am–12;30pm and 4:00pm–7:00pm; admission E5*) which houses a fine collection of Greek ceramics, paintings, pottery and more. My favorite is the *Portrait of an Unknown Man* by the 15th century artist Antonello de Messina.

To get a great view of the city and its harbor, take the half-hour walk up the mountain to **The Rocca**. Follow the steps of the Salita Saraceni, and the signs that start near the Piazza Garibaldi just off the Via Ruggero. On the mountain you'll be following walkways lined with medieval walls that lead to the **Temple of Diana**. Built in the 5th century BCE, it was first used as a place of worship and sacrifice, then later was employed in defense of the city.

Sports & Recreation
You can catch a bus to the best **beaches** in front of the train station or from the Piazza Garibaldi, halfway to the center of town. The cost to go to either **Spiaggia Mezzaforno** or **Spiaggia Settefrati**, two of the better beaches, is E3 each way.

Practical Information
Local Festivals & Holidays
During the summer months there are many music, dance, and performing arts exhibitions on the beaches of Cefalu and in the Cathedral. The best celebration is the **Festa di San Salvatore**, the town's patron saint, which includes fireworks and marching bands and singers.

Postal Services
The **central post office** in Cefalu is on the Via Vazzana off of Via Roma (*Tel. 0921/215-28*) near the station. *Open Monday through Friday 8:30am–5:00pm, Saturdays 9:00am–noon*. But if you're in a hurry, stamps can be bought at any tobacconist (stores indicated by a **T** sign outside), and mailed at any mailbox, which are red and marked with the word *Poste* or *Lettere*.

Tourist Information & Maps
• **Tourist Office**, *Via Corso Ruggero 77 (Tel. 0921/21-050) in the old city. Open Monday–Friday, 8:30am–2:00pm, 4:30pm–7:30pm, and Saturdays 9:00am–2:00pm.* They can supply you with useful maps of the city and area, information about bus schedules to get to the beaches around

Cefalu, and more. They also help with finding accommodations if you arrive without reservations.

Palermo

Palermo started off as a Phoenician city, which the Greeks referred to as Panormos. The city then came under Roman rule during the two **Punic Wars** in 254 BCE. After that they endured Byzantine rule (353–830 CE), then Saracen domination (830-1072), and finally Norman (1072-1194) influence placed its stamp on the city. These conquerors were succeeded by the Hohenstaufens in 1194, then the House of Anjou ruled from 1266 until a popular uprising in 1282.

After that, Palermo came under Argonese and Spanish rule and eventually passed to the Bourbons in the 18th century. It finally became part of Italy on May 27, 1860, when it was liberated by Garibaldi. Today Palermo is Italian but, some say the real rulers are the Mafia.

Palermo is large, busy, noisy, congested and polluted and is completely controlled by Mafia interests. Today there is the beginning of a popular backlash against *La Cosa Nostra's* influence in the city, evidenced by anti-Mafia posters appearing periodically on the walls. But as a tourist you have little to worry about from the Mafia. In Palermo you need to protect yourself against pickpockets and purse snatchers, especially if you roam away from the *centro storico*, but the Mafia has no interest in tourists other than to encourage them to come and spend money.

Centuries ago the city was divided into four quarters, which all merged at the square known as the **Quattro Canti** (four corners) in the center of town. This square is at the intersection of **Corso Vittorio Emanuele** and **Via Maqueda**. The **Albergheria** is northwest of the *quattro canti*, **Capo** is southwest, **Vucciria** is northeast and **La Kalsa** is southeast. Each of these quarters had distinct dialects, cultures, trading practices and markets for their products. There was limited intermingling since intermarriage would result in being ostracized.

Today, the area around the Quattro Canti is where most of the sights are located. Everything here is an eclectic mix of medieval streets and Norman, Oriental, and Baroque architecture, broad modern avenues and large buildings, and bombed-out vacant lots from World War II.

As such it is not nearly as charming as Florence or Venice, and it also has less historical architecture and museums than Rome; but Palermo is still an interesting city to explore. There's a heavy Middle Eastern influence, almost a *souk*-like atmosphere at some markets that differentiates Palermo from other Italian cities. Stay to see Palermo's sights, marvel in its sounds and smells, and then hop on a train and go explore some other less hectic part of Sicily.

To know what's happening now in Palermo, check out the official website: *www.comune.palermo.it/*.

Arrivals & Departures

By Air

You can fly into Palermo from Rome or Milan. The fare is changing all the time, but at last check it was $300 from Rome. It may be even higher by the time you read this, but look for various excursion fares or even package deals with **Alitalia** or **Lufthansa**, the major airlines flying in and out of Sicily. You can also get direct flights from London or Dublin to Palermo, so this could be an option if you are crossing the Atlantic.

By Train

Palermo is about one hour away from Cefalu by train.

Other Options

Bus will be your best budget travel option, but you can also get here by ferry or hydrofoil from other parts of Sicily or the mainland. Consult the various schedules from the town you plan to depart from for the most up-to-date information.

Getting Around Town

Palermo is a city you can enjoy walking in, but getting from one end of it to another can be tiring. That's why we recommend using the **public buses** whenever you can. They cost E1 for a ticket that lasts an hour. You buy them at *Tabacchi* (stores marked with a blue **T**) or at AMAT's kiosks. If you know you're going to be taking the bus a lot, buy an all day pass for E3. Remember to stamp a single ticket or a day ticket in the machines as you get on the bus. The day pass only needs to be stamped once and kept on your person in case an inspector shows up. If you don't have a ticket you will be immediately fined E25.

If you don't want to deal with the push and pull of public transport, simply flag down a taxi, but be prepared to get caught in traffic and watch your fare sky-rocket.

Where To Stay

1. CRISTAL PALACE, *Via Roma 477, 90139 Palermo. Tel. 091/611-2580, Fax 091/611-2589. 90 rooms, 39 with bath, 51 with shower. Single E90-105; Double E115-130. All credit cards accepted. Breakfast included. ****

Located on the busy and noisy Via Roma, this is a completely modern building made almost entirely of glass. Besides super clean and comfortable rooms with air conditioning and satellite TV, the hotel offers a restaurant, a piano bar, a disco, an American-style bar and a gymnasium. Each room has a separate level for work. The bathrooms are smallish with hairdryers and a minimal courtesy toiletry set. This is a good place to stay.

2. **EXCELSIOR**, *Via Marchese Ugo 3, 90139 Palermo. Tel. 091/625-6176, Fax 091/342-139. 128 rooms all with bath. Single E120-140; Double E140-160. All credit cards accepted. Breakfast included.* ★★★★

Centrally located, this hotel's former glory was resurrected in 1987 with a complete renovation of the premises. Near the English gardens for relaxing

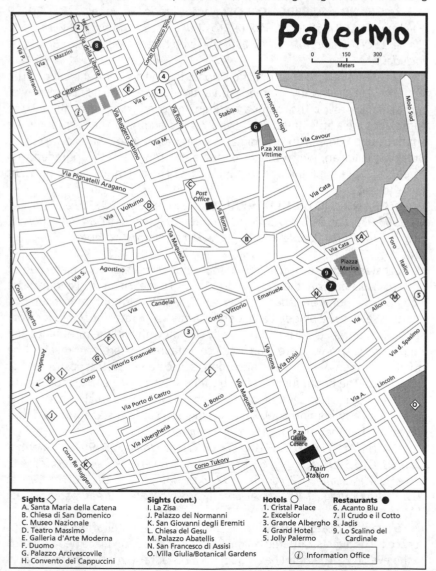

Sights ◇	Sights (cont.)	Hotels ○	Restaurants ●
A. Santa Maria della Catena	I. La Zisa	1. Cristal Palace	6. Acanto Blu
B. Chiesa di San Domenico	J. Palazzo dei Normanni	2. Excelsior	7. Il Crudo e il Cotto
C. Museo Nazionale	K. San Giovanni degli Eremiti	3. Grande Albergho	8. Jadis
D. Teatro Massimo	L. Chiesa del Gesu	4. Grand Hotel	9. Lo Scalino del
E. Galleria d'Arte Moderna	M. Palazzo Abatellis	5. Jolly Palermo	Cardinale
F. Duomo	N. San Francesco di Assisi		
G. Palazzo Arcivescovile	O. Villa Giulia/Botanical Gardens		
H. Convento dei Cappuccini		ⓘ Information Office	

walks and the Via della Liberta for shopping at their pricey boutiques. In the entrance and other public rooms the lamps are from the island of Murano, off Venice. The rooms are large, and come with soundproof windows to block out the traffic noise, but for some reason only 18 rooms have mini-bars. The best rooms are on the second floor with their beautiful bordeaux bedspreads and wall coverings. The bathrooms are a little small but have everything you need. If you need more room, the 16 suites offer it for about E50 more. And to top it off the service is professional and attentive. A great place to stay.

3. GRANDE ALBERGHO SOLE, *Via Vittorio Emanuele 291, 90139 Palermo. Tel. 091/581-811, Fax 091/611-0182. 154 rooms 138 with bath. Single E90-105; Double E115-130. All credit cards accepted. Breakfast included.* ***

Located a few paces from the Duomo in a hectic central location. The entrance hall is elegantly adorned with antiques along with a small display of archaeological relics. The rooms are adequately comfortable even though the furnishings are a little dated and have TV, radio and A/C. The bathrooms are spacious and come with a minimal courtesy toiletry set, but no hairdryer. Breakfast is Italian, which means coffee and a roll. Recently upgraded to a three star, but I think the designation is a bit of a stretch. But still a pleasant place to stay.

4. GRANDE HOTEL ET DES PALME, *Via Roma 398, 90139 Palermo. Tel. 091/583-933, Fax 091/331-545. 187 rooms, 103 with bath, 84 with shower. Single E140-160; Double E180-220. All credit cards accepted. Breakfast included.* ****

Located on the busy Via Roma, the windows here are double-paned so you are insulated from the traffic noise. This is a huge, clean, and comfortable hotel whose rooms are adequately sized. The ones with bathtubs instead of showers seem to be bigger. Each room also has a separate floor/area for work space. The entrance hall is magnificently elegant with antique furnishings and huge Doric columns. There is an in-house restaurant where your meal will be good but expensive. There is also room service and an American-style bar downstairs. The bountiful breakfast buffet is served in a 'yellow' room with a beautiful floral arrangement on the center table. One major plus is the presence of a swimming pool. Recently upgraded to four star status and they deserve it, but the prices have gone through the roof.

5. JOLLY HOTEL DEL FORO ITALICO, *Foro Italico 22, 90133 Palermo. Tel. 091/616-5090, Fax 091/616-1441. E-mail: palermo@jollyhotels.it. Web: www.jollyhotels.it. 277 rooms, 207 with bath, 70 with shower. Single E120-140; Double E140-170. All credit cards accepted. Breakfast included.* ****

Since it is located a ways from the center, the hotel offers shuttle bus service for its guests. Situated on the Foro Italico, it's a fun place people watch in the evenings. The hotel has a pool, nice restaurant, room service, laundry service, air conditioning and satellite TV in the rooms. The place, like all Jolly hotels, is as modern as they come, but it is mainly a businessman's hotel – meaning the rooms are medium sized. The bathrooms are comfortable and come with a complete courtesy toiletry set and a hairdryer. The buffet breakfast is a rich international spread in a room filled with mirrors and lamps made on the island of Murano near Venice. In summer breakfast is served in the gazebo in the interior garden

Where To Eat

6. **ACANTO BLU**, *Via F Guardinone 19, Tel. 091/326-258. Closed Sundays and September. No credit cards accepted. Dinner for two E30.*

A small little place that serves basic rustic cuisine. You can either enjoy the air conditioning inside or the terrace outside. Try some of the extensive *antipasto* table, especially the fried vegetables with a spicy hot sauce. Next try what they call *riso dei poeti* (rice of the poets), which contains apple, radish and fish. It is quite delectable. Then save the best for last, *funghi infornati cotti nella mollica condita con olio e peperoncini* (fresh mushrooms baked in a mold of bread served up with fresh olive oil and peperoncini).

7. IL CRUDO E IL COTTO, *Piazza Marina 45a, Tel. 091/616-9261. Closed Tuesdays and variable holidays. No credit cards accepted. Dinner for two E35.*

In the beautiful Piazza Marina you can get a great meal at this tiny family run *trattoria*. You have Laura in the kitchen and Franchino and Giovanni greeting people and working as waiters. Get a seat outside so you can enjoy the view. Try their *riso ai frutti di mare* (rice with mixed seafood) then a succulent *bistecca* (steak) or *pesce spada alla griglia* (grilled swordfish) for seconds. To wash it all down get some of their house wine, which comes from the local mountains.

8. **JADIS**, *Via Liberta 121, Tel. 091/349-323. Closed Sundays and Mondays and August. Open only at night. No credit cards accepted. Dinner for two E36.*

Located a few blocks north of the Museum of Modern Art, this is a very popular place with the arts crowd as well as with people who appreciate good food. You have a choice of outside seating, which is wonderful on cool evenings. Try their *carpaccio di vitello* or their *carpaccio di pesce spada* (steak of veal or swordfish)

9. **LO SCALINO DEL CARDINALE**, *Via Bottai 18, Tel. 091/3310124. Closed Mondays, for Lunch, and the last half of September. Credit cards accepted. Dinner for two E38.*

A great local place that is always packed during the week. With its terrace in use in the summer there seems to be plenty of space, but in the winter it's difficult to find a spot to eat. Try some of their *crocchette al latte* (croquets with milk) or *al primo sale fritto* (fried with a local cheese). For seconds, try their *pesce spada al profumo di Cardinale* (swordfish with a creamy sauce with sliced bell peppers).

Seeing the Sights
North of Corso Vittorio Emanuele

As you move from the east of Corso Vittorio Emanuele to the west, you may want to catch rides on the frequent **bus #27** to quicken your pace.

A. SANTA MARIA DELLA CATENA

Via Vittorio Emanuele. Open 8:00am–11:30am and 3:30pm–7:00pm.

Built in the early 16th century, this church is named after the chain that used to be dragged across the old harbor, **La Cala**, at night to protect the vessels inside. This used to be the main port of Palermo until it started silting up in the late sixteenth century. The main industrial shipping moved north and this little inlet was left to the fishermen. It's a great place to take a short stroll and take in the sights, smells, and sounds of the Sicilian seafarers.

Not far away, located almost at the eastern part of the city, is the **Porta Felice**, which was built in 1582 to compliment the slightly older **Porta Nuova**, which is all the way to the west. Since these two gates were once the ancient boundaries of old Palermo, this is a good place to start your tour, because from here you can get a good feel for the true extent of ancient Palermo.

Past Porta Felice is the popular promenade, **Foro Italico**, with its own little **amusement park**. On summer nights residents come out here to sit, talk, walk, stare, and share the beautiful evenings with each other.

B. CHIESA DI SAN DOMENICO

Piazza San Domenico. Open 7:30am–noon.

Walk down Via Vittorio Emanuele towards the Porta Nuova and take a right on Via Roma to get to the Piazza San Domenico and the church of the same name. This beautiful 17th century church with an 18th century facade is the burial site of many famous Sicilians. At night the facade and the statue-topped marble column are lit up, creating quite a spectacle. The perfect spot to sip an *aperitivo* at one of the outdoor cafés surrounding the piazza.

Just behind the church is the **Oratorio del Rosario di San Domenico**, which contains some interesting stucco work created by Giacomo Serpotta as well as a magnificent altar piece by Van Dyke (*Via dei Bambinai #16, open 7:30am–noon).*

C. MUSEO NAZIONALE

Piazza Olivella. Tel. 662-0220. Open Monday–Saturday 9:00am–1:30pm, Tuesdays and Fridays also open 3:00pm–5:30pm. Sundays and holidays only open 9:00am–12:30pm. Admission E3.

Go back to the Via Roma and walk north to the **National Museum**. Also known as the Museo Archeologico Regionale, if you've been out discovering Sicily's archaeological sites or intend to do so, you'll love this museum. Located in a former monastery, their collection of pre-historic relics, Etruscan, Greek, Egyptian and Roman pieces is quite extensive and well-presented.

The museum has frescoes from Pompeii, bronze works from Greece, Roman sculptures, and much more. Especially imposing are the 56 lion head water spouts taken from 5th century BCE Himera. This is one of the finest antiquities museums in all of Italy.

D. TEATRO MASSIMO
Piazza Verdi, 90139 Palermo. Tel 091/605-3111, Fax 091/605-3325 or 605-3324. Hours 9:00am–1:00pm and 4:00pm–7:00pm. Admission E3.

The **Teatro Massimo** is down Via Maqueda from the National Museum. Also known as Teatro Vittorio Emanuele, this theater was built from 1875 to 1897 and can seat 3,200 attendees. As such it is the second largest theater in Europe, second only to the opera house in Paris. Currently under renovation, you probably will not be able to get a tour inside, but it doesn't hurt to ask.

E. GALLERIA D'ARTE MODERNA
Gallery open Tuesday–Sunday 9:00am–1:00pm and 3–6:00pm. Admission E5.

I know you didn't come to Sicily to look at modern art, but a trip to the **Modern Art Museum** is a breath of fresh air after looking at relics all day long. Italy's art treasures don't all belong to the past, so visit here and see some beautiful and interesting modern works.

Nearby is the main **tourist office**, past the English gardens in front and past the equestrian statue of Garibaldi in the square. Stop here to get ideas about current happenings and what else to see in Palermo and elsewhere in Sicily.

Walk back down Via Roma to the **Quattro Canti** (The Four Corners) – Via Roma, Via Vittorio Emanuele and Via Maqueda – which converge here at what is the center of the old city.

F. DUOMO
Piazza del Cattedrale. Open 7:00am–noon and 4:00pm–7:00pm.

The **Duomo** is three hundred meters past the Quattro Canti on the Via Vittorio Emanuele. The church was begun by the Normans in 1185, and thereafter underwent many architectural transformations from the 13th century to the 18th, though the Norman towers and triple-apsed eastern side remain today. With its many styles, the intricate exterior is a joy to study. The same can't be said for the interior, which was recreated in a bland neoclassic style.

To the left as you enter you'll find six imposing tombs contains the bodies of past kings of Palermo, including Frederick II and Roger II. In the chapel to the right of the choir is the silver sarcophagus that contains the remains of the city's patron saint, Rosalia. The **treasury**, located to the right of the apse, is infinitely more interesting since it contains some exquisite, jewel-encrusted ancient clothing (E1 to enter). You also find remains of some saints preserved here.

G. PALAZZO ARCIVESCOVILE

Via Papireto Bonnello. Open Tuesday–Sunday 9:00am–1:00pm and 3:00pm–6:00pm.

Immediately southwest of the cathedral is the one-time **Archbishop's Palace** that contains the **Dioclesan Museum**. The museum features many works of art that were salvaged from other churches during the Allied bombings of World War II. If this is closed check out the **Mercato delle Pulci**, just up Via Bonello (next to the Palace) in **Piazza Peranni**. This is a great junk/antique market held everyday from 8:00am to 2:00pm.

A little further down the Via Vittorio Emanuele is the **Porta Nuova**, which was erected in 1535 to commemorate the Tunisian exploits of Charles V.

H. CONVENTO DEI CAPPUCCINI

Open Monday–Saturday 9:00am–noon and 3:00pm–5:00pm. The visit is free but a donation of about E2 per person is expected.

No, this isn't a shrine to that wonderful frothing espresso product, though it is a bizarre yet fascinating place, in a morbid kind of way. To get here, walk 1.5 km west past the Porta Nuova or catch bus #27 going west from the Via Vittorio Emanuele to the Via Pindemonte. After you get off, it's a short walk to the convent. Just follow the signs.

This is like something out of a horror movie. Bodies stacked everywhere. Almost 800 of them. For many centuries this convent was the burial place not only for church members but also for rich laymen. You'll find bodies preserved with a variety of methods with differing results. Some bodies still have their hair and skin. Others have decomposed completely. The saddest sight here, though, are the remains of the tiny infants and young children. A gruesome place to visit, yes; but an experience you will never forget.

I. LA ZISA

Open Monday –Saturday 9:00am–2:00pm. Sundays 9:00am–1:00pm. The visit is free.

Since you're already out here, you might as well walk a short way north to **La Zisa**, a huge palace begun by William I in 1160 and finished by his son William II. Go down the Via Corradino di Svevia, take a right on Via Eugenio L'Emiro (the first road), take an immediate left onto Via Edersi, then take the second right onto Viale Luigi Castiglia and you'll turn left after about fifty meters into the *piazza* that houses La Zisa. This is a wonderful replica of an Arabian palace (Zisa means *magnificent* in Arabic) and was used as a retreat for the king where he had lush exotic gardens tended and wild animals housed.

South of Corso Vittorio Emanuele
J. PALAZZO DEI NORMANNI
Open Monday-Friday 9:00am-noon and 3:00pm-5:00pm and Saturdays and Sundays 9:00am-11:00am. The chapel is closed Sundays.

The **Norman** or **Royal Palace**, just past the Porta Nuova going east on Corso Vittorio Emanuele, is a terrific place. Originally built by the Saracens and remodeled and reinforced by the Normans, this is an imposing fortress-like building that sits on the high ground overlooking the city below. Since the *palazzo* is the current seat of the Sicilian Parliament, you must be escorted by a guide through the rooms. Don't playfully attempt to sneak off; security is pretty tight because of the Mafia problems.

One room you can't miss is the **Cappella Palatina** which contains some of the best **mosaics** outside of Istanbul and Ravenna. The tile art describes scenes from the Old Testament. Another room adorned with mosaics, with a flora and fauna motif, is the **Sala di Ruggero**, King Roger's Hall.

K. SAN GIOVANNI DEGLI EREMITI
Corso Re Ruggero. Open 9:00am-1:00pm. On Tuesdays, Wednesdays, and Fridays also open 3-5:00pm.

Founded by Roger II, and built in 1132, the architecture of **St. John of the Hermits** has quite a bit of Arabic influence. Just down the road from the Norman Palace, this church was built over a mosque and is dominated by five Arab-looking domes. To get to the church you must walk up a path lined with citrus trees, behind which are some 13th century cloisters. A beautiful sight to see.

L. CHIESA DEL OF GESU
Via Porto di Castro. Open 7:00am-noon and 5:00pm-6:30pm.

Follow Via Porto di Castro from the Norman Palace to this small church with its green mosaic dome. It has a multicolored marble interior and an almost surreal interpretation of the *Last Judgment*. In the church's small courtyard, you can still see the effect of Allied bombings during World War II. You can see this same bombing effect near the **Palazzo Abatellis** that is home to the **Galleria Nazionale Siciliana** (see below).

M. PALAZZO ABATELLIS
Via Alloro. Open 9:00am-1:30pm and also open on Tuesdays, Thursdays and Fridays 4:00pm-7:00pm. Sundays and holidays open 9:00am-12;30pm. Admission E4.

This palace houses the **Galleria Nazionale Siciliana**, one of Sicily's wonderful regional art museums. The gallery gives a comprehensive insight into Sicilian painting and sculpture. Some of the work is quite crude, some is magnificent, but if you've never been exposed to Sicilian art, this is your chance to learn.

N. CHURCH OF SAN FRANCESCO DI ASSISI
Via Paternostro. Open only from 7:00am-11:00am every day.

You have to be an early bird to catch this sight: the church is known for its intricate rose window that looks magnificent from the inside when the early morning sun streams through it. The zig-zag design on its exterior is common to many of the churches in the area. Built in the 13th century, there were two side chapels added in the 14th and 15th centuries.

O. VILLA GIULIA PARK & BOTANICAL GARDENS
Via Lincoln. Park open until dark. Botanical Gardens open Monday-Friday 9:00am-noon and Saturdays 9:00am-11:00am. Admission E2.

This is Palermo's best and most centrally-located park, which gives you a respite from the pace of this hectic city. Besides wildlife roaming around, there are gardens, a small kiddy train and a pretty **Botanical Gardens**. The gardens feature tropical plants from all over the world. It's an uplifting spot after a few days touring through Palermo.

Nightlife & Entertainment

There is plenty to do at night in Palermo, but I recommend that you enjoy a nice meal, then retire to your room. Crime is a problem and I don't want you walking down the wrong street. If just having dinner is too boring for you, locate a restaurant near your hotel and stop there for after-dinner drinks before making the short walk back to your hotel. But as always, Palermo is much safer than any comparably sized American city.

Opera

If you are in Palermo from December to June, the traditional opera season, have the proper attire (suits for men, dresses for women), and have a taste for something out of the ordinary, try the spectacle of the opera.
• **Teatro Massimo**, *Piazza Verdi, 90139 Palermo. Tel 091/605-3111, Fax 091/605-3325 or 605-3324*

Shopping

Food shopping can be done at the markets that are located off Via Roma on the **Via Divisi**, as well as between the **Palazzo dei Normani** and the train station at **Piazza Ballaro**.

For inexpensive clothing, try the **Via Bandiera** near Chiesa San Domenico. For more expensive clothing, try along the main thoroughfares of **Via Roma** and **Via Maqueda**.

Practical Information

Local Festivals & Holidays
- **July 11-15**, Festival of Santa Rosalia with fireworks and general insanity
- **September 4**, pilgrimage-like walk to Monte Pelligrino in honor of Santa Rosalia
- **Last week in September**, International Tennis Tournament

Postal Services

The **central post office** in Palermo is at *Via Roma 322. Open Monday through Friday 8:30am–5:00pm, Saturdays 9:00am–noon*. But if you're in a hurry, stamps can be bought at any tobacconist (stores indicated by a **T** sign outside), and mailed at any mailbox, which are red and marked with the word *Poste* or *Lettere*.

Tourist Information & Maps
- **Main Information Office**, *Piazza Castelnuovo 34 (Tel. 091/583-847) across from the Modern Art Museum*
- **Information Office**, *in the train station, open Monday–Friday, 8:00am–8:00pm*. If the office at the station is out of information and/or maps, take bus #101 to the *piazza* and the main office. They both supply detailed maps and information about Palermo and other places of interest. There is also a tourist office in the Stazione Maritima and at the airport.

Trapani

Located on a sickle-shaped peninsula on the northwest coast of Sicily, **Trapani** is the island's largest fishing port. The city, called *Drapanon* (which means sickle) by locals, used to be the main port for the ancient Greek city of **Eryx** (Erice – see next section). Trapani flourished as a trading center, mainly with customers in Africa and the Middle East. The town has an ancient elegant *centro storico* out on the end of the sickle of a peninsula.

Today the city's lifeblood still depends on the trading of salt, wine, and fish. It's a modern city, developed after most everything else was destroyed during Allied bombing in World War II. Trapani is a friendly city and should definitely be one of your destinations while in Sicily.

Arrivals & Departures

Located 94 km from Palermo as the crow flies, the journey by car is about 110 km; by train you will end up putting in closer to 130 km since the tracks wind along the coast until Castellammare del Golfo then turn inland to follow the main roads. The train usually stops at every town along the way, which means that your journey will take about 3 hours.

By car there are a number of options. The journey along highway 186 out of Palermo, which connects with highway 113, will take about 2 hours. After Alcamo you will be able to get on Autostrada A29 which can shorten the time. The best route but the longest would be to take highway 113 to 187. This runs along the coast until Castellammare del Golfo, then heads inland and passes by Erice along the way.

Getting Around Town

The *centro storico* occupies about a square kilometer on the peninsula, so everything in it is within walking distance. The **train station** lets you off just on the edge of the old town, and the docks along **Via Ammiraglio Staiti** (which runs half the southern length of the old town) are where you can catch ferries to the **Egadi Islands**. To get to the city's museum in the new section of town, you'll need to catch bus #1 or #10 from the train station.

Where To Stay

Most of the hotels in Trapani are located in the new city. The two below are the best and closest to the town's old city.

1. CRISTAL, *Piazza Umberto 1, 9100 Trapani. Tel. 0923/20000, Fax 0923/25555. 70 rooms all with bath. Single E115. Double E150. All credit cards accepted. Breakfast included* ****

Located right next to the train station, it is a lovely experience to spend the night here in the heart of Trapani. Strangely peaceful, quiet and calm, this modern hotel offers all necessary amenities and conveniences to make your stay pleasant and relaxing. The common areas are bright and accommodating. The rooms are large and comfortable, and the bathrooms are clean with all necessities, including a telephone. You also have an excellent restaurant and an ambient garden here.

2. VITTORIA, *Via F. Crispi 4, 91100 Trapani. Tel. 0923/873-0444, Fax 0923/29870. 65 rooms all with bath. Single E100; Double E140. All credit cards accepted. Breakfast included.* ***

Located about two blocks from the train station. Exit and walk to the right down Via F. Crispi and you'll run right into it. Really the only good hotel in the

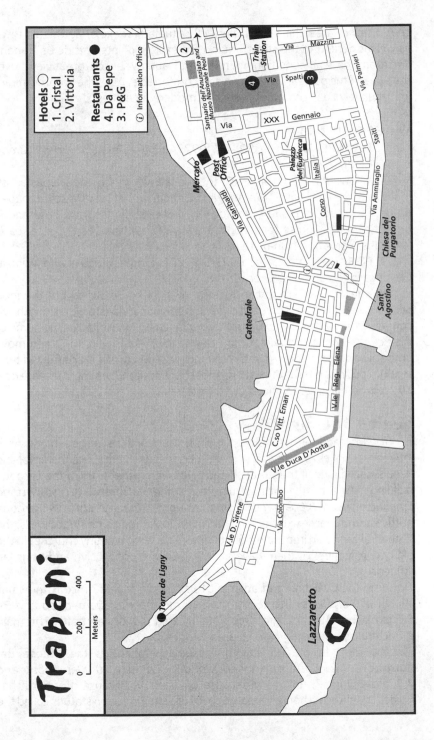

Trapani

0 200 400
Meters

Hotels ○
1. Cristal
2. Vittoria

Restaurants ●
4. Da Pepe
3. P&G

ⓘ Information Office

Santuario dell'Anunziata and Museo Nazionale Peoli

Via Mazzini

Train Station

Via Spalti

Via Palmieri

Via Gennaio

XXX

Mercato

Post Office

Via Garibaldi

Palazzo del Guidecca

Italia

Corso

Via Ammiraglio

Spalti

Chiesa del Purgatorio

Cattedrale

Sant' Agostino

V.le Reg. Elena

C.so Vitt. Eman

V.le Duca D'Aosta

V.le D. Sirene

Via Colombo

● Torre de Ligny

Lazzaretto

centro storico area, this place is perfectly situated for exploring the old town as well as getting to the station quickly to explore points outside of Trapani. The rooms have air conditioning, room and laundry service, great views over the sea and the park, and are clean and comfortable. Also, the bathrooms are immaculately kept and have necessary modern amenities.

Where To Eat

4. DA PEPE, *Via Spalti 50, Tel. 0923/28246. Closed Mondays. Credit cards accepted. Dinner for two E45.*

Just down the road from P&G, they're known for their house pasta dish made with the local pasta, *busiati*, which is actually just *fusilli*, a spiral-shaped pasta. The sauce is made with cooked garlic, tomatoes, and basil and is fantastic. And of course for seconds try any of their varieties of *pesce spada* (swordfish) or *tonno* (tuna) steaks.

3. P&G, *Via Spalti 1, Tel. 0923/547-701. Closed Sundays and August. Credit cards accepted. Dinner for two E45.*

The decorations are not something to write home about, but the food here is excellent. Once you start digging into your antipasto, your mouth will come alive with the flavors of the Mediterranean, not just Italian. Try some of their *cuscus con la cernia* (couscous with stone bass) for *primo*, then move onto some *tonno al forno* (oven cooked tuna steak) or *alla brace* (grilled tuna steak). You should have at least one meal here while in Trapani. There are only 50 seats so make reservations or come early.

Seeing the Sights

The look and feel of this medieval port city, with its European and Arab influences, makes it seem as if you've stepped back in time. The medieval and Renaissance fabric of the streets blends well with the tapestry of the Baroque buildings. One of the best structures is the **Cathedral** (*Corso Vittorio Emanuele, open 8:00am–noon and 3:00pm-6:00pm*). With its Baroque portico and immense exterior, and with its colorful dome and stucco walls, the Cathedral can be an imposing sight compared to the other tiny churches in the old city. A number of them have an interesting mix of Muslim and Christian influences.

Near the cathedral and adjacent to the main tourist office is the small church of **Sant'Agostino** (*Piazzetta Saturno, open 8:00am–noon and 3–6:00pm*). This 14th century church is mainly used as a **concert hall** and its main attraction is its stunning rose colored window.

The most fascinating church to see in Trapani, is the **Chiesa del Purgatorio** (*Via Cassaretto, open Monday–Saturday 10:00am–noon and 4:30pm-6:30pm.*), not really because of itself but because of what it has inside. The church is home to a large set of life-sized wooden statues called the

Misteri that have been paraded through town during Good Friday celebrations every year for the past 600 years. Each statue represents a member of one of the trades, such as fishermen, cobblers, etc. It's quite a sight to see.

The **Torre de Ligny** is a great spot to watch the sunset. Located at the most eastern point of the city the tower also houses the surprisingly interesting **Museo di Preistoria** *(open Monday–Saturday 9:00am-1:00pm and 4:00pm to 8:00pm; admission E2.5)*, which contains Neanderthal bones, skulls and tools, as well as the remains of prehistoric animals. A must see when here in Trapani.

Located in the heart of Trapani's old **Jewish Ghetto** that was established during the medieval oppression of the Jews, is the 16th century **Palazzo della Guidecca** *(Via della Guidecca 43, open 9:00am-1:00pm and 4:00pm-7:00pm)*. It has a plaque-studded facade with some Spanish-style windows, and is an elaborate and intricate architectural piece.

Walk up the Via Mura di Tramontana Ovest on the north side of the peninsula from the tower and you'll come to the bustling **Mercato di Pesce** (Fish Market). Here you can see fishermen selling their catch, and fruit and vegetable vendors clamoring for your attention. But remember to get here in the morning, because it shuts down by 1:30pm.

Really the only reason to venture into the new city is to come see these last two sights. If you don't want to hike 3 km down a large boulevard, catch either bus #1 or #10 from the station. Remember to buy a ticket at a newsstand or *tabacchaio* first (Euro 75 cents).

This 14th century convent and church, **Santuario dell'Anunziata** *(Via Conte Pepoli, open 8:30am–noon and 4-6:00pm; no charge)* contains the town's main treasure, the smiling *Madonna and Child*. This statue has supposedly been responsible for a number of miracles, so it is kept secured here and is usually surrounded by many kneeling worshipers.

Fans of numismatics (that's the study of coins to you and me), hang on to your hats! Beside to the convent and church is the **Museo Nazionale Pepoli** *(Via Conte Pepoli; open Monday–Saturday 9:00am-1:30pm, Sundays until 12:30pm; on Tuesdays, Thursdays and Saturdays also open 4:00pm-6:30pm; admission E3)* that contains a wide variety of artifacts, including an extensive Roman, Greek, and Arab coin collection. Don't miss the 18th century guillotine, the local coral carvings, or the quaint folk-art figurines. It's a great museum for kids of all ages, but remember to come during the day since the lighting isn't quite adequate in the evening.

Nightlife & Entertainment

Trapani closes down around 9:00pm, but just after dinner, along the **Via Vittorio Emanuele** the natives emerge for a stroll or a sip of Sambuca at a sidewalk café. If you're interested in sampling a local delicacy try a *biscotto coi fichi*, a very tasty fig newton-like cookie.

Practical Information

Local Festivals & Holidays
• **Good Friday**, Procession of Wooden Statues from 3:00pm to 7:00pm
• **Last Three weeks of July**, Luglio Musicale Trapanese; musical festival in the Villa Margherita at 9:00pm each night

Postal Services
The **central post office** in Trapani is in the *Piazza Vittorio Veneto (Tel. 0923/873-038) at the ends of Via Garibaldi. Open Monday through Friday 8:00am–5:00pm, Saturdays 9:00am–noon.* But if you're in a hurry, stamps can be bought at any tobacconist (stores indicated by a T sign outside), and mailed at any mailbox, which are red and marked with the word *Poste* or *Lettere*.

Tourist Information & Maps
• **Main tourist office**, *Piazza Saturno, Tel. 0923/29000.* They have maps, brochures, and all sorts of information about the town and surrounding area.

Erice

Only a forty-five minute bus ride from Trapani, don't miss **Erice** when in Sicily. It is a walled mountain town that was once the biggest in the area (Trapani was just its port), and is still completely medieval with its winding streets, alleys, and ancient buildings. You may actually want to stay here rather than in Trapani and do the reverse commute into the larger city, then escape back to this town's silent charms at the end of the day.

The views from Erice's terraces are fantastic. You can see all of Trapani as well as the **Egadi Islands** (Isole Egadi) and on a good day the coast of Africa. Besides the views and the charming streets there is little of importance to see in Erice, but these are types of ancient towns you came to Sicily to see. Don't be upset if there's no Michelangelo's *David* to admire – the town is a masterpiece in itself.

Arrivals & Departures

After a 45 minute bus ride from Trapani, the bus will drop you off at the Porta Trapani at the southwest edge of town. From here cross the piazza to the **tourist office** *(open regular business hours, closed Sundays; Tel. 0923/ 869-388)* and pick up any information you think you might need.

Where To Stay

If you want to stay in Erice during the summer months, make reservations well in advance. Listed below are the three hotels in the town.

1. ELIMO, *Via Vittorio Emanuele, 91016 Erice. Tel. 0923/869-377. 21 rooms all with bath. Single E100; Double E150. No credit cards accepted. Full board E100.* ***

A quaint little hotel that is the second best in the city. It has a fine restaurant and a relaxing bar for an evening's refreshments, and quaint old surroundings. The rooms have heat and A/C as well as a TV if you get bored with ambiance and views. The rooms are also smallish but clean and very comfortable with rather eclectic furnishings.

2. MODERNO, *Via Vittorio Emanuele 63, 91016 Erice, Tel. 0923/869-300, Fax 0923/869-139. 40 rooms, 6 with bath, 34 with shower. Single E90; Double E120. American Express and Visa accepted. Full board E90.* **

The best hotel in the city with clean rooms and relatively modern furnishings. They have laundry and room service as well as a good in-house restaurant that is large, elegant, and serves superb food, especially their *cous*

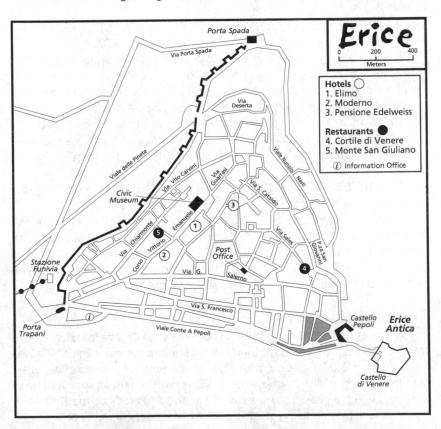

cous di pesce (a Middle Eastern rice dish with fish) or their *vitello al forno* (veal cooked perfectly in the oven). Request a room with a view, since the panorama is spectacular. Each room is laid out and furnished differently from the others. But each is filled with local products, from the carpets to the bed frames. The bathrooms have a small courtesy toiletry set and hairdryers.

3. PENSIONE EDELWEISS, *Cortile Piazza Vincenzo 5, 91016 Erice. Tel. 0923/869-420, Fax 0923/869-252. 13 rooms, 13 with bath. Single E80; Double E95. American Express and Visa accepted. Full board E80.* **

Since there are only three good hotels in Erice, this makes the Edelweiss the third best hotel in town. In a quiet alley off the Piazzetta San Domenico, this is a simple family-run place that is comfortable and clean, even if the furnishings don't seem to match. If you're a budget traveler this is your only option, even though the accommodations are better than budget.

Where To Eat

You're not going to find an inexpensive meal in Erice unless you grab a sandwich at a sidewalk café, but if you try one of these places, at least you'll be eating well.

4. CORTILE DI VENERE, *Via Sales 31, Tel. 0923/869-362. Closed Wednesdays. All credit cards accepted. Dinner for two E50.*

In the summer you can eat in a splendid courtyard surrounded by buildings from the 17th century. The *gamberi marinati* (marinated grilled shrimp), *spaghetti al pesto ericino* (with a pesto sauce Erice-style) and the *tagliolini al uova di tonno* (thin pasta with a sauce of tuna eggs) are all great. For seconds try some of their *involtini di pesce spada* (rolled swordfish steaks stuffed with spices), *calamari ripieni* (stuffed calamari), or a *costata di Angus alla brace* (an Angus steak grilled over an open flame). Definitely the best food and atmosphere in town.

5. MONTE SAN GIULIANO, *Via San Rocco 7, Tel. 0923/869-595. Closed Mondays. All credit cards accepted. Dinner for two E50.*

If you want to get one of the tables that looks out over the water and the Isole Egadi, you need to get here early or reserve in advance. Their *busiati con pesto ericino* (twisted pasta made with almond paste, garlic, tomatoes, and basil) is exquisite. For seconds, I love their *grigliata di calamari, gamberi e pesce spada* (grilled calamari, shrimp, and swordfish).

Seeing the Sights

As you enter the town you'll be confronted by the **Chiesa Matrice**, whose tower served as a lookout post, then a prison before getting religion (*Via Vito Carvini, open 8:00am–noon and 3:00pm–6:00pm*). There are five other churches, much smaller in scale, in Erice. When you find them, stick your head inside and take a peek. They are definitely not St. Peter's or the Duomo in Florence, but they do help you step back in time to medieval Erice.

There's a small, really insignificant **museum** (*Corso Vittorio Emanuele, open Monday–Saturday 8:30am–1:30pm, Sunday 9:00am–noon*) but the town is a museum in and of itself. After wandering through the streets, avoiding the hordes of tourists in the summertime, walk up past the public gardens and the ancient **Torretta Pepoli**, a restored 15th century tower, and go to the **Castello San Venere** (*open Saturday–Thursdays 10:00am–1:00pm and 3:00pm–5:00pm*). Built on the site of an ancient temple to the Greek god Aphrodite and later the Roman god Venus, from here you can get the great views we spoke of earlier. Don't forget your camera.

Agrigento

Even though **Agrigento** is filled with quaint medieval streets and buildings, where butchers and bakers share storefronts with Fendi, nobody comes here just for that experience. Even though the city is not more than 4 km from pristine beaches tourists don't visit for that reason either. The reason people come to Agrigento is for some of the most captivating and well-preserved set of Greek remains and Doric temples outside of Greece – the **Valley of Temples**.

These temples were erected during the 5th century BCE, below the Greek town of Akragas, the forerunner to Agrigento, as testament to the wealth and prosperity of the community. Today Agrigento survives as a result of the tourist trade, and, it is rumored, through Mafia money. But that is the rumor everywhere in Sicilia.

Arrivals & Departures

Since Agrigento is off by itself in the southern part of the island along the coast, with few other towns of tourist interest around, getting here can be quite a haul either by car or by train. To get here by car follow route 115 along the coast, route 640 from Enna (which is on the way from Catania or Messina), or route 189 from Palermo.

Getting Around Town

You can easily walk everywhere in the town itself. The tiny medieval streets are fun to explore. To get the Valley of Temples, you'll need to catch either bus #8, 9 or 10 from the train station. Ask to be let off at the **Museo** (the museum). This a good starting point since it will be able to give you an overview of the entire dig.

Where To Stay

1. **BELVEDERE**, *Via San Vito 20, 92100 Agrigento. Tel. 0922/20051. 35 rooms, 5 with bath, 13 with shower. Single without E45-55; Single E55-65; Double without E55-65; Double E65-80. American Express and Visa accepted.* **

Located near the train station, I would advise getting a bathroom of your own because there are not many in the halls and they aren't too inviting. Little or no amenities, except a good view from some of the rooms. Try to reserve room #30, which has a large balcony where you can relax in the evenings. A good budget traveler's hotel.

2. **DELLE VALLE**, *Via dei Templi 94, 92100 Agrigento, Tel. 0922/26966, Fax 0922/26412. E-mail: dellavalle@italyhotel.com. 140 rooms all with bath. Single E100-140; Double E140-180. Full board E120. All credit cards accepted. Breakfast included.* ****

Located on the road to the temples, you need to take bus #8, 9, or 10 from the station to get here. They have a swimming pool, tranquil and extensive gardens filled with palm and olive trees, four fine restaurants (two of which are in the garden area); and accommodating rooms with all manner of four star amenities. The bathrooms are medium size and come with hairdryer and courtesy toiletry set.

3. **VILLA ATHENA**, *Via dei Templi 33, 92100 Agrigento. Tel. 0922/596-288, Fax 0922/598-770. Web: www.venere.com/it/sicilia/agrigento/villaathena/. 40 rooms, 8 with bath, 32 with shower. Single E100-140; Double E140-180. Full board E120. All credit cards accepted. Breakfast included.* ****

Located in the Valley of the Temples itself, this place has all the amenities you could want, including a pool surrounded by tranquil gardens, a good restaurant, laundry and room service, air conditioning and more. Located in a quaint old romantic building, your rooms are clean as are the bathrooms. The rooms are comfortable and the view from many of the rooms, onto the temples, is exquisite, especially at night, when they are all lit up.

Where To Eat

There are plenty of little bars and cafés at which you can grab a snack, as well as some local restaurants. Below is the one I feel is the best.

4. **KALOS**, *Piazza San Calogero, Tel. 0922/26389. Closed Sunday Nights. Credit cards accepted. Dinner for two E40.*

Located in the small *piazza* near the station and the church of San Calogero, this is a clean, modern looking place, with professional service. Try their *macceroncelli al pistacchio* (macaroni with pistachio sauce, gorgonzola and parmesan cheese). For seconds, get any of their succulent fish or meat cooked on the grill. Great food in a wonderful local environment.

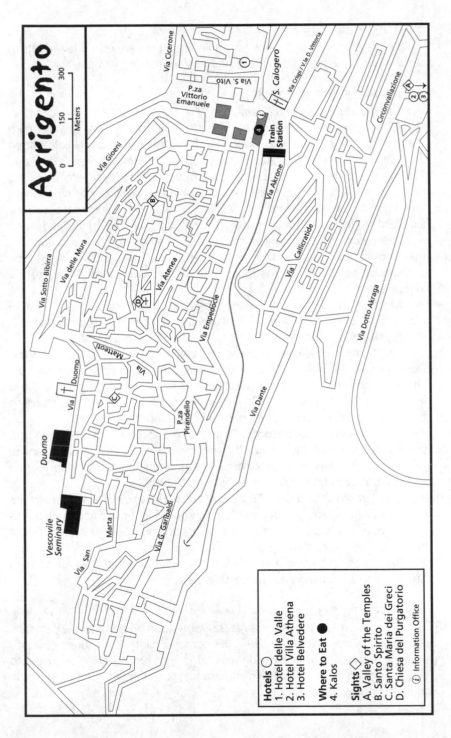

Agrigento

0 150 300
Meters

Via Cicerone
Via S. Vito
P.za Vittorio Emanuele
S. Calogero
Via Crispi / Via D. Vittoria
Circonvallazione
Train Station
Via Akrone
Via Gioeni
Via Sotto Bibirra
Via delle Mura
Via Atenea
Via Empedocle
Via Callicratide
Via Dotto Akraga
Via Matteot
Via Duomo
P.za Pirandello
Via Dante
Duomo
Via G. Garibaldi
Vescovile Seminary
Via San
Marta

Hotels ○
1. Hotel delle Valle
2. Hotel Villa Athena
3. Hotel Belvedere

Where to Eat ●
4. Kalos

Sights ◇
A. Valley of the Temples
B. Santo Spirito
C. Santa Maria dei Greci
D. Chiesa del Purgatorio

ⓘ Information Office

Seeing the Sights

Besides the winding streets and staircases there are only a few sights to see in town. The main show is out at The Valley of the Temples.

A. THE VALLEY OF THE TEMPLES

Open Sunday-Friday 8:00am-dusk.

After being dropped off by the bus #8, 9, or 10 from town, walk down the hill to the **Museo Nazionale Archeologico di San Nicola** *(open Tuesday-Friday 9:00am-1:30pm and 3:00pm-5:00pm, weekends 9:00am-12:30pm)* to admire the artifacts removed from the ruins for safekeeping. This museum will help give you a feel for the people that used to worship at these temples. You can find vases, candlestick holders, lion's head water spouts, excellent model reconstructions of the site below, coins, sarcophagi and more.

The **church** that the museum is named after is next door and contains many Roman sarcophagi with intricate relief work. The church isn't open too often. Walking down the road in front will lead you to the Valley of the Temples.

Most of these temples were destroyed by earthquakes and human destruction. Despite the state of the temples, it's still awe-inspiring to walk among structures that once stood erect in the 5th century BCE.

The **Tempio di Giove** (**Temple of Zeus**) would have been the largest Doric temple ever built had it been completed. It was to be dedicated to the Olympian god Zeus, as you can guess from its name (Jove in English, or *Giove* in Latin, is Zeus). You can still see the remains of one of the standing *telemones*, human figures that were to be the support columns.

The **Tempio della Concordia** (**Temple of Concord**) is probably the best preserved, most probably because it was converted to a Christian church in the 6th century CE. It has been fenced off to keep scavenging tourists from tearing it apart. But even from a distance it is a joy to behold.

The **Tempio di Giunone** (**Temple of Juno/Hera**) is not as well preserved but it is still an engaging structure. You may notice some red and black marks in the stone. These could be remnants of fires that were set when the temple was sacked many centuries ago.

Remember to come out and view the temples at night. They are all lit up offering you a stunning and memorable view.

B. SANTO SPIRITO

Piazza Santo Spirito. Accessible 9:00am-noon and 3:00pm-6:00pm.

Built by Cisterian nuns in 1290, this complex contains a church, convent, and charter house. The church contains some fine stucco work. You'll need to ring the bell on the church to gain admittance. Be patient. It's considered rude to keep ringing the bell.

C. CHURCH OF SANTA MARIA DEI GRECI
Via Santa Maria dei Greci. Open 8:00am–noon and 3:00pm–5:00pm.
Built on a 5th century BCE Greek temple, you can still see evidence of the columns in the walls, as well as the base of the columns in the foundation below the church. Make time to search out the entrance in the courtyard. Also inside are some interesting Byzantine frescoes.

D. CHIESA DEL PURGATORIO
Via Fodera. Open 8:00am–noon and 4:00pm–7:00pm.
The main draw for this church are the eight statues inside that represent the eight virtues. Next to the church is the entrance to a network of underground avenues and courtyards, built by the Greeks in the 5th century BCE. This is a must-see adventure while in Agrigento.

Nightlife & Entertainment
The bars and cafés along **Via Atenea** and in the **Piazzale Aldo Moro** is where the town congregates for its evening *passegiatta* (stroll). Come out with the Italians after dinner, sit at a café and sip an *aperitivo*, or stroll among the natives enjoying the relaxing evenings in Agrigento.

Practical Information
Local Festivals & Holidays
• **First Sunday of February**, Almond Blossom Festival in the Valley of The Temples
• **Late July/Early August**, *Settimana Pirandelliana*. A weeklong festival of plays, opera and ballets all performed in the Piazza Kaos

Postal Services
The **central post office** in Agrigento is in the circular building in *Piazza Vittorio Emanuele. Open Monday through Friday, 8:30am–5:00pm, Saturdays 9:00am–noon.* But if you're in a hurry, stamps can be bought at any tobacconist (stores indicated by a T sign outside), and mailed at any mailbox, which are red and marked with the word *Poste* or *Lettere*.

Tourist Information & Maps
• **Tourist Office**, *Piazza Aldo Moro #123 (Tel. 0922/20391)*, just to the left as you exit the train station. Here you can get free maps and information about the town and the Valley of the Temples.

Siracusa

Most of the old city of **Siracusa (Syracuse)** is situated on an island separated by a narrow channel off the southeastern coast of Sicily. Because of this quaint older town, the scenic **Bay of Porto Grande**, its beautiful natural surroundings, and the monuments and relics of a glorious past, Siracusa is one of the most frequented spots in Sicily.

Founded in 743 BCE by a few colonists from Corinth, **Ortygia** (later to be named Siracusa) grew into a feared and powerful city in the Greek world. In 415 BCE, the city was drawn into the conflict between Athens and Sparta, but when a military expedition from Athens in 413 BCE was completely annihilated the Greeks left the locals alone. To ensure this peace, Siracusa detained over 7,000 Athenians in squalid conditions for over 7 years. Over time, Siracusa's power increased and until 212 BCE, Siracusa was arguably the greatest and most powerful city in the world.

Just after that time, the city expanded from its easily defensible island to the mainland. The ruler at the time, Gelon, built the market area and necropolis which is now the famous **Archaeological Park** with its preserved buildings, temples, and theaters that people from all over the world come to see.

After the first Punic War, in which Siracusa was allied with the Romans, the city changed its alliance in the second Punic War to the Carthaginians. Big mistake. The Romans attacked and conquered the city in 212 BCE, and thus began the city's decline. During this two year assault, the city defended itself with an ingenious variety of devices created by the famous scientist and inventor **Archimedes**. After the Romans finally sacked the city, this last great thinker of the Hellenic world was hacked to death in retribution for the many deaths he caused by his ingenious but deadly defensive devices.

After its occupation, the city never really recovered its past glory, but it did remain the main port in Sicily. It also briefly became the capital of the Byzantine Empire in 663 CE, when the Emperor Constans moved his court here. After that the city, like much of Sicily, was overrun by waves of Arab, Norman, and other conquerors. In conjunction the area has been repeatedly devastated by earthquakes and other natural disasters. Despite all the catastrophes, Siracusa is a great city to visit.

Arrivals & Departures

Nestled down by the southeastern tip of Sicily, Siracusa is a long haul either by car or train. By car the best route to follow is along the coast road, route 115, from Catania. Both by train and by car will take in excess of an hour to traverse the 60 kilometers from Catania.

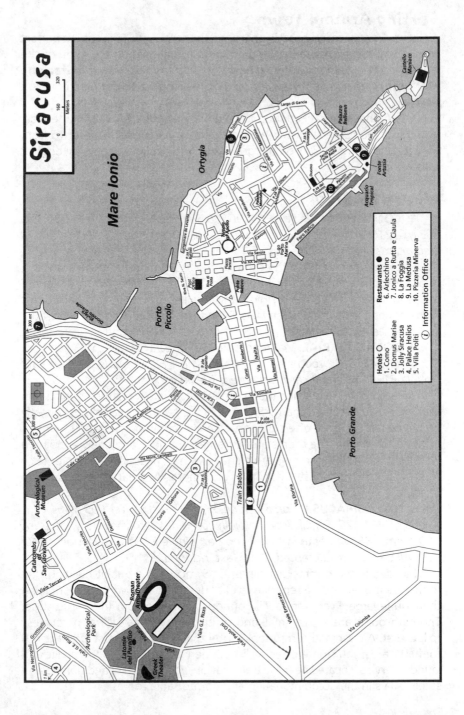

Siracusa

Mare Ionio

Ortygia

Porto Piccolo

Porto Grande

Hotels ○
1. Como
2. Domus Mariae
3. Jolly Siracusa
4. Palace Helios
5. Villa Politi

Restaurants ●
6. Arlecchino
7. Jonica a Rutta e Ciaula
8. La Foggia
9. La Medusa
10. Pizzeria Minerva

ⓘ Information Office

Castello Maniace

Palazzo Bellomo

Fonte Artusa

Acquario Tropical

Largo di Gancia

Tempio d'Apollo

Post Office

Ponte Nuovo

Train Station

P.zza Marconi

Archeological Museum

Catacombs of San Giovanni

Roman Amphitheater

Latomie del Paradiso

Greek Theater

Archeological Park

Getting Around town

If you're staying in a hotel in or around the center city, Siracusa is a perfect city for walking. From the train station, located almost on the edge of the island, you are within walking distance of the *centro storico* and **Stazione Maritima** on the island, as well as the **Archaeological Park** to the north on the mainland.

The Archaeological Park and Museum are about a fifteen minute walk away, so if you're tired you may want to catch either bus # 4, 5 12, or 15 from the Piazza della Poste or from Largo XXV Luglio, which will pass by both of these stops.

Where To Stay

1. COMO, *Piazza Stazione 10, 96100 Siracusa. Tel. 0931/464-055, Fax 0931/61210. 14 rooms all with shower. Single E75-95; Double E110-120. All credit cards accepted. Breakfast E5.* ***

Recently upgraded to a three star hotel, this wonderful little place is in a good location near the station, has air conditioning, satellite TV, room service and laundry service. Near everything, this small hotel has spotless bathrooms with phones and courtesy toiletry kits. Everything has been recently renovated so it still has a luster about it. Good for budget travelers and above.

2. DOMUS MARIAE, *Via Veneto 76, 96100 Siracusa. Tel. 0931/24854, Fax 0931/24858. 12 rooms all with bath. Single E80; Double without E90; Double E120. No credit cards accepted. Breakfast included.* ***

Located in an old building that has been successfully restored to maintain the original architectural charm. Situated in the *centro storico* almost directly on the water, this place offers the service and accommodations of a four star at three star prices. The rooms are extremely spacious and finely appointed with antiques. The bathrooms are elegant with all necessary amenities such as toothbrush, toothpaste, hairdryer and more. A great place to stay in Siracusa.

3. JOLLY SIRACUSA, *Corso Gelone, 96110 Siracusa. Tel. 0931/461-111, Fax 0931/461-126. E-mail: siracusa@jollyhotels.it. Web: www.jollyhotels.it/. 100 rooms, 56 with bath, 44 with shower. Single E100-125; Double E140-160. All credit cards accepted. Breakfast included.* ****

Located in the commercial center of Syracuse in a quaint building, the rooms are modern with a separate level to designed as a work space, making them quite large. Every window is soundproof to keep out the traffic noise. The bathrooms are a little small and offer hairdryers as well as a courtesy toiletry set. A clean and comfortable hotel that has a good restaurant (E140 for full board if you're interested), a little American-style bar, room service and laundry service. Located near the train station, you'll find air conditioning and satellite TVs in the accommodating and comfortable rooms.

4. **PALACE**, *Viale Scala Greca 201, 96100 Siracusa. Tel. 0931/491-566, Fax 0931/756-612. 136 rooms, 39 with bath, 97 with shower. Single E100-125; Double E140-160. All credit cards accepted. Breakfast included.* ****

Located outside of town and north of the Greek Theater in the Archaeological Park, this place is somewhat isolated, so getting the E100 full board option at their in-house restaurant would be a good idea. The rooms are old but comfortable and the darker furniture contrasts well with the white floors. The bathrooms come complete with phone and courtesy toiletry kit.

5. **VILLA POLITI**, *Via M Politi Laudien 2, 96100 Siracusa. Tel. 0931/412-121, Fax 0931/36061. Web: www.initaly.com/agri/hotels/politi/politi.htm. 94 rooms, 85 with bath, 9 with shower. 2 Suites. Single E150; Double E220-280. All credit cards accepted. Breakfast included.* ***

This is another great place to stay while in Siracusa. The rooms are clean and comfortable, the restaurant offers great local cuisine (E86 full board), and the hotel is located in a quaint historic building. You have air conditioning in the rooms, a disco for dancing at night, a swimming pool surrounded by flowers and vegetation, tennis courts, *bocce* courts, and great views over the sea. It's located a short distance outside of town, but is about equidistant from the town and the Archaeological Park. For a three star, this place offers many four star options and their prices reflect that.

Where To Eat

6. **ARLECCHINO**, *Via del Tolomei 5, Tel. 0931/66386. Closed Mondays. All credit cards accepted. Dinner for two E50.*

Located in Ortygia, from the entrance you have a great view of the sea. This modern, well-lit place is huge; over 260 people can be seated at the same time. It caters to tourists, but mainly of the Italian variety so the food is good. Try their *antipasto* buffet table for starters that is overflowing with seafood. Then for more seafood with the *spaghetti ai ricci di mare* (with the riches of the sea) or the *tortelloni con scampi allo zafferano* (large cheese stuffed pasta with a shrimp and sauce). For seconds try any of their oven roasted fish as well as their many meat dishes.

7. **JONICO A RUTTA E CIAULU**, *Riviera Rionisio il Grande 194, Tel. 0931/ 65540. Closed Tuesdays, the end of the year and Easter. All credit cards accepted. Dinner for two E55.*

Located up the coast near the Villa Politi, the best place to eat is on the terrace where you have a fine view of the Ionian Sea. Here you can get some good local dishes at somewhat high prices. Try some of their *spaghetti alla siracusano* (with anchovies and scraped toasted bread sauce), which doesn't sound too appetizing but I like it, or some *spaghetti con tonno fresca* (with fresh tuna sauce). For seconds they serve some great tuna and swordfish steaks.

8. LA FOGLIA, *Via Capodieci 29, Tel. 0931/66233. Closed Tuesdays. All credit cards accepted. Dinner for two E40.*

Located in Ortygia, this is a small local place that changes its menu daily based on whatever ingredients chef Nicoletta was able to get at the market. Usually the *antipasto* will be vegetables, like *fritelle di finocchietto* (fried small fennel). Try one of their soups for your *primo* to save yourself for their exquisite fish dishes. Only 25 seats, so make a reservation.

9. LA MEDUSA, *Via San Teresa 21, Tel. 0931/61403. Closed Mondays and August 15 to September 15. American Express accepted. Dinner for two E30.*

Another restaurant in the Ortygia district, this place is run by a Tunisian who has been in Siracusa for over 20 years. You can get some great couscous with either *pesce* or *carne* (a rice-based dish with either fish or meat) for *primo*. The *antipasto* is good too with the *pesce spada marinata* (marinated swordfish), *gamberetti* (small shrimp) and more. For seconds try their *arrosto misto di pesce* (mixed roast fish). Great atmosphere and good food.

10. PIZZERIA MINERVA, *Piazza Duomo 20, Tel. 0931/69404. Closed Mondays and November. No credit cards accepted. Dinner for two E25.*

In the summer this is the perfect pace to end a long walk through Ortygia. The place seats over 130 people, but not all outside in the *piazza* facing the Duomo. Try and get one of these outside seats. You can get any pizza imaginable here, but if you want it American-style you have to order *doppio mozzarella* (double cheese).

Seeing the Sights

The archaeological park and museum is the big draw here, but there are some lovely squares and churches in town that are great for poking around.

ORTYGIA

On the island of **Ortygia**, the ancient nucleus of Siracusa, you can find remains from over 2,500 years of history. A small area, almost half a kilometer across and only one in length, this little parcel of land contains much of the charm and adventure from all of those centuries.

TEMPLE OF APOLLO

Just over the **Ponte Nuovo** from the mainland is the oldest Doric temple in Sicily. Built in the 7th century BCE, little remains of this once glorious temple except for two pillars and parts of some walls. To really get an idea of what it used to look like, go to the Archaeological Museum for a scale model.

PIAZZA ARCHIMEDE

This is Ortygia's **central piazza** and as such is the place to come any time day or night. The square has some bars and cafés with outside seating where you can sit and enjoy the sight of the 12th century fountain with a woodland nymph cavorting under a cover of modern moss. Down a small road from the square is the **Via del Montalto** on which you can find the **Palazzo Montalto** (*not open to public*), with its fabulous double and triple arched windows. The building's construction was begun in 1397 and is constantly undergoing renovations.

PIAZZA DEL DUOMO

A *piazza* surrounded by some beautiful 17th and 18th century *palazzos* and dominated by the impressive Baroque **Duomo**. The square was built over and encompasses an earlier Greek temple, the 5th century BCE Ionic Temple of Athena. You can still see evidence of the previous structure in the walls, where 26 of the original 34 columns remain. Because much of its earlier wealth was stolen and a majority of it was destroyed in the earthquake of 1693, this cathedral contains a wide variety of differing architectural styles, from Greek to Byzantine to Baroque.

The **Palazzo Benevantano** *(at #24 on the piazza, not open to the public)* is worth a look because of its attractive 18th century facade and serpentine balcony. At the far end of the *piazza* is the small church of **Santa Lucia alla Badia** built from 1695 to 1703 (*open 8:00am-noon and 3:30pm-6:00pm*). The church is significant because it contains the remains of the city's patron saint, Santa Lucia.

GALLERIA DI PALAZZO BELLOMO

Via Capodieci 14. Open Tuesday-Sunday 9:00am-1:00pm. Admission E3.

Almost behind **Santa Lucia alla Badia** is the **Palazzo Bellomo**, a 15th century palazzo that contains a wonderful gallery of all kinds of artwork, including ancient bibles, medieval carriages, sculptures, tombs, paintings and more. The most famous painting is the *Annunciation* by Antonello da Messina.

Walk down to the Via Capodieci to arrive at the **Foro Italico**, the main promenade for the citizens of Ortygia. On this tree-lined promenade you'll find rows of bars and cafés on the land side, and rows of yachts lining the water. It's where the local citizens come to enjoy the evenings before they retire home. At the beginning of this promenade is the fresh water fountain **Fonte Aretusa**. Just past the fountain is the **Aquario Tropical** *(open Saturday-Thursdays 9:00am-1:00pm, admission E3)* that offers 35 different species of tropical fish for your aquarium-viewing pleasure.

CATACOMBS

Via San Giovanni. Open 9:00am-1:00pm and 2:00pm-7:00pm. Closed Wednesdays. Guide tours of catacombs cost E3.

The **catacombs of San Giovanni** are located under the basilica of the same name, and contain a quantity of faded frescoes. This is an ominous tour through a labyrinth of passageways, most of which were destroyed by looters and their riches stolen, so to see a sarcophagus you need to go to the Archaeological Museum.

ARCHAEOLOGICAL MUSEUM
Viale Teocrito. Open Tuesday–Saturday 9:00am–1:00pm and Sunday 9:00am–12:30pm.

To get to the museum, you can take the 15-minute walk or catch bus #4, 5 12, or 15 from the Piazza della Poste or from Largo XXV Luglio. Since this museum is the most extensive antiquities museum in Sicily, you should spend some time browsing through the collection. The museum contains fossils, skeletons, figurines, sarcophagi and more, but the collection's tour de force is the *Venus Anadiomene*, the coy statue of Venus rising from the sea. If you're into antiquities, this is a great place to spend a few hours.

ARCHAEOLOGICAL PARK
Open Tuesday–Sunday 9:00am to an hour before sunset. Admission E3.

To get to the park, you can take the 15-minute walk or catch bus #4, 5 12, or 15 from the Piazza della Poste or from Largo XXV Luglio. The structures preserved here were constructed between 475 BCE and the 3rd century CE and many remain somewhat intact. An example of this preservation is the **Greek Theater**, originally made from the side of the hill around 475 BCE. The structure was enlarged in 335 BCE and could seat up to 15,000 people. If you want to see a performance here, come in May and June on the alternate year when classical Greek plays are staged. They are quite stirring mainly because of the ancient backdrop.

Next door to the Greek Theater is the **Latomie del Paradiso**, the **Paradise Quarry**, so named because many of the 7,000 Athenians captured in 413 BCE went to the afterlife from here. In the quarry are two interesting caves: **Grotta dei Cordari**, where rope makers used to work at their craft because the damp cave kept the strands of rope from breaking, and the **Orecchio di Dionisio** (Ear of Dionysis), so called because the entrance resembles an ear, and the cave has amazing acoustic qualities.

Up from the grotto is the **Roman Amphitheater** which was built in the 3rd century CE. Here they held their vicious gladiatorial games. Just one hundred and forty meters long, it's not quite as impressive as the Colosseum in Rome, but is a treasure in and of itself.

Nightlife & Entertainment
The only real nightlife to speak of is along the **Foro Italico** promenade. Sip a drink, have a light meal, and watch the citizens of Siracusa walk by.

Practical Information

Local Festivals & Holidays
• **May to June**, every even numbered year classical Greek drama is performed at the Greek theater; reservations required

Postal Services
The **central post office** in Siracusa is in the *Piazza delle Poste (Tel. 0931/ 684-16)* located in the *centro storico* island just over the bridge from the mainland. *Open Monday through Friday 8:30am–6:30pm, Saturdays 9:00am– noon.* But if you're in a hurry, stamps can be bought at any tobacconist (stores indicated by a **T** sign outside), and mailed at any mailbox, which are red and marked with the word *Poste* or *Lettere*.

Tourist Information & Maps
• **Tourist office**, *on the island at Via Maestranza 33, Tel. 0931/652-01, on the mainland near the catacombs at Via San Sebastiano 45, Tel. 093/677-10.* There is also one outside of the train station. All three locations can offer you maps of the area and the Archaeological Park, as well as brochures and information about hotels.

Catania

Catania is the second largest city in Sicily and a main point of arrival for many international travelers, who land at the airport just outside the city. The city was destroyed by an earthquake in 1693, but even so there is a mix of architectural influences and sights to be seen. Catania is best enjoyed as a stopover for a few days from which you can visit **Mt**. **Etna**, or rest for a day and then pop over to the beautiful **Taormina**.

Don't get me wrong – Catania is a pleasant city with many 17th century sights to see, and can offer an enjoyable few days – but it is not the safest city and can appear dirty and crowded after a few days.

The city was founded about 729 BCE and was named **Katana** by Greek settlers. Throughout its history it has been occasionally destroyed by **Mount Etna** then rebuilt. As a Greek city it was of small importance compared to Siracusa, but under Roman rule the city was built into one of the largest towns in Sicily. After their rule ended, the city went into a decline that can be seen today.

Be cautious here as you would in most other cities, especially port cities, in Sicily: women should not walk alone in Catania at night, and no one should walk around the area near the train station or the harbor after dark. Your best bet is to stay close to the streets around the Duomo where you'll find people out and about. As usual, beware of deserted streets and use common sense whenever you're out at night.

Arrivals & Departures

By Air

You can fly to **Fontarossa Airport** in Catania from Milan, Rome, and quite a few other Italian cities. The best fares usually are on either **Alitalia** or **Lufthansa**, but it's usually cheaper to fly into Palermo. You can get direct flights from London to Catania, so this could be an option for you when traveling from North America or Australia. There are also direct flights from Dublin to Catania.

Getting In From the Airport

Located only five kilometers south of the city, Fontarossa is easily accessible. Bus #24 leaves from right outside the international terminal and drops you off at the Piazza Duomo in twenty minutes. You can get tickets for the bus (E1.5) at the *Tabacchi* in the Departure Hall. If you want to take a taxi it will cost about E20, depending on how much traffic there is.

By Other Options

Bus and train are your best travel options, but you can get here by ferry or hydrofoil from other parts of Sicily or the mainland as well. Consult the various schedules from the town you plan to depart from for the most up-to-date information.

Getting Around Town

Most of the sights you will want to see are located around the **Piazza Duomo**, so you can easily walk around the city (during the day, never at night) with a map, since the city is laid out haphazardly. The Piazza Duomo is about a twenty minute walk from the train station; to get there from the station, make a left down **Via VI Aprile** to the plant-covered semi-circular **Piazza del Martiri**, then right along the **Via Vittorio Emanuele**.

If you don't want to walk or lug your bag that far, catch one of the following buses: #27, 29, 33, 36, and 39 that will take you from the station to the *piazza*. Tickets cost E1.5 and can be bought at any newsstand or *Tabacchi*.

Where To Stay

As Sicily's second largest city, don't be shocked to discover that hotel accommodations are quite expensive.

CENTRAL PALACE, *Via Etnea 218, 95131 Catania. Tel. 095/325-344, Fax 095/715/8939. Web: www.sars.it/centralpalace/. 99 rooms all with bath. Single E95; Double E140. Credit cards accepted. Breakfast included.* ****

Located in the center of the city near the train station and Duomo, other than the Excelsior this is the place to stay while in Catania. The rooms have air conditioning and TV and are clean, modern, and comfortable. Service is impeccable. Meals are good at their in-house restaurant and you're located in the middle of everything.

EXCELSIOR, *Piazza G Verga 39, 95129 Catania. Tel. 095/537-071, Fax 095/537-015. E-mail: excelsior@cormorano.net. Web: www.cormorano.net/ sgas/excelsior/. 150 rooms all with bath. Single E155-185; Double E185-235. Credit cards accepted. Breakfast E18.* ****

This is the best luxury hotel Catania has to offer. The rooms are large, well-tended, clean and comfortable with a sprinkling of antiques to give them an alluring air. Of course there's air conditioning, TV, and mini-bar, as well as fast room service and competent laundry service. They have a bus to shuttle to the airport, train station, or wherever. Centrally located to all the sights and best of all they have a swimming pool. Their in-house restaurant is quite good but expensive, and their bar is a comfortable place at which to relax in the evenings.

SAVONA, *Via Vittorio Emanuele 210, 95124 Catania. Tel. 326-982, Fax 095/715-8169. 25 rooms, 20 with bath. Single without E45; Single E65; Double without E50-70; Double E60-80. No credit cards accepted. Breakfast included.* **

Smack dab in the middle of town, ideally located for touring. A small clean hotel with little to no amenities except TV and phone in the rooms, a small bar downstairs, and laundry service. But the price is right for budget travel and the service is good.

VILLA DINA, *Via Caronda 129, 95128 Catania. Tel. 095/447-103, Fax the same. 22 rooms all with bath. Single E80; Double E120. Credit cards accepted. Breakfast E7.* ***

Located near everything, this place is situated in a quaint old building and comes with a beautiful garden. It has virtually everything you could want except for air conditioning and an in-house restaurant. I think that's why it's still a three star, since the rooms are kept immaculate and they are very comfortable.

Where To Eat

There are plenty of little *trattoria* and restaurants located in the *centro storico* and all over Catania. I've chosen three of the best for you.

FINOCCHIARO, *Via E. Reina 13, Tel. 095/234-765. Closed Sundays. No credit cards accepted. Dinner for two E43.*

Located just off the Piazza dell'Universita, this place is set back in a courtyard making your meal quite relaxing. This is a place frequented by professors and students with some money. Try their extensive appetizer table complete with seafood and vegetables. You can get the Catania special, *spaghetti alla Norma*, here. The sauce is made with tomatoes, garlic, ricotta cheese, basil and eggplant and is fantastic. They also have plenty of meat and fish cooked on the grill.

I VICERE, *Via Grotte Bianche 97, Tel. 095/320-188. Closed Sundays and June 15 to September 15. Open only at night. All credit cards accepted. Dinner for two E46.*

Located near the north end of the Villa Bellini, it is always a joy to return to this restaurant. The ambiance is refined, the attention of the waiters attentive, and the food created by the chef Saverio is sublime. For appetizers, try any and all available at the huge antipasto table. For *primi*, try some *finocchietto e gamberi* (fennel with shrimp), or a *minestra di fave* (fava bean soup), or *ravioli fusi al ragu* (molded ravioli with a tasty ragu sauce). For seconds try any of their creative meat dishes like the *filletini di maiale al mandarino* (small filets of pork with an orange sauce) or one of the normal grilled or roasted varieties.

LA SICILIANA, *Viale Marco Polo 52a, Tel. 095/376-6400. Closed Sunday nights and Mondays and the first two weeks of August. All credit cards accepted. Dinner for two E68.*

You'll need to take a taxi back and forth to this place (about E5 each way) but if you have the money, this is the most famous restaurant in and around Catania. Operated by three brothers (Vito, Salvo, and Ettore La Rosa) this is a wonderful place to come for a relaxing evening on their garden terrace under an awning. Their seafood antipasti are magnificent. Ask Ettore, who works the floor, which one is best that day. For *primo*, try their *Ripiddu Nivicatu* (rice with cuttlefish and ricotta cheese and a touch of tomato sauce). For seconds try *il tonno con le cipole* (tuna steak made with onions) or the fantastic *lo spiedino di pesce spada e gamberoni gratinati alla brace* (swordfish and large shrimp au gratin cooked on a spit over an open fire).

Seeing the Sights

The best place to start any tour of Catania is in the **Piazza del Duomo**. This is Catania's main square, and from here everything is within walking distance. The central feature of the square is the **Fontana dell'Elefante** in the center. This is an 18th century fountain made from lava that supports an Egyptian obelisk on its back. On the east side of the piazza is the **Duomo** itself (*open 8:00am–noon and 5:00pm–7:00pm*), of which only the medieval apses survived the earthquake of 1693. The facade has incorporated some of the granite columns 'borrowed' from the Roman Amphitheater.

Inside the church the ornate Baroque interior contains a beautiful **Cappella dell Madonna** in which resides a Roman sarcophagus and a statue of the Virgin. As you leave, take note of **Bellini's tomb** located to the left of the entrance.

The **Castello Ursino** is a slight walk south from the Piazza del Duomo, which used to be the castle of Frederick II. The whole area is quite dilapidated since it has been almost completely neglected after the last earthquake. Just recently they've restored as much as they can and removed truck loads of junk thrown into the moat. A small but interesting museum has also just opened inside that focuses on historical artifacts from Catania.

If you head back north up the twisting streets just past the Via Vittorio Emanuele, you'll end up at the **Teatro Romano** and the **Odeon** (*Via Teatro Greco, open 9:00am–1:00pm*). Both were built from marble in the second century CE, most of which was pilfered to make other buildings, and today both sites have been covered with lava from the last eruption.

North up the Via Etnea are the magnificent **Bellini Gardens** (*Via S Tomaselli, open Monday–Saturday 9:00am–1:00pm*). Here you can take a relaxing walk through their serpentine promenades. A great place to come for a picnic and escape the hectic pace of Catania. Just before you arrive at the gardens there is a **Roman Amphitheater** located just below street level. Built in the 3rd century CE, it is the grandest of Catania's Roman remains. This amphitheater could hold close to 16,000, even though it is hard to tell since most of the structure is covered up by surrounding buildings. You can enter the vaults under the buildings to see a little more of the structure.

Nightlife & Entertainment

As a university city, Catania has an entertaining nightlife, but I would not recommend wandering the streets at night unless you've been here before and know where you are going. For entertainment it's best to take a late dinner, then return home early to bed.

Opera

If you are in Catania from December to June, the traditional opera season, have the proper attire (suits for men, dresses for women), and have a taste for something out of the ordinary, try the spectacle of the opera.
• **Teatro Massimo Bellini**, *Via G. Perrotta 12, 95131 Catania. Tel. 095/321-830, Fax the same*

Practical Information

Local Festivals & Holidays
• **February 3-5**, *Festa di Sant'Agata*. Fireworks, procession with statue of saint and long candles, stalls selling sweets
• **November to April**, Catania Jazz Festival

Postal Services

The **central post office** in Catania is at *Via Etnea 215 (Tel. 095/311-506)* near the Duomo. *Open Monday–Friday, 8:30am–5:00pm, Saturdays 9:00am–noon*. But if you're in a hurry, stamps can be bought at any tobacconist (stores indicated by a **T** sign outside), and mailed at any mailbox, which are red and marked with the word *Poste* or *Lettere*.

Tourist Information & Maps
• **Tourist Office**, at the Train Station, Tel. 095/531-802
• **Tourist Office**, at the Airport, Tel. 095/341-900

Both are open Monday–Saturday, 9:00am–noon and 1:00pm–8:00pm. They can offer you free hotel listings, city maps, and information about Catania and the surrounding area.

Mount Etna

One of the world's largest active volcanoes, **Mount Etna's** presence dominates the skyline of the entire coastal area. The last three eruptions - in 1985, 1992 and 2001 - have destroyed local roads and threatened local villagers, who, for some reason, continue to live at the base of this accident waiting to happen. Despite the possibility that the volcano could erupt at any time, Mount Etna is still a great tourist draw.

There are two ways to see the volcano, from the safety of a train that tours the base or from the volcano itself.

Arrivals & Departures
By Train Around the Volcano

You can ride the private railway **Ferrovia Circumetnea**, which goes from Catania around Mount Etna to **Riposto**, up north along the coast. This three hour ride is quite scenic, even if you're not going up the side of the volcano. The train passes through small towns and settlements along the way (**Adrano**, **Randazzo**, and **Giarre**) complete with castles and medieval walls. If you wish, you can disembark, walk around for a while then catch the next train for the coast. But remember there are only three trains a day. Ask the conductor if another is coming along behind so you don't get left at the station.

You can catch this private train – that does not accept Eurorail or Italorail passes – in Catania at **Stazione Borgo** (*Via Coraonda 350 just north of the Bellini Gardens; cost is E6 one way*). Once you reach **Riposto**, you'll need to catch a one-way regular local train back to Catania which should cost E4 and tack another half an hour onto your trip.

By Bus To the Volcano

Skirting the base of the volcano will give you perspective on this natural landmark and afford you some nice views, but actually ascending to the top first-hand will give you a better feel for the awesome strength of this volcano.

To get to the mountain, catch a bus from Catania's central train station at 8:00am and return at 4:00pm. The round-trip ticket costs E5. Buy it inside the train station at the AST window. The bus reaches its destination at the **Rifugio Sapienza**, 1,440 meters below the summit.

Seeing the Sights
Ascending Mt. Etna
You have three options to get near the top: walk, cable car, or mini-van. The highest you're allowed to go is to the **Torre del Filosofo**, a lava tower built by the Romans to commemorate Hadrian's climb to the top. From this spot you're not far from the top and should be treated to gaseous explosions and molten rocks being spit up from the crater. The whole landscape is otherworldly in appearance.

The **cable car** option, if working (this is Italy remember), costs E25 per person, takes two hours, and gives you about 45 minutes of time to wander around. The **minivan option** costs E20 and gives you about the same amount of time. **Walking** can be tiring and treacherous, since the footing is not too secure with lava pebbles hindering your traction. You'll also be climbing a little over 1,000 meters in oxygen-thin air, so you must be prepared.

Taormina

Despite being Sicily's main vacation spot, **Taormina** still retains much of its medieval hill town charm to make it worth a visit. This town is situated in a place of unsurpassed beauty. Located on a cliff top with two coves below, I am hard pressed to imagine a more beautiful sight. Lately some high-rise hotels have sprung up along some of the outlying beaches below, but if you stay in the old town you'll see none of that. But you will see tourists, in numbers that make Taormina uncomfortable in the summer. So the best time to come here is between October and March, when you'll have the whole place, almost, to yourself.

The town is tiny and filled with 15th to 19th century buildings along its main street and in its twisting alleys. Besides wandering through the town's medieval beauty, you can also visit the quiet hill town of **Castelmola**, or frequent the beaches below. There is a cable car that runs between Taormina and its closest beach, **Mazzaro**.

Arrivals & Departures
If you took the train around the base of Mount Etna to Riposto and are not returning to Catania, Taormina is only a short train ride away. If you're leaving from Catania, there are 30 trains a day that take 45 minutes each way and cost E5.

The train station is located far below the town of Taormina and you must catch one of the frequent buses up the mountain. They run until 10:30pm.

Where To Stay

Since this is a tourist town there are plenty of places to stay, but if you arrive in the peak months from April through September without a reservation, you may not be able to find a room or you'll have to settle for less than stellar accommodations.

Below are the best options in each category.

1. CAPARENA LIDO, *Locanda Spisone, Via Nazionale 189, 98039 Taormina. Tel. 0942/652-033, Fax the same. 88 rooms all with bath. Double E130-200. All credit cards accepted. Breakfast included.* ****

This place is a beauty. Settled in by the water and surrounded by greenery, this hotel has a private beach, a swimming pool, satellite TV, a good restaurant serving typical Sicilian dishes, a great bar area, exercise facilities and a tennis court. The rooms are large and comfortable and the bathrooms have every imaginable convenience, including telephone and hairdryer. Breakfast is served in a wonderful room on the top floor with large windows offering a fantastic view of the sea. At the beach you have your own gazebo bar, paddle boats, umbrellas for shade, deck chairs, and musical entertainment in the evenings. A wonderful place to stay.

2. EXCELSIOR PALACE, *Via Toselli 8, 98039 Taormina. Tel. 0942/23975, Fax 0942/23978. 87 rooms all with bath. Single E100-130; Double E130-200. All credit cards accepted. Breakfast included.* ****

Located in the center of town but with great views of both Etna and the sea. A truly tranquil place to stay. Established in 1903 and renovated in the 1980s, this hotel is filled with antiques and every modern convenience. The rooms are more recently renovated and are filled with modern furnishings and all have a view of either the sea or the gardens that surround the hotel. The bathrooms are small but accommodating, with hairdryer and courtesy toiletry kits. There is also a large pool in the middle of the hotel's park that opens in the beginning of spring. The restaurant is also the breakfast room where you are served an abundant buffet of fresh fruit, juice, croissant, cakes, pies, eggs, yogurt, milk, coffee and tea.

3. PRESIDENT HOTEL SPLENDID, *Via Dietro Cappuccini 10, 98039 Taormina. Tel. 0942/23500, Fax 0942/625-289. 50 rooms all with bath. Single E50-65; Double E80-100. American Express, Visa accepted.* **

A fantastic place to stay for any budget. A little run down in places, but the rooms at the front have great panoramic views and most have balconies from which you can sit, enjoy room service, and enjoy the view. The restaurant serves superb local food (the full board for only E50 is a steal) and the view from most of the tables is magnificent. They also have an outside pool and a relaxing bar downstairs. Located about 150 meters from the center of town,

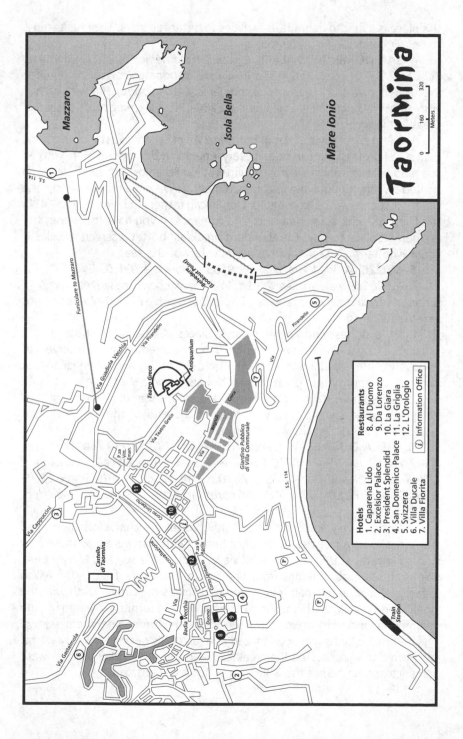

Taormina

Mazzaro

Isola Bella

Mare Ionio

S.S. 114

Funiculare to Mazzaro

Belvedere Point
(Lookout Point)

Via Guadiola Vecchia

Via Pirandello

Via Pirandello

Teatro Greco

Antiquarium

Via Teatro Greco

Via Pirandello

Via Croce

Via Bagnoli Croce

Giardino Pubblico
di Villa Communale

P.za
Vitt.
Eman.

S.S. 114

Via Cappucini

Corso Umberto

Circonvallazione

Castello
di Taormina

P.za 9
Aprile

Corso Umberto

Via Gastelmola

Via
Badia Vecchia

Duomo

Train
Station

0   160   320
Meters

Hotels
1. Caparena Lido
2. Excelsior Palace
3. President Splendid
4. San Domenico Palace
5. Svizzera
6. Villa Ducale
7. Villa Fiorita

Restaurants
8. Al Duomo
9. Da Lorenzo
10. La Giara
11. La Griglia
12. L'Orologio

(i) Information Office

this place is trying to upgrade its facilities to get three stars. Their next step is to get air conditioning in the rooms.

4. SAN DOMENICO PALACE, *Piazza San Domenico 5, 98039 Taormina. Tel. 0942/23701, Fax 0942/625-506. E-mail: sandomenico@cormorano.net. Web: www.cormorano.net/sgas/sandomenico/. 101 rooms, 100 with bath, 1 with shower. Single E210-260; Double E280-430. All credit cards accepted. Breakfast included.* *****

This is the best place to stay in Taormina. An excellent five star deluxe hotel with super professional service and every amenity under the sun. Here you can rub elbows with some of Europe's glitterati while enjoying superb dining, a heated swimming pool, tennis courts, a great view, and a private beach. The hotel is located in an old convent for Dominican fathers that was built in 1430. It is filled with character, ambiance and romance. If you have the money this is a perfect place to stay. The abundant breakfast buffet is served in a classic room with terra cotta tiles with a perfect view of the sea.

5. SVIZZERA, *Via L Pirandelo 26, 98039 Taormina. Tel. 0942/23970, Fax 0942/625-906. E-mail: svizzera@tao.it. Web: www.pensionesvizzera.com/. 16 rooms, 4 with bath, 12 with shower. Single E55; Double E70-90. No credit cards accepted.* *

I just love these small pensione style places. A quaint little hotel on the outskirts of town near the water. Only 16 rooms so remember to reserve well in advance. Here you'll find a relaxing garden setting and some clean and comfortable rooms all at great prices. They also have a shuttle service to pick you up at the train station. No air conditioning or TV in the rooms, but they are pretty good spots to rest your head at the end of the day. A budget travelers paradise. Definitely a hidden gem.

6. VILLA DUCALE, *Via Leonardo da Vinci 60, 98039 Taormina. Tel. 0942/28153, Fax 0942/28710. E-mail: villaducale@tao.it. Web: www.tao.it/villaducale/. Closed Dec 4 - Feb 22. 10 rooms all with bath. Single E190-330; Double E280-460. All credit cards accepted. Breakfast included.* ****

A lovely, lovely, lovely little hotel that has all the character, charm and amenities to be a five star – and it has finally been discovered, as these new prices indicate. You have wonderful views of both the sea and Mount Etna. The rooms are all different from one another and are filled with Sicilian ceramics, locally made bed frames and bed covers of damask cloth with the hotel's logo in gold on them. Some have handmade furniture created by Tino Giammona, and all have wonderful terraces with stunning panoramic views. The bathrooms are super-accessorized and tastefully decorated with ceramic tile from Cattagirone. And the breakfast is absolutely excellent. If you want romance and ambiance this is the place. But it will cost you.

7. **VILLA FIORITA**, *Via L. Piarandello 39, 98039 Taormina. Tel. 0942/ 24122, Fax 0942/625-967. 26 rooms all with bath. Double E120. All credit cards accepted. Breakfast included.* ***

In the three star category, the Villa Fiorita distinguishes itself because of the charm of its location. Virtually engulfed by lavish gardens with a small pool, the hotel also has great views. The entrance hall is small and is paved with authentic Sicilian terra-cotta tiles. The rooms are large and well-decorated with antique furniture and vases, paved with tiles from Cattagirone, and the wall and bed coverings are coordinated white and blue. Some rooms have only small terraces; the rest have balconies and all have deck chairs. The service is professional and courteous. Breakfast is either served out on the terrace or in a lovely and romantic room, an abundant buffet of croissant, jams, and other breakfast rolls all baked and prepared in-house, with many different types of bread, and eggs made to order.

Where To Eat

As a tourist town, there are plenty of little places to eat. Listed below are the restaurants I think are best.

8. **AL DUOMO**, *Vico Erbrei 11, Tel. 0942/625-656. Closed Wednesdays. All credit cards accepted. Dinner for two E40.*

In the summer the best place to eat is on their little terrace facing the Piazza Duomo. They have a small antipasto plate of cheese and salad that I can't recommend. But their pasta dishes are superb, especially the *pennette vecchia Taormina* (little macaronis with a spicy tomato and vegetable sauce). For seconds, try their *polpette arrostite nelle foglie di limone* (roasted meatballs with a touch of lemon sauce).

9. **DA LORENZO**, *Via M Amari 4, Tel. 0942/23480. Closed Wednesdays and November 15 to December 15. All credit cards accepted. Dinner for two E45.*

Situated a stone's throw away from the Piazza Duomo, during the summer the best place to eat is out on their patio. In this small intimate restaurant that only seats around 45 people, the best *antipasto* samplings are the *ricci di mare* (a large plate of mixed seafood), *occhie di bue* (oxen eyeballs - go ahead, be adventurous, they're much better than mountain oysters), or *calamaretti fritti* (fried small squid). For *primo* try their *fusilli al carciofo* (pasta with a tasty artichoke sauce) and for seconds try any of their roasted or grilled meat or fish.

10. **LA GIARA**, *Vico La Floresta 1, Tel. 0942/23360. Closed Mondays but not from July to October. Only open on weekends in November, February and March. All credit cards accepted. Dinner for two E60.*

Elegant and sophisticated, this large place is located in the heart of the old town, and has a great terrace that is used year round with wonderful views all the way to the beach at Giardini Naxos two kilometers away. The cooks create regular local dishes here, as well as creative adaptations of them. Try the *foie gras* for an antipasto or the *insalatina di crostacei* (little salad with crustaceans). For *primo* try the *raviolini di Crostacei in salsa di scampi* (ravioli stuffed with crustaceans in a shrimp sauce). For seconds try any of their regularly prepared meats or fish, or *mignon di carne al tartufo nero* (filet mignon covered with black truffles). You can prolong the evening after dinner by getting a drink at their piano bar.

11. LA GRIGLIA, *Corso Umberto 54, Tel. 0942/23980. Closed Tuesdays and November 20 - December 20. All credit cards accepted. Dinner for two E55.*

On the main street in Taormina, this place is known for their aquarium stuffed with lobsters and fish that you can choose for your meal. This is a rustic but refined place, with professional service preparing you for fine Sicilian food. Try the *vermiccelli incasciati* (fried vermicelli pasta made with a tomato sauce) or the classic *penne con sarde e finicchietto* (tubular pasta with sardines and fennel). For seconds try anything they have on the grill – after all, the name of the place means "The Grill."

12. L'OROLOGIO, *Via Don Bosco 37a, Tel. 0942/625-572. Closed Mondays and November. All credit cards accepted. Dinner for two E50.*

You can sit outside on their enclosed terrace year round. For *antipasto* try their *gamberetti con rucola* (small shrimp with cheese), or *il prosciutto di porcellino* (ham from a young pig) that comes with *bruschette* (garlic and oil smothered bread covered with tomatoes). Next try their *ravioli di carne di cinghiale al finocchietto* (ravioli stuffed with wild boar meat in a fennel sauce). Then for seconds try their excellent *Fantasia dell'Orologio* (mixed fried seafood, meats and cheeses).

Seeing the Sights

Taormina's main attractions are the steep-stepped medieval streets, quaint old buildings, and scenic views over the water, but you will also enjoy the **Teatro Greco** (*Via Teatro Greco. Open 9:00am–1 hour before sunset; admission E3*). Founded by the Greeks in the 3rd century BCE, this theater was almost completely redone by the Romans in the 1st century CE to accommodate their gladiatorial displays. It's so well-preserved that tourists are still allowed to clamber around on the stone seats still in existence today.

Directly in front of the Greek theater are **giardini pubblici** of the **Villa Comunale** (*Via Bagnoli Croce. Open during daylight hours*), where you can enjoy a peaceful stroll or relax on a bench sunk into a flower bush. From the walls there are some wonderful views over the water and the beach areas. Back in town there is a smaller **Teatro Romano** (*Via Corso Umberto, open all the time*), that is partially covered under the **Church of Santa Caterina**. You can peer down from the railings in the street or enter the church to see more of the theater through the floor. Located right next to the tourist office.

If you're in the mood to climb small steep steps up a mountainside for about 30 minutes, then you can enjoy the best views of the area. Located above town, this tumble-down medieval **castello** (*open to the public 9:00am–1:00pm and 4:00pm–7:00pm*) isn't much in itself, but the panoramic views are superb.

Nightlife & Entertainment

There are plenty of discos to choose from, all of which will cost you between E5 and E10 just to get in. If you want a more relaxing evening there is nothing better than sipping a good Sicilian wine at one of the outdoor cafés and watching the world go by. That will be a little expensive too, about E3 per glass, but your eardrums will still be intact.

Practical Information

English Language Bookstore
• **Libreria Interpress**, *Corso Umberto 37, Tel. 0942/24989.* Open regular business hours; not exclusively an English-language bookstore, but they do carry a few popular titles in English

Local Festivals
• **May**, *Sfilato del Carretto.* A dazzling display of colorful Sicilian carts
• **July to September**, *Taormina Arte.* Theatrical, film and musical productions all over the city
• **Christmas**, Festive parade

Moped Rental
• **Sicily on Wheels**, *Via Bagnoli Croce 90, Tel. 0942/625-657.* Must be over 16 to rent. Open daily from 9:00am–1:00pm and 4:00pm–7:00pm. You can also rent cars here, but driving a car in crowded Taormina is not advised. A great way to see the countryside or just go for a spin down to the beach is by moped.

Postal Services
The central post office in Taormina is *at Piazza San Antonio, Tel. 0942/23010. Open Monday through Saturday 8:30am–5:00pm, and since this is a tourist town Sundays 9:00am–noon.* Stamps can be bought at any tobacconist (stores indicated by a **T** sign outside), and mailed at any mailbox, which are red and marked with the word *Poste* or *Lettere*.

Tourist Information & Maps
• **Tourist Office**, *Piazza Santa Caterina, Tel. 0942/232-43.* Can help you find a place to stay and give out maps and other information. *Open Monday–Saturday, 8:30am–2:00pm and 4:00pm–7:00pm.*

Isole Eolie

The **Isole Eolie**, named after the Greek God of the Wind, are seven inhabited islands in total that lie between 30 and 80 km off the north coast of Sicily. Also known as the **Lipari Islands** in reference to the largest island in the chain, the population of the islands today is about 14,000.

Once used as an ancient penal colony, today the islands attract people interested in scuba diving and snorkeling, as well as those wishing to enjoy one of the most unspoiled settings in Italy. This is a vacation paradise. Here you will be on beautiful islands, in a deep blue sea, isolated from everything, with all the peace and tranquility you can find.

The main island, **Lipari**, is more prepared for dealing with tourists and is where the best hotels are located. It also has a beautiful castle, archaeological ruins, and a variety of churches. **Vulcano** is aptly named since it is basically a bubbling volcano itself. **Stromboli** is also an active volcano and is the most scenic of all the islands. These three islands are terribly crowded in the summertime with tourists, but you can visit the other four – **Panarea**, **Salina**, **Filicudi** and **Alicudi** – and enjoy a bit of solitude.

For more information about the islands, check out the official website: *www.isole-eolie.com/*.

Arrivals & Departures

Access to the islands is easiest from **Milazzo** on the north shore of Sicily. There are year-round ferries and hydrofoils that leave several times a day.

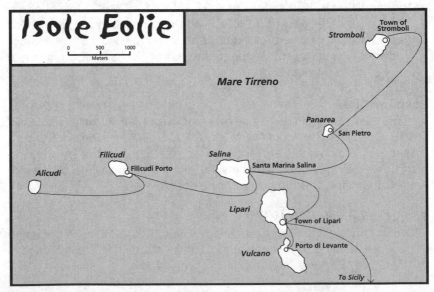

These ferries stop first at Vulcano, then at the main island Lipari. Here you can disembark and catch a smaller local ferry to any of the other islands.

But you can also catch ferries and hydrofoils to the islands from cities in Sicily (**Palermo, Cefalu,** and **Messina**) as well as **Naples** and **Reggio di Calabria** on the mainland, and **Cagliari** in Sardinia.

Ferries & Hydrofoil Companies in Milazzo
• **SNAV**, *Via L. Rizzo 14, Tel. 090/928-4509.* Hydrofoils (E20) only.
• **Siremar**, *Via dei Mille 32, Tel. 090/928-3242.* Ferries (E16) and hydrofoils (E20).
• **Navigazione Generale Italiano**, *Via dei Mille 26 Tel. 090/928-4091.* Ferries (E16) only.

Lipari

The island of **Lipari** is the most visited since it is the largest and most beautiful. The main town of the same name has quaint little pastel-colored houses, and is surrounded by the medieval **Castello** that crowns the small town. Inside the castle walls there are four churches, the town's **Duomo**, and an **archaeological park**, which reveals that there were people in Lipari as far back as 1600 BCE.

Getting Around Town

There are buses every 45 minutes or so that leave Lipari and traverse the island. Any of the other villages are no more than half an hour away by bus. If you're feeling adventurous, rent a moped and ride around the island. They can be rented at one of the many rental shops along the **Via Marina Lunga**.

North of the town of Lipari is the village of **Cannetto**. Visitors come to enjoy the **Spiaggia Bianca**, a small walk north of the village, where topless and bottomless bathing abounds. If you're looking for some exercise, walk the four kilometers uphill to **Quattroochi**. From here you get a magnificent view of the town of Lipari, and the island of **Vulcano** in the background. Remember to bring your camera.

Where To Stay

CARASCO, *Porto delle Genti, 98055 Lipari. Isole Eolie. Tel. 090/981-1605, Fax 090/981-1828. E-mail: info@carasco.it. Web: www.carasco.com/. 89 rooms, 20 with bath, 69 with shower. Per person E50-85. Per person with balcony E60-90. Visa accepted. Full board E70-90.* ***

Located out of reach of Lipari and even the smaller villages on the island, this is truly a resort type environment. Set in a romantic old building, the Carasco has a swimming pool, disco, piano bar, a private beach, great views of the water and other islands, a great restaurant and an accommodating bar. The rooms are relatively large, very clean, quite charming, and extremely comfortable. This is the place where Italians come to relax in the Isole Eolie. Expensive for a three star ... but they're worth it.

MACOMBO, *Via C. Battisti 192, 98055 Lipari. Isole Eolie. Tel. 090/981-1442, Fax 090/981-1062. 14 rooms all with shower. Single E50-80; Double E80-130. No credit cards accepted.* **

Located in the village of Canneto north of the town of Lipari, this is an expensive place that has easy access to the area's beaches. The hotel's rooms are quaint, comfortable, and clean but are not luxurious. They have their own little restaurant from which you can get full board for E50, the price of one meal for two elsewhere. They also have a small bar and, importantly, air conditioning in the summertime.

ORIENTE, *Via G. Marconi 35, 98055 Lipari. Isole Eolie. Tel. 090/981-1493, Fax 090/988-0198. E-mail: info@isolelipari.it. Web: www.isolelipari.it/hoteloriente/. 24 rooms all with shower. Single E50-80; Double E80-130. Visa Accepted.* **

A cute little place in the town of Lipari that is geared to the budget traveler, but which has wonderful amenitiews. They have air conditioning – a rarity in two stars – a beautiful little private park/garden, and a comfortable downstairs bar. The rooms are small and clean but have few other amenities. A nice place to stay.

VILLA MELIGUNIS, *Via Marte 7, 98055 Lipari. Isole Eolie. Tel. 090/981-2426, Fax 090/988-0149. E-mail: villameligunis@netnet.it. Web: www.lineafutura.it/sponsor/meligunis/home.htm. 32 rooms all with shower. Double E150-300. Credit cards accepted. Full board E80-120.* ****

Not far outside of the town of Lipari, this place has a private beach area, their own restaurant, a tranquil little garden area, a wonderful bar and first class service. The rooms are luxurious and comfortable with mini-bar, TV, and air conditioning. They also have a shuttle bus that runs guests back and forth all over the island.

Where To Eat

There are plenty of family-run restaurants all over the island. Most are open only in the high season to fleece the tourists. Below you'll find the best choice on any of the seven islands.

FILIPPINO, *Piazza del Municipio, Tel. 090/911-002. Closed Mondays (but not in high season) and all November 15 to December 15. Credit cards accepted. Dinner for two E50.*

Great local food, especially the *maccaruna alla Filippino*, a tasty home-made pasta dish with a sauce of tomatoes, eggplant, mozzarella and ham, as well as other culinary delights. You can expect to sample some of the best prepared fish anywhere. I don't know what they do or how they do it but any fish you try, whether it's baked, fried, or grilled will melt in your mouth. They also make their own bread in-house and it is stupendous.

Practical Information
Postal Services
The **central post office** in Lipari is on the *Corso Vittorio Emanuele 207, Tel. 090/981-1379. Open Monday through Friday 8:30am–5:00pm, Saturdays 9:00am– noon.* Stamps can also be bought at any tobacconist (stores indicated by a **T** sign outside), and mailed at any mailbox, which are red and marked with the word *Poste* or *Lettere.*

Tourist Information & Maps
• **Tourist Office**, *Via Vittorio Emanuele 202, Tel. 090/988-0095,* and is open regular business hours. You can get free information on buses, sights, and a not very useful map.

Vulcano
Some geologists think this small volcano of an island will erupt sometime around 2002, so beware when you go. Despite the pungent sulfurous smell, you can enjoy a relaxing bath in the heated bubbling water around the island, or coat yourself in the famous **fanghi**, or mud baths. These are located just up the Via Provinciale from the Porto di Levante, where the ferries dock on the east side of the island on the way to the beach. The mud is slightly radioactive, so don't sit in it too long, and pregnant women and small children shouldn't even think of going in.

If caking yourself with mud is not your style, walk down to the beach and immerse yourself in the bubbling **aquacalda** (hot water). You can also go up and peer into the **Gran Crater** (Great Crater) that simmers and boils. You need to be in reasonable shape to get up to the top. Once there you'll have some fabulous photo opportunities of the surrounding islands. You'll need to go in the early morning or late afternoon, since the face of the volcano gets quite hot from the sun and the lava inside at midday.

Almost everything on the island is closed before June and after September, so if you want to stay on the island or grab a bite to eat when it's low season, you may be out of luck.

Where To Stay
CONTI, *Porto Ponente, 98050 Vulcano. Isole Eolie. Tel. 090/985-2012, Fax 090/988-0150. 62 rooms, only 61 with shower. Single with or without shower E60-70; Double E90-110. Visa accepted.* ******
One of the bigger establishments on the island. They have their own

private beach, a fine restaurant, a relaxing garden, a shuttle bus service, but no air conditioning and that may be why they are a two star. Stay here if you can stand the heat. The rooms are relatively large, with inconsistent furnishings, but they are clean and quite comfortable.

EOLIAN HOTEL, *Porto Ponente, 98050 Vulcano. Isole Eolie. Tel. 090/985-2151, Fax 090/985-2153. 88 rooms all with bath. Single E70-100; Double E140-170. Credit cards accepted. Full board E80-100.* ***

Tennis courts, outdoor pool, relaxing garden, a fine restaurant, and more. This place is definitely a good deal. Why the three star rating? The hotel is older than Les Sables Noirs, is well maintained but not quite as polished, and a private beach means much in the rating games on the islands. But other than that absence this is a great place to stay.

LES SABLES NOIRS, *Porto Ponente, 98050 Vulcano. Isole Eolie. Tel. 090/985-2461, Fax 090/985-2454. E-mail: ricevimento.lsn@framon-hotels.it. Web: www.framon-hotels.com/lesablesnoirs/. 33 rooms. 8 with bath. 25 with shower. Per person E80-130. Credit cards accepted. Full board E110-160.* ****

Quite an exclusive establishment located in a truly romantic setting. They have their own private beach where you can rent snorkeling equipment. The hotel also has an outdoor swimming pool, a sun deck, a beautiful view, a piano bar and really good hotel restaurant that serves local cuisine as well as dietetic food. They also have bus service that can take you around the island. The rooms are quaint and comfortable. This place deserves its four star rating.

Stromboli

Another volcano in this chain of islands, **Stromboli** is the furthest from Sicily. This place is super-crowded in high season and is almost completely shut down in the low season. If you want to stay here you need to make reservations well in advance. The year round population of the island is only about 400, but when the tourists come you can have as many as 3,000 or more staying here and many more coming to visit or to camp.

There are two towns on the island, tiny Ginostra on the southern end, and a combination of Piscita, Fiocogrande, San Vincenzo, and Scari which make up what is popularly called **Villaggio Stromboli** (**Stromboli Town**). You'll find most places to eat and stay in Stromboli Town, with only one small no-star pensione in Ginostra.

The only real attraction here is the climb up the **volcano**. To legally do this you need to go with an official guide, who can be hired from the **Club Alpino Italiano** at their offices in Piazza Vincenzo *(Tel. 090/986-263)*. The cost will be between E15 and E20, depending on how well you bargain. You start off in Piscita and the trip should take around three hours up and two hours down, so you have to be in really good shape. You'll also need to wear well-soled boots and bring along at least 1.5 liters of water. Don't drink it all at once. You'll want it later.

About halfway up you'll come across the **Sciara del Fuoco**, the volcanic trail that vents the lava directly into the sea. At the top, be careful not to lean over too far. Once you drop in you'll be hard-boiled forever. On your descent from the top you may decide to go down the other side to **Ginostra** (follow the red, yellow and orange marked rocks) where you can enjoy a less touristy environment. There are ferries from here back to Stromboli Town, as well as Lipari.

Another fun side trip here is a visit to the **lighthouse** on the small rock island of **Strombolicchio**. From Via Marina and the ferry dock, you can hire a boat to take you out there for between E15 and E25.

Where To Stay

LA SCIARA RESIDENCE, *Via Soldato Cincotta, 98050 Stromboli. Isole Eolie. Tel. 090/986-121, Fax 090/986-284. Web: http://spazioweb.inwind.it/ eolie/hotels/stromboli/sciara/sciara.htm. 62 rooms, only 59 with shower. Per person E55-95, room & breakfast included. Per person E85-135, room & full board. All credit cards accepted. ****

A truly romantic and relaxing place to stay. They have their own private beach, a swimming pool, tennis courts, magnificent views and a good hotel restaurant. The one thing they do not have is air conditioning, but try to get a sea view room, open your window, and the sea breeze will cool down the place quickly. A quaint, clean, and comfortable place in an amazingly romantic environment.

LA SIRENETTA PARK HOTEL, *Via Marina 13, 98050 Stromboli. Isole Eolie. Tel. 090/986-025, Fax 090/986-124.43 rooms all with bath. Per person E55-90, room & breakfast included. Per person E85-130, room & full board. Credit cards accepted. ****

Established in 1952 and renovated in 1983, this place is quaint and comfortable. The relaxing garden and outdoor swimming pool add to the ambiance. Besides all the regular amenities for a three star, they also have a nursery to care for your child while you frolic around the island. One item missing is air conditioning, but the breezes from the water usually alleviate any problems.

Salina

Salina is an uncrowded alternative to the three main islands, but that may soon change, so come here now to see the peaceful tranquillity of a place where time stands still. You arrive at **Porto Santa Maria**, the island's main port, where you can rent mopeds or bicycles to traverse the island, or take one of the many buses to any of your destinations.

Just three kilometers south of the port is the little village of **Lingua**, which is really only a small clean beach and a tiny cluster of *pensione* and *trattorie* with great views of Lipari. A nice place to grab a bite to eat. If you head north from the port you'll pass through **Malfa**, a quaint little village that has a backdrop of decaying fishermen's huts. There is also a good beach here. Further along you come to **Pollara**, the site of the last eruption on the island back some 12,500 years ago. The village sits on a crescent-shaped crater from that eruption.

If you arrive on the island on August 15, you will be surrounded by pilgrims celebrating the Assumption of the Virgin festival enroute to the **Sanctuary of the Madonna del Terziot** in **Valdichiesa**.

Where To Stay

If you really want to get away from it all, here's one of the better little hotels on the island:

LA MARINARA, *Via Alfieri, Lingua. Salina. Isole Eolie. Tel. 090/984-3022. 14 rooms all with bath. Single E50; Double E75. No credit cards accepted.* *

A small place with a great restaurant. You can get full board for E50 per person. But since there are a few other restaurants in Lingua you may want to sample some of these. The rooms are simple and rustic but if you decided to stay on this island you should be expecting this. They also have a relaxing little garden where you can enjoy the evenings.

Panarea

Located between Lipari and Stromboli, **Panarea** is the smallest of the seven islands as well as the prettiest. That's why it is slowly becoming the hangout for more and more members of the jet set. From this island you can venture to some smaller islets that surround the east side for some great swimming. You should be able to hire a boat at the ferry dock at **San Pietro** for about E15 per person.

At **Punta Milazzese**, you can explore an archaeological dig of a Bronze Age settlement. There is little else to do on the island except eat, drink, and relax.

Where To Stay

CINCOTTA, *Via San Pietro, 98050 San Pietro. Panarea. Isole Eolie. Tel. 090/993-014, Fax 090/983211. E-mail: info@isolelipari.it. Web: www.isolelipari.it/hotel-panarea-cincotta/. 29 rooms all with showers. Single E90-210. Double E120-230. Credit cards accepted.* ***

What a great location and view. This rustic place that has comfortable yet spartan rooms. You can get half board at their fine local-style restaurant for between E80-140 per person dependeing on the season; and you won't do any better anywhere else on the island. They have a swimming pool surrounded by lush gardens, patios galore and charm and ambiance to spare. A great place to get away to.

RAYA, *Via San Pietro, 98050 Panarea, Isole Eolie. Tel. 90/983013 or 983029, Fax 90/983103. 30 rooms all with bath. Single E100-200; Standard Double E200-250; Exclusive Double E250-300. All credit cards accepted.* *******

What a stunning hotel. Set up on the charming island of Panarea, this internationally renowned hotel is one of the gems of the Mediterranean, and caters to a select clientele. This place has as much peace and privacy as anyone could wish for, with ample sun terraces offering a panorama of astonishing beauty. Each room has its own private terrace with a breathtaking view of volcano Stromboli, softly erupting twice per hour. A park of lush Mediterranean vegetation surrounds the complex. Full board required in high season and is included in the price. This is the place to stay on the Isole Eolie if you want to get away from it all but still have all possible luxury available.

Filucidi

From the **Porto Filucida** where the ferry docks, take a walk north up to the almost abandoned village of **Valdichiesa**. If you keep walking all the way to the west side of the island, you'll be able to see the huge phallic rock formation **La Canna** thrusting out of the sea. If you don't want to walk all the way there, you can hire a boat at the ferry pier to take you for about E15 per person.

You can also go across the island over the thin peninsula to the other coast to the tiny village of **Pecorino**. If you walk along the peninsula east, you'll come to the archaeological site of **Capo Graziano**, where there is a site of Bronze Age structures that predates those on Panarea. One last place to see here is the **Grotta del Bue Marino** (**The Seal Grotto**), which can only be reached by boat.

Where To Stay

PHENICUSA, *Via Porto, 98050 Filicudi. Isole Eolie. Tel. 090/984-4185, Fax 090/988-9966. 36 rooms, 2 with bath, 34 with shower. Single E86; Double E125. No credit cards accepted.* *******

Located at the ferry port, this place has its own private beach and a really good restaurant. Take the option of the full board for E90 per person since you only have one or two other options on the entire desolate island. The rooms with bathtubs (as compared to showers) are the best, but there are only two of them, so reserve early. The other bathrooms are tiny but clean. The rooms are all decorated in a pleasant manner and are comfortable and clean.

Alicudi

This is the place to go if you really want to get away from it all. There are only 125 inhabitants, one hotel, electricity only recently installed, and no paved roads. This tiny island used to be a rocky penitentiary maintained by the Italian government, but now the island is all but abandoned. From the island's only town and the ferry dock, **Alicudi Porto**, you can follow a path north to the ruins of a **castle** that used to house the prisoners. Other than that, and swimming along the rocky shore, there's nothing to do here except relax and enjoy the escape from the system.

On your way here you will pass by the large rock phallus, **La Canna**, off the west coast of Filucidi.

Where To Stay

ERICUSA, *Via Regina Elena, 98050. Alicudi. Isole Eolie. Tel. 090/988-9902. 12 rooms all with shower. Double E80. No credit cards accepted. Full board E80.* *

I suggest you take the full board of breakfast, lunch, and dinner, since your options will be limited on Alicudi. Besides small but comfortable rooms, and tiny but clean bathrooms, the hotel has little else to offer. Very rustic, but oh-so-peaceful and relaxing.

Chapter 27

Sardinia

Roughly oblong in shape, **Sardinia** is the second largest island after Sicily in the Mediterranean Sea. It is located just south of the French island of Corsica. Sardinia is rugged, wild, and rather remote from Italy. Because of this isolation, even more so than Sicily, many of the old Sardinian customs and traditions live on today. The Sardinian language, which developed independently from Italian, still retains many old characteristics, despite the modernizing of the island in more recent years.

What is today an autonomous region in the Republic of Italy started off as home to Bronze Age refugees cast onto Sardinia's shores about 2,000 BCE. Evidence of their existence is seen in the over 700 remaining **nuraghi** – massive towers built with large stones without mortar – that still dot the island. The **Phoenicians** were the first to invade this pristine isle in the 9th century BCE. Later **Rome** was attracted to the island's mineral riches needed to maintain her Legions, and a Roman fleet invaded in 238 BCE.

Around 455 CE, Sardinia fell into the hands of the **Vandals**, then later was fused into the **Byzantine empire**. But repeated **Saracen** attacks weakened the empire's hold so that four independent districts emerged on Sardinia called **Guidacati** that were governed by popular decree. These four independent states remained even after the seafaring cities of Pisa and Genoa, with the Pope's backing, claimed the island as their own. For the next several centuries Sardinia became a protectorate of many different nations including Aragon, Spain, and Austria. **Vittorio Emanuele**, who became king of Italy in 1863, started his campaign to unite the country from Sardinia with the help of a native of the island, **Giuseppe Garibaldi**.

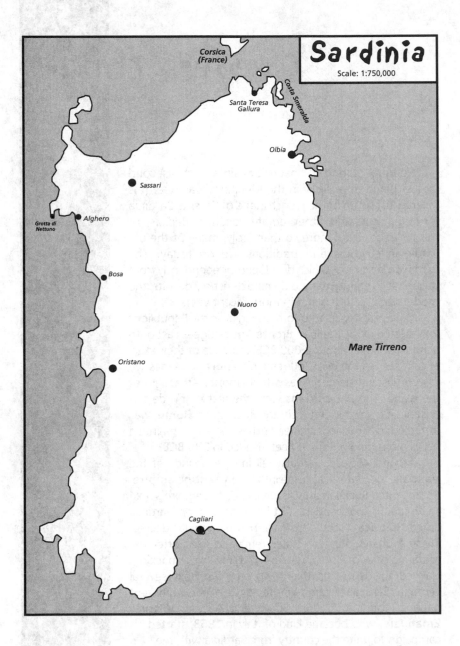

Sardinia

Scale: 1:750,000

Corsica
(France)

Costa Smeralda

Santa Teresa
Gallura

Olbia

Sassari

Grotta di
Nettuno

Alghero

Bosa

Nuoro

Mare Tirreno

Oristano

Cagliari

Sardinia today lags economically behind much of the rest of Europe. Their main industry is pastoral farming, as well as fishing, but recently the island has begun to succumb to the siren call of tourism. Sardinia is also a mining center. It produces four-fifths of Italy's lead. The island's large mineral deposits are largely found in the southwest and include zinc, lignite, fluorite, bauxite, copper, silver, antimony, manganese, and iron.

The island is divided into four provinces: **Cagliari**, **Nuoro**, **Oristano**, and **Sassari** and each province is named for its capital city. Most tourists visit the northern Sassari Province, which includes the famous **Costa Smeralda**, or **Emerald Coast**. But there are also many rustic sights to sea in Sardinia besides the beach, most of which are off the beaten path in the mountains. If you decide to search these out, however, be careful. This is a poor island and if you roam into the mountains, remember to be aware and alert. Women traveling alone in particular could be targets, so please be careful.

For more information, check out the Sardinian website: *http://sardinia.net.*

Arrivals & Departures
By Air

Cagliari has an international airport but it does not yet accept flights from North America. But you can get a flight from most European capitals and a number of Italian cities directly to Cagliari.

From the airport you can take a bus directly to the city center near the train station. The bus leaves every twenty minutes from outside the international terminal and drops you off at the Piazza Matteoti. The ride is free. Check with your travel agent for details.

By Ferry

The most popular way to get to Sardinia is by ferry from one of the ports in Italy, especially **Civitavecchia**, whose ferries land in **Olbia**. If you're traveling in the high season – May to September – you need to book passage on your ferry weeks in advance, since there are so many people going over to Sardinia and there are not that many ferries.

The company **Tirrenia** operates the majority of ferries to and from the destinations below. You can purchase tickets from most travel agents:
• **Civitavecchia** (just north of Rome) **to Olbia**, 7 hours, fare is E25
• **Genoa to Olbia**, 13 hours, E35
• **Naples to Cagliari**, 16 hours, E40
• **Palermo to Cagliari**, 13 hours, E30
• **Trapani to Cagliari**, 11 hours, E30

Climate & Weather

Anytime is a good time to travel to Sardinia. The climate doesn't vary greatly, making Sardinia a pleasant trip any time of year – with the following caveats: November to March is not prime beach weather, and the summers can sometimes be overbearingly hot. For the best weather, visit between early September and the first week in November.

Getting Around Sardinia

By Car

The most prized and thus the most remote sites to visit on the island simply cannot be visited unless you go by car. If this is your first time to Sardinia, I would recommend taking the train until you get a feel for Sardinia and its customs. Rental car listings are in each city's section.

By Train

Service by train has been upgraded in recent years but still remains light years behind the rest of Europe (this is a third world country in many respects). Unlike Italy's mainland, there are frequent delays. But the views you'll see from the train are stupendous. And you won't have to worry about driving on the treacherous mountain roads.

Basic Information

Banking Hours

Banks in Sardinia are open Monday through Friday, 8:35am–1:35pm and only the larger branches are open in the afternoons from 3:00pm–4:00pm. All are closed Saturdays and Sundays and on national holidays. In some cities, the afternoon hour may not even exist. Even if the banks are closed, most travelers checks can be exchanged for Italian lire at most hotels and shops and at the foreign exchange offices in railway stations and at airports.

If you arrive without Italian currency, the **airport** at Cagliari has a few banks and monetary exchange offices *(Ufficio di Cambio)*.

Business Hours

Store hours are usually Monday through Friday, 9:00am–1:00pm, 3:30/4:00pm –7:30/8:00pm, and Saturdays 9:00am–1:00pm. Most stores are closed on Sundays and on national holidays. Don't expect to find any 24-hour convenience stores just around the corner. If you want to have some soda in your room after a long day of touring, you need to plan ahead. Don't expect to get a lot done from 1:00pm to 4:00pm, except find a nice restaurant and enjoy a pleasant afternoon.

Consulates
As you have probably surmised, there are no embassies or consulates on Sardinia, so if you need their assistance you'll have to make do with the embassies in Rome (see Chapter 7, *Basic Information*, for a full list of embassies and consulates).

Public Holidays in Sardinia
Offices and shops in Sardinia are closed on certain dates, so prepare for the eventuality of having virtually everything closed. For more details, see the Sicily chapter; the same holidays are observed here in Sardinia.

Food & Wine
Food
As in Sicily, most Sardinian food is cooked with fresh ingredients raised or caught a short distance from the restaurant, so the food is healthy and satisfying. The traditional Sardinian meal has been influenced by the Middle East, France, and Spain as a result of the past conquests of the island. Other influences include the sea and the climate, perfect for growing many herbs and spices, as well as vegetables and fruits.

Suggested Sardinian Cuisine
These are traditional Sardinian dishes. Enjoy!

Antipasto - Appetizer
• **Antipasto di mare** – Mixed seafood appetizer plate; differs from restaurant to restaurant
• **Pane frattau** – The local thin unleavened bread *carta di musica* covered with eggs and tomato sauce
• **Minestre di pesce** – Fish soup. Varies by region and restaurant.

Primo Piatto - First Course
Pasta
• **Sa fregula** – Pasta in broth with saffron
• **Culurgione** – Ravioli stuffed with beet roots, local cheese, and covered with tomato sauce and sausage made from lamb

Secondo Piatto - Entrée
Carne – Meat
• **Maiale arrosto** – Pig roasted on a spit
• **Capra arrosto** – Goat roasted on a spit
• **Cordula** – Lamb entrails baked with saffron and other spices

Pesce – Fish
• **Aragosta** – Lobster
• **Sogliola alla griglia** – Grilled sole

Dolce - Dessert
• **Sebada** – Dough stuffed with cheese, sugar and honey

Cagliari

Cagliari is the capital of Sardinia, the island's main port, and the main commercial and trade center on the island. The city was founded by the Phoenicians, who called it Caralis, and was later taken over by the Romans and renamed Carales. Eventually it passed through the rule of Spaniards and Pisans and was overrun by Saracens. The town's nickname is *Castello*, which in Sardinian is pronounced *Castedu*, which is the official name for the city.

The old city sits picturesquely on the slopes of a large hill, at the base of which away from the water are the newer suburbs and developments. In the *centro storico* you can find a charming blend of Roman ruins, Spanish churches and medieval streets, castle walls and old town gates.

Arrivals & Departures

See *Arrivals & Departures* at the beginning of this chapter (for all of Sardinia) and choose your preferred mode of transportation.

Getting Around Town

By Bus

The buses all depart from the central location of Piazza Matteoti and cost E1 one way. You can purchase tickets at any newsstand or *Tabacchi*. There is a newsstand in the train station and the bus station. Bus #8 goes up the hill to the old town.

By Foot

Besides getting to the beach, Cagliari is a walkable city even though the sights you're going to see are uphill from the harbor. Once you're at the top the going gets easier.

By Rental Car
• **Hertz**, *Tel. 07/024-0037, office located at the airport. Open Monday– Friday, 9:00am–6:00pm and Saturdays 9:00am–1:00pm.* You need to reserve at least a week in advance. Renting a car is an expensive option, especially if you're renting only for one day. Rates start at E75 per day for their smallest sedan.

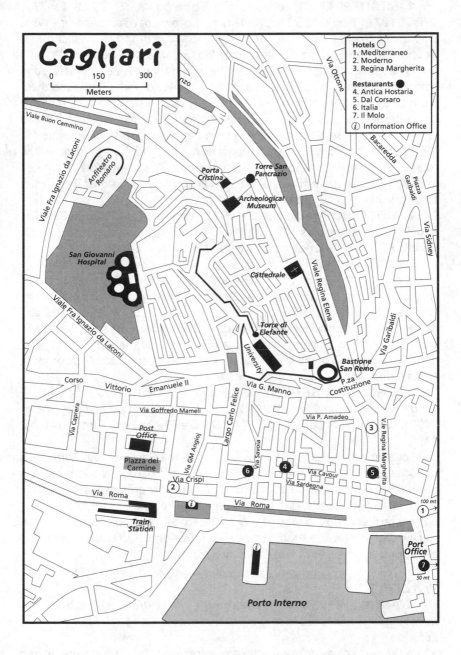

Where To Stay

1. MEDITERRANEO, *Lungomare C. Colombo 46, 09125 Cagliari. Tel. 070/301271, Fax 070/301-274. E-mail: hotelmedyt@tiscalinet.it. Web: web.tiscali.it/hotelMediterraneo/. 136 rooms, all with shower. Single E125; Double E160-180. All credit cards accepted. Breakfast included.* ****

Located about one kilometer from the train station near the cemetery and along the sea. The entrance is guarded by a variety of rare plants, and there are tropical plants inside too. This is a tranquil spot to stay as it is surrounded by gardens. Their restaurant is worth trying and their downstairs bar is a relaxing place to settle down after a long day. The rooms, all renovated in 1991, offer everything you would expect from a four star hotel and more. The rooms with a view over the water are wonderful. The bathrooms, decorated in white and gray are well-accessorized. A good place to stay just if you want to be outside the city center.

2. MODERNO, *Via Roma 159, 09124 Cagliari. Tel. 070/660-286, Fax 070/660-260. 93 rooms, 47 with bath, 46 with showers. Single E70-85; Double E80-100. All credit cards accepted. Breakfast E8 extra.* ***

What a quaint hotel! Situated in an old building near the train station, try to get one of the rooms with a tub since these are the oldest and best. The showers were added later to the other rooms making the bathrooms a little cramped. Overall the accommodations are a little below the three star category but the ambiance makes up for it. The windows are soundproof and from the restored balconies you get a good view of the port. There is air conditioning and TV in the rooms. Laundry and room service too. A good place to stay for a night when in transit elsewhere.

3. REGINA MARGHERITA, *Viale Regina Margherita 44, 09124 Cagliari. Tel. 070/670-342, Fax 070/668-325. Web: www.sardegnasud.com/reg_marg/ . 100 rooms, all with bath. Single E140; Double E170. Credit cards accepted.* ****

Located near the marble steps leading to the Bastione San Remo, this hotel has great views of the old town as well as the harbor. It doesn't have a restaurant, which means that after a tough day of touring you will still have to go out to get something to eat. They try to make up for it with a piano bar, but you can only drink so much. Every other service you should expect in a four star, like laundry service, room service and professional staff is in evidence. The bathrooms are pleasantly large with nice big tubs.

Where To Eat

4. ANTICA HOSTARIA, *Via Cavour 60, Tel. 070/665-870. Closed Sundays, August and national holidays. All credit cards accepted. Dinner for two E65.*

It's always a pleasure to eat at this terrific seafood place. You can get shrimp cocktail, *antipasto di mare* (mixed seafood antipasto) and great grilled steaks of *pesce spada* (swordfish) They also serve a tasty local stew made with lamb called *ghisau*. Their house wine is a superb local wine, but if your palate is more refined their list contains many mainland Italian labels also.

5. DAL CORSARO, *Viale Regina Margherita 28, Tel. 070/664-318. Closed Sundays and December. All credit cards accepted. Dinner for two E80.*

In my opinion this is the best restaurant in Cagliari. You get great food but you also have to pay well for it. It has a wonderful selection of menu options, a perfect selection of local, national and international wines, and the service is impeccable. All this is thanks to Giancarlo and Gianliugi Deidda, who make it their mission in life to give you the best meal possible. If you want something that's not on the menu they will try their best to have the cooks make an equivalent for you. You should try some of their home-made pastas, especially the delicious *tagliolini freschi con zucchine e vongole* (pasta with zucchini and clams) or the *lasagna ai filetti di scorfano e pomodoro fresco* (lasagna with scorpion fish and fresh tomato sauce).

6. IL MOLO, *Calata dei Trinitari, Tel. 070/308959. Closed Sunday and Monday nights, and November. All credit cards accepted. Dinner for two E50.*

Located almost right on the water, this place was a nautical club for many years, but today it is one of the best places to go to savor the seafood of the region. The *menu digestivo* is inviting, offering you a different seafood dish for every course. If you don't want to eat that much, try the flavorful and filling *grigliate miste di pesce* (mixed grilled fish).

7. ITALIA, *Via Sardegna 30, Tel. 070/657-9870. Closed Sundays. All credit cards accepted. Dinner for two E50*

Located by the hotel of the same name, this place has a committed clientele. The Italia serves many local specialties and the menu is equally divided between surf and turf. Start off with the *insalata di polpo* (octopus salad), and move to the *zuppetta di cozze* (muscle soup) so you can save room for the tasty and large *spiedino di carne miste* (mixed meat grilled on a spit). If you want to stick with fish they make excellent grilled and fried of all varieties.

Seeing the Sights

To get to the old town from the harbor, walk past the tree-lined Via Roma up the hill to the **Piazza Costituzione**. Walk up the flight of marble steps to the **Bastione San Remo**, which offers you magnificent views over the city, the harbor, and beyond. These medieval bastions are partially restored and are the best place to begin your exploration of Cagliari's old town.

Pass through the **Porta dei Due Leoni** to the Via Universita and go past the **University** *(open 8:00am–7:00pm)*. If you're so inclined, stop in and see for yourself what a Sardinian university is like. They have peaceful gardens in the back of the main building. As you pass the University, take note of the massive tower, **Torre di Elefante**, on the right hand side of the street. Take a right past the tower and enter the steep lanes, dark alleys, and imposing archways that make up the streets of the old city.

Weave your way up to the **Piazza del Palazzo** where you can find the 14th century **Cattedrale** on the right. Built by the Pisans in 1312, the cathedral (*Piazza Palazzo, open 8:00am–noon and 3:00pm–7:00pm*) is a prime example of their expressive architectural style. On either side of the entrance are two pieces of a pulpit that was created by the Pisan master Gugliemo Pisano, whose family worked on the cathedral and leaning tower in Pisa. The pulpit is covered with magnificent New Testament scenes. Make sure you visit the crypt where the remains of many Sardinian saints are stored.

Exit the cathedral and walk to your right to get to the **Museo Nazionale Archeologico** (*Piazza Indipendenza, open 9:00am–7:00pm; admission E5*). The museum contains some well-preserved, and some not so well preserved, relics and artifacts from Greece and Rome, as well as the largest collection of Sardinian antiquities anywhere. On the upper floors is the **National Painting Museum** that contains pictures from the 14th through the 18th centuries.

In the same piazza as the museum is the **Torre San Pancrazio**. Together with the aforementioned Torre di Elefante, they were part of the defense structure of Cagliari's castle. From the tower, pass through the **Porta Cristina** to get the Viale Buon Cammino. This will lead you to the **Anfiteatro Romano** (*Viale Fra Ignazio Da Laconi, open 9:00am–7:00pm*), which was constructed in the 2nd century CE in a natural depression in the rock. It is definitely one of the most imposing and well-preserved Roman ruins in Sardinia. Today the structure is used for open air concerts and theater presentations. Just south of the theater are the lush **Botanical Gardens** where you can go and relax among a variety of flowers and plants (*Viale Fra Ignazio Da Laconi, open 8:30am–8:00pm, admission E2*).

Excursions & Day Trips
SPIAGGIA DI POETTO

This is Cagliari's most popular bathing beach. **Spiaggia di Poetto** is a white sand paradise which extends 10 km along the **Golfo di Quarta**. On summer weekends, the place is packed with people so try and get here during the week. Take bus **P** from a *fermata* on the south side (harbor side) of Via Roma. It will take about 25 minutes to get here. Remember to buy a bus ticket for E1.5 first from a *Tabacchi* or newsstand first.

NURAGHI DI SAN NURAXI

These are the best preserved complex of **nuraghi** (tall stone structures held together without mortar) in all of Sardinia. Located on the top of a hill, these structures were obviously placed together for defensive purposes, giving us some insight into the culture of the ancient prehistoric civilization that built them. The only easy way to get here is to rent a car or get on a tour to ride the 60 km through rolling countryside.

NORA

Settled by the Phoenicians around 850 BCE, and later taken over by the Romans, the strategic town of Nora sits at the end of peninsula. After a series of disastrous Saracen raids, the stronghold was abandoned to the elements. Today there are some well-preserved Roman ruins, including a forum, amphitheater, temples, and villas with mosaic tiles on the floors. This sight is only easily accessible by car. Public transportation in Sardinia is not up to par with the rest of Italy.

Practical Information

Laundry Services
• **Lavanderia Erica**, *Via Ospedale 109*. Located across from the hospital on the way up the hill to the Roman Amphitheater. Bus #8 goes right up there from the Piazza Matteoti. *Open Monday through Saturday 8:00am to 8:00pm.* E6 for drop-off service that will wash, dry, and fold your clothes.

Postal Services
The **central post office** in Cagliari is *in the Piazza del Carmine, Tel. 070/ 668-356,* near the train station. *Open Monday through Saturday 8:30am– 5:00pm.* But if you're in a hurry, stamps can be bought at any tobacconist (stores indicated by a T sign outside), and mailed at any mailbox, which are red and marked with the word *Poste* or *Lettere*.

Travel Agencies
• **Cosmorama**, *Piazza Repubblica 8, Tel. 070/49-78-72, Fax 070/49-78-73*. If you don't want to rent a car, but you still want to see the sights outside of the city, contact this excellent travel agency to arrange for a private tour. Some of the staff speak decent English.

Tourist Information & Maps
• **Tourist Office**, outside of the train station in the *Piazza Matteoti, Tel. 070/ 669-255, open from 8:30am–8:00pm Monday through Friday, and Saturday 9:00am–1:00pm*. Pick up tourist information about the surrounding areas and useful city and area maps.

Alghero

Bypass the large and industrial city of Sassari altogether and make your way to **Alghero**, one of the most romantic medieval villages by the sea you'll ever find. There really is not too much to do or see in Alghero, but it is so beautiful that visiting here should be your main reason for coming to Sardinia. You'll find tiny alleyways, fantastic vistas, medieval towers, Gothic churches, wonderful restaurants and an ambiance and environment that can't be beat.

Arrivals & Departures

By train it is three hours from Cagliari and an hour from Olbia. Trains leave three times a day from Cagliari and four times a day from Olbia.

If you don't want to wait that long, you can catch a flight into the small domestic **Fortilia Airport** just outside of town. Small commuter flights from mainland Italy, Cagliari, and Sicily fly into this airport.

Renting A Car

• **Avis**, *Fortilia Airport, Tel. 079/935-064.* E55 per day, must be at least 21 years old.
• **Budget**, *Fortilia Airport, Tel. 079/986-050.* E50 per day, must be at least 21 years old.

Where To Stay

1. EL BALEAR, *Lungomare Dante 32, 07041 Alghero. Tel. 079/975-229, Fax 079/974-847. Web: www.algherovacanze.com/hotels/balear.htm. 57 rooms all with bath. Single E65-70; Double E75-86. Credit cards accepted. Breakfast E10 extra.* ***

A respectable three star just on the edge of the old town with wonderful views over the water from their garden terrace. The rooms are nice size and have just recently, thank god, had air conditioning installed. The bathrooms are clean and modernized. Their restaurant serves authentic local food prepared very well and there is a downstairs piano bar for your evening's entertainment.

2. MANNU, *Viale Alghero, Bosa 08013. Tel. 0785/375306, Fax 0785/375-308. 22 rooms all with shower. Single E65-70; Double E75-85. Breakfast included. Credit cards accepted.* ***

If you decide you want to stay in nearby Bosa, a very quiet but incredibly charming small town about a 45 km day trip from Alghero, this is the place for you. It's located in a building of recent construction in a quiet tranquil area with great romantic panoramic views and wonderful service. The rooms are large with high ceilings and the bathrooms are kept immaculate. They have air conditioning, TV, rooms and laundry service and more. The restaurant serves excellent food and is featured below.

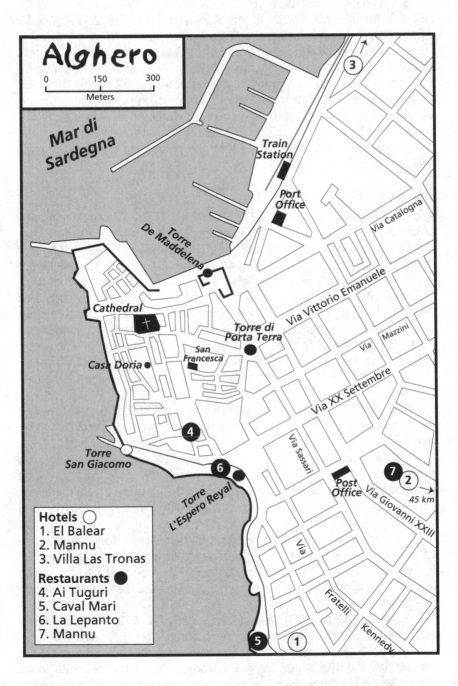

Alghero

0   150   300
Meters

Mar di Sardegna

Train Station

Port Office

Via Catalogna

Torre De Maddelena

Via Vittorio Emanuele

Cathedral

Torre di Porta Terra

Via Mazzini

San Francesca

Via XX Settembre

Casa Doria

4

Via Sassari

Torre San Giacomo

6

Torre L'Espero Reyal

7 2

Post Office   Via Giovanni XXIII

45 km

Via

Hotels ○
1. El Balear
2. Mannu
3. Villa Las Tronas

Restaurants ●
4. Ai Tuguri
5. Caval Mari
6. La Lepanto
7. Mannu

Fratelli Kennedy

5 1

3. VILLA LAS TRONAS, *Lungomare Valencia 1, 07041 Alghero. Tel. 079/ 981-818, Fax 079/981-044. 30 rooms all with bath. Single E120-130; Double E130-170. Breakfast included. Credit cards accepted.* ****

This place was the vacation home of the Italian royal family when they traveled to Sardinia. Now it is a quaint old hotel housed in a romantic old building and run ever so smoothly by Dirretore Antonio La Spina. Here you have access to the old town of Alghero as well as the privacy of your own beach, a swimming pool, great views over the water, bocce courts, and a fine restaurant that serves local cuisine. The service and care given you here makes it feel like a home away from home. Recently upgraded to four star status and their prices now reflect that change.

Where To Eat

4. AL TUGURI, *Via Maiorca 113, Tel. 079/976-722. Closed Sundays and December 20 to January 20. Visa accepted. Dinner for two E50.*

This is a small place spread out over three floors with just enough room to seat about 35 people, and because of this it has an authentic local Algherese feel to it. The owner, Enrico Carbonella, walks among the tables making all feel welcome. The menu isn't extensive, but what they do serve is prepared perfectly. For a*ntipasto* try the *code di gamberi e nuvole di funghi* (shrimps tails and mushroom heads) or the *marinate di pesce fresca* (marinated fresh fish). For pasta you simply must try the *linguine bianche* (made with an oil, garlic and pepper sauce). For seconds their huge *aragosta alla catalana con cipole e pomodorini freschi* (lobster Catalan-style with onions and tomatoes) is terrific.

5. CAVAL MARI, *Lungomare Dante, Tel. 079/981-570. Closed Tuesdays (not in summer) and 15 days in November. Credit cards accepted. Dinner for two E60.*

Located near the Hotel El Belear, this restaurant has a large verandah on the rocks near the water where you can admire the Bay of Alghero. The large dining room is subdivided into sections, giving the place a more intimate feel. The food is a mix of regional traditional, meaning it has some Ligurian and Catalan influences, as well as being a bit creative.

Try their *polpo tiepido all'olio e aglio* (warm roasted octopus served in an oil and garlic sauce) or the *spigola marinata* (seafood grilled on a skewer). But first you must try their many versions of spaghetti, especially *alle cozze* (with mussels) and *ai ricci di mare* (with the riches of the sea, i.e., mixed seafood). The grilled meats are also good.

6. LA LEPANTO, *Via Carlo Alberto 135, Tel. 079/979-116. Closed Mondays in the winter. All credit cards accepted. Dinner for two E70.*

A fine place with a quaint terrace located in the heart of old city, but the preparation of dishes is haphazard. Sometimes it's great, other times so-so. Maybe it's because they try to do too much. The menu is extensive and seems to have everything that surf and turf could offer. I've always been pleased with the *i polpi tiepido con le patate* (roasted octopus in an oil and garlic sauce with roasted potatoes) and the *spaghetti con gamberi e melanzane* (with shrimp and eggplant). For *antipasto* try the exquisite *antipasto misto di pesce spada affumicato* (smoked swordfish) or the *insalata mista* (mixed salad) with fresh vegetables from the region.

7. **MANNU**, *Viale Alghero, Bosa 08013. Tel. 0785/375306. Visa accepted. Dinner for two E50.*

Located inside the Mannu Hotel in the town of Bosa, the decor is classic modern. There aren't many options on the menu and most of the selections are seafood. Try their *gattuccio e la razza in agliata* (dogfish grilled with an oily garlic sauce) for seconds. For *primo*, try either the *risotto alla pescatora* (rice with seafood), *penne alle cozze* (tubular pasta with a mussel sauce), or *spaghetti all'aragosta* (with a lobster sauce).

Seeing the Sights

In town, you'll find the **Chiesa di San Francesco** *(Via Carlo Alberto, open 8:00am–noon and 3:00pm–5:00pm)*, begun in the 14th century and completed in the 16th. The different color stones give a clear indication where work recommenced. The **Casa Doria** *(Via Principe Umberto #7, not open to the public)* is a beautiful 16th century building built by the Doria family of Genoa who played a large part in the fortification and development of the city.

Down the street is the **Cathedral** *(Via Principe Umberto, open 8:00am–noon and 3:30pm–6:00pm)*, which is a jumble of architectural styles that can be seen from its Gothic/Catalan/Renaissance facade. There are three medieval towers located around the town: the **Torre di Porta Terra** to the east that was once one of only two access points into Alghero; the **Torre de L'Espero Reyal** to the south that is circular in design and once served as prison; and the **Torre de San Giacomo** facing the sea that once served as an 18th century dog pound.

In the vicinity of Alghero you can find quaint mountain towns, a necropolis, *nuraghi*, and more. The best sight outside of town are the **Grotte di Nettuno**, eerie but beautiful caverns complete with stalactites and stalagmites that can either be reached by car or by sea. Boats leave from the port near the train station hourly in the summertime. Round-trip takes about 2 1/2 hours and costs E10 per person. If you go by car, the admission is E6 and you'll have to descend over 600 steps to get down to the sea.

Also, only 10 km west of Alghero near the **Capo Caccia** (where there are great beaches, incidentally) are the **Nuraghi di Palmavera** that date back to 1500 BCE. In another direction, just 10 km north of Alghero are the famous **Necropolis di Aghelu Ruju**, a group of 38 tombs built around 3000 BCE.

Then if you go 45 km south of Alghero, you'll stumble upon the most quaint medieval hill town you'll ever find, **Bosa**. If you want to stay the night, or just for a meal to soak up more of the pristine beauty, see the *Where to Stay* and *Where to Eat* sections above. If you want the taste and feel of Sardinia's past merged with its present, Alghero and its environs is the place to visit. But you better hurry before everybody else finds out.

Practical Information
Postal Services
The **central post office** in Alghero is on the corner of *Via Carducci and Via Giovanni XIII*. *Open Monday through Friday, 8:30am–5:00pm, Saturday 9:00am–noon*. Stamps can also be bought at any tobacconist (stores indicated by a **T** sign outside), and mailed at any mailbox, which are red and marked with the word *Poste* or *Lettere*.

Tourist Information & Maps
• **Tourist Office**, *Piazza Porta Terra, Tel. 097/979-054*. You can get maps, a list of possible accommodations, and bus and train schedules.

Olbia

Olbia is like Messina in Sicily, in that you have to come here because this is where the ferry docks – but you don't really want to stay. I'm mentioning it since it is a trans-shipment point and you may have to pass through if you take one of the ferries from **Civitavecchia**. If worse comes to worst and you have to spend the night here, I've listed some decent lodgings and good restaurants.

There are two real sights, **Chiesa San Simplicio** (*Via San Simplicio, open 9:00am–noon and 3:00pm–6:00pm*), a 12th century Pisan Romanesque church, and the **Chiesa Primaziale** (*Piazza Primaziale, accessible 9:00am–noon and 4:00pm–6:00pm*), a 14th century convent complex that you can gain entrance to just by asking. From Olbia you can head south by bus to the beaches around **San Teodoro**, hop the train to **San Teresa Gallura** for a ferry over to the French island of **Corsica**, or start your journey by train across Sardinia to **Alghero** or south to **Cagliari**.

Put simply, since all traces of Olbia's Greek, Roman, and medieval past have been obliterated for the sake of modernization, this place has little of interest for visitors.

Arrivals & Departures
Olbia is the main port on Sardinia, and as such you'll most likely arrive by ferry from any number of mainland Italian ports. See *Arrivals & Departures* in the beginning of this chapter for more information.

Getting Around Town

When you disembark from your ferry, the **train station** is only a couple hundred meters northeast of you. Follow the main road Corso Umberto I until you see the station on your right. The **bus station** is at the end of Corso Umberto I conveniently near the port.

You can walk anywhere, but if you need a taxi late at night there should be some around the port. Or call the **24-hour taxi line**, *Tel. 0789/31039.*

Renting a Car
• **Avis**, *at the airport in Loiri, 10 kilometers outside of town. Tel. 0789/22420.*
Call beforehand to have them send a van to pick you up at the ferry.

Where To Stay

If you don't stay in a three or four star hotel, the accommodations you get will be rather poor here. The three below are my picks for their service and convenience.

1. CENTRALE, *Corso Umberto I 85, 07026, Tel. 0789/23017, Fax 0789/ 26464. Web: www.hotelcentraleolbia.it/. 23 rooms all with shower. Single E95; Double E115. Breakfast E6 extra. Diners Club accepted.* ***

Simply a place to lay your head for a night's rest. The rooms are small but they do have air conditioning, TV, and a phone. There's a small area they call a bar downstairs, as well as meeting rooms. Other than that, this place is an empty shell. Clean, nondescript, but aptly named since it is in the center of things in Olbia.

2. MARTINI, *Via G D'Annunzio, 07026 Olbia. Tel. 0789/926-066, Fax 0789/926-418. Web: http://sardinia.net/tirso/alberg/martini.htm. 66 rooms all with shower. Single E100-120; Double E135-165. Credit cards accepted. Breakfast included.* ****

Certainly the best hotel in Olbia near the center of town. The rooms are large, beautifully appointed, well-lit and some have a view over the bay and the old roman port. Others have a view of the city and the sports center. The communal terrace comes complete with deck chairs and umbrellas. The hotel have air conditioning, TV, laundry service, room service, minibar and more. A restful place a short distance from the train station.

3. PRESIDENT, *Via Umberto 9, 07026 Olbia. Tel. 0789/27501, Fax 0789/ 21551. 44 rooms all with bath. Single E100; Double E140. Credit cards accepted. Breakfast included.* ****

They have a bus service that will pick you up at the ferry if you call and tell them when you're arriving. Located in a plush garden setting, this place has all the necessary four star amenities at low Sardinia prices. They have a fine restaurant of their own, so you don't have to leave the place if you don't want to. The rooms have air conditioning, TV, and mini-bar, and are decently sized and immaculately maintained.

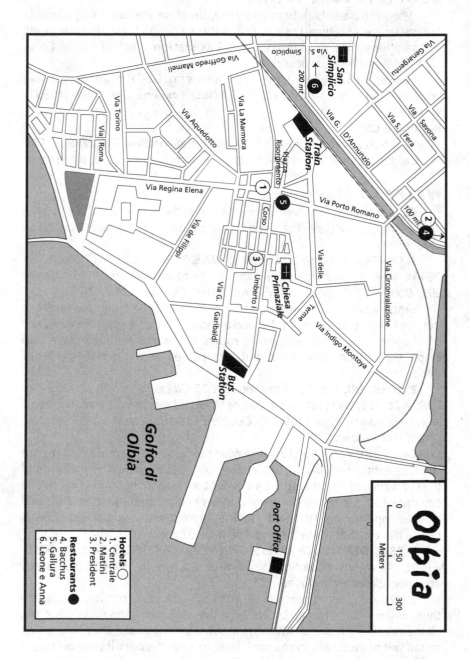

Olbia

0
150
300

Meters

Golfo di Olbia

Hotels ○
1. Centrale
2. Matini
3. President

Restaurants ●
4. Bacchus
5. Gallura
6. Leone e Anna

Via Genargentu

Via S. Simplicio

San Simplicio

200 mt

Via G. D'Annunzio

Via Savona

Via S. Fera

Via Goffredo Mameii

Via Aquedotto

Via La Marmora

Via Torino

Via Roma

Piazza Risorgimento

Train Station

Via Regina Elena

Corso

Via Porto Romano

100 mt

Via de Filippi

Via G. Umberto I

Chiesa Primaziale

Via delle Terme

Via Circonvalazione

Via G. Garibaldi

Via Indigo Montoya

Bus Station

Port Office

Where To Eat

4. **BACCHUS**, *Via G. D'Annunzio 2p, Centro Martini, Tel. 0789/21612. Closed Sundays, but in the summer only Sunday lunch, and 20 days in January. Credit cards accepted. Dinner for two E60.*

Located on the bay of the old Porta Romana, there are nice views from their terrace dining area over the water and the Isola Bianca. The atmosphere inside is grandiose with a touch of elegance, and the food, mainly seafood, is perfectly fresh and appetizing. If you want an *antipasto* try the *calamaro ripieno al profumo di basilico* (large squid stuffed with the taste of basil) – it is truly delicious. For *primo* try any of their fantastic pasta options, especially the *spaghetti ai gamberoni* (with small shrimp sauce). For seconds don't leave without sampling the *filetto di triglia con dadolata di pomodoro* (filet of mullet covered with diced tomatoes).

5. **GALLURA**, *Corso Umberto 145, Tel. 0789/24648. Closed Mondays, 10 days in November and 20 days between December and January. All credit cards accepted. Dinner for two E80.*

Ouch. The prices here really hurt. The atmosphere is nice, a little stuffy and formal but comfortable. If you don't want to spend too much but also get a great meal try the following: *zuppa di verdure* (vegetable soup) as an appetizer, then jump straight to an entrée. This way your meal will be about E45. For entrée, avoid the pricey fish and try either the *l'agnello in tegame* (pan-fried lamb) or the *cinghiale in agrodolce* (sweet and sour wild boar). To finish things off sample some of their succulent *pecorino*. They have a selection of this cheese at different aged stages, each tasting wonderful and amazingly different from one another.

6. **LEONE E ANNA**, *Via Barcellona 90, Tel. 0789/26333. Closed Wednesdays (not in the summer) and January. Credit cards accepted. Dinner for two E80.*

Ouch again. But here, too, if you avoid the fish dishes you can get a great meal at a more reasonable price. This place has regained the vitality, energy, and warmth it used to have years ago. Skip the *antipasto*, most of the seafood, and get some *pappardelle ai funghi porcini*, a scrumptious pasta dish made with olive oil and *porcini* mushrooms. Then for seconds dig into either the succulent *porcetto al forno* (baby pork on the grill) or the *capretto al forno* (baby goat on the grill).

Practical Information

Postal Services

The **central post office** is on the *Via Aquadotte, Tel. 0987/22251*, near the open air market that takes place each the morning. *Open Monday through Saturday 8:30am–5:00pm*. But if you're in a hurry, stamps can be bought at any tobacconist (stores indicated by a **T** sign outside), and mailed at any mailbox, which are red and marked with the word *Poste* or *Lettere*.

Tourist Information & Maps

• **Tourist Office**, *just off the Corso Umberto I on the Via Piro, Tel. 0789/ 21453. Open from 8:30am-1:00pm and 4:00pm-7:00pm Monday through Friday, and 9:00am-1:00pm Saturdays.* If the town is not much to see, the tourist office makes up for it with all the information you can get here: maps of the city and surrounding areas; itineraries for exploring Sardinia's lush beaches and ancient archaeological sites, and most importantly a list of hotels in Sardinia including almost all the little towns and villages.

Costa Smeralda

The **Emerald Coast (Costa Smeralda)** is located just north of Olbia. This coastline at one time used to be nothing but a vibrant community of small fishing villages. Then in 1962 it began to be developed as the playground for the rich and famous. Now all you can see for miles are high-rise luxury and some not-so-luxury hotels. My advice to you is to avoid the congestion and rank consumerism that this area is known for. There is little to see except lots of people crammed like sardines next to each other on the beach, and anything you do costs a small fortune. If you want to experience contrived ambiance, stay close to home and go to Cancun.

The same avoidance warning goes for the once beautiful islands of **La Maddalena** and **Caprerra**, which are now nothing but one big tourist trap. Some of the smaller outlying islands, like **Santa Maria** and **Budelli**, have not yet succumbed completely but they are on their way. If you are so inclined they can all be reached from the port at **Palau**.

One reason you may be interested, but only for a short period of time, in visiting La Maddelena is that in the small town of **Caprera** lie the remains of the Italian and Sardinian hero Giussepe Garibaldi. You can catch a bus from the port to take you over. Other than that, if you decide to visit here, welcome to tacky beach life, Italian-style.

Italy Guide

index

Open Road Travel Guides to Italy

Hey, this is the book you're holding right now, so unless you want to buy one for your friends, look below and on the next page for other great Open Road guides to *la bella Italia!*

Doug Morris takes you to Florence and beyond, to the great towns and villages of Tuscany and Umbria: Lucca, Fiesole, Siena, Assisi, Pisa, plus much more in Orvieto, Spoleto, Gubbio, San Gimignano, Fiesole, Todi and Perugia. $14.95

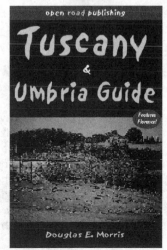

See ordering information on the last page of this book.

Rome Guide
$14.95

The only guide you'll need to the Eternal City! Doug Morris takes you to his favorite restaurants, hotels, special sights, unique pubs and nightlife, and terrific area excursions.

We doubt you'll find another country in the world that is as welcoming and friendly to the bambini, and the number of family-friendly hotels and activities is incredible!

Italy With Kids
$14.95

Eating & Drinking in Italy
$9.95

How many times have you walked into a foreign restaurant and stared blankly at the menu? No more – this comprehensive yet compact 'menu-reader' will guide you through any Italian dining experience with ease!

See ordering information on the last page of this book.

Things Change!

Phone numbers, prices, addresses, quality of food, etc, all change. If you come across any new information, we'd appreciate hearing from you. No item is too small! Drop us an email note at: Jopenroad@aol.com, or write us at:

Italy Guide
Open Road Publishing, P.O. Box 284
Cold Spring Harbor, NY 11724

Travel Notes

Travel Notes

Travel Notes